# College Student Development Theory

## Second Edition

### ASHE Reader Series

Edited by
Maureen E. Wilson
Bowling Green State University

Series Editor
Jerlando F. L. Jackson
University of Wisconsin

**Learning Solutions**

New York  Boston  San Francisco
London  Toronto  Sydney  Tokyo  Singapore  Madrid
Mexico City  Munich  Paris  Cape Town  Hong Kong  Montreal

Cover Art: *Contemplative Figures*, by Robin McDonald-Foley

Pearson Learning Solutions, 501 Boylston Street, Suite 900, Boston, MA 02116
A Pearson Education Company
www.pearsoned.com

Printed in the United States of America

1 2 3 4 5 6 7 8 9 10 V036 16 15 14 13 12 11

0002000102706047297

SB/CB

ISBN 10: 0-558-92973-7
ISBN 13: 978-0-558-92973-2

22 2020

# COPYRIGHT ACKNOWLEDGMENTS

# TABLE OF CONTENTS

# ACKNOWLEDGMENTS

The editor thanks the late Len Foster of Washington State University with whom I first worked in his role as ASHE Reader Series Editor and Jerlando F. L. Jackson, who now serves in that role, for their support and assistance. We also thank Karen Whitehouse, executive editor for Pearson Learning Solutions, for her help in tackling the details required to publish this volume. I am also grateful to my colleagues who served on the advisory board and helped make the difficult choices in compiling this resource.

Elisa S. Abes, Miami University

Marcia B. Baxter Magolda, Miami University

Jennifer Buckley, Indiana University

Tracy L. Davis, Western Illinois University

John P. Dugan, Loyola University Chicago

Florence Hamrick, Rutgers, The State University of New Jersey

Dawn R. Johnson, Syracuse University

Susan R. Jones, Ohio State University

Patricia M. King, University of Michigan

Peter Mather, Ohio University

Matthew Mayhew, New York University

Raechele L. Pope, University at Buffalo

Stephen John Quaye, University of Maryland

Robert Reason, Pennsylvania State University

Lori Reesor, University of Kansas

Vasti Torres, Indiana University

Lisa E. Wolf-Wendel, University of Kansas

## EDITED BY

Maureen E. Wilson, Bowling Green State University

# A NOTE TO THE READER

I anticipate that this edition of the *ASHE Reader on Student Development Theory* will be in print for about three years, at which time a revised edition is expected. Your assistance in shaping the contents (e.g., what is particularly useful, what should be added) will be appreciated.

Please send your suggestions, comments, and recommendations to the *ASHE Reader* to the editor:

Maureen E. Wilson
Associate Professor and Chair
Department of Higher Education and Student Affairs
Bowling Green State University
Bowling Green, OH 43403

mewilso@bgsu.edu

Suggestions about other topics that might be addressed by the *ASHE Reader Series*, or other comments about the series should be sent to the ASHE Reader Series Editor:

Jerlando F. L. Jackson, Ph.D.
Associate Professor of Higher and Postsecondary Education
Educational Leadership and Policy Analysis
University of Wisconsin–Madison
270-K Education Building
1000 Bascom Mall
Madison, WI 53706-1326

jjackson@education.wisc.edu

# INTRODUCTION

## Background of the Reader

Courses in college student development theory examine ways in which students and other adults make meaning of their experiences and how faculty and administrators can promote their learning, growth, and development. The Council for the Advancement of Standards in Higher Education (CAS Standards) includes student development theory as one of five required areas of study for master's level graduate programs for student affairs professionals. These theories examine a wide range of development in college students.

Student development theory is a foundation upon which the profession of student affairs administration rests. Many of the policy and practice decisions made by professionals in the field are based on the belief that students learn, develop, and grow in certain predictable ways and that it is the responsibility of colleges and universities to create environments that facilitate that development. Faculty in student affairs and higher education graduate programs have the responsibility of educating their students about these theories and their application. The students in higher education and the developmental issues they confront are more diverse and complex than ever. The growing body of literature on student development reflects these changes, but comes from a variety of disciplinary areas and therefore is not readily accessible by faculty who teach these subjects, by graduate students who study them, or by professionals in the field who use them. This reader compiles some of the best work available on student development theory.

Choosing an organizing framework for the reader was a great challenge and reflects new conceptualizations in the study of student development theory. In his oft-cited chapter, Rodgers (1991) described four major families of theories: psychosocial, cognitive-structural, person-environmental interaction, and topological [sic]. The first edition of *Student Development in College* (Evans, Forney, & Guido-DiBrito, 1998) had three major sections on theory: 1) psychosocial and identity development theories, 2) cognitive-structural theories, and 3) typology theories. In the second edition of that book (Evans, Forney, Guido, Patton, & Renn, 2010) there are also three main theory sections, but they are different than those in the first edition: 1) foundational (e.g., psychosocial identity, Chickering, Perry, moral development, later cognitive structural theories, and Kolb); 2) integrative theories (i.e., ecological approaches, self-authorship, faith and spirituality, and transition theory); and 3) social identity development (e.g., race, ethnicity, multiracial, sexual, gender, and gender identity development). Baxter Magolda, Abes, and Torres (2008) described epistemological, intrapersonal, and interpersonal development. Jones and Abes (2011 and in this volume) addressed psychosocial, cognitive, and social identity theories, emerging theoretical perspectives (e.g., critical race theory, queer theory, and intersectionality), and theories emphasizing holistic development (e.g., Kegan, Baxter Magolda). They also include other theories not focused directly on student development theory. Clearly, how scholars conceptualize student development is evolving and this volume reflects that evolution. The discussion among advisory board members that led to the current structure was lively. The organization of this reader is similar to the first edition, but has fewer subsections and includes a new section on critical theory. The framework is described in greater detail in the "Overview of the Reader," in the next section.

Another challenge that faces all ASHE Reader editors is deciding which readings to include and which to exclude. Working with the advisory board, I selected key and representative pieces highlighting different theories and theory types. Some classics that laid a foundation upon which others built are included as newer works that show the current status of student development theory. Many advisory board members felt strongly that a section on critical theory was important to include. When possible, I use primary sources but concerns for length and cost resulted in the selection of some summary pieces that include the work of many scholars. The explosion of work on social identity theories is truly noteworthy and is reflected in the length of the recommended readings list in that section. Based on my searches, it appears the volume of work in this area in recent years is greater than in any other.

Space constraints also led to the exclusion of other important theories not directly addressing student *development* such as typology, student success, organizational development, and campus environments theories. In terms of selecting among individual pieces addressing similar themes within sections, I typically chose the more recent article and/or included pieces that were more difficult to find. Each Unit of the Reader concludes with a list of additional recommended readings, some of which present empirical studies based on a variety of theories.

## Purpose of the Reader

This reader is intended to serve as a resource of primary source literature on college student development theory and as a text for courses on student development theory. Graduate students and other scholars and practitioners are introduced to a wide variety of student development theories by reading original works of theorists, contemplating the context in which development occurs, and considering how theory can be applied to practice and how practice can inform theory. The reader is also useful in on-going professional development efforts for student affairs practitioners who lack formal study of student development theory or who wish to become familiar with more recent work on the topic. Professionals who work with college students and want to create programs and services to promote their learning, growth, and development will find a wealth of resources here to aid in those efforts.

Baxter Magolda, M. B., Abes, E., & Torres, V. (2008). Epistemological, intrapersonal, and interpersonal development in the college years and young adulthood. In M. C. Smith & N. DeFrates-Densch (Eds.), *Handbook of research on adult learning and development* (pp. 183–219). New York, NY: Routledge.

Evans, N. J., Forney, D. S., & Guido-DiBrito, F. (1998). *Student development in college: Theory, research, and practice*. San Francisco, CA: Jossey-Bass.

Evans, N. J., Forney, D. S., Guido, F. M., Patton, L. D., & Renn, K. A. (1998). *Student development in college: Theory, research, and practice* (2nd ed.). San Francisco, CA: Jossey-Bass.

Jones, S. R., & Abes, E. S. (2011). The nature and uses of theory. In J. Schuh, S. R. Jones, S. R. Harper, & Associates. *Student services: A handbook for the profession* (5th ed., pp. 149–167). San Francisco, CA: Jossey-Bass.

Rodgers, R. F. (1991). Using theory in practice in student affairs. In T. K. Miller & R. B. Winston (Eds.), *Administration and leadership in student affairs* (pp. 203–251). Muncie, IN: Accelerated Development.

# OVERVIEW OF THE READER

## Unit 1: Introduction to the Study of Student Development Theory

The first unit of the reader provides an overview of student development theory, particularly as a field of study. The two chapters in the unit provide an overview of the nature and uses of theory within a student affairs context, discuss the evolution of the concept of student development, and present a framework of propositions as an agenda for scholars and practitioners in the field.

## Unit 2: Integrated Developmental Models

One of the major advances in contemporary student development theory is work that considers development from a more holistic or integrated fashion, rather than focusing on individual aspects of development without considering how it is affected by other factors. For instance, is cognitive development impacted by one's race or gender? How are psychosocial tasks influenced by one's sexual orientation? Integrated developmental models are presented in this unit. The theory section of the reader is introduced with these integrated or holistic models because they provide an overarching framework through which to understand the more specific dimensions of development that follow.

In Chapter 3, Baxter Magolda discusses a holistic perspective on college student development. Next, King and Baxter Magolda address the development of one desired outcome of college, intercultural maturity. Kegan and Lahey discuss mental capacity and the challenge of change, followed by Abes, Jones, and McEwen's updated Model of Multiple Dimensions of Identity. Love's piece on spiritual development and cognitive development concludes this section.

## Unit 3: Intrapersonal and Interpersonal Development: Psychosocial and Social Identity Theories

Intrapersonal dimensions of development address how individuals actively construct their sense of self while interpersonal dimensions relate to the sense of self in relation to others. As noted in the introduction to this text, the volume of work on social identity theories in particular is massive. This growth is reflected in this ASHE Reader as this unit contains one-third of the chapters in the book and the recommended reading list is quite lengthy. In contrast to early theories that were often developed using samples of White men, contemporary work has expanded considerably to address the roles of race, ethnicity, gender, sexual orientation, disability, social class, first-generation student status, and other factors in developing identity and in other dimensions of development.

In Chapter 8, Torres, Jones, and Renn focus on understanding how identity development is conceptualized in student affairs and how this understanding can help practitioners better promote students' learning and development. The revision of Chickering's classic seven vectors of development is presented next. Then, Arnett argues that emerging adulthood (ages 18–25) is a distinct developmental period. The remaining chapters focus on a range of characteristics and their role in identity development. Chapter 11 addresses models of racial oppression and sociorace followed by a review of research on ethnic identity. Women's and men's identity are considered next. Bilodeau and Renn analyze lesbian, gay, bisexual, and transgender identity development models and Hoffman tackles heterosexual identity development. The final three chapters of this unit focus on identity development of students with disabilities, students of different social classes, and first-generation college students.

## Unit 4: Cognitive Dimensions of Development (Intellectual and Moral)

Cognitive theories address how people come to know and believe. The first half of the unit is focused on cognitive development and includes models developed by Perry, Clinchy (along with Belenky, Goldberger, and Tarule), King and Kitchener, and Baxter Magolda. The unit concludes with moral development as presented by Kohlberg, Gilligan, and Rest, Narvaez, Thoma, and Bebeau.

## Unit 5: Critical Theoretical Perspectives on Development

In content new to the reader, critical theoretical perspectives are addressed in Unit 5. Abes lays the foundation, arguing that the use of multiple theoretical perspectives can be used to challenge inequitable power structures in student development theory. Next, Sólorzano, Villalpando, and Oseguera employ critical race theory in analyzing the educational progress of Latina/o undergraduate students. Finally, Zaytoun examines the relationship between Kegan's theory and the capacity for social consciousness and action.

## Unit 6: Theory to Practice

An important aspect of student development theory is applying it to practice and exemplars of theory-based practice are included in this unit. The unit begins with Parker's classic piece reflecting on how theory can be useful to practitioners, which is followed by Strange and King's chapter on the purposes and functions of student development theory in professional practice. Next, Ortiz and Rhoads present a theoretical framework advancing a multicultural perspective from which to explore and deconstruct Whiteness. Finally, Baxter Magolda describes the Learning Partnerships Model, a framework for promoting self-authorship.

# FOREWORD

## MARCIA B. BAXTER MAGOLDA
### DISTINGUISHED PROFESSOR OF EDUCATIONAL LEADERSHIP
### AT MIAMI UNIVERSITY OF OHIO

Higher education promotes the free exchange of ideas, critical analysis of complex problems, and exploration of diverse perspectives in the process of learning to construct and judge knowledge claims. Effective participation in these learning opportunities requires certain capacities: the epistemological capacity to acknowledge multiple points of view, the intrapersonal capacity to construct an internal identity to guide belief formation, and the interpersonal capacity to mutually negotiate relationships in which beliefs differ. These meaning making capacities, which developmental psychologist Robert Kegan (1994) coined as the mental demands of modern life, undergird adults' ability to learn, lead, and live in the complexity of contemporary society. These capacities develop when adults engage in complex work and life challenges, particularly when others around them: respect their thoughts and feelings, work collaboratively with them to address these challenges, and encourage them to generate their own solutions (Baxter Magolda, 2009). Jack Mezirow described this as transformational learning:

> . . . the process by which we transform our taken-for-granted frames of reference (meaning perspectives, habits of mind, mind-sets) to make them more inclusive, discriminating, open, emotionally capable of change, and reflective so that they may generate beliefs and opinions that will prove more true or justified to guide action. (2000, pp. 7–8)

Some students arrive at college with these capacities; however, more collegians arrive on campuses dependent on authorities for knowledge and peers for identity and relationship formation. College student development theories portray the multitude of possibilities for how collegians make meaning and the processes that enable them to develop the complex epistemological, intrapersonal, and interpersonal capacities to meet the demands of college and adult life. This ASHE *Reader* offers a diverse body of research on these meaning making capacities to help educators promote them during college.

Demands for meaning making vary across contexts. Some educational contexts reward learners for uncritically adopting authority's views whereas others reward learners for constructing their own views by critically analyzing existing evidence. Some collegians come from privileged backgrounds in which others shielded them from life's complexities and authority figures supported their interests. Others come from marginalized backgrounds in which life's complexities emerged from oppression and authority figures did not support their interests. Support for developing the capacities to handle life's complexities also differs across contexts. Families and educators who solve problems constrain opportunities for collegians to develop complex meaning making capacities. Families and educators who help collegians solve their own problems offer opportunities to develop more complex meaning making capacities. Collegians' personal characteristics—gender, race, ethnicity, sexual orientation, faith traditions, social class—intertwine with these contextual variations to shape their experiences and how they approach life's challenges. These layers of complexity require a nuanced vision of college student development theory—a vision of theory as *possibility*.

Robert Coles' (1989) story about his psychiatric residency illustrates this vision of theory as possibility. Coles struggled during his medical internship to reconcile diverse perspectives of his two supervisors—one who encouraged him to formulate theories to explain his patients and another who encouraged him to listen and understand as their stories unfolded. The latter supervisor introduced him to the Greek derivation of the word *theory* as meaning *to behold*, leading Coles to arrive at the insight, "theory is an enlargement of observation" (p. 20). College student development theories emerge from "observations" (often in the form of interviews) of students' meaning making and are thus interpretations of what the observer witnessed. As Coles' supervisor astutely pointed out, "what you are hearing . . . is to some considerable extent a function of *you,* hearing" (p. 15). Many pioneers in college student development theorizing emphasized these notions by explicitly articulating that the foundations of their theories were particular students, in particular contexts, and shaped by their own interpretive lenses. For example, William Perry (1970), Mary Belenky and colleagues (1986), and Carol Gilligan (1982) all explicitly addressed these notions in the prefaces or beginning chapters of their seminal books. Yet educators, often with the good intent to understand and facilitate students' development, inappropriately generalized these theories to students whose experiences differed from these scholars' research participants.

I, too, struggled with this tendency to generalize when I first studied student development theories in graduate school. In my eagerness to apply theories in my residence life work I paid insufficient attention to theorists' cautions. However, I came face-to-face with the limits of generalizing in the midst of conducting my own longitudinal study of college student development. Rereading the cautions in seminal texts prompted me to interpret my data as particular to its context and to explicitly address the contextual nature of my theorizing (Baxter Magolda, 1992). Now that my longitudinal study is in its 25th year, I am increasingly aware of how my participants' unique lives, *me* hearing, and the theoretical grounding of my work intersect to shape my interpretations. Despite my emphasizing these nuances over the years, well-intentioned educators continue to inappropriately generalize this and other work beyond its context.

Contemporary theorists, many of whose work the editor includes in this *Reader*, have extended the observation to multiple contexts and student populations (something William Perry advocated in the preface of his 1970 book), yielding new possibilities for understanding students' meaning making. Some of these theorists have also brought to the foreground socially constructed assumptions that mediate our ability to hear and interpret students' stories to further emphasize the limits of our hearing and thus our theorizing. To effectively construct and apply student development theories, we have to resist the tendency to generalize beyond particular contexts and avoid static categorizing of students' meaning making. To fully respect students' meaning making, we should construct theory "in situ" *with* students, that is, to co-construct how we interpret our observations. Developing theory as possibility and as co-constructed with particular students alleviates the concern many educators share about overgeneralization and applying theory *to* students. The partnerships interwoven through many of the *Reader*'s chapters articulate this vision of the relationship of theory and practice.

This vision of *theory as possibility* makes a mental demand on the meaning making of theorists and educators. This vision requires openness to possibility, critical examination of one's socialization and ideology, willingness to explore one's biases, integrating theoretical perspectives to understand holistic development, and embracing the complexity of sharing authority with learners to name a few. To fashion integrative theoretical perspectives, to generate new theoretical possibilities, and to work across seemingly inconsistent theoretical perspectives—as many of the chapter authors represented here do—necessitates these complex meaning making capacities. It necessitates facing what Kegan and Lahey (2009) call our immunity to change and working to transform our meaning making into the interdependent forms that allow authentic partnerships with others, including our research participants. This *Reader* supports educators in understanding students and supports us in understanding ourselves and fostering our own development.

This ASHE *Reader* offers an eclectic array of student development research to support a vision of theory as possibility. The editor's inclusion of primary sources helps readers access the parameters theorists outline in their original work that are sometimes lost when other scholars synthesize large bodies of research. The editor's inclusion of multiple theoretical perspectives and work on using multiple perspectives in an intersectional way honors the complexity of college student development theories and their use in creating inclusive educational practice. Their balance of integrative perspectives with work that brings forward the nuances of particular student populations enhances our vision of the possibilities. The *Reader* places contemporary work in a historical context and reveals the current status of student development theorizing.

Sustaining a vision of *theory as possibility* necessitates viewing theory as continually evolving through the interaction of student characteristics and contexts, mediated by the theorists who enlarge those observations. Becoming overly attached to any one interpretation constrains our ability to see new possibilities. For example, just because we currently have not observed high numbers of students entering college with strong internal voices does not mean it is impossible, particularly if we reframed education to support it. At the same time, becoming overly attached to new possibilities constrains our ability to see existing theoretical threads that may weave through students' development. Holding multiple possibilities together, searching for meaningful intersections, and exploring new interpretations by using one perspective to look at another in a new way are necessary to sustain and expand theory as possibility. The ASHE *Reader* offers the opportunity to think differently about our theoretical foundations.

## References

Baxter Magolda, M. B. (1992). *Knowing and reasoning in college: Gender-related patterns in students' intellectual development*. San Francisco, CA: Jossey-Bass.

Baxter Magolda, M. B. (2009). *Authoring your life: Developing an internal voice to navigate life's challenges*. Sterling, VA: Stylus.

Belenky, M., Clinchy, B. M., Goldberger, N., & Tarule, J. (1986). *Women's ways of knowing: The development of self, voice, and mind*. New York, NY: Basic Books.

Coles, R. (1989). *The call of stories: Teaching and the moral imagination*. Boston, MA: Houghton Mifflin.

Gilligan, C. (1982). *In a different voice*. Cambridge, MA: Harvard University Press.

Kegan, R. (1994). *In over our heads: The mental demands of modern life*. Cambridge, MA: Harvard University Press.

Kegan, R., & Lahey, L. L. (2009). *Immunity to change: How to overcome it and unlock potential in yourself and your organization*. Boston, MA: Harvard Business Press.

Mezirow, J. (Ed.). (2000). *Learning as transformation: Critical perspectives on a theory in progress*. San Francisco, CA: Jossey-Bass.

Perry, W. G. (1970). *Forms of intellectual and ethical development in the college years: A scheme*. Troy, MO: Holt, Rinehart, & Winston.

# Unit 1

# Introduction to the Study of Student Development Theory

# CHAPTER 1
## THE NATURE AND USES OF THEORY

### SUSAN R. JONES AND ELISA S. ABES

Students who are involved in student organizations and leadership positions are more satisfied with their overall college experience.

First generation students struggle with their transition from high school to college because they have parents who do not understand what they are going through.

Black students hang out together in the cafeteria because the campus climate is a chilly one for them.

Living on campus, especially in living learning communities, improves retention of students participating in these programs.

## Introduction: *"Nothing as Useful as a Good Theory"*

These statements all represent a point of view that a student affairs educator may hold about students. But are they theories? Student affairs educators may hold perspectives grounded in their own experiences and informed by observations that clearly influence their practice. Indeed, we all carry with us, whether explicitly stated or implicitly implied, ideas, beliefs, and prior experiences that directly influence how we make sense of ourselves and the students with whom we interact. Do these constitute theories? What "theories" do you have about college students? And from where do these "theories" come? What questions about college students do your "theories" address—are they questions about college student development, about campus environments, about institutions and organizations? These are all questions for which there may be theoretical considerations.

Although well-known social psychologist Kurt Lewin suggested that there is nothing so practical as a good theory, theories represent more than common-sense or a particular point of view based upon one's own experiences, assumptions, and beliefs. As student affairs educators, it is important to distinguish between informal assumptions we hold (such as those noted at the beginning of the chapter) and those more formal theories that attempt to explain complex phenomena related to the college student experience. Theories have long served and equipped the student affairs profession. Whether focused on individual college student development, campus environments, student learning, student engagement, or organizational functioning, theories are thought to provide a "common language" (Knefelkamp, 1982, p. 379) for those interested in understanding college students and their experiences on campus. However, it is important to also note that the content of this "common language" has shifted over the years. While many of the early theories of the 1950s and 1960s continue to serve as guiding principles, newer theories have emerged that shift the discourse of theory

Jones, S. R., & Abes, E. S. (2011). The nature and uses of theory. In J. Schuh, S. R. Jones, S. R. Harper, & Associates. *Student services: A handbook for the profession* (5th ed., pp. 149–167). San Francisco, CA: Jossey-Bass.

in student affairs and influence how we understand both the process and content of student development and the student experience.

Our hope in this chapter is to illuminate both the more traditional approaches to theory, focusing on families of theories in particular, while also introducing readers to newer theoretical conceptualizations that extend, reframe, or reconceptualize foundational theoretical perspectives. More specifically, the purposes of this chapter are the following: (1) to provide the foundation for the theory chapters that follow by defining theory and distinguishing formal theory from those informal assumptions we use in our daily practice, (2) to explore current conceptualizations of families of theories and the characteristics of each family, including emerging theoretical conceptualizations; (3) to describe paradigmatic influences on the construction of theories, with attention to how and why theories evolve; and, (4) to consider the relationship between theories and student affairs practice.

## What Is Theory?

Noted author, Robert Coles, recounts an anecdote about himself as a young medical resident eager to treat a psychiatric patient (Coles, 1989). After spending a short amount of time with the patient and asking specific questions related to her medical history, he quickly diagnosed her condition. Still, the patient neither responded to him nor improved. Under the tutelage of a supervisor, Coles learns the importance of not only using medical shorthand to diagnose and categorize the condition of his patient, but truly listening to the patient's story in order to understand her and relate to her experiences. When he understood her unique stories, he found that the patient was more than a medical category. And consequently a caring connection was developed that allowed him to more effectively help her.

Through this anecdote, Coles illustrates the relationship between a theory and a story. How often do student affairs professionals quickly try to make sense of students by assigning theoretical language (in Coles's case, medical shorthand) based on brief observations or experiences rather than listening to stories? By doing so, are we "diagnosing" students and categorizing them with broad theories rather than honoring their individuality? Is it possible to learn, plan for, and respond to numerous and diverse students' individual stories without the benefit of theories to inform our understanding? Coles's anecdote asks us to think about the meaning of theory. What is a theory? How do we both honor individual stories and apply the abstract theories upon which they are based? These questions are woven throughout this chapter, but it is up to each of us to determine how to strike this artful balance.

Theories help to simplify and make sense of the complexities of life and represent "an attempt to organize and integrate knowledge and to answer the question 'why?'" (Patterson, 1986, p. xix). Although this is generally also true of our informal assumptions, the theories we describe in this text are different from the informal assumptions we carry about students and student affairs practice. Rodgers (1980) defined formal theory as "a set of propositions regarding the interrelationship of two or more conceptual variables relevant to some realm of phenomena. It provides a framework for explaining the relationship among variables and for empirical investigations" (p. 81). Strange and King (1990) defined a theory as "an abstract representation based on a potentially infinite number of specific and concrete variations of a phenomenon" (p. 17).

Starting with the Greek origin of theory, meaning "I behold," Coles (1989) explained that just as we behold a scene at a theater, when working with people we "hold something visual in our minds; presumably the theory is an enlargement of observation" (p. 20). Theory also offers a framework for understanding more than what is obvious from our observations. As Rabbi Abraham Heschel (n.d.) illuminated, "It is far easier to see what we know than to know what we see." In essence, theories in student affairs are grounded in the particularities of individual stories and experiences, and serve as a way to make sense of the diverse and complex nature of phenomena by reducing many aspects of a phenomenon into a more integrated representation (McEwen, 2003).

Although we try to construct theories that are true to the stories upon which they are based, empirical research does not mean the objective creation of theory. Coles (1989) recollected: "Remember, what you are hearing . . . is to some considerable extent a function of *you*, hearing" (p. 15, emphasis in original). Indeed, Knefelkamp suggested that all theory is autobiographical—that is, "theory represents the knowledge, experience, and worldviews of the theorists who construct it" (McEwen, 2003, p. 165). As socially constructed ideas, theories are developed within changing sociological, historical, and political contexts (McEwen). Depending on the worldview of the theorist, theory can therefore reinforce the status quo or societal power relationships, such as racism, heterosexism, and classism.

When applied with the understanding that theories are socially constructed and do not capture the diversity of all stories, theories serve at least six purposes. Theory is used to describe, explain, predict, influence outcomes, assess practice, and generate new knowledge and research (Knefelkamp, Widick, & Parker, 1978; McEwen, 2003; Moore & Upcraft, 1990). Sometimes one theory is appropriately applied in some respects for all six purposes, although some theories might serve some of these six purposes more effectively than others. For example, Cross's (1995) theory of black racial identity, an example of a student development theory, *describes* several stages that African American students experience as they develop a more complex understanding of their racial identity. Through its description of developmental stages, this theory also *explains* why students might behave in certain ways, for instance why some African American students might frequent Black cultural centers or prefer to sit together in the cafeteria (Tatum, 2003). Through this description and explanation, student affairs professionals can *predict* behavior and provide educational contexts that allow for this intentional gathering that Cross's theory espouses as integral to Black racial identity development. In this way, the theory can also be used to *influence outcomes* by encouraging particular educational contexts that intentionally foster the development of a student's Black identity, often with the assumption that a more complex identity is beneficial to the student. The theory can then be used to *assess* the educational contexts that are intended to foster development by determining whether or not educational contexts are indeed promoting development toward the more complex stages. Scholar-practitioners might see limitations to the stages Cross uses to describe Black racial identity development and choose to conduct research that builds upon his theory, thus *generating new knowledge and research*.

Student affairs professionals have numerous theories from which to choose, yet not all theories are of the same value or usefulness. Patterson (1986) described criteria to evaluate the value of a theory. Accordingly, theories should be: (1) important and relevant to everyday life; (2) precise and understandable; (3) simple and parsimonious; (4) comprehensive; (5) able to be operationalized; (6) empirically valid or verifiable; (7) able to generate new research and ideas; and (8) useful to practitioners (McEwen, 2003; Patterson). When determining a theory's value, it is also important to ask upon what population that theory is based. Does the theory apply only to individuals with those characteristics or more generally to other individuals (Knefelkamp et al., 1978)? This last consideration is especially important for considering how theories apply to diverse students and learning contexts. Indeed, Coles (1989) reminds us that theories need to be true to the stories of the individuals and situations upon which they are based.

## Theories in Student Affairs

A diverse array of theories provide the foundation for student affairs practice and are typically grouped together in what are referred to as "families" of theories or "theory clusters" (Knefelkamp et al., 1978, p. xi). This umbrella term incorporates those theories that are developmental and focus on the individual, including social identities; those that examine students in the collegiate context such as student success, engagement, and learning; theories that explain the relationship of campus environments to student development and success; and those focused on organizations and institutions of higher education.

The chapters that follow reflect this conceptualization of families of theories and each explores more fully a particular family and representative theories within each family. Although this conceptualization of theories as families is useful as an organizing heuristic, newer theories provide alternative theoretical explanations for understanding students, such as critical and poststructural approaches to student development (e.g., critical race theory and queer theory) or those grounded in a more holistic conception of overlapping theory families and intersecting theories (e.g., self-authorship and intersectionality). These theoretical frameworks push the boundaries of the more traditional template and offer new lenses through which to interpret student development and the student experience.

What follows is a brief summary of each of the theory families, including those newer theories that were not represented in the original conceptualization of theory families. Because they are foundational to the profession of student affairs and central to the philosophical commitment to the development of the whole person, student development theories are emphasized in this section.

## Developmental Theories

Theories of student development serve as a foundation for student affairs practice. The term *student* refers to the specific focus on those who are enrolled in higher education settings and *development* suggests that some kind of positive change occurs in the student (e.g., cognitive complexity, self-awareness, racial identity, and/or engagement). One of the earliest contributors to the scholarship on student development, Sanford (1967), defined development as the "organization of increasing complexity" (p. 47) and Rodgers (1990) extended this definition to focus on students, defining student development as: "the ways that a student grows, progresses, or increases his or her developmental capabilities as a result of enrollment in an institution of higher education" (p. 27). The focus of developmental theories gives us a lens for examining both the content of development (e.g., psychosocial theories) and the process of development (e.g., cognitive-structural theories). A few concepts are central to developmental theories and are briefly introduced here.

*Challenge and support.* One of the most fundamental theories to student development is Sanford's (1966) theory of challenge and support. Sanford suggested that students need an optimal balance of challenge and support for development to occur. That is, too much support and students are able to stay comfortable with what they know and experience, and too much challenge and the student becomes overwhelmed. In articulating the need for both challenge and support, Sanford implies that the campus environment interacts with the individual student in both putting into place people, policies, and programs that support students' development or impedes it with the imposition of too much challenge. As the scholarly base of student development theory evolved, we now understand that what constitutes challenge and support for different populations of students may vary. For example, what constitutes support for first generation college students may be distinct from those with parents who attended college. Further, differing cultural background among first generation students may also influence how support is constructed and perceived.

*Dissonance.* Nearly all developmental theories suggest that for development to occur, the individual must experience dissonance or "crisis." This crisis, as Widick et al. (1978) pointed out "is not a time of panic or disruption: It is a decision point—that moment when one reaches an intersection and must turn one way or the other" (pp. 3–4). The resulting interest in resolving the dissonance or crisis creates the conditions for development to occur. Dissonance may emerge from environmental forces, internal processes, or a combination of these.

*Stages, phases, statuses, vectors.* Many of the theories most often utilized in student affairs practice include terminology that suggests a placement or location along a continuum or on a map. Some of the language to convey these locations includes stages (e.g., Erikson, 1959/1980), statuses (e.g., Helms, 1995), vectors (e.g., Chickering, 1969), positions (e.g., Perry, 1968), perspectives (e.g., Belenky et al., 1986), types (e.g., Holland, 1966), frames (e.g., Bolman & Deal, 1991), dimensions (e.g., Jones & McEwen, 2000), or elements (e.g., Baxter Magolda, 2008). The differential language used signals the categorization of theories into specific "families," but also conveys underlying ideas about the process of development and worldviews about how students and their experiences are best understood. For example, Helms (1995) revised the terminology she used for her racial identity theories from stage to status in order to more adequately capture the fluid and dynamic nature of development. Likewise, poststructural theorists resist the use of terminology that suggests the possibility of categorizing or compartmentalizing something as complex as identity.

Regardless of the terminology used, the intent of these theorists was never to posit that the totality of a student's experiences and development could be understood through knowledge only of one's stage or dimension. Each is intended to capture some defining feature of an individual. Presumably, if a student affairs educator is able to assess where a student is cognitively or in relation to racial identity, for example, then the educator knows something about how that student understands oneself and the environment. Similarly, organizations or campus environments can be examined for central characteristics such as culture or climate and defined accordingly. For example, a campus culture that is defined as highly engaged or one described as possessing a chilly climate for women will provide clues to student affairs professionals about key areas for attention.

*Epigenetic principle and developmental trajectory.* One of the foundational principles in Erik Erikson's work on identity development is the epigenetic principle or the idea that "anything that grows has a ground plan . . . and out of this ground plan the parts arise, each part having its time of special ascendancy until all parts have arisen to form a functioning whole" (Erikson, 1959, p. 52). During the traditional college years, the epigenetic plan calls for the individual to address core identity questions such as "Who am I?" (Widick, Parker, & Knefelkamp, 1978). Although Erikson's work is specific to psychosocial development, the idea of a "ground plan" is consistent across and embedded in many theories of student development. That is, development occurs along a trajectory of simple to complex and in predictable stages or sequences. The content of development and the process of development will look different depending on the actual theory (e.g., cognitive, racial identity, psychosocial), but developmental movement is characterized by sequential movement along a trajectory. Newer theoretical frameworks for understanding student development, particularly the influence of the larger structures of privilege and oppression, question the centrality of a trajectory, who names the trajectory, and the role of context in defining progress.

What follows is a brief overview of what we consider to be the major clusters of theories within the family of developmental theories. It is important to note that some of the theories that focus on social identities (e.g., race, ethnicity, and sexuality) are developmental (e.g., GLBT identity), but not all are (e.g., queer theory); and newer conceptualizations suggest the importance of viewing social identities as intersecting and representing the overlap of psychosocial and cognitive domains of development.

## Psychosocial Development Theories

Psychosocial development theories are rooted in the work of Erik Erikson and as the term psychosocial implies, focus on the interaction of the individual with his/her social world. Psychosocial theories examine the content of development; that is what individuals are most concerned about in different time periods of the life cycle. These include values, identity, relationships, career and work, and family. Because of the emphasis on development across the life span, psychosocial theories include those that focus on adolescents, college students, and adults (e.g., Arnett, 2004; Chickering & Reisser, 1993; Erikson, 1959; Josselson, 1987, 1996; Levinson, 1986; Marcia, 1966).

## Cognitive Development Theories

Cognitive-structural theories, anchored in the work of Jean Piaget, focus on the structure of thinking applied to the content of those psychosocial issues identified above. This structure provides an information processing filter that enables the individual to make sense of experiences and new encounters in the world and evolves from more simple to increasing complexity (King, 1978; McEwen, 2003). Most cognitive-structural theories are hierarchical and sequential with each stage representing a more complex way of making meaning. In student affairs, the work of William Perry serves as the foundation for many of the cognitive-structural theories in use. In addition, theories of moral development and faith development are also considered cognitive-structural (e.g., Fowler, 1981; Gilligan, 1993; Kohlberg, 1972).

## Social Identity Theories

Theories comprising the category of social identities are those that focus on "those roles *or* membership categories that a person claims as representative" (Deaux, 1993, p. 6) and include theories of racial identity (e.g., Helms, 1995), ethnic identity (e.g., Phinney, 1990; Torres, 2003), cultural identity (e.g., Yon, 2000); sexual identity (e.g., Cass, 1979; Fassinger & Arseneau, 2007), gender identity (e.g., Downing & Roush, 1985; Kimmel, 2008); religion (e.g., Parks, 2000), disability (e.g., Fine & Asch, 2000; Gibson, 2006), and social class (e.g., hooks, 2000). A number of these particular social identities are under-researched; however, new insights into social identities are gleaned from theoretical frameworks that incorporate the influence of structures of power and oppression on development and the student experience. Further, a number of social identity scholars are emphasizing the importance of examining social identities in relation to one another, rather as discrete units of analysis (e.g., Dill, McLaughlin, & Nieves, 2007; Weber, 2001).

## Emerging Theoretical Perspectives

Although not created with college students in mind, several theoretical perspectives are emerging as useful to new interpretations of college student development and the college experience. Examples include critical race theory (e.g., Delgado & Stefancic, 2001), queer theory (e.g., Sullivan, 2003), and intersectionality (Dill et al., 2007) and each may be used to both critique and reconceptualize existing theoretical frameworks. Although theoretically distinct, these theories share in common an interest in problematizing the "grand narratives" (Lyotard, 1984) and taken for granted dimensions of the college experience. They also emphasize the centrality of power and the importance of social change. For example, an intersectional approach foregrounds the individual's simultaneous location in multiple social identities such as race, class, and gender and suggests that individuals operate within systems of both privilege and oppression (e.g., Dill et al.). Understanding the experience of a White male student with a disability requires examining both the privilege associated with gender and the oppression attached to disability, as well as the interplay between the two. Intersectionality both illuminates the individual lived experience but necessarily situates the individual within larger structures of inequality.

## Theories Emphasizing Holistic Development

Extending the work of Robert Kegan (1982, 1994) Baxter Magolda (2001, 2008), based upon extensive longitudinal research, crafted a theory of self-authorship that is defined as "a developmental capacity" (Baxter Magolda, 2008, p. 269) and as holistic because of the interrelated domains of interpersonal, identity, and cognitive development (Baxter Magolda, 2008). Additional research, using diverse samples, (e.g., Abes, Jones, & McEwen, 2007; Torres & Hernandez, 2007) highlights the promise of conceptualizing development as holistic in order to illuminate the importance of contextual influences such as privilege and oppression (Jones, 2009). In these studies, confronting racism as a developmental task and integral to holistic development (Torres & Hernandez), the role of context in prompting a more fluid and complex intersection of cognitive, interpersonal, and identity domains of development (Abes, Jones, & McEwen), and the interaction of privileged and oppressed identities in relation to holistic development (Jones, 2009) all emerged as significant findings.

## Theories of Organizations and Campus Environments

Theories that focus on organizations, organizational behavior, and campus environments (e.g., Banning, 1989; Bolman & Deal, 1991; Strange & Banning, 2001) emphasize the influence of these larger entities on student development and the student experience as well as the interactions among these. For example, the ways in which campus policies are created reflect particular views of organizations and come together to create a campus culture and an environment that promotes or impedes student success.

## Student Success Theories

New research builds upon what is known about student involvement (e.g., Astin, 1984) and student success (e.g., Braxton, 2003; Perna & Thomas, 2008; Tinto, 1993) to illuminate student engagement (e.g., Kuh, Kinzie, Schuh, & Whitt, 2005). That is, what is it that institutions can do to promote student success along outcomes determined to be central to the student experience, such as student development?

## Typology Models

Typology models (covered only very briefly in this text) differ from many of the other theories useful in student affairs practice because they emphasize what are considered to be more persistent individual traits and characteristics such as personality type (e.g., Jung, 1923/1971), learning style (e.g., Kolb, 1984) and vocational choice (e.g., Holland, 1966). Although it is tempting to identify a person by their type, typology models are nonevaluative (Evans, 2003) and not meant to suggest rigidity in type.

## Paradigmatic Influences on the Construction and Application of Theory

How is it that we move from the particularities of individual stories to the construction of the formal theories used in student affairs practice? Unlike our informal assumptions, empirical research, both qualitative and quantitative, is used to generate and validate formal theories. For instance, grounded theory methodology is one qualitative approach to constructing a theory (Strauss & Corbin, 1990). The art and science of grounded theory, which is an inductive approach to theory creation using stories gathered through interviews and other sources, is to create a theory that is general enough to describe the experiences of all of the participants, but also stays true to the particularities of each individual's stories. Quantitative research, which relies on statistical analysis of numerical data typically accessed through surveys or questionnaires, is a more deductive approach and can also be used to generate theory. Derived usually from large samples, these theories offer a broad perspective on college students and their experiences.

Regardless of the research method used to create theory, our identities, experiences, and worldviews, also known as subjectivities (Fine, 1994), influence theory construction. To the extent possible, theorists should be aware of this influence and, although they cannot entirely know the influence of their subjectivities, since we are all often unaware of perspectives beyond our field of vision (much like a fish unaware of the water in which it swims), there are certain subjectivities about which it is important to be explicit. Specifically, it is important to make clear the research paradigm that guided the theory construction. In addition to reviewing paradigms that have traditionally been used in the creation of student affairs theories, we emphasize in this section paradigms that address social inequities in student affairs and move toward intercultural theories (Tanaka, 2002).

A paradigm, often referred to as a worldview, is a "set of interconnected or related assumptions or beliefs" that guides thinking and behavior (Jones, Torres, & Arminio, 2006, p. 9). Every research paradigm consists of assumptions about the nature of reality (ontology), knowledge (epistemology), and how knowledge is accessed (methodology) (Guba & Lincoln, 2005). Depending on the nature of these assumptions, a paradigm influences the questions guiding the research from which a theory is created; whose stories are included in the research; how the researcher hears the stories; and how the researcher retells the stories. In his notable work, *The Structure of Scientific Revolution*, Kuhn (1962) described how new paradigms emerge as the limitations of previous ones become apparent. With the emergence of new paradigms, contemporary student affairs theorists are diversifying the assumptions behind theory construction, resulting in more inclusive theories that challenge dominant or normative understandings of students and student affairs practice.

We briefly review and provide examples of a few of the traditional and emerging paradigms that have been used to create theories about college students. Whether creating theory, applying theory in practice, or developing and refining one's professional philosophy, it is important to be aware that the worldviews that guide theory creation are not merely scholarly terms saved for rigorous research, but philosophical beliefs that shape our practice as we apply theory to understand diverse student populations. Theory construction is a dynamic process that informs and is informed by practice and therefore matters to all who work with college students.

Two of the paradigms that have traditionally been used in the context of student affairs are positivism and constructivism. Here we review some of their basic elements, as well as strengths and limitations that are important to consider when creating and applying theories.

*Positivism:* Positivism assumes the existence of one reality and that knowledge is objectively knowable, measurable, and predictable through inquiry in which the researcher is removed from the object of study (Lincoln & Guba, 2000). For instance, in the early phases of her longitudinal study, Baxter Magolda used a positivist framework as she began her study of epistemological development (Baxter Magolda, 2004). She assumed an objective stance separate from the research participants to categorize students into developmental stages. She put the theory in the foreground and students in the back, seeking to fit the participants into an unchanging theory. Although this framework offers predictability, consistency, and a timeless nature in research results, (which is considered a strength to some), it does not allow for differences in interpretation based on diverse identities and perspectives or allow for the influence of changing contexts on interpretation.

*Constructivism:* In later phases of her longitudinal research, Baxter Magolda (1992, 2001) transitioned to a constructivist paradigm. She explained that constructivism allows her to understand students' experiences and ways of making meaning in more depth than the positivist approaches that boxed students into preexisting categories (Baxter Magolda, 2004). Constructivism, also sometimes referred to as interpretivism, is grounded in the notion that multiple realities exist and that knowledge is co-constructed between the researcher and participants (Lincoln & Guba, 2000). Methodologically, constructivist research typically seeks to understand reality through dialogue (Lincoln & Guba). Using a constructivist approach, Baxter Magolda put the students' stories before existing theories, allowing her to see multiple possibilities in how to interpret students' stories based on their individuality, changing contexts, and her own subjectivities. She found that she was able to reshape existing theory rather than only testing it. With the limitations of positivism becoming more apparent, much of the contemporary research on student development is grounded in constructivist perspectives.

Although constructivist theories allow for the participants' voices to more prominently make their way into theory, this paradigm, however, does not intentionally address how power structures, such as racism, classism, and heterosexism, have shaped theory. Here we review how two theoretical frameworks that address these concerns have emerged as a way to interpret student experiences and deconstruct theories used in student affairs:

*Critical Theory:* Critical perspectives uncover how invisible power structures shape whose stories are told and how they are heard in the construction of student affairs theories. Critical theory calls for a "radical restructuring [of] society toward the ends of reclaiming historic cultural legacies, social justice, the redistribution of power and the achievement of truly democratic societies" (Lincoln & Denzin, 2000, p. 1056). The goal of critical theory is "a society in which all people, regardless of their economic and cultural backgrounds have a voice in decisions affecting their lives" (Rhoads & Black, 1995, p. 416). An important element of critical theory is its praxis component, meaning that research should be tied into action that changes society in a socially just way. Examples of the use of critical theory to critique student affairs practice include work that unpacks the power dynamics associated with service-learning (Butin, 2005); fraternities (Rhoads, 1995); and the rituals associated with campus tours (Magolda, 2000).

One critical perspective especially worth noting is critical race theory. Critical race theorists seek to illuminate how society is structured along racial lines and then transform this condition. Among its central tenets are that racism is an inherent part of society, that race is a social construction, and that addressing racism depends on hearing the narratives of people of color (Delgado & Stefancic, 2001). Examples of the use of critical race theory to understand student affairs practice include a study of Chicana/o student peer groups (Villalpando, 2003) and facilitating dialogues about racial realities (Quaye, 2008); and both demonstrate the centrality of race in daily practices and interactions.

*Poststructural Theories*: Poststructural theories explore how the power structures that are invisibly woven into society construct reality and the meaning of normal (Lather, 2007). Unlike critical theorists who seek to transform society in a particular way, poststructuralists assume there are multiple possibilities for how society ought to be structured (Rhoads & Black, 1995). Poststructural theories therefore describe identity as a fluid process (Sullivan, 2003) and suggest that a singular story of development is impossible to tell and that, in fact, "refusing definition is part of the theoretical scene" (Lather, p. 5).

Queer theory is one example of a poststructuralist theory. Queer theory brings poststructural concerns to sexuality studies and is effective for addressing power dynamics because of its focus on challenging the heteronormativity in identity constructions. Heteronormativity is the unexamined and prevalent societal assumption that normal is defined through heterosexuality (e.g., Britzman, 1997). Still an emerging perspective, queer theory has been used to challenge heteronormative assumptions about how college students develop and suggests multiple and fluid possibilities for how development might be conceptualized (Abes & Kasch, 2007).

## How Theories Evolve

Representing one worldview, all paradigms are incomplete (Kuhn, 1962). The use of emerging paradigms or even multiple paradigms is therefore one way in which theories evolve to more effectively help us understand college students (Abes, 2009). As the nature of college students evolve, so too must theories used in student affairs. New research questions must be asked and new methodological approaches utilized, both as critiques of the limitations of existing theories and as ways to build upon these theories as new insights are generated. Not only are students and student affairs practice changing, but also are the identities of the theorists. Researcher subjectivities drive the nature of the research questions asked, and the identities of those applying these theories in practice reveals both strengths and limitations in theory development, prompting the need for continuous inquiry into this complex field.

## Relationships of Theories to Student Affairs Practice

Student affairs educators are frequently faced with complex decisions in their daily practice. Consistent with the goals of student affairs, our roles often include overlapping responsibilities and obligations to promote student development, design campus environments that are educationally purposefully, and understand higher education as an organization (McEwen, 2003). Theories provide an important and necessary lens through which to engage our roles and responsibilities and make decisions. Theories do not inform us about what exactly to do, but provide student affairs educators with a way to think about how to interpret individuals, environments, and organizations. Although some may argue that student affairs educators could be effective without using theory to guide their practice, an important indicator of professional competence is knowledge of the theoretical foundation of the field (Pope & Reynolds, 1997).

When applying theory to practice in student affairs it is important to remember, as Perry (1981) cautioned, students always remain larger than their categories. Theories are meant to provide an interpretive lens for what a student affairs educator is anticipating, witnessing, or planning. Let's look at an example:

## Scenario

During the week-long Resident Assistant training, one session on "appreciating diversity" utilized the well-known "Privilege Walk" activity. The facilitator, a White woman and new residence hall director fresh out of graduate school believed it was a great way to help students understand the concepts of privilege, racism, and oppression. Lining up the RAs, she instructed the group to take a step forward or backward, to represent their responses to a series of statements. She begins:

> If your ancestors were forced to come to the U.S. take one step back.
>
> If you were raised in a rented apartment, or house, take one step back.
>
> If you were ever called names because of your race, ethnicity, or sexual orientation, take one step back.
>
> If you were taken to plays or art galleries by your parents, take one step forward.

As she moved through her list, the resident director noticed that the RAs who were members of underrepresented racial/ethnic groups appeared to not be paying attention any more and chatting about other things. Meanwhile, the White males were competing with one another for "first place." At the conclusion of the activity, the resident director began processing the Privilege Walk and almost immediately conflict in the group erupted.
An American Indian male began:

> I don't know why we need yet another activity to remind students of color of "their place" in this world. This activity seems designed to reinforce all kinds of stereotypes and assumptions about who I am and where I come from.

To which a White female RA responded:

> I think you are taking this way too personally. I think it is so good that we are talking about these issues.

And a Latina student retorted:

> Well, this is easy for you to say. You have the luxury of obliviousness. I do take this personally, because it is personal, it is my life! (Jones, 2008)

How might a student affairs educator utilize theories to make sense of what took place in this scenario and then develop an appropriate response? First, it is very important for a practitioner to evaluate the assumptions brought to an interpretation of a particular situation. When thinking about identifying and applying theories to practice, it behooves student affairs educators to look inward and consider how their own experiences, biases, and assumptions may predispose them to one set of theories over others. This scenario might be interpreted through the theoretical lens of racial or ethnic identity theory. However, an emphasis given to individuals alone may miss the larger consideration of the organizational culture in residence life that perpetuates training activities that promote learning for some at the expense of others.

Second, because of the complexity of much of our work it is rare that one theory will carry enough explanatory power for a particular phenomenon so that when applying theory to practice, theories often are used in combination. In this scenario, a student affairs educator might begin by considering the racial identity of each individual (e.g., Helms' theories of White Racial Identity and People of Color Racial Identity) as well as the other social identities that may be salient for each individual (e.g., Jones & McEwen's Model of Multiple Dimensions of Identity). This might help explain why the White woman was not attuned to the emotional impact of the Privilege Walk activity and why the American Indian man was perceived as lashing out. Further understanding may be gleaned from adding a cognitive theory dimension to the application as the White woman appears to be viewing this situation in a less cognitively complex way than are the students of color, perhaps the result of differing lived experiences. In addition, an organizational analysis provides another lens as this activity may both be reflective of a particular organizational culture and impact the climate of the R.A. staff. Drawing from a critical race theory interpretation necessitates an analysis of this situation in relation to the omnipresence of racism and discrimination in the U.S. It is important to recognize that in this scenario, as in practice, student affairs educators rarely possess all there is to know about a particular situation, individual, or dilemma. Therefore, theories guide us toward potential and plausible interpretations, but these should never be viewed as *the* one way to understand what is going on. Consulting with trusted colleagues is very helpful in applying theories to practice, especially when doing so with someone who might not share the same social identities or background experiences.

Third, applying theories to practice takes practice. Because no situation or individual is ever exactly the same, no precise recipes exist for which theories to use under which set of circumstances. Surely, there are clear indicators of fit and mismatch, but each theory applied to a particular phenomenon will illuminate a different part of the story. Theories evolve so staying current with theory generation and scholarly literature is important to applying theory to practice. Student affairs educators now have far greater and deeper repertoire of theories from which to choose than was the case 20 years ago.

## Conclusion

The chapters that follow provide more in depth descriptions of theories that provide the foundation for the student affairs profession. We have a rich and varied body of theory from which to draw and it is important to read primary sources rather than to only rely on summaries of these theories. As noted in this chapter, theories continue to evolve because of new questions, new students, new methodological approaches, and in relation to who is developing and applying theories. However, those early theories that guided the field need not be discarded completely. As you continue to study, understand, and apply theories and theoretical perspectives that inform student affairs research and practice you will discern those constructs and themes that are enduring as well as important points of departure. Finally, as your knowledge of theories becomes more robust, you will see that indeed, there is nothing as useful as a good theory.

## References

Abes, E. S. (2009). Theoretical borderlands: Using multiple theoretical perspectives to challenge inequitable power structures in student development theory. *Journal of College Student Development, 50,* 141–156.

Abes, E. S., & Kasch, D. (2007). Using queer theory to explore lesbian college students' multiple dimensions of identity. *Journal of College Student Development, 48,* 619–636.

Abes, E. S., Jones, S. R., & McEwen, M. K. (2007). Reconceptualizing the Model of Multiple Dimensions of Identity: The role of meaning-making capacity in the construction of multiple identities. *Journal of College Student Development, 48,* 1–22.

Arnett, J. J. (2004). *Emerging adulthood: The winding road from the late teens through the twenties.* New York: Oxford University Press.

Astin, A. W. (1984). Student involvement: A developmental theory for higher education. *Journal of College Student Personnel, 25,* 297–308.

Banning, J. (1989). Creating a climate for successful student development: The campus ecology manager role. In U. Delworth, G. Hanson, & Associates, *Student services: A Handbook for the profession* (2nd ed., pp. 304–322). San Francisco: Jossey-Bass.

Baxter Magolda, M. B. (1992). *Knowing and reasoning in college: Gender-related patterns in students' intellectual development* (1st ed.). San Francisco: Jossey-Bass.

Baxter Magolda, M. B. (2001). Making their own way: Narratives for transforming higher education to promote self-development. Sterling, Va.: Stylus.

Baxter Magolda, M. B. (2004). Evolution of a constructivist conceptualization of epistemological reflection. *Educational Psychologist, 39*(1), 31–42.

Baxter Magolda, M. B. (2008). Three elements of self-authorship. *Journal of College Student Development, 49,* 269–284.

Belenky, M. F., Clinchy, B. M., Goldberger, N. R., & Tarule, J. M. (1986). *Women's ways of knowing: The development of self, voice, and mind.* New York: Basic Books.

Bolman, L. & Deal, T. (1991). *Reframing organizations.* San Francisco: Jossey-Bass.

Braxton, J. M. (2003). Student success. In S. R. Komives, D. B. Woodard, Jr., & Associates (Eds.), *Student services: A handbook for the profession* (pp. 317–335). San Francisco: Jossey-Bass.

Britzman, D. P. (1997). What is this thing called love?: New discourses for understanding gay and lesbian youth. In S. de Castell & M. Bryson (Eds.), *Radical in(ter)ventions: Identity, politics, and difference/s on educational praxis* (pp. 183–207). Albany: State University of New York Press.

Butin, D. W. (2005). Disturbing normalizations of service-learning. In D. W. Butin (Ed.), *Service-learning in higher education* (vii–xx). New York: Palgrave Macmillan.

Cass, V. C. (1979). Homosexual identity formation: A theoretical model. *Journal of Homosexuality, 4,* 219–235.

Chickering, A. W. (1969). *Education and identity*. San Francisco: Jossey-Bass.

Chickering, A. W., & Reisser, L. (1993). *Education and identity, second edition*. San Francisco: CA: Jossey-Bass.

Coles, R. (1989). *The call of stories: Teaching and the moral imagination*. Boston, MA: Houghton Mifflin.

Cross, W. E., Jr. (1995). The psychology of Nigrescence: Revising the Cross model. In J. G. Ponterotto, J. M. Casas, L. A. Suzuki, & C. M. Alexander (Eds.). *Handbook of multicultural counseling* (pp. 93–122). Thousand Oaks, CA: Sage Publications.

Deaux, K. (1993). Reconstructing social identity. *Personality and Social Psychology Bulletin, 19,* 4–12.

Delgado, R., & Stefancic, J. (2001). *Critical race theory: An introduction*. NY: New York University Press.

Dill, B. T., McLaughlin, A. E., & Nieves, A. D. (2007). Future directions of feminist research: Intersectionality. In S. N. Hesse-Biber (Ed.), *Handbook of feminist research* (p. 629–637). Thousand Oaks, CA: Sage.

Downing, N. E., & Roush, K. L. (1985). From passive acceptance to active commitment: A model of feminist identity development for women. *Counseling Psychologist, 13,* 695–709.

Erikson, E. H. (1980). *Identity and the life cycle*. New York: W. W. Norton & Company. (Original work published 1959).

Evans, N. J. (2003). Psychological, cognitive, and typological perspectives on student development. In S. R. Komives, D. B. Woodard, Jr., & Associates (Eds.), *Student services: A handbook for the profession* (pp. 179–202). San Francisco: Jossey-Bass.

Fassinger, R. E., & Arseneau, J. R. (2007). "I'd rather get wet than be under that umbrella": Experiences and identities of lesbian, gay, bisexual, and transgender people. In K. J. Bieschke, R. M. Perez, & K. A. DeBord (Eds.), *Handbook of counseling and psychotherapy with lesbian, gay, bisexual, and transgender clients* (pp. 19–49). Washington, DC: American Psychological Association.

Fine, M. (1994). Working the hyphens: Reinventing self and other in qualitative research. In N. K. Denzin & Y. S. Lincoln (Eds.), *Handbook of qualitative research* (pp. 70–82). Thousand Oaks, CA: Sage.

Fine, M., & Asch, A. (2000). Disability beyond stigma: Social interaction, discrimination, and activism. In M. Adams, W. J. Blumenfeld, R. Castaneda, H. W. Hackman, M. L. Peters, & X. Zuniga (Eds.), *Readings for diversity and social justice* (pp. 330–339). New York: Routledge.

Fowler, J. (1981). *Stages of faith: The psychology of human development and the quest for meaning*. New York: Harper & Row.

Gibson, J. (2006). Disability and clinical competency: An introduction. *The California Psychologist, 39,* 6–10.

Gilligan, C. (1993). *In a different voice: Psychological theory and women's development*. Cambridge, MA: Harvard University Press. (Original work published in 1982.)

Guba, E. G., & Lincoln, Y. S. (2005). Paradigmatic controversies, contradictions, and emerging confluences. In N. K. Denzin & Y. S. Lincoln (Eds.). *The SAGE handbook of qualitative research* (pp. 191–215). Thousand Oaks, CA: SAGE Publications.

Helms, J. E. (1995). An update of Helms's white and people of color racial identity models. In J. G. Ponterotto, J. M. Casas., L. A. Suzuki, & C. M. Alexander (Eds.), *Handbook of multicultural counseling* (pp. 181–198). Thousand Oaks, CA: Sage.

Holland, J. (1966). *The psychology of vocational choice*. Waltham, MA: Blaisdell.

hooks, bell. (2000). *Where we stand: Class matters*. New York: Routledge.

Jones, S. R. (2008). Student resistance to cross-cultural engagement: Annoying distraction or site for transformative learning? In S. R. Harper (Ed.), *Creating inclusive campus environments* (pp. 67–85). Washington, DC: NASPA.

Jones, S. R. (2009). Constructing identities at the intersections: An autoethnographic exploration of multiple dimensions of identity. *Journal of College Student Development, 50,* 287–304.

Jones, S. R., & McEwen, M. K. (2000). A conceptual model of multiple dimensions of identity. *Journal of College Student Development, 41,* 405–414.

Jones, S. R., Torres, V., & Arminio, J. (2006). *Negotiating the complexities of qualitative research in higher education: Fundamental elements and issues*. New York: Routledge.

Josselson, R. (1987). *Finding herself: Pathways to identity development in women*. San Francisco: Jossey-Bass.

Josselson, R. (1996). *Revising herself: The story of women's identity from college to midlife*. San Francisco: Jossey-Bass.

Jung, C. (1923/1971). *Psychological types.* Volume 6 of *The collected works of C. G. Jung.* Princeton, NJ: Princeton University Press.

Kegan, R. (1982). *The evolving self: Problem and process in human development.* Cambridge, MA: Harvard University Press.

Kegan, R. (1994). *In over our heads: The mental demands of modern life.* Cambridge, MA: Harvard University Press.

Kimmel, M. (2008). *Guyland: The perilous world where boys become men.* New York: Harper Collins.

King, P. M. (1978). William Perry's theory of intellectual and ethical development. In L. L. Knefelkamp, C. Widick, & C. A. Parker (Eds.), *Applying new developmental findings* (New Directions for Student Services, No. 4, pp. 35–51). San Francisco: Jossey-Bass.

Knefelkamp, L. L. (1982). Faculty and student development in the '80s: Renewing the community of scholars. In H. F. Owens, C. H. Witten, & W. R. Bailey (Eds.), *College student personnel administration: An anthology* (pp. 373–391). Springfield, IL: Charles C. Thomas.

Knefelkamp, L., Widick, C., & Parker, C. (1978). *Applying new developmental findings* (New Directions for Student Services, No. 4). San Francisco: Jossey-Bass.

Kohlberg, L. (1972). A cognitive-developmental approach to moral education. *Humanist, 6,* 13–16.

Kolb, D. A. (1984). *Experiential learning: Experience as the source of learning and development.* Englewood Cliffs, NJ: Prentice Hall.

Kuh, G. D., Kinzie, J., Schuh, J. H., Whitt, E. H., & Associates (2005). *Student success in college: Creating conditions that matter.* San Francisco: Jossey-Bass.

Kuhn, T. S. (1962). The structure of scientific revolutions. Chicago: University of Chicago Press.

Lather, P. (2007). *Getting lost: Feminist efforts toward a double(d) science.* Albany, NY: State University of New York Press.

Levinson, D. J. (1986). A conception of adult development. *American Psychologist, 41,* 3–13.

Lincoln, Y. S., & Denzin, N. K. (2000). The seventh movement: Out of the past. In Denzin, N. K. & Lincoln, Y. S. (Eds.), *Handbook of qualitative research* (2nd ed., pp. 1047–1065). San Francisco: Sage.

Lincoln, Y. S., & Guba, E. G. (2000). Paradigmatic controversies, contradictions, and emerging confluences. In Denzin, N. K. & Lincoln, W. S. (Eds.), *Handbook of qualitative research* (2nd ed., pp. 163–188). San Francisco: Sage.

Lyotard, J-F. (1984). *The postmodern condition: A report on knowledge (theory and history of literature, volume 10).* Manchester, United Kingdom: Manchester University Press.

Magolda, P. M. (2000). The campus tour ritual: Exploring community discourses in higher education. *Anthropology and Education Quarterly, 31*(1), 24–36.

Marcia, J. E. (1966). Development and validation of ego-identity status. *Journal of Personality and Social Psychology, 3,* 551–558.

McEwen, M. K. (2003). The nature and uses of theory. In S. R. Komives, D. B. Woodard, Jr., & Associates (Eds.), *Student services: A handbook for the profession* (pp. 153–178). San Francisco: Jossey-Bass.

Moore, L. V., & Upcraft, M. L. (1990). Theory in student affairs: Evolving perspectives. In L. V. Moore (Ed.), *evolving theoretical perspectives on students* (New Directions for Student Services, No. 51, pp. 3–23). San Francisco: Jossey-Bass.

Parks, S. D. (2000). *Big questions, worthy dreams: Mentoring young adults in their search for meaning, purpose, and faith.* San Francisco: Jossey-Bass.

Patterson, C. H. (1986). *Theories of counseling and psychotherapy* (4th ed.). New York: Harper & Row.

Perna, L. W., & Thomas, S. L. (2008). *Theoretical perspectives on student success: Understanding the contribution of the disciplines.* ASHE Higher Education Report (Vol. 34, No. 1). San Francisco: Jossey-Bass.

Perry, W. G., Jr. (1968). *Forms of intellectual and ethical development in the college years: A scheme.* New York: Holt, Rinehart, & Winston.

Perry, W. G., Jr. (1981). Cognitive and ethical growth: The making of meaning. In A. W. Chickering and Associates (Eds.), *The modern American college: Responding to the new realities of diverse students and a changing society* (pp. 76–116). San Francisco: Jossey-Bass.

Phinney, J. S. (1990). Ethnic identity in adolescents and adults: Review of research. *Psychological Bulletin, 108,* 499–514.

Pope, R. L., & Reynolds, A. L. (1997). Student affairs core competencies: Integrating multicultural awareness, knowledge, and skills. *Journal of College Student Development, 38,* 266–277.

Quaye, S. J. (2008). *Pedagogy and racialized ways of knowing: Students and faculty engage racial realities in postsecondary classrooms.* Unpublished doctoral dissertation, The Pennsylvania State University.

Rhoads, R. A. (1995). Whale tales, dog piles, and beer goggles: An ethnographic case study of fraternity life. *Anthropology and Education Quarterly, 26,* 306–323.

Rhoads, R. A., & Black, M. A. (1995). Student affairs practitioners as transformative educators: Advancing a critical cultural perspective. *Journal of College Student Development, 36,* 413–421.

Rodgers, R. F. (1980). Theories underlying student development. In D. G. Creamer (Ed.), *Student development in higher education* (pp. 10–95). Cincinnati, OH: American College Personnel Association.

Rodgers, R. F. (1990). Recent theories and research underlying student development. In D. G. Creamer & Associates, *College student development: Theory and practice for the 1990s* (pp. 27–79). Alexandria, VA: American College Personnel Association.

Sanford, N. (1966). *Self and society.* New York: Atherton Press.

Sanford, N. (1967). *Where colleges fail: A study of the student as a person.* San Francisco: Jossey-Bass.

Strange, C. C., & Banning, J. (2001). *Educating by design: Creating campus learning environments that work.* San Francisco: Jossey-Bass.

Strange, C. C., & King, P. M. (1990). The professional practice of student development. In D. G. Creamer (Ed.), *College student development: Theory and practice for the 1990s* (pp. 9–24). Alexandria, VA: American College Personnel Association.

Strauss, A., & Corbin, J. (1990). *Basics of qualitative research: Grounded theory procedures and techniques.* Newbury Park, CA: Sage.

Sullivan, N. (2003). *A critical introduction to queer theory.* New York: New York University Press.

Tanaka, G. (2002). Higher education's self-reflexive turn: Toward an intercultural theory of student development. *The Journal of Higher Education, 73*(2), 263–296.

Tatum, B. D. (2003). *Why are all the Black kids sitting together in the cafeteria* (2nd ed.). New York: Basic Books.

Tinto, V. (1993). *Leaving college: Rethinking the causes and cures of student attrition* (2nd ed.) Chicago: University of Chicago Press.

Torres, V. (2003). Influences on ethnic identity development of Latino college students in the first two years of college. *Journal of College Student Development, 44,* 532–547.

Torres, V., & Hernandez, E. (2007). The influence of ethnic identity on self-authorship: A longitudinal study of Latino/a college students. *Journal of College Student Development, 48,* 558–573.

Villalpando, O. (2003). Self-segregation or self-preservation? A critical race theory and Latino/a critical theory analysis of a study of Chicano college students. *Qualitative Studies in Education, 16,* 619–646.

Weber, L. (2001). *Understanding race, class, gender, and sexuality: A conceptual framework.* New York: McGraw-Hill.

Widick, C., Parker, C., & Knefelkamp, L. L. (1978). Erik Erikson and psychosocial development. In L. L. Knefelkamp, C. Widick, & C. A. Parker (Eds.), *Applying new developmental findings* (New Directions for Student Services, No. 4, pp. 1–17). San Francisco: Jossey-Bass.

Yon, D. (2000). *Elusive culture: Schooling, race, and identity in global times.* New York: State University of New York Press.

# CHAPTER 2
# STUDENT DEVELOPMENT: THE EVOLUTION
# AND STATUS OF AN ESSENTIAL IDEA

## CARNEY STRANGE

This article illustrates the evolution of the concept of student development in the higher education and student affairs literature. The current status of this concept is presented in a framework of 14 propositions as an agenda for scholars and practitioners in the field.

From the early Colonial colleges to the current era of the multiversity, American higher education has concerned itself with the development of individual students for positions of societal leadership and influence. In the "age of the college" (Hofstadter, 1955), a period from the first institutions in America until just prior to the Civil War, preparation of the "gentleman scholar" was compelled by a vision of character development emphasizing command of the classics and refinement of civilized graces. With the inception of modern behavioral sciences in the subsequent "age of the university" (Metzger, 1955), a vision of human development emerged that focused on complex, measurable traits and systems of thought, emotions, motivations, and capacities, presumed to culminate in an integrated state of maturity. The human personality was seen as a function of numerous underlying dimensions that manifested themselves in a variety of observable behaviors and actions. This view was given further credence in the growth of the occupational aptitude assessment movement following the First World War as concepts of human personality traits were applied to the selection and training of personnel in industry and the vocational advisement of students on the college campus. It is this latter vision of development, grounded in the study of human psychology and sociology, that has persisted into the last decade of the Twentieth Century. Over the last 50 years in particular, this vision has been proffered in the academy by professionals in student affairs under the rubric of "student development."

What are the philosophical and educational roots of this vision? What are the implications of its knowledge base for the design and practice of education, both in and out of the classroom, in our American system of higher learning? These questions are addressed in a sequence of five articles. First, I identify what I believe to be some of the foundations of student development in the form of a very brief historical outline of two principal educational movements of the Twentieth Century; I then summarize the current status and meaning of the extant student development knowledge base in the form of propositional statements emanating from a collective of exemplary models and theories in the literature. Second, Patricia King addresses the adequacy and relevance of this knowledge base as a theoretical

---

Strange, C. (1994). Student development: The evolution and status of an essential idea. *Journal of College Student Development*, 35, 399–412.

framework for understanding students and their interactions with our higher education systems. Third, Patrick Terenzini examines the implications of this knowledge base for shaping a future research agenda in American higher education. Fourth, Michael Coomes explores the meaning of these propositions for how campus administrators conceive and implement educational policies. Fifth, Lee Upcraft addresses the dilemmas and challenges of transferring these propositions to the design and conduct of student affairs practice in higher education.

## A Recent Historical Overview

Although rooted in the fundamental tenets of Neohumanism (emphasizing the primary importance of human interests, values, and dignity), Instrumentalism (emphasizing the value of ideas in human experience and progress), and Rationalism (emphasizing self-evident propositional forms of knowledge), student development, as constructed by current scholars, has been fueled particularly by several key philosophical and educational movements of the Twentieth Century. From the Progressive Education Movement of the 1920s (Mayhew, 1977) came an emphasis on student self-direction, the importance of experiential learning techniques, the role of educators as resource guides rather than task masters, the importance of establishing comprehensive evaluative records, and the need for education to work closely with other societal institutions to effect the total development of students. It was within this context that the American Council on Education commissioned the Student Personnel Point of View (American Council on Education, 1937), advocating attention to holistic learning and individual differences in responding to college student needs. Reflecting this same orientation, campus educators and professional association leaders began to call attention to the implications of these tenets for campus personnel practices and for student learners. For example, Jack E. Walters, Director of Personnel in the School of Engineering at Purdue University, and President of the American College Personnel Association from 1930 to 1933, authored monographs entitled *Student Development: How to Make the Most of College Life* (Walters, 1931) and *Individualizing Education by Means of Applied Personnel Procedures* (Walters, 1935), extolling further the importance of holistic development and student responsibility in the educational process. These same themes were underscored once again, following the Second World War, as requisites for global democratic reform in *The Student Personnel Point of View, 1949* (American Council on Education, 1949).

Postulates of the Nontraditional Education Movement of the 1960s (Mayhew, 1977) continued to further shape this student development framework in higher education. Emphasizing the importance of student interests and needs in the design of curriculum and learning, the merits of self-direction, and the relevance of real-life experiences for learning and development, this movement challenged higher education to examine further the nature of student differences and the relationship of these differences to the outcomes of college attendance. Scholars such as Sanford (1962), in *The American College*, focused attention on the connection between formal education and the transition between late adolescence and young adulthood. Researchers such as Trent and Medsker (1968), in *Beyond High School*, and Feldman and Newcomb (1969) in *The Impact of College on Students*, began to methodically address questions about how the college experience influences personality development and student attitudes and beliefs. Observers of college student growth, such as Heath (1968), Perry (1970), Kohlberg (1969), and Chickering (1969), building upon previous analyses of identity and youth (e.g., Erikson, 1963; Keniston, 1965; White, 1958), published seminal models charting patterns of human development during the college years. In the latter part of the decade, professional organizations such as the American College Personnel Association (ACPA) and the National Association of Student Personnel Administrators (NASPA) embraced the concept of student development and reflected this new focus in a variety of professional venues. Student development emerged in their journals, as it did for the first time in 1966 in the *NASPA Journal* (Trent, 1966); in their professional organization agendas, as it first did in 1968 with the initiation of Phase I of ACPA's Tomorrow's Higher Education (T.H.E.) Project; and in their professional conferences, as it first did in 1968 in a collaborative meeting between NASPA and the Berkeley Center for Research and Development in Higher Education. The goal of student development in higher education also caught the attention of national foundations and councils during this period. The Hazen Foundation, for example, issued a report calling for a reaffirmation of the developmental teaching mission of postsecondary education (The Committee on the Student in Higher Education, 1968), and the Commission on Professional Development of the Council of Student Personnel Associations in Higher Education (COSPA) began the process of describing student development services in higher education, authoring a paper which was subsequently distributed and published as the "COSPA Statement" (Commission on Professional Development of COSPA, 1975).

The decade of the 1970s was equally powerful in advancing higher education's attention to the development of students. Bowen (1977), in a comprehensive summary of developmental outcomes, argued the many benefits of college attendance to individuals and society alike. Brown (1972), Parker (1978), and Cross (1976) also played significant roles during this time in bringing student development to the forefront of the student affairs agenda in higher education. Under the aegis of the T.H.E. Project, Brown (1972) authored his *Student Development in Tomorrow's Higher Education: A Return to the Academy*, a monograph invoking student development as a unifying mission of higher education. Parker (1978) brought a number of key student development educators together for purposes of addressing relationships between theories of human development and educational practice, publishing *Encouraging Development in College Students*. During this same period, others such as Banning (1978) and Morrill, Hurst, and Oetting (1980) began conducting studies and writing on the consequences of campus environments for various dimensions of student growth and development. Also during this decade Cross (1971, 1976) emerged as a leader in alerting higher education to the developmental needs and concerns of nontraditional students in *Beyond the Open Door* and *Accent on Learning*. In response to Cross' caution, and to new sensitivities highlighted by the work of theorists like Gould (1978) and Levinson and Associates (1978), higher education began to take notice of the importance of incorporating models of life span development in understanding college students.

From the early 1980s to the present the "science" of student development, although some have challenged such a description (see Bloland, Stamatakos, & Rogers, 1994), continued to evolve and mature with the emergence of a full range of psychosocial, cognitive developmental, typological, and person-environment interaction models (Rodgers, 1980). The connections between personal development and formal education were further enhanced with the appearance of works like: Chickering and Associates' (1981) *Modern American College*, which explored the relevance of the developmental model for the teaching mission in a variety of disciplines; Cross' (1981) *Adults as Learners*, which further iterated a model for understanding needs of returning adult students in higher education; Pascarella and Terenzini's (1991) *How College Affects Students*, which summarized, in the legacy of Feldman and Newcomb (1969), 20 years of research on the outcomes of college attendance; and Kuh et al.'s (1991) *Involving Colleges*, which examined the role of student experiences outside the classroom in attaining stated or espoused educational missions. Advocates such as Knefelkamp (1981, 1984, 1986), a frequent keynote speaker at various professional conferences during this period, continued to focus the attention of the higher education community on the preeminence of the student development mission. Researchers such as Winston, Miller, and Prince (1979) focused on developing instruments to measure the outcomes of student development (e.g., The Student Development Task Inventory); and scholars like Pace (1984) continued work on assessing the nature and impact of institutional environments with The College Student Experiences Questionnaire.

The student development movement, though, was not without its critics during this period, with scholars such as Gilligan (1982), Josselson (1987), and Belenky, Clinchy, Goldberger, and Tarule (1986) identifying perceived biases of extant developmental models, especially as they pertained to patterns of women's growth and development. Others like Moore (1990) and Evans and Wall (1991) also directed attention to questions about the applicability of the student development knowledge base to increasingly diverse student populations, emphasizing the need to reconceptualize knowledge of various campus subpopulations and minority groups. More recently Bloland, Stamatakos, and Rogers (1994) have formulated a comprehensive ideological critique of student development with prescriptions for a realignment of the field with the educational mission of institutions and a refocusing on the facilitation of learning.

## Current Status

Although the goal of human development has long served as a foundation for liberal learning in higher education (see Kuh, Shedd, & Whitt, 1987; Newman, 1973), the history of student development as outlined here has been a relatively brief one in the scheme of American postsecondary education. In that brief period, however, it has posited a body of literature that is both complex and rich in ideas about college students and their educational environments. The current status of this knowledge base is presented here as a framework of theoretical propositions and concepts addressing the growth and development of individual college students, the features and impacts of educational environments, and the dynamics of person-environment interaction. From the perspective of Lewin's (1936) differential interactionist paradigm [B=f(P,E)], this knowledge base emphasizes the importance of both the person and the environment in understanding human behavior. Knefelkamp, Widick, and Parker (1978) edited one of the first summaries of this emerging student development knowledge base and challenged the student affairs profession with the goal of establishing developmental communities in higher education. Accordingly, they argued that such a goal requires a theoretical knowledge base capable of describing four areas:

1. Who the college student is in developmental terms. We need to know what changes occur and what those changes look like.

2. How development occurs. We need to have a grasp of the psychological and social processes which cause development.

3. How the college environment can influence student development. We need to know what factors in the particular environment of a college or university can either encourage or inhibit growth.

4. Toward what ends development in college should be directed. (Parker, Widick, & Knefelkamp, 1978, p. x)

"Knowledge in these four areas," the authors further claimed "would allow us to establish feasible developmental goals; to design interventions that take into account 'where students are'; and to draw on the processes underlying developmental change." They concluded that "making student development theory work involves identifying how and to what extent a theory describes the nature of young adult/adult development and explains the process of developmental change in a higher education context" (p. x).

Within the framework of these four questions, the student development knowledge base has continued to evolve and mature over the past 20 years, yielding a number of propositions about college students and their campus environments. As "propositions," these are constructed as tentative, and sometimes conflicting, distillations of thought emerging in the literature on college student development and are presented here for purposes of challenging practitioners and scholars to examine their relevance for what they practice and for how they come to inquire about and understand the college experience. What "truths" guide and define these propositions? What is their meaning and value to the design of educational policy and the conduct of educational practice?

## The Student in Developmental Terms

Within the context of Parker, Widick, and Knefelkamp's (1978) first question ("Who is the college student in developmental terms?"), four propositions are identified, each illustrated by exemplary theorists, and followed by a brief discussion of their potential implications for higher education:

*Proposition 1: Students differ in age-related developmental tasks that offer important agendas for "teachable moments" in their lives.* This proposition underscores the importance of aspects of students' psychosocial life span and their definition as age-related developmental challenges that culminate into age-appropriate states of maturity or resolution at each chronological phase. The works of Chickering (1969), Chickering and Reisser (1993), Neugarten (1968), Erikson (1950, 1959), and Levinson and Associates (1978) address human development from this perspective; and their concepts are important for understanding the needs of traditional as well as nontraditional students. A key implication of this perspective is that, when learning tasks are relevant (or closely related) to developmental choices embedded in students' current life phase, a highly motivating experience, which Havighurst (1972) identified as a "teachable moment," occurs. For example, a course in ethics and philosophy may be an especially powerful experience for a student who is formulating a personalized set of values for the first time ("Developing Integrity," as Chickering labels the task), or participating in an interpersonal skills workshop in a residence hall may be a highly relevant learning experience for a student engaged in a new significant relationship.

Another implication from this psychosocial-developmental-task perspective emanates from its conception of the progression of human life through repeated structural phases of stability and transition (Levinson & Associates, 1978). During periods of stability closure is sought, firm choices are made, and life proceeds in response to a framework of significant commitments, usually related to various occupational and relational aspects of the life span. In contrast, during periods of transition, questions are paramount; and previous life structures must be dissolved, evaluated, and considered for inclusion in (or exclusion from) the next life structure. The import of this is that educators need to understand and make connections (and encourage students to do so) between what they are learning and the psychosocial developmental tasks they are addressing in their lives. Furthermore, during periods of stability, education must serve to enhance commitments rather than challenge them; and at points of transition, education best serves to frame important questions rather than to insist on firm conclusions.

*Proposition 2: Students differ in how they construct and interpret their experiences, and such differences offer important guides for structuring the education process.* This proposition underscores the importance of cognitive structures, or patterns of meaning-making, that students bring to their educational experiences. Theoretical models that exemplify this perspective include Perry (1970), Kohlberg (1969), Gilligan (1982), and King and Kitchener (1994). According to these models, individuals progress through a sequence of hierarchical stages or positions, each characterized by greater complexity and qualitatively different assumptions about how the world functions with respect to a particular domain. Early simplistic assumptions are gradually replaced by more advanced assumptions, as individuals seek new meanings for the events and experiences in their lives. For example, Kohlberg's model (1969) addresses the domain of moral reasoning, describing how individuals resolve issues of fairness and justice, with reference to the consequences of their actions, their membership in society, and the principles, norms, and rules that define systems of social order. Thus, an individual exhibiting characteristics of earlier stages of moral reasoning tends to interpret issues of justice egoistically, with concerns for the potential gains or losses to self that might result from a particular course of action. In contrast, a person constructing meaning from more advanced stages might understand justice as a matter of fidelity to self-chosen principles that underlie systems of social order and that are codified in the form of laws delineating participants' contracted rights and responsibilities.

In the domain of intellectual reasoning, the work of King and Kitchener (1994) shares a similar set of assumptions about the course of human development. According to their model of reflective judgment, individuals progress through increasingly complex forms (or stages) of reasoning as they advance in their ability to resolve problems of an "ill-structured" nature, with reference to experts in the field, to the compelling quality of available evidence, and to established rules of inquiry. Thus, a person holding assumptions characteristic of early stages of reasoning might argue that the "truth value" of one point of view is established unquestionably by concurrence of an authority, or simply because one "believes it to be so," acknowledging that all points of view are equally valid since "no one knows for sure." At more advanced stages, though, a person acknowledges the difference between facts, opinions, and interpretations, reflecting a complex understanding of inquiry as an inherently fallible process of critical review over a long period of time, involving many sources of input from many individuals, and yielding solutions only approximate in their truth value.

Whether referring to the cognitive structures delineated by Kohlberg (1969) or, those identified by King and Kitchener (1994), understanding such differences is important for educators in responding to students effectively. For instance, assuming that growth along a dimension of cognitive-intellectual development similar to that described in King and Kitchener is an appropriate goal of education, it is important to remember that students in the earlier stages benefit more from learning tasks that emphasize diverse viewpoints and employ experiential modes, supported by a high degree of structure and a personal atmosphere (Widick & Simpson, 1978). At more advanced stages, students thrive on tasks that are abstract, ambiguous, and self-directed in nature, when also supported by a high degree of personalism. Dimensions, like those described in Kohlberg, that emphasize social roles and responsibilities as well as the systems of rules established to define and maintain those roles and responsibilities, serve to challenge students appropriately at the early stages of development. Emphasis on principles that underlie such systems is more appropriate at the more advanced stages.

   *Proposition 3: Students differ in the styles with which they approach and resolve challenges of learning, growth and development, and such differences are important for understanding how and why students function in characteristic manners.* This third proposition underscores the importance of concurrent stylistic differences among students and how such differences reveal themselves in consistent patterns with which students approach a variety of tasks. Theoretical models that exemplify this proposition describe styles or patterns of behaviors with respect to a variety of dimensions in students' lives, such as their career interests (Holland, 1973), their personalities (Myers, 1980), their learning orientations (Kolb, 1983), or their preferred style for processing information (Witkin, 1976). These approaches recognize that as individuals mature they develop consistent patterns in how they interpret and resolve various learning challenges. In that respect, they become somewhat predictable as others recognize their "usual way of doing things." For example, from the widely recognized work of Carl Jung, as modified by Isabel Myers and Katherine Briggs, readers have learned how various "Myers-Briggs types" exhibit preferred ways of using "their minds, specifically the way they perceive and the way they make judgments" (Myers, 1980, p. 1). Some perceive primarily through the senses, whereas others rely upon intuition; some use a logical process of thinking to arrive at judgments, whereas others judge out of their appreciation and feelings for the event or situation. According to the model, either kind of perception can team up with either kind of judgment. Furthermore, depending on individuals' relative interest in their outer world (extraversion) or inner world (introversion), as well as their preference for a perceptive versus a judging attitude, a variety of 16 combinations emerge reflecting "different kind[s] of personality, characterized by [differing] interests, values, needs, habits of mind, and surface traits" (Myers, 1980, p. 4). In a similar vein, Holland (1973) identified six vocational interest types (Realistic, Investigative, Artistic, Social, Enterprising, and Conventional), each with a different pattern of values, interests, expectations, and skills suited to the challenges of different occupational work environments. For example, "social types" enjoy working with people, prefer "activities that entail the manipulation of others to inform, train, develop, cure, or enlighten" (p. 16), and use their social competencies to solve problems. In contrast, "realistic types" prefer "activities that entail the explicit, ordered, or systematic manipulation of objects, tools, machines, [or] animals" (p. 14), and oftentimes lack ability in human relations. Kolb (1983) described various learning orientation preferences individuals acquire as they exhibit differing cognitive processes. Thus, "accommodative learners" rely primarily on concrete experience and active experimentation as their preferred processes, in contrast to "assimilative learners" who prefer reflective observation and abstract conceptualization. In a final example, Witkin (1976) identified a continuum of two contrasting cognitive styles, each with its own preferred mode of learning: "field dependence," with a capacity and preference for wholistic approaches to problem solving; and "field independence," with an orientation and attraction toward analytic reasoning.

   An important implication of these perspectives on human differences is that students develop relatively stable and consistent styles of behavior and performance that need to be taken into account when designing educational practice. Cognitive and personal styles function much like software systems in computers; in order to "run them" effectively, knowledge of the software system is paramount. Strategies incompatible with the software system in use simply will not work. In designing educational experiences compatible with students' identified styles, educators should allow students to exercise their strengths and preferred modes of functioning. On the other hand, as Cross (1976) warned, educators may not be serving students well by feeding them a steady diet of their own predilections. Rather, given the challenges of a complex and changing world, perhaps they should focus on strategies that encourage students to "stretch" and develop their nonpreferred strategies as well. Achieving flexibility in that respect may be the most important and desirable outcome of learning.

*Proposition 4: Students differ in the resolution of tasks of individuation according to their gender, culture-ethnicity, and sexual orientation; such differences offer important contexts for understanding the challenges students face in their search for personal identity.* This fourth proposition has emerged out of recent critiques that have identified various sources of perceived bias and limitation attributed to many current student development models. The works of Josselson (1987) and Gilligan (1982) have drawn attention to the claim that women's perspectives and issues have not been sufficiently accounted for in the constructs and models of human development. Within such a critique, current models of growth and development are challenged as products of male conception, treating concerns and issues important to women's lives as aberrations, delays, or evidence of lack of development. For example, models of psychosocial development have been criticized for their failure to acknowledge adequately the importance of family in charting the life cycles of women; models of intellectual or moral reasoning have also been challenged for falling short in acknowledging the role of intuitive processes or the importance of relational aspects to women in arriving at various judgments and conclusions. Atkinson, Morten, and Sue (1983), among others, have examined the applicability of current models of growth and development to the experiences of cultural ethnic minorities. They concluded that, as a consequence of minority status, various racial ethnic groups experience unique, as well as common, patterns of identity development (e.g., conformity, dissonance, immersion, and introspection) as they progress toward a state of synergy with the dominant culture. Development of a healthy self-concept is inescapably involved with the development of a positive cultural identity. Cass (1979, 1984) leveled similar criticism, arguing that, because of a heterosexual bias in the dominant culture, gay men and lesbians focus on substantially different developmental issues in their resolution of identity. Much like cultural ethnic minorities, gay, lesbian, and bisexual persons are portrayed as progressing through discrete stages of development toward an advanced level of identity synthesis within the dominant culture.

In light of this proposition, educators must consider more carefully the consequences of majority-minority dynamics and interactions as a critical context for understanding the growth and development of students. Concepts and assumptions of "normalcy" and "average" are inevitably products of dominant culture and values. Individuals who do not share those values or participate in that culture are challenged often by a press toward conformity in two divergent cultures: one (a subculture) that acknowledges and supports their identities as members of a minority, and another that challenges their identities for their failure to match commonly held expectations and norms. Rejection of the subculture removes an important source of support; rejection of the dominant culture results in barriers to achievement. In effect, for these individuals, success often entails a dual existence, capable of sustaining both the minority and dominant culture. Consequently, issues and tasks of development may be accompanied by additional degrees of stress and difficulty.

In summary, the "college student in developmental terms" is a person who is engaged in a variety of age-related developmental tasks; who constructs meaning from and approaches the challenges of learning in characteristic patterns or styles; and who must resolve issues of individuation within a dynamic cultural context of gender, ethnicity, and sexual orientation. Individual differences in these aspects are to be expected and accommodated if the full potential of an educational experience is to be realized.

## The Nature of Development

In response to Parker, Widick, and Knefelkamp's (1978) second question ("How does development occur?"), five propositions emerge:

*Proposition 5: Development occurs as individuals reach points of readiness and respond to timely and appropriate learning experiences.* This view of growth and change underlies many of the psychosocial models of human development (e.g., Erikson, 1950, 1959). According to this "epigenetic perspective," the human organism essentially "unfolds" over time as developmental issues and choices ascend and recede at predictable points in the life span. These points of time or "phases," each with a respective list of "age-appropriate tasks," evolve as individuals interact with important others in their psychosocial environments (e.g., family, school, workplace). For example, in American culture, establishing independent living arrangements, going away to college, starting a full-time job, and selecting a mate are typical developmental tasks associated with the transition from late adolescence to young adulthood (for most, between ages 18 and 22). Others' expectations relative to these tasks, as well as self-expectations, serve as both brakes and prods on behavior (Neugarten, 1968), at times admonishing individuals with a sense of urgency ("Isn't it about time you settle down and get a job?") and at other times warning that a person may not be quite ready yet for whatever appears on the horizon (e.g., retirement, independence, or a commitment of marriage). All of this suggests that timing is a critical factor in understanding the outcome of any educational opportunity. Simply put, people are most receptive to learning when they are ready developmentally to address the learning task at hand. For example, the experience of learning about self-interests, skills, and values is most powerful for a person when the task of becoming an independent, self-reliant adult is imminent. Conversely, learning associated with a task already completed, or one not yet encountered, such as identifying an entry-level job objective, does little to stimulate interest, motivation, or desire to pursue it further.

An implication of this proposition is that educational interventions are not likely to have a significant impact if they are untimely (i.e., too early or too late). In such cases, waiting for the right time to capitalize on a "teachable moment," or forfeiting an opportunity altogether by being too late, are perhaps the most appropriate strategies. Readiness to learn, develop, and grow is a function of timing.

*Proposition 6: Development occurs as individuals respond to novel situations and tasks that challenge their current level or capacity.* This proposition underscores the importance of challenge and response in the process of human development (Sanford, 1966). Quite different from the epigenetic view in the previous proposition, this "homeostatic" understanding of growth suggests that human beings intentionally seek and maintain a sense of stability, where preferences, choices, and tasks are extensions of the familiar and comfortable; in other words, individuals prefer and enjoy most doing what they already know how to do. When given the choice, they will choose what is compatible with and familiar to their current structures of understanding and competence. New situations threaten current stability, and due to the inevitable discomfort accompanying such experiences, they are usually resisted or avoided. A consequence of this perspective is the assumption that change and development of people entails exposure to the unfamiliar, in Sanford's (1966) words, situations "to which they cannot adapt with the use of devices already present" (p. 44), experiences that "upset the existing equilibrium, produce instability, [and] set in motion activity leading to stabilization on a higher level" (p. 37). This view of change has been underscored more recently under the guise of "system theory" and "chaos theory," where unpredicted new levels of self-organization emerge from creative fluctuations in the free exchange of energy between an organism and its environment (Caple, 1987a, 1987b). Accordingly, disequilibrium rather than stability offers the most fertile condition for growth and development. One important implication of such views is that growth and change are inherently unsettling and perhaps even disturbing processes. Resistance, discomfort, and stress are to be expected as new challenges are introduced. A steady diet of the familiar, although satisfying and comforting, is rarely growth-producing.

*Proposition 7: Development occurs as individuals evaluate a learning task to be sufficiently challenging to warrant change and sufficiently supportive to risk an unknown result.* This proposition further articulates the essential processes of growth and development, underscoring the notion of developmental dissonance. Building upon Festinger's (1957) concepts of cognitive dissonance, Sanford's (1966) notions of challenge and support, and Rodger's (1991) integration of these perspectives in the context of person-environment interactions, this proposition suggests that, for development to occur, learning experiences must contain elements that are both unsettling as well as reassuring to individuals engaged in them. There is a potential range of dissonance, both supportive and challenging, that encourages a person to risk something new and, therefore, to develop a response at a higher level, employing skills, abilities, or ways of making meaning she or he never before exhibited. This range of opportunity has been labeled "developmental or optimal dissonance" (Rodgers, 1980, p. 41). The extent to which learning opportunities are developmentally dissonant is a matter of personal construction that, in turn, is usually a function of developmental level. For example, drawing from illustrations of developmental instruction in Widick and Simpson (1978), students, on the one hand, who hold "dualistic" assumptions about knowledge are challenged by multiple, conflicting perspectives moderated (i.e., supported) by higher degrees of structure in the learning environment. On the other hand, students who hold "relativistic" assumptions are challenged by learning environments requiring intellectual commitments moderated by lower degrees of structure. Failure to accurately gauge and provide appropriate levels of either dimension (challenge or support), according to this proposition, results in reinforcement of the individual's current assumptions and ways of making meaning (assimilation). To further illustrate, from the same example, high structure, in the absence of multiple perspectives, simply confirms the expectations of certainty held by the "dualist;" and low structure, in the absence of a challenge to make commitments of some sort, allows the "relativist" to exploit the freedom of multiple perspectives. In both cases, the individual simply reinterprets the learning environment in the context of assumptions already held and, thus, fails to change. Challenging and supportive elements are simultaneously required for change and development to occur.

*Proposition 8: Development proceeds through qualitative and cyclical changes of increasing complexity.* The nature of this proposition derives from both the cognitive-structural and psychosocial perspectives on human development. "Development" might be distinguished from "change" as more complex in nature and involving the achievement of qualitatively different and presumably more adequate degrees of integration. These degrees of integration are most often understood in the context of a hierarchical sequence, where each step or level represents an inherently more complex structure and therefore reflects a greater degree of maturity. For example, from a cognitive-structural perspective (e.g., Kohlberg, 1969), how individuals resolve questions of fairness and justice proceeds from early levels of integration, involving the simplest reflections on power and fear of the consequences of an action (a "punishment and obedience orientation," in the parlance of Kohlberg's model), to more advanced levels with consideration for the interplay of self and society, adjudicated by a principled system of mutual rights and responsibilities (a perspective of "social cooperation"). This latter form of justification represents a qualitatively different and more advanced level of integration in that it is more complex, taking into consideration a greater number of concerns and issues than earlier forms. From Rest (1979) it is learned that these changes occur across levels simultaneously, as preferences for earlier forms of meaning recede gradually and new forms ascend. Thus, evidence of "development" is apparent in new and integrated structures, higher consciousness and greater autonomy (Caple, 1987a, 1987b; Kuh, Whitt, & Shedd, 1987) involving multiple complex changes.

Chickering (1969) described the path of human development as a revolving course through cycles of differentiation and integration. Phases of "differentiation," where things previously seen as unitary are challenged by questions and insights of new subtleties and distinctions, yield to phases of "integration," when things previously seen as different are now seen as unitary. What may have appeared to an individual as an adequate resolution (or integration) of a particular issue at one time in his or her life may appear to that same individual at another point in time as simplistic and inadequate. For example, achieving autonomy (Chickering's third vector of development) for the first time may require leaving home, establishing a sense of independence, and making new friends in an unfamiliar place. At another point in the life cycle, that same issue of autonomy may express itself more complexly in purchasing a home or venturing into a new career or business with responsibility for support of a family or other dependents. In this case, the issue of autonomy remains essentially the same; however, its manifestations are different and more complex as development and maturity proceed. And so it is with other issues of human development, such as developing competence, managing emotions, establishing identity, freeing interpersonal relationships, and establishing purpose and integrity (Chickering & Reisser, 1993). This view of development underscores the importance of recurring, yet more complex, themes and issues throughout the life span.

"Settling an issue" is only a temporary, situational resolution at one point in time, likely to be followed by subsequent resolutions of different quality and greater complexity.

*Proposition 9: Development occurs as an interactive and dynamic process between persons and their environments.* This proposition is grounded in Lewin's (1936) differential interactionist paradigm of human behavior. Two assumptions are important in this proposition. First, human development cannot be understood adequately by reference to individual human differences alone. Rather, it must be examined within the context of environmental differences as well. Second, it is assumed that although environments influence the characteristics of individuals, at the same time, individuals influence the nature and characteristics of their environments. Human development results from this dynamic process of mutual shaping and influence, an assumption that is central to the emergent view of student development (Kuh, Whitt, & Shedd, 1987). For example, the patterned stylistic differences discussed in Proposition 3 (e.g., Myers-Briggs Types or Holland Types) illustrate how various environments might exact differing responses from individuals, depending upon their characteristics, as well as how individuals of differing characteristics might influence the environment in different ways. A Holland "Realistic" type will likely respond to a quiet, introverted environment with a certain degree of comfort, because such an environment may reinforce that individual's preference for time alone dedicated to more introspective activities. That person's response will tend to reinforce the quiet, introverted characteristics of the setting. A "Social" type, on the other hand, due to individual preferences for more extroverted, people-oriented activities, may express displeasure with such an environment and proceed to organize it to encourage more social activities that have potential for reinforcing his or her outgoing nature. Thus, both individuals are influenced by the totality of their environment, and each, in turn, continues to shape various aspects of that environment.

In summary, development takes place at recurring points of personal readiness, when conditions of sufficient novelty and familiarity engage individuals to construct new forms of differing quality and greater complexity. This process is dynamic and a result of the interactive mutual shaping of persons and environments.

## Influence of Campus Environments

In response to Parker, Widick, and Knefelkamp's (1978) third question ("How does the college environment influence student development?"), four propositions are articulated, each addressing respectively one of four different aspects influencing the nature and characteristics of a campus environment: (a) its natural and synthetic physical features; (b) the people who inhabit the environment; (c) the manner in which it is organized; and (d) the meaning that members of the campus environment attach to these aspects (i.e., the physical features, the inhabitants, and the organizational structures).

*Proposition 10: Educational environments restrict and enable individuals by the form and function of their natural and synthetic physical characteristics.* This proposition emerges from a wealth of material across a variety of fields. Concepts from diverse disciplines such as art and architecture (e.g., Dober, 1992; Gaines, 1991; Sommer, 1969), ecological psychology (e.g., Barker, 1968), and cultural anthropology (e.g., Moffatt, 1989) have contributed to an understanding of the college campus as a "place apart" (Stern, 1986), whose physical features interact with and influence a range of behaviors, attitudes, and outcomes relative to its educational mission. The knowledge base supporting this proposition underscores the importance of natural features, such as location, terrain, and climate; and synthetic features, such as architectural design, space, amenities, and distance. These features combine, through varying conditions of light, density, noise, temperature, air quality, and accessibility, to create a powerful influence on students' attraction to, satisfaction, and stability within a particular setting. From an intercampus perspective, for example, the natural wooded setting providing the environmental backdrop for a University of the Redlands may influence students to behave in ways very different (e.g., whether or not to walk about alone or in groups) from those at a University of Chicago, ensconced in the middle of a large urban metropolis. From an intracampus perspective, there's a different "feel" to the design and spatial arrangement of a

15 story, high-rise hall with 1200 residents, in comparison to a much smaller "house" arrangement where 15 students occupy a single floor structure. Likewise, a small, flexible seminar room presents a much different atmosphere than a tiered, theater-style lecture hall. Such features of the physical environment set broad limits on the phenomena that can occur in any given setting, making some behaviors more or less likely to occur (Michelson, 1970).

When considered in light of campus social systems (e.g., student groups, departments, living units, classes), this proposition gives rise to issues of facilities usage and control, human interaction, territoriality, privacy and personal space, community, isolation, noise, access, identity, and comfort. These issues, in turn, depending upon how they may or may not be resolved, are important for the quality of students' campus experiences and can serve as prohibitive or positive forces for development in students' lives (Strange, 1983).

*Proposition 11: Educational environments exert a conforming influence through the collective, dominant characteristics of those who inhabit them.* This proposition draws from many of the same models and theories discussed in Proposition 3 (e.g., Holland, 1973; Myers, 1980). Recognizing that individuals differ in the characteristic ways they approach a variety of tasks, Proposition 11 examines such differences from a human aggregate (or group) focus, asserting that environments are transmitted collectively through their inhabitants. The dominant features of any particular environment, therefore, are simply a reflection of the dominant characteristics of the people within that environment (Astin, 1962, 1968; Astin & Holland, 1961). Using descriptors from Holland's (1973) model, for example, "social" environments are characterized by a predominant number of social types, and "conventional" aggregates of individuals create characteristically "conventional" environments.

According to Holland (1973), human aggregates may be conceived of as highly "differentiated" (i.e., they are comprised of individuals primarily of one given type or characteristic such as enterprising) or "undifferentiated" (i.e., composed of individuals of many different types) and "consistent" (i.e., sharing a high degree of type similarity such as artistic and social) or "inconsistent" (i.e., having fewer similarities such as conventional and investigative). Highly differentiated and consistent aggregates are homogeneous in character and therefore exhibit a high degree of focus. The dynamics of human aggregates attract, satisfy, and retain individuals who are most similar in type to the dominant characteristics of those individuals comprising the aggregate. In other words, artistic individuals are attracted to, satisfied within, and retained more readily by artistic human aggregates. Conversely, individuals who are dissimilar to the dominant type are more likely to be repelled by, dissatisfied within, and rejected by a particular aggregate. Consequently, since human aggregates are more attractive to individuals congruent with the existing dominant type, they reinforce and accentuate their own characteristics over time. Individuals within the aggregate, in turn, are encouraged and rewarded for exhibiting those dominant characteristics and are discouraged from exhibiting dissimilar or incongruent characteristics. One implication of these dynamics is that, if attraction, satisfaction, and stability are to be maximized, congruence of persons and environments (human aggregates) must be achieved; and homogeneous aggregates are the most effective arrangement for facilitating such ends. The importance of this "person-environment fit" is reflected in a variety of policies and practices on most college campuses, where admissions and recruitment personnel search for the "right kind of student;" fraternity, sorority, and student organizations look for new members who will "fit in;" and academic and career advisors explore department majors or job placements that are most "compatible" with students' interests, values, and skills.

*Proposition 12: Educational environments, as purposeful and goal directed settings, enable or restrict behavior by how they are organized.* All educational environments, whether classrooms, academic departments, student groups, residence halls, or entire campuses, share characteristics of organized systems. In each of these settings, certain goals or outcomes are established (explicitly or implicitly) by participants and constituents; and these goals shape decisions about the use of various resources and strategies. To facilitate such decisions, it is common practice to "get organized" for purposes of establishing plans, rules, and guidelines of group functioning; for allocating resources; and for identifying those who will share authority and responsibility for making various substantive or procedural decisions (Etzioni, 1964). Thus, faculty develop syllabi to outline course goals and assignments; departments define procedural guidelines and degree requirements; student groups plan for and implement programs; residence life staff create structures for encouraging student participation and leadership; and campus administrators establish rules for effective and efficient use of limited resources.

How such systems are organized can be thought of as primarily "dynamic" in character, or "static" (Hage & Aiken, 1970). Dynamic environments respond to change; static environments tend to resist change. Although all organized systems contain elements of both, whether a system exhibits an overall dynamic or static pattern is a function of various organizational structures, such as the degree of centralization (how power is distributed) or formalization (the number and specificity of enforced rules) in a system. A highly formalized (i.e., having many rules) and centralized organization (i.e., power is highly concentrated in only a few participants) establishes a static pattern where the status quo is preserved, and innovation and opportunities for meaningful involvement of participants are discouraged or restricted. Dynamic organizations, maintained by lower degrees of centralization and formalization, exhibit characteristics of "self-organizing systems" as they evolve toward nonequilibrium (Caple, 1987b, p. 101), encouraging substantive involvement, responsibility, and creativity on the part of members. Providing such opportunities in organized educational environments offers an important key for stimulating students' growth and development (Astin, 1985; Strange, 1981, 1983).

*Proposition 13: The effects of educational environments are a function of how members perceive and evaluate them.* The notion that environments exert their influence through participants' perceptions forms the basis of this proposition. Environmental features are actively constructed or interpreted by members; thus, one person may evaluate a setting as "friendly," "warm," and "unrestricted," whereas another person may evaluate that same environment as "distant," "cool," and "confining." The importance of this distinction is that such perceptions are thought to be predictive of how individuals might likely respond to a given environment. Negative perceptions and interpretations are likely to contribute to dissatisfaction, instability, and the desire to leave a particular environment; positive perceptions are usually predictive of satisfaction, stability, and the desire to remain in an environment.

The constructs implicit in this proposition emerged from some of the earliest systematic studies of college students (e.g., Murray, 1938; Pace & Stem, 1958), where environments were understood in terms of "presses," inferred from consensual self-reports of participants' activities, which, in turn, encourage certain behaviors (e.g., studying quietly) or discourage others (e.g., playing loud music). Such "presses" are constructed by those within as well as those outside of the environment. The extent to which the dominant press of an environment corresponds to an individual's "need" (e.g., to study quietly) is presumed to be predictive of attraction to that environment, if outside, and satisfaction and stability, if within. When environmental press is congruent with individual need, growth is encouraged; a need-press mismatch is more likely to be growth inhibiting.

Within a similar but more recent line of inquiry, Moos (1979) constructed a model of social climates, or environmental personalities, which exert their influence on participants through relationship dimensions, personal growth and development dimensions, and system maintenance and change dimensions. The nature and quality of these dimensions become important as participants evaluate their expectations of environments, their perceptions of ideal environments, and their actual experiences with environments. Thus, individuals may expect a high level of relationship dimensions (e.g., emotional support and involvement of participants) in a particular environment, but find the reality discrepant with their expectations or ideals; in such cases, they are more likely to leave the environment. When environmental expectations, ideals, and realities are congruent, satisfaction and persistence in the environment is much more likely.

Last, this line of inquiry has been enriched with a focus on elements of organizational and institutional culture (Chaffee & Tierney, 1988; Kuh, 1993; Kuh & Whitt, 1988). From this perspective, campus cultures are social constructions (that is, they are invented, discovered, or developed) reflected in various cultural artifacts, including traditions, stories, ceremonies, history, myths, heroines and heroes, interactions among members, policies and practices, symbols, and mission and philosophy. The importance of these cultural artifacts is taught to new members as a means of integrating them into the environment and assisting them in interpreting and understanding the meaning of events and actions. Failure to understand or embrace key elements of campus culture may jeopardize participants' satisfaction or stability in that setting. Like the other two models discussed in the context of this proposition, need-press and social climate, models of institutional culture underscore the importance of examining environments from the perspective and meaning of the members of those environments. Participants' perceptions and constructions are an important source of information for designing responsive educational environments, and educators must be particularly sensitive to any discrepancies between their views of institutional environments and those of students.

In summary, these four propositions suggest that the college environment positively influences student development through physical features that are enabling; aggregate characteristics that are attractive, satisfying, and reinforcing; and organizational structures that are open and dynamic. However, the nature of the effects of these campus environment features is a function of the meanings attached to them and sustained by participant members.

## The Goals of Education

In response to the fourth question posed by Parker, Widick, and Knefelkamp (1978) ("Toward what ends should development in college be directed?"), a final proposition is considered, emphasizing the axiological (value) dimensions of education.

*Proposition 14: Educational systems are embedded in various contexts of select values and assumptions that shape their expectations, processes, and outcomes.* Education by its very nature is both a purveyor and process of culture. In that sense, all educational systems embrace certain values and assumptions (to the exclusion of others) thought to be important in a particular culture, and, on that basis, establish goals (explicit or implicit) for purposes of directing educational programs and interventions. Educational success is gauged then by how well those goals (or goals that emerge in the process) are achieved. American higher education, and its orientation toward student development discussed here, is certainly not an exception to this phenomenon of cultural embedment. For example, the preoccupation with individual rights and practicality of results dominant in American culture lends itself to a higher education system that places increasing value on consumer rights and expectations; and that frequently underscores education as a means to an end—more specifically, to a job or career.

In American culture, definitions of growth and maturity, key constructs in any student development model, are also embedded in a premium placed on independence and autonomy as signs of having reached an advanced level of development. This stands in sharp contrast to Eastern cultures, for example, where individual goals and achievement are usually superseded by group or community needs as the more desirable value. In a similar fashion, the emphasis on maintenance of harmony in Eastern societies may preempt the exercise of candor and directness (Garner, 1989), qualities that might be more appreciated in American society. Such differences map contrasting directions of what it means to be an educated person and the manner in which the knowledge and skills associated with such a state are assessed.

Cultural values also establish parameters for the means and methods of education. For example, Lipset (1989) and Skolnik (1990) distinguished cultural differences between Canada and the United States, noting that the United States is a product of revolution whereas Canada emerged from a process of counterrevolution. Consequently, the United States "devolved a political culture characterized by antistatism, individualism, populism, and egalitarianism," in contrast to Canada, which has developed as a "more class-conscious, elitist, law-abiding, statist, collectivity-oriented, and particularistic [society]" (Skolnik, 1990, p. 82). Thus, Canadian universities tend to be more elitist in their orientation, with less attention being given to how residential communities or cocurricular activities on campus can serve in the education of students. The character of the U.S. system is more egalitarian, at least in its espoused values, and, consistent with its more holistic view of students, is much more likely to include on-campus residential experiences and cocurricular activities as important components of campus culture.

The importance of this proposition is that educators must be more observant of the values and assumptions that form the context of their policies and practices. Especially as they attempt to encourage a more global, multicultural perspective among students, educators must also increase their sensitivity to a wider range of assumptions and values about the "educated person" and the means by which such a goal can be achieved. Heightened awareness in that respect can yield a greater range of options for students. The student development models addressed in these propositions represent a limited context of values and assumptions, primarily embedded in Western rationalism and American pragmatism. There are other legitimate contexts that warrant thoughtful consideration as well.

## Summary and Conclusion

I have argued previously (Strange, 1983; Strange & King, 1990) that what distinguishes professionals at work is their ability to bring reasoned explanations, grounded in evidence, to the phenomena about which they claim expertise. These explanations, in turn, become the basis for implementing action, in the form of various policies, practices, and interventions; and they serve as a framework for evaluating the effectiveness of such action. Student affairs professionals bring to the academy an espoused expertise on students' development, and their explanations are derived from theories about how students learn, grow, and mature during the college experience. Over the past several decades, considerable insight into these phenomena has been gained, the core of which I have attempted to capture here in propositional form under the rubric of student development.

Is this knowledge base sufficient for a comprehensive explanation of how students develop? What might be the points of contradiction and redundancy here, and are there gaps where further conceptual work is warranted? What researchable questions are suggested by these propositions? Is there adequate evidence to support these claims? What is the import of these claims for what is required of students as reflected in accepted educational policies and codes? Are the expectations of educators appropriate and sufficient in light of these propositions? What is the meaning of this student development framework for how professionals on campus go about their work? Do these claims about student growth and development, and about campus environments, support the continuance of current programs and practices? Do they call into question others that may have been long accepted without challenge? These are illustrative of questions that map an agenda to be pursued if a new level of understanding of the power of higher education to effect change in students' lives is to be realized. I have provided the foil here; now I turn to my colleagues for further insight. There is much yet to be mined.

## References

American Council on Education. (1937). *The student personnel point of view* (American Council on Education Studies, Series 1, Vol. 1, No. 3). Washington, DC: Author.

American Council on Education, Committee on Student Personnel Work. (E. G. Williamson, Chair). (1949). *The student personnel point of view* (rev. ed.) (American Council on Education Studies, Series 6, No. 13). Washington, DC: Author.

Astin, A. W. (1962). An empirical characterization of higher educational institutions. *Journal of Educational Psychology, 53,* 224–235.

Astin, A. W. (1968). *The college environment.* Washington, DC: American Council on Education.

Astin, A. W. (1985). *Achieving educational excellence: A critical assessment of priorities and practices in higher education.* San Francisco: Jossey-Bass.

Astin, A. W., & Holland, J. L. (1961). The environmental assessment technique: A way to measure college environments. *Journal of Educational Psychology, 52,* 308–316.

Atkinson, D., Morten, G., & Sue, D. (1983). *Counseling American minorities: A cross-cultural perspective* (2nd ed.). Dubuque, IA: Brown.

Banning, J. H. (Ed.). (1978). *Campus ecology: A perspective for student affairs* (National Association of Student Personnel Administrators Monograph). Cincinnati, OH: National Association of Student Personnel Administrators.

Barker, R. G. (1968). *Ecological psychology: Concepts and methods for studying the environment of human behavior.* Stanford, CA: Stanford University Press.

Belenky, M. F., Clinchy, B. M., Goldberger, N. R., & Tarule, J. M. (1986). *Women's ways of knowing: The development of self, voice, and mind.* New York: Basic Books.

Bloland, P. A., Stamatakos, L. C., & Rogers, R. R. (1994). *Reform in student affairs: A critique of student development.* Greensboro, NC: ERIC Counseling and Student Services Clearinghouse.

Bowen, H. R. (1977). *Investment in learning: The individual and social value of American higher education.* San Francisco: Jossey-Bass.

Brown, R. D. (1972). *Student development in tomorrow's higher education: A return to the academy.* Washington, DC: American College Personnel Association.

Caple, R. B. (1987a). The change process in developmental theory: A self-organization paradigm, part 1. *Journal of College Student Personnel, 28,* 4–11.

Caple, R. B. (1987b). The change process in developmental theory: A self-organization paradigm, part 1. *Journal of College Student Personnel, 28,* 100–104.

Cass, V. C. (1979). Homosexual identity formation: A theoretical model. *Journal of Homosexuality, 4,* 219–235.

Cass, V. C. (1984). Homosexual identity formation: Testing a theoretical model. *Journal of Sex Research, 20,* 143–167.

Chaffee, E. E., & Tierney, W. G. (1988). *Collegiate culture and leadership strategies.* New York: American Council on Education/Macmillan.

Chickering, A. W. (1969). *Education and identity.* San Francisco: Jossey-Bass.

Chickering, A. W., & Associates. (1981). *Modern American college.* San Francisco: Jossey-Bass.

Chickering, A. W., & Reisser, L. (1993). *Education and identity* (2nd ed.). San Francisco: Jossey-Bass.

Commission on Professional Development of COSPA. (1975). Student development services in post secondary education. *Journal of College Student Personnel, 16,* 524–528.

Cross, K. P. (1971). *Beyond the open door: New students to higher education.* San Francisco: Jossey-Bass.

Cross, K. P. (1976). *Accent on learning: Improving instruction and reshaping the curriculum.* San Francisco: Jossey-Bass.

Cross, K. P. (1981). *Adults as learners.* San Francisco: Jossey-Bass.

Dober, R. P. (1992). *Campus design.* New York: Wiley.

Erikson, E. H. (1950). Growth and crisis of the healthy personality. In M. J. E. Senn (Ed.), *Symposium on the healthy personality,* Supplement II (pp. 91–146). New York: Josiah Macy, Jr., Foundation.

Erikson, E. H. (1959). *Identity and the life cycle* (Psychological Issues Monograph 1). New York: International Universities Press.

Erikson, E. H. (1963). *Childhood and society.* New York: Norton.

Etzioni, A. (1964). *Modern organizations.* Englewood Cliffs, NJ: Prentice-Hall.

Evans, N. J., & Wall, V. A. (1991). *Beyond tolerance: Gays, lesbians and bisexuals on campus.* Alexandria, VA: American College Personnel Association.

Feldman, K. A., & Newcomb, T. M. (1969). *The impact of college on students. Volume 1: An analysis of four decades of research.* San Francisco: Jossey-Bass.

Festinger, L. (1957). *A theory of cognitive dissonance.* New York: Row, Peterson.

Gaines, T. A. (1991). *The campus as a work of art.* New York: Preager.

Garner, B. (1989). Southeast Asian culture and classroom culture. *Journal of College Teaching, 37,* 127–130.

Gilligan, C. (1982). *In a different voice: Psychological theory and women's development.* Cambridge, MA: Harvard University Press.

Gould, R. (1978). *Transformations: Growth and change in adult life.* New York: Simon & Schuster.

Hage, J., & Aiken, M. (1970). *Social change in complex organizations.* New York: Random House.

Havighurst, R. J. (1972). *Developmental tasks and education* (3rd ed.). New York: McKay.

Heath, D. H. (1968). *Growing up in college.* San Francisco: Jossey-Bass.

Heilweil, M. (1973). The influence of dormitory architecture on residence behavior. *Environment and Behavior, 5,* 377–412.

Hofstadter, R. (1955). *Academic freedom in the age of the college.* New York: Columbia University Press.

Holland, J. L. (1973). *Making vocational choices: A theory of careers.* Englewood Cliffs, NJ: Prentice Hall.

Josselson, R. (1987). *Finding herself: Pathways to identity development in women.* San Francisco: Jossey-Bass.

Keniston, K. (1965). Social change and youth in America. In E. H. Erikson (Ed.), *The challenge of youth* (pp. 191–222). New York: Doubleday.

King, P. M., & Kitchener, K. S. (1994). *Developing reflective judgment: Understanding and promoting intellectual growth and critical thinking in adolescents and adults*. San Francisco: Jossey-Bass.

Knefelkamp, L. L. (1981, March). *Future promises*. Keynote speech presented at the annual meeting of the American College Personnel Association, Cincinnati, OH.

Knefelkamp, L. L. (1984, April). *Renewal of intellect*. Keynote speech presented at the annual meeting of the American College Personnel Association, Baltimore, MD.

Knefelkamp, L. L. (1986, April). *Generativity*. Keynote speech presented at the annual meeting of the American College Personnel Association, New Orleans, LA.

Knefelkamp, L. L., Widick, C., & Parker, C. A. (Eds.). (1978). *Applying new developmental findings* (New directions in student services, no. 4). San Francisco: Jossey-Bass.

Kohlberg, L. (1969). Stage and sequence: The cognitive developmental approach to socialization. In D. Goslin (Ed.), *Handbook of socialization theory and research* (pp. 347–480). Chicago: Rand McNally.

Kolb, D. (1983). *Experiential learning: Experience as the source of learning and development*. Englewood Cliffs, NJ.: Prentice-Hall.

Kuh, G. D. (Ed.). (1993). *Cultural perspectives in student affairs work*. Washington, DC: American College Personnel Association.

Kuh, G. D., Schuh, J. H., Whitt, E. J., Andreas, R. E., Lyons, J. W., Strange, C. C., Krehbiel, L. E., & MacKay, K. A. (1991). *Involving colleges: Encouraging student learning and personal development through out-of-class experiences*. San Francisco: Jossey-Bass.

Kuh, G. D., Shedd, J. D., & Whitt, E. J. (1987). Student affairs and liberal education: Unrecognized (and unappreciated) common law partners. *Journal of College Student Personnel, 28*, 252–60.

Kuh, G. D., & Whitt, E. J. (1988). *The invisible tapestry: Cultures in American colleges and universities* (ASHE-ERIC Higher Education Report Series, No. 1). Washington, DC: Association for the Study of Higher Education.

Kuh, G. D., Whitt, E. J., & Shedd, J. D. (1987). *Student affairs work, 2001: A paradigmatic odyssey*. Alexandria, VA: American College Personnel Association.

Levinson, D. J., & Associates. (1978). *Seasons of a man's life*. New York: Ballantine.

Lewin, K. (1936). *Principles of topological psychology*. New York: McGraw-Hill.

Lipset, S. M. (1989). *Continental divide: The values and institutions of the United States and Canada*. Toronto: C. D. Howe Institute.

Mayhew, L. B. (1977). *The legacy of the seventies*. San Francisco: Jossey-Bass.

Metzger, W. P. (1955). *Academic freedom in the age of the university*. New York: Columbia University Press.

Michelson, W. (1970). *Man and his urban environment: A sociological approach*. Reading, MA: Addison-Wesley.

Moffatt, M. (1989). *Coming of age in New Jersey: College and American culture*. New Brunswick, NJ: Rutgers University Press.

Moore, L. V. (Ed.). (1990). Evolving theoretical perspectives on students. *New Directions for Student Services, No. 51*. San Francisco: Jossey-Bass.

Moos, R. H. (1979). *Evaluating educational environments*. San Francisco: Jossey-Bass.

Morrill, W., Hurst, J., & Oetting, E. (1980). *Dimensions of intervention for student development*. New York: Wiley.

Murray, H. (1938). *Exploration in personality*. New York: Oxford University Press.

Myers, I. B. (1980). *Gifts differing*. Palo Alto, CA: Consulting Psychologists Press.

Neugarten, B. L. (1968). Adult personality: Toward a psychology of the life cycle. In B. L. Neugarten (Ed.), *Middle age and aging* (pp. 137–147). Chicago: University of Chicago Press.

Newman, J. H. (1973). *The idea of a university*. Westminster, MD: Christian Classics.

Pace, C. R. (1984). *Measuring the quality of college student experiences: An account of the development and use of The College Student Experiences Questionnaire*. Los Angeles: University of California Higher Education Research Institute.

Pace, C. R., & Stern, G. G. (1958). An approach to the measurement of psychological characteristics of college environments. *Journal of Educational Psychology, 49*, 269–277.

Parker, C. A. (Ed.). (1978). *Encouraging development in college students*. Minneapolis: University of Minnesota Press.

Parker, C., Widick, C., & Knefelkamp, L. (Eds.). (1978). Editors' notes: Why bother with theory. In L. L. Knefelkamp, C. Widick, & C. A. Parker (Eds.), *Applying new developmental findings* (New directions in student services, no. 4). San Francisco: Jossey-Bass.

Pascarella, E. T., & Terenzini, P. T. (1991). *How college affects students*. San Francisco: Jossey-Bass.

Perry, W. G. (1970). *Forms of intellectual and ethical development in the college years: A scheme*. New York: Holt, Rinehart, & Winston.

Rest, J. R. (1979). *Development in judging moral issues*. Minneapolis: University of Minnesota Press.

Rodgers, R. F. (1980). Theories underlying student development. In D. G. Creamer (Ed.), *Student development in higher education: Theories, practices & future directions* (ACPA Media Publication Number 27). Alexandria, VA: ACPA Media.

Rodgers, R. F. (1991). Using theory in practice in student affairs. In T. K. Miller, R. B. Winston, Jr., & Associates (Eds.), *Administration and leadership in student affairs: Actualizing student development in higher education* (pp. 203–251). Muncie, IN: Accelerated Development.

Sanford, N. (Ed.). (1962). *The American college: A psychological and social interpretation of the higher learning*. New York: Wiley.

Sanford, N. (1966). *Self and society: Social change and individual development*. New York: Atherton Press.

Skolnik, M. L. (1990). Lipset's *Continental Divide* and the ideological basis for differences in higher education between Canada and United States. *Canadian Journal of Higher Education, XX-2*, 81–93.

Sommer, R. (1969). *Personal space*. Englewood Cliffs, NJ: Prentice-Hall.

Stern, R. A. (1986). *Pride of place: Building the American dream*. New York: Houghton Mifflin.

Strange, C. (1981). Organizational barriers to student development. *National Association of Student Personnel Administrators Journal, 19*, 12–20.

Strange, C. (1983). Human development theory and administrative practice in student affairs: Ships passing in the daylight? *National Association of Student Personnel Administrators Journal, 21*, 2–8.

Strange, C., & King, P. (1990). The professional practice of student development. In D. Creamer & Associates (Eds.), *College student development: Theory and practice for the 1990's* (pp. 9–24; ACPA Media Publication No. 49). Alexandria, VA: American College Personnel Association.

The Committee on the Student in Higher Education. (1968). *The student in higher education*. New Haven, CT: The Hazen Foundation.

Trent, J. W. (1966). Encouragement of student development. *NASPA Journal, 4*, 35–45.

Trent, J. W., & Medsker, L. L. (1968). *Beyond high school*. San Francisco: Jossey-Bass.

Walters, J. E. (1931). *Student development: How to make the most of college life*. New York: Pitman.

Walters, J. E. (1935). *Individualizing education by means of applied personnel procedures*. New York: Wiley.

White, R. W. (1958). *Lives in progress*. New York: Dryden Press.

Widick, C., & Simpson, D. (1978). Developmental concepts in college instruction. In C. A. Parker (Ed.), *Encouraging development in college students* (pp. 27–59). Minneapolis: University of Minnesota Press.

Winston, R. B., Jr., Miller, T. K., & Prince, J. S. (1979). *Student Development Task Inventory* (2nd ed.). Athens, GA: Student Development Associates.

Witkin, H. A. (1976). Cognitive style in academic performance and in teacher-student relations. In S. Messick & Associates (Eds.), *Individuality in learning* (pp. 38–89). San Francisco: Jossey-Bass.

Note: The author acknowledges with appreciation reviews and comments on drafts of this manuscript by Robert Brown, George Kuh, and Louis Stamatakos. Earlier versions of this paper were presented at the annual meetings of the American College Personnel Association, Kansas City, March, 1993 and the Association for the Study of Higher Education, Pittsburgh, November, 1993.

## Unit 1 Additional Recommended Readings

King, P. M. (1994). Theories of college student development: Sequences and consequences. *Journal of College Student Development, 35*, 413–421.

Parker, C. A. (1999). Student development: What does it mean? *Journal of College Student Development, 40*, 494–503. (Originally published July 1974).

Stage, F. K. (1991). Common elements of theory: A framework for college student development. *Journal of College Student Development, 32*, 56–61.

# UNIT 2

## *INTEGRATED DEVELOPMENTAL MODELS*

# CHAPTER 3
# THE ACTIVITY OF MEANING MAKING: A HOLISTIC PERSPECTIVE ON COLLEGE STUDENT DEVELOPMENT

## MARCIA B. BAXTER MAGOLDA

The student affairs profession embraced student development theory as its guiding philosophy in the 1970s, a move articulated explicitly in Brown's (1972) *Student Development in Tomorrow's Higher Education—A Return to the Academy*. Brown reiterated student affairs' commitment to the whole student, a commitment outlined as early as 1937 in the *Student Personnel Point of View* (National Association of Student Personnel Administrators, 1989), and argued for collaboration among student affairs and faculty to promote students' development. Although the profession adopted student development theory as a philosophy to augment its whole student stance, theorists focused on separate strands of theory that complicated emphasizing the whole student.

Knefelkamp, Widick, and Parker (1978) synthesized the student development research literature into five clusters, noting that they "did not find, nor could we create, the comprehensive model of student development" (p. xi). The five clusters—psychosocial theories, cognitive developmental theories, maturity models, typology models, and person–environment interaction models—have remained as separate lines of theorizing through much of the student development literature. Although Knefelkamp and her colleagues portrayed all five clusters as valuable, research tended to further each cluster with insufficient attention to their intersections. Research in the psychological tradition tended to focus on the person; research in the sociological tradition focused on the environment. Literature on student success, outcomes, and learning is often separated from literature on student development. To complicate matters further, research within clusters to create theory in the context of gender, race, ethnicity, and sexual orientation typically resulted in separate silos rather than interconnected possibilities. Although the student affairs profession moved to explicitly embrace the link between development and learning with the *Student Learning Imperative* (American College Personnel Association, 1994) and *Learning Reconsidered* (Keeling, 2004), the learning and student development literatures are rarely integrated (Wildman & Baxter Magolda, 2008). Thus, higher education in general and student affairs in particular lack a holistic, theoretical perspective to promote the learning and development of the whole student.

Constructing a holistic theoretical perspective requires focusing on intersections rather than separate constructs. Robert Kegan, a pioneer in moving toward a holistic theoretical perspective, advocated "moving from the dichotomous *choice* to the dialectical *context* which brings the poles into being in the first place" (1982, p. ix, italics in original). He argued that the questions

Baxter Magolda, M. B. (2009). The activity of meaning making: A holistic perspective on college student development. *Journal of College Student Development, 50*, 621–639.

"Which is to be taken as the master in personality, affect or cognition?" or "Which should be the central focus, the individual or the social?" or "Which should be the primary theater of investigation, the intrapsychic or the interpersonal?" or even "Which is to be taken as the more powerful developmental framework the psychoanalytic or the cognitive structural?" (pp. viii–ix)

should be reconstructed to focus on the context rather than the polarities. He offered the construct of meaning making as the context that would enable "a sophisticated understanding of the relationship between the psychological and the social, between the past and the present, and between emotion and thought" (1982, p. 15).

Another arena to focus on intersections revolves around addressing tensions and intersections between existing theoretical frameworks and new ones generated from specific populations. Nesting new ideas generated from particular student populations in larger concepts, critiquing and extending existing theory rather than ignoring it, and blending particulars and existing overarching ideas would promote integration toward a holistic perspective. The intersections of learning and development are another major area in which integration is warranted. Conducting contemporary research in ways that explore these tensions and intersections is necessary to construct a holistic theoretical perspective that depicts the complexity and variability of development.

In this article, I briefly trace the academic traditions that have formed the major body of student development literature, highlighting the evolution of separate rather than integrated constructs. I then summarize Kegan's conception of a metapsychology that integrates many of these separate lines of research. Next, I offer a holistic framework for student development theory based on contemporary research that takes a holistic approach. I conclude by outlining the kind of future research that is needed to develop and refine an integrated, holistic theoretical foundation for promoting student development.

## Academic Traditions and the Theoretical Clusters

Grounded in the Piagetian tradition, the cognitive-developmental cluster of research articulated the increasingly complex assumptions or structures people use to make meaning of their experience. These assumptions about the nature, limits, and certainty of knowledge (Kitchener, 1983) guide *how* people think rather than *what* they think. As Piaget (1950) described, people use a set of assumptions to guide how they make meaning of their experience until they encounter dissonance. Experiences that conflict with their assumptions are often assimilated into their current structure. If the dissonance is substantial enough that it cannot be easily assimilated into the current structure, individuals revise their assumptions to accommodate the new experience, resulting in growth toward more complex meaning making. Perry (1970) sketched the first trajectory of these structures in college students' intellectual development. He described a trajectory from assuming knowledge is certain and authorities possess it (dualism), through increasing awareness that knowledge is sometimes uncertain and authorities are working to resolve the uncertainties (multiplicity), to accepting that knowledge is constructed in context by those evaluating relevant evidence (relativism). These three major phases of epistemological development have been reaffirmed, expanded, and refined by longitudinal studies of college students and adults. King and Kitchener (1994, 2004) clarified how college students viewed knowledge and how to justify their views across this trajectory, which they defined as pre-reflective, quasi-reflective, and reflective judgment. Belenky, Clinchy, Goldberger, and Tarule (1986) refined the trajectory by introducing connected and separate styles of meaning making based on their study of college and adult women. Baxter Magolda (1992, 2001, 2002) further refined these two styles as gender-related patterns among college students within dualistic and multiplistic phases that merged in the relativistic phase.

Separate and connected styles also emerged in moral development research, another line of research in the cognitive–developmental cluster. Kohlberg's (1969) trajectory from egocentric to conventional to postconventional moral reasoning emphasized the separate or justice orientation, whereas Gilligan's (1970) trajectory from egocentric to self-sacrifice to equality between self and others emphasized the connected or care orientation. Although this line of research clearly addressed the relationship of self and other, the focus remained on moral assumptions and reasoning. Similarly, although both Perry and Belenky and associates explicitly addressed the role of the self in meaning making, the epistemological line of research kept assumptions about knowledge in the forefront. A more detailed synthesis of the cognitive–developmental cluster appears in Patricia King's article in this issue.

Simultaneously, psychosocial theorists developed the story of how adults construct their sense of self. Much of the research on college populations was grounded in Erikson's (1968) psychosocial conceptualization of identity stemming from the interaction of physical and cognitive growth and the demands of the environment. Chickering (1969) and Chickering and Reisser (1983) sketched the particular developmental demands facing college students as they balanced autonomy and interdependence. Josselson (1987, 1996) used James Marcia's framework to study identity based on the combination of exploration and commitment. Some of Josselson's identity statuses portray identity as shaped largely by external forces (i.e., Guardians), whereas others portray identity as interdependent with external others (i.e., Pathmakers). These theories emphasized the intersections between how we see ourselves and how we see relationships with others and again the notions of connection and separation arose as adults negotiated self in the context of relationships. Concern about the relevance of identity theories constructed on white majority populations led to theory construction on various social identities (e.g., race, ethnicity, gender, and sexual orientation). A more detailed synthesis of this cluster appears in the Torres, Jones, and Renn article in this issue.

The remaining three clusters Knefelkamp and colleagues (1978) identified received less attention in the ongoing student development literature. The maturity models largely disappeared from compendiums of student development theory, which is unfortunate; Douglas Heath's (1978) model explicitly identified the cognitive, intrapersonal, and interpersonal dimensions of development. Typology models got some attention, primarily aimed at understanding individual differences, but were regarded as "not truly developmental" (Evans, Forney, & Guido-DiBrito, 1998, p. 204) owing to their lack of a developmental progression. Person–environment interaction models also got little attention in the mainstream developmental literature and became a separate literature on campus environment and ecology. Ethnographic studies of college students, emerging from an anthropological tradition, focused on student culture. The way these lines of research developed separated the psychology of the student mind from the social context in which it developed. This is ironic because the foundational theories of Piaget and Erikson, as well as many who built on their work (e.g., Belenky et al., 1986; Josselson, 1987, 1996; Perry, 1970) clearly emphasized the person in context.

Kegan's (1982) conceptualization of a metapsychology that brought together psychoanalytic and constructive–developmental traditions offered the means to integrate separate clusters of developmental theory into a holistic framework. Bringing together the big ideas of constructivism (i.e., that humans organize meaning) and developmentalism (i.e., that systems evolve through eras based on principles of stability and change), Kegan placed the activity—and evolution—of meaning making at the core of development. Kegan described the subject–object relationship as the deep structure of principles of mental organization. Our meaning-making structures are a combination of elements over which we have control (what Kegan calls *object*) and elements that have control over us (what Kegan calls *subject*). Object is "distinct enough from us that we can do something with it" (Kegan, 1994, p. 32), whereas subject "refers to those elements of our knowing or organizing that we are identified with, tied to, fused with, or embedded in. We *have* object; we *are* subject" (p. 32, italics in original). What is subject and object, or what we have control over, changes over time. Each principle of mental organization, or phase of development, stands on a particular subject–object relationship. These principles guide *how* we construct our thinking, feeling, and social relating. As some aspect that was subject becomes object, we move to a more complex principle. For example, in what Kegan calls the socializing mind, we are subject to the expectations of others and thus we construct our identity to align with those expectations (Kegan & Lahey, 2009). When we can take others' expectations as object, we are able to stand apart from them to construct an internal voice (Baxter

Magolda, 2009) to coordinate external expectations. Kegan calls this new principle the self-authoring mind (Kegan & Lahey, 2009). Because the underlying subject–object relationship undergirds thinking, feeling, and social relating, it intertwines cognitive, intrapersonal, and interpersonal dimensions of development. How we come to know, how we see ourselves, and how we see ourselves in relation to others are all hinged on the same underlying subject–object relationship. Kegan (1994) described growth as "liberating ourselves from that in which we were embedded, making what was subject into object so that we can 'have it' rather than 'be had' by it" (p. 34). This portrayal of self-evolution integrates thinking and feeling, cognition and affect, self and other. Although Kegan referred to this as growth of the mind, he is explicit that the word mind refers to "the person's meaning-constructive or meaning-organizational capacities. I am referring to the selective, interpretive, executive, construing capacities that psychologists have historically associated with the 'ego' or the self'" (p. 29).

Kegan's metapsychology, with its emphasis on the activity of meaning making, also sets the stage for linking development and learning. Bruner (1990) noted that a "more interpretive approach to cognition concerned with 'meaning-making'" (p. 2) proliferated in many disciplines. Bruner articulated learning as construction of meaning about the world and about self. This portrayal of learning is synonymous with Kegan's portrayal of self-evolution in which cognition, identity, and relationships are intertwined. Despite these obvious links, the science of learning evolved separately from even the intellectual development literature (Wildman, 2007). Wildman (2007) articulated three major theoretical shifts in conceptions of learning: "behavior analysis, to information processing, to cultural participation" (p. 20). The shift to learning as cultural participation in the 1980s acknowledged that people made meaning of their experience by acting in a social context. For example, Wenger's (1998) *Communities of Practice* portrays learning as the interconnection of acting within a practice context, making meaning of one's experiences in that context, and developing an identity in the context of belonging to that community. This model of learning incorporates Dewey's (1916) emphasis on experience, Piaget's (1970) emphasis on meaning making, and core concepts from constructivist, feminist, liberatory, and culturally relevant pedagogy (see Baxter Magolda [1999] for an integration of these approaches). The goal of such approaches to learning is greater complexity of meaning making. Mezirow described this as transformative learning:

> The process by which we transform our taken-for-granted frames of reference (meaning perspectives, habits of mind, mindsets) to make them more inclusive, discriminating, open, emotionally capable of change, and reflective so that they may generate beliefs and opinions that will prove more true or justified to guide action. (2000, pp. 7–8)

This expansion of meaning making also hinged on "how we learn to negotiate and act on our own purposes, values, feelings, and meanings rather than those we have uncritically assimilated from others" (p. 8). In describing transformation learning this way, Mezirow described the developmental process of moving away from external authority toward self-authorship that is the central focus of Kegan's (1994) and Baxter Magolda's (2001, 2009) developmental theories.

Kegan's concept of growth of the mind, reflecting an integration of cognitive with intrapersonal and interpersonal development, resonates with Bruner's construction of meaning and Mezirow's transformative learning. When learning is defined as participation in meaningful social practices, all three developmental dimensions are central to learning. The integrative efforts of these lines of scholarship set the stage for creating a more holistic perspective on student development theory.

## Key Constructs, Conceptualizations, and Research That Frame a Holistic Theoretical Perspective on College Student Development

Constructing a holistic theoretical perspective on college student development requires exploring key ideas that ground such a perspective, existing conceptual integrations, and integrative research efforts.

## Key Constructs

What forms does meaning making take in the college years? Parks (2000) noted,

> in the years from seventeen to thirty a distinctive mode of meaning making can emerge . . . [that] includes (1) becoming critically aware of one's own composing of reality, (2) self-consciously participating in an ongoing dialogue toward truth, and (3) cultivating a capacity to respond—to act—in ways that are satisfying and just. (p. 6)

Referring to this same time period as emerging adulthood, Tanner, Arnett, and Leis (2008) suggested it is a time of gaining self-sufficiency and recentering from childhood and adolescent contexts to adult contexts "which nourish adult interdependence" (p. 38). These overarching concepts capture the thread of evolution from external to internal definition that has run through much of the cognitive and social identity student development literature. Contemporary research, however, clarifies that this evolution is not simply a matter of increasing individuation. As young adults begin to compose their own realities and recenter into adult contexts, they renegotiate the relationship of their internal voices and external influence. External forces, initially in the foreground of meaning making, move to the background as internal forces move to the foreground of meaning making. Thus, the internal voice becomes the coordinator of external influence (Baxter Magolda, 2001; Kegan, 1994). This renegotiation is mediated by what Parks calls "'two great yearnings': the yearning for exercise of one's own distinct agency (one's own power to make a difference) and the yearning for belonging, connection, inclusion, relationship, and intimacy" (p. 91). This balancing of agency and communion (Bakan, 1966) is an ongoing quest for young adults as they compose their own realities in connection with important others in their lives in multiple contexts.

These renegotiations come about when people have experiences that are discrepant with or challenge their current meaning-making structure. Piaget (1950) explained that people initially try to assimilate these discrepant experiences into their current meaning making. When this is no longer possible, people accommodate or alter their meaning making to account for the new experiences. Through this process, individuals come to see their meaning making structure as object. Revising this subject–object relationship and moving to increasingly complex principles of mental organization depends on the nature and intensity of the challenge, the persons' individual characteristics, and the degree of support available for facing the challenge of reorganizing meaning making (Kegan, 1994; Sanford, 1962).

## Existing Integrative Efforts

Many college student development theories inherently include person in context by integrating cognitive, intrapersonal, and interpersonal dimensions, and placing making meaning in the context of the social environment. Abes, Jones, and McEwen's (2007) recent reconceptualization of their Model of Multiple Dimensions of Identity offers a clear vision of the interconnections of contextual influences, meaning making, and self-perceptions of multiple identity dimensions. Their model draws out connections between the three dimensions of development yet offers them as one possibility rather than a prescribed model. Their incorporation of social constructionist, feminist, and postmodern theoretical frameworks yields a perspective that describes a *possible process* through which students socially construct their identities, respecting the multiple forms those can take, given the complex interplay between contextual influences, meaning making, and social identities. As such, this revised model reflects Kegan's notion of focusing on the core activity of how we make meaning rather than on the particular meanings we make.

Renn (2003, 2004) explicitly makes the connection between social context and personal meaning making in her use of Bronfenbrenner's ecology model in which "the environment and the individual shape—and are shaped by—one another; the model represents a dynamic, shifting relationship of reciprocal influence" (2004, p. 29). Although Renn's work is addressed in more depth in the Torres, Jones, and Renn article (this issue), it is important to highlight here because of its contribution to contemporary holistic perspectives of college student development. Grounding her exploration of mixed-race students' identity development in this model revealed the complexity of individual development in the context of student culture and institutional milieu.

Using Renn's work as a frame, Taylor (2008) merged environmental and personal variables to construct an "integrated map of young adult's development journey from external reliance to internal definition" (p. 219), thus merging the ecology model with self-evolution. Taylor's visual map highlights the reciprocal influence Renn (and Bronfenbrenner) emphasized and reveals how various meaning-making structures mediate the influence of the environment and vice versa. The prominence of the environment at external meaning making gradually recedes as internal meaning making strengthens and moves to the foreground. Taylor's conceptualization intertwines contemporary cognitive theories into the cognitive dimension, and identity theories into the intrapersonal and interpersonal dimensions. King and Baxter Magolda (2005) offered a similar synthesis in their work on intercultural maturity and developmentally effective experiences (King, Baxter Magolda, Barber, Kendall Brown, & Lindsay, 2009). Abes, Jones, and McEwen (2007) reconceptualized their Model of Multiple Identity Development to integrate the cognitive dimension. These conceptualizations show the potential of integrating multiple theories into a coherent holistic perspective.

## Explicitly Holistic Research Studies

Contemporary research focused specifically on holistic college student development (i.e., that intentionally integrates the three dimensions of development) in social contexts refines these conceptual integrations. I highlight six longitudinal or extensive cross-sectional research efforts and use these theories to create a contemporary holistic perspective on college students' development.[1] Four longitudinal studies trace college students' self-evolution in general, and self-authorship in particular, acknowledging the crucial role of social context in the developmental journey. Baxter Magolda's 22-year study (1992, 2001, 2008, 2009) sketched the journey toward and into self-authorship from age 18 to 40, emphasizing both individual and contextual dynamics that mediate the journey. Torres's (2003; Torres & Baxter Magolda, 2004; Torres & Hernandez, 2007) 5-year study portrays the journey toward self-authorship for Latino/a college students with particular emphasis on how cultural expectations and racism shape the journey. Abes's (2003, 2009; Abes & Jones, 2004) 4-year study of lesbian college students reveals the role of heteronormativity in these students' journey toward self-authorship, a dynamic I return to in the discussion of future directions of theoretical research. The Wabash National Study, a 4-year longitudinal study involving diverse students on six campuses, traces the journey toward self-authorship acknowledging students' individual histories and characteristics, their educational environments, and how they make meaning of their educational experiences (Baxter Magolda, King, Taylor & Perez, 2008; Baxter Magolda, King, Taylor, & Wakefield, 2009; King & Baxter Magolda, 2007; King et al., 2009; King, Baxter Magolda, & Masse, 2008; King, Kendall Brown, Lindsay, & VanHecke, 2007). Drawing on 30 years of formal and informal research, Parks (2000) sketched the evolution of faith development, which she defined as meaning making, from adolescence to adulthood. Her portrayal integrates forms of knowing, dependence, and community that I take to reflect the cognitive, intrapersonal, and interpersonal developmental dimensions. Finally Pizzolato's (2003, 2004, 2005; Pizzolato, Chaudhari, Murrell, Podobnik, & Schaeffer, 2008) research program addresses self-evolution and self-authorship in multiple young adult populations in diverse social contexts. Organizing the particulars of these studies around the thread of evolution from external to internal definition makes a coherent perspective possible without losing the particulars of each theoretical contribution. It also focuses, like Kegan's work and Abes and colleague's (2007) reconceptualized model, on the underlying *activity* of meaning making rather than the specific meaning people make.

Baxter Magolda, Abes, and Torres (2008) blended the findings of their three longitudinal studies to construct an integrated view of college student and young adult development that encom-

---

[1]  I focus this article on research that explicitly incorporates all three dimensions of development. Identity, cognitive, and moral theoretical perspectives are addressed in other articles in this issue.

passed three major phases: following external formulas, crossroads, and self-authorship. I start with that integration and expand it using the Wabash National Study's microsteps within external formulas and crossroads, Baxter Magolda's (2008, 2009) identification of three elements within self-authorship, Parks's faith development perspective, and Pizzolato's findings. I frame this integrated, holistic perspective with the language from my longitudinal study because Torres, Abes, and the Wabash National Study researchers all found this framework useful in their work. It is crucial to note, however, that this holistic perspective is not an attempt to create a grand narrative or truth about student development theory. Rather, it is an attempt to chart the prevailing winds over a continent, recognizing that they do not affect each item in the landscape the same way (Frye, 1990).

## A Holistic Theoretical Perspective

The underlying thread of all six holistic research programs (and of many cognitive and social identity theories) is a gradual emergence of an internal voice to coordinate external influence and manage one's life. Before the cultivation of this internal voice, one's personal voice is an echo of the voice of external authority.

## Following External Formulas

The phrase 'following external formulas' captures the approach many of my longitudinal participants (who were predominantly White) used to decide what to believe, how to view themselves, and how to construct relationships with others throughout college and into their twenties (Baxter Magolda, 1992, 2001). They recorded knowledge provided by their college instructors (sometimes literally), chose majors that advisors or parents suggested, chose social activities and behaviors that yielded peer approval, and defined relational success by meeting others' needs and expectations. Similarly, Torres found that many of her Latino/a participants used external formulas to decide what to believe, make sense of their ethnic identities, and adopt cultural orientations (Torres & Hernandez, 2007). They relied heavily on family to make sense of their ethnic identities and often believed negative stereotypes about Latinos. They identified with either an Anglo or Latino culture, unaware of the possible blending of orientations, and did not venture from the comfort of their orientation. Although they distrusted authorities in general, they trusted their family and known peers. Abes (Abes & Jones, 2004) also reported that some of her participants used external expectations to make sense of their sexual orientation. In their concern to be considered "normal," to fit in with their peers, and to find identity labels that met others' expectations, they sometimes adopted labels without question and without considering how their various social identities intersected. Abes, Jones, and McEwen (2007) described this formulaic meaning making as a filter that allowed contextual influences to be largely accepted as encountered.

Although Parks did not use the language of following external formulas, she captured the phenomenon in her description of adolescent/conventional faith. She noted that "unexamined trust in sources of authority located outside the self" (2000, p. 55) led young adults to compose their reality through others. Adopting beliefs from authorities, depending on assurance from relationships for one's confidence, and participating in community with like-minded others characterized those who had yet to critically examine their faith. Parks made clear that young adults with conventional faith could be strongly committed to their beliefs despite their lack of internal origins. Similarly, longitudinal participants in the studies noted here were often highly committed to their beliefs and identities despite the lack of internal sources for them.

We found this same trust in authorities outside the self and following external formulas across diverse students in the Wabash National Study, which began following college students at six campuses in 2006 (King & Baxter Magolda, 2007; King et al., 2008). Because 86% of the 315 students used external meaning making in their first year of college and 57% of the 228 interviewed in their second year continued to use it (Baxter Magolda et al., 2009), we were able to identify three "microsteps"— early, middle, and late—within external formulas (Baxter Magolda et al., 2008). We identified the key characteristics of early external meaning making as "assuming authorities had the answers, identifying [one] self through external expectations, and deferring to others in relationships" (p. 18). Consistent and completely uncritical acceptance of external authority suggested no awareness of uncertainty on these students' part, much like Baxter Magolda's (1992) participants' early use of absolute knowing. Encountering uncertainty led to middle external meaning making, characterized by "discomfort with uncertainty, lack of clarity of [one's] own perspective, and a sense of obligation to live up to expectations" (Baxter Magolda et al., 2008, p. 20). Although uncertainty arose here, students did not know what to do with it and continued to look to authorities to resolve it, much like Baxter Magolda's (1992) transitional knowers did throughout college. Awareness of multiple perspectives sometimes led to using different formulas for different contexts owing to the lack of ability to integrate multiple perspectives. Shifting identities sometimes resulted from pursuing affirmation from others whose expectations conflicted. Rising tension among multiple perspectives and expectations, or among external formulas, led to late external meaning making characterized by "an increasing openness to uncertainty, recognition of the need to be oneself, and an awareness of the potential conflict of one's own and other's expectations" (Baxter Magolda et al., 2008, p. 24). The important development in late external meaning making was the recognition of the shortcomings of following external formulas. This awareness of following external formulas and the shortcoming of doing so reflects formulas moving from subject to object.

Pizzolato's work with college students at risk of dropping out identified this recognition of the shortcoming of external formulas as the primary reason her participants exhibited crossroads or self-authored ways of knowing early in college (2003, 2004). These students' college aspirations often conflicted with their peers' and communities' external formulas, forcing them to abandon those to create their own formulas for going to college. This path stands in contrast with Baxter Magolda's participants, for whom college attendance was the external formula they were expected to follow. This contrast of experiences highlights the role of context in shaping meaning making. Recognizing the shortcomings of external formulas, whether about career directions, relationships, faith systems, racial or ethnic identity, or sexual orientation, led participants in these studies to enter a crossroads where their internal voices began to emerge.

## Crossroads

The timing and ways in which young adults enter the crossroads varies widely based on individual and environmental variables. Parks described the unraveling of held assumptions as a "shipwreck, what has dependably served as shelter and protection and held and carried one where one wanted to go comes apart. What once promised trustworthiness vanishes" (2000, p. 28). No longer able or willing to depend on the unexamined trust in authority, young adults push away from the dock of external authority to explore the waters for themselves.

Sometimes the shipwreck is a jarring one, like Torres's participants encountered when they recognized racism and the need to work through negative stereotypes about their ethnicity. They often encountered new perspectives and definitions of Latino/a that differed from those of their family. As they became increasingly aware of multiple perspectives about race and ethnicity, they were faced with choosing how to view their own ethnicity. Similarly, Abes reported that her participants started to "realize the limitations of stereotypes; feel frustrated by identity labels insufficient to describe how they made sense of who they were; and challenge other people's expectations for whom they ought to or were allowed to be" (Abes & Jones, 2004, p. 621). For Baxter Magolda's participants, who for the most part encountered shipwrecks after college, these occurred around disappointing relationships, unsatisfying careers, major health crises, or the recognition that they had to find some basis upon which to construct their own beliefs and values internally. Many described these experiences as producing some kind of pain that needed to be resolved. Part of the discomfort of the crossroads stems from the knowledge that one needs to construct one's own beliefs and values yet at the same time one has not formed internal criteria to use to do so.

Two phases of the crossroads emerged in Baxter Magolda's participants' stories. The first was listening to their internal voices. They explored "identifying what made them happy, examining their own beliefs, finding parts of themselves that were important to them, and establishing a distinction between their feelings and external expectations" (Baxter Magolda, 2009, p. 7). Working to hear their own voices prompted the second phase—cultivating their voices—which "involved developing parts of themselves they valued, establishing priorities, sifting out beliefs and values that no longer worked, and putting pieces of the puzzle of who they were together" (p. 7). These tasks were difficult and took various forms depending on how participants approached them, the support available, and the particular tensions in their lives.

Similar crossroads microsteps are beginning to emerge from the Wabash National Study interviews. Some students in their second year interviews described a growing awareness of their own ideas in class, their own values or identity orientations, or their internal understanding of relationships. This emerging internal voice was not yet strong enough to outweigh external influence so they were not consistently able to act on it (Baxter Magolda et al., 2009). A few students who had cultivated their internal voices were able to bring them into tension with external influences. The shift to the exit of the crossroads requires bringing the internal voice to the foreground to coordinate (and perhaps reconstruct) external influence.

Pizzolato's participants encountered the crossroads, and often navigated it, earlier than most because of their need to develop their own voices to justify attending college. Tension between their community and peers' expectations and the possibility of attending college unraveled external assumptions early, as did seeing the effects of street life. These provocative moments, as Pizzolato called them, had the potential to lead out of the crossroads depending on students' volitional efficacy, self-regulation, and coping skills (Pizzolato, 2004, 2005). When they believed in their ability to persist in goal-directed behavior, were the primary source of regulating their own behavior, and coped with challenges via social relationships, they were most likely to solve disequilibrium by moving toward internal self-definitions. Thus, experiencing pain or shipwreck, listening to and cultivating their internal voices, and engaging in supportive relationships helps young adults to strengthen their internal voices sufficiently to author their lives across a variety of circumstances.

## Self-Authorship

Baxter Magolda's longitudinal participants' stories of their 20s and 30s provide rich contexts for identifying the nuances of self-authorship, or the internal capacity to define one's beliefs, identity, and relationships (Baxter Magolda, 2001, 2008, 2009). Baxter Magolda identified three elements of self-authorship from their stories: trusting the internal voice, building an internal foundation, and securing internal commitments (2008, 2009).

*Trusting the Internal Voice.* The key insight Baxter Magolda's participants reported as instrumental in their beginning to trust their internal voices was the distinction between reality and their reaction to it. "They recognized that reality, or what happened in the world and their lives, was beyond their control, but their reactions to what happened was within their control" (Baxter Magolda, 2008, p. 279). This realization, a reflection of reality moving from subject to object, set them on the road to taking responsibility for choosing how to interpret reality, how to feel about their interpretation, and how to react. Dawn, who was beginning to trust her own voice in managing her Multiple Sclerosis diagnosis at age 33, shared that it enabled being more flexible to work with obstacles. Some of Torres's participants began to trust their internal voices to make cultural choices to define their cultural reality and create their own principles to frame it (Torres & Hernandez, 2007). Similarly, some of Abes's participants began to trust their internal voices in making sense of discrimination. Jacky, who experienced discrimination on a number of fronts, researched the issues, "reading in-depth about all sides of an issue and then reaching her own conclusions after a logical analysis of multiple perspectives" (Abes et al., 2007, p. 11). Abes and associates described this process as participants using a complex meaning-making filter (e.g., trusting their internal voices) to analyze the cultural messages coming at them from social contexts. Thus, they were interpreting reality and choosing how to react to it.

Pizzolato's participants who entered college already trusting their internal voices encountered realities that called this trust into question (2004). They sometimes felt deficient compared with their peers in academic work, felt that faculty perceived them as unprepared for college work, and encountered negative reactions to their race or ethnic identities. Some avoided these issues and returned to formula following, whereas those who were able to interpret these realities and choose how to react to them returned to trusting their internal voices. Dawn captured this cyclical nature of trusting one's internal voice as she described numerous trips through the "shadow lands" where confusion reigned. She noted that, "it was not possible to be 'in the light' all the time" (Baxter Magolda, 2008, p. 280).

This uneasiness in coming to trust one's internal voice may be what Parks called the "ambivalence" of probing commitment. She described probing commitment as:

> a serious, critically aware exploration of the adult world and the potential versions of a future that it offers (which the adolescent, in contrast, receives uncritically), through which society's vulnerability, strength, integrity, and possibilities are assessed. A corresponding self-probing tests the strength, vulnerability, and capacity of the self to withstand or use what society will make, ask, and allow. (2000, pp. 67–68)

Parks linked this probing commitment with a fragile inner-dependence, thus connecting the cognitive and intrapersonal developmental dimensions. She translated fragile as newly formed yet vulnerable. Her distinction between inner-dependence and independence (see p. 77) is also informative in clarifying that trusting one's internal voice does not translate to isolation from others. Continued exploration and making choices about one's reaction to reality leads to the next element of self-authorship, building an internal foundation.

*Building an Internal Foundation.* As Baxter Magolda's participants strengthened their trust in their internal voices, they began to organize their choices into commitments that formed a philosophy, or an internal foundation, to guide their ongoing reactions to reality. Mark noted the importance of this foundation when he said, "It's either get a philosophy that's going to be able to provide a foundation or undergirding for what could happen in your life, or when it does hit, you're going to be lost" (Baxter Magolda, 2009, p. 86). As Mark and his peers dealt with career dilemmas, relationship disappointments, parenting, health crises, and finding meaning in a post 9/11 world, those who were building their internal foundations used their commitments to guide their reactions and choices. Torres noted that a few of her participants built internal foundations late in college as they considered choices "within the context of their internal values, culture, and life path" (Torres & Hernandez, 2007, p. 563). They were no longer intimidated by differences and able to maintain their cultural values in diverse contexts. Abes offered another example of a college junior building an internal foundation through integrating her religious, sexual orientation, class, and racial social identities into a complex system to guide her beliefs, identity, and relationships (Baxter Magolda et al., 2008).

Parks's form of knowing called tested commitment resonates with building an internal foundation, as does her form of dependence called confident inner-dependence. Of tested commitment she wrote, "One's form of knowing and being takes on a tested quality, a sense of fittingness, a recognition that one is willing to make one's peace and to affirm one's place in the scheme of things (though not uncritically)" (p. 69). Organizing one's choices into commitments to form an internal foundation results in a centeredness that Parks and many of Baxter Magolda's participants called being "at home" with oneself. Despite this centeredness, Baxter Magolda's participants still shared experiences in the shadow lands, and in retrospect, noted that they held their internal foundations in their heads before they held them in their hearts.

*Securing Internal Commitments.* Some of Baxter Magolda's participants, often in their 30s, recognized that they had constructed commitments in their heads but sometimes fell short of living them in their everyday lives. When these commitments shifted from being under construction to being a "home" in which participants could live, they became second nature (Baxter Magolda, 2008, 2009). When commitments became second nature, they were so natural that participants often did not think consciously about them. These commitments automatically came into play as participants navigated the challenges of their lives, making them comfortable with the chaos they encountered. These commitments also offered a sense of security that led to a greater sense of freedom. Trusting that they could use their foundations to make the best of what happened to them, they were more open to taking risks and to reevaluating their internal foundations. Thus, securing their internal commitments led simultaneously to a sense of security and a sense of possibility.

Baxter Magolda's participants' descriptions sound similar to Parks's (2000) definition of interdependence, which she suggested typically occurred after midlife. Parks described interdependence as the ability "to depend upon others without fear of losing the power of the self" (p. 87), which opened the door to repatterning truth and faith. This interdependence is connected with convictional commitment, or the ability to hold a deep conviction of truth in the context of paradox in the "ongoing motion of meaning-making and faith" (p. 60). A few of Baxter Magolda's participants used the same word Parks used—wisdom—to describe this element of self-authorship. This openness to further grown, to reevaluating one's center, and to embracing paradox seems to set the stage for Kegan's self-transforming mind.

## Caveats

The six research programs I have used to construct this holistic perspective primarily use a constructive–developmental lens. Moving toward integration with other academic traditions is a direction I explore next. Before turning to those directions, I want to reemphasize the point of the holistic perspective I just described. My intent is to point out key threads and possibilities in the underlying activity of meaning making that reappear across many theoretical approaches and that seem relevant (albeit in different times and ways) to a wide range of college students. Our task, if we are to make student development theorizing useful in practice, is to balance identifying new possibilities with the underlying activity of meaning making in a way that allows us to explore the intersections across these theoretical perspectives. Our task is to continue to critique, refine, and enhance our understanding of the possibilities of young adults' meaning making as their personal characteristics intersect with college and societal environments.

# Future Directions and Possibilities

Just as the perspectives I have highlighted here call for dialectic rather than dichotomy, the future of student development theorizing depends on dialectic. It requires bringing multiple perspectives into dialogue, maintaining a context (which I have proposed based on Kegan's work is the activity of meaning making) in which to nest and integrate these perspectives, and conducting developmental research in ways that enlighten holistic development. In arguing for a context and a holistic approach, I am not arguing for a grand narrative or theory. I am advocating exploring the intersections among multiple dimensions of development from multiple perspectives, openly identifying and exploring tensions among these perspectives. Creating one grand theory of holistic development is not possible or desirable; however, placing theoretical frameworks in dialectic to inform a holistic view of development is necessary, as I elaborate next.

## The Need for Holistic Perspectives

As Abes and colleagues (2007) noted, "Few models or theories exist to understand the holistic development of college students" (p. 16). Although research on particular dimensions of development is important, grounding it in a more holistic perspective that incorporates social context and epistemological, intrapersonal, and interpersonal developmental dimensions would contribute to creating more holistic theories. Nesting research on particular dimensions, or on particular aspects of the intersection of person and context, within a larger holistic perspective would help to organize student development theories into a coherent whole rather than the numerous "families" or separate silos into which they are currently organized. Hopefully, the integrative approach taken in the articles in this issue will help to move theoretical research in that direction.

Intentional exploration of the intersections among developmental dimensions is also crucial to understanding the activity of meaning making. King (2010) makes this point in offering evidence for both an "equal partners" perspective and a perspective that the cognitive dimension is the "strong partner" of the three. Torres offered evidence that the cognitive dimension helped her participants make sense of racist stereotypes (Torres, 2010; Torres & Baxter Magolda, 2004), but viewed them as interrelated because "no student ever progressed more than one phase without development in the other dimensions moving forward" (Torres & Hernandez, 2007, p. 570). Pizzolato (2010) also argued for keeping all three in constant connection, saying, "It is through cues from the interpersonal dimension that participants are compelled to question who they are and how they know" (p. 200). Baxter Magolda (2009) traced multiple relationships of the three dimensions in her participants' lives. Some tended to rely on their epistemological dimension when sorting through challenges in all three dimensions. Others who were naturally self-reflective often began with their intrapersonal dimension. Some who were intensely concerned about how others perceived them placed their interpersonal dimension in the forefront. Collectively, they often described holding their convictions initially in their heads rather than in their hearts, suggesting the possibility that convictions were constructed cognitively before they were implemented intrapersonally and interpersonally. Further understanding of the nuances of these intersections would enlighten the individual and societal characteristics that mediate development.

Linking traditional college student development theory with adult development literature and to adolescent meaning making would also contribute to a holistic perspective. Kegan's self-evolution theory has spawned extensive work (e.g., Berger 2004; The Adult Development Research Group, 2001) on adult development involving a wide range of ages and socioeconomic and cultural backgrounds. An entire literature on adult development exists, summarized in numerous handbooks (e.g., Smith & DeFrates Densch, 2009; Hoare, 2006), and informs and intersects with the development of adults attending college. Work with adolescents that highlights their meaning making before college (e.g., Laughlin & Creamer, 2007; Meszaros & Lane, 2010) would also inform college students' meaning making possibilities.

## Using Multiple Theoretical Frameworks to Enhance Holistic Perspectives

Considering student development theories in the context of and in interaction with multiple theoretical frameworks from academic traditions outside of student affairs and higher education is another crucial future direction. Abes, Jones, and McEwen (2007) model this direction by incorporating the social construction of identity, feminist conceptualizations of intersectionality, and the postmodern conceptualization of queer theory into their reconceptualized model. These theoretical frameworks emphasize the fluidity of identity construction, the role dominant social forces play in constructing relationships among multiple social identities, and the role performance of identity plays in shaping identity and dominant structures. As I noted, incorporating these perspectives leads to a holistic perspective that focuses on the underlying process or activity of meaning making rather than specifying the particular constructions that arise from it.

Abes's use of queer theory to reinterpret her longitudinal data (Abes, 2009; Abes & Kasch, 2007) underscores the value of using multiple interpretative lenses to understand the complexity and fluidity of college students' development. Concerned that her constructive–developmental theoretical perspective masked possibilities in her interpretation and did not sufficiently take power structures into account, Abes (2009) advocated "bringing together multiple and even seemingly conflicting theoretical perspectives to uncover new ways of understanding the data" (p. 141). She and a colleague created a borderland between constructivist and queer theory from which they were able to tell a richer story that "brings to life students' lived experiences through constructivism while simultaneously deconstructing them through queer theory" (p. 148). As Abes and Kasch (2007) reinterpreted Abes' longitudinal transcripts from the vantage point of queer theory, they described one participant as "reconstructing external authority by resisting heteronormativity and destabilizing structures it created" (p. 629). This analysis reveals the role of resisting power structures in cultivating one's own voice. They also noted that participants performed new versions of their sexuality, gender, religion, social class, and the intersections of these identities to resist heteronormative structures, thus continuously redefining the meanings of these identities (Abes & Kasch, 2007). Development of these identities is therefore a process of "becoming" that is not assessed as more or less complex. This queer interpretation focuses on the continuously changing interaction between self and society and among social identities unbounded by external or internal definition. Although their queer interpretation does not use the external to internal framework of constructive–developmental theory, it does reveal students' capacity to reconstruct their social identities and the power structures in their social contexts. Recognizing that this queer interpretation was more nuanced when partnered with a constructivist interpretation, Abes offered a rich and insightful exploration of the implications for researchers simultaneously using seemingly contradictory theoretical frameworks.

Zaytoun (2003, 2006, 2010) also advocated integrating multiple theoretical frameworks and illuminated that some of their contradictions may not be incompatible. Zaytoun (2006) integrated feminist, post-structural, and constructive–developmental frameworks in her exploration of "how development results from experiencing the world from within particular social locations" (p. 53). Drawing upon the work of Paula Gunn Allen, Gloria Anzaldúa, and Patricia Hill Collins, Zaytoun (2006) wrote,

> Self is intricately embedded in relationships not only to other people, but to aspects of the world that include social groups, communities, and inanimate and spiritual entities that are deemed important to the individual according to social influence and identity categories within which they relate. As social location plays a role in construction of self, it can also influence how an individual makes meaning and develops psychologically. (p. 59)

Zaytoun (2006) further explored how social identity categories mediate the process of psychological development, how personal consciousness is linked to social consciousness, and how the growth of both personal and social consciousness occurs within the tensions of particular social locations. Drawing on feminist phenomenology, Zaytoun argues that concepts of multiplicity and relationality of self "resonate with Kegan's orders of consciousness, particularly fifth order, and how Kegan's subject–object approach complicates yet appreciates and complements goals of phenomenology" (2010, p. 155). She views Anzaldúa's (2002) concept of *conocimiento* as consistent with Kegan's self-transformation and believes that both help to elucidate the relationship between personal and social consciousness. Taylor (2008), whose conceptual integration was noted earlier, also linked Anzaldúa's seven stages of *conocimiento* to the journey toward self-authorship, noting how Anzaldúa's descriptions enriched understanding of leaving external formulas, experiencing the crossroads, and self-authorship. Both Zaytoun and Taylor point out that Anzaldúa's stages are not linear but cyclical, yet they resonate with the underlying activity of meaning making.

Working with multiple theoretical frameworks helps to address nagging questions in student development theory. Feminist, postmodern, and phenomenological perspectives aid in Kegan's suggestion that we integrate person and context, self, and other in dialectic rather than a dichotomy. Exploring meaning making in the context of social location enlightens questions about how culture, power structures, and oppression shape and are shaped by individual meaning making. Jones (2010) used intersectionality to explore self-authorship in the context of social location thus "connecting individuals to groups and society and exploring the relational and mutually constitutive nature of these relationships" (pp. 240–241). Pizzolato (2010) explored how cultural selfways, or the "socialization of individual selves toward the culturally agreed upon ways of being and knowing" (p. 192), mediate meaning making. Her explorations led her to advocate for greater focus on the interpersonal dimension within meaning making. Baxter Magolda (2010) synthesized the work of numerous authors to address questions about the role of culture and making culture and context object in the evolution of self-authorship.

Using multiple theoretical perspectives also helps to illuminate myths that abound by highlighting inherent, but often underemphasized, aspects of existing student development theories. For example, pairing Anzaldúa's cyclical model with the journey toward self-authorship reveals the possibilities for experiencing the journey cyclically just as Baxter Magolda's (2008) participants reported. Because most theories about self-evolution present it as a trajectory without explicitly emphasizing cyclical possibilities, readers often assume theorists are arguing for a lock-step linear trajectory when most have not. In the same vein, self-evolution in general and self-authorship in particular are often assumed to privilege self over other and separation over connection. Kegan's and Baxter Magolda's integration of the three dimensions clearly emphasizes the connection between self and other throughout self-evolution. Both theories also convey that self-authorship refers to internal rather than separate authorship and heightens the potential for authentic connection with others rather than isolation. Considering multiple theoretical perspectives and their links to constructive–developmental frameworks helps to highlight these linkages in ways that are masked when individual meaning making is placed in the foreground. Of course, use of multiple methodologies and methods, a topic beyond the focus of this article, is also needed to capture the complexity of integrated development.

## Constructing Theory in Context: Theory and Practice as Dialectic

Student development theorizing could also benefit from eliminating the typical dichotomy between theory and practice in the student affairs profession. To understand students in their diverse social contexts and locations requires building theory in practice, intentionally and systematically gathering and interpreting how students make meaning of their experience. Using these observations and interpretations to guide practice creates the opportunity to refine existing theories and identify new possibilities while pursuing the profession's goal—developing the whole student.

*Correspondence concerning this article should be addressed to Marcia B. Baxter Magolda, 304 McGuffey Hall, Miami University, Oxford, OH 45056; baxtermb@ muohio.edu*

# References

Abes, E. S. (2003). *The dynamics of lesbian college students' multiple dimensions of identity.* Unpublished Dissertation, The Ohio State University, Columbus, OH.

Abes, E. (2009). Theoretical borderlands: Using multiple theoretical perspectives to challenge inequitable power structures in student development theory. *Journal of College Student Development, 50*(2), 141–156.

Abes, E. S., & Jones, S. R. (2004). Meaning-making capacity and the dynamics of lesbian college students' multiple dimensions of identity. *Journal of College Student Development, 45*(6), 612–632.

Abes, E. S., Jones, S. R., & McEwen, M. K. (2007). Reconceptualizing the Model of Multiple Dimensions of Identity: The role of meaning-making capacity in the construction of multiple identities. *Journal of College Student Development, 48*(1), 1–22.

Abes, E. S., & Kasch, D. (2007). Using Queer Theory to explore lesbian college students' multiple dimensions of identity. *Journal of College Student Development, 48*(6), 619–636.

American College Personnel Association. (1994). *The Student Learning Imperative.* Washington, DC: Author.

Anzaldúa, G. (2002). Now let us shift. In A. Keating & G. Anzaldúa (Eds.), *This bridge we call home: Radical visions for transformation* (pp. 540–578). New York: Routledge.

Bakan, D. (1966). *The duality of human existence: An essay on psychology and religion.* Chicago: Rand McNally & Company.

Baxter Magolda, M. B. (1992). *Knowing and reasoning in college: Gender-related patterns in students' intellectual development.* San Francisco: Jossey-Bass.

Baxter Magolda, M. B. (1999). *Creating contexts for learning and self-authorship: Constructive-developmental pedagogy.* Nashville: Vanderbilt University Press.

Baxter Magolda, M. B. (2001). *Making their own way: Narratives for transforming higher education to promote self-development.* Sterling, VA: Stylus.

Baxter Magolda, M. B. (2002). Epistemological reflection: The evolution of epistemological assumptions from age 18 to 30. In B. K. Hofer & P. R. Pintrich (Eds.), *Personal epistemology: The psychology of beliefs about knowledge and knowing* (pp. 89–102). Mahwah, NJ: Lawrence Erlbaum Associates.

Baxter Magolda, M. B. (2008). Three elements of self-authorship. *Journal of College Student Development, 49*(4), 269–284.

Baxter Magolda, M. B. (2009). *Authoring your life: Developing an internal voice to navigate life's challenges.* Sterling, VA: Stylus Press.

Baxter Magolda, M. B. (2010). Future directions: Pursuing theoretical and methodological issues in the evolution of self-authorship. In M. B. Baxter Magolda, E. G. Creamer & P. S. Meszaros (Eds.), *Development and assessment of self-authorship: Exploring the concept across cultures* (pp. 267–284). Sterling, VA: Stylus.

Baxter Magolda, M. B., Abes, E., & Torres, V. (2008). Epistemological, intrapersonal, and interpersonal development in the college years and young adulthood. In M. C. Smith & N. DeFrates Densch (Eds.), *Handbook of research on adult learning and development* (pp. 183–219). Mahwah, NJ: Lawrence Erlbaum Associates.

Baxter Magolda, M. B., King, P. M., Taylor, K. B., & Perez, R. J. (2008, November). *Developmental steps within external meaning making*. Paper presented at the annual meeting of the Association for the Study of Higher Education, Jacksonville, FL.

Baxter Magolda, M. B., King, P. M., Taylor, K. B., & Wakefield, K. (2009, April). *Decreasing authority-dependence during the first year of college*. Paper presented at the annual meeting of the American Educational Research Association, San Diego, CA.

Belenky, M., Clinchy, B. M., Goldberger, N., & Tarule, J. (1986). *Women's ways of knowing: The development of self, voice, and mind*. New York: Basic Books.

Berger, J. G. (2004). Dancing on the threshold of meaning: Recognizing and understanding the growing edge. *Journal of Transformative Education, 2,* 336–351.

Brown, R. D. (1972). *Student development in tomorrow's higher education: A return to the academy*. Alexandria, VA: American College Personnel Association.

Bruner, J. (1990). *Acts of meaning*. Cambridge, MA: Harvard University Press.

Chickering, A. W. (1969). *Education and identity*. San Francisco: Jossey-Bass.

Chickering, A. W., & Reisser, L. (1993). *Education and identity, second edition*. San Francisco: Jossey-Bass.

Dewey, J. (1916). *Democracy and education*. New York: The Free Press.

Erikson, E. (1968). *Identity, youth, and crisis*. New York: Norton.

Evans, N. J., Forney, D. S., & Guido-DiBrito, F. (1998). *Student development in college: Theory, research, and practice*. San Francisco: Jossey-Bass.

Frye, M. (1990). The possibility of feminist theory. In D. L. Rhode (Ed.), *Theoretical perspectives on sexual difference* (pp. 174–184). New Haven, CT: Yale University Press.

Gilligan, C. (1982). *In a different voice*. Cambridge, MA: Harvard University Press.

Heath, D. H. (1978). A model of becoming a liberally educated and mature student. In C. A. Parker (Ed.), *Encouraging development in college students* (pp. 189–212). Minneapolis: University of Minnesota Press.

Hoare, C. (Ed.). (2006). *Handbook of adult development and learning*. New York: Oxford University Press.

Jones, S. R. (2010). Getting to the complexities of identity: The contributions of an autoethnographic and intersectional approach. In M. B. Baxter Magolda, E. G. Creamer & P. S. Meszaros (Eds.), *Development and assessment of self-authorship: Exploring the concept across cultures* (pp. 223–244). Sterling, VA: Stylus.

Josselson, R. (1987). *Finding herself: Pathways to identity development in women*. San Francisco: Jossey-Bass.

Josselson, R. (1996). *Revising herself: The story of women's identity from college to midlife*. New York: Oxford University Press.

Keeling, R. P. (Ed.). (2004). *Learning reconsidered: A campus-wide focus on the student experience*. Washington, DC: National Association of Student Personnel Administrators and American College Personnel Association.

Kegan, R. (1982). *The evolving self: Problem and process in human development*. Cambridge, MA: Harvard University Press.

Kegan, R. (1994). *In over our heads: The mental demands of modern life*. Cambridge, MA: Harvard University Press.

Kegan, R., & Lahey, L. L. (2009). *Immunity to change: How to overcome it and unlock potential in yourself and your organization*. Boston: Harvard Business Press.

King, P. M. (2010). The role of the cognitive dimension of self-authorship: An equal partner or the strong partner? In M. B. Baxter Magolda, E. G. Creamer & P. S. Meszaros (Eds.), *Development and assessment of self-authorship: Exploring the concept across cultures* (pp. 167–185). Sterling, VA: Stylus.

King, P. M., & Baxter Magolda, M. B. (2005). A developmental model of intercultural maturity. *Journal of College Student Development, 46*(6), 571–592.

King, P. M., & Baxter Magolda, M. B. (2007, November). *Experiences that promote self-authorship among first year students of color: Understanding and negotiating multiple perspectives*. Paper presented at the annual meeting of the Association for the Study of Higher Education, Louisville, KY.

King, P. M., Baxter Magolda, M. B., Barber, J. P., Kendall Brown, M., & Lindsay, N. K. (2009). Developmentally effective experiences for promoting self-authorship. *Mind, Brain, and Education, 3*(2), 108–118.

King, P. M., Baxter Magolda, M. B., & Masse, J. (2008, October). *And now what? Effects of initial interaction with diverse peers.* Paper presented at the Diversity, Learning, and Inclusive Excellence: Accelerating and Assessing Progress Conference, Long Beach, CA.

King, P. M., Kendall Brown, M., Lindsay, N. K., & VanHecke, J. R. (2007). Liberal arts student learning outcomes: An integrated approach. *About Campus: Enriching the Student Learning Experience, 12*(4), 2–9.

King, P. M., & Kitchener, K. S. (1994). *Developing reflective judgment: Understanding and promoting intellectual growth and critical thinking in adolescents and adults.* San Francisco: Jossey-Bass.

King, P. M., & Kitchener, K. S. (2004). Reflective judgment: Theory and research on the development of epistemic assumptions through adulthood. *Educational Psychologist, 39*(1), 5–18.

Kitchener, K. S. (1983). Cognition, metacognition, and epistemic cognition. *Human Development, 26*, 222–232.

Knefelkamp, L., Widick, C., & Parker, C. A. (Eds.). (1978). *Applying new developmental findings. New Directions for Student Services* (No. 4). San Francisco: Jossey-Bass.

Kohlberg, L. (1969). Stage and sequence: The cognitive developmental approach to socialization. In D. A. Goslin (Ed.), *Handbook of socialization theory and research* (pp. 347–480). Chicago: Rand McNally.

Laughlin, A., & Creamer, E. G. (2007). Engaging differences: Self-authorship and the decision making process. In P. S. Meszaros (Ed.), *Self-Authorship: Advancing students' intellectual growth, new directions for teaching and learning* (Vol. 109, pp. 43–51). San Francisco: Jossey-Bass.

Meszaros, P. S., & Lane, C. D. (2010). An exploratory study of the relationship between adolescent risk and resilience and the early development of self-authorship. In M. B. Baxter Magolda, E. G. Creamer & P. S. Meszaros (Eds.), *Development and assessment of self-authorship: Exploring the concept across cultures* (pp. 85–99). Sterling, VA: Stylus.

Mezirow, J. (Ed.). (2000). *Learning as transformation: Critical perspectives on a theory in progress.* San Francisco: Jossey-Bass.

National Association of Student Personnel Administrators. (1989). *Points of view.* Washington, DC: Author.

Parks, S. D. (2000). *Big questions, worthy dreams: Mentoring young adults in their search for meaning, purpose, and faith.* San Francisco: Jossey-Bass.

Perry, W. G. (1970). *Forms of intellectual and ethical development in the college years: A scheme.* Troy, MO: Holt, Rinehart, & Winston.

Piaget, J. (1950). *The psychology of intelligence,* trans, M. Piercy & D. Berlyne. London: Routledge & Kegan Paul.

Piaget, J. (1970). *Structuralism.* New York: Basic Books.

Pizzolato, J. E. (2003). Developing self-authorship: Exploring the experiences of highrisk college students. *Journal of College Student Development, 44*(6), 797–812.

Pizzolato, J. E. (2004). Coping with conflict: Self-authorship, coping, and adaptation to college in first-year, high-risk students. *Journal of College Student Development, 45*(4), 425–442.

Pizzolato, J. E. (2005). Creating crossroads for self-authorship: Investigating the provocative moment. *Journal of College Student Development, 46*(6), 624–641.

Pizzolato, J. E. (2010). What is self-authorship? A theoretical exploration of the construct. In M. B. Baxter Magolda, E. G. Creamer & P. S. Meszaros (Eds.), *Development and assessment of self-authorship: Exploring the concept across cultures* (pp. 187–206). Sterling, VA: Stylus.

Pizzolato, J. E., Chaudhari, P., Murrell, E. D., Podobnik, S., & Schaeffer, Z. (2008). Ethnic identity, epistemological development, and academic achievement in underrepresented students. *Journal of College Student Development, 49*(4), 301–318.

Renn, K. (2003). Understanding the identities of mixed-race college students through a developmental ecology lens. *Journal of College Student Development, 44*(3), 383–403.

Renn, K. A. (2004). *Mixed race students in college: The ecology of race, identity, and community on campus.* Albany: State University of New York Press.

Sanford, N. (1962). Developmental status of the entering freshman. In N. Sanford (Ed.), *The American college: A psychological and social interpretation of the higher learning* (pp. 253–282). New York: Wiley & Sons.

Smith, M. C., & DeFrates-Densch, N. (Eds.). (2009). *Handbook of research on adult learning and development.* New York: Routledge.

Tanner, J. L., Arnett, J. J., & Leis, J. A. (2008). Emerging adulthood: Learning and development during the first stage of adulthood. In M. C. Smith & N. DeFrates-Densch (Eds.), *Handbook of research on adult learning and development* (pp. 34–67). New York: Routledge.

Taylor, K. B. (2008). Mapping the intricacies of young adults' developmental journey from socially prescribed to internally defined identities, relationships, and beliefs. *Journal of College Student Development, 49*(3), 215–234.

The Adult Development Research Group. (2001). *Toward a new pluralism in ABE/ESOL classrooms: Teaching to multiple "cultures of mind."* National Center for the Study of Adult Learning and Literacy Report #19. Cambridge, MA: Harvard University Graduate School of Education.

Torres, V. (2003). Influences on ethnic identity development of Latino college students in the first two years of college. *Journal of College Student Development, 44*(4), 532–547.

Torres, V. (2010). Investigating Latino ethnic identity within the self-authorship framework. In M. B. Baxter Magolda, E. G. Creamer & P. S. Meszaros (Eds.), *Development and assessment of self-authorship: Exploring the concept across cultures* (pp. 67–84). Sterling, VA: Stylus.

Torres, V., & Baxter Magolda, M. B. (2004). Reconstructing Latino identity: The influence of cognitive development on the ethnic identity process of Latino students. *Journal of College Student Development, 45*(3), 333–347.

Torres, V., & Hernandez, E. (2007). The influence of ethnic identity development on self-authorship: A longitudinal study of Latino/a college students. *Journal of College Student Development, 48*(5), 558–573.

Wenger, E. (1998). *Communities of practice: Learning, meaning, and identity.* Cambridge, UK: Cambridge University Press.

Wildman, T. M. (2007). Taking seriously the intellectual growth of students: Accommodations for self-authorship. In P. S. Meszaros (Ed.), *Self-authorship: Advancing students' intellectual growth. New directions for teaching and learning* (Vol. 109, pp. 15–30). San Francisco: Jossey-Bass.

Wildman, T. M., & Baxter Magolda, M. B. (2008, November). *Bridging learning and development.* Paper presented at the annual meeting of the Association for the Study of Higher Education, Jacksonville, FL.

Zaytoun, K. (2003). *Theorizing at the borders: A feminist, interdisciplinary exploration of the development of adult consciousness.* Miami University, Oxford, Ohio.

Zaytoun, K. (2006). Theorizing at the borders: Considering social location in rethinking self and psychological development. *National Women's Association Journal, 18*(2), 52–72.

Zaytoun, K. (2010). Beyond self-authorship: Fifth order and the capacity for social consciousness. In M. B. Baxter Magolda, E. G. Creamer & P. S. Meszaros (Eds.), *Development and assessment of self-authorship: Exploring the concept across cultures* (pp. 151–166). Sterling, VA: Stylus.

# CHAPTER 4
# A DEVELOPMENTAL MODEL
# OF INTERCULTURAL MATURITY

PATRICIA M. KING AND MARCIA B. BAXTER MAGOLDA

This article focuses on the development of intercultural maturity, which is frequently cited as a desired collegiate outcome. We position our work on intercultural maturity in the context of a holistic approach to human development using Kegan's (1994) model as a foundation and relating this outcome to other collegiate learning outcomes. We introduce a multidimensional framework that describes the development of intercultural maturity. We first explicate the three dimensions of the framework, link these to existing theory and research on student development and intercultural competence, and then illustrate the developmental levels of the framework using examples from interviews with college students.

In times of increased global interdependence, producing interculturally competent citizens who can engage in informed, ethical decision-making when confronted with problems that involve a diversity of perspectives is becoming an urgent educational priority (Gurin, Dey, Hurtado, & Gurin, 2002). For example, when a group of Fortune 500 companies filed a brief in support of the University of Michigan's affirmative action policies (*Fortune 500 corporations*, 2000), they noted that students with an appreciation for diversity:

> are better prepared to understand, learn from and collaborate with others from a variety of racial, ethnic and cultural backgrounds; demonstrate creative problem solving by integrating differing perspectives; exhibit the skills required for good teamwork; and demonstrate more effective responsiveness to the needs of all types of consumers. (¶ 6)

Colleges and universities are in many ways well suited to foster the development of these skills; however, "they are what corporations find in shortest supply among entry-level candidates" (Bikson & Law, 1994, p. 26). Levine and Cureton (1998) provided evidence that appreciation for diversity is also in short supply on college campuses: In their discussion of the growing tension on U.S. campuses around multicultural issues, they noted that "multiculturalism remains the most unresolved issue on campus [in the US] today" (p. 91). Further, persistent reports of racially-motivated hate crimes on college campuses suggest that this remains an unresolved issue and that there is a strong need to find better ways to help students achieve this desired collegiate outcome.

How do people come to understand cultural differences in ways that enable them to interact effectively with others from different racial, ethnic, or social identity groups? How can institutions of higher learning better address the seemingly intractable problems associated with educating for in-

King, P. M., & Baxter Magolda, M. B. (2005). A developmental model of intercultural maturity. *Journal of College Student Development*, 46, 571–592.

tercultural understanding? Finding ways to answer these questions lies at the heart of national and institutional efforts to achieve diversity outcomes and at the center of research designed to better understand how students achieve this important collegiate outcome.

Several scholars have proposed conceptual models to describe intercultural (or multicultural) competencies (e.g., Howard-Hamilton, Richardson, & Shuford, 1998; Ottavi, Pope-Davis, & Dings, 1994; Pope & Reynolds, 1997; Pope, Reynolds, & Mueller, 2004; Pope-Davis, Reynolds, Dings, & Ottavi, 1994). These models provide useful starting points for identifying the attributes that are associated with this ability. For example, Pope and Reynolds include among their listing of multicultural skills "the ability to identify and openly discuss cultural differences and issues," to "differentiate between individual differences, cultural differences, and universal similarities," and "to use cultural knowledge and sensitivity to make more culturally sensitive and appropriate interventions" (p. 271). Unfortunately, theory development on multicultural competence has been limited by heavy reliance on the assessment of attitudes as a proxy for competence.

Landreman (2003) conducted a comprehensive review of the intercultural competence literature, drawing from the fields of intercultural communication, multicultural competence, and developmental psychology, and literature on critical-, stratum-, and ethnic-consciousness. In her critique of this literature, she offered the following observations:

> Definitions of "competence" are theoretically and empirically inconsistent, and do not address the *application* of one's understanding and skills to intergroup relationships or social justice issues; the heterogeneity of cultural groups, the multiplicity, complexity, and intersectionality of identity, and individuals' relationship to institutional and societal power and their social location have been minimally considered . . . as well as the influence these factors have on the individual's experiences, perspectives and presenting problems; absent from the competence literature are considerations concerning students' underlying assumptions about intergroup differences. . . . (p. 39)

She suggested that intercultural consciousness is a more appropriate educational goal than multicultural competence; the prefix "inter" encompasses both domestic and international contexts and implies cultures interacting. She also noted that "achieving consciousness implies an understanding of self and identity (intrapersonal), while interacting with others in a historical and socio-cultural-political context (interpersonal), leading to reflection (cognitive) that motivates action" (pp. 41–42). These observations illustrate that intercultural competence is a complex, multifaceted construct, and that educating for this outcome requires a broader, more comprehensive approach than that suggested by training for knowledge or skills alone.

Similarly, several national reports on undergraduate education have called for the achievement of outcomes that are complex, multi-faceted abilities that require a wide variety of attributes that are interdependent and mutually reinforcing; these include the Association of American Colleges and Universities' (2002) *Greater Expectations* and the ACPA/NASPA (Keeling, 2004) report entitled *Learning Reconsidered*. Using a holistic lens to examine scholarship on intercultural or multicultural competencies allows one to identify underlying capacities that may guide (or at least affect) a learner's ability to integrate knowledge, skills, and awareness, and to act in interculturally mature ways. We argue that the developmental ability that undergirds regarding another culture favorably is grounded in the same ability that undergirds one's ability to regard an interpersonal difference favorably. That is, the developmental complexity that allows a learner to understand and accept the general idea of difference from self without feeling threat to self enables a person to offer positive regard to others across many types of difference, such as race, ethnicity, social class, gender, sexual orientation, and religion. Without this foundation, students may be able to learn about cultural differences; however, this model suggests that they will find it difficult if not impossible to use this knowledge in an intercultural interaction. In other words, less complex levels of cognitive and intrapersonal (identity) development may hinder one's ability to use one's intercultural skills. Similarly, having a sense of identity driven predominantly by others' expectations may diminish one's capacity to apply cognitive and interpersonal attributes in intercultural contexts.

Many scholars of human development have argued that a more holistic approach to educational research and practice is required to help students develop the array of skills that will enable them to tackle complex contemporary problems, especially those with an intercultural dimension (Baxter Magolda, 1997, 1999, 2001, 2003; Baxter Magolda & King, 2004; M. Bennett, 1993; Bidell, Lee, Boucie, Ward, & Brass, 1994; Jones & McEwen, 2000; Kegan, 1994; King & Baxter Magolda, 1996; Knefelkamp, 2005; Mentkowski & Associates, 2000; Ortiz, 2000; Storti, 1990). Looking at intercultural maturity using a holistic perspective provides a possible explanation for the ineffectiveness of simpler, more superficial approaches to intercultural competence that rely on dispensing information and teaching desirable behavior and skills: Perhaps they are ineffective because they fail to consider one or more domains (cognitive, identity, interpersonal) of development. For example, omitting the cognitive component in conflict resolution risks being ineffective with students who see the world in "either/or" terms and who are thus cognitively unable to analyze an intercultural conflict from the perspective of both parties involved. Similarly, omitting the interpersonal component risks being ineffective with students who decide how to act based on others' expectations rather than on the interculturally appropriate criteria that educators may have tried to teach them.

In this article, we argue that educators could be more effective in achieving diversity outcomes if they could organize their goals and programs using a conceptual framework that provides a more holistic approach to defining diversity outcome goals and how students progress toward these goals. In particular, we propose a multidimensional framework that describes how people become increasingly capable of understanding and acting in ways that are interculturally aware and appropriate; we call this capacity intercultural maturity. We first describe our proposed framework and then illustrate the developmental levels of the framework using examples from interviews with college students. We conclude with a discussion of implications for educational practice and for further research.

## A Multidimensional Framework of the Development of Intercultural Maturity

Our proposed model of intercultural maturity draws from several genres of research in multicultural education (see C. Bennett, 2001 for a comprehensive analysis) as it attempts to integrate three major domains of development (cognitive, intrapersonal, and interpersonal). We draw our conceptualization of intercultural maturity primarily from the literature on college student and adult development and, in particular, from Kegan's (1994) model of lifespan development.

According to Kegan, mature individuals are better equipped to approach and respond to complex life tasks because they exemplify what he has termed "self-authorship" (p. 185). Using this way of organizing one's life, individuals act as authors of their lives (not just the stage on which their lives are played out), balancing external influences with their individual interests and those of others around them (Baxter Magolda, 2000a). Many demands placed on adults in contemporary society "require self-authorship because they require the ability to construct our own visions, to make informed decisions in conjunction with coworkers, to act appropriately, and to take responsibility for those actions" (Baxter Magolda, 2001, p. 14). Self-authorship requires complex ways of making meaning of experience, drawing on one's understanding in all three dimensions of development.

Kegan's (1994) model is holistic in that it incorporates and integrates three dimensions of development. The cognitive dimension focuses on how one constructs one's view and creates a meaning-making system based on how one understands knowledge and how it is gained. The intrapersonal dimension focuses on how one understands one's own beliefs, values, and sense of self, and uses these to guide choices and behaviors. The interpersonal dimension focuses on how one views oneself in relationship to and with other people (their views, values, behaviors, etc.) and makes choices in social situations. Kegan argued that development in all three dimensions is required for a person to be able to use one's skills. Those for whom development in one or more dimensions does not provide an adequate basis for coping with the complex life tasks they face often report being overwhelmed or "in over their heads."

Our framework for discussing intercultural maturity encompasses Kegan's (1994) three dimensions of development (cognitive, intrapersonal, and interpersonal), as well as their interconnections. Our choice of the word "maturity" in the name of this educational goal refers to the developmental capacity that undergirds the ways learners come to make meaning, that is, the way they approach, understand, and act on their concerns. Thus, demonstrating one's intercultural skills requires several types of expertise, including complex understanding of cultural differences (cognitive dimension), capacity to accept and not feel threatened by cultural differences (intrapersonal dimension), and capacity to function interdependently with diverse others (interpersonal dimension). In other words, through this proposed model, we are building on Kegan's contention that producing interculturally competent citizens requires helping students achieve intercultural maturity in all three dimensions.

This conceptual framework is designed to reflect two elements that are not apparent in most of the existing literature on collegiate outcomes. First, in recognition that this is a complex collegiate outcome, we define intercultural maturity as multi-dimensional and consisting of a range of attributes, including understanding (the cognitive dimension), sensitivity to others (the interpersonal dimension), and a sense of oneself that enables one to listen to and learn from others (the intrapersonal dimension). Second, acknowledging that students typically learn and become capable of more complex learning by taking a series of steps (whether gradually or quickly), the framework proposed here not only identifies the desired outcome itself, but also includes two steps that lead to the achievement of the outcome, benchmarks along a developmental continuum. For example, being aware of cultural differences is an important first step in cultural competence; respectfully demonstrating this awareness in a conversation with a coworker or community member is a more compelling indication of the achievement of this outcome. Each of these examples shows a basic developmental progression, with the application of one's learning in changing contexts as the more stringent criterion of educational success.

The three proposed developmental levels are offered here as general descriptions of these benchmarks, not as detailed, comprehensive lists of capacities at each level. We also wish to note that the framework is the result of our attempts to integrate insights from existing theories of human development, prior research on student development and intercultural competence, and from our own experience teaching graduate students and researching college student development. The framework has not yet been subjected to empirical analysis. This framework appears in the form of a 3 × 3 matrix, linking the three domains of development (cognitive, intrapersonal, and interpersonal) with three levels of development (initial, intermediate, and mature). Table 1 thus consists of nine cells that show how development in each domain unfolds across three developmental benchmarks, the last of which (the far right column) describes the kind of maturity that is consistent with the description of intended collegiate outcomes noted above. Next, we discuss each dimension separately, and then make some observations about their interrelationships.

## Role of the Cognitive Dimension in Intercultural Maturity

The first row of Table 1 describes the trajectory of the cognitive dimension and how it mediates the way people think about and understand diversity issues. For example, the assumption in the initial level that knowledge is certain and that knowledge claims can be readily judged as right or wrong serves as a barrier to learning about or accepting differing perspectives. At this level, beliefs tend to be adopted from authorities rather than being internally constructed, so challenges to beliefs are often ignored or quickly determined to be wrong. Differing cultural perspectives that do not agree with one's view of what is true are often considered wrong rather than different. This phase has been characterized in several theories of cognitive development as dualistic thinking (Perry, 1968), received knowing (Belenky, Clinchy, Goldberger, & Tarule, 1986), absolute knowing (Baxter Magolda, 1992), pre-reflective thinking (King & Kitchener, 1994), ethnocentric reasoning (M. Bennett, 1993), and as the use of representational skills (Fischer, 1980).

**TABLE 1**

**A Three-Dimensional Developmental Trajectory of Intercultural Maturity**

| Domain of Development and Related Theories | Initial Level of Development | Intermediate Level of Development | Mature Level of Development |
|---|---|---|---|
| **Cognitive** (Baxter Magolda, 1992, 2001; Belenky et al., 1986; M. Bennett, 1993; Fischer, 1980; Kegan, 1994; King & Kitchener, 1994, 2004; Perry, 1968) | Assumes knowledge is certain and categorizes knowledge claims as right or wrong; is naïve about different cultural practices and values; resists challenges to one's own beliefs and views differing cultural perspectives as wrong | Evolving awareness and acceptance of uncertainty and multiple perspectives; ability to shift from accepting authority's knowledge claims to personal processes for adopting knowledge claims | Ability to consciously shift perspectives and behaviors into an alternative cultural worldview and to use multiple cultural frames |
| **Intrapersonal** (Cass, 1984; Chickering & Reisser, 1993; Cross, 1991; D'Augelli, 1994; Helms, 1995; Josselson, 1987, 1996; Kegan, 1994; Marcia, 1980; Parks, 2000; Phinney, 1990; Torres, 2003) | Lack of awareness of one's own values and intersection of social (racial, class, ethnicity, sexual orientation) identity; lack of understanding of other cultures; externally defined identity yields externally defined beliefs that regulate interpretation of experiences and guide choices; difference is viewed as a threat to identity | Evolving sense of identity as distinct from external others' perceptions; tension between external and internal definitions prompts self-exploration of values, racial identity, beliefs; immersion in own culture; recognizes legitimacy of other cultures | Capacity to create an internal self that openly engages challenges to one's views and beliefs and that considers social identities (race, class, gender, etc.) in a global and national context; integrates aspects of self into one's identity |
| **Interpersonal** (M. Bennett, 1993; Chickering & Reisser, 1993; Gilligan, 1982; Kegan, 1994; Kohlberg, 1984; Noddings, 1984) | Dependent relations with similar others is a primary source of identity and social affirmation; perspectives of different others are viewed as wrong; awareness of how social systems affect group norms and intergroup differences is lacking; view social problems egocentrically, no recognition of society as an organized entity | Willingness to interact with diverse others and refrain from judgment; relies on independent relations in which multiple perspectives exist (but are not coordinated); self is often overshadowed by need for others' approval. Begins to explore how social systems affect group norms and intergroup relations | Capacity to engage in meaningful, interdependent relationships with diverse others that are grounded in an understanding and appreciation for human differences; understanding of ways individual and community practices affect social systems; willing to work for the rights of others |

In the intermediate phase of the trajectory, views about knowledge shift from seeing knowledge as certain to increasingly acknowledging the uncertainty associated with making a knowledge claim. This shift is accompanied by decreasing reliance on authority's knowledge claims and increasing reliance on personal processes for adopting knowledge claims. Increasing uncertainty yields more openness to differing perspectives, while personal processing of knowledge claims yields the notion that different people can hold different views for legitimate reasons. The intermediate phase has been characterized as multiplistic thinking (Perry, 1968), subjective and procedural knowing (Belenky et al., 1986), transitional and independent knowing (Baxter Magolda, 1992), quasi-reflective thinking (King & Kitchener, 1994), the beginning stages of ethnorelative reasoning (M. Bennett, 1993), and as the coordination of representational systems and abstract mapping (Fischer, 1980).

The mature phase of the trajectory is marked by the shift to knowledge as constructed and as grounded in context. The ability to consciously shift perspectives emerges because judgments derive from personal experience, evidence from other sources, and others' experience. The ability to entertain multiple perspectives in multiple contexts leads to the ability to use multiple cultural frames. This mature phase has been described as relativistic thinking (Perry, 1968), constructed knowing (Belenky et al., 1986), contextual knowing (Baxter Magolda, 1992), reflective thinking leading to the ability to make reflective judgments (King & Kitchener, 1994), integration, the final ethnorelative stage of M. Bennett's (1993) model, and coordination of abstract systems (Fischer, 1980; see also Fischer & Bidell, 1998; Kitchener, 2002; Kitchener & Fischer, 1990).

Milton Bennett's (1993) model specifically explicates the role of cognitive complexity in the development of intercultural competence, focusing on the ways individuals come to understand cultural differences. This model is grounded in constructivism (how individuals make meaning of experience) and, in particular, how individuals interpret their experiences with diverse others in intercultural situations. It also delineates six major markers that indicate increasing sophistication in complexity of understanding intercultural issues, from ethnocentric (three stages) to ethnorelative (three stages) perspectives. The two forms of adaptation (the second ethnorelative stage) illustrate this link particularly well. The first form is "cognitive frame-shifting," or taking a cultural perspective different from one's own; the second form is "behavioral code-shifting," in which the individual can act from another frame of reference. Both require the cognitive complexity to hold at least two cultural perspectives in mind at the same time.

Since there is cognitive complexity in the presence of diverse worldviews, accepting ambiguity and understanding the basis of differing worldviews require complex thinking skills. Perry (1968), Baxter Magolda (1992, 2001), Fischer (1980), and King and Kitchener (1994, 2004) all posit that earlier, more simplistic levels of cognitive development involve concrete thinking and a belief in absolute knowledge, whereas later, more complex levels reflect an ability to consider knowledge grounded in context, deriving judgments from personal experiences, evidence from other sources, and from the perspectives of others. This raises the distinct possibility that complexity in thinking is a prerequisite for mature understanding of culturally different worldviews (M. Bennett, 1993; King & Shuford, 1996). Intercultural perspective taking, another cognitive task, also has application as students are able to develop the ability to consider both cognitive and affective elements that affect culturally different students (Kappler, 1998; Steglitz, 1993). Evidence of the role of cognitive complexity in the development of intercultural maturity is provided in a study of U.S. students who had studied abroad: Moore and Ortiz (1999) found that interculturally competent students were critical thinkers who suspended judgment until the evidence was in and who included a diverse range of knowledge in what they considered as evidence. Taken together, these findings suggest that there are strong reasons to include and to continue to explore the role of cognitive development in various aspects of intercultural maturity.

## Role of the Intrapersonal Dimension in Intercultural Maturity

The second row in Table 1 traces ways in which the intrapersonal dimension mediates how people think about and come to understand diversity issues. As noted above, this dimension focuses on how people view themselves; this is variously referred to as identity development, ego development, developing a sense of identity, or self-development. This broad category includes a range of identity-related topics, from ways people use their values and beliefs to make life choices and decisions to how they view and interpret their social identities based on factors such as race, ethnicity, class, sexual orientation, and religious affiliation. Each of these factors has been reported to affect the ways students act in intercultural situations, examples of which are offered below.

Fortunately, there is a wealth of literature on identity development to inform this dimension. In the last two decades, there has been a virtual explosion of literature on identity development. This includes theory and research on general models (e.g., Chickering & Reisser, 1993; Josselson 1987, 1996; Kegan, 1994; Marcia, 1966, 1980) as well as models addressing particular dimensions of identity development, such as racial/ethnic identity (e.g., Cross, 1991; Helms, 1995; Parks, 2000; Phinney, 1990; Thompson & Carter, 1997; Torres, 2003; Torres & Baxter Magolda, 2004; Wijeyesinghe & Jackson, 2001) and sexual orientation (e.g., Cass, 1984; D'Augelli, 1994; Evans & D'Augelli, 1996). In these models, individuals at more complex stages of development have considered and integrated these dimensions into a sense of self that is maintained through interactions with diverse others and through participation in majority-defined and -dominated society. While these models tend to focus on culturally distinct differences, they also contain some noteworthy similarities, especially when examined from a holistic, developmental perspective. For example, these theories tend to describe movement from lack of awareness of one's particular identity, through a period of confusion and exploration, to a complex, internally defined perspective on how one's race, ethnicity, or sexual orientation are integrated into one's view of oneself and the world. In addition, these theories indicate that intercultural competence requires an internally defined sense of self to avoid feeling threatened by difference (Kegan, 1994). In other words, several overarching theoretical perspectives are apparent, perspectives that in some ways subsume or overlap with theories addressing particular dimensions of identity development.

As outlined in Table 1, perspectives on diversity issues at the initial level are characterized in ways that tap a variety of aspects of identity; these include a general lack of awareness about one's own social identity. Among racial/ethnic identity development models, this is reflected in Cross's (1991) Preencounter and Encounter stages; Helm's (1995) Contact and Disintegration statuses; and Phinney's (1990) Diffusion-Foreclosure stage; it is also consistent with Josselson's (1987, 1996) foreclosures/guardians. This level is also characterized as being defined by others' expectations; endorsing cultural beliefs, values, or practices in an unreflective or unconsidered way; and being threatened by different cultural values or by others of different social identity groups. Having an externally defined identity yields externally defined beliefs that regulate interpretation of experiences and guide choices. Thus the "resistance" multicultural educators experience from some students may result not only from their reliance on simplistic cognitive categories that do not accommodate multiple cultural perspectives, but also from a sense of self that is largely defined by others, as described in Kegan's (1994) third order. At this level of intercultural maturity, an individual's sense of self might be defined in a restrictive sense by one's primary social identity group, whether or not the values of that group are internally endorsed.

The tension between an externally derived sense of self (e.g., reliance upon affirmation by others or peer group acceptance) and an internally derived self-definition is heightened at the intermediate benchmark of intercultural maturity. This level is characterized by an intentional self-exploration that allows for the simultaneous examination of one's experiences in one's own cultural contexts and an examination of that culture in broader social contexts. For example, it allows for a more visible expression of one's own cultural values and is reflected in Cross's (1991) Immersion/Emersion stage, Helm's (1995) Reintegration and Pseudo-Independence statuses, Phinney's (1990) Diffusion-Foreclosure stage, and in the ability to take a more candid look at the nature of one's own privilege (McIntosh, 1989).

By contrast, a mature level of intrapersonal development as applied to diversity issues is characterized by a sense of self in which various aspects of one's identity are integrated in ways that provide a culturally-sensitive and well-considered basis for making decisions about intercultural interactions. In the theoretical models noted above, this level of development is reflected in Cross's (1991) Internalization and Internalization-Commitment stages, Helms's (1995) Immersion-Emersion and Autonomy statuses, and Phinney's (1990) Identity Achievement stage. Individuals are still open (indeed, eager) to have their views and perspectives questioned, but are not threatened by this process. This mature level resonates with Kegan's (1994) fourth order meaning making, with achievement of Chickering and Reisser's (1993) identity vector, and with Josselson's (1987, 1996) pathmaker.

Ortiz (1997) noted that in campus communities where culture is expressed, opportunities for learning are enhanced when students successfully integrate their ethnicity into their identity. For example, Howard-Hamilton (2000) showed how a student's level of racial identity development could affect his or her response to and performance on class assignments that call for analysis of issues that involve racial dynamics. Broido (2000) found that students who became social justice allies during college had developed self-confidence, defined as "comfort with one's identity and internal loci or worth and approval" (p. 12), and weren't threatened by being aligned with underrepresented or non-dominant groups. These examples illustrate the central role of identity development in achieving intercultural maturity.

## Role of the Interpersonal Dimension in Intercultural Maturity

The third dimension of intercultural maturity involves the ability to interact effectively and interdependently with diverse others. In particular, this draws on the mature capacity to construct and engage in relationships with others in ways that show respect for and understanding of the other's perspectives and experiences, but that are also true to one's own beliefs and values. Developmental theories informing the social dimension of intercultural maturity tend to show change from an egocentric, individualistic perspective ("I act in ways that serve me"), to a perspective that acknowledges that different social groups have different values, sensitivities, and experiences ("to each her own"), to a perspective that reflects an appreciation for ways in which social systems affect relations between and among culturally different groups. Because members of underrepresented groups have not been treated fairly at a societal level, this is a key concern underlying intergroup relations in the US.

Several theories have described development in this domain. Chickering and Reisser (1993) described the development of mature interpersonal relationships among college students, focusing on how students come to appreciate differences across intercultural and interpersonal boundaries. Kohlberg (1984) developed a theory of moral development based on principles of distributive justice, and other scholars focused on an ethic of care as the ethical imperative (Brabeck, 1989; Gilligan, 1982; Martin, 1985; Noddings, 1984); more recently, Rest, Narvaez, Bebeau, and Thoma (1999a, 1999b) proposed using schema theory to explain changes in moral judgment.

The last row of Table 1 outlines key developmental features as individuals develop mature capacity in social contexts, including intercultural contexts. At the initial level, social relations are grounded in one's primary social identity or affinity group, often using egocentric standards to judge cultural differences ("that's not how my family celebrates that holiday") or to judge social policy issues ("what's in it for me?"). Perspectives and values held by others may be tolerated, but are judged as ignorant or wrong. There is little acknowledgement of or reference to abstract concepts such as social ideals of community or to the goals of organized society. This kind of understanding of one's relationships with others is also apparent in the ethnocentric stages of M. Bennett's (1993) model, the Personal Interests schema (similar to pre-conventional reasoning) of Kohlberg's theory (Rest et al., 1999a), and with Level I of Gilligan's (1982) model, which is characterized by an egocentric, survival orientation where self-interest motivates moral reasoning.

By contrast, there is a much greater capacity to explore the nature and sources of intergroup differences at the intermediate level and to interact effectively with others who are seen as different. Individuals tend to be less judgmental, acknowledging the legitimacy of multiple perspectives. Associated with this broadening perspective that allows for a wider range of views and experiences is a broader understanding of social systems; at this level, students show an early awareness of these systems as social/cultural constructions that include not only social expectations that are codified in law, but also social conventions and community rules governing behavior. This kind of reasoning is consistent with the early ethnorelative stages of M. Bennett's (1993) model and with the Maintaining Norms schema (similar to conventional reasoning) as applied to Kohlberg's (1984) theory, reflecting a more inclusive view of roles, rules, and duties as having society-wide implications. It may also be seen in Level II of Gilligan's (1982) model, where connection with others is highlighted, even to the point of forfeiting one's own view to seek others' acceptance and thus avoid hurting them. However, this openness to new perspectives is mitigated by the continued use of others' approval as a standard for one's decisions about what to believe and how to act, as described in Kegan's (1994) third order reasoning and Gilligan's Level II.

The mature level of the interpersonal dimension is characterized by heightened awareness and capacity to engage in intercultural interactions that are interdependent, respectful, informed by cultural understanding, and mutually negotiated. Instead of experiencing such interactions as compromising or diminishing one's own cultural values and experiences, or as threatening one's own sense of self, they are experienced as enhancing one's identity and role as a member of society. This type of understanding is reflected in M. Bennett's (1993) stage of Integration, in which an individual can integrate disparate aspects of one's identity as one moves between cultural perspectives. It is also consistent with Kohlberg's (1984) description of Postconventional reasoning, where moral criteria (such as respect for human rights) have primacy over social conventions (such as roles or contracts) in making moral decisions. At this level, individuals acknowledge that there are many possible social arrangements, so members' duties and rights should derive from the moral purpose of the arrangement, not from its existence per se. It is also consistent with Gilligan's (1982) Level III reasoning, in which a woman's own needs are added to the mix of those that should be taken into account in resolving a moral conflict. The ways of making meaning of intercultural experiences at this level of development appear to enable individuals to comfortably and more effectively act as advocates or social justice allies across a range of social issues, from civil rights to causes related to specific social identities.

Several studies on moral development have addressed the development of intercultural maturity in the college years. Based on their comprehensive literature review of moral judgment development among college students, King and Mayhew (2002, 2004) reported that students who relied on moral principles to reason about moral dilemmas held more positive attitudes toward diversity issues (e.g., Derryberry & Thoma, 2000) and had a higher level of intercultural sensitivity (Endicott, Bock & Narvaez, 2003). They also found that moral reasoning level was a strong predictor of acting in prosocial ways in that those whose moral reasoning relied on moral principles were more likely to engage in prosocial behaviors. They explained these findings by suggesting that the shift from norm-based to principled reasoning reflects students' ability to examine the fairness of social systems; it also reflects the understanding that social systems are cultural constructions and can be changed. These findings illustrate the connections between moral development and intercultural maturity.

## Interrelationships among the Three Dimensions

Links across the three dimensions of development are evident through findings from several studies. For example, having an internal sense of self supports the cognitive ability to acknowledge that people hold multiple perspectives on many issues, including intercultural issues (Baxter Magolda, 2000b; Ortiz, 2000), and for defensible reasons (King & Shuford, 1996). In a study that directly examined this relationship, Guthrie (1996) found that almost half of the variance in college students' level of tolerance for diversity was explained by their level of cognitive complexity in reflective judgment. Similarly, Kitchener and Fischer (1990) argued that the ability to understand abstract concepts (e.g., White privilege) emerges with the ability to engage in abstract mapping; this ability coincides with Stage 4 of quasi-reflective thinking in the Reflective Judgment Model, where knowledge is first understood as an abstraction (King & Kitchener, 1994). In other words, the capacity to examine one's identity through the lens of privilege requires at least an intermediate level of cognitive development. Endicott et al. (2003) reported a similar link to the cognitive dimension. They examined patterns of correlations between moral judgment and intercultural sensitivity and suggested that the obtained shared variance could be explained by the fact that both postconventional and ethnorelative thinking are "rooted in cognitive flexibility, or the ability to understand, consider, and weigh multiple frameworks, or schemas. In flexible moral thinking one is considering frameworks of moral principles and in flexible intercultural thinking one is considering cultural frameworks" (p. 16). Further evidence that these dimensions are related was recently reported by Torres and Baxter Magolda (2004); they found that among a sample of Latino college students, increased cognitive complexity reduced stereotype vulnerability and enabled more complex constructions of ethnic identity.

As can be seen by looking at Table 1, juxtaposing domains of development with varying levels of development illuminates both similarities and differences among the rows and columns. While each row focuses on a different dimension of development, each column reveals similarities in approaches to meaning making within developmental level. At the early phases of development, learners tend to accept authorities' views (cognitive dimension), define themselves through others' views and expectations (intrapersonal dimension), and act in relationships to acquire approval (interpersonal dimension). In the context of racial, ethnic, or sexual orientation identity development, these characteristics are consistent with the lack of awareness of one's particular identity that stems from accepting external (often dominant) perspectives. Dissonance in various aspects of identity development often stems from marginalization by others, which can call into question the validity of external authority. As learners struggle through the confusion that comes with realizing that all knowledge is not certain and that they must consider establishing their own views (cognitive dimension), they also come to question their reliance on others for self-definition (intrapersonal) and on others' approval in relationships (interpersonal). The particulars of race, ethnicity, or sexual orientation are intertwined in this confusion and exploration. The need to explore these issues for oneself and move away from uncritically accepting authorities' views is consistent with the exploration phases of these layers of identity. In later, more complex phases of development where self-authorship on all three dimensions is achieved, it is possible to construct an internally defined perspective on how one's race, ethnicity, or sexual orientation is integrated into one's view of oneself.

Other researchers have also reported findings that illustrate interrelationships across domains of development. One prominent example was offered by Parks Daloz, Keen, Keen, and Daloz Parks (1996) in a study of 100 individuals who had committed themselves to the public good. They reported the following:

> In sum, many of our interviewees are able to coordinate several cultural perspectives at once, including their own. Thus, they can appreciate what they find worthwhile and are open to what they may not easily grasp in another culture, yet they are forthright in their abhorrence of brutality regardless of where it is found. At the same time, they are conscious of their own cultural frame from which they are rendering their judgment. In effect, their appreciation for cultural difference does not invalidate their sense of a moral compass. On the contrary, their experiences appear to strengthen it by taking them across the boundaries of and beyond the blind spots of their own tribal perspectives. (p. 119)

## Student Reflections across Levels of Intercultural Maturity

In the prior section, we presented a conceptual framework for the development of intercultural maturity. Here, we offer examples from interviews with White and Latino students that informed the identification of these developmental themes and that illustrate these themes. These excerpts are drawn from studies conducted by Baxter Magolda (1992, 2001) and Torres (2003).

## Initial Perspectives on Intercultural Maturity

Lauren, a White participant in Baxter Magolda's (1992) longitudinal study, relied on external authority to define herself during college. Her stance on differences was apparent in this story:

> One thing that living off campus showed me the most is that it's really hard sometimes to live with your friends and be good friends with them at the same time. I lived with my best friend last year, and that might have been a mistake because we fought over trivial matters. But it turned into bigger things. This year, we are in the same house but on different floors. We haven't had a fight yet. It's important to learn that they're your friends; however, you can't eat, breathe, and live twenty-four hours a day with them. (Baxter Magolda, pp. 313–314)

Lauren and her best friend fought about their differences when they lived in the same room, leading Lauren to suspect it might have been a mistake to live together. Lauren's revelation the second year that it was easier to get along with friends when living on different floors or not being together so much suggests that maintaining relationships requires avoiding difference. From the vantage point of external self-definition, others' approval is crucial to maintaining relational bonds; thus difference threatens relationships. Elements of her meaning-making process that support this as a threat include viewing difference as wrong, needing affirmation from dependent relationships with similar others, and lacking awareness of one's own values and social identity. This perspective no doubt contributed to Lauren's focus on building friendships with those who were like her during college. This stance does not reflect the ability to deal effectively with difference, a key aspect of intercultural maturity.

Elizabeth, a participant in Torres's (2003) longitudinal study of Latino students' identity development, offers another example of the initial phase of the trajectory. Despite having grown up in a bicultural family (her father is Latino and her mother is Anglo), she accepted the values and attitudes of the majority culture and identified her cultural orientation as Anglo. Torres reported that Elizabeth initially found the diversity in the college environment created an internal conflict:

> I have felt that I have been more segregated [in college] because when I was in high school, there weren't many Hispanics, and so like I [being Cuban] . . . would be neat, like "Yes, I am Cuban, and this is how we do things."

> And here there are so many Hispanics, but most of them have grown up with both Hispanic parents, or in a Hispanic neighborhood, or in a Hispanic country, and so they are like very, very cultural, and I am like half and half, so sometimes I feel like a . . . an outsider in the Hispanic group, but then like I don't want to be, because that is my culture, but I don't speak fluent Spanish anymore, and they [other Latino students] do things different than I would. (Torres, p. 538)

Torres interpreted Elizabeth's perspective as one of unexamined ethnic identity because of the lack of focus on her Latino culture in her earlier environment. Elizabeth's comments suggest that she relies on external others at college for her self-definition, and her lack of similarity to her peers in terms of parental heritage and speaking Spanish limits her ability to connect with them. She feels segregated because she perceives herself as different from her Hispanic peers.

## Intermediate Perspectives on Intercultural Maturity

Both Lauren and Elizabeth shifted to the intermediate phase of the trajectory over time. Lauren reported a very different perspective on interacting with others after college. She worked in various business contexts during her early twenties. During this time she struggled to shift from relying on her parents for direction to making her own choices. By her mid-twenties she reported changes in her relations with others:

> I also matured in my relationships because people my age were not plentiful, so I did make some new friends that were older. And, also, different types of friends. In high school and college, everybody I hung around with was like me. You should give everybody an opportunity to be your friend regardless of where they work or where they went to school or if they didn't go to school or if their economic

background was different than yours. And I can honestly say that I didn't give the other people a chance [before]. And I don't know why. But coming here opened some doors. You just really realize that everybody's different and everybody's unique in their own way. That doesn't mean that they're less because they don't have a college degree, for example. And I'll tell you, too, I think I'm more appreciative right now because from what I see there are so many other sides and walks of life. Everybody's situation isn't like the situation that I have. So maybe a little bit more open, I guess. (Baxter Magolda, 2001, p. 288)

Lauren's experience with people different from herself in age and economic background helped her understand multiple realities. Her shift from external to internal self-definition allowed her to be open to these new realities, leading her to construct relationships with people she avoided in college. Her own evolving sense of her identity in her twenties allowed her to move beyond dependent relationships with similar others to explore differences in a new way. Because she was able to associate with similar peers during college, this challenge did not present itself until after college.

In contrast, Elizabeth's internal conflict prompted her to begin exploring her ethnic identity early in college. At her second-year interview she identified her cultural orientation as bicultural and described to Torres (2003) why she planned to study abroad for a year. She reported that being in a class in which many of the students were Hispanic had an influence on her plans:

So, in that class, I just really felt whiter than white, like more American than ever, and they would stay afterwards with the professor and speak Spanish and . . . oh, I just hurt. I really want to be able to do that and that's like a really big deal why I am studying [abroad] the entire year, because my Spanish is horrendous and . . . I want to be fluent by the time I get back. I want to be able to read in Spanish, write in Spanish and be good at it. And it's been really hard because the Hispanic kids don't look at me as very Hispanic. But the white kids or the American kids, . . . [with] their racism issue, they'll look at me and they'll hear me sing a Spanish song or listen to Spanish music or, you know, things like that, or I want to eat Spanish food and they look at me like, "Oh, God, she is so Spanish" you know, and I'm not. It's just because it is so different to them. So, I don't know, it's hard. . . . My quest or journey to learn Spanish is a really big deal but also the education I get and the different classes in Latin America . . . they all kind of deal with like the same things, like, cultural identity and that's why I am really, really interested in anthropology. But that's like a really big deal, how people see themselves, how people identify because it really has an effect on your whole outlook on life. (Torres, p. 542)

Subtle changes are evident in Elizabeth's second year story. She drew distinctions between how other students see her and how she identifies herself. Although she still desires the approval and acceptance of her Hispanic peers, she identifies herself separately from their perceptions of her. Her awareness of the importance of how people identify themselves suggests her increasing awareness of multiple perspectives. She has concrete plans to explore her cultural identity further and to develop the language that is central to it.

## Mature Perspectives on Intercultural Maturity

Carlos, also a participant in Torres's (2003) study, grew up in an environment in which he was the majority. Torres regarded this as an important factor in Carlos's comfort with his ethnicity upon entering college and his having achieved a complex understanding of his ethnic identity during his second year. He shared the result of seeking out a diverse group of friends during his second year at college:

I definitely found my place. I know a lot more Hispanic students. That's great—I can speak Spanish with them a lot and love that. Also I've learned to live with like the fact that I am different culturally, myself. I've learned to integrate myself and I've culturalized [adapted]. . . . The way I found it is not by trying to change others, but just by trying to understand and making them understand more about me. The Mexican culture within the Hispanic culture is different and I talk about it in conversation, but I also learned not to focus on the fact that my skin may be a different color or my name might be a lot different than others, but rather that all our blood is red. In a way I have become blind to it, but not completely blind to it . . . In a way I accept it more and I think that through me accepting it like that, I think others accept. (Torres, p. 543)

Carlos describes himself as having become blind to difference, but in a qualified way. He sought out diversity within the Hispanic culture and focused on trying to understand different cultural orientations. He talked about his own cultural orientation in conversation with diverse peers to get them to understand him. In accepting his own cultural orientation and how it differs from that of others, he encourages others to accept difference. His understanding of cultural difference goes deeper than skin color or names. He is able to shift perspectives and use multiple cultural frames to understand his friends, can engage in meaningful relationships with diverse others without seeking their approval, and has an internal identity that allows him to stay true to himself and his culture, while openly engaging with others to discuss diverse views.

Christina was a White participant in Casa de la Solidaridad, a Jesuit-based study abroad program where students work with the poor in El Salvador (Yonkers-Talz, 2004). She developed a mature intercultural perspective by living in a rural village in El Salvador and through her relationships with people in the Salvadoran community. She described how it changed her:

> It has turned my world upside down and has made me more aware of things in the world. Spending time in the communities in Tepecoyo [praxis site] and really talking to the people and hearing what they have to say about political issues, their beliefs, and their spirituality. It opens your eyes, seeing how other people live, and the atmosphere and the setting, but also the Casa students have been a key aspect of my learning, because I looked at them and what they say, and they have a lot of views and have so many wonderful things to share. I'd get so much more out of what they had to say than out of any class. . . . The classes helped solidify it all. (Yonkers-Talz, p. 173)

Having sustained relationships with Salvadorans helped Christina understand multiple cultural frames. She used these frames to challenge her views of herself, as evidenced in these comments:

> I feel like I have been inwardly trying to figure out what this experience means to me and how I'm going to take that back, and how that is going to shape what I do in the future. So I feel right now I am more inwardly focused on myself and on my own development of ideas and thoughts and stuff and political thoughts and things along those lines. . . . Sometimes I wonder why I am so grateful for this experience. Now I can never ever again be the same person I was. Sometimes I think it would be so much easier if I didn't know that people live like this and could go on living in my happy little world, thinking everything is perfect, doing the service project and not questioning things. . . . It has affected what I'm going to do. It affected every action that I take. I'm forever dedicated to these people that I have met here. I am dedicated to them and their struggle for justice. In a way I am pushed to figure out why people are living so awfully in the United States. There is still so much poverty in the United States. . . . I thought I would go into nursing and be a missionary but now I feel drawn towards education—to learn about the realities of the world, to do education. . . . I am more aware of how my little decisions affect the greater population, and how things in the U.S. affect smaller countries like El Salvador. My train of thought is changed, asking questions that I would never have bothered to ask before. When we don't know a lot of this stuff [poverty], you don't think about it. You just think about if there are people living like this here, how are people living in the rest of the world and what is the way to deal with that? (Yonkers-Talz, pp. 173–174)

Christina's reflections illustrate her recognition of the need to define her beliefs internally and to define her role in the larger world. She understands how her actions and community practices affect larger social systems and is willing to work to improve the lives of those whose experience differs from her own.

## Summary

In this section, we have presented verbatim examples of student reflections that illustrate the three levels of development of intercultural maturity described in Table 1. These examples illustrate the ways students reflect on their diversity experiences in ways that show development in their meaning-making over time, and how seemingly separate strands of development (cognitive, intrapersonal, and interpersonal) are interrelated as students develop intercultural maturity.

## Educational Applications and Future Inquiry

The changes in students' intercultural skills being called for today require not just knowing more facts or having more awareness, but a genuine maturity, an individual transformation that enables students to apply their knowledge and skills in a variety of contexts. That is, educators are being asked to produce graduates who see the world, themselves, and their own agency in more sophisticated and enabling ways, and who can appropriately draw upon that understanding as the need arises. To achieve this goal, we argue that promoting intercultural maturity will be more effective if it is approached in a manner that takes into account related aspects of development (that is, defined not only as knowledge or as a set of social skills) and that acknowledges that this type of maturity doesn't emerge fully formed, but unfolds with time and experience. We now turn to ways educators can apply this integrated, developmental model to promote intercultural maturity.

Existing frameworks for educational practice illustrate how this developmental, integrated model can be used to guide practice. For example, Ortiz and Rhoads's (2000) framework for multicultural education outlines a series of five steps that are part of an individual's journey toward intercultural maturity. The first step, understanding culture, acknowledges the dynamics of the initial level of development of intercultural maturity and introduces students to new ways of thinking in a low-risk approach. Many students (especially majority White students) report being afraid to discuss diversity issues, either not feeling comfortable with the language of the topic, or afraid that their comments will be misunderstood and labeled racist; both discourage motivation for cultural learning. Ortiz and Rhoads's framework explicitly starts at a lower threshold of risk to encourage the conversation at a place that challenges but does not overwhelm students at the initial level of maturity. The increasingly complex steps engage students in moving toward the intermediate level of intercultural maturity as they learn about other cultures (step two) and deconstruct White culture (step three). The most complex fourth and fifth steps of recognizing the legitimacy of other cultures and developing a multicultural outlook guide students into the mature level of intercultural maturity. The goals and activities for each step engage students in exploring and gradually reformulating how they see the world (cognitive), how they see themselves (intrapersonal), and how they relate to others (interpersonal).

Hornak and Ortiz (2004) demonstrated the utility of this framework to design a multicultural education class for business students at a community college. They chronicled the challenges that students faced when addressing diversity content and found that the Ortiz and Rhoads (2000) framework provided ways for the course instructor to both challenge and support students' efforts to develop a self-authored multicultural perspective. Fernandez (2002) adapted the Ortiz and Rhoads framework to examine the development of intercultural competence. She explored how students' experiences with culture shock could be used to enhance self-authorship. For each of five developmental steps, she noted specific self-authorship goals, cognitive dissonance caused by culture shock, and the role of the guide in providing support for students trying to make meaning of their experiences. Thus this framework provides a rich illustration of the potential of a developmental, integrated model of intercultural maturity in multiple settings.

A second framework for educational practice in multicultural education is used in intergroup dialogue programs on college campuses (Schoem & Hurtado, 2001); these offer another example of how to implement a developmental, integrated model. Designed to promote student interaction and understanding among students from different social backgrounds, these dialogues are structured to explore students' own experiences and assumptions as the basis for enabling them to understand more fully the idea of socially constructed group distinctions and how these are played out in intergroup interactions in the US. The four-stage design of this approach takes into account the trajectory of initial to mature levels of development. The program opens by establishing the foundations for dialogue, including introductions and guidelines (e.g., no personal attacks, respect confidentiality). This welcomes students whose initial level of development may lead them to be fearful of this exchange. At the second stage, the purpose is to develop a shared vocabulary around issues of social identities and social stratification, and then to introduce and explore concepts such as prejudice, in/out group dynamics, discrimination, and privilege, and how each affects intergroup relationships. Not until the third stage does the dialogue focus on "hot topics," difficult or controversial issues such as separation/self-segregation on campus, or racism on campus. Guiding students gradually in exploring their assumptions and worldviews, hearing from others, and formulating more complex perspectives helps students move forward on each developmental dimension. The last stage is designed to prepare students for post-dialogue experiences, especially for action planning and alliance building. The effects of participation in these dialogues are impressive (see Hurtado, 2001, and Stephan and Stephan, 2001, for details of these studies):

> [D]ialogue participation is linked with positive effects on cognitive outcomes such as knowledge about other groups and discrimination in society, stereotype and prejudice reduction, the development of complex thinking, social awareness of self and others in systems of inequality, and increased understanding about the causes of conflict between social groups. Dialogue participation is also found to reduce anxiety about intergroup contact, and to enhance skills related to communication across differences, conflict exploration, comfort dealing with diversity, and perspective taking. Finally, participation in intergroup dialogues, as a participant or a student facilitator, seems to promote more active involvement in social justice work. (Zúñiga, 2003, p. 18)

These outcomes reflect growth on all three developmental dimensions.

Yonkers-Talz (2004) offers another example of matching educational practice to the continuum of initial to mature intercultural maturity and to all three developmental dimensions. He used Baxter Magolda's (2004) Learning Partnerships Model (LPM) to conceptualize the Casa de la Solidaridad, an opportunity for U.S. college students to live, study, and work in poor communities in El Salvador. One of the goals of the Casa program is for students "to learn to analyze information from a variety of cultural perspectives and use it to make wise decisions for themselves but also for the common good" (Yonkers-Talz, p. 151). This goal encompasses the cognitive, intrapersonal, and interpersonal dimensions, respectively. The Casa's classroom pedagogy, living/learning community, experiential components, and emphasis on reflection validate students' ability to craft complex perspectives and situate learning in their experience to engage them at their varying levels of intercultural maturity. All these components also engage students in sustained reflection and in mutual construction of meaning with each other, students from the University of Central America, staff, faculty, and local Salvadorans. Thus participants are engaged in exploring increasingly complex perspectives, experiences, and notions of themselves and others. Yonkers-Talz shares narratives from Casa participants that reveal meaningful progress toward intercultural maturity.

The successful implementation of strategies designed to promote intercultural maturity is enhanced when educators themselves have a sophisticated understanding and a high level of capacity in regard to intercultural issues. For example, Landreman, Rasmussen, King, and Jiang (2004) examined how multicultural educators applied their own critical consciousness to their efforts on behalf of intercultural education.

Despite the success of these educational practices, focused research would strengthen our understanding of how to best promote the important goal of intercultural maturity. Further study of educational practices aimed at promoting intercultural maturity might address these questions: (a) What educational practices promote the developmental complexity that undergirds intercultural maturity? (b) What educational practices promote growth toward self-authorship in all three dimensions simultaneously to support intercultural maturity? (c) What kinds of educational practices promote intercultural maturity by helping learners apply insights gained or lessons learned in one domain to another domain? (d) What kinds of experiences enhance, hinder, and/or mediate the development of intercultural maturity?

Inquiry to address theoretical and assessment issues arising from the developmental, integrated perspective is also warranted. Rich questions related to theoretical issues include: (a) How do various dimensions of students' development (e.g., cognitive complexity, racial identity status, sense of ownership of one's opinions) contribute to their capacity to become interculturally competent? (b) How does development in one domain relate to development in the other two domains? (c) How does intercultural maturity unfold over time, and what are the steps in this developmental process? (d) Does race, ethnicity, or cultural heritage mediate growth toward intercultural maturity? (e) How do the dimensions of development intertwine in the growth of self-authorship that is directed toward intercultural maturity? (f) In students' journeys toward intercultural maturity, what levels of cognitive, intrapersonal, and interpersonal complexity are required to achieve intercultural maturity?

Many assessment questions are also suggested by this model. Key questions include: (a) How can the three domains of development be measured in ways that capture the qualities of each domain and that, when combined, reflect a holistic approach to development? (b) What aspects of intercultural competence should be assessed in a measure of intercultural maturity? (c) What kinds of research designs are needed to document the development of intercultural maturity from an integrated perspective? Progress in answering these and other assessment questions would assist researchers and educators alike in understanding the development of intercultural maturity.

## Conclusion

In this article we have introduced an integrated model of development that we think has great potential for better understanding the nature of intercultural maturity, how students develop the capacity to achieve collegiate outcomes around diversity issues, and why efforts to promote the achievement of a variety of diversity outcomes have met with mixed success. This model lays a foundation for developing an integrated model of the development of intercultural maturity, one that is multidimensional rather than one-dimensional. We have tried to show how an integrative model provides a more comprehensive, and therefore more powerful, conceptual tool for understanding and promoting development than do models that focus predominantly or exclusively on one domain. Further, we have tried to describe how the development of intercultural maturity unfolds gradually and in a manner that reflects an individual's maturity in each of the three dimensions.

We encourage other scholars to extend and test the model we have proposed here, using strategies that enable the assessment of intercultural maturity both within and across developmental domains, and to explore whether the use of an integrated model yields more effective educational interventions. Research on this topic presents not only conceptual but methodological challenges; nevertheless, national and international events that reflect intercultural tensions suggest an urgency to this agenda.

The need to address intercultural issues personally and with more than one's intellect is not a new insight; in fact, Aldous Huxley captured it eloquently in 1947:

> Proverbs are always platitudes until you have experienced the truth of them. The newly arrested thief knows that honesty is the best policy with an intensity of conviction which the rest of us can never experience. And to realize that it takes all sorts to make a world one must have seen a certain number of the sorts with one's own eyes. There is all the difference in the world between believing academically, with the intellect, and believing personally, intimately, with the whole living self. (*Jesting Pilate*, p. 207; quoted by Storti, 1990, p. 53)

Believing with the intellect or relying on cognitive attributes may be a good first step in the development of intercultural maturity. We propose this integrated framework and identify educational programs that exemplify its major components as steps toward the end of helping students to gain the maturity to believe personally and "with the whole living self."

## References

Association of American Colleges and Universities. (2002). *Greater expectations: A new vision of learning as a nation goes to college*. Washington, DC: Author.

Baxter Magolda, M. B. (1992). *Knowing and reasoning in college: Gender-related patterns in student' intellectual development*. San Francisco: Jossey-Bass.

Baxter Magolda, M. B. (1997). Facilitating meaningful dialogues about race. *About Campus*, 2(5), 14–18.

Baxter Magolda, M. B. (1999). *Creating contexts for learning and self-authorship: Constructive-developmental pedagogy*. Nashville, TN: Vanderbilt University Press.

Baxter Magolda, M. B. (2000a). Interpersonal maturity: Integrating agency and communion. *Journal of College Student Development, 41*(2), 141–156.

Baxter Magolda, M. B. (2000b). Teaching to promote holistic learning and development. In Baxter Magolda, M. B. (Ed.), *Teaching to promote intellectual and personal maturity: Incorporating students' worldviews and identities into the learning process*, New Directions for Teaching and Learning. 82, 88–98. San Francisco: Jossey-Bass.

Baxter Magolda, M. B. (2001). *Making their own way: Narratives for transforming higher education to promote self-development*. Sterling, VA: Stylus.

Baxter Magolda, M. B. (2003). Identity and learning: Student affairs' role in transforming higher education. *Journal of College Student Development, 44*(1), 231–247.

Baxter Magolda, M. B. (2004). Self-authorship as the common goal of 21st century education. In M. B. Baxter Magolda & P. M. King (Eds.), *Learning partnerships: Theory and models of practice to educate for self-authorship* (pp. 1–35). Sterling, VA: Stylus.

Baxter Magolda, M. B., & King, P. M., (Eds.). (2004). *Learning partnerships: Theory and models of practice to educate for self-authorship*. Sterling, VA: Stylus.

Belenky, M., Clinchy, B. M., Goldberger, N., & Tarule, J. (1986). *Women's ways of knowing: The development of self, voice, and mind*. New York: Basic Books.

Bennett, C. (2001). Genres of research in multicultural education. *Review of Educational Research, 71*(2), 171–217.

Bennett, M. (1993). Towards ethnorelativism: A developmental model of intercultural sensitivity. In M. Paige (Ed.), *Education for the intercultural experience* (pp. 21–71). Yarmouth, ME: Intercultural Press.

Bidell, T. R., Lee, E. M., Boucie, N., Ward, C., & Brass, D. (1994). Developing conceptions of racism among young white adults in the context of cultural diversity coursework. *Journal of Adult Development, 1*(3), 185–200.

Bikson, T. K., & Law, S. A. (1994). *Global preparedness and human resources: College and corporate perspectives*. Santa Monica, CA: Rand Corporation.

Brabeck, M. (Ed.) (1989). *Who cares? Theory, research, and educational implications of the ethic of care*. New York: Praeger.

Broido, E. M. (2000). The development of social justice allies during college: A phenomenological investigation. *Journal of College Student Development, 41*(1), 3–18.

Cass, V. C. (1984). Homosexual identity formation: Testing a theoretical model. *Journal of Sex Research, 20,* 143–167.

Chickering, A. W., & Reisser, L. (1993). *Education and identity* (2nd ed.). San Francisco: Jossey-Bass.

Cross, W. E. J. (1991). *Shades of Black: Diversity in African-American identities*. Philadelphia: Temple University Press.

D'Augelli, A. R. (1994). Identity development and sexual orientation: Toward a model of lesbian, gay, and bisexual development. In E. J. Trickett, R. J. Watts, & D. Birman (Eds.), *Human diversity: Perspectives on people in context* (pp. 312–333). San Francisco: Jossey-Bass.

Derryberry, P., & Thoma, S. (2000). The friendship effect: Its role in the development of moral thinking in students. *About Campus, 5*(2), 13–18.

Endicott, L, Bock, T., & Narvaez, D. (2003). Moral reasoning, intercultural development, and multicultural experiences: Relations and cognitive underpinnings. *International Journal of Intercultural Relations, 27,* 403–419.

Evans, N. J., & D'Augelli, A. R. (1996). Lesbians, gay men, and bisexual people in college. In R. C. Savin-Williams & K. M. Cohen (Eds.), *The lives of lesbians, gays, and bisexuals: Children to adults* (pp. 201–226). Fort Worth, TX: Harcourt Brace.

Fernandez, E. (2002). Framing incidents of culture shock: A growth process for intercultural maturity. Unpublished paper, University of Michigan. Available from the author, Center for the Study of Higher and Postsecondary Education, 2117 Education Building, 610 East University Avenue, Ann Arbor, MI 49109.

Fischer, K. W. (1980). A theory of cognitive development: The control and construction of hierarchies of skills. *Psychological Review, 87*(6), 477–531.

Fischer, K. W., & Bidell, T. R. (1998). Dynamic development of psychological structures in action and thought. In W. Damon (Ed.) and R. Lerner (Series Editor), *Handbook of child psychology, Vol. 5, Theoretical models of human development* (pp. 467–561). New York: Wiley.

*Fortune 500 corporations file brief in support of diversity in higher education*. (2000, October 16). [On-line press release]. Retrieved March 1, 2004, from: http://www.umich.edu/~urel/admissions/releases/fortune.html

Gilligan, C. (1982). *In a different voice: Psychological theory and women's development.* Cambridge, MA: Harvard University Press.

Gurin, P., Dey, E. L., Hurtado, S., & Gurin, G. (2002). Diversity and higher education: Theory and impact on student outcomes. *Harvard Educational Review, 72*(3), 330–366.

Guthrie, V. L. (1996). *The relationship of levels of intellectual development and levels of tolerance for diversity among college students.* Unpublished doctoral dissertation, Bowling Green State University, Bowling Green, KY.

Helms, J. E. (1995). An update of Helms's White and people of color racial identity models. In J. G. Ponterotto, J. M. Casas, L. A. Suzuki, & C. M. Alexander (Eds.), *Handbook of multicultural counseling* (pp. 188–198). Thousand Oaks, CA: Sage.

Hornak, A. M., & Ortiz, A. M. (2004). Creating a context to promote diversity education and self-authorship among community college students. In M. B. Baxter Magolda & P. M. King (Eds.), *Learning partnerships: Theory and models of practice to educate for self-authorship* (pp. 91–123). Sterling, VA: Stylus.

Howard-Hamilton, M. F. (2000). Creating a culturally responsive learning environment for African American students. In M. B. Baxter Magolda (Ed.), *Teaching to promote intellectual and personal maturity: Incorporating students' worldviews and identities into the learning process. New Directions for Teaching and Learning, 82,* 45–53. San Francisco: Jossey-Bass.

Howard-Hamilton, M. F., Richardson, S., & Shuford, B. C. (1998). Promoting multicultural education: A holistic approach. *College Student Affairs Journal, 18*(1), 5–17.

Hurtado, S. (2001). Research and evaluation on intergroup dialogues. In D. Schoem & S. Hurtado (Eds.), *Intergroup dialogue: Deliberative democracy in school, college, community and workplace* (pp. 22–36). Ann Arbor: The University of Michigan Press.

Jones, S. R., & McEwen, M. K. (2000). A conceptual model of multiple dimensions of identity. *Journal of College Student Development, 41*(4) 405–414.

Josselson, R. (1987). *Finding herself: Pathways to identity development in women.* San Francisco: Jossey-Bass.

Josselson, R. (1996). *Revising herself: The story of women's identity from college to midlife.* New York: Oxford University Press.

Kappler, B. J. (1998). *Refining intercultural perspective-taking.* Unpublished doctoral dissertation, University of Minnesota, Minneapolis.

Keeling, R. P. (Ed.). (2004). *Learning reconsidered: A campus-wide focus on the student experience.* Washington, DC: National Association of Student Personnel Administrators and American College Personnel Association.

Kegan, R. (1994). *In over our heads: The mental demands of modern life.* Cambridge, MA: Harvard University Press.

King, P. M., & Baxter Magolda, M. B. (1996). A developmental perspective on learning. *Journal of College Student Development, 37*(2), 163–173.

King, P. M., & Kitchener, K. S. (1994). *Developing reflective judgment: Understanding and promoting intellectual growth and critical thinking in adolescents and adults.* San Francisco: Jossey-Bass.

King, P. M., & Kitchener, K. S. (2004). Reflective judgment: Theory and research on the development of epistemic assumptions through adulthood. *Educational Psychologist, 39*(1), 5–18.

King, P. M., & Mayhew, M. J. (2002). Moral judgement development in higher education: Insights from the Defining Issues Test. *Journal of Moral Education, 33*(3), 247–270.

King, P. M., & Mayhew, M. J. (2004). Theory and research on development of moral reasoning among college students. In J. C. Smart (Ed.) *Higher education: Handbook of theory and research, Vol. XIX* (pp. 375–440). New York: Springer.

King, P. M., & Shuford, B. C. (1996). A multicultural view is a more cognitively complex view. *American Behavioral Scientist, 40*(2), 153–164.

Kitchener, K. S. (2002). Skills, tasks, and definitions: Discrepancies in the understanding and data on the development of folk epistemology. *New Ideas in Psychology, 20,* 309–328.

Kitchener, K. S., & Fischer, K. W. (1990). A skill approach to the development of reflective thinking. In D. Kuhn (Ed.), *Contributions to human development: Developmental perspectives on teaching and learning, 21* (pp. 48–62). Basel, Switzerland: Karger.

Knefelkamp, L. L. (2005, January). *Educational encounters in the intersection: Student intellectual, intercultural, and identity development.* Presentation made at the Annual Meeting of the Association of American Colleges and Universities, Washington, DC.

Kohlberg, L. (1984). *Essays on moral development: Vol. II. The psychology of moral development*. San Francisco: Harper and Row.

Landreman, L. (2003, November). *A multidimensional model of intercultural consciousness: A reconceptualization of multicultural competence*. Paper presented at the Annual Meeting of the Association for the Study of Higher Education, Portland, OR.

Landreman, L., Rasmussen, C., King, P. M., & Jiang, C. (2004, November). *Exploring the development of multicultural educators' critical consciousness: A phenomenological study*. Paper presented at the Association for the Study of Higher Education, Kansas City, KS.

Levine, A., & Cureton, J. S. (1998). *When hope and fear collide*. San Francisco: Jossey-Bass.

Marcia, J. (1966). Development and validation of ego-identity status. *Journal of Personality and Social Psychology, 3*, 551–558.

Marcia, J. (1980). Identity in adolescence. In J. Adelson (Ed.), *Handbook of adolescent psychology* (pp. 159–187). New York: Wiley.

Martin, J. (1985). *Reclaiming a conversation*. New Haven, CT: Yale University Press.

McIntosh, P. (1989, July–August). White privilege; Unpacking the invisible knapsack. *Peace and Freedom*, 10–12.

Mentkowski, M. and Associates (2000). *Learning that lasts: Integrating learning, development, and performance in college and beyond*. San Francisco: Jossey-Bass.

Moore, K. A., & Ortiz, A. M. (1999). *The intercultural competence project: Site visit and focus group report*. A Report to the Institute on the International Education of Students. East Lansing:. Michigan State University.

Noddings, N. (1984). *Caring: A feminine approach to ethics and moral education*. Berkeley: University of California Press.

Ortiz, A. M. (1997). *Defining oneself in a multicultural world: Ethnic identity in college students*. Unpublished doctoral dissertation, University of California Los Angeles.

Ortiz, A. M. (2000). Expressing cultural identity in the learning community: Opportunities and challenges. In M. B. Baxter Magolda (Ed.), *Teaching to promote intellectual and personal maturity: Incorporating students' worldviews and identities into the learning process. New Directions for Teaching and Learning, 82,* 67–79. San Francisco: Jossey-Bass.

Ortiz, A. M., & Rhoads, R. A. (2000). Deconstructing whiteness as part of a multicultural educational framework: From theory to practice. *Journal of College Student Development, 41*(1) 81–93.

Ottavi, T., Pope-Davis, D., & Dings, J. (1994). Relationship between White racial identity attitudes and self-reported multicultural counseling competencies. *Journal of Counseling Psychology, 41*(2), 149–154.

Parks, S. D. (2000). *Big questions, worthy dreams: Mentoring young adults in their search for meaning, purpose, and faith*. San Francisco: Jossey-Bass.

Parks Daloz, L., Keen, C. H., Keen, J. P., & Daloz Parks, S. (1996). *Common fire: Lives of commitment in a complex world*. Boston: Beacon Press.

Perry, W. G. (1968). *Forms of intellectual and ethical development in the college years: A scheme*. New York: Rinehart and Winston.

Phinney, J. S. (1990). Ethnic identity in adolescents and adults: Review of research. *Psychological Bulletin, 108*(3), 499–514.

Pope, R. L., & Reynolds, A. L. (1997). Student affairs core competencies: Integrating multicultural awareness, knowledge, and skills. *Journal of College Student Development, 38,* 266–277.

Pope, R. L., & Reynolds, A. L., & Mueller, J. (2004). *Multicultural competence in student affairs*. San Francisco: Jossey-Bass.

Pope-Davis, D. B., Reynolds, A. L., Dings, J. G., & Ottavi, T. M. (1994). Multicultural competencies of doctoral interns at university counseling centers: An exploratory investigation. *Professional Psychology: Research and Practice, 25,* 466–470.

Rest, J. R., Narvaez, D., Bebeau, M., & Thoma, S. J. (1999a). *Postconventional moral thinking: A neo-Kohlbergian approach*. Mahwah, NJ: Lawrence Erlbaum.

Rest, J. R., Narvaez, D., Bebeau, M., & Thoma, S. J. (1999b). A Neo-Kohlbergian approach: The DIT and schema theory. *Educational Psychology Review, 11,* 291–324.

Schoem, D., & Hurtado, S. (2001). *Intergroup dialogue: Deliberative democracy in school, college, community, and workplace*. Ann Arbor, MI: University of Michigan Press.

Stephan, W., & Stephan, C. W. (2001). *Improving intergroup relations*. Thousand Oaks, CA: Sage.

Storti, C. (1990). *The art of crossing cultures*. Yarmouth, ME: Intercultural Press.

Steglitz, I. (1993). *Intercultural perspective-taking: The impact of study abroad*. Unpublished doctoral dissertation, University of Minnesota, Minneapolis.

Thompson, C. E., & Carter, R. T. (1997). An overview and elaboration of Helms's racial identity development theory. In C. E. Thompson & R. T. Carter (Eds.), *Racial identity theory: Applications to individual, group, and organizational interventions* (pp. 15–32). Mahway, NJ: Lawrence Erlbaum.

Torres, V. (2003). Factors influencing ethnic identity development of Latino college students in the first two years of college. *Journal of College Student Development, 44*(4), 532–547.

Torres, V., & Baxter Magolda, M. B. (2004). Reconstructing Latino identity: The influence of cognitive development on the ethnic identity process of Latino students. *Journal of College Student Development, 45*(3), 333–347.

Wijeyesinghe, C. L., & Jackson, B. W. III. (2001). *New perspectives on racial identity development: A theoretical and practical anthology*. New York: New York University Press.

Yonkers-Talz, K. (2004). A learning partnership: U.S. college students and the poor in El Salvador. In M. B. Baxter Magolda & P. M. King (Eds.), *Learning partnerships: Theory and models of practice to educate for self-authorship* (pp. 151–184). Sterling, VA: Stylus.

Zúñiga, X. (2003). Bridging differences through intergroup dialogue. *About Campus, 7*(6), 8–16.

# CHAPTER 5
## RECONCEIVING THE CHALLENGE OF CHANGE

### ROBERT KEGAN AND LISA LASKOW LAHEY

What will distinguish your leadership from others' in the years ahead? As the subtitle of this book suggests, we believe it will be your ability to develop yourself, your people, and your teams. Throughout the world—and this is as true in the United States and Europe as it is in China and India—human capability will be the critical variable in the new century. But leaders who seek to win a war for talent by conceiving of capability as a fixed resource to be found "out there" put themselves and their organizations at a serious disadvantage.

In contrast, leaders who ask themselves, "What can I do to make my setting the most fertile ground in the world for the *growth* of talent?" put themselves in the best position to succeed. These leaders understand that for each of us to deliver on our biggest aspirations—to take advantage of new opportunities or meet new challenges—we must grow into our future possibilities. These leaders know what makes that more possible—and what prevents it.

The challenge to change and improve is often misunderstood as a need to better "deal with" or "cope with" the greater complexity of the world. Coping and dealing involve adding new skills or widening our repertoire of responses. We are the same person we were before we learned to cope; we have simply added some new resources. We have learned, but we have not necessarily *developed*. Coping and dealing are valuable skills, but they are actually insufficient for meeting today's change challenges.

In reality, the experience of complexity is not just a story about the world. It is also a story about people. It is a story about the fit between the demands of the world and the capacity of the person or the organization. When we experience the world as "too complex" we are not just experiencing the complexity of the world. We are experiencing a mismatch between the world's complexity *and our own at this moment*. There are only two logical ways to mend this mismatch—reduce the world's complexity or increase our own. The first isn't going to happen. The second has long seemed an impossibility in adulthood.

We (the authors of this book) have spent a generation now studying the growth of mental complexity in adulthood. We think what we have learned may help you to better understand yourself and those who work with you and for you. In gaining that awareness, you will begin to see a new frontier of human capabilities, the place where tomorrow's most successful leaders will focus their leadership attention.

---

Kegan, R. & Lahey, L. L. (2009). Reconceiving the challenge of change. In *Immunity to change* (pp. 11–30). Boston, MA: Harvard Business Press.

## An Updated View of Age and Mental Complexity

The ideas and practices you will find in this book begin by identifying a widespread misconception about the potential trajectory of mental development across the lifespan. When we began our work, the accepted picture of mental development was akin to the picture of physical development—your growth was thought fundamentally to end by your twenties. If, thirty years ago, you were to place "age" on one axis and "mental complexity" on another, and you asked the experts in the field to draw the graph as they understood it, they would have produced something similar to Figure 1: an upward sloping line until the twenties and a flat line thereafter. And they would have drawn it with confidence.

When we began reporting the results of our research in the 1980s, suggesting that some (though not all) adults seemed to undergo qualitative advances in their mental complexity akin to earlier, well-documented quantum leaps from early childhood to later childhood and from later childhood to adolescence, our brain-researcher colleagues sitting next to us on distinguished panels would smile with polite disdain.

"You might think you can infer this from your longitudinal interviews," they would say, "but hard science doesn't have to make inferences. We're looking at *the real thing*. The brain simply doesn't undergo any significant change in capacity after late adolescence. Sorry." Of course, these "hard scientists" would grant that older people are often wiser or more capable than younger people, but this they attributed to the benefits of experience, a consequence of learning how to get more out of the same mental equipment rather than any qualitative advances or upgrades to the equipment itself.

Thirty years later? Whoops! It turns out everybody was making inferences, even the brain scientists who thought they were looking at "the thing itself." The hard scientists have better instruments today, and the brain doesn't look to them the way it did thirty years ago. Today they talk about neural plasticity and the phenomenal capacities of the brain to keep adapting throughout life.

If we were to draw the graph showing age and mental complexity today? On the basis of thirty years of longitudinal research by our colleagues and us—as a result of thoroughly analyzing the transcripts of hundreds of people, interviewed and reinterviewed at several-year intervals—the graph would look like Figure 2.

Two things are evident from this graph:

- With a large enough sample size you can detect a mildly upward-sloping curve. That is, looking at a population as a whole, mental complexity tends to increase with age, throughout adulthood, at least until old age; so the story of mental complexity is certainly *not* a story that ends in our twenties.

- There is considerable variation within any age. For example, six people in their thirties (the bolded dots) could all be at different places in their level of mental complexity, and some could be *more* complex than a person in her forties.

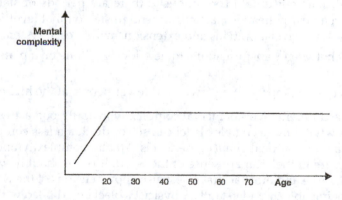

**Figure 1**    Age and mental complexity: The view thirty years ago.

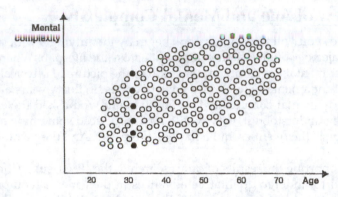

**Figure 2**    Age and mental complexity: The revised view today.

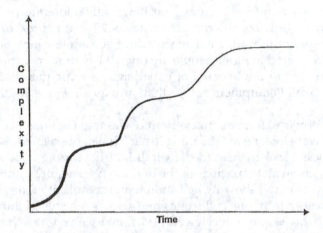

**Figure 3**    The trajectory of mental development in adulthood.

If we were to draw a quick picture of what we have learned about the individual trajectory of mental development in adulthood, it might look something like Figure 3. This picture suggests several different elements:

- There are qualitatively different, discernibly distinct levels (the "plateaus"); that is, the demarcations between levels of mental complexity are not arbitrary. Each level represents a quite different way of knowing the world.

- Development does not unfold continuously; there are periods of stability and periods of change. When a new plateau is reached we tend to stay on that level for a considerable period of time (although elaborations and extensions within each system can certainly occur).

- The intervals between transformations to new levels—"time on a plateau"—get longer and longer.

- The line gets thinner, representing fewer and fewer people at the higher plateaus.

But what do these different levels of mental complexity in adulthood actually look like? Can we say something about what a more complex level can see or do that a less complex level cannot? Indeed, we can now say a great deal about these levels. Mental complexity and its evolution is not about how smart you are in the ordinary sense of the word. It is not about how high your IQ is. It is not about developing more and more abstract, abstruse apprehensions of the world, as if "most complex" means finally being able to understand a physicist's blackboard filled with complex equations.

# Three Plateaus in Adult Mental Complexity

Later on in this book we will say more about these levels, but for now, let's begin with a quick overview of three qualitatively different plateaus in mental complexity we see among adults, as suggested in Figures 4 and 5.

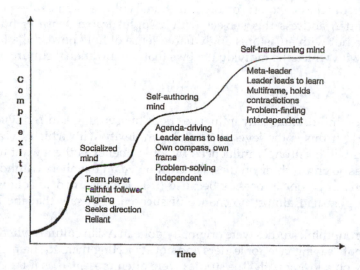

**Figure 4**   Three plateaus in adult mental development.

---

**The socialized mind**

- We are shaped by the definitions and expectations of our personal environment.
- Our self coheres by its alignment with, and loyalty to, that with which it identifies.
- This can express itself primarily in our relationships with people, with "schools of thought" (our ideas and beliefs) or both.

**The self-authoring mind**

- We are able to step back enough from the social environment to generate an internal "seat of judgment" or personal authority that evaluates and makes choices about external expectations.
- Our self coheres by its alignment with its own belief system/ideology/personal code; by its ability to self-direct, take stands, set limits, and create and regulate its boundaries on behalf of its own voice.

**The self-transforming mind**

- We can step back from and reflect on the limits of our own ideology or personal authority; see that any one system or self-organization is in some way partial or incomplete; be friendlier toward contradiction and opposites; seek to hold on to multiple systems rather than projecting all but one onto the other.
- Our self coheres through its ability not to confuse internal consistency with wholeness or completeness, and through its alignment with the dialectic rather than either pole.

**Figure 5**   The three adult plateaus described.

These three adult meaning systems—the socialized mind, self-authoring mind, and self-transforming mind—make sense of the world, and operate within it, in profoundly different ways. We can see how this shows up at work by focusing on any significant aspect of organizational life and seeing how the very same phenomenon—for example, information flow—is completely different through the lens of each perspective.

The way information does or does not flow through an organization—what people "send," to whom they send it, how they receive or attend to what flows to them—is an obviously crucial feature of how any system works. Experts on organizational culture, organizational behavior, or organizational change often address this subject with a sophisticated sense of how systems impact individual behavior, but with an astonishingly naive sense of how powerful a factor is the level of mental complexity with which the individual views that organizational culture or change initiative.

## Socialized Mind

Having a socialized mind dramatically influences both the sending and receiving aspects of information flow at work. If this is the level of mental complexity with which I view the world, then what I think to send will be strongly influenced by what I believe others want to hear. You may be familiar with the classic group-think studies, which show team members withholding crucial information from collective decision processes because (it is later learned in follow-up research) "although I knew the plan had almost no chance of succeeding, I saw that the leader wanted our support."

Some of these groupthink studies were originally done in Asian cultures where withholding team members talked about "saving face" of leaders and not subjecting them to shame, even at the price of setting the company on a losing path. The studies were often presented as if they were uncovering a particularly cultural phenomenon. Similarly, Stanley Milgram's famous obedience-to-authority research was originally undertaken to fathom the mentality of "the good German," and what about the German culture could enable otherwise decent, nonsadistic people to carry out orders to exterminate millions of Jews and Poles.[1] But Milgram, in practice runs of his data-gathering method, was surprised to find "good Germans" all over Main Street, U.S.A., and although we think of sensitivity to shame as a particular feature of Asian culture, the research of Irving Janis and Paul t'Hart has made clear that group-think is as robust a phenomenon in Texas and Toronto as it is in Tokyo and Taiwan.[2] It is a phenomenon that owes its origin not to culture, but to complexity of mind.

The socialized mind also strongly influences how information is *received* and *attended to*. When maintaining alignment with important others and valued "surrounds" is crucial to the coherence of one's very being, the socialized mind is highly sensitive to, and influenced by, what it picks up. And what it picks up often runs far beyond the explicit message. It may well include the results of highly invested attention to imagined subtexts that may have more impact on the receiver than the intended message. This is often astonishing and dismaying to leaders who cannot understand how subordinates could possibly have "made *that* sense out of *this*" communication, but because the receiver's signal-to-noise detector may be highly distorted, the actual information that comes through may have only a distant relationship to the sender's intention.

## Self-Authoring Mind

Let's contrast all this with the self-authoring mind. If I view the world from this level of mental complexity, what I "send" is more likely to be a function of what I deem others need to hear to best further the agenda or mission of my design. Consciously or unconsciously, I have a direction, an agenda, a stance, a strategy, an analysis of what is needed, a prior context from which my communication arises. My direction or plan may be an excellent one, or it may be riddled with blind spots. I may be masterful or inept at recruiting others to invest themselves in this direction. These matters implicate other aspects of the self. But mental complexity strongly influences whether my information sending is oriented toward getting behind the wheel in order to drive (the self-authoring mind) or getting myself included in the car so I can be driven (the socialized mind).

We can see a similar mindset operating when "receiving" as well. The self-authoring mind creates a filter for what it will allow to come through. It places a priority on receiving the information it has sought. Next in importance is information whose relevance to my plan, stance, or frame is immediately clear. Information I haven't asked for, and which does not have obvious relevance to my own design for action, has a much tougher time making it through my filter.

It is easy to see how all of this could describe an admirable capacity for focus, for distinguishing the important from the urgent, for making best use of one's limited time by having a means to cut through the unending and ever-mounting claims on one's attention. This speaks to the way the self-authoring mind is an advance over the socialized mind. But this same description may also be a recipe for disaster if one's plan or stance is flawed in some way, if it leaves out some crucial element of the equation not appreciated by the filter, or if the world changes in such a way that a once-good frame becomes an antiquated one.

## Self-Transforming Mind

In contrast, the self-transforming mind also has a filter, but is not fused with it. The self-transforming mind can stand back from its own filter and look *at* it, not just *through* it. And why would it do so? Because the self-transforming mind both values and *is wary about* any one stance, analysis, or agenda. It is mindful that, powerful though a given design might be, this design almost inevitably leaves something out. It is aware that it lives in time and that the world is in motion, and what might have made sense today may not make as much sense tomorrow.

Therefore, when communicating, people with self-transforming minds are not only advancing their agenda and design. They are also making space for the modification or expansion of their agenda or design. Like those with self-authoring minds, what they send may include inquiries and requests for information. But rather than inquiring only *within* the frame of their design (seeking information that will advance their agenda), they are also inquiring about the design itself. They are seeking information that may lead them or their team to enhance, refine, or alter the original design or make it more inclusive. Information sending is not just on behalf of driving; it is also to remake the map or reset the direction.

Similarly, the way the self-transforming mind receives information includes the advantages of the self-authoring mind's filter, but is not a prisoner of that filter. People at this level of mental complexity can still focus, select, and drive when they feel they have a good map. But they place a higher priority on information that may also alert them to the limits of their current design or frame. They value their filter and its ability to separate the wheat from the chaff, but they know it can also screen out "the golden chaff," the unasked-for, the anomaly, the apparently inconsequential that may be just what is needed to turn the design on its head and bring it to the next level of quality.

Those with self-transforming minds are more likely to have the chance even to consider such information, because people are more likely to send it to them. Why is this? Because those with self-transforming minds not only attend to information once it gets to their door; they also realize their behavior can have a big effect, *upstream*, on whether people decide to approach the door. Others are not left guessing whether to send potentially "off-mission" communication they judge to be important. They send it because people with self-transforming minds have found ways to let them know such information will be welcomed.

## Mental Complexity and Performance

These descriptions, focusing on just a single important element of organizational life—information flow—should begin to make the different levels of mental complexity a little clearer. They also suggest a value proposition for mental complexity. Each successive level of mental complexity is formally higher than the preceding one because it can perform the mental functions of the prior level as well as additional functions. But the discussion of how information flow is conceived and handled also suggests that these formal mental properties translate into real actions with real consequences for organizational behavior and work competence. The implication is that a higher level of mental complexity outperforms a lower level.

Is this just a hypothesis, albeit with some plausible face validity, or has it actually been tested and systematically demonstrated? There are now a number of studies correlating measures of mental complexity with independent assessments of work competence or performance. We will consider these results in greater depth later in this book, but for now let's just take a peek at what these studies show.

Keith Eigel assessed the level of mental complexity of twenty-one CEOs of large, successful companies, each company an industry leader with average gross revenue of over $5 billion.[3] (He used a ninety-minute interview assessment measure that we and our colleagues developed. The Subject-Object Interview, described in "How Do We Assess Level of Mental Complexity?", has been used all over the world, across all sectors, over the last twenty years. It discriminates developmental

---

## How Do We Assess Level of Mental Complexity?

Our assessment tool is a ninety-minute interview we call the Subject-Object Interview, so named because the complexity of a mindset is a function of the way it distinguishes the thoughts and feelings we have (i.e., can look at, can take as *object*) from the thoughts and feelings that "have us" (i.e., we are run by them, are *subject* to them). Each different level of mindset complexity differently draws the line between what is subject and what is object. Greater complexity means being able to *look* at more (take more as *object*). The blind spot (what is *subject*) becomes smaller and smaller. The assessment instrument has proven to be quite subtle: it can identify, with high degrees of interrater reliability, fully five different transitional places between any two mindsets.

The interview begins by handing the subject ten index cards, upon which are written the following cues:

- Angry
- Anxious, nervous
- Success
- Strong stand, conviction
- Sad
- Torn
- Moved, touched
- Lost something, farewells
- Change
- Important

In the first fifteen minutes, we ask the interviewee to make notes on each card in response to questions of the following form: "Think of some times, over the last few days or weeks, when you found yourself feeling really mad or angry about something [or nervous, scared, anxious, etc.], and jot down what comes to mind." The interview then proceeds as a systematic exploration: the interviewee tells us the *whats* (what made him feel angry, successful, etc.) and we probe to learn the *whys* (why would that make him feel angry or successful; just what is at stake?). We chose these prompts because earlier research showed them to be highly successful at eliciting the boundaries and contours of people's current way of constructing reality. A trained interviewer can probe such material to learn the underlying principle governing what the person can and cannot see (the blind spot).

The interviews are transcribed and analyzed according to a uniform process. Thousands of these interviews have now been conducted with people all over the world, with people of all ages and from all walks of life. Most people find the interview a highly engaging experience.

*Source:* L. Lahey, E. Souvaine, R. Kegan, et al., *A Guide to the Subject-Object Interview: Its Administration and Analysis* (Cambridge, MA: The Subject-Object Research Group, Harvard University Graduate School of Education, 1988).

movement between, and within, the levels of mental complexity with high degrees of interrater reliability.) Using separate performance assessments, Eigel also evaluated the CEOs' effectiveness in terms of the ability to:

- Challenge existing processes
- Inspire a shared vision
- Manage conflict
- Solve problems
- Delegate
- Empower
- Build relationships

In addition, for comparison, Eigel did similar assessments in each of the same companies, interviewing promising middle managers nominated by their respective CEOs. Figure 6 summarizes his findings.

Several results stand out. The first obvious one is the clearly discernible upward slope, signifying that increased mental complexity and work competence, assessed on a number of dimensions, are correlated. So not only is it possible to reach higher planes of mental complexity, but such growth correlates with effectiveness, for both CEOs and middle managers. This finding has been replicated in a variety of fine-grained studies of small numbers of leaders, assessed on particular competencies.[4] Taken together, the cumulative data speaks anew to the problem of complexity: we begin to see how being at a given level of mental complexity can make a "complex world" more or less manageable.

## Shifts in the Demands on Followers and Leaders

We can also take a more sweeping view of the same issue by considering the new demands on leaders and their subordinates in the faster, flatter, more interconnected world in which we live. Take another look at Figure 4, the chart of the various plateaus in adult mental complexity.

Now let's consider what was asked, and is now asked, of subordinates. In the world in which we *used to* live, it was enough in most cases if people were good team players, pulled their weight, were loyal to the company or organization where they worked, and could be counted on to follow conscientiously the directions and signals of their boss. In other words, the socialized mind would be perfectly adequate to handle the nature of yesterday's demands upon subordinates.

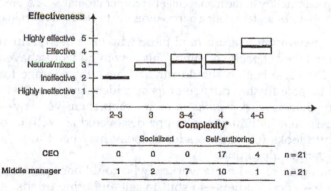

**Figure 6**    Individual mental capacity and business effectiveness: Eigel's results.

*Source:* K. Eigel, "Leader Effectiveness" (PhD diss., University of Georgia, 1998).
*3 = socialized mind; 4 = self-authoring mind; 5 = self-transforming mind

And today? Nathaniel Branden writes:

> In the past two or three decades, extraordinary developments have occurred in the American and global economies. The United States has shifted from a manufacturing society to an information society. We have witnessed the transition from physical labor to mind work as the dominant employee activity. We now live in a global economy characterized by rapid change, accelerating scientific and technological breakthroughs, and an unprecedented level of competitiveness. These developments create demand for higher levels of education and training than were required of previous generations. Everyone acquainted with business culture knows this. What is not understood is that these developments also create new demands on our psychological resources. Specifically, these developments ask for a greater capacity for innovation, self-management, personal responsibility, and self-direction. This is not just asked at the top, it is asked at every level of a business enterprise, from senior management to first-line supervisors and even to entry-level personnel . . . Today, organizations need not only an unprecedentedly higher level of knowledge and skill among all those who participate but also a higher level of independence, self-reliance, self-trust, and the capacity to exercise initiative.[5]

What is Branden—and many others who write about what we are now looking for from our workforce—really saying, as it relates to level of mental complexity? He is saying, without realizing it, that it used to be sufficient for workers to be at the level of the socialized mind, but today we need workers who are at the level of the self-authoring mind. In effect, *we are calling upon workers to understand themselves and their world at a qualitatively higher level of mental complexity.*

And what is the picture if we look not at subordinates but at bosses and leaders? Organizational theorist Chris Argyris raises similar issues about the ever-growing insufficiency of traditional conceptions of managerial and leadership effectiveness that still dominate our thinking today. There may have been a day when it was enough for leaders to develop worthy goals and sensible norms, cultivate alignments around them, and work "to keep organizational performance within the range specified"—all the while exercising the strength of character to advocate for one's position and hold one's ground in the face of opposition.[6] Skillful as such managers may be, their abilities will no longer suffice in a world that calls for leaders who can not only run but reconstitute their organizations—its norms, missions, and culture—in an increasingly fast-changing environment. For example, a company that chooses to transform itself from a low-cost standardized-products organization to a mass customizer or a provider of organization-wide solutions will need to develop a whole new set of individual and team capabilities.

Argyris and Schön described the challenges of a similar organizational transition thirty years ago:

> This, in turn, requires that members of the corporation adopt new approaches to marketing, managing, and advertising; that they become accustomed to a much shorter product life cycle and to a more rapid cycle of changes in their pattern of activities; that they, in fact, change the very image of the business they are in. And these requirements for change come into conflict with another sort of corporate norm, one that requires predictability in the management of corporate affairs . . . A process of change initiated with an eye to effectiveness under existing norms turns out to yield a conflict in the norms themselves.[7]

For more than a generation, Argyris (and those who have been influenced by him) has unwittingly been calling for a new capacity of mind. This new mind would have the ability not just to *author* a view of how the organization should run and have the courage to hold steadfastly to that view. It would also be able to step outside of *its own* ideology or framework, observe the framework's limitations or defects, and *re-author* a more comprehensive view—which it will hold with sufficient tentativeness that its limitations can be discovered as well. In other words, the kind of learner Argyris rightly looks for in the leader of today may need to be a person who is making meaning with a *self-transforming* mind.

Thus, we are asking more and more workers who could once perform their work successfully with socialized minds—good soldiers—to shift to self-authoring minds. And we are asking more and more leaders who could once lead successfully with self-authoring minds—sure and certain captains—to develop self-transforming minds. In short, we are asking for a quantum shift in individual mental complexity across the board.

So how big *is* the gap between what we now expect of people's minds and what their minds are actually like? Are we expecting something that is so big a reach? After all, if the world has gotten more complex over the last half century, then perhaps the world has become a better incubator of mental complexity as well, and the supply of mental complexity has risen with the demand.

We now have two sophisticated, reliable, and widely used measures for assessing mental complexity along the lines we are talking about here. (This is something quite different, obviously, from IQ testing, which has only the most modest correlation with mental complexity; you can have an above average IQ, say 125, and be at any of the three plateaus.) These are the Washington University Sentence Completion Test (SCT) and the Subject-Object Interview (SOI) we introduced earlier.[8] Two large meta-analyses of studies using one or the other of these measures have now been performed, with several hundred participants in each study. Figure 7 presents a quick summary of results.

Two observations stand out from the data in Figure 7:

- Both studies, each done with completely different samples, arrive at the same finding—that in a majority of respondents, mental complexity is not as far along as the self-authoring mind (in fact, in each study exactly 58 percent are not at this level)—and since both studies are skewed toward middle-class, college-educated professionals, the actual percentage in the general population is likely even higher.

- The percentages of people *beyond* the plateau of the self-authoring mind are quite small.

These data suggests that the gap between what we now expect of people's minds (including our own minds) and what our minds are actually like is quite large. We expect most workers to be self-authoring, but most are not. We expect most leaders to be more complex than self-authoring, and very few are.

We can see these same macro trends confirmed at the micro level if we return for a moment to the Eigel study (have another look at Figure 6). Note here that only about half of the "promising middle managers" are self-authoring (and those who are do better than those who are not), and only four of the twenty-one CEOs from industry-leading companies are beyond self-authoring (and those who are do better than those who are not).

## Mental Complexity and "Technical" Versus "Adaptive" Challenges

Our colleague and friend Ronald Heifetz makes an important distinction that helps us summarize the central points we have made so far. Heifetz distinguishes between two kinds of change challenges, those he calls "technical" and others he calls "adaptive."[9] Technical changes are not

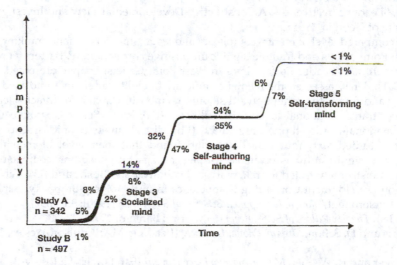

**Figure 7**   Results from two large-scale studies of the distribution of levels of mental complexity among adults.

*Sources:* Study A: R. Kegan, *In Over Our Heads* (Cambridge, MA: Harvard University Press, 1994). Study B: W. Torbert, *Managing the Corporate Dream* (Homewood, IL: Dow-Jones, 1987).

necessarily easy, nor are their results necessarily unimportant or insignificant. Learning how to remove an inflamed appendix or how to land an airplane with a stuck nose wheel are examples of largely technical challenges, and their accomplishment is certainly important to the patient on the surgeon's table or the nervous passengers contemplating a crash landing.

They are nonetheless "technical" from Heifetz's point of view because the skill set necessary to perform these complicated behaviors is well known. The routines and processes by which we might help an intern or novice pilot become an accomplished practitioner are well practiced and proven. While it is entirely possible that an intern or a pilot in training will become qualitatively more complex over years of training, such mental growth is beyond the scope of their technical training. Novice surgeons, for example, become sufficiently skilled surgeons without anyone worrying about their adult development or mental growth.

However, many, if not most, of the change challenges you face today and will face tomorrow require something more than incorporating new technical skills into your current mindset. These are the "adaptive challenges," and they can only be met by transforming your mindset, by advancing to a more sophisticated stage of mental development.

Heifetz says the biggest error leaders make is when they apply technical means to solve adaptive challenges. In other words, we may be unable to bring about the changes we want because we are misdiagnosing our aspiration as technical, when in reality it is an adaptive challenge. The implication is that we must find *adaptive* (nontechnical) means of supporting ourselves and others to meet adaptive challenges.

Distinguishing adaptive challenges from technical ones again brings our attention back from the "problem" to the "person having the problem." We've said that "complexity" is really a story about the relationship between the complex demands and arrangements of the world and our own complexity of mind. When we look at this relationship we discover a gap: our own mental complexity lags behind the complexity of the world's demands. We are in over our heads.

This naturally brings us to a next question: can we actually do something to incubate mental complexity, and to accelerate it? We have spent more than twenty years actively exploring this question in a "laboratory" that has taken us all over the world. In the next chapter we bring you into this laboratory to show you what we have found.

## Notes

1. S. Milgram, *Obedience to Authority* (New York: Harper and Row, 1974).
2. I. Janis, *Groupthink* (Boston: Houghton Mifflin, 1982). P. t'Hart, *Groupthink in Government* (Baltimore: Johns Hopkins University Press, 1990).
3. K. Eigel, "Leader Effectiveness: A Constructive-Developmental View and Investigation" (PhD diss., University of Georgia, 1998).
4. Bartone compared level of mental complexity and leadership performance rankings among graduating West Point cadets and found a significant positive correlation. (P. Bartone et al., "Psychological Development and Leader Performance in West Point Cadets," paper presented at AERA, Seattle, April 2001). Benay assessed the mental complexity of eight leaders in a midsized food distribution company and found the same upward-sloping relationship with a multifactor leadership measure assessing "transformational leadership abilities." (P. Benay, "Social Cognitive Development and Transformational Leadership: A Case Study" (PhD diss., University of Massachusetts, 1997)). Bushe and Gibb studied sixty-four consultants and found that their level of mental complexity was strongly and significantly associated with peer ratings for consulting competence via a seventy-seven-item instrument tested for reliability and validity. (G.R. Bushe and B.W. Gibb, "Predicting Organization Development Consulting Competence from the Myers-Briggs Type Indicator and Stage of Ego Development," *Journal of Applied Behavioral Science* 26 [1990]: 337–357).
5. N. Branden, *The Six Pillars of Self-Esteem* (New York: Bantam, 1995), 22–23.
6. C. Argyris and D. Schön, *Organizational Learning* (Reading, MA: Addison-Wesley, 1978), 21.
7. Ibid.
8. J. Loevinger and R. Wessler, *Measuring Ego Development* (San Francisco: Jossey-Bass, 1970).
9. R. Heifetz, *Leadership Without Easy Answers* (Cambridge, MA: Harvard University Press, 1998).

# CHAPTER 6
## RECONCEPTUALIZING THE MODEL OF MULTIPLE DIMENSIONS OF IDENTITY: THE ROLE OF MEANING-MAKING CAPACITY IN THE CONSTRUCTION OF MULTIPLE IDENTITIES

ELISA S. ABES, SUSAN R. JONES, AND MARYLU K. MCEWEN

We reconceptualize Jones and McEwen's (2000) model of multiple dimensions of identity by incorporating meaning making, based on the results of Abes and Jones's (2004) study of lesbian college students. Narratives of three students who utilize different orders of Kegan's (1994) meaning making (formulaic, transitional, and foundational, as described by Baxter Magolda, 2001) illustrate how meaning-making capacity interacts with the influences of context on the perceptions and salience of students' multiple social identities. Implications for theory, research, and professional practice are discussed.

Recent scholarship in the area of college student identity development has begun to address the complexities of the relationships among three primary domains of development: interpersonal, intrapersonal, and cognitive (e.g., Baxter Magolda, 2001; King & Baxter Magolda, 2005; Torres & Baxter Magolda, 2004). Within the intrapersonal domain, the model of multiple dimensions of identity (Jones & McEwen, 2000) provided one of the first conceptualizations of relationships among social identities (e.g., race, gender, social class, sexual orientation), as well as between personal identity and social identities. Although acknowledged as a contribution to a more complex understanding of identity (e.g., Chavez, Guido-DiBrito, & Mallory, 2003; Davis, 2002; Stevens, 2004), the model does not incorporate other domains such as cognitive development. Abes and Jones (2004), however, in a study of lesbian identity development and meaning making, applied the model of multiple dimensions of identity in conjunction with constructivist–developmental theory. The purpose of this article is to propose, based on Abes and Jones's study, a more complex conceptualization of the model of multiple dimensions of identity that integrates intersecting domains of development.

Because the focus of our work is on developing a more complex conceptualization of the multiple identities model, we position this study within contemporary theorizations of multiple and intersecting identities. To do so, we provide an overview of identity as social construction, feminist and postmodern conceptualizations of intersectionality, and the model of multiple dimensions of identity. We then explore Kegan's (1994) theory of lifespan development and Baxter Magolda's

Abes, E. S., Jones, S. R., & McEwen, M. K. (2007). Reconceptualizing the Model of Multiple Dimensions of Identity: The role of meaning-making capacity in the construction of multiple identities. *Journal of College Student Development, 48*, 1–22.

(2001) research on young adult development toward self-authorship, which is incorporated into our reconceptualization of the multiple identities model.

## Social Construction of Identity

Weber (1998) identified social constructionism as a common theme within scholarship exploring relationships among race, class, gender, and sexuality. A social constructionist perspective on identity challenges the essentialist position that reifies dominant–subordinate binaries presumed to be grounded in biology (e.g., White–non-White, men–women, heterosexual—homosexual; Weber). Instead, social constructionism considers identity to be socially, historically, politically, and culturally constructed at both the institutional and individual levels (Omi & Winant, 1994; Weber). The meaning of social identities cannot be fully captured as they change with evolving contexts and relationships (Omi & Winant). Although essentialism provided the basis for much of the earlier research and resulting theoretical perspectives on student development, contemporary student affairs researchers are increasingly relying on social constructionism as they explore the meanings of identity (McEwen, 2003).

## Conceptualizations of Intersectionality

### Feminist Conceptualizations

Much of the theorizing on multiple identities developed in women's studies literature, often through personal narratives (Weber, 1998). A significant body of this literature grew out of Black feminist scholarship that challenged feminism's Eurocentric assumptions (e.g., hooks, 1984; Smith, 1982). This feminist literature introduced a "framework of intersectionality" that recognized how socially constructed identities are experienced simultaneously, not hierarchically (McCann & Kim, 2002, p. 150). Collins (1990) termed this framework a "matrix of domination" and explained that viewing relationships from an intersecting perspective "expands the focus of analysis from merely describing the similarities and differences distinguishing these systems of oppression and focuses greater attention on how they interconnect" (p. 222).

Autobiographical narratives from two feminist scholars, Lorde (1984) and Anzaldua (1999), illustrated a wholeness associated with integrating multiple identity dimensions within a matrix of domination. Lorde, a "Black lesbian feminist socialist mother of two . . . and a member of an interracial couple" (p. 114), explained that her "fullest concentration of energy is available . . . only when I integrate all the parts of who I am . . . without the restrictions of externally imposed definition" (pp. 120–121). Discussing her experiences as a Mexican American lesbian, a mestiza, Anzaldua offered her theory of mestiza consciousness, or her ability to bring together multiple identities into a new, integrated identity where "the self has added a third element which is greater than the sum of its severed parts. That element is a new consciousness" (pp. 101–102).

Despite its complex explorations of boundary-crossing identities, a conundrum exists within this feminist literature. By studying how aspects of identity, such as race and social class, create differences within women's experiences, an unintended presumption of unity arises within the categories introduced to demonstrate differences (McCann & Kim, 2002). Just as feminists have urged that there is not a singular meaning associated with the experiences of women, so too there is not a singular meaning associated with the experiences of women by nature of the socially constructed categories of race, social class, or sexual orientation. To fully embrace individual experiences, it is necessary to explore differences within each aspect of identity as each is influenced by the simultaneous experience of the other dimensions (McCann & Kim).

### Postmodern Conceptualizations

The impossibility, due to difference, of capturing all experiences associated with identity categories is at the heart of a postmodern theorization of multiple identities. Postmodernism abandons "grand narratives" because they ignore the influence of social, political, and cultural power in people's lives (Tierney & Rhoads, 1993, p. 315). In their place, postmodernists stress "differences between and within groups—race, class, gender, and sexual orientation, for example" (Tierney & Rhoads, p. 315). Informed by the writing of French philosopher Jacques Derrida, a postmodern conceptualization of difference suggests that this construct cannot be easily "dismantled" into "oppositional predicates" and is "neither this not that; but rather this *and* that" (Kearney, 1984, p. 110). Grounded in these principles, a postmodern critique of identity challenges the stability of identity categories.

Of particular relevance to our reconceptualization of the model of multiple identities is the postmodern perspective of queer theory, which suspends the classifications of lesbian, gay, bisexual, masculine, and feminine (Tierney & Dilley, 1998). Principles of queer theory disrupt traditional identity categories based on the suppositions that identity is performed and therefore unstable (Butler, 1991) and comprised of fluid differences rather than a unified essence (Fuss, 1989). Fuss explained that the failure to study identity as difference implies a unity in identity that overlooks variations within identity, such as race and class. Categories are insufficient because differences within those categories cause them to have "multiple and contradictory meanings" (Fuss, p. 98).

## Model of Multiple Dimensions of Identity

Much of the recent literature on multiple identities in student affairs scholarship references Jones and McEwen's (2000) model of multiple dimensions of identity (e.g., Chavez et al., 2003; Davis, 2002; Love, Bock, Jannarone, & Richardson 2005; Miville, Darlington, Whitlock, & Mulligan, 2005). The model (Figure 1) offers a conceptual depiction of relationships among college students' socially constructed identity dimensions, recognizing that each dimension cannot be fully understood in isolation. Building on the work of Reynolds and Pope (1991) and Deaux (1993) and based on the results of grounded theory research with women college students (Jones, 1997), the model of multiple dimensions of identity describes the dynamic construction of identity and the influence of changing contexts on the relative salience of multiple identity dimensions, such as race, sexual orientation, culture, and social class. The model portrays identity dimensions as intersecting rings around a core, signifying how "no one dimension may be understood singularly; it can be understood only in relation to other dimensions" (Jones & McEwen, p. 410). At the center of the model is a core sense of self, comprising "valued personal attributes and characteristics" (Jones, p. 383). Surrounding the core and identity dimensions is the context in which a person experiences her life, such as family, sociocultural conditions, and current experiences. The salience of each identity dimension to the core is fluid and depends on contextual influences (Jones & McEwen).

## Constructivist–Developmental Theory and Multiple Identities

Constructivist–developmental theory considers intrapersonal, cognitive, and interpersonal domains of development as part of a single, integrated mental activity and describes the interrelated development of each domain from simple to complex (Kegan, 1994). Kegan's integrated theory consists of five "orders of consciousness," representing increasingly complex "meaning-making structures," which are sets of assumptions that determine how an individual perceives and organizes one's life experiences (Kegan).

In her extensive longitudinal research, Baxter Magolda (2001) explored Kegan's (1994) work in the context of college students and young adults. Baxter Magolda (2001) suggested that Kegan's third order of consciousness is the most prevalent meaning-making structure among traditional-aged college students. The third order is characterized by making meaning through concrete relationships to which one's own interests are subordinated (Kegan). Relationships define identity, and no process exists for negotiating conflicting relationships. Baxter Magolda (1999a) described this as "formulaic" meaning making. Fewer college students make meaning at the fourth order, or "foundational" meaning making (Baxter Magolda, 1999a), which is characterized by self-authorship.

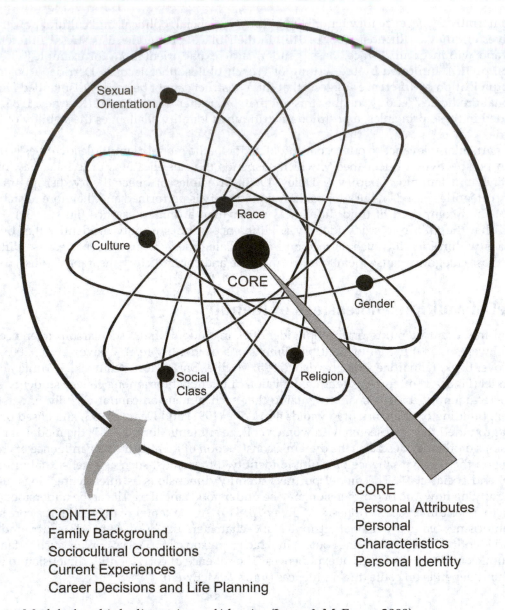

**Figure 1**    Model of multiple dimensions of identity (Jones & McEwen, 2000).

Requiring complexity in all three domains (interpersonal, intrapersonal, and cognitive), self-authorship occurs through "an ability to construct knowledge in a contextual world, an ability to construct an internal identity separate from external influences, and an ability to engage in relationships without losing one's internal identity" (Baxter Magolda, 1999b, p. 12). Students making a transition between formulaic and foundational meaning making are at a "crossroads" (Baxter Magolda, 1999b, p. 38). During this transitional period dominated by tensions and unresolved conflicts between their developing internal voices and external influences, students gradually question formulas increasingly incongruent with developing internal values.

Little research has been conducted exploring self-authorship in the context of how students make meaning of their socially constructed identities, such as race and sexuality. No published research has explored a relationship between self-authorship and intersectionality of social identities. Torres and Baxter Magolda (2004) offered evidence of the role of cognitive complexity in the development of ethnic identity among Latino/a students. Results of their longitudinal study indicated that increased cognitive complexity related to less reliance on stereotypes, authorities, and the approval of others to shape their ethnic identity. King and Baxter Magolda (2005) developed a conceptual framework for intercultural maturity grounded in the integration of cognitive, interpersonal, and intrapersonal development. The intrapersonal dimension of their framework presents a relationship between Kegan's (1994) orders of consciousness and theories of social identity development. In the only study to consider the relationship between college students' meaning-making capacity and perceptions of relationships among their multiple social identity dimensions, Abes and Jones (2004) simultaneously considered Kegan's constructivist–developmental theory and the model of multiple dimensions of identity (Jones & McEwen, 2000). The purpose of this article is to analyze the results of Abes and Jones's study in the context of the model of multiple dimensions of identity and offer, based on this analysis, a reconceptualized model that more aptly captures the complexity of intersecting domains of development.

## Overview of Abes and Jones's (2004) Study

The purpose of Abes and Jones's (2004) study was to explore how lesbian college students perceived their sexual orientation identity and its interaction with other dimensions of identity, such as race, religion, social class, and gender. The design and rationale of the study are detailed in Abes and Jones; we provide an overview here.

Abes and Jones's (2004) study was grounded in a constructivist theoretical framework, which assumes that knowledge is mutually constructed between the researchers and participants (Denzin & Lincoln, 2000). To understand how the participants made meaning of their identities, this study utilized narrative inquiry methodology. The purpose of narrative inquiry is to understand the wholeness of human experience through data collected in the form of stories (Clandinin & Connelly, 2000; Lieblich, Tuval-Mashiach, & Zilber, 1998). This methodological approach is well suited to identity studies because stories offer revealing glimpses into inner selves (Lieblich et al.; Riessman, 2002). Stories not only reveal, but also shape identity because identity stories are "told, revised, and retold throughout life. We know or discover ourselves, and reveal ourselves to others, by the stories we tell" (Lieblich et al., p. 7).

Purposeful sampling was used to obtain information-rich cases (Patton, 1990). All 10 participants, ages 18–23, attended a large, public research university in the Midwest. Five were students of color (one Black, one Latina, one Puerto Rican-Caucasian, one Trinidadian-Caucasian, and one African American-Caucasian); five were Caucasian. There were two Jewish women, one Agnostic, one Pagan, one Agnostic Pagan, one Christian, one Catholic, and three who did not identify with a religion. Eight identified as female, two as androgynous. Six women identified as middle class, one temporarily poor, one working class, and two upper-middle class.

Data were collected through three open-ended interviews with each participant. During the latter part of the second interview, each participant was asked to map her identity onto the model of multiple dimensions of identity (Jones & McEwen, 2000). For data analysis, Abes and Jones (2004) used primarily a categorical content approach, which utilizes constant comparative analysis (Lieblich et al., 1998). Results of the analysis were used to construct much of the participants' narratives. Abes and Jones also considered the structure of the participants' stories, including "the gaps, the silences, the tensions" (Ritchie & Wilson, 2000, p. 21).

Results of Abes and Jones's (2004) study suggested that meaning-making capacity served as a filter through which contextual factors are interpreted prior to influencing self-perceptions of sexual orientation identity and its relationship with other identity dimensions. How context influenced these perceptions depended on the complexity of the meaning-making filter. Participants with complex meaning-making capacity were able, more so than those with less developed capacity, to filter contextual influences, such as family background, peer culture, social norms, and stereotypes, and determine how context influenced their identity. Complex meaning making also facilitated the ease with which sexual orientation was integrated or peacefully co-existed with other dimensions and the extent to which participants' perceptions of their identity dimensions were consistent with the sense of self they hoped to achieve.

## Incorporating Meaning-Making Capacity into the Model of Multiple Dimensions of Identity

Revisiting the model of multiple dimensions of identity through the results of Abes and Jones's (2004) study suggests that incorporating meaning-making capacity into the model would more thoroughly depict the relationship between context and salience (and self perceptions) of identity dimensions, as well as the relationship between social identities and the core of identity. The reconceptualized model (Figure 2), unlike the original model, portrays in two dimensions the interactive nature of the relationships among components of the identity construction process: context, meaning making, and identity perceptions. Contextual influences are drawn in Figure 2 as arrows external to identity. The social identity dimensions are represented similarly to the Jones and McEwen (2000) model. Meaning-making capacity is drawn as a filter. How contextual influences move through the filter depends on the depth and permeability of the filter. The depth (thickness) and permeability (size of openings) of the filter depend on the complexity of the person's meaning-making capacity. To illustrate complex meaning making, the filter would be drawn with increased depth and smaller grid openings; less complex meaning-making capacity would be illustrated through a narrower filter with wider grid openings. Regardless of differences in meaning making, context influences identity perceptions; differences in the depth of the filter and size of the grid openings incorporate contextual influences in qualitatively different ways.

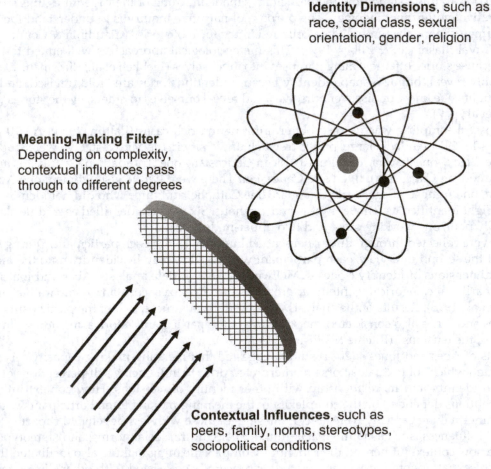

**Self-Perceptions of Multiple Identity Dimensions**, such as race, social class, sexual orientation, gender, religion

**Meaning-Making Filter** Depending on complexity, contextual influences pass through to different degrees

**Contextual Influences**, such as peers, family, norms, stereotypes, sociopolitical conditions

**Figure 2**    Reconceptualized model of multiple dimensions of identity.

Through narratives of three research participants, we offer possibilities of how their identity perceptions might be illustrated through the model with meaning-making capacity integrated into it. The three participants, Amy, Carmen, and Jacky, provide examples of formulaic, transitional, and foundational meaning making. The selections from the narratives describe these participants' perceptions of relationships among their multiple identity dimensions. These selections represent only small parts of a much more in-depth analysis of these three women's detailed narratives, which allowed us to assess meaning-making capacity (Abes, 2003).

## Formulaic Meaning Making and Multiple Dimensions of Identity

Because minimal filtering occurs in formulaic meaning making, contextual influences and perceptions of identity are closely connected. Participants infrequently saw relationships between or among their multiple identities. For instance, they perceived their sexual orientation as separate from their ethnicity if that was what they learned from their family; they perceived their sexual orientation as incompatible with their religion if this is how religious leaders taught them to interpret the major teachings of their religion; and they perceived their gender as either too masculine or too feminine if that is what friends and stereotypes told them.

*Amy's Story.* Amy, a 23-year-old senior, who prides herself on her unwavering opinions and "flaunts her individuality," exemplifies formulaic meaning-making capacity. Amy, who explained that there are two types of lesbians, "coffee shop lesbians and bar lesbians," and never the two shall mix, appeared to unknowingly define her identity in direct opposition to stereotypes, which laced her stories. A self-described bar lesbian, Amy refused to be like the people who attend gay and lesbian student organizations, whom she described as "the same kind of people that are like save the world. . . . I refuse to be anywhere near that." Amy's story demonstrates that formulaic meaning making might result in an identity that is constructed in direct and seemingly unanalyzed opposition to stereotypes. Even though Amy did not construct her identity in a manner consistent with stereotypes, stereotypes still dictated how she perceived her identity. Amy defined herself through who she is not, rather than through who she is.

Believing she was rejecting stereotypes, Amy announced she "flaunted her originality," which meant rejecting most environmental influences. She explained:

> I don't put myself into one group of people. I consider myself one of a kind and that's it. I'm me. I'm my own class, group, genre, everything, like that's how I look at things. . . . I don't seek to relate to other people. I don't because I'm me, I'm myself.

One implication of her desire to be unique was that she denied the possibility that aspects of her identity, such as sexual orientation, race, and social class, affected who she was as a person. As a result, she saw few relationships among her identity dimensions. Because connections with other people were not a primary concern, Amy did not allow her family's expectations to influence how she thought about being gay. For instance, Amy, who was Trinidadian-Caucasian, felt that some of her Trinidadian family members disapproved of her sexual orientation because it did not meet their cultural expectations. She rejected their opinions, not because of internal meaning making, but because she rejected other people's opinions in general, explaining, "I'm not that close to other people . . . and I don't really care. I was like, whatever, it's who I am."

However, not seeming to realize the influence of stereotypes on her thinking, Amy described a relationship between her social class and sexual orientation. Explaining her generally unwavering opinion about the social class of lesbians, she observed:

> I think lesbians are poor in general. . . . The ones that are wealthy, they're few and far between. You usually see lesbians who are bar flies, UPS delivery workers, or the lesbian that's the construction worker. You see the lumberjack. You never see the lawyer or the doctor in these bars. You never see the professional lesbian. . . . I think it's because the lesbians I'm in contact with are young. They're all just out of college or in college. And then the other ones you see at the bars are the old tired lesbians that are really gross and old in their 40s and 50s and sipping on their whiskey.

Although Amy wanted to achieve a higher social class than the women she saw in the bars, these stereotypes had a relatively unfiltered influence on how she understood the relationship between sexual orientation and social class.

*Amy's Model.* When Amy depicted her identity in relationship to the model, she placed most of the dimensions, including culture, race, sexual orientation, and gender, approximately the same distance from her core. Social class was further from her core. Religion, which she described as "hooey," was not relevant to her identity perceptions. Always defining her identity in opposition to stereotypes, she was adamant that none of these social identities influenced who she was as a person. Depicted on the reconceptualized model, Amy's meaning-making filter would be relatively simple. Contextual influences would pass through the filter without Amy making her own meaning of them.

## Transitional Meaning Making and Multiple Dimensions of Identity

Several of the participants were making a transition or on the brink of a transition between formulaic and foundational meaning making. Their stories reflected tensions and conflicts within their identity. As their meaning making grew more complex, these participants were starting to realize the limitations of stereotypes, feel frustrated by identity labels insufficient to describe how they made sense of whom they were, and challenge other people's expectations that caused difficulties integrating multiple identity dimensions. Still, they relied on comfortable formulaic ways of knowing at the same time that they started to see some of the shortcomings of doing so. For instance, they simultaneously believed that it was acceptable to pass as straight when their sexual orientation clashed with their ethnicity and that there was no reason why their ethnicity and sexual orientation needed to be separate; and they believed, but with lingering doubts as a result of stereotypes, that lesbians could achieve upper-class economic status.

*Carmen's Story.* Carmen, a 19-year-old Puerto Rican-Caucasian sophomore, whose meaning making appeared to be at the crossroads between formulaic and foundational, defined her identity though external influences at the same time that she started to realize the limitations of doing so. Although increasingly frustrating to her, she still allowed relatively unfiltered influences from her family, stereotypes, and social norms to determine relationships among her sexual orientation, gender, religion, and culture.

Carmen, for whom identifying with Christianity was important, explained that she did not allow her family's insistence that she would go to hell for being gay influence her attitude about her sexual orientation. She thought it hypocritical to use religion, which teaches the importance of loving everybody, as a basis for disapproving of gay people and explained:

> God made me this way. . . . even if it is a flaw . . . it's a flaw that He's created. . . . I just don't think that because I love differently He doesn't want me to follow his religion or anything like that. . . . The only person that should be concerned with that is me and God. Our relationship is whatever I want it to be.

At the same time, Carmen was uncertain she would ever practice her religion because of the opinions of other people. She explained:

> I think it's difficult just because some religions aren't accepting of my lifestyle and stuff like that. . . . Christianity, they don't accept it, it's not viewed as normal. It makes it harder for me to relate to religion, equate religion in my life.

However, dating a woman would not necessarily exclude being religious. She explained that this would also depend on whether the woman portrayed her gender as "butch or femme," terms she defined through stereotypes:

> If I ended up with a femme girl, and she was Christian, I'd guess we would go to church and we'd try to lead like decent lives . . . according to the Bible. If I settle down with a butch girl, chances are she's not going to feel comfortable, or the Church isn't going to feel comfortable. Finding the right fit is going to be harder in my life I guess.

Carmen expressed frustration with these expectations that did not coincide with her evolving internal beliefs. Still, she relied on external influences, allowing them to strongly influence her perceptions of the relationship among her gender, sexual orientation, and religious identities.

Similarly, Carmen's perceptions of the relationship between her ethnicity and sexual orientation wavered, revealing inner conflict between wanting to be her own person and resigning herself to the expectations of others. Some of Carmen's closest relatives disapproved of her sexual orientation, based in part, she believed, on traditional Puerto Rican values. Carmen's father questioned why she would want to be gay when it added to the "strikes" she already had against her as a Puerto Rican woman. Based on their opinions, Carmen resigned herself to believing that her sexual orientation and culture will unlikely be integrated and attempted to convince herself she was satisfied with that relationship. She explained:

> When I'm around a bunch of Puerto Ricans, I'm not going to be like, yeah I'm gay. . . . If we're getting together, if the focus is more towards my culture or doing something with that aspect of my life . . . then I guess the two are separate there. . . . Eventually I hope when my kids' kids are alive it's not such a big issue. And I don't see it happening. . . . Not that I don't think I can make a difference with a few of my relatives' opinions or anything but . . . I don't see why the two really need to come together.

At the same time that she stated these two dimensions of her identity don't have to come together, it was hard for her to understand why they cannot.

*Carmen's Model.* When Carmen depicted her identity onto the model, she explained that sexual orientation touches her core sense of self as it was the aspect of her identity to which she gave the most thought and that influenced her behavior. She explained this was because she was "abnormal" in society's eyes. Similarly, Carmen explained that her gender was close to her core, but only because of social norms with which she didn't agree but from which she did not believe she could escape. This perceived bind was a result of transitional meaning making. At the same time that she "just wants to be myself and it shouldn't matter," typically wearing men's clothes and exhibiting masculine mannerisms, she also acknowledged that she worried about what other people thought about her gender expression. If it were up to Carmen, who stated: "I don't think about my gender without taking into account social norms," her gender would have been the least important aspect of her identity. She was not sure, though, this was possible.

Also a result of transitional meaning making, she depicted religion in two different ways. She drew religion as a separate identity ring apart from the others, given the complications involved in understanding how religion fits into her life. On the same model, she also drew religion in her core sense of self because she believed that once she has religion in her life, it would be central to her identity. She believed religion would change in salience more than any other aspect of her identity. This dual role of religion, caused by her new and tentative questioning of external influences, is shown in her active questioning of and disagreement with her family's reaction that she would go to hell for being gay. Also illustrative of the transition in meaning-making capacity is her growing internal belief that she could define her own relationship with God despite her family's opinion.

Depicted on the reconceptualized model, Carmen's meaning-making filter would be more complex than Amy's. The filter would have varying depths, allowing some contextual influences to pass through reinterpreted and reshaped by Carmen, and others defined externally and relatively unchanged.

## Foundational Meaning Making and Multiple Dimensions of Identity

With a complex meaning-making filter, participants with foundational meaning-making capacity, or approaching such capacity, had greater ability to determine the relationship between context and perceptions of identity. These women were adept at resisting stereotypes and typically presented their identity in a consistent manner regardless of the environment. Movement toward an internally generated identity allowed some participants to define for themselves relationships among multiple identity dimensions such that they peacefully co-existed. For instance, they understood their sexual orientation to be consistent with their religious beliefs, regardless of how others defined their religion; and they understood their sexual orientation and gender expression as consistent, even when their peers told them otherwise.

*Jacky's Story.* Jacky's story illustrates foundational meaning making. A self-described "temporarily poor, Black, gay, female, Agnostic Pagan, liberal, communist, socialist," Jacky was an academically and politically inquisitive 21-year-old junior. She was keenly aware of her lack of multiple privileges, as well as the privileges she did have, and the numerous reasons for people to discriminate against her. She spent much time researching various political and identity-based issues, reading in-depth about all sides of an issue and then reaching her own conclusions after a logical analysis of multiple perspectives.

Personal and societal discrimination influenced Jacky's thinking about the multiple dimensions of her identity. These contextual factors, however, influenced her identity perceptions in a qualitatively different manner from the ways in which context influenced Amy's and Carmen's self-perceptions. Jacky did not perceive discrimination as determining the meaning she made of each dimension, but rather, discrimination fueled her political fire. To understand how we interpret Jacky's meaning-making capacity, it is important to realize the depth of her political commitment. Jacky, for whom personal is political, considered politics as central to her identity, typically more salient than socially constructed identities, such as race and gender. She explained: "[Social identities] influence my political leanings, and my political leanings influence [social identities], it goes both ways. [Politics] informs a lot of my beliefs, just, I'm a political science major, so I study current topics, or current events." It was the centrality of her political commitments that drove her politically charged and personally meaningful response to personal and societal discrimination relevant to her socially constructed identities. Her response to discrimination grew out of her political beliefs, but did not determine self-perceptions of her socially constructed identities.

For instance, a lack of domestic partnership benefits caused her to be "temporarily poor," serving as a catalyst for her to focus on the relationship between her sexual orientation and social class. Jacky's anger regarding the lack of benefits provoked her to take actions to fight this inequality but did not necessarily influence the way in which she understood her sexual orientation and social class identities. She explained:

> It doesn't make me feel sorry that I'm gay or anything like that, but it makes me wish I could be more able to change the system. . . . I'm Black, gay, and female, and leftist . . . and I'm not a Christian. . . . It makes me follow politics that much more. . . . It helped me shape my opinions and my politics and my point of view.

Likewise, Jacky was aware of discrimination based on her gender. She attributed this to her professional interests in computers, a male-dominated field. Although it was not a pressing matter to her, Jacky explained that her gender does not "fit into the boxes very well. . . . gender is performance . . . and I've never really picked up on social norms . . . I'm just a chick who likes drums and computers." Rather than discrimination altering how she perceived her identity, she became more intrigued by the politics of gender.

Raised in a Catholic household, Jacky used her complex thinking to research and critically analyze numerous religions before identifying a practice she felt fit her best. Even as a young child, before considering her sexual orientation, she never connected with Catholicism yet was intrigued by religion. After she conducted extensive research and tried on various religious practices, she eventually identified as an Agnostic Pagan "who's an atheist when in a bad mood," because she felt it was an expression of herself despite expectations from others for a more traditional religious identity. Although Jacky gave much thought to both her sexual orientation and religion, she rarely thought of the two together. With the capacity to filter out other people's negative perceptions of her identity as a Pagan gay woman, she made her own meaning of this identity. Jacky explained:

> I'm gay, and I'm a Pagan. I'm not necessarily a gay Pagan or a Pagan gay person. They're not against each other . . . but they're two different parts of my identity. Usually if I'm thinking about one, I'm not thinking about the other.

In fact, Jacky typically thought of her multiple identities as parallel rather than intersecting. The few times she considered them to intersect were when she was discriminated against and could not determine which aspect of her identity triggered the behavior. She explained:

> I guess [dimensions of my identity] are not completely parallel, some of them do cross or confound, but I think of them more as I'm a lesbian, I'm Black, I'm a Pagan, atheist, whatever. But then sometimes it will be like I'm a Black lesbian . . . or I'm a Pagan lesbian . . . I think it's situation related. . . . I think about it more as these are parts of me, and it just happens to be that they're all like not the norm. . . . Most of the time if I'm discriminated against, I can tell if it's for a certain reason, like this person doesn't like me because I'm gay, this person doesn't like me because I'm Black . . . and then there's the times when I'm not quite sure why the person doesn't like me, or why I'm getting treated in such a way. And I think that's when it becomes intermingled.

When intermingled, discrimination still influenced her politics more so than identity perceptions. Jacky's capacity to richly analyze the relationship between discrimination and her identity perceptions and maintain some ownership over the dynamic saliency of these dimensions illustrates the complexity of her meaning-making capacity.

*Jacky's Model.* Jacky depicted her identity through the model with sexual orientation and gender closest to her core; race, religion, social class, and disability (she lived with attention deficit disorder) were further away. Sharply aware of discrimination as a contextual influence, Jacky explained that the salience of her identity dimensions is quite fluid. This fluidity did not change how she understood her identity, but rather, where she would devote her political energy. Jacky explained that that there was a "range of saliency" along which each dimension of her identity moved closer or further away from her inner sense of self, depending on the nature of the discrimination she was experiencing.

Always cognizant of constant discrimination based on her sexual orientation, she stated: "Sexuality is the biggest part of my identity that affects me as far as discrimination. . . . I feel that constantly every single day, day in and day out." Consistently close to the core, sexual orientation's range of saliency was narrow. She explained that her religion probably had the greatest range along which it moves. Jacky, who was "not raised in Black culture," explained that race typically was not an aspect of her identity to which she gave much thought. But her race traveled along its saliency range over the course of the study, at one point coming in as close to her inner sense of self as she believed it ever would. The movement was precipitated by how infuriated she was about current arguments against race-sensitive affirmative action.

The meaning-making filter in Jacky's model is more complex than in Amy's or Carmen's models. The filter has more depth, and the grid openings are smaller and less porous. Jacky reinterprets the contextual influences as they pass through the filter, ascribing her own internal meaning onto the context. For instance, as contextual influences, which Jacky described as discrimination and her political upbringing, pass through the filter, she makes meaning of them by determining how to translate them into political thought or action.

# Discussion

## A Reconceptualized, Integrated Model

As illustrated through the narratives of Amy, Carmen, and Jacky, relationships among socially constructed identities represent a complex interaction among multiple domains of development. Although the model of multiple dimensions of identity (Jones & McEwen, 2000) offered for the first time in the literature on student development theory a conceptual framework for understanding relationships among students' personal and socially constructed identities, we are reconceptualizing the model to incorporate meaning-making capacity. This reconceptualization adds to contemporary student development literature that integrates students' intrapersonal, cognitive, and interpersonal domains of development (Abes & Jones, 2004; King & Baxter Magolda, 2005; Torres & Baxter Magolda, 2004). Incorporating meaning-making capacity into the model provides a richer portrayal of not only *what* relationships students perceive among their personal and social identities, but also *how* they come to perceive them as they do. By incorporating personal and multiple social identities, Jones and McEwen's model provides a holistic representation of the intrapersonal domain; with the inclusion of meaning-making capacity, the reconceptualized model provides a holistic representation of the integration of intrapersonal development with the cognitive and interpersonal domains.

Integrating meaning-making capacity into the model of multiple dimensions of identity (Jones & McEwen, 2000) also addresses a question regarding distinctions in the model between the core self (personal identity) and the surrounding social identities, especially social identities typically lacking privilege in dominant–subordinate hierarchies. Although this distinction between social identities and core was apparent in the data from which the original model was conceptualized (Jones, 1997), several of the participants in Abes and Jones's (2004) study included social identities, most often sexual orientation, as part of their core. Their reasons for doing so differed and were related in some measure to meaning-making capacity.

Some participants with complex meaning-making capacity considered sexual orientation part of their core because they perceived this dimension as internally defined and fully incorporated into their identity. In contrast, others considered sexual orientation as core because they perceived their core to be influenced by external factors; these participants resisted the notion that core could be wholly defined internally. Utilizing transitional meaning-making capacity, these participants recognized that social norms were catalysts for sexual orientation to be in their core, regardless of whether it was something they wanted to be central to their identity. For example, Carmen reluctantly perceived her sexual orientation and gender as core because she realized that external influences caused these aspects of her identity to be central to whom she was as a person. Reconceptualizing Jones and McEwen's (2000) model by integrating meaning-making capacity opens up possibilities for understanding not only relationships between context and identity, but also between social identities and the core. Doing so also provides a reminder that high salience of a social identity in relationship to the core does not always imply positive self-perceptions of that identity. An externally defined identity could be salient to one's sense of self but for negative reasons, such as family or religious disapproval. Thus, incorporating meaning making into the model contributes to a more developmental and dynamic understanding of how persons negotiate complexities of personal and social identities.

## Queer Theory and Multiple Identities

An inherent irony emerges in the study of multiple dimensions of identity, which is highlighted in our reconceptualized model. Our interest in capturing the complexities of identity development when multiple domains are considered is bolstered by theoretical frameworks such as intersectionality, which includes both feminist conceptualizations and the postmodern perspective of queer theory. However, these theoretical frameworks, especially queer theory, argue against the very notion that identity can be "captured" and that a core identity exists. Britzman (1997) described this tension well:

> In terms of educational research, now more often than not, the idea of identity still remains tied to the mistaken view that identities are either given or received and not negotiated socially, politically, and within specific historical conditions. These absences result in the pinning of identity onto a straight continuum. . . . I want to argue for a more complex and historically grounded notion of identity, one interested in identity as fluid, partial, contradictory, nonunitary, and very social matters. (pp. 184–185)

The three narratives of Amy, Carmen, and Jacky illustrate the performative and fluid nature of identity construction. As performative, participants' actions were not representative of identity; instead, actions created identity (Butler, 1991). Decisions regarding their manner of dress, choice of partners, religious practices, and political involvement became the meaning of their identity dimensions. Participants who utilized more complex meaning making demonstrated an awareness of the performative nature of their identity rather than a reliance on fixed and externally defined meanings. Those utilizing less developed meaning making were not always aware of the performative nature of their identity; still, it was this unacknowledged performativity that lay beneath their attempts to fit into others' socially constituted expectations and navigate the resulting tensions and ambiguities associated with crossing multiple borders.

In proposing a reconceptualized model, queer theory causes us to revisit the meaning of the core sense of self found in the multiple identities model. Jones (1997) described the core as an inner-defined personal sense of self, incorporating "valued personal attributes and characteristics" (p. 383). It is important at this juncture to clarify that participants in Abes and Jones's (2004) study described the core and some of their social identities as interacting dynamically. For instance, socially constructed identities might move in and out of the core depending on contextual influences and the changing meaning individuals make of these identities. Although fluid in nature, the core includes personal values and aspects of identity that individuals perceive as central to their sense of self. This conceptualization of the core is consistent with queer theory. Although queer theory suggests that identities are always in a state of movement (e.g., Talburt, 2000), queer theory also suggests that repeating enactments of identity creates one's identity; this is performativity (Butler, 1991). Although the continuous repetition is a "copy" that never had an "original" (Butler), the repetition creates a sense of self, including a core sense of personal values, however fluid that sense of self might be.

In applying the tenets of queer theory to an illustration of multiple identities, we work to present both the fluid nature of identity and the lived experience of conflict and negotiation as described by the participants. Given the fluid differences within identity (Fuss, 1989), our reconceptualized model is not intended to illustrate a linear, stable, and predictable relationship between meaning-making capacity and the salience and self-perceptions of identity dimensions. We do not believe such an orderly relationship exists. We introduce meaning making into the model as only one key consideration in how students understand their multi-faceted identities. Meaning making neither predicts nor proscribes relative salience or the nature of the relationships among social identities. Meaning making does, however, provide one explanation for how students perceive their identities as they do. With queer principles in mind, the revised model should be interpreted as one possibility for identity construction rather than an orderly, predictable pattern.

Queer theory principles, for example, challenge Jacky's perceptions of identity dimensions as generally parallel to one another. Fuss (1989) argued that differences should not be seen as space between identities, but instead, space within identities. Here lies one of the tensions of pairing queer theory with college students' lived experiences interpreted through a constructivist lens. Abes (in press) explored this sometimes contradictory relationship and found that, although queer theory might not always describe college students' identity perceptions, analyzing relationships among students' multiple identities through a queer lens revealed how "participants continuously redefined the meaning they made of their identity. They rethought labels they had previously used to describe their identity, considered dimensions of their identity previously taken for granted, and challenged assumptions about what is normal." With queer principles in mind, the revised model should be interpreted as one possibility for identity construction rather than an orderly, predictable pattern.

# Implications for Theory, Research, and Practice

## Theory Development and Interpretation

Implications for student development theory are suggested by the reconceptualized model, which incorporates meaning making with personal and social identities. Although a wide array of student development theories is available to student affairs professionals to understand students and guide practice (McEwen, 2003), most theories fall within one of the families of psychosocial, cognitive, and social identity development theories. Few models or theories exist to understand the holistic development of college students. In an early model of maturity in college students (although based on a study only of college men), Heath (1968, 1980) considered development through a matrix of four domains of development (cognitive, self-concept, values, and personal relations) and five sets of developmental tasks. Baxter Magolda (2001), in her longitudinal study of college students into adulthood and their development of self-authorship, and King and Baxter Magolda (2005), in their model of intercultural maturity, provide contemporary perspectives of the intersection of epistemological, intrapersonal, and interpersonal dimensions of development. The reconceptualized model presented here, incorporating meaning making into the model of multiple dimensions of identities (Jones & McEwen, 2000), is placed within the context of few models of holistic development in the student development theory literature. (We note that we are using two sets of words to describe domains of development: psychosocial, cognitive, and social identity, because these terms are in common use in the student development literature; and epistemological, interpersonal, and intrapersonal as they are used by Kegan, 1994, Baxter Magolda, e.g., 2001, and King and Baxter Magolda. Collectively each set of terms represents holistic development; individually, both interpersonal and intrapersonal are components of psychosocial and social identity development, and vice versa.)

We focus on three specific implications related to student development theory. First is the importance of incorporating contemporary perspectives of fluidity, performativity, and salience in theory development and use, particularly related to multiple social identities. The reconceptualization of the model of multiple dimensions of identity (Jones & McEwen, 2000) and the voices of lesbian college students from Abes and Jones's study (2004) illustrate the great fluidity and varying salience of students' multiple identities and the performative nature of students' identity. Abes and Jones captured the ways in which identity salience changed for participants in their study, often depending on contextual influences and participants' meaning-making capacity. The introduction of these ideas, some of which stem from queer theory, suggests the possibility of exploring the role of heteronormativity, and other privileging societal structures, in students' negotiations of their multiple social identities (Abes, in press). D'Augelli's (1994) theory of gay, lesbian, and bisexual identity development is one of the few theories that consider the relationship between societal power structures and the fluidity of identity formation. D'Augelli called for theory development that starts with the assumption that identity is "mutable" and a "dynamic process of interaction and exchange between the individual and the many levels of social collectives during the historical period of her or his life" (p. 330). Similarly, King (1994) drew attention to "complex stage models of development [that] . . . take intraindividual variability into account" (p. 418) and noted complex stage models, according to Rest (1979), "as depicting a much messier and complicated picture of development" (p. 65). Although some researchers have applied D'Augelli's dynamic theory of sexual orientation development (e.g., Renn & Bilodeau, 2005), student development theory in general has been slow to move in a direction that considers relationships between power structures and the fluidity of development. The reconceptualized model builds on D'Augelli's perspective by demonstrating the importance of developmental theories considering contextual influences and the dynamic development of socially constructed identities.

Second is the need to create theories addressing students' holistic development, that is, the complex and fluid intersection of epistemological (or cognitive), psychosocial, and social identity domains of development. Many student development theories focus primarily on one domain of development, such as psychosocial (e.g., Chickering & Reisser, 1993), cognitive (e.g., Perry, 1981), racial identity (e.g., Helms, 1995), and sexual identity (e.g., McCarn & Fassinger, 1996). A small amount of research and only two contemporary theories, specifically those of Baxter Magolda (2001) and King and Baxter Magolda (2005), have considered the intersection of two or more of these domains of development. This reconceptualization of the model of multiple dimensions of identity (Jones & McEwen, 2000) offers one specific example of incorporating epistemological development with interpersonal and intrapersonal development. Although we acknowledge that empirical theory generation and validation involve significant research endeavors, this reconceptualized model suggests the importance of creating theories, based on diverse samples, that integrate the domains of epistemological, interpersonal, and intrapersonal development. Creating complex holistic developmental models may mark the significant challenge for development of student development theory in the 21st century.

A third implication related to theory is the responsibility of professionals to have an in-depth knowledge of the complexities and holistic aspects of existing theories. Perhaps because many of the current student development theories focus primarily on one domain of development, little attention is paid to other developmental domains incorporated in various theories. We highlight two specific examples of developmental models that are more comprehensive than they appear on the surface. First, although Perry's (1981) scheme is considered a cognitive–structural development theory, Perry actually named his scheme one of "intellectual and ethical development." Intellectual development (positions 1–6) corresponds to the epistemological or cognitive domain, but in the ethical domain (commitment within relativism, positions 7–9), Perry extended cognitive development to intrapersonal and interpersonal domains (for instance, commitments about one's career, lifestyle, values). Second, Helms (1995), in her models of racial identity development for people of color and for White persons, not only addresses the development of the social identity of race, but also incorporates how one processes socioracial information (epistemological domain). Indeed, in both of her racial identity models, Helms stated that "maturation [in racial identity] is triggered by a combination of cognitive–affective complexity within the individual and race-related environmental stimuli" (p. 184). So, in both of these examples, student affairs professionals seem to focus on the central developmental domain (cognitive or racial identity), often to the exclusion of acknowledging and using each theory in its full complexities. The incorporation of meaning making in the model of multiple dimensions of identity (Jones & McEwen, 2000) illustrates the value of complex models incorporating more than one domain. It is noteworthy that some current theories, such as Perry's and Helms's, are more complex than how they may be used in practice.

## Challenges and Directions for Designing Research on Multiple Identities

Important to an understanding of multiple and intersecting dimensions of identity is discussion about the difficulty in studying complexity in social identity development. Weber (1998), in her presentation of a conceptual framework for understanding the intersections of race, class, gender, and sexuality, wrote:

> When we say that race, gender, and sexuality are social constructs, not fixed biological traits, we also mean that we cannot *fully* capture their meaning in everyday life in the way that social scientists often attempt to do by employing them as variables in traditional quantitative research. When race, gender, and sexuality are treated as discrete variables, individuals are typically assigned a single location along a dimension, which is defined by a set of presumably mutually exclusive and exhaustive categories. (p. 18)

However, designing studies that capture the complexity of inhabiting multiple locations simultaneously is difficult (McCall, 2005). Participants in those studies may not understand that their social identities are continuously shaped by systems of race, class, gender, and sexuality (Weber). Without this context, they perceive some dimensions of their identities as less salient, at different times and under differing circumstances. Integrating the meaning-making filter into the model helps to understand these apparent differences in self-perceptions. For instance, transitional meaning-making capacity provides one explanation for the discrepancy between Carmen's statements that no relationship existed between her sexual orientation and ethnicity, and the stories she shared in which the two were intertwined.

Still, research on multiple identities seems to privilege the researchers' points of view and interpretation at the expense of the participants' lived experiences. In studies of identity, researchers necessarily point participants in a specific direction with their line of questioning. Abes and Jones (2004) were aware of this possibility in their study and explained to participants that they need not discuss dimensions of their identity they did not believe were salient to their sense of self or to which they gave little thought. Nevertheless, the questioning prompted thinking and often the sharing of stories the participants might not have considered relevant to their sense of self absent the prompting. Despite best attempts, the difference between imposing and understanding became complicated as the participants' stories sometimes belied their assertions regarding lack of salience of some identity dimensions (Abes, in press; Abes & Jones).

Some of the limitations of this study suggest areas for further research. As with Jones and McEwen's (2000) model, the possibilities for the updated model are based on a developmental snapshot of a student's journey toward self-authorship. Longitudinal research will provide a more comprehensive exploration of the relationships between meaning-making capacity and perceptions of relationships among multiple dimensions of identity. Although not in the context of multiple identities, Torres and Baxter Magolda (2004) illustrate the rich understanding of social identities that emerges from longitudinal research.

Likewise, the data upon which these illustrations are drawn were the stories of 10 women who identified as lesbian. Although the interviews with these women included stories about multiple dimensions of their identity, the focus was on perceptions of their sexual orientation identity; other dimensions were explored primarily in relationship to their sexual orientation. In-depth explorations of other identity dimensions, such as race, ethnicity, and religion, in relationship to one another, might provide a more comprehensive picture of the nature of the meaning-making filter and the relationships among context, meaning making, and content.

Meaning-making capacity is just one possibility for understanding students' perceptions of the salience and meaning of their social identities. Further research should address other factors that are part of the mix, including the role of particular contextual influences, such as campus culture, and the challenges posed by the particulars of students' unique multiple identities, which might account for how students perceive certain contextual influences, such as family norms and faith-based expectations.

## Professional Practice

Although the purpose of our scholarship is to extend a theoretical model, we also offer a few implications for practice. Including meaning-making capacity in the model of multiple dimensions of identity (Jones & McEwen, 2000) provides a lens to understand more clearly how students see themselves. As illustrated through the stories of Amy, Carmen, and Jacky, the role of meaning-making capacity enables educators to more effectively see students as they see themselves by understanding not only *what* they perceive their identity to be, but also *how* they make meaning of their identity dimensions as they do, how they come to perceive identity dimensions as salient or relatively unimportant, and to what degree they understand their social identities as integrated or distinct. Knowing the relationship between meaning-making capacity and identity perceptions provides professionals who work with college students a deeper awareness of how students understand themselves. In turn, this knowledge allows professionals to more effectively engage in meaningful and individualized educational partnerships with students to help them develop a more complex understanding of their identity and the power associated with defining identity for oneself.

Given that complex meaning-making capacity better enables students to self-author (Baxter Magolda, 2001) how they understand their sexual orientation identity and its relationship with other identity dimensions, one practical implication of the reconceptualized multiple identities model is the attention it focuses on helping students create more complex meaning-making filters. In her description of the learning partnership model, Baxter Magolda (2001) offers a strategy for fostering meaning-making capacity through the use of three design principles: validate students' capacity to know, situate learning in students' experience, and define learning as mutually constructing meaning. The reconceptualized model of multiple identities suggests the importance of applying these three principles in the context of students' multiple identities. The many ways this might be accomplished include the incorporation of experiential and reflective components into identity-based academic courses and cocurricular advising, counseling, and programming. Whether in group contexts, such as first-year seminars, community service, or identity-based student organizations and student centers, or in individualized contexts, such as career counseling and academic advising, the design principles can be used to create conditions where multiple truths about identity perceptions are assumed; students bring their own identity-based experiences and stories into the mix to co-construct with peers, advisors, counselors, and instructors new truths, understandings, and perspectives about their sense of self.

Along with meaning making, another key consideration in understanding students' multiple identities is for student affairs professionals to acknowledge and understand the nature of the contextual influences. One responsibility of professionals is to know and be aware of the campus culture and how the culture relates to students' representation and development of their multiple identities. By way of example, saliency of sexual orientation for a lesbian college student might depend on campus culture. For instance, sexual orientation might be more (or less) salient for a student at a women's college that has a feminist culture and support for lesbian students than for a student attending a public research institution in a conservative state with little visible support for students who are not heterosexual. Also, the nature of each dimension of one's identity might play a role in the salience of the other dimensions. A Latina student, for example, might perceive family influences important as a result of values associated with her culture (Torres, 2003) as well as her meaning-making complexity (Torres & Baxter Magolda, 2004). Further, student affairs professionals should consider students' meaning-making capacity in relation to campus culture and other contextual influences. For example, students may not always apply their full meaning-making capacity to all aspects of their identity, in part a result of contextual influences. For instance, a White student who is a complex meaning-maker might not make meaning of her racial identity in a complex manner if the contextual influences by which she is surrounded have not yet caused her to recognize her racial privilege (Helms, 1992).

The reconceptualized model not only draws attention to fostering complexity in students' self-perceptions of their multiple identities but also serves as a reminder of the importance of professionals developing their own meaning-making capacity. As student affairs professionals work with college students to help them develop more complex and empowered identities, it is important that professionals develop toward self-authoring their own multiple identities. Similar to Helms's (1995) discussion of racial identity in interpersonal environments, the more complex professionals' meaning-making capacity and self-understanding, the more effectively professionals can understand and foster the identity development of college students. Thus, an implication of this reconceptualized model integrating multiple identities and meaning-making capacities suggests the importance of professionals understanding themselves and engaging in and reflecting on contexts where the way they understand their own identities is challenged (McEwen, 2003).

## Conclusion

This reconceptualized model incorporating meaning-making capacity into the model of multiple dimensions of identity (Jones & McEwen, 2000), based on Abes and Jones's (2004) study, provides an illustration of the integration of the multiple facets of college students' development. Perhaps this model and that of King and Baxter Magolda (2005) suggest directions for a new generation of student development theory formulation and research. Models of students' holistic development and ways to integrate students' cognitive, intrapersonal, and interpersonal development offer the potential for more complex understanding of college students' development and for designing programs and environments to enhance the complexities of students' development.

## References

Abes, E. S. (2003). *The dynamics of lesbian college students' multiple dimensions of identity*. Unpublished doctoral dissertation, The Ohio State University, Columbus.

Abes, E. S. (in press). Applying queer theory in practice with college students: Transformation of a researcher's and participant's perspectives on identity. *Journal of Gay and Lesbian Issues in Education*.

Abes, E. S., & Jones, S. R. (2004). Meaning-making capacity and the dynamics of lesbian college students' multiple dimensions of identity. *Journal of College Student Development, 45,* 612–632.

Anzaldua, G. (1999). *Borderlands: La frontera* (2nd ed.). San Francisco: Aunt Lute Books.

Baxter Magolda, M. B. (1999a). *Creating contexts for learning and self-authorship: Constructive-developmental pedagogy*. Nashville, TN: Vanderbilt University Press.

Baxter Magolda, M. B. (1999b). The evolution of epistemology: Refining contextual knowing at twentysomething. *Journal of College Student Development, 40,* 333–344.

Baxter Magolda, M. B. (2001). *Making their own way: Narratives for transforming higher education to promote self-development.* Sterling, VA: Stylus.

Britzman, D. P. (1997). What is this thing called love?: New discourses for understanding gay and lesbian youth. In S. de Castell & M. Bryson (Eds.), *Racial in(ter)ventions: Identity, politics, and difference/s on educational praxis* (pp. 183–207). Albany: State University of New York Press.

Butler, J. (1991). Imitation and gender subordination. In D. Fuss (Ed.), *Inside/Out: Lesbian theories, gay theories* (pp. 13–31). New York: Routledge.

Chavez, A. F., Guido-DiBrito, F., & Mallory, S. L. (2003). Learning to value the "other": A framework of individual diversity development. *Journal of College Student Development, 44,* 453–469.

Chickering, A. W., & Reisser, L. (1993). *Education and identity* (2nd ed.). San Francisco: Jossey-Bass.

Clandinin, D. J., & Connelly, F. M. (2000). *Narrative inquiry: Experience and story in qualitative research.* San Francisco: Jossey-Bass.

Collins, P. H. (1990). *Black feminist thought: Knowledge, consciousness, and the politics of empowerment.* New York: Routledge.

D'Augelli, A. R. (1994). Identity development and sexual orientation: Toward a model of lesbian, gay, and bisexual development. In E. J. Trickett, R. J. Watts, & D. Birman (Eds.), *Human diversity: Perspectives on people in context* (pp. 312–333). San Francisco: Jossey-Bass.

Davis, T. L. (2002). Voices of gender role conflict: The social construction of college men's identity. *Journal of College Student Development, 43,* 508–521.

Deaux, K. (1993). Reconstructing social identity. *Personality and Social Psychology Bulletin, 19,* 4–12.

Denzin, N. K., & Lincoln, Y. S. (2000). The discipline and practice of qualitative research. In N. K. Denzin & Y. S. Lincoln (Eds.), *Handbook of qualitative research* (2nd ed., pp. 1–28). Thousand Oaks, CA: Sage.

Fuss, D. (1989). *Essentially speaking: Feminism, nature, and difference.* New York: Routledge.

Heath, D. H. (1968). *Growing up in college: Liberal education and maturity.* San Francisco: Jossey-Bass.

Heath, D. H. (1980). Wanted: A comprehensive model of healthy development. *Personnel and Guidance Journal, 58,* 391–399.

Helms, J. E. (1992). *A race is a nice thing to have: A guide to being a White person, or understanding the White persons in your life.* Framingham, MA: Microtraining Associates.

Helms, J. E. (1995). An update of Helms's White and People of Color racial identity models. In J. G. Ponterotto, J. M. Casas, L. A. Suzuki, & C. M. Alexander (Eds.), *Handbook of multicultural counseling* (pp. 181–198). Thousand Oaks, CA: Sage.

hooks, b. (1984). *Feminist theory: From margin to center.* Boston: South End Press.

Jones, S. R. (1997). Voices of identity and difference: A qualitative exploration of the multiple dimensions of identity development in women college students. *Journal of College Student Development, 38,* 376–386.

Jones, S. R., & McEwen, M. K. (2000). A conceptual model of multiple dimensions of identity. *Journal of College Student Development, 41,* 405–414.

Kearney, R. (1984). *Dialogues with contemporary continental thinkers: The phenomenological heritage.* Manchester, NH: Manchester University Press.

Kegan, R. (1994). *In over our heads: The mental demands of modern life.* Cambridge, MA: Harvard University Press.

King, P. M. (1994). Theories of college student development: Sequences and consequences. *Journal of College Student Development, 35,* 413–421.

King, P. M., & Baxter Magolda, M. (2005). A developmental model of intercultural maturity. *Journal of College Student Development, 46,* 571–592.

Lieblich, A., Tuval-Mashiach, R., & Zilber, T. (1998). *Narrative research: Readings, analysis, interpretation.* Thousand Oaks, CA: Sage.

Lorde, A. (1984). *Sister outsider.* Freedom, CA: Crossing.

Love, P. G., Bock, M., Jannarone, A., & Richardson, P. (2005). Identity interaction: Exploring the spiritual experiences of lesbian and gay college students. *Journal of College Student Development, 46,* 193–209.

McCall, L. (2005). The complexity of intersectionality. *Signs: Journal of Women in Culture and Society, 30,* 1771–1800.

McCann, C. R., & Kim, S. (2002). *Feminist theory reader: Local and global perspectives.* New York: Routledge.

McCarn, S. R., & Fassinger, R. E. (1996). Revisioning sexual minority identity formation: A new model of lesbian identity and its implications for counseling and research. *The Counseling Psychologist, 24,* 508–534.

McEwen, M. K. (2003). The nature and use of theory. In S. R. Komives & D. B. Woodard, Jr. (Eds.), *Student services: A handbook for the profession* (4th ed., pp. 153–178). San Francisco: Jossey-Bass.

Miville, M. L., Darlington, P., Whitlock, B., & Mulligan, T. (2005). Integrating identities: The relationships of racial, gender, and ego identities among White college students. *Journal of College Student Development, 46,* 157–175.

Omi, M., & Winant, H. (1994). *Racial formation in the United States from the 1960s to the 1990s.* New York: Routledge.

Patton, M. (1990). *Qualitative evaluation and research methods* (2nd ed.). Newbury Park, CA: Sage.

Perry, W. G., Jr. (1981). Cognitive and ethical growth: The making of meaning. In A. W. Chickering & Associates, *The modern American college* (pp. 76–116). San Francisco: Jossey-Bass.

Renn, K. A., & Bilodeau, B. (2005). Queer student leaders: An exploratory case study of identity development and LGBT student involvement at a Midwestern research university. *Journal of Gay and Lesbian Issues in Education, 2*(4), 49–71.

Rest, J. R. (1979). *Development in judging moral issues.* Minneapolis: University of Minnesota Press.

Reynolds, A. L., & Pope, R. L. (1991). The complexities of diversity: Exploring multiple oppressions. *Journal of Counseling and Development, 70,* 174–180.

Riessman, C. K. (2002). Analysis of personal narratives. In J. F. Gubrium & J. A. Holstein (Eds.), *Handbook of interview research* (pp. 695–710). Thousand Oaks, CA: Sage.

Ritchie, J. S., & Wilson, D. E. (2000). *Teacher narrative as critical inquiry: Rewriting the script.* New York: Teachers College Press.

Smith, B. (1982). Toward a Black feminist criticism. In G. T. Hull, P. B. Scott, & B. Smith (Eds.), *All the women are White, all the Blacks are men, but some of us are brave* (pp. 157–175). Old Westbury, NY: Feminist Press.

Stevens, Jr., R. A. (2004). Understanding gay identity development within the college environment. *Journal of College Student Development, 45,* 185–206.

Talburt, S. (2000). Introduction: Some contradictions and possibilities of *Thinking Queer.* In S. Talburt & S. R. Steinberg (Eds.), *Thinking queer* (pp. 3–13). New York: Peter Lang.

Tierney, W. G., & Dilley, P. (1998). Constructing knowledge: Educational research and gay and lesbian studies. In W. F. Pinar (Ed.), *Queer theory in education* (pp. 49–71). Mahwah, NJ: Lawrence Erlbaum.

Tierney, W. G., & Rhoads, R. A. (1993). Postmodernism and critical theory in higher education: Implications for research and practice. In J. C. Smart (Ed.), *Higher education: Handbook of theory and research* (Vol. IX, pp. 308–343). New York: Agathon Press.

Torres, V. (2003). Influences on ethnic development of Latino college students in the first two years of college. *Journal of College Student Development, 44,* 532–547.

Torres, V., & Baxter Magolda, M. (2004). Reconstructing Latino identity: The influence of cognitive development on the ethnic identity process of Latino students. *Journal of College Student Development, 45,* 333–347.

Weber, L. (1998). A conceptual framework for understanding race, class, gender, and sexuality. *Psychology of Women Quarterly, 22,* 13–22.

# CHAPTER 7
# COMPARING SPIRITUAL DEVELOPMENT AND COGNITIVE DEVELOPMENT

## PATRICK G. LOVE

Three spiritual development theories and theorists (i.e., Parks, Fowler, and Helminiak) were compared with traditional cognitive development theory and theorists. The analysis reveals both commonalities between the two sets of theories and unique contributions to an understanding of student development on the part of spiritual development theory. Practical and research implications are described.

Theories of spiritual development have existed at the margins of student development theory for about 20 years and have not been given serious consideration as to what they contribute to our understanding of the experiences of college students. Given the expanding interest in spirituality and the increased focus on developmental theory related to spirituality (Love & Talbot, 1999), it makes sense to consider where theories of spiritual development fit into the constellation of student development theories and what, if anything, spiritual development theories uniquely contribute to the discourse of student development. A major focus in this article is to describe the theories of spiritual development and compare them to cognitive development theories. The specific theories of spiritual development used for this analysis are those of Sharon Daloz Parks (1986, 2000), James Fowler (1981, 1996), and Daniel Helminiak (1987, 1996). Given obvious space limitations, the cognitive development theories used in this comparison (Baxter Magolda, 1992; Belenky, Clinchy, Goldberger, & Tarule, 1986; King & Kitchener, 1994; Perry, 1970) are described in less depth due to their status in the "canon" of student affairs literature. Prior to comparing spiritual development and cognitive development it is first necessary to differentiate religion from spirituality, discuss the relationship between faith development and spiritual development, and provide brief descriptions of the spiritual development theories used in this comparison.

## Differentiating Religion and Spirituality

Differentiating the notion of religion from issues of spirituality and faith is important, both because of spirituality's long history as an aspect of theology, and because the terms (i.e., *religion, spirituality, faith*) are often used interchangeably (e.g., "What faith are you?" "I am a Catholic."). According to Rev. David Palmer, Ph.D. (personal communication, June 16, 2001) all religions include three basic elements. First, at the core of religions is the experience of or quest for the "ultimate." A prime biblical example would be the encounter of Moses with the burning bush. This core religious experience is then expressed and communicated to others by means of story (e.g., the Bible, the Koran) and

Love, P. G. (2002). Comparing spiritual development and cognitive development. *Journal of College Student Development*, 43, 357–373.

symbol (e.g., music, dance, images). Story and symbol are key aspects of Sunday school and the worship experience in Christian churches. Finally, reflection on religious experiences is articulated in philosophical terms in the form of doctrine and dogma.

Parks (2000), like Fowler (1981) before her, spoke of faith development as opposed to spiritual development, though throughout this article the terms are treated synonymously. At its core, faith is a process of meaning-making, which is the process of making sense out of the activities of life, seeking patterns, order, coherence, and relation between and among the disparate elements of human living. It is the process of discovering and creating connections among experiences and events. Faith is differentiated from traditional cognitive development theories because it is the activity of seeking and composing meaning involving the most comprehensive dimensions of the human experience. That is, faith is trying to make sense of the "big picture," trying to find an overall sense of meaning and purpose in one's life.

Parks (2000) described spirituality to be a personal search for meaning, transcendence, wholeness, purpose, and "apprehension of spirit (or Spirit) as the animating essence at the core of life" (p. 16). Therefore from this perspective, spirituality is at the core of religion. However, it is important to differentiate these two terms because some religious people may be tied so closely to dogma and doctrine as to be disconnected from issues of the spirit, and those who fail to distinguish story (e.g., the Bible) from dogma and doctrine. Other people disavow any notion of or connection with religion, yet are deeply involved in a search for meaning, wholeness, and purpose.

## Faith Development and Spiritual Development

Parks described faith as both transcendent and immanent. That is, in the experience and activity of faith, it both lies beyond the range of ordinary perception and experience (i.e., transcendent) and, thus, is ultimately unknowable, and it remains within the individual and the particulars of individual experience (i.e., immanent). Parks also differentiated the notion of faith from belief. Although faith development is a dynamic and active process of meaning-making and faith "undergoes transformation across the whole life span," (p. 16) a belief is more static than faith and something accepted as true resulting in a condition where the holder is free from doubt. Faith is also a social phenomenon, dealing with our understanding of our relationships with others, and with the common contexts in which those relationships are embedded (Bee, 1987). Bee pointed out that implicit in this definition of faith is a distinction between the form and structure of one's faith and the specific content. That means that any given level of spiritual development may be expressed in a wide variety of belief systems or religions, which is captured in the framework of religion described above. Parks (2000) indicated that a person of faith may well deny the existence of a supernatural being called God, but that individual would at least be living with confidence in some center of value and with loyalty to some cause. As Helminiak (1996, p. 5) pointed out, "Buddhism, Taoism, Confucianism, and much of Western humanism have obvious spiritual intent without any reference to God."

Helminiak (1987) added several defining factors to spiritual development. As indicated above, he argued that authentic self-transcendence is a prime criterion of spiritual development and it is also the central principle needed to explain spiritual development in a nontheological context. Authentic self-transcendence is a conscious and self-aware process. By "authentic," Helminiak (1987) meant that the individual is motivated by an ongoing personal commitment to openness, questioning, honesty, and goodwill. Helminiak (1987) also argued that spiritual development, because it is rooted in authentic self-transcendence, only begins when an individual reaches a reflectively, critically, and analytically self-aware stage of development, typically in or near adulthood. He differed from both Parks and Fowler on this point, though he recognized the cognitive developmental changes that occur prior to this stage.

Another factor that Helminiak (1987) added is the individual's openness to the spiritual and to developing spiritually. To develop spiritually, one must desire wholeness, authenticity, and genuineness. All spiritual development theorists recognize that at some point in the developmental scheme, further development is not guaranteed. Finally, Helminiak (1987) was specific in arguing that spiritual development involves the whole person; it entails personal integrity and wholeness, meaning an integration of multiple developmental domains, including emotional, social, and cognitive.

## Spiritual Development Theorists and Theories

### Sharon Daloz Parks

Sharon Daloz Parks is a theologian who has worked as a teacher, counselor, and minister in a collegiate environment. Her work provided the framework for this theoretical comparison. Parks grounded her work in both the psychosocial and cognitive-structural traditions of student development theory. Her theory grew from her dissertation research on the meaning-making of college students. She foregrounded and emphasized the interrelatedness of cognitive development; affective states; and interpersonal, social, and cultural influences. Parks's first major work in the area of spirituality—faith development—was her book, *The Critical Years: Young Adults and the Search for Meaning, Faith, and Commitment*, published in 1986, before the current surge of interest in spirituality. Consequently, it generally was ignored in student affairs. In fact, the book went out of print. In the mid-1980s, spirituality-related issues such as faith development were still strongly taboo on many college campuses, in academe in general, and in student affairs in particular. Since the mid-1990s, however, there has been a surge in the quest for meaning, or for spiritual or religious fulfillment both within society and among traditional-aged college students. Given this growing focus on issues of the spirit, Parks (2000) revisited her earlier work on faith development, further elaborated her theory, and published a new book on the topic: *Big Questions, Worthy Dreams: Mentoring Young Adults in Their Search for Meaning, Purpose, and Faith.*

Parks's work was used as the foundation of this synthesis for three reasons. First, her original work built on Fowler's (1981) theory of faith development. In fact, she extended Fowler's work by proposing another stage of faith development between Adolescent and Adult, which she called "Young Adult," thereby more clearly focusing on traditional-aged college students. Second, she used and compared her work to the theories and research of Jean Piaget, William Perry, Robert Kegan, Erik Erikson, Lawrence Kohlberg, and Carol Gilligan. The origins of virtually all theories of student cognitive development can be traced to Piaget's work. All the others in this list are considered student development theorists, so her work was actually grounded in traditional student development theory. Third, her work is the most recent and, therefore, incorporated the most current research conducted in cognitive and psychosocial theory.

Because her work formed the foundation of this comparison, my description of it in this section is brief. Parks asserted that most stage-related developmental theories jump directly from adolescent to adult and attribute any "noise" or anomalies between those two stages to the transition from adolescence to adulthood. Parks argued instead that there is actually another stage of development between adolescence and adulthood that she labeled young adult. She also differentiated in adulthood between tested adults and mature adults. This results in a four-stage model of development: Adolescent/Conventional, Young Adult, Tested Adult, and Mature Adult. Each stage is comprised of three components (See Table 1 for the model and comparison to other theories): forms of knowing (a cognitive aspect of faith development), forms of dependence (an affective and social aspect of faith development), and forms of community (a social aspect of faith development). Forms of knowing refers to the relationships of self to authority (including self-authority) and self to knowledge. This cognitive component of spiritual development was built on the work of William Perry (1970) and James Fowler (1981), and the forms of knowing and their development correspond quite closely with the structures that Perry, Fowler, and other cognitive-structural theorists have posited.

Parks described forms of dependence as affective aspects of faith development; they are focused on how people feel. However, in her description of the various stages of dependence she also described interpersonal interactions, which are social aspects of development, and the view of oneself as an authority figure, which is an aspect of cognitive development. She described the dependence part of her model as focusing on the relationships through which we discover and change our views of knowledge and faith. More than the other two elements of her model, the forms of dependence demonstrate the interactive and holistic nature of her model.

Forms of community address a "neglect" (Kegan, 1982) in many cognitive development theories or in the synopses of cognitive development theories, namely, the failure to give adequate recognition to the influence of interpersonal, social, and cultural contexts on one's development. Piaget (1969) was clear about the influence that interaction with the environment had on cognitive development, but it was a fact often overlooked by theorists who followed him or who sought to extend his theory (Parks, 2000). Parks's model was focused particularly on community to more clearly identify the tension between the desire for agency and autonomy and the desire for belonging, connection, and intimacy. Taken together, Parks's interacting components of faith development bring together the cognitive, affective, and interpersonal elements of human existence. The addition of the dependence and community components draws somewhat on the work of Erik Erikson (1968) and especially on the work of Robert Kegan (1994), the only other major student development theorist who proposed a theory integrating the cognitive, affective, and social aspects of development (Love & Guthrie, 1999).

## James Fowler

James Fowler focused on the intersection of theology, human development, and psychology. He was among the first to extend human development theory (especially Piaget and Erikson) to the understanding of spiritual development. Fowler conducted research on the stages of faith development in Boston in the 1970s, and although he first articulated his theory in *Life Maps: Conversations on the Journey of Faith* (1978), it was in *Stages of Faith: The Psychology of Human Development and the Quest for Meaning* (1981) that he presented the first comprehensive description of the theory and the research upon which it is based.

Fowler's theory includes seven stages of faith development that cover the life span (actually six stages plus a prestage describing infants). Table 1 shows the three stages most likely to be experienced by college students: Mythic-Literal, Synthetic-Conventional, and Individuative-Reflective, plus his two additional advanced stages—Conjunctive and Universalizing. Briefly, Fowler (1996) compared the Mythic-Literal stage to Piaget's Concrete Operational stage of cognitive development in that the ability to adopt a perspective emerges, as does rational, linear, and logical thinking. The name of the stage comes from the fact that the narrative, stories, symbols, and concepts of the particular religious or spiritual context are seen as literally true by someone at this stage. Fowler indicated that this stage usually emerges in middle childhood, but like all subsequent stages can persist far into the life span. The Synthetic-Conventional stage usually does not appear before adolescence. In this stage, "capable of using and appreciating abstract concepts, young persons begin to think about their thinking, to reflect upon their stories, and to name and synthesize their meanings" (Fowler, 1996, p. 61). He also wrote:

> During this stage youths develop attachments to beliefs, values, and elements of personal style that link them in conforming relations with the most significant others among their peers, family, and other adults. Identity, beliefs, and values are strongly felt, even when they contain contradictory elements. However, they tend to be espoused in tacit rather than explicit formulations. At this stage, one's ideology or worldview is lived and asserted; it is not yet a matter of critical and reflective articulation. (1996, p. 61)

The centerpiece of the Individuative-Reflective stage is the taking on of authority by individuals for defining values, goals, and meanings that they had previously abdicated to other individuals and groups. The individual is able to reflect on one's own existence and process of development and begins to self-define and to self-construct roles and relationships. It is in Conjunctive Faith where limits and contradictions within one's experience become evident. Truths, beliefs, and faith are recognized to contain paradoxes, contradictions, and multiple perspectives. Finally, Universalizing Faith represents the normative endpoint of spiritual development (Fowler, 1981). Simply, it is the lived perfection of Conjunctive Faith attained by relatively few. Fowler identified Mahatma Gandhi,

Martin Luther King, and Mother Theresa as exemplars of this stage. Although the last two stages would be rare even in college staff, no less college students, they do establish the trajectory of spiritual development as conceptualized by Fowler.

## Daniel Helminiak

With a background in psychology and theology, Daniel Helminiak has focused of much of his work on understanding the relationships among the spiritual, intellectual, emotional, and social aspects of human development. Helminiak (1987) proposed a five-stage model of spiritual development; however, in his own description only the last three stages represent spiritual development, which he described as strictly an adult phenomena. This model was based on analysis and integration of both human development theory and theology, and not on empirical research. The first two stages he borrowed from Loevinger's (1977) theory of ego development. They are Conformist and the transitional stage labeled Conscientious/ Conformist. These two stages represent the experience of adolescents who are moving from the stage of seeking approval and being directed externally in their meaning making to self-awareness and self-determination. According to Helminiak (1987) the Conscientious stage is the first stage of spiritual development:

> It is characterized by the achievement of significantly structuring one's life according to one's own understanding of things, by optimism over one's newly accepted sense of responsibility for oneself and one's world, and by a rather unbending commitment to one's principles. (p. 85)

In the Compassionate stage one learns to surrender some of the world one has constructed for oneself. "One's commitments are no less intense, but they are more realistic, more nuanced, and more supported by deeply felt and complex emotion. One becomes more gentle with oneself and with others" (p. 85). Finally, the Cosmic stage is related to Maslow's self-actualization:

> [An] on-going actualization of potentials, capacities, talents, as fulfillment of a mission (or call, fate, destiny, vocation), as a fuller knowledge of, and acceptance of, the person's own intrinsic nature, as an increasing trend toward unity, integration, or synergy within the person. (Helminiak, 1987, p. 86)

# Theoretical Comparisons

The theoretical comparisons are conducted through Parks's four stages of spiritual development and the components of forms of knowing, dependence, and community.

## Adolescent/Conventional

Before students embark on the developmental journey to adulthood, Parks (2000) saw their faith—the meaning they make of the world—existing first in a form that is based in and dependent on authority in the context of a monolithic community that defines "us" (in the community) and "them" (those outside the community). During this stage of development, the absolute form of knowing breaks down and other perspectives are heard and recognized, the individual grows in self-awareness, authorities may be resisted, and the definition and experience of the community becomes more diffuse. This is a time of great ambiguity and uncertainty for individuals in their journey of spiritual development.

*Forms of knowing.* Faith development is the process of making meaning and the changes in that process over time. Cognitive development theorists described the process of change in the cognitive structures that students use to make meaning of their world by focusing on how meaning is structured, not on what is known or believed. The forms of knowing in Parks's (2000) model basically reflect the cognitive developmental aspect of spiritual development.

The forms of knowing that Parks (2000) identified in the Adolescent/Conventional stage of faith development are the authority-bound and dualistic form of knowing and the unqualified relativism form of knowing. Authority-bound and dualistic knowing is grounded in some form of authority that exists outside of oneself. It can be easily recognizable as an element within one's life (e.g., one's religion, the Bible, the Constitution) or a person or group (e.g., parents, teachers, clergy). It can also be more socially pervasive and subtle, such as the unquestioned authority of media, culturally affirmed roles and personalities (e.g., experts, artists, entertainers), and customs (e.g., conventions of thought, feeling, and behavior) (Parks, 2000). This is similar in focus to Fowler's (1981) stage of Mythic-Literal faith, which is based on a linear, orderly, and predictable universe, governed by a predictable God. In this stage, faith is composed of the stories, rules, and implicit values of the community in which one exists. Parks pointed out that when an authority-bound form of knowing "prevails, people cannot stand outside of their own perspective, or reflect upon their own thought" (p. 55). As individuals experience the breakdown in the absolute nature of authorities in their life, they shift to the form of knowing that Parks labeled unqualified relativism. The unqualified relativism form of knowing is the recognition on the part of the knower that "all knowledge is shaped by, and thus relative to, the context and relationships within which it is composed . . . and every opinion and judgment may be as worthy as any other" (p. 57).

Like Parks, Perry (1970) labeled the first position in his scheme of intellectual development Dualism. However, from her description of the Unqualified Relativism form of knowing, Parks (2000) appears to have collapsed the distinctions between Perry's positions of Multiplicity and his position of Relativism. Where Perry described three positions (i.e., Early Multiplicity, Late Multiplicity, and Relativism), Parks (2000) described only one. In fact, Perry also differentiated between two forms of Late Multiplicity (i.e., Multiplicity Correlate and Relativism Subordinate). This lack of differentiation in Parks's theory becomes evident because her next form of knowing (Probing Commitment) is more closely related to Perry's position of Initial Commitment in Relativism. The point of this comparison is that Parks appears to have downplayed a significant transition that occurs in students' forms of sense-making at this stage of development. Perry, on the other hand, differentiated Multiplicity and Relativism due to their distinctively different sets of underlying assumptions. While recognizing the existence of ambiguity and uncertainty, Perry described Multiplicity as still being grounded in the basic assumptions of Dualism—that ultimately there is one truth, one right answer to all questions, and the hope that the world would be ultimately knowable. Relativism, on the other hand, is grounded in different assumptions (i.e., the acceptance that the world is inherently ambiguous, complex, and unknowable). This lack of clarity in Parks's form of knowing makes comparisons to other theories more difficult, because all other theories follow Perry's distinction in forms of knowing based on these two radically different sets of assumptions. The gap between Unqualified Relativism and Probing Commitment is represented by a cell with a question mark in Table 1.

Additionally, other cognitive development theorists perceived greater gradations in the form and structure of knowing within this particular period of development than did Parks (2000). For example, Baxter Magolda (1992) identified Absolute Knowing (akin to Authority-Bound/Dualistic knowing), Transitional and Independent knowing (two aspects of the multiplistic aspect of Unqualified Relativism), and Contextual knowing (similar to aspects of Perry's position of Relativism). Belenky, Clinchy, Goldberger, and Tarule (1986) identified Received knowing (also akin to Authority-Bound/Dualistic knowing), Subjective knowing (an aspect of Unqualified Relativism), Procedural knowing (not evident in Parks's scheme), and Constructed knowing (like Baxter Magolda's Contextual knowing, it is similar to aspects of Perry's [1970] position of Relativism). King and Kitchener's Reflective Judgment Model (1994) has seven stages, the first five of which relate to Parks's forms of dualism and unqualified relativism. King and Kitchener also describe three basic positions in their model, the first two of which (Pre-reflective and Quasi-reflective) relate (though not precisely) to Parks's first two forms of knowing. Love and Guthrie (1999) in a synthesis of major cognitive development theories (i.e., Baxter Magolda; Belenky et al.; Kegan, 1994; King & Kitchener; Perry) also identified two basic forms of knowing that correspond somewhat with Parks's first two forms. They labeled their forms of knowing Unequivocal knowing and Radical Subjectivism. Radical Subjectivism differs from Unqualified Relativism in that it is grounded in the same assumptions as Perry's position of Multiplicity and does not correspond to Relativism.

*Forms of dependence.* The adolescent/conventional forms of dependence are Dependent and Counterdependent. According to Parks (2000), *dependence* means "a person's sense of self and truth depends upon his or her immediate relational and affectional ties in a primary way" (p. 74). One's form of knowing during this time is especially dependent on whatever and whoever the authority is in one's life. Other cognitive development theorists (e.g., Baxter Magolda, 1992; Belenky et al., 1986; and King & Kitchener, 1994), either directly or indirectly described the dependence of authority-bound knowers. In addition to the dependence exhibited by women in the received knowing position, Belenky et al. described a particularly pernicious form of dependence in their Silence status, where women had no voice and any sense of self was absolutely dependent upon the domineering authorities in their lives, such as authoritarian parents, or abusive spouses or partners. Highlighting Parks's assertion relating dependence to affective aspects of faith development, Belenky et al.'s silenced women lived in fear and without hope, very negative emotions that make the process of spiritual development practically impossible.

Counterdependence is movement in opposition to Authority. Parks (2000) indicated that this is an aspect of the adolescent stage, without indicating that it follows directly from dependence or necessarily has to occur at all. In a manner of speaking, Counterdependence is also a form of dependence in that the individual pushes away from the pattern of meaning-making that is familiar and dominant in her or his life. The individual is moving away from or against the authority she or he knows, rather than actively moving toward a new authority or new truth. They are still dependent on the former truth because, absent a new truth, what they know to be true is that it is *not* what they formerly held to be true: "I don't know what I want (or believe), but I know it isn't this." Perry (1970) identified a pattern similar to Parks's notions of Dependence and Counterdependence. Perry's "adherents" tended to identify and agree with authorities through a dualistic structure of the world. Those identified as being in "opposition" set themselves apart from authorities.

*Forms of community.* Parks (2000) identified two forms of community that take place during a person's journey through the adolescent stage of faith development. The first form of community is Conventional and the second is Diffuse. A conventional community is one in which conformity by members to cultural norms, interests, and assumptions is expected and enforced. It is homogenous in that the core expectation is that the community is made up of people who are "like us," however "like us" is defined.

Just as absolute authority and dependence on a single authority eventually breaks down, the monolithic nature of the community breaks down as well, or at least a person's willingness to define themselves solely as a member of one particular community declines. Just as in Multiplicity (Perry, 1970) each opinion or truth claim is granted equivalent status, so are relationships as one enters the Diffuse stage of development. One becomes more open to expanding the notion of community, but one's commitment to any particular community weakens.

*Summary of adolescent/conventional.* How one makes sense of the world, and how one answers the ultimate questions we face as sentient beings (e.g., Why am I here?) during adolescence usually begins with simple answers representing a simple view of a straightforward and knowable world. These questions have answers that can be found in the authorities in individuals' lives and the answers are shared among those in their community. Along the way this innocent view of the world comes under stress. Authorities are found to be in error, undependable, or in conflict. Communities other than those that support a conventional view are experienced and discovered to have some validity or worth. These experiences can result in a loss of faith, though it is a loss of a naive faith, and a loss that actually signals a developmental movement forward. Parks (2000) described the experiences that alter our view of the world in some dramatic way, and especially in this stage of development, as "shipwrecks." The world (or our view of it) is found to be untrustworthy. We struggle to make sense of competing authorities, of our own growing sense of self-awareness and self-authority, and of the multiple communities we experience. We embark upon the most significant transition of spiritual development—that stage that Parks has labeled Young Adult.

## Young Adult

Parks (2000) pointed out that as the expected life span of humans increased, as our society became more complex, and as preparation for adulthood grew longer (e.g., the addition of college and, more recently, graduate school as a requirement for many occupations), the developmental phases from childhood to adulthood lengthened and differentiated. In fact, the phase of development labeled adolescence is a product of the 20th century. Parks suggested that there is another distinguishable phase between adolescence and full adulthood, which she has labeled young adult. Parks (2000) indicated that most developmental psychologists do not recognize such a stage, and instead, refer to it as the process of transition between adolescence and full adulthood. Helminiak (1987), however, does appear to recognize such a stage in his understanding of spiritual development. He sees Loevinger's (1977) Self-Aware level of ego development, as the appropriate transition stage between Fowler's Synthetic-Conventional and Individuative-Reflective stages. In their synthesis of cognitive development theories focused on college students, Love and Guthrie (1999), identified what they labeled "The Great Accommodation." They argued that among the variety of accommodations a person's cognitive structures make during development, this is the most radical. It is the accommodation of cognitive structures where a person transitions from seeing the world as ultimately knowable and certain to seeing the world as complex, ambiguous, and not completely knowable. This notion of The Great Accommodation applied to spiritual development appears to correspond closely to the theological concept of metanoia, which is a conversion that involves a radical reorientation of one's whole being.

As described by cognitive development theorists, this transition is the time when the individual's own role as knower and authority emerges (Baxter Magolda, 1992). Love and Guthrie (1999) located this great transitional phase at about the place where Parks has added the Young Adult stage. Parks added a dimension to this great accommodation or stage. She emphasized that the most important element of this stage is the emergence of a critical self-awareness—a self-conscious and self-aware self. During adolescence the individual comes to realize the existence of the self as a self and can then hold both one's own perceptions and those of another at the same time. However, in young adulthood one takes ownership, authority, and responsibility for shaping one's own ongoing development. There are actually two elements at play in Parks's theory. The first is the critical self-awareness and the second is the willingness and motivation to respond to the self-awareness by shaping one's own ongoing development. Helminiak (1987) pointed out that many people never completely transcend this stage—they are self-aware, aware of their development, yet actively or passively choose to not continue to develop spiritually or cognitively. As he says, "spiritual growth has been stifled and one may well have settled for a lifetime of spiritual mediocrity" (p. 84).

*Forms of knowing.* Parks (2000) labeled the form of knowing in the Young Adult stage Probing Commitment. One who is at the Young Adult stage recognizes that in the complex and contextual nature of the world one must take action, choose a path, shape one's own future—one constructs a faith, one constructs meaning. She adds Probing Commitment between Fowler's (1981) third stage (Synthetic-Conventional) and his fourth stage (Individuative-Reflective) of faith development, which is why a gap has been placed in Table 1 between Fowler's third and fourth stages. In the Synthetic-Conventional stage, an individual is developing an integrated identity; however, that identity is based on tacit elements of the culture in which the individual is embedded. The transition to the Individuative-Reflective stage requires a leap to where one becomes able to critically choose one's beliefs, values, and commitments. Parks argued the existence of a stage in between where an individual makes and learns from tentative commitments. This stage corresponds quite closely to Perry's (1970) position of Initial Commitment in Relativism.

The cognitive development theorists who followed Perry's lead explored other aspects of advanced cognitive development. King and Kitchener (1994) elaborated structural and epistemological aspects of development beyond relativism, focusing on the use of critical inquiry and probabilistic justification to guide knowledge construction. Belenky et al. (1986) described an integration of subjective and objective strategies for knowing. Baxter Magolda (1992) focused on the merging of the gender-related patterns evidenced in her earlier ways of knowing to produce a knower capable of constructing an individual perspective by judging evidence in context. Parks, Perry, and the rest of the theorists recognized the fact that the knower comes into a sense of agency in the knowing process. Students recognize their active role in considering context, in comparing and evaluating viewpoints to assess relative merit, and in constructing an individual perspective on issues.

*Forms of dependence.* Parks (2000) described the form of dependence at the young adult stage as fragile inner-dependence. By "fragile" she did not mean weak, feeble, or puny. Instead, she used the term in the way someone would describe a tree sapling—vulnerable, but healthy, vital, and full of promise. Parks compared this emerging sense of self-authority to the notion of subjective knowing where a trust in one's own knowledge and experience is recognized (Belenky et al., 1986). In complex modern society, emerging adults experience a slow and sporadic transition from full dependence upon parents or authorities to independence and autonomy. One can recognize one's ability to shape one's future and make decisions, while recognizing, for example, the financial resources received from parents that allows one to continue in school. In the multiple contexts through which young adults must navigate, they will at times feel like, and be treated like, children (i.e., dependent, without responsibility) and other times and circumstances, they will be treated as adults (i.e., independent, responsible).

*Forms of community.* Parks (2000) labeled the form of community needed by a young adult to help with the development of a complex adult faith as a mentoring community. She argued that a critical, cognitive self-aware perspective of one's familiar value orientation alone is not enough to precipitate a transformation in faith. She also believed that critical self-awareness combined with a single mentoring figure may still be insufficient to reorder faith itself. The growth that comes with critical self-awareness must be grounded in the experience of a compatible social group, what she termed a mentoring community.

> [A mentoring community] offers a network of belonging in which young adults feel recognized as who they really are, and as who they are becoming. It offers both challenge and support and thus offers good company for both the emerging strength and the distinctive vulnerability of the young adult. (Parks, 2000, p. 95)

As adolescents and young adults struggle to emerge from the ambiguity of Unqualified Relativism, a mentoring community gives them the hope and expectation that a new robust faith will emerge from the process. Although Parks cited residence halls as potential mentoring communities, her description of this type of community more readily brings to mind learning communities and living-learning centers that are proliferating on campuses. It also appears that the culture, the underlying values, beliefs, norms, and expectations, that form potential mentoring communities need to be considered. The stronger the culture, the less one is able to deviate from the norms, the less one is able to tentatively probe a commitment, instead commitment may be demanded. One need only think of some of the unhealthy aspects of the pledging experiences of fraternities and sororities, organizations with very powerful cultures, to realize the damaging potential of strong cultures that demand commitment while inhibiting critical self-awareness.

This notion of a mentoring community exhibits the element of personal choice in the developmental process. Although the activities in which we choose to partake and the groups we choose to join throughout our life span (including as children) shape the developmental process, it is the self-aware selection of groups and activities and the awareness of the possible influence on our development that distinguishes these choices from previous choices.

*Summary of young adult.* Young Adult is the stage at which most traditional age college students find themselves. In the process of spiritual development, students new to college may experience "functional regression," (Love & Guthrie, 1999) where students who undertake new learning in a new environment appropriately regress to previous, more comfortable, stages until they feel comfortable in the new environment. Upon entering college, students may regress to authority-bound truth as provided by professors or administrators, return to a greater dependence on others in authority, and experience college as a diffuse and confusing set of communities or latch on to a single authoritarian community—cults being a most extreme example. College will also be a time where initial probing commitments are made and remade, where one's emerging sense of inner-dependence is tested, and where one may have the opportunity to experience one or more mentoring communities.

## Tested Adult and Mature Adult

Parks (2000) described the development that occurs beyond the Young Adult stage. Those individuals who reach the Tested Adult stage may very well be undergraduates, but they are more likely to be postgraduates, graduate students, or beyond. Parks argued that a Mature Adult faith rarely is in evidence before midlife.

*Forms of knowing.* Parks (2000) did not describe the stages of Tested Commitment and Convictional Commitment in much depth. As she indicated with Tested Commitment, "one's form of knowing and being takes on a tested quality, a sense of fittingness, a recognition that one is willing to make one's peace and to affirm one's place in the scheme of things" (p. 69). There is a reduction in the ambiguity and dividedness that marked the early period of Probing Commitment. Perry's Commitment in Relativism (Positions 6 through 9 of his scheme) was the least developed aspect of his theory (Love & Guthrie, 1999). In a way, Parks (2000) suffered the same drawback in her model (though it must be stated that the focus of her work was on young adults).

Building on the work of Jane Loevinger (1977) and Fowler, Helminiak (1987) provided more detail about what he perceived to be the postconventional forms of knowing in spiritual development. As indicated above, his first stage of spiritual development is labeled the Conscientious stage. This is followed by the Compassionate stage. He indicated that it is aligned, though imperfectly, with Fowler's Conjunctive stage.

> [In the Compassionate stage] one learns to surrender some of the world one has so painstakingly constructed for oneself. One's commitments are no less intense, but they are more realistic, more nuanced, and more supported by deeply felt and complex emotion. One becomes more gentle with oneself and with others. (Helminiak, p. 85)

In the more advanced stages of spiritual development, untangling the influence of cognition, affect, and interpersonal relationships becomes much more difficult.

*Forms of dependence.* In the last two stages of Parks's (2000) model, the individual moves from a fragile inner-dependence to a confident inner-dependence to interdependence. The movement in faith development she described is from an external focus (dependence on an external authority) to an internal focus (inner-dependence) to an interaction and healthy integration of the two and to a recognition that throughout one's life there has existed interdependence. Parks pointed out that "what is new, however, is one's awareness of the depth and pervasiveness of the interrelatedness of all of life and the important yet limited strength of one's own perceptions" (pp. 86–87). The movement described above is reminiscent of Chickering's (Chickering & Reisser, 1993) vector of moving through autonomy toward interdependence. He also described an external to internal to integration movement.

*Forms of community.* Finally, there are the forms of community in which the individual developing in faith finds one's self. At the Tested Adult stage, the tendency is to feel most comfortable in a self-selected class or group. This tends to be a group that shares the meanings of the tested adult.

> [With a confident inner-dependence,] the adult faith can sustain respectful awareness of communities other than its own; it can tolerate, if not embrace, the felt tensions between inevitable choices. . . . [However,] though one's new network of belonging may be much more diverse in some respects, its members may nevertheless hold similar political, religious, and philosophical views and values and share the loyalties of a particular economic class. Even the most cosmopolitan and liberal of mind often discover, upon close examination of their own network of belongings, that those who count are also of like mind. (Parks, 2000, p. 100)

Parks then described the movement of the individual from these homogeneous communities to seeking participation in communities that are open to and seeking others holding views and perspectives different from one's own. This is similar to Fowler's (1981) stage of Conjunctive faith where there is genuine openness to the truths and traditions and communities other than one's own. It is a disciplined openness to truths of those who are "other."

*Summary of tested adult and mature adult.* "Spiritual development is human development when the latter is conceived according to a particular set of concerns: integrity or wholeness, openness, self-responsibility, and authentic self-transcendence" (Helminiak, 1987, pp. 95–96). The movement toward a mature adult faith is one of greater connection to, interaction with, and belonging to the broader world. It involves a recognition of one's interdependence and interconnectedness with communities and individuals beyond one's perceptual scope. It involves growing comfortable with and actually welcoming the ambiguity and doubt that exists even within one's tested convictions.

## Spiritual Development's Contribution to the Discourse of Student Development

One's level of cognitive development need not be similar to one's spiritual development, though because they both relate to the development of meaning-making, it is hard to imagine a situation where they would be significantly divergent in an individual. Given the focus on meaning-making, there are many ways in which theories of spiritual development and cognitive development overlap and are mutually informing. However, it is also important to identify the ways in which spiritual development theories focus on particular dimensions or contribute unique elements to our understanding of the process of human development.

### Integration of Cognitive, Social, and Affective Dimensions of Development

Love and Love (1995) argued for a greater focus on the integration of the cognitive, social, and affective dimensions of development. To date, no cognitive development theorist has argued against the role of affect and social interaction in development. In fact, Piaget was quite explicit about the role of environment on development. However, the dominant focus in cognitive development theories concerning college students has been on meaning-making and the development of its structures. Parks (2000) argued that spiritual development cannot only focus on the structures of meaning-making and has created a three-part model that incorporates the cognitive, affective, and social dimensions. Among other student development theorists Kegan (1994) is the only one who actively integrated cognitive, affective, and social dimensions in his theorizing.

### Impact of Social and Cultural Context

Again, all theorists to some degree address the role of the environment. However, Parks (2000), Fowler (1996), and Helminiak (1987) actually built it into their theories. The impact of the social and cultural context is seen in Fowler's work by his recognition that starting at the Mythical-Literal Stage of faith development the environment can either serve to contribute to development or can serve to obstruct or retard development. He pointed out that some fundamentalist faith communities (both conservative and liberal) serve to restrict the spiritual development of their members.

### Postconventional Forms of Meaning-Making

As Table 1 makes clear, much of the work of the spiritual development theorists in the realm of theorizing about meaning making focuses on the development that occurs beyond "The Great Accommodation." Again, according to at least one theorist (Helminiak, 1987) spiritual development really only begins at that point. Perry's (1970) notion of intellectual and ethical development recognized that much of the focus beyond relativism was on valuing, choosing, commitment—what he termed ethical development. Unfortunately, the last four positions of his model encompassing Commitment in Relativism were the least developed aspects of his theory. As the table shows, those who followed Perry's work, such as Baxter Magolda (1992), Belenky et al. (1986), were no more successful than Perry in elaborating the developmental stages beyond the great accommodation, with each identifying only one stage beyond that point. King and Kitchener (1994) were more successful in identifying three. Parks (2000), Fowler (1981, 1996), and Helminiak (1987) not only differentiated three additional stages beyond the great accommodation (though, as pointed out, Parks's are not very well elaborated), but they also recognized the possibility of development beyond those.

**TABLE 1**

**Spiritual Development Theories Compared With Cognitive Development Theories**

| | Adolescent/Conventional | | | Young Adult | | Tested Adult | | Mature Adult |
|---|---|---|---|---|---|---|---|---|
| **Forms of Knowing** | Authority-bound, dualistic | Unqualified relativism | | ? | Probing commitment | Tested commitment | | Convictional commitment |
| **Forms of Dependence** | Dependent/counter-dependent | | | Fragile inner-dependence | | Confident inner-dependence | | Interdependence |
| **Forms of Community** | Conventional | | Diffuse | Mentoring community | | Self-selected class/group | | Open to other |

Fowler: Mythic-literal | Synthetic-conventional | Individuative-reflective | Conjunctive | Universalizing

Helminiak: Conscientious | Compassionate | Cosmic

Perry: Dualism 1 2 | Multiplicity 3 4 | Relativism 5 6 | Commitment in relativism 7 8 9

Baxter Magolda: Absolute | Transitional | Independent | Contextual

Belenky, Clinchy, Goldberger, and Tarule: Silence | Receiv'd | Subjective | Procedural | Constructed

King and Kitchener: Pre-reflective 1 2 3 | Quasi-reflective 4 5 | Reflective 6 7

The Great Accommodation (Love & Guthrie, 1999)

# Implications

## Practice Implications

*Student affairs professionals need to reflect on their own spiritual development.* If spirituality and spiritual development is inherent in all people (and not just "religious" people), then student affairs professionals need to consider this developmental process in their own lives. This means considering how they create meaning, purpose, and direction in their lives, the forms of dependence that exist in their relationships, and the types of communities to which they belong.

*Differentiate spiritual development from religious practice.* Student affairs professionals need to recognize the spiritual aspects of everyday life and not just associate spirituality with religious practice. However, it also means recognizing that religious activity and other spiritually related activities may be manifestations of students searching for meaning and faith.

*Focus on the enhancement of students' cognitive development, which will in all likelihood contribute to their spiritual development.* Given the close relationship between faith development and cognitive development theory, experiences, activities, and environments that are designed to enhance students' cognitive development will in all likelihood contribute to students' spiritual development as well.

*Create mentoring communities and review current student groups and organizations as potential mentoring communities.* Parks described the potential of communities to greatly influence the spiritual development of students. In addition to trying to create such communities on campus, student affairs professionals should assess already existing communities to see in what ways they can be encouraged to become mentoring communities.

## Research Implications

Given that the spiritual development of college students has been a fairly recent focus in the student affairs literature, a number of issues need to be explored by student affairs researchers.

*Explore the intersection and interaction between faith development and cognitive development.* In this article I have examined and compared existing research and conceptual work related to cognitive and spiritual development. One of the most important next steps is for research to be conducted specifically looking at both cognitive development and spiritual development in college students to better understand their relationship and mutual influence in individuals.

*Explore the interaction between faith/spiritual development and one's cultural context.* Although some research has explored the role of society and culture on cognitive development (Kegan, 1994), not enough cross-cultural research on cognitive development has been conducted (Hofer & Pintrich, 1997; Kegan, 1994). The same can certainly be said about the study of spiritual development. The need for such research is further heightened by the increasingly global nature of higher education and the college experience. That is, as Western, positivistic culture, characterized by a mind-body split is influenced by Eastern, nonpositivistic culture characterized by mind-body integration, there may very well be an influence on the spiritual development of college students.

# Conclusion

The work of Sharon Daloz Parks (2000), James Fowler (1981, 1996), and Daniel Helminiak (1987) has reinforced the relationship of spiritual development theories and traditional developmental theories, especially cognitive-structural theories. Both sets of theories have been focused on the ways in which people make meaning of the world they live in and the experiences they have. Parks and Fowler both have contributed ways of viewing issues of the spirit as involved in the developmental experiences of all people, not just those who choose to practice a religion or who participate in nontraditional spiritual practices. Parks especially described the developmental process in such a way that addresses the cognitive, affective, and social aspects of faith development. Through her framework one can view both the structures and the content of meaning making.

# References

Baxter Magolda, M. B. (1992). *Knowing and reasoning in college: Gender-related patterns in students' intellectual development*. San Francisco: Jossey-Bass.

Bee, H. L. (1987). *The journey of adulthood*. New York: Macmillan.

Belenky, M., Clinchy, B., Goldberger, N., & Tarule, J. (1986) *Women's ways of knowing: The development of self, voice, and mind*. New York: Basic Books.

Chickering, A., & Reisser, L. (1993). *Education and identity* (2nd ed.). San Francisco: Jossey-Bass.

Collins, J. R., Hurst, J. C., & Jacobsen, J. K. (1987). The blind spot extended: Spirituality. *Journal of College Student Personnel, 28*(3), 274–76.

Erikson, E. H. (1968). *Identity: Youth and crisis*. New York: Norton.

Fowler, J. W. (1978). *Life maps: Conversations on the journey of faith*. Waco, TX: Word Books.

Fowler, J. W. (1981). *Stages of faith: The psychology of human development and the quest for meaning*. San Francisco: Harper Collins.

Fowler, J. W. (1996). *Faithful change: The personal and public challenges of postmodern life*. Nashville, TN: Abingdon Press.

Helminiak, D. A. (1987). *Spiritual development: An interdisciplinary study*. Chicago: Loyola University Press.

Helminiak, D. A. (1996). *The human core of spirituality: Mind as psyche and spirit*. Albany: SUNY Press.

Hofer, B. K., & Pintrich, P. R. (1997). The development of epistemological theories: Beliefs about knowledge and knowing and their relation to learning. *Review of Educational Research, 67*(1), 88–140.

Kegan, R. (1982). *The evolving self: Problem and process in human development*. Cambridge, MA: Harvard University Press.

Kegan, R. (1994). *In over our heads: The mental demands of modern life*. Cambridge, MA: Harvard University Press.

King, P. M., & Kitchener, K. S. (1994). *Developing reflective judgment: Understanding and promoting intellectual growth and critical thinking in adolescents and adults*. San Francisco: Jossey-Bass.

Loevinger, J. (1977). *Ego development*. San Francisco: Jossey-Bass.

Love, P. G., & Love, A. G. (1995). *Enhancing student learning: Intellectual, social, and emotional integration*. ASHE-ERIC Higher Education Report No. 4. Washington, DC: George Washington University, Graduate School of Education and Human Development.

Love, P. G., & Guthrie, V. L. (1999). *Understanding and applying cognitive development theory* (New Directions for Student Services No. 88). San Francisco: Jossey-Bass.

Love, P. G., & Talbot, D. (1999). Defining spiritual development: A missing consideration for student affairs. *NASPA Journal, 37*(1), 361–375.

Parks, S. (1986). *The critical years: Young adults and the search for meaning, faith, and commitment*. San Francisco: Harper Collins.

Parks, S. (2000). *Big questions, worthy dreams: Mentoring young adults in their search for meaning, purpose, and faith*. San Francisco: Jossey-Bass.

Pascarella, E., & Terenzini, P. (1991). *How college affects students*. San Francisco: Jossey-Bass.

Perry, W. G., Jr. (1970). *Forms of intellectual and ethical development in the college years: A scheme*. New York: Harcourt Brace Javanovich College.

Piaget, J. R. (1969). *Science of education and the psychology of the child*. New York: Viking Compass.

# Unit 2 Additional Recommended Readings

Abes, E. S., & Jones, S. R. (2004). Meaning-making capacity and the dynamics of lesbian college students' multiple dimensions of identity. *Journal of College Student Development, 45*, 612–632.

Baxter Magolda, M. B. (1998). Developing self-authorship in young adult life. *Journal of College Student Development, 39*, 143–156.

Baxter Magolda, M. B. (2001). *Making their own way: Narratives for transforming higher education to promote self-development*. Sterling, VA: Stylus

Baxter Magolda, M. B. (2008). Three elements of self-authorship. *Journal of College Student Development, 49*, 269–284.

Baxter Magolda, M. B. (2009). *Authoring your life: Developing an internal voice to navigate life's challenges.* Sterling, VA: Stylus.

Baxter Magolda, M. B., Creamer, E. G., & Meszaros, P. S. (Eds.). (2010). *Development and assessment of self-authorship: Exploring the concept across cultures.* Sterling, VA: Stylus.

Debold, E. (2002, Fall–Winter). Epistemology, fourth order consciousness, and the subject-object relationship or how the self evolves with Robert Kegan [Electronic Version]. *EnlightenNext Magazine, 22.* Retrieved from http://www.enlightennext.org/magazine/

Drago-Severson, E. (2010). *Leading adult learning.* Thousand Oaks, CA: Corwin Press.

Kegan, R. (1982). *The evolving self: Problem and process in human development.* Cambridge, MA: Harvard University Press.

Kegan, R. (1994). *In over our heads: The mental demands of modern life.* Cambridge, MA: Harvard University Press.

Love, P. G., & Guthrie, V. L. (1999). Kegan's orders of consciousness. In *Understanding and applying cognitive development theory* (New Directions for Student Services No. 88, pp. 65–76). San Francisco, CA: Jossey-Bass.

Parks, S. D. (2000). *Big questions, worthy dreams: Mentoring young adults in their search for meaning, purpose, and faith.* San Francisco, CA: Jossey-Bass.

Pizzolato, J. E. (2003). Developing self-authorship: Exploring the experiences of high-risk college students. *Journal of College Student Development, 44,* 797–812.

Taylor, K. B. (2008). Mapping the intricacies of young adults' developmental journey from socially prescribed to internally defined identities, relationships, and beliefs. *Journal of College Student Development, 49,* 215–234.

Torres, V., & Hernandez, E. (2007). The influence of ethnic identity on self-authorship: A longitudinal study of Latino/a college students. *Journal of College Student Development, 48,* 558–573.

# UNIT 3

# *INTRAPERSONAL AND INTERPERSONAL DEVELOPMENT: PSYCHOSOCIAL AND SOCIAL IDENTITY THEORIES*

# CHAPTER 8
## IDENTITY DEVELOPMENT THEORIES IN STUDENT AFFAIRS: ORIGINS, CURRENT STATUS, AND NEW APPROACHES

VASTI TORRES, SUSAN R. JONES, AND KRISTEN A. RENN

Enhancing the development of students has long been a primary role of student affairs practitioners. Identity development theories help practitioners to understand how students go about discovering their "abilities, aptitude and objectives" while assisting them to achieve their "maximum effectiveness" (American Council on Education, 1937, p. 69). The tasks involved in discovering abilities, goals, and effectiveness are part of creating a sense of identity that allows the student to enter adult life. Identity is shaped by how one organizes experiences within the environment (context) that revolves around oneself (Erikson, 1959/1994). Across academic disciplines, the view of how individuals organize experiences takes on varying definitions. Within the student affairs literature, *identity* is commonly understood as one's personally held beliefs about the self in relation to social groups (e.g., race, ethnicity, religion, sexual orientation) and the ways one expresses that relationship. Identity is also commonly understood to be socially constructed; that is, one's sense of self and beliefs about one's own social group as well others are constructed through interactions with the broader social context in which dominant values dictate norms and expectations (see Gergen, 1991; McEwen, 2003). Examples of these broader social contexts include both institutions such as education and work, as well as systems of power and inequality such as race, social class, and gender (Anderson & Collins, 2007).

Social construction of identity occurs in different contexts on campus such as in how student organizations are created and which students are drawn to them, or in the social identities among those in leadership positions and those not, as well as in issues of institutional fit within access and retention. One of the components of identity development that arises quickly on most campuses is the process of students learning how to balance their needs with those of others (Kegan, 1982, 1994; Kroger, 2004). In working to create community and mutual respect on campus, student affairs professionals help students to understand this balance between self and others as well as expose students to the varied nature of what is encompassed in the "other." A common program used to illustrate this process revolves around diversity issues. These programs often focus on exposure to other social groups and an understanding of how history supports society's view of these groups. This influence of the other contributes to the social construction of identity; in other words, the context and interactions with others—including other people, societal norms, and/or expectations that evolve from culture—influence how one constructs one's identity (Jones, 1997; McEwen, 2003; Torres, 2003; Weber, 1998). In addition, several researchers embrace a developmental approach to

Torres, V., Jones, S. R., & Renn, K. A. (2009). Identity development theories in student affairs: Origins, current status, and new approaches. *Journal of College Student Development, 50,* 577–596.

describe the shift that occurs when students move from accepting simple definitions of self based on external factors to more complex understandings of self within context (e.g., Baxter Magolda, 2001; Pizzolato, 2010; Taylor, 2008; Torres & Hernandez, 2007).

This article focuses on understanding how identity development is conceptualized in student affairs. The need to understand the person, context, and interactions between the two advances identity theories as relevant to student affairs practice. The more practitioners understand how students make meaning of their identities, the better they are able to assist in promoting student learning and development in higher education institutions.

Although much of the research on college student development that informs student affairs practice originated in psychology, other disciplines contribute different lenses that can add to a more nuanced understanding of how identity evolves. Identity is often conceptualized as a developmental construct, and this conceptualization persists in current identity research. However, newer conceptualizations in both psychology and other disciplines resist the notion of identity as a developmental and linear process, instead emphasizing the fluid, dynamic, and performative nature of identity. Performativity illuminates the more contingent nature of identity and suggests that individuals create and recreate identity through their actions, which are constantly shifting (Abes & Kasch, 2007). The review that follows includes both of these perspectives on identity. In addition, because identity is influenced by students' many roles, expectations, and beliefs, we also address the intersectionality of identity dimensions. Finally, we explore five future directions for research on identity development in college students.

## Disciplinary Origins of the Study of Identity

Although college student development theories draw largely from developmental psychology, the study of identity also has a rich tradition in sociology, social psychology, and human ecology. In addition, postmodern and poststructural theories (e.g., queer theory, feminist poststructuralism, and critical race theory [CRT]) also contribute substantially to the multidisciplinary approach necessary to understanding identities and identity development. Each field locates the study of identity within its own disciplinary lens, but they share commitments to understanding the individual, his or her social context, the influence of social groups, and various dimensions of identity (e.g., race, ethnicity, gender, sexual orientation). This section summarizes the disciplinary origins of the study of identity.

## Psychology

Student affairs practice, and the student development theories that have supported it since the middle of the twentieth century, grew from a counseling and vocational psychology approach (Miller & Prince, 1976). Therefore, it is not surprising that the most commonly taught theories related to identity and identity development are rooted in psychology. Psychological definitions of identity focus on understanding of self, or personal identity. Erik Erikson (1959/1994) expanded on Freud's thinking about the development of "ego identity," a concept that posits identity as a stage of ego growth (Marcia, 1993). Taking a lifespan approach, Erikson identified eight stages/phases in which individuals address a series of crises to arrive at more or less healthy resolutions to major developmental tasks. He proposed that development is governed in part by the epigenetic principle, a combination of genetic and environmental influences that governs the direction and timing of development (Erikson, 1959/1994).

A key middle stage in ego identity development is the adolescent identity crisis, and because the vast majority of college students at the time were adolescents, Arthur Chickering (1979) focused on this stage to propose seven "vectors" specific to college student identity within the Eriksonian stage of identity crisis. The legacy of Freud's and Erikson's thinking appears in Chickering's focus on resolution of specific developmental tasks in each vector (e.g., managing emotions, developing purpose). Yet Chickering (1979) departed significantly from his forebears when he proposed that vectors differed from stages, because although they built on one another, they were not mutually exclusive or unilinear. The revision of Chickering's student identity development theory (Chickering & Reisser, 1993) elaborated further on its intellectual roots by focusing on dimensions of identity (race, gender, and to a much lesser extent sexuality) in the more contemporary context of a radically changed student body. Since Chickering's first foray into describing student identities, the college student population in the United States has undergone a substantial diversification, from majority male to majority female, to include a higher proportion and diversity of students of color, and to include visible populations of adult students, immigrants, students with disabilities, and lesbian, gay, bisexual, and transgender students (Thelin, 2004).

Challenged to understand the identities of the new student population, student affairs as a field turned to emerging identity theories from psychology. Scholars and professionals brought into the field theories of racial and ethnic identity development (Cross, 1995; Helms, 1990, 1994; Phinney, 1993), women's identities and moral development (Gilligan, 1979, 1982; Josselson, 1996), and sexual orientation (Cass, 1979; D'Augelli, 1994). In keeping with the psychological tradition, most of the early theories were stage based and linear, although some provided for the possibility of the developing person cycling back through earlier stages. These theories also adhered to their discipline's focus on the individual and his or her sense making in development.

## Sociology

Sociological perspectives on identity generally consider an individual's identification with a given social group. Sociologists focus on the identities and roles of individuals in groups, and on interactions among groups, including studies of identity politics and social movements. Important sociologists of identity include George Herbert Mead and Sheldon Stryker.

Within higher education, sociologists Kenneth Feldman and Theodore Newcomb (Feldman & Newcomb, 1969) laid the foundation for applying sociology to the study of college students. They viewed:

> the college as an arena of social interaction in which the individual comes in contact with a multitude of actors in a variety of settings, emphasizing that through these social interactions and other social influences the identities of individuals are, in part, constituted. (Kaufman & Feldman, 2004, p. 464)

Sociologists emphasize the role of higher education institutions in creating contexts for the development of situated "felt" identities, which may endure to become more permanent felt identities. Felt identities include those that encompass personal traits (e.g., intelligence, race) and roles (e.g., music major, college student, athlete). Sociological approaches to identity help to explain, from a broader perspective than does psychology, the forces that act on individuals as they make their way into adulthood and form self-concepts of, allegiances to, and aspirations toward various identities.

## Social Psychology

Social psychologists who study identity focus, as the name of their field suggests, on where groups and individuals interact in theory and in practice. Many social psychologists use the term *identity formation*, instead of identity development, and emphasize questions of what drives individuals to adopt group identities and to express those identities through behaviors, alone or in the collective. Social psychologists in general may adopt a perspective that is more psychological or more sociological, but those who study identity typically understand that positive self-esteem from belonging to groups contributes to individual wellbeing, sense of community, and belonging. As Adams and Marshall (1996) stated, "Individuals need a sense of uniqueness and a sense of belonging" (p. 429), a personal identity that includes group membership.

James Côté and Charles Levine (2002) synthesized sociological and psychological theories of identity formation/development to posit that identities are the result of processes of culture and individual agency. Côté and Levine rooted their synthesis on the psychology side in Erikson's ego identity formation and on the sociological side in the personality and social structure perspective. The personality and social structure perspective relies on three levels of analysis to examine social behavior: personality, interaction with others, and broader social structure. Day-to-day interactions filter expectations, socialization, and social control to the individual, who in turn broadcasts his or her presentation of self into a socially constructed reality. So when a student is coming out as lesbian, the everyday interactions she has with family, friends, and community shape her understanding of what it means to be lesbian, and then as she projects that identity into those interactions through her world, she socially constructs the reality of her lesbian identity. Combining ego identity formation and the personality and social structure perspective, formation of the student's lesbian identity proceeds through a series of crises and commitments experienced and enacted through daily interactions.

Social psychologists bring two important concepts to studying identity development that have not typically been included in the study of college students: *emerging adulthood* and *possible selves*. We introduce them briefly here to draw attention to them, recognizing that each has become a substantial research area beyond the scope of this article to describe in full. Emerging adulthood, as it sounds, represents a time in development after adolescence and before full adulthood (Arnett, 2004). The overlap of this time with so-called traditional college age (eighteen to twenty-four years) is undeniable, especially in the ways that college is sometimes said to buffer students from the realities of life and to forestall adult responsibilities and decisions (see Baxter Magolda, 2001). Possible selves represent an individual's hoped for or feared future self, and thus link cognition, motivation, and behavior (Markus & Nurius, 1986). In terms of identity development, students' hoped for and feared possible selves may lead them into groups who share and reinforce, for example, racial identity, or groups that discourage the growth of certain identities. Only a few studies (e.g., Pizzolato, 2003, 2005; Pizzolato, Chaudhari, Murrell, Podobnik, & Schaeffer, 2008) have applied concepts of emerging adulthood and possible selves to the study of college students, but a number of researchers used them in the study of identity formation (e.g., Dunkel & Anthis, 2001; Schwartz, Côté, & Arnett, 2005; Syed & Azmitia, 2008), and demonstrate their value to the study of student development.

## Human and Developmental Ecology

Human and developmental ecology frames identity as an individual characteristic that plays a role in influencing interactions between the developing person and his or her environment, and identity development as an interactive process between individual and environment that leads to increasingly complex understandings of self and self in context (Bronfenbrenner, 1979, 1993; Bubolz & Sontag; 1993). All ecology theories are not developmental per se, because they do not focus on particular outcomes of developmental processes (e.g., identity, cognition, physical skills), but some can be used to explain the ways that personal characteristics interact with environments to promote or inhibit development (Renn, 2003; Renn & Arnold, 2003). Human and developmental ecology thus can legitimately be considered as a field that concerns itself, at least in part, with identity development.

Human and developmental ecologists (Bronfenbrenner, 1979, 1993; Bubolz & Sontag, 1993) locate personal identities within a nested context of individuals and the immediate, more distal, and broader societal settings in which they are located. For college students, those immediate settings might include a roommate, athletic team, clubs, classmates, faculty, and family. More distal settings could be the academic administration and federal agencies that make policy decisions that impact students' opportunities for learning and development (e.g., curriculum, study abroad offerings, financial aid). In the example of multiracial identity development, Renn (2003, 2004) demonstrated that the ability and propensity of mixed race students to identify with one or more of their racial heritage groups is influenced by immediate settings (e.g., campus racial climate and attitudes of students from various backgrounds), more distal settings (e.g., policies that determine what racial categories are available on institutional and government forms), and society as a whole (e.g., the end of laws against interracial marriage, attitudes about mixed race people, role models). Conversely, the visible presence of mixed race people on campus and in society exerts a force that changes the environment from the immediate campus climate to the decennial census. The environment influences identity development and expressed identities in turn influence the environment.

## Postmodernism and Poststructuralism

Brought to the social sciences from literary studies, postmodernism and poststructuralism are philosophies that provide theoretical context for research into and interpretation of students' identities. These philosophies are based on the idea that "there are no objective and universal truths, but that particular forms of knowledge, and the ways of being that they engender, become 'naturalised' in culturally and historically specific ways" (Sullivan, 2003, p. 39). Identity, then, is socially constructed and naturalized in temporal and cultural contexts. The study of identity, which is already acknowledged as socially constructed in psychology, sociology, and developmental ecology, becomes nearly impossible if postmodernism and poststructuralism are carried to their theoretical extreme, a condition in which identities are so constantly under construction and reconstruction that they cannot be fixed long enough to be measured or interpreted. Yet some psychologists, sociologists, and student development scholars (e.g., Abes, 2009; Gergen, 1991; Renn, 2004) incorporated postmodern approaches in their work on identities and identity development. Queer theory, CRT, and postmodern feminism (which are described elsewhere in this article) are among the perspectives that are gaining ground in research on student identities, and they represent important foundations for the emergent research described in the next section.

# Present Status of Identity Development Theories

In the past 15 years, research on identity evolved to be more inclusive, nuanced, and interdisciplinary in its approach. It is beyond the scope of this article to provide an overview of all existing identity development theories; we focus here on three key elements of current understandings of identity development. First, it is important to understand the commonalities that emerge among theories. Second, new perspectives on identity elaborate multiple theoretical lenses used to consider identity development. And finally, we describe the role of social status on identity to exemplify how theories can assist in understanding the growing population of diverse students in higher education.

## Commonalities Among Theories

Identity development theories share some characteristics and assumptions about the nature of development, the social construction of identity, and the importance of considering environmental influences. Many of the theories used in student affairs focus on identity as a developmental progression from simple, conferred ideas about oneself to more complex understandings of what makes up identity (see Marcia, 1993; Quintana, 2007). A number of theories (e.g., Cass, 1979; Cross & Vandiver, 2001; Helms, 1990, 1994) mark development through progressive, linear stages or statuses that lead to an end point in which identities are internalized, synthesized, and permanent. The term *stage* has been criticized for representing an identity state that is rigid, stable, and defined externally to the individual (see Helms, 1994). Statuses take into account previous modes of coping while also acknowledging progress toward more internalized ways of seeing self. This more nuanced understanding of how individuals develop complexity prompted Helms (1994) to change her terminology to *statuses* rather than *stages*. Still, both statuses and stages can be critiqued for being narrow and not taking broader contextual issues into consideration as individuals move from simpler to more complex understandings of self and identity (Côté & Schwartz, 2002).

A second common characteristic of identity development theories is the general understanding that identity is socially constructed and reconstructed. Previous sections of this article defined social construction and its influence on understanding identity. Through a social constructionist lens, identity development is not necessarily considered a linear phenomenon. Rather, development may involve a set of tasks that may be undertaken in any order (e.g., D'Augelli, 1994) or a revisiting of identity statuses that allows for identity reconstruction (Marcia, 2002). This process of identity reconstruction is typically initiated as a result of disequilibrium, a psychological state of mismatch between individual sense making and perceptions of self in context (environment), or life changes that can initiate dissonance between perception of self and attainment of possible selves (Marcia, 2002; Markus & Nurius, 1986; Pizzolato, 2003, 2005). Disequilibrium prompts the individual to enter a reformation period that does not disintegrate his or her established identity; instead, the cognitive process of making meaning of changes prompts reconstruction of identity that incorporates change in environment, social status, or other life events.

A third characteristic common to identity development theories entails consideration of the environment or context, a complex system that influences behaviors, attitudes, and cognition (Bronfenbrenner, 1979, 1993; Wozniak & Fischer, 1993). Because identity is socially constructed, societal changes, including changes in the campus environment, are major influences on how one views one's own identity and others' identities. As ecology theories make clear, the context in which a person lives is determined by societal norms, values, and behaviors (Bronfenbrenner, 1979, 1993). The influence of culture and societal norms creates an intricate web of unstated expectations on the individual. As society changes this web may expand or change, but it is always present. Individuals express their understanding of these expectations through a series of assumed behaviors or beliefs and are often unnoticed by most individuals. Yet this web dictates behavior and determines who or what is seen as appropriate (Collins, 2000).

As a result, members of the majority culture are in a position to determine what the norm is, what is valued, and what is socially appropriate. The power to determine the definition of a healthy identity, therefore, represents a privilege given to people with dominant social status. For this reason, examining the role that culture and dominance play in personal and societal beliefs about identity is critical to understanding socially constructed identities.

## New Approaches

Although it is important to recognize commonalities among existing theories, several newer theoretical approaches to understanding identity are emerging. These approaches foreground both marginalized populations (e.g., by race, ethnicity, disability, or sexuality) as well as the societal structures and dynamics that produce and perpetuate marginalization and oppression (e.g., racism, heterosexism, ableism). Using these theoretical frameworks not only sheds light on particular populations but also on how power and privilege shape identity theories more generally (Abes, 2009). As Anderson and Collins (2007) noted, "Using a social structural analysis of race, class, and gender turns your attention to how they work as systems of power—systems that differentially advantage and disadvantage groups depending on their social location" (p. 61). Three new approaches gaining in utility for student affairs are CRT, Latino critical theory (LatCrit), and queer theory. These approaches help researchers and practitioners to highlight the experiences of marginalized populations. Consistent with other approaches, identity is viewed as socially constructed. Yet, these newer approaches make critical a closer examination of how society defines the norm in relation to understanding of race, ethnicity, and sexuality.

CRT places the influence of culture, with an acknowledgement of the importance of race and ethnicity, at the center of what is being researched or considered (Delgado & Stefancic, 2001). Three underlying tenets characterize CRT: (a) structures that oppress must be deconstructed to understand how they influence others; (b) the value of every human being must be considered in the reconstruction; and (c) society should promote value in equal power among all involved (Ladson-Billings, 1998). Using this lens supports a belief that there is no such thing as colorblind research and that failure to recognize social identities perpetuates inequality (Parker, 1998).

CRT originated in legal studies and is broadly connected with critical theory (Habermas, 1987; Tierney & Rhoads, 1993) as a philosophical school of thought because of the shared interest in critiquing social realities and liberation from oppressive societal structures and redistribution of power through the challenging of these structures (Lincoln & Denzin, 2000). However, CRT focuses on the centrality of race and the omnipresence of racism in U.S. society (Delgado & Stefancic, 2001).

The use of CRT among Latinos is called LatCrit, which gives "credence to critical raced-gendered epistemologies that recognize students of color as holding and creators of knowledge" (Delgado Bernal, 2002, p. 107). In addition to placing race and ethnicity at the center, LatCrit considers contrasting European influenced perspectives against those that are Latino oriented. By acknowledging the power held by the majority European culture, researchers expand on the influence that marginalization has on a group of minorities. In expanding the influence, LatCrit also highlights the interconnectedness between societal norms and how norms can be used to oppress certain identities.

Queer theory considers identity and gender as fluid and recognizes the beliefs that historically categorized some behaviors and attractions as nonconforming (Bilodeau & Renn, 2005; Halperin, 2003). In addition, "Queer theory creates complex intersections of identity through multiple strategies of resistance" (Abes & Kasch, 2007, p. 622). The opposition of power structures defines these strategies of resistance. By acknowledging that those in the majority tend to define norms according to their own privilege (typically White, heterosexual, and middle class values), researchers who use queer theory question the social construction of acceptable behaviors, the so-called normal and abnormal. Like CRT and LatCrit, queer theory enriches the study of identity development by drawing attention to previously unexplored perspectives—those from socially constructed margins and experiences. CRT, LatCrit, and queer theory draw attention to the critical role of social status of different identity groups in the construction of identities.

## Potential Role of Social Status on Identity

Research that considers social status focuses on the relationship between context and developing person while acknowledging the influence of a person's group membership within the larger societal context. For example, those in the majority may retain power without acknowledging it (Helms, 1990, 1994). White racial identity theories posit that individuals who are members of the majority culture must understand and acknowledge the privilege their social status gives them to achieve an appreciation of diversity in their life and not impose majority culture on others (Helms, 1990, 1994). A different process occurs for those who are not in the majority and thus have limited power in deciding what is socially accepted.

Societal views of a privileged majority can influence how the identities of minority group members are seen and valued. The majority's views are often associated with historical biases and can promote a negative image of the minority group and its members, thus prompting a tension between a minority group's beliefs and societal views of the group. This majority view can be seen as oppressing identities that are nonmajority and therefore not consistent with definitions of the norm. Understanding and acknowledging the role oppression plays in the lives of marginalized populations is important to understanding how social status of different groups influences identity development (Torres, 2009). For example, Cross and Vandiver (2001) described the process involved in understanding racial and ethnic identity for people of color as moving from negative images that promote a desire to "fit in" and be more like the majority (Whites within U.S. culture) to a more internalized and integrated sense of self with positive views about one's race or ethnic background. This more internalized sense of self includes valuing differences in society as well as within one's own close circle of friends. Whether primarily a member of a majority or minority group, people of all racial and ethnic groups must understand the role social status plays in how individuals view race in the United States. Although racism is talked about, it is the acknowledgement or experiencing of racism that more clearly prompts the understanding that race is central to the context within society (Torres & Hernandez, 2007).

Social status differences exist not only between monoracial groups, but also between individuals who are monoracial (of one racial heritage) and those who are biracial or multiracial (of more than one racial heritage). Students of mixed race or ethnicity may be keenly aware of the ways that their multiple heritages place them at odds with norms of appearance and cultural knowledge expressed by their monoracial peers (Renn, 2008). Older theories about racial and ethnic identity assumed that one race or ethnicity is nurtured in childhood, whereas multiracial development theories recognize the processes involved with growing up in a home that may encompass cultural aspects of multiple heritage groups. In the face of societal expectations that an individual belong to one racial category, multiracial youth may feel pressure to choose between races (Renn, 2008; Root, 2003; Wijeyesinghe, 2001). Theories focused on multiracial students support a sense of self within and across multiple races and the integration of complex understandings of race as a part of identity.

These theoretical understandings of multiple races also highlight intersections that occur among the many roles, beliefs, and choices an individual makes within his or her context. Identities are constructed and expressed differently according to what values, norms, and expectations are made more or less salient (Abes, Jones, & McEwen, 2007; Gergen, 1991; Renn, 2004; Stewart, 2009; Weber, 1998). For this reason, it is important to consider the intersections of identities.

## Identity and Intersections

Ruthellen Josselson, noted identity scholar, captures the dynamic tension that characterizes research on identity development by stating:

> Living our identities is much like breathing. We don't have to ask ourselves each morning who we are. We simply are. . . . Identity is never fixed; it continually evolves. But something in it stays constant; even when we change, we are recognizably who we have always been. Identity links the past, the present and the social world into a narrative that makes sense. It embodies both change and continuity. (Josselson, 1996, p. 29)

As the previous sections of this article documents, the focus of research on identity shifts with historical perspectives, discipline, and context, including the relationship between the parts and the whole of the self. The tension characterized by Josselson illustrates the competing conceptualizations of identity and the "split between theory and lived experience" (Zambrana & Dill, 2009, p. 279). Intersectionality is a new heuristic that addresses this tension by bringing together both the parts and the whole of self as well as the individual in context. In this section, research on multiple identities and intersectionality is explored for its potential to bring theory and lived experience more closely together and to capture the complexities of identity in contemporary times.

Hall (1992) provided an organizational framework to represent the evolution of thinking about identity (he used the term *subject* to describe the self) that reflects the tensions in differing conceptualizations of how the self is understood over time. He delineated three competing conceptualizations of the subject: the enlightenment subject, the sociological subject, and the postmodern subject. Each conceptualization conveys the way in which the self is understood and measured. For example, identity as enlightenment subject is presumed to be innate, described as the core self and revealed along a linear trajectory. The social world is foregrounded in the sociological self and identity develops through the interaction and mediation between the self and sociocultural contexts. And assumptions behind the conceptualization of the postmodern self challenge the very notion of a stable, fixed, unified self, instead emphasizing fragmentation, fluidity, and performativity (Gergen, 1991; Hall, 1992; Yon, 2000).

As previous sections of this article describe, these conceptualizations are evidenced in the evolution of student development research on identity. For example, the epigenetic principle, a central tenet of Erikson's concept of identity development, reflects the enlightenment model; recognition of sociocultural influences and theories focused on specific social identities, as well as those that incorporate environmental and contextual factors reveal elements of the sociological model; and more recent identity work that questions whether or not an essence is even possible and that interrogates structures of power and oppression in relation to identity signals the postmodern subject. Researchers with an interest in more fully and explicitly addressing the larger social categories and contexts in which individuals are situated produced studies that more directly explore social identities and their intersections. Further, this research enabled a return to holistic development, albeit in new form—that is, capturing the whole of an individual more complexly, by emphasizing both social identities and the overlapping domains of identity, cognitive, and interpersonal development. Because another article addresses holistic development or the intersections of intrapersonal, interpersonal, and cognitive development, this article discusses the emerging scholarship examining intersecting identities, highlighting the "postmodern subject." In particular, the concepts of identity salience and contextual influences that inform an understanding of social identities, the analytic lens of intersectionality as a promising framework for identity research, and the challenges in conducting research that investigates identity intersections are explored.

Much of the earlier scholarship in the area of social identities examined social identities independently, as discrete units of analysis (Jones & McEwen, 2000). Further, as Weber (1998) pointed out, the view of individuals in identity scholarship was as "typically assigned a single location along a dimension, which is defined by a set of presumably mutually exclusive and exhaustive categories" (p. 18). This approach resulted in a rich set of developmental theories that examined, for example, the particulars of racial identity, ethnic identity, gender identity, and sexual identity. However, rarely were these brought together in a way that acknowledged that an individual's lived experience is not grounded in only one social identity, but more so in the way in which these identities intersect (Jones, 1997). Even when bringing social identities together, approaches resulted in additive strategies, rather than truly integrative ones (Bowleg, 2008) that would reflect more closely individuals' lived experiences. As a way to convey this distinction Bowleg titled her article addressing methodological challenges with symbols that represent additive and intersectional approaches: "When Black + Lesbian + Woman ≠ Black Lesbian Woman" (p. 312). What Bowleg suggested is that most research presumes that each identity dimension exists independently and thus can be understood singularly. Rather, as Bowleg wrote, an approach that examines these identities together illustrates that "being Black and lesbian confers a unique experience, above and beyond being Black or lesbian" (p. 319).

## Multiple Dimensions of Identity

Research addressing the possibility of intersecting social identities in student development was introduced in the model of multiple dimensions of identity (MMDI; Jones & McEwen, 2000). Drawing on the work of social psychologist Deaux (1993) and Reynolds and Pope's (1991) model of multiple oppressions, the MMDI distinguished between social identities (e.g., race, class, gender, religion) and a personal identity, depicted as a "core sense of self" (personal characteristics and attributes that the individual claims). The MMDI highlighted the notion of identity salience in the context of multiple identities suggesting that the more salient a social identity is to the individual, the closer to the core it moved; in other words, the more integrated that social identity was to a core sense of self. What contributed to the salience of social identities was depicted in the model as contextual influences, such as family background, sociocultural influences, and current experiences, all of which shift with changing circumstances.

The MMDI was reconceptualized first based upon data from a narrative inquiry exploring lesbian college students' identity development (Abes & Jones, 2004), and again with the integration of a cognitive filter to explore the role of meaning making in perceptions of self, the relationships of context to salience and between social identities and the core were further illuminated (Abes et al., 2007). This analysis and resulting reconceptualized model also raised additional questions about what constitutes the core identity, how social identities variously interact, and the role of larger structures of power and privilege operating in individuals' lives, in ways of which these individuals may not be aware.

Although some may suggest that these approaches to studying and conceptualizing identity are still grounded in the basic Eriksonian tenets of psychosocial identity, what distinguishes earlier theories and models from those that followed is the explicit attention given to context and the interactions between these contexts and social identities. That is, contexts are patterned by larger structures of power and oppression that interact with individual identities in both particular and systematic ways. An example of this dynamic is found in the work of Torres (2009), who argues that dealing with racism is a developmental task central to identity development of Latino students. Abes (2009) provided another example by illuminating limitations in the use of constructivist approaches in identity research on lesbian college students for their failure to question the power of heteronormativity in a way that acknowledges the societal rather than individual forces at work. Therefore, it is not enough to simply acknowledge that all individuals possess multiple identities and these identities interact. Rather, as developmental ecologists posit, multiple identities must be connected to the larger social structures in which they are embedded. Further, although much of the research on multiple identities emerged from the study of oppressed identities, this focus brings to light the ways in which majority and minority identities interact and the reality that many individuals possess both privileged and oppressed identities. This perspective is reflected in the analytic lens of intersectionality.

## Intersectionality

Intersectionality, as a framework for the study and understanding of identity, grew out of the field of critical legal studies (e.g., Crenshaw, 1991) and the scholarship of women of color (e.g., Collins, 2000; Dill, McLaughlin, & Nieves, 2007). Seeking to address the absence of representation of their experiences in the literature and to put forward the lived experiences of marginalized individuals, intersectionality expands the analytic lens to include both multiple identities and larger social structures of power and inequality (Dill & Zambrana, 2009; Shields, 2008). Intersectionality is described as "an innovative and emerging field of study that provides a critical analytic lens to interrogate racial, ethnic, class, physical ability, age, sexuality, and gender disparities and to contest existing ways of looking at these structures of inequality" (Dill & Zambrana, p. 1). Interdisciplinary by design and in its application, intersectionality provides a framework for new approaches to understanding and researching identity and student identity development. Intersectionality is also squarely focused on praxis. That is, the intent and outcomes of an intersectional approach and analysis is the transformation of practice to address inequalities and promote social change (Dill, personal communication, September 11, 2008) and, thus, may be applied to a full range of issues in student affairs, including the understanding of student identity development and other diversity issues.

Dill et al. (2007) noted, "To a large extent, intersectional work is about identity" (p. 630), and a central tenet of intersectionality is that "individual identity exists within and draws from a web of socially defined statuses some of which may be more salient than others in specific situations or at specific historical moments" (Dill & Zambrana, 2009, p. 4). More specifically, Dill and Zambrana suggested that intersectionality is:

> Characterized by the following four theoretical interventions: (1) Placing the lived experiences and struggles of people of color and other marginalized groups as a starting point for the development of theory; (2) Exploring the complexities not only of individual identities but also group identity, recognizing that variations within groups are often ignored and essentialized; (3) Unveiling the ways interconnected domains of power organize and structure inequality and oppression; and (4) Promoting social justice and social change by linking research and practice to create a holistic approach to the eradication of disparities and to changing social and higher education institutions. (p. 5)

Dill and Zambrana's intentional use of the term *theoretical intervention* is significant because it suggests that intersectionality is not a theory itself, but an analytic lens through which theories may be viewed and which results in a shifting frame of reference. Intervention implies both this movement and that the use of intersectionality will result in an improved analysis and greater understanding. It is important to note that intersectionality provides a lens both for investigating identity development and for bringing a focus on identity (e.g., dynamics of race, class, gender) to a full range of questions relevant to student development, such as retention, student involvement, campus community, and equity. For example, given the theoretical interventions noted here, student affairs educators could design programs or develop policy with the experiences of underrepresented students at the center of the process, rather than assuming majority student experiences apply to everyone. Family weekend programs, for instance, presume a traditional family structure and the financial resources to attend. Another example of viewing policy making through an intersectional lens suggests attentiveness to within-group differences rather than advocating for only one student organization focused on "Asian American students," which runs the risk of ignoring the many cultural, generational, and immigrant status identity differences in this monolithic category.

Although intersectionality emerged primarily from the scholarship women of color and is intended to focus on the experiences of marginalized individuals and groups by highlighting structures of inequality that influence these experiences, as Collins (2000) suggested, a "matrix of domination" exists which entangles structures of domination with those of privilege. Thus, intersectionality makes way for the examination of both privileged and oppressed identities and acknowledges the possibility of individuals' inhabiting both (Dill et al., 2007). Much of the earlier research on identity and student development left this distinction untouched. In other words, scholarship typically addressed identity as though the developmental process was the same for all (e.g., psychosocial, cognitive, moral) or it delved more deeply into the process of specific groups (e.g., Asian Americans, Latino/as, lesbian, gay, bisexual, and transgender students). The result is a lack of sophistication and complexity in understanding how these identity processes interact and the substantive within group differences. This lack of complexity leads to the problem of essentializing groups and failure to question the ways in which power operates differently in the lives of certain individuals and groups. However, studying identity using an intersectional lens is quite challenging.

## Methodological Challenges

Studying identities as discrete, independent variables is far easier to accomplish methodologically and is one way of "managing the complexity" of intersecting identities (McCall, 2005). Some researchers moved toward embracing this complexity through qualitative methodological strategies that allow for a closer examination of the realities of lived experience. However, studying intersecting identities is not without challenges and is difficult to work out methodologically. The challenge, as Bowleg (2008) captured, is "how to ask questions about experiences that are intersecting, interdependent, and mutually constitutive, without resorting, even inadvertently, to an additive approach" (p. 314). What this means for student affairs educators is that the presence of intersecting identities (e.g., Asian American students with disabilities) does not necessarily constitute an intersectional approach. Indeed, all individuals possess multiple social identities. However, each is typically treated as distinct and independent. Rather, intersectionality centers analysis on how students' experiences are enmeshed in systems of power and inequality. This analysis results in foregrounding an issue (e.g., sexual health, campus violence, academic achievement, campus community) rather than demographic categories and how understanding such an issue is enhanced by looking at the intersections of race, class, gender, and other social structures. Designing studies that are able to get to both micro and macro levels of analysis is very challenging and there are currently few good examples.

Jones (2009) recently used intersectionality as a theoretical framework for analyzing the self-authoring process. What such a lens provided to the discussion of self-authorship was a more explicit emphasis on social identities and the challenges involved in securing an internal identity when contextual influences of power and privilege are considered. Abes (2009) called for the use of multiple theoretical perspectives to explore student identities and expose the power structures that shape both identities and the student development theories formulated to explain those identities. Both of these examples also illustrate another methodological challenge of intersectionality and that is the role of implicit data (Abes & Kasch, 2007; Bowleg, 2008; Jones, 2010). Just as it is challenging to design intersectional research, it is also difficult for participants to fully articulate intersectional identities. This leaves considerable authority to the researcher to interpret mutually constitutive identities when participants may not yet acknowledge these themselves and could also hinder the ability to accurately convey and represent their lived experiences. Research designs must contain mechanisms that illustrate the researcher's effort to interpret implicit data. These strategies include reflection on researcher positionality, member checking with participants, and other measures consistent with assuring trustworthiness of findings (Jones, Torres, & Arminio, 2006). As with all research, costs and benefits accompany researcher decisions. However, intersectionality holds great potential to more completely reflect the whole of self in context while also tending to the structures of inequality that exert powerful influences on the constructions of both privileged and oppressed identities.

## Future Research on Identity Development Theories

As evidence in this manuscript makes clear, substantial literature on college student identity development now exists to guide practice and inform the generation of new theory. By maintaining the multidisciplinary roots of identity development studies and by being alert to emerging theoretical approaches in social science research, student affairs researchers and practitioners are in a position to consider new ways of examining identities and identity development. Among these possibilities are the continued emphasis on intersectionality and the tension of examining both the whole student and his or her constituent parts; greater fluidity within identity categories (e.g., race, gender, sexual orientation); a more nuanced exploration of environments; the influence of technology on developmental context, self-presentation, and identity construction; and the role of globalization on identities.

### Examining the Whole Student and the Constituent Parts

The holistic approach of student affairs (American Council on Education, 1937) was echoed in early studies (e.g., Chickering, 1979) of student identity, which provided a foundation for understanding college student development and its place in Erikson's (1959/1994) life cycle. As college populations became more diverse and social scientists attended to racial and sexual orientation identity development in the 1970s, 1980s, and 1990s, student development theory evolved to focus tightly on identity development of specific student populations (e.g., racial and ethnic groups, lesbian, gay, bisexual, and transgender students, and women). In the last decade, although studies of specific populations have continued to enrich knowledge of identity development in distinct domains considered more or less in isolation, some scholars (Abes, 2009; Abes et al., 2007; Jones, 2010; Stewart, 2009) have begun to put the pieces back together to consider the whole student again, in all of his or her complex and intersecting identities.

   This new way of focusing on the whole student brings the field full circle from a two-dimensional student to a fully three-dimensional, developing person in an ever-changing context. As Abes (2009) pointed out, student development researchers are unaccustomed to working across theoretical boundaries in the ways that may be necessary to fully understand wholeness through intersectionality. The tensions between understanding the whole without erasing its distinctive parts and between working with postmodern and critical theories in tandem with some of the useful and informative structural theories will become central to the study of college student identities in the next decade. We expect that studies of, for example, identity and identity development in emerging adulthood, the presence of "college student" possible selves, and the influence of cultural milieu on identity development will inform theory and student affairs practice.

### Greater Fluidity Within Identity Categories

In addition to expanding understanding and use of intersectionality, identity development researchers are beginning to take seriously the ways that students describe greater fluidity within identity categories (e.g., race, gender, sexual orientation). Rather than view a biracial student who identifies herself situationally in the different heritage groups of her parents as less than fully developed because she has not selected one identity group (in many theories meaning the non-White heritage), a fluid approach to racial identity allows for the student's racial identity to shift over time and place, even to the extent that she may deconstruct and reconstruct racial categories as they have been understood (Renn, 2004). A fluid approach to gender allows not only for transgender students to move across the spectrum of gender expression and identity, but for the acknowledgement that systematic genderism (the social structures and norms that require individuals to be one and only one gender, expressed as a woman or a man) affects people of all genders (Bilodeau, 2009). These examples point to the ways that social constructions privilege some identities over others within a category (expressed in racism, sexism, and homophobia, among other oppressions), and also privilege the concept of fixed identities within categories as opposed to fluid conceptions of racial groups, gender identities, and sexuality.

Queer theory (Halperin, 2003; Sullivan, 2003) offers language and tools for understanding how student development theorists might adopt more fluid approaches to identity. Abes (2009) and Abes and Kasch (2007) offer good examples of how to study college student development without reinforcing heteronormativity (in their example) and fixed notions about identity and identity categories. Other scholars using queer theory provide additional examples of how to decenter identities related to the normalization of certain kinds of bodies (see Sherry [2004] for a discussion of queer theory and disability studies). Expansion of this kind of work will benefit the study of college student identities and the practice of student affairs.

## More Nuanced Exploration of Environments

Throughout this article, we have emphasized the importance of environment, both micro and macro, in the development of identities. Yet the tools with which student development scholars currently assess and understand environments are not adequate to support the theoretical advancements currently underway in the field. In the person–environment system, the study of the person (student) has evolved to be much more sophisticated than the study of the environment. Currently, environmental assessment consists of small-scale studies of individual institutions, as in campus climate studies for gender, race, and sexual orientation or campus-level assessments of student involvement and outcomes, and large-scale studies of student engagement (e.g., with faculty, libraries, peers). Although these studies provide valuable information about the student experience and outcomes, they are not designed to facilitate the exploration of student identities or identity development. The role of environment in identity development remains undertheorized and understudied.

Promising work in this area is emerging from studies that use developmental ecology and those that use in-depth, longitudinal data collection (qualitative or quantitative) to examine the influence of changing environments on identity development (e.g., Guardia & Evans, 2008; Renn, 2004; Taylor, 2008; Torres & Hernandez, 2007). In the next decade, these studies and others underway may contribute substantively to what is known about how specific environments and changes in the environment interact with identity development processes.

## Influence of Technology

Without a doubt, technology—specifically the Internet, but also telecommunications—has changed the nature of the college environment for student development. The World Wide Web has created new venues for identity exploration and online social networks (e.g., Facebook, Myspace) create new venues for identity expression. Before their emergence, young people from any identity group could find themselves isolated before college and even on campus; now, any student with access to the Internet can find media, blogs, entertainment, support groups, political groups, and polemics related to any identity he or she wishes to explore. The influence of information by and about people of different identities on identity development in college students is not well understood, but some qualitative studies have shown that students believe it plays some role (see Gasser, 2008; Martínez Alemán & Wartman, 2009).

Because online information is unfiltered, not always of reliable quality, and not necessarily affirming of all identities, more research is needed to understand how technology can influence identity.

Better understood are the ways that students use technology to present and construct their identities in online forums. Martínez Alemán and Wartman (2009) studied online student culture, and in the process uncovered the ways students talked and wrote about their evolving identity expression in online social networking sites.

Students' identities on Facebook and Second Life, for example, are constructed and kept more or less consistent with their "in-person" identities by the ways that students affiliate online with people who are friends in "real life." Greater congruence between online and "real-life" friendship groups results in greater consistency between online identity and "real" identity; identity development in "real life" is reflected in shifting expressions of self online through changing choice of images, quotes, group memberships, and so forth. So identity development may be observed through online expression of self, a potentially rich research approach. Additional research on the intersections between technology and identity offer much promise for future research and might be easily based on growing institutional practices using online social networks and simulations in, for example, recruiting, orientation, and advising.

## Globalization and Identity Development

Finally, increasing internationalization and globalization of higher education and society are prompting interesting new research on student identity development. The meaning of, for example, ethnic and racial identities are different in the United States and in global perspective. Connecting African-American identity with a global reference group including Africans in diasporas and on the African continent provides a new dimension to racial identity. It does not, of course, reduce the impact of racism in the lives of African-American students or on their identity development as understood through the lens of CRT. International experiences (e.g., study or service abroad, having an international student roommate or instructor) may create disequilibrium, providing impetus for identity exploration that leads to further development (see King & Baxter Magolda, 2005; Martínez Alemán, 2000). Discussions of international issues such as global poverty, clean water, human rights, and immigration may expose students to opposing and supporting viewpoints that can also stimulate identity development (Miller & Fernández, 2007; Ortiz, 2000). Studies of identity development in international students are uncommon and often entail small-sample, single campus investigations of students from one country or region (e.g., Diangelo, 2006; Koehne, 2005). Research on the impact of globalization on identity development of domestic students in higher education is nascent and these areas are ripe for high-quality inquiries.

In conclusion, the study of identity development has a promising future that can build on a strong, multidisciplinary foundation. Student development scholars and student affairs professionals should be open to new theoretical approaches and to exploring new combinations of well-known theories. Critical race theory, LatCrit, queer theory, and theories of intersectionality have much to contribute to understanding student identity development, yet further investigation of the ways that individuals and their environments interact in the social construction of both identity categories and individual identities is needed. It is impossible to predict precisely what direction identity development theory will take, but it seems likely that the productive tension between understanding the whole student and understanding what identities constitute that whole will stimulate new ways of understanding students and their development.

## References

Abes, E. S. (2009). Theoretical borderlands: Using multiple theoretical perspectives to challenge inequitable power structures in student development theory. *Journal of College Student Development, 50*, 141–156.

Abes, E. S., & Jones, S. R. (2004). Meaning-making capacity and the dynamics of lesbian college students multiple dimensions of identity. *Journal of College Student Development, 45*, 612–632.

Abes, E. S., Jones, S. R., & McEwen, M. K. (2007). Reconceptualizing the Model of Multiple Dimensions of Identity: The role of meaning-making capacity in the construction of multiple identities. *Journal of College Student Development, 48*, 1–22.

Abes, E. S., & Kasch, D. (2007). Using queer theory to explore lesbian college students' multiple dimensions of identity. *Journal of College Student Development, 48*, 619–636.

Adams, G. R., & Marshall, S. K. (1996). A developmental social psychology of identity: Understanding person in context. *Journal of Adolescence, 19*, 429–442.

American Council on Education. (1937). The student personnel point of view. In A. L. Rentz (Ed.), *Student affairs a profession's heritage* (2nd ed.). 66–77. Washington, DC: American College Personnel Association.

Anderson, M. L., & Collins, P. H. (2007). Systems of power and inequality. In M. L. Anderson & P. H. Collins (Eds.), *Race, class, & gender: An anthology* (6th ed.; pp. 61–90). Belmont, CA: Thomson Wadsworth.

Arnett, J. J. (2004). *Emerging adulthood: The winding road from the late teens through the twenties.* New York: Oxford University Press US.

Baxter Magolda, M. B. (2001). *Making their own way: Narratives for transforming higher education to promote self-development.* Sterling, VA: Stylus.

Bilodeau, B. L. (2009). *Genderism: Transgender students, binary systems and higher education.* Saarbrücken, Germany: VDM Verlag.

Bilodeau, B. L., & Renn, K. A. (2005). Analysis of LBGT identity development models and implications for practice. In R. L. Sanlo (Ed.), *Gender identity and sexual orientation: Research, policy, and personal perspectives* (New Directions for Student Services, no. 111, pp. 25–39). San Francisco, Jossey-Bass.

Bowleg, L. (2008). When Black + lesbian + woman ≠ Black lesbian woman: The methodological challenges of qualitative and quantitative intersectionality research. *Sex Roles, 59*, 312–325.

Bronfenbrenner, U. (1979). *The ecology of human development: Experiments by nature and design.* Cambridge, MA: Harvard University Press.

Bronfenbrenner, U. (1993). The ecology of cognitive development: Research models and fugitive findings. In R. H. Wozniak & K. W. Fischer (Eds.), *Development in context: Acting and thinking in specific environments* (pp. 3–44). Hillsdale, NJ: Lawrence Erlbaum Associates.

Bubolz, M. M., & Sontag, M. S. (1993). Human ecology theory. In P. Boss, W. J. Doherty, R. LaRossa, W. R. Schumm, & S. K. Steinmetz (Eds.), *Sourcebook of family theories and methods: A contextual approach* (pp. 419–447). New York: Plenum.

Cass, V. C. (1979). Homosexual identity formation: A theoretical model. *Journal of Homosexuality, 4*, 219–235.

Chickering, A. R. (1979). *Education and identity.* San Francisco: Jossey-Bass.

Chickering, A. W., & Reisser, L. (1993). *Education and identity* (2nd ed.). San Francisco: Jossey-Bass.

Collins, P. H. (2000). *Black feminist thought: Knowledge, consciousness, and the politics of empowerment.* New York: Routledge.

Côté, J. E., & Levine, C. G. (2002). *Identity formation, agency, and culture: A social psychological synthesis.* Hillsdale, NJ: Lawrence Erlbaum Associates.

Côté, J. E., & Schwartz, S. J. (2002). Comparing psychological and sociological approaches to identity: Identity status, identity capital, and the individuation process. *Journal of Adolescence, 25*, 571–586.

Crenshaw, K. (1991). Mapping the margins: Intersectionality, identity politics, and violence against women of color. *Stanford Law Review, 43*, 1241–1299.

Cross, W. E., Jr. (1995). The psychology of Nigrescence: Revisiting the Cross model. In J. G. Ponterotto, J. M. Casas, L. A. Suzuki, & C. M. Alexander (Eds.), *Handbook of multicultural counseling* (pp. 93–122). Thousand Oaks, CA: Sage.

Cross, W. E., & Vandiver, B. J. (2001). Nigrescence theory and measurement: Introducing the cross racial identity scale (CRIS). In J. G. Ponterotto, J. M. Casas, L. A. Suzuki, & C. M. Alexander (Eds.), *Handbook of multicultural counseling* (pp. 371–393). Thousand Oaks, CA: Sage.

D'Augelli, A. R. (1994). Identity development and sexual orientation: Toward a model of lesbian, gay, and bisexual development. In E. J. Trickett, R. J. Watts, & D. Birman (Eds.), *Human diversity: Perspectives on people in context* (pp. 312–333). San Francisco: Jossey-Bass.

Deaux, K. (1993). Reconstructing social identity. *Personality and Social Psychology Bulletin, 19*, 412.

Delgado, R. & Stefancic, J. (2001). *Critical race theory: An introduction.* New York: New York University Press.

Delgado Bernal, D. (2002). Critical race theory, Latino critical theory, and critical racedgendered epistemologies: Recognizing students of color as holders and creators of knowledge. *Qualitative Inquiry, 8,* 105–126.

Diangelo, R. J. (2006). The production of whiteness in education: Asian international students in a college classroom. *Teachers College Record, 108,* 1983–2000.

Dill, B. T., McLaughlin, A. E., & Nieves, A. D. (2007). Future directions of feminist research: Intersectionality. In S. N. Hesse-Biber (Ed.), *Handbook of feminist research* (pp. 629–637). Thousand Oaks, CA: Sage.

Dill, B. T., & Zambrana, R. E. (2009). *Emerging intersections: Race, class, and gender in theory, policy, and practice.* New Brunswick, NJ: Rutgers University Press.

Dunkel, C. S., & Anthis, K. S. (2001). The role of possible selves in identity formation: A shortterm longitudinal study. *Journal of Adolescence, 24,* 765–776.

Erikson, E. H. (1959/1994). *Identity and the life cycle.* New York: W. W. Norton & Company.

Feldman, K. A., & Newcomb, T. M. (1969). *The impact of college on students.* San Francisco: Jossey-Bass.

Gasser, H. S. (2008). Being multiracial in a wired society: Using the internet to define identity and community on campus. In K. A. Renn & P. Shang (Eds.), *Biracial and multiracial students* (New Directions for Student Services, no. 123, pp. 63–71). San Francisco: Jossey-Bass.

Gergen, K. J. (1991). *The saturated self: Dilemmas of identity in contemporary life.* New York: Basic Books.

Gilligan, C. (1979). Woman's place in man's life cycle. *Harvard Educational Review, 49,* 431–446.

Gilligan, C. (1982). *In a different voice: Psychological theory and women's development.* Cambridge, MA: Harvard University Press.

Guardia, J. R., & Evans, N. J. (2008). Factors influencing the ethnic identity development of Latino fraternity members at a Hispanic Serving Institution. *Journal of College Student Development, 49,* 163–181.

Habermas, J. (1987). *The theory of communicative action volume two lifeworld and system: A critique of functionalist reason.* Boston: Beacon Press.

Hall, S. (1992). The question of cultural identity. In S. Hall, D. Held, & T. McGrew (Eds.), *Modernity and its futures* (pp. 273–315). Cambridge: Policy Press.

Halperin, D. M. (2003). The normalization of queer theory. *Journal of Homosexuality, 45,* 339–343.

Helms, J. E. (1990). *Black and white racial identity theory, research, and practice.* Westport, CT: Praeger.

Helms, J. E. (1994). The conceptualization of racial identity and other "racial" constructs. In E. J. Trickett, R. J. Watts, & Birman, D. (Eds.) *Human diversity perspectives on people in context* (pp. 285–311). San Francisco: Jossey-Bass.

Jones, S. R. (1997). Voices of identity and difference: A qualitative exploration of the multiple dimensions of identity development in women college students. *Journal of College Student Development, 38,* 376–386.

Jones, S. R. (2009). Constructing identities at the intersections: An autoethnographic exploration of multiple dimensions of identity. *Journal of College Student Development, 50,* 287–304.

Jones, S. R. (2010). Getting to the complexities of identity: The contributions of an autoethnographic and intersectional approach. In M. B. Baxter Magolda, E. Creamer, & P. Meszaros (Eds.), *Development and assessment of self-authorship: Exploring the concept across cultures* (pp. 223–244). Sterling, VA: Stylus.

Jones, S. R., & McEwen, M. K. (2000). A conceptual model of multiple dimensions of identity. *Journal of College Student Development, 41,* 405–414.

Jones, S. R., Torres, V., & Arminio, J. (2006). *Negotiating the complexities of qualitative research in higher education: Fundamental elements and issues.* New York: Routledge.

Josselson, R. E. (1996). *Revising herself: The story of women's identity from college to midlife.* New York: Oxford University Press.

Kaufman, P., & Feldman, K. A. (2004). Forming identities in college: A sociological approach. *Research in Higher Education, 45,* 463–496.

Kegan, R. K. (1982). *The evolving self: Problem and process in human development.* Cambridge, MA: Harvard University Press.

Kegan, R. (1994). *In over our heads: The mental demands of modern life.* Cambridge, MA: Harvard University Press.

King, P. M., & Baxter Magolda, M. B. (2005). A developmental model of intercultural maturity. *Journal of College Student Development, 46,* 571–592.

Koehne, N. (2005). (Re)construction: Ways international students talk about their identity. *Australian Journal of Education, 49,* 104–119.

Kroger, J. (2004). *Identity and adolescence: The balance between self and other* (3rd ed.). London: Routledge.

Ladson-Billings, G. (1998). Just what is critical race theory and what's it doing in a nice field like education? *Qualitative Studies in Education, 11,* 724.

Lincoln, Y. S., & Denzin, N. K. (2000). The seventh movement: Out of the past. In N. K. Denzin & Y. S. Lincoln (Eds.), *Handbook of qualitative research* (2nd ed., pp. 163–188). Thousand Oaks, CA: Sage.

Marcia, J. (2002). Identity and psychosocial development in adulthood. *Identity: An International Journal of Theory and Research, 2*(1), 7–28.

Marcia, J. E. (1993). The status of the statuses: Research review. In J. M. Marcia, A. S. Waterman, D. R. Matteson, S. L. Archer, & J. L. Oflofshy (Eds.), *Ego identity: A handbook for psychosocial research* (pp. 22–41). New York: Springer-Verlag.

Markus, H., & Nurius, P. (1986). Possible selves. *American Psychologist, 41,* 954–969.

Martínez Alemán, A. M. (2000). Race talks: Undergraduate women of color and female friendships. *Review of Higher Education, 23,* 133–152.

Martínez Alemán, A. M., & Wartman, K. L. (2009). *Online social networking on campus: Understanding what matters in student culture.* New York: Routledge.

McCall, L. (2005). The complexity of intersectionality. *Signs: Journal of Women in Culture and Society, 30,* 1771–1800.

McEwen, M. K. (2003). The nature and uses of theory. In S. R. Komives, D. B. Woodard, Jr., & Associates (Eds.), *Student services: A handbook for the profession* (pp. 153–178). San Francisco: Jossey-Bass.

Miller, A. T., & Fernández, E. (2007). New learning and teaching from where you've been: The global intercultural experience for undergraduates. In M. Kaplan & A. T. Miller (Eds.), *Scholarship of multicultural teaching and learning* (New Directions for Teaching and Learning, no. 111, pp. 55–62). San Francisco: Jossey-Bass.

Miller, T. K., & Prince, J. S. (1976). *The future of student affairs.* San Francisco: Jossey-Bass.

Ortiz, A. M. (2000). Expressing cultural identity in the learning community: Opportunities and challenges. In M. B. Baxter Magolda (Ed.), *Teaching to promote intellectual and personal maturity incorporating students' worldviews and identities into the learning process* (New Directions for Teaching and Learning, no. 82, pp. 67–79). San Francisco: Jossey-Bass.

Parker, L. (1998). Race is . . . race ain't: An exploration of the utility of critical race theory in qualitative research in education. *Qualitative Studies in Education, 11,* 43–55.

Phinney, J. S. (1993). A three-stage model of ethnic identity development in adolescence. In M. E. Bernal & G. P. Knight (Eds.), *Ethnic identity formation and transmission among Hispanic and other minorities* (pp. 61–79). Albany: State University of New York Press.

Pizzolato, J. E. (2003). Developing self-authorship: Exploring the experiences of high-risk college students. *Journal of College Student Development, 44,* 797–812.

Pizzolato, J. E. (2005). Creating crossroads for self-authorship: Investigating the provocative moment. *Journal of College Student Development, 46,* 624–641.

Pizzolato, J. E. (2010). What is self-authorship? A theoretical exploration of the construct. In M. B. Baxter Magolda, E. Creamer, & P. Meszaros (Eds.), *Development and assessment of self-authorship: Exploring the concept across cultures* (pp. 187–206). Sterling, VA: Stylus.

Pizzolato, J. E., Chaudhari, P., Murrell, E. D., Podobnik, S., & Schaeffer, Z. (2008). Ethnic identity, epistemological development, and academic achievement in underrepresented students. *Journal of College Student Development, 49,* 301–318.

Quintana, S. M., (2007). Racial and ethnic identity: Developmental perspectives and research. *Journal of Counseling Psychology, 54,* 259–270.

Renn, K. A. (2003). Understanding the identities of mixed race college students through a developmental ecology lens. *Journal of College Student Development, 44,* 383–403.

Renn, K. A. (2004). *Mixed race students in college: The ecology of race, identity, and community.* Albany: State University of New York Press.

Renn, K. A. (2008). Research on biracial and multiracial identity development: Overview and synthesis. In K. A. Renn & P. Shang (Eds.), *Biracial and multiracial students* (New Directions for Student Services, no. 123, pp. 13–32). San Francisco: Jossey-Bass.

Renn, K. A., & Arnold, K. D. (2003). Reconceptualizing research on peer culture. *Journal of Higher Education, 74,* 261–291.

Reynolds, A. L., & Pope, R. L. (1991). The complexities of diversity: Exploring multiple oppressions. *Journal of Counseling and Development, 70*, 174–180.

Root, M. P. P. (2003). Racial identity development and persons of mixed race heritage. In M. P. P. Root & M. Kelley (Eds.) *Multiracial child resource book living complex identities* (pp. 34–41). Seattle, WA: Mavin Foundation.

Schwartz, S. J., Côté, J. E., & Arnett, J. J. (2005). Identity and agency in emerging adulthood: Two developmental routes in the individuation process. *Youth & Society, 37*, 201–209.

Sherry, M. (2004). Overlaps and contradictions between queer theory and disability studies. *Disability & Society, 19*, 769–783.

Shields, S. (2008). Gender: An intersectionality perspective. *Sex Roles, 59*, 301–311.

Stewart, D. L. (2009). Perceptions of multiple identities among Black college students. *Journal of College Student Development, 50*, 253–270.

Sullivan, N. (2003). *A critical introduction to queer theory*. New York: New York University Press.

Syed, M., & Azmitia, M. (2008). A narrative approach to ethnic identity in emerging adulthood: Bringing life to the identity status model. *Developmental Psychology, 44*, 1012–1027.

Taylor, K. B. (2008). Mapping the intricacies of young adults' development journey from socially prescribed to internally defined relationships, and beliefs. *Journal of College Student Development, 49*, 215–234.

Thelin, J. R. (2004). *A history of American higher education*. Baltimore, MD: The Johns Hopkins University Press.

Tierney, W. G., & Rhoads, R. A. (1995). Postmodernism and critical theory in higher education: Implications for research and practice. In J. C. Smart (Ed.), *Higher education: Handbook of theory and research* (Vol. IX, pp. 308–343). New York: Agathon Press.

Torres, V. (2003). Influences on ethnic identity development of Latino college students in the first two years of college. *Journal of College Student Development, 44*, 532–547.

Torres, V. (2009). The developmental dimensions of recognizing racism. *Journal of College Student Development, 50*, 504–520.

Torres, V., & Hernandez, E. (2007). The influence of ethnic identity on self-authorship: A longitudinal study of Latino/a college students. *Journal of College Student Development, 48*, 558–573.

Weber, L. (1998). A conceptual framework for understanding race, class, gender, and sexuality. *Psychology of Women Quarterly, 22*, 13–22.

Wijeyesinghe, C. L. (2001). Racial identity in multiracial people an alternative paradigm. In C. L. Wijeyesinghe & B.W. Jackson, III (Eds.), *New perspectives on racial identity development: A theoretical and practical anthology* (pp. 129–152). New York: New York University Press.

Wozniak, R. H., & Fischer, K. W. (1993). Development in context: An introduction. In R. H. Wozniak & K.W. Fischer (Eds.), *Development in context: Acting and thinking in specific environments* (pp. xi–vi). Hillsdale, NJ: Lawrence Erlbaum Associates.

Yon, D. A. (2000). *Elusive culture: Schooling, race, and identity in global times*. Albany: State University of New York Press.

Zambrana, R. E., & Dill, B. T. (2009). Conclusion: Future directions in knowledge building and sustaining institutional change. In B. T. Dill & R. E. Zambrana (Eds.), *Emerging intersections: Race, class, and gender in theory, policy, and practice* (pp. 274–290). New Brunswick, NJ: Rutgers University Press.

# CHAPTER 9
## THE SEVEN VECTORS
### ARTHUR W. CHICKERING AND LINDA REISSER

Our model does not portray development as one predominant challenge or crisis resolution after another, each invariably linked to specific ages. Development for college students, which today includes persons of virtually all ages, is a process of infinite complexity. Just as students are notorious for not proceeding through the institution according to schedule, they rarely fit into oversimplified paths or pigeonholes. We propose the seven vectors as maps to help us determine where students are and which way they are heading. Movement along any one can occur at different rates and can interact with movement along the others. Each step from "lower" to "higher" brings more awareness, skill, confidence, complexity, stability, and integration but does not rule out an accidental or intentional return to ground already traversed. We assume that "higher" is better than "lower," because in adding the skills and strengths encompassed by these vectors, individuals grow in versatility, strength, and ability to adapt when unexpected barriers or pitfalls appear.

We also recognize that developmental patterns described by psychosocial theorists may have been skewed by the exclusivity of their samples, as was the case for cognitive theorists. Women were less prominent in Erikson's thinking, and males were initially excluded from Loevinger's sample. Nontraditional students and members of minority groups often were left out altogether. These deficiencies are now being corrected. For example, there have been studies on identity formation for women (Josselson, 1987), on nonwhite students (Cross, 1971; Helms, 1990; Sue and Sue, 1971; Martinez, 1988; Johnson and Lashley, 1988; Atkinson, Morten, and Sue, 1983; Ho, 1987; Branch-Simpson, 1984), and on homosexual students (Cass, 1979; Coleman, 1981–1982; Dank, 1971; Minton and McDonald, 1983–1984; Plummer, 1975; Troiden, 1979). Many of these studies seem to be turning up variations in style and sequence, but the fundamental themes reappear and continue to serve as foundations for the seven vectors.

The vectors describe major highways for journeying toward individuation—the discovery and refinement of one's unique way of being—and also toward communion with other individuals and groups, including the larger national and global society. We propose that while each person will drive differently, with varying vehicles and self-chosen detours, eventually all will move down these major routes. They may have different ways of thinking, learning, and deciding, and those differences will affect the way the journey unfolds, but for all the different stories about turning points and valuable lessons, college students live out recurring themes: gaining competence and self-awareness, learning control and flexibility, balancing intimacy with freedom, finding one's voice or vocation, refining beliefs, and making commitments.

Since we refrained from describing development in terms of Erikson's age-specific crises, we are hesitant to portray it as movement from one stage or position to the next. Rest (1979) differentiated

Chickering, A. W., & Reisser, L. (1993). The seven vectors. In *Education and identity* (2nd ed., pp. 34–52). San Francisco, CA: Jossey-Bass.

between "simple-stage models" and "complex-stage models." Using simple-stage models, a typical assessment question was, "What stage is a person in?" Assuming one stage at a time with no overlapping, no skipping of stages, and no steps backward, it should be easy to pinpoint where a student is and design challenges to foster the next step. Loevinger, Perry, and Kohlberg, following Piaget's lead, envisioned cognitive structures that evolved in an orderly fashion. Like windows built into a house, they became relatively fixed lenses for interpreting reality and screening input. Major remodeling was needed to change the windows. Once the new model was installed, it was as hard to go back to the old structure as to replace stained glass with a plain windowpane. Furthermore, the brain would not move from windowpane to stained glass in one leap. A sliding glass door had to come next, and then beveled, leaded designs, perhaps with inset mirrors and magnifying glasses. Perry differed from his colleagues in allowing for escape, retreat, and delay in his theory of intellectual development. For others, it was onward and upward, and while it was easy for a student to look back with disdain on an earlier way of thinking, it was hard to see beyond the next level of complexity, let alone understand an instructor who was teaching two or more stages ahead.

King (1990, pp. 83–84) warns against an overly simplified description of cognitive processes, which are inconsistent with many research findings. "For example, people don't seem to change from the exclusive use of one set of assumptions to the exclusive use of those of the next adjacent stage; rather, the use of assumptions characteristic of several stages at once often has been found. Stage usage seems to be influenced by a variety of individual factors (e.g., consolidation of existing structures, fatigue, readiness for change) and environmental factors (e.g., whether one is asked to create one's own solution to a problem or to critique someone else's solution, explaining one's beliefs verbally or in writing)." Different test characteristics and demands call forth different cognitive structures. Rest (1979, p. 63) proposes that instead of trying to assess what stage the person is in, we should ask, "To what extent and under what conditions does a person manifest the various types of organizations of thinking?"

A linear perspective may also frustrate those who want to help students achieve the upper reaches of stage theories. Pascarella and Terenzini (1991, p. 35) found no evidence of college students functioning at any of the final three stages of Loevinger's model. Kohlberg (1972) found that stage 4 (law and order) was the predominant stage in most societies. Perry (1970) was more optimistic, saying that perhaps 75 percent of the seniors in his study had reached positions 7 and 8. Subsequent research found Perry position scores ranging from 2 to 5, with no students scoring at the committed positions (Kurfiss, 1975; Pascarella and Terenzini, 1991, p. 30). This does not mean that higher levels are not present or possible. In fact, as our student populations diversify, the likelihood that all the stages will be represented increases. It may mean that the strategies for assessing developmental levels still need refining, or it may mean that the journey is a more logical priority than the destination.

Given the limitations of sequential models, we have proposed a sequence in order to suggest that certain building blocks make a good foundation (see Table 1). Some tasks are more likely to be encountered early in the journey. College students, regardless of age, will be challenged to develop intellectual competence. If the college does nothing else, it will try to move students along this vector. If it requires physical education or encourages athletics and if it supports participation in music, art, drama, or dance, it will foster physical and manual competence. Unless the new student makes a serious effort to remain isolated, the experience of meeting new people inside and outside of class will stimulate interpersonal competence. Whether leaving home for the first time or returning to college late in life, students will face loneliness, anxiety, frustration, and conflict. They will be required to make decisions, set goals, and develop greater autonomy. While younger students may be more obsessed with sex and romance, older students may be forming new relationships and perhaps reexamining earlier ones in light of what they are reading and whom they are meeting. Therefore, it is likely that a college will move students along these first four vectors, and growth in each area helps construct identity. Most students also experience greater clarity about purposes, values, and ways of thinking. If they are lucky, they will discover interests and people they care deeply about and will make lasting commitments. And they will expand their awareness of who they are and of how valuable they are.

**TABLE 1**

**The Seven Vectors: General Developmental Directions**

| From | To |
| --- | --- |
| **Developing Competence** | |
| Low level of competence (intellectual, physical, interpersonal) | High level of competence in each area |
| Lack of confidence in one's abilities | Strong sense of competence |
| **Managing Emotions** | |
| Little control over disruptive emotions (fear and anxiety, anger leading to aggression, depression, guilt, and shame, and dysfunctional sexual or romantic attraction) | Flexible control and appropriate expression |
| Little awareness of feelings | Increasing awareness and acceptance of emotions |
| Inability to integrate feelings with actions | Ability to integrate feelings with responsible action |
| **Moving Through Autonomy Toward Interdependence** | |
| Emotional dependence | Freedom from continual and pressing needs for reassurance |
| Poor self-direction or ability to solve problems; little freedom or confidence to be mobile | Instrumental independence (inner direction, persistence, and mobility) |
| Independence | Recognition and acceptance of the importance of interdependence |
| **Developing Mature Interpersonal Relationships** | |
| Lack of awareness of differences; intolerance of differences | Tolerance and appreciation of differences |
| Nonexistent, short-term, or unhealthy intimate relationships | Capacity for intimacy which is enduring and nurturing |
| **Establishing Identity** | |
| Discomfort with body and appearance | Comfort with body and appearance |
| Discomfort with gender and sexual orientation | Comfort with gender and sexual orientation |
| Lack of clarity about heritage and social/cultural roots of identity | Sense of self in a social, historical, and cultural context |
| Confusion about "who I am" and experimentation with roles and lifestyles | Clarification of self-concept through roles and lifestyle |
| Lack of clarity about others' evaluation | Sense of self in response to feedback from valued others |
| Dissatisfaction with self | Self-acceptance and self-esteem |
| Unstable, fragmented personality | Personal stability and integration |
| **Developing Purpose** | |
| Unclear vocational goals | Clear vocational goals |
| Shallow, scattered personal interests | More sustained, focused, rewarding activities |
| Few meaningful interpersonal commitments | Strong interpersonal and family commitments |
| **Developing Integrity** | |
| Dualistic thinking and rigid beliefs | Humanizing values |
| Unclear or untested personal values and beliefs | Personalizing (clarifying and affirming) values while respecting others' beliefs |
| Self-interest | Social responsibility |
| Discrepancies between values and actions | Congruence and authenticity |

Few developmental theories have paid much attention to emotions and relationships. More work has been done on thoughts and values. Our theory assumes that emotional, interpersonal, and ethical development deserve equal billing with intellectual development.

How does this revision differ from the earlier version of *Education and Identity?*

1. The fifth vector, *freeing interpersonal relationships,* had been retitled *developing mature interpersonal relationships* and moved back in sequence, prior to *establishing identity.* We did this primarily to recognize the importance of students' experiences with relationships in the formation of their core sense of self.

2. The chapter on the *managing emotions* vector has been broadened beyond the earlier focus on aggression and sexual desire to address anxiety, depression, anger, shame, and guilt, as well as more positive emotions.

3. We have placed more emphasis on the importance of interdependence, while not denying the significance of learning independence and self-sufficiency. Instead of retaining the term *developing autonomy*, we have renamed this vector *moving through autonomy toward interdependence.*

4. More emphasis has been placed on the intercultural aspects of tolerance as a component of developing mature interpersonal relationships, which also entails a growing capacity for intimacy.

5. We have added more complexity to the *developing identity* vector. We have noted issues raised by recent researchers concerning differences in identity development based on gender, ethnic background, and sexual orientation.

6. More current research findings have been cited as they relate to the vectors (although this book is not meant to contain a thorough review of the literature).

7. We have added illustrative statements from students to reflect greater diversity. Where earlier statements reinforce the text, they have been left in.

Like many humanistic models, this one is founded on an optimistic view of human development, assuming that a nurturing, challenging college environment will help students grow in stature and substance. Erikson believed in an epigenetic principle. Rogers saw a benign pattern at work in human beings, similar to the process that turns acorns into oak trees. The ancient Greeks had a concept alien to our modern-day emphasis on specialization and fragmentation between body and mind, between the physical and the spiritual. It is called *aretê.* According to the Greek scholar H. D. F. Kitto (1963, pp. 171–172), it was their ideal:

> When we meet it in Plato we translate it "Virtue" and consequently miss all the flavour of it. "Virtue," at least in modern English, is almost entirely a moral word; *aretê* on the other hand is used indifferently in all the categories and means simply "excellence." It may be limited of course by its context; the *aretê* of a race-horse is speed, of a cart-horse strength. If it is used, in a general context, of a man it will connote excellence in the ways in which a man can be excellent—morally, intellectually, physically, practically. Thus the hero of the *Odyssey* is a great fighter, a wily schemer, a ready speaker, a man of stout heart and broad wisdom who knows that he must endure without too much complaining what the gods send; and he can both build and sail a boat, drive a furrow as straight as anyone, beat a young braggart at throwing the discus, challenge the Phraecian youth at boxing, wrestling, or running; flay, skin, cut up, and cook an ox, and be moved to tears by a song. He is in fact an excellent all-rounder; he has surpassing *aretê.*

Kitto says that "this instinct for seeing things whole is the source of the essential sanity in Greek life" (p. 176). Institutions that emphasize intellectual development to the exclusion of other strengths and skills reinforce society's tendency to see some aspects of its citizens and not others. Just as individuals are not just consumers, competitors, and taxpayers, so students are not just degree seekers and test takers. To develop all the gifts of human potential, we need to be able to see them whole and to believe in their essential worth. In revising the seven vectors, we hope to offer useful tools to a new generation of practitioners who want to help students become "excellent all-rounders." We also hope to inspire experienced faculty, administrators, and student services and support staff to recommit to the mission of nurturing mind, body, heart, and spirit.

## An Overview

Lasting personality changes may not occur in a blinding flash. As Dylan Thomas (1939, pp. 29–30) said, "Light breaks where no sun shines . . . Dawn breaks behind the eyes . . . Light breaks on secret lots . . . On tips of thought. . . ." While some epiphanies are dramatic and sudden, most occur gradually and incrementally. We may not know for years that a single lecture or conversation or experience started a chain reaction that transformed some aspect of ourselves. We cannot easily discern what subtle mix of people, books, settings, or events promotes growth. Nor can we easily name changes in ways of thinking, feeling, or interpreting the world. But we can observe behavior and record words, both of which can reveal shifts from hunch to analysis, from simple to complex perceptions, from divisive bias to compassionate understanding. Theory can give us the lenses to see these changes and help them along.

The challenges students, faculty, and administrators face today can be overwhelming. While the 1960s brought protest marches, drug busts, demands for curricular relevance, and students insisting on shared power, it was also an era of expanding budgets, new construction, and innovative programs. The boom lasted through the 1970s, and longer in some states. The resources were there to support adequate staffing, burgeoning specialization, and bold experiments. Perhaps we should have foreseen the pendulum swinging backward. Now administrators spend a great deal of time stretching dollars, consolidating services, and managing crises. Faculty are teaching larger classes or worrying about too few enrollees, fretting about retirement, relying on adjunct instructors, scrutinizing contracts, and going to union meetings. Students are facing higher tuition, longer lines, and fewer seats in the classroom. With higher costs, bleaker job prospects, and more evident crime statistics, students may focus more on security than on self-improvement.

Student development theory must apply to this generation of students as well as to future ones. It must be useful to institutional leaders as they cope with retrenchment as well as expansion. Without a developmental philosophy at the core of the college, it can become a dispensary of services, a training ground for jobs that may not exist, or a holding tank for those not sure what to do next. Institutions that impart transferable skills and relevant knowledge, bolster confidence and creativity, and engender social responsibility and self-directed learning are needed more than ever. To be effective in educating the whole student, colleges must hire and reinforce staff members who understand what student development looks like and how to foster it.

The seven vectors provide such a model. Though they were originally proposed as major constellations of development during adolescence and early adulthood, we have attempted to apply the vectors to adults as well. We have tried to use language that is gender free and appropriate for persons of diverse backgrounds. The vectors have stood the test of time as conceptual lenses. They have enabled higher education practitioners to view their students, their courses, and their programs more clearly and to use them as beacons for change. Those who have kept up to date on research, or who want more specificity and complexity, may be frustrated by our level of generality. Yet we believe that the original version of the model has been useful precisely because of its broad conceptual nature, leaving practitioners the options of putting their own understanding and interpretation into it and applying it within their own contexts.

We have also attempted to tie this model to student perceptions of their experience. We have drawn excerpts from student self-assessments, short reflection exercises, and papers on developmental theories where autobiographical examples were included. Over a period of three years, I (Reisser) invited students in my classes and professionals attending my presentations to complete a "developmental worksheet" by writing anonymous responses to the following:

1. Briefly describe a change in yourself that had a major impact on how you lived your life. What was the "old" way of thinking or being, vs. the "new" way? What did you move *from* and what did you move *to*? How did you know that a significant change had occurred?

2. What were the important things (or persons) that *helped* the process? What did the person *do*? What was the experience that catalyzed the shift? Were there any *feelings* that helped or accompanied the process?

In all, 120 worksheets were collected, and though they were not based on carefully designed sampling procedures, the statements excerpted from them bring to life the potentially dry formality of theory. When students' research or reflection papers included relevant examples, I (Reisser) asked to keep copies for future writing projects on student development. Students' statements from the 1969 edition were also used here to illustrate developmental stages.

The seven vectors are summarized below.

**1. *Developing competence.*** Three kinds of competence develop in college—intellectual competence, physical and manual skills, and interpersonal competence. Intellectual competence is skill in using one's mind. It involves mastering content, gaining intellectual and aesthetic sophistication, and, most important, building a repertoire of skills to comprehend, analyze, and synthesize. It also entails developing new frames of reference that integrate more points of view and serve as "more adequate" structures for making sense out of our observations and experiences.

Physical and manual competence can involve athletic and artistic achievement, designing and making tangible products, and gaining strength, fitness, and self-discipline. Competition and creation bring emotions to the surface since our performance and our projects are on display for others' approval or criticism. Leisure activities can become lifelong pursuits and therefore part of identity.

Interpersonal competence entails not only the skills of listening, cooperating, and communicating effectively, but also the more complex abilities to tune in to another person and respond appropriately, to align personal agendas with the goals of the group, and to choose from a variety of strategies to help a relationship flourish or a group function.

Students' overall sense of competence increases as they learn to trust their abilities, receive accurate feedback from others, and integrate their skills into a stable self-assurance.

**2. *Managing emotions.*** Whether new to college or returning after time away, few students escape anger, fear, hurt, longing, boredom, and tension. Anxiety, anger, depression, desire, guilt, and shame have the power to derail the educational process when they become excessive or overwhelming. Like unruly employees, these emotions need good management. The first task along this vector is not to eliminate them but to allow them into awareness and acknowledge them as signals, much like the oil light on the dashboard.

Development proceeds when students learn appropriate channels for releasing irritations before they explode, dealing with fears before they immobilize, and healing emotional wounds before they infect other relationships. It may be hard to accept that some amount of boredom and tension is normal, that some anxiety helps performance, and that impulse gratification must sometimes be squelched.

Some students come with the faucets of emotional expression wide open, and their task is to develop flexible controls. Others have yet to open the tap. Their challenge is to get in touch with the full range and variety of feelings and to learn to exercise self-regulation rather than repression. As self-control and self-expression come into balance, awareness and integration ideally support each other.

More positive kinds of emotions have received less attention from researchers. They include feelings like rapture, relief, sympathy, yearning, worship, wonder, and awe. These may not need to be "managed" so much as brought into awareness and allowed to exist. Students must learn to balance self-assertive tendencies, which involve some form of aggressiveness or defensiveness, with participatory tendencies, which involve transcending the boundaries of the individual self, identifying or bonding with another, or feeling part of a larger whole.

**3. *Moving through autonomy toward interdependence.*** A key developmental step for students is learning to function with relative self-sufficiency, to take responsibility for pursuing self-chosen goals, and to be less bound by others' opinions. Movement requires both emotional and instrumental independence, and later recognition and acceptance of interdependence.

Emotional independence means freedom from continual and pressing needs for reassurance, affection, or approval. It begins with separation from parents and proceeds through reliance on peers, nonparental adults, and occupational or institutional reference groups. It culminates in diminishing need for such supports and increased willingness to risk loss of friends or status in order to pursue strong interests or stand on convictions.

Instrumental independence has two major components: the ability to organize activities and to solve problems in a self-directed way, and the ability to be mobile. It means developing that volitional part of the self that can think critically and independently and that can then translate ideas into focused action. It also involves learning to get from one place to another, without having to be taken by the hand or given detailed directions, and to find the information or resources required to fulfill personal needs and desires.

Developing autonomy culminates in the recognition that one cannot operate in a vacuum and that greater autonomy enables healthier forms of interdependence. Relationships with parents are revised. New relationships based on equality and reciprocity replace the older, less consciously chosen peer bonds. Interpersonal context broadens to include the community, the society, the world. The need to be independent and the longing for inclusion become better balanced. Interdependence means respecting the autonomy of others and looking for ways to give and take with an ever-expanding circle of friends.

**4. Developing mature interpersonal relationships.** Developing mature relationships involves (1) tolerance and appreciation of differences (2) capacity for intimacy. Tolerance can be seen in both an intercultural and an interpersonal context. At its heart is the ability to respond to people in their own right rather than as stereotypes or transference objects calling for particular conventions. Respecting differences in close friends can generalize to acquaintances from other continents and cultures. Awareness, breadth of experience, openness, curiosity, and objectivity help students refine first impressions, reduce bias and ethnocentrism, increase empathy and altruism, and enjoy diversity.

In addition to greater tolerance, the capacity for healthy intimacy increases. For most adolescent couples, each is the pool and each the Narcissus. Satisfying relationships depend on spatial proximity, so that each can nod to the other and in the reflection observe himself or herself. Developing mature relationships means not only freedom from narcissism, but also the ability to choose healthy relationships and make lasting commitments based on honesty, responsiveness, and unconditional regard. Increased capacity for intimacy involves a shift in the quality of relationships with intimates and close friends. The shift is away from too much dependence or too much dominance and toward an interdependence between equals. Development means more in-depth sharing and less clinging, more acceptance of flaws and appreciation of assets, more selectivity in choosing nurturing relationships, and more long-lasting relationships that endure through crises, distance, and separation.

**5. Establishing identity.** Identity formation depends in part on the other vectors already mentioned: competence, emotional maturity, autonomy, and positive relationships. Developing identity is like assembling a jigsaw puzzle, remodeling a house, or seeking one's "human rhythms," a term that Murphy (1958) illustrated by photic driving. A person watching an instrument that emits flashes at precise intervals eventually hits a breaking point—the point at which the rhythm induces a convulsion. If, for example, the number is sixteen, the observer may rapidly lose consciousness as this number is presented in the standard time interval. Seventeen and fifteen, however, are safe numbers. It is not until thirty-two or some other multiple of sixteen reached that a breakdown recurs. Like the piano wire that hums or like the glass that shatters, we all have our critical frequencies in a variety of areas. Development of identity is the process of discovering with what kinds of experience, at what levels of intensity and frequency, we resonate in satisfying, in safe, or in self-destructive fashion.

Development of identity involves: (1) comfort with body and appearance, (2) comfort with gender and sexual orientation, (3) sense of self in a social, historical, and cultural context, (4) clarification of self-concept through roles and life-style, (5) sense of self in response to feedback from valued others, (6) self-acceptance and self-esteem, and (7) personal stability and integration. A solid sense of self emerges, and it becomes more apparent that there is an *I* who coordinates the facets of personality, who "owns" the house of self and is comfortable in all of its rooms.

College student concern with appearance is obvious. Though gowns no longer prevail except at Oxford and Cambridge, town residents recognize students, especially younger ones who don emblems of student culture. Whatever the limitations or prescriptions, experimentation occurs. With clarification of identity, however, it diminishes. By graduation, most of the early creative—or bizarre—variations are given up. Experimentation with dress and appearance herald pathways to sexual identity. Looking at old high school yearbooks confirms the evolution of hairstyles. Macho, androgynous, or femme fatale "looks" come and go, but identity hinges on finding out what it means to be a man or a woman and coming to terms with one's sexuality.

Establishing identity also includes reflecting on one's family of origin and ethnic heritage, defining self as a part of a religious or cultural tradition, and seeing self within a social and historical context. It involves finding roles and styles at work, at play, and at home that are genuine expressions of self and that further sharpen self-definition. It involves gaining a sense of how one is seen and evaluated by others. It leads to clarity and stability and a feeling of warmth for this core self as capable, familiar, worthwhile.

**6. *Developing purpose.*** Many college students are all dressed up and do not know where they want to go. They have energy but no destination. While they may have clarified who they are and where they came from, they have only the vaguest notion of who they want to be. For large numbers of college students, the purpose of college is to qualify them for a good job, not to help them build skills applicable in the widest variety of life experiences; it is to ensure a comfortable life-style, not to broaden their knowledge base, find a philosophy of life, or become a lifelong learner.

Developing purpose entails an increasing ability to be intentional, to assess interests and options, to clarify goals, to make plans, and to persist despite obstacles. It requires formulating plans for action and a set of priorities that integrate three major elements: (1) vocational plans and aspirations, (2) personal interests, and (3) interpersonal and family commitments. It also involves a growing ability to unify one's many different goals within the scope of a larger, more meaningful purpose, and to exercise intentionality on a daily basis.

We use the term *vocation* in its broadest sense—as specific career or as broad calling. Vocations can include paid work, unpaid work, or both. We discover our vocation by discovering what we love to do, what energizes and fulfills us, what uses our talents and challenges us to develop new ones, and what actualizes all our potentials for excellence. Ideally, these vocational plans flow from deepening interests, and in turn, lend momentum to further aspirations that have meaning and value. Considerations of life-style and family also enter the equation. As intimate relationships increasingly involve the question of long-term partnership and as formal education and vocational exploration draw to a close, next steps must be identified. It is difficult to construct a plan that balances life-style considerations, vocational aspirations, and avocational interests. Many compromises must be made, and clearer values help the decision-making process.

**7. *Developing integrity.*** Developing integrity is closely related to establishing identity and clarifying purposes. Our core values and beliefs provide the foundation for interpreting experience, guiding behavior, and maintaining self-respect. Developing integrity involves three sequential but overlapping stages: (1) humanizing values—shifting away from automatic application of uncompromising beliefs and using principled thinking in balancing one's own self-interest with the interests of one's fellow human beings, (2) personalizing values—consciously affirming core values and beliefs while respecting other points of view, and (3) developing congruence—matching personal values with socially responsible behavior.

Humanizing values involves a shift from a literal belief in the absoluteness of rules to a more relative view, where connections are made between rules and the purposes they are meant to serve. Thus, the rules for a ball game can change to accommodate limited numbers of players or other unusual conditions; rules concerning honesty, sex, or aggressiveness can vary with circumstances and situations, while overriding principles (such as the Golden Rule) become more important. This change has also been called "liberalization of the superego" or "enlightenment of conscience"—the process by which the rigid rules received unquestioned from parents are reformulated in the light of wider experience and made relevant to new conditions (Sanford, 1962, p. 278).

Students bring to college an array of assumptions about what is right and wrong, true and false, good and bad, important and unimportant. Younger students may have acquired these assumptions from parents, church, school, media, or other sources. When others' values are internalized, most behavior conforms even when the judge is absent. Disobedience produces either diffuse anxiety or specific fear of discovery and punishment. Most of the values are implicit and unconsciously held; therefore, they are hard to identify or explain. With humanizing of values, much of this baggage comes to light. The contents are examined. Many items are discarded on brief inspection, sometimes with later regret. Some items are tried and found unsuitable. A few are set aside because they still fit and can be incorporated into a new wardrobe.

Personalizing of values occurs as the new wardrobe is assembled. Ultimately, the items selected are those required by the characteristics of the wearer, by the work expected to be done, by the situations to be encountered, and by the persons who are seen as important. In short, individuals select guidelines to suit themselves and to suit the conditions of their lives. In time, the components of this wardrobe are actively embraced as part of the self and become standards by which to flexibly assess personal actions.

Personalizing of values leads to the development of congruence—the achievement of behavior consistent with the personalized values held. With this final stage, internal debate is minimized. Once the implications of a situation are understood and the consequences of alternatives seem clear, the response is highly determined; it is made with conviction, without debate or equivocation.

These, then, are the seven major developmental vectors for college students. Each has additional components, and more detailed study reveals further ramifications. This overview, however, suggests the major configurations.

## References

Atkinson, D. R., Morten, G., and Sue, D. W. *Counseling American Minorities: A Cross-Cultural Perspective.* (2nd ed.) Dubuque, Iowa: Brown, 1983.

Branch-Simpson, G. "A Study of the Patterns in the Development of Black Students at The Ohio State University." Unpublished doctoral dissertation, Ohio State University, Columbus, 1984.

Cass, V. C. "Homosexual Identity Formation: A Theoretical Model." *Journal of Homosexuality*, 1979, 4, 219–235.

Coleman, E. "Developmental Stages of the Coming Out Process." *Journal of Homosexuality*, 1981–1982, 7(2/3), 31–43.

Cross, K. P. *Beyond the Open Door: New Students to Higher Education.* San Francisco: Jossey-Bass, 1971.

Dank, B. M. "Coming Out in the Gay World." *Psychiatry*, 1971, 34, 180–197.

Helms, J. "An Overview of Black Racial Identity Theory." In J. Helms (ed.), *Black and White Racial Identity: Theory, Research, and Practice.* New York: Greenwood Press, 1990.

Ho, M. *Family Therapy with Ethnic Minorities.* Newbury Park, Calif.: Sage, 1987.

Johnson, M., and Lashley, K. "Influence of Native-Americans' Cultural Commitment on Preferences for Counselor Ethnicity." *Journal of Multicultural Counseling and Development*, 1988, 17, 115–122.

Josselson, R. *Finding Herself: Pathways to Identity Development in Women.* San Francisco: Jossey-Bass, 1987.

King, P. M. "Assessing Development from a Cognitive-Developmental Perspective." In D. G. Creamer and Associates, *College Student Development: Theory and Practice for the 1990's.* Alexandria, Va.: American College Personnel Association, 1990.

Kitto, H. D. F. *The Greeks.* Baltimore, Md.: Penguin Books, 1963.

Kohlberg, L. "A Cognitive-Developmental Approach to Moral Education." *Humanist*, 1972, 6, 13–16.

Kurfiss, J. "Sequentiality and Structure in a Cognitive Model of College Student Development." *Developmental Psychology*, 1975, 13(6), 565–571.

Martinez, C., Jr. "Mexican Americans." In L. Comas-Diaz and E. Griffith (eds.), *Clinical Guidelines in Cross-Cultural Mental Health.* New York: Wiley, 1988.

Minton, H. L., and McDonald, G. J. "Homosexual Identity Formation as a Developmental Process." *Journal of Homosexuality*, 1983–1984, 9(2/3), 91–104.

Murphy, G. *Human Potentialities.* New York: Basic Books, 1958.

Pascarella, E. T., and Terenzini, P. T. *How College Affects Students: Findings and Insights from Twenty Years of Research*. San Francisco: Jossey-Bass, 1991.

Perry, W. G. *Forms of Intellectual and Ethical Development in the College Years: A Scheme*. Troy, Mo.: Holt, Rinehart & Winston, 1970.

Plummer, K. *Sexual Stigma: An Interactionist Account*. London: Routledge, 1975.

Rest, J. *Development in Judging Moral Issues*. Minneapolis: University of Minnesota Press, 1979.

Sanford, N. *The American College*. New York: Wiley, 1962.

Sue, S., and Sue, D. "Chinese-American Personality and Mental Health." *Amerasia Journal*, 1971, 1, 36–49.

Thomas, D. "Light Breaks Where No Sun Shines." In D. Thomas, *Collected Poems*. New York: New Directions Books, 1939.

Troiden, R. R. "Becoming Homosexual: A Model of Gay Identity Acquisition." *Psychiatry*, 1979, 42, 362–373.

# CHAPTER 10
## EMERGING ADULTHOOD
### A THEORY OF DEVELOPMENT FROM THE LATE TEENS THROUGH THE TWENTIES

JEFFREY JENSEN ARNETT

Emerging adulthood is proposed as a new conception of development for the period from the late teens through the twenties, with a focus on ages 18–25. A theoretical background is presented. Then evidence is provided to support the idea that emerging adulthood is a distinct period demographically, subjectively, and in terms of identity explorations. How emerging adulthood differs from adolescence and young adulthood is explained. Finally, a cultural context for the idea of emerging adulthood is outlined, and it is specified that emerging adulthood exists only in cultures that allow young people a prolonged period of independent role exploration during the late teens and twenties.

When our mothers were our age, they were engaged. . . . They at least had some idea what they were going to do with their lives. . . . I, on the other hand, will have a dual degree in majors that are ambiguous at best and impractical at worst (English and political science), no ring on my finger and no idea who I am, much less what I want to do. . . . Under duress, I will admit that this is a pretty exciting time. Sometimes, when I look out across the wide expanse that is my future, I can see beyond the void. I realize that having nothing ahead to count on means I now have to count on myself; that having no direction means forging one of my own. (Kristen, age 22; Page, 1999, pp. 18, 20)

For most young people in industrialized countries, the years from the late teens through the twenties are years of profound change and importance. During this time, many young people obtain the level of education and training that will provide the foundation for their incomes and occupational achievements for the remainder of their adult work lives (Chisholm & Hurrelmann, 1995; William T. Grant Foundation Commission on Work, Family, and Citizenship, 1988). It is for many people a time of frequent change as various possibilities in love, work, and worldviews are explored (Erikson, 1968; Rindfuss, 1991). By the end of this period, the late twenties, most people have made life choices that have enduring ramifications. When adults later consider the most important events in their lives, they most often name events that took place during this period (Martin & Smyer, 1990).

Sweeping demographic shifts have taken place over the past half century that have made the late teens and early twenties not simply a brief period of transition into adult roles but a distinct period of the life course, characterized by change and exploration of possible life directions. As

Arnett, J. J. (2000). Emerging adulthood: A theory of development from the late teens through the twenties. *American Psychologist, 55*, 469–480.

recently as 1970, the median age of marriage in the United States was about 21 for women and 23 for men; by 1996, it had risen to 25 for women and 27 for men (U.S. Bureau of the Census, 1997). Age of first childbirth followed a similar pattern. Also, since midcentury the proportion of young Americans obtaining higher education after high school has risen steeply from 14% in 1940 to over 60% by the mid-1990s (Arnett & Taber, 1994; Bianchi & Spain, 1996). Similar changes have taken place in other industrialized countries (Chisholm & Hurrelmann, 1995; Noble, Cover, & Yanagishita, 1996).

These changes over the past half century have altered the nature of development in the late teens and early twenties for young people in industrialized societies. Because marriage and parenthood are delayed until the mid-twenties or late twenties for most people, it is no longer normative for the late teens and early twenties to be a time of entering and settling into long-term adult roles. On the contrary, these years are more typically a period of frequent change and exploration (Arnett, 1998; Rindfuss, 1991).

In this article, I propose a new theory of development from the late teens through the twenties, with a focus on ages 18–25. I argue that this period, *emerging adulthood*, is neither adolescence nor young adulthood but is theoretically and empirically distinct from them both. Emerging adulthood is distinguished by relative independence from social roles and from normative expectations. Having left the dependency of childhood and adolescence, and having not yet entered the enduring responsibilities that are normative in adulthood, emerging adults often explore a variety of possible life directions in love, work, and worldviews. Emerging adulthood is a time of life when many different directions remain possible, when little about the future has been decided for certain, when the scope of independent exploration of life's possibilities is greater for most people than it will be at any other period of the life course.

For most people, the late teens through the midtwenties are the most *volitional* years of life. However, cultural influences structure and sometimes limit the extent to which emerging adults are able to use their late teens and twenties in this way, and not all young people in this age period are able to use these years for independent exploration. Like adolescence, emerging adulthood is a period of the life course that is culturally constructed, not universal and immutable.

I lay out the theoretical background first and then present evidence to illustrate how emerging adulthood is a distinct period demographically, subjectively, and in terms of identity explorations. Next, I explain how emerging adulthood can be distinguished from adolescence and young adulthood. Finally, I discuss the economic and cultural conditions under which emerging adulthood is most likely to exist as a distinct period of the life course.

## The Theoretical Background

There have been a number of important theoretical contributions to the understanding of development from the late teens through the twenties. One early contribution was made by Erik Erikson (1950, 1968). Erikson rarely discussed specific ages in his writings, and in his theory of human development across the life course he did not include a separate stage that could be considered analogous to emerging adulthood as proposed here. Rather, he wrote of development in adolescence and of development in young adulthood. However, he also commented on the *prolonged adolescence* typical of industrialized societies and on the *psychosocial moratorium* granted to young people in such societies "during which the young adult through free role experimentation may find a niche in some section of his society" (Erikson, 1968, p. 156). Thus, Erikson seems to have distinguished—without naming—a period that is in some ways adolescence and in some ways young adulthood yet not strictly either one, a period in which adult commitments and responsibilities are delayed while the role experimentation that began in adolescence continues and in fact intensifies.

Another theoretical contribution can be found in the work of Daniel Levinson (1978). Levinson interviewed men at midlife, but he had them describe their earlier years as well, and on the basis of their accounts he developed a theory that included development in the late teens and the twenties. He called ages 17–33 the *novice phase* of development and argued that the overriding task of this phase is to move into the adult world and build a stable life structure. During this process, according to Levinson, the young person experiences a considerable amount of change and instability while sorting through various possibilities in love and work in the course of establishing a life structure. Levinson acknowledged that his conception of the novice phase was similar to Erikson's ideas about the role experimentation that takes place during the psychosocial moratorium (Levinson, 1978, pp. 322–323).

Perhaps the best-known theory of development in the late teens and the twenties is Kenneth Keniston's theory of youth. Like Erikson and Levinson, Keniston (1971) conceptualized youth as a period of continued role experimentation between adolescence and young adulthood. However, Keniston wrote at a time when American society and some Western European societies were convulsed with highly visible youth movements protesting the involvement of the United States in the Vietnam War (among other things). His description of youth as a time of "tension between self and society" (Keniston, 1971, p. 8) and "refusal of socialization" (p. 9) reflects that historical moment rather than any enduring characteristics of the period.

More importantly, Keniston's (1971) application of the term *youth* to this period is problematic. *Youth* has a long history in the English language as a term for childhood generally and for what later became called adolescence (e.g., Ben-Amos, 1994), and it continues to be used popularly and by many social scientists for these purposes (as reflected in terms such as *youth organizations*). Keniston's choice of the ambiguous and confusing term *youth* may explain in part why the idea of the late teens and twenties as a separate period of life never became widely accepted by developmental scientists after his articulation of it. However, as I argue in the following sections, there is good empirical support for conceiving this period—proposed here as emerging adulthood—as a distinct period of life.

## Emerging Adulthood Is Distinct Demographically

Although Erikson (1968), Levinson (1978), and Keniston (1971) all contributed to the theoretical groundwork for emerging adulthood, the nature of the period has changed considerably since the time of their writings more than 20 years ago. As noted at the outset of this article, demographic changes in the timing of marriage and parenthood in recent decades have made a period of emerging adulthood typical for young people in industrialized societies. Postponing these transitions until at least the late twenties leaves the late teens and early twenties available for exploring various possible life directions.

An important demographic characteristic of emerging adulthood is that there is a great deal of demographic variability, reflecting the wide scope of individual volition during these years. Emerging adulthood is the only period of life in which nothing is normative demographically (Rindfuss, 1991; Wallace, 1995). During adolescence, up to age 18, a variety of key demographic areas show little variation. Over 95% of American adolescents aged 12–17 live at home with one or more parents, over 98% are unmarried, fewer than 10% have had a child, and over 95% are enrolled in school (U.S. Bureau of the Census, 1997). By age 30, new demographic norms have been established: About 75% of 30-year-olds have married, about 75% have become parents, and fewer than 10% are enrolled in school (U.S. Bureau of the Census, 1997).

In between these two periods, however, and especially from ages 18 to 25, a person's demographic status in these areas is very difficult to predict on the basis of age alone. The demographic diversity and unpredictability of emerging adulthood is a reflection of the experimental and exploratory quality of the period. Talcott Parsons (1942) called adolescence the *roleless role*, but this term applies much better to emerging adulthood. Emerging adults tend to have a wider scope of possible activities than persons in other age periods because they are less likely to be constrained by role requirements, and this makes their demographic status unpredictable.

One demographic area that especially reflects the exploratory quality of emerging adulthood is residential status. Most young Americans leave home by age 18 or 19 (Goldscheider & Goldscheider, 1994). In the years that follow, emerging adults' living situations are diverse. About one third of emerging adults go off to college after high school and spend the next several years in some combination of independent living and continued reliance on adults, for example, in a college dormitory or a fraternity or sorority house (Goldscheider & Goldscheider, 1994). For them, this is a period of semiautonomy (Goldscheider & Davanzo, 1986) as they take on some of the responsibilities of independent living but leave others to their parents, college authorities, or other adults. About 40% move out of their parental home not for college but for independent living and full-time work (Goldscheider & Goldscheider, 1994). About two thirds experience a period of cohabitation with a romantic partner (Michael, Gagnon, Laumann, & Kolata, 1995). Some remain at home while attending college or working or some combination of the two. Only about 10% of men and 30% of women remain at home until marriage (Goldscheider & Goldscheider, 1994).

Amidst this diversity, perhaps the unifying feature of the residential status of emerging adults is the instability of it. Emerging adults have the highest rates of residential change of any age group. Using data from several cohorts of the National Longitudinal Study, Rindfuss (1991) described how rates of residential mobility peak in the midtwenties (see Figure 1). For about 40% of the current generation of emerging adults, residential changes include moving back into their parents' home and then out again at least once in the course of their late teens and twenties (Goldscheider & Goldscheider, 1994). Frequent residential changes during emerging adulthood reflect its exploratory quality, because these changes often take place at the end of one period of exploration or the beginning of another (e.g., the end of a period of cohabitation, entering or leaving college, or the beginning of a new job in a new place).

School attendance is another area in which there is substantial change and diversity among emerging adults. The proportion of American emerging adults who enter higher education in the year following high school is at its highest level ever, over 60% (Bianchi & Spain, 1996). However, this figure masks the expanding diversity in the years that follow. Only 32% of young people ages 25–29 have completed four years or more of college (U.S. Bureau of the Census, 1997). For emerging

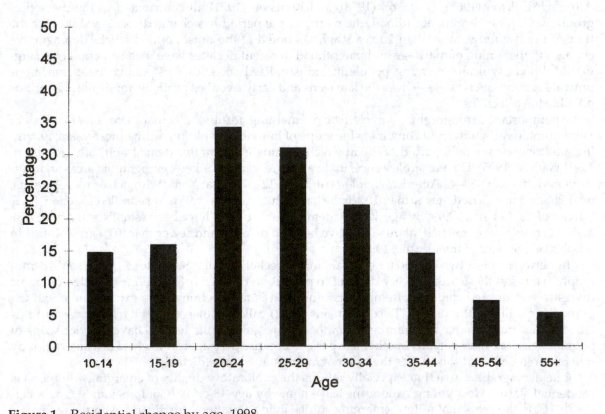

**Figure 1**    Residential change by age, 1998.

*Note.* Data are from "Geographic Mobility: March 1997 to March 1998," by the U.S. Bureau of the Census, 2000, *Current Population Reports* (Series P-20, No. 520), Washington, DC: U.S. Government Printing Office.

adults, college education is often pursued in a nonlinear way, frequently combined with work, and punctuated by periods of nonattendance. For those who do eventually graduate with a four-year degree, college is increasingly likely to be followed by graduate school. About one third of those who graduate with a bachelor's degree are enrolled in postgraduate education the following year (Mogelonsky, 1996). In European countries too, the length of education has become extended in recent decades (Chisholm & Hurrelmann, 1995).

Overall, then, the years of emerging adulthood are characterized by a high degree of demographic diversity and instability, reflecting the emphasis on change and exploration. It is only in the transition from emerging adulthood to young adulthood in the late twenties that the diversity narrows and the instability eases, as young people make more enduring choices in love and work. Rindfuss (1991) called the period from ages 18 to 30 "demographically dense" (p. 496) because of the many demographic transitions that take place during that time, especially in the late twenties.

## Emerging Adulthood Is Distinct Subjectively

Emerging adults do not see themselves as adolescents, but many of them also do not see themselves entirely as adults. Figure 2 shows that when they are asked whether they feel they have reached adulthood, the majority of Americans in their late teens and early twenties answer neither *no* nor *yes* but the ambiguous *in some respects yes, in some respects no* (Arnett, in press). This reflects a subjective sense on the part of most emerging adults that they have left adolescence but have not yet completely entered young adulthood (Arnett, 1994a, 1997, 1998). They have no name for the period they are in—because the society they live in has no name for it—so they regard themselves as being neither adolescents nor adults, in between the two but not really one or the other. As Figure 2 shows, only in their late twenties and early thirties do a clear majority of people indicate that they feel they have reached adulthood. However, age is only the roughest marker of the subjective transition from emerging adulthood to young adulthood. As illustrated in Figure 2, even in their late twenties and early thirties, nearly one third did not feel their transition to adulthood was complete.

One might expect emerging adults' subjective sense of ambiguity in attaining full adulthood to arise from the demographic diversity and instability described above. Perhaps it is difficult for young people to feel they have reached adulthood before they have established a stable residence, finished school, settled into a career, and married (or at least committed themselves to a long-term love relationship). However, perhaps surprisingly, the research evidence indicates strongly that these demographic transitions have little to do with emerging adults' conceptions of what it means

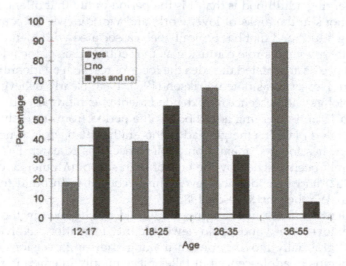

**Figure 2**  Subjective conceptions of adult status in response to the question, do you feel that you have reached adulthood?

*Note. N* = 519. Data are from Arnett (in press).

to reach adulthood. Consistently, in a variety of studies with young people in their teens and twenties, demographic transitions such as finishing education, settling into a career, marriage, and parenthood rank at the *bottom* in importance among possible criteria considered necessary for the attainment of adulthood (Arnett, 1997, 1998, in press; Greene, Wheatley, & Aldava, 1992; Scheer, Unger, & Brown, 1994).

The characteristics that matter most to emerging adults in their subjective sense of attaining adulthood are not demographic transitions but individualistic *qualities of character* (Arnett, 1998). Specifically, the two top criteria for the transition to adulthood in a variety of studies have been *accepting responsibility for one's self* and *making independent decisions* (Arnett, 1997, 1998; Greene et al., 1992; Scheer et al., 1994). A third criterion, also individualistic but more tangible, *becoming financially independent*, also ranks consistently near the top.

The prominence of these criteria for the transition to adulthood reflects an emphasis in emerging adulthood on becoming a self-sufficient person (Arnett, 1998). During these years, the character qualities most important to becoming successfully self-sufficient—accepting responsibility for one's self and making independent decisions—are being developed. Financial independence is also crucial to self-sufficiency, so it is also important in emerging adults' conceptions of what is necessary to become an adult. Only after these character qualities have reached fruition and financial independence has been attained do emerging adults experience a subjective change in their developmental status, as they move out of emerging adulthood and into young adulthood. For most young people in American society, this occurs some time during the twenties and is usually accomplished by the late twenties (Arnett, in press).

Although emerging adults do not view demographic transitions as necessary for attaining adulthood, it should be noted that parenthood in particular is often sufficient for marking a subjective sense of adult status. Parenthood ranks low in young people's views of the essential criteria for adulthood for people in general, but those who have had a child tend to view becoming a parent as the most important marker of the transition to adulthood for themselves (Arnett, 1998). The explorations that occur in emerging adulthood become sharply restricted with parenthood, because it requires taking on the responsibilities of protecting and providing for a young child. With parenthood, the focus of concern shifts inexorably from responsibility for one's self to responsibility for others.

## Emerging Adulthood Is Distinct for Identity Explorations

A key feature of emerging adulthood is that it is the period of life that offers the most opportunity for identity explorations in the areas of love, work, and worldviews. Of course, it is adolescence rather than emerging adulthood that has typically been associated with identity formation. Erikson (1950) designated identity versus role confusion as the central crisis of the adolescent stage of life, and in the decades since he articulated this idea the focus of research on identity has been on adolescence (Adams, 1999). However, as noted, Erikson (1950, 1968) clearly believed that industrialized societies allow a prolonged adolescence for extended identity explorations. If adolescence is the period from ages 10 to 18 and emerging adulthood is the period from (roughly) ages 18 to 25, most identity exploration takes place in emerging adulthood rather than adolescence. Although research on identity formation has focused mainly on adolescence, this research has shown that identity achievement has rarely been reached by the end of high school (Montemayor, Brown, & Adams, 1985; Waterman, 1982) and that identity development continues through the late teens and the twenties (Valde, 1996; Whitbourne & Tesch, 1985).

The focus on identity issues in emerging adulthood can be seen in the three main areas of identity exploration: love, work, and worldviews. Identity formation involves trying out various life possibilities and gradually moving toward making enduring decisions. In all three of these areas, this process begins in adolescence but takes place mainly in emerging adulthood. With regard to love, American adolescents typically begin dating around ages 12 to 14 (Padgham & Blyth, 1991). However, because any serious consideration of marriage is a decade or more away for most 12- to 14-year-olds, young people view the early years of dating as primarily recreational

(Roscoe, Dian, & Brooks, 1987). For adolescents, dating provides companionship, the first experiences of romantic love, and sexual experimentation; however, their dating relationships typically last only a few weeks or months (Feiring, 1996), and few adolescents expect to remain with their "high school sweetheart" much beyond high school.

In emerging adulthood, explorations in love become more intimate and serious. Dating in adolescence often takes place in groups, as adolescents pursue shared recreation such as parties, dances, and hanging out (Padgham & Blyth, 1991). By emerging adulthood, dating is more likely to take place in couples, and the focus is less on recreation and more on exploring the potential for emotional and physical intimacy. Romantic relationships in emerging adulthood last longer than in adolescence, are more likely to include sexual intercourse, and may include cohabitation (Michael et al., 1995). Thus, in adolescence, explorations in love tend to be tentative and transient; the implicit question is, Who would I enjoy being with, here and now? In contrast, explorations in love in emerging adulthood tend to involve a deeper level of intimacy, and the implicit question is more identity focused: Given the kind of person I am, what kind of person do I wish to have as a partner through life?

With regard to work, a similar contrast exists between the transient and tentative explorations of adolescence and the more serious and focused explorations of emerging adulthood. In the United States, the majority of high school students are employed part-time (Barling & Kelloway, 1999). Although adolescents often report that their work experiences enhance their abilities in areas such as managing their time and money (Mortimer, Harley, & Aronson, 1999), for the most part their jobs do not provide them with knowledge or experience that will be related to their future occupations (Greenberger & Steinberg, 1986; Steinberg & Cauffman, 1995). Most adolescents are employed in service jobs—at restaurants, retail stores, and so forth—in which the cognitive challenges are minimal and the skills learned are few. Adolescents tend to view their jobs not as occupational preparation but as a way to obtain the money that will support an active leisure life—paying for compact discs, concerts, restaurant meals, clothes, cars, travel, and so forth (Bachman & Schulenberg, 1993; Shanahan, Elder, Burchinal, & Conger, 1996; Steinberg & Cauffman, 1995).

In emerging adulthood, work experiences become more focused on preparation for adult work roles. Emerging adults begin to consider how their work experiences will lay the groundwork for the jobs they may have through adulthood. In exploring various work possibilities, they explore identity issues as well: What kind of work am I good at? What kind of work would I find satisfying for the long term? What are my chances of getting a job in the field that seems to suit me best?

Emerging adults' educational choices and experiences explore similar questions. In their educational paths, they try out various possibilities that would prepare them for different kinds of future work. College students often change majors more than once, especially in their first two years, as they try on possible occupational futures, discard them, and pursue others. With graduate school becoming an increasingly common choice after an undergraduate degree is obtained, emerging adults' educational explorations often continue through their early twenties and midtwenties. Graduate school allows emerging adults to switch directions again from the path of occupational preparation they had chosen as undergraduates.

For both love and work, the goals of identity explorations in emerging adulthood are not limited to direct preparation for adult roles. On the contrary, the explorations of emerging adulthood are in part explorations for their own sake, part of obtaining a broad range of life experiences before taking on enduring—and limiting—adult responsibilities. The absence of enduring role commitments in emerging adulthood makes possible a degree of experimentation and exploration that is not likely to be possible during the thirties and beyond. For people who wish to have a variety of romantic and sexual experiences, emerging adulthood is the time for it, because parental surveillance has diminished and there is as yet little normative pressure to enter marriage. Similarly, emerging adulthood is the time for trying out unusual work and educational possibilities. For this reason, short-term volunteer jobs in programs such as Americorps and the Peace Corps are more popular with emerging adults than with persons in any other age period. Emerging adults may also travel to a different part of the country or the world on their own for a limited period, often in the context of a limited-term work or educational experience. This too can be part of their identity explorations, part of expanding their range of personal experiences prior to making the more enduring choices of adulthood.

With regard to worldviews, the work of William Perry (1970/1999) has shown that changes in worldviews are often a central part of cognitive development during emerging adulthood. According to Perry, emerging adults often enter college with a worldview they have learned in the course of childhood and adolescence. However, a college education leads to exposure to a variety of different worldviews, and in the course of this exposure college students often find themselves questioning the worldviews they brought in. Over the course of their college years, emerging adults examine and consider a variety of possible worldviews. By the end of their college years they have often committed themselves to a worldview different from the one they brought in, while remaining open to further modifications of it.

Most of the research on changes in worldviews during emerging adulthood has involved college students and graduate students, and there is evidence that higher education promotes explorations and reconsiderations of worldviews (Pascarella & Terenzini, 1991). However, it is notable that emerging adults who do not attend college are as likely as college students to indicate that deciding on their own beliefs and values is an essential criterion for attaining adult status (Arnett, 1997). Also, research on emerging adults' religious beliefs suggests that regardless of educational background, they consider it important during emerging adulthood to reexamine the beliefs they have learned in their families and to form a set of beliefs that is the product of their own independent reflections (Arnett & Jensen, 1999; Hoge, Johnson, & Luidens, 1993).

Although the identity explorations of emerging adulthood make it an especially full and intense time of life for many people, these explorations are not always experienced as enjoyable. Explorations in love sometimes result in disappointment, disillusionment, or rejection. Explorations in work sometimes result in a failure to achieve the occupation most desired or in an inability to find work that is satisfying and fulfilling. Explorations in worldviews sometimes lead to rejection of childhood beliefs without the construction of anything more compelling in their place (Arnett & Jensen, 1999). Also, to a large extent, emerging adults pursue their identity explorations on their own, without the daily companionship of either their family of origin or their family to be (Jonsson, 1994; Morch, 1995). Young Americans ages 19–29 spend more of their leisure time alone than any persons except the elderly and spend more of their time in productive activities (school and work) alone than any other age group under 40 (Larson, 1990). Many of them see the condition of the world as grim and are pessimistic about the future of their society (Arnett, 2000b). Nevertheless, for themselves personally, emerging adults are highly optimistic about ultimately achieving their goals. In one national poll of 18- to 24-year-olds in the United States (Hornblower, 1997), nearly all—96%—agreed with the statement, "I am very sure that someday I will get to where I want to be in life."

## Other Notable Findings on Emerging Adulthood

The three areas outlined above—demographics, subjective perceptions, and identity explorations—provide the most abundant information on the distinctiveness of emerging adulthood. However, evidence is available from other areas that suggests possible lines of inquiry for future research on emerging adulthood. One of these areas is risk behavior. Although there is a voluminous literature on adolescent risk behavior and relatively little research on risk behavior in emerging adulthood (Jessor, Donovan, & Costa, 1991), the prevalence of several types of risk behavior peaks not during adolescence but during emerging adulthood (ages 18–25). These risk behaviors include unprotected sex, most types of substance use, and risky driving behaviors such as driving at high speeds or while intoxicated (Arnett, 1992; Bachman, Johnston, O'Malley, & Schulenberg, 1996). Figure 3 shows an example for binge drinking.

What is it about emerging adulthood that lends itself to such high rates of risk behavior? To some degree, emerging adults' risk behaviors can be understood as part of their identity explorations, that is, as one reflection of the desire to obtain a wide range of experiences before settling down into the roles and responsibilities of adult life. One of the motivations consistently found to be related to participation in a variety of types of risk behavior is sensation seeking, which is the desire

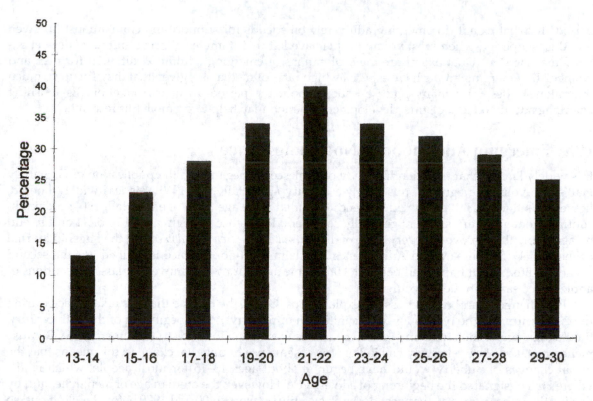

**Figure 3**   Rates of binge drinking (five or more alcoholic drinks in a row) in the past two weeks at various ages.

*Note.* Data are from "Transitions in Drug Use During Late Adolescence and Young Adulthood," by J. G. Bachman, L. D. Johnston, P. O'Malley, and J. Schulenberg, in *Transitions Through Adolescence: Interpersonal Domains and Context* (p. 118), by J. A. Graber, J. Brooks-Gunn, and A. C. Petersen (Eds.), 1996, Mahwah, NJ: Erlbaum. Copyright 1996 by Erlbaum. Used with permission. Data also available at http://www.monitoringthefuture.org/data/99data/pr99t1c.pdf.

for novel and intense experiences (Arnett, 1994b). Emerging adults can pursue novel and intense experiences more freely than adolescents because they are less likely to be monitored by parents and can pursue them more freely than adults because they are less constrained by roles. After marriage, adults are constrained from taking part in risk behavior by the responsibilities of the marriage role, and once they have a child, they are constrained by the responsibilities of the parenting role. In one example of this, Bachman et al. (1996) used longitudinal data to show how substance use rises to a peak in the early twenties during the role hiatus of emerging adulthood, declines steeply and sharply following marriage, and declines further following the entry to parenthood. The responsibilities of these roles lead to lower rates of risk behavior as emerging adulthood is succeeded by young adulthood.

Research on family relationships among emerging adults has also been conducted. For American emerging adults in their early twenties, physical proximity to parents has been found to be *inversely* related to the quality of relationships with them. Emerging adults with the most frequent contact with parents, especially emerging adults still living at home, tend to be the least close to their parents and to have the poorest psychological adjustment (Dubas & Petersen, 1996; O'Connor, Allen, Bell, & Hauser, 1996). In European studies, emerging adults who remain at home tend to be happier with their living situations than those who have left home; they continue to rely on their parents as a source of support and comfort, but they also tend to have a great deal of autonomy within their parents' households (Chisholm & Hurrelmann, 1995). Thus, for emerging adults in both the United States and Europe, *autonomy* and *relatedness* are complementary rather than opposing dimensions of their relationships with their parents (O'Connor et al., 1996).

These findings provide a foundation for research into development during emerging adulthood. Of course, much more work remains to be done on virtually every aspect of development during this period. To what extent do emerging adults rely on friends for support and companionship, given that this is a period when most young people have left their families of origin but have not yet entered marriage? To what extent are the explorations of emerging adulthood different for men and women? Do emerging adults have especially high rates of media use, given that they spend so much time alone? These and many other questions about the period await investigation. Establishing emerging adulthood as a distinct developmental period may help to promote this research.

## Why Emerging Adulthood Is Not Adolescence

It is widely known that the scientific study of adolescence began with the publication of G. Stanley Hall's two-volume magnum opus nearly a century ago (Hall, 1904). What is less widely known, however, is that in Hall's view adolescence extended from age 14 to age 24 (Hall, 1904, p. xix). In contrast, contemporary scholars generally consider adolescence to begin at age 10 or 11 and to end by age 18 or 19. The cover of every issue of the *Journal of Research on Adolescence*, the flagship journal of the Society for Research on Adolescence, proclaims that adolescence is defined as "the second decade of life." What happened between Hall's time and our own to move scholars' conceptions of adolescence earlier in the life course?

Two changes stand out as possible explanations. One is the decline that has taken place during the 20th century in the typical age of the initiation of puberty. At the beginning of the 20th century, the median age of menarche in Western countries was about 15 (Eveleth & Tanner, 1976). Because menarche takes place relatively late in the typical sequence of pubertal changes, this means that the initial changes of puberty would have begun at about ages 13–15 for most people, which is just where Hall designated the beginning of adolescence. However, the median age of menarche (and by implication other pubertal changes) declined steadily between 1900 and 1970 before leveling out, so that now the typical age of menarche in the United States is 12.5 (Brooks-Gunn & Paikoff, 1997). The initial changes of puberty usually begin about 2 years earlier, thus the designation of adolescence as beginning with the entry into the second decade of life.

As for the age when adolescence ends, the change in this age may have been inspired not by a biological change but by a social change: the growth of high school attendance that made high school a normative experience for adolescents in the United States. In 1900, only 10% of persons ages 14–17 were enrolled in high school. However, this proportion rose steeply and steadily over the course of the 20th century to reach 95% by 1985 (Arnett & Taber, 1994). This makes it easy to understand why Hall would not have chosen age 18 as the end of adolescence, because for most adolescents of his time no significant transition took place at that age. Education ended earlier, work began earlier, and leaving home took place later. Marriage and parenthood did not take place for most people until their early twenties or midtwenties (Arnett & Taber, 1994), which may have been why Hall designated age 24 as the end of adolescence. (Hall himself did not explain why he chose this age.)

In our time, it makes sense to define adolescence as ages 10–18. Young people in this age group have in common that they live with their parents, are experiencing the physical changes of puberty, are attending secondary school, and are part of a school-based peer culture. None of this remains normative after age 18, which is why it is not adequate simply to call the late teens and early twenties *late adolescence*. Age 18 also marks a variety of legal transitions, such as being allowed to vote and sign legal documents.

Although some scholars have suggested that the late teens and early twenties should be considered late adolescence (e.g., Elliott & Feldman, 1990), for the most part scholars on adolescence focus on ages 10–18 as the years of adolescent development. Studies published in the major journals on adolescence rarely include samples with ages higher than 18. For example, in 1997, 90% of the studies published in the *Journal of Research on Adolescence* and the *Journal of Youth & Adolescence* were on samples of high school age or younger. College students have been the focus of many research studies, but most often as "adults" in social psychology studies. Sociologists have studied the late teens and the twenties for patterns of demographic events viewed as part of the transition to adulthood (e.g., Hogan & Astone, 1986; Rindfuss, 1991). However, few studies have recognized the late teens through the twenties as a distinct developmental period.

## Why the Forgotten Half Remains Forgotten

In 1987, a distinguished panel of scholars and public policy officials was assembled by the William T. Grant Foundation and asked to address the life situations of young people who do not attend college after high school, especially with respect to their economic prospects. They produced an influential and widely read report entitled *The Forgotten Half: Non-College-Bound Youth in America* (William T. Grant Foundation Commission on Work, Family, and Citizenship, 1988), which contained an analysis of the circumstances of the "forgotten half" and a set of policy suggestions for promoting a successful transition from high school to work.

Over a decade later, the forgotten half remains forgotten by scholars, in the sense that studies of young people who do not attend college in the years following high school remain rare. Why did the Grant commission's widely acclaimed report not inspire more enduring scholarly attention to young people not attending college in this age period? One reason is practical. Studies of college students are ubiquitous because college students are so easy to find—most scholars who teach at colleges or universities have ready access to them. Studying young people who are not in college is more difficult because they are not readily accessible in any institutional setting. Other ways of obtaining research participants in this age period must be used, such as contacting community organizations or taking out newspaper ads, and these samples often have the liability of being nonrepresentative. The same conditions apply to research on college students after they leave college. Few studies exist of young people in their midtwenties to late twenties, in part because they are not available in any institutional setting. Notable exceptions to this rule include some excellent longitudinal studies (the National Longitudinal Studies, e.g., Rindfuss, 1991; the Monitoring the Future studies, e.g., Bachman et al., 1996; O'Connor et al., 1996; Offer & Offer, 1975).

However, the dearth of studies on young people in their late teens and twenties is not due only to the difficulty of finding samples in this age group. It also arises from the lack of a clear developmental conception of this age group. Scholars have no clearly articulated way of thinking about development from the late teens through the twenties, no paradigm for this age period, so they may not think about young people at these ages as a focus for developmental research. Emerging adulthood is offered as a new paradigm, a new way of thinking about development from the late teens through the twenties, especially ages 18–25, partly in the hope that a definite conception of this period will lead to an increase in scholarly attention to it.

## Why Emerging Adulthood Is Not Young Adulthood

But (some might object) is there not already a paradigm for the years of the late teens and the twenties? Is that not what young adulthood is? The answer is *no*. There are a number of reasons why *young adulthood* is unsatisfactory as a designation for this developmental period.

One reason is that the use of *young adulthood* implies that adulthood has been reached at this point. As we have seen, most young people in this age period would disagree that they have reached adulthood. They see themselves as gradually making their way into adulthood, so *emerging adulthood* seems a better term for their subjective experience. More generally, the term *emerging* captures the dynamic, changeable, fluid quality of the period.

Also, if ages 18–25 are young adulthood, what would that make the thirties? Young adulthood is a term better applied to the thirties, which are still young but are definitely adult in a way that the years 18–25 are not. It makes little sense to lump the late teens, twenties, and thirties together and call the entire period *young adulthood*. The period from ages 18 to 25 could hardly be more distinct from the thirties. The majority of young people ages 18–25 do not believe they have reached full adulthood, whereas the majority of people in their thirties believe that they have (Arnett, in press). The majority of people ages 18–25 are still in the process of obtaining education and training for a long-term adult occupation, whereas the majority of people in their thirties have settled into a more stable occupational path. The majority of people ages 18–25 are unmarried, whereas the majority of people in their thirties are married. The majority of people ages 18–25 are childless, whereas the majority of people in their thirties have had at least one child. The list could go on. The point should be clear. Emerging adulthood and young adulthood should be distinguished as separate developmental periods.

It should be emphasized, however, that age is only a rough indicator of the transition from emerging adulthood to young adulthood. Eighteen is a good age marker for the end of adolescence and the beginning of emerging adulthood, because it is the age at which most young people finish secondary school, leave their parents' home, and reach the legal age of adult status in a variety of respects. However, the transition from emerging adulthood to young adulthood is much less definite with respect to age. There are 19-year-olds who have reached adulthood—demographically, subjectively, and in terms of identity formation—and 29-year-olds who have not. Nevertheless, for most people, the transition from emerging adulthood to young adulthood intensifies in the late twenties and is reached by age 30 in all of these respects.

Emerging adulthood differs both from adolescence and from young adulthood in that it is, to some extent, defined by its heterogeneity. As noted, in emerging adulthood, there is little that is normative. Emerging adulthood is very much a transitional period leading to adulthood, and different emerging adults reach adulthood at different points. Also, the possibility of devoting the late teens and early twenties to explorations of various kinds is not equally available to all young people, and in any case, people vary in the degree of exploration they choose to pursue.

The heterogeneity of emerging adulthood represents both a warning and an opportunity for those who wish to study this age period. The warning is to be cautious in making sweeping statements about emerging adults. Almost always, such statements need to be qualified by mentioning the heterogeneity of emerging adulthood. The opportunity is that this heterogeneity makes emerging adulthood an especially rich, complex, dynamic period of life to study.

## Emerging Adulthood Across Cultures

Thus far, the focus of this article has been on emerging adulthood among young people in the West, especially in the United States. Is emerging adulthood a period of life that is restricted to certain cultures and certain times? The answer to this question appears to be *yes.* For example, Schlegel and Barry (1991), in their comprehensive integration of information on adolescence in 186 traditional non-Western cultures, concluded that adolescence as a life stage is virtually universal, but that a further period between adolescence and adulthood (*youth,* in the terminology they used) existed in only 20% of the cultures they studied. In the cultures in their sample, adulthood was typically signified by entry into marriage, and marriage usually took place at about ages 16 to 18 for girls and at about ages 18 to 20 for boys. This early timing of marriage allowed for a period of adolescence but not for a period of emerging adulthood.

Emerging adulthood, then, is not a universal period but a period that exists only in cultures that postpone the entry into adult roles and responsibilities until well past the late teens. Thus, emerging adulthood would be most likely to be found in countries that are highly industrialized or postindustrial. Such countries require a high level of education and training for entry into the information-based professions that are the most prestigious and lucrative, so many of their young people remain in school into their early twenties and midtwenties. Marriage and parenthood are typically postponed until well after schooling has ended, which allows for a period of exploration of various relationships before marriage and for exploration of various jobs before taking on the responsibility of supporting a child financially. Table 1 shows the median ages of marriage in a range of highly industrialized countries, contrasted with the median ages of marriage in selected developing countries.

Although median marriage ages are typically calculated on a countrywide basis, it should be noted that emerging adulthood is best understood as a characteristic of cultures rather than countries. Within some highly industrialized countries, members of minority cultures may have cultural practices that lead to a shortened period of emerging adulthood or no emerging adulthood at all. For example, in the United States, members of the Mormon church tend to have a shortened and highly structured emerging adulthood. Because of cultural beliefs prohibiting premarital sex and emphasizing the desirability of large families, considerable social pressure is placed on young Mormons to marry early and begin having children. Consequently, the median ages of marriage and

## TABLE 1

### Median Marriage Age of Women in Selected Countries

| Industrialized Countries | Age | Developing Countries | Age |
| --- | --- | --- | --- |
| United States | 25.2 | Egypt | 21.9 |
| Canada | 26.0 | Morocco | 22.3 |
| Germany | 26.2 | Ghana | 21.1 |
| France | 26.1 | Nigeria | 18.7 |
| Italy | 25.8 | India | 20.0 |
| Japan | 26.9 | Indonesia | 21.1 |
| Australia | 26.0 | Brazil | 22.6 |

*Note.* Data are from *The World's Youth,* by J. Noble, J. Cover, and M. Yanagishita, 1996, Washington, DC: Population Reference Bureau. Copyright 1996 by the Population Reference Bureau. Reprinted with permission.

first childbirth are much lower among Mormons than in the American population as a whole (Heaton, 1992), and young Mormons are likely to have a much briefer period of exploration before taking on adult roles.

Limitations in educational and occupational opportunities also influence the extent to which young people can experience their late teens and twenties as a volitional period. The young woman who has a child outside of marriage at age 16 and spends her late teens and early twenties alternating between welfare and low-paying jobs has little chance for exploration of possible life directions, nor does the young man who drops out of school and spends most of his late teens and early twenties unemployed and looking unsuccessfully for a job (Cote & Allahar, 1996). Because opportunities tend to be less widely available in minority cultures than in the majority culture in most industrialized countries, members of minority groups may be less likely to experience ages 18–25 as a period of independent exploration of possible life directions (Morch, 1995). However, social class may be more important than ethnicity, with young people in the middle class or above having more opportunities for the explorations of emerging adulthood than young people who are working class or below. Alternatively, it may be that explorations are not fewer in the working class but different, with more emphasis on work explorations and less emphasis on education. These are possibilities to be investigated.

In economically developing countries, there tends to be a distinct cultural split between urban and rural areas. Young people in urban areas of countries such as China and India are more likely to experience emerging adulthood, because they marry later, have children later, obtain more education, and have a greater range of occupational and recreational opportunities than young people in rural areas. In contrast, young people in rural areas of developing countries often receive minimal schooling, marry early, and have little choice of occupations except agricultural work. Thus in developing countries emerging adulthood is often experienced in urban areas but rarely in rural areas.

However, it should also be noted that emerging adulthood is likely to become more pervasive worldwide in the decades to come, with the increasing globalization of the world economy. Between 1980 and 1995, the proportion of young people in developing countries who attended secondary school rose sharply, and the median ages of marriage and first childbirth rose in these countries as well (Noble et al., 1996). As developing countries are becoming more integrated into a global economy, there is an increasing number of higher-paying jobs in these countries, jobs that require young people to obtain higher education. At the same time, as technology becomes increasingly available in these countries, particularly in agriculture, the labor of young people is becoming less and less necessary for family survival, making it possible for many of them to attend school instead.

These changes open up the possibility for the spread of emerging adulthood in developing countries. Economic development makes possible a period of the independent role exploration that is at the heart of emerging adulthood. As societies become more affluent, they are more likely to grant young people the opportunity for the extended moratorium of emerging adulthood, because they have no urgent need for young people's labor. Similarly, economic development is usually accompanied by increased life expectancy, and devoting years to the explorations of emerging adulthood becomes more feasible and attractive when people can expect to live to be at least 70 or 80 rather than 40 or 50. Thus it seems possible that by the end of the 21st century emerging adulthood will be a normative period for young people worldwide, although it is likely to vary in length and content both within and between countries (Arnett, 2000a). The growth and variability of emerging adulthood in countries and cultures around the world would make an important and fascinating topic for a nascent scholarly field of emerging adulthood.

## Conclusion

Emerging adulthood has become a distinct period of the life course for young people in industrialized societies. It is a period characterized by change and exploration for most people, as they examine the life possibilities open to them and gradually arrive at more enduring choices in love, work, and worldviews. Not all young people experience their late teens and twenties as years of change and exploration, even in industrialized societies. Some lack the opportunities to use those years as a volitional period; others may be inclined by personality or circumstances to limit their explorations or to seek a relatively early resolution to them. Nevertheless, as scholars we can characterize emerging adulthood as a period when change and exploration are common, even as we recognize the heterogeneity of the period and investigate this heterogeneity as one of emerging adulthood's distinguishing characteristics.

Emerging adulthood merits scholarly attention as a distinct period of the life course in industrialized societies. It is in many respects the age of possibilities, a period in which many different potential futures remain possible and personal freedom and exploration are higher for most people than at any other time. It is also a period of life that is likely to grow in importance in the coming century, as countries around the world reach a point in their economic development where they may allow the prolonged period of exploration and freedom from roles that constitutes emerging adulthood.

## References

Adams, G. R. (1999). *The objective measure of ego identity status: A manual on theory and test construction.* Guelph, Ontario, Canada: Author.

Arnett, J. (1992). Reckless behavior in adolescence: A developmental perspective. *Developmental Review, 12,* 339–373.

Arnett, J. J. (1994a). Are college students adults? Their conceptions of the transition to adulthood. *Journal of Adult Development, 1,* 154–168.

Arnett, J. (1994b). Sensation seeking: A new conceptualization and a new scale. *Personality and Individual Differences, 16,* 289–296.

Arnett, J. J. (1997). Young people's conceptions of the transition to adulthood. *Youth & Society, 29,* 1–23.

Arnett, J. J. (1998). Learning to stand alone: The contemporary American transition to adulthood in cultural and historical context. *Human Development, 41,* 295–315.

Arnett, J. J. (2000a). *Emerging adulthood: Prospects for the 21st century.* Manuscript submitted for publication.

Arnett, J. J. (2000b). High hopes in a grim world: Emerging adults' views of their futures and of "Generation X." *Youth & Society, 31,* 267–286.

Arnett, J. J. (in press). Conceptions of the transition to adulthood from adolescence through midlife. *Journal of Adult Development.*

Arnett, J. J., & Jensen, L. A. (1999, November). *A congregation of one: The individualization of religious beliefs among people in their twenties.* Paper presented at the annual meeting of the Society for the Scientific Study of Religion, Boston, MA.

Arnett, J., & Taber, S. (1994). Adolescence terminable and interminable: When does adolescence end? *Journal of Youth & Adolescence, 23,* 517–537.

Bachman, J. G., Johnston, L. D., O'Malley, P., & Schulenberg, J. (1996). Transitions in drug use during late adolescence and young adulthood. In J. A. Graber, J. Brooks-Gunn, & A. C. Petersen (Eds.), *Transitions through adolescence: Interpersonal domains and context* (pp. 111–140). Mahwah, NJ: Erlbaum.

Bachman, J. G., & Schulenberg, J. (1993). How part-time work intensity relates to drug use, problem behavior, time use, and satisfaction among high school seniors: Are these consequences or just correlates? *Developmental Psychology, 29*, 220–235.

Barling, J., & Kelloway, E. K. (1999). *Young workers: Varieties of experience.* Washington, DC: American Psychological Association.

Ben-Amos, I. K. (1994). *Adolescence and youth in early modern England.* New Haven, CT: Yale University Press.

Bianchi, S. M., & Spain, D. (1996). Women, work, and family in America. *Population Bulletin, 51*(3), 1–48.

Brooks-Gunn, J., & Paikoff, R. (1997). Sexuality and developmental transitions during adolescence. In J. Schulenberg, J. L. Maggs, & K. Hurrelmann (Eds.), *Health risks and developmental transitions during adolescence* (pp. 190–219). New York: Cambridge University Press.

Chisholm, L., & Hurrelmann, K. (1995). Adolescence in modern Europe: Pluralized transition patterns and their implications for personal and social risks. *Journal of Adolescence, 18*, 129–158.

Cote, J. E., & Allahar, A. L. (1996). *Generation on hold: Coming of age in the late twentieth century.* New York: New York University Press.

Dubas, J. S., & Petersen, A. C. (1996). Geographical distance from parents and adjustment during adolescence and young adulthood. *New Directions for Child Development, 71*, 3–19.

Elliott, G. R., & Feldman, S. S. (1990). Capturing the adolescent experience. In S. S. Feldman & G. R. Elliott (Eds.), *At the threshold: The developing adolescent* (pp. 1–14). Cambridge, MA: Harvard University Press.

Erikson, E. H. (1950). *Childhood and society.* New York: Norton.

Erikson, E. H. (1968). *Identity: Youth and crisis.* New York: Norton.

Eveleth, P., & Tanner, J. (1976). *Worldwide variation in human growth.* New York: Cambridge University Press.

Feiring, C. (1996). Concepts of romance in 15-year-olds. *Journal of Research on Adolescence, 6*, 181–200.

Goldscheider, F., & Davanzo, J. (1986). Semiautonomy and leaving home during early adulthood. *Social Forces, 65*, 187–201.

Goldscheider, F., & Goldscheider, C. (1994). Leaving and returning home in 20th century America. *Population Bulletin, 48*(4), 1–35.

Greenberger, E., & Steinberg, L. (1986). *When teenagers work: The psychological and social costs of adolescent employment.* New York: Basic Books.

Greene, A. L., Wheatley, S. M., & Aldava, J. F., IV. (1992). Stages on life's way: Adolescents' implicit theories of the life course. *Journal of Adolescent Research, 7*, 364–381.

Hall, G. S. (1904). *Adolescence: Its psychology and its relation to physiology, anthropology, sociology, sex, crime, religion, and education* (Vol. 1). Englewood Cliffs, NJ: Prentice-Hall.

Heaton, T. B. (1992). Demographics of the contemporary Mormon family. *Dialogue, 25*, 19–34.

Hogan, D. P., & Astone, N. M. (1986). The transition to adulthood. *Annual Review of Sociology, 12*, 109–130.

Hoge, D. R., Johnson, B., & Luidens, D. A. (1993). Determinants of church involvement of young adults who grew up in Presbyterian churches. *Journal of the Scientific Study of Religion, 32*, 242–255.

Hornblower, M. (1997, June 9). Great Xpectations. *Time, 149*, 58–68.

Jessor, R., Donovan, J. E., & Costa, F. M. (1991). *Beyond adolescence: Problem behavior and young adult development.* New York: Cambridge University Press.

Jonsson, B. (1994, March). *Youth life projects and modernization in Sweden: A cross-sectional study.* Paper presented at the biennial meeting of the Society for Research on Adolescence, San Diego, CA.

Keniston, K. (1971). *Youth and dissent: The rise of a new opposition.* New York: Harcourt Brace Jovanovich.

Larson, R. W. (1990). The solitary side of life: An examination of the time people spend alone from childhood to old age. *Developmental Review, 10*, 155–183.

Levinson, D. J. (1978). *The seasons of a man's life.* New York: Ballantine.

Martin, P., & Smyer, M. A. (1990). The experience of micro- and macroevents: A life span analysis. *Research on Aging, 12*, 294–310.

Michael, R. T., Gagnon, J. H., Laumann, E. O., & Kolata, G. (1995). *Sex in America: A definitive survey.* New York: Warner Books.

Mogelonsky, M. (1996, May). The rocky road to adulthood. *American Demographics, 18,* 26–36, 56.

Montemayor, R., Brown, B., & Adams, G. (1985). *Changes in identity status and psychological adjustment after leaving home and entering college.* Paper presented at the biennial meeting of the Society for Research on Child Development, Toronto, Ontario, Canada.

Morch, S. (1995). Culture and the challenge of adaptation: Foreign youth in Denmark. *International Journal of Comparative Race and Ethnic Studies, 2,* 102–115.

Mortimer, J. T., Harley, C., & Aronson, P. J. (1999). How do prior experiences in the workplace set the stage for transitions to adulthood? In A. Booth, A. C. Crouter, & M. J. Shanahan (Eds.), *Transitions to adulthood in a changing economy: No work, no family, no future?* (pp. 131–159). Westport, CT: Praeger.

Noble, J., Cover, J., & Yanagishita, M. (1996). *The world's youth.* Washington, DC: Population Reference Bureau.

O'Connor, T. G., Allen, J. P., Bell, K. L., & Hauser, S. T. (1996). Adolescent–parent relationships and leaving home in young adulthood. *New Directions in Child Development, 71,* 39–52.

Offer, D., & Offer, J. B. (1975). *From teenage to young manhood.* New York: Basic Books.

Padgham, J. J., & Blyth, D. A. (1991). Dating during adolescence. In R. M. Lerner, A. C. Petersen, & J. Brooks-Gunn (Eds.), *Encyclopedia of adolescence* (pp. 196–198). New York: Garland.

Page, K. (1999, May 16). The graduate. *Washington Post Magazine, 152,* 18, 20.

Parsons, T. (1942). Age and sex in the social structure of the United States. *American Sociological Review, 7,* 604–616.

Pascarella, E., & Terenzini, P. (1991). *How college affects students: Findings and insights from twenty years of research.* San Francisco: Jossey-Bass.

Perry, W. G. (1999). *Forms of ethical and intellectual development in the college years: A scheme.* San Francisco: Jossey-Bass. (Original work published 1970)

Rindfuss, R. R. (1991). The young adult years: Diversity, structural change, and fertility. *Demography, 28,* 493–512.

Roscoe, B., Dian, M. S., & Brooks, R. H. (1987). Early, middle, and late adolescents' views on dating and the factors influencing partner selection. *Adolescence, 22,* 59–68.

Scheer, S. D., Unger, D. G., & Brown, M. (1994, February). *Adolescents becoming adults: Attributes for adulthood.* Poster presented at the biennial meeting of the Society for Research on Adolescence, San Diego, CA.

Schlegel, A., & Barry, H., III. (1991). *Adolescence: An anthropological inquiry.* New York: Free Press.

Shanahan, M., Elder, G. H., Jr., Burchinal, M., & Conger, R. D. (1996). Adolescent earnings and relationships with parents: The work–family nexus in urban and rural ecologies. In J. T. Mortimer & M. D. Finch (Eds.), *Adolescents, work, and family: An intergenerational developmental analysis* (pp. 97–128). Thousand Oaks, CA: Sage.

Steinberg, L., & Cauffman, E. (1995). The impact of employment on adolescent development. In R. Vasta (Ed.), *Annals of child development* (Vol. 11, pp. 131–166). London: Kingsley.

U.S. Bureau of the Census. (1997). *Statistical abstracts of the United States: 1997.* Washington, DC: Author.

U.S. Bureau of the Census. (2000). *Geographic mobility: March 1997 to March 1998* (Current Population Reports, Series P-20, No. 520). Washington, DC: U.S. Government Printing Office.

Valde, G. A. (1996). Identity closure: A fifth identity status. *Journal of Genetic Psychology, 157,* 245–254.

Wallace, C. (1995, April). *How old is young and young is old? The restructuring of age and the life course in Europe.* Paper presented at Youth 2000: An International Conference, Middlesborough, UK.

Waterman, A. L. (1982). Identity development from adolescence to adulthood: An extension of theory and a review of research. *Developmental Psychology, 18,* 341–358.

Whitbourne, S. K., & Tesch, S. A. (1985). A comparison of identity and intimacy statuses in college students and alumni. *Developmental Psychology, 21,* 1039–1044.

William T. Grant Foundation Commission on Work, Family, and Citizenship. (1988). *The forgotten half: Non-college-bound youth in America.* Washington, DC: William T. Grant Foundation.

# CHAPTER 11
## MODELS OF RACIAL OPPRESSION AND SOCIORACE

### JANET E. HELMS AND DONELDA A. COOK

It is impossible for us to provide a thorough review of the socioracial group issues of each of the five major groups. Nevertheless, in previous chapters, we sought to provide enough of a flavor of the tensions so that therapists can have a basis for thinking about possible socioracial tensions that might impact the therapy process with themselves as the symbolic catalyst. Social scientists of various theoretical persuasions and orientations have attempted to provide explanations of racism's impact on individuals and/or intergroup relations, but rarely (with the possible exception of psychoanalytic theorists) have they considered the impact of racial factors on the therapy process per se.

Most contemporary theories of race and culture have tended to focus on the societal structural dynamics and implications of race and (occasionally) culture, but have rarely examined their intrapsychic and interpersonal consequences at the level of the individual. Yet therapists ought to be concerned about the interplay between the person's objective reality or circumstances (e.g., conditions of oppression) and her or his subjective well-being (e.g., manner in which experiences are interpreted).

Moreover, it is important to realize that although both race and culture involve person-environment socialization, for each individual client, psychorace and psychoculture may be differentially salient to the client in any given situation. For some people, racial socialization will be a more important aspect of their personality development, and for others, cultural socialization will be more important. In this chapter, we examine models of racial oppression and sociorace for their usefulness in assessing client dynamics.

## Socioracial Racial Theory

In order to maintain control over a group, it is necessary for the group in power to psychologically debilitate the target group's members. Not only must the members of the VREGs (in this case) be convinced that the inferior status of their group is preordained or deserved, but the benefactors, beneficiaries, and perpetrators of the psychological and systemic oppression must also convince members of their own group that their superior status is justly deserved and that they bear no personal responsibility for the inferior status of the other socioracial out-groups.

Of course, one set of strategies that White Americans collectively have used to achieve and maintain functional control over visible racial and ethnic groups (VREGs) is differential dispensation and

Helms, J. E., & Cook, D. A. (1999). Models of racial oppression and sociorace. In *Using race and culture in counseling and psychotherapy: Theory and process* (pp. 69–100). Boston: Allyn & Bacon.

allotment of social, political, and economic power according to White-defined racial criteria. The efficient use of such strategies requires that mutually exclusive racial categories be created, regardless of whether these categories have any biogenetic basis in fact.

Moreover, members of the oppressed group(s) must be "de-culturated," by which we mean exposed to pervasive, systematic, ongoing indoctrination to the effect that their traditional culture as well as the members of that cultural group are inferior and worthless. The resulting cultural vacuum is then filled with the dominant group's stereotypical depictions of the various socioracial groups.

Also, members of the deculturated groups must be taught to which "racial" group they belong, and what observable socially undesirable characteristics define their group membership. That is, they must be "racinated" (see Cross, Parham, & Helms, 1991). This sequence of events makes it possible for the dominating group to maintain control over those groups considered to be threats to the status quo. In this society, groups of color (ALANAs) have been the primary focus of societies' demoralizing deculturation and racination tactics.

Whites, the preservers of the racial status quo and definers of the dominative group, must also be taught the fabricated observable criteria for innately belonging to or earning membership in the privileged group. As mentioned in the previous chapter, the racination process for them involves learning the sociopolitical rules of the dominant group (a process that presumably begins at birth); it also requires replacement of traditional European and Asian cultures with amalgamated (White) American culture. In addition, they must create and/or learn the rationale for why VREGs do not have or deserve equivalent status in this country.

For both Whites and VREGs, a discernible manifestation of the deculturation-racination process is the internalization of racial stereotypes. The mental health professions as well as politicians have contributed mightily to the content of existing racial stereotypes. Thus, in their analysis of racism in the mental health literature, Thomas and Sillen (1972) outlined the following racial stereotypic assumptions: (a) Blacks are endowed with "less gray matter" and smaller brains and consequently, are more prone (than Whites) to "insanity"; (b) social protest by People of Color is an infallible symptom of mental derangement; (c) less evolved or "lower races" (on the racial hierarchy) have not evolved sufficiently beyond their "simian past" to practice appropriately the conventions of civilized society (e.g., monogamous marriage); (d) VREGs cannot control their emotions and demonstrate a lack of morality, particularly with respect to sexuality; (e) VREGs are inappropriate candidates for psychoanalysis because of their "simplistic minds," but make excellent research specimens; and (f) living in close proximity to Blacks and other "lower races" (especially Asians and Native Americans) contaminates Whites, and so forth.

Perhaps not surprisingly, these stereotypes do not differ markedly from the racial stereotypes that prevail in contemporary society more widely. However, perhaps more surprising is the fact that the themes underlying the stereotypes are still a strong aspect of the conceptualization of racial dynamics in mental health and psychotherapy literature.

Interestingly, as Axelson (1993) noted, there is no consensual derogatory stereotype of Whites as a *racial* group. Their superiority is assumed. White stereotypes, such as they are, pertain to particular "deviant" ethnic groups (e.g., Polish jokes) or White subgroups who otherwise are assumed (without evidence) to differ in major ways from most White people (e.g., "rednecks").

For both the oppressors and oppressed, internalized racial stereotypes about oneself as well as others are a major component of what is meant by the term *internalized racism*, or psychological reactions to racial oppression. Among mental health practitioners, personalized psychological reactions are assumed to have major therapeutic implications, although they typically only discuss these implications as they pertain to Blacks and other VREGs.

For example, Landrum and Batts (1985) proposed a variety of related symptoms including poor self-concept, misdirected anger, in-group discord, drug addiction, and so forth as the potential focus of race-related interventions. When internalized racism is expressed overtly, it can have implications for the quality of a person's interactions with others. In the case of therapists and clients, in particular, the quality of the therapy process may be detrimentally influenced by the nature of the psychological reactions to race that each party has internalized.

## Models of Racial Oppression

Feagin (1984) divides the existing explanatory models of racism and ethnocentricism into two categories—*order* and *power-conflict*. The focus of these models tends to differ depending on whether they were intended to explain the life circumstances of the dominative group (Whites) or one or more of the dominated groups. In the former case, one typically sees a greater emphasis on describing White people's negative reactions to "non-White" or "non-American" others; in the latter, one sees most emphasis on explaining adaptations of African, Latina/Latino, Asian, and Native Americans (ALANAs) to societal racism and ethnocentricism.

According to Feagin (1984), order theories generally emphasize the outcomes of assimilation and/or racism, that is, the manner by which nondominant groups adapt to or become like the dominant group. Power-conflict theories focus on the social control and conflict associated with subordinating other groups, in this case, White strategies for controlling other groups.

Nevertheless, virtually none of the models discussed by Feagin is of much use in analyzing the psychological implications of race in the psychotherapy process because they tend to treat race as group or structural dynamic rather than individual-difference dimensions. Structural dynamics pertain to societal conditions of racial classification (such as racial integration in housing and schools), and differential access to power (such as voting patterns and numbers of elected officials), whereas individual difference dimensions pertain to subjective reactions to one's conditions of racism (such as depression, exhilaration, and so forth). Using our terminology, structural models identify distal or sociological characteristics, whereas psychological models describe psychological (subjective) or proximal reactions to race.

In this chapter, some models that pertain specifically to issues of structural conditions of racism and ethnocentricism, that is, power-conflict and order models, are briefly summarized. We think these models are most useful for forming hypotheses about the societal racial conditions under which individual members of the various socioracial groups may exist. We also present models of racial identity development (Helms, 1990a) as one manner of conceptualizing clients' psychological adaptations to racism that we have found useful for explaining client and therapist racial dynamics in individual and group psychotherapy.

## White Power-Conflict Models

The central question driving the quest for White models of racial oppression has concerned the group's propensity to seek and maintain dominative relationships with people who are assumed to be of a different race. At least up until 1964, when the first Civil Rights Act was signed, the relationship of Whites to groups of color was unapologetic domination, segregation, and oppression. Again the details of the domination differed depending on which group one considers.

However, the common thread running through race relations involving Whites as the protagonists is that Whites considered themselves to be superior to *all* non-White groups, and therefore entitled by birthright to "life, liberty, and the pursuit of happiness." Naturally, all groups of color were considered subservient and inferior and were expected to earn any of the rights to life, liberty, or justice that White society was willing to accord them.

Even the White people who are often portrayed as being sympathetic to the causes of people of color often were practitioners of racism. Abraham Lincoln, the "Great Emancipator," reveals his level of personal and institutional racism in the following quote: "I will say, then that I am not, nor ever have been, in favor of bringing about in any way the social and political equality of the white [sic] and black [sic] races (applause); that I am not, nor ever have been, in favor of making voters or jurors of negroes [sic], nor of qualifying them to hold office, nor to intermarry with white [sic] people . . .

And inasmuch as they cannot so live, while they do remain together there must be the position of superior and inferior, and I as much as any other man am in favor of having the superior position assigned to the white [sic] race" (cited in Zinn, 1980, p. 184).

Most social scientists have been unable to explain why Whites have adhered to the principles of White supremacy, privilege, and domination for so long and so consistently with so many socioracial groups. Several theoretical explanations have been offered and we briefly summarize them here, not necessarily because we subscribe to them, but because therapists should be aware of the theories that may underlie their clients' expectations of them.

Theoretical explanations of Whites' dominative status can be categorized approximately as follows: (a) racial superiority; (b) racial inferiority; and (c) circumstantial. We intend only to describe these perspectives briefly, and consequently, in the case of those perspectives that are purported to be theories of "development" or "evolution," we may have done the perspectives a disservice. Therefore, the reader is referred to the original sources for a fuller elaboration of the perspectives.

## White Racial Superiority

The general premise of White superiority explanations is that Whites deserve their dominant sociopolitical status because they are genetically, intellectually, and/or culturally superior to those whom they have dominated. Consequently, the characteristics of the White group are the standards by which members of other groups are evaluated.

In psychology more specifically, White superiority explanations have existed in both implicit and explicit versions. To the extent that they are based on the experiences of White people and their culture, universalistic perspectives are implicit White superiority perspectives (see Wrenn, 1962). Explicit models typically are founded on principles of sociobiology and directly base their premises on racial classifications, but not necessarily measurable physiological "racial" characteristics.

## Universalistic Perspectives

In a sense most of the traditional theories of counseling and psychotherapy are based on universalistic principles. According to Ridley, Mendoza, and Kanitz (1994), universalistic perspectives are of two types—*generic* and *etic* or *true universalistic*. Proponents of generic perspectives argue that there are principles, aspects, or processes of human existence that transcend (socio)racial and cultural boundaries and, therefore, are applicable to all human beings. Proponents of etic universalistic frameworks contend that aspects of traditional theories are universally applicable to all people or that new culturally inclusive models can be created that will be applicable to everyone regardless of socioracial and/or cultural boundaries.

Generic models, theories, and principles are implicitly White racial and/or cultural superiority perspectives because they typically are explanations of human adaptations using the socialization experiences of White westerners and Europeans as the basis of such interpretations. Such perspectives rarely consider the possibility that different life circumstances might contribute to alternate adaptations, which might be equally "healthy" for members of those groups to whom they pertain.

Consequently, the behavior of Whites is considered to be normative for other groups, and deviations from such norms are considered to be deficits. Explanations for these alleged deficits are then presumed to lie in the group's genetic makeup (in reality, racial classifications) or environmental deprivation. Hypothetical "group deficiencies" then become the justification for a wide range of dominative behaviors on the part of Whites.

With regard to the history of intergroup racial and cultural relations in general, group deficiencies of various sorts were used to justify the domination of all of the visible racial and ethnic groups. According to Hacker (1992), "From the premise of genetic inferiority, there follows the corollary that members of a lesser race should be content to perform tasks unsuited to other strains. This was the rationale for slavery, and it has by no means disappeared. (There are even hints of this in the plea to create more blue-collar jobs for black [sic] men.)" (p. 28). In the mental health professions more specifically, alleged ALANA inferiority has been used consistently to explain why ALANAs' behaviors supposedly do not conform to White-based standards in most aspects of the helping process.

## Sociobiology

The basic premise of race-related sociobiological theory is that the racial-classification groups can be aligned along a superiority/inferiority hierarchy based on their presumed ancestry regardless of national or continental boundaries. Franklin (1991) contends that the underlying "scientific" basis of this perspective is Social Darwinism, and suggests that it was the philosophy underlying much of the "founding fathers'" and their descendants' mistreatment of VREGs in this country (see Helms, 1994).

According to Hutnik (1991) and Spikard (1992), some of the earliest spokespersons in U.S. society for this perspective were Madison Grant (1916), Henry Pratt Fairchild (1926), Howard C. Hill (1919), and Ellwood P. Cubberly (1929). In psychology, some spokespersons have been G. Stanley Hall (1904), J. Phillip Rushton (1990, 1995), and Arthur Jensen (1969). Originally, as previously noted, advocates of the racial sociobiological perspective argued that the northern and western European "races" were superior to all other racial groups, including southern and eastern Europeans. Although the order of the alignment of the racial categories shifted slightly over the ensuing decades, with Asians occasionally replacing Whites at the top of the hierarchy (see, for example, Rushton, 1995), according to Spikard (1992, p. 14), the typical order devised by the dominant European group was as follows: ". . . Caucasians at the top, Asians next, then Native Americans, and Africans at the bottom—in terms of both physical abilities and moral qualities [such as dishonesty, poverty, uncleanliness]."

The notion that psychological characteristics (e.g., physical abilities, personality characteristics) were inherited provided the justification for White Americans' domination and exploitation of other groups. Each racial group was assumed to be defined by a distinctive combination of psychological characteristics, and consequently, to occupy a different rung on the Darwinian evolutionary ladder. Since they were presumably the most evolved, Anglo-Saxon Americans had the right to force other groups to conform to their standards and/or to take from misfits that which was necessary (e.g., land, life, personhood, culture) to ensure the dominance and unity of the White American group.

## White Racial Inferiority Models

White inferiority models attribute Whites' history of other-group domination to inherent aspects of the condition of being White, such as physiological or environmental deficits relative to other socioracial groups. Both psychoanalytic and cultural explanations of the "White personality" have been offered, according to which the sociopolitical characteristics of the White group are attributed to physiological or evolutionary deficiencies, and consequent psychological impairment resulting therefrom.

As is true of the other perspectives, our rationale for presenting these perspectives is not necessarily because we endorse them wholeheartedly, but rather because many clients will have internalized them as a form of folk psychology, a way of ameliorating the pain of institutional and cultural racism. The therapist who first hears about these views of White people from the mouths of her or his client is likely to be caught unawares.

*Psychoanalytic.* Although psychoanalytic theory often has been used to account for White racism (Comer, 1991; P. Katz, 1976), psychiatrist Frances Cress Welsing (1974) is probably the first person to use this theoretical orientation to account for Whites' propensity to dominate other socioracial groups. Psychoanalytic theory originated with Sigmund Freud. In general, psychoanalytic theorists locate the motivation for human behavior in (usually) unconscious drives and instincts as Freud did. In many versions of psychoanalytic theory, these motivations have themes of sexuality and/or aggression.

For Welsing, the conscious or unconscious force that motivates Whites' domination of others is the drive to compensate for their whiteness; that is, their "color inadequacy" or "albinism." Thus, the basic premises of Cress's "Color-Confrontation Theory" are as follows: (a) When white people encounter any part of the massive numbers of peoples of color of the world, they become painfully aware of their minority status with respect to their own relative lack of color and number; and (b) in response to the wounded sense of identity that is based on an unchangeable part of themselves—

their external appearance—they develop a number of defensive reactions and mechanisms to protect themselves from their own feelings of inadequacy.

Among the reactions are uncontrollable hostility and aggression, and defensive feelings that continuously have had peoples of color as their target throughout history. Among the defense mechanisms are repression of feelings and awareness of their genetic color inferiority; reaction formation in which the valued and desired skin color is psychologically imbued with opposite characteristics such as dirtiness, evil, and so forth; and "compensatory logic" (also a form of reaction formation) in which the lack of color or genetic deficiency is transformed into White supremacy. Thus, according to Welsing, White supremacy then becomes Whites' justification for their participation in the varieties of institutional and cultural racism that prevail in the society.

*Environmental.* Michael Bradley (1978), an anthropologist, proposed the theory of the "ice-man inheritance." According to his theory, White people are the descendants of Africans of color who migrated into the Northern Hemisphere, where their efforts to survive during the Ice Age (from 100,000 to 10,000 years Before the Present, B.P., which he defines as beginning in 1950) resulted in the evolution of definitive physiological and psychological characteristics, vestiges of which were transmitted to successive generations.

Thus, Bradley (1978, p. 26) contends that "glacial evolution demanded certain special adaptations of Neanderthal man [sic] and that present-day Caucasoids still show vestiges of these adaptations. *These special adaptations had incidental side effects which resulted in an exceptionally aggressive psychology, an extreme expression of the cronos complex, and a higher level of psychosexual conflict compared to all other races of men* [sic]."

In Bradley's thesis, "Caucasoid" refers to "White peoples." By *cronos complex,* he means territorial behaviors designed to protect one's identity and status across time (past, present, and future). In other words, people compete with their ancestral past (i.e., one must achieve more than one's ancestors), the present (i.e., one should accomplish more than the living including one's own offspring), and the future (i.e., one attempts to leave a legacy that others cannot surpass). Whereas Bradley contends that the cronos complex is a theme in all human societies, he argues that it is stronger in White groups because they were the only group to have evolved in a glacial environment, and consequently, they alone developed the exceptionally high level of aggression used to impose their identity on others. Unlike other racial groups, evolution in such austere circumstances allegedly narrowed the range of physical (e.g., sexual enjoyment) and psychological (e.g., empathy) options available to Whites for sublimating their self-protective aggressiveness.

## Circumstantial

These explanations generally attribute Whites' exploitation of other groups to the circumstance of Whites' being the political majority in the country. Most such perspectives tend to begin the search for descriptions of the White condition post Civil War. More often than not, some simplistic form of racism or other manner of out-group prejudice is seen as the cause of Whites' self-aggrandizement. Richardson (1989) pointed out that these theories of racism generally treat VREG people as stressors to White people rather than conversely. Nevertheless, based on their reviews of racism literature, various authors (e.g., Allport, 1958; Katz, 1976; Richardson, 1989; Singer, 1962) have classified existing power-conflict racism-prejudice theories as follows:

*Historical.* The root causes of contemporary interracial-group conflict are located in the histories of the visible racial and ethnic groups (VREGs) that are participants in the conflict. Recall that the opportunity to convert and save the souls of African and Native Americans was frequently used as a rationale for slavery, an option that presumably is no longer available. Therefore, if ALANAs are discriminated against, it is because the options to civilize them are no longer readily available, and/or they no longer take maximal advantage of existing remedies. In other words, to understand Whites' anti-Black or anti-Native sentiments, then one needs to examine the histories of enslavement of these groups. Typically such perspectives do not explicate the reasons why or the manner in which the historical experiences of VREGs are responsible for shaping White people's feelings, attitudes, or behaviors.

*Sociocultural.* Societal and cultural (actually racial) trends cause people's individual racism. So, for example, urbanization (the tendency of large groups of especially People of Color to move into cities) has been hypothesized to account for Whites' antipathy toward Blacks because it promotes racial isolation and segregation, and because the incoming group does not share the same cultural values as the host group. Yet as Richardson (1989) notes, such explanations disregard the fact that even people who are not involved in the societal trend (e.g., urbanization) may express or experience the same types and levels of racism as those who are involved.

*Earned reputation.* Alleged offensive characteristics of VREGs (e.g., bad odor, diminishment of property values, intellectual deficits) may provoke White people's abhorrence and aggression. Then these racial stereotypes may be used to justify Whites' negative attitudes toward other socioracial groups. This perspective is implicit in much of the psychotherapy literature pertaining to racial factors.

## White Order Models

Although race- and culture-focused theorists have tended to be oblivious to the impact of White racism and Anglo-Saxon ethnocentrism on White people, if we stretch our imaginations some, we can adapt a couple of the existing frameworks to discuss Whites' potential adaptations to racism at the individual level.

*Frustration-aggression hypothesis.* Originally proposed by Dollard (1957; Dollard, Doob, Miller, Mowrer, & Sears, 1939), this explanation of the causes of racism and ethnocentrism continues to exist in the psychotherapy literature in sometimes modified forms. The basic premise here is that people respond to frustration, hostility, or unpleasant feelings of day-to-day arousal by taking them out on (displacing) convenient substitutes (scapegoats) for the more powerful aggressors or uncontrollable events. In this case, people of other perceived races or cultures become the scapegoats or targets for the frustration-reducing expressions of racism-ethnocentrism.

According to McLemore (1983), any guilt aroused by recognition that one is displacing aggression is assuaged by using racial stereotypes to rationalize former behaviors as well as new feelings of adverse arousal to daily frustrations, resulting in a cycle of out-group aggression. Since Whites are in the numerical majority and hold the institutional power, it is more likely that their frustration-aggression cycle will be overtly expressed, whereas VREGs are assumed to use covert forms of expression such as passive aggression or urban riots (Simpson & Yinger, 1972).

Although the frustration-aggression hypothesis was proposed as a universally applicable explanation of the manner by which people acquire personal racism, we think it may be more useful for understanding some, but not all, White people's racial reactions. In our experience, some White clients use a race-specific lay version of the frustration-aggression hypothesis to explain their antipathy toward other groups. "Some (fill in the socioracial group) person was mean (fill in a specific act) to me and ever since then, I have hated (or other appropriate affective verb) all (fill in the blank) people."

Obviously, a certain amount of personal racism and inadequate skills for managing one's emotions underlie such assertions. The therapist can use the frustration-aggression hypothesis to aid her or him in identifying the client's specific manner of resolving daily frustrations, and to assist the client in learning more competent strategies for coping explicitly with life in general, and incidentally, other racial groups.

## VREG Models

Interestingly, theories of VREGs' adaptation to their group's particular conditions of exploitation and domination have generally focused on describing the circumstances of African Americans. This singular focus on African Americans when addressing matters of race, and the other groups (i.e.,

Asian, Latino/Latina, and Native Americans) when examining issues concerning cultural adaptation, probably has occurred for two reasons.

First, throughout mental health history until the mid-1970s, all of the groups of color were generally considered to be no different than Blacks for all practical purposes (Thomas & Sillen, 1972). Consequently, theoretical formulations that pertained to one group were considered to be applicable to members of the other socioracial groups as well.

As it became expedient for economic and political reasons to expand the varieties of socioracial groups to accommodate differential prejudices and discrimination against immigrants of color and/or from undesirable parts of Europe and Asia, mental health theorists, practitioners, and researchers joined the rest of society in focusing on cultural differences as the justification for their alleged psychopathology rather than the maladaptive racial climate. Moreover, because Native Americans were generally considered to have a distinct culture whereas African Americans were not (Shuffleton, 1993), the effect of racism on Native people's well being has been as absent as the study of cultural incompatibility has been for people of African descent in the United States.

Thus, with respect to theoretical perspectives, one finds some allegedly racial psychological models with Black Americans as their focus, and some cultural models with Native, Latino/Latina, and Asian Americans as their focus. One rarely sees cultural factors addressed with respect to African Americans or racial factors addressed vis-à-vis the other groups of color. Consequently, in our experience, we have found that many of our colleagues and students have difficulty realizing that both cultural and racial factors might be of concern to VREG clients, regardless of their particular socioracial membership group.

In this chapter, we discuss racial sociological and psychological models. In the next chapter, we focus more explicitly on group-relevant cultures.

## Sociological Perspectives

Most of these theories are intended to explain the psychological consequences of and/or the psychological motivations (i.e., internal mechanisms) for what is considered to be group-specific antisocial or deviant behavior. Most locate the stimuli for these consequences in the conditions of institutional racism and personality deficits of African Americans.

Geschwender (1968; cited in McLemore, 1983) proffered three theoretical models based on the proposition that civil disturbance is a reaction to people's increased dissatisfaction as they compare their real circumstances to their ideal circumstances. They are as follows: (a) Rising-expectation hypothesis—in response to improving group-related conditions, people begin to hope and believe that significant change is possible. Discontent occurs when the hoped-for ideal and one's reality are too discrepant, and consequently, collective action may occur; (b) Relative-deprivation hypothesis—People of Color compare their lives to those of Whites, and if the gap between one's group's real status and the status of Whites is not perceived to be narrowing, then discontent may occur. Such discontent would not be based entirely on one's group's objective circumstances, but rather one's circumstances relative to the more advantaged group(s); (c) Rise-and-drop hypothesis—if an era of improvement for one's group is perceived as being followed by a period of stagnation or decline, then frustration and anger may result from unfulfilled expectations, even if individual members of the group are better off than before.

Note that each of these models infers individual psychological reactions (e.g., frustration, discontent, anger) from one's ascribed socioracial membership group.

## Psychological Models

Some theorists have presented the perspective that all Black people are irrevocably scarred by their circumstances of being the victims of the societal conditions of racism (see Helms, 1990b, for an overview). Contemporary versions of this perspective conceivably can find their antecedents in the work of Kardiner and Ovesey (1951). Therefore, we believe that it might be useful to examine their formulation in some detail.

*Mark of oppression.* Kardiner and Ovesey contend that the "central problem" of personality adaptation for "Negro" people is racial discrimination. Racial discrimination creates chronically low self-esteem among members of this population because they are constantly receiving negative images of themselves from other people's behavior toward them. Because the pain of racial discrimination is unremitting and constant, the person adopts "restitutive maneuvers" (defense mechanisms) to maintain internal equilibrium. Some of these defenses protect the person's intrapsychic status by preventing her or him from being overwhelmed by the pain of discrimination; some enable the person to present an acceptable social facade so that he or she can interact with the relevant social environments, albeit in a maladaptive manner. All of this self-management requires a constant expenditure of psychic energy that deprives the person of the psychological resources necessary to build a more healthy personality structure.

Figure 1 illustrates the personality structure of Black people as conceptualized by Kardiner and Ovesey. In the model, (racial) discrimination fuels development of the Black personality constellation of low self-esteem (the self-focused consequence of discrimination) and aggression (the other focused reaction to discrimination).

The figure portrays the primacy of low self-esteem and aggression in the Black personality, but was intended to be only a skeletal outline of the ways in which these dynamics manifest themselves. Thus, not only is low self-esteem evident in Black people's allegedly high levels of anxiety and tendencies to have higher aspirations than society will permit them to realize, but

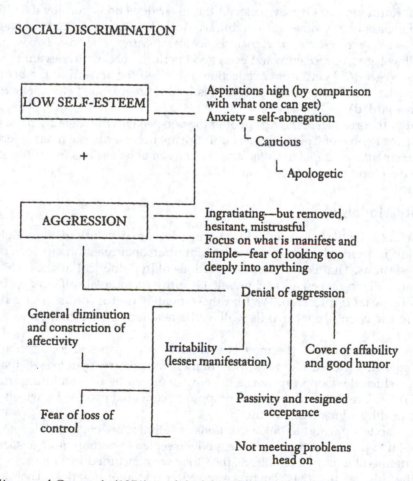

**Figure 1**    Kardiner and Ovesey's (1951) model of the Black personality.

From THE MARK OF OPPRESSION: A Psychosocial Study of the American Negro by Abram Kardiner and Lionel Ovesey. Copyright 1951. Reprinted by permission of W. W. Norton & Company, Inc.

also in their self-contempt, idealization of Whites, and "frantic efforts to be white [sic]," hostility, apathy, hedonism, "living for the moment," "criminality," and hatred of oneself and other members of one's racial group.

Similarly, not only are anxiety, ingratiation, simplistic thinking, and denial of aggression symptoms of Black people's underlying aggression, but so too are the following: (a) rage and fear, which eventually become interchangeable because of the societal prohibitions against expressing the former if one is Black; (b) submission or compliance, which become increasingly more abject with greater levels of rage and hatred; (c) laughter, gaiety, or flippancy, which, of course, are evidence of denied rage; and (d) masochism, depression, migraine headaches, and hypertension resulting from repressed rageful feelings toward a loved object.

It is fairly easy to find the psychological themes proposed by Kardiner and Ovesey reverberating throughout the mental health literature in which visible racial and ethnic groups are depicted. For example, Smith (1980) noted the overwhelming focus on the alleged psychopathology of Black people rather than of society in the career development literature.

Moreover, even the cursory overview of Kardiner and Ovesey's perspective that we have presented reveals that their (and similar) perspectives make "healthy personality" and (especially) Black people oxymorons. In addition, although we will not present the rest of their perspective here, suffice it to say that the contemporary themes of restricted emotionality, family pathology, absentee fathers, emotionally ungratifying mothers, lack of positive Black "role models," and so forth may not necessarily have begun with Kardiner and Ovesey, but were certainly embellished by them.

In addition, Kardiner and Ovesey believed that their depictions pertained to Black people regardless of social class or any other life conditions. According to them, ". . . the Negro [sic] has *no possible basis for a healthy self-esteem and every incentive for self-hatred.* The basic fact is that in the Negro [sic] aspiration level, good conscience and even good performance are irrelevant in face of the glaring fact that the Negro [sic] gets a poor reflection of himself [or herself] in the behavior of whites [sic], no matter what he [or she] does or what his [or her] merits are" (Kardiner & Ovesey, 1951, p. 197, underlines added).

Racial identity theorists were the first to offer the perspectives that healthy personality development is possible for People of Color, White people are not necessarily the main objects of identification and reinforcement for People of Color, and that racism in its various forms has implications for the personality development of White people.

## Racial Identity Models

In actuality, racial (in fact "socioracial") identity models are psychological models because they intend to explain individuals' intrapsychic and interpersonal reactions to societal racism in its various manifestations. That is, they are descriptions of hypothetical intrapsychic pathways for overcoming internalized racism and achieving a healthy socioracial self-conception under varying conditions of racial oppression. We find these models useful for assessing the influence of racial factors on the client's concerns as well as the reactions of the client and therapist to one another.

Table 1 summarizes some of the models that have been proposed to describe the socioracial adaptations of specific socioracial groups. Most of these models are "typologies" that propose static character types, which develop in response to being deprived by or benefitting from racism in its various forms. A few are stage theories that propose a sequential process by which an individual's growth toward healthy adjustment occurs.

Many of the models purport to be descriptions of "ethnic" or "cultural" development or adaptation. However, if to us, the particulars of the models seemed to pertain more to socioracial dynamics as we have defined them than to culture, then they were included in Table 1. In some instances, we modified the original theorists' language to reflect our interpretation. Therefore, we include them here as exemplars of racial rather than cultural psychological models.

## TABLE 1

### Selected Summary of Visible Racial or "Ethnic" Group (VREG)

| Author | Kind | Group | Description of Types/Stages |
|---|---|---|---|
| Banks (1981) | Stage | African American | **Ethnic Psychological Captivity**—Person internalizes society's negative view of his/her socioracial group. **Ethnic Encapsulation**—Person participates primarily with own socioracial group, which is idealized. **Ethnic Identity Clarification**—Person learns self-acceptance. **Biethnicity**—Person possesses healthy sense of socioracial identity and can function in own group and in White culture. **Multiethnicity**—Person is self-actualized and can function beyond superficial levels in many cultures. |
| Cross (1971) | Stage | African American | **Preencounter**—Person identifies with White people and culture, and rejects or denies kinship with Black people and culture. **Encounter**—Person repudiates previous identification with Whites, seeks identification with Blacks. **Immersion-Emersion**—Person completely identifies with Blacks and abhors Whites. **Internalization**—Person incorporates a positive Black identity and transcends psychological effects of racism. **Internalization-Commitment**—Person maintains Black identity while resisting the various forms of societal oppression. |
| Dizard (1970) | Typology | African Americans | **Assimilated**—Person moves as comfortably and easily in White environments as White prejudice will permit. **Pathological**—Person exhibits some form of psychopathology as the primary response to life's hardships. **Traditional**—Person attempts to preserve one's own-group identity, integrity and dignity. |
| Gay (1984) | Stage | African American | **Preencounter**—Person's socioracial identity is subconscious or subliminal or dominated by Euro-American conceptions of one's group. **Encounter**—Person's perceptions of her/his socioracial group are shattered by an event, which initiates search for new group conceptions. **Post-Encounter**—Person experiences and exudes inner security, self-confidence, and pride in one's socioracial group. |
| Carney & Kahn (1984) | Stage | White American | **Stage 1**—Person's perceptions of VREG people are based on societal stereotypes. **Stage 2**—Person recognizes own-group embeddedness, but deals with other groups in a detached scholarly manner. **Stage 3**—Person either denies the importance of race or expresses anger toward one's own group. **Stage 4**—Person attempts to blend aspects of White culture with aspects of VREG cultures. **Stage 5**—Person has commitment to promoting social equality and cultural pluralism. |

## TABLE 1 (continued)

| Author | Kind | Group | Description of Types/Stages |
|---|---|---|---|
| Hardiman (1982) | | White Americans | **Acceptance**—Person shows active or passive endorsement of White superiority.<br>**Resistance**—Person has initial conscious awareness of racial identity.<br>**Redefinition**—Person attempts to redefine Whiteness from a nonracist perspective.<br>**Internalization**—Person internalizes nonracist White identity. |
| Terry (1977) | | White Americans | **Color blind**—Person equates acknowledgment of color with racism; feels one can exonerate oneself from being White by asserting one's "human-ness."<br>**White Blacks**—Person abandons Whiteness by overidentifying with Blacks and rejecting one's Whiteness.<br>**New Blacks**—Person recognizes that racism is a White problem and ascribes to a pluralistic racial world view. |

*Note:* More extensive versions of this table appear in Helms (1990a, 1990b).

The majority of the models summarized have single sociracial groups as their focus (either African American or White American). Although some models attempt to describe the adaptations of a variety of groups exposed to similar conditions of oppression (e.g., Atkinson, Morten, & Sue, 1989; Myers et al., 1991), these latter theories presumably are examples of what Ridley et al. (1994) mean by etic-universal perspectives.

Still other theories not summarized in Table 1 are either efforts to integrate existing theories with similar themes and constructs (e.g., Sabnani, Ponterotto, & Borodovsky, 1991) or derivatives or restatements of those theories (e.g., Rowe, Bennett, & Atkinson, 1994). Despite the many versions of racial identity theory from which one might choose, we will use Helms's (1984; 1990a; 1994) version of racial identity theory because that is the perspective that we have found most useful in our own work with therapists, clients, and ourselves.

## Helms's Racial Identity Theory

Helms (1984; 1990a) originally proposed White and Black racial identity models and used them to describe the psychotherapy process involving these two groups. Subsequently, she expanded the Black model to pertain to other VREGs in recognition of the commonalities of experience with respect to racial (but not necessarily cultural) societal forces.

Thus, as is our central premise, the models are based on the assumption that racial classifications are sociopolitical constructions whose existence signals sociracial groups' differential rankings or access to resources in the political and economic societal hierarchy. Predictable psychological consequences (e.g., internalized racism) are assumed to result from being socialized as a member of one group rather than another; that is, either a dominant or nondominant collective.

The racial identity models are intended to describe the process of development by which individual members of the various sociracial groups overcome the version of internalized racism that typifies their group in order to achieve a self-affirming and realistic racial-group or collective identity. The need for such development exists because society differentially rewards or punishes members of societally ascribed racial groups according to their racial classifications.

## Common Themes

The two racial identity models (as well as her gender identity model) share some common themes, which are summarized in Table 2. However, to discuss these, it is necessary to take note of another alteration in Helms's Black/White model, which is the replacement of the construct of "stages" with "ego statuses" (Helms, 1996). Statuses are cognitive-affective-conative intrapsychic principles for responding to racial stimuli in one's internal and external environments. Helms (1996) contends that the change was necessary to encourage mental health workers who use racial identity models to conceive of the process of development as involving dynamic evolution rather than static personality structures or types. Therapists presumably cannot modify types whereas they may be able to alter processes.

For both models, the developmental process involves successive differentiations of increasingly more sophisticated racial identity ego statuses whose objective or measurable manifestations are schema or information-processing strategies. The maturation or evolution of the more sophisticated statuses makes it possible for the person to perceive and respond to racial information in one's internal and external environments in increasingly more complex ways. Thus, Helms makes a distinction between racial identity *development* and racial identity *expression.* Development or maturation refers to the sequence by which racial identity statuses potentially become available for self-expression, and schema or expression is the manner(s) in which a person's available statuses actually are manifested.

Although the general process of developing a racial identity (that is, self-referential commitment to a societally ascribed racial group) is considered to share some similarities, the content of the developmental process within the two models differs markedly because of group differences in access to social, economic, political, and numerical resources. Thus, although the underlying thematic content of the models as described is susceptible to change as the racial dynamics of the global society change, it seems to require major societal cataclysms for societal racial dynamics to be transformed—at least in positive directions.

## People of Color (POC) Racial Identity

In the POC model, a basic assumption is that, in the United States, the symptoms or consequences of racism directed toward one's racial group are a negative conception of one's racial group and oneself as a member of that group. In this model, *POC* refers to Asian, African, Latino/Latina, and Native Americans of color living in the United States regardless of the original continental origins of their ancestry. Even our cursory overview of the history of race (rather than ethnic) relations in the United States (e.g., Takaki, 1993; Zinn, 1990) reveals that peoples of the so-designated groups have been subjected to similar (but not necessarily identical) deplorable political and economic conditions because they were not perceived to be "pure" white.

### TABLE 2

#### Summary of Common Ego Status Themes in Helms's Racial Identity Models

| Themes |
| --- |
| Persons must overcome societal definitions of one's socioracial group by redefining oneself in personally meaningful terms. |
| Self-redefinition involves a sequential differentiation or maturation of ego statuses. |
| Simplest or least complex statuses develop first. |
| The seeds of more complex statuses are inherent in earlier statuses. |
| Statuses that are most consistently reinforced in the environment become strongest and potentially dominant. |
| Status is dominant when it occupies the largest percentage of the ego and is used most frequently for interpreting racial material. |
| Statuses that are not reinforced recede in importance and become recessive. |
| Successive statuses are infrequently used to govern responses to racial stimuli. |
| Ego statuses are hypothetical constructs that cannot be measured. |
| The strength of ego statuses is inferred from their behavioral expressions—schemata. |
| Schemata typically reflect the themes that are present in the person's socioracial environment(s). |
| Environments can be internal (psychological) or external (environmental). |

Moreover, as Alba (1990) notes, the conditions of oppression that "undesirable" White ethnic immigrants to this country originally faced virtually had disappeared by their third generation in this country. Yet racism continues to follow members of the visible racial groups well beyond the third generation in this country, and has become a "tradition" that they must learn to survive.

Thus, a primary collective identity developmental task for them all is to overcome or abandon socialized negative racial-group conceptions (that is, internalized racism) as previously discussed in order to develop a realistic self-affirming collective identity. Therefore, abandonment of internalized racism involves similar processes for each of the groups of color, regardless of the specific group to which they have been relegated.

Helms's model to explain the process by which this adaptation potentially occurs is a derivative and integration of aspects of Cross's (1971) Negro-to-Black conversion model, Atkinson et al.'s (1989) Minority Identity Development model, and Erikson's collective identity model, with some influence from Kohut's (1971) self psychology. Table 3 summarizes the sequence by which the ego statuses as well as the correlated schema become differentiated for VREGs. The labels for the ego statuses in parentheses are the names appropriated from Cross (1971), and Helms tends to use them when only African American people are the population being assessed.

*Conformity.* Accordingly, *Conformity*, the original or least sophisticated status and schema, involves the person's adaptation and internalization of White society's definitions of one's group(s), either by conforming to the existing stereotypes of one's own group(s) or attempting to become White and assimilated into White culture. Thus, this status tends to foster information processing in which White people and their culture are idealized and anything other than White is denigrated. When the person is using the Conformity schema or information processing strategy (IPS), he or she is oblivious to the racial dynamics in her or his environment, and if they are forced into the person's awareness, he or she may respond with selective perception in which information is nonconsciously distorted and minimized to favor the White group.

The Conformity speaker in Table 3 illustrates the manner in which those aspects of oneself that are perceived to be White (heritage, culture) are elevated and those that are not are devalued or ignored. However, she also demonstrates a basic principle of racial identity development—the seeds of latter statuses are present in the original status. Thus, that part of herself that is proud of her White heritage will still be present if she develops the status of Integrative Awareness, but she will be able to demonstrate equal pride in her African American heritage.

*Dissonance.* *Dissonance*, the ego status characterized by disorientation, confusion, and unpredictable responses to racial events, begins to evolve as the person begins to acknowledge her or his lack of fit in the White world. Notice that the speaker in Table 3 seems to be caught between two cultures, Black and White, in this instance. A common theme underlying the Dissonance schema is the ambivalence and anxiety caused by the lack of familiarity with the nature of one's own group's cultural and sociopolitical battles and accomplishments and the lack of positive material about one's own group with which to replace one's waning idealization of the White group.

*Immersion.* The *Immersion* status evolves in response to the person's need to replace the group-specific negativity that resides in her or his identity constellation with positive group information, and thereby alleviate the anxiety triggered by awareness of the lack of a viable racial self-definition in a society that so values racial classifications. When a person is using the Immersion status, he or she idealizes everything considered to be of his or her group and denigrates everything considered to be of the "White world." When this schema is operative, the person maintains stability and predictability by indulging in simplistic thinking in which race or racism is virtually always a central theme, and one's own group members are always right as long as they conform to externally defined standards of group-appropriate behaviors. In Table 3, Nelson demonstrates the seemingly mindless conformity to stereotypic ideals of Blackness, whether or not those ideals are personally meaningful.

## TABLE 3

**Summary of ALANA Racial Identity Ego Statuses, Examples, and Information Processing Strategies (IPS)**

**Status and Example**

**Conformity (Pre-encounter)**—External self-definition that implies devaluing of own group and allegiance to White standards of merit. Person probably is oblivious to socioracial groups' sociopolitical histories. IPS: Selective perception, distortion, minimization, and obliviousness to socioracial concerns.
*Example:* "If you are a mixed race [Black-White] person, don't deny your European heritage just because Black people [in the U.S.] try to force you to choose. We are special because of our White heritage! We can be mediators of peace between these two warring peoples."

**Dissonance (Encounter)**—Ambivalence and confusion concerning own socioracial-group commitment and ambivalent socioracial self-definition. Person may be ambivalent about life decisions. IPS: Repression of anxiety-evoking racial information, ambivalence, anxiety, and disorientation.
*Example:* "I talked 'white,' moved 'white,' most of my friends were white. . . . But I never really felt accepted by or truly identified with the white kids. At some point, I stopped laughing when they would imitate black people dancing. I distanced myself from the white kids, but I hadn't made an active effort to make black friends because I was never comfortable enough in my 'blackness' to associate with them. That left me in sort of a gray area. . . ." (Wenger, 1993, p. 4).

**Immersion**—Idealization of one's socioracial group and denigration of that which is perceived as White. Use of own-group external standards to self-define and own-group commitment and loyalty is valued. May make life decisions for the benefit of the group. IPS: Hypervigilence and hypersensitivity toward racial stimuli and dichotomous thinking.
*Example:* "So there I was, strutting around with my semi-Afro, studiously garbling the English language because I thought that 'real' Black people didn't speak standard English, . . . contemplating changing my name to Malika, or something authentically black . . ." (Nelson, 1993, p. 18).

**Emersion**—A euphoric sense of well-being and solidarity that accompanies being surrounded by people of one's own socioracial group. IPS: Uncritical of one's own group, peacefulness, joyousness.
*Example:* "A jubilant [Black] scream went up . . . we had a feeling, and above all we had power . . . So many whites [sic] unconsciously had never considered that blacks [sic] could do much of anything, least of all get a black [sic] candidate this close to being mayor of Chicago" (McClain, 1983, cited in Helms, 1990, p. 25).

**Internalization**—Positive commitment to and acceptance of one's own socioracial group, internally defined racial attributes, and capacity to objectively assess and respond to members of the dominant group. Can make life decisions by assessing and integrating socioracial group requirements and self-assessment. IPS: Intellectualization and abstraction.
*Example:* "By claiming myself as African-American and Black, I also inherit a right to ask questions about what this identity means. And chances are this identity will never be static, which is fine with me" (L. Jones, 1994, p. 78).

**Integrative Awareness**—Capacity to value one's own collective identities as well as empathize and collaborate with members of other oppressed groups. Life decisions may be motivated by globally humanistic self-expression. IPS: Flexible and complex.
*Example:* "[I think of difference not] as something feared or exotic, but difference as one of the rich facts of one's life, a truism that gives you more data, more power and more flavor . . . [You need a variety of peoples in your life.] . . . so you won't lapse into thinking you're God's gift to all knowledge as North American Negro" (L. Jones, 1994, p. 80).

*Note:* Descriptions of racial identity statuses are adapted from Helms (1994). Statuses are described in the order they are hypothesized to evolve.

*Emersion.* Thematically, community, communalism, and commitment to one's own group are the driving forces of the *Emersion* status. The appearance of this status is the recognition of the person's need for positive group definition. When the person is using this status, he or she feels grounded when surrounded by members of her or his own group. As is the case for the Dissonance status, Emersion is primarily an affective status (e.g., joyousness and euphoria in response to the presence or accomplishments of one's own group).

The example in Table 3 demonstrates the joyousness that may be experienced when a member of one's groups accomplishes something of note. The solidarity is often evident in people's clustering with people of their own group, particularly in predominantly White environments.

*Internalization.* A positive commitment to one's group, internally defined racial attributes and perspectives, as well as the capacity to objectively assess and respond differentially to members of one's own as well as the dominant racial group characterize the *Internalization* status. When using this status, the person uses abstract reasoning or intellectualization and is capable of weighing and integrating complex racial information.

The speaker using the Internalization schema in Table 3 illustrates the person's ability to be self-analytic, self-exploratory, and flexible with respect to her identity. She also illustrates the principle that one's manner of resolving racial dilemmas becomes more complex as one gains access to increasingly more sophisticated ego statuses.

*Integrated awareness.* The most sophisticated status and schema (i.e., *Integrative Awareness*) involve the capacity to express a positive racial self and to recognize and resist the multiplicity of practices that exist in one's environment to discourage positive racial self-conceptions and group expression. In addition, when this status is accessible, the person is able to accept, redefine, and integrate in self-enhancing ways those aspects of herself and himself that may be deemed to be characteristic of other socioracial and cultural groups. Furthermore, her or his conceptualization of other people and environmental events can be as complex as needed to ensure healthy intrapsychic and interpersonal functioning. When speaking from this status, L. Jones demonstrates the thirst for diversity that often characterizes this status.

*Summary.* To summarize, the evolution of ego statuses for People of Color begins with the most primitive status whereby the person primarily interprets and responds to racial information in a manner that suggests negative own-group identification, endorsement of societal prejudices toward one's group, and uncritical esteem for the White group. The last status to evolve permits the person to resist many types of oppression of one's own and others' collective identity groups without abandoning one's primary commitment to one's own group(s). The end goal of the maturational process is to acquire the latter status and be able to use it most of the time in coping with a racially complex world in which one's integrated and positive sense of self is frequently at risk.

## White Racial Identity

In the White model, it is assumed that being a member of the acquisitive sociracial group contributes to a false sense of racial-group superiority and privilege. Thus, the process of overcoming internalized racism for Whites is assumed to require the individual to replace societally ordained racial group entitlement and privilege with a nonracist and realistic self-affirming collective (racial) identity. Helms and Piper (1994) define *White people* as follows: "those Americans who self-identify or are commonly identified as belonging exclusively to the White racial group regardless of the continental source (e.g., Europe, Asia) of that racial ancestry" (p. 126).

As a consequence of growing up and being socialized in an environment in which members of their group (if not themselves personally) are privileged relative to other groups, Whites learn to perceive themselves (and their group) as being entitled to similar privileges. In order to protect such privilege, individual group members and, therefore, the group more generally, learn to protect their privileged status by denying and distorting race-related reality, and aggressing against perceived threats to the racial status quo. Consequently, healthy identity development for a White person involves the capacity to recognize and abandon the normative strategies of White people for coping with race.

Helms's (1984, 1990a, 1994) theory proposes a process by which White people develop racial identity. As shown in Table 4, for White people, the maturation process of recognition and abandonment of White privilege begins with the ego's avoidance or denial of the sociopolitical implications of one's own and others' racial-group membership (Contact status) and concludes with its capacity to strive for non-racist own-group membership and humanistic racial self-definition and social interactions (Autonomy status).

## Contact

The racial identity evolutionary process for Whites begins with *Contact*, a primitive status, primarily characterized by simplistic reactions of denial and obliviousness to the ways in which one benefits

## TABLE 4

**Summary of White Racial Identity Ego Statuses, Examples, and Information Processing Strategies (IPS)**

**Status and Example**

**Contact**—Satisfaction with racial status quo, obliviousness to racism and one's participation in it. If racial factors influence life decisions, they do so in a simplistic fashion. IPS: Obliviousness, denial, superficiality, and avoidance.

*Example:* "... The Balls have prided themselves on the ancestral image of compassion, emphasizing that masters tried as best they could not to separate slave families in sale; that no Ball masters perpetrated violence or engaged in master-slave sex. Ed Ball's research is viewed by some family members, especially the elderly ones, as a threat to long-held beliefs. Some would prefer not to know too many details about their ancestors' slave practices, one relative says" (Duke, 1994, p. 12).

**Disintegration**—Disorientation and anxiety provoked by unresolvable racial moral dilemmas that force one to choose between own-group loyalty and humanism. May be stymied by life situations that arouse racial dilemmas. IPS: Suppression, ambivalence, and controlling.

*Example:* "I was upset. I couldn't do anything for a couple of weeks ... Was I causing more pain than healing? Was this somebody else's history, not mine? Was I an expropriator, as Stefani Zinerman [a Black woman newspaper editor] accuses me of being? Should I just stop [investigating my family's history of slave ownership] and let black [sic] people do their own history?" (Duke, 1994).

**Reintegration**—Idealization of one's socioracial group; denigration and intolerance for other groups. Racial factors may strongly influence life decisions. IPS: Selective perception and negative outgroup distortion.

*Example:* "When someone asks him, 'Don't you feel bad because your ancestors owned slaves?' his response is 'No, I don't feel bad because my ancestors owned slaves. I mean, get over it. If Ed wants to go around and apologize, Ed's free to go around and apologize. But quite frankly, Ed didn't own any slaves. He isn't responsible for slavery or anybody's misfortunes ...' " (Duke, 1994, p. 24).

**Pseudo-Independence**—Intellectualized commitment to one's own socioracial group and subtle superiority and tolerance of other socioracial groups as long as they can be helped to conform to White standards of merit. IPS: Selective perception, cognitive restructuring, and conditional regard.

*Example:* "He has also said to them [the descendants of his family's slaves]: I am sorry ... his mother, brother and a few other relatives believe the apology had a healing effect ..." (Duke, 1994, p. 12).

**Immersion**—The searching for an understanding of the personal meaning of Whiteness and racism and the ways by which one benefits from them as well as a redefinition of Whiteness. IPS: Hypervigilance, judgmental, and cognitive-affective restructuring.

*Example:* "I'm interested to look at whiteness [sic] as carefully as white [sic] people look at blackness [sic]. As a white [sic] person, I'm interested to understand how my ethnicity [sic] has produced me as an individual ... and how whiteness [sic] produces the majority experience of Americans. My plantation research might be a way for me to do this intellectually as a writer" (Duke, 1994, p. 12).

**Emersion**—A sense of discovery, security, sanity, and group solidarity and pride that accompanies being with other White people who are embarked on the mission of rediscovering Whiteness. IPS: Sociable, pride, seeking positive group-attributes.

*Example:* "But Ed's apology [for his family's ownership of slaves] produced positive reactions as well. Janet and Ted Ball, Ed's mother and brother, both were moved by [his apology]: 'I was crying too,' says Janet Ball ... Ted Ball ... says he whispered a private 'thank you' to his little brother. .... He feels grateful to Ed 'for doing the hard work it took to get to the apology.' " (Duke, 1994, p. 24).

**Autonomy**—Informed positive socioracial-group commitment, use of internal standards for self-definition, capacity to relinquish the privileges of racism. Person tries to avoid life options that require participation in racial oppression. IPS: Flexible and complex.

*Example:* "... It's [the exploration of his familial history of slave ownership] about me personally trying to find some way as a white [sic] person, quite apart from my family's history, to acknowledge what's happened in this country. I mean during the time that English-speaking people have been in this country, for more years were black [sic] people enslaved than not enslaved" (Duke, 1994, p. 25).

*Note:* Descriptions of racial identity statuses are adapted from Helms (1994). Racial identity ego statuses are listed in the order that they are hypothesized to evolve.

from membership in the entitled group and only superficial acknowledgement of one's membership in the White group. Thus, when this status is dominant, the person reacts to racial stimuli with denial, obliviousness, or avoidance of anxiety-evoking racial information, especially when such information implies something derogatory about the White group or the person as a member of that group.

Notice that in the example, the historian's family rejects him when he attempts to move from the family's pie-in-the-sky romanticization of its ancestors' slave ownership. Their obliviousness serves a protective function in that those family members who can avoid facing their ancestors' history of ownership of Black people can also avoid present-day responsibility for doing something to make amends.

*Disintegration.* *Disintegration* begins to evolve when one can no longer escape the moral dilemmas of race in this country and one's participation in them. Sometimes it is initiated by People of Color's reactions to one's naivete or superficiality, but usually it evolves and becomes stronger as one is continuously exposed to circumstances where one cannot afford to ignore one's Whiteness and the socialization rules that characterize the group because of the risk of ostracism by the White group.

The basic nature of the moral dilemmas is that one is continuously forced to disassociate with respect to race and racism while acting toward People of Color in inhumane ways in order to be loved, accepted, and valued by significant members of the White group. When this status is in charge of the person, it is expressed as disorientation, confusion, general (sometimes debilitating) distress, and nonreceptivity to anxiety-evoking information.

In the example in Table 4, the speaker illustrates the type of disintegration that frequently follows the White person's rebuffed attempts to "do good" for People of Color. Whereas the speaker thinks his turmoil is attributable to a Black person's animosity, a more likely explanation is that family members' antipathy is causing him to question whether the costs of being beneficent outweigh the benefits.

*Reintegration.* The *Reintegration* status evolves as a system for mitigating the anxiety that occurs when one's Disintegration status is dominant. The person reduces pain and avoids personal anxiety by adopting the version of racism that exists in her or his socialization environments, which then relieves her or him of the responsibility for doing anything about it. The general theme of this status and correlated schema is idealization of one's own socioracial group, denigration and intolerance toward other groups, and protection and enhancement of the White group and thereby the maintenance of the racism status quo. Thus, selective perception and distortion of information in an own-group enhancing and out-group debasing manner describe this status and correlated schema.

The need to avoid personal responsibility for racism is evident in the Reintegration example. By minimizing the significance of his family's role in perpetuating slavery, and consequently, his personal advancement because of it, he eliminates his own and his entire family's responsibility to do anything about it.

*Pseudo-independence.* The *Pseudo-Independence* status is characterized by an intellectualized commitment to one's racial group in which one identifies with the "good" nonracist Whites and rejects the "bad" racists. Identification and commitment are made possible by acknowledgement of superficial group (rather than personal) culpability for Whites' racial wrongdoing, and by not necessarily conscious efforts to resolve "the race problem" by assisting People of Color to become more like Whites. Schematic expression or information-processing strategies involve reshaping racial stimuli to fit one's own "liberal" societal framework, avoidance of negative information about oneself, and selective perception.

*Immersion.* The *Immersion* status involves the search for a new, humanistic, nonracist definition of Whiteness. When this status is operative, the person attempts to recover from prior distorted racial socialization and seeks accurate information about race and racism and their pertinence to oneself. The information-processing strategies operative here are searching for internally defined racial standards or reeducating oneself, hypervigilence, and activism.

In Table 4, the Immersion schema is expressed by the person's frenetic search for the meaning of Whiteness to himself or herself as well as to other White people in society. Although he or she is not certain where his or her inquiry will end, it is fueled by the inexplicable belief that such self- and other exploration is virtually ordained. This sensation of being on a mission of recovery characterizes the Immersion status and its schematic expression.

*Emersion.* The *Emersion* status is the appreciation of and withdrawal into the community of reeducated White people for the purposes of rejuvenating oneself and solidifying one's goals of seeking new self-knowledge. This is primarily an affective status and so one finds a variety of emotional themes including the joyous tears and prayerful gratitude toward kindred sojourners described in Table 4.

*Autonomy.* The last and most advanced status to evolve permits complex humanistic reactions to internal and environmental racial information based on a realistic, nonracist self-affirming conception of one's racial collective identity. When a person is operating from the *Autonomy* status, he or she no longer has to impose arbitrary racial definitions on others nor must succumb to others' arbitrary racial criteria. The Autonomy schema permits flexible analytic self-expression and responses to racial material.

## Racial Identity Expression

As previously discussed, the model describes the development or process by which the statuses come into being. Consequently, the highlights or distinguishable aspects of the statuses and related schemata are described. However, most individuals develop more than one status, and if multiple statuses exist, then they can operate in concert. That is, they may each influence a person's reactions to racial stimuli.

Thus, in Tables 3 and 4, although we have categorized the examples according to what appears to be the strongest status-schema theme, it seems to us that aspects of other status-schema are present in virtually every instance. For example, in Table 4, the Reintegration segment is classified as *primarily* Reintegration because of the person's subtle dehumanizing and unwillingness to acknowledge even his ancestors' role in perpetuating slavery and racism. However, the minimization and intellectualization of racial tensions that characterize the Contact and Pseudo-Independence statuses also waft through this example. Similar blends of statuses can be found in the other examples as well, and presumably blends describe people's reactions more often than do "pure" statuses.

Also apparent in the examples in Tables 3 is the fact that racial identity themes may be blended in the individual's reactions to racial catalysts regardless of their socioracial classification. As we just observed with respect to White identity development, most people probably do not express their racial identity in pure forms. Thus, the second example in Table 3 illustrates expression of both the Conformity and Dissonance statuses in that the VREG speaker acknowledges his White cultural socialization and consequent greater familiarity with White people on one level (Conformity), but also is able to describe his lack of fit with either the Black or White socioracial group (Dissonance).

Nevertheless, each of the examples has a racial identity theme that seems to be stronger than the others, and to determine which is a person's strongest status, one would need to analyze the themes inherent in several samples of a person's race-related behavior. Themes that frequently occur presumably signal stronger underlying statuses, and conversely, stronger statuses conceivably contribute to more consistent thematic race-related expressions.

However, more often than not, researchers have attempted to develop quantitative paper-and-pencil inventories for assessing racial identity. Burlew and Smith (1991) and Ponterotto and Casas (1991) critically reviewed some of them. Of these measures, the ones used most frequently are the Black and White racial identity research scales developed by Helms and her associates (Helms & Parham, 1996; Helms & Carter, 1990; Carter, 1996; Corbett, Helms, & Reagan, 1992). From these measures, Helms (1996) proposed racial identity assessment inventories, which she suggests might be useful in mapping the person's racial identity expression.

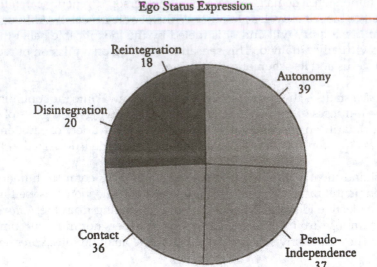

**Figure 2**   Linda's White racial identity profile.

Linda's profile suggests that her strongest expressed statuses are a combination of Contact, Autonomy, and Pseudo-Independence. Her weakest statuses are Disintegration and Reintegration. Subscales followed by asterisk(s) are higher (single) or very much higher (double) than the subsequent subscale. The ordering of Linda's scores is similar whether one examines subscale scores relative to her immediately adjacent clockwise raw score (see pie), or her scores as compared to Carter's (1996) percentile norms (% tile column). Pie slices of the same shade do not differ significantly. Contact (i.e., lack of sophistication about the significance of race) appears to be a strong influence in her interpretation and reaction to racial information. For more information about interpreting racial identity profiles, see Helms (1996).

| Mode of Expression | Raw Score | % tile | Comment |
|---|---|---|---|
| Contact | 36* | 81 | Contact is stronger than Disintegration |
| Disintegration | 20 | 19 | Disintegration does not differ significantly from Reintegration |
| Reintegration | 18** | 11 | Reintegration is much weaker than Pseudo-Independence |
| Pseudo-Independence | 37 | 70 | Pseudo-Independence does not differ significantly from Autonomy |
| Autonomy | 39 | 70 | Autonomy does not differ significantly from Contact |
| Total | 150 | | Profile appears to be valid |

Using the scoring procedures Helms proposed for the assessment of Whites' racial identity expression (WRIAS Social Attitudes Inventory), we generated a racial identity profile for the White female group leader (see Figure 2). The profile suggests that this person's racial identity resting-state expression is characterized by equally strong Contact, Pseudo-Independent, and Autonomy schemata. Thus, she does not have a clearly dominant schemata, although Disintegration and Reintegration appear to be recessive for her. In response to race-related stimuli other than the paper-and-pencil inventory, one would expect her to be rather naive about such matters, but to express her naivete in a liberal and intellectualized manner with traces of personal independence and nonconformity to derogatory group norms.

## Conclusions and Implications for Therapy

As symbolized in Figure 3, the first question one needs to ask is whether issues of commitment to a sociracial group are germane to the problem for which the client is seeking assistance. The possibilities are: (a) yes, either implicitly or explicitly the client's problem involves race, racism, or racial identity; (b) maybe, the possibility exists that such factors are relevant, but if so, their manner of influence is not unambiguously evident; (c) no, the person is experiencing a "universal" life problem for which racial tensions and/or dynamics in particular do not seem to be relevant.

In the case of the first two options, the general sociological models of oppression *might* provide some insight into the racial life conditions experienced by clients and/or therapists. However, inferring that any particular circumstances or characteristics of a group necessarily pertain to individual members of the group is ill-advised. Rather one might use such perspectives to form hypotheses about the relevant dynamics in the person's life, but these should be confirmed or disconfirmed in one's actual interactions.

Moreover, the content of one's own or one's client's racial stereotypes might reveal the racial perspective on which they are based. It may be easier to countermand such stereotypes when one understands their origins. In any case, one dimension of our perspective concerns examining whether the client has *personally* experienced socioracial oppression or benevolence because of her or his racial classification, and, if so, in what form. Remember that cues to such experiences can be factors so subtle as differential treatment due to skin color differences within and between socioracial groups, or so overt as job promotions accorded on the basis of racial classification.

The psychological perspectives might be more useful in conceptualizing the race-related dynamics of clients with respect to any of the three options, although we think that the early historical perspectives that we summarized (e.g., frustration-aggression) might pertain to certain clients rather than all clients. For example, if one's client is clearly aggressing against someone of another socioracial group, then one should look initially toward daily life frustrations to identify provocations or socialization experiences.

However, if the client is the target of the aggression, then it is not certain that any of the power-conflict or most of the traditional psychological race-related models will be of benefit to her or him. Particularly, if the client is a VREG person, such models may be inapplicable because for the most part, they were created to assist White people in comprehending People of Color.

In our experience, client's reactions to socioracial dynamics tend to be complex on the cognitive, affective, and behavioral levels regardless of the person's socioracial group. Therefore, we tend to

Excerpt: "We're special because of our European ancestry."
Therapist considerations: ARE SOCIORACIAL DYNAMICS RELEVANT?

| | Yes | Maybe | No |
|---|---|---|---|
| Relevant Sociological Factors | | | |
| Psychological Reactions | | | |
| Interventions | | | |

| Relevant Sociological Factors | Psychological Reactions | Interventions |
|---|---|---|
| Apparent racial classification | Anger | Empathy |
| Skin color | Defensiveness Conformity status | Factual race-related information |
| Parents' differential experiences of sociorace | Naivete | Communication skills |

**Figure 3**    Some socioracial dimensions of clients and therapists.

prefer the more complex psychological (i.e., racial identity) theories for making sense of these dynamics because they make it possible to conceptualize racial reactions as common human responses in the racial environment(s) of the United States rather than as inexplicable peculiarities of the visible racial and ethnic groups.

If one thinks that history of oppression-domination is relevant, then one needs to specify the kinds that are relevant for this particular client and perhaps her or his social system. Next, one attempts to move inside the client by choosing some psychological model (e.g., racial identity) for describing her or his reactions to these stimuli. Then one shapes one's interventions according to what seems appropriate for the client's conditions. Several authors, some of whom are summarized in Table 2, have proposed interventions matched to the client's levels of expressed racial identity (Carney & Kahn, 1984; Gay, 1984; Helms, 1990a; Sabnani et al., 1991). These may need to be modified somewhat to match the client's needs.

Figure 3 is an example of how one might perform such an analysis using the first example in Table 3. The comment suggests that the person is experiencing anxiety, anger, and perhaps confusion (psychological reactions) apparently in response to others' communications about her racial classification (sociological), and perhaps her own manner of communicating about her socioracial group allegiances.

Others might intuit from her statement that she devalues membership in the African American group, and that she is ignorant of the racial histories of both of her parents' socioracial groups. Moreover, she is attempting to resolve her Conformity status issues with respect to the two groups—Blacks and Whites—that have the longest continuous history of racial conflict in this country, perhaps without the conceptualization and communication skills necessary to do so.

Thus, in her case, a racially sensitive therapist would need to understand the multiple ways in which issues of racial oppression and dominance might be expressed within the client (e.g., Does she perceive that she acquires higher or lower status because of her parentage?) as well as her significant socialization environments (e.g., How does each parent cope with race?), and communicate this understanding to the client in an empathic manner. Moreover, since the client may be caught in a familial and societal war that is not of her making, the therapist will need to help her acquire information and teach her communication strategies to help her disentangle herself, as well as help her learn to explore and recognize the complex racial dynamics that seem to be playing themselves out in her environment.

The issues presented in the figure for discursive purposes are based on a rather small excerpt of this person's behavior and may not be accurate even for her. Therefore, they should not automatically be generalized to someone else who makes a similar comment. Rather the framework should be used to suggest the kind of investigation in which the therapist should engage in order to be appropriately responsive to racial dynamics.

Also, at the risk of being redundant, let us remind the reader that information about a person's racial identity does not reveal anything about her or his cultural socialization, except perhaps how much the person values her or his socioracial group's traditional culture. That is, a person may have developed a positive racial identity (e.g., have positive feelings about her or his socioracial group) without ever having been socialized in the relevant culture. Conversely, a person may have been socialized in a particular culture, and consequently, be capable of practicing its customs, traditions, and so forth without having any understanding of the sociopolitical racial dynamics that the groups consider to be central to their survival.

# References

Alba, R. D. (1990). *Ethnic identity: The transformation of White America*. New Haven: Yale University Press.

Allport, G. (1958). *The nature of prejudice* (abridged edition). New York: Doubleday Anchor Books.

Atkinson, D. R., Morten, G., & Sue, D. R. (1989). *Counseling American minorities: A cross-cultural perspective* (3rd ed.). Dubuque, IA: Wm. C. Brown.

Axelson, J. A. (1993). *Counseling and development in a multicultural society* (2nd ed.). Pacific Grove, CA: Brooks/Cole Publishing Company.

Banks, J. A. (1981). The stages of ethnicity: Implications for curriculum reform. In J. A. Banks (Ed.), *Multi-ethnic education: Theory and practice* (pp. 129–139). Boston: Allyn & Bacon.

Bradley, M. (1978). *The iceman inheritance: Prehistoric sources of Western man's racism, sexism, and aggression.* New York: Warner Books.

Burlew, A. K., & Smith, L. R. (1991). Measures of racial identity: An overview and a proposed framework. *Journal of Black Psychology, 17*(2), 53–71.

Carney, C. G., & Kahn, K. B. (1984). Building competencies for effective cross-cultural counseling: A developmental view. *The Counseling Psychologist, 12*(1), 111–119.

Carter, R. T. (1996). Exploring the complexity of racial identity attitude measures. In G. R. Sodowsky & J. Impara (Eds.), *Multicultural assessment* (pp. 193–223). Lincoln, NE: Buros Institute of Mental Measurement.

Comer, J. P. (1991). White racism: Its root, form, and function. In R. L. Jones (Ed.), *Black Psychology* (pp. 591–596). Berkeley, CA: Cobb & Henry.

Corbett, M., Helms, J. E., & Regan, A. (1992). The development of a White racial identity immersion scale. Paper presented at the American Psychological Association Convention, Washington, D.C.

Cross, W. E., Jr. (1971). The Negro-to-Black conversion experience: Toward a psychology of Black liberation. *Black World, 20*(9), 13–27.

Cross, W. E., Jr., Parham, T. A., & Helms, J. E. (1991). The stages of Black identity development: Nigresence models. In R. L. Jones (Ed.), *Black Psychology* (pp. 319–338). Berkeley, CA: Cobb & Henry Publishers.

Cubberly, E. P. (1929). *Changing conceptions of education.* Boston: Houghton & Mifflin.

Dizard, J. E. (1970). Black identity, social class, and Black power. *Journal of Social Issues, 26*(1), 195–207.

Dollard, J. (1957). *Caste and class in a Southern town* (3rd ed.). Garden City, NY: Doubleday.

Dollard, J., Doob, L., Miller, N., Mowrer, O. H., & Sears, R. R. (1939) *Frustration and aggression.* New Haven: Yale University Press.

Duke, L. (1994, August 28). This harrowed ground. *The Washington Post Magazine,* pp. 8–13; 20–25.

Fairchild, H. P. (1926). *The melting pot mistake.* Boston: Little, Brown and Company.

Feagin, J. R. (1984). *Racial and ethnic relations.* Englewood Cliffs, NJ: Prentice-Hall, Inc.

Franklin, V. P. (1991). Black social scientists and the mental testing movement, 1920–1940. In R. L. Jones (Ed.), *Black Psychology* (pp. 207–224). Berkeley, CA: Cobb & Henry.

Gay, G. (1984). Implications of selected models of ethnic identity development for educators. *The Journal of Negro Education, 54*(1), 43–52.

Geschwender, J. A. (1968). Explorations in the theory of social movements and revolutions. *Social Forces, 47,* 127–135.

Grant, M. (1916). *The passing of the great race.* New York: Scribner.

Hacker, A. (1992). *Two nations: Black and White, separate, hostile, unequal.* New York: Charles Scribner's Sons.

Hall, G. S. (1904). *Adolescence.* New York: Appleton.

Hardiman, R. (1982). *White identity development: A process oriented model for describing the racial consciousness of White Americans.* Unpublished doctoral dissertation, University of Massachusetts, Amherst.

Helms, J. E. (1984). Toward a theoretical explanation of the effects of race on counseling: A Black and White model. *The Counseling Psychologist, 12,* 153–165.

Helms, J. E. (1990a). *Black and White racial identity: Theory, research, and practice.* Westport, CT: Greenwood Press.

Helms, J. E. (1990b). Three perspectives on counseling and psychotherapy with visible racial/ethnic group clients. In F. C. Serafica, A. I. Schwebel, R. K. Russell, P. D. Isaac, & L. B. Myers (Eds.), *Mental Health of Ethnic Minorities* (pp. 171–201). New York: Praeger.

Helms, J. E. (1994). Racial identity and other "racial" constructs. In E. J. Trickett, R. Watts, & D. Birman (Eds.), *Human Diversity* (pp. 285–311). San Francisco: Jossey Bass.

Helms, J. E. (1996). Toward a methodology for assessing "racial identity" as distinguished from "ethnic identity." In G. R. Sodowsky & J. Impara (Eds.), *Multicultural Assessment.* Lincoln, NE: Buros Institute of Mental Measurement.

Helms, J. E., & Carter, R. T. (1990). Development of the White racial identity attitude scale. In J. E. Helms (Ed.), *Black and White racial identity: Theory, research, and practice* (pp. 67–80). Westport, CT: Greenwood Press.

Helms, J. E., & Parham, T. A. (1996). The Racial Identity Attitude Scale. In R. L. Jones (Ed.), *Handbook of tests and measurements for Black populations* (Vol. 2), (pp. 167–174). Hampton, VA: Cobb & Henry Publishers.

Helms, J. E., & Piper, R. E. (1994). Implications of racial identity theory for vocational psychology. *Journal of Vocational Psychology, 44,* 124–138.

Hutnik, N. (1991). *Ethnic minority identity: A social psychological perspective.* Oxford: Oxford University Press.

Jensen, A. R. (1969). How much can we boost IQ and scholastic achievement? *Harvard Educational Review, 39,* 1–123, 126.

Jones, L. (1994, May). Mama's White. *Essence Magazine,* pp. 78, 80, 148.

Kardiner, A., & Ovesey, L. (1951). *The mark of oppression: Explorations in the personality of the American Negro.* Cleveland, OH: Meridian Books.

Katz, P. A. (1976). The acquisition of racial attitudes in children. In P. A. Katz (Ed.), *Toward the elimination of racism* (pp. 125–150). New York: Pergamon.

Kitano, H. H. (1982). Mental health in the Japanese American community. In E. E. Jones & S. J. Korchin (Eds.), *Minority Mental Health* (pp. 149–164). New York: Praeger.

Kohut, H. (1971). *Analysis of the self.* New York: International University Press.

Landrum, J., & Batts, V. A. (1985). *Internalized racial oppression.* Unpublished working paper. Cited in J. Landrum-Brown, Black mental health and racial oppression. In D. S. Ruin (Ed.), *Handbook of mental health and mental disorder among Black Americans* (pp. 113–132). New York: Greenwood Press.

McClain, L. (1983, July 24). How Chicago taught me to hate Whites. *Washington Post, Section C,* 1, 4.

McLemore, S. D. (1983). *Racial and ethnic relations in America.* Boston, MA: Allyn and Bacon.

Myers, L. J., Speight, S. L., Highlen, P. S., Cox, C. I., Reynolds, A. L., Adams, E. M., & Hanley, C. P. (1991). Identity development and worldview: Toward an optimal conceptualization. *Journal of Counseling and Development, 70,* 54–63.

Ponterotto, J. G., & Casas, J. M. (1991). *Handbook of racial/ethnic minority counseling research.* Springfield, IL: Charles C. Thomas.

Richardson, T. Q. (1989). White racial consciousness and the counseling profession. Unpublished paper, LeHigh University, Bethlehem, PA.

Ridley, C. R., Mendoza, D. W., & Kanitz, B. E. (1994). Multicultural training: Reexamination, operationalization, and integration. *The Counseling Psychologist, 22,* 227–289.

Rowe, W., Bennett, S. K., & Atkinson, D. R. (1994). White racial identity models: A critique and alternative proposal. *The Counseling Psychologist, 22,* 129–146.

Rushton, J. P. (1990). Differential K theory: The sociobiology of individual and group differences. *Personality and Individual Differences, 6,* 441–452.

Rushton, J. P. (1995). *Race, evolution, and behavior: A life history perspective.* New Brunswick, NJ: Transaction Publishers.

Sabnani, H. B., Ponterotto, J. G., & Borodovsky, L. G. (1991). White racial identity development and cross-cultural counselor training: A stage model. *The Counseling Psychologist, 19* (1), 76–102.

Shuffleton, F. (1993). *A mixed race: Ethnicity in early America.* New York: Oxford University Press.

Simpson, G. E., & Yinger, J. M. (1972). *Racial and cultural minorities* (4th ed.). New York: Harper and Row.

Singer, L. (1962). Ethnogenesis and Negro Americans today. *Social Research, 29,* 419–432.

Smith, E. J. (1980). Profile of the Black individual in vocational literature. In R. L. Jones (Ed.), *Black Psychology* (pp. 324–357). New York: Harper & Row.

Spikard, P. R. (1992). The illogic of American racial categories. In M. P. P. Root (Ed.), *Racially mixed people in America* (pp. 12–23). Newbury Park, CA: Sage Publications.

Takaki, R. (1993). *A different mirror. A History of multicultural America.* Boston: Little, Brown.

Terry, R. W. (1977). *For Whites only.* Grand Rapids, MI: William B. Erdmans.

Thomas, A., & Sillen, S. (1972). *Racism and Psychiatry.* New York: Brunner/Mazel, Inc.

Welsing, F. C. (1974). The Cress theory of color-confrontation. *The Black Scholar, May,* 32–40.

Wenger, J. (1993). Just part of the mix. *Focus, 21*(9), 3, 4.

Wrenn, G. C. (1962). The culturally encapsulated counselor. *Harvard Educational Review, 32*(4), 444–449.

Zinn, H. (1980). *A history of the United States.* New York: Harper & Row.

# CHAPTER 12
# ETHNIC IDENTITY IN ADOLESCENTS AND ADULTS: REVIEW OF RESEARCH

## JEAN S. PHINNEY

Ethnic identity is central to the psychological functioning of members of ethnic and racial minority groups, but research on the topic is fragmentary and inconclusive. This article is a review of 70 studies of ethnic identity published in refereed journals since 1972. The author discusses the ways in which ethnic identity has been defined and conceptualized, the components that have been measured, and empirical findings. The task of understanding ethnic identity is complicated because the uniqueness that distinguishes each group makes it difficult to draw general conclusions. A focus on the common elements that apply across groups could lead to a better understanding of ethnic identity.

The growing proportion of minority group members in the United States and other Western countries has resulted in an increasing concern with issues of pluralism, discrimination, and racism in the media. However, psychological research on the impact of these issues on the individual is uneven. Most of the research dealing with psychological aspects of contact between racial or ethnic groups has focused on attitudes toward racial or ethnic groups other than one's own and particularly on stereotyping, prejudice, and discrimination. The emphasis has been on attitudes of members of the majority or dominant group toward minority group members; this is a research area of great importance in face of the daily evidence of ethnic tensions and racial violence.

A far less studied aspect of diversity has been the psychological relationship of ethnic and racial minority group members with their own group, a topic dealt with under the broad term *ethnic identity*. The study of attitudes about one's own ethnicity has been of little interest to members of the dominant group, and little attention has been paid by mainstream, generally White researchers to the psychological aspects of being a minority group member in a diverse society.

Recent concern with ethnic identity has derived in part from the ethnic revitalization movements in the 1960s. Growing awareness in society of differences associated with ethnic group membership (e.g., lower educational and occupational attainment) has been accompanied by social movements leading to increased ethnic consciousness and pride (Laosa, 1984). Attitudes toward one's ethnicity are central to the psychological functioning of those who live in societies where their group and its culture are at best poorly represented (politically, economically, and in the media) and are at worst discriminated against or even attacked verbally and physically; the concept of ethnic identity provides a way of understanding the need to assert oneself in the face of threats to one's identity (Weinreich, 1983). The psychological importance of ethnic identity is attested to by numerous literary

Phinney, J. S. (1990). Ethnic identity in adolescents and adults: Review of research. *Psychological Bulletin, 108*, 499–514.

writings of ethnic group members about the struggle to understand their ethnicity (e.g., Du Bois, 1983; Kingston, 1976; Malcolm X, 1970; Rodriguez, 1982).

The issue of ethnic identity has also been brought to the fore by changing demographics, including differential birthrates and increasing numbers of immigrants and refugees throughout the world. Projections suggest that by the mid-1990s, minority youth will constitute more than 30% of the 15- to 25-year-olds in the United States (Wetzel, 1987). The topic not only has important implications within psychology (e.g., Ekstrand, 1986) but also has broad political significance. In response, Canada has developed an explicit policy of multiculturalism and supports continuing study of the issue (Berry, Kalin, & Taylor, 1977). Many European countries will be dealing for years to come with struggles of ethnic minorities to maintain or assert their identities (Kaplan, 1989).

Within the social sciences, many writers have asserted that ethnic identity is crucial to the self-concept and psychological functioning of ethnic group members (e.g., Gurin & Epps, 1975; Maldonado, 1975). Critical issues include the degree and quality of involvement that is maintained with one's own culture and heritage; ways of responding to and dealing with the dominant group's often disparaging views of their group; and the impact of these factors on psychological well-being. These issues have been addressed conceptually from a variety of perspectives (e.g., Alba, 1985; Arce, 1981; Atkinson, Morten, & Sue, 1983; Dashefsky, 1976; DeVos & Romanucci-Ross, 1982; Frideres & Goldenberg, 1982; Mendelberg, 1986; Ostrow, 1977; Parham, 1989; Staiano, 1980; Tajfel, 1978, 1981; Weinreich, 1988; Yancey, Ericksen, & Juliani, 1976; Zinn, 1980).

However, the theoretical writing far outweighs empirical research. Most of the empirical work on ethnic identity has concentrated on young children, with a focus on minority children's racial misidentification or preference for White stimulus figures. This work has been widely discussed and reviewed (e.g., Aboud, 1987; Banks, 1976; Brand, Ruiz, & Padilla, 1974) and is not addressed here. Far less work has been done on ethnic identity beyond childhood and particularly the transition from childhood to adulthood; this gap has been recently noted (Kagitcibasi & Berry, 1989). In published studies on ethnic identity in adolescents and adults, researchers have generally focused on single groups and have used widely discrepant definitions and measures of ethnic identity, which makes generalizations and comparisons across studies difficult and ambiguous. The findings are often inconclusive or contradictory.

The topic is of sufficient importance to warrant serious research attention, but in order for the research to yield useful and meaningful results, greater conceptual and methodological clarity is needed. The primary goal of this article is to provide such clarity through a review of the empirical literature on ethnic identity in adolescents and adults. I describe the definitions and conceptual frameworks that have guided empirical research, the way in which the construct has been defined and measured, and the empirical findings. The article concludes with recommendations for future research.

In order to review the literature, an extensive search was carried out to locate journal articles from psychology, sociology, and allied social sciences, published since 1972, that dealt empirically with ethnic or racial identity in adolescents (12 years or older) or adults. The material reviewed was limited in several ways. In order to focus on research that had been subject to peer review and that was accessible to readers, only published journal articles were included. Books, chapters, dissertations, and unpublished papers were excluded, with some noted exceptions. Also excluded were (a) articles that dealt only with social identity (social class, political affiliation, national and religious identity) and did not include ethnicity and (b) articles in which the term *ethnic identity* was used to mean simply the ethnic group membership of the subjects (e.g., Furnham & Kirris, 1983). Only English-language articles were examined. Conceptual articles that included no empirical data were reviewed and are referred to but are not included in the analyses.

Seventy empirical articles dealt substantively with ethnic identity beyond childhood. The authors of those articles examined many ethnic groups and presented widely differing approaches to the meaning, the measurement, and the study of ethnic identity in adolescents and adults. The articles varied widely both in conceptualization and in the terminology applied to ethnic identity and its components. They differed in whether ethnic identity was simply described or was considered a variable whose antecedents, correlates, or outcomes were studied. However, all dealt with ethnic identity in minority or non-dominant group members, including White ethnics. Ethnic identity among members of a dominant group in society, although it can be conceptualized (Helms, 1985), has apparently not been studied empirically. The next section is an overview of the studies.

## Overview: Studies of Ethnic Identity

The articles reviewed focused on a variety of ethnic groups. The largest group of studies, nearly half the total, dealt with White ethnic groups, such as Greek and Italian Americans or French Canadians. These articles included (in order of frequency) studies from the United States, Canada, the United Kingdom, Israel, and Australia. Within White ethnic groups, Jews have been the subgroup most studied. In a few studies, White subjects were included primarily as a group in contrast to an ethnic minority group (Hispanic, Black, or Asian); in these cases the White subjects were undifferentiated as to ethnic origin.

The second largest group of studies involved Black subjects; these studies were mostly from the United States. A smaller group of studies, entirely from the United States, dealt with Hispanic subjects. A few studies focusing on Asians were primarily from the United States, but some were from Canada and Great Britain; the studies from Great Britain dealt with East Indians, mostly Pakistanis. The distribution of studies has been very uneven; many studies focused on White ethnic groups and Black Americans, but few on Asian Americans, Hispanics, or American Indians.

The articles represented research from a diversity of fields, published in 36 different journals; the majority were from psychology but some were from sociology, anthropology, social work, and education. Researchers often appeared unaware of previous work; that is, they did not cite relevant prior work. Therefore, there was much duplication of effort as researchers developed new measures independently.

The research overall presented a picture of fragmented efforts by many researchers working individually with particular ethnic groups and developing measures of limited generality. Rarely have researchers conducted follow-up studies to develop or extend a measure or to elaborate on concepts developed in a study. Nevertheless, the studies provided a starting point for understanding how different researchers have sought to understand and study ethnic identity.

## Definitions of Ethnic Identity

Ethnic identity was defined in many ways in the research reviewed. The fact that there is no widely agreed-on definition of ethnic identity is indicative of confusion about the topic. A surprising number of the articles reviewed (about two thirds) provided no explicit definition of the construct. The definitions that were given reflected quite different understandings or emphases regarding what is meant by *ethnic identity*.

In a number of articles, ethnic identity was defined as the ethnic component of social identity, as defined by Tajfel (1981): "that part of an individual's self-concept which derives from his knowledge of his membership of a social group (or groups) together with the value and emotional significance attached to that membership" (p. 255). Some writers considered self-identification the key aspect; others emphasized feelings of belonging and commitment (Singh, 1977; Ting-Toomey, 1981; Tzuriel & Klein, 1977), the sense of shared values and attitudes (White & Burke, 1987, p. 311), or attitudes toward one's group (e.g., Parham & Helms, 1981; Teske & Nelson, 1973). In contrast to the focus by these writers on attitudes and feelings, some definitions emphasized the cultural aspects of ethnic identity: for example, language, behavior, values, and knowledge of ethnic group history (e.g., Rogler, Cooney, & Ortiz, 1980). The active role of the individual in developing an ethnic identity was suggested by several writers who saw it as a dynamic product that is achieved rather than simply given (Caltabiano, 1984; Hogg, Abrams, & Patel, 1987; Simic, 1987).

In summary, researchers appeared to share a broad general understanding of ethnic identity, but the specific aspects that they emphasized differed widely. These differences are related to the diversity in how researchers have conceptualized ethnic identity and in the questions they have sought to answer; these issues are reviewed in the next section.

## Conceptual Frameworks for the Study of Ethnic Identity

About a quarter of the studies suggested no theoretical framework, but most of the studies were based on one of three broad perspectives: social identity theory, as presented by social psychologists; acculturation and culture conflict, as studied by social psychologists, sociologists, or anthropologists; and identity formation, drawn from psychoanalytic views and from developmental and counseling psychology. There is considerable overlap among the frameworks on which the studies were based, as well as great variation in the extent to which the relevant framework or theory was discussed and applied to the research. However, these three approaches provide a background for understanding the empirical research.

### Ethnic Identity and Social Identity Theory

Much of the research on ethnic identity has been conducted within the framework of social identity as conceptualized by social psychologists. One of the earliest statements of the importance of social identity was made by Lewin (1948), who asserted that individuals need a firm sense of group identification in order to maintain a sense of well-being. This idea was developed in considerable detail in the social identity theory of Tajfel and Turner (1979). According the theory, simply being a member of a group provides individuals with a sense of belonging that contributes to a positive self-concept.

However, ethnic groups present a special case of group identity (Tajfel, 1978). If the dominant group in a society holds the traits or characteristics of an ethnic group in low esteem, then ethnic group members are potentially faced with a negative social identity. Identifying with a low-status group may result in low self-regard (Hogg, Abrams, & Patel, 1987; Ullah, 1985). An extensive literature deals explicitly with the notion of "self-hatred" among disparaged ethnic groups, generally with reference to Black Americans (Banks, 1976; V. Gordon, 1980). Much of the research reviewed was concerned with this issue: that is, whether or to what extent membership in, or identification with, an ethnic group with lower status in society is related to a poorer self-concept. A number of studies addressed these issues (Grossman, Wirt, & David, 1985; Houston, 1984; Paul & Fischer, 1980; Tzuriel & Klein, 1977; White & Burke, 1987); the specific findings are discussed later in the article.

Tajfel (1978) asserted that members of low-status groups seek to improve their status in various ways. Individuals may seek to leave the group by "passing" as members of the dominant group, but this solution may have negative psychological consequences. Furthermore, this solution is not available to individuals who are racially distinct and are categorized by others as ethnic group members. Alternative solutions are to develop pride in one's group (Cross, 1978), to reinterpret characteristics deemed "inferior" so that they do not appear inferior (Bourhis, Giles, & Tajfel, 1973), and to stress the distinctiveness of one's own group (Christian, Gadfield, Giles, & Taylor, 1976; Hutnik, 1985).

Social identity theory also addresses the issue of potential problems resulting from participation in two cultures. Both Lewin (1948) and Tajfel (1978) discussed the likelihood that identification with two different groups can be problematic for identity formation in ethnic group members because of the conflicts in attitudes, values, and behaviors between their own and the majority group (Der-Karabetian, 1980; Rosenthal & Cichello, 1986; Salgado de Snyder, Lopez, & Padilla, 1982; Zak, 1973). The issue in this case is whether individuals must choose between two conflicting identities or can establish a bicultural ethnic identity and, if so, whether that is adaptive.

A distinct but related approach to ethnic identity is based on symbolic interactionism and identity theory (Stryker, 1980). Research in this framework emphasizes the importance of shared understandings about the meaning of one's ethnic identity, which derive both from one's own group and from a "countergroup" (White & Burke, 1987).

### Acculturation as a Framework for Studying Ethnic Identity

Ethnic identity is meaningful only in situations in which two or more ethnic groups are in contact over a period of time. In an ethnically or racially homogeneous society, ethnic identity is a virtually meaningless concept. The broad area of research that has dealt with groups in contact is the acculturation literature.

The term *ethnic identity* has sometimes been used virtually synonymously with *acculturation*, but the two terms should be distinguished. The concept of acculturation deals broadly with changes in cultural attitudes, values, and behaviors that result from contact between two distinct cultures (Berry, Trimble, & Olmedo, 1986). The level of concern is generally the group rather than the individual, and the focus is on how minority or immigrant groups relate to the dominant or host society. Ethnic identity may be thought of as an aspect of acculturation, in which the concern is with individuals and the focus is on how they relate to their own group as a subgroup of the larger society.

Two distinct models have guided thinking about these questions: a linear, bipolar model and a two-dimensional model. In the linear model, ethnic identity is conceptualized along a continuum from strong ethnic ties at one extreme to strong mainstream ties at the other (Andujo, 1988; Makabe, 1979; Simic, 1987; Ullah, 1985). The assumption underlying this model is that a strengthening of one requires a weakening of the other; that is, a strong ethnic identity is not possible among those who become involved in the mainstream society, and acculturation is inevitably accompanied by a weakening of ethnic identity.

In contrast to the linear model, an alternative model emphasizes that acculturation is a two-dimensional process, in which both the relationship with the traditional or ethnic culture and the relationship with the new or dominant culture must be considered, and these two relationships may be independent. According to this view, minority group members can have either strong or weak identifications with both their own and the mainstream cultures, and a strong ethnic identity does not necessarily imply a weak relationship or low involvement with the dominant culture.

This model suggests that there are not only the two acculturative extremes of assimilation or pluralism but at least four possible ways of dealing with ethnic group membership in a diverse society (Berry et al., 1986). Strong identification with both groups is indicative of integration or biculturalism; identification with neither group suggests marginality. An exclusive identification with the majority culture indicates assimilation, whereas identification with only the ethnic group indicates separation. Table 1 is an illustration of this model and some of the terms that have been used for each of the four possibilities in empirical research. A number of the studies reviewed were based on this model (e.g., M. Clark, Kaufman, & Pierce, 1976; Hutnik, 1986; Ting-Toomey, 1981; Zak, 1973), and in some the authors explored empirical evidence for the bipolar versus the two-dimensional models (e.g., Elias & Blanton, 1987; Zak, 1976). Research on this issue is summarized later.

An important empirical issue in this area has been the question of the extent to which ethnic identity is maintained over time when a minority ethnic group comes in contact with a dominant majority group (DeVos & Romanucci-Ross, 1982; Glazer & Moynihan, 1970; M. Gordon, 1964) and

**TABLE 1**

**Terms Used for Four Orientations, Based on Degree of Identification With Both One's Own Ethnic Group and the Majority Group**

| Identification with Majority Group | Identification with Ethnic Group | |
|---|---|---|
| | Strong | Weak |
| Strong | Acculturated Integrated Bicultural | Assimilated |
| Weak | Ethnically identified Ethnically embedded Separated Dissociated | Marginal |

the impact of the process on psychological adjustment (e.g., Berry, Kim, Minde, & Mok, 1987). Underlying both these issues is the theme of culture conflict between two distinct groups and the psychological consequences of such conflicts for individuals. How such conflicts are dealt with at the individual level is part of the process of ethnic identity formation.

## Ethnic Identity Formation

Both the social identity and the acculturation frameworks acknowledge that ethnic identity is dynamic, changing over time and context. In a similar vein, several of the definitions cited earlier include the idea that ethnic identity is achieved through an active process of decision making and self-evaluation (Caltabiano, 1984; Hogg et al., 1987; Simic, 1987). In a conceptual chapter, Weinreich (1988) asserted that ethnic identity is not an entity but a complex of processes by which people construct their ethnicity. However, in research based on the social identity or acculturation frameworks, investigators in general have not examined ethnic identity at the level of individual change—that is, developmentally.

A developmental framework was provided by Erikson's (1968) theory of ego identity formation. According to Erikson, an achieved identity is the result of a period of exploration and experimentation that typically takes place during adolescence and that leads to a decision or a commitment in various areas, such as occupation, religion, and political orientation. The ego identity model, as operationalized by Marcia (1966, 1980), suggests four ego identity statuses based on whether people have explored identity options and whether they have made a decision. A person who has neither engaged in exploration nor made a commitment is said to be *diffuse;* a commitment made without exploration, usually on the basis of parental values, represents a *foreclosed* status. A person in the process of exploration without having made a commitment is in *moratorium;* a firm commitment following a period of exploration is indicative of an *achieved identity* (see Table 2). Although Erikson alluded to the importance of culture in identity formation, this model has not been widely applied to the study of ethnic identity.

The formation of ethnic identity may be thought of as a process similar to ego identity formation that takes place over time, as people explore and make decisions about the role of ethnicity in their lives. A number of conceptual models have described ethnic identity development in minority adolescents or adults. Cross (1978) described a model of the development of Black consciousness in college students during the Civil Rights era. In a dissertation, Kim (1981) described Asian-American identity development in a group of young adult Asian-American women. A model of ethnic identity formation based on clinical experience was proposed by Atkinson et al. (1983), and Arce (1981) conceptualized the issues with regard to Chicanos.

In a recent article, Phinney (1989) examined commonalities across various models and proposed a three-stage progression from an unexamined ethnic identity through a period of exploration to an achieved or committed ethnic identity (see Table 2). According to this model, early adolescents and perhaps adults who have not been exposed to ethnic identity issues are in the first stage, an unexamined ethnic identity. According to Cross (1978) and others (e.g., Atkinson et al., 1983; Kim, 1981), this early stage is characterized for minorities by a preference for the dominant culture. However, such a preference is not a necessary characteristic of this stage. Young people may simply not be interested in ethnicity and may have given it little thought (their ethnic identity is diffuse). Alternatively, they may have absorbed positive ethnic attitudes from parents or other adults and therefore may not show a preference for the majority group, although they have not thought through the issues for themselves—that is, are foreclosed (Phinney, 1989).

A second stage is characterized by an exploration of one's own ethnicity, which is similar to the moratorium status described by Marcia (1980). This may take place as the result of a significant experience that forces awareness of one's ethnicity ("encounter," according to Cross, 1978, or "awakening," according to Kim, 1981). It involves an often intense process of immersion in one's own culture through activities such as reading, talking to people, going to ethnic museums, and participating actively in cultural events. For some people it may involve rejecting the values of the dominant culture.

**TABLE 2**

**Marcia's Ego Identity Statuses (Top) and Proposed Stages of Ethnic Identity (Bottom)**

| Marcia (1966, 1980) | Identity Diffusion | Identity Foreclosure | Identity Crisis[a] | Moratorium | Identity Achievement |
|---|---|---|---|---|---|
| Cross (1978) | | Pre-encounter | Encounter | Immersion/ emersion | Internalization |
| Kim (1981) | | White identified | Awakening to social political awareness | Redirection to Asian American consciousness | Incorporation |
| Atkinson et al. (1983) | | Conformity: Preference for values of dominant culture | Dissonance: Questioning and challenging old attitudes | Resistance and immersion: Rejection of dominant culture | Synergetic articulation and awareness |
| Phinney (1989) | Unexamined ethnic identity: Lack of exploration of ethnicity. Possible subtypes: Diffusion: Lack of interest in or concern with ethnicity | Foreclosure: Views of ethnicity based on opinions of others | Ethnic identity search (Moratorium): Involvement in exploring and seeking to understand meaning of ethnicity for oneself | | Achieved ethnic identity Clear, confident sense of own ethnicity |

[a] Identity crisis is not one of Marcia's original four statuses.

The stage model suggests that as a result of this process, people come to a deeper understanding and appreciation of their ethnicity—that is, ethnic identity achievement or internalization. This culmination may require resolution or coming to terms with two fundamental problems for ethnic minorities: (a) cultural differences between their own group and the dominant group and (b) the lower or disparaged status of their group in society (Phinney, Lochner, & Murphy, 1990). The meaning of ethnic identity achievement is undoubtedly different for different individuals and groups because of their different historical and personal experiences. However, achievement does not necessarily imply a high degree of ethnic involvement; one could presumably be clear about and confident of one's ethnicity without wanting to maintain one's ethnic language or customs. A recent conceptual article suggested that the process does not necessarily end with ethnic identity achievement but may continue in cycles that involve further exploration or rethinking of the role or meaning of one's ethnicity (Parham, 1989). A similar idea has been suggested with regard to ego identity (Grotevant, 1987).

Empirical research based on these models has involved describing changes over time in a person's attitudes and understanding about his or her ethnicity. In addition, researchers have looked at factors related to ethnic identity formation, such as parental attitudes and social class, and at correlates, including self-esteem or adjustment and attitudes toward counselors. Results of research on these questions are discussed later.

## Components of Ethnic Identity

In order to examine questions that derive from theory or to address research questions of current interest, it is necessary to begin with a measure of ethnic identity. In this section, the various aspects of ethnic identity that were selected for study are reviewed. The majority of the studies focused on components related to what might be called the *state* of ethnic identity—that is, a person's identification at a given time. In studies of this type, the components most widely studied were self-identification as a group member, a sense of belonging to the group, attitudes about one's group membership, and ethnic involvement (social participation, cultural practices and attitudes). A much smaller group of studies emphasized *stages* of ethnic identity, or changes over time in a person's identification. In the following section, I examine these components and the ways in which they have been assessed.

## Ethnicity and Ethnic Self-Identification

*Self-identification* (also called *self-definition* or *self-labeling*) refers to the ethnic label that one uses for oneself. Research with children has been concerned largely with the extent to which children "correctly" label themselves—that is, whether the label they choose corresponds to the ethnicity of their parents (Aboud, 1987). A related issue has been whether "incorrect" labeling is associated with a poor self-concept (Cross, 1978). Beyond childhood, the concerns are different. Adolescents and adults can be assumed to know their ethnicity; the issue is thus one of choosing what label to use for oneself. Although this appears to be a simple issue, it is in fact quite complex, inasmuch as one's ethnicity, as determined by descent (parental background), may differ from how one sees oneself ethnically.

In countries settled by Europeans (where much of the research under review was conducted), the use of an ethnic label, for example, Polish American, is for the most part optional for people of European descent. Many Whites under these circumstances use no ethnic label and may in fact be unable to identify their country of origin (Singh, 1977).

However, among those who are racially distinct, by features or skin color, or whose culture (language, dress, customs, etc.) clearly distinguishes them from the dominant group, self-identification is at least partly imposed. Calling oneself Black or Asian American is less self-categorization than recognition of imposed distinctions, and the issue is less *whether* to use an ethnic label than *which* ethnic label to adopt. For example, people whose parents or grandparents came from Mexico can call themselves Mexican American, Hispanic, Latino, or Chicano (among others), each of which has a different connotation (Buriel, 1987).

Regardless of whether an ethnic label is chosen or imposed, people may feel that a single label is inaccurate, inasmuch as they are part of two or more groups. Ethnic groups members may identify themselves as only partly ethnic and partly mainstream. For example, among a group of second-generation Irish adolescents in England, about half considered themselves part English and part Irish; the remainder called themselves either English or Irish (Ullah, 1985, 1987). Selection of a label is particularly problematic for those whose parents are from two or more distinct groups; they may, for example, call themselves mixed, such as half Hispanic and half White, or they may ignore part of their heritage and call themselves either White or Hispanic (Alipuria & Phinney, 1988).

Although ethnic self-identification is clearly an essential starting point in examining ethnic identity, it was not specifically assessed in about half the studies reviewed. In some cases, subjects were recruited from groups whose ethnicity was known to the researchers (e.g., Jewish student groups were recruited by Davids, 1982, and by Lax & Richards, 1981; students at Armenian schools were recruited by Der-Karabetian, 1980). In other studies, the subjects were simply defined as group members without explanation of how this was determined. None of the studies with Black subjects included self-identification. The failure to assess self-definition with any group raises the possibility that the studies included subjects who did not consider themselves members of the group in question.

When self-identification was assessed, items were presented in a variety of ways. If the participants were assumed to be from a given group or groups, it was possible to provide multiple-choice items appropriate for the particular group (e.g., Ullah, 1985, 1987) or to have subjects rate themselves or match labels of themselves in terms of similarity to individuals with particular labels (Christian et al., 1976; Giles, Llado, McKirnan, & Taylor, 1979; Giles, Taylor, & Bourhis, 1977; Giles, Taylor, Lambert, & Albert, 1976; Rosenthal & Hrynevich, 1985).

However, to use these sorts of questions, the researcher must preselect participants of known ethnicity. Determining ethnicity for research purposes is in itself a methodological problem that has often been ignored. An alternative is to use an unselected sample and determine ethnicity by asking participants about their parents' ethnicity. Ethnic self-identification can then be assessed with open-ended questions or multiple-choice items with a wide range of possible alternative labels, or both. However, the responses of some subjects will vary, depending on whether they are forced to choose from a list of labels provided or are simply given a blank to fill in.

In summary, ethnic self-identification is an important but complex aspect of ethnic identity, and the way in which it is assessed needs to be considered when the results obtained are interpreted.

## Sense of Belonging

People may use an ethnic label when specifically asked for one and yet may not have a strong sense of belonging to the group chosen. Therefore, it is important to assess the feeling of belonging. However, a sense of belonging was evaluated in only about a quarter of the studies reviewed, perhaps because of the difficulty of accurately tapping this subtle feeling. Researchers have devised a number of approaches to this problem; some examples are the following: "I am a person who (never, seldom, sometimes, often, very often) feels strong bonds toward [my own group]" (Driedger, 1976); "My fate and future are bound up with that of [my own group]" (Der-Karabetian, 1980; Zak, 1973, 1976); "I feel an overwhelming attachment to [my own group]" (Krate, Leventhal, & Silverstein, 1974; Parham & Helms, 1981, 1985a, 1985b). The subject may express a sense of "peoplehood" (Lax & Richards, 1981) or present self with an ethnic label (M. Clark et al., 1976; Elizur, 1984). A variation of this attitude is the importance attributed to one's ethnicity (Davids, 1982; Zak, 1973, 1976) or a feeling of concern for one's culture (Christian et al., 1976).

A sense of belonging to one's own group can also be defined in contrast to another group—that is, the experience of exclusion, contrast, or separateness from other group members (Lax & Richards, 1981): for example, "How much difference do you feel between yourself and [members of another group]?" (Ullah, 1987) or "[How similar are you to] kids from other countries who don't fit in well?" (Rosenthal & Hrynevich, 1985).

## Positive and Negative Attitudes Toward One's Ethnic Group

In addition to their self-identification and a sense of a belonging, people can have both positive and negative attitudes toward their own ethnic group. These attitudes were examined in more than half the studies reviewed. Positive attitudes include pride in and pleasure, satisfaction, and contentment with one's own group. They are assessed by items such as "[I am] proud to identify with [my own group]" and "[I] consider [my own] culture rich and precious" (Driedger, 1976) and "[I am similar to] people who feel good about their cultural background" (Rosenthal & Hrynevich, 1985) or by questions such as "How much pride do you feel towards [your own group]?" (Phinney, 1989; Ullah, 1987).

The term *acceptance* is frequently used for positive attitudes, particularly in studies involving Black subjects (Paul & Fischer, 1980). Typical items include "I believe that being Black is a positive experience" and "I believe that because I am Black I have many strengths" (Parham & Helms, 1981, 1985a, 1985b) and "I feel excitement and joy in Black surroundings" (Krate et al., 1974; Parham & Helms, 1981, 1985a, 1985b). Acceptance of being Black is often phrased in contrast to White culture: "When I think of myself as a Black person, I feel I am more attractive and smarter than any White person" (Morten & Atkinson, 1983). Acceptance of being Black has also been assessed indirectly, through having subjects draw figures and determining whether they include Black characteristics. Although this method has been used commonly with children, it has also been employed in studies with adults (Bolling, 1974; Kuhlman, 1979).

Two indirect ways of measuring positive (and negative) attitudes are to have subjects rate themselves and their group in relation to adjectives with good and bad connotations (Grossman et al., 1985) or to rate a speech that had been tape-recorded in different languages and accents (Bourhis et al., 1973). The latter case included adjectives such as "arrogant," "friendly," "self-confident," and "snobbish."

The absence of positive attitudes, or the presence of actual negative attitudes, can be seen as a denial of one's ethnic identity. They include "displeasure, dissatisfaction, discontentment" with one's ethnicity (Lax & Richards, 1981); feelings of inferiority; or a desire to hide one's cultural identity (Driedger, 1976; Ullah, 1985). An item used to tap negative feelings is "[I am like/unlike] kids from other countries who try to hide their background" (Rosenthal & Hrynevich, 1985). Negative feelings may be a normal aspect of ethnic identity for some groups; Lax and Richards (1981) stated that "Jewish identity by itself does not imply acceptance of one's Jewishness. . . . Being Jewish stirs up many ambivalent feelings" (pp. 306–307). An indirect but presumably powerful way of assessing negative attitudes is to determine whether the subject would remain a group member if given the choice. Several researchers asked whether the subject, if given a chance to be born again, would wish to be born a member of their ethnic group (Der-Karabetian, 1980; Tzuriel & Klein, 1977; Zak, 1973).

In studies with Black subjects, the negative attitudes are phrased both as denial of Blackness and as preference for White culture (Morten & Atkinson, 1983; Paul & Fischer, 1980; Phinney, 1989): "Most Black people I know are failures" (Parham & Helms, 1981, 1985a, 1985b); "I believe that large numbers of Blacks are untrustworthy" (Krate et al., 1974); "Sometimes I wish I belonged to the White race"; and "I believe that White people are intellectually superior to Blacks" (Krate et al., 1974; Parham & Helms, 1981, 1985a, 1985b).

In summary, the terms and phrasing vary with the groups under study, particularly in assessments of negative attitudes. Items for most White ethnic groups are more likely to make reference to hiding or denying one's group; for Blacks and Jews, lack of acceptance or wishing to change groups suggest negative attitudes.

## Ethnic Involvement (Social Participation and Cultural Practices)

Involvement in the social life and cultural practices of one's ethnic group is the most widely used indicator of ethnic identity but also the most problematic. As long as measures are based on specific practices that distinguish an ethnic group, it is impossible to generalize across groups; this issue is explored in detail later. The indicators of ethnic involvement that are most commonly assessed are language, friendship, social organizations, religion, cultural traditions, and politics.

*Language.* Language is the most widely assessed cultural practice associated with ethnic identity, but it was included in less than half of the studies. Language was most intensively assessed in studies of White subjects. Most of these studies dealt with subjects who had emigrated from Continental Europe to an English-speaking country (the United States, Canada, England, or Australia) and had the option of retaining their language; some were living in their country of origin (Wales) where English is dominant. Language was also assessed in a study involving American Jews in Israel, and of the nine studies of Hispanics in the United States, seven included assessment of the use of Spanish. In addition, several researchers examined the desire of adults to have their children learn their ethnic language (Caltabiano, 1984; Leclezio, Louw-Potgieter, & Souchon, 1986; Teske & Nelson, 1973).

Although language has been considered by some as the single most important component of ethnic identity, its importance clearly varies with the particular situation, and it is inappropriate for some groups. None of the studies of Black identity have included language, even though familiarity with Black English is considered an important marker of Black identity (Kochman, 1987).

*Friendship.* In roughly a fourth of the studies, the researchers assessed friendship, using items such as ratings of "importance of ingroup friends" and "ingroup dating" (Driedger, 1975), "ethnic background of friends" (Garcia, 1982), or other measures of ethnic friendships. Friendship was included as an aspect of ethnic identity in studies with most groups; however, only a few studies with Black subjects include this component.

*Religious affiliation and practice.* This component was assessed in less than a fourth of the studies; the researchers used items related to church membership, attending religious ceremonies, parochial education, and religious preference. The subjects of those studies came largely from White ethnic groups, from some Hispanic groups, and from one Jewish group; no studies of Blacks included religion as an aspect of ethnic identity.

*Structured ethnic social groups.* Participation in ethnic clubs, societies, or organizations was included as a component of ethnic identity in studies involving primarily White subjects; Asians and Hispanics were also represented, but no Black groups were.

*Political ideology and activity.* Involvement in political activities on behalf of one's ethnic group was included in a few studies; a disproportionately large number of those studies focused on Blacks. Typical items were "I frequently confront the system and the man" (Krate et al., 1974; Parham & Helms, 1981, 1985a, 1985b); "A commitment to the development of Black power dominates my behavior" (Krate et al., 1974); and "I constantly involve myself in Black political and social activities" (Parham & Helms, 1981, 1985a, 1985b). One measure of Black identity focused primarily on political ideology (Terrell & Taylor, 1978).

A study of Mexican-Americans included the question "Are you active in any political organization which is specifically Mexican-American oriented?" (Teske & Nelson, 1973). Some studies with White ethnics mentioned involvement with the politics of one's country of origin as an indicator of ethnic identity (Constantinou & Harvey, 1985).

*Area of residence.* In a few studies, the subject's area of residence was included. In some cases, the geographical region was assessed (Giles et al., 1977, 1976; Taylor, Bassili, & Aboud, 1973). In others, items tapped the number or proportion of in-group members in one's neighborhood (Der-Karabetian, 1980)—for example, "[Subject] chooses to live in an area where others [ingroup members] have settled" (Caltabiano, 1984)—or were worded to assess "[subject's] readiness to live in an integrated neighborhood" (Tzuriel & Klein, 1977). This component has not been included in studies of Blacks.

*Miscellaneous ethnic/cultural activities and attitudes.* In addition to those elements already mentioned, a wide variety of specific cultural activities and attitudes were assessed. Half the studies, distributed across all the groups studied, included one or more of the following miscellaneous cultural items: ethnic music, songs, dances, and dress; newspapers, periodicals, books, and literature; food or cooking; entertainment (movies, radio, TV, plays, sports, etc.); traditional celebrations; traditional family roles, values, and names; visits to and continued interest in the homeland; the practice of endogamy or opposition to mixed marriages; and knowledge about ethnic culture or history. These items were most often assessed by direct questions. However, in one study (of Chinese Americans), subjects were asked to rate themselves on attitudes or values that were presumed to be characteristic of a group: for example, agreement with the statement that "A good child is an obedient child" (Ting-Toomey, 1981).

## Reliability of Measures

Specific measures of ethnic identity as a state have included various combinations of the aforementioned elements; differing numbers of items have been used to assess each one. The reliability of measures is often not reported or is low enough to raise questions about conclusions based on the measure. Of the studies analyzed, less than a fifth furnished reliability information on the measures used. The reliability coefficients cited (usually Cronbach's alpha) ranged widely (from .35 to .90), and many were quite low. Rarely was the same measure used in more than one study in order to establish reliability with different samples, and in no studies was there evidence for test–retest reliability with the same subjects. A reliable measure of ethnic identity is clearly essential to the further study of this topic.

## Ethnic Identity Development

Measuring stages of ethnic identity development presents quite different problems. In only a small number of the studies reviewed did researchers attempt to deal with individual changes in ethnic identity over time; they used one of two basic approaches.

One group of studies was based on the model of Black identity formation described by Cross (1978). The researchers used variations of the Racial Identity Attitude Scale (RIAS), developed by Parham and Helms (1981) on the basis of Cross's earlier work. This scale is essentially an attitude scale, aimed at tapping negative, positive, or mixed attitudes of Blacks toward their own group and toward the White majority, attitudes that are assumed to change as the person moves through the stages. Items tap each of the four proposed stages—pre-encounter, encounter, immersion, and internalization—with reliabilities of .67, .72, .66, and .71, respectively (Parham & Helms, 1981).

Issues related to the reliability of the scale were addressed in two articles (Helms, 1989; Ponterotto & Wise, 1987). Ponterotto and Wise found support for the existence of all the stages except the second, the encounter stage. However, Akbar (1989) questioned whether ethnic or racial identity, as a core personality trait, could be assessed by an attitudinal measure such as the RIAS.

A second group of studies was aimed at developing measures of stages of ethnic identity that can be applied across ethnic groups. This approach, which was based on the ego identity measures of Marcia (1966) and Adams, Bennion, and Huh (1987), focused on the two components of the process of identity formation: (a) a search for the meaning of one's ethnicity and (b) a commitment or a decision about its place in one's life. A questionnaire used with college students from four groups (Asian American, Black, Mexican American, and White) yielded reliabilities of .69 for ethnic identity search and .59 for ethnic identity commitment (Phinney & Alipuria, 1990). In a subsequent study, interviews were used to assess ethnic identity among high school students from three minority groups (Asian American, Black, and Mexican American); raters then judged each subject as being in one of three stages of ethnic identity (Phinney, 1989). Absolute agreement between raters on stage assignment was .80 (Cohen's kappa = .65).

The variety of components of ethnic identity in the research reviewed makes it difficult to summarize or draw conclusions about exactly what ethnic identity consists of. Most researchers have acknowledged its complex, multidimensional nature and have tried to understand this complexity in some way, as is examined in the next section.

## Interrelationships, Salience, and Generality of Components

Researchers have approached the complexity of ethnic identity by attempting to identify its essential components, their interrelationships, and their relative salience. One common approach has been factor analysis. However, because of the variety of types and the numbers of items used, factor analysis has yielded widely discrepant results in different studies. Researchers have found a single factor for ethnic identity (Garcia & Lega, 1979); two factors, differing widely among the studies (Constantinou & Harvey, 1985; Driedger, 1976; Leclezio et al., 1986); three factors (Hogg et al., 1987); or four or more factors, again different in each study (Caltabiano, 1984; Driedger, 1975; Garcia, 1982; Makabe, 1979; Rosenthal & Hrynevich, 1985). When several groups were studied, the factors varied, depending on the group (Driedger, 1975; Rosenthal & Hrynevich, 1985).

### Interrelationships of Components

A specific question that has concerned researchers is the relationship between what people say they are (ethnic self-identification) and what they actually do (ethnic involvement) or how they feel (ethnic pride). In a study of Irish adolescents in England, Ullah (1987) found a close relationship between ethnic self-definition and indices of ethnic group behavior, as did Der-Karabetian (1980) in a study with Armenian Americans. In contrast, a study of East Indian adolescents in England (Hutnik, 1986) revealed little relation between ethnic identification and behavior. In a comprehensive study in which a variety of components of ethnicity for Chicanos were measured separately, Garcia (1982) found a complex set of relationships, including a negative relationship between ethnic self-identification and preference for various ethnic practices. Pride in their Irish background, among second-generation Irish adolescents in England, was related to self-identification as Irish; those who called themselves English were more likely to hide the fact of their Irish background (Ullah, 1985).

### Salience of Components

Assumptions regarding salience were implicit in the components of ethnic identity selected for study with particular groups, and these components differed widely among groups. For White ethnic groups, language and a variety of miscellaneous cultural activities were most widely used as indicators of ethnic identity, and attitudes were considered somewhat less important. In the assessment of Jewish identity, ethnic affirmation and denial were included far more than with other

White groups, whereas language was less frequently included. In studies with Hispanics, language was treated as a dominant component. A distinctive pattern emerges from the studies of American Blacks: Attitudes were the most widely used element, and the measures generally included both pro-Black and anti-White attitudes. Also, political activity was more evident as a criterion for Black identity than for the other groups, but assessment of language, friends, social groups, and neighborhood were almost completely absent.

A number of studies have suggested that language is one of the most important elements of ethnic identity (Giles et al., 1976, 1977; Leclezio et al., 1986; Taylor et al., 1973). However, a study carried out in a different setting showed that language was not salient (Giles et al., 1979). Language was seldom included in studies involving particular groups, such as Blacks.

Furthermore, salience can be manipulated. When salience of ethnicity was increased through an experimental manipulation, Welsh subjects expressed closer affiliation with their group (Christian et al., 1976).

## General Versus Specific Aspects of Ethnic Identity

The widely differing results from attempts to define the components and structure of ethnic identity raise a fundamental conceptual question: Is it possible to study ethnic identity in general terms, or, because each group and setting is unique, must each be studied separately? It is interesting that in the theories and definitions presented by researchers, ethnic identity was treated as a general phenomenon that is relevant across groups. Yet researchers have attempted to answer theoretical and definitional questions almost exclusively in terms of one group or, sometimes, a few specific groups.

A starting point in resolving this dilemma is to recognize that there are elements that are both common across groups and unique to ethnic identity for any group. On the basis of the research reviewed, it appears that self-identification, a sense of belonging, and pride in one's group may be key aspects of ethnic identity that are present in varying degrees, regardless of the group. Furthermore, the developmental model postulates that all ethnic group members have the option to explore and resolve issues related to their ethnicity, although they may vary in the extent to which they engage in this process, at both the individual and the group levels. A focus on these common elements would allow for comparisons across groups and permit one to determine whether general conclusions can in fact be drawn. A measure aimed at assessing common aspects of ethnic identity requires both selection of common components and wording of items in general rather than specific terms. Such a measure has recently been proposed as a start toward studying ethnic identity as a general phenomenon (Phinney, 1990).

On the other hand, the specific cultural practices, customs, and attitudes that distinguish one group from another are essential for understanding individual groups and the experience of members of those groups in particular settings and time frames (e.g., Keefe & Padilla, 1987). The study of ethnic identity at this more specific level may be of particular value for education, counseling, and therapeutic applications.

## Empirical Findings

Because of the different conceptualizations, definitions, and measures that have been used in the study of ethnic identity, empirical findings are difficult or impossible to compare across studies. Not surprisingly, the findings are often inconsistent.

### Self-Esteem, Self-Concept, and Psychological Adjustment

A key issue in conceptual writing about ethnic identity has been the role of group identity in the self-concept: Specifically, does a strong identification with one's ethnic group promote a positive self-concept or self-esteem? Or, conversely, is identification with an ethnic group that is held in low regard by the dominant group likely to lower one's self-esteem? Furthermore, is it possible to hold negative views about one's own group and yet feel good about oneself?

Early interest in these questions stemmed from the work of K. Clark and Clark (1947), which showed that young Black children tended to prefer White dolls to Black dolls. The meaning of such findings continues to be debated, and a number of reviewers have discussed the findings (Aboud, 1987; Banks, 1976; Brand et al., 1974; V. Gordon, 1980). However, this controversy has been dealt with almost entirely in studies with children, and there has been little extension of the work into adolescence and adulthood, the topic of the current review. Given the theoretical importance of this issue, it is surprising that in only 11 of the studies reviewed, the researchers assessed self-esteem or a related construct and examined its relationship to some measure of ethnic identity. The researchers who did address this question presented conflicting results.

Three of the studies suggested positive effects of ethnic identity, although the measures used were different in each case. Among Black early adolescents (ages 13–14) of low socioeconomic status (SES), "acceptance of racial identity," as measured by six items (no reliability given), was found to be significantly related to self-concept as measured by the Tennessee Self Concept Scale (Paul & Fischer, 1980). A study with Anglo-American and Mexican-American junior high school students revealed a positive relationship between self-esteem, assessed by Rosenberg's (1979) Self-Esteem Scale, and ethnic esteem, as measured by adjective ratings of one's own group (Grossman et al., 1985). Among Israeli high school students, ego identity, which is suggestive of good adjustment, was higher among those with high ethnic group identification than among those with low identification (on a scale with reliability of alpha equal to .60), especially among the Oriental Jews, a minority group in Israel (Tzuriel & Klein, 1977).

Four studies revealed no relationship between ethnic identity and various measures of adjustment. A study of Black and White college students revealed no relationship between self-esteem (Rosenberg scale) and ethnic identity, measured in terms of similarity-to-group scores on semantic differential ratings of Blacks and Whites—that is, similarity to a stereotype of one's own group (White & Burke, 1987). Also, for Black college students, "Black consciousness," measured by attitudes toward Blacks and Whites, was unrelated to two measures of self-esteem (Houston, 1984). Among Arab-Israeli college students, self-esteem (Rosenberg scale) was not related to measures of Arab identity (scale reliability = .81) or Israeli identity (scale reliability = .83; Zak, 1976). Finally, a study of Italian Australians revealed "Italian identity" (scale reliability = .89) to be unrelated to psychosocial adjustment, according to the Offer Self-Image Questionnaire and the Erikson Psychosocial Stage Inventory (Rosenthal & Cichello, 1986). In summary, these studies of ethnic identity, in which a variety of measures of ethnic identity as a state were used, permit no definitive conclusion about its role in self-esteem.

In contrast to the preceding studies, researchers in four studies examined self-esteem in relation to the stage model of ethnic identity. By analogy with the ego-identity literature, in which positive psychological outcomes have been associated with an achieved identity (Marcia, 1980), the developmental model predicts higher self-esteem in subjects with an achieved ethnic identity. This prediction was supported in a study with 10th-grade Black, Asian-American, and Mexican-American adolescents, in which subjects at higher stages of ethnic identity, as assessed by interviews, were found to have significantly higher scores on all four subscales of a measure of psychological adjustment (self-evaluation, sense of mastery, family relations, and social relations), as well as on an independent measure of ego development (Phinney, 1989). A similar relationship between ethnic identity search and commitment (scale reliabilities = .69 and .59, respectively) and self-esteem was found among college students from four ethnic groups (Asian American, Black, Mexican American, and White); the relationship was stronger among minority group students than among their White peers (Phinney & Alipuria, 1990). A study with Black college students, which was based on Cross's (1978) process model, revealed that low self-esteem was related to the earliest (pre-encounter) stage and to the immersion (moratorium) stage, whereas high self-esteem was associated with the encounter stage, which involves events that precipitate a search or immersion (Parham & Helms, 1985a). In a related study, the pre-encounter and immersion stages were found to be related to feelings of inferiority and anxiety (Parham & Helms, 1985b). These studies suggest that a positive self-concept may be related to the process of identity formation—that is, to the extent to which people have come to an understanding and acceptance of their ethnicity.

## Ethnic Identity in Relation to the Majority Culture

The acculturation framework for studying ethnic identity suggests that for understanding ethnic identity, it is necessary to consider also the individual's relationship to the dominant or majority group. Whereas a number of the studies reviewed focused on a single ethnic group, without reference to the dominant group (e.g., Asbury, Adderly-Kelly, & Knuckle, 1987; Constantinou & Harvey, 1985; Garcia & Lega, 1979; Keefe, 1986; Masuda, Hasegawa, & Matsumoto, 1973), many researchers took into consideration the relationship to the dominant group.

A central question, as discussed earlier, is whether ethnic identity is directly related to degree of acculturation or whether, conversely, it is independent, so that, for example, one could have a strong ethnic identification and also have strong ties to the dominant culture (see Table 1). Several studies suggest that the two are independent. In a study with adolescent girls of East Indian extraction who were living in England, Hutnik (1986) assessed separately self-identification (as Indian or British) and Indian and British cultural behaviors; the results showed the two dimensions to be unrelated. A similar picture emerged from a study of seven White ethnic groups in Canada (Driedger, 1976). Group scores demonstrated varying degrees of ethnic affirmation and denial for each group, which resulted in three types of ethnic identity, depending on degree of ethnic identification or denial: majority assimilator, ethnic identifiers, and ethnic marginals. Similarly, studies of Armenian Americans (Der-Karabetian, 1980), Jewish Americans (Zak, 1973), and Chinese Americans (Ting-Toomey, 1981) revealed ethnic identity and American identity to be independent dimensions.

However, other studies gave different results. A comparison of bipolar and orthogonal models of ethnic identity among Israelis living in the United States suggested that attitudes and behaviors relative to being Israeli, Jewish, or American were not independent (Elias & Blanton, 1987). Affective measures of the three aspects of identity were positively intercorrelated, whereas behavioral measures were negatively related; subjects who engaged in many typical American behaviors showed fewer Israeli behaviors. In another study of Israelis residing in the United States (Elizur, 1984), Jewish and American identity tended to be negatively related.

More complex results emerged from two studies in which qualitative data were used. An extensive study of Mexican-American and Asian-American adults (M. Clark et al., 1976) revealed six profiles representing different combinations of attitudes, behaviors, and knowledge relative to one's own culture and American culture. A qualitative study of Mexican-American high school students (Matute-Bianchi, 1986) demonstrated five types of ethnic identity, depending on the students' degree of involvement in their own ethnic culture and in the mainstream culture of the high school. Moreover, the types of identity were related to school achievement. Those students who were more embedded in the barrio culture were the least successful academically.

The value of studies such as these, in which mainstream as well as ethnic orientation is assessed, has been in emphasizing that ethnic identity is not necessarily a linear construct; it can be conceptualized in terms of qualitatively different ways of relating to one's own and other groups. A problem in using this more complex conceptualization is in assessing the attributes of the contrast group. The characteristics of mainstream culture are far more difficult to define than those of a particular subculture. The issue of measurement of mainstream attitudes belongs properly to the topic of acculturation; these measurement issues were thoroughly discussed by Berry et al. (1986).

The two-dimensional model provides some clarification of the importance of ethnic identity to the self-concept. Some of the contradictions and inconsistencies noted in this review may be a function of differences in the degree to which researchers have considered identification with both the ethnic group and the mainstream culture. For example, although ethnic identity, in the sense of identification with one's ethnic group, can range from strong to weak, an understanding of how ethnic identity is related to self-concept may require also determining an individual's relationship to the majority group. There is some evidence that the acculturated or integrated option may be the most satisfactory and the marginal, the least (Berry et al., 1987). However, the other two possibilities, assimilation and separation, may also provide the basis for a good self-concept, if the person is comfortable with these alternatives and is in an environment that supports them (Phinney et al., 1990).

## Changes in Ethnic Identity Related to Generation of Immigration

A second focus of research within the acculturation framework is the way in which ethnic identity changes with contact with another group. Writers generally have agreed that ethnic identity is a dynamic concept, but relatively few have studied it over time. However, a number of researchers have examined changes related to generational status among immigrant groups.

Studies of generational differences in ethnic identity have shown a fairly consistent decline in ethnic group identification in later generations descended from immigrants (Constantinou & Harvey, 1985; Fathi, 1972). Ethnic identity was found to be similarly weaker among those who arrived at a younger age and had lived longer in the new country (Garcia & Lega, 1979; Rogler et al., 1980) and among those with more education (Rogler et al., 1980). However, a study of third- and fourth-generation Japanese-American youth revealed virtually no generational difference (Wooden, Leon, & Toshima, 1988), and a study of Chinese Americans suggests a cyclical process whereby ethnic identity became more important in third- and fourth-generation descendents of immigrants (Ting-Toomey, 1981). A recent study (Rosenthal & Feldman, in press) found that among adolescent Chinese immigrants, ethnic knowledge and behavior decreased between the first and second generations, but that there was no change in the importance or positive valuation of ethnicity. The authors suggest that although some behavioral and cognitive elements of ethnic identity decline, immigrants retain a commitment to their culture. Furthermore, specific programs can foster ethnic identity (Zisenwine & Walters, 1982).

A study of three age groups in Japan (Masuda et al., 1973) illustrates the possible confounding of generation with age and cultural change. Older Japanese scored higher than did younger people in a measure of Japanese identification, in results similar to the generational differences among Japanese immigrants. Comparisons between younger (second-generation) and older (first-generation) subjects may thus tap age as well as cohort differences. In a retrospective interview study with elderly Croatians, Simic (1987) noted an intensification of ethnic sentiments during later life.

## Ethnic Identity and Gender

Gender may be a variable in acculturation in those cultures in which men are more likely to get jobs in the mainstream culture while the women remain at home. There may also be different cultural expectations for men and women, such as the assumption that women are the carriers of ethnic traditions. The very little research that addresses this issue suggests a greater involvement in ethnicity by women than by men. Research with Chinese-American college students revealed women to be more oriented to their ancestral culture than were men (Ting-Toomey, 1981), and a drawing study showed higher Black identification in women (Bolling, 1974). Among Irish adolescents in England, girls were significantly more likely than boys to adopt an Irish identity (Ullah, 1985). Japanese girls and women tended to score higher than boys and men on Japanese ethnic identity (Masuda et al., 1973).

In contrast, Jewish boys in Canada were found to show greater preference for Jewish norms than did girls (Fathi, 1972), a fact that the author suggested may be related to the Jewish emphasis on male dominance. Among East Indian and Anglo-Saxon adolescents in England, girls were more inclined than boys to mix with their own group, but they were also more willing to invite home someone from a different group (Hogg et al., 1987). Gender was found to interact with ethnic identity on attitudes toward counseling (Ponterotto, Anderson, & Grieger, 1986) and on a measure of visual retention (Knuckle & Asbury, 1986).

In the sparse literature on identity formation, Parham and Helms (1985b) found that Black men were more likely than Black women to endorse attitudes from the earliest stages and less likely to show evidence of the highest stage. A similar trend among Black adolescents was noted by Phinney (1989). These fragmentary results clearly allow no conclusions about sex differences in ethnic identity.

## Contextual Factors in Ethnic Identity

Ethnic identity is to a large extent defined by context; it is not an issue except in terms of a contrast group, usually the majority culture. The particular context seems to be an essential factor to consider, yet relatively few researchers have examined it in any detail. There is some evidence that ethnic identity varies according to the context (e.g., Vermeulen & Pels, 1984) and the characteristics of the group (Rosenthal & Hrynevich, 1985). Adolescents report that their feelings of being ethnic vary according to the situation they are in and the people they are with (Rosenthal & Hrynevich, 1985). Ethnic identity is positively related to the ethnic density of the neighborhood (Garcia & Lega, 1979) and negatively to the occupational and residential mobility of subjects (Makabe, 1979); it varies among communities within the same state (Teske & Nelson, 1973).

Some writers have suggested that ethnic identity is less likely to be maintained among middle-SES than among lower-SES ethnic group members. Among second-generation Irish adolescents in England, those from lower socioeconomic backgrounds were significantly more likely to identify themselves as Irish than were middle-SES youth, perhaps because they lived in areas with a higher concentration of Irish immigrants. However, research based on the developmental model has revealed no relationship between stages of ethnic identity and social class among high school students (Phinney, 1989) or college students (Phinney & Alipuria, 1990), and racial identity attitudes were not predictive of socioeconomic status among Black college students (Carter & Helms, 1988).

The impact of the context on Black identity has been investigated through studies of transracial adoption. Racial identity was more of a problem for Black children and adolescents adopted into White homes than for those adopted by Black parents, although the self-esteem of the two groups did not differ (McRoy, Zurcher, Lauderdale, & Anderson, 1982). Transracially adopted Hispanic adolescents were similarly likely to identify themselves as Americans, whereas those adopted by Mexican-American couples overwhelmingly called themselves Mexican American (Andujo, 1988). Furthermore, the parental attitudes and perceptions had an important impact on the racial identity of transracial adoptees (McRoy, Zurcher, & Lauderdale, 1984).

There has been little research on such presumably important factors as the relative size of the ethnic group (at the local or the national level) or its status in the community.

## Ethnic Identity Formation

The developmental model assumes that with increasing age, subjects are more likely to have an achieved ethnic identity. Although there is little empirical support for this assumption, some results suggest that there is a developmental progression. In an interview study with Black and White 8th graders, about a third of the subjects showed evidence of ethnic identity search (Phinney & Tarver, 1988); among 10th graders in a related study, the comparable figure was about half (Phinney, 1989). Thus it appeared that the older students had done more searching. In a study based on Cross's (1978) model, Black college students reported their perceptions of themselves over the past, present, and future as shifting from lower to higher levels of Black identity (Krate et al., 1974). Both longitudinal and cross-sectional studies are needed to examine changes toward higher levels of ethnic identity formation.

Although the process model of ethnic identity has not been validated, it provides an alternative way of thinking about ethnic identity. Both attitudes and behaviors with respect to one's own and other groups are conceptualized as changing as one develops and resolves issues and feelings about one's own and other groups. Differing ethnic attitudes and behaviors may therefore reflect different stages of development, rather than permanent characteristics of the group or the individuals studied. Some discrepancies in the findings regarding relationships among components of ethnic identity, reported earlier in this review, may result from studying subjects at different stages of development.

Another topic of interest in this area has been the impact of ethnic identity stages on attitudes regarding the ethnicity of counselors. Black college students in the early stages preferred White counselors (Parham & Helms, 1981), whereas those in the intermediate stages showed a preference for Black counselors (Morten & Atkinson, 1983; Parham & Helms, 1981). Results for subjects at the highest stage are mixed; they may show Black preference (Parham & Helms, 1981) or no preference (Morten & Atkinson, 1983). Stages of ethnic identity development in Blacks are also related to perceptions of White counselors (Pomales, Claiborn, & LaFromboise, 1986).

In examining the relationship of stages of Black identity to Black value orientations, Carter and Helms (1987) found that certain values could be predicted from the stages; for example, the highest stage, internalization, was associated with a belief in harmony with nature.

The study of stages of ethnic identity is at present rudimentary; however, a developmental perspective may be able eventually to provide a more complete understanding of this phenomenon across age.

## Recommendations for Future Research

The most serious need in ethnic identity research is to devise reliable and valid measures of ethnic identity. To accomplish this, it is important to distinguish between general aspects of ethnic identity that apply across groups and specific aspects that distinguish groups. General measures would be valuable in addressing the important questions about ethnic identity that are raised by theory.

A key question is the implication of ethnic identity for psychological adjustment. The relationship is complex, and a clarification requires consideration not only of the strength of ethnic identity but also of the relationship to the majority culture, as outlined in Table 1, and of the stages of ethnic identity development suggested in Table 2. A specific question to be answered is whether self-esteem can be equally high in people who are acculturated, ethnically embedded (or dissociated), or even assimilated. The extent to which these alternatives are equally healthy forms of ethnic identity may depend on whether a person has an achieved ethnic identity—that is, has explored the issues and made a conscious decision.

Another critical issue is the impact of ethnic identity on attitudes toward both the dominant group and other minority groups. Is it the case that feeling good about one's own group is associated with positive attitudes toward other groups? The answer to this question could have important policy implications, as is seen in the case of Canada (Berry et al., 1977).

The role of the context—family, community, and social structure—needs further study. In particular, past researchers have generally neglected socioeconomic status as a variable and, like most psychological researchers, has mostly used middle-SES samples. Because some ethnic minority groups are substantially underrepresented in the middle class, findings based on college students or other middle-class samples may lack generality. Even data from high school surveys may be distorted because lower-class students are more likely not to obtain parental permission to participate, to be absent from school, or to have reading problems (Phinney & Tarver, 1988). The confounding of socioeconomic status and ethnicity as a personal identity issue was eloquently stated by Steele (1988).

The vast majority of the research on ethnic identity is descriptive or correlational; only a very few investigators have used experimental manipulations (e.g., Rosenthal, Whittle, & Bell, 1988). As long as purely descriptive approaches are used, ethnic identity may be confounded with other personality characteristics, and it will be impossible to identify the effect of ethnic identity on behavior and attitudes.

A significant problem that has been virtually ignored in research is that of people from mixed backgrounds. There has been little documentation of this growing phenomenon, and it has been difficult to study, as many subjects identify themselves as members of one group even though they in fact have a mixed background (Alba & Chamlin, 1983; Salgado de Snyder et al., 1982; Singh, 1977). Anecdotal evidence indicates that in some cases women who have married Hispanics are considered to be Hispanic because of their surnames, as are children whose father is Hispanic, regardless of their mothers' ethnicity. In general, persons with one minority-group parent are considered to belong to that group. The responses of all such persons to items assessing aspects of ethnic identity may well distort the findings. Collecting data on the ethnicity of both parents and distinguishing subjects who are from mixed backgrounds is an essential step in dealing with this problem.

## Summary

In a world where the populations of most countries are increasingly diverse, both ethnically and racially, it is essential to understand the psychological impact of such diversity (Albert, 1988). Although attitudes of the majority toward minority ethnic groups have received most attention, it is equally important to understand how ethnic group members deal with being part of a group that may be disparaged or discriminated against, that must struggle to maintain its own customs and traditions, and that is not well represented in the media, among other problems. The task of understanding ethnic identity is complicated by the fact that the uniqueness that distinguishes each group and setting makes it difficult to draw general conclusions across groups.

There are important research questions to be addressed, such as the role of ethnic identity in self-esteem, its relationship to acculturation, and its place in the development of personal identity. Currently, researchers can offer few answers to these questions because of widely differing approaches to the study of ethnic identity, including lack of agreement on what constitutes its essential components, varying theoretical orientations that have guided the research, and measures that are unique to each group. It is hoped that this article brings some conceptual clarity to this important area and stimulates further research on ethnic identity.

## References

Aboud, F. (1987). The development of ethnic self-identification and attitudes. In J. Phinney & M. Rotheram (Eds.), *Children's ethnic socialization: Pluralism and development* (pp. 32–55). Newbury Park, CA: Sage.

Adams, G., Bennion, L., & Huh, K. (1987). *Objective measure of ego identity status: A reference manual.* Logan: Utah State University Laboratory for Research on Adolescence.

Akbar, N. (1989). Nigrescence and identity: Some limitations. *The Counseling Psychologist, 17,* 258–263.

Alba, R. (1985). *Ethnicity and race in the U.S.A.* London: Routledge & Kegan Paul.

Alba, R., & Chamlin, M. B. (1983). A preliminary examination of ethnic identification among Whites. *American Sociological Review, 48,* 240–242.

Albert, R. (1988). The place of culture in modern psychology. In P. Bronstein & K. Quina (Eds.), *Teaching a psychology of people: Resources for gender and sociocultural awareness* (pp. 12–18). Washington, DC: American Psychological Association.

Alipuria, L., & Phinney, J. (1988, April). *Ethnic identity in mixed-ethnic college students in two settings.* Paper presented at the meeting of the Western Psychological Association, Burlingame, CA.

Andujo, E. (1988). Ethnic identity of transethnically adopted Hispanic adolescents. *Social Work, 33,* 531–535.

Arce, C. (1981). A reconsideration of Chicano culture and identity. *Daedalus, 110*(2), 177–192.

Asbury, C., Adderly-Kelly, B., & Knuckle, E. (1987). Relationship among WISC-R performance categories and measured ethnic identity in Black adolescents. *Journal of Negro Education, 56,* 172–183.

Atkinson, D., Morten, G., & Sue, D. (1983). *Counseling American minorities.* Dubuque, IA: Wm. C. Brown.

Banks, W. (1976). White preference in Blacks: A paradigm in search of a phenomenon. *Psychological Bulletin, 83,* 1179–1186.

Berry, J., Kalin, R., & Taylor, D. (1977). *Multiculturalism and ethnic attitudes in Canada.* Ottawa, Canada: Minister of Supply and Services.

Berry, J., Kim, U., Minde, T., & Mok, D. (1987). Comparative studies of acculturative stress. *International Migration Review, 21,* 491–511.

Berry, J., Trimble, J., & Olmedo, E. (1986). Assessment of acculturation. In W. Lonner & J. Berry (Eds.), *Field methods in cross-cultural research* (pp. 291–324). Newbury Park, CA: Sage.

Bolling, J. (1974). The changing self-concept of Black children. *Journal of the National Medical Association, 66,* 28–31, 34.

Bourhis, R., Giles, H., & Tajfel, H. (1973). Language as a determinant of Welsh identity. *European Journal of Social Psychology, 3,* 447–460.

Brand, E., Ruiz, R., & Padilla, A. (1974). Ethnic identification and preference: A review. *Psychological Bulletin, 86,* 860–890.

Buriel, R. (1987). Ethnic labeling and identity among Mexican Americans. In J. Phinney & M. Rotheram (Eds.), *Children's ethnic socialization: Pluralism and development* (pp. 134–152). Newbury Park, CA: Sage.

Caltabiano, N. (1984). Perceived differences in ethnic behavior: A pilot study of Italo-Australian Canberra residents. *Psychological Reports, 55,* 867–873.

Carter, R., & Helms, J. (1987). The relationship of Black value-orientations to racial identity attitudes. *Measurement and Evaluation in Counseling and Development, 19,* 185–195.

Carter, R., & Helms, J. (1988). The relationship between racial identity attitudes and social class. *Journal of Negro Education, 57,* 22–30.

Christian, J., Gadfield, N., Giles, H., & Taylor, D. (1976). The multidimensional and dynamic nature of ethnic identity. *International Journal of Psychology, 11,* 281–291.

Clark, K., & Clark, M. (1947). Racial identification and preference in Negro children. In T. Newcomb & E. Hartley (Eds.), *Readings in social psychology* (pp. 551–560). New York: Holt.

Clark, M., Kaufman, S., & Pierce, R. (1976). Explorations of acculturation: Toward a model of ethnic identity. *Human Organization, 35,* 231–238.

Constantinou, S., & Harvey, M. (1985). Dimensional structure and intergenerational differences in ethnicity: The Greek Americans. *Sociology and Social Research, 69,* 234–254.

Cross, W. (1978). The Thomas and Cross models of psychological nigrescence: A literature review. *Journal of Black Psychology, 4,* 13–31.

Dasheksky, A. (Ed.) (1976). *Ethnic identity in society.* Chicago: Rand McNally.

Davids, L. (1982). Ethnic identity, religiosity, and youthful deviance: The Toronto computer dating project. *Adolescence, 17,* 673–684.

Der-Karabetian, A. (1980). Relation of two cultural identities of Armenian-Americans. *Psychological Reports, 47,* 123–128.

DeVos, G., & Romanucci-Ross, L. (1982). *Ethnic identity: Cultural continuities and change.* Chicago: University of Chicago Press.

Driedger, L. (1975). In search of cultural identity factors: A comparison of ethnic students. *Canadian Review of Sociology and Anthropology, 12,* 150–161.

Driedger, L. (1976). Ethnic self-identity: A comparison of ingroup evaluations. *Sociometry, 39,* 131–141.

Du Bois, W. E. B. (1983). *Autobiography of W. E. B. Du Bois.* New York: International Publishing.

Ekstrand, L. (1986). *Ethnic minorities and immigrants in a cross-cultural perspective.* Lisse, Netherlands: Swets & Zeitlinger.

Elias, N., & Blanton, J. (1987). Dimensions of ethnic identity in Israeli Jewish families living in the United States. *Psychological Reports, 60,* 367–375.

Elizur, D. (1984). Facet analysis of ethnic identity: The case of Israelis residing in the United States. *Journal of General Psychology, 111,* 259–269.

Erikson, E. (1968). *Identity: Youth and crisis.* New York: Norton.

Fathi, A. (1972). Some aspects of changing ethnic identity of Canadian Jewish youth. *Jewish Social Studies, 34,* 23–30.

Frideres, J., & Goldenberg, S. (1982). Myth and reality in Western Canada. *International Journal of Intercultural Relations, 6,* 137–151.

Furnham, A., & Kirris, R. (1983). Self-image disparity, ethnic identity and sex-role stereotypes in British and Cypriot adolescents. *Journal of Adolescence, 6,* 275–292.

Garcia, J. (1982). Ethnicity and Chicanos: Measurement of ethnic identification, identity, and consciousness. *Hispanic Journal of Behavioral Sciences, 4,* 295–314.

Garcia, M., & Lega, L. (1979). Development of a Cuban ethnic identity questionnaire. *Hispanic Journal of Behavioral Sciences, 1,* 247–261.

Giles, H., Llado, N., McKirnan, D., & Taylor, D. (1979). Social identity in Puerto Rico. *International Journal of Psychology, 14,* 185–201.

Giles, H., Taylor, D., & Bourhis, R. (1977). Dimensions of Welsh identity. *European Journal of Social Psychology, 7,* 165–174.

Giles, H., Taylor, D., Lambert, W. E., & Albert, G. (1976). Dimensions of ethnic identity: An example from northern Maine. *Journal of Social Psychology, 100,* 11–19.

Glazer, N., & Moynihan, D. (1970). *Beyond the melting pot.* Cambridge, MA: Harvard University Press.

Gordon, M. (1964). *Assimilation in American life.* London: Oxford University Press.

Gordon, V. (1980). *The self-concept of Black Americans.* Lanham, MD: University Press America.

Grossman, B., Wirt, R., & Davids, A. (1985). Self-esteem, ethnic identity, and behavioral adjustment among Anglo and Chicano adolescents in West Texas. *Journal of Adolescence, 8,* 57–68.

Grotevant, H. (1987). Toward a process model of identity formation. *Journal of Adolescent Research, 2,* 203–222.

Gurin, P., & Epps, E. (1975). *Black consciousness, identity, and achievement.* New York: Wiley.

Helms, J. (1985). Toward a theoretical explanation of the effects of race on counseling: A Black and White model. *The Counseling Psychologist, 12,* 153–165.

Helms, J. (1989). Considering some methodological issues in racial identity counseling research. *The Counseling Psychologist, 17,* 227–252.

Hogg, M., Abrams, D., & Patel, Y. (1987). Ethnic identity, self-esteem, and occupational aspirations of Indian and Anglo-Saxon British adolescents. *Genetic, Social, and General Psychology Monographs, 113,* 487–508.

Houston, L. (1984). Black consciousness and self-esteem. *Journal of Black Psychology, 11,* 1–7.

Hutnik, N. (1985). Aspects of identity in a multi-ethnic society. *New Community, 12,* 298–309.

Hutnik, N. (1986). Patterns of ethnic minority identification and modes of social adaptation. *Ethnic and Racial Studies, 9,* 150–167.

Kagitcibasi, C., & Berry, J. (1989). Cross-cultural psychology: Current research and trends. In M. Rosenzweig & L. Porter (Eds.), *Annual review of psychology* (Vol. 40, pp. 493–531). Palo Alto, CA: Annual Reviews.

Kaplan, R. (1989, July). The Balkans: Europe's third world. *The Atlantic, 263,* 16–22.

Keefe, S. (1986). Southern Appalachia: Analytical models, social services, and native support systems. *American Journal of Community Psychology, 14,* 479–498.

Keefe, S., & Padilla, A. (1987). *Chicano ethnicity.* Albuquerque: University of New Mexico Press.

Kim, J. (1981). *The process of Asian-American identity development: A study of Japanese American women's perceptions of their struggle to achieve positive identities.* Unpublished doctoral dissertation, University of Massachusetts.

Kingston, M. (1976). *The woman warrior.* South Yarmouth, MA: J. Curley.

Knuckle, E., & Asbury, C. (1986). Benton revised visual retention test: Performance of Black adolescents according to age, sex, and ethnic identity. *Perceptual and Motor Skills, 63,* 319–327.

Kochman, T. (1987). The ethnic component in Black language and culture. In J. Phinney & M. Rotheram (Eds.), *Children's ethnic socialization: Pluralism and development* (pp. 219–238). Newbury Park, CA: Sage.

Krate, R., Leventhal, G., & Silverstein, B. (1974). Self-perceived transformation of Negro-to-Black identity. *Psychological Reports, 35,* 1071–1075.

Kuhlman, T. (1979). A validation study of the Draw-a-Person as a measure of racial identity acceptance. *Journal of Personality Assessment, 43,* 457–458.

Laosa, L. (1984). Social policies toward children of diverse ethnic, racial and language groups in the United States. In H. Stevenson & A. Siegel (Eds.), *Child development research and social policy* (pp. 1–109). Chicago: University of Chicago Press.

Lax, R., & Richards, A. (1981). Observations on the formation of Jewish identity in adolescents: Research report. *Israel Journal of Psychiatry and Related Sciences, 18,* 299–310.

Leclezio, M. K., Louw-Potgieter, J., & Souchon, M. B. S. (1986). The social identity of Mauritian immigrants in South Africa. *Journal of Social Psychology, 126,* 61–69.

Lewin, K. (1948). *Resolving social conflicts.* New York: Harper.

Makabe, T. (1979). Ethnic identity scale and social mobility: The case of Nisei in Toronto. *The Canadian Review of Sociology and Anthropology, 16,* 136–145.

Malcolm X, (1965). *Autobiography of Malcolm X.* New York: Golden Press.

Maldonado, D., Jr. (1975). Ethnic self-identity and self-understanding. *Social Casework, 56,* 618–622.

Marcia, J. (1966). Development and validation of ego-identity status. *Journal of Personality and Social Psychology, 3,* 551–558.

Marcia, J. (1980). Identity in adolescence. In J. Adelson (Ed.), *Handbook of adolescent psychology* (pp. 159–187). New York: Wiley.

Masuda, M., Hasegawa, R., & Matsumoto, G. (1973). The ethnic identity questionnaire: A comparison of three Japanese age groups in Tachikawa, Japan, Honolulu, and Seattle. *Journal of Cross-Cultural Psychology, 4,* 229–244.

Matute-Bianchi, M. (1986). Ethnic identities and pattern of school success and failure among Mexican-descent and Japanese-American students in a California high school: An ethnographic analysis. *American Journal of Education, 95,* 233–255.

McRoy, R., Zurcher, L., & Lauderdale, M. (1984). The identity of transracial adoptees. *Social Casework, 65,* 34–39.

McRoy, R., Zurcher, L., Lauderdale, M., & Anderson, R. (1982). Self-esteem and racial identity in transracial and inracial adoptees. *Social Work, 27,* 522–526.

Mendelberg, H. (1986). Identity conflict in Mexican-American adolescents. *Adolescence, 21,* 215–222.

Morten, G., & Atkinson, D. (1983). Minority identity development and preference for counselor race. *Journal of Negro Education, 52,* 156–161.

Ostrow, M. (1977). The psychological determinants of Jewish identity. *Israel Annals of Psychiatry and Related Disciplines, 15,* 313–335.

Parham, T. (1989). Cycles of psychological nigrescence. *The Counseling Psychologist, 17,* 187–226.

Parham, T., & Helms, J. (1981). The influence of Black students' racial identity attitudes on preferences for counselor's race. *Journal of Counseling Psychology, 28,* 250–257.

Parham, T., & Helms, J. (1985a). Attitudes of racial identity and self-esteem of Black students: An exploratory investigation. *Journal of College Student Personnel, 26,* 143–147.

Parham, T., & Helms, J. (1985b). Relation of racial identity attitudes to self-actualization and affective states of Black students. *Journal of Counseling Psychology, 32,* 431–440.

Paul, M., & Fischer, J. (1980). Correlates of self-concept among Black early adolescents. *Journal of Youth and Adolescence, 9,* 163–173.

Phinney, J. (1989). Stages of ethnic identity in minority group adolescents. *Journal of Early Adolescence, 9,* 34–49.

Phinney, J. (1990). *The Multigroup Ethnic Identity Measure: A new scale for use with adolescents and adults from diverse groups.* Manuscript submitted for publication.

Phinney, J., & Alipuria, L. (1990). Ethnic identity in older adolescents from four ethnic groups. *Journal of Adolescence, 13.*

Phinney, J., Lochner, B., & Murphy, R. (1990). Ethnic identity development and psychological adjustment in adolescence. In A. Stiffman & L. Davis (Eds.), *Ethnic issues in adolescent mental health.* Newbury Park, CA: Sage.

Phinney, J., & Tarver, S. (1988). Ethnic identity search and commitment in Black and White eighth graders. *Journal of Early Adolescence, 8,* 265–277.

Pomales, J., Claiborn, C., & LaFromboise, T. (1986). Effect of Black students' racial identity on perceptions of White counselors varying in cultural sensitivity. *Journal of Counseling Psychology, 33,* 57–61.

Ponterotto, J., Anderson, W., & Grieger, I. (1986). Black students' attitudes toward counseling as a function of racial identity. *Journal of Multicultural Counseling and Development, 14,* 50–59.

Ponterotto, J., & Wise, S. (1987). Construct validity study of the Racial Identity Attitude Scale. *Journal of Counseling Psychology, 34,* 218–223.

Rodriguez, R. (1982). *Hunger of memory.* Boston: Godine.

Rogler, L., Cooney, R., & Ortiz, V. (1980). Intergenerational change in ethnic identity in the Puerto Rican family. *International Migration Review, 14,* 193–214.

Rosenberg, M. (1979). *Conceiving the self.* New York: Basic Books.

Rosenthal, D., & Cichello, A. (1986). The meeting of two cultures: Ethnic identity and psychosocial adjustment of Italian-Australian adolescents. *International Journal of Psychology, 21,* 487–501.

Rosenthal, D., & Feldman, S. (in press). The nature and stability of ethnic identity in Chinese youth: Effects of length of residence in two cultural contexts. *Journal of Cross-Cultural Psychology.*

Rosenthal, D., & Hrynevich, C. (1985). Ethnicity and ethnic identity: A comparative study of Greek-, Italian-, and Anglo-Australian adolescents. *International Journal of Psychology, 20,* 723–742.

Rosenthal, D., Whittle, J., & Bell, R. (1988). The dynamic nature of ethnic identity among Greek-Australian adolescents. *Journal of Social Psychology, 129,* 249–258.

Salgado de Snyder, N., Lopez, C. M., & Padilla, A. M. (1982). Ethnic identity and cultural awareness among the offspring of Mexican interethnic marriages. *Journal of Early Adolescence, 2,* 277–282.

Simic, A. (1987). Ethnicity as a career for the elderly: The Serbian-American case. *Journal of Applied Gerontology, 6*, 113–126.

Singh, V. (1977). Some theoretical and methodological problems in the study of ethnic identity: A cross-cultural perspective. *New York Academy of Sciences: Annals, 285*, 32–42.

Sommerlad, E., & Berry, J. (1970). The role of ethnic identification in distinguishing between attitudes towards assimilation and integration of a minority racial group. *Human Relations, 13*, 23–29.

Staiano, K. (1980). Ethnicity as process: The creation of an Afro-American identity. *Ethnicity, 7*, 27–33.

Steele, S. (1988). On being Black and middle class. *Commentary, 85*, 42–47.

Stryker, S. (1980). *Symbolic interactionism: A social structural version.* Menlo Park, CA: Benjamin Cummings.

Tajfel, H. (1978). *The social psychology of minorities.* New York: Minority Rights Group.

Tajfel, H. (1981). *Human groups and social categories.* Cambridge, England: Cambridge University Press.

Tajfel, H., & Turner, J. (1979). An integrative theory of intergroup conflict. In W. Austin & S. Worchel (Eds.), *The social psychology of intergroup relations* (pp. 33–47). Monterey, CA: Brooks/Cole.

Taylor, D. M., & Bassili, J. N., & Aboud, F. E. (1973). Dimensions of ethnic identity: An example from Quebec. *Journal of Social Psychology, 89*, 185–192.

Terrell, F., & Taylor, J. (1978). The development of an inventory to measure certain aspects of Black nationalist ideology. *Psychology, 15*, 31–33.

Teske, R., & Nelson, B. (1973). Two scales for the measurement of Mexican-American identity. *International Review of Modern Sociology, 3*, 192–203.

Ting-Toomey, S. (1981). Ethnic identity and close friendship in Chinese-American college students. *International Journal of Intercultural Relations, 5*, 383–406.

Tzuriel, D., & Klein, M. M. (1977). Ego identity: Effects of ethnocentrism, ethnic identification, and cognitive complexity in Israeli, Oriental, and Western ethnic groups. *Psychological Reports, 40*, 1099–1110.

Ullah, P. (1985). Second generation Irish youth: Identity and ethnicity. *New Community, 12*, 310–320.

Ullah, P. (1987). Self-definition and psychological group formation in an ethnic minority. *British Journal of Social Psychology, 26*, 17–23.

Vermeulen, H., & Pels, T. (1984). Ethnic identity and young migrants in The Netherlands. *Prospects, 14*, 277–282.

Weinreich, P. (1983). Emerging from threatened identities. In G. Breakwell (Ed.), *Threatened identities* (pp. 149–185). New York: Wiley.

Weinreich, P. (1988). The operationalization of ethnic identity. In J. Berry & R. Annis (Eds.), *Ethnic psychology: Research and practice with immigrants, refugees, native peoples, ethnic groups and sojourners* (pp. 149–168). Amsterdam: Swets & Zeitlinger.

Wetzel, J. (1987). *American youth: A statistical snapshot.* Washington, DC: William T. Grant Foundation.

White, C., & Burke, P. (1987). Ethnic role identity among Black and White college students: An interactionist approach. *Sociological Perspectives, 30*, 310–331.

Wooden, W., Leon, J., & Toshima, M. (1988). Ethnic identity among Sansei and Yonsei church-affiliated youth in Los Angeles and Honolulu. *Psychological Reports, 62*, 268–270.

Yancey, W., Ericksen, E., & Juliani, R. (1976). Emergent ethnicity: A review and reformulation. *American Sociological Review, 41*, 391–403.

Zak, I. (1973). Dimensions of Jewish-American identity. *Psychological Reports, 33*, 891–900.

Zak, I. (1976). Structure of ethnic identity of Arab-Israeli students. *Psychological Reports, 38*, 239–246.

Zinn, M. (1980). Gender and ethnic identity among Chicanos. *Frontiers, 5*, 18–24.

Zisenwine, D., & Walters, J. (1982). Jewish identity: Israel and the American adolescent. *Forum on the Jewish People, Zionism, and Israel, 45*, 79–84.

# CHAPTER 13
# FROM PASSIVE ACCEPTANCE TO ACTIVE COMMITMENT: A MODEL OF FEMINIST IDENTITY DEVELOPMENT FOR WOMEN

NANCY E. DOWNING AND KRISTIN L. ROUSH

This article presents a model of feminist identity development for women. The model is derived, in part, from Cross's (1971) theory of Black identity development and is based on the premise that women who live in contemporary society must first acknowledge, then struggle with, and repeatedly work through their feelings about the prejudice and discrimination they experience as women in order to achieve authentic and positive feminist identity. The stages in this process include passive acceptance, revelation, embeddedness-emanation, synthesis, and active commitment. Implications of the model are outlined for women, nonsexist and feminist psychotherapies and contemporary society.

Much of the literature on feminist counseling and psychotherapy has focused on definitions (e.g., Rawlings & Carter, 1977) and comparisons with traditional paradigms. Inherent in many of these writings is an adherence to the "uniformity myths" of psychotherapy (Keisler, 1966), the assumption that a particular approach will work for most, if not all, clients, presenting problems, and under most circumstances. Feminist authors have attended minimally, if at all, to issues of appropriateness for different clients and client receptiveness to feminist interventions. The purpose of this article is to address these issues by describing a developmental model of feminist identity and delineating the implications of this model for women, feminist and nonsexist psychotherapies, and contemporary society.

This model has been developed by drawing upon the authors' clinical and personal experience, the meager literature in the area (Avery, 1977; Gurin, 1982; Moreland, 1976), and the developmental theories describing the acquisition and maintenance of a positive minority (specifically, Black) identity. The authors wrote this article from a feminist perspective, believing that any model that attempts to describe accurately events in women's lives must acknowledge the prejudice and discrimination that are a significant part of their life experiences. Hence, the authors feel that in contemporary society women share some of the developmental experiences of a minority population (as defined by Yetman & Steele, 1975); therefore, the literature on the identity development of minorities is considered relevant for women as well.

Downing, N. E., & Roush, K. L. (1985). From passive acceptance to active commitment: A model of feminist identity development for women. *The Counseling Psychologist, 13*, 695–709.

Specifically, this article will describe (1) a representative theory of positive Black identity development (Cross, 1971), (2) the application of Cross's theory to a developmental model of feminist identity, (3) the interface between this model and other selected developmental theories, and (4) the implications of this model for women, feminist and nonsexist psychotherapies, and contemporary society.

## Theories of Positive Black Identity Development

Of the major theories of positive Black identity development (Cross, 1971, 1978; Jackson, 1976/1977; Thomas, 1970, 1971), the one most relevant and applicable to a model of feminist identity is that outlined by Cross (1971). He delineates a five-stage theory: preencounter, encounter, immersion-emersion, internalization, and internalization-commitment.

In Cross's first stage, that of *preencounter*, individuals consciously or unconsciously support individual, institutional, and cultural oppression and accept their oppression as if it were justified. This acceptance of oppression often results in a very negative self-concept. In addition, people in this stage believe that the minority group should strive to assimilate itself into the majority culture. Jackson (1976/1977) describes a similar phenomenon that he labels the passive acceptance stage.

The second stage, *encounter*, is actually a two-step process. First, the individual has a profound experience, a crisis, and, second, the person begins to reinterpret the world as the result of this experience. Cross points to the slaying of Martin Luther King as just such a significant catalyzing experience for many Blacks in the later 1960s. The predominant feelings experienced during this stage are guilt over previous passive acceptance of cultural oppression and anger for being "brainwashed" by society. Cross's second stage is similar to Jackson's (1976/1977) active resistance stage in which the individual consciously rejects the manifestations of oppression and experiences intense anger.

The third stage, *immersion-emersion*, is inevitable because individuals cannot tolerate the intensity of their feelings generated in the encounter stage for prolonged periods of time. Individuals in this stage initially withdraw from the dominant culture and immerse themselves in the minority subculture. The theme "Black is beautiful" is characteristic of Afro-Americans in the immersion stage; they develop "an idealistic, superhuman expectancy toward practically anything Black" (Cross, 1971, p. 21).

During the emersion phase of this stage, feelings of guilt and anger begin to dissipate, ego involvement in "being Black" begins to decrease, and there is an increasing sense of pride. The emersion phase is also characterized by a greater openness to alternate viewpoints. The individual's perspective begins to mellow from the dualistic thinking that "Black is good; non-Black is bad" to a more relativistic perspective. We again find parallels with Jackson's theory; he describes this stage as one of redirection in which individuals define their minority identity in positive terms independent of the values of the dominant culture and sublimate their anger by immersing themselves in the minority subculture and heritage.

Cross's fourth stage, *internalization*, is characterized by the resolution of the conflicts between the old and new identities, an increased self-confidence about one's Blackness, and movement toward a "pluralistic, nonracist perspective." Jackson's fourth stage, which he also labels internalization, is similar, with the addition that individuals integrate the positive aspects of their newly found minority identity with their unique, individual qualities.

Cross adds a fifth stage, *internalization-commitment*, which is characterized by the struggle to translate one's new, integrated identity into meaningful action for the benefit of the minority community. Implicit in this stage is Cross's belief that the development of a positive minority identity cannot remain an individual experience in isolation from a commitment to the minority community.

## A Model of Feminist Identity

Cross's theory has heuristic value for the development of a model of positive feminist identity. The proposed model, outlined in Table 1, has five stages: passive acceptance, revelation, embeddedness-emanation, synthesis, and active commitment. The model addresses feminist identity development specifically for women; implications for men are included when relevant.

## TABLE 1

### Parallels Between the Identity Development Stages for Women and Blacks

#### Stages for Women

| Passive Acceptance | Revelation | Embeddedness-Emanation | Synthesis | Active Commitment |
|---|---|---|---|---|
| Passive acceptance of traditional sex roles and discrimination; belief that traditional roles are advantageous; men are considered superior. | Catalyzed by a series of crises, resulting in open questioning of self and roles and feelings of anger and guilt; dualistic thinking; men are perceived as negative. cautious interaction with men. | Characterized by connectedness with other select women, affirmation and strengthening of new identity. Eventually more relativistic thinking and | Development of an authentic and positive feminist identity; sex-role transcendence; "flexible truce" with the world; evaluate men on an individual basis. not the same as women. | Consolidation of feminist identity; commitment to meaningful action, to a nonsexist world. Actions are personalized and rational. Men are considered equal but |

#### Stages for Blacks

| Preencounter | Encounter | Immersion-Emersion | Internalization | Internalization-Commitment |
|---|---|---|---|---|
| The unaware person; acceptance of oppression as justified; values assimilation into majority culture; negative self-concept. | Catalyzed by profound event(s) resulting in increased awareness, rejection of oppression, and feelings of guilt and anger. | Initially characterized by withdrawal from the dominant culture, immersion in one's heritage and hostility toward whites. Eventually greater cognitive flexibility and pride emerge. | Development of an integrated, more positive self-image; adoption of a pluralistic, nonracist perspective. | Commitment of the new self to meaningful action for the benefit of the minority community. |

*Note:* The data on the stages for Black women were adapted from Cross (1971).

214

*Stage I, passive acceptance.* Our first stage, passive acceptance, parallels Cross's theory and describes the woman who is either unaware of or denies the individual, institutional, and cultural prejudice and discrimination against her. As Schaef (1981) describes it, this is the woman who accepts the white male system, the perspective of the dominant, majority culture. This woman carefully selects associates and experiences so as to avoid contact with ideas that may upset her sense of equilibrium as a woman (Avery, 1977). Traditional sex-role stereotypes are accepted (Moreland, 1976); the Stage I woman believes the traditional roles to be advantageous and considers men to be superior to women. An example of a woman in this stage is a student enrolled in one of the author's "Psychology of Women" course who, after the instructor encouraged class members to use the terms "men" and "women" for college-age males and females, responded by saying that she did not want to consider herself a woman because she liked the advantages of thinking of herself as a girl.

Toward the end of this stage there appears to be an important element of readiness (e.g., Erickson, 1950; Helms, 1984), a receptivity or openness to change or risk. Denial and selective perception diminish and the woman becomes increasingly open to alternative conceptualizations of herself and the world. This readiness helps facilitate the transition into the revelation stage and may be related to higher levels of ego development and/or self-esteem.

*Stage II, revelation.* Stage II, revelation, is precipitated by one or a series of crises or contradictions that the woman can no longer ignore or deny. Although the events that precipitate this stage vary widely, some typical ones include consciousness-raising groups, realization of discrimination against female children, ending of a relationship, divorce, or denial of credit or job application, or involvement in the women's movement (Cherniss, 1972). It is likely that movement from passive acceptance to revelation is a function of not only the quality, frequency, and intensity of such significant events but also the readiness of the individual to change her frame of reference.

Some women make the transition into the revelation stage suddenly, but for most it is a gradual and difficult shift. Unlike the process for Blacks in the late 1960s, as outlined by Cross, most women make the transition through a series of events less monumental than the death of a major leader like Martin Luther King. In fact, it may be the absence of generally agreed-upon, highly publicized, significant events relevant to women that has contributed to the difficulty of this transition and the seemingly small percentage of women who enter the revelation stage (Gurin, 1982). Transition may be further complicated by the perceptual distortions so characteristic of women in the passive acceptance stage. Traditional female socialization includes a distrust of one's perceptions, a mechanism that helps perpetuate the woman's subordinate status (Miller, 1976). A growing sense of trust in one's perceptions is necessary to begin the process of questioning oneself and one's role in order to make the transition to the revelation stage.

During revelation, women experience primarily feelings of anger and secondarily feelings of guilt. "Women describe themselves as having been duped, sold out, betrayed and raped by the universe," and their response is often anger and rage in cosmic proportions (Avery, 1977). Women in this stage often experience feelings of guilt over the ways they have participated in their own oppression in the past. Another characteristic is very dualistic thinking (Knefelkamp, Widick, & Stroad, 1975). They see all (or most) men as negative and all women as positive; one woman labeled these perceptions as "female chauvinism." Frequently, a woman in this stage restricts her social contacts to a small number of people who are comfortable and accepting of her intense feelings (Moreland, 1976).

Often women in the revelation stage are perceived by other women in this stage as having a mature, positive identity, when in reality they have developed a "pseudo-identity" based on the negation of traditional femininity and the dominant culture. In Erickson's (1968b) terms, these women have developed a negative identity rather than an identity based on an affirmation of the strengths of being female (see Miller, 1976; Moreland, 1976, for clarification).

*Stage III, embeddedness-emanation.* The embeddedness phase of the third stage is most likely more difficult for Caucasian women than for Blacks in this culture. The barriers for women to attaining this stage seem more subtle in nature, are chronic in duration, and may be posed by significant others as well as by society. Most women are so integrally involved in the dominant culture through marriage, work, and children that it is difficult for them to withdraw and to find and embed themselves in a "female is beautiful" subculture. As Gurin (1982, p. 5) writes, "And this [development of gender consciousness] is very uncomfortable because women are, after all, the mothers, wives, lovers, sisters and daughters of men. There is no other subordinate group that has such an intimate relationship with the dominant group." Some marriages end in divorce when the woman feels the need to withdraw from the dominant culture in order to immerse herself, feeling that she cannot do so within the context of her marriage. Women's centers, women's studies classes, and women's support groups are some of the few havens that exist for women experiencing embeddedness.

This phase is a time for "discovery of sisterhood" (Avery, 1977) and for much creative activity (art, music, drama) depicting the oppressed role of women. When a woman is able to experience embeddedness, she often develops a close emotional connection with other, similar women. This connectedness provides the woman with a reflection of her new frame of reference, the opportunity to discharge her anger in a supportive environment, and affirmation and strength in her new identity. Lesbians who have a supportive female-oriented subgroup with which to identify may often have an easier transition to the embeddedness phase.

Although embeddedness may be more difficult for Caucasian women than for Blacks, their continued interconnection with the dominant culture may result in the greater ease with which women seem to experience the latter part of this stage, emanation—the beginnings of an openness to alternate viewpoints and to a more relativistic versus dualistic perspective. Although the need to reduce dissonance between one's newly emerging identity and the repeated experience of being treated as subordinate may result in women reverting to earlier stages, some women are able to tolerate these discrepancies and emerge from this uncomfortable state with a healthier, multidimensional, and adaptive perspective. Women in the emanation phase typically interact cautiously with men.

Factors that likely influence the transition to emanation include the realization that one's rage has limited effects upon the factors that produce and maintain the oppressive dominant culture, an awareness that one has adopted as rigid a belief system in the embeddedness phase as one assumed during the passive acceptance stage, a willingness to grieve the loss of the self as defined by either traditional sex roles or the rigid beliefs of the embeddedness phase, and the capacity to separate from the strong female friendships developed in Stage III.

*Stage IV, synthesis.* Women in Stage IV, synthesis, increasingly value the positive aspects of being female and are able to integrate these qualities with their unique personal attributes into a positive and realistic self-concept. They are able to transcend traditional sex roles, make choices for themselves based on well-defined personal values, and evaluate men on an individual, rather than stereotypic, basis. Women in this stage accept both oppression-related explanations for events and other causal factors and are able to make accurate attributions. They have struck "a flexible truce" (Avery, 1977) with the world, one that allows them to channel their energies productively but also to respond appropriately to experiences of oppression and discrimination. Miller (1976) alludes to internalization when she writes about the "new way" (p. 41) women can value their psychological qualities and live life with authenticity, and Moreland (1976) labels this stage as one of celebration.

*Stage V, active commitment.* The fifth stage, active commitment, involves the translation of the newly developed consolidated identity into meaningful and effective action. There is a "deep and pervasive commitment to social change" (Avery, 1977) aimed at creating a future in which sex-role transcendence is a valued and encouraged goal. Women in this stage select issues carefully based on their unique talents and the possibility of both personal gratification and effecting societal change. Few women truly evolve to the active commitment stage, and the authors believe that most women who are dedicated to working for women's rights may actually be functioning out of needs from earlier stages, particularly revelation and embeddedness-emanation.

As with some more recent developmental theories (e.g., Loganbill, Hardy & Delworth, 1982), it is assumed that women may recycle through these stages, each time experiencing the challenge of that stage more profoundly and using previously learned skills to work through the particular stage again. It is also assumed that women may stagnate in a specific stage, most often in the revelation or embeddedness periods. In addition, women may revert to earlier stages when their skills are insufficient to respond to the demands of current life stresses. Furthermore, progress from stage to stage is determined not only by the woman's readiness, but also by the unique interpersonal and environmental context of her life (see Helms, 1984, for clarification).

## Research

There has been virtually no research directly addressing the development of a positive feminist identity. The most closely related research is on group consciousness for women. Gurin (1982) identified four essential components of group consciousness: (1) group identification, (2) discontentment with the group's power, (3) recognition of the disparity in status between one's group and other groups, and (4) approval of collective action. She collected data from representative national samples in 1972, 1976, and 1979 and found (1) increased group identification for women over time; (2) low and unchanged feelings of discontentment with the group's power; (3) increased recognition of the disparity between groups (e.g., in 1972, 33% of the women surveyed attributed status differences to discrimination rather than to individual deficiencies; by 1979 the proportion had risen to 55%); and (4) low and unchanged endorsement of collective action. In addition, Gurin found that greater labor force participation, education, and political activism were related to higher levels of group consciousness, whereas religious activism and marital status (being married or widowed) were related to lower group consciousness. Overall, Gurin's sociological study suggests that some progress has been made in women's collective journey toward a positive feminist identity, but the road ahead appears to be a long and difficult one.

Research is sorely needed that explicitly addresses the development of a positive feminist identity. Specifically, future research should address (1) the development of assessment methods to identify and distinguish the stages; (2) longitudinal studies to discover the optimal sequence of stages and the predicted length of each stage; (3) the identification of precipitating events and moderator variables that maximize and impede movement through the stages; and (4) the impact of various therapist-client stage combinations on a variety of psychotherapeutic process and outcome variables.

## Interface with Other Developmental Theories

The proposed model of feminist identity development is most closely related to the general literature on identity development, with Erickson's (1950) work, "The Eight Stages of Man (sic)," being central to this literature. According to Erickson, identity versus role confusion (Stage 5) precedes intimacy versus isolation (Stage 6). Although not clearly stated, Erickson's stages focused on male, not female, development (Downing, 1983). More recently, numerous authors (Chodorow, 1973; Douvan & Adelson, 1966; Gilligan, 1982; Josselson, 1973; Marcia & Friedman, 1970; Williams, 1977) have concluded that identity and intimacy are concurrent, not sequential stages for females and that females find their identity within the context of relationships. Thus Erickson's stage theory cannot serve as a broader developmental context in which to place the proposed model of feminist identity development.

More germane to this model is Erickson's (1968a) notion of a "passive identity," a total reliance on personal identity in an effort to transcend the culture and its available psychosocial identity patterns, expectations, and constraints (e.g., social identity). Passive identity can be nonadaptive or pathological when a new coherent social identity fails to be established and one remains absorbed within a personal world (see Marcia & Friedman's [1970] descriptions of moratorium, foreclosed, and diffused identity statuses for clarification). Passive identity can also be an adaptive regression, leading to an ability to forge actively a new social identity through redefining the existing world and one's role within it in ways that allow for congruence with one's personal identity (Lichtenstein, 1977). The proposed model of feminist identity development serves as a blueprint for women to transcend their passive identity and to integrate both personal and social identities into a coherent whole (Stage IV, synthesis).

Unlike Erickson, Kegan (1982) provides a broader developmental framework in which to place this model of feminist identity development. He proposes a six-stage model of the development of the self, which he describes as a lifelong process of differentiation from embeddedness. Of interest here is Kegan's description of Stages 5 and 6: institutional balance and interindividual balance. With the attainment of institutional balance, individuals lose their embeddedness in relationships (similar to the latter part of the emanation phase) and develop a coherent self across space and time and apart from others (necessary for successfully completing the synthesis stage). Institutional balance is followed by interindividual balance, in which one can acknowledge being an individual among individuals and in which groups are important to meeting the needs of people, rather than being an end in themselves (similar to the latter part of the synthesis and the active commitment stages). Although further elaboration of these parallels is needed, it seems quite likely that movement through the feminist identity stages is dependent, in part, on successful mastery of the stages of general identity development as outlined by Kegan.

In addition, this model of feminist identity development appears to overlap and have implications for Rebecca, Hefner, and Oleshansky's (1976) theory of sex-role transcendence. Their three-stage theory describes the evolution from a nondiscriminating position to a polarized stage and finally to a transcendent sex-role identity. Individuals in the polarized stage adopt and value traditional sex-role attitudes and behaviors (similar to the women in the passive acceptance stage). Individuals who have reached sex-role transcendence are described as feeling "free to express their human qualities without fear of retribution for violating sex-role norms. There has been a transcendence of stereotypes and a reorganization of possibilities learned in Stage II (polarized) into a more personally relevant framework" (p. 204). The characteristics of this sex-role transcendence stage are strikingly similar to those ascribed to Stage IV, synthesis. Thus the proposed feminist identity model may prove useful in further elaborating the transition between a polarized and a transcendent sex-role identity.

## Implications for Psychotherapy

This model has a number of implications for psychotherapy with women. First, viewing female clients' presenting problems within the context of this developmental framework will add richness to the therapist's understanding of clients' concerns. For example, a woman in the embeddedness-emanation stage who presents with feelings of loneliness and isolation, of feeling unconnected to a similar peer group, is likely to have a very different phenomenological field than a woman in the passive acceptance stage who describes herself as isolated and lonely. Thus this model provides a useful assessment tool for therapists to gain a greater contextual understanding of their clients' experiences.

The model also has implications for intervention strategies. Therapists who are familiar with the sequence of stages can better plan interventions, using such techniques as plus-one staging (Knefelkamp et al., 1975), thereby lessening client resistance and confusion and increasing the possibility of successful therapeutic outcome. For example, encouraging the isolated, lonely woman who is in the embeddedness-emanation stage to seek out a woman's support group or to get involved in her local chapter of NOW will most likely be effective interventions. Similar suggestions for the passive acceptance woman who lacks the readiness to move on to revelation are more likely to be counterproductive. Likewise, if a female client wishes to work through her intense feelings of anger at all men, the model provides guidance regarding the sequence of feelings and experiences necessary for the client to gain a more flexible, individualistic perspective on this issue. In addition, therapists who are familiar with this model can provide anticipatory guidance to clients regarding the sequence of stages they will likely experience. By providing a clear goal, an understandable endpoint, the model may also assist both the therapist and client to tolerate better the erratic progress (two steps forward, one step back) that is so characteristic of psychotherapy.

Furthermore, the theory suggests that clients who progress from one stage to the next may experience some feelings of loss as they discard the familiarity and security of an earlier stage for the unknown, new stage. The therapist can be alerted to these feelings of loss and facilitate the grieving process.

In addition to having implications for assessment and intervention, this model also provides a developmental framework for feminist therapy. The tenets of feminist therapy as outlined by Rawlings and Carter (1977) can be viewed as reactions to the predominant paradigms of psychotherapy. Thus many of the principles of feminist therapy have evolved antithetically to these traditional paradigms, rather than from a thorough understanding of the life experiences of women (Gilligan, 1982, is a notable exception). In contrast, this theory represents a proactive, observation-based contribution to the theory of feminist therapy.

Finally, the model provides one yardstick to measure therapists' potential effectiveness when working with particular client issues. Cross (1971) and Helms (1984) both believe that individuals who have experienced Stage V, internalization-commitment, have a greater capacity for understanding, supporting, and showing compassion for individuals who are struggling with earlier stages. In our opinion, female therapists can be most beneficial to female clients with sex-role issues when they themselves have cycled through the first five stages at least once. In addition, this model has implications for feminist therapy training programs; such programs should consider this developmental sequence in the design and implementation of the curriculum and its experiential components in order to produce well-qualified feminist therapists.

## Implications for Contemporary Society

In addition to having important implications for psychotherapy with women, this model is also relevant to the women's movement and society in general. Although the five-stage process has been described in the context of individual life experience, the women's movement could also be viewed as experiencing these stages. Considering recent history, the 1950s were a time of passive acceptance of the feminine mystique. The 1960s and early 1970s constituted the revelation stage in which women in the movement expressed anger and demanded that their rights be unrestricted (Rosenthal, 1984). The late 1970s and the beginning of this decade have brought with it a realization that the expression of anger is not the ultimate goal (*Notes from the Third Year*, 1970) and an increasing, yet tentative, sense of pride in what it means to be female (e.g., Miller, 1976; Schaef, 1981). The movement appears to be immersing itself in its cultural roots and heritage. This model suggests that emanation is the next task for the movement to master collectively; it is likely to take many years before great numbers reach the synthesis or active commitment stages (Gurin, 1982).

This model also has implications for men. Specifically, males who are familiar with this model may be more understanding and supportive of the feelings and needs of women with whom they are intimately involved. Knowledge of this model may also help the unfortunate male who becomes the focus of the anger of the Stage II woman. Understanding the revelation experience may help the male separate his responsibility for the woman's anger from that which is the result of many years of prejudice and discrimination. In addition, this theory may have some relevance for the development of gender consciousness in males, although extensive work is needed to discern the similarities and differences between the sexes in this area.

There are also several limitations of this model as it has been proposed. First, the issue of possible class, age, racial, and ethnic differences in the development of a feminist identity has not been addressed here (e.g., Giddings, 1984; Malson, 1983) and requires much more attention. Second, greater attention needs to be focused on the intrapersonal, interpersonal, institutional, and cultural forces that both catalyze and impede progress through the stages. Third, a better understanding of the recycling process through the stages (what Schaef [1981] would call "a higher level of truth" [understanding]) is needed. Fourth, greater elaboration of the similarities and differences between our proposed model and other developmental theories is needed. Finally, and most important, much research is needed to substantiate the various components of this theory. It is hoped that future theoretical and empirical efforts will address these and other important implications of the model.

Cross (1971, p. 25) points out that until Blacks understand, control, and direct the process of positive identity development they "will continue to rely on the jolting consequences of fortuitous events"; the same applies to women. It is our hope that continued exploration of this model will increase our collective understanding of the process and lessen "the jolting consequences of fortuitous events" in women's lives.

## References

Avery, D. M. (1977). The psychosocial stages of liberation. *Illinois Personnel and Guidance Association Quarterly, 63*, 36–42.

Cherniss, C. (1972). Personality and ideology: A personological study of women's liberation. *Psychiatry, 35*, 190–225.

Chodorow, N. (1973). *The reproduction of mothering*. Berkeley: University of California Press.

Cross, W. E. (1971). Negro-to-Black conversion experience: Toward a psychology of Black liberation. *Black World*, 20(9), 13–27.

Cross, W. E. (1978). The Thomas and Cross models of psychological nigrescence: A review. *Journal of Black Psychology*, 5, 13–31.

Douvan, E., & Adelson, J. (1966). *The adolescent experience*. New York: John Wiley.

Downing, S. D. (1983). *The emerging female self: An exploration of personal identity, social identity and the conflict of coalescence*. Unpublished manuscript, University of Denver, School of Professional Psychology.

Erickson, E. H. (1950). *Childhood and society*. New York: Norton.

Erickson, E. H. (1968a). *Identity, youth and crisis*. New York: Norton.

Erickson, E. H. (1968b). *Young man Luther: A study in psychoanalysis and history*. New York: Norton.

Giddings, P. (1984). *When and where I enter: The impact of Black women on race and sex in America*. New York: Morrow.

Gilligan, C. (1982). *In a different voice: Psychological theory and women's development*. Cambridge: Harvard University Press.

Gurin, P. (1982). Group consciousness. *Institute for Social Research Newsletter*, 10(1,2), 4–5.

Helms, J. E. (1984). Toward a theoretical explanation of the effects of race on counseling: A Black and White model. *The Counseling Psychologist*, 12, 153–165.

Jackson, B. W. (1977). The function of a Black identity development theory in achieving relevance in education for Black students (Doctoral dissertation, University of Massachusetts, Amherst, 1976). *Dissertation Abstracts International*, 37, 5667A.

Josselson, R. (1973). Psychodynamic aspects of identity formation in college women. *Journal of Youth and Adolescence*, 2, 3–52.

Kegan, R. (1982). *The evolving self: Problem and process in human development*. Cambridge: Harvard University Press.

Keisler, D. (1966). Some myths of psychotherapy research and the search for a paradigm. *Psychological Bulletin*, 65, 110–136.

Knefelkamp, L. L., Widick, C. C., & Stroad, B. (1975). Cognitive-developmental theory: A guide to counseling women. In L. Harmon, J. Birk, L. Fitzgerald, & M. Tanney (Eds.), *Counseling women*. Monterey, CA: Brooks/Cole.

Lichtenstein, H. (1977). *The dilemma of human identity*. New York: Jason Aranson.

Loganbill, C., Hardy, E., & Delworth, U. (1982). Supervision: A conceptual model. *The Counseling Psychologist*, 10, 3–42.

Malson, M. R. (1983). Black women's sex-roles: The societal context for a new ideology. *Journal of Social Issues*, 39, 101–113.

Marcia, J. E., & Friedman, M. L. (1970). Ego identity status in college women. *Journal of Personality*, 38, 249–263.

Miller, J. B. (1976). *Toward a new psychology of women*. Boston: Beacon.

Moreland, J. R. (1976). Facilitator training for consciousness raising groups in an academic setting. *The Counseling Psychologist*, 6(3), 66–68.

*Notes from the third year*. (1970). New York: The Herstory Collection [Microfilm].

Rawlings, E. T., & Carter, D. K. (1977). Feminist and nonsexist psychotherapy. In E. I. Rawlings & D. K. Carter (Eds.), *Psychotherapy for women*. Springfield, IL: Charles C. Thomas.

Rebecca, M., Hefner, R., & Oleshansky, B. (1976). A model of sex-role transcendence. *Journal of Social Issues*, 32, 197–206.

Rosenthal, N. B. (1984). Consciousness raising: From revolution to re-evaluation. *Psychology of Women Quarterly*, 8, 309–326.

Schaef, A. W. (1981). *Women's reality: An emerging female system in a white male society*. Minneapolis: Winston.

Thomas, C. (1970). Different strokes for different folks. *Psychology Today*, 4(4), 48–53, 78–80.

Thomas, C. (1971). *Boys no more*. Encino, CA: Glencoe.

Williams, J. (1977). *Psychology of women: Behavior in a biosocial context*. New York: Norton.

Yetman, N., & Steele, C. (Eds.). (1975). *Majority and minority: The dynamics of racial and ethnic relations*. Boston: Allyn & Bacon.

# CHAPTER 14
## VOICES OF GENDER ROLE CONFLICT: THE SOCIAL CONSTRUCTION OF COLLEGE MEN'S IDENTITY

### TRACY L. DAVIS

The purpose of this constructivist inquiry was to explore the impact of socially prescribed gender roles on college men's identity development. Ten White, traditionally-aged students were interviewed and data from the interviews were analyzed using hermeneutic phenomenology. Students discussed communication restrictions associated with scripted gender roles, fear of femininity, feelings of being overly challenged, and a sense of confusion about masculinity.

Gilligan's (1982) landmark self-in-relation theory of women's development inspired important challenges to traditional views of human development and led to the reevaluation of many of the theories that undergird the practice of student development. Student affairs scholars and practitioners no longer rely solely on theories that have been constructed primarily by and about men. Belenky, Clinchy, Goldberger, & Tarule (1986), for example, developed a conceptual framework that helped student affairs practitioners better understand women's cognitive development. Josselson's (1987, 1996) and Jones's (1997) investigations allow student affairs professionals to hear women's voices in the context of identity development. The findings in these studies demonstrate the need for student affairs practitioners to become familiar with the ways that gender affects development.

Although researchers have begun to investigate how gender affects women's identity development, there has been relatively little written about such impact on the psychosocial development of college men. One reason for this lack of research may be based on a faulty assumption that most traditional scholarship regarding human development has already been about men. At first glance, this assumption seems obvious and well-founded. After all, Gilligan (1982) and others have convincingly argued that developmental research has too often viewed the male sex as representative of humanity. However, as Meth and Pasick (1990) point out,

> although psychological writing has been androcentric, it has also been gender blind [and] it has assumed a male perspective but has not really explored what it means to be a man any more than what it means to be a woman. (vii)

Researchers need, therefore, to more closely examine the development of men through the lenses of gender.

Davis, T. L. (2002). Voices of gender role conflict: The social construction of college men's identity. *Journal of College Student Development, 43,* 508–521.

Researchers' understanding of identity formation is commonly attributed to Erikson's (1968) developmental theory. According to Erikson, individuals gain a sense of who they are by confronting a universal sequence of challenges or crises (e.g., trust, intimacy, etc.) throughout their lives. Marcia (1966) operationalized Erikson's original theory and similarly suggested that identity formation is the most important goal of adolescence. Marcia viewed identity development as a process of experiencing a series of crises with one's ascribed childhood identity and subsequently emerging with new commitments. That is, as individuals consider new ideas that are in conflict with earlier conceptions, they weigh possibilities, potentially experiment with alternatives, and eventually choose commitments that become the core of a newly wrought identity. Those successfully transcending crises and making commitments are said to have an achieved identity. Individuals avoiding the process altogether, neither experiencing crises nor making commitments, are in a state of identity diffusion. Individuals may also be somewhere between these two possibilities by either simply maintaining a parentally derived ideology (foreclosed) or by actively experimenting with and resolving identity-related questions prior to commitment (moratorium).

Josselson's longitudinal research (1987, 1996), based upon Marcia's framework, investigated women's identity development. Josselson (1987) categorized participants into all four identity statuses and found that women

> internalize the central priorities of their mothers as the issues to feel the same or different about. As college-age, late adolescents, these women judge their distance from their families by whether and how much they carry on family religious traditions, whom they choose as friends, what sexual values they adopt, how they dress, whether and when and whom they plan to marry. These were the central points of negotiation in the separation-individuation drama. (p. 172)

For the women in her study, relationships with primary family, partners, children, and friends were what Josselson (1987) called key "anchors" (p. 176) that mediated making new commitments.

Whereas Marcia (1966) found decisions involving occupational choice, religious beliefs, and political ideology to be predictive of overall identity statuses, especially with men, Josselson (1987) and Schenkel and Marcia (1972) each found that crises and commitments in the areas of religion and sexual values to be more indicative of women's identity statuses.

Recent models of identity development have gone beyond these more epigenetic conceptualizations, with their emphasis on cognitive processes of development, to increasingly focus on the dynamic interaction between individuals and the social systems in which they function. Chickering and Reisser (1993), for example, in an update of Chickering's (1969) work, added a section to the establishing identity chapter entitled "sense of self in a social, historical, and cultural context" (p. 181). In addition, Josselson (1996) recently suggested that identity is "not just a private, individual matter . . . [but] a complex negotiation between the person and society" (p. 31). Similarly, D'Augelli (1994) conceived identity as "the dynamic processes by which an individual emerges from many social exchanges experienced in different contexts over an extended historical period" (p. 324). The construction of identity also depends, therefore, on the cultural, social, and political context in which these processes occur. A recent model offered by Jones and McEwen (2000) reinforces this idea. In their model, sexual orientation, race, culture, class, religion, and gender are identity dimensions that circulate around one's core identity. The salience of a particular dimension to one's core identity depends on changing contexts that include current experiences, family background, sociocultural conditions, career decisions, and life planning. In the current investigation, we examined one of these dimensions—gender—in an attempt to understand how college men internally experience externally defined gender roles.

Gender role conflict is defined as "a psychological state occurring when rigid, sexist, or restrictive gender roles learned thorough socialization, result in personal restriction, devaluation, or violation of others or self" (O'Neil, 1990, p. 25). Numerous studies using a common measure of men's gender role conflict, the Gender Role Conflict Scale (GRCS) (O'Neil, Helms, Gable, David, & Wrightsman, 1986) resulted in four underlying Factors: Restrictive Emotionality; Success, Power, and Competition; Restrictive Affectionate Behavior Between Men; and Conflict Between Work and Family Relations. In a review of the gender role literature, Thompson, Pleck, and Ferrera (1992) concluded that "gender role conflict provides an important link between societal norms scripting traditional masculinities and an individual's adaptation" (p. 598). Exploring men's gender role conflict, therefore, may provide rich information about college men's identity development.

Gender role conflict has been correlated with higher levels of anxiety and lower capacity for intimacy (Sharpe & Heppner, 1991). In addition, research has found that gender role conflict is related to negative attitudes toward seeking help (Good & Wood, 1995), low self-esteem (Cournoyer & Mahalik, 1995), negative attitudes and intolerance toward homosexuals (Rounds, 1994), depression (Good & Mintz, 1990), and endorsement of a traditional masculine ideology (Good, Braverman, & O'Neil, 1991). Results of these studies illustrate the importance of understanding male gender role conflict and its effects on the healthy development of men.

The purpose of this study was to explore conflicts related to socially constructed gender roles that may impact men's identity development. Given the increasing emphasis on the social construction of identities and the negative impacts that gender role conflict have on men, it seemed critical to examine how college men are coping with culturally defined notions of what it means to be a man. That is, assuming identity develops as one interacts with society and that gender is a central dimension of one's conception of self, it would be helpful to investigate how societal gender role expectations are influencing college men. Although the underlying concepts of identity development and gender role conflict assisted in making sense of the interviews, interpretations were allowed to emerge from the data.

## Method

General identity development models and theories offer descriptions of a wide array of experiences for diverse populations of individuals. To more clearly understand how gender roles influence college men's identity development, unconstrained by current deterministic conceptualizations, I used a constructivist approach (Lincoln & Guba, 1985). The purpose of constructivist inquiry is "to produce depth of understanding about a particular topic or experience" (Manning, 1999, p. 12). The constructivist perspective, based largely on the research of Piaget (1954) and Vygotsky (1978), suggests that knowledge does not and cannot produce representations of an independent reality, but instead is rooted in the perspective of the knower. As such, identity development is not the result of stage development related to maturation; rather, it is understood as a construction by the individual through social learning and interpretive reorganization. There has been a recent debate about constructivism among those who place more emphasis on the individual cognitive structuring processes and those who emphasize the sociocultural effects of learning. In this study, I assumed a more social constructivist approach with emphasis on (a) the social context in which development occurs and (b) the importance of social interaction and negotiation.

Consistent with the epistemological assumptions of constructivism is the phenomenological methodology employed in this study. Phenomenology addresses experience from the perspective of the individual and is based on the assumption that people have a unique way of making meaning of their experience. That is, for people to understand a phenomenon, they must grasp it from another's perspective.

In addition to constructivist epistemological assumptions and a phenomenological methodology, this investigation is informed by a hermeneutic philosophical position. Hermeneutics is the science of interpretation. According to van Manen (1990), meanings are often hidden and must be brought to the surface through reflection. Hermeneutic phenomenology, thus, can "bring explicitness out of implicitness, to unveil the essence of the lived experience of a few, which allows for insight into the possible lived experience of others" (p. 316).

Consistent with these paradigmatic assumptions, interviews were conducted at Western Illinois University (WIU). Western Illinois University enrolls approximately 12,000 students, about half of whom are men. WIU is a public regional institution with popular ROTC and law enforcement programs, and high student participation in Greek life and intramurals. WIU is also a politically conservative and rural campus. Interviews were conducted between Spring 2000 and Spring 2001.

## Participants

Participants in this study were 10 male undergraduate students who ranged in age from 18 to 21 years old. Five were in their last semester of their senior year, 4 were juniors, and 1 was a sophomore. All participants in this study were White and heterosexual. Three individuals were enrolled in the College of Liberal Arts, two in Business, two in Communications, one in Education, one in Agriculture, and one in Law Enforcement. Each participant was extensively involved in leadership of at least one of the following organizations: Interfraternity Council, Student Alumni Council, University Housing and Dining Services, or the Bureau of Cultural Affairs.

## Procedure

Participants were purposefully selected through snowball or chain sampling (Patton, 1990). This approach "identifies cases of interest from people who know people who know people who know what cases are information-rich, that is, good examples for study" (p. 182). These exemplar cases were identified based on the recommendations of student affairs professionals and graduate assistants who work directly with students. The referral contact people were asked to identify students who were reflective about gender or currently struggling with gender-related issues. They were also given a description of gender role conflict and asked if they knew men who might be grappling with socially scripted gender expectations.

Interviews were conducted by a male investigator and three graduate students (one male and two female). Each researcher was skilled at conducting interviews and trained in microcounseling and listening skills. Interviewers were also knowledgeable about gender-related developmental issues in general and men's issues, in particular.

## Interviews

Prior to individual interviews, prospective participants were given a description of the study and its methods, a clarification of the commitment required for participation, and an informed consent form describing procedures to ensure confidentiality. After consent was given, participants provided basic demographic information.

Individual interviews were conducted in a private room by one of the four interviewers. According to Lincoln and Guba (1985), interviewing is one strategy for examining an individual's constructions and reconstructions of "persons, events, activities, organizations, feelings, motivations, claims, concerns, and other entities." (p. 268). Interviews lasted between 45 minutes and 70 minutes and were tape-recorded. Following each session, interviewers noted their experience and specifically commented on general impressions of the meeting, their reactions to the participant, and any notable or peculiar aspects of the interview. These journals were included in the data set and used in the analysis.

The interviewers used a set of questions adapted from Josselson's (1996) study of women's identity development. The protocol focused on how participants see themselves, important factors in their lives that shape who they are, how they have changed and what has stimulated that change, how they imagine their future, and what it is like being a man on campus. According to Kavale (1996), "an interview is literally an *inter view*, an inter-change of views between two persons conversing about a theme of mutual interest" (p. 14). Although the interview protocol was structured, interviewers were given latitude to explore responses in more depth. This open-ended questioning helps to "minimize the imposition of predetermined responses when gathering data" (Patton, 1990, p. 295).

## Data Analysis

One of the greatest difficulties I had in analyzing the data was negotiating the Self-Other dynamic. Susan Jones warns qualitative researchers to check their "own subjectivity and theoretical stance so that decisions are indeed rooted in the research process as it unfolds rather than in the researchers' own points of view." For me, this meant being aware that I might try to make the interview data fit my preconceptions (Self) rather than allowing the participants (Other) to speak for themselves. I am drawn to the study of gender and men due to my own curiosity about the impact of gender on men's development, but I also have political, social, and cultural views related to this topic. I also clearly have biases associated with my own development as a White, heterosexual, Italian American male. As I read transcripts and listened to participants, for example, I had to intentionally avoid relying on initial intuitive interpretations rooted in my own experience. Negotiating interpretations with other interviewers helped me routinely assess whose story was being told. My own theoretical filter of knowledge, based in developmental gender role conflict and identity theory, also influenced my interpretations. In addition to the fact that these interpretations were subjected to the scrutiny of other members of the research team, I use participants' own language to illustrate our interpretations. These and several strategies listed below are aimed at "working the hyphen" (Fine, 1994, p. 72) in the Self-Other split to try to maintain the integrity of the participants' stories.

The data set for this study consisted of the 10 interviews, which were transcribed verbatim, and the interviewer journals. Following procedures outlined by Coffey and Atkinson (1996), the first step in the analysis was for each investigator to independently read the interview transcripts and mark concepts, words, phrases, or sentences that seemed interesting or important. We then met to compare categories, negotiate and reconcile discrepancies, and develop a set of meaning categories or themes. As the transcripts were read and reread, the meaning categories were refined by analyzing the concepts that the data were organized around, comparing concepts across transcripts, and adding new themes that emerged only after seeing similar concepts in multiple transcripts. As Miles and Huberman (1994) pointed out, this refinement process illustrated critical nuances and generated awareness of previously unnoticed and seemingly unremarkable units of data.

This technique of reexamination continued throughout the data analysis and interpretation processes. The major themes that emerged from this process were identified, discussed among analysts, and compared to literature related to men's psychosocial development. These themes and comparisons are reported in the following sections.

Trustworthiness of these findings was enhanced through peer debriefing, keeping a methodological journal, and member checking. Lincoln and Guba (1985) defined peer debriefing as "a process of exposing oneself to a disinterested peer in a manner paralleling an analytic session and for the purpose of exploring aspects of the inquiry that might otherwise remain only implicit within the inquirer's mind" (p. 308). The peer debriefer for this study was a doctoral candidate in the University of Iowa College of Education. Lincoln and Guba also maintained that member checks, a process through which participants verify data and the resulting interpretations, are necessary to establish credibility. Participants in this study were given an opportunity to review the categories and summative interpretations for review, clarification, and suggestions. Due to the length of the study, graduation, and in one case, failure to show up for scheduled sessions, only two respondents participated in member checks.

Dependability and confirmability added to the trustworthiness of this study and were assessed through an auditor. According to Lincoln and Guba (1985), dependability can be established as the auditor examines the processes by which the various stages of the study, including analytic techniques, were conducted. The auditor, an advanced doctoral candidate well versed in qualitative methodologies, confirmed that the analytic processes were applicable to this study and that the data analysis strategies were applied consistently. To demonstrate confirmability, a journal of the inquiry process, copies of all taped interviews, notes from interviewer reflections and discussions, and hard copies of all transcripts were maintained.

In addition to peer debriefing, limited member checks, auditor review, and keeping a methodological journal, this study provided information regarding transferability of findings. The standard of transferability is a measure of whether or not the reader is given enough information about the setting to evaluate the extent to which the study's findings might be transferred to other contexts (Lincoln & Guba, 1985). According to Patton (1990), this can be accomplished through "thick description" and solid descriptive data. In this article, the context of the investigation is described and readers are given rich descriptions of participants' characteristics, including direct quotes from the interviews.

## Results

Five themes emerged from the data: the importance of self-expression, code of communication caveats, fear of femininity, confusion about and distancing from masculinity, and a sense of challenge without support.

### Importance of Self-Expression

Contrary to the popular image of the inexpressive male, participants felt that self-expression and communication were very important to them. It was clear, however, that being comfortable with self-expression was something recently learned and not a behavior that was routinely practiced earlier in life. For example, one man reflected,

> What I enjoy the most is having good conversations with people, like interacting with people. It's something I really enjoy—especially—this is a really new thing for me too. I didn't really do it a lot in the past and it's something I'm starting to [do] a little more. I'd say right now that's probably something that I enjoy most.

Moreover, participants rarely mentioned how they communicate with others without indicating some awareness that what they were doing was somehow outside of the boundaries of traditional masculinity. One participant reported:

> It just seems like it's amazing how different men and women are regarding handling stress and things. It's kind of a role confusion for me, because I'm the kind of person that likes to talk it out. It's difficult when you're supposed to keep things in.

Whereas verbal interaction was seen as personally important, the awareness of how others might view expressivity seemed to shape these participants' reflections on their behavior.

### Code of Communication Caveats

There were three important caveats that seemed to affect these students' styles and levels of communication. These caveats are related to feelings of safety, worrying about how others will perceive them, and learned, socially appropriate ways of interacting, particularly with other men.

*Communication with women.* Men seemed to be able to express themselves more freely with women than with other men. One participant put it this way, "I like to talk to friends. I like to talk and chat—I'll talk about anything, I'm especially a chatterbox with girls [sic]. We'll just sit around and watch TV, we'll discuss like relationships, life, anything." Opening up to women as friends was seen as safer and easier than being vulnerable to other men. Although this appeared to be true with female friends, there was some fear that expressive and relational behavior might be penalized if women were seen as potential partners. According to one man:

> You've got to be jerky to women, I know that. They say they want nice guys but they really don't. The thing that bugs me is that I've always been the ideal husband rather than the ideal boyfriend, which bothers me. They're like, "you're the type of guy I'd like to marry, not the type of guy I'd want to date." I just think it's because I'm too nice.

Messages that these men received from women affected their attitudes about dating. Although communication was less inhibited with female friends than with male friends, it appears to be more affected by sex-typed assumptions with potential female mates.

*One-on-one communication with other men.* Participants also felt that their style of communication was quite different in groups than it was with one other person. When these men were with a group of other men, even friends, there was some level of performance associated with their communication. Humorous comments and "put-downs" were the norm. On the other hand, respondents felt able to become more intimate and direct in the context of just one other friend. One man commented:

> Men don't communicate unless they have their secure circle of friends and they can talk with this one guy. I mean they all hang out and drink beer and have a good time, but after everyone leaves, Stan's going to stay behind and we're going to have a great talk. There's always that one guy that stays behind and there's always going to be that connection too.

These students sent a strong message that they were conscious of gendered rules associated with when and how relational communication can occur. Another student talked about limiting what he said during discussions with groups of men until he was confident they were accepting and that he would not have to worry about what they were going to think.

*Nonverbal and side-by-side communication.* The way that participants communicated affection to other men took a form that could easily be missed or misunderstood. These men talked about indirectly showing affection through both verbal and nonverbal means. One participant, for example, discussed how he relates to his father.

> The way I show affection, like the first thing I do is come in the house and he just grabs a hold of my shoulder, squeezes it a little bit and then I punch him in the stomach a little bit and that's—I mean I've told my dad I love him like maybe four times in my entire life—I mean that's just how we show affection. And that's basically the way I am with all guys too, like if I don't feel like I can punch you, you're not my friend. . . . It's like a love tap, you know, that's basically what it amounts to.

When participants did verbally express themselves with other men, they often did so in a "side-by-side," as opposed to a "face-to-face," manner. One student shared that his most memorable bonding experience with his best friend occurred as they sat next to each other and talked about their fears and problems during a long trip in the car. Similarly, other participants discussed taking a trip to a casino or getting together to watch World Wrestling Federation (WWF) as activities that created opportunities to communicate and relate to other men. On the surface, these activities might appear to be anything but relational, but note *how* two participants described their activity: "One of the big things me and Nick do is play Playstation. We get out of class and we can play for like 8 hours and just—it's kind of like a bonding experience between us." or "Like when I go gambling. It's the trip down and talking with somebody that kind of knows at the same level as what I'm doing, it's sorting things out, you know at the same level as me." These men discussed their connection to and relationship with other men in the context of an activity, but their story was not about the activity itself.

## Fear of Femininity

Although participants described ways that they were able to express themselves to other men, some communicated both fear and frustration related to the narrow boundaries of that expression. At the root of this frustration was a fear of being seen as "feminine" or somehow "unmanly." One student said, "You know if at the bar someone bumps into you, you have to be the tough guy. You can't have guys thinking weird things about you, you know you got to prove yourself." Participants also discussed how even seemingly nongendered activities raised questions about how others interpret their sexual orientation. Openness to talking, wearing a lot of cologne, and clothing choices were each actions mentioned by participants that made other people question their sexual orientation. One student, for example, said, "People have thought I am gay. I think it's because I talk, but, I'll sit there and listen too, and I'll put input into other people's problems like friends do or gay guys do." This connection between ostensibly feminine activities and being gay sent a clear message to these students that to avoid certain labels, they had to restrict their behavior.

## Confusion About and Distancing from Masculinity

Each participant was asked about what it was like being a man on campus. This question, more than any other, was generally met with a long silence before a response was given. It was as if these men had given very little thought to this part of their identity. Several students replied by saying, "I really don't think about it too much," or, "I really don't pay attention to differences." Students were clear, however, that they did not see themselves as typical of most men. One man said, for example, "I'm not a stereotypical male macho kind of person. I talk about lots of things, and I really value my relationships with people." Participants communicated a general sense of unease with masculinity. They were simultaneously unreflective about what being a guy means and aware that masculinity was something with which they did not want to identify.

## Sense of Challenge without Support

For those respondents who did answer the question about what it was like being a man on campus, there was a common theme of feeling left out. Several students mentioned the existence of support services designed specifically for women (e.g., women's center, women's leadership programs) without a corresponding focus on men. One student gave a specific example of feeling challenged, whereas female students were supported.

> I know a lot of men because I'm in a lot of math and physics classes and there are not a whole lot of girls [sic] in them. It seems like they get more attention, I don't know why. Our male teachers, it seems like they are more apt to give them help. If we don't get it, it's like "I don't understand how you don't understand this—you should be understanding this." I'm like "OK, fine, I don't understand." Then the girl goes up there and he talks quieter and he's more apt to listen to her. I don't know, it just seems he's more understanding of why a girl would not understand. I don't see why girls and guys are different that way.

# Discussion

The finding that these men did not often think of themselves in terms of their gender is not surprising. This is consistent with Levine and Cureton's (1998) study, which found that "males were neither as eloquent nor as thoughtful in describing gender differences. In the main, it was simply not on the male radar screen" (p. 111). It is, however, problematic if men do not see themselves as men. If identity development is fostered by experiencing crises and choices, as Marcia (1966) suggested, gender and sex need to at least be a blip on the radar screen before reflective commitment can occur. The lack of gender awareness may also be explained by Jones and McEwen's (2000) multiple identity model. According to this model, privilege and inequality are least visible and least understood by those who are most privileged by cultural systems. Like White people who do not see themselves as having a race (Helms, 1992), these men may not have been conscious of their sex. This may be particularly true within university cultures like WIU, where profeminist influences are not as visible as they are on many college campuses.

It was similarly noticeable that these men did not mention anything about their racial identity in the interviews. Existing in a cultural context where their gender and race are not "on the radar screen" is both a privilege and a problem. That is, being in an environment where one's race and gender are routinely affirmed promotes a foreclosed identity where crisis is absent and commitments are not explored. To reach an achieved identity, important aspects of one's identity (such as race, gender, and religion) need to be explored.

Although gender and race identity issues were generally unconsidered, men in this study had a sense that they were not being supported. Consistent with Pollack's (1999) research, this study found that men felt pushed or challenged without sufficient empathy or support. One participant's story about feeling that female students were supported whereas male students were challenged is particularly poignant. Not only is it outside the traditional male role for an individual to express a need for help (Good & Wood, 1995), but also educators may misunderstand this lack of expression as a lack of need. Osherson (1986), moreover, described the archetypal scene of a distressed little boy crying out for emotional soothing only to experience both the minimizing of his pain and disapproval for showing such unmanly behavior. The common phrase "take it like a man" is an artifact of this deeper cultural script.

This research also illuminates the importance of gender role conflict on college men's identity development. Students described several instances where they were fearful about how other people might interpret their behavior. According to O'Neil (1981), fear of femininity is at the center of men's gender role conflict. In this study, fear manifested itself through stories of homophobia, restricted emotional expression (e.g., no crying), and limits on verbal expression and communication. These heterosexual men were afraid, essentially, that others would view them as feminine, gay, or somehow other than a man. Thus, when others' assumptions about their sexual orientation did not fit with their own sense of self, participants felt a need to alter their behavior. Men's self-expression may be mediated by what this behavior means, or might mean, to other people. In other words, being less expressive had the benefit of helping to avoid labels they wanted to evade. This may also help to explain findings that male students tend to exhibit more homophobic attitudes and perpetrate significantly more hate-motivated assaults than women do (D'Augelli, 1991).

The finding that participants felt restrictions associated with expression is problematic in a number of ways. First, gender-related limits on men's self-expression have been linked to negative emotional outcomes (Blazina, 2001; Brody, 1996). Second, one of the central findings in this study was that these students clearly felt that self-expression was important to them. The fact that they valued self-expression even though they were aware that this behavior was sometimes penalized illustrates the tensions causing gender role conflict. In other words, these men wanted to give voice to certain emotions but were acutely cognizant of the parameters in which these feelings could be expressed. The expression of certain feelings or certain behaviors is quite simply outside of what Pollack (1999) calls "the boy code." Not wanting to appear vulnerable to other men, fear of being seen as gay, and wanting to avoid the "just friend-not boyfriend" label all shaped how and what men in this study communicated.

Students also described communication with their male friends in a way that could easily be misunderstood. Stories about playing video games, traveling in a car to go gambling, and watching WWF wrestling were initially overlooked by investigators. When, however, we suspended our assumptions and more carefully listened to the participant's descriptions, it became clear that they were describing these activities in relational terms. Although communication was "side-by-side" and "doing oriented," the stories being told were about relationship building and connection. This finding is similar to Pollack's (1999) investigation into male development which found that "many mothers find that if they engage in action-oriented activities with their sons, their boys began to open up and talk" (p. 101). Although various activities that men do together may appear on the surface to be incongruent with intimacy, the actions may in fact be rooted in forging relationships and building "buddyship."

Interestingly, the interviewers felt that some of these communication patterns were evident during the interviews. The female researchers noted that men were generally more comfortable expressing themselves than the interviewers anticipated. Several men in this study felt that expressing themselves to women was generally easier than talking with men, as long as the women were viewed as friends and not potential partners. This was true about most topics, although female interviewers felt that discussions about sex and relationships were sometimes awkward. The male interviewers felt that the participants were generally very expressive. This may be, in part, due to the one-on-one nature of the interaction. Men in this study mentioned that it was easier to express themselves with just one other male as opposed to groups of men.

## Implications for Student Affairs

Results of this study suggest that student affairs professionals need to provide programming and learning interventions aimed at putting gender on the radar screen for men. Just as we need to help White students see themselves as racial beings, we need to facilitate men learning about themselves as men. Helping men become more aware of their gender should help to promote identity development to the extent that unconsidered gender roles are keeping them from making reflective identity commitments. One strategy that I have used with undergraduate men is to show commercial, movie, and sitcom video clips that have gender-related messages. I then follow these clips with questions to focus attention on both how gender roles are constructed and how to become a critical consumer of these messages. The goal is to help students select for themselves who they are and who they want to become.

In addition to the need for student development professionals to facilitate reflection regarding gender identity, participants' stories also suggest that we may need to give college men more support. In a patriarchal culture, men are privileged, but that should not keep us from treating men developmentally. Pollack (1990), for example, challenged us to "be sensitively aware (and less countertransferentially critical) of the particular forms of affiliative needs and capacities shown by men" (p. 318). Student affairs professionals need to be alert to any disposition to rely on sex role expectations in deciding on developmentally appropriate challenges and supports. Similarly, in this study, several men noticed institutional supports for women, but no such safety net or safe harbor for men on campus. It is important to offer direct services to men, as men, on campus.

Student affairs professionals should also understand that certain forms of men's communication might be more relational than we initially realize. Gender-related restrictions regarding verbal expression clearly influenced *how* men in this study communicated. The students generally preferred one-on-one communication, felt more comfortable communicating with women, and expressed intimacy "side-by-side" or in the context of doing. Certain developmental interventions may, therefore, be more effective outside of the context of groups. For example, resident assistants (RAs) trying to confront a male student may meet less resistance if the confrontation is handled one-on-one.

It is similarly important for male RAs to be aware that men may have a hard time expressing certain feelings to them. Activity-based or "doing" strategies may help facilitate such expression. According to Pollack (1999), the following approaches are critical to facilitating discussion with men: create a safe space, give men time to feel comfortable with expression, seek out and provide alternative pathways for expression (i.e., relate while engaging in action-oriented activities), listen without judging, and give affirmation and affection. Student affairs professionals should consider engaging men in action-oriented activities such as going for a walk or some other "doing" activity in order to get beyond the mask of masculinity.

## Conclusion

Research into women's identity development grew out of a belief that women must be understood within the context of their role expectations and restrictions. To understand men's identity development, student affairs professionals need to explore how men see themselves as men within "the context of the restraints, constraints, and expectations of the male gender role" (Scher, 1990, p. 325). Identity models that are focused on naturally occurring developmental tasks may tell only a portion of the story. Researchers and student affairs practitioners would be well advised to consider models that reflect the idea that identities are also socially constructed (e.g., Jones & McEwen, 2000). Participants in this research clearly articulated conflicts between behaviors that they personally valued (e.g., self-expression) and how they felt others interpreted that behavior. To the extent that people accept scripted gender roles either blindly or due to perceived sanctions for acting outside of these roles, their identity is less self-authored and more socially constructed.

O'Neil's (1981) concept of gender role conflict provides a useful framework for understanding how a man may see himself in the context of culturally transmitted role expectations. Fear of femininity, restricted expression, and restricted affectionate behavior among men were evident in the stories told by students in this study. The themes emerging from these stories suggest ways for student affairs professionals to design developmentally appropriate interventions for men, especially those experiencing gender role conflict.

The findings from this study must be interpreted within the limitations of the phenomenological methodology, participants, and context in which the research was conducted. Consistent with the constructivist tradition, the participants' voices and research team's interpretations are not intended to be representative of all men. Clearly, the fact that the research was based on a nondiverse group of men, especially in terms of important identity dimensions of sexual orientation and race, limits the transferability of findings. Information is given, however, regarding the research context and participant interviews to assist the reader in applying the results.

Future researchers should consider implementing longitudinal qualitative studies to get a sense of the events that promote or inhibit development, how other components of self (e.g., sexual orientation, cultural heritage, etc.) might impact growth, and how identity development progresses over time. It is also important to vary the contexts in which studies are implemented. In addition, more research is clearly necessary for various populations of men, including gay men, men with disabilities, and men from various cultural backgrounds.

## References

Belenky, M. F., Clinchy, B. M., Goldberger, N. R., & Tarule, J. M. (1986). *Women's ways of knowing*. New York: Basic Books.

Blazina, C. (2001). Analytic psychology and gender role conflict: The development of the fragile masculine self. *Psychotherapy, 38*(1), 50–59.

Brody, L. R. (1996). Gender, emotional expression, and the family. In R. Kavanaugh, B. Zimmerberg-Glick, and S. Fein (Eds.), *Emotion: Interdisciplinary Perspectives*. Hillsdale, NJ: Lawrence Erlbaum.

Chickering, A. W., (1969). *Education and identity*. San Francisco: Jossey-Bass.

Chickering, A. W., & Reisser, L. (1993). *Education and identity (2nd ed.)*. San Francisco: Jossey-Bass.

Coffey, A., & Atkinson, P. (1996). *Making sense of qualitative data: Complementary research strategies*. Thousand Oaks, CA: Sage.

Cournoyer, R. J., & Mahalik, J. R. (1995). Cross-sectional study of gender role conflict examining college-aged and middle-aged men. *Journal of Counseling Psychology, 42*(1), 11–19.

D'Augelli, A. R. (1991). Gay men in college: Identity processes and adaptations. *Journal of College Student Development, 32,* 140–146.

D'Augelli, A. R. (1994). Identity development and sexual orientation: Toward a model of lesbian, gay, and bisexual development. In E. J. Trickett, R. J. Watts, & D. Birman (Eds.), *Human diversity: Perspectives on people in context* (pp. 312–333). San Francisco: Jossey-Bass.

Erikson, E. (1968). *Identity, youth, and crisis*. New York: Norton.

Fine, M. (1994). Working the hyphens: Reinventing self and other in qualitative research. In N. R. Denzin & Y. S. Lincoln (Eds.), *Handbook of Qualitative Research* (pp. 70–82). Thousand Oaks, CA: Sage Publications.

Gilligan, C. (1982). *In a different voice*. Cambridge, MA: Harvard University Press.

Good, G. E., Braverman, D., & O'Neil, J. M. (1991). *Gender role conflict: Construct validity and reliability*. Paper presented at the annual meetings of the American Psychological Association, San Francisco, CA.

Good, G. E., & Mintz, L. B. (1990). Gender role conflict and depression in college men: Evidence for compound risk. *Journal of Counseling and Development, 69,* 17–21.

Good, G. E., & Wood, P. K. (1995). Male gender role conflict, depression, and help seeking: Do college men face double jeopardy? *Journal of Counseling & Development, 74*(1), 70–75.

Helms, J. E. (1992). *A race is a nice thing to have: A guide to being a White person or understanding the White persons in your life*. Topeka, KS: Content Communications.

Jones, S. R. (1997). Voices of identity and difference: A qualitative exploration of the multiple dimensions of identity development in women college students. *Journal of College Student Development, 38*(4), 376–385.

Jones, S. R., & McEwen, M. K. (2000). A conceptual model of multiple dimensions of identity. *Journal of College Student Development, 41*(4), 405–414.

Josselson, R. (1987). *Finding herself: Pathways to identity development in women*. San Francisco: Jossey-Bass.

Josselson, R. (1996). *Revising herself: The story of women's identity from college to midlife*. New York: Oxford University Press.

Kavale, S. (1996). *Interviews: An introduction to qualitative research interviewing*. Thousand Oaks, CA: Sage.

Levine, A., & Cureton, J. (1998). *When hope and fear collide*. San Francisco: Jossey-Bass.

Lincoln, Y., & Guba, E. (1985). *Naturalistic inquiry*. Thousand Oaks, CA: Sage.

Manning, K. (1999). *Giving voice to critical campus issues: Qualitative research in student affairs*. Lanham, MD: University Press of America.

Marcia, J. (1966). Development and validation of ego-identity status. *Journal of Personality and Social Psychology, 3*, 551–559.

Meth, R. L., & Pasick, R. S. (1990). *Men in therapy: The challenge of change*. New York: Guilford Press.

Miles, M. B., & Huberman, A. M. (1984). *Qualitative data analysis*. Beverly Hills, CA: Sage.

O'Neil, J. M. (1981). Patterns of gender role conflict and strain: Sexism and fear of femininity in men's lives. *The Personnel and Guidance Journal, 60*, 203–210.

O'Neil, J. M. (1990). Assessing men's gender role conflict. In D. Moore & F. Leafgren (Eds.), *Problem-solving strategies and interventions for men in conflict* (pp. 23–38). Alexandria, VA: American Counseling Association.

O'Neil, J. M., Helms, B. J., Gable, R. K., David, L., & Wrightsman, L. S. (1986). Gender role conflict scale: College men's fear of femininity. *Sex Roles, 14*, 335–350.

Osherson, S. (1986). *Finding our fathers*. New York: Fawcett Columbine.

Patton, M. Q. (1990). *Qualitative evaluation and research methods* (2nd ed.). Newbury Park, CA: Sage.

Piaget, J. (1954). *The construction of reality in the child* (M. Cook, Trans.). New York: Basic Books.

Pollack, W. S. (1990). Men's development and psychotherapy: A psychoanalytic perspective. *Psychotherapy, 27*, 316–321.

Pollack, W. S. (1999). *Real boys: Rescuing our sons from the myths of boyhood*. New York: Holt.

Rounds, D. (1994). *Predictors of homosexual intolerance on a college campus: Identity, intimacy, attitudes toward homosexuals and gender role conflict*. Unpublished master's thesis, Department of Psychology, University of Connecticut.

Schenkel, S., & Marcia, J. E. (1972). Attitudes toward premarital intercourse in determining ego identity status in college women. *Journal of Personality, 40*(1), 472–482.

Scher, M. (1990). Effect of gender role incongruities on men's experience as clients in psychotherapy. *Psychotherapy, 27*, 322–326.

Sharpe, M. J., & Heppner, P. P. (1991). Gender, gender-role conflict, and psychological well-being in men. *Journal of Counseling Psychology, 38*, 323–330.

Thompson, E. H., Pleck, J. H., & Ferrera, D. L. (1992). Men and masculinities: Scales for masculinity ideology and masculinity-related constructs. *Sex Roles, 27*, 573–607.

van Manen, M. (1990). *Researching lived experience: Human science for an action sensitive pedagogy*. Albany, NY: State University of New York Press.

Vygotsky, L. S. (1978). *Mind in society: The development of higher psychological processes*. Cambridge, MA: Harvard University Press.

# CHAPTER 15
# ANALYSIS OF LGBT IDENTITY DEVELOPMENT MODELS AND IMPLICATIONS FOR PRACTICE

BRENT L. BILODEAU AND KRISTEN A. RENN

In their efforts to serve all students more effectively, many student affairs professionals seek to understand how students come to have and enact lesbian, gay, bisexual, and transgender (LGBT) identities. In the past two decades, student affairs professionals have adopted psychosocial models of sexual orientation identity development (Cass, 1979, 1984), and a handful of scholars (D'Augelli, 1994; Evans and Broido, 1999; Rhoads, 1994) have attempted to describe LGBT identity in higher education settings. This chapter presents an overview of literature regarding models of LGBT identity development, including stage models of sexual orientation identity development, theories specific to LGBT people of color, a life span approach to LGBT identity development, and approaches to transgender identity development. Thematic similarities and differences as well as implications for educational practice and research are discussed.

## Stage Models of Gay and Lesbian Identity Development

In the United States, the 1970s marked a new era in research regarding sexual orientation identity development with the emergence of theoretical stage models describing homosexual identity. These models focused on the resolution of internal conflict related to identification as lesbian or gay, and informed what is commonly termed the *coming-out* process (see, for example, Cass, 1979, 1984; Fassinger, 1991; Savin-Williams, 1988, 1990; Troiden, 1979, 1988). Based on studies with small sample sizes, most often of men, these theoretical perspectives assert that non-heterosexuals move through a series of identity development stages, usually during the teenage years or early twenties. Though the number of stages and their names vary across theories, they share common characteristics. Gonsiorek (1995) described shared aspects of these models as follows.

Typically, these models begin with a stage in which individuals use multiple defense strategies to block recognition of personal homosexual feelings. These defensive strategies are maintained for an unspecified time period in an attempt to minimize an individual's same-gender feelings. The process of expending energy to deny and minimize feelings may have negative consequences for overall emotional health. Yet, for many individuals, a gradual recognition and tentative acceptance of same-gender feelings emerge as they come to accept that their feelings are not heterosexually oriented. According to the stage models, this emergence of same-gender feelings is followed

Bilodeau, B. L., & Renn, K. A. (2005). Analysis of LGBT identity development models and implications for practice. In R. L. Sanlo (Ed.), *Gender identity and sexual orientation: Research, policy, and personal development* (New Directions for Student Services No. 111, pp. 25–39). San Francisco, CA: Jossey-Bass.

by a period of emotional and behavioral experimentation with homosexuality, often accompanied by a growing sense of personal normality. Some models describe the ending of a first relationship as a time of identity crisis in which negative feelings about being gay or lesbian return. As the individual again begins to accept non-heterosexual feelings, a sense of identity as lesbian or gay becomes internally integrated and is viewed as a positive aspect of self. While most scholars describe the coming-out process in clear stages, they also note that it is generally more fluid, with stops, starts, and backtracking (Cass, 1979, 1984; Troiden, 1979; Savin-Williams, 1990).

Differences among the stage models illustrate the difficulty of using only one model to understand a complex psychosocial process (the development of sexual orientation identity). Yet, the predominance and persistence of stage models in the research literature and in current educational practice suggest that they represent with some accuracy the developmental process. In contrast, Ryan and Futterman (1998) noted that most of lesbian, gay, and bisexual identity development models were based on research on adults reflecting on their experience. Few models exist that specifically address developmental issues of lesbian, gay, and bisexual adolescents.

## Adolescence and Sexual Orientation Identity Development

Research on adolescents and sexual orientation supplements the stage models with information specific to youth and college students. Research on teenage youth notes a trend in which self-identification as lesbian, gay, or bisexual happens at increasingly earlier ages (Troiden, 1998). It is therefore more likely that students will enter college having already begun—or completed—the coming-out process.

When considering developmental issues of adolescents and sexual orientation, it is also important to note that these years may be characterized by sexual experimentation as well as by confusion about identity (Ryan and Futterman, 1998; Savin-Williams, 1990). Same-gender adolescent sexual experiences do not necessarily signal a lesbian, gay, or bisexual identity (Blumenfeld and Raymond, 1993). Conversely, adolescents may identify as lesbian, gay, or bisexual without having had any sexual experience (Ryan and Futterman, 1998; Savin-Williams, 1990). The diversity of individual adolescents' experiences of identifying as lesbian, gay, or bisexual highlights the need to consider multiple developmental models.

## Research on LGBT Identities in Bisexuals, People of Color, and Women

There is growing scholarly recognition of the experience and diversity of sexual orientation beyond "heterosexual," "gay," and "lesbian" identities, and this recognition has led to challenges to the traditional stage models of sexual orientation identity development. Scholars have found that bisexuals experience identity processes differently from the way lesbians and gay men do (Fox, 1995; Klein, 1990, 1993). For example, some individuals may come to bisexual identity after self-labeling as lesbian or gay. Others may identify bisexual feelings from childhood onward. Still others may not become aware of bisexual feelings until after experiencing heterosexual relationships or marriages. Further, stage models do not account for ways in which the boundaries between Eurocentric notions of culture, sexual orientation, and gender identity are blurred and reconstructed in non-Western contexts (Brown, 1997; Gonsiorek, 1995). One such example is the existence of "Two Spirit" identities that blend Western notions of gender identity and sexual orientation within Native American communities (Brown, 1997). Across cultures, LGBT identities have different names and meanings.

Researchers are providing new perspectives on the experience of multiple and intersecting identities related to race and ethnicity, nationality, and sexuality. Research regarding the ways race and culture interact with the experience of LGBT identities in the United States has expanded (Boykin, 1996, on African Americans; Diaz, 1997, and Espin, 1993, on Latinos; Manalansan, 1993, on Asian Americans; Crow, Brown, and Wright, 1997, and Wilson, 1996, on Native Americans). Beyond the United States, scholarship on the intersections of LGBT identities and nationality is expanding as well, particularly in reference to Africans, Latin Americans, Middle Easterners, and South and East Asians (Ben-Ari, 2001; Kapack, 1992; Kovac, 2002; McLelland, 2000).

Additional research addresses the influence of gender, socioeconomic class, ability, and spirituality on LGBT identity development. Regarding gender differences, women's non-heterosexual identity processes have most often been presented as paralleling those of men, yet a number of scholars indicate that women may come out and have intimate same-gender experiences at somewhat later ages (Brown, 1995; Sears, 1989). Recent research explores LGBT identities related to social class and class systems, posing questions about how non-heterosexual identities intersect with class privilege and oppression (Becker, 1997; Raffo, 1997; Vanderbosh, 1997). Scholarship is emerging that addresses ways that identities of people with disabilities are influenced by LGBT identity processes (Clare, 1999). DuMontier (2000) hypothesized interactions between sexual orientation and faith development, and other authors discuss specific religious traditions and sexual orientation identity (Love, 1998).

By expanding the theoretical bases for understanding LGBT identities beyond those represented by white, Western men in the foundational models of homosexual identity formation (such as Cass, 1979 and 1984, and Troiden, 1979), researchers provide a complex picture of non-heterosexual identity. They highlight the social context of non-heterosexual identities across cultures and draw attention to the diversity that exists within LGBT communities.

## Alternatives to Stage Models: A Life Span Approach to Sexual Orientation and Gender Identity Development

As more scholars describe the development of non-heterosexual identity as a fluid and complex process influenced by other psychosocial identities, it becomes apparent that stage models are not adequate to describe all non-heterosexual identity processes. In addition, bisexual and transgender experiences, with their emphasis on identities existing outside traditional binary constructions of gender and sexuality, pose unique challenges to stage models. Though no identity development model can fully address the intersections and complexities of non-heterosexual identity, D'Augelli (1994) offered a "life span" model of sexual orientation development that takes social contexts into account in ways that the early stage models did not. As well, D'Augelli's model has the potential to represent a wider range of experiences than the theories relating to specific racial, ethnic, or gender groups.

The D'Augelli framework addresses issues often ignored in other models, presenting human development as unfolding in concurring and multiple paths, including the development of a person's self-concept, relationships with family, and connections to peer groups and community. This model suggests that sexual orientation may be very fluid at certain times in the life span and more fixed at others and that human growth is intimately connected to and shaped by environmental and biological factors. The D'Augelli model describes six "identity processes" that operate more or less independently and are not ordered in stages:

- Exiting heterosexuality
- Developing a personal LGB identity
- Developing an LGB social identity
- Becoming an LGB offspring
- Developing an LGB intimacy status
- Entering an LGB community

An individual may experience development in one process to a greater extent than another; for example, he or she may have a strong LGB social identity and an intimate same-sex partner, but not have come out as LGB to family (become an LGB offspring). Furthermore, depending on the context and timing, he or she may be at different points of development in a given process, such as when an openly LGB person enters a new work setting and chooses not to express his or her LGB identity.

Developed to represent sexual orientation identity development, D'Augelli's model has also been used for understanding corresponding processes in the formation of transgender identity (Renn and Bilodeau, 2005). In a recent study of transgender identity development in college students, Bilodeau (2005) noted that participants described their gender identities in ways that reflect the six processes of the D'Augelli model. Research on transgender college students is rare, and differences between sexual orientation and gender identity are not always well understood (Bilodeau, 2005).

## Definitions of Transgender Identities

The term *gender identity* has been used to describe an individual's internal sense of self as male, female, or an identity between or outside these two categories (Wilchins, 2002). Individuals whose biological sex assignment matches male or female gender identity and the range of related behavioral expressions deemed acceptable by societal norms may be referred to as "traditionally gendered." The term *transgender* focuses on individuals whose gender identity conflicts with biological sex assignment or societal expectations for gender expression as male or female (Bornstein, 1994; Elkins and King, 1996; Wilchins, 1997, 2002).

The term *transgender* is often used as an inclusive category for a wide range of identities, including transsexuals, transvestites, male and female impersonators, drag kings and queens, male-to-female (MTF) persons, female-to-male (FTM) persons, cross-dressers, gender benders, gender variant, gender nonconforming, and ambiguously gendered persons (Bornstein, 1994; Feinberg, 1996; O'Keefe and Fox, 1997; Wilchins, 1997, 2002). While these terms are more commonly used in the United States, it is important to note that in a number of non-Western societies, transgender identities are defined with a unique terminology reflecting cultural norms (Besnier, 1993; Brown, 1997; Johnson, 1997). In these contexts, gender identity and sexual orientation are presented as more integrated identities, compared with the Western medical and psychiatric tradition of segmenting sexual orientation and gender identity into distinctive categories.

## Western Psychiatric and Medical Perspectives on Transgender Identities

As Western psychiatric and medical traditions have set the standards for the diagnosis and care of transgender persons in the United States, it is important to consider their impact. While various scholars, as well as members of the transgender community, regard these traditions as invaluable for addressing the needs of transgender persons (Brown and Rounsley, 1996), others suggest that medical and psychiatric perspectives are dominated by themes of transgender identities as forms of mental illness and biological malady (Califia, 1997). The term *disorder* dominates the literature. Medical and psychiatric literature focuses primarily on a binary construction of transgender identity (all individuals should be assigned to either male or female categories), with an emphasis on "correcting" gender deviance through reassignment to the "appropriate" gender. This focus makes transsexuals—individuals who often choose to transition from one gender to another with medical assistance—of primary concern.

A section on Gender Identity Disorder (GID) appears for the first time in the American Psychiatric Association's 1980 publication, *Diagnostic and Statistical Manual of Mental Disorders, 3rd Edition* (*DSM-III*). GID is described as incongruence between biological sex assignment and gender identity. Three different types of GID diagnoses are discussed: transsexualism, non-transsexualism type, and not otherwise specified (American Psychiatric Association, 1980). In *DSM III*, treatments described vary from psychotherapy to sex reassignment surgery (SRS). Three more editions of DSM have appeared since 1980.

The current edition, *Diagnostic and Statistical Manual of Mental Disorders, 4th Edition, Text Revision* (*DSM-IV-TR*) (American Psychiatric Association, 2000), continues the use of the GID classification, but expands diagnosis standards introduced in *DSM-III*. In *DSM-IV-TR*, there are four major criteria that must be present to make a diagnosis. First, there must be evidence of a strong and persistent cross-gender identification, which is the desire to be, or the insistence that one is, of the other gender (Criteria A). This cross-gender identification must not merely be a desire for any perceived cultural advantages of being the other gender. Second, there must also be evidence of persistent discomfort about one's assigned gender (based on biological anatomy) or a sense of inappropriateness in the gender role of that assigned gender (Criteria B). Third, the individual must not have a concurrent physical intersex condition (referring to conditions in which a person is born with a reproductive or sexual anatomy that does not fit the typical definitions of female or male) (Criteria C). Fourth, there must be evidence of clinically significant distress or impairment in social, occupational, or other important areas of functioning (Criteria D). In the case of transsexuality, individuals are further categorized under primary transsexualism (emerging in early childhood) or secondary transsexualism (emerging during or after puberty). GID is used primarily to diagnose conditions related to transsexual identities, while another classification, Gender Identity Disorder Not Otherwise Specified (GIDNOS), applies to conditions such as intersex anatomy or cross-dressing behavior (American Psychiatric Association, 2000).

*DSM-IV-TR* is complemented by the fifth edition of the *Harry Benjamin Standards of Care for Gender Identity Disorders*, which outlined a treatment framework, including therapeutic and medical guidelines, as well as standards for ongoing evaluation of patients who are undergoing sex reassignment surgery (Harry Benjamin International Gender Dysphoria Association, 2001). A number of scholars (including Bornstein, 1994; Carter, 2000; Mallon, 1999b) are highly critical of *DSM-IV-TR* and the *Harry Benjamin Standards of Care*, citing their negative, stigmatizing nature. Using these two frameworks, an individual must in essence be documented as having a mental illness (using *DSM-IV-TR*) in order to access sex reassignment surgery (as specified by the *Harry Benjamin Standards of Care*) (Carter, 2000).

Literature consistently identifies a growing outrage in transgender communities regarding the GID diagnosis (see Califia, 1997; Carter, 2000; Wilchins, 2002). Pressure to remove gender identity disorders from *DSM-IV-TR* has been compared to the 1973 removal of homosexuality as a mental illness diagnostic classification from the 1973 edition of the *DSM* (Carter, 2000). Pauline Parks, a transgender activist, argues that every psychiatrist who diagnoses GID in a patient merely by virtue of the individual's transgender identity is complicit in the manipulation and control of transgender people and their bodies. Parks asserts that in diagnosing someone with a so-called illness that the person does not have, the psychiatrist engages in behavior that not only is unethical, but also constitutes medical malpractice (Cooper, 1999).

Further, medical and psychiatric literature focuses primarily on a binary construction of gender identity. Normality is defined as a biological and gender identity match as either male or female. The majority of medical and therapeutic approaches are designed to assist individuals in moving from one gender to another. These approaches do not fully address the needs of individuals who, for a variety of reasons, may forgo gender reassignment surgery or may define gender identity as existing outside binary notions of male or female identities. In reaction to binary identities, one transgender college student described self as follows:

> I'd use the word transgender. I'd also use "non-operational female to male." I'd also use the word "genderqueer." I identified as a feminist before identifying as trans. It was really embedded in me. It played a big part in my decision not to have surgery. I've tried with my identity to not reinforce the gender binary system, and options have been limited to the trans community by focusing so much on transsexualism (involving gender reassignment surgery). The only option is, if you're male, to become female, or vice-versa. Transgender youth have felt that binary gender system is not for them. We want to increase the number of genders. [Bilodeau, 2005]

Though medical and psychiatric approaches comprise the dominant paradigm for addressing the concerns and needs of transgender persons in the United States, it is apparent that these perspectives provide only partial understanding of the range of ways transgender identities are expressed.

## Feminist, Postmodern, and Queer Theory Perspectives on Gender Identity

Feminist, postmodern, and queer theoretical scholars present significant alternatives to medical and psychiatric perspectives on gender identity. A number of these scholars suggest that gender identity is not necessarily linked to biological sex assignment at birth, but is created through complex social interactions and influenced by the dynamics of institutionalized power inequalities (Butler, 1990, 1993; Halberstam, 1998; Wilchins, 2002). Further, this framework takes issue with binary male or female constructions of gender and transgender expression as mental illness, favoring more fluid notions of gender identity (Butler, 1990, 1993; Creed, 1995; Feinberg, 1996, 1998; Halberstam, 1998, Wilchins, 2002). Regarding systemic power and gender, Bornstein (1994) suggested that gender is essentially a binary, male or female class system. This system leads to negation of the existence of more fluid gender identities increasingly expressed by transgender youth (Bilodeau, forthcoming; Wilchins, 2002). The systemic privileging of the binary, two-gender system has been described by the term *genderism* (Wilchins, 2002).

As alternatives to binary gender identity constructions and related oppressive systems, a number of feminist, postmodern, and queer theorists posit transgender identities and gender fluidity as normative and cite as evidence centuries of global traditions of gender-nonconforming identities (Butler, 1990, 1993; Creed, 1995; Feinberg, 1996, 1998; Halberstam, 1998). As examples, Feinberg (1996) documented several instances in Western European history where gender variance and transgression existed, including Joan of Arc, Amelia Earhart, and Rebecca's Daughters (cross-dressing Welsh resistance fighters in World War II). Beyond normalizing support of transgender identities, a number of feminist, postmodern, and queer theorists suggest that all individuals may benefit from the dismantling of dual gender systems, promoting greater freedom from rigid gender roles (Feinberg, 1996; Wilchins, 2002). Themes reflecting these perspectives are also emerging in human development spheres.

## Human Development and Transgender Identities: A Call for New Theoretical Models

A notable contribution in the human development field is the volume *Social Services with Transgendered Youth* (Mallon, 1999a), which primarily focuses on adolescent populations. In particular, the book addresses problematic issues of *DSM-IV* and broadens attention to ways youth construct gender identity outside binary systems. In another publication, Mallon (1999b) argued that it is inappropriate for social service practitioners to use traditional human development models, including those of Erikson (1950) and Marcia (1980), because these theorists posit concepts of gender role identification in traditionally gendered, biologically based constructions. Though an increasing number of studies of transgender persons are emerging (Denny, 1998; Devor, 1997), Mallon (1999b) suggested that this work has yet to propose the creation of healthy, nonstigmatizing models of transgender identity development. He calls upon human service practitioners to create such models and to develop an in-depth understanding of cross-disciplinary trends regarding sexual orientation and gender identity concerns.

## Multiple Perspectives Related to Sexual Orientation and Gender Identity

To summarize the theoretical lenses presented in this chapter, models and theories related to sexual orientation and gender identity development differ in scope, format, and underlying epistemological assumptions. These perspectives range from being based on assumptions of a universal linear experience of identity development to relying more on the social context of the developing person. Some models assume that sexual orientation and gender identity have distinctive natures, separate from the interplay of identity characteristics related to race, nationality, disability, spirituality, and socioeconomic class.

Other models view diverse identity characteristics as inextricably linked to the development and expression of sexual orientation and gender identity. In addition, some models assume an essentialized, biologically determined nature of sexual orientation and gender identity, while others focus on the social construction of identity. These assumptions, as well as the nature of the research sample (if any) on which the model was based, influence the general characteristics of families of theories. Table 1 summarizes some of these characteristics, origins, strengths, and criticisms.

## Implications for Student Affairs Practice and Scholarship

The choice of a particular theoretical model influences educational practice and research. Practitioners and scholars must take into account the value-laden nature of theories related to sexual orientation and gender identity development. As an example, a worthy student affairs goal is to support LGBT students in ongoing self-work surrounding personal identity. Basing educational interventions intended to promote development on linear models, however, may imply that there is an ideal endpoint that students should be prompted to attain. The educational initiative could imply that to be at any stage other than the endpoint is inferior.

Alternatively, if the theoretical family selected as the basis to design LGBT student support initiatives is feminist, postmodern, or queer, design considerations should address the social construction of LGBT identities within systems of campus power. Example questions and related issues are as follows:

When considering the design of LGBT student support initiatives, what is the nature of the university's political and sociohistorical contexts and how do these influence current levels of LGBT student "outness" and visibility? The student expression of sexual orientation and gender identity at a small, private, politically liberal institution may be very different from that at a large public land-grant institution with a conservative board of regents.

Given political and sociohistorical contexts, how supportive will institutional leadership be of implementing a range of LGBT student support initiatives?

What type of strategic advocacy for LGBT student support initiatives is the best match to secure institutional support?

Are advocacy strategies selected in collaboration with LGBT students in a manner that empowers identity construction and expression?

These questions mirror assumptions of feminist, postmodern, and queer theory perspectives, reflecting ways in which choice of theoretical model may influence decisions about design of campus LGBT student support initiatives.

Beyond the work of student affairs practitioners, the impact of the operating assumptions of an LGBT theoretical framework is also revealed by faculty engaged in teaching and research. Using a feminist perspective in a study of transgender student identity may result in very different conclusions from those drawn from research based on a medical model. For example, a feminist study may reveal ways in which the voices of transgender students are systematically silenced on campus. A medically based study may focus on ways that transitioning from one gender to another may aid transgender students in being more comfortable on campus.

Theoretical operating assumptions may at times be explicit, at others unnamed, but some form of bias is always involved. It is critical that student affairs professionals and scholars are fully conscious of the potential impact that these assumptions bring to their work.

Based on the models presented in this chapter, related student affairs practice and research may express a wide range of assumptions and values. These include such notions as "biology is destiny," "social change occurs only through grassroots empowerment," and "human life unfolds in stages." Regardless of the models of sexual orientation or gender identity selected as the basis for practice and research, it is important that they be thoughtfully examined. Practitioners and scholars have an ethical responsibility to understand what the underlying assumptions of the models are, what each purports to describe, on what populations or premises the models were based, and whose interests are served by different models and their uses.

**TABLE 1**

**Comparison of Sexual Orientation and Gender Identity Development Theories**

| | Stage Models of Sexual Orientation Identity Development | Life Span and Other Nonlinear Models of Sexual Orientation Identity Development | Diverse Perspectives on Sexual Orientation and Gender Identity | Medical and Psychiatric Perspectives on Gender Identity | Feminist, Postmodern and Queer Perspectives on Gender Identity |
|---|---|---|---|---|---|
| Examples of Theorists or Sources | Cass, Fassinger, Savin-Williams, Troiden | D'Augelli, Fox, Klein, Rhoads | Boykin, L. S. Brown, Clare, Diaz, Raffo, Wilson | *Diagnostic and Statistical Manual of Mental Disorders, Fourth Edition, Text Revision; Harry Benjamin Standards of Care* | Butler, Creed, Feinberg, Halberstam, Wilchins |
| General characteristics of models | Linear progression from lack of awareness of sexual orientation through immersion in identity to integration of identity. | Focus on specific processes of identity development within sociocultural and life span context. | Describe LGBT identity and development in relation to other psychosocial identities (gender, race, culture, class, ability, and so on). | Posit "normal" gender identity as that in which gender identity corresponds in traditional ways to biological sex; transgenderism and transsexuality are viewed as psychiatric disorders. | Posit gender identity as socially constructed within system of power based on gender, race, class, sexual orientation, ability, and other socially constructed categories. |
| Samples on which models were based | General adult population, clinical or incarcerated populations (Cass) | College students, general adult population | Subpopulations of adults, adolescents, college students | Clinical populations | None; scholarship and theories not typically derived from empirical research |

| | | | | |
|---|---|---|---|---|
| Strengths of these models for higher education practice | • Offer parallel theories of human development (such as Erikson, 1950) in progression from less to more complex ways of understanding self and society<br>• Conceptualize development in a way that can be understood and applied in campus settings | • Account for context of identity development<br>• Illuminate processes as well as outcomes of identity development<br>• Some were developed specific to college context | • Enrich theoretical basis for understanding LGBT identity in multicultural contexts<br>• Challenge universalized notions of LGBT identity<br>• Support development of programs and services that meet needs of diverse student populations | • Provide legal basis for provision of services to transgender individuals under the Americans with Disabilities Act | • Account for context of identity development<br>• Illuminate psychosocial elements of college environment that may influence gender identity<br>• Account for structural differences in power |
| Criticisms of these models | • Appear to prescribe a universal linear developmental trajectory that does not fit the experience of many individuals<br>• Imply an endpoint and appear to value achievement of that endpoint as most healthy outcome of identity development<br>• Ignore individual differences (gender, race, class, culture, and so on) that may influence or interact with sexual orientation identity<br>• Many are not specific to college environment or experience<br>• Many were developed with small empirical samples or were not based on empirical data | • Many are not specific to college environment or experience<br>• Many were developed with small empirical samples or were not based on empirical data | • Some appear to assume fixed notions of socially constructed categories (gender, race, class, and so on) and universality of experience of LGBT people within those categories<br>• Many were developed with small empirical samples or were not based on empirical data<br>• Many are not specific to college environment or experience | • Appear to ignore social contexts of gender identity development and enactment<br>• Tend to pathologize as mentally ill individuals whose gender identity does not conform to their biological sex<br>• Most are not specific to college environment or experience<br>• Ignore individual differences (race, class, culture, and so on) that may influence or interact with gender identity | • Do not provide theoretical background on identity development per se<br>• Most are not specific to college environment or experience |

# References

American Psychiatric Association. *Diagnostic and Statistical Manual of Mental Disorders*. (3rd ed.) Washington, D.C.: American Psychiatric Press, 1980.

American Psychiatric Association. *Diagnostic and Statistical Manual of Mental Disorders*. (4th ed., text revision) Washington, D.C.: American Psychiatric Association, 2000.

Becker, D. "Growing Up in Two Closets: Class and Privilege in the Lesbian and Gay Community." In S. Raffo (ed.), *Queerly Classed*. Boston: South End Press, 1997.

Ben-Ari, A. T. "Experiences of 'Not Belonging' in Collectivistic Communities: Narratives of Gays in Kibbutzes." *Journal of Homosexuality*, 2001, 42(2), 101–124.

Besnier, N. "Polynesian Gender Liminality Through Time and Space." In G. Herdt (ed.), *Third Sex, Third Gender: Beyond Sexual Dimorphism in Culture and History*. New York: Zone Books, 1993.

Bilodeau, B. "Beyond the Gender Binary: A Case Study of Transgender College Student Development at a Midwestern University." *Journal of Gay and Lesbian Issues in Education*, 2005, 2(4).

Blumenfeld, W. J., and Raymond, D. *Looking at Gay and Lesbian Life*. (2nd ed.) Boston: Beacon Press, 1993.

Bornstein, K. *Gender Outlaw: On Men, Women and the Rest of Us*. New York: Routledge, 1994.

Boykin, K. *One More River to Cross: Black and Gay in America*. New York: Anchor Books, 1996.

Brown, L. B. "Women and Men, Not-Men and Not-Women, Lesbians and Gays: American Indian Gender Style Alternatives." In L. B. Brown (ed.), *Two Spirit People: American Indian Lesbian Women and Gay Men*. New York: Harrington Park Press, 1997.

Brown, L. S. "Lesbian Identities: Concepts and Issues." In A. R. D'Augelli and C. J. Patterson (eds.), *Lesbian, Gay and Bisexual Identities over the Lifespan*. New York: Oxford University Press, 1995.

Brown, M. L., and Rounsley, C. A. *True Selves: Understanding Transsexualism for Families, Friends, Coworkers, and Helping Professionals*. San Francisco: Jossey-Bass, 1996.

Butler, J. *Bodies That Matter: On the Discursive Limits of "Sex."* New York: Routledge, 1993.

Butler, J. *Gender Trouble: Feminism and the Subversion of Identity*. New York: Routledge, 1990.

Califia, P. *Sex Changes: The Politics of Transgenderism*. San Francisco: Cleis Press, 1997.

Carter, K. A. "Transgenderism and College Students: Issues of Gender Identity and Its Role on Our Campuses." In V. A. Wall, and N. J. Evans (eds.), *Toward Acceptance: Sexual Orientation Issues on Campus*. Washington, D.C.: American College Personnel Association, 2000.

Cass, V. C. "Homosexual Identity Formation: A Theoretical Model." *Journal of Homosexuality*, 1979, 4, 219–235.

Cass, V. C. "Homosexual Identity Formation: Testing a Theoretical Model." *Journal of Sex Research*, 1984, 20, 143–167.

Clare, E. *Exile and Pride: Disability, Queerness, and Liberation*. Boston: South End Press, 1999.

Cooper, K. "Practice with Transgendered Youth and Their Families." In G. P. Mallon (ed.), *Social Services with Transgendered Youth*. Binghamton, N.Y.: Harrington Park Press, 1999.

Creed, B. "Lesbian Bodies: Tribades, Tomboys, and Tarts." In E. Grosz and E. Probyn (eds.), *Sexy Bodies: The Strange Carnalities of Feminism*. New York: Routledge, 1995.

Crow, L., Brown, L. B., and Wright, J. "Gender Selection in Two American Indian Tribes." In L. B. Brown (ed.), *Two Spirit People: American Indian Lesbian Women and Gay Men*. New York: Harrington Park Press, 1997.

D'Augelli, A. R. "Identity Development and Sexual Orientation: Toward a Model of Lesbian, Gay, and Bisexual Development." In E. J. Trickett, R. J. Watts, and D. Birman (eds.), *Human Diversity: Perspectives on People in Context*. San Francisco: Jossey-Bass, 1994.

Denny, D. (ed.). *Current Concepts in Transgender Identity*. New York: Garland, 1998.

Devor, H. *FTM: Female-to-Male Transsexuals in Society*. Bloomington: Indiana University Press, 1997.

Diaz, R. "Latino Gay Men and Psycho-Cultural Barriers to AIDS Prevention." In M. Levine, J. Gagnon, and P. Nardi (eds.), *In Changing Times: Gay Men and Lesbians Encounter HIV/AIDS*. Chicago: University of Chicago Press, 1997.

DuMontier, V. L., II. "Faith, the Bible, and Lesbians, Gay Men, and Bisexuals." In V. A. Wall and N. J. Evans (eds.), *Toward Acceptance: Sexual Orientation Issues on Campus*. Washington, D.C.: American College Personnel Association, 2000.

Elkins, R., and King, D. "Blending Genders—An Introduction." In R. Elkins and D. King (eds.), *Blending Genders: Social Aspects of Cross-Dressing and Sex Changing*. New York: Routledge, 1996.

Erikson, E. *Childhood and Society.* New York: Norton, 1950.

Espin, O. M. "Issues of Identity in the Psychology of Latina Lesbians." In L. S. Garnets and D. C. Kimmel (eds.), *Psychological Perspectives on Lesbian and Gay Male Experiences.* New York: Columbia University Press, 1993.

Evans, N. J., and Broido, E. M. "Coming Out in College Residence Halls: Negotiation, Meaning Making, Challenges, and Supports." *Journal of College Student Development,* 1999, *40,* 658–668.

Fassinger, R. E. "The Hidden Minority: Issues and Challenges in Working with Lesbian Women and Gay Men." *Counseling Psychologist,* 1991, *19*(2), 157–176.

Feinberg, L. *Transgender Warriors: Making History from Joan of Arc to Dennis Rodman.* Boston: Beacon Press, 1996.

Feinberg, L. *Trans Liberation: Beyond Pink or Blue.* Boston: Beacon Press, 1998.

Fox, R. "Bisexual Identities." In A. R. D'Augelli and C. J. Patterson (eds.), *Lesbian, Gay, and Bisexual Identities over the Lifespan: Psychological Perspectives.* New York: Oxford University Press, 1995.

Gonsiorek, J. C. "Gay Male Identities: Concepts and Issues." In A. R. D'Augelli and C. J. Patterson (eds.), *Lesbian, Gay, and Bisexual Identities over the Lifespan: Psychological Perspectives.* New York: Oxford University Press, 1995.

Halberstam, J. *Female Masculinity.* Durham: Duke University Press, 1998.

Harry Benjamin International Gender Dysphoria Association. "The HBIGDA Standards of Care for Gender Identity Disorders, Sixth Version." 2001. http://www.hbigda.org/soc.cfm. Accessed Oct. 20, 2004.

Johnson, M. *Beauty and Power: Transgendering and Cultural Transformation in the Southern Philippines.* New York: Berg, 1997.

Kapack, J. S. "Chinese Male Homosexuality: Sexual Identity Formation and Gay Organizational Development in a Contemporary Chinese Population." Unpublished doctoral dissertation, University of Toronto, 1992.

Klein, F. *The Bisexual Option.* (2nd ed.) New York: Haworth Press, 1993.

Klein, F. "The Need to View Sexual Orientation as Multivariable Dynamic Process: A Theoretical Perspective." In D. P. McWhirter, S. A. Sanders, and J. M. Reinisch (eds.), *Homosexuality/Heterosexuality: Concepts of Sexual Orientation.* New York: Oxford University Press, 1990.

Kovac, A. L. "Africa's Rainbow Nation." *Journal of Southern African Studies,* 2002, *28*(2), 74–82.

Lev, A. I. *Transgender Emergence: Therapeutic Guidelines for Working with Gender-Variant People and Their Families.* New York: Haworth Press, 2004.

Love, P. G. "Cultural Barriers Facing Lesbian, Gay, and Bisexual Students at a Catholic College." *Journal of Higher Education,* 1998, *69,* 298–323.

Mallon, G. P. (ed.). *Social Services with Transgendered Youth.* Binghamton, N.Y.: Harrington Park Press, 1999a.

Mallon, G. P. "Preface: An Ecological Perspective of Social Work Practice with Transgendered Persons." In G. P. Mallon (ed.), *Social Services with Transgendered Youth.* Binghamton, N.Y.: Harrington Park Press, 1999b.

Manalansan, M. "(Re)Locating the Gay Filipino: Resistance, Postcolonialism, and Identity." *Journal of Homosexuality,* 1993, *26*(2/3), 53–73.

Marcia, J. E. "Identity in Adolescence." In J. Adelson (ed.), *Handbook of Adolescent Psychiatry.* New York: Wiley, 1980.

McLelland, M. *Male Homosexuality in Modern Japan: Cultural Myths and Social Realities.* Richmond, Va.: Corson Press, 2000.

O'Keefe, T., and Fox, K. *Trans-x-u-all: The Naked Difference.* London: Extraordinary People Press, 1997.

Raffo, S. "Introduction." In S. Raffo (ed.), *Queerly Classed.* Boston: South End Press, 1997.

Renn, K. A., and Bilodeau, B. "Queer Student Leaders: A Case Study of Identity Development and Lesbian, Gay, Bisexual, and Transgender Student Involvement at a Midwestern Research University." *Journal of Gay and Lesbian Issues in Education,* 2005, *3*(1).

Rhoads, R. A. *Coming Out in College: The Struggle for a Queer Identity.* Westport, Conn.: Bergin and Garvey, 1994.

Ryan, C., and Futterman, D. *Lesbian and Gay Youth: Care and Counseling.* New York: Columbia University Press, 1998.

Savin-Williams, R. C. "Gay and Lesbian Adolescents." *Marriage and Family Review,* 1990, *14,* 197–216.

Savin-Williams, R. C. "Theoretical Perspectives Accounting for Adolescent Homosexuality." *Journal of Adolescent Health,* 1988, *9*(6), 95–104.

Sears, J. T. "The Impact of Gender and Race on Growing up Lesbian and Gay in the South." *National Women's Studies Association Journal,* 1989, *1,* 422–457.

Troiden, R. R. "Becoming Homosexual: A Model of Gay Identity Acquisition." *Psychiatry*, 1979, 42, 362–373.

Troiden, R. R. "Homosexual Identity Development." *Journal of Adolescent Health Care*, 1988, 9, 105–113.

Vanderbosh, J. "Notes from the Working Class." In S. Raffo (ed.), *Queerly Classed*. Boston: South End Press, 1997.

Wilchins, R. A. "Queerer Bodies." In J. Nestle, C. Howell, and R. A. Wilchins (eds.), *Genderqueer: Voices from Beyond the Sexual Binary*. Los Angeles: Alyson, 2002.

Wilchins, R. A. *Read My Lips: Sexual Subversion and the End of Gender*. New York: Firebrand Books, 1997.

Wilson, A. "How We Find Ourselves: Identity Development in Two-Spirit People." *Harvard Educational Review*, 1996, *66*(2), 303–317.

# CHAPTER 16
# CONCEPTUALIZING HETEROSEXUAL IDENTITY DEVELOPMENT: ISSUES AND CHALLENGES

## ROSE MARIE HOFFMAN

This article summarizes the work of R. L. Worthington and J. J. Mohr (2002); R. L. Worthington, H. B. Savoy, F. R. Dillon, and E. R. Vernaglia (2002); and J. J. Mohr (2002) on heterosexual identity development that constituted the Major Contribution section of the July 2002 issue of *The Counseling Psychologist*. The author provides an overview of the 2 independently developed models of heterosexual identity development presented in these articles and discusses implications for counseling practice, training, and research. The author also offers a personal perspective on aspects of this body of work, including points raised by L. A. Gilbert and J. Rader (2002) and K. J. Bieschke (2002) in their reaction papers that followed these articles.

Models of identity development specifically intended for majority groups (e.g., Whites, men, heterosexuals) are considerably less prominent in the literature than are models developed for nondominant groups. To a large extent, this is understandable in that exploring the various developmental processes experienced by individuals who are oppressed because of membership in a particular group (e.g., Blacks, women, gay men, and lesbians) may be integral to their ultimate well-being. Such a focus further reflects the progress in counseling and related fields over the past 30 years in recognizing the importance of multicultural awareness and diversity issues. Yet, majority identity development models are integral to a true understanding of the nature of privilege and one's membership in an oppressive group (Worthington & Mohr, 2002), concepts that also need to be explored if we are to more fully understand and appreciate multiculturalism. An additional problem with the relative lack of attention to identity development for majority group members is that it may inadvertently serve to perpetuate the status of minority group members as the "other," as the ones who need explaining.

Regarding sexual orientation, Worthington and Mohr (2002); Worthington, Savoy, Dillon, and Vernaglia (2002); and Mohr (2002) have successfully turned this tide. Their innovative work on heterosexual identity development constituted the Major Contribution section of the July 2002 issue of *The Counseling Psychologist*. The purpose of this article is to provide a brief review of the two independently developed models presented in this work, with particular attention to implications for counseling practice, training, and research. Some of the points raised by Gilbert and Rader (2002) and Bieschke (2002) in their reaction papers that followed these articles are addressed, and my own perspectives on aspects of this body of work are offered.

Hoffman, R. M. (2004). Conceptualizing heterosexual identity development: Issues and challenges. *Journal of Counseling and Development, 82*, 375–380.

## Heterosexual Identity Development

As an element of identity development, sexual orientation is typically considered only in relation to processes that homosexual individuals experience as they work through statuses toward internalization and synthesis. Yet, just as White racial identity development has been recognized as a unique process that those privileged regarding race need to examine, heterosexual identity development merits attention as an equally salient process for those privileged in this area.

In their introductory article, Worthington and Mohr (2002) discussed essentialism and social constructivism as competing paradigms for understanding sexual orientation and clarified their position concerning this debate. This was particularly important in framing their independent articles that followed. They noted that growing support for conceptualizing sexual orientation as a socially constructed phenomenon (i.e., that sexual orientation categories are somewhat arbitrary demarcations as opposed to viewing sexual orientation as more rigid or fixed) has been misconstrued by anti-LGB (lesbian, gay, and bisexual) groups and conversion/reparative therapy advocates as suggesting that individuals *choose* their sexual orientation rather than simply *are* who they are. Worthington and Mohr further noted that, although both of the models of heterosexual identity development presented in their articles incorporate constructivist assumptions, they were unequivocally opposed to conversion therapy practices and clearly stated that their work should not be used to support such approaches. Worthington and Mohr also referred the reader to the article by Worthington et al. (2002) that followed their introductory article for a discussion of the distinctions made between *sexual orientation*, *sexual identity*, and *sexual orientation identity*, which provides a solid basis for appreciating sexual orientation as a stable component of one's overall sexual identity.

## A Multidimensional Model of Individual and Social Identity

Worthington et al. (2002) proposed a multifaceted model of heterosexual identity development, grounded in a comprehensive literature base spanning a variety of areas, that includes majority and minority group identity development, heterosexuality, and contextual influences on development and integrates feminist, multicultural, and LGB perspectives. The model includes developmental statuses, as most identity development models do, but also integrates biopsychosocial influences and dimensions of individual as well as social identity, aspects that are typically absent in other models. Each of the components of their model is outlined as follows.

### Biopsychosocial Influences

Worthington et al. (2002) identified six biopsychosocial influences that affect sexual identity development: biology; microsocial context; gender norms and socialization; culture; religious orientation; and systemic homonegativity, sexual prejudice, and privilege. For the purposes of this review, they are mentioned rather than discussed here; however, readers interested in a specific component of the model are referred to the original source for a detailed discussion.

### Processes and Dimensions of Heterosexual Identity Development

Worthington et al. (2002) posited that heterosexual identity development is characterized by parallel processes of individual identity development and social identity development, each occurring within the biopsychosocial context outlined earlier. As previously noted, the distinct definitions that Worthington et al. proposed for sexual orientation, sexual orientation identity, and sexual identity provide a basis for understanding the scope of their work. Specifically, they distinguished between sexual orientation, defined as one's "sexuality-related predispositions" (p. 497), and sexual orientation identity, a "more precise term regarding one's acceptance and recognition of [one's] sexual orientation" (p. 497). As their definition suggests, sexual orientation identity is a conscious identification with one's sexual predispositions. Worthington et al. further distinguished these constructs from sexual identity, defined as "the comprehensive process involving self-definition more broadly as a sexual being" (p. 497). An important feature of their model is that individual sexual identity includes, but is not limited to, sexual orientation identity. The process of individual heterosexual identity development includes six dimensions:

> (a) identification and awareness of one's sexual needs [one's sexual orientation is included in this category], (b) adoption of personal sexual values, (c) awareness of preferred sexual activities, (d) awareness of preferred characteristics of sexual partners, (e) awareness of preferred modes of sexual expression, and (f) recognition and identification with sexual orientation (i.e., sexual orientation identity). (p. 512)

The six dimensions of heterosexual individual identity development "evolve and interact" (p. 512) with the process of heterosexual social identity development, which includes two dimensions: (a) group membership identity and (b) attitudes toward sexual minorities.

## Statuses of Heterosexual Identity Development

Worthington et al. (2002) theorized that, for heterosexual individuals, the processes of individual identity development and social identity development occur within five identity development statuses. From *unexplored commitment* to a heterosexual identity, heterosexual individuals may enter *active exploration*—described as "purposeful exploration [cognitive or behavioral], evaluation, or experimentation of one's sexual needs, values, orientation and/or preferences for activities, partner characteristics, or modes of sexual expression" (p. 516)—*diffusion* (similar to active exploration but often resulting from crisis and therefore lacking in goal-directed intentionality), or move directly to a status characterized by *deepening and commitment* to a heterosexual identity. Worthington et al. suggested that it is not uncommon for heterosexually identified individuals to bypass both active exploration and diffusion, because of the prevalence of social and cultural contexts in which heterosexuality is the norm. Thus, individuals frequently enter deepening and commitment simply as a result of maturational development, as opposed to a process of experimentation regarding sexual identity. Worthington et al.'s model includes a *synthesis* status, distinguished by "a sense of congruence among the dimensions of individual identity as well as the three developmental processes" (p. 519); note that the three developmental processes Worthington et al. refer to are individual sexual identity, group membership identity, and attitudes toward sexual minorities. Worthington et al. theorized that synthesis is a difficult status to achieve, given the complexity of the model, and hypothesized that it may require active exploration. They further hypothesized that an individual may move out of synthesis into either active exploration or diffusion. Individuals who move into diffusion from any of the statuses will subsequently need to go through a process of active exploration as a pathway to another status. Because entrance into diffusion is likely to be precipitated by a crisis, experience in this status is frequently accompanied by psychological distress and may require counseling to progress to active exploration.

## Heterosexual Identity and the Heterosexual Therapist

Mohr (2002) presented a model of sexual orientation identity that he offered as a framework for examining the effectiveness of heterosexual-identified therapists' work with LGB clients. Underlying Mohr's model is his belief that biased practice displayed by heterosexual therapists can be conceptualized as a "manifestation of their efforts to process and respond to sexual orientation issues in ways that foster a positive and coherent identity" (p. 533). A key element of his model is the existence and interplay of both a personal identity and a public identity as components of heterosexual identity. Personal identity reflects the heterosexual individual's inner experience and understanding of his or her heterosexual orientation. Public identity, on the other hand, includes the manner in which individuals express and demonstrate their experience of their heterosexuality in interpersonal arenas.

Similar to Worthington et al.'s (2002) position, Mohr (2002) differentiated between heterosexuality and heterosexual identity, suggesting that heterosexual identity represents the understanding that one has of his or her sexual orientation, its meaning for the individual, which is different from the sexual orientation itself. Mohr conceptualized heterosexual identity as a "product of the inter-play between individuals' sexual orientation schemas and their motivation to fulfill basic needs for social acceptance and psychological consistency" (Worthington & Mohr, 2002, p. 492). Heterosexual identity is depicted in his model as having three primary components: (a) precursors of adult het-erosexual identity, (b) determinants of adult heterosexual identity, and (c) determinants of identity states.

## Precursors of Adult Heterosexual Identity

Mohr (2002) posited two categories of precursors of adult heterosexual identity. He identified the first as *experiences with personal sexuality*, which include attractions, fantasies, and sex experiences. The second category reflects *exposure to information about sexual orientation*, through the influences of the media, peers, family, school, and church.

## Determinants of Adult Heterosexual Identity

The aforementioned precursors contribute to what Mohr (2002) referred to as the individual's *work-ing models of sexual orientation*, identified as the first determinant of adult heterosexual identity. The purpose of these working models is to provide prototypes by which individuals can enhance their understanding of sexual orientation, their own as well as that of others. As such, they serve as cog-nitive sexual orientation schemas. Mohr presented and described the four working models included in the model: (a) *democratic heterosexuality*, in which people of all sexual orientations are viewed as essentially the same (analogous to the color-blind stance of some White individuals); (b) *compulsory heterosexuality*, in which heterosexuality is the only acceptable sexual orientation; (c) *politicized het-erosexuality*, in which homosexual or bisexual individuals are seen as oppressed but valiant sur-vivors of a hostile society or culture; and (d) *integrative heterosexuality*, in which all individuals are viewed as participants in an oppressive system, with no one person being "all good or all bad with regard to her or his stance on sexual orientation issues" (p. 545).

One's working models of sexual orientation affect, and are affected by, one's core motivations, which Mohr (2002) identified as the second determinant of adult heterosexual identity. Core motiva-tions include *social acceptance*, or the need to "fit in" with one's reference groups, and *psychological consistency*, or the need to have an internally consistent sense of self.

## Determinants of Identity States

Mohr (2002) theorized that working models and core motivations operate synergistically to give heterosexual individuals a fairly stable sense of themselves in relation to their sexual orientation identities, although day-to-day fluctuations in both the expression and the salience of one's hetero-sexual identity are likely to occur. Mohr interpreted these fluctuations as indications of changes in heterosexual identity states. According to Mohr, the identity state is determined by a *sexual orienta-tion stimulus* in conjunction with the *immediate context* in which the stimulus is perceived.

# Implications for Counseling Practice, Training, and Research

The heterosexual identity development models presented by Worthington et al. (2002) and Mohr (2002) have extensive implications for the counseling profession. Ways in which these models may be applied or used in counseling practice, education and supervision of counselors-in-training, and counseling research are discussed as follows.

## Counseling Practice

The work of Worthington et al. (2002) and Mohr (2002) is groundbreaking in that it shifts the focus from one in which the heterosexual counselor must only be knowledgeable about gay and lesbian identity development in working with LGB clients to one in which the sexual identity development of both parties becomes relevant. Examples provided in Mohr's in-depth discussion of counselors' working models of sexual orientation will facilitate heterosexual counselors' insight into dynamics with LGB clients. Whereas Mohr's model is specific to counseling relationships in which the counselor is heterosexual and the client is lesbian, gay, or bisexual, Worthington et al.'s model is likely to have implications for the counseling process whenever the counselor and/or client is heterosexual. Worthington et al.'s model also has relevance for counselors working with clients whose sexual identity is unknown or unachieved.

Worthington et al. (2002) hypothesized that the level of sexual identity achievement of the heterosexual counselor is related to several desired counselor characteristics, including

> level of affirmativeness regarding LGB issues, . . . recognition of and comfort with sexually-related material in counseling, . . . ability to recognize and address erotic transference and countertransference in the context of counseling, . . . avoidance of sexual exploitation of clients, . . . and . . . ability to prevent sexual values from unduly influencing one's work with clients. (p. 523)

Although these hypotheses are yet to be tested, the importance of these outcomes is such that counselors need to seriously consider the potential this model may hold for enhancing their effectiveness.

In addition to separately considering the sexual identity development of counselor and client, Worthington et al. (2002) further addressed the importance of examining the interaction of both. Acknowledging the parallel between racial identity development theory and sexual identity development theory, they noted that counseling dyads in which the counselor's level of identity development is generally well integrated and not below that of the client are preferred.

## Counselor Training

Given that the majority of counselors-in-training are likely to be heterosexual-identified, both Worthington et al.'s (2002) and Mohr's (2002) models have important implications for counselor education. By providing a mechanism by which heterosexual counselors-in-training may examine their own sexual identity development, both models may serve as tools to enhance the competence of counseling trainees who are privileged with respect to their sexual orientation.

Mohr (2002) provided a table of questions for exploration of heterosexual identity designed for supervisors to use with their supervisees as well as with themselves. Questions are presented in relation to the different components of his model (e.g., working models of sexual orientation, core motivations), providing a valuable framework for the supervisor to apply and explore various aspects of the model.

Worthington et al. (2002) and Mohr (2002) stressed the importance of creating and maintaining LGB-affirmative training environments, and both models may be appropriately used as pathways to those goals. Mohr specifically challenged individuals involved with training programs to guard against discouraging the exploration of antigay attitudes, noting that an unanticipated effect of this may be that students with fundamentalist religious beliefs may retreat and lose any motivation that they may have had to honestly explore their sexual identities. As Mohr indicated, a commitment to developing an environment in which diverse perspectives of sexual orientation may be freely shared is likely to facilitate trainees' ability to discover creative ways of negotiating the intricacies of sexual-identity-related conflicts.

An emphasis on heterosexual identity development issues in counselor education programs must accompany and not overshadow an emphasis on LGB sexual identity development in preparing both heterosexual and LGB counselors to work effectively with LGB clients. An understanding of both minority and majority sexual identity development on the part of both LGB and heterosexual counselors is necessary and currently very likely to receive insufficient attention. As Worthington et al. noted, however, self-knowledge is fundamental to an understanding of others; thus, facilitating heterosexual students' self-awareness in this area, particularly regarding their privileged status, may be best viewed as a prerequisite to their readiness to more fully understand the LGB sexual identity development models currently being taught. In addition, creating an environment in which counselors-in-training can safely develop this self-knowledge requires that counselor educators and supervisors need to be open to their own self-exploration.

## Research

As indicated in the discussion of implications for counseling practice, Worthington et al. (2002) proposed a number of plausible hypotheses regarding possible links between desirable characteristics of counselors and a well-integrated level of sexual identity achievement of the heterosexual counselor. These hypotheses need to be tested. Before such hypotheses, or even the validity of the model itself, can be empirically examined, however, researchers must develop a number of measures. As Worthington et al. suggested, instruments that operationalize the model's key constructs are needed. Measures designed to assess the proposed dimensions of individual sexual identity must be developed, and improved measures of heterosexual attitudes toward sexual minorities are needed. Worthington et al. proposed that their model may provide the basis for extensive research opportunities and offered a number of suggestions and possible applications. Although all the possibilities they identified are exciting and viable, the impact of the development of appropriate heterosexual identity measures on current research on intersecting identities (e.g., ethnicity/race, gender, sexual orientation, and age) may be one with some of the most far-reaching implications.

Similarly, Mohr's (2002) model also requires that appropriate measures be developed to assess its constructs and processes. Mohr acknowledged that such research will most likely be quite challenging, given the complexity of the model. He suggested that in examining his model, researchers may wish to use qualitative approaches, such as essay analysis and interviews, to enhance their ability to convey some of this complexity. Although Worthington et al.'s (2002) model also is quite complex, its components may lend themselves more easily to empirical investigation. Mohr, like Worthington et al., advocated examination of his model in terms of multiple identities and suggested investigating working model accessibility in relation to multiple social reference group memberships (race, gender, religion, disability, etc.).

Finally, both Worthington et al.'s (2002) and Mohr's (2002) models may result in increased attention to building majority identity development models in other areas. For example, a male identity development model might be proposed that incorporates a parallel to Worthington et al.'s premise that an integrated level of heterosexual identity development entails an understanding of one's membership in an oppressive majority group and its concomitant attitudes and beliefs about members of sexual minority groups. Applied to male identity development, this suggests that an integrated level of male identity development would also require an understanding of one's membership in an oppressive majority group, as well as attitudes, values, and beliefs about women. Such a model of male development might also resemble one or more current models of White identity development.

## Reactions

Gilbert and Rader (2002) and Bieschke (2002) provided the two reaction articles that come after Worthington and Mohr (2002), Worthington et al. (2002), and Mohr (2002). No rejoinder was written by the authors of the major contribution articles; however, in this section, I offer my comments regarding some of the content of their critiques and include additional personal reactions to the major articles.

### The Missing Discourse of Gender?

Although they acknowledged many of the merits of these articles, Gilbert and Rader (2002) voiced a great deal of concern about what they identified as the "silence" of the models regarding gender theory. As a gender theorist myself, I too am attentive to lack of appropriate consideration of gender as a key aspect of identity. And, as much as I agree with many of Gilbert and Rader's arguments, I am not convinced that the lack of formal inclusion of gender in models developed to conceptualize heterosexual identity development is necessarily a deficit.

Sexism and heterosexism are indeed "partners in crime" in counseling practice that ignores some of the needs of heterosexual and LGB clients, as Gilbert and Rader (2002, p. 569) suggested; however, racism, able-body-ism, ageism, and classism also are partners in this process. Ideally, models of identity development might be constructed that explicitly consider all possible areas of diversity, including gender, ethnicity/race, sexual orientation, age, disabilities, religion, class, and so on. However, models focused on one of these areas can already be extremely complex. How do we make an identity development model fully inclusive without it becoming unwieldy and overwhelming? That is a real challenge. Given that this challenge remains unmet, it may be helpful to keep in mind that using a model that focuses on one aspect of identity does not presuppose that the user will ignore all other aspects.

Somewhat ironically, Bieschke (2002) commended Worthington et al.'s (2002) model for "its explicit focus on gender" (Bieschke, 2002, p. 579). In her praise of its breadth, Bieschke stated that "[t]he focus on gender is particularly noteworthy, and the ability of the model to include transgendered individuals is groundbreaking" (p. 577). This comment addressed Worthington et al.'s in-depth description of gender norms and socialization (pp. 504–506) as one of the six biopsychosocial influences in their model. Bieschke focused on the import of Worthington et al.'s point that "one must understand oneself as a man or a woman before one can understand one's heterosexuality" (Bieschke, p. 577), and she suggested that this comment had the potential to change the way individuals approach their sexuality. (For a detailed discussion of gender self-concept, gender self-confidence, gender self-definition, and gender self-acceptance, see Hoffman, Borders, & Hattie, 2000.)

Bieschke's praise for Worthington et al.'s (2002) attention to transgendered individuals is well-deserved. A real strength of their work is its transcendence of dichotomous conceptions of both gender and sexual orientation. In their discussion of gender norms and socialization as a biopsychosocial influence on heterosexual identity development, they cited evolving theory related to transgenderism (see Cole, Denny, Eyler, & Samons, 2000). Of particular relevance is the 9-point gender continuum, developed by Eyler and Wright (as cited in Cole et al., 2000), that "describes current gender self-concept and evolution over time, ranging from female-based identities through nontraditional identities to male-based identities" (Worthington et al., 2002, p. 506). (See Worthington et al. for a description of these categories.) A particularly salient point reiterated by Worthington et al. is that despite the confusion regarding the relationship between sexual orientation and transgenderism, transgendered individuals can be any sexual orientation.

## Sexual Identity Development or Heterosexual Identity Development?

Bieschke's (2002) recommendation to Worthington et al. (2002) was that they consider expanding their model to include all of sexual identity. My view is that this would obfuscate its standing as a majority identity development model at whose core is the acknowledgment of a privileged status. One's developmental experiences as a member of an oppressive group do not parallel the experiences of those who are oppressed because of their membership in a particular group. I also believe that Bieschke misinterpreted Worthington et al.'s position, to some degree, by suggesting that they already seem to be heading in the direction of extending their model to include LGB as well as heterosexual identity development. Worthington et al. did use the terms *heterosexual identity* and *sexual identity* interchangeably at times, as Bieschke noted; however, such instances are within their discussion of heterosexual identity development and, thus, "heterosexual" is understood. Bieschke pointed to Worthington et al.'s third footnote as further support for applying the model to LGB individuals; however, the wording of the footnote actually seems to suggest the opposite position. Yet, Worthington et al. also suggested in their conclusion that integration of heterosexual and LGB identity models may be possible.

Bieschke (2002) noted that "much of the work the authors have done is in naming what they have discovered and, by naming, . . . point the way to further exploration" (p. 575). Worthington et al. (2002) and Mohr's (2002) work should be lauded for its careful articulation of many terms that now may be used more precisely, and thus more appropriately and meaningfully, in discussions of heterosexual identity and related constructs.

## Conceptualizing Identity Intersections

It is one thing to acknowledge that each of us has multiple identities, as racial, gendered beings of different ages, sexual orientations, religions, and so on, with privileged status in some areas and nonprivileged status in others (although conceivably an individual may be privileged, or not, regarding all areas). It is more difficult to constantly keep in mind that when conceptualizing majority or minority identity development as it pertains to any one area, we are simultaneously considering people who differ regarding the other areas. To illustrate, in their discussion of systemic homonegativity, sexual prejudice, and privilege as one of the six biopsychosocial influences on heterosexual identity development, Worthington et al. (2002) described the system of privilege that heterosexual individuals enjoy, "including the right to marry, death benefits for life partners, partner health benefit packages from employers, the protection of custody and visitation rights, and the protection from hate crimes, just to name a few" (p. 509). Although this is true regarding sexual orientation, it is not necessarily accurate regarding other aspects of one's identity. For example, a heterosexual man or woman may be the target of a hate crime if he or she is Black (or a member of other oppressed groups). This reality suggests that even though an identity development model may be appropriately limited to one issue and may focus on either the minority or majority status regarding that area, as the developers and users of such models, we must accept the challenge to work to maintain a perspective that recognizes the complexity of the identity intersections within our clients and within ourselves.

## Conclusion

Worthington et al. (2002) and Mohr (2002) presented two complex models of heterosexual identity development. Both of these models are reflective of the permeability and fluidity of human development, of which identity is a major part. In so doing, they succeeded in extending our conceptualization of sexual identity far beyond the limits of sexual orientation.

On an even broader level, this work has the potential to serve as a catalyst for positive societal change by challenging people to more closely examine the injustice inherent in heterosexual privilege. As such, it constitutes an extraordinarily significant contribution to counseling professionals, both to our knowledge base and to the development of attitudes that may help to ameliorate this injustice. Finally, the possible applications of this body of work to other majority identity development areas (e.g., male development) holds promise for evolution of an expanded understanding of additional areas of privilege.

## References

Bieschke, K. J. (2002). Charting the waters. *The Counseling Psychologist, 30,* 575–581.

Cole, S. S., Denny, D., Eyler, A. E., & Samons, S. L. (2000). Issues of transgender: Terminology, gender diversity, and the primacy of gender. In L. T. Szuchman & F. Muscarella (Eds.), *Psychological perspectives on human sexuality* (pp. 149–195). New York: Wiley.

Gilbert, L. A., & Rader, J. (2002). The missing discourse of gender? *The Counseling Psychologist, 30,* 567–574.

Hoffman, R. M., Borders, L. D., & Hattie, J. A. (2000). Reconceptualizing femininity and masculinity: From gender roles to gender self-confidence. *Journal of Social Behavior and Personality, 15,* 475–503.

Mohr, J. J. (2002). Heterosexual identity and the heterosexual therapist: Using identity as a framework for understanding sexual orientation issues in psychotherapy. *The Counseling Psychologist, 30,* 532–566.

Worthington, R. L., & Mohr, J. J. (2002). Theorizing heterosexual identity development. *The Counseling Psychologist, 30,* 491–495.

Worthington, R. L., Savoy, H. B., Dillon, F. R., & Vernaglia, E. R. (2002). Heterosexual identity development: A multidimensional model of individual and social identity. *The Counseling Psychologist, 30,* 496–531.

# CHAPTER 17
## DISABLED STUDENTS IN HIGHER EDUCATION
### NEGOTIATING IDENTITY

SHEILA RIDDELL, TERESA TINKLIN, AND ALASTAIR WILSON

## Introduction

In this penultimate chapter, we draw on recent theoretical developments in the field of disability studies to question whether a simple conceptualisation of disability as a unitary category is empirically sustainable and whether it is supported by the subjective experiences of the case study students.

For many disabled people, such as those labelled as having learning difficulties or mental health difficulties, the category of disability has been assigned to them by others with little or no negotiation. For many, the category signals a spoilt identity and as a result it has not necessarily been incorporated into their sense of self. Indeed, many people with learning difficulties actively reject the label, preferring to see themselves as having a physical impairment or as not being disabled at all (Riddell *et al.*, 2001). Disabled students in higher education are different from this, in that they have chosen to disclose an impairment on their UCAS form or at some time during their studies. For some, the fact that their impairment is visible and restrictive means that declaring it is essential to obtaining the support they require. However, for the majority of disabled students, who have dyslexia or a hidden impairment such as ME, disclosure is less essential to everyday survival and the invisibility of their impairment means that it might be possible to avoid disclosure. Interesting questions therefore arise as to why disabled students choose to disclose an impairment and whether they see this as an essential part of their identity, or whether it is viewed as transient and contingent on the particular context in which they find themselves.

## Understanding Identity

Watson (2002) notes that identity has become a highly contested field of theorising and research in recent years. According to Hall (1996), there are two distinct approaches to understanding identity. In the first model, identity is viewed as essential, natural or intrinsic. An individual is born with a given identity, which remains with them throughout life, structuring their biography and experience. Much thinking characterised as 'modernist', such as versions of feminism, anti-racism and nationalism, is implicitly or explicitly based on an essentialist understanding of identity. The second model denies the existence of any identity based on a shared origin or experience, suggesting instead that identity is multiple and temporal. Often associated with postmodernism, this version of

Riddell, S., Tinklin, T., & Wilson, A. (2005). Disabled students in higher education: Negotiating identity. In *Disabled students in higher education: Perspectives on widening access and changing policy* (pp. 130–147). London: Routledge.

identity is based on the notion of an evolving and 'endlessly performative self' (Hall, 1996: 1). These multiple selves are viewed as 'incoherently, actively and playfully assembled and negotiated with those relevant at any particular point in time' (Baron *et al.*, 1999). Within the second reading of identity, different views are expressed with regard to the extent of individual agency and external power structures. Riddell *et al.* (2001), in their discussion of people with learning difficulties within the context of a learning society, concluded that the parameters for negotiating identity available to this group were distinctly limited as a result of many factors including the stigma associated with learning difficulties, the lack of financial power and the restrictions imposed by the repertoire of available services. A different vision is presented by Beck (1992) in his discussion of the 'risk society' in late modernity. According to Beck:

> Increasingly everyone has to choose between different options, including as to which group or subculture one wants to be identified with. In fact one has to choose and change one's social identity as well and take the risks in doing so. (Beck, 1992: 88)

Instead, risks have to be navigated by individuals, and the process of identity construction and maintenance is inextricably linked with the negotiation of risk, with some forms of identity having a privileged social status and others attracting 'an abundance of risks' (Beck, 1992). A paradox in Beck's view of identity is that the act of choosing and changing one's social identity implies an active agent, which might be viewed as approximating to the modernist version of the essential self.

## Disability and Identity

Early writing in disability studies tended to assume that impairment was a fixed attribute, whereas disability was a relative construct in that it was contingent on the particular environment in which an impairment was experienced. This argument was powerfully set out by Oliver (1990) in his book *The Politics of Disablement*. The front cover exemplified this idea by depicting a wheelchair user attempting to access a polling station, approachable only by steep steps. Whilst the individual was clearly capable of exercising his democratic right to vote, he was prevented from doing so by the physical barrier. Abberley (1987) described impairment as 'the bedrock' which has to be taken into account in understanding the experience of disability. There is a strong current in disability studies and in public policy which continues to see the presence of impairment as the key element in defining who should be described as disabled, and indeed, it is difficult to conceive of a legal definition of disability which could be divorced from the notion of impairment. This type of thinking corresponds with Hall's first model of identity, based on a modernist understanding of the self as fixed and essential, 'unfolding from beginning to end through all the vicissitudes of history without change' (Hall, 1996: 3).

Recently, however, postmodern and poststructuralist writers have mounted serious challenges to the basis of disability studies, critiquing the taken-for-granted distinction between disabled and non-disabled people, which is seen as perpetuating Enlightenment fallacies that social categories and constructions are 'real' (Corker, 2003; Corker and Shakespeare, 2002). Whilst the construction of a binary line between disabled and non-disabled people may be useful politically and legally, these writers argue that such a hierarchy may simply not accord with people's experience, as impairments fluctuate and are experienced in different ways over an individual's life course. In addition, what is constructed as an impairment at one point in time may be viewed differently at another. This is well illustrated by a historical analysis of many categories, such as hysteria, which plagued middle class Victorian females, and dyslexia and attention deficit disorder, which appear to be affecting growing numbers of school children in the western world. These examples suggest that, whilst the reality of some impairments cannot be denied (e.g. a serious spinal injury), others are the product of historically contingent social constructions. Such views are clearly challenging to the development of a movement based on a common identity, but nonetheless have to be addressed in order to develop a better understanding of the relationship between disability, impairment and identity.

In this chapter, we draw on case studies to understand the way in which disabled students understand disability and reconcile it with other aspects of their identity. Key themes emerging from students' accounts included a critical recognition of the complexity of identity and a deep ambivalence about identifying themselves as disabled, partly as a result of fear of stigma and a rejection of victim status. In the following paragraphs, we illustrate some of the ways in which disabled students made sense of the category.

## Disability as an Equivocal Identity

As noted above, although the case study students were aware that they had voluntarily placed themselves within the category of disability, many continued to express uncertainty about the adequacy of the label to reflect their perception of self. This ambivalence was particularly evident in the case of the dyslexic students, who described their struggle for recognition whilst at the same time questioning the congruence between dyslexia and disability.

### Maurice: Scottish University 2

Maurice was a second year medical student at Scottish University 2 who had previously completed a degree in Physiology and Sports Science. His parents were both teachers, but his dyslexia was not formally diagnosed until the second year of his first degree. At school, he was regarded as 'a bit slow':

> I went through school—everything was never fine—I was always slow. Always from the start of primary school, my mother and father would have been brought in because my reading wasn't very good, my reading was always very slow. Both my parents were teachers, so I think what really happened was that they sort of worked with me a bit. Nothing was ever diagnosed except that 'Maurice's a bit slow', do you know what I mean, and I must have just muddled through school to be honest. English was never a strong point and I don't know if that was why I went down the science route, because it wasn't structured essays, factual learning. It was understanding, and I was always better with diagrams and thing like that.

Maurice was prompted to go to the disabled students adviser for a diagnosis because of the problems which emerged in his second year with assignment writing. A lecturer noted the discrepancy between his oral and written performance:

> He stood out from the very beginning in class. He usually led the questioning and in all oral interchange he was outstanding ... but it wasn't coming through in his written work, that similar ability to construct concepts, to critically handle them.

Just as he had been labelled 'slow' at school, university staff began to see him as a lazy, disorganised student. When he asked why he had been given a poor grade for an assignment, he would be told: 'Well, Maurice, it just doesn't look—it looks like you've done it the night before . . . It doesn't flow, there is not a structure to the essay'.

Following a visit to an educational psychologist, Maurice was told that he was dyslexic, and described a feeling of relief at being able to exchange a negative identity for a more positive one:

> Initially my diagnosis was 'You are dyslexic' and at that time that was a relief to me. I didn't take it to heart, I didn't think I was retarded or something like that. I think some people do take it to heart. I thought, 'Well, that's quite a relief' and I was quite happy with the position that the university was going to give me some extra time in exams and I thought, 'Oh that's good, it will take a bit of the pressure off me a bit more in writing essays'.

In reality, the extra time in exams was experienced as a mixed blessing, but the sense of release from blame meant that Maurice was able to finish his first degree and embark on a second.

However, the negotiation of identity with significant others was ongoing. When he enquired about entering Medicine, he received a slightly frosty response from the medical faculty:

> I came to enquire about it and they were a bit standoffish about the whole dyslexic thing. . . . Their point of view is that they see it as an excuse and they say, 'Why do you want extra time in an exam, you wouldn't get extra time during a surgery or extra time in resuscitation.'

Fellow students were also likely to look down on anyone who might be regarded as less able:

> I know it is better being dyslexic, I can feel my medical friends saying 'And how did you fail that test Maurice?' There are a few people think that.

Whilst having the diagnosis of dyslexia is important to Maurice in bolstering his self-esteem, he is reluctant to discuss this with other students:

> There's about three other people in my year who are dyslexic in Medicine and I've bumped into them as we've arrived at the exam hall 25 minutes early, you can work it out, but that's the only way. Sometimes it comes up in the conversation, 'Where were you?' 'Seeing the special needs adviser.' 'Oh, what's that about?' It never gets brought up in conversation with any academic members of staff.

Maurice continued to struggle with the idea that he shared a common identity with someone with more significant impairments:

> I don't like thinking of myself as disabled, I don't even like, when you started talking, I don't even like that you almost put me in the category with someone in a wheelchair. I almost find that offensive. No. I mean, God, I'm glad I'm not and it's almost a relief that I don't have to deal with a physical or other disability. I really don't like holding it up or shouting about it at all. I like that it's been identified and I'm not stupid, I rather look on it like that.

Despite his ambivalence about the category of dyslexia, Maurice maintained a sense of himself as a person who was discriminated against by the university assessment system, which prioritised mastery of the written word and 'tested my weakness'. Rather than extra time in exams, Maurice considered that an alternative form of assessment based on oral work should be permitted. At the very least, he felt that 'people who are marking my exam scripts or marking my course work should know that I am dyslexic, so that allowances could be made'.

## Sheena, English University 1

Sheena was a 32-year-old mature student studying for an MPhil in Psychology following a first degree in Psychology at a post-92 university. She had embarked on a PhD at English University 1, but had been told at the end of her first year that this was not realistic due to her difficulties in writing. This had been a severe blow and she felt that she had suffered an injustice. Sheena's early education involved many changes of school, since her father was in the armed forces. Like Maurice, she grew up with a sense of herself as slow and uncoordinated, although dyslexia was not diagnosed formally until much later:

> No, I didn't know that I had it. I've always had a sense of feeling different. I was the last kid, for example, in my class to move out of pumps because I couldn't tie my bloody laces. I was sixteen before I could use a normal clock. I always knew there were things I couldn't do that other people could, but I always thought I must be horrendously stupid and that. I was also one of three and I was the only daughter to fail my 11 plus and that kind of reinforced the whole idea that I must just be incredibly stupid. . . . I did think, 'Well, why am I good at this and why am I crap at that and why am I so clumsy all the time?'

Sheena managed to get through her first degree without major difficulties as a result of 'overlearning', but 'there were a few times that they had to re-read my exam scripts as my writing is absolutely appalling and for my tutors to allow me to do that was very nice'. Problems became more apparent when she left university to begin work:

> I'm a pretty bright person who had managed to compensate in a variety of ways for these problems but I was very aware of it and I was having a chat with a friend when I was 21 and saying, 'There's something wrong, I don't know what it is, but there is something different and there's something wrong but I just don't know what it is' . . . I went out to work for a while and did very, very well. Kept getting little things on my desk about time management and I thought, 'Cheeky buggers, I'm working my nuts off here, working hard and what's this time management about?' I didn't realise then that I was working hard but working pretty inefficiently as well because of my organisational problems.

The identification of dyslexia seems to have happened in a somewhat roundabout way. Whilst she was working with young offenders, her difficulties with spelling kept on being pointed out to her. Subsequently, a conversation with a young man who had just received a diagnosis made her realise that she had exactly the same set of difficulties:

> I think the boys noticed. 'Miss, how come you spell crap miss, miss, why can't you spell? Miss, why don't you know the correct way round for H, Y and Z?' So in a way the boys picked up on it but nobody else seemed to. But it wasn't until I went to see my supervisor because I met somebody I had been testing and he came in to see me and told me he was dyslexic and I said, 'How do you know you're dyslexic?' and I thought, 'Oh my God, that's what it is, I'm dyslexic'.

Sheena described the shift that happened in her sense of self when it was suggested for the first time that she might have dyslexia:

> You know you have these problems and you suspect that you have these problems but you spend your whole life covering up and compensating for them and you get to a point when you wonder if it's just your paranoia and then somebody goes, 'Yes, you were right, you do have a learning disability or learning difficulty or whatever' and it's like all of those things that you quite suspected but weren't quite sure. All of those things that you thought made you slightly more cracked up than everybody else is true and that was the hard part. I think that was the hard part for me getting the diagnosis and feeling different as well, and all of a sudden I had a legitimate reason.

Like many of the students in our study, the diagnosis of dyslexia was experienced as a form of absolution, altering their self-perception in such a way as to free them from a sense of guilt and failure. However, during the first year of her second degree, disclosure became a major issue. It transpired that her supervisor had discussed the possibility of dyslexia with other people, including the disabled students adviser, without including Sheena in the conversation. As a result, Sheena experienced a sense of betrayal and loss of control over the management of her own identity:

> If you disclose something to one tutor, . . . it then becomes public knowledge and at some point I think it did. That worried me hugely because it does undermine your confidence in the institution where you study. But yeah, I think there was an element of control there, I don't mind admitting that control is important because control allows you to predict what's going to happen next and give you structure and it gives you some certainty at least.

For Sheena, the diagnosis of dyslexia did not imply an acceptance of disability as an essential part of identity:

> I don't see myself as disabled. I ask myself the question, 'Has it stopped me from doing anything?' and the answer is 'No'. My only worry is that if I had known earlier it would have become self-limiting so I'm very pleased that I didn't find out that I had it before I went off and did things that I found challenging.

> I don't identify with the notion of disability, I do identify with the notion of difficulty. Because difficulties can be overcome. Disability, I think it feels much more like a life sentence, do you know what I mean, it seems much worse to have a disability than to have a difficulty that you have some kind of notion, some capacity for overcoming. I don't think of myself as disabled.

One reason for Sheena's rejection of the idea of herself as a disabled person was that it conflicted with her self-image as a determined and competent individual:

> It [being identified as someone with a learning difficulty] just makes me proud or stubborn but I don't want people to kind of think, 'Poor you', because you get on with it, don't you. You don't make a drama out of a crisis, you just get on with it.

The department's refusal to allow Sheena to progress with the PhD had made her very unhappy and she believed this was attributable in part to a lack of support:

> I think it does ultimately affect your relationships, but your mental state and how much support you get affects your mental state as well. I think it depends ultimately on how good your self-esteem is as well. A lot of your self-esteem is derived through your ability to be successful and your ability to do a good job, and when you feel that you're failing, that's a huge issue, a huge issue.

Some people in the university continued to have doubts about the validity of a diagnosis of dyslexia, an attitude she had also encountered in relation to ME, which was seen as 'a hysterical hormones thing'. Ultimately, her own ambivalence about dyslexia and disability was reflected in uncertainty about whether to disclose a disability in a job application:

> I wouldn't, I would not tick the disabled box—I think maybe I did actually rein in my pride and tick the disability box and I rang them and said, 'I'm dyslexic and if I'm coming to your centre then I need access to a word processor'. So yeah, I think in that instance I made it work for me and then I thought, well, damn it, why should I handicap myself? In other instances I haven't because I'm very suspicious, despite the fact that the Disability Discrimination Act exists. I'm very, very suspicious of people making a judgement about who you are depending on whether you tick a box or you don't. Because I think people don't understand that you can have dyslexia and be completely, perfectly affable, perfectly bright person who just has a few problems in these areas over here.

## Disability as a Misplaced Identity

### Terry, English University 4

Terry was a 27-year-old student studying for an MSc in Deaf Studies at English University 4, an elite pre-92 institution. His father was a physician and he described the family as 'middle class' and 'not rich but privileged'. At the time of the research, Terry was an active member of the deaf community both within and outside the university. He was diagnosed as having hearing difficulties at a relatively early age, but was not allowed to learn sign language or connect with the deaf community:

> As I said before, when I was growing up I was kind of kept separate from the deaf community. I remember growing up and asking if I could learn sign language and kind of being refused time and time again. I remember at the age of 12 and 14 and 16 kind of being insistent about learning sign language and again, as I said, being refused.

> I kind of arrived in the deaf community late and I suppose that was because I grew up in an oral environment and there are quite a lot of deaf people who are like that and they don't identify as deaf people, you know, they see themselves as a person with a hearing problem, rather than growing up in a deaf community. And you know the oral system can kind of in a way brainwash people into thinking, 'Oh no, no, there is nothing relevant about me being deaf and using sign language'. And if you don't learn sign language the oral system kind of labels you as a failure, or has done in the past, you know, as somebody who can't speak, or somebody who can't lip-read, so it can be quite a negative connotation. So people kind of internalise that so it can be quite difficult to reject that and then actually go out and learn sign language.

On leaving school, Terry went to a university in London and there learnt sign language, which rapidly opened up new possibilities:

> So at the end of that course I started meeting more deaf people and I started learning sign language and that was kind of a real epiphany, it was amazing and it was the first time that I could really express myself and just chat in a group and the first time that I really started having complete access to an academic environment. So that was a very positive experience.

After a brief period in another university, he moved to English University 4 and was extremely active in university politics, representing disabled students in the students' union and also for the National Union of students. However, he continued to experience ambivalence about whether he was primarily a disabled person or a deaf person, and eventually he decided to put his energies into establishing a new union for deaf students.

At University 4, some of Terry's lecturers could use BSL, but others required sign language interpreters and these were not always available. As a result, Terry had taken advice from two solicitors and was planning to bring a case against the university under DDA Part 4, on the grounds that it had failed to make reasonable adjustments. Despite this very high level of involvement, Terry still felt isolated from wider university life:

> I feel cut off from university life as though I can't really participate socially within groups. I can't go along to open lectures . . . here at the Centre for Deaf Studies it's easy because there are other

deaf students and within the corridors there are academics I can talk to but other students in other departments won't necessarily be able to do that. Even students here might have an informal chit chat when they are having coffee or whatever and talk about the course and obviously as deaf students we are not able to participate in those discussions. So you kind of feel, and I do feel, quite cut off from the wider participation of the university and I think that's an important part of university life. That was definitely how it felt at [other universities], I just felt really quite isolated from everybody else.

According to the director of the access unit, having a peer group was essential to the building and maintenance of strong identity and sense of self, which might otherwise be undermined by an institution geared towards the needs of 'standard' students:

Deaf students, particularly those students who use sign language, will have a sense of identity with each other but also with the deaf community, so they will have a connection into that community as well as making contact with each other and having a sense of a group of students who actually meet regularly on social occasions. They will often be students who are studying on their own in a department and that's one of the major difficulties, for deaf students in particular, but other disabled students as well, that is often the case, they will be the only deaf student in their year and that does create enormous difficulties of isolation. My own view is that the university, because of its overall ethos, tends to deal better with those students who are nearest to the normal and the further away the student is from the norm the more difficult it is for other students and the more informal university, if you like, to deal with it.

## Robbie, Scottish College 1

Experiences of pedagogy and curriculum in higher education and, using the experiences of Robbie by way of illustration, noted the emphasis on learning support in the Scottish College of Further and Higher Education compared with the approach in older universities, where learning support was a relatively novel concept. Robbie felt that his college experience had been a positive one partly as a result of the presence and support of a deaf community, reinforcing the points made by Terry. With regard to his identity, Robbie commented:

It's not something that I walk around thinking about, but I kind of know that I'm disabled, but in some recess of my brain I don't call myself disabled. Sometimes you think that this word is more applicable to someone who can't walk properly or maybe they are blind or something. Because you probably know that a lot of hearing people think of deaf people as being stupid or deaf and dumb and things like that, and that's something I don't like.

We [deaf students] don't talk about these sort of issues, about disablement: Are we disabled? Are we deaf? We wouldn't use the word disabled to describe ourselves, the word we use to describe ourselves is deaf. I don't mean that I hate the word or reject it, it's just something that we don't use.

Unlike Terry, who had struggled with significant others, including parents and teachers, to be recognised as deaf, Robbie grew up with a positive sense of himself as a deaf person who was a member of a deaf family and a deaf community. For both, using sign language was essential to the maintenance of this identity. For other case study students who were deaf and were not sign language users, there was a sense of double exclusion both from the hearing community and from the deaf community. The prioritising of a deaf over a disabled identity, described by both Terry and Robbie, is important and resonates with Sheena's and Maurice's view of themselves as people with dyslexia rather than disabled people.

## Disability as a Resisted Identity

### Leslie, Scottish University 3

Leslie was in his first year at Scottish University 3 studying History. He had left his local comprehensive school to work as an apprentice fitter and turner. After six years undertaking 'heavy work', including a spell in a restaurant which left him 'hacked off', he decided to come to university and enrolled in an Access course at the local FE college. The university was 'on the doorstep so it seemed straightforward to come here.' However, just before he was due to start, Leslie was involved in a serious accident which left him with major head injuries. The university disability service had provided a very high level of support, ensuring that assessments were conducted quickly, a DSA claim was made and note-takers engaged. Leslie was provided with a small laptop computer and note-takers for each lecture. Overall, he felt that the university had provided him with excellent support. However, he described himself as 'generally quite dull' and his life at university as 'quite boring'. Fellow students were described thus:

> . . . these people are all very clever people, you know what I mean. Which makes them seem a lot older than 18. Especially since they are all the same, you know.

They were contrasted with people from the small town where he grew up and still returned to:

> It's fine when I go home. I still see some people I knew ten years ago, they know what happened to me . . . they make allowances for it anyway.

Overall, Leslie felt alienated from the university. In addition to his head injury, which he recognised had caused him major physical and psychological problems, other factors such as age and social class may have had an effect. Although he had a problem with balance and walking, Leslie did not see himself as disabled, an identity he associated with people who were, in his view, more seriously impaired, such as wheelchair users.

## Karla, Scottish University 2

Karla, a mature student, was in the fourth year of a Sociology and Politics degree at Scottish University 2, an ancient institution taking 85 per cent of its intake from state schools or colleges. Karla had a physical impairment, acquired as an adult, which meant that she had difficulty walking and sometimes used a wheelchair. Karla was from a working-class background and left school with no qualifications. After travelling, she spent two years at college before entering university. Karla's perception was that her status as a single parent with money problems was more salient than having an impairment. She complained, for example, that a course in Women's Studies was held from three to five o'clock in the afternoon, which made it inaccessible to those with childcare responsibilities:

> I can't get back to get my little girl after school. Now I pay excessively for the childcare service. Classes that are late I can't do . . . I've had to see lecturers more about asking for extensions and they are never very forthcoming and it's got nothing to do with disability. I've got a child, I get her to bed, I sleep with her from 8.00–10.00 p.m. and I set an alarm and get up and work until two at night . . . I don't believe in the assessment system. I know it's meant to be fair assessment and everyone's got the same chance, but that's rubbish. Some of my friends are out working every hour God will send. Others, their parents pay for everything.

Karla perceived there to be a difference in identity and awareness between those born with an impairment and people like her who acquired it later in life:

> From what I've seen of my friends who are born disabled, they are very comfortable with it and call me a guest sometimes. 'Oh, here's the guest'. And my uncomfortableness is wrong. Well, not wrong . . . it's the whole thing of becoming disabled once you have developed as a person or been born disabled . . . If there was a group, I'm sure that you would find that most people had been born disabled in it.

She particularly objected to being grouped into a special area with other disabled people in cinemas and theatres:

> Sometimes when you get out somewhere because it's accessible, you almost feel like it's 'Freakers' Ball'. It's horrible.

Karla was clearly at a critical point in her life, when existing aspects of her identity, such as being working class, were being held up for critical scrutiny and either rejected or incorporated into a new narrative. Being a single parent was regarded as the most important aspect of her identity, which would continue to play a key role in structuring her biography. Reflecting a sense of how disability is socially constructed, Karla tended to see herself as a 'guest' rather than a core member of this group.

## Maureen, English University 2

Maureen was a mature student in her 60s who was studying History on a part-time basis. She had spent the majority of her adult life in the home, bringing up three children and undertaking the majority of household work including decorating. When she reached the age of 55 she decided there was a need to 'turn my life around and do something with it, and just set myself a couple of goals'. One of these was to get a degree, and as a first step she enrolled on an Access course. Maureen had a diagnosis of rheumatoid arthritis and was obliged to use powerful drugs to keep the condition under control. She described the way in which she saw the idea of disability as being imposed on her by others:

> *Do you see yourself as disabled at all?*

> No, no, not at all. It's weird because the lecturer I was talking about earlier, who was brilliant and helped me through, we were having a chat one day and I said that I had never thought that I was disabled and she said 'Who put the label on you?' sort of thing and I said 'The hospital really'. The hospital and different people at the hospital gave me leaflets and said that I could apply for different things from social security and I was thinking 'I'm not disabled'. But I don't like it, I don't like it at all and I don't think anybody else does really.

Even applying for disability-related benefits had been difficult for Maureen as she felt that disability was a term reserved for people with more severe impairments. When she came to the university, for example, she was reluctant to speak to the disabled students adviser about claiming the DSA:

> I felt I was taking something that I shouldn't be. Like when I go to the hospital, and I go every two weeks because they monitor my blood, I sit there and if you didn't see my hands, you would say, 'What's wrong with her?' type of thing. And I see people who are really fantastic but they are really crippled and I think, 'I'm wasting their time'. So I don't feel very comfortable, I feel a bit of a cheat, but on the other hand I couldn't have done without it . . . I feel there is someone more worthy than me, you know. It's like my disabled parking bay, I've got my blue badge, I'm registered disabled. I didn't register myself as disabled. There is no way I will go into a disabled parking bay because someone with a wheelchair might need it more than me so if there is another parking bay I will use that. I've talked to [partner] about this and he says, 'Don't be silly, look at the state of your hands'. As I say, I feel there are people a lot worse off than me and I don't see myself as disabled.

# Disability as Political Identity

## Phil, Scottish University 1

Phil, at Scottish University 1 (a post-92, inner-city institution), was in the second year of an undergraduate degree leading to a professional qualification in social work. He had a visual impairment from birth which he described thus:

> I'm registered blind, macular degeneration, very poor central vision. I have very poor vision generally but I have blind spots in the middle so I do tend to look out of the side of my eyes. But I just have very poor vision and I can get about as long as I cross at the green man and all that kind of stuff. I'm not very good at night and everything I have to read has to be magnified, speech by computer and so on.

Phil had received little support in his mainstream school and left with no qualifications, in large part because of his visual impairment:

> So I kind of bluffed my way through school. I couldn't see the board, I couldn't read the books, you know, I just managed to get through it somehow, but I never got any qualifications. I nearly got an O level in English but I didn't pass. I think I left quite disenchanted.

After marriage and a period studying in his local FE college, Phil decided to stay at home to look after his new-born daughter since his wife had a fulltime job. He described this time in his life as rather demotivating:

> I was in the house . . . I didn't do very much apart from personal reading and playing sports. Not basically doing a lot, I just kind of gave up. I think I was quite disillusioned by the way the various systems act against you. I thought I was missing the educational system, I didn't get any real help.

However, just as educational failure contributed to his low self-esteem and loss of purpose, a later period of education at a local university was instrumental in the development of a much more positive sense of self:

> It's been a gradual confidence-building thing, probably one of the greatest things education has given me is confidence in myself again and obviously enhanced self-esteem.

In part, this positive sense of himself as a disabled person came about as a result of his first encounter with the social model of disability:

> When I came to university I started looking at the social model of disability. We had a lecturer who came in for the day who was blind and he started talking about the social model of disability . . . he went on about the social model of disability and he had a couple of books about it and then I sort of became more aware of it. I always remember one thing which stood out at me when I was reading, it was about the issuing of ramps. You know how that's viewed as a special requirement and the article said, well, stairs are provided for people. If there were no stairs to some buildings no one would get in, but there was nothing about society providing stairs, they are just provided and that's that. And that turned a wee light on in my head, and another one was that people can't do anything without glasses, but because of the cost of them, glasses are widely available to people, but computer equipment is expensive so people don't get it.

At this point in his life, Phil described himself as a highly politicised disabled person who was willing to argue for his rights:

> I probably do think of myself as a disabled person, but disabled in the sense that I'm disabled by society, not by my physical disability. So it's more a kind of political definition I would give. I don't tend to see myself as disabled in the negative sense. But I think a lot of it has come from my education.

Because of his commitment to his course and his young family, Phil was not able to get involved in student politics as a disabled activist, but he believed his understanding of disability infused all aspects of his life, and he intended to develop his thinking further in his future employment as a social worker. At Scottish University 1, there was an established tradition of student activism and another mature student, Fiona, who had a diagnosis of cerebral palsy, continued her earlier work as a disability activist within the university, sitting on the Student Representative Council.

## Conclusion

It is evident from the accounts above that the experience of higher education plays a critical part in identity formation. For some people, higher education allows them to shed aspects of their former self. For example, Karla saw university as offering the opportunity to forge a new identity as a middle class person. For others, life as a student requires the melding of existing aspects of identity with emerging aspects of self. For example, Phil had to incorporate his identity as a parent and mature student into his new understanding of disability as a social construction. A striking finding of the research was that the majority of students were ambivalent about owning disability as a key facet of their identity.

Students' relationship with the category of disability was, to some extent, linked with the nature of their impairment. Those diagnosed with dyslexia tended to embrace this category as preferable to the spoilt identity associated with generic learning difficulties, a negative label which had often been attached to them at school. This is consistent with earlier research (Riddell *et al.*, 1994) which described parents' struggles to have their children diagnosed as dyslexic in school in the face of opposition from educational psychologists. In their study of policy and provision for children with specific learning difficulties in Scottish schools, Riddell *et al.* found that parents often insisted that children with dyslexia were a discrete group, whilst educational psychologists maintained that learning difficulties occur on a continuum, and with no qualitative distinction between dyslexia and 'common or garden' types of learning difficulty. Whilst dyslexic students were willing to categorise themselves as disabled in order to obtain support, they found it difficult to identify with others in this group. Deaf students were equally ambivalent about the category of disability, seeing themselves as a linguistic minority and rejecting the deficit connotations associated with the term.

Students who had acquired an impairment as a result of accident, injury or the ageing process saw themselves as qualitatively different from those who were born with an impairment. Those with acquired impairments represent the majority of disabled people, since the incidence of impairment increases with age, and only 17 per cent of disabled people have a congenital impairment (Riddell and Banks, 2001). As a result of the demographic profile of disabled people, the understandings of people with acquired impairments are likely to be particularly salient in influencing future policy. Indeed, a recurring theme emerging from the case studies was that students saw other people as being 'more disabled' than they were, even when their impairments had a significant impact on their daily lives. In the light of the new public sector duty to positively promote equality for disabled people, this ambivalence towards disability as a key facet of identity is important.

In relation to theories of identity which we outlined at the start of this chapter, it is evident that disabled students' construction of self appears to coincide with Hall's second model of identity as temporal, contingent and negotiated. This is consistent with Watson's (2002) finding that disabled people may not prioritise disability in developing and maintaining their sense of self. Watson suggests that impairment, and hence the fixed identity of being a disabled person, is generally viewed negatively in a society which 'denigrates disabled people'. As a result, people with impairment reject the identity of being a disabled person, since this is experienced as something which others wish to impose, rather than arising as an embedded part of lived experience. This explanation resonates with the accounts given by disabled students in this study.

# References

Abberley, P. (1987) 'The concept of oppression and the development of a social theory of disability', *Disability, Handicap and Society* 2: 5–19.

Baron, S., Riddell, S. and Wilson, A. (1999) 'The secret of eternal youth: identity, risk and learning difficulties', *British Journal of Sociology of Education* 20 (4): 483–99.

Beck, U. (1992) *The Risk Society*, London: Sage Publications.

Corker, M. (2003) 'Deafness/Disability—problematising notions of identity, culture and structure', in S. Riddell and N. Watson (eds) *Disability, Culture and Identity*, London: Pearson Education.

Corker, M. and Shakespeare, T. (2002) 'Mapping the terrain', in M. Corker and T. Shakespeare (eds) *Disability/Postmodernism*, London: Continuum.

Hall, S. (1996) 'Introduction: who needs identity?', in S. Hall and P. Du Gay (eds) *Questions of Cultural Identity*, London: Sage.

Oliver, M. (1990) *The Politics of Disablement*, Basingstoke: Macmillan.

Riddell, S. and Banks, P. (2001) *Disability in Scotland: A Baseline Study*, Edinburgh: Disability Rights Commission.

Riddell, S. and Banks, P. (2005) *Disability and Employment in Scotland: A Review of the Evidence Base*, Edinburgh: Scottish Executive.

Riddell, S., Brown, S. and Duffield, J. (1994) 'Conflicts of policies and models: the case of specific learning difficulties', in S. Riddell and S. Brown (eds) *Special Educational Needs Policy in the 1990s: Warnock in the Market Place*, London: Routledge.

Watson, N. (2002) 'Well, I know this is going to sound very strange to you, but I don't see myself as a disabled person: identity and disability', *Disability & Society* 17 (5): 509–29.

# CHAPTER 18
# THE ROLE OF SOCIAL CLASS IN THE FORMATION OF IDENTITY: A STUDY OF PUBLIC AND ELITE PRIVATE COLLEGE STUDENTS

## ELIZABETH ARIES AND MAYNARD SEIDER

The authors explored the influence of social class on identity formation in an interview study of 15 lower income students and 15 affluent students from a highly selective liberal arts school and 15 lower income students from a state college. Students ranked occupational goals as 1st in importance to identity and social class as 2nd. The affluent students regarded social class as significantly more important to identity than did the lower income students, were more aware of structural factors contributing to their success, and had higher occupational aspirations. Social class was an area of exploration for half the students, with higher levels of exploration shown by the lower income private school students than by the state college students. Lower income students developed an ideology that rationalized their social class position.

Social identity theory and self-categorization theory have taught social scientists that a social group can become a part of the self (Smith, 1999; Tajfel, 1981; Turner, 1982) and that knowledge of group memberships and the emotional significance that are attached to them make up an important component of the self-concept (Tajfel). In the last two decades, researchers have paid attention to many of the social groups that shape individuals' selves, especially sex, race or ethnicity, and sexual orientation (e.g., Bilsker, Schiedel, & Marcia, 1988; Frable, 1997; Phinney, 1990), but researchers have paid relatively little attention to social class in the understanding of the self and identity (Argyle, 1994; Frable, 1997; Lott & Bullock, 2001; Ostrove & Cole, 2003; Phillips & Pittman, 2003; Wentworth & Peterson, 2001). Researchers have conceptualized *class* in nonpsychological terms as a material location that is based on economic and material resources, on income, education, and occupation (Domhoff, 1967) or "as a set of differential positions on a scale of social advantage" (Ortner, 1991, p. 168), but researchers have paid relatively little attention to what social class signifies in psychological terms (Ostrove & Cole; Stewart & Ostrove, 1993; Wentworth & Peterson). Ostrove and Cole organized a recent volume of the *Journal of Social Issues* on social class in the context of education to "expand the possibilities for psychologists to see ourselves as responsible for understanding the implications of class at both the individual and group levels" (p. 678).

Aries, E., & Seider, M. (2007). The role of social class in the formation of identity: A study of public and elite private college students. *Journal of Social Psychology, 147*, 137–157.

Social class position differentiates people's experiences and the ways in which they view and experience the world (Ostrove & Cole, 2003; Phoenix & Tizard, 1996). Social class constrains "the possibilities they face and the decisions they make" (Massey, Gross, & Eggers, 1991, p. 397), and it "provides the possibilities and limits for his or her personal identity (i.e., only a certain range of possibilities will occur because of prior socialization specific to role location, or social customs and conventions)" (Côté & Levine, 2002, p. 135). Although identity achievement involves choice, power and privilege are what dictates the choices that one has (Côté, 1996). Class can "shape, constrain, and mediate the development and expression of knowledge, beliefs, attitudes, motives, traits, and symptoms" (Stewart & Ostrove, 1993, p. 476).

Constructing an identity involves occupational choice, but those choices are shaped by the people who are available in one's environment for identification as well as the work opportunities (Erikson, 1968). Numerous researchers have demonstrated the relationship between socioeconomic status and career aspirations (Alix & Lantz, 1973; Cook et al., 1996; MacLeod, 1995; Rojewski & Kim, 2003; Rojewski & Yang, 1997). In a study of 5th–12th graders from school districts in a rural, economically depressed area, Alix and Lantz found that high occupational aspirations varied positively with socioeconomic status. Cook et al. examined the occupational aspirations of two groups of elementary and junior high school boys: inner-city minority boys and White boys from more advantaged homes. Although race and class were confounded in that study, the researchers found that "from second grade on, the jobs boys expect to hold recreate the system of class- and race-based occupational differentiation found in the United States today. That is, economically advantaged boys disproportionately expect to be doctors or lawyers, the ghetto boys disproportionately expect to be policemen or firemen" (p. 3375). Rojewski and Yang's analysis of data from the National Educational Longitudinal Study of 1988 (NELS: 88) revealed that "the longitudinal effects of socioeconomic status on occupational aspirations indicate that approximately 10% of the variance of occupational aspirations can be accounted for conceptually by this variable" (p. 402). In an extension of this study that was based on NELS: 88–94, Rojewski and Kim further demonstrated the considerable influence of socioeconomic status on occupational aspirations. MacLeod (1995) conducted an ethnographic study of the aspirations of a group of Black adolescent boys and a group of White adolescent boys living in a housing project. He argued that the fact that "many boys from both groups do not even aspire to middle-class jobs is a powerful indication of how class inequality is reproduced in American society" (p. 112).

Researchers can also approach how social class shapes the self and identity through Bourdieu's (1977) construct of *cultural capital*, which refers broadly to "knowledge of or competence with 'highbrow' aesthetic culture" (Lareau & Weininger, 2003, p. 568) and to skills or abilities that "provide access to scarce rewards" (p. 587). Middle class competencies and knowledge differ from those of the working class and are perceived to be superior (Lawler, 1999). From the middle class perspective, the working classes "do not *know* the right things, they do not *value* the right things, they do not *want* the right things" (Lawler, p. 11). Sennett and Cobb (1972, p. 3) spoke of the "hidden injuries of class," the conflicting and often negative judgments affecting working class identity.

However, empirical support is lacking for the argument that social class necessarily has a negative impact on feelings of self-worth. A meta-analytic review of the literature (Twenge & Campbell, 2002) revealed that social class had only a small effect on self-esteem ($d = .15$). Membership in a low-status group does not necessarily lead to lower feelings of self-worth because people develop self-protective strategies to buffer themselves from the prejudice of others (Crocker & Major, 1989). People are motivated to maintain a positive self-evaluation (Turner, Hogg, Oakes, Reicher, & Wetherell, 1987). Researchers have shown that even homeless individuals, at the bottom of the status system, develop strategies to construct and affirm personal identities that provide a sense of self-worth and self-respect (Snow & Anderson, 1987). The need for positive identity may promote "selective accentuation of intergroup differences that favour the in-group" (Abrams & Hogg, 1990, p. 3). Although an important aspect of identity formation is the adoption of an ideology (Erikson, 1968) and a worldview (Arnett, 2000), researchers know little about the ideologies that members of lower classes may develop to affirm self-respect.

Social class may operate not only as an independent variable that shapes the self, but also as a domain of identity exploration. The literature on working class individuals who move into more privileged positions (e.g., entering universities or becoming university professors) suggests that social mobility has significant effects on one's sense of self because identities must be renegotiated and that social class is an important domain of identity exploration for upwardly mobile individuals (Baxter & Britton, 2001; Dews & Law, 1995; Jones, 2003; Lawler, 1999; Ostrove, 2003; Skeggs, 1997; Tokarczyk & Fay, 1993; Wentworth & Peterson, 2001). Movement between classes involves changes in judgment, taste, opinions, preferences, and practices (Stewart & Ostrove, 1993). Upwardly mobile working class individuals struggle to establish a sense of continuity between who they were and who they are becoming (Lawler; Reay, 1996), because "class is embedded in people's history" (Lawler, p. 6) and working class childhoods go on being lived in the present (Reay). Upwardly mobile working class individuals struggle with alienation from their own pasts, families, and cultural backgrounds, yet they lack a feeling of belongingness in the middle class worlds that they have entered (Lubrano, 2004; Wentworth & Peterson, 2001).

Our goal in the present study was to examine the role that social class may play in the formation of identity, both as an independent variable that shapes identity (e.g., class position may shape choices, self-conceptions, and ideologies) and as a domain of importance and personal relevance to identity (i.e., a domain that may be actively explored). To assess identity, we drew on Marcia's (1966, 1993) operationalization of Erikson's (1968) construct of identity by using Marcia's Identity Status Interview (ISI). The ISI examines the presence of identity exploration and commitment in the domains of occupation, ideology (i.e., politics and religion), and sex-role attitudes. Following the lead of researchers who have added ethnicity to the ISI as a domain of importance in studying ethnic minority adolescents (e.g., Aries & Moorehead, 1989; Phinney, 1989), we added the domain of social class to the ISI as a potential area of importance and exploration in the identity formation process. Although researchers have used Marcia's methodology to examine identity in students from differing social class backgrounds (Morash, 1980; Munro and Adams, 1977), none have considered social class to be a domain of potential identity exploration. Phillips and Pittman (2003) theorized that the stress and limited opportunities that are associated with poverty will inhibit identity exploration, and the present research extends their theorizing to a wider spectrum of social classes. In the present research, we focused on four questions:

*Research Question 1:* How does social class compare to occupational goals, political and religious beliefs, and sex-role attitudes in its importance to identity? Does its importance vary depending on social class background?

*Research Question 2:* To what extent is the domain of social class an area of identity exploration, and does exploration vary by social class background?

*Research Question 3:* Is social class background related to occupational strivings?

*Research Question 4:* What are the ideologies that people of different social class backgrounds develop to understand class-based aspects of identity?

## Method

### Participants

Participants were 45 undergraduates that we drew from three groups. Each group had 15 participants. Two groups (one affluent and one lower income) of students attended a highly selective liberal arts college (labeled Little Ivy). The third group, which comprised lower income students, attended a state liberal arts college (labeled State College). We limited participation in the study to students who were White to avoid confounding race and class. Students at Little Ivy were all of traditional college age, so we limited our sample at State College to students of traditional age. All participants were 1st- or 2nd-year students. Finally, we balanced each group by gender.

In nearly all the cases, the samples of affluent and lower income student differed not only by parental income, but also by parental education and occupation, grandparents' education, and self-perceived social class. For the vast majority of the students from all three samples, the income, education, and occupational categories tended to correlate well, but, as with social class in general, these indicators were not always consistent. The difficulties with categorizing can be exemplified by looking at two cases. A student who reported the lowest parental income had two parents who had graduated from college. Another student's subjective identification was with the "upper middle class," yet the bulk of the data that he provided suggested a lower class category. Neither of his parents had graduated from college, suggesting a status that was much more in line with the lower income students than with the affluent students. Also, his father's occupation, mechanic, fell more squarely within the lower income sample, whereas his mother's occupation, "small business owner/secretary" was more ambiguous.

*Affluent sample.* We recruited affluent students at Little Ivy from an introductory psychology class. This group self-reported family income of at least $110,000 with several respondents answering over $250,000. They all reported their class identity as at least upper middle class with several choosing upper class. In a pattern that sociologists have noted for about 40 years (Marger, 2005), those students objectively on the top of the income or wealth pyramid identified downward as upper middle class or middle class, whereas those students with low incomes more likely presented themselves as middle class. In an essay on teaching at Little Ivy, Dizard (1991) reported that although the majority of Little Ivy students came from the wealthiest 5–10% of U.S. families, they tended to subjectively identify as slightly above middle class to upper middle class.

Although one may question self-reported family income and subjective class standing when they occur by themselves, the educational backgrounds and occupational levels of the parents of this group help solidify their affluent, solidly upper middle class (if not upper class) objective class status. Both parents of all the students were college graduates, and in fact most parents had graduate or professional degrees. More than half of the parents had graduated from elite liberal arts colleges much like Little Ivy, including four who had preceded their children at Little Ivy. In fact, 13 of the 15 students in this group were at least the third generation of their family to attend college, most claiming at least two grandparents who were college graduates. Occupationally, the parents (in most cases both fathers and mothers) held solid professional and managerial positions, including that of attorney, investment banker, director of a scientific lab, and corporate vice president.

*Lower income Little Ivy sample.* We recruited lower income students at Little Ivy via the director of financial aid, who sent letters to all 1st- and 2nd-year White students receiving financial aid whose parental incomes were under $50,000, telling them that they qualified for a study of identity. When this procedure did not produce enough students, we raised the income level to $60,000. On subjective social class, 6 students described themselves as middle class, 5 described themselves as lower middle class, 2 described themselves as working class, 1 self-described as lower class, and 1 self-described as upper middle class (in an aforementioned case). On educational background, this sample differed significantly from the affluent group. Only half of their mothers and fathers had completed college, and a third of this group comprised first generation college students. Most had none or only one grandparent who had graduated from college. Occupationally, their parents generally held blue-collar (e.g., truck driver, mechanic, taxi driver, waitress, bricklayer) or middle level white-collar positions (e.g., high school teacher, graphic designer).

*State College sample.* We recruited State College students from introductory social science or sociology classes. In the State College group, all but 1 student reported parental incomes under $50,000. Of all the State College students, 8 self-reported their class as middle class, 4 self-reported their class as working class, 2 self-reported it as lower middle class, 1 self-reported it as low-to-lower class, and 0 self-reported it as upper middle class or higher class. Only about a third of these students had a mother or father who had completed college, and 60% were first generation college students.

Almost none had grandparents who had graduated from college. Occupationally, their parents were comparable to the lower income Little Ivy students' parents, although the State College students were more solidly blue collar. On the whole, researchers should consider this group as somewhat lower in objective social class than the lower income Little Ivy sample.

## Procedure

Both authors conducted interviews at both schools. Before the interviews, participants read and signed informed consent forms. Interviews ranged from 1 hr to 2 hr in length and were tape recorded for later coding. Participants received $20 for participation. After payment, debriefing consisted of informing participants that the central focus of the study was social class and identity.

## Measures

The late adolescent college form of Marcia's Identity Status Interview (ISI; Marcia & Archer, 1993) served as the basis of a structured identity interview.

Marcia (1966) designed the ISI to determine whether individuals fall into one of four identity statuses: *achieved*, *moratorium*, *foreclosed*, or *diffused*. Researchers determine identity status by two variables: whether the person has undergone a period of exploration and whether a commitment has been made. Individuals who have undergone a period of exploration and made occupational and ideological commitments are *identity achieved*. Those who are still in a period of exploration and have not made commitments are *identity moratorium*. Those who have made commitments without examination of the values and goals that have been endorsed by parents and parent surrogates are *identity foreclosed*. Those who have no clear direction in terms of occupation or ideology and have not actively explored these areas are *identity diffused*.

The interview included questions in the domains traditionally assessed: vocational plans, religious beliefs, political beliefs, and sex-role attitudes (Marcia & Archer, 1993). We added a fifth domain, social class, to the interview to parallel the other four areas of the interview. In the section on social class, we asked participants what differences social class had made in their lives, whether class was something that they discussed with their parents, whether they had questioned or changed their ideas about social class and their class identity, what started them thinking about these questions, and whether they expected their ideas on the role of social class in their lives to change at all. Both authors coded responses in each domain into one of the four identity statuses: achieved, moratorium, foreclosed, or diffused. Interrater reliability (Cohen's Kappa) was .72. According to the interview protocol (Marcia & Archer), at the end of each section we asked participants to rate how important that domain was in their life on a 7-point scale ranging from 1 (*not at all important*) to 7 (*extremely important*).

We added two additional questions to the interview to assess the ideologies that individuals developed to deal with their class position and to understand their place in society: (a) "What would you say the major factors are that lead to a person's success in the United States?" (b) "Suppose it were possible for you and your family to be born all over again, would you want to be born in the same social class or a different social class?"

## Results

*Question 1: How Does Social Class Compare to Occupational Goals, Political and Religious Beliefs, and Sex-Role Attitudes in Its Importance to Identity? Does Its Importance Vary Depending on Social Class Background?*

Across the total sample, participants rated occupational goals as most important to identity ($M = 5.33$, $SD = 0.84$), followed by social class ($M = 4.77$, $SD = 1.23$), sex roles ($M = 4.60$, $SD = 1.51$), politics ($M = 4.31$, $SD = 1.51$), and religion, which received the lowest importance ratings ($M = 3.93$, $SD = 2.06$). We calculated a one-way analysis of variance to compare the three groups (affluent Little Ivy, lower income Little Ivy, lower income State College) on ratings of the importance of social class to identity. We found significant differences between the groups, $F(2, 42) = 3.94$, $p = .027$, $\eta^2 = .16$. Fisher least significant differences (LSD) tests revealed that the affluent Little Ivy students ($M = 5.43$, $SD = 0.96$) rated social class as significantly more important to identity than did both the State College students ($M = 4.30$, $SD = 1.14$) and the lower income Little Ivy students ($M = 4.57$, $SD = 1.33$). The two lower income groups did not differ significantly from each other.

The affluent students seemed well aware of the role that their economically privileged status had played in forming their identities and of the accrued benefits that shaped the self. As one affluent student said, "I could say that if I was born into a completely different class, my life would probably be completely different. So to that extent, [social class] has been completely important." The affluent students recognized that their class status was related to the quality of education that they had received (see Fine & Burns, 2003). Affluence had given them access to excellent schooling at either private schools or public schools that were well funded. One student reported that at her public high school, $14,000 of tax money per student went into the school, an amount at the high end of public school per capita spending (Kozol, 2005). The affluent students realized their educational opportunities had put them on a different path in life: for example, "There's a big difference between the track you're put on by going to [Little Ivy], and the track you're put on by going to [a state school]." They also spoke of their opportunities to travel. For example, one student said,

> I think [my social class position] certainly opened up so many opportunities to me that I wouldn't have had if I'd come from another background. I mean especially things like spending time in Europe. . . . I did an exchange program in France. My family's been to Europe a couple of times. You know we've gone on other various trips, like to Hawaii.

Affluence had opened up opportunities for them to develop skills and interests (e.g., "[My social class] has allowed me to do things that I am interested in regardless of financial restraints").

The lower income students were more likely than the affluent students to push class aside in their conception of their own identities (Seider & Aries, 2004). As one lower income Little Ivy student stated,

> I don't think that [social class] played a part in my life, that it's made me not be able to do things that I want. I don't think my life would have been significantly different if I had all the money in the world.

Other lower income Little Ivy students echoed similar themes: one student claimed, "I don't feel like it has made such a big difference to me. I have had enough"; another said,

> I don't think social class had any influence. I just always took advantage of any opportunities that I was given. I guess I have more of an appreciation for certain opportunities. We never had an extreme amount of money, but I always had what I needed and mostly what I wanted. I was pretty spoiled.

Likewise, the responses of State College students downplayed the importance of social class. One State College student said, "I don't think social class had any influence." Other State College students made similar responses. For example, a student commented, "I don't think about [social class]. It's not been a factor in my life so I don't know where it could come in to being important". Another said,

> I don't really see [class] as having made a difference. I don't, but that's just because I've been through it. I don't know what it's like to be poor or what it's like to be rich. . . . I think that's the only reason that [social class] didn't affect me was because I never got the spoils of being rich, and I never really had the want of being poor.

*Question 2: To What Extent Is the Domain of Social Class an Area of Identity Exploration, and Does Exploration Vary by Social Class Background?*

Students who had undergone a period of exploration of the meaning of social class to identity are found in both the achieved status and the moratorium status. Significant differences emerged between the three groups in the percentage of students for whom social class was a domain of exploration, $\chi^2(2, N = 44) = 10.20$, $p = .006$, Cramér's $V = .48$. The highest degree of exploration in the realm of social class was among lower income Little Ivy students (78.6%), the lowest degree by State College students (26.7%), with affluent Little Ivy students in the middle (53.3%). Post hoc comparisons with a series of chi-square tests (with continuity correction) on each of the pairs with a Bonferroni correction ($\alpha = .017$) showed that the two lower income groups significantly differed from each other, $\chi^2(1, N = 29) = 7.96$, $p = .005$, Cramér's $V = .59$.

In response to questions about whether they had ever questioned or changed their ideas about social class or their class identity, the following responses from State College students were typical: "No"; "I don't think so"; and "No, not really. I never really put much thought into it." The percentage of State College students (26.7%) who were in diffusion in regard to social class was twice that of the affluent Little Ivy students (13.3%) and three times that of the lower income Little Ivy students (7.1%). A few State College students had given considerable thought to the role that social class had played in their lives, but such responses were infrequent. For example, one student said,

> When I was younger, I was naive: You had the poor, you had us, and then you had the rest. Now I can see things on a deeper level, the more I look. Deeper that I can see reasons, the socialization, how people grew up, how people learn. I can see there are barriers in terms of social class as to how far you can go. You have rights to go anywhere you want in America the land of opportunity, but if you are raised in a very poor neighborhood and a very poor family you don't learn, "Oh, I am going to go on to college"; you learn that I am going to grow up and get a job so that I can survive.

By contrast, lower income Little Ivy students had given a great deal of thought to class-based aspects of their identities. Lower income students at Little Ivy found themselves surrounded by students from predominantly affluent families, whereas such students at State College found themselves surrounded by students from class backgrounds similar to their own. Many of the lower income Little Ivy students had given considerable thought to how their world view was influenced by their class backgrounds. One student reported,

> I've never been with people who are as wealthy as some people here. And it just made me, it just made me realize that people are different, and they have this whole other outlook on life. I'd say [the wealthy students] have no clue as to what 90% of the people in this country live with.

Another talked about the conflicts that were raised by coming to Little Ivy:

> I will say that it was difficult coming here in that it's a very different world from home, and I definitely felt like I didn't want to betray my parents as far as, you know, looking on that kind of income level as inferior or trying to change myself completely from that and trying to assimilate completely into the more wealthy kind of mindset.

Many lower income Little Ivy students felt their class-based identity was in flux. One student reported, "I think I'm part of a different social class than I came in here with, I was socialized to be part of." Another was struggling with class membership: "I say at this point in my life, I am kind of trying to figure out what I want to be as far as class wise." A third student had come to terms with class origins but thought that "My class is always going change as I grow older and get into a profession. That's going to bring up whole new issues about class, because I'll potentially be in a different class than my parents were. So it's always going to be an issue."

For some students, their thinking about social class had led to a sense of clarity on their social class position:

> I think that I've come to terms with who I am in my social class. And I mean, if I, I can't imagine myself falling below where I am now. I mean I can see myself maybe, you know, moving up some. But in terms of how important it is, or I'm happy like where I am. I can't imagine it changing dramatically.

Half of the affluent students had explored questions of social class and class-based aspects of their identities. Some affluent families had taught their children to be aware of class differences and their obligations to give back. Some affluent students gained an awareness of social class through exposure to people from different class backgrounds either at Little Ivy (e.g., "I get to see people from different backgrounds, and I can see that there are differences, and it is a significant aspect of society."). Volunteer work made some

> more conscious of the problems of people who are poor, what they have to deal with. . . . It made me think not everyone has what I have, and like I should be a lot more thankful for it. I should be thankful for the family situation I have. I think it just made me think of what they would have to deal with every day, sort of, and like what you could maybe do to change that.

For some students, academic studies exposed them to the importance of class to identity:

> The more that I learn about separations of the wealthiest 1% and the poorest 1% in the country, it makes you sort of doubt the American Dream at this point. You can't get a good job if you don't have an education, and you cannot get the education that you need from a public high school any more.

Finally, for some wealthy students, thoughts about their affluence made them uncomfortable and guilty. One student spoke of having developed

> sort of a negative idea of affluence in general. . . . Just the fact that I saw people buying stuff that they didn't need and flaunting their wealth in the forms of SUVs and stuff like that. I just thought that a lot of it was just such a waste and that really a lot of people could make much better use of their money by not having it.

Another reported,

> I mean I am so grateful for what I have. I'm so grateful to being born there. But I'm also on some level uncomfortable with it. Not like I want anything else, and not like I don't think everyone should be born at the same level, but there is definitely a discomfort zone.

*Question 3: Is Class Background Related to Occupational Strivings?*

Through the section of the ISI that concerns occupational goals, we asked students to speak about their occupational aspirations. We coded occupational aspirations for the presence or absence of occupations that required a doctorate or professional degree. A chi-square test revealed significant differences between the three groups, $\chi^2(2, N = 44) = 8.65, p = .013$, Cramér's $V = .44$. Two thirds of the affluent Little Ivy students aspired to occupations requiring a doctorate or professional degree, whereas one third of the lower income Little Ivy students did, and 14.3% of the State College students did. Post hoc comparisons with a series of chi-square tests (with continuity correction) on each of the pairs and with a Bonferroni correction showed that the affluent and State College groups differed significantly from each other, $\chi^2(1, N = 29) = 6.17, p = .013$, Cramér's $V = .53$.

The aspirations of the affluent students are consistent with the educational and occupational levels of their parents. The affluent group's occupational goals tended to be occupations that would award them much more power, income, and status than those of either of the lower income groups. For example, 60% of this group expected to be lawyers, and 20% expected to be physicians (Seider & Aries, 2004, pg. 12). The lower income Little Ivy group anticipated occupations that would elevate them over their parents, because one third wanted to teach, and 20% wanted to practice law or medicine. The State College group's reach was not as high, although their goals would bring them above their parents in status and income. They tended to be vaguer about their goals and also to focus on entry-level positions in professions such as teaching and counseling.

Approximately half the students in each group were in moratorium, in the midst of an exploration of occupational identity: affluent Little Ivy, 46.7%; lower income Little Ivy, 53.3%; State College, 42.9%. Few were in diffusion: affluent Little Ivy, 6.7%; lower income Little Ivy, 0.0%; State College, 7.1%. The affluent Little Ivy students showed the highest levels of foreclosure in the domain of occupation (26.7%), whereas the lower income students showed little evidence of foreclosure in this area (lower income Little Ivy, 6.7%; State College, 0.0%). Both lower income groups showed more evidence of achievement in the domain of occupation (lower income Little Ivy, 40%; State College, 50%) than did the affluent group (20%) and were more likely to have made occupational choices before entering college.

Some of the affluent students based occupational goals on identifications with family members. One student, whose father and older brother were lawyers, stated that "I'm just imagining, based on my personality and my family history, I'm sure I'll go to law school at some time." An economics major who was interested in law and investment banking decided on his major before college "because of my parents; my dad is an investment banker." When considering occupational goals, this student thought, "Maybe law school. Maybe go into the side of business my dad is in." One of the affluent group's most progressive and politically active students, a political science major, anticipated working in politics for an elected official or a think tank. He already had experience working for a candidate and may want to be one himself someday. As he put it, "Bill Bradley was told from age 10 he was supposed to be president. I wasn't told that, but it was one of those things all along that I wanted to do."

The lower income Little Ivy students' occupational aspirations tended to focus on teaching and mostly on college teaching. Most were very engaged with their academic work, enjoyed and appreciated their classes, and wanted to go on to graduate school and to teach at the college or university level. When asked what she would enjoy about being an academic, one student responded, "I love teaching. I love working with people who are passionate about what they want to do and want to learn." Like most of the Little Ivy students, no matter their economic background, she showed no doubts that she would achieve her degree goals. One student, who was less certain of his occupational goals, nonetheless tried to connect various possibilities to his strong interests. An accomplished musician who had been playing an instrument since the age of 5 years, he indicated that his ideal goal would be to be able to make a living by "playing music and performing." He also had plans for graduate school in English and for teaching high school English, depending on how his music career would go.

On the whole, the lower income State College students seemed less certain of their occupational goals and were less likely to see graduate school as an option in the near future. One student who really loved theater but was not able to break into it in college talked about a business major. At that point, he could not articulate what his focus would be in that area. When he was asked whether his parents had plans for him regarding an occupation, he answered, "No, my dad told me never to be a truck driver because that is what he is, but they never told me to be a lawyer." In fact, a Cooperative Institutional Research Program (Higher Education Research Institute, 1999) survey among 1st-year students at the state college revealed that more male students chose "police officer" than "lawyer" as a career goal. As compared with men, 1st-year women more frequently chose entry-level careers in education and human services, bypassing additional education for advanced work or management positions in those areas (Seider, 2002). Pressure from family members and additional economic concerns worked to focus many of the students' attention to occupations that they could fill soon after graduation. However, one psychology major did not fit that pattern. He very much enjoyed psychological research ("I took a psychology course in high school in my junior year, and I just loved it so much that I want to pursue it") and had some opportunities to work in a lab at the college. Very knowledgeable about graduate school and opportunities in the field, he seemed confident that he would go on and receive his doctorate. What differentiated this student from most at the state college was the educational background of his family; both parents had completed graduate school and both had taught at the high school and college levels.

*Question 4. What Are the Ideologies That People of Different Social Class Backgrounds Develop to Understand Class-Based Aspects of Identity?*

We coded answers to the question "What would you say the major factors are that lead to a person's success in the United States?" for the presence or absence of two types of responses: personal factors (i.e., hard work, motivation, determination) and structural factors (i.e., social class position, opportunities, connections, education). Chi-square tests comparing the three groups on the presence or absence of personal factors revealed no significant differences between the groups, $\chi^2(2, N = 43) = 2.60$, *ns*, Cramér's $V = .25$. Approximately three quarters of students in each group named personal factors as important to success. However, significant differences emerged in whether students mentioned structural variables as major determinants of success, $\chi^2(2, N = 43) = 9.73$, $p = .008$, Cramér's $V = .48$. Ninety-three percent of affluent Little Ivy students, 69.2% of lower income Little Ivy, and 40% of State College students noted the importance of structural factors to success. Post hoc comparisons with a series of chi-square tests (with continuity correction) on each of the pairs with a Bonferroni correction showed the difference between the affluent and State College groups to be significant, $\chi^2(1, N = 30) = 7.35$, $p = .007$, Cramér's $V = .57$.

When asked, "Suppose it were possible for you and your family to be born all over again, would you want to be born in the same social class or a different social class?" the affluent students (92%) were more likely to say the same social class than the lower income students, $\chi^2(2, N = 41) = 4.70$, $p = .095$, Cramér's $V = .34$. However, 69% of lower income Little Ivy students and 57% of State College students said the same social class. One lower income Little Ivy student said,

> When we didn't have money, it was really hard. I am not upset with anything that has happened in my life. If anything, I think it has made me a better person. Having my experiences has been an advantage for seeing the world from.

A second lower income Little Ivy student also wanted "definitely" to be born in the same class.

> It doesn't matter how much money you have or anything like that. . . . You know, whatever doesn't kill you only makes you . . . stronger. I wouldn't want to live this really posh life and be really spoiled and have whatever I want. You know, I wouldn't appreciate anything. It wouldn't be special to me.

Also typical of the lower income students was a third lower income Little Ivy student, who felt that his lower income status helped him to learn "to value the dollar, learn . . . how to work hard. I also learned that if I do work hard and I do make money and stuff, what I can get from it."

Slightly more than half of the State College sample echoed the responses of the lower income Little Ivy students. "I think I would like to stay the same. I think that the experiences that I have had and where I come from all . . . have . . . influenced my character." Added another, "I like being in the middle class. Because if I was born in a higher class, I would probably end up being a little more spoiled." However, nearly half of the group would have liked to have been born in a higher class. One student, who left no doubt about his wishes, put it this way: "I'd want to be rich. I'd want to see what it's like. . . . I just want money, and people might think it's greedy . . . , but you know, I just want to have money to do what I want." Another student responded in a more subtle manner:

> I think it would be nicer to have more money. It seems like you would have more opportunities. But I don't know if that would make me any happier. But I think you'd be able to do more . . . like take trips . . . , like have nicer things, be able to pay for a better school.

Finally, one student replied, "Probably [a] different [class], a little higher up the chain, middle class. It just would be easier for everyone—no worries at all."

Nearly all the affluent Little Ivy students would have wanted to be born in the same class. They generally recognized their privilege, but also stated that they would do good work, taking advantage of their comfortable status. As one student put it,

> You can be in the upper class and still teach your kids, as my parents taught me, that there is a level of difference and that you need to respect and not discriminate based on that level of difference. But be aware of it. Given the opportunities . . . I was given, I wouldn't trade for anything. But also if you can make yourself aware of the differences, then it's worth it. That you can make a difference then, because you can use your knowledge and the power or money you have, to do something about it.

## Discussion

The present data reveal that social class plays an important role both as an independent variable that shapes the formation of identity and as a domain of identity exploration. When asked to rate the importance of five domains of identity—occupational goals, political beliefs, religious beliefs, sex-role attitudes, and social class—college students gave occupational goals the highest ratings and social class the next highest ratings. However, affluent students perceived social class as significantly more important to identity than did the lower income students from both private and state colleges. The affluent students were well aware of the educational benefits that had accrued from their economically privileged status and of the opportunities that they had to travel and pursue their interests. The lower income students were more likely to downplay class in their conception of their own identities than were the affluent students (Seider & Aries, 2004). It is striking that social class held lower salience for the lower income students, who had been given the least capital. Just as some Blacks have social identities that accord only minor significance to race (Cross, Strauss, & Fhagen-Smith, 1999), some lower income students appeared to have social identities that accorded low significance to social class.

Social class was an area of exploration for half the affluent students, contributing to their understanding of the advantages that their social class position had given them. Exposure to people of different social classes either at Little Ivy or through volunteer work, coursework that addressed unequal distributions of wealth in this society, and reflections on their own privileged position all contributed to this exploration. By contrast, and consistent with their lower ratings of the importance of social class to identity, almost three quarters of State College students indicated no exploration or questioning of the domain of social class and instead showed the highest level of diffusion in this domain. However, of particular interest is the finding that social class was an area of identity exploration for three quarters of the lower income Little Ivy students. These lower income private college students were three times more likely to have explored the domain of social class than the State College students, despite the fact that they rated social class as similar in importance to identity. The data suggest that social class becomes an important area of exploration when individuals encounter people from very different social class backgrounds (Aries & Seider, 2005; Ostrove, 2003). The lower income Little Ivy students were exposed to a majority of students who were highly affluent and whose class backgrounds diverged widely from their own, making their own class backgrounds salient (consistent with distinctiveness theory: McGuire, 1984) and pushing them to think about their class status and to find a rationalization for how things had turned out. The State College students, who were in a more homogeneous setting where they were surrounded by other working class students, had less stimulation to think about class-based aspects of their identities. The exploration of social class by the lower income elite college students led not to anger or resentment, but to ideologies to rationalize their class status, as we will discuss later in this article.

The data support previous findings that class position limits occupational strivings (Cook et al., 1996; MacLeod, 1995; Rojewski & Kim, 2003; Rojewski & Yang, 1997). Erikson (1968) held that during childhood, individuals develop a set of expectations about what they will be as an adult, and the people available to them for identification shape those expectations. In the present study, it was the affluent Little Ivy students who aspired to occupations that require a doctorate or professional degree and that would lead to greater income, power, or prestige. Two thirds of the group expected to be lawyers, physicians, or college professors. Some of the affluent students based these occupational goals on identifications with family members. The aspirations of the affluent students were consistent with the educational and occupational levels of their parents.

There were no doctors or lawyers among the parents of the lower income students. From the lower income Little Ivy group, the modal occupational expectation centered on teaching at the college and high school levels, with a minority of students considering law or medicine. Neither law, medicine, nor college professorship appeared as an aspiration of any State College student; instead such students emphasized teaching and counseling. Researchers may well account for the "lower" aspirations of the State College students by their somewhat lower economic status and their lack of cultural capital as compared with those of the lower income Little Ivy students. Further, the fact that the lower income Little Ivy students were indeed at Little Ivy and recognized the avenues that their privileged status opened for them more than likely raised their confidence in their ability to move much higher than did their parents. However, it is notable that the lower income Little Ivy students' choice of occupations (teaching, particularly at the college level) rested considerably on their intellectual capabilities and accomplishments, factors that they did have control over. Their more affluent classmates had disproportionately chosen occupations such as law and politics, positions they are well familiar with given their families' standings and positions, which relied more on the social capital that they and their families already possessed. For the lower income students, to choose those occupations and to hope to move upward in them would represent a much less certain gamble for the future. Given their class statuses and differential social and cultural capital, all of the students' aspirations seem well within the range of their respective groups and provide evidence for the reproduction of social class (Bowles & Gintis, 1976; MacLeod, 1995).

In the area of occupational goals, 93% of both lower income groups had already explored identity, whereas two thirds of the affluent Little Ivy students had. For lower income students, many of whom were the first generation to go to college, new areas of study and occupational horizons had opened up to them for the first time, and they had been encouraged to explore new interests. Yet, despite the new opportunities that had opened up to them, their aspirations remained lower than those of the affluent students.

The students' responses to the question of whether—if they could be born again—they would want to be born in the same social class revealed the ideologies that the students developed to understand class-based aspects of identity and to protect themselves from the injuries of class inequalities. It is not surprising that the affluent students were more likely to say that they would want to be born in the same social class than were the lower income students. However, it was somewhat unexpected that two thirds of the lower income Little Ivy students and slightly over half of the State College students also would choose to be born again in the same social class. Many of the lower income students protected themselves from the injuries of class (Sennett & Cobb, 1972) and downplayed the importance of money by emphasizing the positive aspects of their class upbringing. Many lower income students would want no change in class position because they valued the character traits that they believe they had developed by virtue of the economic struggles of their family. In fact, the lower income students from both schools seemed remarkably similar in this regard. They highlighted the positive virtues that they derived from their class position. They showed pride in their resourcefulness, having learned to find ways to get what they needed. They saw themselves as more independent because they could not rely on their parents. They appreciated what they had and exhibited the motivation to succeed and to take advantage of opportunities. Also, Ostrove and Long (2001) found that lower income college women expressed pride in their social class, despite the difficulties that it posed in their lives. However, it is important to note that nearly half of the State College students wanted more money, more opportunities to travel and to buy things, and access to better schooling.

Erikson (1968, p. 190) argued that adolescents need to find an ideology that "later can serve as rationalizations for what has come about." The lower income students had developed an ideology that rationalized and minimized the disadvantages they had faced. The data support the contention that members of groups with less power or status develop self-protective strategies and navigate a route to positive identity (Crocker & Major, 1989; Snow & Anderson, 1987; Turner et al., 1987). The data help to explain the finding that social class is unrelated to self-esteem (Twenge & Campbell, 2002). Lower income students seem to have protected themselves both through the lower salience they accord to social class in its importance to identity and in the positive view that they develop of members of their social class.

The students' beliefs about the criteria for success in the United States revealed further information about their ideologies about class. Three quarters of all students focused on personal character traits such as motivation, hard work, and determination as important to success, accepting the ideology of the American Dream. However, the elite students were significantly more likely than the state college students to cite structural factors—for example, individuals' position in society, the opportunities available to them, and the connections they can make—as important to a person's success. Thus the elite college students, who had been given more opportunities, had more awareness of the importance of these opportunities for success. The state college students seemed less aware that they have not been given the same chances for entrée into positions of power and wealth. Rather than articulating any anger toward any structural inequalities, the state college students interpreted their present status and life style as a success.

Lower income students also used the self-protective strategy of positioning themselves in the middle of the social structure and, therefore, as privileged in relation to the poor. Thus, their class position could be seen as an advantage. It kept them from being spoiled like the rich, but they had not struggled like the poor. They had things easier than those below them and had made it to college. They ignored the privileges of the upper class and seemed neither envious nor jealous of those who had been given more. As one State College student put it, "I think the only reason that [social class] didn't affect me was because I never got the spoils of being rich and I never really had the want of being poor."

Researchers should keep in mind the historical period in which these interviews were done, a time of conservative ascendancy in the United States, a time when social programs to aid the poor were being cut, a time when unions and the working class were under attack, and a time when relatively little class mobility was occurring. Thus, the finding that both lower income groups showed a contentment with their statuses, a rationalization of their position, and a lack of anger or jealousy toward the upper class or the more affluent students may well be a reflection of the times and a reaction that could change if the political climate changes (see Perrucci & Wysong, 2003).

Because of the nature of the sample, researchers should note several important limitations of the present study. Students who attend college come from better educated families with higher incomes than do those that do not attend college, and the sample excluded individuals who grew up in poverty. Because the lower income students in this study were upwardly mobile, they were likely to have different perspectives and identity statuses than lower income young adults who went directly into the workforce. For example, it is likely that individuals who do not make it to college would show less evidence of exploration (Morash, 1980; Phillips & Pittman, 2003). Although our sample allowed us to examine the influence of social class on the perspectives of White college students, future researchers need to pursue the interactions of sex, race or ethnicity, and social class because "social identities are always experienced in conjunction with each other" (Ostrove & Cole, 2003, p. 681; see also Bettie, 2000; Cole & Omari, 2003). We hope that the present exploratory study has shed some light on the role that social class plays in higher education and that it will stimulate further research on class-based aspects of identity.

# References

Abrams, D., & Hogg, M. A. (1990). An introduction to the social identity approach. In D. Abrams (Ed.), *Social identity theory: Constructive and critical advances* (pp. 1–9). New York: Springer-Verlag.

Alix, E. K., & Lantz, H. R. (1973). Socioeconomic status and low occupational aspirations: Resignation as an orientational variable. *Social Science Quarterly, 54,* 596–607.

Argyle, M. (1994). *The psychology of social class.* London: Routledge.

Aries, E., & Moorehead, K. (1989). The importance of ethnicity in the development of identity of black adolescents. *Psychological Reports, 65,* 75–82.

Aries, E., & Seider, M. (2005). The interactive relationship between class identity and the college experience: The case of lower income students. *Qualitative Sociology, 28,* 419–443.

Arnett, J. J. (2000). Emerging adulthood: A theory of development from the late teens through the twenties. *American Psychologist, 55,* 469–480.

Baxter, A., & Britton, C. (2001). Risk, identity and change: Becoming a mature student. *International Studies in Sociology of Education, 11,* 87–102.

Bettie, J. (2000). Women without class: Chicas, cholas, trash and the presence/absence of class identity. *Signs: Journal of Women in Culture and Society, 26,* 1–35.

Bilsker, D., Schiedel, D., & Marcia, J. E. (1988). Sex differences in identity status. *Sex Roles, 18,* 231–236.

Bourdieu, P. (1977). Cultural reproduction and social reproduction. In J. Karabel & A. Halsey (Eds.), *Power and ideology in education* (pp. 487–511). New York: Oxford University Press.

Bowles, S., & Gintis, H. (1976). *Schooling in capitalist america.* New York: Basic Books.

Cole, E. R., & Omari, S. R. Race, class and the dilemmas of upward mobility for African Americans. *Journal of Social Issues, 59,* 785–802.

Cook, T. D., Church, M. B., Ajanaku, S., Shadish, W. R., Kim, J., & Cohen, R. (1996). The development of occupational aspirations and expectations among inner-city boys. *Child Development, 67*, 3368–3385.

Côté, J. (1996). Identity: A multidimensional analysis. In G. R. Adams, R. Montemaayor, & J. P. Gullotta (Eds.), *Psychosocial development during adolescence: Progress in developmental contextualism* (pp. 130–180). Thousand Oaks, CA: Sage.

Côté, J. E., & Levine, C. G. (2002). *Identity formation, agency, and culture: A social psychological synthesis.* Mahwah, NJ: Erlbaum.

Crocker, J., & Major, B. (1989). Social stigma and self-esteem: The self-protective properties of stigma. *Psychological Review, 96*, 608–630.

Cross, W. E., Strauss, L., & Fhagen-Smith, P. (1999). African American identity development across the life span: Educational implications. In R. Hernandez-Sheets & E. R. Hollins (Eds.), *Racial and ethnic identity in school practices: Aspects of human development* (pp. 29–47). Mahwah, NJ: Erlbaum.

Dews, C. L. B., & Law, C. L. (Eds.). (1995). *This fine place so far from home: Voices of academics from the working class.* Philadelphia: Temple University Press.

Dizard, J. E. (1991). Achieving place: Teaching social stratification to tomorrow's elite. In *Teaching what we do: Essays by Amherst College faculty* (pp. 145–162). Amherst, MA: Amherst College Press.

Domhoff, G. W. (1967). *Who rules America.* Englewood Cliffs, NJ: Prentice Hall.

Erikson, E. H. (1968). *Identity: Youth and crisis.* New York: Norton.

Fine, M., & Burns, A. (2003). Class notes: Toward a critical psychology of class and schooling. *Journal of Social Issues, 59*, 841–860.

Frable, D. E. S. (1997). Gender, racial, ethnic, sexual, and class identities. *Annual Review of Psychology, 48*, 139–162.

Higher Education Research Institute. (1999). *Cooperative Institutional Research Program Freshman Survey Institutional Profile.* Los Angeles: University Of California.

Jones, S. J. (2003). Complex subjectivities: Class, ethnicity, and race in women's narratives of upward mobility. *Journal of Social Issues, 59*, 803–820.

Kozol, J. (2005). *The shame of the nation: Restoration of apartheid schooling in America.* New York: Crown.

Lareau, A., & Weininger, E. B. (2003). Cultural capital in educational research: A critical assessment. *Theory and Society, 32*, 567–606.

Lawler, S. (1999) "Getting out and getting away": Women's narratives of class mobility. *Feminist Review, 63*, 3–24.

Lott, B., & Bullock, H. E. (2001). Who are the poor? *Journal of Social Issues, 57*, 189–206.

Lubrano, A. (2004). *Limbo: Blue-collar roots, white-collar dreams.* Hoboken, NJ: Wiley.

MacLeod, J. (1995). *Ain't no makin' it: Aspirations & attainment in a low-income neighborhood.* Boulder, CO: Westview.

Marcia, J. E. (1966). Development and validation of ego identity status. *Journal of Personality and Social Psychology, 3*, 551–558.

Marcia, J. E. (1993). The status of the statuses: Research review. In J. E. Marcia, A. S. Waterman, D. R. Matteson, S. L. Archer, & J. L. Orlofsky (Eds.), *Ego identity: A handbook for psychosocial research* (pp. 22–41). New York: Springer-Verlag.

Marcia, J. E., & Archer, S. L. (1993). Identity status interview: Late adolescent college form. In J. E. Marcia, A. S. Waterman, D. R. Matteson, S. L. Archer, & J. L. Orlofsky (Eds.), *Ego identity: A handbook for psychosocial research* (pp. 303–317). New York: Springer-Verlag.

Marger, M. M. (2005). *Social inequality: Patterns and processes* (3rd ed.). Boston: McGraw-Hill.

Massey, D. S., Gross, A. B., & Eggers, M. L. (1991). Segregation, the concentration of poverty, and the life chances of individuals. *Social Science Research, 20*, 397–420.

McGuire, W. J. (1984). Search for the self: Going beyond self-esteem and the reactive self. In R. A. Zucker, U. Aronoff, & A. I. Rabin (Eds.), *Personality and the prediction of behavior* (pp. 73–120). San Diego, CA: Academic Press.

Morash, M. A. (1980). Working class membership and the adolescent identity crisis. *Adolescence, 15*, 313–320.

Munro, G., & Adams, G. R. (1977). Ego-identity formation in college students and working youth. *Developmental Psychology, 13*, 523–524.

Ortner, S. B. (1991). Reading America: Preliminary notes on class and culture. In R. G. Fox (Ed.), *Recapturing anthropology: Working in the present* (pp. 163–189). Sante Fe, NM: School of American Research Press.

Ostrove, J. M. (2003). Belonging and wanting: Meanings of social class background for women's constructions of their college experiences. *Journal of Social Issues, 59*, 771–784.

Ostrove, J. M., & Cole, E. R. (2003). Privileging class: Toward a critical psychology of social class in the context of education. *Journal of Social Issues, 59*, 677–692.

Ostrove, J. M., & Long, S. M. (2001, August). *White women's social class identity and the college experience.* Paper presented at the Annual Convention of the American Psychological Association, San Francisco, CA.

Perrucci, R., & Wysong, E. (2003). *The new class society: Goodbye American Dream?* (2nd ed.). Oxford, England: Roman & Littlefield.

Phillips, T. M., & Pittman, J. F. (2003). Identity processes in poor adolescents: Exploring the linkages between economic disadvantage and the primary task of adolescence. *Identity: An International Journal of Theory and Research, 3*, 115–129.

Phinney, J. S. (1989). Stages of ethnic identity development in minority group adolescents. *Journal of Early Adolescence, 9*, 34–49.

Phinney, J. S. (1990). Ethnic identity in adolescents and adults: A review of research. *Psychological Bulletin, 108*, 499–514.

Phoenix, A., & Tizard, B. (1996). Think through class: The place of social class in the lives of young Londoners. *Feminism & Psychology, 6*, 427–442.

Reay, D. (1996). Dealing with difficult differences: Reflexivity and social class in feminist research. *Feminism and Psychology, 6*, 443–456.

Rojewski, J. W., & Kim, H. (2003). Career choice patterns and behavior of work-bound youth during early adolescence. *Journal of Career Development, 30*, 89–108.

Rojewski, J. W., & Yang, B. (1997). Longitudinal analysis of select influences on adolescents' occupational aspirations. *Journal of Vocational Behavior, 51*, 375–410.

Seider, M. (2002). Inequities in higher education: The experiences of State College and Little Ivy students. *Mind's Eye: A Liberal Arts Journal*, (Fall), 35–57.

Seider, M., & Aries, E. (2004, August). *Pushing class aside: How college students legitimize the class structure.* Paper presented at the meeting of the American Sociological Association, San Francisco, CA.

Sennett, R., & Cobb, J. (1972). *The hidden injuries of class.* New York: Knopf.

Skeggs, B. (1997). *Formations of class and gender: Becoming respectable.* London: Sage.

Smith, E. R. (1999). Affective and cognitive implications of a group becoming part of the self: New models of prejudice and of the self-concept. In D. Abrams & M. A. Hogg (Eds.), *Social identity and social cognition* (pp. 183–196). Oxford, England: Blackwell.

Snow, D.A., & Anderson, L. (1987). Identity work among the homeless: The verbal construction and avowal of personal identities. *American Journal of Sociology, 6*, 1336–1371.

Stewart, A. J., & Ostrove, J. M. (1993). Social class, social change, and gender. *Psychology of Women Quarterly, 17*, 475–497.

Tajfel, H. (1981). *Human groups and social categories: Studies in social psychology.* Cambridge, England: Cambridge University Press.

Tokarczyk, M. M., & Fay, E.A. (Eds.). (1993). *Working-class women in the academy: Laborers in the knowledge factory.* Amherst: University of Massachusetts Press.

Turner, J. C. (1982). Towards a cognitive redefinition. In H. Tajfel (Ed.), *Social identity and intergroup relations* (pp. 15–40). New York: Cambridge University Press.

Turner, J. C., with Hogg, M.A., Oakes, P. J., Reicher, S. D., & Wetherell, M. S. (1987). *Rediscovering the social group: A self-categorization theory.* Oxford, England: Blackwell.

Twenge, J. M., & Campbell, W. K. (2002). Self-esteem and socioeconomic status: A meta-analytic review. *Personality and Social Psychology Review, 6*, 59–71.

Wentworth, P. A., & Peterson, B. E. (2001). Crossing the line: Case studies of identity development in first-generation college women. *Journal of Adult Development, 8*, 9–21.

# CHAPTER 19
# NEGOTIATING MULTIPLE IDENTITIES WITHIN MULTIPLE FRAMES: AN ANALYSIS OF FIRST-GENERATION COLLEGE STUDENTS

MARK P. ORBE

This article draws from narratives, collected from 79 first-generation college (FGC) students across several different campuses, to explore the saliency of FGC student status and the various ways in which it is enacted during interactions with others. Communication theory of identity serves as the study's theoretic foundation. Multiple points of analysis capture the complex nature of identity negotiation for FGC students. Findings warrant three conclusions: (1) the salience of FGC status in their daily interactions varies considerably among students; (2) FGC status appears to be more important for individuals who also identify as co-cultural group members; and (3) FGC students appear to lack any significant sense of communal identity.

First-generation college (FGC) students are enrolling in U.S. colleges and universities in increasing numbers, yet we know little of how this aspect of identity is negotiated in their communication with others. Research has documented that FGC students have entered colleges and universities—particularly within community colleges (Shor, 1987)—at a growing proportion since the 1920s (Billson & Terry, 1982; National Center for Education Statistics, 1998). Yet, little has been written on the experiences of FGC students (Hertel, 2002; Riehl, 1994). Conducting such research is especially difficult because of incomplete data regarding the number of FGC students in higher education (Padron, 1992), as well as the great heterogeneity associated with the group.

To be sure, FGC students often overlap with those who fall under the rubrics of "nontraditional" (Query, Parry, & Flint, 1992), "under-prepared" (Bartholomae, 1985; Rose, 1989), or "disadvantaged" students (Rodriguez, 1975). In fact, research that describes how higher education has, or has not, been true to its commitment to provide accessible public education to these groups (Shor, 1987) serves as an important backdrop for current research on FGC students. However, it is important to recognize that not all FGC students enter college from nontraditional, disadvantaged backgrounds. Some, as described by Orbe (2003) come from families with considerable "cultural capital" (Karabel & Halsey, 1977) that, in the absence of a college education, still provide significant support for FGC students.

Orbe, M. P. (2004). Negotiating multiple identities within multiple frames: An analysis of first-generation college students. *Communication Education, 53*, 131–149.

Lavin and Hyllegard's (1996) longitudinal study of the City University of New York's (CUNY) open admissions program serves as one of the most extensive treatments regarding the long-term benefits that come with a college education—especially those who are the first in their family to earn a college education. These scholars make a strong argument about the short- and long-term benefits of greater accessibility to higher education. Yet, they recognize that not all of those who took advantage of open admissions at CUNY during the years in which it was in operation were FGC students (p. 19). In this regard, Lavin and Hyllegard's (1996) study, and others like it, do not provide precise data regarding FGC students. The small amount of research that does focus solely on FGC students typically examines statistical relations with other important variables related to college success. For instance, FGC students (as compared to students whose parents had some college experience) have lower SAT scores (Riehl, 1994), make the decision to attend college later in their high-school careers (Fallon, 1997), and choose less selective colleges (MacDermott, Conn, & Owen, 1987). Once enrolled, they tend to experience more difficulties adjusting to college and "have less commitment to the role of student" (Orozco, 1999, p. 70). Some of these difficulties can be tied to lack of support at home (Bartels, 1995; York-Anderson & Bowman, 1991). FGC students typically do not participate in student organizations, interact with other students or faculty, or study hard (Billson & Terry, 1982), when compared to those whose parents had some college experience.

Given this information, it should come as no surprise that FGC students on average have lower first-semester grades, are more likely to drop out the first semester, or do not return for their second year (Brooks-Terry, 1988; Riehl, 1994). Billson and Terry (1982) suggest that this academic achievement gap may be in part due to the tendency for FGC students to spend almost twice as much time working part-time or full-time jobs (as compared to their second-generation counterparts). While some of the studies cited here were conducted in the 1980s, their findings were mirrored by recent longitudinal research conducted by the National Center for Education Statistics (1998). According to Rose (1995), the strength of this type of data lies in its ability to sample widely and generalize broadly. Yet, he adds that "the weakness is that detail gets lost" (p. 6).

In 1992, Zwerling and London produced an edited volume dedicated to the experiences of FGC students. While the volume's focus was primarily on the community college experience, the studies collected therein nonetheless constitute the most comprehensive treatment of FGC students to date. Within this volume, education scholars explored the similarities and differences among FGC students (based on age, race/ethnicity, gender and class; Kiang, 1992; Rendon, 1992; Richardson & Skinner, 1992), and also described some existing programs designed to enhance the success of FGC students (Chaffe, 1992; Padron, 1992; Stein, 1992). In addition, several chapters (e.g., Lara, 1992; London, 1992) described how the ongoing negotiation of home and college life results in "trying to live simultaneously in two vastly different worlds" (Rendon, 1992, p. 56). The consistent conclusion that FGC students may feel like outsiders at school as well as home is especially relevant to research regarding multiple-identity negotiation.

In fact, some scholars have described the experiences of FGC students as similar to entering an "alien culture" (Chaffe, 1992; Rose, 1989) complete with peculiar ways of seeing, doing, and communicating about things (Bartholomae, 1985). While the transition from high school/full-time employment to college involves some adaptation for all students (in terms of learning a new set of academic and social rules; see Terenzini et al., 1994), FGC students do not have the benefit of parental experience to guide them, either in preparing for college or in helping them understand what will be expected of them after they enroll (Riehl, 1994). In addition to attempting to learn an "alien culture" of academic and social rules, FGC students must also negotiate issues of marginality—on both ends—as they work to bridge the worlds of their homes/families/neighborhoods and college life (Brooks-Terry, 1988; Orbe, 2003). A central aspect of this ongoing process involves negotiating multiple layers of identity.

The increasing number of FGC students on college campuses across the U.S. therefore presents itself as a valuable point of analysis for research that seeks insight into how multiple aspects of identity are negotiated in an educational environment. Specifically, emerging research on FGC students can benefit from scholarship that explores how multidimensional sense of identity is constructed and enacted with others across various contexts. This type of study is also responsive to recent mandates for studies that pay increasing attention to intersections of race, class, and gender and their conjoined impact on communication behaviors (e.g., Allen, 2002; Jackson, 1999). Houston (2002), for example, criticizes existing research in which one aspect of identity is "conceived as universally 'more important' than the others" (p. 37). It is thus incumbent on studies focusing on identity negotiation among FGC students to acknowledge that the salience of FGC student status will vary among participants. Research that takes such an approach can apply and extend current communication theories regarding identity negotiation, as well as offer practical guidance to educators who are interested in maximizing the educational experiences of all of their students.

## Theoretical Framework

Michael Hecht (1993) outlined the initial conceptualization of the Communication Theory of Identity (CTI) more than a decade ago. Since that time, he and colleagues have used the theory to study identity negotiation among different cultural groups, including Jewish Americans (Golden, Niles, & Hecht, 2002; Hecht & Faulkner, 2000; Hecht, Jackson, Lindsley, Strauss, & Johnson, 2001) and African Americans (Hecht, Jackson, & Ribeau, 2003). According to CTI, identity is "inherently a communication process and must be understood as a transaction in which messages and values are exchanged" (Hecht et al., 2003, p. 230). Identity is located within four different "frames": (1) within individuals, (2) within relationships, (3) within groups, and (4) communicated between relational partners and group members (Golden et al., 2002). It is important to recognize that these frames permeate all discussions of identity and should not be seen as static or linear (Hecht et al., 2003). Studies of identity should include an awareness of the "interpenetration of frames" (Hecht, 1993, p. 80)—or the ways in which frames can be studied simultaneously. Such analyses can illustrate how frames of identity are competing and/or complementary with one another (Golden et al., 2002) and, consequently, capture the intricate ways that the communication of identity is a complex, multidimensional process. In this regard, each of the frames discussed here serves as a "frame of reference" for a person's identity (Hecht et al., 2003).

The first frame of identity is the personal frame. Within this context, identity is the result of a person's self-cognitions, self-concept, and sense of well-being (Golden et al., 2002). The second frame of identity involves the enactment of identity to others. According to CTI, identities are enacted to others through communication (Hecht et al., 2003); thus, the second frame focuses on messages that a person sends that express his or her identity. Individuals can use either direct or indirect messages to reveal their identity to others (Hecht & Faulkner, 2000). A relationship frame of identity, the third in the model, focuses on how identity emerges through our relationships with others, as well as how relationships themselves construct their own identities (Golden et al., 2002; Hecht et al., 2003). The fourth location of identity, identity as a communal frame, occurs in the context of a larger community. "Identity is something held in the collective or public memory of a group that, in turn, bonds the group together" (Hecht et al., 2003, p. 237). In this regard, a community possesses a group identity that represents a shared identity of all of its members.

Most of the current work drawing on CTI (e.g., Golden et al., 2002; Hecht et al., 2003) has focused primarily on identity-negotiation processes with specific racial and ethnic groups. However, the theory's utility for studying other types of cultural identification (age, gender, class, disability, and sexual orientation)—and the ways that each of these may be simultaneously negotiated in different ways—is clear. For example, Orbe (2003) focused on the communicative experiences of African American FGC students. His research found that these students' communicative experiences varied significantly; in many instances, the divergence could be attributed to how FGC status intersected with other characteristics such as age, gender, and class. Accordingly, being an FGC student may be highly salient to one person's identity, not important at all to another, or somewhere in between for a third, depending on the situation. (See Hecht & Faulkner, 2000, for a similar discussion of varying ethnic salience among Jewish Americans.) Given the lack of research on the identity messages of FGC students, and the usefulness of CTI in studying negotiations of multiple identities, the following two research questions were posed:

RQ1: How central is FGC status to the identities of FGC students on different college campuses?

RQ2: How, if at all, is FGC identity negotiated at the personal, enacted, relational, and communal frames of identity?

## Methods

### Participants

Data for this study were part of a larger project that focused on the communicative experiences of FGC students. Over the course of a two-year period (Summer 1999–Summer 2001), I conducted 13 focus group discussions and four individual in-depth interviews with a total of 71 FGC students and eight FGC graduates. This group comprised 46 women and 33 men. Thirty-four were European Americans, 29 African Americans, 12 Hispanic/Latinos, and four Asian Americans. Fifty-five were traditionally aged and 24 were nontraditionally aged students.

Focus groups and in-depth interviews were conducted on six different campuses across three Midwestern states. Participants were drawn from one mid-sized competitively selective university ($n = 16$), one mid-sized public state university ($n = 6$), one large public state university ($n = 27$), one small public university ($n = 6$), one small commuter regional campus ($n = 10$), and one small commuter college focusing on business and legal studies ($n = 14$). At each campus, a faculty/staff liaison assisted in identifying potential study participants. These campus liaisons made announcements to classes and campus organizations. The announcements included a definition of FGC status, and some study volunteers indicated that this announcement was the first time they had consciously thought of themselves as FGC students. Thus, this solicitation procedure was apparently successful in recruiting a sample for which FGC status held varying levels of salience.

### Procedures

Lasting approximately 45–75 minutes, focus-group discussions and in-depth interviews used an interview guide (topical protocol) to generate a conversation about "what it's like to be a first-generation college student." Consistent with the practices of qualitative research (e.g., van Manen, 1990), open-ended and broadly structured questions were used to allow participants to give attention to issues they regarded as most significant. The interview protocol included questions such as, "How would you describe your transition to college during your first year?", "What has been the most difficult part of your adjustment?", "What advice would you give other first-generation college students preparing to attend college?", "How conscious are you about being the first in your family to attend college?", and "What are some specific things that made your transition more or less successful?" All in-depth interviews and focus group discussions, which each included between four and ten participants, were audiotaped and later transcribed verbatim.

### Analysis

I utilized McCracken's (1988) guidelines in order to discover emerging themes within the interview transcripts. According to McCracken (1988, p. 19), analysis can follow these steps: (a) initial sorting out of important from unimportant data; (b) examination of the slices of data for logical relationships and contradictions; (c) rereading of transcripts to confirm or disconfirm emerging relationships and beginning recognition of general properties of the data; (d) identification of general themes and sorting of the themes in a hierarchical fashion, while discarding those that prove useless in the organization; and (e) a review of the emergent themes for each of the transcripts and determination of how these can be synthesized into themes. Van Manen (1990) describes the thematization process as an attempt to give "shape to the shapeless" (p. 88). Therefore, while the procedures can be described in a clear, linear manner, the actual process is often one which is less clear cut and more spiraling (Wright & Orbe, 2003). For example, in the case of some participants' comments, a single narrative was classified within multiple general themes. Multiple classification was especially common for accounts that were lengthy, as well as for those that, regardless of length, reflected multiple points of analysis.

Following procedures for identifying emerging themes in qualitative data (McCracken, 1988), narratives that focused on identity negotiation were isolated from those discussing other FGC communicative experiences. Three criteria—repetition, recurrence, and forcefulness (Owen, 1984)—helped shape the next step in the analysis process. The *repetition* criterion refers to the repetition of keywords and phrases, and words that are "special" or significant in describing a certain experience or feeling. The *recurrence* criterion examines the meanings that were threaded throughout the text, even if the participants used different wording to represent the same meaning. The *forcefulness* criterion enables the researcher to understand the importance or uniqueness of certain words or phrases. Forcefulness is typically displayed through vocal inflection, volume, or emphasis. Transcription conventions indicated vocal forcefulness within the interview and focus group transcripts by using all capital letters or boldface type.

To allow participants to provide meaningful feedback on how their narratives were analyzed and interpreted, focus groups facilitated at the later stages of data collection were used as a source of member checking (Scheibel, 1992). Replicating a naturalistic inquiry process utilized by Bauer and Orbe (2001), I divided data collection into two parts. Initially, nine focus groups were conducted, and their discussions transcribed and analyzed to reveal 18 different preliminary themes. Once these preliminary topical ideas were established, four additional focus groups were facilitated. The same topical protocol was used for these discussions as for the first nine, but in addition, I also asked participants in these latter groups to provide feedback on the preliminary themes that were beginning to emerge from the thematization process. In this regard, I was able to understand the narratives from participants within a contextual framework broader than any one particular focus-group discussion.

# Findings

The analysis of transcripts generated a number of themes regarding the identity of FGC students. Utilizing the four identity frames of CTI (Hecht, 1993), the findings are organized into two major sections. The first describes various levels of FGC student status among participants (RQ1), while the second shares accounts of how the personal frame of identity is enacted relationally with others (RQ2).

## Centrality of Identity via Personal Frames

*High-salience FGC student identity.* When asked, "How conscious are you about being the first in your family to attend college?", many participants stated that it was something that they thought about "every day." One African American male FGC student attending a selective university explained:

> It sits in my head every day. It's like I know that I'm the first one to get this far for my family . . . I know that my mom is depending on me to make a very good example for my little brother. So, I have to do my best at all times.

Many of the participants described how their FGC student status helped to motivate them at college. Several students of color were particularly adamant in describing how this aspect of their identity is important because it serves as an important link to others in their families who can build on their collegiate success. One African American woman who was excelling at a selective Midwestern university explained:

> Sometimes it gets really hard—What keeps me going is that I am the first in my family [to attend college]. And I have four younger brothers and sisters that look up to me . . . That's what keeps me going instead of just shutting down or throwing a temper tantrum. I just keep going. I can't do anything else but finish.

For some, the centrality of their FGC student identity served as a key motivator for success. However, other participants acknowledged the pressure that this status exerted on their college experiences. Like the student who earlier described his FGC student status as like "sitting in his head everyday," a Latina student from a public university also shared the weight that sometimes accompanied this aspect of her identity:

> I think about it a lot. I stress a lot about classes, knowing that it is all of my family's hopes and dreams . . . everything that they couldn't do, that my brothers and sisters could not do. I'm doing it for everyone. I'm the youngest of four and the first person to graduate from high school, first and only one to attend the university. My dad is one of 12 and my mom is one of 13. Out of all of my dad's side and all of my mom's side, I'm actually the second person to go to the university.

Another European American woman at a more selective university in the same state described how she attempted to avoid the extra pressure that came with being an FGC student:

> I know that I think about it all of the time. Sometimes I try to avoid thinking about it, in terms of being a first generation college student. I just think that, okay, I'm here, I have to do this. I have to get it done. I have to do what I want [to] do—my goals. Okay, I'm the only one. I'm the last one in my family. So, I have to do this. I have to get my college degree and bring it back home to my parents.

For a number of participants, FGC student status functioned as a salient aspect of their identity because of the hardships that they experienced, compared to students who had the benefits of parents who had gone to college. While this was an issue across a number of different focus group students, it seemed most relevant to students who were attending a selective university "where students had a lot of money." Several of the students remarked that "they [had] pretty much put themselves through school," a reality that situated their FGC status as a salient part of their personal identity frame—especially when they lacked the privilege afforded to non-FGC students. One Latina student offered the following example:

> I think about it all the time, especially because they [students whose parents went to college] have so many more benefits than us [FGC students]. Take my one friend, for example. She got the same score on the ACT test that I did. But then her dad made her take that Princeton Review course—paid $800 for her—and then had her retake the test. She got a 27 on it after she scored an 18. I couldn't believe it. I just remember telling my mom, and she was like, "I wish that I could do it for you, but is it that important?"

Another Latina student at the same selective university enumerated additional privileges that non-FGC students unconsciously benefited from:

> Those kids have their own computers in their rooms . . . you stand in line at the computer lab forever—late at night whenever you can get on a computer. But they can get up whenever they want and work on their computer. I don't know . . . they just have that extra edge on everything. I mean they get their books right then and there, but we have to wait until the financial aid checks come in. So, we have to usually spend extra money on the new books. I don't know . . . It's a lot of small things.

*Variable-salience FGC student identity.* Not all participants described their FGC student status as central to their personal frames of identity, however. A focus group comprising women at a large Midwestern public university manifested considerable difference of opinion about FGC status. For example, one European American woman stated, "If I were to describe myself, [FGC student status] wouldn't be the first thing that I would say about myself. It would come closer to the end of the list. It's not a big deal for me. When I talk with other people, it just doesn't come up." However, another European American woman confessed, "I do think about it. I think about it a lot when I start thinking about my family. I am the only one who ever went to college."

When asked directly about the salience of FGC student status on their identity, many participants described it as highly situational. In other words, it was contingent on other things that were going on in their lives. This was most evident when participants discussed different periods of their college years. For example, when asked about how central being an FGC was to her identity, one

European American nontraditional student who was currently working part-time on her Ph.D. at a mid-sized selective university said:

> It depends on what is happening in my life . . . when taking certain classes, I always felt like I didn't know what the heck they were talking about. I felt like I started on a different level than a lot of people. And I was always trying to catch up.

Another student thought about his family's lack of previous experience in college when he chose to attend a local branch campus instead of going away to college. "I thought it would be easier to be at home," he shared.

Two occasions in particular seem to trigger a greater consciousness for FGC students regarding their identities as the first in their families to attend college. The first occasion was during their initial experiences on campus. One Hispanic man, who was attending a large public university, explained the surreal nature of actually being on campus during his first semester:

> I used to think about it a lot at the beginning. I kept thinking about it probably like the entire first month. "Wow, I'm in college. Wow, I'm the first one to go. Wow, I'm going to classes. I have my backpack and everything. I look like those people on TV that go to school."

Another student remembers thinking about being an FGC student during the first few days of class. The normal anxiety of being able to complete the work was magnified by feelings that "people like me don't go to college." She shared with the focus group that she "definitely felt out of place." In fact, she recalled, "looking around at all of the people in the room and thinking: 'I bet all of their parents went to college.'" For many of these participants, becoming acclimated to college life resulted in a reduced level of consciousness of their FGC student status. However, graduation was the second occasion that typically triggered a resurgence in terms of their identity of FGC students. One European American student, who relied on student loans throughout his tenure at a large public university, described how his FGC student status "hit him" when he received notification that he would be "paying the loans back until 2026!" Another FGC student, a Latina from the same university, shared that her feelings of being at a disadvantage resurfaced while she completed graduate school applications. She described "being amazed at the amount of support that her boyfriend [a non-FGC student] got from his family . . . something completely lacking from [her] own family." For many participants, graduation represented a time when they were able to witness exactly how much their accomplishments at college meant to their families. One European American man at a small public university reflected:

> The time that I thought about it most was at graduation. My parents and grandparents were there . . . just seeing the smiles on their faces and how much they enjoyed that . . . that was the most rewarding thing that I had ever gone through.

*Nonsalient FGC student status.* While the vast majority of participants described the central or variable ways in which FGC student status functioned as part of their identity, a small but significant number of participants reported that they had never really thought about being the first in their family to go to college. Most of these individuals reported that the first time they had recognized this aspect of their identities was when they were informed of the study. As one European American man, who attended a community college explained:

> I never thought about it. When I heard about the study . . . that was the first time I thought about [being an FGC student]. I don't think that there is a big difference. Everyone comes to college not knowing any one . . . And we are all here, going to class on the first day. It's all the same.

FGC students who described their status as nonsalient were attending, or had attended, less prestigious campuses (e.g., a local two-year business college). Student comments from students at these schools revealed that being surrounded by students from similar circumstances reduced the likelihood that FGC status served as a point of differentiation in their educational experiences.

In addition, an analysis of the narratives across saliency levels revealed that certain types of students were more likely to regard their FGC status as more salient than others. Students of color, students from a lower socioeconomic status, and nontraditional female students most often described a high saliency regarding their FGC status. In comparison, those FGC students who were White, from a middle to high socioeconomic status, and of traditional college age were more likely to experience being a first-generation college student with variable salience. Interestingly, the only four-year university participants to describe their FGC status as nonsalient were traditionally aged European American male students.

## Enacted and Relational Frames of FGC Student Identity

According to CTI, individuals reveal their identities to others within the enacted frame of identity (Hecht et al., 2003). Decisions about disclosing identity, however, are situated in the context of other frames (or layers) of identity. The interpenetration of layers, or the ways in which each layer is present in one or multiple frames (Golden et al., 2002), made it extremely difficult to thematize FGC student identity messages via four separate sections. Therefore, instead of utilizing the four frames of identity as an organizational structure to address RQ2, I discuss the identity messages of FGC students by comparing and contrasting those that occur at home and on campus in the context of these frames of identity.

*Identity enactment at home.* By definition, being an FGC student is initially manifested with the relational frame of identity. In other words, being a first-generation college student is contingent on the fact that those to which you are relationally tied did not attend college. This is an important consideration given that many participants described that their FGC student status was enacted at home—a context where being a FGC student often emerged as a salient point of difference for family members and friends. This section describes the identity negotiation process, sometimes mutual, sometimes not, that FGC students are challenged by within their home environments.

In several focus-group discussions, participants explained how they were given "special attention" during weekend trips home. Specifically, some FGC students explained that, while they were home, they benefited from special meals, shopping trips, monetary gifts, and extra attention from relatives. One African American student at a large public university explained how he was typically "treated like a king":

> I think about it [being an FGC student] a lot, especially when I go home and visit on the weekends. When I go home, I get treated like a king! I hear that my mom hadn't cooked the whole week, but as soon as I make it in town she's in there cooking up a storm! It definitely comes with its perks. My siblings definitely think that I get more attention now.

Another African American male student from the same university explained that, during his last trip home, his church acknowledged his presence and took up a special offering for him. He went on to explain how others—past classmates and younger children in the neighborhood—always want to talk with him to see how he is doing, something that is tied to "the neighborhood that [he] grew up in . . . only a select few make it out."

African American and Latino FGC students were especially likely to feel that they were representing the larger community back home. One African American man related a story that illustrated how many members of his community regarded him as a liaison to college life:

> So, now when I go home, my mother is quick to say, "Come to work with me." I would go to work with her, but I would basically sit in a chair and watch her do people's hair. All the women will say, "Oh, you are so-so's boy. You are so handsome. You go to college?" . . . They talk to you like you are not a regular person any more. They talked to you like you are—not a superstar—but like you came back from outer space or something. "So what was it like there?"

For several students, additional attention from family and friends was less direct. Some, for instance, described how they would not receive direct messages from family members about the significance of their identity as college students. Instead, they would hear from others that those very family members frequently told them how proud they were. One European American man explained:

> It's weird . . . my older brothers and sisters tell me that my dad keeps telling everyone else how proud he is of me. But I've never heard it from him . . . It's like he's keeping a secret from me that he's proud. He'll tell my brother how proud he is of me. And then I'll walk in the room, [and he'll scream]: "Hey your football team sucks!"

While several individuals described how their FGC student status was enacted at home in positive ways, such was not the case for all participants. Some explained that college was not a topic that was discussed in their home, and they received clear messages that it was to be avoided. One woman explained that part of this, for her, related to sex roles in her culture:

> When you get home, it's like, okay, you are not in this Latina college student identity any more. You are now back home where your college life doesn't matter . . . you have to do what everyone tells you . . . you have to learn to bite your lip.

Several nontraditional female FGC students also explained how they explicitly avoided behaviors that would give prominence to their college studies. For some, including one European American woman who had begun her doctoral studies at a mid-sized selective university, this included avoiding studying around certain family members:

> My husband is still against college . . . I don't really tell him a lot about it. It's like my own little world. He complains when I stay up late studying for tests. For a while I couldn't bring a book out if he was home. He had to be at work or out.

Despite attempts to downplay their identity as FGC students, several participants described instances where it remained a point of contention with others who were perceived to be "threatened by," or "jealous of" their accomplishments. One European American woman explained how this was the case when communicating with one of her older brothers:

> I try to—to be honest with you—avoid acting like I've got all this new information in my head because they don't like it. I have a brother and we usually talk about different things. I can't remember the specific topic, but I asked him, "Where did you read that? Where did you get that statistic from?" He just got irate! "The big college woman wants proof!" He thinks that I've changed, [and am] trying to act better than the rest of them.

While FGC student identity is defined in terms of family, it also impinges on nonfamilial friendships. A European American woman at a mid-sized public university shared a story involving her best friend.

> I have a best friend, and she never went to college. She could paint very well—and she could have had such a great career. But I get . . . I don't know if it is being resentful . . . but it seems as if she just gets mad at me because I am at school trying to do things. When I do go home, she wants to go out to the bar where she works. I usually go for a little while, but when I'm ready to leave, she'll say, "Oh, are you going to get your degree? Too good to hang out with us now?" . . . You do get that friction sometimes which makes it easy to just NOT go home.

***Identity enactment on campus.*** At home, being an FGC student was nearly always salient. Whether communicated overtly or covertly, family and friends would insist on identity negotiation regardless of the students' preference. On campus, however, FGC student identity was enacted mostly at the discretion of the FGC student, since there were no overt identifying markers. Out of the total number of participants, only one (a European American woman) explained that she was proud to disclose that she was an [FGC student] in her conversations with others. Being an FGC student was central to her self-concept and gave her accomplishments particular importance. In comparison, a handful of students stated that they typically did not enact their identity as FGC students to others. For some, especially those who were attending the more selective universities, coming from a family without college degrees was "embarrassing." One African American woman, for example, explained that she didn't want others to think that her parents didn't value education.

> I do think about it [being an FGC student] a lot, but I don't just go around and announce it. I do think about it a lot, and I do know and understand the reasons why neither one of my parents could go. But I don't know if others will understand . . . they may think that my parents don't value what goes on at college.

For these students, a negative stigma was attached to being an FGC student. However, decisions to avoid enacting this aspect of identity were made based on other reasons as well. One European American student at a large public university was clear that the reason why he did not disclose that part of his identity is because he didn't want to be defined primarily as an FGC student.

> I don't really tell other people that I'm first generation, it's something that I just keep to myself . . . but for no particular reason. I just don't feel that they need to know. I don't feel a need to share. I don't want pity or praise for that, I want it for me. First-generation college student . . . that's not how I want to be known. I just want to be known as me, myself.

As revealed in the transcripts, many FGC students assume that most—if not all—of the students that they come into contact with come from families with a legacy of college experience. Such was the case with one nontraditional female student who was attending a community college.

> I definitely felt out of place. I'm looking around at all of the people in the classroom and thinking: "I bet all of their parents went to college." I don't want to tell them that mine didn't . . . I would not tell people . . . I still haven't told people that my mom and dad didn't graduate from high school. I bet I've only told 2–3 people total . . . I kinda wait to see what they are going to say. But, I don't know. I don't want to be the only one in the group whose parents didn't attend college.

Making decisions based on the situational elements inherent in the communication setting (relationship with the other person, timing, context of particular discussion) is common to the identity messages within the enacted frame of identity (Hecht & Faulkner, 2000). For FGC students, this was reflected in explicit identity messages that were enacted once they learned that others were FGC students themselves, or displayed some sensitivity to their experiences. However, in other instances, identity messages were expressed to others who were not aware of the privilege that was associated with having parents who went to college. Such was often the case for FGC students whose roommates seemed to take college less seriously because "it was handed to them on a silver platter by their parents." Within each focus group discussion, participants described their disbelief in terms of how non-FGC roommates treated their college experience. Many recounted how roommates would "sleep until noon," "miss class all the time," and "not study at all," while they "never missed a class despite holding down two jobs to help pay for school." In several instances, FGC students would get so frustrated with these types of roommates that they would confront them by "telling them how lucky they were to have so much family support." Such conversations typically included disclosures about their own backgrounds, reaffirming the vigor in which the FGC students maximized their college experiences.

## Discussion

Results indicated considerable variability among FGC students in terms of the centrality of that aspect of their identities. One of the most important determinants of that salience may have been the demographic composition of the student body on their campus. For example, the two participants quoted in the section on nonsalient FGC student identity both attended a regional campus that served a large proportion of FGC students. In short, these two traditionally aged students—and others like them—less frequently discussed the saliency of being an FGC student than their nontraditionally aged counterparts. Especially during the morning and afternoon hours when these two participants took most of their classes, they were no different than most of the classmates: 18–25-year-old European American FGC students. In this context, they were not "others," but they were members of the predominant group.

The findings highlight three specific points of conclusion. First, the saliency of FGC student status in the overall construction of identity varied greatly. The centrality of FGC student identity was largely influenced by situational context (home versus school) and type of campus (selective, public, community college, or university). Second FGC student status appeared to be more salient when it intersected with other aspects of a person's co-cultural identity, especially those based on race/ethnicity, age, socioeconomic status, and gender. For some FGC students, the privilege associated with being male, European American, middle/upper class, and/or within the traditional age for college students enables FGC student status to remain on the margins of their self-concepts. Third, and finally, FGC students appear to lack any sense of community with other groups of FGC students. The findings reveal that first-generation college students are more likely to feel more comfortable in sharing their experiences with other FGC students; yet, this did not occur as frequently as one would expect. When FGC students did support one another, it was most often done within the context of one or two individuals. For the vast majority of participants, being a part of the study's focus group was the very first time that they knowingly found themselves within a large group of FGC students. In the absence of any particular form of a collective "we," individual relationships with others—family, friends, and roommates—have a greater influence in terms of how their identity is enacted. Each of these three points has clear implications in terms of research, theory, and practice.

## Theoretical Implications

Communication Theory of Identity (CTI) represents a theoretical framework that has great utility for explorations of how multiple identities are negotiated across various contexts. At the core of the theory is the idea that "communication shapes identity while identity shapes communication" (Golden et al., 2002, p. 46). The research described in this manuscript extends a small, but growing, body of research by communication scholars who have used the theory to study the complex ways in which identity is negotiated at multiple layers of interaction. While the study has demonstrated the utility of CTI in framing the identity messages of FGC students, it also has prompted a number of questions. Due to space limitations, I highlight two of the most pressing here.

Unlike most aspects of cultural identity studied by communication scholars, FGC student status does not exist within the context of a larger community with which individuals can identify. Many of the participants of this study were conscious of the unique challenges that came with being the first in the family to attend college, yet were unaware (until learning of the study) of the existing language and research surrounding this phenomenon. This scenario generates a number of questions for scholars interested in studying identity in educational contexts. First, how is identity negotiation affected when a salient aspect of a student's identity exists without any form of communal association? Second, since the communal frame of identity is one of four levels of analysis that are central to the CTI paradigm (e.g., Hecht et al., 2002), does the absence of a communal frame of identity in the case of FGC student identity point to a fundamental flaw of CTI? Does CTI offer some alternate interpretation of this scenario that accommodates and explains a lack of a communal frame of identity? In the context of this study, FGC students appeared to rely more heavily, in the absence of a larger sense of community, on relational frames of identity. Does the same occur for other groups with salient identity markers that may be invisible to others?

A second pressing issue, which has not explicitly been explored in previous CTI studies, involves instances when a person has little choice to enact an aspect of their identity because it is directly or indirectly enacted by others. In more traditional identity theory terms, attributed identity as a college student is often inescapable when FGC students return to their communities of origin, regardless of whether the student chooses to avow such an identity. CTI, through the concept of interpenetration, allows researchers to look simultaneously at the personal, enacted, and relational frames of identity. However, the enacted frame of identity connotes agency on behalf of the individual (i.e., he or she makes decisions to send explicit or implicit messages regarding their identity to others). How would CTI scholars explain interactions where a person has less/no control over when a certain aspect of their identity is enacted within interactions by others?

## Recognizing FGC Identity Negotiation in Classrooms

For those of us who experience higher education from the standpoint of an FGC student, it is clear that the academy changes "foreigners" who enter its culture, more so than being changed by them (Rendon, 1992). While a number of different programs have been developed to increase the enrollment and matriculation of FGC students (Chaffe, 1992; Padron, 1992; Stein, 1992), the impact of these support services on the larger cultural framework of most universities is questionable (Shor, 1987). What has been largely absent from most discussions regarding this issue is the role that faculty members can play in facilitating a cultural environment that enhances the success of FGC students. Accordingly, this final section draws from the findings of this study to discuss how teachers can figure into identity negotiation processes for FGC students. First, I discuss how FGC student status can be added to existing discussions on how various forms of privilege are enacted in the classroom. Second, I identify several challenges faced by professors who are interested in enhancing their communication effectiveness with all students.

In the past ten to 15 years, the concept of privilege has been used to enlighten educators to the small, but significant, ways in which majority group members benefit from existing social, organizational, and societal structures. Initially, this work focused on White privilege and male privilege (e.g., McIntosh, 1988). Recently, Martin and Davis (2001) have offered specific guidelines as to how whiteness can be incorporated into intercultural communication courses. While their work points to an important area of application with communication curricula, I would argue that educators need to gain a greater awareness of various locations of privilege and conduct self-examinations of the current practices, in terms of both pedagogy and curricula. Some current treatments (e.g., Orbe & Harris, 2001) do explain how educators can expand traditional discussions of privilege beyond that which is closely associated with gender and race. By expanding the conversation about relative privilege in society in such a manner, students of all backgrounds can achieve greater consciousness regarding the dynamics of privileges as applied to FGC student status, as well as to age, disability, socioeconomic status, and sexual orientation. Instructors in all manner of classes—not simply those that focus on issues of power, difference, or culture—can find ways to implement such conversations.

As articulated by McIntosh (1989), "unless we study what we haven't noticed, we will never understand what we think we have noticed" (p. 11). Traditionally, the issues of race, ethnicity, and/or gender have taken center stage in terms of research that seeks to make connections between diversity issues and effective communication practices. Research on FGC students can extend this body of research and create new opportunities to explore the complexities regarding multiple-identity negotiation in the college classroom. It also can help sensitize educators to consider the diversity in their classrooms in the broadest possible terms. With an increased awareness of the multidimensional nature of students' identities, teachers can then begin to discern what their role should be in terms of increasing their students' sense of agency as those students negotiate multiple aspects of their identity.

I close this article by identifying several challenges for classroom teachers who are committed to embracing new conceptualizations of multiple diversities. First, acknowledge the diversity within your class beyond that which is most obvious in terms of race, gender, and age. This translates into giving attention to both the visible, and less visible, aspects of each student's identity. Second, do not automatically assume that one aspect of a student's identity is naturally more salient to his or her overall self-concept than others. This is only possible if individuals acknowledge the diversity within cultural group experiences (e.g., not all FGC students come from lower socioeconomic backgrounds). Third, listen carefully to the identity messages that students send in their verbal, nonverbal, and written messages. This process can provide a productive point of reflection in terms of identifying course readings, assignments, and practices that may privilege certain group experiences over others. Each of these challenges speaks specifically to the experiences of FGC students but is also simultaneously applicable to general issues regarding identity, difference, and effective communication—each of which remains crucially important for communication education scholarship.

# References

Allen, B. J. (2002). Goals for emancipatory communication research on black women. In M. Houston & O. I. Davis (Eds.), *Centering ourselves: African American feminist and womanist studies of discourse* (pp. 21–34). Cresskill, NJ: Hampton Press.

Bartels, K. (1995). *Psychosocial predictors of adjustment to the first year of college: A comparison of first-generation and SGCs*. Unpublished doctoral dissertation, University of Missouri-Columbia.

Bartholomae, D. (1985). Inventing the university. In M. Rose (Ed.), *When a writer can't write* (pp. 134–165). New York: Guilford.

Bauer, K., & Orbe, M. (2001). Networking, coping, and communicating about a medical crisis: A phenomenological inquiry of transplant recipient communication. *Health Communication, 13,* 141–161.

Billson, J. M., & Terry, M. B. (1982). In search of the silken purse: Factors in attrition among first-generation students. *College and University, 58,* 57–75.

Brooks-Terry, M. (1988). Tracing the disadvantages of first-generation college students: An application of Sussman's option sequence model. In S. K. Steinmetz (Ed.), *Family support systems across the life span* (pp. 121–134). New York: Plenum Press.

Chaffe, J. (1992). Transforming educational dreams into education reality. In L. S. Zwerling & H. B. London (Eds.), *First-generation students: Confronting the cultural issues* (pp. 81–88). San Francisco, CA: Jossey-Bass.

Fallon, M. V. (1997). The school counselor's role in first generation students' college plans. *The School Counselor, 44,* 384–393.

Golden, D. R., Niles, T. A., & Hecht, M. L. (2002). Jewish American identity. In J. N. Martin, T. K. Nakayama, & L. A. Flores (Eds.), *Readings in intercultural communication: Experiences and contexts* (pp. 44–52). New York: McGraw-Hill.

Hecht, M. L. (1993). 2002—A research odyssey: Toward the development of a communication theory of identity. *Communication Monographs, 60,* 76–81.

Hecht, M. L., & Faulkner, S. (2000). Sometimes Jewish, sometimes not: The closeting of Jewish American identity. *Communication Studies, 51,* 372–387.

Hecht, M. L., Faulkner, S. L., Meyer, C., Niles, T. A., Golden, D. A., & Cutler, M. (2002). Jewish American identity: A communication theory of identity analysis of the television series "Northern Exposure." *Journal of Communication, 52,* 852–869.

Hecht, M. L., Jackson, R. L., Lindsley, S., Strauss, S., & Johnson, K. (2001). Language and ethnicity: Layering identities as frames. In H. Giles & W. P. Robinson (Eds.), *The new handbook of language and social psychology* (2nd ed., pp. 429–450). New York: Wiley.

Hecht, M. L., Jackson, R. L., & Ribeau, S. A. (2003). *African American communication: Exploring identity and culture*. Mahwah, NJ: Lawrence Erlbaum.

Hertel, J. B. (2002). College student generational status: Similarities, differences, and factors in college adjustment. *Psychological Record, 52*(l), 3–18.

Houston, M. (2002). Seeking difference: African Americans in interpersonal communication research, 1975–2000. *Howard Journal of Communications, 13,* 25–41.

Jackson, R. L. (1999). *The negotiation of cultural identity*. Westport, CT: Praeger.

Karabel, J., & Halsey, A. H. (1977). Educational research: A review and interpretation. In J. Karabel & A. H. Halsey (Eds.), *Power and ideology in education* (pp. 323–347). New York: Oxford University Press.

Kiang, P. N. (1992). Issues of curriculum and community for first-generation Asian Americans in college. In L. S. Zwerling & H. B. London (Eds.), *First-generation students: Confronting the cultural issues* (pp. 97–112). San Francisco: Jossey-Bass.

Lara, J. (1992). Reflections: Bridging cultures. In L. S. Zwerling & H. B. London (Eds.), *First-generation students: Confronting the cultural issues* (pp. 65–70). San Francisco: Jossey-Bass.

Lavin, D. E., & Hyllegard, D. (1996). *Changing the odds: Open admissions and the life chances of the disadvantaged*. New Haven, CT: Yale University Press.

London, H. B. (1992). Transformations: Cultural challenges faced by first-generation students. In L. S. Zwerling & H. B. London (Eds.), *First-generation students: Confronting the cultural issues* (pp. 5–12). San Francisco: Jossey-Bass.

MacDermott, K. G., Conn, P. A., & Owen, J. W. (1987). The influence of parental education level on college choice. *Journal of College Admissions, 115,* 3–10.

Martin, J., & Davis, O. I. (2001). Conceptual foundations for teaching about whiteness in intercultural communication courses. *Communication Education, 50,* 298–313.

McCracken, G. (1988). *The long interview*. Newbury Park, CA: Sage.

McIntosh, P. (1988). White privilege and male privilege: A personal account of coming to see correspondence through work in women's studies. *Wellesley College Center for Research on Women Working Paper Series, 189,* 1–19.

McIntosh, P. (1989). Feeling like a fraud: Part Two. *Wellesley College Center for Research on Women Working Paper Series, 37,* 1–14.

National Center for Education Statistics (1998). First-generation students: Undergraduates whose parents never enrolled in postsecondary education. Retrieved December 15, 2002, from http://nces.ed.gov/pubs98/98082.html

Orbe, M. (2003). African American first generation college student communicative experiences. *Electronic Journal of Communication/La Revue Electronique de Communication, 13*(2/3).

Orbe, M., & Harris, T. M. (2001). *Interracial communication: Theory into practice.* Belmont, CA: Wadsworth.

Orozco, C. D. (1999). Factors contributing to the psychosocial adjustment of Mexican American college students. *Dissertation Abstracts International, 59,* 4359.

Owen, W. (1984). Interpretive themes in relational communication. *Quarterly Journal of Speech, 70,* 274–287.

Padron, E. J. (1992). The challenge of first-generation college students: A Miami-Dade perspective. In L. S. Zwerling & H. B. London (Eds.), *First-generation students: Confronting the cultural issues* (pp. 71–80). San Francisco: Jossey-Bass.

Query, J. M., Parry, D., & Flint, L. J. (1992). The relationship among social support, communication competence, and cognitive depression for nontraditional students. *Journal of Applied Communication, 20,* 78–94.

Rendon, L. I. (1992). From the barrio to the academy: Revelations of a Mexican American "scholarship girl." In L. S. Zwerling & H. B. London (Eds.), *First-generation students: Confronting the cultural issues* (pp. 55–64). San Francisco: Jossey-Bass.

Richardson, R. C., & Skinner, E. F. (1992). Helping first-generation minority students achieve degrees. In L. S. Zwerling & H. B. London (Eds.), *First-generation students: Confronting the cultural issues* (pp. 29–44). San Francisco: Jossey-Bass.

Riehl, R. J. (1994). The academic preparation, aspirations, and first-year performance of first-generation students. *College and University, 70,* 14–19.

Rodriguez, R. (1975). Going home again: The new American scholarship boy. *American Scholar, 44,* 15–28.

Rose, M. (1989). *Lives on the boundary: The struggles and achievements of America's underprepared.* New York: The Free Press.

Rose, M. (1995). *Possible lives: The promise of public education in America.* New York: Houghton Mifflin.

Scheibel, D. (1992). Faking identity in clubland: The communicative performance of "fake ID." *Text and Performance Quarterly, 12,* 160–175.

Shor, I. (1987). *Critical teaching and everyday life.* Chicago: University of Chicago Press.

Stein, W. J. (1992). Tribal colleges: A success story. In L. S. Zwerling & H. B. London (Eds.), *First-generation students: Confronting the cultural issues* (pp. 89–96). San Francisco: Jossey-Bass.

Terenzini, P. T., Rendon, L. I., Upcraft, M. L., Millar, S. B., Allison, K. W., Gregg, P. L., & Jalomo, R. (1994). The transition to college: Diverse students, diverse stories. *Research in Higher Education, 35*(1), 57–73.

van Manen, M. (1990). *Researching the lived experience: Human science for action sensitive pedagogy.* Albany: State University of New York Press.

Wright, T. J., & Orbe, M. (2003). Turning the tables of analysis in intercultural communication research: Studying the facework strategies used by "anonymous" European American reviewers. *Howard Journal of Communications, 14,* 1–14.

York-Anderson, D. C., & Bowman, S. L. (1991). Assessing the college knowledge of first-generation and second-generation college students. *Journal of College Student Development, 32,* 116–122.

Zwerling, L. S., & London, H. B. (Eds.) (1992). *First-generation students: Confronting the cultural issues.* San Francisco, CA: Jossey-Bass.

## Unit 3 Additional Recommended Readings*

Alvarez, A. N. (2002). Racial identity and Asian Americans: Supports and challenges. In M. K. McEwen, C. M. Kodama, A. N. Alvarez, S. Lee, & C. T. H. Liang (Eds.), *Working with Asian American college students* (New Directions for Student Services No. 97, pp. 33–43). San Francisco, CA: Jossey-Bass.

Arminio, J. (2001). Exploring the nature of race-related guilt. *Journal of Multicultural Counseling and Development, 29,* 239–252.

Bilodeau, B. (2005). Beyond the gender binary: A case study of two transgender students at a Midwestern research university. *Journal of Gay & Lesbian Issues in Education, 3,* 29–44.

Borrego, S. E. (2004). *Class matters: Beyond access to inclusion.* Washington, DC: NASPA.

Bray, B. (1997). Refuse to kneel. In A. Garrod & C. Larimore (Eds.), *First person, first peoples: Native American college students tell their life stories* (pp. 23–42). Ithaca, NY: Cornell University Press.

Bryant, A. N., Choi, J. Y., & Yasuno, M. (2003). Understanding the religious and spiritual dimensions of students' lives in the first year of college. *Journal of College Student Development, 44,* 723–745.

Carter, K. A. (2000). Transgenderism and college students: Issues of gender identity and its role on our campuses. In V. A. Wall & N. J. Evans (Eds.), *Toward acceptance: Sexual orientation issues on campus* (pp. 261–282). Washington, DC: American College Personnel Association.

Cass, V. C. (1979). Homosexual identity formation: A theoretical model. *Journal of Homosexuality, 4,* 219–235.

D'Augelli, A. R. (1994). Identity development and sexual orientation: Toward a model of lesbian, gay, and bisexual development. In E. J. Trickett, R. J. Watts, & D. Birman (Eds.), *Human diversity* (pp. 312–333). San Francisco, CA: Jossey-Bass.

Davis, T., & Kimmel, M. (in press). The construction of masculinities in guyland. In J. Laker & T. Davis (Eds). *Masculinities in higher education: Theoretical and practical considerations.* New York, NY: Routledge.

Edwards, K. E., & Jones, S. R. (2009). "Putting my man face on": A grounded theory of college men's gender identity development. *Journal of College Student Development, 50,* 210–228.

Eliason, M. J. (1995). Accounts of sexual identity formation in heterosexual students. *Sex Roles, 32,* 821–834.

Erikson, E. H. (1980). *Identity and the life cycle.* New York: W. W. Norton & Company. (Original work published 1959)

Evans, N. J., Assadi, J. L., & Herriott, T. K. (2005). Encouraging the development of disability allies. In R. D. Reason, E. M. Broido, T. L. Davis, & N. J. Evans (Eds.). *Increasing students' development of social justice attitudes and actions* (New Directions for Student Services No. 110, pp. 67–79). San Francisco, CA: Jossey-Bass.

Evans, N. J., & Broido, E. M. Coming out in college residence halls: Negotiation, meaning making, challenges, supports. *Journal of College Student Development, 40,* 658–668.

Evans, N. J., & Herriott, T. K. (2009). Disability theory and its implications for student affairs practice. In J. Higbee & A. Mitchell (Eds.). *Making good on the promise: Student affairs professionals with disabilities.* Lanham, MD: American College Personnel Association.

Fassinger, R. E. (1998). Lesbian, gay, and bisexual identity and student development theory. In R. L. Sanlo (Ed.), *Working with lesbian, gay, bisexual, and transgender college students: A handbook for faculty and administrators* (pp. 13–22). Westport, CT: Greenwood.

Fassinger, R. E., & Arseneau, J. R. (2007). "I'd rather get wet than be under that umbrella": Experiences and identities of lesbian, gay, bisexual, and transgender people. In K. J. Bieschke, R. M. Perez, & K. A. DeBord (Eds.), *Handbook of counseling and psychotherapy with lesbian, gay, bisexual, and transgender clients* (2nd ed., pp. 19–49). Washington, DC: American Psychological Association.

Fhagen-Smith, P. E. (2010). Social class, racial/ethnic identity, and the psychology of "choice". In K. Korgen (Ed.). *Multiracial Americans and social class: The influence of social class on racial identity.* New York, NY: Routledge.

Fhagen-Smith, P. E., Vandiver, B. J., Worrell, F., & Cross, W. E. (in press). (Re)examining racial identity differences across gender, community type, and socioeconomic status among African American college students. *Identity: An International Journal of Research and Theory.*

Fine, M., & Asch, A. (2000). Disability beyond stigma: Social interaction, discrimination, and activism. In M. Adams, W. J. Blumenfeld, R. Castaneda, H. W. Hackman, M. L. Peters, & X. Zuniga (Eds.), *Readings for diversity and social justice* (pp. 330–339). New York: Routledge.

Fox, R. C. (1996). Bisexuality in perspective: A review of theory and research. In B. Firestein (Ed.), *Bisexuality: The psychology and politics of an invisible minority* (pp. 3–50). Thousand Oaks, CA: Sage.

Fries-Britt, S. (2000). Identity development of high-ability Black collegians. In M. B. Baxter Magolda (Ed.), *Teaching to promote intellectual and personal maturity: Incorporating students' worldviews and identities into the learning process* (New Directions for Teaching and Learning No. 82, pp. 55–65.) San Francisco, CA: Jossey-Bass.

Furstenberg, F. F. (2008). The intersections of social class and the transition to adulthood. In J. T. Mortimer (Ed.), *Social class and transitions to adulthood* (New Directions for Child and Adolescent Development No. 119, pp. 1–10.) San Francisco, CA: Jossey-Bass.

Gibson, J. (2006). Disability and clinical competency: An introduction. *The California Psychologist, 39,* 6–10.

Harper, S. R., Harris, F. H., & Mmeje, K. (2005). A theoretical model to explain the overrepresentation of college men among campus judicial offenders: Implications for campus administrators. *NASPA Journal, 42*(4), 565–588.

Harper, S., & Harris, F. (2010). *College men and masculinities: Theory, research, and implications for practice*. San Francisco, CA: Jossey-Bass.

Harris III, F. (2010). College men's meanings of masculinities and contextual influences: Toward a conceptual model. *Journal of College Student Development, 51*, 297–318.

Helms, J. E. (1990). Introduction: Review of racial identity terminology. In J. E. Helms (Ed.), *Black and White racial identity: Theory, research, and practice* (pp. 3–8). Westport, CT: Greenwood Press.

Helms, J. E. (1995). An update of Helms' White and people of color racial identity models. In J. G. Ponterotto, J. M. Casas, L. A. Suzuki, & C. M. Alexander (Eds.), *Handbook of multicultural counseling* (pp. 181–198). Thousand Oaks, CA: Sage.

hooks, b. (2000). *Where we stand: Class matters*. New York, NY: Routledge.

Horse, P. G. (2005). Native American identity. In M. J. T. Fox, S. C. Lowe, & G. S. McClellan (Eds.), *Serving Native American students* (New Directions for Student Services No. 109, pp. 61–68). San Francisco, CA: Jossey-Bass.

Jones, S. J. (1998). Subjectivity and class consciousness: The development of class identity. *Journal of Adult Development, 5*, 145–162.

Jones, S. J. (2003). Complex subjectivities: Class, ethnicity, and race in women's narratives of upward mobility. *Journal of Social Issues, 59*, 803–820.

Jones, S. R. (2009). Constructing identities at the intersections: An autoethnographic exploration of multiple dimensions of identity. *Journal of College Student Development, 50*, 287–304.

Jordan, J. V. (1997). The relational self: A new perspective for understanding women's development. In J. Strauss & G. R. Goethals (Eds.). *The self: Interdisciplinary approaches* (pp. 136–149). New York: Springer-Verlag.

Josselson, R. (1987). *Finding herself: Pathways to identity development in women*. San Francisco, CA: Jossey-Bass.

Josselson, R. (1996). *Revising herself: The story of women's identity from college to midlife*. San Francisco, CA: Jossey-Bass.

Kimmel, M. (2008). *Guyland: The perilous world where boys become men*. New York: Harper Collins.

Kodama, C. M., McEwen, M. K., Liang, C. T. H., & Lee, S. (2002). An Asian American perspective on psychosocial student development theory. In M. K. McEwen, C. M. Kodama, A. N. Alvarez, S. Lee, & C. T. H. Liang (Eds.), *Working with Asian American college students* (New Directions for Student Services No. 97, pp. 45–60). San Francisco, CA: Jossey-Bass.

Korgen, K. O. (Ed.). (2010). Multiracial Americans and social class: The influence of social class on racial identity. London: Routledge.

Laker, J., & Davis, T. (in press). *Masculinities in higher education: Theoretical and practical considerations*. New York: Routledge.

Leach, M. M., Behrens, J. T., & LaFleur, N. K. (2002). White racial identity and White racial consciousness: Similarities, differences, and recommendations. *Journal of Multicultural Counseling and Development, 30*, 66–80.

Levine, H., & Evans, N. J. (1991). The development of gay, lesbian and bisexual identities. In N. J. Evans & V. A. Wall, *Beyond tolerance: Gays, lesbians and bisexuals on campus*. Alexandria, VA: American College Personnel Association.

Levinson, D. J. (1986). A conception of adult development. *American Psychologist, 41*, 3–13.

Marcia, J. E. (1966). Development and validation of ego-identity status. *Journal of Personality and Social Psychology, 3*, 551–558.

McCarn, S. R., & Fassinger, R. E. (1996). Revisioning sexual minority identity formation: A new model of lesbian identity and its implications for counseling and research. *The Counseling Psychologist, 24*, 508–534.

McEwen, M. K., Roper, L. D., Bryant, D. R., & Langa, M. J. (1990). Incorporating the development of African-American students into psychosocial theories of student development. *Journal of College Student Development, 31*, 429–436.

McKinney, J. S. (2005). On the margins: A study of the experiences of transgender college students. *Journal of Gay & Lesbian Issues in Education, 3*, 63–75.

Miville, M. L., Darlington, P., Whitlock, B., & Mulligan, T. (2005). Integrating identities: The relationships of racial, gender, and ego identities among White college students. *Journal of College Student Development, 46*, 157–175.

Mueller, J. A., & Cole, J. (2009). A qualitative examination of heterosexual consciousness among college students. *Journal of College Student Development, 50*, 320–336.

Nash, R. (2001). One group many truths: Constructing a moral conversation. In *Religious Pluralism in the Academy: Opening the Dialogue* (pp. 165–206). New York, NY: Peter Lang.

Nash, R. J. (2007). Understanding and promoting religious pluralism on college campuses. *Spirituality in Higher Education Newsletter, 3*(4), 1–9.

Orbe, M. P. (2008). Theorizing multidimensional identity negotiation: Reflections on the lived experiences of first-generation college students. In M. Azmitia, M. Syed, & K. Radmacher (Eds.), *The intersections of personal and social identities* (New Directions for Child and Adolescent Development No. 120, pp. 81–95). San Francisco, CA: Jossey-Bass.

Ostrove, J. M., & Long, S. M. (2007). Social class and belonging: Implications for college adjustment. *Review of Higher Education, 30*, 363–389.

Phinney, J. S. (1990). Ethnic identity in adolescents and adults: Review of research. *Psychological Bulletin, 108*, 499–514.

Pope, R. L. (1998). The relationship between psychosocial development and racial identity of Black college students. *Journal of College Student Development, 39*, 273–282.

Pope, R. L. (2000). The relationship between psychosocial development and racial identity of college students of color. *Journal of College Student Development, 41*, 304–314.

Quintana, S. M. (2007). Racial and ethnic identity: Developmental perspectives and research. *Journal of Counseling Psychology, 54*, 259–270.

Reeves, P. M. (1999). Psychological development: Becoming a person. In M. C. Clark & R. S. Caffarella (Eds.), *An update on adult development theory: New ways of thinking about the life course* (New Directions for Adult and Continuing Education No. 84, pp. 19–27). San Francisco, CA: Jossey-Bass.

Renn, K. A. (2000). Patterns of situational identity among biracial and multiracial college students. *The Review of Higher Education, 23*, 399–420.

Renn, K. A. (2003). Understanding the identities of mixed race college students through a developmental ecology lens. *Journal of College Student Development, 44*, 383–403.

Renn, K. A. (2007). LGBT student leaders and queer activists: Identities of lesbian, gay, bisexual, transgender, and queer-identified college student leaders and activists. *Journal of College Student Development, 48*, 311–330.

Renn, K. A., & Shang, P. (Eds.). (2008). *Biracial and multiracial students* (New Directions for Student Services No. 123). San Francisco, CA: Jossey-Bass.

Reynolds, A. L., & Pope, R. L. (1991). The complexities of diversity: Exploring multiple oppressions. *Journal of Counseling and Development, 70*, 174–180.

Root, M. P. P. (1995). Resolving "other" status: Identity development of biracial individuals. In N. R. Goldberger & J. B. Veroff (Eds.), *The culture and psychology reader* (pp. 575–593). New York, NY: New York University Press.

Sanford, N. (1962). Developmental status of the entering freshman. In N. Sanford (Ed.), *The American College* (pp. 253–282). New York, NY: Wiley.

Schwartz, J. L., Donovan, J., & Guido-DiBrito, F. (2009). Stories of social class: Self-identified Mexican male college students crack the silence. *Journal of College Student Development, 50*, 50–66.

Seifert, T. A., & Holman-Harmon, N. (2009). Practical implications for student affairs professionals' work in facilitating students' inner development. In S. K. Watt, E. E. Fairchild, & K. M. Goodman (Eds.). *Special issue: Intersections of religious privilege: difficult dialogues and student affairs practice* (New Directions for Student Services No. 125, pp. 13–21) San Francisco, CA: Jossey-Bass.

Small, J. (2008). College student religious affiliation and spiritual identity: A qualitative study (Doctoral dissertation, University of Michigan). Retrieved from http://hdl.handle.net/2027.42/60817

Stamm, L. (2006). The dynamics of spirituality and the religious experience. In A. W. Chickering, J. C. Dalton, & L. Stamm, *Encouraging authenticity and spirituality in higher education* (pp. 37–65). San Francisco, CA: Jossey-Bass.

Stewart, D. L. (2002). The role of faith in the development of an integrated identity: A qualitative study of Black students at a White college. *Journal of College Student Development, 43*, 579–596.

Stewart, D. L. (2009). Perceptions of multiple identities among Black college students. *Journal of College Student Development, 50,* 253–270.

Syed, M., & Azmitia, M. (2008). A narrative approach to ethnic identity development in emerging adulthood: Bringing life to the identity status model. *Developmental Psychology, 44,* 1012–1027.

Taub, D. J., & McEwen, M. K. (1991). Patterns of development of autonomy and mature interpersonal relationships in Black and White undergraduate women. *Journal of College Student Development, 32,* 502–508.

Taub, D. J., & McEwen, M. K. (1992). The relationship racial identity attitudes to autonomy and mature interpersonal relationships in Black and White undergraduate women. *Journal of College Student Development, 33,* 439–446.

Torres, V. (2003). Influences on ethnic identity development of Latino college students in the first two years of college. *Journal of College Student Development, 44,* 532–547.

Torres, V., Howard-Hamilton, M. F., & Cooper, D. L. (2003). *Identity development of diverse populations: Implications for teaching and administration in higher education* (ASHE-ERIC Higher Education Report, 29). San Francisco, CA: Wiley.

Weber, L. (2009). *Understanding race, class, gender, and sexuality: A conceptual framework. (2nd ed.).* New York, NY: McGraw-Hill.

Wentworth, P. A., & Peterson, B. E. (2001). Crossing the line: Case studies of identity development in first-generation college women. *Journal of Adult Development, 8,* 9–21.

Wijeyesinghe, C. L., & Jackson, B. W. (Eds.) (2001). *New perspectives on racial identity development: A theoretical and practical anthology.* New York, NY: New York University Press.

Wilson, A. (1996). How we find ourselves: Identity development and two-spirit people. *Harvard Educational Review, 66,* 303–317.

Worthington, R. L., Savoy, H. B., Dillon, F. R., & Vernaglia, E. R. (2002). Heterosexual identity development: A multidimensional model of individual and social identity. *The Counseling Psychologist, 30,* 496–531.

Yon, D. (2000). *Elusive culture: Schooling, race, and identity in global times.* New York, NY: State University of New York Press.

---

* Given the abundance of recommendations in this unit, sources that address this content as well as another aspect of development (e.g., sexual orientation and cognitive development) are included in the other unit (e.g., cognitive).

# UNIT 4

## COGNITIVE-DIMENSIONS OF DEVELOPMENT (INTELLECTUAL AND MORAL)

# CHAPTER 20
# PATTERNS OF DEVELOPMENT IN THOUGHT AND VALUES OF STUDENTS IN A LIBERAL ARTS COLLEGE

### A Validation of a Scheme

## WILLIAM G. PERRY, JR.
PROJECT DIRECTOR

## CONTRIBUTORS:
## NORMAN A. SPRINTHALL
## JOHN W. WIDEMAN
## FRANK J. JONES

Final Report
Project No. 5-0825
Contract No. SAE-8973

Bureau of Study Counsel
Harvard University
Cambridge, Massachusetts
April 1968

The research reported herein was performed pursuant to a contract with the Office of Education, U.S. Department of Health, Education, and Welfare. Contractors undertaking such projects under Government sponsorship are encouraged to express freely their professional judgment in the conduct of the project. Points of view or opinions stated do not, therefore, necessarily represent official Office of Education position or policy.

U.S. Department of
Health, Education, and Welfare
Office of Education
Bureau of Research

Perry, W. G., Jr. (1970). *Forms of intellectual and ethical development in the college years: A scheme.* Fort Worth, TX: Holt, Reinhart, Winston.

*Note*

Certain sentences, paragraphs and materials pertaining to work completed before the initiation of Contract SAE-8973 are included in the introduction of this report as they appear in W. G. Perry, Jr., *Forms of Intellectual and Ethical Development in the College Years,* Copyright President and Fellows of Harvard College, 1968. For any such sentences, paragraphs and materials appearing in this report: Reproduction in whole or in part is permitted for any purpose of the United States Government.

## Introduction

We summarize here the derivation and nature of the developmental scheme which is tested by the work covered by the report proper. A full account is available in W. G. Perry, *Forms of Intellectual and Ethical Development in the College Years.*\* We refer the reader to that full account for such matters as the historical setting of the study, its philosophical assumptions, its problems of conceptualization, its psychological derivations, its own assumptions about values, its techniques of data gathering, and its relation to the work of the researchers. In this summary, all such matters—including notation of references—will be kept at a minimum in order to present a concise outline of substance fundamental to this report.

## 1. Origins of the Developmental Scheme

In 1954 the staff of the Bureau of Study Counsel at Harvard College undertook to explore the experience of the generality of undergraduates over and beyond those who applied to us for counsel. Our purpose was purely descriptive: to sample the great variety of experience we felt to be represented in the student body. Our work as counselors had, however, given us a particular interest in one aspect of this variety: the great range in the ways in which different students appeared to address the diversity and relativism of thought and values that characterized their liberal education in the setting of a pluralistic university. Our initial intent was simply to collect the accounts of twenty or thirty quite different students as they might tell us about their experience in open interviews at the end of each of their four years in college.

*Procedure*

We started out, then, to illustrate the variety in students' response to the impact of intellectual and moral relativism. Wishing to secure this variety in a small sample of students, we felt it best to obtain the largest possible range between those freshmen bringing with them a strong preference for dualistic, right-wrong thinking and those bringing with them a strong affinity for more qualified, relativistic and contingent thinking. We considered such differences as manifestation of differences in "personality" (in keeping with much psychological thinking of the time). It had not yet occurred to us that it might be more fruitful, at least for our purpose, to consider such differences primarily as expressions of stages in the very experience we were setting out to explore.

Starting, then, from the research on the authoritarian personality (Adorno and Brunswik, *et al.,* 1950) and G. G. Stern's work at Chicago using the *Inventory of Beliefs* (Stern, 1953), we devised a measure which we called *A Checklist of Educational Views* (CLEV). In preliminary trials in 1953 to 1954, the measure promised to identify students along the dimension we desired.

We administered CLEV to a random sample of 313 freshmen in the fall of 1954 and to the same students in the spring of 1955. On the basis of their scores on the measure, we then sent invitations to 55 students, 31 of whom volunteered to tell us in interview about their college experience. Among these freshman were some who had scored at the extreme of dualistic thinking, some at the extreme of contingent thinking, some from the mean, and some who had changed their scores markedly from fall to spring.

---

\*Bureau of Study Counsel, Harvard University, Copyright President and Fellows of Harvard College, 1968.

Our interviews with these students in late May and June of each of their college years resulted in 98 tape-recorded interviews, including 17 complete four-year records. We conducted the interviews themselves in as open-ended a way as possible so as to avoid dictating the structure of a student's thought by the structure of our questions. That is, we asked only for what seemed salient in the student's own experience, beginning interviews with an invitation of the form: "Would you like to say what has stood out for you during the year?" After the student's general statements, we then asked: "As you speak of that, do any particular instances come to mind?" (Cf. Merton, Fiske and Kendall, 1952.)

Perhaps as a consequence of these procedures, the variety in the form and content of the students' reports appeared at first to exceed our expectations and to exclude any possibility of orderly comparison. However, *we gradually came to feel that we could detect behind the individuality of the reports a common sequence of challenges to which each student addressed himself in his own particular way.* For most of the students, their address to these challenges as they experienced them in their academic work, in the social life of the college, and in their extra-curricular activities or employment, seemed to represent a coherent development in the forms in which they functioned intellectually, in the forms in which they experienced values, and the forms in which they construed their world. The reports of those few students who did not evidence this development seemed meaningful as descriptions of deflection from some challenge in the sequence. In this sequence, tendencies toward dualistic thinking and tendencies toward contingent thinking now appeared less as the personal styles we had originally conceived them to be and more saliently as characteristics of stages in the developmental process itself.*

At this point we radically extended the purpose of our study and committed ourselves to experimental as well as descriptive procedures. We undertook 1) to abstract the sequence we had detected in the students' reports to form an articulated developmental scheme, 2) to obtain a larger sample of students' reports of their experience over their four years of college, 3) to prepare the developmental scheme for a test of validity.

1)   We first spelled out the development we saw in the students' reports in first-person phenomenological terms—that is, in the words that might be used by an imaginary "modal" student moving along the center line of that generalized sequence of challenges and resolutions which we thought we saw behind all the variegated reports of our individual volunteers. We then described in abstract terms, from the outside, the structure of each of the major stages (i.e., the more enduring or stable forms in which the students construed the world). Concomitantly, we attempted to articulate those transitional steps (i.e., the more conflicted and unstable forms) which appeared to lead from stage to stage, transforming one structure to the next. With the main theme roughed out, we then traced around it the major variations which our data suggested to us, or which our scheme suggested through its own logic. Among these variations were included those deflections and regressions which we had interpreted as "opting out" or alienation from the course of maturation presumed by the scheme.

2)   To obtain a second and enlarged sample, we sent invitations to 50 freshmen from the Class of '62 and 104 freshmen from the Class of '63. These freshmen were drawn from a random third of their classmates who had filled out a revised form of the *Checklist of Educational Views* in fall and spring. In this instance, however, we ignored their scores on this instrument and selected those we would invite through a random procedure. A total of 109 students responded, resulting later, in June of 1963, in 366 interviews, including 67 complete four-year reports.

3)   Concurrently with sending out invitations to the Second Sample, we returned once again to our developmental scheme in order to reduce its form and terminology to a kind of scale which would be amenable to the tests of validation which are the subject of this report. These efforts resulted in a Glossary of twenty terms to which we ascribed special meanings and a Chart of Development expressing the scheme through a layout on a single sheet. The reader will find this Chart and Glossary at the end of this chapter for reference in connection with the following resumé of the scheme.

---

*The developmental aspect of these tendencies was observed by other researchers of the period (Loevinger, 1959), (Sanford, 1956, 1962), (Harvey, *et al.*, 1961).

## 2. Outline of the Developmental Scheme

### General

The process traced by the scheme may be considered roughly analogous to that which Piaget calls "de-centering" at each of his several "periods" of development (Flavell, 1963). In parallel with Piaget theories also, this "de-centering" will be considered as mediated by "assimilations" and "accommodations" in those structures (roughly Piaget's "schema") through which the person finds meaning in his experiences. Here this process of developing an "equilibrium" between the person and the environment would be considered as occurring at a level or "period" as yet unexplored in Piaget's publications—a period of philosophizing in which the capacity for *meta*-thinking emerges. This capacity provides for detachment, enabling the person to become "his own Piaget" (Bruner, 1959), and involves the person in radical redefinitions of responsibility.

Our scheme departs in major ways from Piagetian forms, but the analogy will serve for initial orientation and will explain in particular why our scheme begins, in Positions 1 and 2, with a recapitulation of highly simplistic and egocentric forms at a philosophical level.*

### Overview of the Scheme

The Chart outlines the nine Positions of development of our scheme, and below these the three conditions of deflection: Temporizing, Escape and Retreat.

Most broadly, the development may be conceived in two major parts centering on Position 5. The outlook of Position 5 is that in which a person first perceives man's knowledge and values as generally relative, contingent and contextual. The sequence of structures preceding this Position describes a person's development from a dualistic absolutism and toward this acceptance of generalized relativism. The sequence following this Position describes a person's subsequent development in orienting himself in a relativistic world through the activity of personal Commitment.

In a somewhat more detailed way of conceiving the scheme, it may be seen in three parts each consisting of three Positions. In Positions 1, 2 and 3, a person modifies an absolutistic right-wrong outlook to make room, in some minimal way, for that simple atomistic pluralism we have called Multiplicity. In Positions 4, 5 and 6 a person accords the diversity of human outlook its full problematic stature, next perceives in the simple pluralism of Multiplicity the patternings of contextual Relativism, and then comes to foresee the necessity of personal Commitment in a relativistic world. Positions 7, 8 and 9 then trace the development of Commitments in the person's actual experience.

The Positions of deflection (Temporizing, Escape and Retreat) offer alternatives at critical points in the development. The scheme assumes that a person may have recourse to them whenever he feels unprepared, resentful, alienated or overwhelmed to a degree which makes his urge to conserve dominant over his urge to progress. In the first three Positions in the development, the challenge is presented by the impact of Multiplicity, in the middle three Positions by the instability of self in a diffuse Relativism, and in the final Positions by the responsibilities of Commitment.

### Layout of the Chart

The main line of development extends from left to right as Position 1, Position 2 through Position 9. Above these headings, overlapping bands group these Positions by the most generalized character-

---

*The most interesting parallel to our scheme lies in the work of Harvey, Hunt and Schroeder (1961) and D. E. Hunt (in Harvey, 1966), work of which we were quite ignorant while completing our formulations in 1960. Terminology differs but the similarities of conceptualization are confirmatory.

istics of their structure: Simple Dualism, Complex Dualism, Relativism and Commitment in Relativism. Each Position is then given its own descriptive title directly below its number. This is followed by a brief outline and diagrammatic representation of the major structure of the Position and its alternates or substructures. The alternatives and substructures of a given Position express the major variations of the central theme as we found them in the students' reports. Or to use another metaphor, various linkages of these options offer alternative routes and by-ways through which the development can be achieved.

Positions departing front the main line of development are represented in parallel to the development, below it on the chart: Temporizing, Escape, and Retreat. The structures of these special categories may have the form of any of the main Positions directly above, with some addition, subtraction, or alteration which functions as a delay, detachment, or rejection of the movement expressed in the main line.

As we expected, no freshman in the study was found to express the structure of Position 1 at the time of his interview in June. A few did attempt to describe themselves as having arrived at college in just such a frame of mind, but none could have remained in it and survived the year. Position 1 is therefore an extrapolation generated by the logic of the scheme. At the end of the year, freshmen normatively expressed the outlooks of Positions 3, 4, or 5. Host seniors were found to function in Positions 6, 7, and 8. The Position at which a student was rated as a freshman was not predictive of the Position at which he would be rated in his senior year.

Position 9 expresses a maturity of outlook and function beyond the level we expected the experience of a college senior to make possible for him, though he might have intimations of it. Like Position 1, it is an extrapolation rounding out the limits of the scheme. On rare occasions, however, one or another of our judges was so impressed with some senior's report that he did rate the student at Position 9. In discussion, the judge would reveal that the rating was a kind of tribute made in humble, and even somewhat envious, respect.

The tests of the scheme's validity covered by the present study concern the reliability of the judges' agreement solely as to the *number of the Position* (and special category of Temporizing, Escape and Retreat) most expressive of a given student's report. The tests do not extend to the judges' agreement about the substructures and stylistic distinctions coded on the Chart. In addition to rating each report as to numerical Position (and special category) the judges did note on their rating forms the coding of the substructure and style they felt to be most evident. Inspection of these ratings suggests to the eye that the judges were in reliable agreement about these finer distinctions, but the demonstration of this reliability required a number of ratings and a complexity of analysis beyond the limits of the present study.

In the summary of the scheme that follows, therefore, we shall describe the abstract outlines of each Position and its major substructures rather baldly, with a minimum attention to particular variations. This generalized description will serve the reader for his purposes in this report, but it will leave each Position rather static and reduce the sense of the scheme's experiential flow. For a livelier portrayal of the students' experience we again refer the reader to the full account (Perry, *op. cit.*) where the richness of the data is explored for its own sake.

### Position 1, Basic Duality

The outlook of Position 1 is one in which the world of knowledge, conduct and values is divided as the small child divides his world between the family and the vague inchoate outside. From this Position, a person construes all issues of truth and morality in the terms of a sweeping and unconsidered differentiation between in-group vs. out-group. This division is between the familiar world of Authority-right-we, as against the alien world of illegitimate-wrong-others. In the familiar world, morality and personal responsibility consist of simple obedience. Even "learning to be independent," as Authority asks one to, consists of learning self-controlled obedience. In the educational aspect of this world, morality consists of committing to memory, through hard work, an array of discrete items—correct responses, answers, and procedures, as assigned by Authority.

This set of assumptions may indeed be the simplest which a person in our culture may hold on epistemological and axiological matters and still be said to make any assumptions at all.

Only three or four of our students seem to have come to college while still viewing the world from this Position's epistemological innocence. Furthermore its assumptions are so incompatible with the culture of a pluralistic university that none of these few could have maintained his innocence and survived to speak to us directly from it in the Spring of his freshman year. Within the confines of our data, therefore, our portrayal of this Position involves inferences beyond those required for structures from which our students spoke directly. The inferences are derived in two ways: 1) by examination of students' efforts to describe the outlook in retrospect, 2) by considering the outlook of students in slightly more advanced positions with the question: What would the world seem like to these students without what they describe as new discoveries?

Our construction from these inferences, however, finds confirmation outside of these data. In our counseling practice we have consulted with entering freshmen who have spoken directly from this structure in sharing with us their efforts to make sense of their new milieu. The outlook is also quite familiar in school settings where it sometimes receives explicit or implicit institutional support. Indeed, there is so little that is novel about it that it finds an almost full expression in the *Book of Genesis*. A freshman looks back:

> S. When I went to my first lecture, what the man said was just like God's word, you know. I believed everything he said, because he was a professor, and he's a Harvard professor, and this was, this was a respected position. And—ah, ah, people said, "Well, so what?" . . . and I began to—ah, realize.

A salient characteristic of this structure, and the source of its innocence, is its lack of any alternative or vantage point from which the person may observe it. Detachment is therefore impossible, especially regarding one's own thought. A person therefore cannot explicitly describe such an outlook while embedded in it. This quality is evident in the difficulty our students experienced in trying to describe the state even in retrospect. Most students who made the effort could shape only such brief summaries as, "Well, *then* I just wouldn't have thought at all," or "These questions [of different points of view] just weren't there to worry over, sort of; I mean, I guess everything seemed too settled. But I wouldn't have even thought of saying *that*."

The following excerpt is from a senior's effort at retrospect:

> S. I certainly couldn't—before that I was, you know, I wouldn't ask. /Yeah/ I wouldn't have—I wouldn't be able to *talk* on this subject at *all*. I mean, the—these four years have really sort of set this all up, because I never read any—well, I've practically never read any philosophies or theologies before, so that what I have is just—well, was *there* you know.

The extraordinary stability of this structure—expressed by the student's remark "I wouldn't *ask*"—results from the consignment of all that might contradict Authority to the outer-darkness of the illegitimate-wrong-other. This dualism leaves the world of Authority free of conflict. All differences from Authority's word, being lumped together with error and evil, have no potential for legitimacy. As illegitimate, they complement and confirm the rightness of Authority instead of calling it into question:

> S. Well I come, I came here from a small town. Midwest, where, well, ah, everyone believed the same things. Everyone's Methodist and everyone's Republican. So, ah, there just wasn't any . . . well that's not quite true . . . there are some Catholics, two families, and I guess they, I heard they were Democrats, but they weren't really, didn't seem to be in town really, I guess. They live over the railroad there and they go to church in the next town.

This structuring of the world is clearly the prototype of the structure of bigotry and intolerance; but in its naive origins, as the above excerpt makes clear, it may simply be the derivative of a homogeneous cultural setting. A person with this kind of outlook, then, cannot be termed intolerant or bigoted until he is confronted with the challenge of change, as he will be in the later Positions.

Epistemologically, the outlook assumes that knowledge consists of a set of right answers known by the Authorities and existing in the Absolute. There is assumed to be a right answer for everything, and all answers are either right or wrong. There are no better or worse answers. In an educational setting, therefore, the comparative merit of students is presumed to be determined by the sum of their right answers minus the sum of their wrong answers, as on spelling tests. From this and the next two Positions, therefore, instructors' efforts to get students to think relativistically will be consistently misperceived, as: "He wants me to put in *more* generalizations," or, conversely, "He wants me to put in *more* facts."

Knowledge and value are closely intertwined. A right answer is valid only if it has been obtained by hard work, and Authority is presumed to know whether the work has been done or not. Against this background the perception that some students receive high grades for little work will precipitate a moral crisis. Acts, like propositions, are also either right or wrong rather than better or worse, and virtue is a quantitative accretion of good deeds balanced by not too many bad deeds, as in "how good I've been this week." Truly qualitative distinctions of better and worse would involve contingent judgments by the observer that are incompatible with the structure. In the same sense there can be nothing truly neutral, only things which are "all right," meaning approved or condoned by Authority and therefore "not wrong." A category for the intrinsically neutral, which opens a domain into which Authority has "no right" to intrude, is a later development (see Multiplicity in Position 4). Here at the outset "all right" means "permitted" and though the category opens some area of freedom and diversity, as for play, it remains strictly within Authority's domain. Obedience, therefore, solves all moral problems.

> S. Well the only thing I could say to a prospective student is just say, "If you come here and do everything you're supposed to do, you'll be all right," that's just about all.

In our records the first loosening and accommodation in this structure will arise from the pressing need to assimilate diversity in the peer group, especially in conversations in the dormitory. This is seconded by a more gradual realization of pluralism in the ranks of society itself. This latter accommodation is facilitated, however, by a differentiation that can be made within the bounds of the structure itself. In its earliest form, no distinction may be made between Authority and Knowledge-in-the-Absolute: "the truth" and "what they want" may be synonymous. However, the very fact that Authorities themselves constantly refer to truth as outside themselves and as binding even upon them—this fact tends to separate out the Absolute from Authority and to give it an existence of its own in a kind of Platonic world of ideas. The system then becomes vulnerable from within, as was the Garden of Eden. The Tree of Knowledge sooner or later may be approached directly without the mediation of Authority. Until this radical approach is made, however, the structure places Authority, especially in educational settings, as the mediator between the student and the Absolute. And if the task of Authority is to mete out knowledge in manageable and digestible portions, this makes instructors vulnerable to judgment as good or bad mediators between the students and the Absolute.

In this distinction, Authorities—as mediators—can even be indulged somewhat by being granted their peculiar interest in "theories" and "interpretations" but only so far as these do not seriously obscure the solid truths it is their duty to communicate:

> S. A certain amount of theory is good but it should not be dominant in a course. I mean theory might be convenient for them, but it's nonetheless—the facts are what's *there*. And I think that should be, that *should* be the main thing.

An instructor can be perceived as failing of adequate mediation on two grounds. The older and admittedly "experienced" instructors are usually perceived as "knowing their subject" but may be criticized for failing of that "teaching method" which outlines procedure:

> S. He must have taught it for the past thirty years. He uses books, but they were, they were very bad. And the teacher himself didn't eluci-, didn't help us much at all. He came in and he would do problems on the board without thinking of whether the, it was ever getting through to the class. And it usually wasn't.

The young teaching assistant, however, is liable to perception as an outright fraud, a kind of older-brother pretender who arrogates the perquisites of Authority without its justification in knowledge:

> S. I don't know how many guys feel that way, but I, I (laughs) feel, I think a lot of the students do. Just—ah, well, they don't have much respect for these men. No kidding, they just don't. They really, they really think, they think sometimes that they just are, the worse things in the world. They ah, and, and I think some of them are not as, half as smart as some of the students there. The students can talk circles around these guys. And it doesn't really do your, do them any good. For one thing, Professor Black who taught us [previously] . . . Christmas! you couldn't lose him on one point. Man, he wouldn't, you couldn't, you couldn't *find* a question *he* couldn't answer. I doubt. And you respected him for it. Not that you're trying to trick the, the section man, but you, when you come up with any kind of a reasonable question, *he* can answer it for you, and he can answer it *well*. Whereas the section men dwiddle around and, and talk a lot of nonsense.

One might suppose that this distinction between good and bad Authority might make possible the direct perception of pluralism in Authority's ranks. In the records expressive of the early Positions in our scheme, however, the assumption that there is one right answer to all questions seems too firm to allow of this assimilation. A revered professor who actually teaches a pluralistic or relativistic address to his own subject is initially misunderstood; he is perceived as "teaching us to think independently," meaning "to find the right answer on our own" (see Positions 2 and 3).

In our records, the confrontation with pluralism occurs most powerfully in the dormitory. Here diversity emerges within the in-group with a starkness unassimilable to the assumptions of Position 1 by any rationalizations whatever. The accommodations of structure forced by this confrontation make possible a more rapid and clear perception of pluralism in the curriculum:

> S. So in my dorm I, we've been—ah, a number of discussions, where, there'll be, well, there's quite a variety in our dorm, Catholic, Protestant, and the rest of them, and a Chinese boy whose parents— ah follow the teachings of Confucianism. He isn't, but his folks are. . . . And a couple of guys are complete—ah agnostics, agnostics. Of course, some people are quite disturbing, they say they're atheists. But they don't go very far, they say they're atheists, but they're not. And then there are, one fellow, who is a deist. And by discussing it—ah, it's the, the sort of thing that, that really—ah awakens you to the fact that—ah . . . (words lost)

Pluralism seems to be perceived next in the readings assigned by Authority in the curriculum.

> S. Well the one thing, I would say, that strikes *me* most, ahh, of course just, just one point—ah, there are many other ones, but I would say that course—ah Philosophy 1b takes up, we've been—ah discussing the modern philosophers, introduction to modern philosophy, it includes—ah the reading of Descartes, Spinoza—Descartes, Spinoza, Hume, Kant and James, and so there, you see it right there, it's the same, same thing, it's, it's a very *wide range*.

In short it appears that it is the extension of potential legitimacy to "otherness" that brings the implicit background of Position 1 into foreground where transformations in its structure may occur. Otherness in the implicit, unquestioned structure had been consigned to an unconsidered limbo— on the other side of the tracks. Pluralism forcefully demands legitimacy in the peer group or is more gradually accorded its legitimacy in the curriculum offered by Authority itself. Its assimilation requires accommodations in the most fundamental assumptions of outlook. These changes can be rapid or extended through time, but our records suggest that there are a limited number of paths through which these changes can lead coherently from Position 1 to a relativistic view of man's predicament. The linkages among the variant structures within Positions 2, 3, and 4 reveal these sequences. The progression is from thinking to meta-thinking, from man as knower to man as critic of his own thought.

### Position 2, Multiplicity Pre-Legitimate

Looking outward through the structural assumptions of Position 1, a student will first perceive such matters as contingencies of thought, contextual considerations, diverse interpretations and relative values as an undifferentiated, unpatterned mass of discrete impedimenta which seem to becloud what should be a direct view of the Right Answers. Where this complexity is presented by Authority itself, which is expected to elucidate the Right Answers, the anomaly may be assimilated to the assumptions of Position 1 in either of two ways. Both of these assimilations reduce complexity to the status of a mere artifact without real epistemological significance. No accommodations need therefore be made in the basic assumptions about the nature of the Truth which is presumed to be "really there" behind the complexity.

The choice between these two assimilations which form the alternative substructures of Position 2 appears to be dictated by the student's temperamental and developmental tendency toward either compliance (Adherence) or revolt (Opposition) in relation to Authority. In the Oppositional alternative, the student perceives the Authorities in question as bad and as failing of their mediational role:

> S. One comes to Harvard expecting all sorts of great things, and then one hits these, these Gen. Ed. courses which are extremely, ah, I don't know, they're just *stupid*, most of them. I've taken two, I'm taking Nat. Sci. and Hum. both of which I found, well, it's an extremely confused sort of affair, nobody seems to know anything. . . . [about Nat. Sci.] It's supposed to teach you to—ah, reason better. That seems to be the, the excuse that natural science people give for these courses, they're supposed to teach you to arrive at more logical conclusions and look at things in a more scientific manner. Actually what you get out of that course is you, you get an idea that science is a terrifically confused thing in which nobody knows what's coming off anyway.

In contrast the more trusting Adherent student sees Authority as presenting complexities for his own good—to help him learn to find the Right Answer on his own:

> S. I found that you've got to find out for yourself. You get to a point where you, ah, see this guy go through this rigamarole and everything and you've got to find out for yourself what he's talking about and think it out for yourself. Then try to get to think on your own. And that's something I never had to do, think things out by myself, I mean. In high school two and two was four; there's nothing to think out there. In here they try to make your mind work, and I didn't realize that last year until the end of the year.

> I. You kept looking for the answer and they wouldn't give it to you . . .?

> S. Yeah, it wasn't in the *book*. And that's what confused me a lot. *Now* I know it isn't in the book for a purpose. We're supposed to think about it and come *up* with the answer!

These two perceptions are equivalent in providing no legitimate place, in their common, epistemological assumptions, for human uncertainty. Truth is not perceived as inherently problematical. Even that procedure which the students will later refer to as "interpretation" is here perceived either as needless confusion or a mere exercise. It is in this sense that we saw them as developmentally equivalent structures in our scheme.*

### Position 3, Multiplicity Subordinate

A Sophomore-to-be is speaking of his preference for physics:

> S. I'd feel (laughs) rather insecure thinking about these philosophical things all the time and not coming up with any definite answers. And definite answers are, well, they, they're sort of my foundation point. In physics you get definite answers to a point. Beyond that point you know there *are* definite answers, but you can't reach them.

---

*In the sense of personal individuation, however, the Oppositional alternative is more advanced: the student taking this stand has dared to set himself apart from Authority in a recapitulation, at a philosophical level, of primary adolescent revolt. Our records reveal, however, a paradox in the consequences of this forward step. In the early Positions of the scheme, a student taking a firm stand in Opposition to Authority rejects the tools of relativistic thinking which his instructors in a modern liberal university are endeavoring to teach. He then has no recourse, but to entrench himself in all-or-none dualistic thought. Ironically, then, the student who is more compliant in these earlier Positions acquires more rapidly the tools of rational and productive dissent. This irony may be shown to result from the revolution in the university's own epistemological assumptions in the past fifty years (see Perry, *op. cit.*) and its consequences will be remarked on below under Retreat and in the Conclusion of this report.

In the concession "but you can't reach them," this student makes room in his epistemology for a legitimate human uncertainty. It is a grudging concession and does not affect the nature of truth itself (only man's relation to it!), but the accommodation has loosened the tie between Authority and the Absolute. Uncertainty is now unavoidable, even in physics. As a consequence, a severe procedural problem becomes unavoidable too. How, in an educational institution where the student's every answer is evaluated, are answers judged? Where even Authority doesn't know the answer yet, is not any answer as good as another?

So far Authority has been perceived as grading on amount of right-ness, achieved by honest hard work, and as adding an occasional bonus for neatness and "good expression." But in the uncertainty of a legitimized Multiplicity, coupled with a freedom that leaves "amount" of work "up to you" and Authority ignorant of how much you do, rightness and hard work vanish as standards. Nothing seems to be left but "good expression":

S. If I present it in the right manner it is well received. Or it is received . . . I don't know, I still haven't exactly caught onto what, what they want.

Authority's maintenance of the old morality of reward for hard work is called into serious question:

S. A lot of people noticed this throughout the year, that the mark isn't proportional to the work. 'Cause on a previous paper I'd done a lot of work and gotten the same mark, and on this one I wasn't expecting it. . . . I just know that you can't, ah, expect your mark in proportion to the amount of work you put in. . . . In prep school it was more of a, more, the relationship was more personal and the teacher could tell whether you were working hard, and he would give you breaks if he knew you were working. It wasn't grading a student on his aptitude, it was grading somewhat on the amount of work he put in.

This amount of uncertainty can again raise Opposition:

S. This place is all full of bull. They don't want anything really honest from you. If you turn in something, a speech that's well written whether it's got one single fact in it or not is beside the point. That's sort of annoying at times, too. You can put things over on people around here; you're almost given to try somehow to sit down and write a paper in an hour, just because you know that whatever it is isn't going to make any difference to anybody.

And temptation is set in the way:

S. It looks to me like it's (laughs) kind of not very good, you know? I mean you can't help but take advantage of these things.

A legitimate though still subordinate place has been accorded for diversity of opinion in Authority's domain. The anomaly of Authority's continuing to grade one's opinions, even in areas of legitimate uncertainty as to the Right Answer, is not satisfactorily resolved by the notion of "good expression." The tension of the guest to find out "what They want" is high.

### Position 4, Multiplicity Correlate or Relativism Subordinate

The students' accounts reveal that in finding some resolution of the question left unanswered by Position 3 they again split into two groups, depending on their tendency toward Opposition or Adherence.

The Oppositional students seize on the notion of legitimate uncertainty as a means of raising Multiplicity to the status of a realm of its own, correlate with and over against the world of Authority in which Right Answers are known. In the new realm, freedom is, or should be, complete: "Everyone has a right to his own opinion," and "They have no right to say we're wrong":

S. I mean if you read them [critics], that's the great thing about a book like *Moby Dick*. [Laughs] *Nobody* understands it!

This new structure, consisting of two domains, represents an accommodation of earlier structures which preserves their fundamental dualistic nature. Instead of the simple dualism of the right-wrong world of Authority, we now have the complex or dual-dualism of a world in which the Authority's dual right-wrong world is one element and Multiplicity is the other. The categorization of all epistemological and moral propositions in accordance with this structure remains atomistic and all-or-none.

The student has thus succeeded in preserving a categorical dualism in his world and at the same time has carved out for himself a domain promising absolute freedom. Here again, then, it is difficult to see how the Oppositional student can assimilate from this structure a perception of contextual relativistic thought. However the structure does derive strength from the daring behind its creation, and it is a strength that can serve the student well in the future. The establishment of a domain separate and equal to that of Authority, in which the self takes a stand in chaos, will provide (once contextual thought is discovered to provide some order) a platform from which certain Authorities, and knowledge itself, may be viewed with entirely new eyes.

By whatever means it is discovered, the bridge to the new world of comparative thought will lie in the distinction between *an* opinion (however well "expressed") and a *supported* opinion:

> S. Well—it's an opinion, but it's got to be an educated opinion. Have something behind it, not just a hearsay opinion. I mean, you can't form an opinion unless you have some knowledge behind it, I suppose.

In this transitional statement it is not yet clear that a better opinion would not still be one which simply has "more" knowledge behind it in the purely quantitative sense; and yet an "educated" opinion is surely something else than a right answer or a wrong answer or *any* opinion. The step to truly qualitative comparison is now a short one.

There is, however, another pathway from Position 3 to the vision of general Relativism in Position 5. This path, which the majority of our students followed, does not involve setting Multiplicity, as a world of its own, over against the world of Authority. Rather, it allows the discovery of Relativism in Multiplicity to occur in the context of Authority's world where Multiplicity is still a subordinate to Authority as something "They want us to work on" (Relativism Subordinate):

> S. Another thing I've noticed about this more concrete and complex approach—you can get away without . . . trying to think about what they want—ah, think about things the *way* they want you to think about them. But if you try to use the approach the course outlines, then you find yourself thinking in *complex terms*: weighing more than one factor in trying to develop your own opinion. Somehow, for me, just doing that has become extended beyond the courses. . . . Somehow what I think about things now seems to be more—ah, it's hard to say right or wrong—but it seems (pause) more *sensible.*

Here the correction from "what they want" to "the *way* they want you to think" signals the discovery of the articulation of the "concrete" with the "complex" in "weighing" in Multiplicity—a mode of thought which is the structural foundation of Relativism. The weighing of "more than one factor," or, as this student later explained, "more than one approach to a problem," forces a comparison of patterns of thought, that is, a thinking about thinking. For most students, as for this student, the event seems to be conscious and explicit; that is, the initial discovery of meta-thought occurs vividly in foreground, as figure, against the background of previous ways of thinking, and usually as an item in the context of "what They want."

Now the capacity to compare different approaches to a problem in "developing one's own opinion" is presumably the ordinary meaning of "independent thought." The paradox for liberal education lies in the fact that so many of our students learned to think this way because it was "the way They want you to think," that is, out of a desire to conform. The challenge of a more genuine independence then confronted these students in the revolutionary perception of the general relativism of all knowledge, including the knowledge possessed by Authority itself (Position 5).

### Position 5, Relativism Correlate, Competing, or Diffuse

Up to this point the students have been able to assimilate the new, in one way or another, to the fundamental dualistic structure with which they began. The new, to the extent that it has been anomalous or contradictory, has naturally forced them to make certain accommodations in the structure, but these have been achieved either by the elaboration of dualism into a dual dualism or by the addition of a new subcategory of "critical thinking" to the general category of "what Authority wants."

The students now achieve a revolution in their view of the world by making a transposition in the hierarchy or forms of Position 4. They promote Relativism from its status as a special case (or subordinate part within a broad dualistic context) to the status of context, and within this new context they consign dualism to the subordinate status of a special case.

A student makes a transitional statement in which the revolution is all but complete; in context his word "complexity" refers to a relativistic approach to knowledge:

> S. I don't know if complexity itself is always necessary. I'm not sure. But if complexity is *not* necessary, at least you have to find that it *is* not necessary before you can decide, "Well, this particular problem needs only the simple approach."

Here it is the "simple" right-or-wrong that has become a special case. The student now finds it safer to assume complexity as a general state and then to discover simplicity if it happens to be there. The statement would represent the fully-developed structure of Position 5 except for the fact that the "simple," when it occurs, is still assumed to *be* simple and not itself a derivative of complexity (e.g., 2 + 2 *does* equal 4; the simplicity of the proposition is not perceived as a derivative within a relativistic theory of sets).

The notion that some or most knowledge may be relativistic while some remains absolute and dualistic is the structuring we termed Relativism Correlate. In other records, where the student wavered between absolutistic and relativistic assumptions without appearing to notice that he held two incompatible generalized frames, we called the structure Relativism Competing. Both of these structures may be considered partly transitional. The complete revolution, expressed in the assumption of general Relativism in all knowledge, we named Relativism Diffuse.

The nature of this revolution of outlook—through a transposition between the structure of part and the structure of context—has been revealed as a major strategy in the development of scientific theory (Kuhn 1962). As a strategy of personal growth it would seem to deserve a prominent place not only in theory of cognitive development but also in consideration of emotional maturation and the formation of identity.

The vision of generalized Relativism, and of the procedural skills of contextual analysis and comparison appropriate to it, provides students with a new sense of having "caught on" in their studies and of possessing a new way of looking at life:

> S. It's a method that you're dealing with, not, not a substance. It's a method, a purpose—ah, "procedure" would be the best word I should imagine, that you're, that you're looking for. And once you've developed this procedure in one field, I think the important part is to be able to transfer it to another field, and the example that I brought up about working with this, this crew of men. It's probably—ah, the most outstanding at least one of the achievements that I feel that I've been able to make as far as transferring my academic experience to the field of everyday life.

It presents a serious problem, however. This is the problem of identity and decision making in a world devoid of certainty, a world in which differing values may be legitimate on differing grounds:

> S. It has involved the tearing away of a lot of beliefs in what has been imposed by convention and I think that it does come down to you tearing away your faith in the fact that—ah . . . [seeing that] conforming to any standard, that other people have decided, is selfish. I'm (laughs) not trying to drum it up into an emotional issue, but it's that on the important questions of what you're going to do, well, then I think you do see that ideals that have been set up elsewhere aren't necessarily the right thing. And you're exposed to more—ah, perfect ways of life that contradict each other. And you sort of wonder how could *all* the things be perfect?
>
> You know, in the past months, it's been a matter of having really . . . having reduced to the level where I really wasn't sure there was anything in particular to follow. I, you do begin to wonder on what basis you'd judge *any* decision at all, 'cause there really isn't—ah . . . too much of an absolute you can rely on as to . . . and even as to whether . . . there are a lot of levels that you can tear it apart, or you can base an ethical system that's a, presupposes that there are men who . . . or you can get one that doesn't presuppose that anything exists . . . and try and figure out of what principles

you're going to decide any issue. Well, it's just that right now I'm not sure that, . . . of what the—ah, what those de—, how to make any decision at all. When you're here and are having the issues sort of thrust in your face at times . . . that is, just seeing the thinking of these men who have pushed their thought to the absolute limit to try and find out what was their personal salvation, and just seeing how that fell short of an all-encompassing answer to, for everyone. That those ideas really are individualized. And you begin to have respect for how great their thought could be, without its being absolute.

It is this problem, then, that confronts the student with the realization that he, too, faces the challenge of taking a stand, of affirming his own values and decisions through acts of personal Commitment, and that these Commitments will require of him not only all the reason at his disposal but the courage of something beyond the security which reason alone can provide.

### Position 6, Commitment Foreseen

In this study the word Commitment refers to a person's affirmative acts of choice and orientation in a relative world. The upper case "C" is used to distinguish such acts from unconsidered commitments deriving solely from familial and cultural absorptions in a dualistic world. The difference has its analogy in the theological distinction between Faith, affirmed in doubt, and simple belief. An illustration from our records would be a student who had always shared the familial expectation that he would go to medical school, and, when admitted, suddenly faced for the first time the real decision of whether he wished to become a doctor.

In common usage the word often refers more narrowly to the object or content of Commitment alone rather than to the whole act or relation. Thus, "a man's commitments" may suggest his wife, children, job, and whatever obligations or causes or expectancies he has undertaken. If, however, one includes not only these external objects but also a man's acts of choice, and the personal investment he makes in them, the word refers to an affirmatory experience through which the man continuously defines his identity and his involvements in the world (cf. Polanyi, 1958).*

This experience is then characterized by its stylistic qualities as well as by content. These qualities involve decisions as to balance in dimensions such as: narrowness vs. breadth, number vs. intensity, wholeheartedness vs. tentativeness, stability vs. flexibility, continuity vs. diversity, etc. Space will not allow of illustrations of these stylistic issues here, but it is important to note their importance for the person. Identity derives from both the content and the forms, or stylistic aspects, of commitments, e.g., "I am a politician" and "I find I really prefer a wide range of acquaintances to narrowing down to one or two close friends." The stylistic, however, often feels to the person more proximal to the self, being experienced as the origin of choices in content, e.g., "I'm just the kind of person who ought never to get married." Being proximal, stylistic affirmations usually feel less open to alternatives than the area in which they find expression: "It doesn't matter what I'm doing so long as I feel I'm building something."

For the purposes of this scheme, Commitments are considered creative acts of structuring in that through them the individual orients himself in a world perceived as relativistic in knowledge and values. In Position 6 Commitments are foreseen as necessary to a responsible life, but they have not yet been made and experienced:

S. A lot of people must go through a phase of sort of finding themselves alone in the world, in a way. Sort of splitting away from their family to some extent, if it's only geographically. Sometimes not geographically; he could be at home and the same thing might happen, but geography emphasizes it. And, and then they must work out new relationships to the world, I think.

---

*There are, of course, aspects of identity that appear to be passively acquired and none of one's doing, such as one's height, one's limp, or the fact that as a child one was never schooled in the arts. The question is, however, one's address to these facts: One can refuse to "accept" them, investing one's honor in stubborn battle against the irremediable; one can "resign" oneself, denying any responsibility; or one can affirm, "I *am* one who is so high, limps, and wishes he had been schooled in the arts as a child. This is part of who I am."

S. There was one other thing I expected—I expected that when I got to Harvard—I was—ah slightly ahead of my time in that I was an atheist before I got here—I came up here expecting that Harvard would teach me one universal truth . . . (pause). Took me quite a while to figure out . . . that if I was going for a universal truth or something to believe in, it had to come within me.

The initial intimation of the need for Commitment may come in any content area: vocation, standards of conduct, involvement in academic work, extra-curricular activities, or religion. It usually awakens a fear of a "narrowing" which is too reminiscent of the old dualistic narrowness from which the student has so recently emerged:

S. Just have to sort of make the most of it, as it comes, and I say that's one thing you learn out of college that life is, is not one set narrow little plain. You just have to sort of, it's a very big thing, you just sort of have to ma—make your way through it as best you can after you've, experience of course is always the best teacher. That's just a question of, well, say, broadening your outlook and learning to be yourself. Everybody they say as they get older tends to get more set in their ways but we hope not. If, if we can stay flexible as much as you can, it's better. It's not good to get too narrow-minded or set in your ways.

One must somehow hold one's breath and plunge, trusting:

S. You just have to jump into it, that's all, before, before it can have any effect on you. And the farther in you force yourself to get in the first place, the more possibilities there are, the more ideas and concepts there are that can impinge on you and so the more likely you are to get involved in it. Actually you have to make some kind of an assumption in the first place that it's worthwhile to get into it, and that you're capable of doing something once you get into it.

### Position 7, Initial Commitment

This Position is marked quite simply by the student's report of some first experience of Commitment:

S. This may sound sort of silly, but I've developed a sense of, ah, a set of morals. I never had to use them before I got here, but since I got here and, ah, have seen what goes on—they may be unusual, sort of but I don't think so—I, ah, had to develop them because it's something I never ran into before. It's, well, I'm out of high school now, I'm out of that sort of thing, kid stuff I might call it now. I'm a freshman in college, I find that kid stuff kind of ridiculous. Ah, here I'm out in the big world, more or less. And I've come to things and decisions I've never had to make before, and I've made them. And afterwards, thinking it over, I've said I've done this because, well, it was right, and the alternative wouldn't have suited me and I wouldn't have felt good about it. Ah, maybe somebody else wouldn't have cared, maybe somebody else would have told me just the opposite.

From this experience there begins to evolve a more intimate realization of its nature:

S. There are so many values you can't possibly line up all of them. Maybe what you do is pick out one, or two, or three, after a while. It's not a fast thing. It's slow. But you pick out something that you kind of like after a while, rather than trying to do what you see is being liked. I mean, you come here, and you get a total view of everything, and you see a whole lot of values. I mean, you're confronted with them. Every one of them is a good thing in its own way, and so you instinctively want to be at least a little bit aware and take part in all of them. But you can't. I mean, it's impossible just from a pure mechanical point of spending time. You kind of focus on the type of career you want and when you think about that, then if you're going to work toward it, it has its own imperatives. It means that you have to drop certain things and focus more on others. If you want to teach, that means you emphasize studies and drop clubs, and a certain amount of social life and some athletics. You just let these things become peripheral. (Pause) And you're sure about that.

The further unfolding of the personal meaning of Commitment as an on-going activity—particularly in that balancing of its qualitative aspects from which one creates one's life style—will be represented in Positions 8 and 9.

### Position 8, Orientation in Implications of Commitment
### Position 9, Developing Commitments

In these last Positions of development the steps are qualitative rather than structural, representing degrees of ripeness in an art of living. Position 8 represents a period of exploration of the implications of Commitment(s) made. The initial Commitment, say of "deciding what I want to do," does not solve as many problems as was hoped; indeed it raises others:

> S. I don't think it reduces the number of problems I face or uncertainties, it just was something that troubled me that I thought was—I always thought that it was an unnecessary problem and based on my limited experience with a broadened world . . . (Now) I don't see it as something that is passed; it is something I have to decide continually.

Many of these new problems are the stylistic issues mentioned above, such as those of tentativeness vs. certainty:

> S. [correcting his own word] Well "tentative" implies . . . perhaps, I mean, uncertainty and, and, readiness to change to anything, and—ah, it's not that. It's openness to change but, but not looking for change, you know—ah. . . . At the same time—ah, believing pretty strongly in what you do believe, and so it's not, you know, it's not tentative. . . .

And again:

> S. So it's a commitment. It's a real, definite commitment, with a possibility of (laughs) of withdrawing from the commitment, which I think is the only realistic kind of commitment I can make, because there *is* a possibility of change here.

And between contemplative awareness and action:

> S. I don't . . . I don't brood. . . . I think that's a waste of time (laughing), I mean I'd rather do something than just sit around and . . . brood about it. Sometimes I . . . I'm just about . . . sometimes you do hasty things . . . it's a certain amount of relief to . . . just . . . just to do something. But . . . now the only . . . the only broodiness is sort of an inward broodiness . . . about whether . . . whether I'm on the right track . . . the right field. There are all kinds of pulls, pressures and so forth . . . parents . . . this thing and that thing . . . but there comes a time when you just have to say, "Well . . . I've got a life to live . . . I want to live it this way. I welcome suggestions. I'll listen to them. But when I make up my mind, it's going to be me. I'll take the consequences."

The elaborations of these evolving experiences require illustration by excerpts too lengthy to include here. Their destiny is clearly suggested in several of our students' records: a way of life in which the person finds in the development of his Commitments, and in the style of his responsibility, a sense not only of his identity but of his community. Position 9, representing this open and developing maturity, rounds out the scheme. We had thought the Position might lie beyond that reach which experience could provide a college student, but the judges did in fact use the rating on occasion. The average rating for one senior placed him between Positions 8 and 9.

In view of popular notions of this particular generation of students as "uncommitted," "alienated," or "silent," the following finding of this study seems impressive: on the basis of their average rating by the judges, *seventy-five per cent of our sample were judged to have attained the degree of Commitment characterized by Positions 7 and 8.* A sense of the meaningfulness with which the judges used the concept of Commitment to describe the maturation evident in the students' reports may be derived from two tables:

## TABLE 1

### Number of Seniors with Average Rating in Positions of Commitment
(Total Sample N=20)

|  | Position | N |
|---|---|---|
| Average rating | 6.5–7.4 | 8 seniors |
| Average rating | 7.5–8.4 | 7 seniors |
| Total |  | 15 |

## TABLE 2

### Instances of Individual Ratings in Positions of Commitment
(Six Judges, 20 Students = 120 Ratings per Year)

| Position | Fresh | Soph | Junior | Senior |
|---|---|---|---|---|
| 7 (Initial Commitment) | 3 | 11 | 48 | 42 |
| 8 (Experience of Implications) | 0 | 0 | 14 | 55 |
| 9 (Developing Commitment) | 0 | 0 | 0 | 13 |
| Totals | 3 | 11 | 62 | 110 |

(*Note:* the reliability of ratings was proved to be independent of the judge's knowledge of a student's year in college.)

### *Alternatives to Growth: Temporizing, Retreat, Escape*

In any of the Positions in the main line of development a person may suspend, nullify, or even reverse the process of growth as our scheme defines it: 1) He may pause for a year or more often quite aware of the step that lies ahead of him, as if waiting or gathering his forces (Temporizing). 2) He may settle for exploiting the detachment offered by some middle Position on the scale, in the avoidance of personal responsibility known as alienation (Escape). 3) He may entrench himself, in anger and hatred of "otherness," in the white vs. black dualism of the early Positions (Retreat).

*Temporizing*, defined as a pause in growth over a full academic year, does not itself involve alienation, even though it may contain that potential. Sometimes it is even a time of what one might call lateral growth—a spreading out and a consolidation of the structure of a Position recently attained. At other times it seems more fallow, suspended, poised. Often enough a student will say, "I'm just not ready yet."

The destiny of such periods—whether they will terminate in a resumption of growth or in a drifting into Escape—seems to be foretold in the tone in which a student waits. He may speak as one waiting for agency to rise within himself, for himself to participate again in responsibility for his growth. Or he may speak as one waiting for something to happen to him, something to turn up that will interest him enough to solve all problems.

Temporizing can occur at any Position on our scale. Here, for example, a sophomore finds himself still wandering, after two years, in the diffuse relativism of Position 5 into which his opposition to Authority had led him in high school:

S. Well, I can't say much except a complete ah, relativistic outlook on everything. I used to be a very militant agnostic in high school, and though I'm no longer militant, I'm . . . still an agnostic, I don't do the debating with anybody any more, probably because I've come to the conclusion that in many respects the other side is quite worthwhile for a great many people . . . and . . . even for me perhaps thirty years from now. But not right at the moment. I've become, my whole dominant theme has been sort of just a pragmatic approach to everything. At times I feel this is highly inadequate and it perhaps is just all an excuse for . . . thinking what you want to think.

But I can't see any other answer to the problem. It doesn't seem possible to, to, to determine any absolute, so . . . so I'm sort of stuck with the relativism that leaves me a little bit dissatisfied. . . . It's still basically the same relativism that I, that I had when I was back in high school.

Waiting for experience to inform one can slip toward letting fate be responsible:

S.  Well, I've got a pretty—well my problem is that I've got a clear view of three or four things that I'd like to be doing. Can't for the life of me figure out which one I want to follow. Ah, foreign service, college teaching, politics. . . . I don't know which one I want to follow. Again here is the—ah . . . the problem, I think, is . . . one between activism and detached analysis, and I can't figure out which one, ah, I'm best for, and whether I can figure out a synthesis of both in some field. I don't know, perhaps I'll wait and see what, see what time brings, see if I pass the foreign service exam. Let that decide.

Followed a few steps further, the temptation leads into the style of alienation and irresponsibility we call *Escape*. "Temptation" and "irresponsibility" are moral terms, and I use them advisedly. In our records, students who speak from Escape express guilt—a malaise they experience not so much in regard to the social responsibilities from which they are alienated as in regard to their own failure toward themselves.

Our records reveal two roads leading to two forms of Escape which differ in quality and structure. The following excerpts illustrate mid-points along each of these roads. The first leads toward a limp dissociation:

S.  It ah, . . . well, I really, I don't know, I just, I don't get particularly worked up over things. I don't react too strongly. So that I can't think. I'm still waiting for the event, you know, everyone goes through life thinking that something's gonna happen, and I don't think it happened this year. So we'll just leave that for the future. Mainly you're, you're waiting for yourself to change, see after you get a good idea, continued trial and effort, exactly how you're going to act in any period of time, once you get this idea, then you're constantly waiting for the big change in your life. And, it certainly didn't happen this year. . . .

"Dissociation," the term we used to denote the potential of this "drifting," refers to a passive delegation of all responsibility to fate. Its tone is depressed, even when pleasure is still possible in irresponsibility. The sense of active participation as an agent in the growth of one's identity is abandoned. Its final destiny lies in the depersonalized looseness of Multiplicity (Multiplicity Correlate, Position 4) dissociated from the challenge of meaning.

In contrast, the more strenuous intellectual demands of Relativism provide an escape in which a vestigial identity can be maintained in sheer competence. Here the self is a doer, or a gamesman, and its opportunism is defended by an encapsulation in activity, sealed off from the implications of deeper values.

S.  I know that I had trouble—ah first of all in just listening to the lectures, trying to make out what they meant. . . . These—ah—ah, the pursuit of the absolute first of all. . . . And then I . . . (laughs) sort of lost the absolute, and stuff like that. I think that gradually it sunk in, and, I don't know, maybe it's just. . . . Well, it came to me the other night: if relativity is true on most things, it's an easy way out. But I don't think that's . . . maybe that's just the way I think now. . . . Well, in, in a sense I mean that you don't have to commit yourself. And maybe that's just the push button I use on myself . . . right now, because I am uncommitted.

The sense of full alienation in either of these modes of Escape cannot be conveyed by short excerpts, but the following are suggestive if considered as expressive of the tone of an entire report: Dissociation:

S.  I never get particularly upset about anything, but my father feels I'm wasting my time and potential and his money, and all that. But I don't know, I don't really see any way this thing can be resolved; I've just accepted it. . . . But I would like to make my peace with the family.

S.  I can always rationalize my way out of anything. I mean, if I ever start to feel this way, I feel that it's all sort of futile; I haven't done anything yet and it's too late, why start now? . . . defeated, and all that. Oh, I can always find something to do to forget about it, or just tell myself it's ridiculous, and it never really bothers me for any length of time.

S. I've thought quite a bit about this: I've never really identified myself definitely with anything. I hadn't permitted myself to so far as grades were concerned or as far as friends—particularly in a few isolated cases. I had just a sort of "I'm me, and I just like to stand out there and look things over" attitude, and I don't know whether this is good or bad.

S. It turns out to be tough because of the fact that, that you have these courses that tempt you to, to not do anything at all about them and therefore you're apt to, ah, get slightly lower grades than you would anyway, and it was, you know, what the heck, I wasn't interested anyway—next year, you know, it'll all be different when I'll be able to take almost all courses that I want to take, and so forth and so forth.

Encapsulation:

S. It seems to me that the security that you gain from knowing how you're going to handle . . . a situation which isn't really that important now . . . is completely overshadowed by the worry . . . that it causes if you try to ascertain what you're going to do. And I think . . . oh, if you have, if your development is such that you can handle situations as they arise . . . and that you have more or less an intelligent point of view and a rational outlook, that you could solve any problem that comes up with a minimum of time, trouble, and . . . I don't think that it's necessary to worry about things so far in the future. I mean, opportunities may present themselves, or completely change my life, and the, the, and of course my wife and baby's life, too, I may be offered who knows what, right after I graduate, you know, you never know, and there's no chance of really—ah . . . planning so far ahead as to take into account; you can't do it. . . .

It's just like, I mean, it's just like playing football. As long as you have the right position and the right balance now, you're ready for anything that may come, . . . whereas, if you plan for one special move, a change of plan on the opponent's side and you're right off on left field, and get faked out. As long as you're ready for anything and, and, and, and in good condition, more or less, and in football it takes a good body and a clear mind, and the same thing applies to . . . anything in general and being alert you're ready to . . . handle any situation as it arises and that's more or less the "full philosophy," unquote, that I've, that I've used throughout my life . . . if I may be so bold as to say that; and . . . since I, it has been successful for me, and I've, I've found it very satisfactory to me, I . . . that's, that's just the way it is with me. And I don't think I recommend it for anyone, of course. I, I'd be a fool to, but I do think it has its merits, and for me it's the, the one way to do things.

S. So the best thing I have to do is just forget about deciding, and try to . . . I mean, not give up on any scheming or any basic set of ideas . . . that'll give myself, they'll give me a direction. Just give up completely, and when it comes down to individual choices, make them on what I feel like doing emotionally at the moment.

A particular form of Escape, long recognized by philosophers and theologians, is "escape into commitment." The distinction between Commitment as a step of growth *in* a relativistic world and commitment as an escape *from* complexity is usually quite clear in our records. In the latter, commitment is yearned for as a reinstitution of embeddedness. The hope seems to be that through intensity of focus, all ambivalences will be magically resolved. The event is envisaged either as something one hurls oneself into through despair of choosing, or as some "interest" that emerges from the environment to absorb one totally, and blessedly.

S. It would be great if a bolt of lightning comes down, in some way I could be tested, and find out that I have a great talent for music (laughs) and then really just drop everything and go into that. But I'm sure it won't happen, or I'm almost sure. But it could just as well be anything as music.

And yet, one can be aware of the irresponsibility of the principle that *any* commitment is *better* than *no* Commitments:

S. I've seen this all along: withdraw into your shell; this is the easy way, I mean you could take a basic, just a fundamental commitment and be done with it.

C. And be done with it. Yes. There you are.

S. That's an easy way out. The other way is pretty frustrating.

Perhaps, though, it only seems as if it would be easy, or *easier*. Some one all-encompassing "shell" of a "commitment" would promise protection from all the complexity, all the competing responsibilities that threaten to overwhelm one's freedom with their demands, or to leave one paralyzed, as a student put it "like a donkey between forty bales of hay." However the sustained denial of one's realization is known to require immense energy.

This energy is evident in the dogmatic moral intensity of that reactive entrenchment in Positions 2 or 3 which we termed *Retreat*. In Position 1, we noted, "prejudice" and intolerance were inherent structurally, but the enemy of "bad others" was far away. The main line of development has traced the growing person's assimilation of the diversity of others' views and the evolution of a rational basis for tolerance in the midst of Commitment in a relativistic world. In this tolerance one may fight for one's own beliefs but in full respect for the rights of others.

Under stress (of fear, anger, extreme moral arousal, or simple overburden of complexity) it is possible to take refuge in the all-or-none forms of early dualism. At this point reactive adherence to Authority (the "reactionary") requires violent repudiation of otherness and of complexity. Similarly, reactive opposition to Authority (the "dogmatic rebel") requires an equally absolutistic rejection of any "establishment." Threatened by a proximate challenge, this entrenchment can call forth in its defense hate, projection, and denial of all distinctions but one.

In this structure of extreme proprietary "right-ness," others may be perceived as so wrong and bad as to have no "rights," and violence is justified against them.

Retreat is rare in our records and where it occurs it cannot be illustrated by concise excerpts. In recent years its structure is exemplified vividly in the forms of thought of the extreme "radical" left in student revolt. These forms may be examined in the statements of the "radical" as opposed to the "liberal" students speaking in *Students and Society* (Center for the Study of Democratic Institutions, 1968). The forms are of course identical with those employed by persons and groups of the extreme radical right.

### A Note on Resumption of Growth

Alienation in Escape or Retreat need not be permanent. It may be for some persons a vital experience in growth—part of the very temptation in the wilderness that gives meaning to subsequent Commitment. Emergence may start in any affirmation of responsibility.

Briefly put:

S. Just saying, "O.K., well; that's what I can do, and that's what I can't do," in a way, and to be satisfied with my potential and not dream about other things and to try to develop what I have found that I have and not to worry about the things I don't have.

Often recovery occurs as a kind of "lifting" of depression, or a resurgence of care:

S. Emotionally I think I was trying to find some sort of rationalization for my feeling that I wasn't going to achieve anything. These are certainly not the values I have now. They're not the goals I want now. I don't think I'm going to be happy unless I can feel I'm doing something in my work.

S. I was sort of worried when I came back, wondering if, "Well, shucks, am I just going to lie down on the job or am I going to do it because it has to be done?" I found out that I wasn't doing it because it *had* to be, but because things interested me. Some things didn't interest me so much, but I felt I couldn't let them slide and I took them as best I could, in what order I could.

Alienation cannot be prevented. And indeed it should not be. If it could be prevented, so could that detachment which is man's last recourse of freedom and dignity *in extremis*. The educator's problem is therefore certainly not to prevent alienation, or even to make the option less available. His problem is to provide as best he can for the sustenance of care.

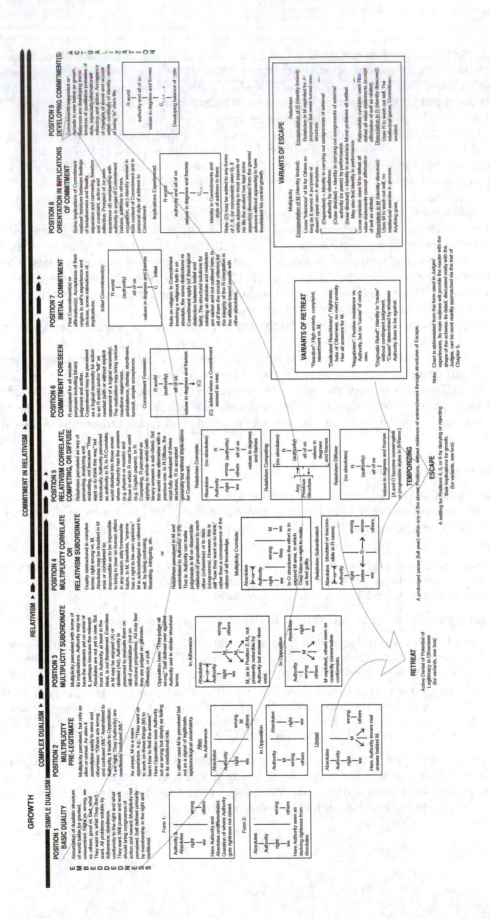

# Glossary

The following glossary is reproduced from the Judge's Manual. It provides a reference for certain terms appearing in the text, and on the Chart, to which a particular meaning is assigned.

**Absolute**   The established Order: The Truth, conceived to be the creation and possession of the Deity, or simply to exist, as in a Platonic world of its own; The Ultimate Criterion, in respect to which all propositions and acts are either right or wrong.

**Accommodation**   The modification or reorganization of a structure in response to incongruities produced by assimilations.

**Adherence**   Chart code: A (contrast Opposition)

1) Alignment of self with Authority in a Dualistic structuring of the world; or

2) In parentheses: (A), a "conservative" preference in a relativistic structuring of the world.

**Assimilation**  Chart code: parentheses ( )   The connection of a new percept to an extant structure. This may require various degrees of subordination of the implications of the new percept to the demands of an extant structure, and/or various degrees of accommodation of the structure.

On the Chart, the quantity within the parentheses is to be read as assimilated to the structure preceding the parenthesis; for example, 4A (M) reads "Multiplicity assimilated to Adherence in structure of Position 4."

**Authority** (upper-case A)   The possessors of the right answers in the Absolute, or the mediators of same (as viewed in Adherence); or the false or unfair pretenders to the right answers in the Absolute (as viewed in Opposition).

**authority** (lower-case a)   An aspect of social organization and interaction in a relative world, with many differentiations (e.g., power, expertise, etc.).

**Commitment**  Chart code: C   An affirmation of personal values or choice in Relativism. A conscious act or realization of identity and responsibility. A process of orientation of self in a relative world.

The word Commitment (capital C) is reserved for this integrative, affirmative function, as distinct from 1) commitment to an unquestioned or unexamined belief, plan, or value, or 2) commitment to negativistic alienation or dissociation.

**defensive** (adjective descriptive of Adherence or Opposition) Chart code: Ad or Od   Adherence or Opposition functioning in internal structures of emotional control so as to produce high resistance to qualification, ambiguity, or change.

**Dualism or Duality** (upper-case D)   A bifurcated structuring of the world between Good and Bad, Right and Wrong, We and Others.

Complex Dualism—a Dualism in which one element is itself dualistically structured.

**dualism or duality** (lower-case d)   Any binary function in a relative world, e.g., the right/wrong quality of a proposition in a specified context.

**Escape**   The denial of the implications for growth in Positions 4 and 5 by Dissociation or Encapsulation in the structure of these Positions.

**Dissociation**  Chart code: D   Sustained opportunistic denial of responsibilities implied for the self in Multiplicity or Relativism.

**Encapsulation**  Chart code: E   Consolidated assimilation of Multiplicity or Relativism to a Dualistic structure, projecting responsibility on Authority.

**Growth**   Progression from one structure to a higher structure as defined in the scheme.

**Multiplicity**  Chart code: M   A plurality of "answers," points of view, or evaluations, with reference to similar topics or problems. This plurality is perceived as an aggregate of discretes without internal structure or external relation, in the sense, "Anyone has a right to his own opinion," with the implication that no judgments among opinions can be made. (compare Relativism)

**Opposition**  Chart code: O (contrast Adherence)

1) Alignment vs. Authority in a Dualistic structuring of the world; or

2) In parentheses: (O), a preference for change and experimentation, as opposed to conservatism, in a relativistic structuring of the world.

**Position** (1 to 9 etc. on the Chart)   That structure representing the mode, or central tendency, among the forms through which an individual construes the world of knowledge and values at a given time in his life.

**Relativism** Chart code: R   A plurality of points of view, interpretations, frames of reference, value systems and contingencies in which the structural properties of contexts and forms allow of various sorts of analysis, comparison and evaluation in Multiplicity.

**Retreat**   An active rejection of the implications for Growth by entrenchment in a defensive variant of Position 2 or 3.

**Structure**   The relational properties of a world view, with special reference to the forms in which the nature of knowledge and value are construed.

**Temporizing**   A suspension of Growth (for a year) without recourse to the structurings of Escape.

# CHAPTER 21
## SHARING IN THE COSTS OF GROWTH

### WILLIAM G. PERRY, JR.

During my visits to the conference groups and workshops, I had a feeling that developmental this and that (e.g., Perry's Scheme, whatever *that* might be) had been pushed onto people a bit these three days. In one group, a person suddenly broke into the conversation to say, "I don't know what's going on! I wish I knew what this conference was all about. All I'm doing is sitting wondering all the time whether I should sell my house. I shouldn't worry so about such a thing. My parents bought and sold lots of houses when I was young and never thought anything about it. I don't see why I'm so upset about it, but I am. And I can't seem to see how this fits into the Perry Scheme."

I am not about to fit such an experience into anything, much less the Perry Scheme. However, I want to put that experience up on the shelf, for a minute, because I think it may help us to understand something important about development, no matter whose scheme one uses to look at development—something we have not mentioned at this conference.

First, let me review three or four of those little discoveries of the obvious that we all make in life. When we first come into this world, it is obvious that there are authorities and that they know what they are doing, or at least so it seems. They tell us what to do and what not to do, and so they know what they are doing. That is discovery 1.

Discovery 2 is that they do not know what they are doing after all. And since they do not seem to know what they are doing and do not have all the answers, we think, "Hurray! As soon as I can get out from under their tyranny I'm free, and any opinion is as good as any other, mine included."

Discovery 3 is that when I get out from under their tyranny I walk smack into a plate-glass wall and find that I am still subject to a tyranny, not of *they*, but of *fact*. And in that tyranny of reality I discover that, although there are a lot of differences of opinion among reasonable people, not every opinion is as good as any other, including some which I have that are no good at all. And then I have to get to work and start thinking about all these things. I think about various ways in which very reasonable people disagree very reasonably in wide areas. For instance, I am told that all the Euclidian geometry I learned was just a nice little game with its own rules. Of course, one can be right or wrong within the rules of Euclidian geometry, but the chances that Euclidian geometry conforms to anything in this universe, I am now told, are only about one in three billion; there are other geometries that have a better probability of conforming to something in the universe. I also find that in such important matters as religion very reasonable people disagree very intensely. I examine various religions and I find that some of them have as much claim to be more than superstition as anything I believe. Suddenly I realize that it is a little questionable to go around killing other people to the glory of the particular god I believe in. So I have discovered the obvious 3.

Then I make one more discovery, another obvious one, that I am faced with the challenge of affirming myself and my life as a person. Given so many differences of opinion among reasonable

x

people, differences which reason alone cannot resolve, I see that I can never be sure I am making the "right" decisions in life. And yet I must decide. Oh, I have been told never to make a wrong decision lest I regret it all my life, but now I see I have no protection against regret. Unless I am going to weasel out of really living, I must choose what I believe in and own the consequences, and never know what lay down the roads I did not take. I have discovered what Robert Frost meant, and what it means to commit.

Why have I just rehearsed these four obvious discoveries? There has been all this talk at this conference about the Perry Scheme, and if some of you are in doubt about what it is—that is it. I mean, students reported to us about making these discoveries, and that is what the Perry Scheme is, nothing more. It took thirty of us, listening to students for fifteen years to make these obvious discoveries, and then we looked at each other and said, "Fifteen years for *this*?"

So the next questions are, "What's so good about advancing along such a series of discoveries (or any other scheme of development we have been considering)? Why should we educators devote ourselves to promoting discoveries like that? Why should we push or entice or seduce people to go along with discoveries like that?" I know of one reason, and that is that since the world is, indeed, complicated, it is better to have a matching set of complicated ideas to deal with it than to try to use a simple idea that does not fit. Perhaps something more can be said for these discoveries, however. One is that by a considerable study of the different ways in which reasonable people see things, we are put in the position to learn that the most valuable of all the qualities of maturity of which Doug Heath talked this morning is compassion.

I am not about to expand on the social utility of compassion. I want to ask some special questions about this conference: "If development is all so obvious, then *why is it so hard*? If it's all that simple and all that obvious, then what in the world are we here for? Why *is* it so hard to grow? Why is it even harder to help *other* people grow? What have we been talking about for three days?"

Over the past several months, some of the staff in our little office have been asking students about how they learn. We just ask, "Tell us about how you experience learning." The usual response is, "You mean *really* learning?" There seems to be a distinction between "just" learning and "really" learning, which is what the students want to talk about. "Really" learning invariably refers to experiences in which one sees the world and one's self in a new and broader light—in short, to those very discoveries that mark the major steps into maturity I have been talking about.

I want to share with you the response of a young woman, a freshman. She said that so far she had been just learning more things at Harvard—"kind of flat"—and that the last time she had really learned was back in high school. She had a social science teacher whom she admired and he introduced to the class one of the Ames experiments with the revolving window. (You know it: There is this odd-shaped window that revolves on an axis and you see it revolve and you *know* it revolves; but then the lighting is changed and the window does not revolve; it oscillates from side to side, and you *know* it oscillates; and then the lighting is changed back and there the window is, revolving.) She said her teacher looked around and said to no one in particular, "So what do you make of *that*?" and no one said anything. "And all of a sudden I *saw*. I mean I saw how much we bring with us to our perception of things, how much we construct our worlds. And I realized that if this was true of windows, how about people? parents? myself, too? The whole world opened up to me, sort of, how everybody makes their own meanings, how different things can look in a different light, so to speak."

She then went on to say how the same experiment had been demonstrated at Harvard as just one more gimmick of perceptual illusion. The interviewer, bored with this complaint, brought her back to that moment in high school: "How did you feel then?" "Oh it was awful. I mean, my world was shattered. I guess it's sort of naive to use a word like this here, but it was like I lost my innocence. I mean nothing could ever be for sure—like it seems—I mean, again."

Our interviewer then asked, "How come you stayed with it instead of just laughing it off and forgetting it?"

"Oh, that was because of the teacher! You see, I trusted him, and I knew he knew. I mean, we didn't talk about it really, but he just looked at me and I knew he knew—what I'd learned—and what I'd lost! I guess because he knew what I'd lost, I could stay with what I'd seen."

So what I am talking about is something that we have left out in our talk of promoting development: What do we do about the house we leave when we go to a new place? When we leave the way we saw the world, in which everything was just so and just as we thought, and we see it all differently, we move into a world where all of what was solid and known is crumbling. And the new is untried. What do we do about the house we just sold out of? What do we do about the old simple world? It may be a great joy to discover a new and more complex way of thinking and seeing, but what do we do about all the hopes that we had invested and experienced in those simpler terms? When we leave those terms behind, are we to leave hope too?

Does the teacher have a responsibility here, not only to promote growth and development, but to help people to do something with the losses?

I want to go back to the words: "Because he knew what I'd lost, I could stay with what I'd seen." If a loss has been known, if a pain of mine has been known and shared by somebody, if somebody has been aware of one of my pains, then I can go on. I can let that pain die in some way and go on to reinvest the hope. (Not that I ever really get entirely over it, you understand. What happens to the wounds of the past? Theodore Reik was asked that question, you remember. He said, "Well, they ache in bad weather.") But still, if these things have been known and shared, then somehow it is possible for me to do a strange thing called grieving, which I do not pretend to understand. It seems all right to let it hurt.

But if it is not allowed to grieve or to hurt, I have to deny the truth to have my chin up. If my loss has never "lived," socially, then I must keep it alive myself, protect it like a responsibility, even. Then I do not know why it is that I get stuck. It comes to me as a sort of theorem, that when you have taken one step in development, you cannot take another until you have grieved the losses of the first. I wonder how that hypothesis would look in testing. Jessie Taft, who was a therapist, wrote, "The therapist becomes the repository of the outworn self." So too, this teacher of social sciences became the repository of this young woman's innocence.

What about the losses in what we have been calling "career development"? In good times, when there is a world of plenty out there, students can be butcher, baker, candlestick maker; they can be anything. All they have to do is choose. It feels like a narrowing down. It feels as if you are losing all the other selves that you could have been. So I have always wanted to write vocational theory all over again; not about how you choose what you are going to do, but about how you give up all the other selves you are not going to be.

Nowadays, of course, fewer of those opportunities are available out there. So, in the last few years, we have had a different kind of feeling, one of desperation. In order to make it in this competitive world everything becomes contingent on what I do right now. It is an unbroken chain. If I slip any place, I have had it. My whole life rests on this one sentence that I am trying to write, so I cannot finish the sentence.

I do not know what to say about grieving and the teaching of grieving, because I do not understand it. I know it goes by waves. I know that when you take yourself off someplace, and say, "Now I will face this, and grieve," nothing happens. But when you open up a bureau drawer and see something there that reminds you of something, then you have had it. I do not understand it, but I know that we do not allow it enough in our culture and we do not have the legitimizing rituals for the experience; therefore our people cannot grow well. They have to leave parts of themselves behind. Although I do not know how to teach people how to grieve, I have found that the teacher or counselor can make it clear that the pain is legitimate.

Such, then, is surely our responsibility: to stay, as it were, with the student's past and to the very extent that we invite the student to grow beyond it. It is a challenging task. Yet, just as our students can tell us why the obvious is so difficult (were we only to listen), so they may also tell us how we can help them to learn that the pain of growth is not a shame of youth that separates them from us.

I am reminded of a privileged moment I was given recently. A young woman had given me a lovely time all year. This woman, a freshman, is very accomplished; she was the president of her class in school and captain of the swimming team, and she had straight As in one of the most challenging schools in the country. But something was all wrong at college. She came to see me, we chatted, and she worked things out. I found that it was not only my privilege but my duty to enjoy her and to appreciate the trip she gave me on the roller coaster of adolescence. It was marvelous and sometimes very painful, but always somehow beautiful. Of course, she sometimes scared me by carrying too much sail. But I was enjoying it, I knew who I was supposed to be—the good uncle who listened. Then there came a day when she seemed profoundly moved, so I fastened my seatbelt. She had decided to transfer, she said, and she was feeling sad about leaving friends she had taken so long to make. There was a pause. Then she said, "Yesterday I was walking to class, and all of a sudden it came over me, that my days are numbered." I did my best not to stir. She looked at me. "Then it came to me that these days with you are numbered, too. Like, there comes a time when you have to move over and make room for others who need the time more." And then I thought of her as an older sister with her four younger sisters. And I said, "Well, gee, yeh, I know. And I've been thinking how I'll *miss* you." And she said, "Oh, really? Have you been thinking that way, too?" And so she just kept looking at me. It was one of those silences that went on for about fifteen minutes. About every five minutes or so she said softly, "Yes." Now I realized that she was a bright person and was putting things together. One of the things she was looking at was a guy whose days also were numbered, and by a lot smaller number than hers, and she looked me right in the eye for a long time. After a long time we got up. Somehow I decided it was time to say something, and I heard my voice say, "Growing is so bitter, so *bittersweet.*"

I did not hear the condescension in that remark until too late, and my inner critic turned on me in fury. "There you go, ruining the most beautiful moments again with your sappy platitudes." Well, I have learned that when I have made a mistake I am not the best person to try picking up the pieces, so I bit my tongue and waited. She looked at me without wavering and said gently, "And bittersweet for you, too." With that she touched my hand and left.

I have been finding that growing at this conference is bitter, bittersweet, and if I may let that young woman speak for all of us, I think she would say, gently, "And for you, too."

# CHAPTER 22
# REVISITING WOMEN'S WAYS OF KNOWING

## BLYTHE MCVICKER CLINCHY

When Mary Belenky, Nancy Goldberger, Jill Tarule, and I began the project that led eventually to our book on *Women's Ways of Knowing* (WWK, 1986/1997), we called it Education for Women's Development. We set out to interview women varying widely in age, ethnicity, and social class, women who had attended or were attending a variety of educational institutions ranging from small, selective liberal arts colleges to inner city community colleges, as well as several "invisible colleges," social agencies serving mothers of young children living in rural poverty. The question that guided our research continues to guide my research today. I like the way Mary Belenky words the question: "How come so many smart women feel so dumb?" Based on our own experiences in college and graduate school, and experiences recounted by our friends and our students, the four of us suspected that part of the answer might lie in the structure and practices of these educational institutions. Thus, we shared with earlier psychologists such as G. Stanley Hall a concern that higher education might be harmful to women's health. Hall worried that college might shrink women's wombs, rendering them infertile or "functionally castrated" (1917, p. 634); we worried that it might shrink their minds, or at least fail to expand them to their full potential.

In an attempt to explore the nature of the problem and to consider how institutions might be modified to better serve the needs and interests of women, we developed an extensive interview and administered it to 135 women, along with several standard developmental measures. The interview included sections dealing with self-concept, moral judgment, relationships, and educational experiences, as well as one ultimately labeled "ways of knowing." Although, like all of the contributors to this volume, we were familiar with William Perry's "scheme" tracing epistemological development in the college years (1970), and Nancy Goldberger (1981) and I (Clinchy & Zimmerman, 1982; 1985) had used it in previous longitudinal research, epistemology was at first no more salient in our thinking than any other aspect of development. Gradually, however, as we coded responses to what we then called the "Perry part" of the interview and then reread the rest of each woman's interview in the light of the coding, we came to believe, as we say in the preface to the second edition of the book, "that the women's epistemological assumptions were central to their perceptions of themselves and their worlds," and so "epistemology became the organizing principle for our data analysis and for the book that we were beginning to imagine" (WWK, 1997, xviii).

In the book we describe five different perspectives from which women view the world of truth, knowledge, and authority. Perry's scheme provided the scaffolding we used in coding the women's responses, and the perspectives we present are deeply grounded in his "positions," although we emphasize slightly different aspects of epistemology. Perry's positions are defined mainly in terms of the nature of knowledge and truth (truth as absolute, for example, versus multiple), whereas we stress the women's relation to knowledge and truth, their conceptions of themselves as knowers.

Clinchy, B. M. (2002). Revisiting women's ways of knowing. In B. K. Hofer & P. R. Pintrich (Eds.), *Personal epistemology: The psychology of beliefs about knowledge and knowing* (pp. 63–87). Mahwah, NJ: Lawrence Erlbaum Associates.

For instance, do they conceive of the source of knowledge as internal or external, and do they experience themselves as receiving or as creating truth? We listened, too, for deviations from Perry's scheme, for one would not expect the responses of women varying widely in age, class, and educational background to be identical to those of Perry's largely privileged and largely male undergraduate sample. Indeed, we found that while the general outline of Perry's scheme survived, many of the answers the women gave could not be wedged into it, and so, "In this instance, as in others, when the data the women provided diverged from the theories we had brought to the project, we forced ourselves to believe the women and let go of the theories" (WWK, 1997, pp. xii–xiv).

The book plunged us into a lively, wide-ranging conversation: It drew serious attention, often intensely critical, among scholars and researchers from a variety of disciplines, as well as moving testimonials from hundreds of "ordinary" women who saw parallels between their own stories and the stories in the book. I intend this chapter to be a contribution to this continuing conversation. I shall discuss some salient and controversial aspects of each of the perspectives we defined, drawing on the original text and also on research and theoretical speculations that have emerged in the years since its publication.

## Silence

We named this, the least adequate perspective we could discern, "Silence," signifying the voicelessness of women at this position. Asked, "How do you feel about speaking?", Trish responds, "Um. I wonder if I'm using the right words. I can't do it anywhere." These women have difficulty hearing as well as speaking. As Belenky writes, they "see words more as weapons than as a means of passing meanings back and forth between people. They do not believe themselves capable of understanding and remembering what the authorities or anyone else might say to them" (Belenky, 1996, p. 394). Lacking "the most basic tools for dialogue, the Silenced feel voiceless and excluded from the community" (Belenky, 1996, p. 394). They have been excluded, also, from theories of epistemological development, for these theories are based on words—oral or written accounts—produced mainly by people with considerable formal education. Silent women, feeling "incapable of articulating their own thoughts and feelings to others," (Belenky, 1996) make poor research subjects, and they rarely wend their way into institutions of higher learning. All of the women who taught us about Silence came from the invisible colleges, not the visible ones, and most of them could describe the position only because, having moved somewhat beyond it, they could view it retrospectively. For example, Ann said:

> I could never understand what they were talking about. My schooling was very limited. I didn't learn anything. I would just sit there and let people ramble on about something I didn't understand, and I would say "Yup, yup." I would be too embarrassed to ask, "What do you really mean?" . . . I had trouble talking. If I tried to explain something and someone told me that it was wrong . . . I'd just fall apart. (WWK, p. 23)

In fact, the Silence perspective does not belong in accounts of epistemological "development." Silence grows out of a background of poverty, isolation, subordination, rejection, and, often, violence. It is not a step in "normal" development but a failure to develop, "a position of not knowing" (Goldberger, 1996b, p. 4) imposed by a society inattentive to the needs of its members.[1] It should not be seen, as some readers have interpreted it, as the first stage in a developmental sequence.

Still, since the publication of WWK, I have learned that the position, although "abnormal," may not be as rare as I once thought. A few years ago, while outlining the WWK positions for a group of community college faculty, I remarked that we could skip quickly over "Silence" because such people were unlikely to appear in their classes. A flurry of hands went up, and the participants proceeded to disabuse me of my assumption. The position was heavily represented, they said, among the many very poor people who had recently entered their colleges, mostly perforce, as a result of changes in welfare regulations.

Even highly educated articulate women, some of whom make a profession of speaking and writing, have testified to us in hundreds of letters that they resonate to the description of this perspective. Although they are by no means entrapped in (capital "S") Silence, they report that they frequently find themselves in situations in which they are (lowercase "s") silenced. Lewis and Simon offer a fascinating account of a graduate course taught by Simon in which Lewis and the other women students felt silenced by the males in the class. They quote an account by one student that is remarkably similar to Ann's:

> I don't understand what they [the men] are talking about. I feel like I'm not as well educated as them. I haven't done too much reading in this area. They know so much more than I. I just feel that if I said anything, they'd say, what is she doing in this class, she doesn't know anything, so I keep my mouth shut. (Lewis & Simon, 1986, p. 466)

As Simon says,

> Being muted is not just a matter of being unable to claim a space and time within which to enter a conversation. Being muted also occurs when one cannot discover forms of speech within conversation to express meanings and to find validation from others. (Lewis & Simon, 1986, p. 464)

The muting of the women in Simon's class was confined to a particular (although not uncommon) situation, and the women were able to devise strategies for eliminating it. The muting of the profoundly Silent women pervades their entire lives and is much less tractable, but it is not irreversible: The invisible colleges and programs like the "Learning Partners" project directed by Belenky and her colleagues (Belenky, 1996; Belenky, Bond, & Weinstock, 1998), have succeeded in providing settings in which Silent women can "express meanings and find validation from others."

## Received Knowing[2]

From this perspective, built on Perry's (1970) Dualism, truth is absolute and unambiguous. Received Knowers[3] believe that for every question there is a single, correct answer. They see the world in terms of black and white, right and wrong, true and false, good and bad; there is no room for ambiguity. "The stars twinkle for one reason," a student said. "That's why they do it. If something is proven, then there is no other way it could happen." Truth is external; it lies in the hands of Authorities, and one is utterly dependent on Them to dispense it:[4] "How can you learn if the teacher isn't telling you?" In the course of a longitudinal study of epistemological development in young women, based on Perry's scheme, (Clinchy & Zimmerman, 1982; 1985), Claire Zimmerman and I asked Wellesley undergraduates, "Suppose two people disagree on the interpretation of a poem. How would you decide which one is right?" A sophomore replied, "You'd have to ask the poet. It's his poem."

Like many of my colleagues, I grow impatient with students who behave as Received Knowers. These are the students who sit, pencils poised, prepared to record the truths I dispense, the ones who ask exactly how long the paper should be, and exactly which topics will appear on the exam. These students are willing to regurgitate the information they have stored in their heads on a test, but they don't like being asked to apply it. They tend to see knowledge as something to be stored and reproduced, but not to be used and never to be questioned. They like multiple choice exams, and I don't. I can muster some compassion for Received Knowers by recalling how I revert to this position whenever I am faced with something novel, complex, and incomprehensible, like the first time I saw a game of cricket or heard a piece of atonal music. On such occasions I yearn for an expert who will just tell me what it all means.

It was not until I embarked on the WWK research however, that I came to feel genuine respect for Received Knowing. I teach at an academically selective, academically rigorous college, and I see it as my task to help students move beyond received knowing and on to more active, reflective modes of thinking. But through this project we met women for whom Received Knowing was an achievement, rather than something to be "got over," like measles or chicken pox or adolescence. They showed us that the position has virtues. The chief virtue of the Received Knower is that she is receptive. She can listen, even if the listening seems hardly more active than the listening a tape recorder does. Women who rely on received knowledge can take in information, while Ann, looking back on a life in Silence, recalls that she "could never understand what they were talking about." Received Knowers can appreciate expertise and make use of it. Silent women do not perceive authorities as sources of knowledge. "Authorities bellow but do not explain," although they must be obeyed; they cannot be understood.

Ann began to emerge as a knower when she became a mother. She needed to know how to take care of her baby, and she was lucky enough to live in an area serviced by a Children's Health Program, where the staff "knew all the answers," and took the time to spell them out in language she could understand. Unlike many professionals, they continually emphasized her competence, rather than their own.

> I'd walk in there and they would say, "You're wonderful. You're a great mother." . . . I'd walk out of there feeling so good. I'd feel like I could tame the world. . . . I feel like I could go in there and they could hire me, you know, that's how much knowledge they have given me.

While recognizing the virtues of Received Knowing, it is important also to see its limitations. For Received Knowers, as we defined the position, Authority is the only source of knowledge. Judging by the comments of some of our critics, we did not make the "only" point clear. The feminist literary theorist Patrocinio Schweickart, for instance, recalls herself as listening intently and taking careful notes in college and graduate school. We "miss something important," she says, if we assume that in this case she was behaving as a Silent woman or a Received Knower. But the authors of WWK would make no such assumption; we would agree with Schweickart that "silence" in this case might well be "a sign not of passivity, but of the most intense intellectual engagement" (1996, p. 307). It is important to distinguish between (lowercase) received knowing as a "strategy" (Goldberger, 1996a) that one chooses to deploy in a particular situation (during a lecture, say, or a cricket game), because of its adaptive value, and (uppercase) Received Knowing as a compulsory position from which authorities are viewed as the sole source of knowledge, knowledge that is assumed to be absolutely true, and which one simply ingests "as is" without any awareness of active processing. Similarly, we do not assume, of course, that simply because a person is not speaking, she is operating from a position of Silence.

As Goldberger points out, "Relying on experts or yielding to the knowledge of others is not necessarily indicative of the narrowly defined version of Received Knowing we present in WWK. . . . It is the way in which a person 'constructs' authority and expert that helps us understand more fully his or her epistemological stance" (1996a, p. 347). For instance, in her own research with "bicultural" Americans, Goldberger found that although African Americans stressed in their stories the importance of relying on God, "their construal of God as authority is more one of Collaborator and Coknower than Dictator" (1996a, p. 347). Goldberger implies that WWK's treatment of Received Knowledge is culture bound: "Yielding to authorities external to oneself is often characterized in Western culture, which values autonomy and independent judgment, as 'childlike,' 'passive,' or 'dependent'" (1996a, p. 347). I agree, and I think, too, that we were "bound" by the limits of our sample. Most of the women we coded as Received Knowers occupied relatively subordinate positions in terms of age or social class, being either very young undergraduates or very poor older women. Received Knowing might take a different form among, say, a sample of prosperous middle-aged people.

I believe, now, that we paid too little attention to distinctions within our sample of Received Knowers. As it is, our construction of this and the other positions partakes of what might be called "epistemological (or perhaps "positional") essentialism," lumping into the same category perspectives that may differ in significant ways. Received Knowing cannot be quite the same for a first-year student in an elite college who depends on the words of a presumably benign professor, and a fifty-year-old with minimal formal education who is at the mercy of the "information" supplied by an abusive mate. Or consider a milder, but not insignificant contrast: the experiences of a male and a female Received Knower in Perry's sample (Harvard undergraduates in the 1960s) might also differ, for the male knew that he might someday be one of Them, while the female could envision no such possibility.[5]

## Subjectivism

Subjective knowing is in some respects the opposite of received knowledge. Received Knowers believe in universally valid Absolute Truths. Subjectivists adhere to the doctrines of "Multiplicity" (Perry, 1970) and "Subjective Validity" (Clinchy & Zimmerman, 1982): truth (lowercase t) is personal and individual, all opinions are equally valid, and everyone's opinions are right for them. While Received Knowers see knowledge as external and utterly objective, subjectivists look inside themselves for knowledge; for them, truth springs from the heart or the gut. In WWK we tell the story of Inez, a young single mother of three, who (in our terms), had lately moved out of Received Knowing into Subjectivism. She told us, "There's a part of me that I didn't even know I had until recently—instinct, intuition, whatever. It helps me and protects me. It's perceptive and astute. I just listen to the inside of me and I know what to do."

Unlike Received Knowers, Subjectivists tend to be deeply suspicious of the information dispensed by authorities. For most of her life Inez had been abused and exploited by powerful males, first her father and brothers, then her husband. She grew up believing that, as she put it, no woman could "think and be smart." Inez no longer pays any attention to external authorities; she is her own authority. "I can only know with my gut," she said. "I've got it tuned to a point where I think and feel all at the same time and I know what is right. My gut is my best friend—the one thing in the world that won't let me down or lie to me or back away from me."

For Inez, Subjectivism spells liberation, but for Kim, a first-year African American student at a traditional elite college, it almost certainly spells trouble. I asked Kim to read and respond to the following statement: "In areas where the right answers are known, I think the experts should tell us what is right. But in areas where there are no right answers I think anybody's opinion is as good as another's." Kim didn't just agree with the second sentence; she also *dis*agreed with the first, the notion that there are in any area "right answers" that are "known." "I don't like that," she said. "I just don't like that. Who's to say what answer is right and what answer is wrong? They could have been given the wrong information. I'm sure there are a helluva lot of teachers who are walking around being misinformed. . . . I very seldom go by what people say."

Like other Subjectivists, Kim relied on the data supplied by first-hand experience rather than the second-hand information offered by authorities:

> If they were to tell me that there was going to be an earthquake tomorrow, that scientists had gone and studied all the scales and said this, I wouldn't believe them. I'd have to wait and see. The only way I could believe it is for it to actually happen. It is said that the earth goes around the sun. I don't have any proof. It is written in books, sure. But the person who wrote it in books could have been misinformed.

A Subjectivist would not dream of "asking the poet" how to interpret his poem. In her view, it isn't "his poem;" it's hers, and "there isn't any right or wrong. We're all allowed to read into a poem any meaning we want." As one woman said, "Whatever you see in the poem, it's got to be there." Here, the external world seems almost to disappear. The words on the page dissolve into a sort of Rorschach inkblot exerting little constraint on the meaning the reader projects onto the page. What the Subjectivist reader "sees" is likely to resemble closely what she already "knows." Asked how she decided among competing interpretations being discussed in English class, one student said, "I usually find that when ideas are being tossed around I'm usually more akin to one than another. I don't know—my opinions are just sort of there." And another said, "Well, with me it's almost more a matter of liking one more than another. I mean, I happen to agree with one or identify with it more."

Unless she can "identify" with a phenomenon, the Subjectivist cannot deal with it. "I cannot relate to an atom," Kim told me. Asked what she meant by "relate," she said, "I can comprehend it, I can feel it." Some of her classmates, she said, "can see why two positives would connect. I can't see that force, but I can see anger and emotions." How, I wondered, was this young woman going to pass the science distribution requirement?

Subjectivists "just know" what they know; their knowledge is based not on words or inferences but on the immediate apprehension of reality. Mrs. Spender, a character in Angela Thirkell's novel,

*Growing Up*, says, "You only have to mention a thing to me and I seem to see it . . . I don't need to read, I just sense what things are about." Mrs. Spender does not question the validity of her perceptions, nor does she leave room for others to question them. "A person's experience can't be wrong," as one young woman said, and "an idea is right if it feels right"—right for herself, although not necessarily for anyone else. Subjectivists are as tolerant of others' opinions as they are of their own: judge not, that ye not be judged. When Kim told me that she didn't like to call people wrong, I asked, "Would that extend to people like Hitler?" "Absolutely," she replied. "I would never, no—I wouldn't call him wrong. Whatever he has done, I would not call him wrong . . . I value my opinion. I value what I do. I have no right whatsoever to go out and call somebody wrong because it is different from what I do."

At first glance, this passage may strike the reader, as it did me, as amoral mindless relativism. But Kim's next sentence makes it clear that she does have values of her own: "Now I think that the extermination of the Jews was wrong. I am not saying that he was wrong." It is not clear whether Kim means that Hitler's opinion is wrong in some objective or absolute sense, or whether it is simply wrong for her, but it is clear that she distinguishes between persons and the opinions they hold. She knows that, as the anthropologist Clifford Geertz puts it, differences of opinion are not just "clashes of ideas," that "there are people attached to those ideas" (Geertz, quoted in Berreby, 1995). Only if you realize that, Geertz maintains, can you be "open to dialogue with other people."

Kim realizes it, but she is not open to dialogue with other people. She disagrees with Hitler, but she would see no point in exploring the issue with him. She is not interested in why he believes in the extermination of Jews, nor would she care to argue the point: Hitler's opinion may be right for him, but it is irrelevant to her. Subjectivists do not see values—their own or anyone else's—as a subject for reflection, and without reflection there can be no genuine dialogue. Their anemic "discussions" are like parallel play: based on "mere unlikeness" of views, in Geertz's phrase, they are characterized by a "vacuous tolerance that, engaging nothing, changes nothing" (Geertz, 1986, p. 113). As the philosopher Elizabeth Spelman wrote:

> Tolerance is . . . the least of the virtues of people who really want to learn about others and about their lives: to tolerate someone is simply to let her have her say; I needn't listen to her, I needn't respond to her, I needn't engage with her in any way at all. All I have to do is not interfere with her. Prior to and after I've allowed her to make her presence known, I can blot her out of my consciousness. (Spelman, 1988, p. 181)

Although Subjectivists preach "openness," they actually practice a sort of aloof tolerance toward other points of view; they listen politely, but they do not really hear. As the philosopher Iris Murdoch might put it, they are unable to love. "Love," Murdoch said, "is the extremely difficult realisation that something other than oneself is real. Love . . . is the discovery of reality" (1970/1985, p. 51). Genuine dialogue, Geertz says, requires the realization that "other people are as real as you are" (quoted in Berreby, 1995). In some sense, the Subjectivist lacks this realization; she is lost in her own subjectivity. Although she acknowledges in theory the existence and validity of other realities, only her own is really real to her. She can only look out through this subjective reality; she cannot transcend it or detach herself from it.

Subjectivists perceive the world in terms of themselves, ignoring its otherness. The writer/teacher Peter Elbow calls this "projection in the bad sense" (Elbow, 1973, p.149). They hear a person (or a poem) meaning what they would mean, if they said those words, or else they do not hear it at all. In order to perceive otherness, one must acquire a degree of objectivity. To avoid projection in the bad sense, Subjectivists need to acquire techniques for "imaginative entry . . . into an alien turn of mind" (Geertz, 1986, p. 118). They need to learn how to explore and examine ideas—their own and other people's. They must rediscover on a higher plane the insight achieved by children of four and five, that belief and reality do not always coincide.

## The Limits of Preprocedural Knowing

At my college, many students, especially in the first year or two, exhibit a split epistemology. Typically, they perceive science and mathematics from a Received Knowing perspective, and the humanities from a Subjectivist perspective. Students with a strong proclivity for Received Knowledge gravitate toward the first domain, and those who are strongly tilted toward Subjectivism gravitate toward the latter.[6] If they persist in these positions, both groups will run into trouble, especially in advanced courses: Received Knowers may be confronted with Heisenberg's uncertainty principle and Bohr's principle of complementary, and Subjectivists will certainly encounter teachers who insist that only those interpretations that are thoroughly grounded in the text deserve consideration. Unless they are to find themselves "in over their heads" in the psychologist Robert Kegan's (1994) phrase, in college and beyond, they will need to develop more powerful ways of knowing, for both these perspectives, although seemingly so different, share similar serious deficiencies.

Both are uncritical ways of knowing. Ann, the Received Knower, perceives the staff at her invisible college to be infallible, and Inez, the Subjectivist, perceives her own gut as infallible. They do not examine their knowledge; they simply accept it as true and act on it with unquestioning obedience. Both modes are relatively passive. Ann and Inez do not create their knowledge. Ann's opinions come ready-made from the agency; Inez's opinions are, as that student put it, "just there." People who rely solely on received or subjective knowledge are in some sense not really thinking. They have no systematic, deliberate procedures for developing new ideas or for testing the validity of ideas. Judging from longitudinal data and the women's retrospective accounts, this "Procedural Knowing" is for some the next step in development.

## Procedural Knowing

Procedural Knowers no longer believe that one can acquire knowledge or arrive at truth through immediate apprehension. Knowledge does not consist of facts to be stored "as is," nor of the static residue of direct experience. Knowledge is a process, and it requires work. Although no single "answer" may be "right," all interpretations are not equally valid. Knowing requires the application of procedures for comparing and contrasting and constructing interpretations, and the quality of the knowledge depends on the skill of the knower.

In WWK we described two sorts of procedures that we called "separate" and "connected" knowing. Separate Knowing is a detached, impersonal, objective, critical approach, best typified, perhaps, by the model of "hard science." Many people would call it simply "thinking," or maybe "good thinking." Once upon a time, so did I. Elsewhere, I have told how Zimmerman and I stumbled on what we now call "connected knowing" while searching for evidence of what we now call "separate knowing" among Wellesley undergraduates. Some of our interview questions were designed to ascertain whether the students had acquired an appreciation of critical thinking, a component of Perry's Position 4. For example, we asked them to respond to a statement another student had made in an earlier interview that seemed to provide evidence of critical thinking: "As soon as someone tells me his point of view, I immediately start arguing in my head the opposite point of view. When someone is saying something, I can't help turning it upside down" (Clinchy, 1998, p. 770).

Although some of the women agreed heartily with the quotation, some disagreed. One said, "When I have an idea about something, and it differs from the way another person's thinking about it, I'll usually try to look at it from that person's point of view, see how they could say that, why they think they're right, why it makes sense." And another said,

> If you listen to people and listen to what they have to say, maybe you can understand why they feel the way they do. There are reasons. They're not just being irrational. When I read a philosopher I try to think as the author does. It's hard, but I try not to bias the train of thought with my own impressions. I try to just pretend that I'm the author. I try to really just put myself in that person's place and feel why is it that they believe this way.

This young woman would agree with Virginia Woolf (1932/1948) that in reading a book one should "try to become" the author, his "fellow worker" and "accomplice."

In time, as my colleagues and I accumulated more and more responses like these, we began to think that connected knowing might constitute a genuine procedure, and this is how we present it in WWK. In retrospect, this seems to me to have been an audacious, perhaps presumptuous move. Because we had little empirical data of our own to use in constructing the concept, having never asked a single question designed to elicit it, in a sense we "made it up"—not out of whole cloth, to be sure, but out of a necessarily eclectic assortment of ideas. Since the publication of the book, along with various collaborators, I have been attempting through systematic research and conversations with colleagues (alive and dead, in person and in print) to define the components of connected knowing and separate knowing more clearly and to ascertain how the two procedures (or various versions thereof) play out in actual practice. Annick Mansfield and I (1992) developed an interview designed to elicit the ways in which men and women define the two procedures, how they feel about them, what they see as their benefits, drawbacks, and purposes, when and where and with whom they do and do not use each procedure, and how their use of them has changed over time. A number of researchers, including my own students as well as other investigators at various institutions working with widely varying populations, have also used some version of this interview. Because most of this research is still in progress, and because of limitations of space, I shall not dwell on it in detail here, but I have drawn on it in developing the description of the two procedures that I present here.

Table 1 summarizes some contrasting features of separate and connected knowing. The two modes have somewhat different purposes: while Connected Knowers are primarily interested in understanding the object of attention, Separate Knowers are primarily oriented toward its validity. The Connected Knower asks, "What does this poem (person, idea, etc.) mean?" The Separate Knower might ask, "How good is this poem? What are its strengths and weaknesses?" "What is the evidence for and against this theory?" In attempting to get at the meaning of an idea, the Connected Knower adopts a "believing" stance (Elbow, 1973; 1986), using empathy in an attempt to share the experience behind the idea, "feeling with" and "thinking with" the author of the idea. One woman told us that in counseling undergraduates, she is "usually a bit of a chameleon. I try to look for pieces of the truth in what the person's saying instead of going contrary to them, sort of collaborate with them." In

## TABLE 1

### Characteristics of Connected and Separate Knowing

| Aspect | Connected Knowing | Separate Knowing |
|---|---|---|
| The name of the game: | The "Believing Game": looking for what is right; accepting | The "Doubting Game": looking for what is wrong; critical |
| Goals: | Emphasis on meaning: to understand and be understood | Emphasis on validity: to justify, test, refine, convince, and be convinced |
| The relationship between the knowers: | Supportive: reasoning *with* the other | Adversarial, challenging: reasoning *against* the other |
| The knower's relation to the known: | Personal. Attachment & intimacy: "stepping in" | Impersonal. Detachment and distance: "stepping back" |
| The nature of agency: | Active surrender | Mastery and control |
| The nature of discourse: | Narrative | Argument |
| The role of emotion: | Feelings illuminate thought | Feelings cloud thought |
| Procedure for achieving (approximating) "objectivity": | Adopting the perspective of the particular other; empathy | Adopting a neutral perspective, "from no position in particular;" adhering to rules for avoiding bias |
| Basis of authority: | Personal experience (own or vicarious) | Mastery of relevant knowledge and methodology |
| Strengths: | Holistic, inclusive | Narrowing, discriminating |
| Vulnerabilities: | Absence of conviction; loss of identity, autonomy, and power. Danger of always being the listener | Absence of conviction; alienation and absence of care and intimacy. Danger of never listening |

contrast, Separate Knowers take a critical stance, acting as adversaries rather than allies. Instead of stepping into the other's shoes they step back, measuring the quality of the object against impersonal criteria such as the logic of the argument or the fit between the theory and the data.

Both Separate and Connected Knowers exhibit objectivity, but of a different sort. Separate Knowers believe in separating the knower from the known, so as to avoid "contamination." In searching for truth, they try to "weed out the self" using Elbow's (1973, p. 149) phrase, putting their own feelings and values aside and adopting a neutral perspective, "from no position in particular." To avoid bias, they adopt procedures such as "double-blinding" in conducting experiments and "blind grading" in assessing students' work. Connected Knowers also attempt to suspend their own beliefs, but instead of adopting a neutral perspective, they adopt the perspective of the other. When we asked women what "objectivity" meant to them, and why one should be objective, they often said something like, "When you're trying to help a friend decide whether to get an abortion, you have to forget what you think about abortion and see it from her point of view, given her assumptions." Connected Knowers do not "extricate" (Elbow, 1973) the self: convinced that the knower and the known are inextricably related, they use the self to help them connect with the other. To "the strong democrat," wrote the political scientist Benjamin Barber:

> "I will listen" means not that I will scan my adversary's position for weaknesses and potential trade-offs, nor even . . . that I will tolerantly permit him to say whatever he chooses. It means, rather, "I will put myself in his place. I will try to understand, *I will strain to hear what makes us alike* (1984, p. 175; emphasis added).

Connected Knowers take this approach not only to people but to relatively "impersonal" objects. "To understand a poem," an undergraduate said, "You must let the poem pass into you and become part of yourself, rather than something you see outside yourself. . . . there has to be some parallel between you and the poem." And the biochemist portrayed by June Goodfield in *An Imagined World* says, "If you really want to understand about a tumor you've got to *be* a tumor" (Goodfield, 1991/1994, p. 226). In contrast, Separate Knowers adhere to what the feminist philosopher Susan Bordo calls "the Cartesian masculinization of thought"; for them it is "the otherness of nature [that] allows it to be known," and "empathic, associational, or emotional response obscures objectivity, feeling for nature muddies the clear lake of the mind" (Bordo, 1986, p. 452). Connected Knowers, in contrast, believe that emotions can serve as clues. A nursery school teacher once told me that in trying to understand a particular child, she asks herself, "How does this child make me feel?" "I know my reaction says something about me," she says, "and I have to sort that out, but it also tells me something about him."

Separate and connected knowing, as presented here, are inventions, something like ideal types. In our work we have never encountered an individual who exhibited all the aspects of either mode, and it is possible that different categories of individuals will show different patterns, containing some components of a mode and excluding others. In a study of attitudes toward separate and connected knowing among Wellesley and MIT undergraduates, Mansfield and I found that many of the Wellesley undergraduates we interviewed embraced some aspects of Separate Knowing as we presented it (impartial analysis, for example) but strongly objected to its more oppositional aspects, such as playing "devil's advocate," and while most of the women included empathy in delineating their own versions of "connected knowing," not one of the men referred to empathy or, indeed, made any mention of affect (Rabin, 1994). (We suspect that the difference has as much or more to do with the cultural norms of the two institutions as with gender.)

Some of our research participants seem to express more complex versions of the modes than others. As the philosopher Sara Ruddick reminds us, "a 'position' or 'way' allows development within its modality" (Ruddick, 1996, p. 255). In an attempt to trace this development, Mansfield and I are looking for specific differences between versions that seem intuitively more or less sophisticated, and we are examining longitudinal data collected from adolescents in search of developmental change, asking, for instance, whether some components appear to come in earlier than others.

As work continues, particularly in different cultures and subcultures, researchers will surely deconstruct the crude dichotomy presented in Table 1, identifying configurations that contain elements from both its columns. Consider, for instance, Kochman's (1981) intriguing account of the distinctive ways in which urban community Black students and White middle-class students in his Chicago college classroom deal with conflict. The White students seem to adopt a prototypical detached Separate Knowing style: They "relate to their material as spokesmen, not advocates . . . They believe that the . . . merits of an idea are intrinsic to the idea itself. How deeply a person cares about or believes in the idea is considered irrelevant to its fundamental value." Blacks, on the other hand, use an approach that is adversarial, but neither disinterested nor unemotional. They "present their views as advocates. They take a position and show that they care about this position" (p. 20). Whites believe that "caring about one's own ideas" makes a person "less receptive to opposing ideas," but Blacks see no contradiction between attachment to one's own ideas and openness to alternative ideas, which they also value; in fact, they are suspicious of people who present an argument as if they had no personal stake in it. "Whites believe that opinions should be evaluated on their own merits: they are taught to present ideas as though the ideas had an objective life, existing independent of any person expressing them," but Blacks, "because they feel that all views . . . derive from a central set of core beliefs that cannot be other than personal . . . often probe beyond a given statement to find out where a person is 'coming from' in order to clarify [its] meaning and value" (Kochman, 1981, pp. 20–23).

## Connected Knowing Versus Subjectivism

Of all the themes presented in WWK, the concept of Connected Knowing has provoked the most interest, probably the most research, certainly the most controversy, and—in my defensive opinion—the most misunderstanding. As I have written:

> In WWK we defined connected knowing as a rigorous, deliberate, and demanding procedure, a way of knowing that requires work. Contrasting it with . . . "subjectivism," we said, "It is important to distinguish between the effortless intuition of subjectivism (in which one identifies with positions that feel right) and the deliberate imaginative extension of one's understanding into positions that initially feel wrong or remote." (WWK, 1986, p. 121). Many of our readers—friends and foes alike—have ignored the distinction, conflating connected knowing with subjectivism by treating it more as a reflex than a procedure. (Clinchy, 1996, p. 209)

Connected Knowing builds on the positive qualities of Subjectivism, but it transcends its limits. Table 2 presents some of the similarities and differences between the two modes. Connected Knowers retain the Subjectivist's respect for subjectivity and for the lessons that can be learned from firsthand experience, but they are not imprisoned within their own subjectivity or confined to their own narrow slice of experience; they develop techniques for entering into alien subjectivities and making use of vicarious experience. Connected Knowers, like Subjectivists, are reluctant to make judgments; they are in this sense "accepting," but theirs is not the passive acceptance, the "to-each-his-own-indifferentism" (Geertz, 1986, p. 122) of the Subjectivist. Fully developed Connected Knowing requires that one "affirm" or "confirm" the subjective reality of the other, and affirmation is not merely the absence of negative evaluation; it is a positive effortful act. Affirmation of a person or a position means "saying Yes to it" (Elbow, 1986, p. 279), rather than merely offering sympathetic understanding. Confirmation means, in the theologian Martin Buber's wonderful phrases, to "imagine the real," to "make the other present" (Buber, quoted by Friedman, 1985, p. 4). It involves "a bold swinging . . . into the life of the other" (Buber, quoted by Kohn, 1990, p. 112).

We saw that Subjectivists cannot engage in genuine dialogue; although they speak, often they cannot really hear. "What's the point of class discussion," one student asked, "when you have your own thoughts that feel right?" For Connected Knowers knowledge is neither absolutely private nor absolutely certain; hearing other voices becomes not only possible but, because truth is now problematic rather than transparent, essential. Connected Knowers begin to perceive other people's realities not just as "alternatives to" themselves, as Subjectivists do, but as "alternatives for" themselves (Geertz, 1986, p. 111, citing Bernard Williams). Other people's realities become possibilities for them.

Connected Knowers develop techniques for facilitating and eliciting these realities through "active listening" (Rogers & Farson, 1967). Active listening is not a natural capacity, but in Geertz's

## TABLE 2

### Subjectivism and Connected Knowing Similarities and Differences

| Subjectivism | Connected Knowing |
|---|---|
| reflexive, reactive, spontaneous | deliberate, effortful; midwifery |
| locked in one's own perspective | entering another perspective |
| often "projection in the based sense" (Elbow): egocentric assumption that others share one's view | suspending, "bracketin" one's own view |
| Everyone has a right to their own opinion and everyone's opinion is right for them. | Everyone has a right to a considered opinion. People are responsible for their opinions. |
| All opinions are equally valid; an opinion has validity simply because someone holds it. Assertion of validity of one's own opinion for one's self, but only for one's self. | Some opinions are better than others, but one should not evaluate an opinion unless one has tried hard to understand it. |
| Knowledge is derived from first-hand experience. | Knowledge can be acquired through vicarious experience. |
| Only my own subjectivity is really real to me. | One can enter into other subjectivities. |
| One should show tolerance and respect for views that differ from one's own. | One should try to imagine, explore, and understand views that differ from one's own |
| Intuition and feeling are involved, but not empathy. (feeling, but not feeling with) | Intuition and feeling may be involved, especially empathy. |
| little or no reasoning involved; the "gut" or "the heart" predominate. | "thinking with" as well as "feeling with" the other. |
| One need not entertain other views as possible options for the self. (Resistant to change) | One should entertain other people's opinions as possibilities for the self. (Open to transformation) |

phrase, a "skill arduously to be learned" (Geertz, 1986, p. 122), one that is rarely practiced in daily life. Having tried for years with more and less success to learn and to teach the art of interviewing, I know how difficult it is to listen "objectively" in the connected sense, that is, to hear the other in the other's own terms, to act, as the psychoanalyst Evelyne Schwaber puts it, as "an observer from within" (Schwaber, 1983, p. 274). Connected Knowers achieve skill, too, in making themselves understood by finding a route into the other's subjectivity: Kim, the African American student we met earlier, seemed to move outside her normally Subjectivist frame when, in the midst of describing an experience of racial discrimination, she suddenly leaned across the desk and asked, "Are you Jewish?"—searching, it seemed, for some "parallel" between us that would allow her experience to "pass into" me.

Connected Knowing, like Subjectivism (and unlike Separate Knowing), attends to feelings as sources of insight, but it also involves reasoning—feeling with and thinking with. This point is often overlooked, perhaps because the dichotomy between separate and connected knowing that we present is assimilated into the dualism between thinking and feeling that pervades this culture, leading to a fallacious syllogism: If separate knowing involves thinking, and connected knowing involves feeling, connected knowing must not involve thinking. We say that although connected knowing is uncritical it is not unthinking, but in a culture in which the predominant view is that thinking *is* critical thinking, "uncritical thinking" becomes an oxymoron.

## Issues of Gender

Although WWK is based entirely on interviews with women, it has been widely described as a study of "sex differences," perhaps partly because when male and female are perceived as binary opposites, as they typically are, it is difficult to see why one would speak of "women's" ways of knowing except to distinguish them from men's ways. We did not argue that the positions we described applied only to women, although we speculated that for various reasons, the positions might take somewhat different form in men; Marcia Baxter Magolda's research suggests that this might be so. In particular, we did not mean to imply that all women, and only women, are Connected Knowers or that all men, and only men, are Separate Knowers. Because we interviewed only women, the voices we used to illustrate both modes were largely, of course, women's voices. Indeed, we did not attempt to "code" participants as Connected or Separate Knowers, but only as Procedural Knowers, for, having not yet clearly defined the two modes when we began the research, we had asked no questions designed to elicit the relevant data.

Subsequent research, involving men as well as women, and using recently developed survey measures as well as interviews focusing directly on separate and connected knowing, suggests that the two modes may be gender-related, but not gender exclusive. For instance, in two studies involving undergraduates at academically selective colleges, females consistently rated connected knowing statements higher than separate knowing statements, while males' ratings of the two modes did not differ (Galotti, Clinchy, Ainsworth, Lavin, & Mansfield, 1999; Galotti, Drebus, & Reimer, 1999). I know of no studies comparing the frequency of use of the two modes by males and females except in terms of self-report; more objective (observer-based) data would be useful.

However, sex differences were not then and are not now a central interest for me. I resonate to the words of Carol Gilligan: "When I hear my work being cast in terms of whether women and men are really (essentially) different or who is better than whom, I know that I have lost my voice, because these are not my questions" (1993, xiii). They were not our questions either. We did not mean to assert that connected knowing was "better" than separate knowing, only that it was "a different voice," a legitimate and effective voice that deserved to be heard. Like Gilligan and other "different voice" theorists, we "wished to repair an omission in psychological theory and in the society, by bringing into public consciousness a way of seeing, speaking, and knowing that emphasized attachment and interdependence rather than detachment and autonomy" (Clinchy & Norem, 1998, p. 785).

Critics contend that connected knowing is essentially a powerless way of knowing. I argue that it can be a powerful way of constructing knowledge (Clinchy, 1998), but I acknowledge that a society that devalues it will devalue the person who uses it. Until the "omission" of that voice in the institutions of this society is repaired, those who use it will suffer. I was reminded of this recently when I heard a colleague in economics tell how she insists that her students develop "a public voice" for use in class, a confident, decisive, authoritative voice that differs from the hesitant, groping, vague, and uncertain "private" voice they use in the residence hall. "I tell them," she said, "that if the CEO asks them how many factories they should build, and they say" F-i-i—i-ve. . . . ? (with rising inflection), while the guy next to her says firmly "Seven!," seven will be built and the guy will be promoted above them." A bit shaken, I recalled how that very morning I had been urging the students in my seminar not to conduct an interview as if it were an exam, but to say things like "So - o - - o, you mean. . . ? . . . I'm not sure I understand . . . I think maybe . . ." In effect I was asking them to bring their private voices into the public domain. Which of us was right, I asked myself, the economist or me? Both. One voice is more effective in one context, the other in the other. We know from research that these procedures are not mutually exclusive, indeed, measures of the two appear to be orthogonal (David, 1999; Galotti, Clinchy, Ainsworth, Lavin, & Mansfield, 1999; Galotti, Drebus, & Reimer, 1999). Students need to develop skill in both modes, so that they can deploy whichever is appropriate for a given occasion. In time, we might even envision their achieving a way of knowing that integrates the two voices into one. What would such a voice sound like? In WWK, we weren't sure, but we began to sketch it out, and we called it Constructed Knowing.

## Constructed Knowing

The chapter on Constructed Knowing in WWK was by far the most difficult to write. It passed from hand to hand among us for months, as we wrote and revised it, and I, for one, have never been satisfied with it. Because this is the most complex of the positions, it is the most difficult to construct, and because our sample contained so few Constructed Knowers, we had little data to work with. Since the publication of WWK, my students and I have sought out research participants who we believed might help us in constructing a richer portrait of the position—for instance, relatively privileged adults active in professional and community life, and a sample of undergraduates nominated by their professors as "complex thinkers" in their fields (Arch, 1998). In this section, I rely largely on their words, elaborating on several aspects of the position presented in WWK. This research is in its infancy, and my comments should be read as highly speculative.

Constructed knowing has much in common with Perry's Position 5. Complexity and ambiguity are assumed, and "right answers are a special case." Anna, a senior honors student majoring in history, said that in her field, although there were some questions such as "Did this happen on this day?" to which an answer could be true or false, "those aren't the questions that are the important questions." For Amy, another senior, the epistemological "revolution" described by Perry, has clearly occurred: "There's a state of creative confusion, or at least doubt. I think it's always going to be that way." When last she encountered math and science, Amy had assumed that they contained "Truth with a capital T:"

> My experience with [science and math] has been on such a basic level that it's almost like spelling. You can spell right and you can spell wrong . . . I have a sense, though, that [in] higher level mathematics and stuff you get into things where just one answer isn't sufficient or isn't the only way. Things can sort of just diverge off, and there is more than one possibility. . . . I think that exists, you know, it must. Can't all be '2 and 2 is 4.'

When we ask Procedural Knowers to describe their ways of learning and thinking, they often enumerate a linear step-by-step program. Constructivists are less articulate; they struggle to find images to express the process, and the images are more often circular than linear. Amy says "it's hard to explain:"

> You proceed out of confusion. . . . There's just sort of a sense of a mixing bowl where you sort of let— where you are confused and you don't have any solid or stable. . . . I think it's sort of like a whirlpool or something like that. Where you've got a lot of ideas zooming around, and you haven't yet affixed any of them to being right or wrong in your head yet or meshing with all the others. Things are still just sort of whirling around; then you start, pulling them out and filtering things out and making sense out of them.

Similarly, Marie said:

> A lot of it has been lots of passive and then 'Boom!', all of a sudden something comes and really sticks, and I'm very active, and [then] lots of passive again, and then 'Boom!' again. It's like I have to take in a whole lot and sift it all down. You know, put it all in a big sieve and sift it all down and the stuff that falls through I collect and start building with, and then 'Wham!'—all of a sudden the right piece will fall into the sieve and something will be completed.

We gave the Constructed Knowing chapter the subtitle, Integrating the Voices, to capture the women's tales of "weaving together the strands of rational and emotive thought and of integrating objective and subjective knowing" (WWK, p. 134). Amy and Marie weave together the "active surrender" of connected knowing with the "mastery and control" of separate knowing into a single way of knowing. In her practice as a family counselor, Sara tries to combine the empathy of connected knowing with the detachment of separate knowing. Recently, she told us, she canceled an appointment with a client in order to take a needed vacation with her daughter, and the client felt betrayed. "I'm working hard to get to a place where I can really understand how tortured she feels by this," she said. "I want to stay right with her as much as I can. I also have to keep monitoring this whole thing from a professional stance, trying to see it all and keep it all in perspective." Aware that she herself is tilted toward connection, she observes herself carefully: "If I find myself being too much into that close-up stance where I'm completely involved in that person's perspective and maybe lose touch with the professional stance, I need to scramble to get my professional stance back." Although Sara is aware that some therapists find an aggressive approach effective, she knows that it would not work for her. "Even if I have to confront sometimes, I still want to do that within a relationship that I feel is viable and trusting." She has evolved an approach that blends aspects of separate and connected knowing: she will "take an oppositional stance," voicing exceptions to a client's interpretations, but she phrases her comments in connected language, "in a way that hopefully isn't argumentative, but sort of like a confused statement." No one taught Sara this technique; she developed it herself to suit the sort of person she is. As Kegan might put it, while Procedural Knowers are "subject" to their procedures, Constructed Knowers are in control of them; they own them.

At the heart of constructed knowing, as is implicit in Perry's Position 5, is the belief that "All knowledge is constructed, and the knower is an intimate part of the known" (WWK, p. 137). Kegan asks, "Having put our world together, are we awake to the fact that it is an invented reality, a made world? Do we regularly look for some quite different way the same experience could cohere and so render a whole different meaning?" "[W]e 'make sense,' " he goes on, "but we do not always take responsibility for it as made" (Kegan, 1994, p. 205). Although none of us, of course, is always conscious of inventing reality, Constructivists often are, and at least on reflection, they recognize that they are responsible for their constructions and that it is their duty—"an ethical imperative," as one woman put it—to consider alternative constructions. If truth is "an increasing complexity," as the poet Adrienne Rich (1979, p. 187) said, and as our Constructivists believe, there is never a single, crucial experiment or a perfect, "impregnable" argument that will settle the matter. Procedural Knowers stay within a given system—the viewpoint of a particular person or a particular discipline, for example. Constructivists move among systems. Amy, who worried during her sophomore year that she might "mix up" the material from one course with the material from another, and "say the wrong things on the exam," told us, as a senior:

> I think one of the most exciting things is when you're getting different insights into a similar thing. Like when you're taking seventeenth-century literature as well as art you have a sense of a lot of things coming together, a lot of different things that explain each other sometimes . . . And you start getting a much greater sense of what was happening, and why each thing in turn produced the other, and how they all interact.

In WWK we wrote, "[C]onstructivists show a high tolerance for internal contradiction and ambiguity" (p. 137). " 'Dialogue' and 'balance' were key words in [the] epistemological vocabulary" of the "complex thinkers" interviewed by Joanna Arch (1998, p. 53). For example, Karen approaches history, her field of concentration, as "a dialogue" between past and present; although it is important for historians to avoid projecting current assumptions and concerns "blindly back into the past," she said, it is important also to keep them in mind. Philosophers and psychologists refer to this sort of approach as "dialectical thinking" (e.g., Basseches, 1986; Clayton & Birren, 1980; also see Oser & Reich, 1987, on "complementarity"), Karen calls it "my little two-direction thing." (Notice that, like Sara, she "owns" the approach.)

When Constructed Knowers find their thoughts and feelings in conflict, they try to cultivate a "conversation" between the two, instead of allowing one to silence the other. In her "rational mind," Karen said, she is opposed to censorship, but, "intuitively," because of an experience involving the attempted suicide of a friend after reading an assigned book, she is in favor of it:

> There has to be a way for that experience to coincide with thought. And be more than a gut reaction, even though the gut reaction is the strongest thing about it. And I think that's true of all sorts of things. . . . I remain convinced . . . that what's truly right will work on both an emotional and a logical level. And maybe that's not true. But I'd like to think that and pursue that thought.

Although barely twenty one years old, Karen seems to have the beginnings of "wisdom," as defined by Labouvie-Vief: "While *logos* has insisted on the separation of such realms as reason and faith, thinking versus feeling, outer versus inner, or mind versus body, wisdom maintains that these two realms constitute but complementary and interacting poles of thought (1990, p. 78)."

Interviews with older, seemingly "wise" women like Sara have led me to suspect that when constructed knowing reaches its fullest development (probably not before middle age, I would guess), the construction of self and other might look something like Kegan's (1994) "fifth order consciousness." To illustrate the difference between fourth and fifth order consciousness, respectively, Kegan invents two couples, the Ables and the Bakers, both of whom have been married for many years. The Ables respect their differences, and most of the time they are "comfortable" with them. "We're probably more comfortable with each other," they said, "because we're a lot more comfortable with ourselves. . . .

Anyway, we've become a good team. We find that our differences are often complementary. One picks up what the other one misses." For each of the Ables, the self is single and complete: "Mr. Able comes over to discover the world of Mrs. Able, but in all his respectful discovering he never questions the premise that this is not his world." For each of the Bakers, on the other hand, the self is multiple and incomplete, an "evolving self" (Kegan, 1982) composed of contradictory parts. The Bakers have come to see that the differences each experiences between the self and the other are also differences within the self and the other. "When Mr. Baker comes over to try on the perspective he has identified with Mrs. Baker, . . . he is vulnerable to discovering another world within himself." For instance, to an outsider it may appear that one of the Bakers is an activist and the other a contemplative. But "when we are at our best," said the Bakers themselves, "we get a good glimpse of the fact that the activist . . . also has a contemplative living inside him." And when they have a fight, if it's a good fight, "the fight becomes a way for us to recover our own complexity, . . . to leave off making the other into our opposite and face up to our own oppositeness."

The Ables have learned to avoid destructive conflict by treating each other as complements rather than enemies; through respecting each other's points of view, compromising, and taking turns, they have become "a good problem-solving team." But their relationship is not a source of growth: "We are who we are," they say (Kegan, 1994, p. 308). The Bakers' relationship is a source of growth, "a context for a sharing and an interacting in which both are helped to experience their 'multipleness,' in which the many forms or systems that each self is are helped to emerge" (Kegan, 1994, p. 313). When differences between partners are acknowledged as differences within each of the partners, they become similarities between them, and the apparent opposition between similarity and difference is dissolved. Piaget was right, I think, in positing difference and contradiction as powerful forces in development, but I believe that similarity and coincidence can be equally powerful, and that the integration of the two, in constructed knowing, is more powerful still.

## Conclusion

In WWK we could not assert with confidence that the epistemological positions we defined represented a developmental progression, for we had longitudinal data for only the small proportion of our sample whom we had also interviewed in earlier studies; otherwise, we had to rely on retrospective accounts. In any case, I now believe that we should be wary of moving too quickly to embrace theories that postulate a single, acontextual linear direction in epistemological development. Such global theories have been useful in the past, but, the pervasiveness of "domain specificity" has led me to believe that we need to examine development within rather than across domains. For instance, it seems likely that, while in approaching the humanities, students often move from a Subjectivist to a Procedural position, in approaching science they may "skip" Subjectivism, going directly from Received to Procedural Knowing. I believe that microanalytic longitudinal investigations of individuals grappling with a particular discipline or set of issues can be especially illuminating, for example, studies of changes over months or years in students' conceptions of truth within a particular course, as revealed through interviews and essays (e.g., McCarthy, 1987; McCarthy & Fishman, 1991). Besides providing a more detailed account of the nature of development, longitudinal "case studies" of this sort can lead to hypotheses about the kinds of experiences that facilitate epistemological development, for example, Haviland and Kramer's (1991) analysis of the diary of Anne Frank suggests that intensity of emotion about a particular issue can serve as a stimulus to more complex constructions of the issue.

## Notes

1. In this respect, Belenky's (1996) renaming of the position as Silenced seems appropriate.
2. In WWK we call this position "Received Knowledge." All four of the coauthors now prefer the more active verbal form for each of the positions.
3. For convenience, I refer to Received "Knowers" rather than "Knowing," but I do not mean to imply that a given individual always operates out of a single perspective.

4. I borrow the uppercase (A and T) from Perry to connote the power of Authority and the nature of Truth as conceived at this position.

5. Even today, women constitute only about 12% of Harvard's faculty of Arts and Sciences.

6. In a survey distributed as part of the "Pathways Project" (Rayman & Brett, 1993) at Wellesley, students were asked to respond to the statement, "I prefer subject matter with precise answers to subject matter with multiple interpretations." This question discriminated significantly, and more than any other, (a) between those students who said on entering the college that they planned to major in math or science from those who said they planned to major in social sciences or humanities; and (b) between those who at the end of the sophomore year stuck with their plan to major in math or science and those who switched to a non-science major.

# References

Arch, J. (1998). Epistemological assumptions and approaches to learning in three academic disciplines. Unpublished undergraduate honors thesis. Wellesley College, Wellesley, MA.

Barber, B. (1984). *Strong democracy: Participatory politics for a new age.* Berkeley: University of California Press.

Basseches, M. (1986). Dialectical thinking and young adult cognitive development. In R. A. Mines & K. S. Kitchener (Eds.), *Adult cognitive development: Methods and models.* New York: Praeger.

Belenky, M. (1996). Public homeplaces: Nurturing the development of people, families, and communities. In *Knowledge, difference, and power: Essays inspired by* Women's Ways of Knowing, 393–440. New York: Basic Books.

Belenky, M., Bond, L., & Weinstock, J. (1997). *A tradition that has no name: Public homeplaces and the development of people, families, and communities.* New York: Basic Books.

Belenky, M., Clinchy, B., Goldberger, N., R., & Tarule, J. (1986/1997). *Women's ways of knowing: The development of self, mind, and voice.* New York: Basic Books.

Berreby, D. (1995, April 9). Unabsolute truths: Clifford Geertz. *The New York Times Magazine.*

Bordo, S. (1986). The Cartesian masculinization of thought. *Signs, II,* 439–456. Reprinted in S. Harding, & J. O'Barr (Eds.) (1987). Sex and scientific inquiry (pp. 247–264). Chicago: University of Chicago Press.

Clayton, V & Birren, J. (1980). The development of wisdom across the life span: A reexamination of an ancient topic. *Life span development and behavior, 3,* 103–135.

Clinchy, B. (1996). Connected and separate knowing: Toward a marriage of two minds. In N. Goldberger, J. Tarule, B. Clinchy, & M., Belenky (Eds.), *Knowledge, difference, and power: Essays inspired by* Women's Ways of Knowing (pp. 205–247). New York: Basic Books.

Clinchy, B. (1998). A plea for epistemological pluralism. In B. Clinchy and J. Norem (Eds.), *Readings in gender and psychology* (760–777). New York: New York University Press.

Clinchy, B. & Norem, J. (1998). Coda: In-Conclusion . . . In B. Clinchy and J. Norem (Eds.), *Readings in gender and psychology* (778–798). New York: New York University Press.

Clinchy, B., & Zimmerman, C. (1982). Epistemology and agency in the development of undergraduate women. In P. Perun (Ed.), *The undergraduate woman: Issues in educational equity.* Lexington, MA: D. C. Heath.

Clinchy, B., & Zimmerman, C. (1985). Growing up intellectually: Issues for college women. *Work in Progress,* No. 19. Wellesley, MA: Stone Center Working Papers Series.

David, C. (1999). Fear of success and cognitive styles in college women. Unpublished undergraduate honors thesis. Wellesley College, Wellesley, MA.

Elbow, P. (1973). Appendix Essay: The doubting game and the believing game—An analysis of the intellectual enterprise. In *Writing without teachers.* London: Oxford University Press.

Elbow, P. (1986). *Embracing contraries.* New York: Oxford University Press.

Friedman, M. (1985). *The healing dialogue in psychotherapy.* New York: Jason Aronson.

Galotti, K., Clinchy, B., Ainsworth, K., Lavin, B., & Mansfield, A. (1999). A new way of assessing ways of knowing: The attitudes toward thinking and learning survey (ATTLS). *Sex Roles, 40,* 745–766.

Galotti, K., Drebus, D., & Reimer, R. (1999, April). Ways of knowing as learning styles. Research Display presented at the Biennial Meeting of the Society for Research in Child Development, Albuquerque, NM.

Geertz, C. (1986, Winter). The uses of diversity. *Michigan Quarterly Review,* 105–123.

Gilligan, C. (1993). Letter to readers, 1993. In *In a different voice: Psychological theory and women's development,* 2nd ed., ix–xxvii. Cambridge: Harvard University Press.

Goldberger, N. (1981). *Meeting the developmental needs of college students.* Final report presented to the Fund for the Improvement of Post-Secondary Education (FIPSE), Simon's Rock of Bard College, Great Barrington, MA.

Goldberger, N. (1996a). Cultural imperatives and diversity in ways of knowing. In *Knowledge, difference, and power: Essays inspired by* Women's Ways of Knowing, 335–371. New York: Basic Books.

Goldberger, N. (1996b). Looking backward, looking forward. In *Knowledge, difference, and power: Essays inspired by* Women's Ways of Knowing, 1–21. New York: Basic Books.

Goodfield, J. (1991/1994). *An imagined world: A story of scientific discovery.* Ann Arbor: University of Michigan Press.

Hall, G. S. (1917). *Adolescence: Its psychology and its relations to physiology, anthropology, sociology, sex, crime, religion, and education.* New York: D. Appleton & Co.

Haviland, J. M., & Kramer, D. A. (1991). Affect-cognition relationships in adolescent diaries: The case of Anne Frank. *Human Development, 34,* 143–159.

Kegan, R. (1982). *The evolving self.* Cambridge, MA: Harvard University Press.

Kegan, R. (1994). *In over our heads: The mental demands of modern life.* Cambridge, MA: Harvard University Press.

Kochman, T. (1981). *Black and white styles in conflict.* Chicago: University of Chicago Press.

Kohn, A. (1990). *The brighter side of human nature: Altruism and empathy in everyday life.* New York: Basic Books.

Labouvie-Vief, G. (1990). Wisdom as integrated thought: Historical and developmental perspectives. In R. Sternberg (Ed.), *Wisdom: Its nature, origins, and development* (pp. 52–83). Cambridge: Cambridge University Press.

Lewis, M., & Simon, R. (1986). Discourse not intended for her: Learning and thinking within patriarchy. *Harvard Educational Review, 56,* 457–471.

Mansfield, A., & Clinchy, B. (1992, May 28). *The influence of different kinds of relationships on the development and expression of "separate" and "connected" knowing in undergraduate women.* Paper presented as part of a symposium, *Voicing relationships, knowing connection: Exploring girls' and women's development,* at the 22nd Annual Symposium of the Jean Piaget Society: Development and vulnerability in close relationships. Montreal, Qu'bec, Canada.

McCarthy, Lucille P. (1987). A stranger in strange lands: A college student writing across the curriculum. *Research in the Teaching of English, 21,* 233–265.

McCarthy, Lucille P., & Fishman, Stephen M. (1991). Boundary conversations: Conflicting ways of knowing in philosophy and interdisciplinary research. *Research in the Teaching of English, 25,* 419–468.

Murdoch, I. (1970/1985). *The sovereignty of good.* London: ARK Paperbacks, Routledge & Kegan Paul.

Oser, F., & Reich, K. (1987). The challenge of competing explanations: The development of thinking in terms of complementarity of 'theories.' *Human Development, 30,* 178–186.

Perry, W. (1970/1999). *Forms of intellectual and ethical development in the college years.* New York: Holt, Rinehart, and Winston.

Rabin, C. (1994). *Separate and connected knowing in undergraduate men and women.* Unpublished undergraduate honors thesis. Wellesley College, Wellesley, MA.

Rayman, P., & Brett, B. (1993). *Pathways for women in science: The Wellesley report.* Wellesley, MA: Wellesley College.

Rich, A. (1979). *On lies, secrets, and silence: Selected prose (1966–1978).* New York: Norton.

Rogers, C, & Farson, R. (1967). Active listening. In Haney, W. *Communication and organizational behavior: Text and cases,* (81–97). Homewood, IL: Richard D. Irwin, Inc.

Ruddick, S. (1996). Reason's femininity: A case for connected knowing. In *Knowledge, difference, and power: Essays inspired by* Women's Ways of Knowing, 248–273. New York: Basic Books.

Schwaber, E. (1983). Schwaber, E. (1983). Construction, reconstruction, and the mode of clinical attunement. In A. Goldberg, *The future of psychoanalysis.* (pp. 273–291) New York: International Universities Press.

Schweickart, P. (1996). Speech is silver, silence is gold: The asymmetrical intersubjectivity of communicative action. In *Knowledge, difference, and power: Essays inspired by* Women's Ways of Knowing, 305–331. New York: Basic Books.

Spelman, E. (1988). *Inessential woman: Problems of exclusion in feminist thought.* Boston: Beacon Press.

Woolf, V. (1932/1948). How should one read a book? In *The common reader, Series 1 and 2* (pp. 281–295). New York: Harcourt Brace.

# CHAPTER 23
## CONNECTED AND SEPARATE KNOWING
### TOWARD A MARRIAGE OF TWO MINDS

## BLYTHE MCVICKER CLINCHY

In *Women's Ways of Knowing* (WWK, 1986) Mary Belenky, Nancy Goldberger, Jill Tarule, and I described an epistemological position we called *procedural knowledge*, which took two forms, encompassing two "procedures" that many of the women we interviewed seemed to use in searching for truth; we called them "separate" and "connected" knowing. In the ensuing years, observing the varied and often surprising meanings assigned to these notions by some who have befriended them and the abuse that has been heaped upon them by some of their foes, I have occasionally felt like the character played by Woody Allen in the film *Annie Hall*, who, returning to childhood as an invisible presence, observes his parents engaged in one of their customary and (to him) imbecilic arguments. Incensed by the absurdity of both their positions, he shouts, "You're both wrong!" but his shouts are inaudible. In this chapter I want to make my views on separate and especially connected knowing audible.

Connected knowing was originally a serendipitous discovery. We did not ask the women we interviewed to tell us about it; they did so spontaneously, and from their comments we constructed the procedure as a sort of "ideal type." Since then, I have been attempting through systematic research and conversations with colleagues (alive and dead, in person and in print) to ascertain how the two procedures (or various versions thereof) play out in actual practice. My colleague Annick Mansfield and I (1992) developed an interview designed to elicit the ways in which men and women define the two procedures; how they feel about them, what they see as their benefits, drawbacks, and purposes; when and where and with whom they do and do not use each procedure; and how their use of them has changed over time. A number of researchers, including my own students, as well as other investigators at various institutions working with widely varying populations, have also used some version of this interview. Drawing on this work, I shall try in this chapter to clarify and complicate the concepts of separate and connected knowing, and, along the way, contest misreadings of the two modes that seem to me especially pernicious.

## Believing and Doubting

Let me begin by defining the two orientations as we intended to define them in WWK. If you approach this chapter as a separate knower, you examine its arguments with a critical eye, insisting that I justify every point. In the writer Peter Elbow's terms you "play the doubting game" (1973),

Clinchy, B. M. (1996). Connected and separate knowing: Toward a marriage of two minds. In N. R. Goldberger, J. M. Tarule, B. M. Clinchy & M. F. Belenky (Eds.), *Knowledge, difference, and power: Essays inspired by Women's Ways of Knowing* (pp. 205–247). New York, NY: Basic Books.

looking for flaws in my reasoning, considering how I might be misinterpreting the evidence I present, what alternative interpretations could be made, and whether I might be omitting evidence that would contradict my position. The standards you apply in evaluating my arguments are objective and impersonal; they have been agreed upon and codified by logicians and scientists. You need not be a person to apply these rules; you could be a cleverly programmed computer.

If, on the other hand, you take a connected approach to this chapter, you read it with an empathic, receptive eye. Instead of inspecting the text for flaws, you play "the believing game" (Elbow, 1973): if something I say seems to you absurd, you do not ask, " 'What are your arguments for such a silly view as that?' but rather, 'What do you see? . . . Give me the vision in your head. You are having an experience I don't have; help me to have it?' " "The focus," Elbow writes, "is not on propositions and validity of inferences but on experiences or ways of seeing" (1986, p. 261). In asking, "Why do you think that?" connected knowers are not demanding logical or empirical justification; they are asking, "What in your experience has led you to that point of view?" They are concerned not with the soundness of the position but with its meaning to the knower; their aim is not to test its validity but to understand it.[1] Given our present primitive grasp of the "rules" for connected knowing, it would be impossible to program a computer to practice it, and given its "personal" character, it may never be possible.

In fact, of course, you will probably approach this chapter with a mixture of the two orientations. Although for the sake of convenience I will cast separate and connected knowing into dualistic terms, I do not mean to suggest that the two modes are mutually exclusive. "Separate knowers" and "connected knowers" are fictional characters; in reality the two modes can and do coexist within the same individual. Later in the chapter I will try to deconstruct the dualities and complicate the picture. But for the moment, to paraphrase Virginia Woolf (1929/1989), let these lies flow from my lips, and remember that they are lies.

In separate knowing one takes an adversarial stance toward new ideas, even when the ideas seem intuitively appealing; the typical mode of discourse is argument. In WWK we used the following excerpt from an interview with a college sophomore to illustrate the orientation, and we have used it in research and in workshops to stimulate discussion of separate knowing:

> I never take anything someone says for granted. I just tend to see the contrary. I like playing the devil's advocate, arguing the opposite of what somebody's thinking, thinking of exceptions, or thinking of a different train of thought.

People often use images of war in describing separate knowing. Consider, for example, a young man we call Mel,[2] who espouses a sort of Patriot missile epistemology: "If I could get a job shooting holes in other people's [ideas]," he said, "I would enjoy my life immensely."

> If somebody explains [his or her position] to me and I can . . . shoot holes in it, then I won't tend to believe it, and if they can explain away every misgiving that I have about the [position], then I'll tend to believe it. . . . [And] if they seriously believe in something which you think is very wrong, if you—if you shoot enough holes in what they're saying, they'll start doubting it themselves. It could happen to you too. It happens the other way around.

In contrast, in connected knowing one tries to embrace new ideas, looking for what is "right" even in positions that seem initially wrong-headed or even abhorrent. An excerpt from another college sophomore illustrates this approach:

> When I have an idea about something, and it differs from the way another person is thinking about it, I'll usually try to look at it from that person's point of view, see how they could say that, why they think that they're right, why it makes sense.

As an undergraduate we call Cecily said, "If you listen to people and listen to what they have to say, maybe you can understand why they feel the way they do. There are reasons. They're not just being irrational." Virginia Woolf, posing the question "How should one read a book?" (1932/1948), advises the reader to "try to become" the author, and Cecily agrees:

> When I read a philosopher I try to think as the author does. It's hard, but I try not to bias the train of thought with my own impressions. I try to just pretend that I'm the author. I try to really just put myself in that person's place and feel why is it that they believe this way.

Connected knowers act not as adversaries, but as allies, even advocates, of the position they are examining. Become the author's "fellow worker," his "accomplice," Woolf says, and Sheila, one of our research participants, tells us that in counseling undergraduates she is "usually a bit of a chameleon": "I try to look for pieces of the truth in what the person's saying instead of going contrary to them. Sort of collaborate with them."

Some of our research participants and some of our readers perceive the separate knower's argumentative style as a pig-headed attempt to bully the opponent into submission, but I regard this as a primitive or degenerate form of separate knowing. Properly practiced, the procedure requires that one hold one's views loosely, remaining open to competing positions. For Mel, other people's ideas are fair game, but so too are his: "It happens the other way around too," he says. "It could happen to you." For mature separate knowers, the doubting game is a fair game.

Whereas separate knowers are sometimes perceived as stubbornly attached to their own opinions and deaf to the views of others, connected knowers are sometimes perceived as excessively open-minded—indeed, as having no minds of their own, like the "over-empathizers" characterized by the psychologist Robert Hogan as "equivocating jellyfish" (1973, p. 224). But the picture of the connected knower as merely a jellyfish, clone, chameleon, or wimp, like that of the separate knower as merely a bully, is a caricature. It portrays, perhaps, a primitive or regressive form of connected knowing, but it grossly distorts more mature forms. Sheila, one of our most proficient connected knowers, describes herself as only "a *bit* of a chameleon," and is careful to distinguish between understanding a point of view and agreeing with it. She is not gullible. She does not believe everything she hears—at least not for long. She "believes" in a point of view only in order to understand it. "Believing" is a *procedure* that guides her interaction with other minds; it is not the *result* of the interaction.

## Connected Knowing as Procedure

Notice the recurrence of the word *try* in the descriptions connected knowers give of their approach; Cecily, for instance, uses it four times in four sentences. Although some people exhibit a proclivity toward connected knowing that appears to be "natural," those who really seem to understand and use the approach rarely describe it as effortless and often allude to its difficulties. The philosopher Elizabeth Spelman refers to the "strenuousness of knowing other people, even people very much like ourselves" (Spelman, 1988, p. 181), and the poet Adrienne Rich, in a brilliant essay recounting her attempt to enter the mind and heart of Emily Dickinson by journeying to the poet's home, depicts herself as "an insect, vibrating at the frames of windows, clinging to the panes of glass, trying to connect" (Rich, 1979, p. 161). True connected knowing is neither easy nor natural. As the anthropologist Clifford Geertz says:

> Comprehending that which is, in some manner of form, alien to us and likely to remain so, without either smoothing it over with vacant murmurs of common humanity, disarming it with to-each-his-own indifferentism, or dismissing it as charming, lovely even, but inconsequent, is a skill we have arduously to learn, and having learnt it, work continuously to keep alive; it is not a connatural capacity, like depth perception or the sense of balance, upon which we can complacently rely. (Geertz, 1986, p. 122)

In WWK we defined connected knowing as a rigorous, deliberate, and demanding *procedure*, a way of knowing that requires *work*. Contrasting it with the epistemological position we called "subjectivism," we said, "It is important to distinguish between the effortless intuition of subjectivism (in which one identifies with positions that feel right) and the deliberate imaginative extension of one's understanding into positions that initially feel wrong or remote" (WWK, 1986, p. 121). Many of our readers—friends and foes alike—have ignored the distinction, conflating connected knowing with subjectivism by treating it more as a reflex than as a procedure; *connected* and *procedural* become antonyms (*procedural* apparently being synonymous with *separate*), thus seeming to render connected knowing nonprocedural. The philosopher Lorraine Code makes this error, when, in discussing WWK, she describes people behaving "connectedly or procedurally" (Code, 1991, p. 261), and so does a member of my own household, who has read, apparently with care, every draft of everything I have written on this topic.

My immediate reactions to such misreadings are decidedly oppositional: like Mel, I prepare to launch a few verbal missiles. But then I seem to hear Cecily's voice whispering in my ear that perhaps our readers and my housemate are "not being irrational"; perhaps "there are reasons" for their "silly ideas." I resolve to use connected knowing procedures to try to understand why people are unable to see connected knowing as a procedure, why they persistently confuse it with subjectivism. Utilizing one of my favorite defense mechanisms, I transform a source of irritation into a subject for research.

In qualitative research, as methodologist Grant McCracken says, "the investigator serves as a kind of 'instrument' in the collection and analysis of data:" "Detection proceeds by a kind of 'rummaging' process. The investigator must use his or her experience and imagination to find (or fashion) a match for the patterns evidenced by the data" (McCracken. 1988, pp. 18, 19). I did not need to rummage very deeply before coming up with a couple of matches, two occasions on which I had interpreted as subjectivist, and dismissed as relatively mindless, behavior that I now believe might have exemplified connected knowing.

First match: I began teaching at a women's college while still attending graduate school at Harvard, where class discussions followed the ballistic model favored by separate knowers. Although I sometimes found it hard to breathe in this atmosphere, I also found it stimulating, and it became for me the mark of a "good class." When I tried to create the same atmosphere in the classes I was teaching, however, I met with considerable resistance from students like Sue, who said to her interviewer, "In class, when you want to say something, you just want to have it float out in the air and just, you know, stand. You don't want to have it, like, shot down." My students spoke their piece and listened politely as others spoke theirs, but they would not take issue with one another, and, in my opinion, they spent far too much time exchanging anecdotes about their personal experiences. In *Professing Feminism*, Daphne Patai and Norelta Koertge speak scornfully of women's studies groups in which everyone agrees with everyone else, "and everybody feels validated and cozy" (Patai & Koertge, 1994, p. 174). That is how I regarded these classes: It is embarrassing to recall that in a piece written at the time, I dismissed them as "sewing circle classes." (How's that for gender stereotyping?)

A second "match" drawn out of the compost of memory came from a longitudinal study that preceded and overlapped with the WWK research in which my colleague Claire Zimmerman and I (Clinchy & Zimmerman, 1982, 1985) were using William Perry's (1970) "scheme" largely derived from and illustrated by interviews with Harvard males) to trace the epistemological and ethical development of a sample of undergraduate women. Some of the questions we asked were designed to ascertain whether the students had reached a position in Perry's scheme that involves critical thinking. Some clearly had. For instance, during the first year of the project a student made a comment we would now consider prototypical of separate knowing: "As soon as someone tells me his point of view, I immediately start arguing in my head the opposite point of view. When someone is saying something, I can't help turning it upside down." The next year, we converted this response into a stimulus and asked the students to respond to it.[3] To our dismay, most of them said that they didn't much like that approach and they didn't use it much. Grace, for instance, said that even when she disagreed with someone she didn't start arguing in her head; she started trying to imagine herself in the person's situation. She said, "I sort of fit myself into it in my mind and then I say, 'I see what you mean.'" She said, "There's this initial point where I kind of go into the story, you know? And become like Alice in Wonderland falling down the rabbit hole." Search as we might, we could find no place in Perry's scheme for falling down rabbit holes, and so we interpreted Grace's comment as evidence not of a particular way of thinking but of the absence of any kind of thinking. We saw it, as our critics often see connected knowing, as a sort of naïve credulity: Grace, we concluded, was the sort of person who would fall for anything.

It took me a long time to see that people like Grace and the students in those sewing-circle classes might be following some sort of (admittedly tacit) procedure, rather than simply wallowing in subjectivity. Because connected knowing has much in common with subjectivism, the difference can be difficult to discern. Both subjectivists and connected knowers show respect for views that differ from their own: they seem to listen and refuse to criticize. Both value the sort of knowledge that emerges from firsthand experience, and both draw on feelings and intuition as sources of information. In each of these respects, however, connected knowing does not simply incorporate features of subjectivism; it builds on them, and the resulting construction is quite different.

## Validity, Understanding, and Trust in the Knower

Incidents of miscommunication between men and women like the ones the sociolinguist Deborah Tannen (1990) recounts in *You Just Don't Understand* often come about because the men are operating out of a separate knowing perspective, while the women are operating out of a connected knowing perspective. For instance, a wife listens intently and nods encouragingly as she draws from her husband his reasons for wishing to buy a new car; the next day he turns up with the new car and is hurt and astonished by her angry reaction. The husband has taken the wife's uncritical acceptance as evidence of her agreement and approval; the wife, however, was merely trying to understand. Miscommunications between the authors of WWK and their readers take a similar form, especially when the readers are schooled in philosophy, a discipline founded on adversarial reasoning (Moulton, 1983) and, according to the philosopher Richard Rorty, preoccupied with questions concerning the validity of knowledge.[4] This is the separate knowing perspective. Connected knowing is concerned with matters that, as Rorty (cited by Bruner, 1986, p. 12) says, Anglo American philosophy does not often address, questions about the meaning of experience. Lorraine Code believes, as do we, that in dealing with the formula "S knows that P," philosophers have paid too little attention to S, to characteristics of the knower and her situation that can affect what is known, but she argues that we go too far in the other direction, focusing exclusively on the knower—on how she knows— and ignoring *what* she knows, the content and validity of her views.

We invite that charge, I think, by using the word *know*[5] instead of, say, *believe* or *think* or *feel*. For most philosophers, to "know" something is to make some claim to validity. I may believe that Martians are filling my cellar with poison gas, but surely I do not "know" it. Although we were aware that the word *know* was ambiguous and possibly misleading, we decided, nonetheless, to use it, because it seemed the connected thing to do: we wanted as much as possible to hear the women in their own terms, and "knowing" seemed to come closest to what most of them meant. We rejected "thinking" because, given the dichotomy in this culture between cognition and affect, we were afraid that "thinking" might imply absence of feeling, and for many of the women feeling was intimately involved in "knowing." We rejected "belief" because although some of the women we interviewed distinguished between believing and knowing, others did not in subjectivism, for example, the terms are synonymous. The literary theorist Patrocinio (Patsy) Schweickart (see her chapter in this volume) writes, "One cannot assert meaningfully that something is true or valid only for oneself." This, of course, is precisely what subjectivists do assert. "Everyone's opinion is right for him or her," they say, and, although such a statement may not be meaningful in some discourse communities, it is meaningful to them. Schweickart goes on, "I have beliefs, prejudices, or presuppositions; but I *make* validity claims" (Schweickart, 1988, p. 299). Again, although this is a sensible distinction, it is not one that subjectivists make: "Anyone's interpretation is valid, if that's the way he or she sees it. I mean, nobody can tell you that your opinion is wrong, you know."

In interviewing the women and poring over transcripts of their interviews, we relied predominantly on connected knowing, suspending judgment in an attempt to make sense of the women's ways of making sense of their experience. Code regards connected knowing as "epistemologically problematic" (Code, 1991, p. 253) because it precludes evaluation, and she notes with disapproval a presumption shared by subjectivists and connected knowers that, as one student said, "A person's experience can't be wrong." Although she is aware of the damage done in the past by "experts' telling women what they are really experiencing" (Code, 1991, p. 256) and acknowledges that our "quasi-therapeutic" techniques may be useful in "empowering women who have been 'damaged by patriarchal oppression' " (Code, 1991, p. 252), Code argues that our "acritical acceptance" of the women's autobiographical accounts "is not the only—or the best—alternative" (Code, 1991, p. 256). For us, however, at the data-collection stage of our research, there was no alternative. In order to hear a person in her own terms, the listener must suspend judgment. We may object to the lessons a woman has drawn from her experience. We may feel that she is a victim of "false consciousness," that she has been brainwashed by her oppressors, and that the terms in which she casts her experience are not "her own" but have been foisted on her by the patriarchy. Nevertheless, we must put these thoughts aside and accept her reality as her reality, not only accept it but collude with her in its construction. As the social scientist Stephanie Riger says,

> In contrast to traditional social science in which the researcher is the expert on assessing reality, an interpretive–phenomenological approach permits women to give their own conception of their experiences. Participants, not researchers, are considered the experts at making sense of their world. . . . The shift in authority is striking. (Riger, 1992, p. 733)

Psychologist Jill Morawski and literary theorist R. S. Steele show how in traditional psychological research "the power of the psychologist is increased at the cost of the subjects" (Morawski & Steele, 1991, p. 112), offering as an illustration the psychologist Walter Mischel's (1969) pronouncement that while "subjects" perceive continuities in their personality traits over time, statistics prove them wrong.

> According to [Mischel], in so far as the subjects are numbers on "IBM sheets," that is, objects of scientific reductionism, they are reliable. However, as sentient subjects, that is, beings capable of self-reflection and of constructing a personal history, they are untrustworthy. (Morawski & Steele, 1991, p. 113)

Distrust of the "subject" also permeates accounts of traditional psycho-analytic psychotherapy. After perusing this literature, the psychoanalyst Evelyne Schwaber concluded that "analytic listening remains steeped in a hierarchical two-reality view" (Schwaber, 1983a, p. 390), "the one the patient experiences, and the one the analyst 'knows' " (Schwaber, 1983a, p. 386):

> My first supervisor listened by sifting the material through her own perspective—that is, from the vantage point of the analyst's reality—in trying to and the patient's observing ego to recognize the distortions in her perceptions. The second supervisor sharpened the focus from *within* the patient's perspective, to see in it a certain plausibility, however outlandish, unrealistic, entitled, it may have seemed to the outside observer. (Schwaber, 1983a, pp. 379–380)

Schwaber, like the "constructed knowers" in WWK, sees value in the more separate as well as the more connected approach and uses elements of both in her work, but she firmly rejects the notion that the analyst's view is more accurate than the patient's: the two realities, she says, are "relative" rather than hierarchical (1983a, p. 390).

Like the males in Tanner's anecdotes, readers sometimes interpret our "acritical acceptance" of the women's stories as implying approval of their views. To refrain from criticism, however, means to refrain from approval as well as disapproval. (Good critics, after all, illuminate the merits as well as the faults of the things they examine.) Connected knowing shares with subjectivistm an appreciation of subjective reality, but it does not adhere to the subjectivist doctrine of "subjective validity," the view that all opinions are equally valid and "everyone's opinion is right for him or her."[6] Connected knowing does not imply relativism in this sense. When one is using techniques of connected knowing, as in the initial stages of our research, issues of validity are simply irrelevant.

Although both subjectivists and connected knowers might say that "experience can't be wrong," they mean different things when they say it. Subjectivists *are* unmitigated relativists. They do believe that whatever truths have emerged from a person's firsthand experience are valid for that person. They do believe that these truths are unambiguous, in the feminist philosopher M. E. Hawkesworth's (1989) terms, "transparent" and "unmediated" by personal or cultural preconceptions. Asked how she decides what a poem means, a student speaking from this perspective replies, "Whatever you see in the poem, it's got to be there." Although her teacher may feel that such a student has ignored the words on the page, treating the text as a mirror or an inkblot onto which she projects the contents of her own mind, to the student the meaning is simply there on the page. Much (although not all) of Hawkesworth's critique of feminist positions based on intuition can be applied to subjectivism:

> The distrust of the conceptual aspects of thought, which sustains claims that genuine knowledge requires immediate apprehension, presumes not only that an unmediated grasp of reality is possible but

also that it is authoritative. Moreover, appeals to intuition raise the specter of an authoritarian trump that precludes the possibility of rational debate. Claims based on intuition manifest an unquestioning acceptance of their own veracity. . . . Thus, intuition provides a foundation for claims about the world that is at once authoritarian, admitting of no further discussion, and relativist, since no individual can refute another's "immediate" apprehension of reality. Operating at a level of assertion that admits of no further elaboration or explication, those who abandon themselves to intuition conceive and give birth to dreams, not to truth.[7] (Hawkesworth, 1989, p. 545)

Code (1991, p. 258, n. 74), persisting in reading WWK as an endorsement of subjectivism, quotes this passage from Hawkesworth in criticizing what she interprets as our position. In fact, we could have written the passage ourselves, and we nearly did, in describing Minna, a Hispanic woman enrolled in a community college who, in our view, was beginning to struggle out of subjectivism into procedural knowledge. Deserted by her husband and left with an eight-year-old daughter, no money, no employable skills, and no friends, Minna saw now that as Hawkesworth puts it, in abandoning herself to intuition she had "conceived and given birth to dreams, not to truth." "I was confused about everything," she said. "I was unrealistic about things. I was more in a fantasy world. You have to see things for what they are, not for what you want to see them. I don't want to live in a dream world." Now, she says, "I think everything out, and I want to make sure I understand exactly what's going on before I do anything" (WWK, 1986, p. 99). Code warns that "a subjective knower's 'gut' often lets her down," and subjectivism is not necessarily "conducive to empowerment" (Code, 1991, p. 254). This is not news to Minna, nor to the authors of WWK.

Unlike the feminist scholars who are the objects of Hawkesworth's critique, Sue, the student who wished that her words might float out into the air and just stand, does not *choose* to rely on private, intuitive truth; she has not yet developed an alternative method. Encapsulated in her own world, she can only assert her own truth. For many women who speak from a subjectivist perspective conversations, especially with likeminded people, are a source of great pleasure, but for Sue "discussion" in English class is futile: "Because I know I can't see where they're coming from, so why, you know, why keep trying at it if it doesn't feel comfortable to you, but you have your own thoughts that feel right?" With the advent of procedural knowing, epistemological isolation comes to an end, and collaborative construction of knowledge through discussion becomes not only possible but, because truth is now problematic rather than transparent, essential. Separate knowers can engage in "rational debate," rather than mere assertion and counterassertion, in order to adjudicate truth claims. And connected knowers can obtain vicarious experience through mutual "elaboration and explication" of personal narratives.

This is the sort of interchange, I now believe, that was struggling to be born and may occasionally have emerged, although I could not hear it, in those sewing circle classes I perceived as utterly unproductive. It is easy to misperceive active listening as passive and polite, hard to see it as a genuine procedure, a "skill requiring arduously to be learned." Anyone who has tried to teach (or to learn) the art of connected interviewing,[8] however, knows how difficult it is to learn to listen "objectively," in the connected sense, that is, to hear the other in the other's own terms, to become "an observer from within" (Schwaber, 1983b, p. 274).

## Affirming the Knower

In connected knowing it is essential to refrain from judgment "because," as the psychologist Carl Rogers says, "it is impossible to be accurately perceptive of another's inner world if you have formed an evaluative opinion of that person" (Rogers, 1980, p. 152). If you doubt that assertion, Rogers says, try to describe the views of someone you believe is definitely wrong in a fashion that the person will consider accurate. "In the believing game," Elbow writes, "the first rule is to refrain from doubting" (Elbow, 1973, p. 149). For her undergraduate honors thesis, Carolyn Rabin (1994) analyzed interviews on separate and connected knowing with undergraduates from the Massachusetts Institute of Technology and Wellesley College collected in the Clinchy–Mansfield project. She noted that for many of the MIT men this is what "connected knowing" meant—to refrain from criticism—and this is all it meant; they had not progressed beyond the first rule of the game. I argue, however, that fully developed connected knowing requires that one "affirm" or "confirm" the subjective reality of the other, and affirmation is not merely the absence of negative evaluation; it is a positive effortful act. Affirmation of a person or a position means, as Elbow says, "to say Yes to it" (Elbow, 1986, p. 279), rather than merely offering sympathetic understanding. Confirmation means, in the philosopher Martin Buber's wonderful phrases, to "imagine the real," to "make the other present" (Buber, quoted by Friedman, 1985, p. 4). It involves "a bold swinging . . . into the life of the other" (Buber, quoted by Kohn, 1990, p. 112), and as Alfie Kohn says, this other, for Buber, is a particular other, not an "interchangeable someone" (Kohn, 1990, p. 112), and the knower is "not merely avoiding objectification but affirmatively invoking, . . . addressing the other's status as a subject, . . . an actor, a knower, a center of experience" (Kohn, 1990, p. 100).

This "bold swinging into the life of the other" is a far cry from polite tolerance or "to-each-his-own indifferentism," but it is also not to be confused with approval or agreement. It should be obvious that, as Geertz puts it, "Understanding what people think doesn't mean you have to think the same thing" (Geertz, quoted in Berreby, 1995, p. 4). " 'Understanding,' " Geertz writes, "in the sense of comprehension, perception, and insight needs to be distinguished from 'understanding' in the sense of agreement of opinion, union of sentiment, or commonality of commitment. . . . We must learn to grasp what we cannot embrace" (Geertz, 1986, p. 122). From the connected knowing perspective, of course, we must first try very hard to embrace it.

Conversations involving mutual confirmation are not to be confused with the "relatively harmonious situations" described by Patai and Koertge and mentioned earlier, in which "everyone feels validated and cozy" (Patai & Koertge, 1994, p. 174). If "everyone feels validated" in this situation, it is not because they have been told they are right; it is because they have been heard. As one young woman said, "When people [are] interested in why I feel the way I do and why it makes sense to me, . . . I feel that what I have to say might mean something and has some impact." This sort of validation is especially welcome to procedural knowers. Whereas subjectivists are confident that they can arrive at the truth (the truth for them) simply by reading it off from experience (whatever you see in the poem, it's got to be there) or attending to their infallible guts, procedural knowers have no such assurance. Separate knowers need to know whether their views can survive the scrutiny of an outsider's critical eye, and connected knowers need to know whether their thoughts can "mean something" to someone else, even, perhaps, "an attentive stranger" (Ruddick, 1984, p. 148).

In swinging boldly into the mind of another, truly saying yes to it, two perversions of "connected knowing" are prevented. One is to "use it as a weapon," as one woman said, as "when people say, 'Well, I can see how you would say that given your background,' . . . referring to my background as some wacky thing that nobody else has ever experienced." In this patronizing version, known, I am told, as "the California fuck off," one distances one's self from the other's experience, in effect saying "No" to it. A second perversion is to say yes too quickly, to assume without reflection that others feel as we do or as we would feel in their situation, that is, to assimilate the other to the self: "I know just how you feel!" we say, having, in fact, very little idea or quite the wrong idea.

## The Self as Instrument

Whereas separate knowing requires "self-extrication," "weeding out the self," in Elbow's terms, connected knowing requires "self-insertion" or "projection in the good sense" (Elbow, 1973, p. 149) or, to use a more feminine image, "receiving the other into [the] self" (Noddings, 1984, p. 30). Procedures for minimizing "projection in the bad sense" (Elbow, 1973, p. 149), or, as developmental psychologist Jean Piaget puts it, "excluding the intrusive self" (Piaget, 1972, quoted by Keller, 1983b, p. 134), have been well developed and are known to be effective, although of course not perfectly so. For instance, the effects of "bias" are reduced if observers in an experiment are "double-blinded," unaware of both the hypothesis being tested and the treatment to which the subjects have been assigned. Procedures for using the self as an instrument of understanding are less well developed, but practitioners of the increasingly prevalent "new paradigm" research have made considerable progress in developing and articulating them.

This is not the place to inventory these techniques, but I have already mentioned the procedure by which the investigator rummages through her experience in search of a "match." "The diverse aspects of the self," McCracken says, "become a bundle of templates to be held up against the data until parallels emerge" (McCracken, 1988, p. 19). "To understand a poem, an undergraduate said, "You must let the poem pass into you and become part of yourself, rather than something you see outside yourself. . . . There has to be some parallel between you and the poem." This is an active procedure: we must construct the parallels, by conjuring up "metaphorical extensions, analogies, associations" (Elbow, 1973, p. 149), and we need not simply wait for a poem or a person or a patient to strike a chord, for by "fine tuning" (Margulies, 1989, p. 16) the instrument of our subjectivity we can increase the likelihood of its "empathic resonance" (Howard, 1991, p. 189). Instead of simply "letting" the other in, we can prepare our minds to receive it by engaging in arduous systematic "self-reflection." McCracken advises, for instance, that in preparation for qualitative research, the investigator should construct a "detailed and systematic appreciation of his or her personal experience with the topic of interest. . . . The investigator must inventory and examine the associations, incidents and assumptions that surround the topic in his or her mind" (McCracken, 1988, p. 32), thus "preparing the templates with which he or she will seek out 'matches' in the interview data. The investigator listens to the self in order to listen to the respondent" (McCracken, 1988, p. 33).

In conducting the interview, too, one uses the self as an instrument of understanding. The sociologist Marjorie DeVault, who has forcefully urged us to "analyze more carefully the specific ways that interviewers use personal experience as a resource for listening," describes her own procedure as focusing "on attention to the unsaid, in order to produce it as topic and make it speakable." It "involves noticing ambiguity and problems of expression in interview data, then drawing on my own experience in an investigation aimed at 'filling in' what has been incompletely said" (DeVault, 1990, p. 104).[9]

In using the self to understand the other, we risk imposing the self on the other; projection in the good sense can easily degenerate into projection in the bad sense. Patti Lather, a sympathetic practitioner of new paradigm research, worries that "rampant subjectivity" could prove to be its "nemesis" (Lather, 1986, p. 68). How are we to distinguish between the psychoanalyst Heinz Kohut's "empathy," defined as "the recognition of the self in the other" (Kohut, 1978, quoted by Jordan, 1991, p. 68), and the subjectivist's "Whatever you see in the poem, it's got to be there"? How do we ensure that we are not treating the other as a mirror or a blot of ink, a mere receptacle for our own subjectivity? As the psychologist Alfred Margulies says, "Because empathy is by definition the 'imaginative projection of one's own consciousness into another being,' we will unavoidably find ourselves reflected within our gaze toward the other. I look for you and see myself" (Margulies, 1989, p. 58).

Clinicians and qualitative researchers agree that the matches one pulls from one's own experience should serve only as "clues" (DeVault, 1990, p. 104), "merely a bundle of possibilities, pointers, and suggestions that can be used to plumb the remarks of a respondent" (McCracken, 1988, p. 19). "Imagining how one would feel—or actually has felt," says Alfie Kohn, should be regarded as only a "provisional indication" (Kohn, 1990, p. 133), or as Margulies puts it, "a map constructed second-hand from another life's travels, a map that undergoes constant reworking, revision (re-vision), and clarification" (Margulies, 1989, p. 53). One must remain open to "subtle surprises," to emerging discrepancies between the map and the patient's "inscape." Qualitative researchers devise strategies for inviting surprise, often enlisting the cooperation of participants in reworking the map. Indeed, one must move beyond matching to achieve true understanding. In Kohn's terms we must move beyond "imagine-self" to "imagine-other." If we assume that we have reached full understanding once we run out of matches, we are indeed assimilating the other to the self. The psychiatrist Maurice Friedman calls this truncated procedure "identification":

> [T]he therapist resonates with the experiences related by the client only to the extent that they resemble his or her own. It says, in effect, "I am thou," but misses the Thou precisely at the point where its otherness and uniqueness takes it out of the purview of one's own life stance and life experience. (Friedman, 1985, p. 197)

## I, Thou, and It

Some of our readers and research participants conceive of connected knowing as useful only in dealing with people. At worst, they describe it as a way of "being nice," "getting along with people," and "keeping the peace"; at best, they see it as a way of understanding directed only at live and present people. In WWK, however, we said, "When we speak of separate and connected knowing we refer not to any sort of relationship between the self and another person but [to] relationships between knowers and the objects (of subjects) of knowing (which may or may not be persons)" (WWK, 1986, p. 102). We said that "the mode of knowing is personal, but the object of knowing need not be," citing Cecily's comment (WWK, 1986, p. 121) that in reading a philosopher she "tries to think as the author does," and the comment of another student, who said that "you shouldn't read a book [in this case, Dante's *Divine Comedy*] just as something printed and distant from you, but as a real experience of someone who went through some sort of situation" (WWK, 1986, p. 113).

In connected knowing, the "it" is transformed into a "thou," and the "I" enters into relationship with the thou.[10] Scientists use this procedure. The biologist Barbara McClintock says, in words that have grown familiar, that you must have the patience to hear what the corn "has to say to you" and the openness "to let it come to you" (Keller, 1983a, p. 198), and the pseudonymous biochemist portrayed by June Goodfield in *An Imagined World* says, "If you really want to understand about a tumor you've got to *be* a tumor" (Goodfield, 1991/1994, p. 226). According to the psychologist Seymour Papert, even toddlers are capable of a sensorimotor version of connected knowing. Before the age of two, he says, he "fell in love with gears"; indeed, he became a gear. "You can *be* the gear," he writes. "You can understand how it turns by projecting yourself into its place and turning with it" (Papert, 1980, pp. vi–vii). Papert and his colleague Sherry Turkle found that some of the students they observed learning to construct computer programs—especially girls and women—also "reasoned from within" their programs. Anne, for instance, "psychologically places herself in the same space as the sprites" (the objects whose movements she is programming). "She is down there, in with the sprites. . . . When she talks about them her gestures with hand and body show her moving with and among them. When she speaks of them she uses language such as 'I move here' " (Turkle & Papert, 1990, p. 144).[11] Anne treats the computer rather like "a person" (Turkle, 1984, p. 112), "allowing ideas to emerge in the give and take of conversation with it" (Turkle, 1984, p. 104).

Our research participants often describe their way of reading in similar terms. "You should treat the text as if it were a friend," a student said, and she meant, as Schweickart means, not just to treat it nicely, but to regard it as "not a mere object, like a stone, but the objectification of a subject" (Schweickart, 1989, p. 83). Adrienne Rich, Schweickart writes, aims to make the poet Emily Dickinson "live as the substantial palpable presence animating her works" (Schweickart, 1989, p. 50), to "make [her] present" as Buber (quoted by Friedman, 1985, p. 4) would say. Connected reading is an intersubjective procedure: "The reader encounters not simply a text, but a 'subjectified object': the 'heart and mind' of another woman. She comes into close contact with an interiority—a power, a creativity, a suffering, a vision—that is *not* identical with her own." Schweickart contrasts this feminist version of reader response theory with one put forth by literary theorist Georges Poulet. Poulet also takes a personal approach: "To understand a literary work . . . is to let the individual who wrote it reveal [herself] to us *in* us" (Poulet, 1980, p. 46, quoted by Schweickart, 1986, p. 52). But he portrays reader and author as opponents in a zero-sum game. The reader "becomes the 'prey' of what he reads. . . . His consciousness is 'invaded,' 'annexed,' 'usurped.' . . . In the final analysis, the process of reading leaves room for only one subjectivity" (Schweickart, 1986, pp. 52–53).

In the feminist version of the theory (we call it "connected reading"), on the other hand, there is a "doubling" of subjectivity: "One can be placed at the disposal of the text while the other remains with the reader." Schweickart warns, however, that ultimately, because the reader constructs the meaning of the text, "there is only one subject present—the reader. . . . The subjectivity roused to life by reading, while it may be attributed to the author, is nevertheless not a separate subjectivity but a projection of the subjectivity of the reader" (Schweickart, 1986, p. 53). Projection in the bad sense is a very real danger when the author, being absent, cannot speak for herself.[12] Schweickart:

> In real conversation the other person can interrupt, object to an erroneous interpretation, provide further explanations, change her mind, change the topic, or cut off conversation altogether. In reading, there are no comparable safeguards against the appropriation of the text by the reader. (Schweickart, 1986, p. 53)

The best that can be done in connected reading is to encourage absent authors to speak and to join them in a semblance of collaboration. The writer and critic Doris Grumbach recounts a midlife change in her ways of reading that sounds like a transition from a relatively separate to a relatively connected approach. "It is hard work to read more slowly," she says. "But when I slow down, I interlard the writers' words with my own. I think about what they are saying. . . . I dillydally in their views" (Grumbach, 1991, p. 15). Reading becomes a kind of conversation, and the reader apprentices herself to the writer. "Reading in the new way now, I learn. Before, I seemed to be instructing the book with my superior opinions" (Grumbach, 1991, p. 15).[13] ("Do not dictate to your author, try to become him" [Woolf, 1932, p. 282].)

"Subjectivist theories of reading," Schweickart says, "silence the text" (Schweickart, 1989, p. 83). This applies to the informal subjectivist theories of ordinary readers as well as to members of the lit-crit community: "We're all allowed to read into a poem any meaning we want," and "Whatever you see in the poem, it's got to be there," whether the poet likes it or not. Objectivist readings, on the other hand, such as the ones offered by people adhering to the epistemological position we call *received knowing*, silence the reader: to find out what a poem means, "you'd have to ask the poet; it's his poem." For connected readers it is different: A poem does not belong solely to its author. "Poems are written," a student explained, "but you also have to interpret them." A poem is not something "that sits there and does nothing. It has to be interpreted by other people, and those people are going to have their own ideas of what it means." Those ideas, however, must be grounded in the text: interpretation is "a two-person activity," involving the poet as well as the reader.

In sharing with the text the task of interpretation, instead of claiming it as solely their own, connected readers might seem to possess less authority than subjectivist readers. But the authority of subjectivism is, in fact, derivative, and, being derivative, it is fragile. Who is it who "allows" us to interpret poetry for ourselves, and if They have the power to allow it, might They not also have the power to take away the privilege? ("My English teacher lets me have my own opinions," a student said, but she worried that next semester's teacher might be less lenient.)

Authority in subjectivism is limited, as well as tenuous. In one of our studies, we asked students to tell us how they assessed the merits of a poem. "To me," one woman replied, "what makes one poem better than another one is that I can get something from it as a person. That says nothing about the poem itself. I mean, I have no authority." I hear in this comment an appropriate humility, a refusal to lay down the law and speak for the text. But I hear, too, a poignant diffidence: The student is saying that she has no public voice, that, although she is free to make her own judgments, there is no reason for anyone to listen to her. Her judgments have no objective value. They say nothing about the poem—they are just about her; there is no "it" here; subjectivist reading is a one-person activity.

In granting some voice to the text, the connected reader actually increases the power of her own voice. Although acknowledging that the authority of her interpretation is qualified, she asserts that it does have *some* authority, and, because she constructed the interpretation herself, no one can take it away (although she herself may decide to abandon it). Like the subjectivist, the connected reader speaks "as a person," but, because her words concern the poem as well as herself, they are comprehensible to others and worthy of attention. And, far from silencing the author, by speaking as a person the connected reader leaves space for the text to speak. Schweickart astutely observes that although Rich's "use of the personal voice . . . serves as a reminder that her interpretation is informed by her own perspective," it also "serves as a gesture warding off any inclination to appropriate the authority of the text as a warrant for the validity of the interpretation" (Schweickart, 1986, p. 54). Like the subjectivist, the connected reader does not presume to speak for the text, but, unlike the subjectivist, she does not speak only to herself; she assumes that her words might "mean something, and have some impact" on other readers.

## Thinking and Feeling

To adopt the perspective of the other requires thinking (reasoning, inference) as well as empathy. Indeed, although the term *empathy* has come to connote merely an affective "feeling with," the German word from which it was translated, *Einfühlung*, meant, literally, "feeling into," and referred, according to the psychologist M. F. Basch, to "the ability of one person to come to know first-hand, so to speak, the experience of another"; "inference, judgment, and other aspects of reasoning thought" were as central to its meaning as affect (Basch, 1983, p. 110). The loss in translation of these cognitive aspects can be seen as an instance of the Western tendency to treat thinking and feeling as mutually exclusive, the same tendency that has led readers of WWK to assume that because separate knowing involves reasoning, and connected knowing differs from separate knowing, then connected knowing must involve merely feeling. A tendency to place a "separate spin" on essentially connected notions is also evident here. To "feel with" seems to preserve the autonomy of knower and known: their feelings are parallel but not fused. "Feeling into," in contrast, suggests a more intimate relation. In any case, connected knowing and *Einfühlung*, in its original meaning, seem to be close relatives, if not twins.

Kohn writes that "without imagining the reality of the other, empathic feeling is ultimately self-oriented and thus unworthy of the name" (Kohn, 1990, p. 131), and imagining the reality of the other requires responding to its cognitive content as well as its affect. Kohn recalls an incident from his student days when he raised a concern with his instructor, a psychiatrist, about some aspect of the course. "I can see you're angry," the instructor said. Up to that point, Kohn says, he had not been angry, but the instructor's response did anger him, because "it referred only to what he believed was my mood, effectively brushing aside the content of what I had expressed. His exclusively affective focus felt dismissive, even infantalizing, rather than empathic or understanding" (Kohn, 1990, pp. 311–312).

Subjectivism is especially prone to this "noninferential empathy" (Flavell, 1985, p. 139). "I'm very empathic," a student told us, "very sensitive to other peoples' emotions, even if I don't know them. Somebody could be depressed across the room, and I'll be depressed all day because that person's depressed who I don't even know." Emotional contagion is not sufficient for mature connected knowing (although it may constitute a rudimentary basis for it),[14] nor is "situational role-taking," Kohn's "imagine-self," meaning, What would *I* do, given *my* background, personality, values, and so on, in *his* situation? In connected knowing one must "imagine-other" (my rephrasing of Kohn's "imagine-him"), put one's self into the head and heart, as well as the shoes of the other. Kohn:

> The issue is not just how weepy I become upon learning that your spouse has died; it is also whether I am merely recalling and reacting to a comparable loss in my own life or whether I am resonating to your unique set of circumstances—the suddenness of the death, the particular features of this person you loved that are especially vivid for you, your rocky marital history and the resultant prickles of guilt you are now feeling, the way your initial numbness is finally giving way to real pain, the respects in which your unconscious fears of being abandoned are about to be freshly revived by this event, the relationship that you and I have had up to now, and so on. (Kohn, 1990, pp. 132–133)

It is this intense concentration on the unique aspects of the object that characterizes the objectivity of connected knowing. If you act as the author's accomplice, Woolf says, "if you open your mind as widely as possible, then signs and hints of almost imperceptible fineness, from the twist and turn of the first sentences, will bring you into the presence of a human being unlike any other. Steep yourself in this, acquaint yourself with this." In separate knowing one regards the object as an instance of a category (a type of person, say, or a genre) and measures it against objective standards. In connected knowing, the focus is on the object in itself, in all its particularity of detail. Once having constructed a complex constellation of specific circumstances peculiar to the particular worlds of the novelist or the next-door neighbor, or who- or whatever, connected knowers are forced to acknowledge disjunctions between these worlds and their own, and the danger of imagining the other as the self is sharply diminished.

"Nonempathic inference" (Flavell, 1985, p. 139) seems as problematic as noninferential empathy. Kohn asks us to "imagine a continuum; on one side are universal experiences, where imagine-self will do (burning hand); on the other side are things one has not personally experienced, where imagine-him is obviously required (giving birth)" (Kohn, 1990, p. 134). ("Him" seems an odd choice of pronoun in this context.) "The interesting cases," Kohn writes, "are in the middle (death of spouse). One can get away with treating that example as a generic grief, but only at a considerable cost to the integrity of the empathic response" (Kohn, 1990, p. 134). It seems likely that we are especially prone to assimilation to the self concerning the "things in the middle," those "universal" events that appear to be similar but are experienced differently, like the ones listed by the philosopher Elizabeth Spelman: "birth, death, eating, cooking, working, loving, having kin, being friends" (Spelman, 1988, p. 179). Fully to "imagine-other" in these situations seems to me to require feeling as well as thinking, but the MIT men do not seem to think so: in delineating their versions of "connected knowing," not one of them—even among those who claimed to use the procedure—referred to empathy or, indeed, made any mention of affect, whereas many of the Wellesley women did. The difference is rooted not in gender but in epistemology (which, although related to gender, is not synonymous with it). Women who are predominantly separate knowers also practice nonempathic inference, and, perceiving their ideas as autonomous, independent of their persons, they wish that others would do the same with them, Roberta, for instance, said that although she welcomed the opportunity to defend her carefully constructed opinions, when people tried to delve into the experiences behind the opinions instead of treating them on their own merits, she tended to "push [them] away:" "I feel like they're belittling me. . . . Why don't they just ask me straight out why I think my idea, because I've thought my idea through. They don't have to like, beat around the bush about it" (Mansfield & Clinchy, 1992).

To people like Roberta, who present themselves as heavily tipped in the direction of separate knowing, it is especially important that people respond to the impersonal cognitive content of their ideas; they tend to be suspicious of more personal approaches, experiencing them as Kohn experienced his instructor's noninferential empathy, as "belittling" (Roberta), as "infantatizing" and "dismissive" (Kohn). People who present themselves as oriented toward connected knowing, on the other hand, are wary of *impersonal* approaches: like the women in Tannen's accounts, they feel bereft when their listeners (in Tannen's account, men) offer analyses and solutions to the painful problem they have recounted, instead of resonating to their pain. Some adolescent males, observing this response in girls of their acquaintance, have formed a theory about it. "Girls don't want you to fix their problems," eighteen-year-old David Constantine writes to *Parade* magazine. "They just want to talk about them, and they want you to listen. They don't want you to say, 'What do you care?' or 'It's nothing to worry about.'" David infers correctly that girls don't want their worries dismissed, but his grasp of empathy seems limited: "Girls want you to say things like, 'Hmmm . . .' and 'Really?' and 'Wow, I don't blame you.'" According to David, girls just want to feel validated and cozy. "A good 'Hmmm . . .' and a feigned interested look is more important to them than the greatest answer we could come up with to all their troubles" ("What Bothers Me about Girls," 1994). David would claim, as have several of our students and colleagues who appear to be oriented separate knowing, that it is not necessary to feel what a person is feeling in order to understand him. From the connected knowing perspective, however, thinking cannot be divorced from feeling. Those who practice fully developed connected knowing, like those who practice Kohn's fully developed empathy, "truly experience the other as a subject." Kohn uses the word *experience* rather than *understand*—and so, I think, should I—"because something more than an intellectual apprehension is required. . . . [T]he connection . . . must be felt viscerally" (Kohn, 1990, p. 150).

## Connected Knowing with the Self

I first read the words "[T]he connection . . . must be felt viscerally" after teaching an especially intense session of my seminar, and they seemed to me just right, but the next phrase brought me up short: "The connection must be felt viscerally *as surely as one's own humanness and uniqueness are felt*" (Kohn, 1990, p. 150). Whoa. Was Kohn asserting that knowledge of the self is prerequisite to knowledge of others, that we experience others as subjects only by analogy to our experience of ourselves as subjects? My fifteen seminar students had asserted that afternoon with nearly perfect unanimity that they found it far easier to understand other people's beliefs and values and desires than to know their own. They would agree with Addie, an interviewee who said, "It's easy for me to see a whole lot of different points of view on things and to understand why people think those things. The hard thing is sitting down and saying, 'Okay, what do *I* think, and why do *I* think it?' " When in our research we asked young women to "describe themselves to themselves," they said things like "I'm about average" and "My ideas are just sort of like the norms." They seemed often to respond not as compassionate observers from within, but as stern judges from without: "I'm too fat . . . fairly good with people . . . pretty smart . . . not as tolerant as I should be." Psychologists Lyn Brown and Carol Gilligan describe how in adolescence girls who come up against "a wall of shoulds" (Brown & Gilligan, 1992, p. 97); they "come to a place where they feel they cannot say or feel or know what they have experienced" (Brown & Gilligan, 1992, p. 4). For many adult women, the wall remains in place; they cannot seem to connect with their own humanness and uniqueness. Muttering aloud, I reported all this to Kohn, interlarding my words with his, and apparently he heard me, for he went on: "[T]his last formulation gives us pause. . . [I]t is not clear that everyone does experience his or her own subjectivity" (Kohn, 1990, p. 150). It is crystal clear from research results (as well as ordinary observation) that many do not.

In our interviews, Annick and I tried to determine whether our respondents used separate knowing with themselves. We asked, "Do you ever use this approach with yourself—with your own thinking? Play devil's advocate with yourself, or argue with yourself?" Almost all said that they did, some describing the internal critic as a destructive antagonist, others drawing a more benign picture of "a friend behaving as an enemy" (Torbert, 1976), like the one inhabiting the philosopher Alice Koller's head, "thinking up the strongest possible arguments against my own position" in order to "find the flaws in my reasoning, the blunt edges of the ideas I'm trying to sharpen" (Roller, 1990, p. 27). No one was baffled by our question; everyone could make some sense of it.

One day Annick happened to notice that we asked no comparable question about connected knowing, whereas in every other respect we had constructed parallel questions about the two approaches. Although we wanted to repair the omission, we were uncertain how to phrase such a question, or even whether such a question made sense. It seemed nonsensical to ask whether people tried to step into their own shoes; surely they were already in them. Bewildered, we asked our friends, "What would it mean to use connected knowing with yourself?" Ann Stanton (see her chapter, this volume) instantly replied, "It means to treat your mind as if it were a friend." This seemed to make sense. After all, we had ample evidence that the women we had interviewed found it hard to befriend their ideas, hard to "believe" them, to "say yes" to them. And so we added to the interview a question that, after repeated rephrasing, emerged (still a bit awkwardly) as "Do you ever use this approach with yourself? Try to see why you think what you do, what's right about it?" Our respondents had as much trouble answering the question as we had had in formulating it. "Huh? What? What do you mean? I don't get it." Often, they heard the question as asking about not a friend but an enemy in the head: "Oh, yeah," they said. "I'm forever second-guessing myself." Not one of our research participants managed to articulate with much clarity a practice of connected knowing with the self.

For most of the women we interviewed, then, connected knowing with the self was at least as difficult to achieve as connected knowing with the other, and possibly more so. These women were like the patient described by the psychotherapist Judith Jordan who, before therapy, "did not seem able to take her own inner experience as a serious object for interest and attention." "I care for others sometimes like a sheepherder," the woman said. . . . "I put myself in their place and I understand. With myself, though, I used to be like a lion tamer with a bull whip" (Jordan, 1991, p. 78). The clinical literature suggests that "intrapsychic empathy" (Schafer, 1964, p. 251) is a skill arduously to be learned, requiring discipline and practice, usually under the guidance of some sort of tutor (a therapist, perhaps, or a Zen master).

The psychoanalyst Joanna Field tells a compelling story of her own efforts to achieve intrapsychic empathy. Feeling "utterly at sea as to how to live my life," thinking second-hand thoughts, and "whipping" herself in pursuit of second-hand goals, she developed over a period of years her own "method" of "active passivity" that enabled her, ultimately, to step inside her own shoes, to "see through [her] own eyes instead of at second hand." The method requires that one take an active stance toward one's thoughts and feelings, rather than simply letting them run on as a sort of "unconscious monologue" in the background of one's mind, but the activity is the sort practiced by midwives rather than taskmasters. "I began to see," Field writes, "that I must play the Montessori teacher to my thought, must leave it free to follow its own laws of growth, my function being to observe its activities, provide suitable material to enchannel them, but never to coerce it into docility" (Field, 1936/1981, p. 7). The process has much in common with the modes of fostering growth used by the public leader Mary Belenky in her chapter in this volume. Field writes,

> By continual watching and expression I must learn to observe my thought and maintain a vigilance not against "wrong" thoughts, but against refusal to recognize any thought. Further, this introspection meant continual expression, not continual analysis; it meant that I must bring my thoughts and feelings up in their wholeness, not argue about them. (Field, 1936/1981, pp. 204–205)

Field found that one way of bringing her thoughts and feelings up in their wholeness was to let them "write themselves" into the friendly pages of her journal. The journal turns the "I" into an "it," objectifying the knower's subjectivity, and in perusing the journal the knower turns the "it" into a "thou," in effect practicing connected knowing with herself.

But it is difficult to penetrate the wall of shoulds and speak truly, even in the privacy of one's journal, and in public it is even harder. The novelist Mary Gordon says that in striving to develop her own voice as a writer she was haunted by "bad specters" who infused her with a fear of being "trivial" (Gordon, 1980, p. 27), two famous male poets, perhaps, peering over her shoulder as she sat at the typewriter, and murmuring, "Your experience is an embarrassment; your experience is insignificant" (Gordon, 1980, p. 28). "Do you talk much in class?" we asked an undergraduate. "It's hard," she said. "I think—I always think, 'Do I really want to say this or not? Is it important enough to say?'"

Given the presence of strangling self-doubt, most of us find it impossible to achieve intrapsychic empathy on our own. Lacking the skill and stamina to serve as Montessori teachers to ourselves, we depend on external "teachers"—friends and colleagues, as well as certified teachers—who help us to say what we want to say (WWK, 1986, p. 218), reading our early drafts as "sympathetic allies," "trying to see the *validity*" in what we have written, and telling us "the ways in which [it] makes sense" (Elbow, 1986, p. 287).

It is reasonable to argue that without intimate knowledge of one's self one cannot enter into intimacy with another, that one "who is essentially a stranger to himself is unlikely to forge an affective connection to someone else" (Kohn, 1990, p. 152). Without self-knowledge we cannot exploit genuine similarities between self and other, using "templates" in the self to guide us to "matches" in the other. Without self-knowledge we cannot preserve the otherness of the other; he, she, or it becomes a creature of our projections. But how *well* must we know ourselves before we can know another, and must self-knowledge always come first? After all, as the philosopher Iris Murdoch says, "Self is as hard to see justly as other things" (Murdoch, 1970, p. 67)—harder, for people like Addie.

## Fear of Fusion

Addie reports that when she entered her friends' subjective frames of reference, she lost touch with her own: "I felt, 'My God, I'm becoming—I'm not me anymore. I'm not thinking my own ideas anymore.' I was becoming very affected by other people's opinions and ideas." Writers on empathy seem to live in dread of such an event; anxiety over the possibility of "fusion" pervades the literature, expressed at times in hyperbolic terms and seeming to my mind to reach near-phobic proportions. "What happens to the self when it feels into the other?" Kohn asks, and he answers, apparently in an effort to quell anxiety that I was not experiencing, "All is not lost" (Kohn, 1990, p. 153). Kohn reports that Buber rejected the word *empathy* because it connoted "loss of the self in the process of experiencing the other" (Kohn, 1990, p. 153), and Buber was at pains to emphasize that one could experience the other "without forfeiting anything of the felt reality of his [own] reality" (Buber, 1947, p. 62). Schweickart assures us that Adrienne Rich does not "identify" with Dickinson, but merely "establishes an affinity" (Schweickart, 1989 p. 64). Steele warns that "the reader must claim her or his independence as a subject, not allowing her or himself to be subjugated by the text" (Steele, 1986, p. 259). Carl Rogers advises therapists "[t]o sense the client's world as if it were your own, but without ever losing the 'as if' quality" (Rogers, 1961, p. 284). Kohn asserts that empathy does not require that "the self become submerged in the other" or that "its subjectivity be demolished" (Kohn, 1990, p. 153), and Elbow reminds players of the believing game that "it's only a game"; they can quit at any time (Elbow, 1973, p. 174).

Although of course there is truth in the view that the empathic self can (indeed, must) maintain its integrity and need not (indeed, must not) allow itself to be consumed by the other, these statements raise the specter of reducing a paradox—"the paradox of separateness within connection," as Jordan defines it (Jordan, 1991, p. 69)—to a dichotomy: "seeing the self as *either* distinct and autonomous *or* merged and embedded" (Jordan, 1991, p. 72). Words like *forfeit, claim,* and *allow* seem to partake of a "justice" orientation, common among those who conceive of themselves as "separate" rather than "connected" in relationships (Lyons, 1983). Formulations of empathy seem often to begin from a premise of distance and difference—"strain[ing]" after similarity" (Barber, 1984, p. 175) across a divide over an "abyss" (Buber, 1947, p. 175)—rather than solidarity and similarity. Perhaps it is possible to "leave the self *intact* but also leave the self *transformed*" (Kohn, 1990, italics added) if *intact* is defined as "unimpaired," but the word carries traces of its root meaning of "untouched," and so in this context connotes an impregnable self. Indeed, if empathy is defined as projection into the other, as it is in the *Oxford Universal Dictionary* among many others, one may even detect a whiff of castration anxiety in forebodings of fusion.

The women we interviewed used images of reception rather than projection in describing connected knowing (WWK, 1986, p. 122). The biographer Elizabeth Young-Breuhl puts it this way:

> Empathizing involves . . . putting another person *in yourself,* becoming another person's habitat, without dissolving the person, without digesting the person. You are mentally pregnant, not with a potential life but with a person, indeed, a whole life, a person with her history. So the person lives on in you and you can, as it were, hear her in this intimacy. But this depends upon your ability to tell the difference between the subject and yourself, to appreciate the role that she plays in your psychic life. (Young-Breuhl, as quoted by Breslin, 1994, p. 19)

For Young-Breuhl "the other is incorporated as other" (Breslin, 1994, p. 19). There is a "doubling" of subjectivity, as in Schweickart's account of reading, in spite of the (paradoxical) fact that "there is only one subject present" (see my earlier discussion and Schweickart's chapter, this volume). In "caring," says the philosopher Nel Noddings, "I become a duality. . . . The seeing and feeling are mine, but only partly and temporarily mine, as on loan to me" (Noddings, 1984, p. 30). In this "receptive" conception of empathy one need never leave home, and so, perhaps, the risk of being stranded, like Addie, behind the eyes of the other, is diminished.[15] Although Buber's concept of "inclusion" (explicated by Friedman) contains images of moving out ("bold swinging into the life of another"), in (paradoxical) fact, it does not require that one leave one's home ground: "Inclusion . . . does not mean at any point that one gives up the ground of one's own concreteness [or] ceases to see through one's own eyes" (Friedman, 1985, p. 199). Inclusion means "making present." Through "mutual confirmation," Friedman says, "partners" make each other present in their "wholeness, unity, and uniqueness"[16] (Friedman, 1985, p. 4). In this context, connected knowing with the other and connected knowing with the self are reciprocal rather than oppositional processes: neither partner disappears into the other; each makes and keeps the other present.

## Knowing Communities

Both separate and connected knowing achieve their full power when practiced in partnership with other like-minded knowers. Separate knowers benefit from partnership with friends willing to behave as enemies. Francis Crick, one of the discoverers of the structure of DNA, says, "A good scientist values criticism almost more highly than friendship; no, in science criticism is the height and measure of friendship. The collaborator points out the obvious, with due impatience. He stops the nonsense" (Crick, quoted by Bruffee, 1981, p. 178). An MIT student supplied a moving illustration of this process and, incidentally, of the detachment that is, for me, the heart and soul of separate knowing. Ed was one of several summer student interns working in a hospital laboratory on various projects. Each week the students met with the dozen or so scientists who were the "brains of the group," to present their problems and their ideas.

> I would say something like, "You know, we had this spike in the frequency plot here, and I think it's because of this," and before you could blink an eye one of the big older guys would go, "No, no, that's wrong." And I'm like—"Uh, okay." I mean, like, for three or four days I've been thinking that it was this thing. And I thought I was so clever for figuring it out. And the guy will—in—in five seconds shoot it down and say, "No, that's absolutely wrong because of this." And of course he's right.

> It took me a good part of the summer to realize how much it wasn't malicious. And that all these gentlemen were there for the purpose of science and for engineering. And they didn't mean anything personal, when they shot you down right away. But it was—the way they saw it is, they were dismissing a wrong proposition so it wouldn't have time to—They would—they would just take care of it right away.

> I thought it was real neat. To see that happen—I mean, some of these doctors are some of the best doctors or bioengineers around. And they were able to—they didn't see ideas as *possessions*. They saw ideas as ideas. [pause] And ideas were sort of like the group's ideas. You sat there and you formulated something for a project that the group was working on. So it was a group idea. [pause] It just continues to amaze me.[17]

Collaboration may be more essential to connected than to separate knowing. We are better at playing solitaire in the doubting game than in the believing game, Elbow thinks, because we've had more practice at it (Elbow, 1973, p. 175), and certainly the women we've talked with seemed more adept at doubting than believing themselves. It is easier to internalize a partner in the doubting game, because the rules of that game are codified within discourse communities, and anyone who knows the rules will do: the partner, to borrow a phrase from Kohn, is an "interchangeable someone" (Kohn, 1990, p. 112). Psychologists Marvin Berkowitz and Fritz Oser (1987) found that once adolescents reached the highest stage of skill in argumentation, achieving the ability to integrate a partner's argument with their own and to anticipate weaknesses in both, the partner became "superfluous . . . because one can now fully anticipate the other and take a more objective perspective on one's own reasoning, critically examining it as if from an outside perspective" (Berkowitz & Oser, 1987, p. 9).[18]

Because the partners in connected knowing are not interchangeable someones, but particular persons whose unique perspectives cannot be anticipated and so cannot be internalized, connected collaboration would seem to be minimally a two-person activity, although, of course, the external collaborator need not be a real and present person. Jill Tarule examines processes of connected collaboration in detail in her chapter in this volume. Here, I offer only one example, drawn from a famous short story, "A Jury of Her Peers," written by Susan Glaspell and published in 1917. Ed's story illustrates the power of detachment in the collaborative construction of knowledge; Glaspell's story shows how attachment can be an equally powerful force.

In the story, Mrs. Wright, a farmer's wife, has been taken off to jail on suspicion of murder, after apparently tying a rope around her husband's neck and strangling him in his sleep. Mrs. Hale, a neighbor who knew Mrs. Wright as a girl, but has rarely visited her in recent years, and Mrs. Peters, the sheriff's wife, are collecting household articles to take to Mrs. Wright in jail, while their husbands search the bleak homestead for clues to the motive for the crime. It is the women who come upon two crucial clues: a birdcage with its door hinge ripped apart, suggesting that "someone must have been—rough with it" (Glaspell, 1917, p. 273), and a strangled canary, laid in a pretty box. " 'She liked the bird,' " Mrs. Hale says. " 'She was going to bury it in that pretty box.' " Mrs. Peters, recapturing feelings she has trained herself to disown, remembers, " 'When I was a girl . . . my kitten—there was a boy took a hatchet, and before my eyes—before I could get there—. . . If they hadn't held me back I would have—'—hearing the men's footsteps overhead she finishes "weakly,"—'hurt him.' "

" 'Wright wouldn't like the bird," Mrs. Hale says, " 'a thing that sang. She used to sing. He killed that too.' " Thinking of the bleak, childless, cheerless household, dominated by the chilly presence of the stern and silent Mr. Wright, which she has loathed to visit, and recalling Mrs. Wright as "Minnie Foster, when she wore a white dress with blue ribbons and stood up there in the choir and sang" (Glaspell, 1917, p. 278). Mrs. Hale says, " 'If there had been years and years of—nothing, then a bird to sing to you, it would be awful—still—after the bird was still.' " Glaspell writes, "It was as if something within her not herself had spoken, and it found in Mrs. Peters something she did not know as herself." " 'I know what stillness is,' she said, in a queer, monotonous voice. When we homesteaded in Dakota, and my first baby died—after he was two years old—and me with no other then—' " (Glaspell, 1917, p. 278).

The empathic interchange seems to involve not just a "doubling" but at least a tripling of subjectivities: Each woman achieves greater understanding of herself and the other, and both come to understand a crime that had seemed initially inexplicable, especially to Mrs. Peters, a woman who is, after all, "married to the law." Digging down deep, the women find a commonality of experience that dissolves the distance between them and leads to the construction of knowledge. Although Glaspell is aware of distinctions among the three women, it is the similarities she emphasizes. Mrs. Hale says, " 'We live close together and we live far apart. We all go through just a different kind of the same thing! If it weren't,—why do you and I *understand*? Why do we *know*—what we know this minute?' " (Glaspell, 1917, p. 279).

## Transformation of Self and Other

Theories of empathy that stress preservation of an intact self seem irrelevant to Glaspell's story. They connote a conception of the self as "finished" as well as separate—a sort of packaged self that one carts about from one relationship to the next. My (partially) postmodern mind is more comfortable with a notion of selves-in-process, being coconstructed and reconstructed in the context of relationships, and this is the story Glaspell tells: Mrs. Peters, in particular, is transformed by the visions Mrs. Hale shares with her and by her own "retrospective self-empathy" (Blanck & Blanck, 1979, p. 251). Friedman's notion of "mutual confirmation" (adopted from Buber) does seem to imply such a conception: he says that "mutual confirmation is essential to becoming a self" (Friedman, 1985, p. 119), and confirmation, in Buber's terms means "accepting the whole potentiality. . . . 'I accept you as you are' [means that] I discover in you just by my accepting love . . . what you are meant to become' " (Buber, 1966, pp. 181 ff., quoted in Friedman, 1985, p. 136).

In highly developed forms of connected knowing with the other, it becomes possible to view the self from the perspective of the other. As Kohn says, "[i]n order to make the *other* into a subject by taking her perspective, one must . . . make the self into an object . . . come to see ourselves from the outside, the way others see us" (Kohn, 1990, p. 150). Schwaber describes how in becoming a more "connected" (my term) therapist, she moved from a traditional conception of the "transference" as "a phenomenon arising from internal pressures within the patient, from which the analyst, as a blank screen, could stand apart and observe, to that in which the specificity of the analyst's contribution was seen as intrinsic to its very nature" (Schwaber, 1983. p. 381). Taking the patient's reality seriously, "believing" it, forced her to see herself as the patient saw her, and to own (take seriously) her own response, instead of seeing it as merely a reaction to the patient's view, as is implied in the term *counter-transference*.

In one sense, it is not easy to objectify the self, to see one's self as others see us, especially, as Spelman points out, if it means entertaining the view of those whom we have oppressed of ourselves as oppressors (Spelman, 1988, p. 178). (Oppressors objectify the oppressed, of course, in order to prevent such revelations.) In another sense, however, women often find it all too easy to turn themselves into objects: the critic in their heads speaks from a distance, and it speaks in "shoulds," telling them how they ought to be and preventing them from seeing who they are and how they want to be. "Healthy self-objectification," Kohn says, consists of allowing one's self to be "watched and weighed" (Kohn, 1990, p. 151), an uncomfortable experience, but one that can be borne by "someone confident in her subjectivity, unafraid of being object to another." Many of our research participants, however, confess that they are not confident in their subjectivity, and, given the unhealthy objectifications to which they have been subjected in the past, perpetrated by not-so-friendly enemies within and without, they are understandably wary of being "watched and weighed." It is true that we need to face up to friends acting as enemies, but we also need friends acting as friends (Marshall & Reason, 1993), people who will view us with a compassionate rather than a critical eye, and who will invite us to do the same with them. *Subjectification*—joint subjectification—seems a better term than *objectification* to describe this process.

Spelman contrasts people (such as Schwaber) who actively seek out another person's viewpoint, "taking seriously how it represents a critique" of their own, with people who practice mere "tolerance" (Spelman, 1988, p. 183). The former are open to transformation; the latter are not. The subjectivist's spontaneity, her tendency to trust her own judgment and "go with her gut," are sources of genuine power, but they may limit her capacity for transformation. She is likely to emerge from "interactions" with ideas with her own prior positions intact. Asked how she decides among competing interpretations of a poem, a student replied:

> I usually find that when ideas are being tossed around I'm usually more akin to one than another. I don't know—my opinions are just sort of *there*. . . . It's almost more a matter of liking one more than another. I mean, I happen to agree with one or identify with it more.

In connected learning, on the other hand, both the learner and the subject matter are, Elbow says, "deformed":

> Good learning is not a matter of finding a happy medium where both parties are transformed as little as possible. Rather, both parties must be maximally transformed—in a sense deformed. There is violence in learning. We cannot learn something without eating it, yet we cannot really learn it either without being chewed up. (Elbow, 1986, p. 147)

Subjectivism is a form of what the psychologist David Perkins (Perkins, Farady, & Bushey, 1991) calls "makes-sense epistemology." A makes-sense epistemologist "believes that the way to evaluate conclusions is by asking whether they 'make sense' at first blush" (Baron, 1991, p. 177). The person

> only has to get to the point of telling one story about the situation that weaves together the facts in one way, from one point of view, congruent with the person's prior beliefs. Then the model "makes sense." When sense is achieved, there is no need to continue. (Perkins et al., 1991, p. 99)

Both separate and connected knowing are procedures that transcend makes-sense epistemology and meet the criteria for Perkins's "critical epistemology." Both procedures contain the premise that "it is not enough for a particular story to match one's prominent prior beliefs" (Perkins et al., 1991, p. 100), and "it is not enough for a particular story about a situation to hang together. One must consider what other, rather different stories might also hang together" (Perkins et al., 1991, pp. 99–100). In separate knowing one generates arguments that compete with a given position—another person's or one's own—and looks for flaws beneath the apparently sensible surface. In connected knowing one enters into stories beyond the bounds of one's own meager experience, and attempts to make meaning out of narratives that "at first blush" make little sense. Players in the believing game, Elbow says, are anything but credulous.

> The credulous person really suffers from *difficulty* in believing, not ease in believing: give him an array of assertions and he will always believe the one that requires the least expenditure of believing energy. He has a weak believing muscle and can only believe what is easy to believe. . . . The fact that we call this disease credulity when it is really incredulity reflects vividly our culture's fear of belief. (Elbow, 1973, p. 183)

Perhaps it was my own fear of belief, and my addiction to doubt, that made it so hard for me to see that when Grace told us of "falling down the rabbit hole, like Alice in Wonderland," she might be describing a hard-won ability, rather than an involuntary swoon; that an uncritical way of knowing might qualify as a critical epistemology; and that "going into the story" could be a powerful strategy for discovering how "other stories, rather different" from one's own, "might also hang together."

A part of me would like to end this chapter here, leaving you with a picture of connected knowing as a tough-minded, counterintuitive way of knowing, a critical epistemology that is in some sense the absolute opposite of the subjectivist makes-sense epistemology with which it is so often confused. This is how Elbow presents the believing game, as a way of achieving "distance" from one's spontaneous beliefs. And this is how we represent connected knowing in our research: "When I have an idea about something, and it *differs* from the way another person is thinking about it." But I cannot leave it at that. Neither Elbow's concept of the believing game nor the quotation we use in our research captures the full meaning I would like the concept to have.

Although it is important to distinguish the connected knower from the makes-sense epistemologist who accepts without further exploration whatever appears at first blush to be true, it is also important to remember that what appears to be true may in fact *be* true and should not be dismissed out of hand. This is a notion that frightens academicians, who greet with suspicion books like WWK and Gilligan's (1982) *In a Different Voice* precisely because the stories they tell "resonate so thoroughly" with the experience of women readers that they are accepted without further exploration as true and may serve to reinforce sexist stereotypes (Greeno & Maccoby, 1986, p. 315).

Of course it is dangerous to accept without further exploration ideas that seem intuitively right, but it is equally dangerous to dismiss out of hand knowledge gleaned from experience that fails to meet conventional standards of truth. That is what women and other groups marginal to the academy have done for years. We have been taught, to paraphrase Gilligan, "to forget what we know." It is well, I think, to remember what we know, or think we know; to preserve rather than abandon the respect for one's own intuition that is at the heart of subjectivism. Of course, what feels right may be wrong, but it may be right; "They" may be wrong. And although I agree that it is important to subject apparent truths to further exploration, I believe it is important to do so along connected as well as separate paths.

It took me a long time to recognize that there was a connected path. Separate knowing came easily to me, as I believe it does for most academic women, our proclivities in this direction being part of the reason we became academics: we like to argue and, as academics, we're allowed to. I first drifted into graduate school in search of the tough-minded reasoning I had known in college and had found largely missing during the years since college, spent mainly in the company of children under the age of eight and their mothers. I knew I had come to the right place when, at one of the first class meetings, the professor said, "Whenever an idea rings a bell with me, seems intuitively true, I'm immediately suspicious of it"—critical epistemology in a nutshell, and, to mix a couple of metaphors, just my cup of tea!

Like Sara Ruddick (this volume), I too have had a love affair with reason. The affair has endured, and although, as is often the case in long-term relationships, I have grown less starry-eyed and idealistic about this lover than I once was; like Ed, the MIT summer intern, I still find it "real neat" that a group of scientists can treat ideas "not as possessions" but "as ideas." On the twenty-fifth reading, Ed's story still sends thrills down my spine. I want my students, too, to fall in love and stay in love with separate knowing.

Once upon a time, this was my only wish. My pedagogical duty, as I saw it, was to stamp out any sign of reliance on firsthand experience and intuition, and instill a reliance on hard-headed critical thinking. For instance, when, objecting to my pronouncement from on high that males proved to be more adept on tests of spatial intelligence than females, a student in development psychology argued that she had a terrific sense of direction, whereas her brother couldn't find his way out of a paper bag, I would explain, patiently, through gritted teeth (accompanied, sometimes, by a sickly smile, but it's hard to do both at once), that of course there were exceptions, that psychological laws were merely proababilistic statements—saying to the student, in effect, "Your experience is irrelevant; your experience is embarrassing." In a sense, of course, I was "right," but so, in another sense, was she. Elsewhere, I have told how an African American student taught me, before the psychologist Diana Baumrind (1972) did, that parental practices denned as "authoritarian" might have a different meaning and different consequences in African American than in White families (Clinchy, 1995). Experiences such as these have led me to see that my job is not to suppress the lessons students have gained from firsthand experience, but to help them build on them. The other day, a colleague said, "Anecdotes are not data." "Nonsense," I replied, in characteristically connected fashion. "Of course they are."

As this essay attests, my relationship with connected knowing has become a full-blown affair. The procedures that Glaspell's Mrs. Hale and Mrs. Peters bring to bear on their problem are as exciting to me as the ones Ed's bioengineers bring to bear on theirs, and the knowledge they construct is just as powerful; indeed, as Mary Belenky's chapter (this volume) suggests, the Mrs. Hales and Mrs. Peterses might even transform the world.

I now bring to my teaching a polygamous epistemology, and I find that far from disrupting the first marriage, the second has stabilized it: the two are complementary. My students and I are amenable to argument, if we know that people are really listening. We are willing to dilly-dally in one another's embryonic notions, aware that with careful cultivation, these notions might blossom into powerful ideas—possibly even testable hypotheses to be subjected to the rigors of the doubting game. And, whereas once I hoped only that my students might achieve competence in the skills of separate knowing, now I wish for them what has meant so much to me—a marriage of two minds.

## Notes

1. Connected knowing differs in this respect from the believing game, the ultimate purpose of which is to test validity.
2. Unless otherwise indicated, quotations are from participants interviewed in various research projects, and names are pseudonyms.
3. In this research we frequently adopted responses given in one year as stimuli the next year, in an attempt to conduct a sort of quasi conversation among students across the period of the study.
4. Although there have always been less adversarial strains in philosophy and in social science (notably *verstehen*), they have not been dominant.
5. I thank my friend Margaret Osler for helping me to understand this.
6. We may invite misreading by careless use of the terms *subjective knowledge* and *subjectivism*, sometimes using them interchangeably, as Code (1991, p. 255) points out.
7. Subjectivists are not "authoritarian" in the usual sense, however; they make no claim that what is true for them should be true for others or that, as some standpoint theorists assert, their own views are privileged. They are honestly unmitigated relativists.
8. Separate (adversarial) interviewing also has its place, of course, and also requires skill, of a different sort.
9. In another instance of the perhaps inevitable failure of understanding across disciplinary divides, Code speaks of WWK's researchers as taking their respondents' words "literally," "from the surface" (1991, p. 256), a characterization that scarcely does justice to the sort of procedures DeVault describes, nor, indeed, to the complexity of any decent qualitative research procedure.
10. I have borrowed the phrase "I, thou, and it" from the philosopher of science David Hawkins (1967), who uses it in a different but related fashion in discussion of primary education.
11. These "body syntonic" (Turkle & Papert, 1990, note, p. 144) forms of connected knowing should be explored further. Some cultures, Nancy Goldberger says (see her chapter in this volume), support these ways of knowing, but the computer culture does not. Turkle and Papert tell of a fourth-grade boy who, overhearing a classmate speaking of "getting down inside the computer," sneered: "That's baby talk." Instructors in a Harvard programming course were no more hospitable to these "primitive" modes.
12. Spelman (1988), following Jean-Paul Sartre, points out that the danger is not eliminated even when the subject is present. We can "imagine" the person sitting next to us instead of really trying to make her acquaintance.
13. Grumbach's description is reminiscent of Schwaber's account of the shift in her perspective as therapist from external expert, instructing the patient with her superior opinions, to "observer from within," dilly-dallying respectfully in their views.
14. In observations of very young children, psychologist Carolyn Zahn-Waxler and her colleagues found that "self-referential behaviors" such as "pointing to one's own injury when another is injured" and reproducing or imitating others' affective experiences" predicted later "empathic concern" (Zahn-Waxler, Radke-Yurrow, Wagner, & Chapman, 1992, pp. 133, 134).
15. Although this is sheer—perhaps wild—speculation, both "doubling" and the emphasis on receptivity versus projection may have precursors in early childhood. Doubling is reminiscent of the "double-

voiced discourse" in which one attends simultaneously to one's own and one's playmates' agendas, observed by sociolinguist Amy Sheldon (1992) among preschoolers, especially girls. The spontaneous stories of preschool girls are often structured around domestic harmony, whereas boys' stories involve venturing forth into an often frightening and chaotic unknown (Nicoloupoulo, Scales, & Weintraub, 1994).

16. In my view, of course, the partner need not be a person.
17. I thank the student who conducted this interview as part of her work for a seminar I teach. The student must remain anonymous in order to protect Ed's identity, but she knows who she is.
18. "I have always had in my head an adversary," Piaget says (1972, p. 222). Piaget's adversary, usually a logical positivist, seems to me to have been something of a pushover.

# References

Barber, B. R. (1984). *Strong democracy: Participatory politics for a new age.* Berkeley: University of California Press.

Baron, J. (1991). Beliefs about thinking. In J. F. Voss, D. N. Perkins, & J. W. Segal (Eds.), *Informal reasoning and education,* 169–186. Hillsdale, NJ: Lawrence Erlbaum.

Basch, M. F. (1983). The concept of self: An operational definition. In B. Lee & G. Noam (Eds.), *Developmental approaches to the self.* New York: Plenum Press.

Baumrind, D. (1972). An exploratory study of socialization effects on black children: Some black-white comparisons. *Child Development, 43,* 261–267.

Belenky, M., Clinchy, B., Goldberger, N., & Tarule, J. (1986). *Women's ways of knowing: The development of self, voice, and mind.* New York: Basic Books.

Berkowitz, M. W., & Oser, F. (1987, April). *Stages of adolescent interactive logic.* Paper presented at the Biennial Meeting of the Society for Research in Child Development, Baltimore, MD.

Berreby, David. (1995, April 9). Unabsolute truths: Clifford Geertz. *New York Times Magazine.*

Blanck, G. & Blanck, R. (1979). *Ego psychology II: Psychoanalytic developmental psychology.* New York: Columbia University Press.

Breslin, James, E. B. (1994, July 24). Terminating Mark Rothko: Biography is mourning in reverse. *The New York Times Book Review, 3,* 19.

Brown, L. M., & Gilligan, C. (1992). *Meeting at the crossroads: Women's psychology and girls' development.* Cambridge, MA: Harvard University Press.

Bruffee, K. A. (1981). The structure of knowledge and the future of liberal education. *Liberal Education, 67,* 177–186.

Bruner, J. S. (1986). Actual minds, possible worlds. Cambridge, MA: Harvard University Press.

Buber, M. (1947/1965). *Between man and man.* (Ronald G. Smith, Trans.). New York: Macmillan.

Buber, M. (1966). *The knowledge of man: A philosophy of the interhuman.* New York: Harper & Row, Torchbooks.

Clinchy, B. (1995). A connected approach to the teaching of developmental psychology. *Teaching of Psychology, 22,* 100–104.

Clinchy, B., & Zimmerman, C. (1982). Epistemology and agency in the development of undergraduate women. In P. Perun (Ed.), *The undergraduate woman: Issues in educational equity.* Lexington, MA: D. C. Health.

Clinchy, B., & Zimmerman, C. (1985). Growing up intellectually: Issues for college women. *Work in Progress,* No. 19. Wellesley, MA: Stone Center Working Papers Series.

Code, L. (1991). *What can she know?* Ithaca, NY: Cornell University Press.

DeVault, M. L. (1990). Talking and listening from women's standpoint. Feminist strategies for interviewing and analysis. *Social Problems, 37,* 96–116.

Elbow, P. (1973). Appendix essay: The doubting game and the believing game—an analysis of the intellectual enterprise. In *Writing without teachers.* London: Oxford University Press.

Elbow, P. (1986). *Embracing contraries.* New York: Oxford University Press.

Field, J. (1936/1981). *A life of one's own.* Los Angeles: J. P. Tarcher, St. Martin's Press.

Flavell, J. (1985). *Cognitive development* (2nd ed.). Englewood Cliffs, NJ: Prentice Hall.

Friedman, M. (1985). *The healing dialogue in psychotherapy.* New York: Jason Aronson.

Geertz, C. (1986, Winter). The uses of diversity. *Michigan Quarterly Review*, 105–123.

Gilligan, C. (1982). *In a different voice.* Cambridge, MA: Harvard University Press.

Glaspell, S. (1917). A jury of her peers. Reprinted in E. J. O'Brien (Ed.) (1918), *The best short stories of 1917 and the yearbook of the American short story*, 256–281. Boston: Small, Maynard.

Goodfield, J. (1991/1994). *An imagined world: A story of scientific discovery*, Ann Arbor: University of Michigan Press.

Gordon, M. (1980). The parable of the cave or: In praise of watercolors. In J. Sternburg (Ed.), *The writer on her work*, 27–32. New York: W. W. Norton.

Greeno, C. G., & Maccoby, E. E. (1986). On *In a different voice:* An interdisciplinary forum: How different is the "different voice"? *Signs, 11,* 310–316.

Grumbach, D. (1991). *Coming into the end zone: A memoir.* New York: W. W. Norton.

Hawkesworth, M. E. (1989). Knowers, knowing, known: Feminist theory and claims of truth. *Signs, 14,* 533–557.

Hawkins, D. (1967). *I, thou, it.* Reprint of a paper presented at the Primary Teachers' Residential Course, Loughborough, Leicestershire. Cambridge, MA: Elementary Science Study, Educational Services, Inc.

Hogan, R. (1973). Moral conduct and moral character: A psychological perspective. *Psychological Bulletin, 70,* 217–232.

Howard, G. S. (1991). Culture tales: A narrative approach to thinking, cross-cultural psychology, and psychotherapy. *American Psychologist, 46,* 187–197.

Jordan, J. (1991). Empathy and self boundaries. In J. V. Jordan, A. G. Kaplan, J. B. Miller, I. P. Stiver, & J. L. Surrey (Eds.), *Women's growth in connection: Writings from the Stone Center*, 67–80. New York: Guilford Press.

Keller, E. F. (1983a). *A feeling for the organism.* New York: Freeman.

Keller, E. F. (1983b). Women, science, and popular mythology. In J. Rothschild (Ed.), *Machine ex dea*, 131–135. New York: Pergamon Press.

Kohn, A. (1990). *The brighter side of human nature: Altruism and empathy in everyday life.* New York: Basic Books.

Kohnt, H. (1978). The psychoanalyst in the community of scholars. In P. Ornstein (Ed.), *The search for the self: Selected writings of Heinz Kohut,* Vol. 2, 685–724. New York: International Universities Press.

Koller, A. (1990). *The stations of solitude.* New York: William Morrow.

Lather, P. (1986). Issues of validity in openly ideological research: Between a rock and a soft place. *Interchange, 17,* 63–84.

Lyons, N. (1983). Two perspectives on self, relationships, and morality. *Harvard Education Review, 53,* 125–145.

McCracken, G. D. (1988). *The long interview. Qualitative research methods series* (vol. 13). Newbury Park: Sage.

McMillan, C. (1982). *Women, reason and nature.* Princeton, NJ: Princeton University Press.

Mansfield. A., & Clinchy, B. (1992, May 28). The influence of different kinds of relationships on the development and expression of "separate" and "connected" knowing in undergraduate women. Paper presented as part of a symposium, Voicing relationships, knowing connection: Exploring girls' and women's development, at the 22nd Annual Symposium of the Jean Piaget Society: Development and vulnerability in close relationships. Montreal, Québec, Canada.

Margulies, A. (1989). *The empathic imagination.* New York: W. W. Norton.

Marshall, J. & Reason, P. (1993). Adult learning in collaborative action research: reflections on the supervision process. *Studies in continuing education, 15,* 117–133.

May, R. (1969). The emergence of existential psychotherapy. In R. May, E. Angel, & H. F. Ellenberger (Eds.), *Existence.* New York: Simon & Schuster.

Michel, W. (1969). Continuity & change in personality. *American Psychologist, 24,* 1012–1018.

Morawski, J. G., & Steele, R. S. (1991). The one or the other? Textual analysis of masculine power and feminist empowerment. *Theory and Psychology, 1,* 107–131.

Moulton, J. (1983). A paradigm of philosophy: The adversary method. In Harding, S., & Hintikka, M. B. (Eds.), *Discovering reality.* Dordrecht, Holland: Reidel.

Murdoch, I. (1970/1985). *The sovereignty of good.* London: ARK Paperbacks, Routledge & Kegan Paul.

Nicolopoulou, A., Scales, B., & Weintraub, J. (1994). Gender differences and symbolic imagination in the stories of four-year-olds. In A. H. Dyson & C. Genish (Eds.), *The need for story: Cultural diversity in classroom and community.* Urbana, IL: National Council of Teachers of English.

Noddings, N. (1984). *Caring.* Berkeley, CA: University of California Press.

Papert, S. (1980). *Mindstorms.* New York: Basic Books.

Patai, D. & Koertge, N. (1994). *Professing feminism.* New York: Basic Books.

Perkins, D. N., Farady, M., & Bushey, B. (1991). Everyday reasoning and the roots of intelligence. In J. F. Voss, D. N. Perkins, & J. W. Segal (Eds.), *Informal reasoning and education.* Hillsdale, NJ: Lawrence Erlbaum.

Perry, W. (1970). *Forms of intellectual and ethical development in the college years.* New York: Holt, Rinehart, & Winston.

Piaget, J. (1972) *The child's conception of the world.* Totowa, NJ: Littlefield, Adams.

Poulet, G. (1980). Criticism and the experience of interiority (C. Macksey & R Macksey, Trans.). In J. Tomkins (Ed.), *Reader-response criticism: From formalism to structuralism.* Baltimore: Johns Hopkins University Press.

Rabin, C. (1994). *Separate and connected knowing in undergraduate men and women.* Unpublished undergraduate honors thesis, Wellesley College, Wellesley, MA.

Rich, A. (1979). Vesuvius at home: The power of Emily Dickinson. In *On lies, secrets and silence: Selected prose, 1966–1978.* New York: W. W. Norton.

Riger, S. (1992). Epistemological debates, feminist voices: Science, social values, and the study of women. *American Psychologist, 47,* 730–740.

Rogers, C. R. (1951). *Client-centered therapy.* Boston: Houghton Mifflin.

Rogers, C. R. (1961). *On becoming a person: A therapist's view of psychotherapy.* Boston: Houghton Mifflin.

Rogers, C. R. (1980). Empathic: An unappreciated way of being. In *A way of being* (pp. 137–163). Boston: Houghton Mifflin.

Rogers, C. R., & Farson, R. E. (1967). Active listening. In Haney, W. V. *Communication and organizational behavior: Text and cases,* 81–97. Homewood, IL: Richard D. Irwin.

Ruddick, S. (1984). New combinations: Learning from Virginia Woolf. In Asher, C., DeSalvor, L., & Ruddick, S. *Between women.* Boston: Beacon Press.

Schafer, R. (3964). The clinical analysis of affects. *Journal of the American Psychoanalytic Association, 12,* 275–299.

Schwaber, E. (1983a). Psychoanalytic listening and psychic reality. *International Review of Psychoanalysis, 10,* 379–392.

Schwaber, E. (1983b). Construction, reconstruction, and the mode of clinical attunement. In A. Goldberg (Ed.), *The future of psychoanalysis,* 273–291. New York: International Universities Press.

Schweickart, P. P. (1986). Reading ourselves: Toward a feminist theory of reading. In Elizabeth A. Flynn & P. P. Schweickart (Eds.), *Gender and reading: Essays on readers, texts, and contexts,* 31–62. Baltimore: Johns Hopkins University Press.

Schweickart, P. P. (1988). Engendering critical discourse. In C. Koelb & Victor Lokke (Eds.), *The current in criticism: Essays on the present and future of criticism,* 295–317. West Lafayette, IN: Purdue University Press.

Schweickart, P. P. (1989). Reading, teaching, and the ethic of care. In S. L. Gabriel & I. Smithson (Eds.), *Gender in the classroom: Power and pedagogy,* 78–95. Chicago: University of Illinois Press.

Sheldon, A. (1992). Conflict talk: Sociolinguistic challenges to self-assertion and how young girls meet them. *Merrill-Palmer Quarterly, 38,* 95–118.

Spelman, E. V. (1988). *Inessential woman: Problems of exclusion in feminist thought.* Boston: Beacon Press.

Steele, R. S. (1986). Deconstructing histories: Toward a systematic criticism of psychological narratives. In T. R. Sarbin, *Narrative psychology: The storied nature of human conduct,* 256–275. New York: Praeger.

Tannen, D. (1990). *You just don't understand: Women and men in conversation.* New York: Ballantine.

Torbert, W. (1976). *Creating a community of inquiry: Conflict, collaboration, transformation.* New York: Wiley.

Turkle, S. (1984). *The second self: The computer and the human spirit.* New York: Simon & Schuster.

Turkle, S. & Papert, S. (1990). Epistemological pluralism: styles and voices within the computer culture. *Signs, 16*, 128–157.

What bothers me about girls. (1994, March 13). *Parade.*

Woolf, V. (1929/1989). *A room of one's own.* New York: Harvest/HBJ Book, Harcourt Brace Jovanovich.

Woolf, V. (1932/1948). How should one read a book? In *The common reader, Series 1 and 2*, 281–295. New York: Harcourt Brace.

Zahn-Waxler, C., Radke-Yarrow, M., Wagner, E. & Chapman, M. (1992). Development of concern for others. *Developmental Psychology, 28*, 126–136.

# CHAPTER 24
# REFLECTIVE JUDGMENT: THEORY AND RESEARCH ON THE DEVELOPMENT OF EPISTEMIC ASSUMPTIONS THROUGH ADULTHOOD

## PATRICIA M. KING AND KAREN STROHM KITCHENER

The reflective judgment model (RJM) describes the development of complex reasoning in late adolescents and adults, and how the epistemological assumptions people hold are related to the way they make judgments about controversial (ill-structured) issues. This article describes the theoretical assumptions that have guided the development of the RJM in the last 25 years, showing how these ideas influenced the development of assessment protocols and led to the selection of research strategies for theory validation purposes. Strategies discussed here include a series of longitudinal studies to validate the proposed developmental sequence, cross-sectional studies examining age/educational level differences, and studies of domain specificity. Suggestions for assessing and promoting reflective thinking based on these findings are also offered here.

Do the benefits of inoculating health care workers against smallpox outweigh the risks? Will a proposed urban growth policy protect farmland without sacrificing jobs? Is affirmative action an effective tool for promoting genuine access to higher education? Controversial problems such as these about which "reasonable people reasonably disagree" are called ill-structured problems (Churchman, 1971; Wood, 1983); they are characterized by two features: that they cannot be defined with a high degree of completeness, and that they cannot be solved with a high degree of certainty. In the last 25 years, we have investigated how late adolescents and adults come to understand and make judgments about these kinds of controversial problems. In examining the responses that hundreds of individuals across a wide range of age and educational levels have given to such questions, we have made three major observations: (a) there are striking differences in people's underlying assumptions about knowledge, or epistemic assumptions; (b) these differences in assumptions are related to the way people make and justify their own judgments about ill-structured problems; and (c) there is a developmental sequence in the patterns of responses and judgments about such problems. The reflective judgment model (RJM; King & Kitchener, 1994; K. S. Kitchener & King, 1981) provides a theoretical framework for understanding and organizing these observations.

King, P. M., & Kitchener, K. S. (2004). Reflective judgment: Theory and research on the development of epistemic assumptions through adulthood. *Educational Psychologist, 39*, 5–18.

In this article, we begin by presenting the original theoretical grounding and underlying assumptions that have guided the development of the RJM, as well as the influence of subsequent theoretical developments, and then show how these assumptions guided the development of assessment protocols and led to the selection of research strategies for theory validation purposes. The next major section of this article summarizes research on the RJM that tested the theoretical claims about the development of reflective judgment. Last, we explore some of the implications for practice and research based on the theoretical ideas and empirical findings presented here.

## Reflective Judgment Model

The RJM is a model of the development of reflective thinking from late adolescence through adulthood. This construct was first defined by Dewey (1933), who argued that reflective judgments are initiated when an individual recognizes that there is controversy or doubt about a problem that cannot be answered by formal logic alone, and involve careful consideration of one's beliefs in light of supporting evidence. This kind of reasoning remains a central goal of education, especially higher education; this is evident in several recent national reports on undergraduate education, each of which reiterated the need for college graduates to think reflectively (American Association of Colleges and Universities [AAC&U], 2002; American Association of Higher Education, American College Personnel Association [ACPA], & National Association of Student Personnel Administrators, 1998; ACPA, 1994). The RJM describes a progression of seven major steps in the development of reflective thinking leading to the capacity to make reflective judgments; each step represents a qualitatively different epistemological perspective. In defining these perspectives, we use K. S. Kitchener's (1983) definition of epistemic cognition (as distinguished from cognition and metacognition), focusing on individuals' underlying assumptions about knowledge and how it is gained. For each step in this progression (which we call stages, as defined below) the RJM includes a description of individuals' views of knowledge and concepts of justification, showing the relationship between the epistemological assumptions people hold and the way they make judgments about controversial (ill-structured) issues. The model shows how the assumptions are interrelated and how they reflect an internal logic within each stage. (See Table 1.) In the following description, we offer a general overview of these seven stages and offer examples from Stage 4, which is characteristic of the reasoning of a majority of college students, and Stage 7, which is indicative of the kind of reasoning many colleges aspire to teach (AAC&U) and which has been associated with the kind of thinking skills adults need to function effectively in today's complex societies (Baxter Magolda, in press; Kegan, 1994). These examples illustrate how qualitatively different sets of epistemic assumptions are associated with distinctly different ways of justifying beliefs in adulthood. Because a detailed descriptions of each stage is available elsewhere (King & Kitchener, 1994), here we offer only a brief summary of the seven stages.

As an introduction to this developmental progression, consider the seven stages grouped into three levels: prereflective thinking (Stages 1–3), quasi-reflective thinking (Stages 4–5), and reflective thinking (Stages 6–7). We are aware that labels such as these (e.g., "absolutist") risk being interpreted as overly simplistic reflections of complex epistemological perspectives and that similar terms are used to refer to quite different epistemologies (as documented by Hofer & Pintrich, 1997). For this reason, we use numbers to reflect the order in which the epistemological perspective typically emerges and offer these broader categories as a more general introduction to the model. Although clustering qualitatively different stages into levels reduces complexity by collapsing stages within levels and highlighting similarities, this strategy also risks obscuring within-level differences. Thus, the summaries that follow should be read with the understanding that important differences exist between stages, both within and across levels.

A major hallmark of *prereflective thinking* is that knowledge is assumed to be certain, and accordingly, that single correct answers exist for all questions and may be known with absolute certainty, usually from authority figures. Well- and ill-structured problems are not differentiated, as all problems are assumed to be well structured. Further, those using prereflective assumptions do not use evidence to reason toward a conclusion, relying instead on a restatement of beliefs or on unsubstantiated personal opinions. With *quasi-reflective thinking* comes the recognition that uncertainty is a part of the knowing process, the ability to see knowledge as an abstraction, and the recognition that knowledge is constructed. This is a major advance, as it lays a foundation for the construction of beliefs that are internally derived, not simply accepted from others. Further, evidence is now understood as a key part of the knowing process, as it provides an alternative to dogmatic assertions that are characteristic of prereflective thinking. Those using quasi-reflective assumptions are aware that different approaches or perspectives on controversial issues rely on different types of evidence and different rules of evidence, and that factors like these contribute to different ways of framing issues. Here are two examples of Stage 4 reasoning:

### Stage 4 Reasoning, Example 1

*Interviewer* (I): "Can you say that one point of view is better and another worse?"

*Respondent* (R): "No, I really can't on this issue. It depends on your beliefs since there is no way of proving either one."

*I:* "Can you say that one is more accurate than the other?"

*R:* "No, I can't. I believe they're both the same as far as accuracy."

### Stage 4 Reasoning, Example 2

*I:* "Can you say one view of creation is right and one is wrong?"

*R:* "No, because no one can prove how the world was created or how man evolved. Scientists can get close to it—an actual answer. When it comes right down to it, as to the actual change, they don't know because they can't draw a straight relationship between apes and man. There isn't a straight relationship . . ."

In quasi-reflective reasoning, the link between gathering evidence and making a conclusion is tenuous; this link becomes explicit in reflective thinking, the third level of the RJM.

*Reflective thinkers* consistently and comfortably use evidence and reason in support of their judgments. They argue that knowledge claims must be understood in relation to the context in which they were generated, but that they can be evaluated for their coherence and consistency with available information. Because new data or new perspectives may emerge as knowledge is constructed and reconstructed, individuals using assumptions of reflective thinking remain open to reevaluating their conclusions and knowledge claims.

### Stage 7 Reasoning, Example 1

*I:* "Can you ever say you know for sure?"

*R:* "It's [the view that the Egyptians built the pyramids] very far along the continuum of what is probable."

*I:* "Can you say one is right and one is wrong?"

*R:* "Right and wrong are not comfortable categories to assign to this kind of item—more or less like or reasonable—more or less in keeping with what the facts seem to be."

### Stage 7 Reasoning, Example 2

*R:* "It's my belief that you have to be very skeptical about what you read for popular consumption . . . even for professional consumption."

*I:* "How do you ever know what to believe?"

*R:* "I read widely . . . of many points of view. Partly [it's] reliance on people you think you can rely on, who seem to be reputable journalists, who make measured judgments. Then reading widely and estimating where the reputable people line up or where the weight of the evidence lies."

## TABLE 1

### Summary of Reflective Judgment Stages

| Prereflective Thinking | Quasireflective Thinking | Reflective Thinking |
|---|---|---|
| **Stage 1** <br> *View of knowledge:* Knowledge is assumed to exist absolutely and concretely; it is not understood as an abstraction. It can be obtained with certainty by direct observation. <br><br> *Concept of justification:* Beliefs need no justification because there is assumed to be an absolute correspondence between what is believed to be true and what is true. Alternate beliefs are not perceived. <br><br> *"I know what I have seen."* | **Stage 4** <br> *View of knowledge:* Knowledge is uncertain, and knowledge claims are idiosyncratic to the individual because situational variables (such as incorrect reporting of data, data lost over time, or disparities in access to information) dictate that knowing always involves an element of ambiguity. <br><br> *Concept of justification:* Beliefs are justified by giving reasons and using evidence, but the arguments and choice of evidence are idiosyncratic (e.g., choosing evidence that fits an established belief). <br><br> *"I would be more inclined to believe evolution if they had proof. It is just like the pyramids: I do not think we will ever know. Who are you going to ask? No one was there."* | **Stage 6** <br> *View of knowledge:* Knowledge is constructed into individual conclusions about ill-structured problems on the basis of information from a variety of sources. Interpretations that are based on evaluations of evidence across contexts and on the evaluated opinions of reputable others can be known. <br><br> *Concept of justification:* Beliefs are justified by comparing evidence and opinion from different perspectives on an issue or across different contexts and by constructing solutions that are evaluated by criteria such as the weight of the evidence, the utility of the solution, or the pragmatic need for action. <br><br> *"It is very difficult in this life to be sure. There are degrees of sureness. You come to a point at which you are sure enough for a personal stance on the issue."* |
| **Stage 2** <br> *View of knowledge:* Knowledge is assumed to be absolutely certain or certain but not immediately available. Knowledge can be obtained directly through the senses (as in direct observation) or via authority figures. | **Stage 5** <br> *View of knowledge:* Knowledge is contextual and subjective because it is filtered through a person's perceptions and criteria for judgment. Only interpretations of evidence, events, or issues may be known. | **Stage 7** <br> *View of knowledge:* Knowledge is the outcome of a process of reasonable inquiry in which solutions to ill-structured problems are constructed. The adequacy of those solutions is evaluated in terms of what is most reasonable or probable according to the current evidence, and it is reevaluated when relevant new evidence, perspectives, or tools of inquiry become available. |

(continued)

# TABLE 1 (continued)

## Summary of Reflective Judgment Stages

| Prereflective Thinking | Quasireflective Thinking | Reflective Thinking |
|---|---|---|
| Stage 2 (cont.)<br>*Concept of justification:* Beliefs are unexamined and unjustified or justified by their correspondence with the beliefs of an authority figure (such as a teacher or parent). Most issues are assumed to have a right answer, so there is little or no conflict in making decisions about disputed issues.<br><br>*"If it is on the news, it has to be true."*<br><br>Stage 3<br>*View of knowledge:* Knowledge is assumed to be absolutely certain or temporarily uncertain. In areas of temporary uncertainty, only personal beliefs can be known until absolute knowledge is obtained. In areas of absolute certainty, knowledge is obtained from authorities.<br>*Concept of justification:* In areas in which certain answers exist, beliefs are justified by reference to authorities' views. In areas in which answers do not exist, beliefs are defended as personal opinion because the link between evidence and beliefs is unclear.<br>*"When there is evidence that people can give to convince everybody one way or another, then it will be knowledge; until then, it is just a guess."* | Stage 5 (cont.)<br>*Concept of justification:* Beliefs are justified within a particular context by means of the rules of inquiry for that context and by context-specific interpretations of evidence. Specific beliefs are assumed to be context specific or are balanced against other interpretations, which complicates (and sometimes delays) conclusions.<br><br>*"People think differently and so they attack the problem differently. Other theories could be as true as my own, but based on different evidence."* | Stage 7 (cont.)<br>*Concept of justification:* Beliefs are justified probabilistically on the basis of a variety of interpretive considerations, such as the weight of the evidence, the explanatory value of the interpretations, the risk of erroneous conclusions, consequences of alternative judgments, and the interrelations of these factors. Conclusions are defended as representing the most complete, plausible, or compelling understanding of an issue on the basis of the available evidence.<br><br>*"One can judge an argument by how well thought-out the positions are, what kinds of reasoning and evidence are used to support it, and how consistent the way one argues on this topic is as compared with how one argues on other topics."* |

*Note.* From *Developing Reflective Judgment* (p. 14–15), by P. M. King and K. S. Kitchener, 1994, San Francisco: Jossey-Bass. Copyright 1994 by John Wiley & Sons, Inc. Reprinted with permission.

These examples illustrate the kinds of developmentally ordered differences in the way people reason about ill-structured problems that are described in the RJM.

## Theoretical Assumptions Underlying the RJM

We turn next to one of the questions that is the focus of this volume, the paradigmatic assumptions underlying each theory of personal epistemology. Because research on the RJM spans more than 25 years, we will introduce the theoretical assumptions from both historical and contemporaneous perspectives.

*Developmental traditions.* The RJM evolved out of a careful examination of the few models of late adolescent and adult intellectual development that existed in the late 1970s. Our initial conceptualization (K. S. Kitchener & King, 1981) was grounded in the cognitive-developmental tradition of Piaget (1965; Piaget & Inhelder, 1969) and Kohlberg (1969). Other developmental theorists in this tradition whose work informed our early conceptualization of the RJM were Perry (1968, 1970), Broughton (1975, 1978), Loevinger (1976), and Harvey, Hunt, and Schroder (1961). The cognitive-developmental tradition has much in common with more recent constructive-developmental perspectives (e.g., Fischer & Pruyne, 2002; Kegan, 1982, 1994). What these two approaches share are (a) the underlying assumption that meaning is constructed, (b) the emphasis on understanding how individuals make meaning of their experiences, and (c) the assumption that development (not just change) occurs as people interact with their environments. Another central defining feature is that patterns of meaning-making are described in developmental terms, that is, the frameworks people use for interpreting their experiences (e.g., categories and organizing principles) are described as becoming more complex, integrated, and complete over time. These changes do not occur automatically but rather through interaction with an environment that both challenges and supports growth.

However, our data led us to reject two well-known assumptions espoused by prominent theorists from this tradition. First, unlike Piaget, we do not assume that cognitive development is best measured by deductive reasoning, nor do we assume that it is complete with the emergence of formal operations at age 16 (indeed, our data show that this is not the case). And in contrast to Kohlberg, we do not claim cross-cultural universality, and we endorse Rest's (1979) concept of a complex rather than a simple stage model of development.

*Stage theory.* At the time the RJM was being developed in the 1970s, Rest (a faculty member who supervised our initial research) was also working within the cognitive-developmental tradition. As a researcher of moral development, he was beginning to raise questions about the adequacy of what he called the "simple stage" model being advanced by Kohlberg (1969), a critique Rest (1979) later published in his first book. We took the opportunity to ask similar questions based on our initial study (K. S. Kitchener & King, 1981), such as whether there was stage variability or consistency among an individual's responses. Our scoring procedures were intentionally designed to allow for this question to be tested (i.e., allowing raters to record multiple stages if several were apparent in a given interview protocol). We found that Rest's alternative, the "complex stage" model of development, provided a good explanatory framework for our data. That is, we observed that development in reasoning about ill-structured, controversial problems has stage-like properties, but not that it evolves in a lock-step, one-stage-at-a-time fashion. Hence, we refer to the major categories of thinking and interrelated clusters of assumptions as stages, but our use of this term is qualified, based on specific assumptions and definitions that fall outside more traditional usage. Below, we offer data illustrating development across stages that support this approach.

We acknowledge that stage models within the cognitive-developmental tradition have been criticized as providing inadequate conceptual frameworks for describing development (e.g., Flavell, 1971). Two underlying assumptions about stages (traditionally defined) have drawn considerable criticism. The first is that individuals utilize only one organizing framework (stage) at a time and, therefore, that development from stage to stage is abrupt with any overlap between stages occurring briefly only during transitions between stages. At the time of stage consolidation, stage usage is assumed to peak at 100%, consistent with the common phrase used when referring to stage theories, being "in a stage." The second criticism is that the stages constitute an invariant sequence that exists across all cultures. Kohlberg's (1969, 1984) claim to the universality of his sequence of stages of moral development was based on his refutation of moral relativism as an inadequate philosophical framework (Kohlberg, 1991) and on cross-cultural studies indicating that the pattern of development he proposed was also apparent among individuals across several cultures. We do not make these claims. We do, however, support the other claims within this tradition (that meaning is constructed, that these constructions are developmentally ordered, and that development is the result of person-environment interactions).

Rest's (1979) complex stage model better captures the nature of development of reflective judgment because it accounts for the observed patterns in data gathered using the Reflective Judgment Interview (RJI). For example, it is common to find an individual who relies heavily on Stage 4 assumptions while reasoning about a controversial problem, but who also makes statements that are consistent with Stage 3 and Stage 5 assumptions. By contrast, someone who relies heavily on Stage 2 assumptions rarely uses assumptions of any stage higher than Stage 3. As Rest noted, this approach suggests a "much messier and complicated picture of development" (p. 65) than does a simple stage approach.

Does the complex stage model proposed by Rest accurately capture reflective judgment data? We examined variability of scores of those in our 10-year longitudinal sample (described later in the review of RJM research) to answer this question. In only two cases were the RJI ratings limited to a single stage; in the vast majority of cases, a subdominant score was assigned, and this was almost always an adjacent stage. In a small proportion of cases, more than two stage scores were assigned. Wood (1997) examined the variability of RJI scores using data from 15 studies for which raw data were available ($n$ = 1,995 problem scores; reported in Wood, 1993). He constructed a "percent stage utilization score" based on all responses across the four problems; this score indicated the proportion of time each stage was assigned. He then calculated a series of spline regressions (Darlington, 1990), which predicted stage utilization on the basis of overall RJI score. (A graph of these may be found in King & Kitchener, 1994, Figure 6.2.) Here, development is pictured as a series of uneven, overlapping waves, where usage of given stage assumptions rises and falls in different proportions over time. As this figure shows, for those whose modal score was Stage 2, 70% of the ratings were for Stage 2, with less than 20% at Stage 3. About two-thirds of the ratings were at Stage 3 for those with a modal Stage 3 rating, with the remainder fairly equally distributed between Stages 2 and 4. A similar pattern was obtained for those with a modal Stage 4 rating; here, the remaining ratings were split fairly equally between Stages 3 and 5. However, the shape of the "wave" was much flatter for Stage 5, with only about half of the ratings at Stage 5; the remainder were spread two stages higher and lower than the mode. The shape of the curve for Stage 6 was more similar to those for Stages 3 and 4. In other words, variability in reasoning across stages was the norm and not the exception in these ratings. No individuals evidenced non-adjacent utilization patterns (3/5, 4/6, etc.). This evidence is consistent with the assumptions of complex stage theory (Rest, 1979) and adds further evidence that characterizing individuals as being "in" or "at" a single stage is misleading. Based on these patterns, King, Kitchener, and Wood (1994) suggested that development in reflective thinking be characterized as

> . . . waves across a mixture of stages, where the peak of a wave is the most commonly used set of assumptions. While there is still an observable pattern to the movement between stages, this developmental movement is better described as the changing shape of the wave rather than as a pattern of uniform steps interspersed with plateaus. (p. 140)

This shift from simple to complex stage theory represents a radical change in how development is conceptualized; indeed, it may be considered a change of paradigmatic proportions within stage theory.

**Skill theory.** The second theoretical model that has affected our thinking about RJM research is Fischer's skill theory. Fischer and his colleagues (Fischer, 1980; Fischer, Bullock, Rosenberg, & Raya, 1993; Fischer & Lamborn, 1989; K. S. Kitchener & Fischer, 1990) identified seven developmental levels that emerge between ages 2 and 30. These levels are divided into two overlapping tiers, the representational tier and the abstract tier. The focus of the representational tier is on individuals' ability to manipulate concrete representations, objects, people, or events; the focus of the abstract tier is on individuals' ability to integrate, manipulate, and reason using abstract concepts. This portion of skill theory has much in common with Kegan's (1982, 1994) theory of the development of mature capacity toward self-authorship. The upper levels of Fischer's model also have much in common with the RJM; in fact, the seven stages of the RJM can be readily mapped onto Representational Levels 1–4 and Abstract Levels 2–4 (Fischer & Pruyne, 2002; King, 1985; K. S. Kitchener, 2002; K. S. Kitchener & Fischer, 1990). Reflective thinking requires the ability to think abstractly, which explains the correspondence between the abstract levels of skill theory and Stages 4–7. K. S. Kitchener (2002) also suggested that skill theory provides a framework for comparing the multiple models of folk epistemology (R. Kitchener, 2002) and personal epistemology, such as those in Hofer and Pintrich's (1997, 2002) comprehensive reviews.

Another important and influential aspect of Fischer's work is his assumption that no skills exist independent of the environment and that the skill levels a person demonstrates will vary depending on the conditions under which they are assessed. (Notably, the acknowledgement that performance varies with task demands is incompatible with the simple stage assumption that individuals are "in" one stage at a time.) Fischer and his colleagues (Fischer & Pipp, 1984; Lamborn & Fischer, 1988) posited that variability in individuals' responses across tasks reflects the degree of "contextual support" (e.g., memory prompts, feedback, opportunity to practice) available at the time of the assessment. He suggested that tasks that require performance without support elicit a person's *"functional level"* capacity, but that tasks that provide contextual support can elicit performance at levels that are closer to the upper limit of the person's cognitive capacity, called *"optimal level."* Contextual support can be provided by offering participants a high-level example of the skill, the opportunity to ask questions about the example, the chance to practice the skill in a variety of settings, and so on:

> It is the emergence of this general capacity [for abstract thinking] that establishes an upper limit on the level of independent functioning an individual can potentially achieve in reflective thinking or other domains involving advanced abstract thinking. This upper limit of skill development is termed the *optimal* level. (Fischer & Pruyne, 2002, p. 169; italics in original)

The space between functional and optimal levels is called one's "developmental range" and reflects the range of skills that an individual can access and produce depending on the circumstances. That is, the nature of the person's experience—including the structure of the learning and assessment tasks—affects where within this developmental range a person's performance will fall. If courses and other opportunities for student learning do not provide contextual support for developing the skills associated with forming abstract concepts like reflective thinking (a criticism commonly levied at both schools and colleges), students will be more likely to perform at functional rather than optimal levels. Further, those who have access to higher levels of development would also have access to a larger repertoire of responses from which to choose, explaining Fischer's (1980; Kitchener & Fischer, 1990) hypothesis that optimal and functional level will diverge to a greater degree as the person approaches higher levels of development.

Fischer (1980; Kitchener & Fischer, 1990) also hypothesized that functional level performance would improve in a slow, steady fashion, resulting in a gradual, even slope if graphed over time. By contrast, he hypothesized that optimal level performance would be less even and instead be characterized by spurts at given age levels, followed by plateaus between spurts. Thus, researchers would expect different developmental trajectories depending on whether their measures yield data on functional or optimal level performance.

The ability to operate at an optimal level is influenced not only by support and practice, but also by changes in brain activity and the reorganization of neural networks (Fischer & Pruyne, 2002; Fischer & Rose, 1994). The emergence of abstractions and reflective thinking appears to involve brain development that does not occur until late adolescence and early adulthood.

As this brief summary shows, skill theory provides an innovative approach to the study of human development in general and the development of reflective thinking (with its grounding in epistemic cognition) in particular. For example, the concept of developmental range provides an alternative way of addressing the question of being "in" or "at" a single stage on the RJM, and a way of targeting educational interventions to students' developmental levels. Further, its differentiation of functional and optimal level suggests the need to analyze measures of cognitive development or personal epistemology for degree of contextual support, and to develop measures that assess both levels. And although skill theory is certainly consistent with the person-environment interaction assumptions inherent in the cognitive-developmental paradigm, it specifies particular environmental variables (e.g., contextual support) that appear to affect how students learn to engage in the production of more advanced behaviors (here, reflective thinking).

## Measuring Reflective Judgment

Over the last 25 years, we have experimented with several assessment procedures to measure reflective judgment and its underlying epistemic assumptions. In order to illustrate the links between theoretical assumptions stemming from our research paradigm and our assessment approaches, we describe how the development of several assessment procedures was grounded in theoretical considerations.

*The Reflective Judgment Interview.* The RJI was initially designed to measure reflective thinking as described by the RJM and to inform theory development. We used an iterative process between theory development and assessment ("boot-strapping") for much of the first decade of research on the RJM, moving back and forth between theory development and validation efforts. The RJI uses a semistructured interview format to elicit responses from participants regarding how they reason about ill-structured problems. A trained and certified interviewer asks a series of predetermined but open-ended questions regarding their reasoning in order to get at their fundamental assumptions concerning knowledge and how it is gained. The original interview consisted of four controversial problems (the accuracy of news reporting, the creation of human beings, the safety of chemical additives to foods, and the building of the Egyptian pyramids). A dilemma on the safety of nuclear power was added for the 10-year longitudinal retest, and several discipline-specific dilemmas have been used in subsequent studies (business, chemistry, and psychology). The RJI also includes a standardized series of probe questions; each question is designed to elicit comments that reflect individuals' epistemic assumptions (specifically, their assumptions about knowledge, how it is gained, how they decide what to believe). Probe questions ask about the basis for their point of view, the certainty with which they hold that view, whether differing opinions on the topic are right or wrong or better or worse, and how it is possible people (including experts) disagree about the topic. The one-hour interview was designed to yield a picture of how people approach the task of knowing and making judgments about controversial intellectual issues by looking at ways they understand and make meaning of concepts such as evidence, differences of opinion, uncertainty, and interpretation. (For a detailed description of the RJI, see King & Kitchener, 1994, Chapter 5 and Resource A.)

The RJI is scored by trained and certified raters using the Reflective Judgment Scoring Rules (K. S. Kitchener & King, 1985). Consistent with the complex stage assumptions noted above, raters can assign three scores to each dilemma to reflect whatever characteristics of reasoning they observe in the interview; these typically range across two adjacent stages. The stage most clearly or frequently observed is coded first as the dominant stage, followed by the subdominant stage(s). Occasionally, one dilemma includes statements that reflect three different stages; this is rare, but recording all three is an option available to raters if they determine that this best captures the reasoning in the interview. The point here is that scoring is designed to reflect whatever stage-characteristic responses are evident in the transcript and not to assume a priori that consistency (or inconsistency) will be observed. Assigned scores are then weighted across dominant and subdominant stages, and an overall dilemma score is calculated. The training and certification programs for interviewers and raters were put into place to assure comparability across studies and researchers. (We have recently discontinued these programs in order to focus on the development of other measures.)

Fischer's (Fischer & Pruyene, 2002; Kitchener & Fischer, 1990) differentiation of functional and optimal levels of performance raised several questions for research on the RJM. In particular, it called for the consideration of the level of performance characterized by the RJI: because no contextual support is offered, the RJI may be considered a measure of functional level. As such, it may underestimate a person's capacity to engage in reflective thinking, yielding a score at the lower rather than the higher end of the individual's developmental range. Implications of this insight for research and teaching are explored later in the article.

***The Prototypic Reflective Judgement Interview (PRJI).*** As noted earlier, there are several points of correspondence between Fischer's skill theory and the RJM. In order to evaluate whether the developmental patterns Fischer (1980) had predicted occurred for the development of reflective thinking as defined by the RJM (K. S. Kitchener & Fischer, 1990), a measure of optimal level performance was needed. Fischer argued that optimal measures required two qualities: first, there had to be an independent assessment for each step in the developmental sequence. Second, the research design had to vary relevant characteristics of the participants (especially age) as well as characteristics of the environment (e.g., the amount of environmental support provided for a response). Using these criteria, K. S. Kitchener, Lynch, Fischer, and Wood (1993) designed a new measure, the prototypic reflective judgment interview (PRJI) to assess reflective judgment under conditions of support and practice. The study measured both functional level (using the RJI) and optimal level (using the PRJI) to determine whether scores differed between the two measures of reflective thinking and whether there was evidence for age-related spurts and plateaus using the optimal level measure. Because of its theoretical significance, this study is summarized here.

To construct the PRJI, two problems from the RJI were selected, and stage-prototypic responses were written for reflective judgment Stages 2 through 7. These responses were based on answers given by people for the same problems used in the RJI; they were presented in order to give contextual support for high-level responses to the reflective judgment problems. Participants were first asked to complete the RJI, then to read one of the prototypic statements, and to respond to a series of questions that directed their attention to key elements of the statement. They were then asked to explain the prototypic statement in their own words; each answer was scored as a "hit" if it accurately paraphrased the statement and as a "miss" if it did not. This procedure was repeated for each reflective judgment stage and both of the problems. They were then given two prototypic statements addressing a different ill-structured problem; the statements were selected to correspond with the highest and second highest stages they had paraphrased in the interview. Participants were asked to think about these statements prior to the next testing, which took place two weeks later; this strategy provided contextual support in the form of exposure to and the opportunity to think about higher stage responses to ill-structured problems. The procedure was repeated at the next testing, fulfilling the practice component of contextual support.

Three findings from the study are relevant for the current discussion of how stage theory and skill theory as complementary theoretical models have informed research on the RJM. First, participants scored higher on the PRJI than on the RJI. This supports the idea that individuals are not "in" a stage but rather that they have access to several stages, and that this reflects the effects of contextual support and practice. In other words, contextual support appears to increase the individuals' access to higher stage functioning, yielding more advanced levels of performance (here, higher reflective thinking scores). Second, there was an age-related ceiling in the PRJI even after practice, suggesting that optimal levels are age-related. This is consistent with the developmental trends observed in RJM research (described later) but offers new information about the nature and limits of age-related trends. Third, there was evidence of age-related developmental spurts on the PRJI at reflective judgment Stages 4 to 6. This is consistent with Fischer's hypothesis that the emergence of optimal levels is marked by spurts in performance and then plateaus. It also helps explain the growth in reflective thinking that has been observed with samples of traditional-age college students (whether this growth is consistent with collegiate goals is discussed later).

***The Reasoning About Current Issues Test (RCI).*** Although the RJI and PRJI provided extremely rich information for theory development, their expense both in time and money was problematic in terms of conducting the kind of validation and application studies that were of interest to researchers and educators alike. In the process of developing an objectively scored measure of reflective thinking, we developed and tested several different approaches; these are described by Wood, Kitchener, and Jensen (2002). Here, we discuss the most recent measure, the Reasoning About Current Issues Test (RCI). This is an objectively scored instrument that was built on research using prior measures, but using a format that is amenable to large-scale administration. Because this is described elsewhere, the focus of this discussion is on ways our theoretical assumptions guided measurement development.

The RCI was modeled after Rest's Defining Issues Test (DIT) of moral judgment (Rest, 1979, 1986; Rest, Narvaez, Bebeau, & Thoma, 1999). The DIT has been found to be a highly reliable measure of moral judgment, able to detect developmental change over time, and sensitive to macrolevel changes in reasoning about social issues among adults. (For reviews of research using the DIT among college students, see King & Mayhew, 2002, in press.) In the RCI, respondents are asked to read a dilemma similar to those used in the RJI. In addition to the chemicals in foods dilemma, several others have been used that reflect contemporary issues (causes of alcoholism, workforce preparation, immigration policy, determinants of sexual orientation). The RCI first asks respondents to write a short statement describing their response in their own words. These written statements served to "prime the pump" by encouraging respondents to start thinking about their views on the given topics. Respondents are then asked to rate and rank in order a series of short statements to indicate the statements' similarity to the respondents' own views; each statement reflects the epistemic assumptions of one of the reflective judgment stages.

Each statement was based on responses made by respondents taking the RJI and modified from the statements developed for the PRJI. By merit of being a recognition task, this format provides contextual support (in contrast to the RJI). These brief statements are not written to capture an individual's whole network of underlying assumptions on which a judgment is based, nor to yield a nuanced articulation of how the individual approaches making judgments about controversial issues. Rather, it appears that responding to short items serves to activate the internal organizing schemas that individuals use to make judgments about the given issue, but without filling in the details about the specific rationale used and strategies employed, and without articulating the specific epistemic principles underlying the approach. (For a more detailed description of this rationale as applied to the DIT, see Rest et al., 1999.)

In addition, we wished to control for the possibility that the respondents would endorse statements that sounded impressive (e.g., that used sophisticated vocabulary) but that were not similar to the approach they used, or even to an approach they aspired to use. To address this concern, we created a series of statements that are grammatically correct but nonsensical. When these are selected, the responses for that problem are excluded from the analyses. The RCI score is calculated across all dilemma topics based on the statements most often ranked as similar to the participant's own view. Internal consistency reliabilities have been in the low to mid-.70s (depending on the sample). It takes 30 to 45 minutes to complete (Wood et al., 2002).

There are many trade-offs to be made when moving from a production task with open-ended questions (the RJI) to a recognition task where respondents are asked to choose from a limited set of predefined options (the RCI). Although both approaches are designed to tap into related skills required for the production of reflective thinking, the two are not simply different formats that yield comparable scores; rather, each serves a different purpose, makes different demands on respondents, and yields a different "snapshot" of the development of reflective thinking. Having participants evaluate statements provides more contextual support than responding to open-ended interview questions; therefore, we would anticipate that individuals would score higher on the RCI than the RJI, and this has been the case.

## Research on the RJM

In the last 25 years, we have learned a great deal about reflective thinking and how it develops. The centerpiece of our book, *Developing Reflective Judgment* (King & Kitchener, 1994), is a review of this research base. It reports both the results of our 10-year longitudinal study of the development of reflective judgment using three age/educational level cohorts (*n* = 80 at Time 1), other longitudinal studies of 120 other respondents, as well as a review of cross-sectional studies in which more than 1,700 people (high school students, college students, graduate students, and nonstudent adults) completed the RJI. Since the publication of that volume, Wood (1997) has completed a comprehensive secondary analysis of these data, and an updated literature review was published (King & Kitchener, 2002). Interested readers should consult these works for details. Here, we will summarize the major findings from this body of research, especially as they pertain to the focus of this special issue, how our theoretical framework has guided research on reflective judgment.

*Validating the developmental sequence.* RJM was proposed as a model of reflective thinking in the cognitive-developmental tradition, where the major claim is that the stages constitute a developmental sequence. Documenting the existence of this sequence and validating the model requires longitudinal data. Toward this end, we conducted a 10-year longitudinal study using three age/educational cohorts ($n = 80$ at Time 1, $n = 53$ at Time 4). At Time 1, the three gender-balanced cohorts included high school juniors, college juniors, and third-year doctoral students; the younger two groups were matched to the doctoral students on gender and academic aptitude (based on scores from the Minnesota Scholastic Aptitude Test). This was designed as a check of the competing hypothesis that obtained cohort differences on the RJI (e.g., if graduate students scored higher than college students) could be attributed to differences in aptitude. Even with this control, age and educational level remained confounded in this study. By the time of the last testing, all but one of the high school cohort had completed a bachelor's degree, and about half of the college cohort had completed post-baccalaureate degrees. This yielded a well-educated sample and served as a leveling factor for the age/educational level confounding at Time 1.

Mean RJI scores were significantly different between groups at Time 1 (1977), with the doctoral students scoring the highest ($M = 5.67$), followed by the college students ($M = 3.76$), and the high school students ($M = 2.77$). The RJI mean score increased consistently for the high school and college student groups at each subsequent testing (1979, 1983, and 1987). Over the 10-year period, the former high school students' RJI scores increased over 2.5 stages to 5.29, the former college students' scores rose an average of 1.29 stages to 5.05, and the mean scores of the former doctoral students increased an average of .54, to 6.21. The overall rate of increase (less than two stages in two years) suggests that reflective thinking evolves slowly and steadily, even among those engaged in postsecondary education.

To determine whether a developmental sequence existed, we carefully examined the pattern of scores over time—and even reprinted the list of individual RJI scores in their entirety for other researchers to examine (King & Kitchener, 1994, Table B6.2). We found that during the 10 years of this study, the use of higher stage reasoning increased, and the use of lower stage reasoning decreased. This is evident in the individual examples reported by King and Kitchener (1994). For example, listed below are RJI scores for three individuals (a high school student, #105: a college student, #417; and a doctoral student, #310) at Times 1 (1977), 2 (1979), 3 (1983), and 4 (1987). The mean score is given first, followed by the mode (dominant/subdominant stage observed):

105, T1: 3.17; 3(4); T2: 3.96; 4(3); T3: 5.67; 6(5); T4: 6.59; 7(6)

417, T1: 3.92; 4(3); T2: 3.63; 4(3); T3: 4.54; 4(5); T4: 4.96; 5(6/4)

310, T1: 5.29; 5(6); T2: 5.63; 6(5); T3: 5.71; 6(5); T4: 6.02; 6(7/5)

Both types of analyses offer strong support for the claim that the posited reflective judgment stages form a developmental sequence.

Similar patterns of change were obtained in six other longitudinal studies involving an additional 180 individuals who took the RJI (Brabeck & Wood, 1990; Polkosnik & Winston, 1989; Sakalys, 1984; Schmidt, 1985; Van Tine, 1990; Welfel & Davison, 1986) and ranging in duration from 3 months to 4 years. The most noteworthy finding among these studies is that the pervasive pattern is one of growth or stability. As King and Kitchener (1994) reported, "in every sample tested, the scores either stayed the same or increased over time. Further, with two exceptions, the mean score increased significantly for all groups tested at 1- to 4-year intervals" (p. 156). The amount of change was smallest in studies of short duration (3–4 months); significant increases were consistently observed in studies of at least a year's duration. In studies reporting incidence of regressions (Brabeck & Wood; King & Kitchener; Sakalys; Schmidt; Welfel & Davison), 0–16% of the mean scores declined between testings, while 84–100% of the mean scores either remained consistent or increased. This suggests that change in reflective thinking over time is better reflected as stability or development rather than decline, and that earlier stage assumptions are rarely used once they are replaced with more advanced assumptions.

Similarly, longitudinal data based on RCI scores obtained at the beginning and end of the first year of college yielded significant increases of about one third of a standard deviation, with comparable gain scores by gender and ethnicity (K. S. Kitchener, Wood, & Jensen, 2003). These freshmen were tested again as sophomores, and a sample of juniors was retested as seniors; RCI scores again increased significantly over time. These findings provide additional evidence that the RJM describes a developmental sequence. However, the growth correlation coefficient was significantly and negatively correlated with scores at Time 1 for the entire sample, by class and by gender: Those who had the lowest scores at Time 1 gained the most, and those who entered with the highest scores gained the least. The pattern was similar for a small subset of the participants who also completed the RJI (K. S. Kitchener et al., 2003).

**Differences by age/educational level.** Another desirable characteristic of a model of reflective thinking is that it can detect predictable changes in thinking across educational levels (e.g., that graduate students score higher than undergraduate students). Over two dozen cross-sectional studies have been used to examine educational level differences in reflective judgment; these studies include samples of high school students, traditional- and nontraditional-age college students, graduate students, and nonstudent adults. Questions related to educational level differences have been of particular interest to those interested in using reflective thinking as a college outcomes variable. Because promoting intellectual development (and especially skills associated with complex reasoning) is a common goal of higher education, studies documenting complex reasoning among college students have been of interest among many higher education researchers. As these studies have been summarized elsewhere, we present only a brief review of these findings.

King et al. (1994) reviewed 25 studies in which more than 1,500 respondents from across the United States took the RJI. Student RJI scores increased slowly but steadily across educational levels, from high school ($M = 3.2$) to the first year of college ($M = 3.6$) to the senior year of college ($M = 4.0$) to early graduate study ($M = 4.6$) to advanced doctoral study ($M = 5.3$). The average RJI scores for nonstudent adults with and without college degrees were 4.3 and 3.6, respectively. The high school students consistently evidenced the assumptions associated with prereflective thinking, such as making decisions on the basis of beliefs that are not subject to evaluation, especially when a conclusion was consistent with what they wanted to believe. Among the college samples, the shift to Stage 4 reasoning indicates that the students had accepted uncertainty as part of the knowing process and were using evidence more consistently to make judgments. Kroll (1992) eloquently captured the shift from prereflective to quasi-reflective thinking as the movement from "ignorant certainty" (the dogmatic assertions characteristic of prereflective thinking) to "intelligent confusion" (acknowledging what you don't know, and why). Although this represents an important step toward reflective thinking, it is not the kind of thinking that is consistent with intended college outcomes (Brabeck, 1983; King, 1992). Only advanced doctoral students consistently used the assumptions of reflective thinking.

A similar pattern of findings was reported based on studies that used the RCI. Wood, Kitchener, and Jensen (2003) conducted a meta-analysis based on all available studies using RCI data; this yielded a sample of 8,537 students who were enrolled in college, graduate, and professional programs at seven different colleges or universities. They found significant differences by educational level, even after controlling for academic aptitude and prior academic achievement. Graduate students scored significantly higher than did medical students, who scored significantly higher than did undergraduate students ($p<.001$). Among the undergraduate students, significant differences were found between early level college students (freshmen and sophomores) and more advanced students (seniors). Thus, the educational level differences in reflective thinking that were found using the RJI were also found using the RCI; however, scores by educational level were about one stage higher on the RCI than on the RJI.

Data from cross-sectional studies showing upward trends in reflective judgment scores across age/educational levels offer corroborating evidence that the RJM describes a developmental sequence. In addition, this collection of studies (especially those that controlled for age) offers evidence that development in reflective thinking is associated with participation in educational programs.

*Domain specificity.* Do individuals reason using similar sets of epistemic assumptions across domains? That is, do respondents score similarly or differently when reasoning about controversies of different content? We have analyzed score variability using several indices. Internal consistency, as measured by coefficient alpha, has been high, with the median scores in the low .80s (King & Kitchener, 1994). Inter-dilemma correlations have been lower, varying with the heterogeneity of scores in the sample, typically in the mid .40s. King, Kitchener, Wood, and Davison (1989) examined individual modal RJI scores and found that the modal score was consistent across dilemmas 75% of the time. However, Wood et al. (2003) reported a significant main effect for dilemma topic using the RCI, as well as an interaction of topic by education level. Students in all four collegiate class levels (freshman through senior) plus graduate students tended to score higher on the two psychology dilemmas (origins of alcoholism and of homosexuality) than on the other three (artificial sweeteners, curricular reform, and immigration policy); however the class difference was accounted for by the higher scores of the seniors and graduate students. That is, the magnitude of the dilemma differences was more pronounced for the more advanced students. Whether this is an artifact of sampling (e.g., representation of behavioral science majors among the seniors) is not known. Interestingly, the scores within the two sets of dilemmas (psychology and nonpsychology) were quite similar.

These findings suggest that there is a relatively high rate of consistency in people's use of epistemic assumptions when reasoning about ill-structured problems. This could be because the RJM describes development in molar rather than fine-grained terms, and therefore is less sensitive to differences in dilemma content. Alternatively, it may be that epistemic assumptions themselves provide a guiding framework for making interpretive judgments that individuals use across a variety of problems such as those measured by the RJI and RCI.

Another way to consider questions related to domain specificity is to look at whether people reason similarly in terms of reflective thinking as compared with how they reason about issues in other areas. Data from several studies that have examined this question (reviewed in King & Kitchener, 1994) strongly suggest that development in reflective judgement is related to but distinct from development in other aspects of cognitive development (verbal aptitude, formal operations, academic ability, critical thinking) and from moral and identity development, and strongly predictive of tolerance for diversity (Guthrie, King, & Palmer, 2000).

## Implications for Practice and Research

How can educators apply their understanding of the nature of the development of reflective thinking as described by the RJM to educational practice? The theory and research presented here offer many possibilities for answering this question. First, the strong effects associated with education offer a hopeful sign that the educational experiences for many students are effective in promoting growth toward reflective thinking. However, the nature of these practices remains largely unexplored, and there is considerable concern (e.g., Baxter Magolda, in press; King, 1992) that the observed reflective thinking skills are not as developed as those called for in the national reports mentioned at the beginning of this article. Nor are they at the level consistent with college goals for students, nor at the level associated with the complex issues and decisions college students will face upon graduation, whether as employees, citizens, consumers, or parents.

Second, consider the consistent finding that development in reflective thinking appears to unfold in a slow, steady manner following the sequence of stages outlined in the RJM. Without data on specific educational experiences affecting this growth curve, it is reasonable to assume that theoretically grounded interventions would yield increases in performance, but probably not in dramatic proportions. Given that stage assumptions are organizing categories for viewing knowledge and knowing, and given that each stage is more like a molar than a fine-grained unit of analysis for development, slow, steady progress is a more reasonable expectation; after all, each stage is a dramatic shift in world view and one's role as a knower. We have offered a number of suggestions elsewhere for promoting reflective thinking (King, 1992, 2000; King & Kitchener, 1994, 2002; K. S. Kitchener et al., 2003; Wood & Lynch, 1998). These range from intentionally incorporating ill-structured problems into the curriculum to improving discipline-specific contextual support, to structuring opportunities for practice and feedback to stimulate optimal level thinking. In each of these practices, students are encouraged to examine their assumptions, gather and interrogate the available evidence from multiple perspectives, and be responsible for offering their own conclusions of the evidence.

Third, it is noteworthy that virtually all the studies that comprise the database for the RJM have measured functional level, not optimal level. In only one study (Kitchener et al., 1993) did the measure of reflective judgment offer contextual support, and probably not at a level that would elicit performance at the upper reaches of a participant's developmental range. According to skill theory, functional level measures offer a low estimate of individuals' ability to engage in reflective thinking. If the average educational level scores are low estimates, then the concerns indicating deficits in student performance around reflective thinking may be overstated. Kroll (1992) also discouraged educators from directing their efforts toward a student's average performance; instead, he encouraged teachers to focus on the leading edge of development, which would be at a higher level within the student's developmental range. Similarly, the finding of differences in performance with and without contextual support suggests that educators should be encouraged to evaluate the amount and kind of contextual support they offer when assessing reflective thinking, for example, in student papers.

K. S. Kitchener et al. (2003) provided new information on the role of student involvement in an assortment of campus activities in promoting reflective thinking. In addition to the RCI, they also administered the College Student Experiences Questionnaire (CSEQ; Pace, 1990), which asks students to indicate on a 4-point scale how frequently they participated in particular collegiate activities. Findings from the freshman sample highlight the complexity of the relationship between participation in college activities and epistemological thinking. Predictably, those who entered college with higher reflective judgment scores also graduated with higher scores. For freshmen, the relationship between Time 1 and Time 2 scores are consistent with expectations about students with higher and lower reflective scores: Those who entered with higher scores endorsed an appreciation for challenging courses, a willingness to work harder in classes, and a commitment to thinking through ideas themselves. They expressed enthusiasm for being in college and indicated an appreciation for the scientific method and further growth in understanding of science. By contrast, the amount of growth in RCI scores for freshmen was almost always negatively correlated with the educational college activities on the CSEQ, including almost all items having to do with seeking out experiences that were different from prior experiences, or seeking out others who were different from themselves. That is, those who relied on prereflective assumptions were less open to experiences that involved talking about different points of view or interacting with others who are different. These students simply may not seek out these experiences as frequently as students who enter with more advanced epistemological assumptions. Studies such as this that link types of collegiate experiences to patterns of college student growth would be particularly helpful in advancing our understanding of the mechanisms of development in reflective thinking. Baxter Magolda's (1999, 2001) pedagogical framework for promoting development offers a promising conceptual tool for designing interventions to promote not only reflective thinking but also advanced capacities in identity and interpersonal domains (for examples in higher education contexts, see Baxter Magolda & King, in press).

Educators have often reported that they are puzzled by how students defend their beliefs—for example, why some reduce complex controversies to simple, black-and-white terms, and why others are so appreciative of the value of multiple perspectives that they are unable to make their own judgments. Our hope here is that educators can better interpret their observations about student behaviors by understanding how such behaviors are grounded in their epistemic assumptions, and how these assumptions about knowledge and how it is gained are related to the ways students justify their own judgments about controversial issues.

# References

American Association of Colleges and Universities (2002). *Greater expectations: A new vision for learning as a nation goes to college.* National Panel Report. Washington, DC: Author.

American Association of Higher Education, American College Personnel Association, National Association of Student Personnel Administrators (1998). *Powerful partnerships.* Washington, DC: Author.

American College Personnel Association (1994). *The student learning imperative.* Washington, DC: Author.

Baxter Magolda, M. B. (1999). *Creating contexts for learning and self-authorship: Constructive-developmental pedagogy.* Nashville, TN: Vanderbilt University Press.

Baxter Magolda, M. B. (2001). *Making their own way: Narratives for transforming higher education to promote self-development.* Sterling, VA: Stylus Publishing.

Baxter Magolda, M. B. (in press). Self-authorship as the common goal of 21st century education. In M. B., Baxter & P. M. King (Eds.), *Learning partnerships: Educating for self-authorship.* Sterling, VA: Stylus Publications.

Baxter Magolda, M. B., & King, P. M. (Eds.), (in press). *Learning partnerships: Educating for self-authorship.* Sterling, VA: Stylus Publications.

Brabeck, M. (1983) Critical thinking skills and reflective judgment development: Redefining the aims of higher education. *Journal of Applied Developmental Psychology, 4*(1), 23–34.

Brabeck, M., & Wood, P. K. (1990). Cross-sectional and longitudinal evidence for differences between well-structured and ill-structured problem solving abilities. In M. L. Commons, C. Armon, L. Kohlberg, F. A. Richards, R. A. Grotzer, & J. D. Sinnott (Eds.), *Adult development 2: Models and methods in the study of adolescent and adult thought* (pp. 133–146). New York: Praeger.

Broughton, M. (1975). *The development of natural epistemology in years 11 to 16.* Unpublished doctoral dissertation. Graduate School of Education, Harvard University, Cambridge, MA.

Broughton, M. (1978). Development of concepts of self, mind, reality, and knowledge. In W. Damon (Ed.). *Social cognition. New directions for child development* (Vol. 1, pp. 75–100). San Francisco: Jossey-Bass.

Churchman, C. W. (1971). *The design of inquiring systems: Basic concepts of systems and organization.* New York: Basic Books.

Darlington, R. B. (1990). *Regression and linear models.* New York: McGraw-Hill.

Dewey, J. (1933). *How we think: A restatement of the relations of reflective thinking to the educative process.* Lexington, MA: Heath.

Fischer, K. W. (1980). A theory of cognitive development: The control and construction of hierarchies of skills. *Psychological Review, 87,* 477–531.

Fischer, K. W., Bullock, D., Rosenberg, E. J., & Raya, P. (1993). The dynamics of competence: How context contributes directly to skill. In R. Wozniak & K. W. Fischer (Eds.), *Development in context: Acting and thinking in specific environments* (pp. 93–117). Hillsdale, NJ: Lawrence Erlbaum Associates, Inc.

Fischer, K. W., & Lamborn, S. D. (1989). Mechanisms of variation developmental levels: Cognitive and emotional transitions during adolescence. In A. de Ribaupierre (Ed.), *Transitions mechanisms in child development: The longitudinal perspective* (pp. 33–670), Cambridge, England: Cambridge University Press.

Fischer, K. W., & Pipp, S. L. (1984). Processes of cognitive development: Optimal level and skill acquisition. In R. J. Sternberg (Ed.), *Mechanisms of cognitive development* (pp. 45–80). New York: Freeman.

Fischer, K. W., & Pruyne, E. (2002). Reflective thinking in adulthood: Emergence, development, and variation. In J. Demick & C. Andreoletti (Eds.), *Handbook of adult development* (pp. 169–198). New York: Plenum.

Fischer, K. W., & Rose, S. P. (1994). Dynamic development of coordination of components of brain and behavior. In G. Dawson & Fischer K. W. (Eds.), *Human behavior and the developing brain* (pp. 2–66). New York: Guilford.

Flavell, J. (1971). Stage related properties of cognitive development. *Cognitive Psychology, 2,* 421–453.

Guthrie, V. L., King, P. M., & Palmer, C. J. (2000). Cognitive capabilities underlying tolerance for diversity among college students. Manuscript submitted for publication.

Harvey, L. J., Hunt, D., & Schroder, H. M. (1961). *Conceptual systems and personality organization.* New York: Wiley.

Hofer, B. K. & Pintrich, P. R. (1997). The development of epistemological theories: Beliefs about knowledge and knowing and their relation to learning. *Review of Educational Research, 67,* 88–140.

Hofer, B. K., & Pintrich, P. R. (2002). Personal epistemology: The psychology of beliefs about knowledge and knowing. Mahwah, NJ: Lawrence Erlbaum Associates, Inc.

Kegan, R. (1982). *The evolving self.* Cambridge, MA: Harvard University Press.

Kegan, R. (1994). *In over our heads: The mental demands of modern life.* Cambridge, MA: Harvard University Press.

King, P. M. (1985). Choice-making in young adulthood: A developmental double-bind. *Counseling and Human Development, 18*(3), 1–12.

King, P. M. (1992). "How do we know? Why do we believe?" Learning to make reflective judgments. *Liberal Education, 78*(1), 2–9.

King, P. M. (2000). Learning to make reflective judgments. In M. B. Baxter Magolda (Ed.), *Linking student development, learning, and teaching: New directions for teaching and learning* (Vol. 82, pp. 15–26). San Francisco: Jossey-Bass.

King, P. M., & Kitchener, K. S. (Eds.), (1994). *Developing reflective judgment: Understanding and promoting intellectual growth and critical thinking in adolescents and adults.* San Francisco: Jossey-Bass.

King, P. M., & Kitchener, K. S. (2002). The reflective judgment model: Twenty years of epistemic cognition. In B. K. Hofer & P. R. Pintrich (Eds.), *Personal epistemology: The psychology of beliefs about knowledge and knowing* (pp. 37–61). Mahwah, NJ: Lawrence Erlbaum Associates, Inc.

King, P. M., Kitchener, K. S., & Wood, P. K. (1994). Research on the reflective judgment model. *Developing reflective judgment: Understanding and promoting intellectual growth and critical thinking in adolescents and adults.* San Francisco: Jossey-Bass.

King, P. M., Kitchener, K. S., Wood, P. K., & Davison, M. L. (1989). Relationships across developmental domains: A longitudinal study of intellectual, moral and ego development. In M. L. Commons, J. D. Sinnott, F. A. Richards, & C. Armon (Eds.), *Adult development: Vol. 1. Comparisons and applications of developmental models* (pp. 57–72). New York: Praeger.

King, P. M., & Mayhew, M. J. (2002). Moral judgement development in higher education: Insights from the Defining Issues Test. *Journal of Moral Education, 33,* 247–270.

King, P. M., & Mayhew, M. J. (in press). Theory and research on the development of moral reasoning among college students. *Handbook of Higher Education.*

Kitchener, K. S. (1983). Cognition, metacognition and epistemic cognition: A three-level model of cognitive processing. *Human Development, 4,* 222–232.

Kitchener, K. S. (2002). Skills, tasks, and definitions: Discrepancies in the understanding and data on the development of folk epistemology. *New Ideas in Psychology, 20,* 309–328.

Kitchener, K. S., & Fischer, K. (1990). A skill approach to the development of reflective thinking. In D. Kuhn (Ed.), *Contributions to human development: Developmental perspectives on teaching and learning thinking skills* (Vol. 21, pp. 48–62). Basel, Switzerland: Karger.

Kitchener, K. S., & King, P. M. (1981). Reflective judgment: Concepts of justification and their relationship to age and education. *Journal of Applied Developmental Psychology, 2*(2), 89–116.

Kitchener, K. S., & King, P. M. (1985). *The reflective judgment scoring manual.* Unpublished manuscript.

Kitchener, K. S., Lynch, C. L., Fischer, K. W., & Wood, P. K. (1993). Developmental range of reflective judgment: The effect of contextual support and practice on developmental stage. *Developmental Psychology, 29*(5), 893–906.

Kitchener, K. S., Wood, P. K. & Jensen, L. (2003). *Individual differences in gains in reflective judgment and their relationship to college experiences.* University of Denver, CO.

Kitchener, R. (2002). Folk epistemology: An introduction. *New Ideas in Psychology, 20*(2/3), 89–105.

Kohlberg, L. (1969). Stage and sequence: The cognitive-developmental approach to socialization. In D. Goslin (Ed.), *Handbook of socialization theory and research.* (pp. 347–450). Chicago: Rand McNally.

Kohlberg, L. (1984). *The psychology of moral development: The nature and validation of moral stages.* San Francisco: Harper & Row.

Kohlberg, L. (1991). My personal search for universal morality. In L. Kuhmerker (Ed.), *The Kohlberg legacy for the helping professions.* Birmingham, AL: R.E.P. Books.

Kroll, B. (1992). *Teaching hearts and minds: College students reflect on the Vietnam War through literature.* Carbondale, IL: Southern Illinois University Press.

Lamborn, S. D., & Fischer, K. W. (1988). Optimal and functional levels in cognitive development: The individual's developmental range. *Newsletter of the International Society for the Study of Behavioral Development, 2*(Serial No. 14), 1–4.

Loevinger, J. (1976). *Ego development: Conceptions and theories.* San Francisco: Jossey-Bass.

Pace, R. (1990). *College Student Experience Questionnaire: Norms for the third edition.* Bloomington, IN: Center for Postsecondary Research and Planning, Indiana University.

Perry, W. (1968). *Patterns of development in thought and values of students in a liberal arts college: A validation of a scheme* (Final Report, Project No. 5-0825, Contract No. SAE-8973), Washington, DC: Department of Health, Education, and Welfare.

Perry, W. (1970). *Forms of intellectual and ethical development in the college years: A scheme.* Troy, MO: Holt, Rinehart & Winston.

Piaget, J. (1965). *The moral judgment of the child.* New York: Free Press.

Piaget, J., & Inhelder, B. (1969). *The psychology of the child.* New York: Basic Books.

Polkosnik, M. C., & Winston, R. B. (1989). Relationships between students' intellectual and psychological development: An exploratory investigation. *Journal of College Student Development, 30*(1), 10–19.

Rest, J. R. (1979). *Development in judging moral issues.* Minneapolis: University of Minnesota Press.

Rest, J. R. (1986). *Moral development: Advances in research and theory.* New York: Praeger.

Rest, J. R., Narvaez, D., Bebeau, M., & Thoma, S. (1999). *Postconventional moral thinking: A neo-Kohlbergian approach.* Mahwah, NJ: Lawrence Erlbaum Associates, Inc.

Sakalys, J. (1984). Effects of an undergraduate research course on cognitive development. *Nursing Research, 33,* 290–295.

Schmidt, J. A. (1985). Older and wise? A longitudinal study of the impact of college on intellectual development. *Journal of College Student Personnel, 26,* 388–394.

Van Tine, N. B. (1990). The development of reflective judgment in adolescents. *Dissertation Abstracts International, 51,* 2659.

Welfel, E. R., & Davison, M. L. (1986). How students make judgments: Do educational level and academic major make a difference? *Journal of College Student Personnel, 23,* 490–497.

Wood, P. K. (1983). Inquiring systems and problem structure: Implications for cognitive development. *Human Development, 26,* 249–265.

Wood, P. K. (1993). *Context and development of reflective thinking: A secondary analysis of the structure of individual differences.* Unpublished manuscript, University of Missouri at Columbia.

Wood, P. K. (1997). A secondary analysis of claims regarding the Reflective Judgment Interview: Internal consistency, sequentiality and intra-individual differences in ill-structured problem solving. In J. C. Smart (Ed.), *Higher education: Handbook of theory and research* (Vol. 12, pp. 243–312). Edison, NY: Agathon Press.

Wood, P. K., Kitchener, K. S., & Jensen, L. (2002). Considerations in the design and evaluation of a paper-and-pencil measure of epistemic cognition. In B. K. Hofer & P. R. Pintrich (Eds.), *Personal epistemology: The psychology of beliefs about knowledge and knowing* (pp. 277–294). Mahwah, NJ: Lawrence Erlbaum Associates, Inc.

Wood, P. K., Kitchener, K. S., & Jensen, L. (2003). College students' concepts of belief justification regarding open-ended controversies. Manuscript submitted for publication.

Wood, P. K., & Lynch, C. L. (1998). Using guided essays to assess and encourage reflective thinking. *Assessment Update, 10*(2), 14–15.

# CHAPTER 25
## EVOLUTION OF A CONSTRUCTIVIST CONCEPTUALIZATION OF EPISTEMOLOGICAL REFLECTION

### MARCIA B. BAXTER MAGOLDA

The epistemological reflection model offers a constructivist theory of personal epistemology based on a 16-year longitudinal study. Participants' developmental journeys are intertwined with the researchers' journey to trace the evolution of the model and its implications for research and practice to promote personal epistemology.

A friend who is a physics major said he was going to a physics seminar. When I heard the word *seminar*, I thought, "Physics has seminars? I mean, you can debate physics? And not be right and not be wrong?" *Reginald* (Baxter Magolda, 1992, p. 136)

Rereading the data, I became immersed in the students' stories. I lost track of the categorization system that had become so ingrained in my thinking as I listened to their experiences and what they thought about them. The experience transformed my thinking. *Marcia* (Baxter Magolda, 1992, p. 10)

These two quotes, one from a participant in my longitudinal study and the other from my own notes as researcher, illustrate moments of epistemological transformation—questioning existing assumptions and crafting new ones to see the world from a more complex perspective. Reginald conveys his new insights on physics that led him to a new perspective on knowledge. I convey my new way of seeing inquiry that led me to a constructivist conceptualization of epistemological reflection (ER). In this article I narrate the interweaving of two transformational journeys—my own and that of longitudinal participants'—to explain how the ER model and its paradigmatic foundation evolved over the course of a 20-year research program.

The ER model emerged from a 16-year longitudinal interview study of young adults' development from age 18 to 34 (Baxter Magolda, 1992, 2001). I use the term *epistemological reflection* to refer to assumptions about the nature, limits, and certainty of knowledge, and how those epistemological assumptions evolve during young adulthood. Like other developmental theorists (e.g., King & Kitchener, 2004), I view epistemological assumptions about the nature of knowledge—its certainty, complexity, and source—as the core of personal epistemology. I concur with other theorists (e.g., Louca, Elby, Hammer, & Kagey, 2004; Schommer-Aikins, 2004) that beliefs about self, learning, classroom instruction, and domain-specific beliefs are part of personal epistemology. I regard these latter components as intertwined with epistemological assumptions rather than as independent

Baxter Magolda, M. B. (2004). Evolution of a constructivist conceptualization of epistemological reflection. *Educational Psychologist, 39*, 31–42.

beliefs or resources. Thus, epistemological transformation is a shift to a more complex set of episte- mological assumptions rather than the acquisition of particular learning strategies or skills.

The ER model portrays personal epistemology as socially constructed and context-bound. Peo- ple actively construct or *make meaning* of their experience—they interpret what happens to them, evaluate it using their current perspective, and draw conclusions about what experiences mean to them. The meaning they construct depends on their current assumptions about themselves and the world, conflicting assumptions they encounter, and the context in which the experience occurs. De- velopmental transformation stems from the interaction of internal (e.g., assumptions) and external (e.g., experiences) factors. Personal epistemology is intertwined with other dimensions of develop- ment, namely identity and relationships (Baxter Magolda, 2001).

My conceptualization of the construct of personal epistemology evolved over time. My expe- riences mirror the socially constructed and context-bound nature of personal epistemology. I ac- tively made meaning of my experiences based partially on assumptions I had at given points in time, conflicting assumptions I encountered, and the context in which these experiences occurred. Evolution of my conceptualization of the construct is due to a complex interplay between my meaning-making as a researcher, the study participants' meaning-making as young adults, and the implications of the intersection of these two sets of meaning-making for how I conducted the longitudinal study.

Just as young adult development is best understood in the context of the particular young adult's meaning-making, the ER model is best understood in the context of my particular meaning-making— the theoretical and methodological paradigms that guided me during the course of this 20-year re- search program. From my present vantage point, I engage in reflexivity, or "the process of reflecting critically on the self as researcher" (Lincoln & Guba, 2000, p. 183) in tracing the evolution of my meaning-making regarding personal epistemology. The intersections among my evolution as a re- searcher, the participants' evolution as young adults, and the evolving methodology of the longitudi- nal study illustrate the constructivist paradigm and place the ER model in context. I discuss four phases of my research agenda to trace this evolution, clarifying my use of the terms *positivism* and *con- structivism* as the story unfolds.

## Phase 1: Assessing Intellectual Development

My study of intellectual development began when I encountered William Perry's (1970) theory in graduate school. Perry described intellectual development as progressing from a dualistic perspective of knowledge as right or wrong, through a multiplistic perspective in which knowl- edge is uncertain, to a relativistic perspective in which contextual evidence justifies knowledge claims. The richness of his theory and the way it resonated with my experience with college stu- dents prompted me to adopt it as a way to understand students. My undergraduate psychology training, coupled with graduate research courses rooted in positivism, led me to interpret Perry's work using a positivist frame of reference. Lincoln and Guba (2000) described posi- tivism as a perspective that assumes an objective external reality and emphasizes the need for inquirers to be objective in accessing that reality, and focuses on generalization and cause-effect linkages. For example, I interpreted Perry's scheme as the natural order (e.g., objective reality) of intellectual development. The linear nature of the scheme (e.g., linear causal links) seemed logical and born out in my experience. Because the scheme emphasized *how* rather than *what* people think, the core trajectory appeared context- and value-free. In my passion for promoting students' intellectual development. I generalized Perry's scheme to all students. I viewed it as a *grand narrative*, which Clandinin and Connelly (2000) described as timeless, context-free, and certain. Thus, I overlooked the theory's contextual nuances despite Perry's careful articulation of its constructive-developmental nature.

I knew that constructive-developmental theoretical frameworks such as Perry's (1970) were in tension with positivist inquiry methods. Constructive-developmental theorists advanced that peo- ple *construct* reality and "evolve through eras according to regular principles of stability and change" (Kegan, 1982, p. 8). The major constructive-developmental theories highlighted in higher education (e.g., Gilligan, 1982; Loevinger & Wessler, 1970; Perry; Piaget, 1950) in the 1970s stemmed from interview studies to theorize how people constructed reality. These theorists generally translated this rich interview data into stages of development. As other researchers attempted to construct paper-pencil instruments for assessing people's developmental stages, they emphasized that open-ended tasks in which students produced a response provided a more accurate portrayal of development than did tasks in which students selected among options provided (e.g., Gibbs & Widaman, 1982). Scholars devised elaborate rating processes to interpret these production responses to insure a degree of objectivity and accuracy (e.g., Gibbs & Widaman, 1982; Loevinger & Wessler, 1970). These rating processes placed the original theoretical models in the forefront yet included options for identifying new theoretical concepts that might emerge from the data. Thus research attempted to maintain a degree of objectivity to enhance legitimacy while embracing basic tenets of constructive-developmental theory.

It was in this context that I spent the early years of my research program devising a paper-pencil measure of development on the Perry (1970) scheme. My dissertation was the initial validation of the measure of epistemological reflection (MER)—a short-essay production task that posed questions about the role of the instructor, learner, peers, and evaluation in learning, and the nature of knowledge and educational decision-making. These domains were central to Perry's theory. I relied on Loevinger and Wessler's (1970) data analysis processes as well as Gibbs and Widaman's (1982) model of constructing specific coding manuals for each domain. The MER coding system placed Perry's first five positions (ranging from dualism to relativism) in the foreground yet allowed for the inclusion of new categories discovered during data analysis. Subsequent studies to validate the MER resulted in a coding manual based on more than 1,000 MER responses (Baxter Magolda & Porterfield, 1988).

During this time, the question of gender differences in intellectual and moral development arose (Belenky, Clinchy, Goldberger, & Tarule, 1986; Gilligan, 1982). Belenky et al.'s (1986) study of a group of women offered a portrait of intellectual development similar to Perry's (1970) in its array of perspectives from dualistic to relativistic assumptions, yet different in important ways. Participants in both studies relied on authority for knowledge in the early phases of development, but women focused on receiving it rather than mastering it as Perry's men did. Some women used a subjective perspective involving listening to their own internal voices. Belenky et al. also identified two sets of procedures for knowing: one objective and separate from the object to be known, and one involving gaining access or connection to the object to be known. The most complex phase of both portraits was similar in focus on constructing knowledge from relevant evidence in a context. Belenky et al. were explicit about their constructivist approach, emphasizing their five ways of knowing as context-bound and one of many multiple realities. However, it was not the constructivist perspective that created dissonance for me. It was similarities and differences with Perry's scheme that attracted my attention. Belenky et al.'s descriptions of subjectivity and connection resonated with some of the MER responses I had collected that appeared incongruent with Perry's scheme, leading me to identify the next phase of my research as exploring how gender shaped college students' approach to the nature, limits, and certainty of knowledge.

## Phase 2: Encountering Uncertainty

My longitudinal study began in 1986 with 101 first-year college students: 51 women and 50 men. This gender balance was crucial to the goal of tracing the role of gender in intellectual development. Our annual 60- to 90-minute interviews initiated a journey neither my participants nor I anticipated. Their journey as young adults centered on discovering uncertainty in knowledge, themselves, and relationships, and finding paths through uncertainty to author their own beliefs and lives. My journey as a researcher centered on discovering new theoretical and methodological frames of reference and rebalancing my research insights with existing theory. Encountering uncertainty preoccupied both participants and me in the first two years of the study.

## Marcia's Journey: Encountering Uncertainty in Theory and Inquiry

Using my positivist lens on constructive-developmental theory, I began this project with inquiry methods that were "betwixt" positivist and constructivist.

*Theoretical assumptions.* Allowing gender-inclusive possibilities in knowing to emerge required an inductive approach. Yet my positivist theoretical bent shaped this inductive approach. Despite Belenky et al.'s (1986) insistence that their five perspectives (silence, received, subjective, procedural, and constructed knowing) were not necessarily sequential, I quickly connected them to Perry's (1970) first five positions (basic duality, multiplicity prelegitimate, multiplicity subordinate, multiplicity correlate, and relativism). I carried these theoretical constructions in my head during this early phase of the longitudinal study. Although I intended the open-ended interviews to allow for new possibilities, I realize in retrospect that I placed theory in the foreground of my inquiry. This leaned toward testing rather than generating theory, inconsistent with the constructivist notion of beginning "with experience as expressed in lived and told stories" (Clandinin & Connelly, 2000, p. 40).

*Methodological assumptions.* Randomly selecting participants from the population of the freshman class ensured the "representative sample" needed to gain a broad picture of development, the gender balance needed to make claims about the role of gender, and legitimacy. Open-ended questions to address the domains that previous research identified as relevant to intellectual development yielded an interview guide (Patton, 1990) to ensure gathering relevant data. The interview guide thus had face validity and yet was open to new possibilities. For example, to solicit perceptions of instructors, I asked, "What do you expect from instructors to help you learn effectively?" If necessary, I used the follow-up question: "What kinds of relationships do you think instructors and students should have to make learning effective?" I also began with a version of Perry's (1970) broad opening question, asking participants to talk about the most significant aspect of their learning experiences that year, to offer them the freedom to set the interview agenda. I framed the study as an exploration of the role of gender in learning to make the study's purpose meaningful to participants and increase their investment in contributing insights to improve educational practice.

These data collection methods were both beneficial and limiting. The random sample resulted in the gender balance needed and included participants from all six academic divisions of the university. It accounted for numerous extraneous variables, thereby allowing a clearer focus on gender. One of these benefits—acquiring a sample representative of the larger population—was also a limitation. Because students of color comprised three percent of the population, the sample included three students of color. My narrow focus on gender led me to overlook the importance of race. The "guided" interview protocol yielded comprehensive data about key domains of intellectual development yet allowed room for respondents to share their particular experiences and the meaning they made of them. Its structure also led to the inadvertent omission of learning outside the classroom in Year 1 because the participants interpreted the questions as limited to the classroom. Revising the interview for Year 2 remedied this shortcoming yet still limited responses to what students viewed as relevant to the questions. Framing the study as a study about learning overlooked important dimensions of development that were not perceived (either by me or the participants) as central to learning (i.e., identity and relationships).

Collectively these methods yielded rich stories (within the limits noted here). I grounded my initial interpretation of these stories in the MER rating system. I had used Loevinger and Wessler's (1970) developing categories system to analyze more than 1,000 MER responses of both men and women prior to starting the longitudinal study. This process involved categorizing an initial set of MER responses according to Perry's (1970) five positions, using those categories to organize additional responses, and using the additional responses to construct a more extensive explanation of categories based on the empirical data. Using this process over time, I constructed the MER rating system describing young adult epistemological assumptions, empirically grounded in data despite its origins in a priori theory (primarily Perry's first five positions). Using this system as a starting point to interpret interviews balanced a priori theory with emerging theory.

## Participants' Journeys: Encountering Uncertainty in Epistemological Assumptions

My approach was consistent with participants' reliance on authority in the early years of college. Their ways of knowing led them to accept and expect my setting the parameters of the study, guiding the interview, and interpreting their stories without their involvement. They often questioned whether they knew enough about learning to be helpful. Because they did not see themselves as authorities, they rarely responded to my annual summary and invitation to make recommendations to modify the interpretations. I identified two sets of epistemic assumptions, or assumptions about the nature, certainty, and limits of knowledge (Kitchener, 1983), from the first two years' interviews. These two ways of knowing form the initial phases of the ER model.

*Absolute knowing.* Year 1 interviews revealed that two-thirds of the 101 participants assumed that knowledge was certain and known by those designated as authorities. Jim conveyed this way of knowing in his description of learning:

> The information is cut and dried. It is either right or wrong. If you know the information, you can do well. It is easy because you just read or listen to a lecture about the ideas, then present it back to the teacher. (Baxter Magolda, 1992, p. 77)

I called this perspective absolute knowing due to the certainty inherent in it. Absolute knowers translated this core assumption about knowledge to expectations for learning, including: (a) teachers communicate information clearly to students and make sure that students understand it; (b) students obtain knowledge from teachers; (c) peers share material and explain it to each other; (d) evaluation is a means to show the teacher students acquired knowledge. Nearly half the participants continued to use this way of knowing during their sophomore year.

*Transitional knowing.* One third of the interviewees entered college with assumptions more complex than absolute knowing. This group perceived knowledge as absolute in some arenas but uncertain in others. I labeled this perspective transitional knowing to reflect the participants' transition from certainty toward uncertainty. Carl conveyed these sentiments:

> I don't particularly care for humanities, English or stuff. There's a lot of—the answers are—they can vary. There's no right or wrong answer. I like things where there's a right answer. Like in chemistry, there's a right answer, but in other classes there's not. I guess it could be easier if there's not a right answer, but I feel uneasy in classes like that. (Baxter Magolda, 1992, p. 106)

Al spoke in more detail to the dilemma of contexts in which the answers were unclear:

> You do something like accounting; it's not subjective. But marketing is more subjective. When we analyze a case, there are different ways to go about it. At least from the classes I've had, there's a process you go through to analyze the case. In one class, he gave us a process, but we don't know what to do with it because he never gives us a concrete idea of what you should do. There have to be more guidelines or structure. You have to have something more firm there; there's never a straight answer. (Baxter Magolda, 1992, p. 106, 108)

Transitional knowers held many of the same expectations for learning as absolute knowers in the areas where "right" answers existed. In the uncertain areas, transitional knowers shifted from acquiring to understanding knowledge, expected teachers to focus on understanding and application, preferred evaluation focused on understanding rather than on memorization, and used peers to explore different interpretations. Students embraced transitional knowing during their college years. Slightly more than 53% of the participants used this way of knowing their sophomore year, 83% their junior year, and 80% their senior year.

*Gender-related reasoning patterns.* Reviewing interview data, I noted qualitatively different approaches to the two ways of knowing although I had not yet synthesized them into gender-related patterns at this phase of the study. I include the descriptions here because they reflect the participants' journeys even though they were constructed from the revised interpretation processes described in the next phase.

Two distinct versions of absolute knowing emerged in the interviews, reflecting what I came to understand as gender-related reasoning patterns. I use the term gender-related to convey that women or men in the project used one pattern more but the patterns were not exclusive to one gender. The receiving pattern, used more often by women in this group, focused on listening and recording knowledge to learn. Toni's comments exemplify this pattern:

> I like to listen—just sit and take notes from an overhead. The material is right there. And if you have a problem, you can ask him, and he can explain it to you. You hear it, you see it, and then you write it down. (Baxter Magolda, 1992, p. 73)

By contrast, mastery pattern students desired participation, showing the instructor their interest and actively mastering the material. Tim's comments exemplify this pattern:

> I like getting involved with the class. Just by answering questions, asking questions. Even if you think you know everything, there's still questions you can ask. When he asks questions, you can try to answer them to your best ability. Don't just let the teacher talk but have him present questions to you. (Baxter Magolda, 1992, p. 73)

The mastery pattern, used more often by men than women in this study, focused on active involvement yet still hinged on acquiring knowledge from authorities. The emergence of these two patterns clarified that active involvement did not necessarily indicate more complex ways of knowing.

Two distinct patterns emerged in transitional knowing as well. Interpersonal pattern students, more often women than men in this study, attempted to connect to the subject and to others to learn in the uncertain areas. Kris illustrated this pattern:

> I get into discussions. Classroom discussions are better for me to learn. You have an opening lecture, where you have the professor discuss. Then students can contribute. Listening to other students contribute their ideas and putting in my own inputs—that makes learning better for me because it makes me think more and try to come up with more generative ideas as to what I would do in a situation. (Baxter Magolda, 1992, p. 117)

The interpersonal pattern's focus on sharing views and connecting one's perspectives with that of others' contrasted with the impersonal pattern's focus on defending views. Students using the impersonal pattern, more often men in this study, tended to stand at arm's length from others and the subject under study. Scott portrayed this approach:

> The debate and discussion process for me is really interesting; I learn a lot more because I remember questions. And I guess I learn the most when I sit and I'm actually forced to raise my hand and then I have to talk. I have to sit there and think on the spot. I learn it better than in a note-taking class that is regurgitation. (Baxter Magolda, 1992, p. 126)

Interpersonal pattern students tended to focus more on others' perspectives whereas impersonal pattern students tended to focus more on their own perspectives.

## The Journeys' Initial Intersection

I encountered dissonance from multiple directions in Year 3 of the project. The most salient dissonance stemmed from incongruence between my data analysis and the impressions of the participants I gleaned during interviews. This marked the first intersection of our respective journeys as participants and researcher. From the outset of the study I coded interview data with the initial categories from the MER manual, formed new categories from new codes, and kept track of this evolving category system I used to interpret subsequent interviews. To explore the role of gender, I followed Loevinger and Wessler's (1970) system of assigning these categories to positions, translating those to numbers to analyze potential gender differences. This yielded a statistical difference in men and women's intellectual development, with men scoring higher. This difference did not ring true with my impressions during interviews or my interpretation of interview transcripts. Recognizing that the statistical difference still placed participants in the same epistemological position, I reevaluated my data analysis process. The interpretation of gender-related patterns for absolute and transitional knowing emerged as a result.

Simultaneously, I became aware of debates in the higher education community regarding positivist and constructivist research paradigms and quantitative and qualitative inquiry. I began to study the constructivist paradigm and qualitative inquiry, finding both consistent with feminist scholarship I was concurrently reading to inform my perspective on gender. Meanwhile, student development scholars were raising questions about the relevance of existing theory for diverse student populations, suggesting that generalizing theory overlooked gender, race, ethnicity, and sexual orientation. These dynamics, and the increasing legitimacy of qualitative inquiry, prompted me to reframe my theoretical and methodological assumptions in ways that brought constructive-developmental theory, the constructivist paradigm, and qualitative inquiry together. This in turn led me to reframe how I collected and interpreted the longitudinal data.

## Phase 3: Exploring Systems For Managing Uncertainty

Years 4 through 6 of the project focused on exploring systems for managing uncertainty both for participants and me. Participants realized that uncertainty was more pervasive than they had thought earlier in college and that they would have to assume responsibility for deciding what to believe rather than relying on external authorities. I realized that my research program generated new theoretical possibilities, and I would have to assume responsibility for articulating those possibilities rather than relying on existing theories. We all set out in search of systems to help us meet these challenges.

### Marcia's Journey: Exploring the Constructivist Paradigm

*Theoretical assumptions.* I found the assumptions of the constructivist paradigm—realities are multiple, context-bound, and mutually shaped by interaction of the knower and known (Lincoln & Guba, 2000)—a better fit with constructive-developmental theory than were the positivist assumptions (e.g., objective reality, context-free, researcher objectivity) I had superimposed on it. The assumption of multiple realities instead of one objective reality better reflected participants' gender-related patterns. Participants who shared basic epistemic assumptions approached knowing in different ways. What some perceived as an ideal learning environment others perceived as the worst possible one. The constructivist assumption that knowledge is context-bound resonated with participants' unique experiences and varied stories. The assumption that entities shape each other was also evident in the participants' narratives. Because they used various ways of knowing or reasoning patterns, they interpreted learning situations differently. Subsequently, their instructors sometimes altered the nature of learning situations in response to participants' reactions. This mutual shaping was occurring between researcher and participant as well. I realized that I could not separate myself from what I was observing. Participants told me that reflecting on their experience in the interviews changed their thinking about it and made them more aware of it in the intervening year (more about this later). The role of subjectivity in the study became apparent.

I found language to connect these constructivist assumptions to intellectual development in Frye's (1990) notion of naming patterns to understand the diversity of women's experiences. She wrote: "Naming patterns is like charting the prevailing winds over a continent, which does not imply that every individual and item in the landscape is identically affected" (p. 180). Developmental patterns, taken as prevailing winds, chart overarching similarities yet remain open for particularities across individuals. From this vantage point, naming patterns is aimed at generating new possibilities rather than at narrowing theoretical constructs. Considering Perry's (1970) original work from this lens clarified its constructivist nature. It also meant reconstructing my longitudinal study on a constructivist foundation.

*Methodological assumptions.* My gravitation toward constructivism meant aligning my inquiry with qualitative assumptions. Lincoln and Guba (2000) wrote: "Qualitative researchers stress the socially constructed nature of reality, the intimate relationship between the researcher and what is studied, and the situational constraints that shape inquiry" (p. 8). Realizing the need to place participants' stories in the foreground meant moving my theoretical frameworks to the background. From that position they informed my understanding but did not presuppose a particular construction from participants' stories. Rebalancing the role of my perspective and participants' perspectives warranted giving participants more freedom of expression. Loosening the structure of the interview to solicit broader stories and conducting the interview in a more flexible manner achieved a better balance of content that participants and I perceived as relevant.

These changes warranted substantial transformation in my interpretation of participants' stories. Revisiting Loevinger and Wessler's (1970) evolving category system, I noted its similarity to constructing categories based on participants' stories. Exploring alternatives that squarely placed participants' stories in the foreground, I found the grounded formal theory approach a better fit with my constructivist leanings. Glaser and Strauss (1967) proposed this approach to develop theory from systematically gathered data. Addressing the role of existing theory, they wrote:

> In this methodology, theory may be *generated* initially from the data, or, if existing (grounded) theories seem appropriate to the area of investigation, then these may be *elaborated* and modified as incoming data are meticulously played out against them. . . . Researchers can also carry into current studies any theory based on their *previous research*, providing it seems relevant to these—but again the matching of theory against data must be rigorously carried out. (Strauss & Corbin, 1994, p. 273)

Because my initial category system emerged from empirical data from more than 1,000 students, it represented a relevant grounded theory to use in the longitudinal study. Because data collection and interpretation are "guided by successively evolving interpretations made during the course of the study" (Strauss, 1987, p. 10), possibilities would continue to emerge if I rigorously matched data to the grounded theory. Thus, I continued to sort the transcripts by epistemological assumptions but reread them to identify the core aspects of participants' stories. Consciously moving a priori theory to the background enabled me to name patterns, both in ways of knowing and gender-related patterns within them, in ways that were more consistent with the data. I had found a system for managing the uncertainty inherent in viewing personal epistemology through a constructivist lens.

This process yielded the four ways of knowing and reasoning patterns within them reported in *Knowing and Reasoning in College* (Baxter Magolda, 1992). This volume contains the guiding assumptions of my journey as a researcher to that point. These included: Ways of knowing and patterns within them are socially constructed, context-bound, and best understood through naturalistic inquiry, and represent possibilities; and reasoning patterns are fluid and gender-related rather than dictated by gender. These guiding assumptions resonated with Strauss and Corbin's (1994) view of grounded theory as fluid due to its focus on the interaction of multiple actors, temporality, and process.

## Participants' Journeys: Exploring Systems to Guide Beliefs

Uncertainty became increasingly prevalent in the fourth- and fifth-year interviews. Although 80% of the seniors used transitional knowing, it dropped off considerably in light of expectations inherent in life after college. Participants searched for ways to make decisions in the face of increasing uncertainty.

*Independent knowing.* Independent knowing, characterized by viewing most knowledge as uncertain, became the predominant way of knowing for 16% of the seniors. Laura described how it emerged for her:

> I became very skeptical about what the "truth" was. It's amazing how you can influence statistics. Statistics are supposed to be really the truth. You can't manipulate statistics. But then I learned you really can manipulate statistics to have a point of view to be the truth. (Baxter Magolda, 1992, p. 138)

Once Laura realized that statistics could be manipulated to construct a view of the truth, she abandoned the notion that knowledge is certain. Instead, she concluded

> Everything's relative; there's no truth in the world—that sort of thing. So I've decided that the only person that you can really depend on is yourself. Each individual has their own truth. No one has the right to decide. "This has to be your truth, too." (Baxter Magolda, 1992, p. 136)

Independent knowing changed expectations for learning. Independent knowers focused on thinking for themselves, sharing views with peers to expand their thinking, and expecting teachers to promote independent thinking and avoid judging students' opinions.

For participants who had focused on listening to others, the struggle in independent knowing was to learn to listen to oneself. This characterized the interindividual pattern within independent knowing, used most often by women in this group. Alexis' story reveals the tension between listening to others and identifying her own beliefs:

> I like to listen to their arguments for it; then I listen to other people's arguments against it. And then it's just my own personal view, really, whether I can establish the credibility—so I guess it really stems from the credibility of the person who's saying it also, as well as just the opinion on it. I listen to both sides. I usually throw some of my own views into it as well. So I'm influenced by other people—like each member of the group should be influenced by each other. But when the final vote comes in, you should go with what you believe. (Baxter Magolda, 1992, pp. 147–148)

Alexis was so accustomed to subjugating her voice that it was difficult for her to express it. Lowell, on the other hand, could readily bring his voice forward. He struggled to listen to others as he used the individual pattern of independent knowing. His comments illustrate this pattern:

> I'd consider myself conservative. And there was one guy in our group who was quite liberal and acknowledged it. I guess it gave me another viewpoint, another aspect to look at this. Like it or not, we're all kind of ingrained one way or another, whether it's the liberal end or the conservative end. He looked at it in this way, and I looked at it in another way. And everybody in the group had their own ways on it. [You had] to try to get your point across without sounding too dominating—I'm searching for words and not finding them. To try to listen to theirs, to *really* listen, not to just hear it and let it go through. And then to try to take that into account and reach a compromise. There was quite a bit of discussion. But I don't think the attempt was to try to change each other's mind. It was just, "Your point is all right, but you've got to look at this part, too, because this is as relevant." (Baxter Magolda, 1992, pp. 136–137)

Movement into independent knowing occurred more readily in employment and graduate school contexts as evidenced by 57% using it in Year 5 interviews. Interviewees reported that employers and graduate faculty asked them to assume responsibility for their thinking and work. Employers and faculty expected them to evaluate multiple perspectives, to bring their own perspective to their work, and to choose plans of action accordingly. Unfortunately, many had not yet developed criteria for choosing from among alternatives. They soon discovered that everything was not relative.

*Contextual knowing.* Identifying criteria from which to make choices first appeared in contextual knowing, characterized by the belief that knowledge exists in a context and is judged on evidence relevant to that context. Only 2 of the 80 participants who remained in the study their senior year adopted this way of knowing. It replaced earlier ways of knowing gradually in the initial years following college, primarily due to the constant expectation that young adults function in this way. Anne portrayed the experience of many of her peers as she described realizing what was expected of her at work:

> I guess you just do it because you have to. You have to come up with some answers. Just kind of bumble through it I guess, try to rationalize things out. I wrote down some solutions and wrote down pluses of the solutions. Then I'd try to think of what kind of questions my boss would ask, like "What would happen if we did this?" and "Where did you get these numbers?" . . . Before, I would make a decision and take it into my boss. But now I've learned to say to myself, "What's he going to want to know? Have you thought of everything?" And it's made me go back and rethink everything and come up with some other alternatives and just make sure what I'm thinking is good. (Baxter Magolda, 2001, p. 243)

Being challenged to carefully ponder choices and offer defensible solutions simultaneously challenged participants to integrate the reasoning patterns evident in earlier ways of knowing. Contextual knowing required connecting to others and the subject to be known yet at the same time required standing back to analyze the situation. Mark, contemplating a decision about marriage, described contextual knowing involving both patterns:

> As far as firm and personal life, I sit down and I write down things I know, pro and con, "Go into a relationship," "Don't go into a relationship," cost-benefit kind of analysis. Like I said, I don't leave my rationality behind because I think that's really an effective tool. And then I think about all my options, and there's something about it. It carries on its own momentum. . . . So I listen to those feelings, and I come to my room and I sit down and I push all my books away. I grab a sheet of paper or whatever and start writing things down, how I feel. And then when I feel like I've got a handle on those feelings and options, then I talk to the people affected. . . . When you bring other people into it, you push your feelings down just a touch because then you want to be open-minded again at that point. And then you talk to people unaffected by it, too, because obviously when people are affected by it they're invested in it. . . . I don't let my feelings rush me into anything because . . . you're dealing with personal life more—if you do something rash, it can cost you a lot. (Baxter Magolda, 2001, pp. 42–43)

Participants experienced the need to establish criteria for knowing and recognized that they had to decide for themselves. Yet they often continued to look to external sources for guidance.

*External formulas.* Interviews from Years 5 and 6 revealed that many participants used external formulas to guide their lives regardless of their ways of knowing. Mark, whose story was just described as an example of contextual knowing, still approached law school using a formula for success:

> I came here and I tried to figure out what the legal culture figures is success. I knew a Supreme Court clerkship was, so one of my goals was to aim towards that. So I got here to law school and I figured out, "Okay, well, to be a success here you have to get to know some professors who are influential with judges to get a good clerkship, to get in the pipeline, get in the star system here. Also get on *Law Review*. Write a paper here that you can publish." I thought, "Okay, this is kind of the plan then, step by step." The ultimate plan for success in the legal culture, I mean, go to [this] Law School and do these things, then you've got it made. . . . I would be in the *ultimate* position to do whatever I want to do because I will have done *everything* possible, and then I'd be in a position to make a choice that reflected exactly who I was, or at least more clearly. (Baxter Magolda, 2001, p. 41)

Likewise, Gwen, the other contextual knower during her senior year, offered this post-college perspective:

> We're taught to make [our] plan. Plan your work and work your plan and you're going to get where you want to go. . . . I could set my sights on something and it would happen. And I would generally know some of the things I needed to do to get there. If you want this, then do this, this, and this, and it happened. (Baxter Magolda, 2001, p. 43)

On leaving college, longitudinal participants did what they had been taught to do best—follow authorities' leads to manage uncertainty.

## The Journeys Converge at a Crossroads

Initially these interviews confused me. I wondered how so many seniors could construct the world from the vantage point of transitional knowing. Yet I wondered why those who had shifted to independent or contextual knowing still used external formulas to approach life after college. The gender-related patterns merging as the epistemological journey progressed surprised me. Post-college environments prompted movement toward independent and contextual knowing faster than did the college environment, which was disconcerting.

Fortunately, participants' journeys prompted them to infuse their understandings of these dilemmas into interviews. Many volunteered that learning was not a meaningful framework for their post-college experience and asked to talk about their experience in general instead. These broader conversations revealed that other developmental dimensions (e.g., identity and relationships) mediated their intellectual development. My study of Kegan's (1994) theory emphasizing the intertwining of the cognitive, intrapersonal, and interpersonal developmental dimensions informed this interpretation. Participants also addressed specific challenges and supports they found in their work, advanced education, and personal contexts, and their reactions to them. Their rapid transformation in these new environments called into question my theoretical assumptions about the nature of development.

## Phase 4: Rebalancing Existing Knowledge and New Perspectives

As participants were solidifying their beliefs about themselves and the world in the years after college, I was solidifying my constructivist theoretical and methodological assumptions. Our journeys converged into a joint path as we rebalanced existing knowledge with our own voices and experience. Participants' voices moved to the foreground as they authored their own lives. I moved the data and our construction of it to the foreground, authoring new theoretical possibilities. Our journeys again mediated the conduct of the study as we became partners in interpreting the nature of ER.

### Marcia's Journey: Putting Existing Theory in Perspective

*Theoretical assumptions.* The use of external formulas after college by participants who had adopted independent and contextual ways of knowing perplexed me. The post-college interviews revealed that three questions were salient in participants' 20s: How do I know, who am I, and what kind of relationships do I want? These three questions were intertwined in their stories. The stories resonated with Kegan's (1994) portrayal of holistic development as the intertwining of cognitive (i.e., how do I know?), intrapersonal (i.e., who am I?), and interpersonal (i.e., what kind of relationships do I want?) dimensions. Rereading Perry (1970), Belenky, et al. (1986), and Loevinger and Wessler (1970) revealed that they had foreseen this connection years earlier. Interviewees who developed complex ways of knowing often could not live those ways of knowing until they had developed complex ways of seeing themselves and their relations with others. Recognizing the value of interviewees' broader life stories beyond the epistemological dimension led me to explore *narrative inquiry*, "the activities involved in working with the various kinds of stories of life experiences found in life histories, long interviews, . . ." (Schwandt, 1997, p. 98). This solidified the need to move interviewees' narratives to the foreground of my meaning-making.

Following participants' lives for 12 years after their college graduation yielded a wide range of experiences in diverse settings characterized by a broad continuum of challenge and support. The complex interplay of participants' assumptions about themselves and their worlds, the assumptions they encountered, and the contexts in which these encounters took place shaped their particular meaning-making. In some cases transformation was gradual; in other cases it was surprisingly rapid. Analyzing these dynamics led me to abandon my earlier theoretical assumption that development is a gradual process, naturally unfolding in logical sequence. I now view existing developmental models as descriptions of how contexts have shaped young adults (in interaction with young adults' current meaning-making) rather than as descriptions of what is possible in terms of developmental growth. Higher education focused on knowledge acquisition has trained students to be transitional knowers; alternative higher education contexts (e.g., focused on knowledge construction) might make complex meaning-making possible at much earlier ages than I have encountered it to date.

Collectively, these theoretical assumptions form my constructivist interpretation of ER. They also altered the conduct of the longitudinal study.

*Methodological assumptions.* In the years after the participants finished college, my interview protocol steadily moved toward an informal conversational interview (Patton, 1990). Realizing the richness inherent in narratives emerging from participants' sense of what was important, I asked fewer and fewer questions. These unstructured interviews (Fontana & Frey, 1994) invited participants to shape the interview. Participants volunteered topics of importance that emerged in the year between our annual interviews, talked freely about them, and explored their meaning in response to my probing questions about what it meant for them or why they perceived it a particular way. Having read summaries and books about the project, participants knew that how and why they made meaning was a primary focus. My focus on listening to their stories, constantly asking for the meaning behind their thinking or how they arrived at their current perspective, provided opportunities for self-reflection. As Ned shared, the interview was an opportunity for introspection:

> I don't often get the opportunity for someone to ask these tough questions to figure out my framework. It is very parallel to discussions with my close friend—at the beginning I had no idea what I'd say; then I recognize things I need to think more about.

Many interviewees noted that this kind of introspection and discussion to identify how they made meaning was rare in their daily lives. They relished an interview format that encouraged exploration and let them set the agenda. They were most likely shaped by participating in it. The rapport established from our long association enriched these reflections and contributed to participants' comfort in sharing personal details of their lives. Respecting participants' privacy is an important component of building trust and rapport that enables this level of intimacy (Baxter Magolda, 2001). Acknowledging that this partnership affects participants' meaning-making is another aspect of the constructivist nature of the project. The ER model is context-bound by virtue of participants' reports that they are aware of how they make meaning due to their participation in the project. Our intertwining journeys offer insight into the partnerships that promote personal epistemology.

As participants and I became partners in exploring their meaning-making in interviews, we gradually became interpretation partners. My willingness to rebalance existing and new perspectives led to shifting grounded theory methodology (Strauss & Corbin, 1994) to generate theory from the data rather than match data to existing grounded theory. I no longer sorted transcripts by epistemological position. Instead, I reviewed each year's transcriptions of the taped interviews and coded them into units. I then sorted the units into categories to identify themes and patterns from the data. This is what qualitative researchers call "allowing themes to emerge." Rereading data for each participant across years resulted in successively evolving interpretations and further development of patterns. Two research partners joined me to reread and analyze the post-college data. Each of us prepared summaries of themes individually followed by meetings in which we discussed and synthesized our perceptions. This use of multiple analysts helped mediate our subjectivities and increase the adequacy of our interpretations. Prolonged engagement to build trust and understanding and member checking to assure accuracy of interpretations enhanced the credibility of the themes and patterns. Participants were increasingly willing to explore my interpretations and offer their feedback. I shared drafts of publications with participants whose stories were told in-depth and solicited their input on these interpretations. Interviews following the publication of *Making Their Own Way* (Baxter Magolda, 2001) included conversation about their reaction to my construction of the collective group's experience. Participants now routinely refer me to books or articles they have read that inform the project.

## Participants' Journeys: Putting External Authority in Perspective

Participants' experience with external formulas led to crossroads where external and internal influence collided. Moving internal influence to the foreground and becoming authors of their lives was consistent with the partnership emerging in the longitudinal study. As their internal voices emerged and gained strength, they were increasingly willing to join me in making meaning of their experiences.

*Crossroads.* The emergence of the intrapersonal and interpersonal dimensions of development in the post-college interviews led me to shift from placing ways of knowing in the foreground to placing phases in the journey toward self-authorship in the foreground. For the shift to internal decision-making needed for independent and contextual knowing to occur, similar shifts needed to occur in the intrapersonal and interpersonal dimensions. The crossroads marked a phase in which participants recognized the need for internal self-definition and decision making but were struggling to make this shift. Kurt spoke eloquently about this phase:

> I'm the kind of person who is motivated by being wanted, I think. I've gone to a couple of workshops and, either fortunately or unfortunately, I'm the kind of person who gets my self-worth on whether or not other people accept me for what I do or other people appreciate what I'm doing. . . . I'm coming from a position where I get my worth and my value from other people, which is, I think, wrong for me to do. But that's where I am right now. I feel like whether or not I choose to be happy is dependent upon me and only me. . . . The power of choice is mine. I have a choice of how I want to perceive each and every situation in my life. . . . Obviously I'm not to that point yet because I choose to make myself happy and make myself sad on what other people are thinking. (Baxter Magolda, 2001, pp. 98–99)

Arrival at this crossroads stemmed from dissatisfaction with external formulas and environmental challenges to shift the balance of external and internal voices in meaning-making. Shifting the balance to place their internal voices at the center of meaning-making led to self-authorship.

*Becoming the author of one's life.* Becoming the author of one's life meant taking responsibility for one's beliefs, identity, and relationships. The internal voice became the coordinator of meaning-making in all three dimensions of development. Mark's comments illustrate this notion:

> Making yourself into something, not what other people say or not just kind of floating along in life, but you're in some sense a piece of clay. You've been formed into different things, but that doesn't mean you can't go back on the potter's wheel and instead of somebody else's hands building and molding you, you use your own, and in a fundamental sense change your values and beliefs. (Baxter Magolda, 2001, p. 119)

Dawn's narrative reveals how changing values and beliefs involves all three dimensions:

> The more you discover about yourself, the more you can become secure with it. And that obviously leads to greater self-confidence because you become comfortable with who you really are. . . . I'm more willing to express my ideas and take chances expressing my ideas. . . . I'm not as afraid to be willing to say that because of what I am this is how I feel. . . . And I think self-awareness too, because you realize that it doesn't really matter if other people agree with you or not. You can think and formulate ideas for yourself and ultimately that's what's important. You have a mind and you can use it. . . . You can form an opinion that's more important than the opinion itself. So it's kind of a self-confidence and self-awareness thing. (Baxter Magolda, 2001, pp. 152–153)

Because Dawn's internally defined sense of self (intrapersonal) made her more secure, she worried less about how others viewed her (interpersonal). This freed her to express her thinking and recognize her ability to use her mind (epistemological). Framing responses to the questions "how do I know," "who am I," and "what kind of relationships do I want" from this internal perspective yielded self-authorship.

*Internal foundation.* In their late 20s and early 30s, many participants were increasingly comfortable with their identities and beliefs, and how they related to others. As they constructed frameworks to answer the questions about what to believe, who to be, and how to relate to others, the frameworks solidified to form comprehensive belief systems. The framework for "who I am" solidified into a solid sense of self that made participants feel "personally grounded" and able to be true to themselves in all dimensions of their lives. This sense of self contributed to their ability to choose core beliefs and integrate them into an internal belief system that guided their lives. The security of the internal self and belief system afforded them a new vantage point from which to engage in authentic, mutual relationships with others. Solidifying the internal self, belief system, and approach to relationships created both a solid foundation and openness to ambiguity and change. Becoming comfortable with the internal voice yielded a security to explore others' perspectives; complex ways of knowing meant ambiguity and uncertainty would always be commonplace. Sandra's comments convey this phase of the journey:

I have a clearer vision of what I really want to do. I have a stronger image of who I am. I'm not so wrapped up in being a counselor, I'm being Sandra. I have a clearer vision of Sandra and the different things that make up who I am. I went from "I am a counselor" to "I do some social work." I am not afraid to say what I believe in and stand for it. I don't make reckless decisions that hurt my lifestyle or self—like quitting my job—but I am able to say, "This is how it is." . . . To help others, you have to maintain self. Now that I'm out of my old job, I recognize the point where I began to lose myself. If it happens again, I see it and don't do it. I don't worry much. I'm confident that I do a good job; I know this. If others disagree, they can find someone else. I have a lot of feedback that I trust is the truth. I've taken charge and get things done. I am more confident. I am able to recognize signs more quickly now. It sounds nonchalant, but that is how I feel. Some of that was blurry in my old job. I knew some things I wouldn't do, but as we were speeding towards them, I couldn't tell how many I would do. Now I can see the line, and know what I won't do. (Baxter Magolda, 2001, pp. 166, 168)

Because Sandra had a solid internal sense of self and belief system, she functioned authentically in her work environment. She imagined change as acceptable because she knew her foundation would remain intact. Participants built these internal foundations at varying paces in their early thirties depending on the complex interplay between their ways of viewing the world and contexts they encountered.

## Partnerships for Promoting and Researching Personal Epistemology

Longitudinal participants experienced growth in complex, fluid environments that emphasized social construction of knowledge, the participants' role in it, and mutual engagement with experts in knowledge construction. From their descriptions, I developed the learning partnerships model, a framework for constructing these transformational contexts (Baxter Magolda, 2001; Baxter Magolda & King, 2004). The framework reinforces my constructivist interpretation of personal epistemology and self-authorship in its emphasis of the social construction of knowledge and the centrality of personal meaning-making in interpreting experience.

### Learning Partnerships in Educational Practice

Some longitudinal participants experienced learning partnerships during college; more experienced them after college. Their post-college contexts offered substantial challenge accompanied by substantial support. Challenge came in the form of three core assumptions inherent in contexts participants viewed as growth producing: Knowledge is complex and socially constructed; self is central to knowledge construction; and authority and expertise are shared in mutual knowledge construction among peers. Complexity and social construction of knowledge emphasized using multiple perspectives to make choices in context, thus modeling epistemological complexity. Self as central to knowledge construction emphasized that one's identity must come into play in deciding what to believe, thus modeling intrapersonal complexity. Sharing authority and expertise emphasized mutual negotiation of knowledge, thus modeling interpersonal complexity.

Support to meet these demands took the form of three principles: validating learners as knowers, situating learning in learners' experience, and defining learning as mutually constructing meaning. Affirming learners' ability to construct knowledge, although not necessarily the knowledge they had currently constructed, welcomed them into the knowledge construction process. Situating learning in learners' experience gave them a base from which to construct knowledge connecting their experience to the task at hand. Defining learning as mutually constructing meaning affirmed the expectation that learners participate in knowledge construction.

Although these assumptions and principles took diverse forms in diverse contexts, they were prevalent in employment, graduate school, professional school, and community settings. Extensive stories illustrating this model in diverse settings (Baxter Magolda, 2001; Baxter Magolda & King, 2004) reveal rich but fluid possibilities for educational practice. The prevailing winds of the model suggest that educators and learners must be collaborative partners in the journey toward self-authorship. Creating contexts in which learners experience the complexity of the world around them helps them encounter new assumptions. Mutually engaging learners in reflecting on the interplay between new and existing assumptions and inviting them to take responsibility for their beliefs, identities, and relationships enables self-authorship. These partnerships are fluid and evolving, their nature congruent with the constructivist nature of personal epistemology. The evolution of my partnership with longitudinal participants described here is one example that has afforded them and me the opportunity to encounter new assumptions, compare them to existing ones, and reshape beliefs accordingly. They used these experiences to assist in self-authoring their lives; I used these experiences to self-author the construct of personal epistemology. Educational practice using the learning partnerships model would offer similar contexts for transformation to learners.

## Learning Partnerships in Future Research

This special issue raises numerous questions about the nature of personal epistemology, its components and their interconnections, and the interplay of internal and external factors in developmental change. Viewing personal epistemology as complex and socially constructed necessitates future research including the multiple components and clarifying their potential interconnections. Viewing the self as central to knowledge construction suggests future research focused on how people use their current epistemological assumptions to actively construct meaning and new perspectives. Simultaneously, viewing authority and expertise as shared in knowledge construction portends research focused on the interplay between internal and external factors in developmental change. Working collaboratively across paradigms and approaches, as is the intent of this issue, aids in exploring these complex possibilities.

My partnership with my participants over the years has significantly altered my assumptions about personal epistemology and how it develops. One important aspect of this partnership is its longitudinal nature, allowing for tracing transformation over time and context. My study contributes to understanding the personal epistemology of a group of white young adults who attended a selective liberal arts college. Similar studies could contribute to understanding the personal epistemology of groups with varying races, ethnicities, economic classes, and sexual orientations. Conducting these studies in a range of college contexts would enhance understanding of the environmental influence on personal epistemology. Another important aspect is the partnership itself, the interweaving of perspectives and evolving journeys as we pursue understanding. Analyzing our relationships with our participants, their effects on participants and the research, and reflexivity about our own research will enhance our inquiry and the possibilities we are able to generate from it.

# References

Baxter Magolda, M. B. (1992). *Knowing and reasoning in college: Gender-related patterns in students' intellectual development*. San Francisco: Jossey-Bass.

Baxter Magolda, M. B. (2001). *Making their own way: Narratives for transforming higher education to promote self-development*. Sterling, VA: Stylus.

Baxter Magolda, M. B., & King, P. M. (Eds.), (2004). *Learning partnerships: Theory & models of practice to educate for self-authorship*. Sterling, VA: Stylus.

Baxter Magolda, M. B., & Porterfield, W. D. (1988). *Assessing intellectual development: The link between theory and practice*. Alexandria, VA: American College Personnel Association.

Belenky, M., Clinchy, B. M., Goldberger, N., & Tarule, J. (1986). *Women's ways of knowing: The development of self, voice, and mind*. New York: Basic Books.

Clandinin, D. J., & Connelly, F. M. (2000). *Narrative inquiry: Experience and story in qualitative research*. San Francisco: Jossey-Bass.

Fontana, A., & Frey, J. H. (1994). Interviewing: The art of science. In N. K. Denzin & Y. S. Lincoln (Eds.), *Handbook of qualitative research* (pp. 361–376). Thousand Oaks, CA: Sage.

Frye, M. (1990). The possibility of feminist theory. In D. L. Rhode (Ed.), *Theoretical perspectives on sexual difference* (pp. 174–184). New Haven, CT: Yale University Press.

Gibbs, J., & Widaman, K. F. (1982). *Social intelligence: Measuring the development of sociomoral reflection.* Englewood Cliffs, NJ: Prentice-Hall.

Gilligan, C. (1982). *In a different voice.* Cambridge, MA: Harvard University Press.

Glaser, B., & Strauss, A. (1967). *The discovery of grounded theory: Strategies for qualitative research.* Chicago: Aldine.

Kegan, R. (1982). *The evolving self: Problem and process in human development.* Cambridge, MA: Harvard University Press.

Kegan, R. (1994). *In over our heads: The mental demands of modern life.* Cambridge, MA: Harvard University Press.

King, P., & Kitchener, K. S. (2004). Reflective judgment: Theory and research on the development of epistemic assumptions through adulthood. *Educational Psychologist, 39,* 5–18.

Kitchener, K. S. (1983). Cognition, metacognition, and epistemic cognition. *Human Development, 26,* 222–232.

Lincoln, Y. S., & Guba, E. G. (2000). Paradigmatic controversies, contradictions, and emerging confluences. In N. K. Denzin & Y. S. Lincoln (Eds.), *Handbook of qualitative research* (2nd ed., pp. 163–188). Thousand Oaks, CA: Sage.

Loevinger, J., & Wessler, R. (1970). *Ego development* (Vol. 1). San Francisco: Jossey-Bass.

Louca, L., Elby, A., Hammer, D., & Kagey, T. (2004). Epistemological resources: Applying a new epistemological framework to science instruction. *Educational Psychologist, 39,* 57–68.

Patton, M. Q. (1990). *Qualitative evaluation and research methods.* Newbury Park, CA: Sage.

Perry, W. G. (1970). *Forms of intellectual and ethical development in the college years: A scheme.* Troy, MO: Holt, Rinehart, & Winston.

Piaget, J. (1950). *The psychology of intelligence* (M. Piercy & D. Berlyne, Trans.). London: Routledge & Kegan Paul.

Schommer-Aikins, M. (2004). Explaining the epistemological belief system: Introducing the embedded systemic model and coordinated research approach. *Educational Psychologist, 39,* 19–29.

Schwandt, T. A. (1997). *Qualitative inquiry: A dictionary of terms.* Thousand Oaks, CA: Sage.

Strauss, A. (1987). *Qualitative analysis for social scientists.* New York: Cambridge University Press.

Strauss, A., & Corbin, J. (1994). Grounded theory methodology: An overview. In N. Denzin & Y. Lincoln (Eds.). *Handbook of qualitative research* (pp. 273–285). Thousand Oaks, CA: Sage.

# CHAPTER 26
## MORAL STAGES AND MORALIZATION: THE COGNITIVE-DEVELOPMENTAL APPROACH

### LAWRENCE KOHLBERG

In this chapter I shall present an overview of the cognitive-developmental theory of moralization as elaborated in studies of moral stages by myself and my colleagues. I shall first present a theoretical description of the six moral stages, followed by an account of the development of our methods for identifying or scoring stage. Having presented a picture of what moral development is and how to assess it, I shall go on to present the theory of moralization which can best account for this picture of moral development, and then to contrast this theory with approaches which see moral developments as a result of socialization or social learning.

In a sense, this chapter represents an updating of earlier presentations of my theory of moral development stages (Kohlberg, 1969). In this chapter, however, there is no attempt to review research comprehensively, as research reviews have appeared earlier (Kohlberg, 1964, 1969) and are forthcoming (Kohlberg and Candee, in prep.). The philosophic assumptions and implications of our stages are also treated only briefly, having been thoroughly discussed elsewhere (Kohlberg, 1971b, 1981a.)

## The Place of Moral Judgment in the Total Personality

To understand moral stage, it is helpful to locate it in a sequencer of development of personality. We know that individuals pass through the moral stages one step at a time as they progress from the bottom (Stage 1) toward the top (Stage 6). There are also other stages that individuals must go through, perhaps the most basic of which are the stages of logical reasoning or intelligence studied by Piaget (1967). After the child learns to speak, there are three major developmental stages of reasoning: the intuitive, the concrete operational, and the formal operational. At around age 7, children enter the stage of concrete logical thought; they can then make logical inferences, classify things and handle quantitative relations about concrete things. In adolescence, many but not all individuals enter the stage of formal operations, at which level they can reason abstractly. Formal operational thinking can consider all possibilities, consider the relations between elements in a system, form hypotheses, deduce implications from the hypotheses, and test them against reality. Many adolescents and adults only partially attain the stage of formal operations; they consider all the actual relations of one thing to another at the same time, but do not consider all possibilities and do not form abstract hypotheses.

In general, almost no adolescents and adults will still be entirely at the stage of concrete operations, many will be at the stage of partial formal operations, and most will be at the highest stage of formal operations (Kuhn, Langer, Kohlberg, and Haan, 1977). Since moral reasoning clearly is reasoning, advanced moral reasoning depends upon advanced logical reasoning. There is a parallelism

Kohlberg, L. (1984). Moral stages and moralization: The cognitive-developmental approach. In *The psychology of moral development* (Vol. 2, pp. 170–205). San Francisco, CA: Harper Row.

between an individual's logical stage and his or her moral stage. A person whose logical stage is only concrete operational is limited to the preconventional moral stages, Stages 1 and 2. A person whose logical stage is only "low" formal operational is limited to the conventional moral stages, Stages 3 and 4. While logical development is a necessary condition for moral development, it is not sufficient. Many individuals are at a higher logical stage than the parallel moral stage, but essentially none are at a higher moral stage than their logical stage (Walker, 1980).

Next after stages of logical development come stages of social perception or social perspective- or role-taking (see Selman, 1976). We partially describe these stages when we define the moral stages. These role-taking stages describe the level at which the person sees other people, interprets their thoughts and feelings, and sees their role or place in society. These stages are very closely related to moral stages, but are more general, since they do not deal just with fairness and with choices of right and wrong. To make a judgment of fairness at a certain level is more difficult than to simply see the world at that level. So, just as for logic, development of a stage's social perception precedes, or is easier than, development of the parallel stage of moral judgment. Just as there is a vertical sequence of steps in movement up from moral Stage 1 to moral Stage 2 to moral Stage 3, so there is a horizontal sequence of steps in movement from logic to social perception to moral judgment. First, individuals attain a logical stage, say, partial formal operations, which allows them to see "systems" in the world, to see a set of related variables as a system. Next they attain a level of social perception or role-taking, where they see other people understanding one another in terms of the place of each in the system. Finally, they attain Stage 4 of moral judgment, where the welfare and order of the total social system or society is the reference point for judging "fair" or "right." We have found that individuals who move upward in our moral education programs already have the logical capacity, and often the social perception capacity, for the higher moral stage to which they move (Walker, 1980).

There is one final step in this horizontal sequence: moral behavior. To act in a morally high way requires a high stage of moral reasoning. One cannot follow moral principles (Stages 5 and 6) if one does not understand or believe in them. One can, however, reason in terms of such principles and not live up to them. A variety of factors determines whether a particular person will live up to his or her stage of moral reasoning in a particular situation, though moral stage is a good predictor of action in various experimental and naturalistic settings (Kohlberg, 1969).

In summary, moral stage is related to cognitive advance and to moral behavior, but our identification of moral stage must be based on moral reasoning alone.

## Theoretical Description of the Moral Stages

The six moral stages are grouped into three major levels: preconventional level (Stages 1 and 2), conventional level (Stages 3 and 4), and postconventional level (Stages 5 and 6).

To understand the stages, it is best to start by understanding the three moral levels. The preconventional moral level is the level of most children under 9, some adolescents, and many adolescent and adult criminal offenders. The conventional level is the level of most adolescents and adults in our society and in other societies. The postconventional level is reached by a minority of adults and is usually reached only after the age of 20. The term "conventional" means conforming to and upholding the rules and expectations and conventions of society or authority just because they are society's rules, expectations, or conventions. The individual at the preconventional level has not yet come to really understand and uphold conventional or societal rules and expectations. Someone at the postconventional level understands and basically accepts society's rules, but acceptance of society's rules is based on formulating and accepting the general moral principles that underlie these rules. These principles in some cases come into conflict with society's rules, in which case the postconventional individual judges by principle rather than by convention.

One way of understanding the three levels is to think of them as three different types of relationships between the *self* and *society's rules and expectations*. From this point of view, Level I is a preconventional person, for whom rules and social expectations are something external to the self;

Level II is a conventional person, in whom the self is identified with or has internalized the rules and expectations of others, especially those of authorities; and Level III is a postconventional person, who had differentiated his or her self from the rules and expectations of others and defines his or her values in terms of self-chosen principles.

Within each of the three moral levels, there are two stages. The second stage is a more advanced and organized form of the general perspective of each major level. Table 1 defines the six moral stages in terms of (1) what is right, (2) the reason for upholding the right, and (3) the social perspective behind each stage, a central concept to which our definition of moral reasoning now turns.

## Social Perspectives of the Three Moral Levels

In order to characterize the development of moral reasoning structurally, we seek a single unifying construct that will generate the major structural features of each stage. Selman (1976) offers a point of departure in the search for such a unifying construct; he has defined levels of role-taking which parallel our moral stages and which form a cognitive-structural hierarchy. Selman defines role-taking primarily in terms of the way the individual differentiates his or her perspective from other perspectives and relates these perspectives to one another. From our point of view, however, there is a more general structural construct which underlies *both* role-taking and moral judgment. This is the concept of *sociomoral perspective*, which refers to the point of view the individual takes in defining both social facts and sociomoral values, or "oughts." Corresponding to the three major levels of moral judgment, we postulate the three major levels of social perspective as follows:

| Moral Judgment | Social Perspective |
|---|---|
| I. Preconventional | Concrete individual perspective |
| II. Conventional | Member-of-society perspective |
| III. Postconventional, or principled | Prior-to-society perspective |

Let us illustrate the meaning of social perspective in terms of the unity it provides for the various ideas and concerns of the moral level. The conventional level, for example, is different from the preconventional in that it uses the following reasons: (1) concern about social approval; (2) concern about loyalty to persons, groups, and authority; and (3) concern about the welfare of others and society. We need to ask, What underlies these characteristics of reasoning and holds them together? What fundamentally defines and unifies the characteristics of the conventional level is its *social perspective*, a shared viewpoint of the participants in a relationship or a group. The conventional individual subordinates the needs of the single individual to the viewpoint and needs of the group or the shared relationship. To illustrate the conventional social perspective, here is 17-year-old Joe's response to the following question:

Q.—Why shouldn't you steal from store?

A.—It's a matter of law. It's one of our rules that we're trying to help protect everyone, protect property, not just to protect a store. It's something that's needed in our society. If we didn't have these laws, people would steal, they wouldn't have to work for a living and our whole society would get out of kilter.

Joe is concerned about *keeping the law,* and his reason for being concerned is *the good of society as a whole.* Clearly, he is speaking as a member of society. "It's one of *our* rules that *we're making* to protect everyone in *our* society." This concern for the good of society arises from his taking the point of view of "us members of society," which goes beyond the point of view of Joe as a concrete, individual self.

Let us contrast this *conventional member-of-society perspective* with the *preconventional concrete individual perspective.* The latter point of view is that of the individual actor in the situation thinking

**TABLE 1**

**The Six Moral Stages**

| | Content of Stage | | |
|---|---|---|---|
| Level and Stage | What Is Right | Reasons for Doing Right | Social Perspective of Stage |
| *Level I: Preconventional* Stage 1—Heteronomous Morality | To avoid breaking rules backed by punishment, obedience for its own sake, and avoiding physical damage to persons and property. | Avoidance of punishment, and the superior power of authorities. | *Egocentric point of view.* Doesn't consider the interests of others or recognize that they differ from the actor's; doesn't relate two points of view. Actions are considered physically rather than in terms of psychological interests of others. Confusion of authority's perspective with one's own. |
| Stage 2—Individualism, Instrumental Purpose, and Exchange | Following rules only when it is to someone's immediate interest; acting to meet one's own interests and needs and letting others do the same. Right is also what's fair, what's an equal exchange, a deal, an agreement. | To serve one's own needs or interests in a world where you have to recognize that other people have their interests, too. | *Concrete individualistic perspective.* Aware that everybody has his own interest to pursue and these conflict, so that right is relative (in the concrete individualistic sense). |
| *Level II: Conventional* Stage 3—Mutual Interpersonal Expectations, and Interpersonal Conformity | Living up to what is expected by people close to you or what people generally expect of people in your role as son, brother, friend, etc. "Being good" is important and means having good motives, showing concern about others. It also means keeping mutual relationships such as trust, loyalty, respect, and gratitude | The need to be a good person in your own eyes and those of others. Your caring for others. Belief in the Golden Rule. Desire to maintain rules and authority which support stereotypical good behavior. | *Perspective of the individual in relationships with other individuals.* Aware of shared feelings, agreements, and expectations which take primacy over individual interests. Relates points of view through the concrete Golden Rule, putting yourself in the other person's shoes. Does not yet consider generalized system perspective. |

about his interests and those of other individuals he may care about. Seven years earlier, at age 10, Joe illustrated the concrete individual perspective in response to the same question:

Q.—Why shouldn't you steal from a store?

A.—It's not good to steal from the store. It's against the law. Someone could see you and call the police.

Being "against the law," then, means something very different at the two levels. At Level II, the law is made by and for "everyone," as Joe indicates at age 17. At Level I, it is just something enforced by the police, and accordingly, the reason for obeying the law is to avoid punishment. This reason derives from the limits of a Level 1 perspective, the perspective of an individual considering his or her own interests and those of other isolated individuals.

**Table 1** *(continued)*

| Content of Stage | | | |
| --- | --- | --- | --- |
| Level and Stage | What Is Right | Reasons for Doing Right | Social Perspective of Stage |
| Stage 4—Social System and Conscience | Fulfilling the actual duties to which you have agreed. Laws are to be upheld except in extreme cases where they conflict with other fixed social duties. Right is also contributing to society, the group, or institution. | To keep the institution going as a whole, to avoid the breakdown in the system "if everyone did it," or the imperative of conscience to meet one's defined obligations. (Easily confused with Stage 3 belief in rules and authority; see text.) | *Differentiates societal point of view from interpersonal agreement or motives.* Takes the point of view of the system that defines roles and rules. Considers individual relations in terms of place in the system. |
| *Level III: Postconventional, or Principled* Stage 5—Social Contract or Utility and Individual Rights | Being aware that people hold a variety of values and opinions, that most values and rules are relative to your group. These relative rules should usually be upheld, however, in the interest of impartiality and because they are the social contract. Some nonrelative values and rights like *life* and *liberty*, however, must be upheld in any society and regardless of majority opinion. | A sense of obligation to law because of one's social contract to make and abide by laws for the welfare of all and for the protection of all people's rights. A feeling of contractual commitment, freely entered upon, to family, friendship, trust, and work obligations. Concern that laws and duties be based on rational calculation of overall utility, "the greatest good for the greatest number." | *Prior-to-society perspective.* Perspective of a rational individual aware of values and rights prior to social attachments and contracts. Integrates perspectives by formal mechanisms of agreement, contract, objective impartiality, and due process. Considers moral and legal points of view; recognizes that they sometimes conflict and finds it difficult to integrate them. |
| Stage 6—Universal Ethical Principles | Following self-chosen ethical principles. Particular laws or social agreements are usually valid because they rest on such principles. When laws violate these principles, one acts in accordance with the principle. Principles are universal principles of justice: the equality of human rights and respect for the dignity of human beings as individual persons. | The belief as a rational universal moral principles, and a sense of personal commitment to them. | *Perspective of a moral point of view from which arrangements derive.* Perspective is that of any rational individual recognizing the nature of morality or the fact that persons are ends in themselves and must be treated as such. |

Let us now consider the perspective of the *postconventional level*. It is like the preconventional perspective in that it returns to the standpoint of the individual rather than taking the point of view of "us members of society." The individual point of view taken at the postconventional level, however, can be universal; it is that of any *rational moral individual*. Aware of the member-of-society perspective, the postconventional person questions and redefines it in terms of an individual moral perspective, so that social obligations are defined in ways that can be justified to any moral individual. An individual's commitment to basic morality or moral principles is seen as preceding, or being necessary for, his or her taking society's perspective or accepting society's laws and values. Society's laws and values, in turn, should be ones which any reasonable person could be committed to—whatever his or her place in society and whatever society he or she belongs to. The postconventional perspective, then, is *prior to society*; it is the perspective of an *individual who has made the moral commitments or holds the standards on which a good or just society must be based.* This is a perspective by which (1) a particular society or set of social practices may be judged and (2) a person may rationally commit him- or herself to a society.

An example is Joe, our longitudinal subject, interviewed at age 24:

Q.—*Why shouldn't someone steal from a store?*

A.—It's violating another person's rights, in this case, to property.

Q.—*Does, the law enter in?*

A.—Well, the law in most cases is based on what is morally right, so it's not a separate subject, it's a consideration.

Q.—*What does "morality" or "morally right" mean to you?*

A.—Recognizing the rights of other individuals, first to life and then to do as he pleases as long as it doesn't interfere with somebody else's rights.

The wrongness of stealing is that it violates the moral rights of individuals, which are prior to law and society. Property rights follow from more universal human rights (such as freedoms which do not interfere with the like freedom of others). The demands of law and society derive from universal moral rights, rather than vice versa.

It should be noted that reference to the words *rights* or *morally right* or *conscience* does not necessarily distinguish conventional from postconventional morality. Orienting to the morally right thing, or following conscience as against following the law, need not indicate the postconventional perspective of the rational moral individual. The terms *morality* and *conscience* may be used to refer to group rules and values which conflict with civil laws or with the rules of the majority group. To a Jehovah's Witness who has gone to jail for "conscience," conscience may mean God's law as interpreted by his or her religious sect or group rather than the standpoint of any individual oriented to universal moral principles or values. To count as postconventional, such ideas or terms must be used in a way that makes it clear that they have a foundation for a rational or moral individual who has not yet committed him- or herself to any group or society or its morality. "Trust," for example, is a basic value at both the conventional and the postconventional levels. At the conventional level, trustworthiness is something you expect of others in your society. Joe expresses this as follows at age 17:

Q.—*Why should a promise be kept, anyway?*

A.—Friendship is based on trust. If you can't trust a person, there's little grounds to deal with him. You should try to be as reliable as possible because people remember you by this, you're more respected if you can be depended upon.

At this conventional level, Joe views trust as a truster as well as someone who could break a trust. He sees that the individual needs to be trustworthy not only to secure respect and to maintain social relationships with others, but also because as a member of society he expects trust of others in general.

At the postconventional level, individuals take a further step. They do not automatically assume that they are in a society in which they need the friendship and respect of other individuals. Instead they consider why any society or social relationship presupposes trust, and why the individual, if he or she is to contract into society, must be trustworthy. At age 24, Joe is postconventional in his explanation of why a promise should be kept:

I think human relationships in general are based on trust, on believing in other individuals. If you have no way of believing in someone else, you can't deal with anyone else and it becomes every man for himself. Everything you do in a day's time is related to somebody else and if you can't deal on a fair basis, you have chaos.

We have defined a postconventional moral perspective in terms of the individual's reasons *why* something is right or wrong. We need to illustrate this perspective as it enters into making an actual decision or defining *what is right.* The postconventional person is aware of the moral point of view that each individual in a moral conflict situation ought to adopt. Rather than defining expectations and obligations from the standpoint of societal roles, as someone at the conventional level would, the postconventional individual holds that persons in these roles should orient to a "moral point of views." While the postconventional moral viewpoint does also recognize fixed legal-social obligations, recognition of moral obligations may take priority when the moral and legal viewpoints conflict.

At age 24 Joe reflects the postconventional moral point of view as a decision-making perspective in response to Heinz's dilemma about stealing a drug to save his wife:

> It is the husband's duty to save his wife. The fact that her life is in danger transcends every other standard you might use to judge his action. Life is more important than property.
>
> Q.—*Suppose it were a friend, not his wife?*
>
> A.—I don't think that would be much different from a moral point of view. It's still a human being in danger.
>
> Q.—*Suppose it were a stranger?*
>
> A.—To be consistent, yes, from a moral standpoint.
>
> Q.—*What is this moral standpoint?*
>
> A.—I think every individual has a right to live and if there is a way of saving an individual, he should be saved.
>
> Q.—*Should the judge punish the husband?*
>
> A.—Usually the moral and the legal standpoints coincide. Here they conflict. The judge should weigh the moral standpoint more heavily but preserve the legal law in punishing Heinz lightly.

## Social Perspectives of the Six Stages

This section will explain the differences in social perspective at each moral stage within each of the three levels. It will attempt to show how the second stage in each level completes the development of the social perspective entered at the first stage of the level.

We will start with the easiest pair of stages to explain in this way—Stages 3 and 4, comprising the conventional level. In the preceding section we quoted the isolated-individual perspective of Stages 1 and 2 and contrasted it with Joe's full-fledged member-of-society perspective at age 17, a perspective which is Stage 4. Joe's statements about the importance of trust in dealing with others clearly reflect the perspective of someone taking the point of view of the social system. The social perspective at Stage 3 is less aware of society's point of view or of the good of the whole of society. As an example of Stage 3, let us consider Andy's response to a dilemma about whether to tell your father about a brother's disobedience after the brother has confided in you.

> He should think of his brother, but it's more important to be a good son. Your father has done so much for you. I'd have a conscience if I didn't tell, more than to my brother, because my father couldn't trust me. My brother would understand; our father has done so much for him, too.

Andy's perspective is not based on a social system. It is rather one in which he has two relationships: one to his brother, one to his father. His father as authority and helper comes first. Andy expects his brother to share this perspective, but as someone else centered on their father. There is no reference to the organization of the family in general. Being a good son is said to be more important not because it is a more important role in the eyes of, or in terms of, society as a whole or even in terms of the family as a system. The Stage 3 member-of-a-group perspective is that of the average good person, not that of society or an institution as a whole. The Stage 3 perspective sees things from the point of view of shared relationships between two or more individuals—relations of caring, trust, respect, and so on—rather than from the viewpoint of institutional wholes. In summary, whereas the Stage 4 member-of-society perspective is a "system" perspective, the Stage 3 perspective is that of a participant in a shared relationship or shared group.

Let us turn to the proconventional level. Whereas Stage 1 involves only the concrete individual's point of view, Stage 2 is aware of a number of other individuals, each having other points of view. At Stage 2, in serving my interests I anticipate the other person's reaction, negative or positive, and he or she anticipates mine. Unless we make a deal, we each will put our own point of view first. If we make a deal, each of us will do something for the other.

The shift from Stage 1 to Stage 2 is shown by the following change in another subject's response between age 10 and age 13 to a question about whether an older brother should tell his father about a younger brother's misdeed, revealed in confidence. At 10, the subject gives a Stage 1 answer:

> In one way it was right to tell because his father might beat him up. In another way it's wrong because his brother will beat him up if he tells.

At age 13, he has moved to Stage 2:

> The brother should not tell or he'll get his brother in trouble. If he wants his brother to keep quiet for him sometime, he'd better not squeal now.

In the second response, there is an extension of concern to the brother's welfare as it affects the subject's own interests through anticipated exchange. There is a much clearer picture of the brother's point of view and its relationship to his own.

Turning to the postconventional level, a typical Stage 5 orientation distinguishes between a moral point of view and a legal point of view but finds it difficult to define a moral perspective independent of contractual-legal rights. Joe, an advanced Stage 5, says with regard to Heinz's dilemma of whether to steal the drug to save his wife:

> Usually the moral and the legal standpoints coincide. Here they conflict. The judge should weigh the moral standpoint more.

For Joe, the moral point of view is not yet something prior to the legal point of view. Both law and morality for Joe derive from individual rights and values, and both are more or less on an equal plane. At Stage 6, obligation is defined in terms of universal ethical principles of justice. Here is a Stage 6 response to Heinz's dilemma:

> It is wrong legally but right morally. Systems of law are valid only insofar as they reflect the sort of moral law all rational people can accept. One must consider the personal justice involved, which is the root of the social contract. The ground of creating a society is individual justice, the right of every person to an equal consideration of his claims in every situation, not just those which can be codified in law. Personal justice means, "Treat each person as an end, not a means."

This response indicates a very clear awareness of a moral point of view based on a principle ("Treat each person as an end, not a means") which is more basic than, and from which one can derive, the sociolegal point of view.

## Four Moral Orientations and the Shift Toward Greater Equilibrium Within Stages

In discussing social perspectives we have not differentiated *perception* of social fact (role-taking) from *prescription* of the right or good (moral judgment). What are the distinctive features of stages of moral judgment as opposed to social perspective in general?

To define the distinctively moral, we now turn to the moral categories analyzed by moral philosophy. These include "modal" categories (such as rights, duties, the morally approvable, responsibility) and "element" categories (such as welfare, liberty, equality, reciprocity, rules and social order). In describing moral philosophic theories by type, it is customary to analyze the primary moral categories of the theory from which the other categories derive. There are four possible groups of primary categories called *moral* orientations. Found at each of our moral stages, they define four kinds of decisional strategies, each focusing on one of four universal elements in any social situation. These orientations and elements are as follows:

1. *Normative order:* Orientation to prescribed rules and roles of the social or moral order. The basic considerations in decision making center on the element of *rules.*

2. *Utility consequences:* Orientation to the good or bad *welfare consequences* of action in the situation for others and/or the self.

3. *Justice or fairness:* Orientation to *relations* of liberty, equality, reciprocity, and contract between persons.

4. *Ideal-self:* Orientation to an image of actor as a *good self,* or as someone with conscience, and to the self's motives or virtue (relatively independent of approval from others).

In defining the distinctively moral, some writers stress the concept of rule and respect for rules (Kant, Durkheim, Piaget). Others identify morality with a consideration of welfare consequences to others (Mill, Dewey). Still others identify morality with an idealized moral self (Bradley, Royce, Baldwin). Finally, some (Rawls, and myself) identify morality with justice. In fact, individual persons may use any one or all of these moral orientations. As an example, we have the following orientations to the property issue at Stage 3:

*Why shouldn't you steal from a store, anyway?*
1. *Normative order:* It's always wrong to steal. If you start breaking rules of stealing, everything would go to pieces.

2. *Utilitarian:* You're hurting other people. The storeowner has a family to support.

3. *Justice:* The storeowner worked hard for the money and you didn't. Why should you have it?

4. *Ideal-self:* A person who isn't honest isn't worth much. Stealing and cheating are both the same, they are both dishonesty.

While all orientations may be used by an individual, my colleagues and I claim that the most essential structure of morality is a justice structure. Moral situations are ones of conflict of perspectives or interest; justice principles are concepts for resolving those conflicts, for giving each his or her due. In one sense, justice can refer to all four orientations. Sustaining law and order may be seen as justice (normative order), and maximizing the welfare of the group may be seen as justice (utility consequences). In the end, however, the core of justice is the *distribution of rights and duties regulated by concepts of equality and reciprocity.* Justice recognized as a "balance" or equilibrium corresponds to the structural moving equilibrium described by Piaget on logic (1967). Justice is the normative logic, the equilibrium, of social actions and relations.

A person's sense of justice is what is most distinctively and fundamentally moral. One can act morally and question all rules, one may act morally and question the greater good, but one cannot act morally and question the need for justice.

What are the actual developmental findings regarding the four moral orientations? And do they support our theory's assertion of the primacy of justice? A partial answer comes from our longitudinal data. For this purpose, we group the normative order and utilitarian orientations as interpenetrating to form Type A at each stage. Type B focuses on the interpenetration of the justice orientation with an ideal-self orientation. Type A makes judgments more descriptively and predictively, in terms of the given "out there." Type B makes judgments more prescriptively, in terms of what ought to be, of what is internally accepted by the self. A Type B orientation presupposes both awareness of rules and a judgment of their fairness.

Our longitudinal data indeed support the notion that the two types are relatively clear substages. The B substage is more mature than the A substage in the sense that a 3A may move to 3B, but a 3B can never move to 3A (though he or she may move to 4A). Individuals can skip the B substage, that is, move from 3A to 4A; but if they change substage, it is always from A to B. In a sense, then, the B substage is a consolidation or equilibration of the social perspective first elaborated at the A substage. B's are more balanced in perspective. A 3A decides in terms of What does a good husband do? What does a wife expect? A 3B decides in terms of What does a husband who is a partner in a good mutual relationship do? What does each spouse expect of the other? Both sides of the equation are balanced; this is fairness. At 4A, the subject decides in terms of the questions What does the system demand? At 4B the subject asks, What does the individual in the system demand as well as the system, and what is a solution that strikes a balance? Thus, a 4B upholds a system, but it is a "democratic" system with individual rights.

Because of this balance, B's are more prescriptive or internal, centering more on their judgments of what ought to be. They are also more universalistic, that is, more willing to carry the boundaries of value categories, like the value of life, to their logical conclusion. As an example, a Stage 3 subject responded to Heinz's drug-stealing dilemma by giving a standard A response, "A good husband would love his wife enough to do it." Asked whether a friend would steal a drug for a friend, he said, "No, a friend isn't that close that he has to risk stealing." He then added, "But when I think about it, that doesn't seem fair, his friend has just as much right to live as his wife."

Here we see a tendency, based on an orientation to justice, to universalize obligation to life and to distinguish it from role stereotypes. In summary, the full development and consolidation of moral judgment at each stage is defined by the categories and structures of justice, although stage development occurs in all four moral orientations.

## Methodology in Assessing Moral Judgment Development

### The Aspect-Scoring System

In our original formulation (Kohlberg, 1958, 1969), the moral stages were defined in terms of twenty-five "aspects," grouped, in turn, under the following major sets: rules, conscience, welfare of others, self's welfare, sense of duty, role-taking, punitive justice, positive justice, and motives. Each higher stage had a more internalized and autonomous idea of moral rules, a greater concern about the welfare of others, a broader conception of fairness, and so on.

Our first attempt to identify an individual's moral stage from his interview protocol used "aspect scoring." This was done with two methods: sentence scoring and story rating. Sentence scoring used a manual that listed prototypical sentences on each aspect in each moral dilemma. Every statement of a subject was scored by aspect and stage; and these statements were then converted into percentages, generating a profile of stage usage for each subject.

The second method of aspect scoring was story rating. Here the subject's total response to a story was assigned a stage on each aspect in terms of that stage's overall definition. Stage mixtures were handled by intuitively weighting a dominant and a minor stage of response. An example of a story-rating manual illustrating Stage 1 reasoning on seven aspects is presented in Table 2, which refers to the classic example of Heinz's dilemma:

> In Europe, a woman was near death from a rare form of cancer. There was one drug that the doctors thought might save her, a form of radium that a druggist in the same town had recently discovered. The druggist was charging $2,000, ten times what the drug cost him to make. The sick woman's husband, Heinz, went to everyone he knew to borrow the money, but he could only get together about half of what [the drug] cost. He told the druggist that his wife was dying and asked him to sell it cheaper or let him pay later. But the druggist said no. So Heinz got desperate and broke into the man's store to steal the drug for his wife.

> Q.—Should the husband have done that? Why?

To illustrate the aspect-scoring procedure, we present an interview on the dilemma about Heinz and his dying wife, broken down into three statements and scored as Stage 1 by reference to Table 2.

> *Statement 1*
> Q.—Should Heinz have done that?
> A.—He shouldn't do it.
>
> Q.—Why?
> A.—Because then he'd be a thief if they caught him and put him in jail.

## TABLE 2

### Aspect Scoring: Story Rating Manual with Prototypical Stage 1
### Statements on Drug-Stealing Dilemma

**Stage 1**

1. *Rules:* Thinks Heinz should not steal the drug, since it is bad to steal, whatever the motive; it's against external law and is a violation of the superior power of the police.
2. *Conscience:* Concern about the wrongness of stealing is in terms of fear of punishment.
3. *Altruism:* Thinks about his own welfare, not that of other people, like his wife.
4. *Duty:* Duty is only what he has to do, a husband doesn't have to steal for his wife.
5. *Self-interest:* Yields to power and punishment where rational self-interest would say to stick up for himself or to try to get away with it.
6. *Role Taking:* Since Stage 1 doesn't see things from other people's point of view, and doesn't expect them to see things from his, he expects punishment for stealing, no matter why he did what he did.
7. *Justice:* Justice in punishment is simply retribution for committing a crime, for breaking the law.

In terms of Table 2, this statement reveals the following Stage 1 moral conceptions:

1. *Rules:* It's bad to steal or break rules whatever the reason, "he'd be a thief," it's a violation of law and police.
2. *Conscience:* It's wrong because it leads to punishment.

*Statement 2*

Q.—Is it a husband's duty to steal?

A.—I don't think so.

This statement indicates the following Stage 1 thinking:

3. *Altruism:* Doesn't focus on the welfare of the others, such as one's wife.
4. *Duty:* Obligation is limited to what one has to do because of superior power, not obligation to other people as such.

*Statement 3*

Q.—If you were dying of cancer but were strong enough, would you steal the drug to save your own life?

A.—No, because even if you did have time to take the drug, the police would put you in jail and you would die there anyway.

This statement indicates the following:

5. *Self-interest:* In thinking about his own welfare, he is not rational and does not stand up for himself or try to get away with a violation where it would be sensible to, because he believes he cannot escape the power and punishment system.

**The limits of aspect scoring.** In a sense, aspect scoring by story is still the easiest introduction to the stages, and yields sufficient interjudge agreement (.89). This method turned out, however, to contain too much extraneous content to yield a measure or classification meeting the invariant sequence postulate of stage theory. This failure appeared in our original analysis of twelve-year longitudinal data gathered every three years on fifty males aged 10 to 26 (Kohlberg and Kramer, 1969; Kramer, 1968). The most outstanding inversion of sequence was an apparent shift from a Stage 4 society orientation to a Stage 2 relativistic hedonism in some subjects who became "liberated" and "relativized" in their college years. Based on the fact that these subjects eventually moved on to Stage 5 principled thinking, we eventually concluded that this relativistic egoism was a transitional phase, a "Stage 4½"—a no-man's-land between rejection of conventional morality and the formulation of nonconventional or universal moral principles. The social perspective of Stage 4½ was clearly different from that of naive Stage 2. The Stage 4½ questioned society and viewed himself and the rules from an "outside-of-society" perspective, whereas the Stage 2 saw things as a concrete individual relating to other individuals through concrete reciprocity, exchange, and utilities (Turiel, 1977).

A second inversion of sequence was found in a small proportion of individuals who "regressed" from Stage 4 to Stage 3, or skipped from Stage 3 to Stage 5. These inversions, in turn, could be seen as due to an inadequate definition of Stage 4, a definition which equated "law-and-order" ideas (content) with taking a social system perspective (stage structure). As a result, we redefined as Stage 3 (rather than Stage 4) any law-and-order thinking which did not display a social system perspective (for example, an Archie Bunker concept of law and order).

These changes in conceptions of the stages reflected a growing clarity in the distinction between structure and content which led us to abandon aspect scoring. Our aspect scoring was based not on "structure," but on certain statistical or probabilistic associations between structure and content. For example, a social system perspective tends to yield moral judgments whose content is law and order. One can, however, have much of this content at Stage 3 without the social system perspective, or one can have the social system perspective without this content. Accordingly, we decided to generate a new, more structural scoring method, which we call issue scoring.

## Intuitive Issue Scoring

In order to develop a more structural scoring system, the first step was to standardize or analyze types of content used at every stage. These types of content, called issues or values, represent *what* the individual is valuing, judging, or appealing to rather than his *mode of reasoning* about that issue. To analyze stage differences, we must first make sure each stage is reasoning about or from the same values. We had attempted to do this with the aspects, but they were a mixture of formal or structural characteristics of judgment (for example, motives versus consequences and sense of duty) and direct issues or value content (for example, law and rules). Accordingly, we developed the following list of issues, values, or moral institutions found in every society and culture:

1. Laws and rules
2. Conscience
3. Personal roles of affection
4. Authority
5. Civil rights
6. Contract, trust, and justice in exchange
7. Punishment and justice
8. The value of life
9. Property rights and values
10. Truth
11. Sex and sexual love

The new content issues each embody several different moral aspects. For example, thinking about the issue of contract and trust involves formal aspects of altruism, duty, rules, role-taking, fairness, and so on.

Our classification of content in terms of issues also gave rise to a new unit to be rated. This unit is all the ideas a person uses concerning an issue in a story. The old system had rated each separate idea separately (sentence scoring) or else rated the story as a whole (story rating). But the sentence unit had proven too small for structural classification, and the story unit had proven too large for analytic, as opposed to ideal, typological scoring.

## TABLE 3

### Issue Scoring Stages in Heinz's Dilemma

| Stage | What Is Life's Value in the Situation? | Why Is Life Valuable? |
|---|---|---|
| Stage 1 | Wife's life has no clear value here to husband or others when it conflicts with law and property. Does not see that husband would value his wife's life over stealing. | Does not give a reason and does not indicate understanding that life is worth more than property. |
| Stage 2 | It is its immediate value to the husband and to the wife, herself. Assumes the husband would think his wife's life is worth stealing for, but he isn't obligated to if he doesn't like her enough. Life's value to a person other than its possessor depends on relationship; you wouldn't steal to save the life of a mere friend or acquaintance. | Each person wants to live more than anything else. You can replace property, not life. |
| Stage 3 | Life's value is its value to any good, caring, person like the husband. The husband should care enough to risk stealing (even if he does not steal), and a friend should care enough to save the life of a friend or another person. | People should care for other people and their lives. You're not good or human if you don't. People have much more feeling for life than for anything material. |
| Stage 4 | Even though he may think it wrong to steal, he understands the general value or *sacredness* of human life or the rule to preserve life. Sacredness means all other values can't be compared with the value of life. The value of life is general; human life is valuable no matter what your relationship to the person is, though this doesn't obligate you to steal. | Life is valuable because God created it and made it sacred. Or life is valuable because it is basic to society; it is a basic right of people. |
| Stage 5 | One recognizes that in this situation the wife's *right to life* comes before the druggist's right to property. There is some obligation to steal for anyone dying; everyone has a right to live and to be saved. | Everyone or society logically and morally must place each person's individual right to life before other rights such as the right to property. |

Having decided on issues, we then defined stage thinking on each issue. An example is the conception of life issue as worked out for Heinz's dilemma about stealing the drug (Table 3). To illustrate the use of this issue in scoring, here are excerpts from an interview with Tommy, a 10-year-old boy who spontaneously focuses on the life issue.

His wife was sick and if she didn't get the drug quickly, she might die. Maybe his wife is an important person and runs a store and the man buys stuff for her and can't get it any other place. The police would blame the owner that he didn't save the wife.

Q.—Does it matter whether the wife is important or not?

A.—If someone important is in a plane and is allergic to heights and the stewardess won't give him medicine because she's only got enough for one and she's got a sick friend in the back, they should put the stewardess in a lady's jail because she didn't help the important one.

Q.—Is it better to save the life of one important person or a lot of unimportant people?

A.—All the people that aren't important, because one man just has one house, maybe a lot of furniture, but a whole bunch of people have an awful lot of furniture and some of these poor people might have a lot of money and it doesn't look it.

Is Tommy's response Stage 1, Stage 2, or Stage 3 in terms of Why is life valuable? Tommy does not seem to fit Stage 1 in Table 3, since his response indicates that the wife's life does have a value justifying stealing. His response *is* Stage 1, however, because Tommy does not clearly recognize that life is more valuable to an individual than property. He says the lives of a lot of people who aren't important are worth more than the life of one important person because all the ordinary people together have more furniture or property. This is Stage 1 thinking, not Stage 2, because the value of life depends on a vague status of being important, not on the husband's or wife's interests or needs.

## Standardized Issue Scoring

The procedure just discussed is called *intuitive issue scoring* and is theoretically the most valid method of scoring, since it is instrument free, that is, applicable to any moral dilemma. It is adequately reliable (90 percent interrater agreement) in the hands of thoroughly trained or experienced scorers. Reliable intuitive scoring, however, cannot be learned without personal teaching and supervised experience. It also is too intuitive to provide satisfactory test-construction characteristics of item difficulty, item independence, written versus oral interviews, and so on. We are therefore now developing a manual for standardized issue scoring (Colby and Kohlberg, 1984 in press). This manual is based on a standardized interview which probes only two issues on each of three stories. The standard form, Form A, contains three stories covering six issues as follows:

**Story III:** Heinz steals the drug

**Issues:** life, property

**Story III:** the judge must decide whether to punish Heinz

**Issues:** conscience, punishment

**Story I:** the father breaks a promise to his son

**Issues:** contract, authority

There is a second form for retest purposes, Form B, with different stories covering the same issues.

The manual for standardized issue scoring presents criterion judgments defining each stage on each issue for each story. A *criterion judgment* is the reasoning pattern that is most distinctive of a given stage. Theoretically, such reasoning follows from the structural definition of the stage. Empirically, the criterion judgment is actually used by a substantial number of subjects at that stage (as defined by their global score) and not at other stages.

In the old sentence-scoring interview, sentences were matched to "prototypical" sentences of each stage in a manual. In some sense the new system returns to this procedure, but with controls. The first control is for the presence of the response in terms of the content or issue of response. The new system eliminates the problem of whether a criterion judgment at a given stage is not expressed because the subject does not have a stage structure for that concept, or whether it is not expressed because the content (or issue) of response has not been elicited by the interview. The second control distinguishes between matching to a verbal sentence and matching to a criterion judgment. On the unit-of-response side, this implies that the unit of interpretation is bigger than the sentence. It also implies that the stage structure of the criterion judgment is clarified or distinguished from particular examples or exemplars.

The methodology of establishing standardized scoring is like Loevinger's methodology (Loevinger and Wessler, 1970) for scoring ego stage, in that criterion items are defined by reference to their use by individuals who have been intuitively staged. The difference, however, is that the criterion judgments are not the result of sheer empirical item analysis; rather, they must logically fit the theoretical stage description.

In my opinion, this standardized scoring system goes as far toward standardization as is possible while maintaining theoretical validity. We define "validity" as true measurement of development, that is, of longitudinal invariant sequence. A more common notion of test validation is prediction from a test to some criterion external to the test of which the test is presumed to be an indicator. Using the latter notion, some people assume that a moral judgment test should be validated by predicting "moral behavior." In this sense, Hartshorne and May's tests (1928–30) of "moral knowledge" fail to be valid, since they do not predict well to morally conforming behavior in ratings or experiments. We have argued that moral stage development predicts maturity of moral behavior better than Hartshorne and May's measures; but we have also argued that moral behavior is not a proper external criterion for "validating" a moral judgment test. From the point of view of cognitive-developmental theory, the relationship of the development of judgment to action is something to be studied and theoretically conceptualized; the issue is not one of "validating" a judgment test by a quantitative correlation with behavior.

Using the concept of external criterion validation, others have thought that a test of moral development should be validated by its relationship to *age*, a key meaning of the term *development*. While our measure of moral judgment maturity does correlate with chronological age in adolescents aged 10 to 18 ($r = +.71$), such a correlation is not "validating." Many adults are morally immature, so that a test which maximized correlation with age would ecologically relate to age but have little relation to *moral development*. The validity criterion of moral judgment development is construct validity, not prediction to an external criterion. *Construct validity* here means the fit of data obtained by means of the test to primary components of its theoretical definition. The primary theoretical definition of structural moral development is that of an organization passing through invariant sequential stages. The structural stage method meets this criterion in that longitudinal data so rated display invariant steplike change. The criterion for validity for our new standard moral-reasoning test is congruence with, or prediction to, structural scoring.

The construct validity of a moral development measure has a philosophical or ethical dimension as well as a psychological dimension, that is, the requirement that a higher moral stage be a philosophically more adequate way of reasoning about moral dilemmas than a lower stage. This is a judgment about ways of thinking, not a grading of the moral worth of the individual. I claim (Kohlberg, 1971b) that each higher stage of reasoning is a more adequate way of resolving moral problems judged by moral-philosophic criteria. This claim is, again, made for structural scoring stages; a "standardized" test may be said to be valid insofar at it correlates with, or predicts to, structural stage.

An alternative approach to a standardizing measurement of moral development is set forth in Rest's presentation of his Defining-Issues Test (1976). Rest relies primarily on the more usual approach to empirical test construction and validation. Test construction is by empirical item analysis. The test is conceived as assessing a continuous variable of moral maturity rather than discrete qualitative stages. Test validation is primarily defined by correlations with various criteria, such as age, having studied moral philosophy, and so on. Rest, like my colleagues and myself, is interested in construct validity, not simply prediction to an external criterion. His conception of construct validity, however, is the notion of moderate-to-high correlations with other tests or variables expected to be associated with the test or variable in question. Instead, our conception of construct validity implies assignment of individuals to stages in such a way that the criterion of sequential movement is met. In our opinion, Rest's approach does provide a rough estimate of an individual's moral maturity level, as suggested by his reported correlation of .68 between his measure and an issue scoring of moral dilemma interviews.

We believe Rest's method is useful for exploratory examination of the correlates of moral maturity, but not for testing theoretical propositions derived from the cognitive-developmental theory of moral stages. Choice of various methods, then, must weigh facility of data gathering and analysis against relatively error-free tests of structural theory.

## In What Sense Are the Stages "True"?

In claiming that our stages are "true," we mean, first, that stage definitions are rigidly constrained by the empirical criterion of the stage concept: Many possible stages may be conceptualized, but only one set of stages can be manifested as a longitudinal invariant sequence. The claim we make is that anyone who interviewed children about moral dilemmas and who followed them longitudinally in time would come to our six stages and no others. A second empirical criterion is that of the "structured whole," that is, individuals should be consistently at a stage unless they are in transition to the next stage (when they are considered in mixed stages). The fact that almost all individuals manifest more than 50 percent of responses at a single stage with the rest at adjacent stages supports this criterion.

Second, in claiming that the stages are "true," we mean that the conceptual structure of the stage is not contingent on a specific psychological theory. They are, rather, matters of adequate logical analysis. By this we mean the following:

1. The ideas used to define the stages are the subjects', not ours. The logical connections among ideas define a given stage. The logical analysis of the connections in a child's thinking is itself theoretically neutral. It is not contingent on a psychological theory any more than is a philosopher's analysis of the logical connections in Aristotle's thinking.

2. The fact that a later stage includes and presupposes the prior stage is, again, a matter of logical analysis, not psychological theory.

3. The claim that a given child's ideas *cohere* in a stagelike way is a matter of logical analysis of internal connections between the various ideas held by the stage.

In short, the correctness of the stages as a description of moral development is a matter of empirical observation and of the analysis of the logical connections in children's ideas, not a matter of social science theory.

Although *the stages themselves are not a theory*, as descriptions of moral development they do have definite and radical implications for a social science *theory of moralization*. Accordingly, we shall now (1) elaborate a cognitive-developmental theory of moralization which can explain the facts of sequential moral development and (2) contrast it with socialization theories of moralization.

## Types of Moralization Theory: Cognitive-Developmental, Socialization, and Psychoanalytic Theories

A discussion of a cognitive-developmental moral theory immediately suggests the work of Piaget (1932). Piaget's concepts, however, may best be considered as only one example of the cognitive-developmental approach to morality represented in various ways by J. M. Baldwin (1906), Bull (1969), J. Dewey and J. H. Tufts (1932). Harvey, Hunt, and Schroeder (1961), Hobhouse (1906), Kohlberg (1964), McDougall (1908), and G. H. Mead (1934). The most obvious characteristic of cognitive-developmental theories is their use of some kind of stage concept, of some notion of age-linked sequential reorganizations in the development of moral attitudes. Other common assumptions of cognitive-developmental theories are as follows:

1. Moral development has a basic cognitive-structural or moral-judgmental component.

2. The basic motivation for morality is a generalized motivation for acceptance, competence, self-esteem, or self-realization, rather than for the meeting of biological needs and the reduction of anxiety or fear.

3. Major aspects of moral development are culturally universal, because all cultures have common sources of social interaction, role-taking, and social conflict which require moral integration.

4. Basic moral norms and principles are structures arising through experiences of social interaction rather than through internalization of rules that exist as external structures; moral stages are not defined by internalized rules but by structures of interaction between the self and others.

5. Environmental influences in moral development are defined by the general quality and extent of cognitive and social stimulation throughout the child's development, rather than by specific experiences with parents or experiences of discipline, punishment, and reward.

These assumptions contrast sharply with those of "socialization," or "social-learning," theories of morality. The work of Aronfreed (1968), Bandura and Walters (1959), Berkowitz (1964),

Hoffman (1970), Miller and Swanson (1960), Sears, Rau, and Alpert (1965), and Whiting and Child (1953) may be included under this general rubric. The social-learning theories make the following assumptions:

1. Moral development is growth of behavioral and affective conformity to moral rules rather than cognitive-structural change.
2. The basic motivation for morality at every point of moral development is rooted in biological needs or the pursuit of social reward and avoidance of social punishment.
3. Moral development or morality is culturally relative.
4. Basic moral norms are the internalization of external cultural rules.
5. Environmental influences on normal moral development are defined by quantitative variations in strength of reward, punishment, prohibitions, and modeling of conforming behavior by parents and other socializing agents.

Research based on classical Freudian theory can also be included under the socialization rubric. While the classical Freudian psychoanalytic theory of moral development (Flugel, 1955) cannot be equated with social-learning theories of moralization, it shares with these theories the assumption that moralization is a process of internalization of cultural or parental norms. Further, while Freudian theory (like cognitive-developmental theory) postulates stages, these classical Freudian stages are libidinal-instinctual rather than moral, and morality (as expressed by the superego) is conceived as formed and fixed early in development through internalization of parental norms. As a result, systematic research based on Freudian moral theory has ignored stage components of moral development and has focused on "internalization" aspects of the theory (Kohlberg, 1963b).

A forthcoming book (Kohlberg and Candee, eds., in prep.) reports on forty studies which represent an accumulation of replicated findings firmly consistent with a cognitive-developmental theory of moralization and quite inexplicable from the view of socialization theories. The next section elaborates the cognitive-developmental view of how the social environment stimulates moral stage development.

## How Does Cognitive-Developmental Theory Characterize Environmental Stimulation of Moral Development?

Moral development depends upon stimulation defined in cognitive-structural terms, but this stimulation must also be social, the kind that comes from social interaction and from moral decision making, moral dialogue, and moral interaction. "Pure cognitive" stimulation is a necessary background for moral development but does not directly engender moral development. As noted earlier, we have found that attainment of a moral stage requires cognitive development, but cognitive development will not directly lead to moral development. However, an absence of cognitive stimulation necessary for developing formal logical reasoning may be important in explaining ceilings on moral level. In a Turkish village, for example, full formal operational reasoning appeared to be extremely rare (if the Piagetian techniques for intellectual assessment can be considered usable in that setting). Accordingly, one would not expect that principled (Stage 5 or 6) moral reasoning, which requires formal thinking as a base, could develop in that cultural context.

Of more importance than factors related to stimulation of cognitive stage are factors of general social experience and stimulation, which we call *role-taking opportunities*. What differentiates social experience from interaction with things is the fact that social experience involves role-taking: taking the attitude of others, becoming aware of their thoughts and feelings, putting oneself in their place. When the emotional side of role-taking is stressed, it is typically termed *empathy* (or *sympathy*). The term *role-taking*, coined by G. H. Mead (1934), is preferable, however, because (1) it emphasizes the cognitive as well as the affective side, (2) it involves an organized structural relationship between self and others, (3) it emphasizes that the process involves understanding and relating to all the roles in the society of which one is a part, and (4) it emphasizes that role-taking goes on in *all* social interactions and communication situations, not merely in ones that arouse emotions of sympathy or empathy.

Although moral judgments entail role-taking—putting oneself in the place of the various people involved in a moral conflict—attainment of a given role-taking stage, as indicated earlier, is a necessary but not a sufficient condition for moral development. As an example, the role-taking advance necessary for Stage 2 moral reasoning is awareness that each person in a situation can or does consider the intention or point of view of every other individual in the situation. A child may attain this role-taking level and still hold the Stage 1 notion that right or justice is adherence to fixed rules which must be automatically followed. But if the child is to see rightness or justice as a balance or exchange between the interests of individual actors (Stage 2), he or she must have reached the requisite level of role-taking. Role-taking level, then, is a bridge between logical or cognitive level and moral level; it is one's level of social cognition.

In understanding the effects of social environment on moral development, then, we must consider that environment's provision of role-taking opportunities to the child. Variations in role-taking opportunities exist in terms of children's relation to their family, their peer group, their school, and their social status vis-à-vis the larger economic and political structure of the society.

With regard to the family, the disposition of parents to allow or encourage dialogue on value issues is one of the clearest determinants of moral stage advance in children (Holstein, 1968). Such an exchange of viewpoints and attitudes is part of what we term "role-taking opportunities." With regard to peer groups, children high in peer participation are more advanced in moral stage than are those who are low. With regard to status in the larger society, socioeconomic status is correlated with moral development in various cultures (Kohlberg and Candee, eds., in prep.). This, we believe, is due to the fact that middle class children have more opportunity to take the point of view of the more distant, impersonal, and influential roles in society's basic institutions (law, economy, government, economics) than do lower class children. In general, the higher an individual child's participation in a social group or institution, the more opportunities that child has to take the social perspectives of others. From this point of view, extensive participation in any particular group is not essential to moral development but participation in some group is. Not only is participation necessary, but mutuality of role-taking is also necessary. If, for instance, adults do not consider the child's point of view, the child may not communicate or take the adult's point of view.

To illustrate environments at opposite extremes in role-taking opportunities, we may cite an American orphanage and an Israeli kibbutz. Of all environments we have studied, the American orphanage had children at the lowest level, Stages 1 and 2, even through adolescence (Thrower, in Kohlberg and Candee, eds., in prep.). Of all environments studied, an Israeli kibbutz had children at the highest level, with adolescents mainly at Stage 4 and with a considerable percentage at Stage 5 (Reimer, 1977). Both orphanage and kibbutz environments involved low interaction with parents, but they were dramatically different in other ways. The American orphanages not only lacked parental interaction but involved very little communication and role-taking between staff adults and children. Relations among the children themselves were fragmentary, with very little communication and no stimulation or supervision of peer interaction by the staff. That the deprivation of role-taking opportunities caused a retardation in role-taking as well as in moral judgment was suggested by the fact that the orphanage adolescents failed a role-taking task passed by almost all children of their chronological and mental age. In contrast, children in the kibbutz engaged in intense peer interaction supervised by a group leader who was concerned about bringing the young people into the kibbutz community as active dedicated participants. Discussing, reasoning, communicating feelings, and making group decisions were central everyday activities.

Obviously, the kibbutz differed as a moral environment from the orphanage in other ways as well. Beyond provision of role-taking opportunities by groups and institutions, how do we define the *moral atmosphere* of a group or institution? We have said that the core of specifically moral component of moral judgment is a sense of justice. While role-taking defines the conflicting points of view taken in a moral situation, the "principles" for resolving conflicting points of view at each moral stage are principles of justice, of giving each his or her due. The core of the moral atmosphere of an institution or environment, then, is its justice structure, "the way in which social institutions distribute fundamental rights and duties and determine the division of advantages from social cooperation" (Rawls, 1971, p. 7).

It appears from our research that a group or institution tends to be perceived as being at a certain moral stage by its participants. Our empirical work on this has been primarily based on the perception by inmates of the atmospheres of various prisons in which they were incarcerated (Kohlberg, Hickey, and Scharf, 1972). Although for reasons of comprehension inmates cannot perceive an institution as being at a higher level than a stage above their own, they can perceive it as being at lower stages. Thus, Stage 3 inmates perceived one reformatory as Stage 1, another as Stage 2, and a third as Stage 3. An example of a Stage 3 prisoner's perception of staff in the Stage 3 institution is, "They are pretty nice and they show interest. I get the feeling that they care a little more than most people do." An example of a Stage 3 inmate's perception of staff as being Stage 2 in the Stage 2 institution is, "If a guy messes up in a certain way or doesn't brown-nose as much as he should, the counselor won't do a job for him. It's all favoritism. If you go out of your way for a guy, he will go out of his way for you."

Even more extreme perceptions of the subjects' world or institution as being low stage were shown in the orphanage study. With regard to parents, here is a 15-year-old boy's response:

Q.—Why should a promise be kept?

A.—They aren't. My mother called up and says, "I will be up in two weeks," then I don't see her for eight months. That really kills you, something like that.

On the moral judgment test this boy was beginning to show some Stage 3 concern about affection, promises, and so on; but his world was one in which such things meant nothing. This boy's mother is Stage 2, but the orphanage environment presents no higher-stage moral world. While the nuns who direct this particular orphanage are personally conventionally moral, their moral ideology translates into a justice structure perceived as Stage 1 by this boy. He says:

It really breaks your heart to tell the truth because sometimes you get in trouble for it. I was playing and I swung a rock and hit a car. It was an accident, but I told the sister. I got punished for it.

Obviously, prisons and orphanages are exceptional in representing monolithic or homogeneous lower-stage environments. It is plausible in general, however, that the moral atmosphere of environments is more than the sum of the individual moral judgments and actions of its members. It is also plausible that participation in institutions that have the potential of being seen as at a higher stage than the child's own is a basic determinant of moral development.

A notion that a higher-stage environment stimulates moral development is an obvious extension of experimental findings by Turiel (1966) and Rest (1973) that adolescents tend to assimilate moral reasoning from the next stage above their own, while they reject reasoning below their own. The concept of exposure to a higher stage need not be limited to a stage of reasoning, however; it may also include exposures to moral action and to institutional arrangements. What the moral atmosphere studies we have quoted show is that individuals respond to a composite of moral reasoning, moral action, and institutionalized rules as a relatively unified whole in relation to their own moral stage.

Using the notion that creation of a higher-stage institutional atmosphere will lead to moral change, Hickey and Scharf (1980) and I developed a "just community" in a women's prison involving democratic self-government through community decisions as well as small-group moral discussion. This program led to an upward change in moral reasoning as well as to later changes in life-style and behavior.

In addition to the role-taking opportunities and the perceived moral level provided by an institution, a third factor stressed by cognitive-developmental theory is cognitive-moral conflict. Structural theory stresses that movement to the next stage occurs through reflective reorganization arising from sensed contradictions in one's current stage structure. Experiences of cognitive conflict can occur either through exposure to decision situations that arouse internal contradictions in one's moral reasoning structure or through exposure to the moral reasoning of significant others which is discrepant in content or structure from one's own reasoning. This principle is central to the moral discussion program that we have implemented in schools (Blatt and Kohlberg, 1975; Colby 1972). While peer-group moral discussion of dilemmas leads to moral stage change through exposure to the next stage of reasoning, discussion without such exposure also leads to moral change. Colby (1972) found, for example, that a program of moral discussion led to some development of Stage 5 thinking on a posttest in a group of conventional level students who had shown no Stage 5 reasoning on the pretest.

Real-life situations and choices vary dramatically in their potential for moral-cognitive conflict of a personal nature. This conclusion comes from our longitudinal data on the movement of individuals from conventional to principled morality. One factor that appears to have precipitated the beginning of this shift was the college moratorium experience of responsibility and independence from authority together with exposure to openly conflicting and relativistic values and standards. The conflict involved here was between the subject's own conventional morality and a world with potentials for action that did not fit conventional morality. Some of our other subjects changed in more dramatic moral situations which aroused conflict about the adequacy of conventional morality. One subject, for example, moved from conventional to principled thinking while serving as an officer in Vietnam, apparently because of awareness of the conflict between law-and-order "Army morality" and the more universal rights of the Vietnamese.

## Moral Development and Ego Development

As we move from general characteristics of environments to the more individual life experiences that seem to promote moral change, a cognitive-developmental theory begins to seem limited and abstract. At this point, one begins to draw upon theories like Erikson's (1964), which present age-typical emotional experiences as they relate to a developing personality or self. It then becomes useful to look at the individual's ego level as well as his or her moral stage. In this sense, ego-development theories represent possible extensions of cognitive-developmental theory as it moves into the study of individual lives and life histories. There is a broad unity to the development of social perception and social values which deserves the name of "ego development." This unity is perhaps better conceived as a matter of levels than of structural stages, since the unity of ego levels is not that of logical or moral stage structures. The requirements for consistency in logic and morals are much tighter than those for consistency in personality, which is a psychological, not a logical, unity. Furthermore, there are relatively clear criteria of increased adequacy in logical and moral hierarchies, but not in ego levels.

Because moral stages have a tighter unitary structure, it would be a mistake to view them as simply reflections of broader ego levels. Writers such as Peck and Havighurst (1960) and Loevinger and Wessler (1970) have nevertheless treated moral development as part of general stages of ego or character development—indeed, as a bench mark for such development. If ego development is seen as the successive restructuring of the relationship between the self and standards, it is natural for ego-development theorists to use changes in the moral domain as bench marks. Similar restructurings are assumed to hold in the relations of the self to values in other areas, such as work achievement, sociability, art, politics, religion, and so on.

We hold, however, that there is a unity and consistency to moral structures, that the unique characteristics of moral structures are defined by formalistic moral philosophy, and that to treat moral development as simply a facet of ego (or of cognitive) development is to miss many of its special problems and features. We believe that

1. Cognitive development or structures are more general than, and are embodied in, both self or ego structures and in moral judgment.
2. Generalized ego structures (modes of perceiving self and social relations) are more general than, and are embodied in, moral structures.
3. Cognitive development is a necessary but not sufficient condition for ego development.
4. Certain features of ego development are a necessary but not sufficient condition for development of moral structures.
5. The higher the moral stage, the more distinct it is from the parallel ego stage.

While these propositions suggest a high correlation between measures of ego development and measures of moral development, such a correlation does not imply that moral development can be defined simply as a division or area of ego development. Moral structure distinct from ego structures can be found, however, only if moral stages are first defined in ways more specific than the ways used to characterize ego development. If this specification is not made in the initial definition of moral development, one is bound to find moral development to be simply an aspect of ego development, as Peck and Havighurst (1960) and Loevinger and Wessler (1970) have. Loevinger's inability to differentiate moral items from nonmoral items in her measure of ego development simply demonstrates that her criteria of moral development were not more specific than her general criteria of ego development.

In summary, a broad psychological cognitive-developmental theory of moralization is an ego-developmental theory. Furthermore, in understanding moral functioning, one must place the individual's moral stage within the broader context of his or her ego level. To see moral stages as simply reflections of ego level, however, is to lose the ability to theoretically define and empirically find order in the specifically moral domain of the human personality.

# References

Aronfreed, J. *Conduct and Conscience: The Socialization of Internalized Control Over Behavior.* New York: Academic Press, 1968.

Baldwin, J. M. *Social and Ethical Interpretations in Mental Development.* New York: Macmillan, 1906.

Bandura, A., and Walters, R. H. *Adolescent Aggression.* New York: Ronald, 1959.

Bull, N. J. *Moral Education.* London: Routledge, 1969.

Berkowitz, L. *Development of Motives and Values in a Child.* New York: Basic Books, 1964.

Blatt, M., and Kohlberg, L. "The Effects of Classroom Moral Discussion upon Children's Moral Judgment. *Journal of Moral Education 4* (1975):129–161.

Colby, A. "Logical Operational Limitations on the Development of Moral Judgment." Unpublished Ph.D. dissertation, Columbia University, 1972.

Colby, A., and Kohlberg, L. *The Measurement of Moral Judgment*, vols. I and II. New York: Cambridge University Press, 1984, in press.

Dewey, J., and Tufts, J. H. *Ethics.* New York: Holt, 1932.

Erikson, E. H. *Insights and Responsibility: Lectures on the Ethical Implications of Psychoanalytic Insight.* New York: Norton, 1964.

Flugel, J. C. *Man, Morals, and Society: A Psychoanalytic Study.* New York: International Universities, 1955.

Hartshorne, H., and May, M. A. *Studies in the Nature of Character.* Columbia University Teachers College. Vol. 1: *Studies in Deceit.* Vol. 2: *Studies in Service and Self-Control.* Vol. 3: *Studies in Organization of Character.* New York: Macmillan, 1928–30.

Harvey, O. J., Hunt, D., and Schroeder, D. *Conceptual Systems.* New York: Wiley, 1961.

Hickey, J., and Scharf, P. *Toward a Just Correctional System.* San Francisco: Jossey-Bass, 1980.

Hobhouse, J. T. *Morals in Evolution: A Study in Comparative Ethics.* New York: Holt, 1923 (originally published in 1906).

Hoffman, M. L. "Conscience, Personality and Socialization Techniques. *Human Development 13* (1970):90–126.

Holstein, C. "Parental Determinants of the Development of Moral Judgment." Unpublished Ph.D. dissertation, University of California, Berkeley, 1968.

Kohlberg, L. "The Development of Modes of Moral Thinking and Choice in the Years Ten to Sixteen." Unpublished Ph.D. dissertation, University of Chicago, 1958.

Kohlberg, L. "The Development of Children's Orientations Toward a Moral Order: 1. Sequence in the Development of Moral Through." *Vita Humana 6* (1963b):11–33.

Kohlberg, L. "The Development of Moral Character and Ideology." In M. L. Hoffman, ed., *Review of Child Development Research*, vol. 1. New York: Russell Sage Foundation, 1964.

Kohlberg, L. "Stage and Sequence: The Cognitive-developmental Approach to Socialization." In D. A. Goslin, ed., *Handbook of Socialization Theory and Research.* Chicago, Ill.: Rand McNally, 1969.

Kohlberg, L. "From *Is* to *Ought*: How to Commit the Naturalistic Fallacy and Get Away with It in the Study of Moral Development." In T. Mischel, ed., *Cognitive Development and Epistemology*. New York: Academic Press, 1971b.

Kohlberg, L. *Essays in Moral Development. Volume 1: The Philosophy of Moral Development*. New York: Harper & Row, 1981a.

Kohlberg, L. and Kramer, R. "Continuities and Discontinuities in Childhood and Adult Moral Development." *Human Development* 12 (1969):93–120.

Kohlberg, L. and Candee, D., eds., *Research in Moral Development*. Cambridge, Mass.: Harvard University Press, in preparation.

Kohlberg, L., Hickey, J., and Scharf, P. "The Justice Structure of the Prison: A Theory and Intervention." *The Prison Journal* 51(1972):3–14.

Kramer, R. "Moral Development in Young Adulthood." Unpublished Ph.D. dissertation, University of Chicago, 1968.

Kuhn, D., Langer, J., Kohlberg, L., and Haan, N. "The Development of Formal Operations in Logical and Moral Judgment." *Genetic Psychology Monographs* 95 (1977): 97–188.

Loevinger, J., and Wessler, R. *Measuring Ego Development, Col. I: Construction and Use of a Sentence Completion Test*. San Francisco: Jossey-Bass, 1970.

McDougall, W. *An Introduction to Social Psychology*. London: Methuen, 1908.

Mead, G. H. *Mind, Self and Society*. Chicago: University of Chicago Press, 1934.

Miller, D., and Swanson, G. *Inner Conflict and Defense*. New York: Holt, Rinehart & Winston, 1960.

Peck, R. F. and Havighurst, R. J. *The Psychology of Character Development*. New York: Wiley, 1960.

Piaget, J. *The Moral Judgment of the Child*. Glencoe, Ill.: Free Press, 1948, 1965 (originally published in 1932).

Piaget, J. *Six Psychological Studies*. New York: Random House, 1967.

Rawls, J. A. *Theory of Justice*. Cambridge, Mass.: Harvard University Press, 1971.

Reimer, J. "A Study in the Moral Development of Kibbutz Adolescents." Unpublished doctoral dissertation Harvard Graduate School of Education, 1977.

Rest, J. "The Hierarchical Nature of Moral Judgment." *Journal of Personality* 41 (1973):86–109.

Rest, J. "New Approaches in the Assessment of Moral Judgment." In T. Lickona, ed., *Moral Development and Behavior: Theory, Research, and Social Issues*. New York: Holt, Rinehart and Winston, 1976.

Sears. R. R., Rau, L., and Alpert, R. *Identification and Child Rearing*. Stanford, Calif.: Stanford University Press, 1965.

Selman, R. L. "The Development of Social-Cognitive Understanding: A Guide to Education and Clinical Practice." In T. Lickona, ed., *Moral Development and Behavior: Theory, Research, and Social Issues*. New York: Holt, Rinehart and Winston, 1976.

Turiel, E. "Conflict and Transition in Adolescent Moral Development II: The Resolution of Disequilibrium Through Structural Reorganization." *Child Development* 48 (1977):634–637.

Walker, L. J. "Cognitive and Perspective-Taking Prerequisites for Moral Development." *Child Development* 51 (1980):131–140.

Whiting, J. W. M. and Child, I. L. *Child Training and Personality: A Cross-Cultural Study*. New Haven: Yale University Press, 1953.

# CHAPTER 27
# IN A DIFFERENT VOICE: WOMEN'S CONCEPTIONS OF SELF AND OF MORALITY

## CAROL GILLIGAN

As theories of developmental psychology continue to define educational goals and practice, it has become imperative for educators and researchers to scrutinize not only the underlying assumptions of such theories but also the model of adulthood toward which they point. Carol Gilligan examines the limitations of several theories, most notably Kohlberg's stage theory of moral development, and concludes that developmental theory has not given adequate expression to the concerns and experience of women. Through a review of psychological and literary sources, she illustrates the feminine construction of reality. From her own research data, interviews with women contemplating abortion, she then derives an alternative sequence for the development of women's moral judgments. Finally, she argues for an expanded conception of adulthood that would result from the integration of the "feminine voice" into developmental theory.

The arc of developmental theory leads from infantile dependence to adult autonomy, tracing a path characterized by an increasing differentiation of self from other and a progressive freeing of thought from contextual constraints. The vision of Luther, journeying from the rejection of a self defined by others to the assertive boldness of "Here I stand" and the image of Plato's allegorical man in the cave, separating at last the shadows from the sun, have taken powerful hold on the psychological understanding of what constitutes development. Thus, the individual, meeting fully the developmental challenges of adolescence as set for him by Piaget, Erikson, and Kohlberg, thinks formally, proceeding from theory to fact, and defines both the self and the moral autonomously, that is, apart from the identification and conventions that had comprised the particulars of his childhood world. So equipped, he is presumed ready to live as an adult, to love and work in a way that is both intimate and generative, to develop an ethical sense of caring and a genital mode of relating in which giving and taking fuse in the ultimate reconciliation of the tension between self and other.

Yet the men whose theories have largely informed this understanding of development have all been plagued by the same problem, the problem of women, whose sexuality remains more diffuse, whose perception of self is so much more tenaciously embedded in relationships with others and whose moral dilemmas hold them in a mode of judgment that is insistently contextual. The solution has been to consider women as either deviant or deficient in their development.

That there is a discrepancy between concepts of womanhood and adulthood is nowhere more clearly evident than in the series of studies on sex-role stereotypes reported by Broverman, Vogel, Broverman, Clarkson, and Rosenkrantz (1972). The repeated finding of these studies is that the

Gilligan, C. (1977). In a different voice: Women's conceptions of self and morality. *Harvard Educational Review*, 47, 481–517.

qualities deemed necessary for adulthood—the capacity for autonomous thinking, clear decision making, and responsible action—are those associated with masculinity but considered undesirable as attributes of the feminine self. The stereotypes suggest a splitting of love and work that relegates the expressive capacities requisite for the former to women while the instrumental abilities necessary for the latter reside in the masculine domain. Yet, looked at from a different perspective, these stereotypes reflect a conception of adulthood that is itself out of balance, favoring the separateness of the individual self over its connection to others and leaning more toward an autonomous life of work than toward the interdependence of love and care.

This difference in point of view is the subject of this essay, which seeks to identify in the feminine experience and construction of social reality a distinctive voice, recognizable in the different perspective it brings to bear on the construction and resolution of moral problems. The first section begins with the repeated observation of difference in women's concepts of self and of morality. This difference is identified in previous psychological descriptions of women's moral judgments and described as it again appears in current research data. Examples drawn from interviews with women in and around a university community are used to illustrate the characteristics of the feminine voice. The relational bias in women's thinking that has, in the past, been seen to compromise their moral judgment and impede their development now begins to emerge in a new developmental light. Instead of being seen as a developmental deficiency, this bias appears to reflect a different social and moral understanding.

This alternative conception is enlarged in the second section through consideration of research interviews with women facing the moral dilemma of whether to continue or abort a pregnancy. Since the research design allowed women to define as well as resolve the moral problem, developmental distinctions could be derived directly from the categories of women's thought. The responses of women to structured interview questions regarding the pregnancy decision formed the basis for describing a developmental sequence that traces progressive differentiations in their understanding and judgment of conflicts between self and other. While the sequence of women's moral development follows the three-level progression of all social developmental theory, from an egocentric through a societal to a universal perspective, this progression takes place within a distinct moral conception. This conception differs from that derived by Kohlberg from his all-male longitudinal research data.

This difference then becomes the basis in the third section for challenging the current assessment of women's moral judgment at the same time that it brings to bear a new perspective on developmental assessment in general. The inclusion in the overall conception of development of those categories derived from the study of women's moral judgment enlarges developmental understanding, enabling it to encompass better the thinking of both sexes. This is particularly true with respect to the construction and resolution of the dilemmas of adult life. Since the conception of adulthood retrospectively shapes the theoretical understanding of the development that precedes it, the changes in that conception that follow from the more central inclusion of women's judgments recast developmental understanding and lead to a reconsideration of the substance of social and moral development.

## Characteristics of the Feminine Voice

The revolutionary contribution of Piaget's work is the experimental confirmation and refinement of Kant's assertion that knowledge is actively constructed rather than passively received. Time, space, self, and other, as well as the categories of developmental theory, all arise out of the active interchange between the individual and the physical and social world in which he lives and of which he strives to make sense. The development of cognition is the process of reappropriating reality at progressively more complex levels of apprehension, as the structures of thinking expand to encompass the increasing richness and intricacy of experience.

Moral development, in the work of Piaget and Kohlberg, refers specifically to the expanding conception of the social world as it is reflected in the understanding and resolution of the inevitable conflicts that arise in the relations between self and others. The moral judgment is a statement of priority, an attempt at rational resolution in a situation where, from a different point of view, the choice itself seems to do violence to justice.

Kohlberg (1969), in his extension of the early work of Piaget, discovered six stages of moral judgment, which he claimed formed an invariant sequence, each successive stage representing a more adequate construction of the moral problem, which in turn provides the basis for its more just resolution. The stages divide into three levels, each of which denotes a significant expansion of the moral point of view from an egocentric through a societal to a universal ethical conception. With this expansion in perspective comes the capacity to free moral judgment from the individual needs and social conventions with which it had earlier been confused and anchor it instead in principles of justice that are universal in application. These principles provide criteria upon which both individual and societal claims can be impartially assessed. In Kohlberg's view, at the highest stages of development morality is freed from both psychological and historical constraints, and the individual can judge independently of his own particular needs and of the values of those around him.

That the moral sensibility of women differs from that of men was noted by Freud (1925/1961) in the following by now well-quoted statement:

> I cannot evade the notion (though I hesitate to give it expression) that for women the level of what is ethically normal is different from what it is in man. Their superego is never so inexorable, so impersonal, so independent of its emotional origins as we require it to be in men. Character-traits which critics of every epoch have brought up against women—that they show less sense of justice than men, that they are less ready to submit to the great exigencies of life, that they are more often influenced in their judgments by feelings of affection or hostility—all these would be amply accounted for by the modification in the formation of their super-ego which we have inferred above. (pp. 257–258)

While Freud's explanation lies in the deviation of female from male development around the construction and resolution of the Oedipal problem, the same observations about the nature of morality in women emerge from the work of Piaget and Kohlberg. Piaget (1932/1965), in his study of the rules of children's games, observed that, in the games they played, girls were "less explicit about agreement [than boys] and less concerned with legal elaboration" (p. 93). In contrast to the boys' interest in the codification of rules, the girls adopted a more pragmatic attitude, regarding "a rule as good so long as the game repays it" (p. 83). As a result, in comparison to boys, girls were found to be "more tolerant and more easily reconciled to innovations" (p. 52).

Kohlberg (1971) also identifies a strong interpersonal bias in the moral judgments of women, which leads them to be considered as typically at the third of his six-stage developmental sequence. At that stage, the good is identified with "what pleases or helps others and is approved of by them" (p. 164). This mode of judgment is conventional in its conformity to generally held notions of the good but also psychological in its concern with intention and consequence as the basis for judging the morality of action.

That women fall largely into this level of moral judgment is hardly surprising when we read from the Broverman et al. (1972) list that prominent among the twelve attributes considered to be desirable for women are tact, gentleness, awareness of the feelings of others, strong need for security, and easy expression of tender feelings. And yet, herein lies the paradox, for the very traits that have traditionally defined the "goodness" of women, their care for and sensitivity to the needs of others, are those that mark them as deficient in moral development. The infusion of feeling into their judgments keeps them from developing a more independent and abstract ethical conception in which concern for others derives from principles of justice rather than from compassion and care. Kohlberg, however, is less pessimistic than Freud in his assessment, for he sees the development of women as extending beyond the interpersonal level, following the same path toward independent, principled judgment that he discovered in the research on men from which his stages were derived. In Kohlberg's view, women's development will proceed beyond Stage Three when they are challenged to solve moral problems that require them to see beyond the relationships that have in the past generally bound their moral experience.

What then do women say when asked to construct the moral domain; how do we identify the characteristically "feminine" voice? A Radcliffe undergraduate, responding to the question, "If you had to say what morality meant to you, how would you sum it up?," replies:

> When I think of the word morality, I think of obligations. I usually think of it as conflicts between per-
> sonal desires and social things, social considerations, or personal desires of yourself versus personal
> desires of another person or people or whatever. Morality is that whole realm of how you decide these
> conflicts. A moral person is one who would decide, like by placing themselves more often than not as
> equals, a truly moral person would always consider another person as their equal . . . in a situation of
> social interaction, something is morally wrong where the individual ends up screwing a lot of people.
> And it is morally right when everyone comes out better off.*

Yet when asked if she can think of someone whom she would consider a genuinely moral person,
she replies, "Well, immediately I think of Albert Schweitzer because he has obviously given his life
to help others." Obligation and sacrifice override the ideal of equality, setting up a basic contradiction in her thinking.

Another undergraduate responds to the question, "What does it mean to say something is
morally right or wrong?," by also speaking first of responsibilities and obligations:

> Just that it has to do with responsibilities and obligations and values, mainly values. . . . In my life sit-
> uation I relate morality with interpersonal relationships that have to do with respect for the other per-
> son and myself. [Why respect other people?] Because they have a consciousness or feelings that can be
> hurt, an awareness that can be hurt.

The concern about hurting others persists as a major theme in the responses of two other Radcliffe
students:

> [Why be moral?] Millions of people have to live together peacefully. I personally don't want to hurt
> other people. That's a real criterion, a main criterion for me. It underlies my sense of justice. It isn't
> nice to inflict pain. I empathize with anyone in pain. Not hurting others is important in my own pri-
> vate morals. Years ago, I would have jumped out of a window not to hurt my boyfriend. That was
> pathological. Even today though, I want approval and love and I don't want enemies. Maybe that's
> why there is morality—so people can win approval, love and friendship.

> My main moral principle is not hurting other people as long as you aren't going against your own con-
> science and as long as you remain true to yourself. . . . There are many moral issues such as abortion, the
> draft, killing, stealing, monogamy, etc. If something is a controversial issue like these, then I always say
> it is up to the individual. The individual has to decide and then follow his own conscience. There are no
> moral absolutes. . . . Laws are pragmatic instruments, but they are not absolutes. A viable society can't
> make exceptions all the time, but I would personally. . . . I'm afraid I'm heading for some big crisis with
> my boyfriend someday, and someone will get hurt, and he'll get more hurt than I will. I feel an obliga-
> tion to not hurt him, but also an obligation to not lie. I don't know if it is possible to not lie and not hurt.

The common thread that runs through these statements, the wish not to hurt others and the
hope that in morality lies a way of solving conflicts so that no one will get hurt, is striking in that it
is independently introduced by each of the four women as the most specific item in their response
to a most general question. The moral person is one who helps others; goodness is service, meeting
one's obligations and responsibilities to others, if possible, without sacrificing oneself. While the
first of the four women ends by denying the conflict she initially introduced, the last woman anticipates a conflict between remaining true to herself and adhering to her principle of not hurting others. The dilemma that would test the limits of this judgment would be one where helping others is
seen to be at the price of hurting the self.

The reticence about taking stands on "controversial issues," the willingness to "make exceptions all the time" expressed in the final example above, is echoed repeatedly by other Radcliffe students, as in the following two examples:

> I never feel that I can condemn anyone else. I have a very relativistic position. The basic idea that I
> cling to is the sanctity of human life. I am inhibited about impressing my beliefs on others.

> I could never argue that my belief on a moral question is anything that another person should accept.
> I don't believe in absolutes. . . . If there is an absolute for moral decisions, it is human life.

---

* The Radcliffe women whose responses are cited were interviewed as part of a pilot study on undergraduate
moral development conducted by the author in 1970.

Or as a thirty-one-year-old Wellesley graduate says, in explaining why she would find it difficult to steal a drug to save her own life despite her belief that it would be right to steal for another: "It's just very hard to defend yourself against the rules. I mean, we live by consensus, and you take an action simply for yourself, by yourself, there's no consensus there, and that is relatively indefensible in this society now."

What begins to emerge is a sense of vulnerability that impedes these women from taking a stand, what George Eliot (1860/1965) regards as the girl's "susceptibility" to adverse judgments of others, which stems from her lack of power and consequent inability to do something in the world. While relativism in men, the unwillingness to make moral judgments that Kohlberg and Kramer (1969) and Kohlberg and Gilligan (1971) have associated with the adolescent crisis of identity and belief, takes the form of calling into question the concept of morality itself, the women's reluctance to judge stems rather from their uncertainty about their right to make moral statements or, perhaps, the price for them that such judgment seems to entail. This contrast echoes that made by Matina Horner (1972), who differentiated the ideological fear of success expressed by men from the personal conflicts about succeeding that riddled the women's responses to stories of competitive achievement.

> Most of the men who responded with the expectation of negative consequences because of success were not concerned about their masculinity but were instead likely to have expressed existential concerns about finding a "non-materialistic happiness and satisfaction in life." These concerns, which reflect changing attitudes toward traditional kinds of success or achievement in our society, played little, if any, part in the female stories. Most of the women who were high in fear of success imagery continued to be concerned about the discrepancy between success in the situation described and feminine identity. (pp. 163–164)

When women feel excluded from direct participation in society, they see themselves as subject to a consensus or judgment made and enforced by the men on whose protection and support they depend and by whose names they are known. A divorced middle-aged woman, mother of adolescent daughters, resident of a sophisticated university community, tells the story as follows:

> As a woman, I feel I never understood that I was a person, that I can make decisions and I have a right to make decisions. I always felt that that belonged to my father or my husband in some way or church which was always represented by a male clergyman. They were the three men in my life: father, husband, and clergyman, and they had much more to say about what I should or shouldn't do. They were really authority figures which I accepted. I didn't rebel against that. It only has lately occurred to me that I never even rebelled against it, and my girls are much more conscious of this, not in the militant sense, but just in the recognizing sense. . . . I still let things happen to me rather than make them happen, than to make choices, although I know all about choices. I know the procedures and the steps and all. [Do you have any clues about why this might be true?] Well, I think in one sense, there is less responsibility involved. Because if you make a dumb decision, you have to take the rap. If it happens to you, well, you can complain about it. I think that if you don't grow up feeling that you ever had any choices, you don't either have the sense that you have emotional responsibility. With this sense of choice comes this sense of responsibility.

The essence of the moral decision is the exercise of choice and the willingness to accept responsibility for that choice. To the extent that women perceive themselves as having no choice, they correspondingly excuse themselves from the responsibility that decision entails. Childlike in the vulnerability of their dependence and consequent fear of abandonment, they claim to wish only to please but in return for their goodness they expect to be loved and cared for. This, then, is an "altruism" always at risk, for it presupposes an innocence constantly in danger of being compromised by an awareness of the trade-off that has been made. Asked to describe herself, a Radcliffe senior responds:

> I have heard of the onion skin theory. I see myself as an onion, as a block of different layers, the external layers for people that I don't know that well, the agreeable, the social, and as you go inward there are more sides for people I know that I show. I am not sure about the innermost, whether there is a core, or whether I have just picked up everything as I was growing up, these different influences. I think I have a neutral attitude towards myself, but I do think in terms of good and bad. . . . Good—I

try to be considerate and thoughtful of other people and I try to be fair in situations and be tolerant. I use the words but I try and work them out practically. . . . Bad things—I am not sure if they are bad, if they are altruistic or I am doing them basically for approval of other people. [Which things are these?] The values I have when I try to act them out. They deal mostly with interpersonal type relations. . . . If I were doing it for approval, it would be a very tenuous thing. If I didn't get the right feedback, there might go all my values.

Ibsen's play, *A Doll House* (1879/1965), depicts the explosion of just such a world through the eruption of a moral dilemma that calls into question the notion of goodness that lies at its center. Nora, the "squirrel wife," living with her husband as she had lived with her father, puts into action this conception of goodness as sacrifice and, with the best of intentions, takes the law into her own hands. The crisis that ensues, most painfully for her in the repudiation of that goodness by the very person who was its recipient and beneficiary, causes her to reject the suicide that she had initially seen as its ultimate expression and choose instead to seek new and firmer answers to the adolescent questions of identity and belief.

The availability of choice and with it the onus of responsibility has now invaded the most private sector of the woman's domain and threatens a similar explosion. For centuries, women's sexuality anchored them in passivity, in a receptive rather than active stance, where the events of conception and childbirth could be controlled only by a withholding in which their own sexual needs were either denied or sacrificed. That such a sacrifice entailed a cost to their intelligence as well was seen by Freud (1908/1959) when he tied the "undoubted intellectual inferiority of so many women" to "the inhibition of thought necessitated by sexual suppression" (p. 199). The strategies of withholding and denial that women have employed in the politics of sexual relations appear similar to their evasion or withholding of judgment in the moral realm. The hesitance expressed in the previous examples to impose even a belief in the value of human life on others, like the reluctance to claim one's sexuality, bespeaks a self uncertain of its strength, unwilling to deal with consequence, and thus avoiding confrontation.

Thus women have traditionally deferred to the judgment of men, although often while intimating a sensibility of their own which is at variance with that judgment. Maggie Tulliver, in *The Mill on the Floss* (Eliot, 1860/1965) responds to the accusations that ensue from the discovery of her secretly continued relationship with Phillip Wakeham by acceding to her brother's moral judgment while at the same time asserting a different set of standards by which she attests her own superiority:

> I don't want to defend myself. . . . I know I've been wrong—often continually. But yet, sometimes when I have done wrong, it has been because I have feelings that you would be the better for if you had them. If *you* were in fault ever, if you had done anything very wrong, I should be sorry for the pain it brought you; I should not want punishment to be heaped on you. (p. 188)

An eloquent defense, Kohlberg would argue, of a Stage Three moral position, an assertion of the age-old split between thinking and feeling, justice and mercy, that underlies many of the clichés and stereotypes concerning the difference between the sexes. But considered from another point of view, it is a moment of confrontation, replacing a former evasion, between two modes of judging, two differing constructions of the moral domain—one traditionally associated with masculinity and the public world of social power, the other with femininity and the privacy of domestic interchange. While the developmental ordering of these two points of view has been to consider the masculine as the more adequate and thus as replacing the feminine as the individual moves toward higher stages, their reconciliation remains unclear.

## The Development of Women's Moral Judgment

Recent evidence for a divergence in moral development between men and women comes from the research of Haan (Note 1) and Holstein (1976) whose findings lead them to question the possibility of a "sex-related bias" in Kolhberg's scoring system. This system is based on Kohlberg's six-stage description of moral development. Kohlberg's stages divide into three levels, which he designates as preconventional, conventional and postconventional, thus denoting the major shifts in moral perspective around a center of moral understanding that equates justice with the maintenance of existing social systems. While the preconventional conception of justice is based on the needs of the self, the conventional judgment derives from an understanding of society. This understanding is in turn superseded by a postconventional or principled conception of justice where the good is formulated in universal terms. The quarrel with Kohlberg's stage scoring does not pertain to the structural differentiation of his levels but rather to questions of stage and sequence. Kohlberg's stages begin with an obedience and punishment orientation (Stage One), and go from there in invariant order to instrumental hedonism (Stage Two), interpersonal concordance (Stage Three), law and order (Stage Four), social contract (Stage Five), and universal ethical principles (Stage Six).

The bias that Haan and Holstein question in this scoring system has to do with the subordination of the interpersonal to the societal definition of the good in the transition from Stage Three to Stage Four. This is the transition that has repeatedly been found to be problematic for women. In 1969, Kohlberg and Kramer identified Stage Three as the characteristic mode of women's moral judgments, claiming that, since women's lives were interpersonally based, this stage was not only "functional" for them but also adequate for resolving the moral conflicts that they faced. Turiel (1973) reported that while girls reached Stage Three sooner than did boys, their judgments tended to remain at that stage while the boys' development continued further along Kohlberg's scale. Gilligan, Kohlberg, Lerner, and Belenky (1971) found a similar association between sex and moral-judgment stage in a study of high-school students, with the girls' responses being scored predominantly at Stage Three while the boys' responses were more often scored at Stage Four.

This repeated finding of developmental inferiority in women may, however, have more to do with the standard by which development has been measured than with the quality of women's thinking per se. Haan's data (Note 1) on the Berkeley Free Speech Movement and Holstein's (1976) three-year longitudinal study of adolescents and their parents indicate that the moral judgments of women differ from those of men in the greater extent to which women's judgments are tied to feelings of empathy and compassion and are concerned more with the resolution of "real-life" as opposed to hypothetical dilemmas (Note 1, p. 34). However, as long as the categories by which development is assessed are derived within a male perspective from male research data, divergence from the masculine standard can be seen only as a failure of development. As a result, the thinking of women is often classified with that of children. The systematic exclusion from consideration of alternative criteria that might better encompass the development of women indicates not only the limitations of a theory framed by men and validated by research samples disproportionately male and adolescent but also the effects of the diffidence prevalent among women, their reluctance to speak publicly in their own voice, given the constraints imposed on them by the politics of differential power between the sexes.

In order to go beyond the question, "How much like men do women think, how capable are they of engaging in the abstract and hypothetical construction of reality?" it is necessary to identify and define in formal terms developmental criteria that encompass the categories of women's thinking. Such criteria would include the progressive differentiations, comprehensiveness, and adequacy that characterize higher-stage resolution of the "more frequently occurring, real-life moral dilemmas of interpersonal, empathic, fellow-feeling concerns" (Haan, Note 1, p. 34), which have long been the center of women's moral judgments and experience. To ascertain whether the feminine construction of the moral domain relies on a language different from that of men, but one which deserves equal credence in the definition of what constitutes development, it is necessary first to find the places where women have the power to choose and thus are willing to speak in their own voice.

When birth control and abortion provide women with effective means for controlling their fertility, the dilemma of choice enters the center of women's lives. Then the relationships that have traditionally defined women's identities and framed their moral judgments no longer flow inevitably from their reproductive capacity but become matters of decision over which they have control. Released from the passivity and reticence of a sexuality that binds them in dependence, it becomes possible for women to question with Freud what it is that they want and to assert their own answers to that question. However, while society may affirm publicly the woman's right to choose for herself, the exercise of such choice brings her privately into conflict with the conventions of femininity, particularly the moral equation of goodness with self-sacrifice. While independent assertion in judgment and action is considered the hallmark of adulthood and constitutes as well the standard of masculine development, it is rather in their care and concern for others that women have both judged themselves and been judged.

The conflict between self and other thus constitutes the central moral problem for women, posing a dilemma whose resolution requires a reconciliation between femininity and adulthood. In the absence of such a reconciliation, the moral problem cannot be resolved. The "good woman" masks assertion in evasion, denying responsibility by claiming only to meet the needs of others, while the "bad woman" forgoes or renounces the commitments that bind her in self-deception and betrayal. It is precisely this dilemma—the conflict between compassion and autonomy, between virtue and power—which the feminine voice struggles to resolve in its effort to reclaim the self and to solve the moral problem in such a way that no one is hurt.

When a woman considers whether to continue or abort a pregnancy, she contemplates a decision that affects both self and others and engages directly the critical moral issue of hurting. Since the choice is ultimately hers and therefore one for which she is responsible, it raises precisely those questions of judgment that have been most problematic for women. Now she is asked whether she wishes to interrupt that stream of life which has for centuries immersed her in the passivity of dependence while at the same time imposing on her the responsibility for care. Thus the abortion decision brings to the core of feminine apprehension, to what Joan Didion (1972) calls "the irreconcilable difference of it—that sense of living one's deepest life underwater, that dark involvement with blood and birth and death" (p. 14), the adult questions of responsibility and choice.

How women deal with such choices has been the subject of my research, designed to clarify, through considering the ways in which women construct and resolve the abortion decision, the nature and development of women's moral judgment. Twenty-nine women, diverse in age, race, and social class, were referred by abortion and pregnancy counseling services and participated in the study for a variety of reasons. Some came to gain further clarification with respect to a decision about which they were in conflict, some in response to a counselor's concern about repeated abortions, and others out of an interest in and/or willingness to contribute to ongoing research. Although the pregnancies occurred under a variety of circumstances in the lives of these women, certain commonalities could be discerned. The adolescents often failed to use birth control because they denied or discredited their capacity to bear children. Some of the older women attributed the pregnancy to the omission of contraceptive measures in circumstances where intercourse had not been anticipated. Since the pregnancies often coincided with efforts on the part of the women to end a relationship, they may be seen as a manifestation of ambivalence or as a way of putting the relationship to the ultimate test of commitment. For these women, the pregnancy appeared to be a way of testing truth, making the baby an ally in the search for male support and protection or, that failing, a companion victim of his rejection. There were, finally, some women who became pregnant either as a result of a failure of birth control or intentionally as part of a joint decision that later was reconsidered. Of the twenty-nine women, four decided to have the baby, one miscarried, twenty-one chose abortion, and three remained in doubt about the decision.

In the initial part of the interview, the women were asked to discuss the decision that confronted them, how they were dealing with it, the alternatives they were considering, their reasons for and against each option, the people involved, the conflicts entailed, and the ways in which making this decision affected their self-concepts and their relationships with others. Then, in the second part of the interview, moral judgment was assessed in the hypothetical mode by presenting for resolution three of Kohlberg's standard research dilemmas.

While the structural progression from a preconventional through a conventional to a postconventional moral perspective can readily be discerned in the women's responses to both actual and hypothetical dilemmas, the conventions that shape women's moral judgments differ from those that apply to men. The construction of the abortion dilemma, in particular, reveals the existence of a distinct moral language whose evolution informs the sequence of women's development. This is the language of selfishness and responsibility, which defines the moral problem as one of obligation to exercise care and avoid hurt. The infliction of hurt is considered selfish and immoral in its reflection of unconcern, while the expression of care is seen as the fulfillment of moral responsibility. The reiterative use of the language of selfishness and responsibility and the underlying moral orientation it reflects sets the women apart from the men whom Kohlberg studied and may be seen as the critical reason for their failure to develop within the constraints of his system.

In the developmental sequence that follows, women's moral judgments proceed from an initial focus on the self at the *first level* to the discovery, in the transition to the *second level*, of the concept of responsibility as the basis for a new equilibrium between self and others. The elaboration of this concept of responsibility and its fusion with a maternal concept of morality, which seeks to ensure protection for the dependent and unequal, characterizes the *second level* of judgment. At this level the good is equated with caring for others. However, when the conventions of feminine goodness legitimize only others as the recipients of moral care, the logical inequality between self and other and the psychological violence that it engenders create the disequilibrium that initiates the *second* transition. The relationship between self and others is then reconsidered in an effort to sort out the confusion between conformity and care inherent in the conventional definition of feminine goodness and to establish a new equilibrium, which dissipates the tension between selfishness and responsibility. At the *third level,* the self becomes the arbiter of an independent judgment that now subsumes both conventions and individual needs under the moral principle of nonviolence. Judgment remains psychological in its concern with the intention and consequences of action, but it now becomes universal in its condemnation of exploitation and hurt.

## Level I: Orientation to Individual Survival

In its initial and simplest construction, the abortion decision centers on the self. The concern is pragmatic, and the issue is individual survival. At this level, "should" is undifferentiated from "would," and others influence the decision only through their power to affect its consequences. An eighteen-year-old, asked what she thought when she found herself pregnant, replies: "I really didn't think anything except that I didn't want it. [Why was that?] I didn't want it, I wasn't ready for it, and next year will be my last year and I want to go to school."

Asked if there was a right decision, she says, "There is no right decision. [Why?] I didn't want it." For her the question of right decision would emerge only if her own needs were in conflict; then she would have to decide which needs should take precedence. This was the dilemma of another eighteen-year-old, who saw having a baby as a way of increasing her freedom by providing "the perfect chance to get married and move away from home," but also as restricting her freedom "to do a lot of things."

At this first level, the self, which is the sole object of concern, is constrained by lack of power; the wish "to do a lot of things" is constantly belied by the limitations of what, in fact, is being done. Relationships are, for the most part, disappointing: "The only thing you are ever going to get out of going with a guy is to get hurt." As a result, women may in some instances deliberately choose isolation to protect themselves against hurt. When asked how she would describe herself to herself, a nineteen-year-old, who held herself responsible for the accidental death of a younger brother, answers as follows:

> I really don't know. I never thought about it. I don't know. I know basically the outline of a character. I am very independent. I don't really want to have to ask anybody for anything and I am a loner in life. I prefer to be by myself than around anybody else. I manage to keep my friends at a limited number with the point that I have very few friends. I don't know what else there is. I am a loner and I enjoy it. Here today and gone tomorrow.

The primacy of the concern with survival is explicitly acknowledged by a sixteen-year-old delinquent in response to Kohlberg's Heinz dilemma, which asks if it is right for a desperate husband to steal an outrageously overpriced drug to save the life of his dying wife:

> I think survival is one of the first things in life and that people fight for. I think it is the most important thing, more important than stealing. Stealing might be wrong, but if you have to steal to survive yourself or even kill, that is what you should do. . . . Preservation of oneself, I think, is the most important thing; it comes before anything in life.

## The First Transition: From Selfishness to Responsibility

In the transition which follows and criticizes this level of judgment, the words selfishness and responsibility first appear. Their reference initially is to the self in a redefinition of the self-interest which has thus far served as the basis for judgment. The transitional issue is one of attachment or connection to others. The pregnancy catches up the issue not only by representing an immediate, literal connection, but also by affirming, in the most concrete and physical way, the capacity to assume adult feminine roles. However, while having a baby seems at first to offer respite from the loneliness of adolescence and to solve conflicts over dependence and independence, in reality the continuation of an adolescent pregnancy generally compounds these problems, increasing social isolation and precluding further steps toward independence.

To be a mother in the societal as well as the physical sense requires the assumption of parental responsibility for the care and protection of a child. However, in order to be able to care for another, one must first be able to care responsibly for oneself. The growth from childhood to adulthood, conceived as a move from selfishness to responsibility, is articulated explicitly in these terms by a seventeen-year-old who describes her response to her pregnancy as follows:

> I started feeling really good about being pregnant instead of feeling really bad, because I wasn't looking at the situation realistically. I was looking at it from my own sort of selfish needs because I was lonely and felt lonely and stuff. . . . Things weren't really going good for me, so I was looking at it that I could have a baby that I could take care of or something that was part of me, and that made me feel good . . . but I wasn't looking at the realistic side . . . about the responsibility I would have to take on . . . I came to this decision that I was going to have an abortion [because] I realized how much responsibility goes with having a child. Like you have to be there, you can't be out of the house all the time which is one thing I like to do . . . and I decided that I have to take on responsibility for myself and I have to work out a lot of things.

Stating her former mode of judgment, the wish to have a baby as a way of combating loneliness and feeling connected, she now criticizes that judgment as both "selfish" and "unrealistic." The contradiction between wishes for a baby and for the freedom to be "out of the house all the time"—that is, for connection and also for independence—is resolved in terms of a new priority, as the criterion for judgment changes. The dilemma now assumes moral definition as the emergent conflict between wish and necessity is seen as a disparity between "would" and "should." In this construction the "selfishness" of willful decision is counterposed to the "responsibility" of moral choice:

> What I want to do is to have the baby, but what I feel I should do which is what I need to do, is have an abortion right now, because sometimes what you want isn't right. Sometimes what is necessary comes before what you want, because it might not always lead to the right thing.

While the pregnancy itself confirms femininity—"I started feeling really good; it sort of made me feel, like being pregnant, I started feeling like a woman"—the abortion decision becomes an opportunity for the adult exercise of responsible choice.

> [How would you describe yourself to yourself?] I am looking at myself differently in the way that I have had a really heavy decision put upon me, and I have never really had too many hard decisions in my life, and I have made it. It has taken some responsibility to do this. I have changed in that way, that I have made a hard decision. And that has been good. Because before, I would not have looked at it realistically, in my opinion. I would have gone by what I wanted to do, and I wanted it, and even if it wasn't right. So I see myself as I'm becoming more mature in ways of making decisions and taking care of myself, doing something for myself. I think it is going to help me in other ways, if I have other decisions to make put upon me, which would take some responsibility. And I would know that I could make them.

In the epiphany of this cognitive reconstruction, the old becomes transformed in terms of the new. The wish to "do something for myself" remains, but the terms of its fulfillment change as the decision affirms both femininity and adulthood in its integration of responsibility and care. Morality, says another adolescent, "is the way you think about yourself . . . sooner or later you have to make up your mind to start taking care of yourself. Abortion, if you do it for the right reasons, is helping yourself to start over and do different things."

Since this transition signals an enhancement in self-worth, it requires a conception of self which includes the possibility for doing "the right thing," the ability to see in oneself the potential for social acceptance. When such confidence is seriously in doubt, the transitional questions may be raised but development is impeded. The failure to make this first transition, despite an understanding of the issues involved, is illustrated by a woman in her late twenties. Her struggle with the conflict between selfishness and responsibility pervades but fails to resolve her dilemma of whether or not to have a third abortion.

> I think you have to think about the people who are involved, including yourself. You have responsibilities to yourself . . . and to make a right, whatever that is, decision in this depends on your knowledge and awareness of the responsibilities that you have and whether you can survive with a child and what it will do to your relationship with the father or how it will affect him emotionally.

Rejecting the idea of selling the baby and making "a lot of money in a black market kind of thing . . . because mostly I operate on principles and it would just rub me the wrong way to think I would be selling my own child," she struggles with a concept of responsibility which repeatedly turns back on the question of her own survival. Transition seems blocked by a self-image which is insistently contradictory:

> [How would you describe yourself to yourself?] I see myself as impulsive, practical—that is a contradiction—and moral and amoral, a contradiction. Actually the only thing that is consistent and not contradictory is the fact that I am very lazy which everyone has always told me is really a symptom of something else which I have never been able to put my finger on exactly. It has taken me a long time to like myself. In fact there are times when I don't, which I think is healthy to a point and sometimes I think I like myself too much and I probably evade myself too much, which avoids responsibility to myself and to other people who like me. I am pretty unfaithful to myself . . . I have a hard time even thinking that I am a human being, simply because so much rotten stuff goes on and people are so crummy and insensitive.

Seeing herself as avoiding responsibility, she can find no basis upon which to resolve the pregnancy dilemma. Instead, her inability to arrive at any clear sense of decision only contributes further to her overall sense of failure. Criticizing her parents for having betrayed her during adolescence by coercing her to have an abortion she did not want, she now betrays herself and criticizes that as well. In this light, it is less surprising that she considered selling her child, since she felt herself to have, in effect, been sold by her parents for the sake of maintaining their social status.

## The Second Level: Goodness as Self-Sacrifice

The transition from selfishness to responsibility is a move toward social participation. Whereas at the first level, morality is seen as a matter of sanctions imposed by a society of which one is more subject than citizen, at the second level, moral judgment comes to rely on shared norms and expectations. The woman at this level validates her claim to social membership through the adoption of societal values. Consensual judgment becomes paramount and goodness the overriding concern as survival is now seen to depend on acceptance by others.

Here the conventional feminine voice emerges with great clarity, defining the self and proclaiming its worth on the basis of the ability to care for and protect others. The woman now constructs the world perfused with the assumptions about feminine goodness reflected in the stereotypes of the Broverman et al. (1972) studies. There the attributes considered desirable for women all presume an other, a recipient of the "tact, gentleness and easy expression of feeling" which allow the woman to respond sensitively while evoking in return the care which meets her own "very strong need for security" (p. 63). The strength of this position lies in its capacity for caring; its limitation is the restriction it imposes on direct expression. Both qualities are elucidated by a nineteen-year-old who contrasts her reluctance to criticize with her boyfriend's straightforwardness:

> I never want to hurt anyone, and I tell them in a very nice way, and I have respect for their own opinions, and they can do the things the way that they want, and he usually tells people right off the bat. . . . He does a lot of things out in public which I do in private . . . it is better, the other [his way], but I just could never do it.

While her judgment clearly exists, it is not expressed, at least not in public. Concern for the feelings of others imposes a deference which she nevertheless criticizes in an awareness that, under the name of consideration, a vulnerability and a duplicity are concealed.

At the second level of judgment, it is specifically over the issue of hurting that conflict arises with respect to the abortion decision. When no option exists that can be construed as being in the best interest of everyone, when responsibilities conflict and decision entails the sacrifice of somebody's needs, then the woman confronts the seemingly impossible task of choosing the victim. A nineteen-year-old, fearing the consequences for herself of a second abortion but facing the opposition of both her family and her lover to the continuation of the pregnancy, describes the dilemma as follows:

> I don't know what choices are open to me; it is either to have it or the abortion; these are the choices open to me. It is just that either way I don't . . . I think what confuses me is it is a choice of either hurting myself or hurting other people around me. What is more important? If there could be a happy medium, it would be fine, but there isn't. It is either hurting someone on this side or hurting myself.

While the feminine identification of goodness with self-sacrifice seems clearly to dictate the "right" resolution of this dilemma, the stakes may be high for the woman herself, and the sacrifice of the fetus, in any event, compromises the altruism of an abortion motivated by a concern for others. Since femininity itself is in conflict in an abortion intended as an expression of love and care, this is a resolution which readily explodes in its own contradiction.

"I don't think anyone should have to choose between two things that they love," says a twenty-five-year-old woman who assumed responsibility not only for her lover but also for his wife and children in having an abortion she did not want:

> I just wanted the child and I really don't believe in abortions. Who can say when life begins. I think that life begins at conception and . . . I felt like there were changes happening in my body and I felt very protective . . . [but] I felt a responsibility, my responsibility if anything ever happened to her [his wife]. He made me feel that I had to make a choice and there was only one choice to make and that was to have an abortion and I could always have children another time and he made me feel if I didn't have it that it would drive us apart.

The abortion decision was, in her mind, a choice not to choose with respect to the pregnancy—"That was my choice, I had to do it." Instead, it was a decision to subordinate the pregnancy to the continuation of a relationship that she saw as encompassing her life—"Since I met him, he has been my life. I do everything for him; my life sort of revolves around him." Since she wanted to have the baby and also to continue the relationship, either choice could be construed as selfish. Furthermore, since both alternatives entailed hurting someone, neither could be considered moral. Faced with a decision which, in her own terms, was untenable, she sought to avoid responsibility for the choice she made, construing the decision as a sacrifice of her own needs to those of her lover. However, this public sacrifice in the name of responsibility engendered a private resentment that erupted in anger, compromising the very relationship that it had been intended to sustain.

> Afterwards we went through a bad time because I hate to say it and I was wrong, but I blamed him. I gave in to him. But when it came down to it, I made the decision. I could have said, 'I am going to have this child whether you want me to or not,' and I just didn't do it.

Pregnant again by the same man, she recognizes in retrospect that the choice in fact had been hers, as she returns once again to what now appears to have been missed opportunity for growth. Seeking, this time, to make rather than abdicate the decision, she sees the issue as one of "strength" as she struggles to free herself from the powerlessness of her own dependence:

> I think that right now I think of myself as someone who can become a lot stronger. Because of the circumstances, I just go along like with the tide. I never really had anything of my own before . . . [this time] I hope to come on strong and make a big decision, whether it is right or wrong.

Because the morality of self-sacrifice had justified the previous abortion, she now must suspend that judgment if she is to claim her own voice and accept responsibility for choice.

She thereby calls into question the underlying assumption of Level Two, which leads the woman to consider herself responsible for the actions of others, while holding others responsible for the choices she makes. This notion of reciprocity, backwards in its assumptions about control, disguises assertion as response. By reversing responsibility, it generates a series of indirect actions, which leave everyone feeling manipulated and betrayed. The logic of this position is confused in that the morality of mutual care is embedded in the psychology of dependence. Assertion becomes personally dangerous in its risk of criticism and abandonment, as well as potentially immoral in its power to hurt. This confusion is captured by Kohlberg's (1969) definition of Stage Three moral judgment, which joins the need for approval with the wish to care for and help others.

When thus caught between the passivity of dependence and the activity of care, the woman becomes suspended in an immobility of both judgment and action. "If I were drowning, I couldn't reach out a hand to save myself, so unwilling am I to set myself up against fate" (p. 7), begins the central character of Margaret Drabble's novel, *The Waterfall* (1971), in an effort to absolve herself of responsibility as she at the same time relinquishes control. Facing the same moral conflict which George Eliot depicted in *The Mill on the Floss*, Drabble's heroine proceeds to relive Maggie Tulliver's dilemma but turns inward in her search for the way in which to retell that story. What is initially suspended and then called into question is the judgment which "had in the past made it seem better to renounce myself than them" (Drabble, p. 50).

## The Second Transition: From Goodness to Truth

The second transition begins with the reconsideration of the relationship between self and other, as the woman starts to scrutinize the logic of self-sacrifice in the service of a morality of care. In the interview data, this transition is announced by the reappearance of the word selfish. Retrieving the judgmental initiative, the woman begins to ask whether it is selfish or responsible, moral or immoral, to include her own needs within the compass of her care and concern. This question leads her to reexamine the concept of responsibility, juxtaposing the outward concern with what other people think with a new inner judgment.

In separating the voice of the self from those of others, the woman asks if it is possible to be responsible to herself as well as to others and thus to reconcile the disparity between hurt and care. The exercise of such responsibility, however, requires a new kind of judgment whose first demand is for honesty. To be responsible, it is necessary first to acknowledge what it is that one is doing. The criterion for judgment thus shifts from "goodness'" to "truth" as the morality of action comes to be assessed not on the basis of its appearance in the eyes of others, but in terms of the realities of its intention and consequence.

A twenty-four-year-old married Catholic woman, pregnant again two months following the birth of her first child, identifies her dilemma as one of choice: "You have to now decide; because it is now available, you have to make a decision. And if it wasn't available, there was no choice open; you just do what you have to do." In the absence of legal abortion, a morality of self-sacrifice was necessary in order to insure protection and care for the dependent child. However, when such sacrifice becomes optional, the entire problem is recast.

The abortion decision is framed by this woman first in terms of her responsibilities to others: having a second child at this time would be contrary to medical advice and would strain both the emotional and financial resources of the family. However, there is, she says, a third reason for having an abortion, "sort of an emotional reason. I don't know if it is selfish or not, but it would really be tying myself down and right now I am not ready to be tied down with two."

Against this combination of selfish and responsible reasons for abortion is her Catholic belief that

> . . . it is taking a life, and it is. Even though it is not formed, it is the potential, and to me it is still taking a life. But I have to think of mine, my son's and my husband's, to think about, and at first I think that I thought it was for selfish reasons, but it is not. I believe that too, some of it is selfish. I don't want another one right now; I am not ready for it.

The dilemma arises over the issue of justification for taking a life: "I can't cover it over, because I believe this and if I do try to cover it over, I know that I am going to be in a mess, It will be denying what I am really doing." Asking "Am I doing the right thing; is it moral?," she counterposes to her belief against abortion her concern with the consequences of continuing the pregnancy. While concluding that "I can't be so morally strict as to hurt three other people with a decision just because of my moral beliefs," the issue of goodness still remains critical to her resolution of the dilemma:

> The moral factor is there. To me it is taking a life, and I am going to take that upon myself, that decision upon myself and I have feelings about it, and talked to a priest . . . but he said it is there and it will be from now on, and it is up to the person if they can live with the idea and still believe they are good.

The criteria for goodness, however, move inward as the ability to have an abortion and still consider herself good comes to hinge on the issue of selfishness with which she struggles to come to terms. Asked if acting morally is acting according to what is best for the self or whether it is a matter of self-sacrifice, she replies:

> I don't know if I really understand the question. . . . Like in my situation where I want to have the abortion and if I didn't it would be self-sacrificing, I am really in the middle of both those ways . . . but I think that my morality is strong and if these reasons—financial, physical reality and also for the whole family involved—were not here, that I wouldn't have to do it, and then it would be a self-sacrifice.

The importance of clarifying her own participation in the decision is evident in her attempt to ascertain her feelings in order to determine whether or not she was "putting them under" in deciding to end the pregnancy. Whereas in the first transition, from selfishness to responsibility, women made lists in order to bring to their consideration needs other than their own, now, in the second transition, it is the needs of the self which have to be deliberately uncovered. Confronting the reality of her own wish for an abortion, she now must deal with the problem of selfishness and the qualification that she feels it imposes on the "goodness" of her decision. The primacy of this concern is apparent in her description of herself:

> I think in a way I am selfish for one thing, and very emotional, very . . . and I think that I am a very real person and an undemanding person and I can handle life situations fairly well, so I am basing a lot of it on my ability to do the things that I feel are right and best for me and whoever I am involved with. I think I was very fair to myself about the decision, and I really think that I have been truthful, not hiding anything, bringing out all the feelings involved. I feel it is a good decision and an honest one, a real decision.

Thus she strives to encompass the needs of both self and others, to be responsible to others and thus to be "good" but also to be responsible to herself and thus to be "honest" and "real."

While from one point of view, attention to one's own needs is considered selfish, when looked at from a different perspective, it is a matter of honesty and fairness. This is the essence of the transitional shift toward a new conception of goodness which turns inward in an acknowledgement of the self and an acceptance of responsibility for decision. While outward justification, the concern, with "good reasons," remains critical for this particular woman: "I still think abortion is wrong, and it will be unless the situation can justify what you are doing." But the search for justification has produced a change in her thinking, "not drastically, but a little bit." She realizes that in continuing the pregnancy she would punish not only herself but also her husband, toward whom she had begun to feel "turned off and irritated." This leads her to consider the consequences self-sacrifice can have both for the self and for others. "God," she says, "can punish, but He can also forgive." What remains in question is whether her claim to forgiveness is compromised by a decision that not only meets the needs of others but that also is "right and best for me."

The concern with selfishness and its equation with immorality recur in an interview with another Catholic woman whose arrival for an abortion was punctuated by the statement, "I have always thought abortion was a fancy word for murder." Initially explaining this murder as one of lesser degree—"I am doing it because I have to do it. I am not doing it the least bit because I want to," she judges it "not quite as bad. You can rationalize that it is not quite the same." Since "keeping the child for lots and lots of reasons was just sort of impractical and out," she considers her options to be either abortion or adoption. However, having previously given up one child for adoption, she says: "I knew that psychologically there was no way that I could hack another adoption. It took me about four-and-a-half years to get my head on straight; there was just no way I was going to go through it again." The decision thus reduces in her eyes to a choice between murdering the fetus or damaging herself. The choice is further complicated by the fact that by continuing the pregnancy she would hurt not only herself but also her parents, with whom she lived. In the face of these manifold moral contradictions, the psychological demand for honesty that arises in counseling finally allows decision:

> On my own, I was doing it not so much for myself; I was doing it for my parents. I was doing it because the doctor told me to do it, but I had never resolved in my mind that I was doing it for me. Because it goes right back to the fact that I never believed in abortions. . . . Actually, I had to sit down and admit, no, I really don't want to go the mother route now. I honestly don't feel that I want to be a mother, and that is not really such a bad thing to say after all. But that is not how I felt up until talking to Maureen [her counselor]. It was just a horrible way to feel, so I just wasn't going to feel it, and I just blocked it right out.

As long as her consideration remains "moral," abortion can be justified only as an act of sacrifice, a submission to necessity where the absence of choice precludes responsibility. In this way, she can avoid self-condemnation, since, "When you get into moral stuff then you are getting into self-respect and that stuff, and at least if I do something that I feel is morally wrong, then I tend to lose some of my self-respect as a person." Her evasion of responsibility, critical to maintaining the innocence necessary for self-respect, contradicts the reality of her own participation in the abortion decision. The dishonesty in her plea of victimization creates the conflict that generates the need for a more inclusive understanding. She must now resolve the emerging contradiction in her thinking between two uses of the term right: "I am saying that abortion is morally wrong, but the situation is right, and I am going to do it. But the thing is that eventually they are going to have to go together, and I am going to have to put them together somehow." Asked how this could be done, she replies:

> I would have to change morally wrong to morally right. [How?] I have no idea. I don't think you can take something that you feel is morally wrong because the situation makes it right and put the two together. They are not together, they are opposite. They don't go together. Something is wrong, but all of a sudden because you are doing it, it is right.

This discrepancy recalls a similar conflict she faced over the question of euthanasia, also considered by her to be morally wrong until she "took care of a couple of patients who had flat EEGs and saw the job that it was doing on their families." Recalling that experience, she says:

> You really don't know your black and whites until you really get into them and are being confronted with it. If you stop and think about my feelings on euthanasia until I got into it, and then my feelings about abortion until I got into it, I thought both of them were murder. Right and wrong and no middle but there is a gray.

In discovering the gray and questioning the moral judgments which formerly she considered to be absolute, she confronts the moral crisis of the second transition. Now the conventions which in the past had guided her moral judgment become subject to a new criticism, as she questions not only the justification for hurting others in the name of morality but also the "rightness" of hurting herself. However, to sustain such criticism in the face of conventions that equate goodness with self-sacrifice, the woman must verify her capacity for independent judgment and the legitimacy of her own point of view.

Once again transition hinges on self-concept. When uncertainty about her own worth prevents a woman from claiming equality, self-assertion falls prey to the old criticism of selfishness. Then the morality that condones self-destruction in the name of responsible care is not repudiated as inadequate but rather is abandoned in the face of its threat to survival. Moral obligation, rather than expanding to include the self, is rejected completely as the failure of conventional reciprocity leaves the woman unwilling any longer to protect others at what is now seen to be her own expense. In the absence of morality, survival, however "selfish" or "immoral," returns as the paramount concern.

A musician in her late twenties illustrates this transitional impasse. Having led an independent life which centered on her work, she considered herself "fairly strong-willed, fairly in control, fairly rational and objective" until she became involved in an intense love affair and discovered in her capacity to love "an entirely new dimension" in herself. Admitting in retrospect to "tremendous naiveté and idealism," she had entertained "some vague ideas that some day I would like a child to concretize our relationship . . . having always associated having a child with all the creative aspects of my life." Abjuring, with her lover, the use of contraceptives because, "as the relationship was sort of an ideal relationship in our minds, we liked the idea of not using foreign objects or anything artificial," she saw herself as having relinquished control, becoming instead "just simply vague and allowing events to just carry me along." Just as she began in her own thinking to confront "the realities of that situation"—the possibility of pregnancy and the fact that her lover was married—she found herself pregnant. "Caught" between her wish to end a relationship that "seemed more and more defeating" and her wish for a baby, which "would be a connection that would last a long time," she is paralyzed by her inability to resolve the dilemma which her ambivalence creates.

The pregnancy poses a conflict between her "moral" belief that "once a certain life has begun, it shouldn't be stopped artificially" and her "amazing" discovery that to have the baby she would "need much more [support] than I thought." Despite her moral conviction that she "should" have the child, she doubts that she could psychologically deal with "having the child alone and taking the responsibility for it." Thus a conflict erupts between what she considers to be her moral obligation to protect life and her inability to do so under the circumstances of this pregnancy. Seeing it as "my decision and my responsibility for making the decision whether to have or have not the child," she struggles to find a viable basis on which to resolve the dilemma.

Capable of arguing either for or against abortion "with a philosophical logic," she says, on the one hand, that in an overpopulated world one should have children only under ideal conditions for care but, on the other, that one should end a life only when it is impossible to sustain it. She describes her impasse in response to the question of whether there is a difference between what she wants to do and what she thinks she should do:

> Yes, and there always has. I have always been confronted with that precise situation in a lot of my choices, and I have been trying to figure out what are the things that make me believe that these are things I should do as opposed to what I feel I want to do. [In this situation?] It is not that clear cut. I both want the child and feel I should have it, and I also think I should have the abortion and want it, but I would say it is my stronger feeling, and that I don't have enough confidence in my work yet and that is really where it is all hinged, I think . . . [the abortion] would solve the problem and I know I can't handle the pregnancy.

Characterizing this solution as "emotional and pragmatic" and attributing it to her lack of confidence in her work, she contrasts it with the "better thought out and more logical and more correct" resolution of her lover who thinks that she should have the child and raise it without either his presence or financial support. Confronted with this reflected image of herself as ultimately giving and good, as self-sustaining in her own creativity and thus able to meet the needs of others while imposing no demands of her own in return, she questions not the image itself but her own adequacy in filling it. Concluding that she is not yet capable of doing so, she is reduced in her own eyes to what she sees as a selfish and highly compromised fight

> for my survival. But in one way or another, I am going to suffer. Maybe I am going to suffer mentally and emotionally having the abortion, or I would suffer what I think is possibly something worse. So I suppose it is the lesser of two evils. I think it is a matter of choosing which one I know that I can survive through. It is really. I think it is selfish, I suppose, because it does have to do with that. I just realized that. I guess it does have to do with whether I would survive or not. [Why is this selfish?] Well, you know, it is. Because I am concerned with my survival first, as opposed to the survival of the relationship or the survival of the child, another human being . . . I guess I am setting priorities, and I guess I am setting my needs to survive first. . . . I guess I see it in negative terms a lot . . . but I do think of other positive things; that I am still going to have some life left, maybe. I don't know.

In the face of this failure of reciprocity of care, in the disappointment of abandonment where connection was sought, survival is seen to hinge on her work which is "where I derive the meaning of what I am. That's the known factor." While uncertainty about her work makes this survival precarious, the choice for abortion is also distressing in that she considers it to be "highly introverted—that in this one respect, having an abortion would be going a step backward; going outside to love someone else and having a child would be a step forward." The sense of retrenchment that the severing of connection signifies is apparent in her anticipation of the cost which abortion would entail:

> Probably what I will do is I will cut off my feelings, and when they will return or what would happen to them after that, I don't know. So that I don't feel anything at all, and I would probably just be very cold and go through it very coldly. . . . The more you do that to yourself, the more difficult it becomes to love again or to trust again or to feel again. . . . Each time I move away from that, it becomes easier, not more difficult, but easier to avoid committing myself to a relationship. And I am really concerned about cutting off that whole feeling aspect.

Caught between selfishness and responsibility, unable to find in the circumstances of this choice a way of caring which does not at the same time destroy, she confronts a dilemma which reduces to a conflict between morality and survival. Adulthood and femininity fly apart in the failure of this attempt at integration as the choice to work becomes a decision not only to renounce this particular relationship and child but also to obliterate the vulnerability that love and care engender.

## The Third Level: The Morality of Nonviolence

In contrast, a twenty-five-year-old woman, facing a similar disappointment, finds a way to reconcile the initially disparate concepts of selfishness and responsibility through a transformed understanding of self and a corresponding redefinition of morality. Examining the assumptions underlying the conventions of feminine self-abnegation and moral self-sacrifice, she comes to reject these conventions as immoral in their power to hurt. By elevating nonviolence—the injunction against hurting—to a principle governing all moral judgment and action, she is able to assert a moral equality between self and other. Care then becomes a universal obligation, the self-chosen ethic of a postconventional judgment that reconstructs the dilemma in a way that allows the assumption of responsibility for choice.

In this woman's life, the current pregnancy brings to the surface the unfinished business of an earlier pregnancy and of the relationship in which both pregnancies occurred. The first pregnancy was discovered after her lover had left and was terminated by an abortion experienced as a purging expression of her anger at having been rejected. Remembering the abortion only as a relief, she nevertheless describes that time in her life as one in which she "hit rock bottom." Having hoped then to "take control of my life," she instead resumed the relationship when the man reappeared. Now, two years later, having once again "left my diaphragm in the drawer," she again becomes pregnant. Although initially "ecstatic" at the news, her elation dissipates when her lover tells her that he will leave if she chooses to have the child. Under these circumstances, she considers a second abortion but is unable to keep the repeated appointments she makes because of her reluctance to accept the responsibility for that choice. While the first abortion seemed an "honest mistake," she says that a second would make her feel "like a walking slaughter-house." Since she would need financial support to raise the child, her initial strategy was to take the matter to "the welfare people" in the hope that they would refuse to provide the necessary funds and thus resolve her dilemma:

> In that way, you know, the responsibility would be off my shoulders, and I could say, it's not my fault, you know, the state denied me the money that I would need to do it. But it turned out that it was possible to do it, and so I was, you know, right back where I started. And I had an appointment for an abortion, and I kept calling and cancelling it and then remaking the appointment and cancelling it, and I just couldn't make up my mind.

Confronting the need to choose between the two evils of hurting herself or ending the incipient life of the child, she finds, in a reconstruction of the dilemma itself, a basis for a new priority that allows decision. In doing so, she comes to see the conflict as arising from a faulty construction of reality. Her thinking recapitulates the developmental sequence, as she considers but rejects as inadequate the components of earlier-stage resolutions. An expanded conception of responsibility now reshapes moral judgment and guides resolution of the dilemma, whose pros and cons she considers as follows:

> Well, the pros for having the baby are all the admiration that you would get from, you know, being a single woman, alone, martyr, struggling, having the adoring love of this beautiful Gerber baby . . . just more of a home life than I have had in a long time, and that basically was it, which is pretty fantasy-land; it is not very realistic. . . . Cons against having the baby: it was going to hasten what is looking to be the inevitable end of the relationship with the man I am presently with. . . . I was going to have to go on welfare, my parents were going to hate me for the rest of my life, I was going to lose a really good job that I have, I would lose a lot of independence . . . solitude . . . and I would have to be put in a position of asking help from a lot of people a lot of the time. Cons against having the abortion is having to face up to the guilt . . . and pros for having the abortion are I would be able to handle my deteriorating relation with S. with a lot more capability and a lot more responsibility for him and for myself . . . and I would not have to go through the realization that for the next twenty-five years of my life I would be punishing myself for being foolish enough to get pregnant again and forcing myself to bring up a kid just because I did this. Having to face the guilt of a second abortion seemed like, not exactly, well, exactly the lesser of the two evils but also the one that would pay off for me personally in the long run because by looking at why I am pregnant again and subsequently have decided to have a second abortion, I have to face up to some things about myself.

Although she doesn't "feel good about having a second abortion," she nevertheless concludes,

> I would not be doing myself or the child or the world any kind of favor having this child. . . . I don't need to pay off my imaginary debts to the world through this child, and I don't think that it is right to bring a child into the world and use it for that purpose.

Asked to describe herself, she indicates how closely her transformed moral understanding is tied to a changing self-concept:

> I have been thinking about that a lot lately, and it comes up different than what my usual subconscious perception of myself is. Usually paying off some sort of debt, going around serving people who are not really worthy of my attentions because somewhere in my life I think I got the impression that my needs are really secondary to other people's, and that if I feel, if I make any demands on other people to fulfill my needs, I'd feel guilty for it and submerge my own in favor of other people's, which later backfires on me, and I feel a great deal of resentment for other people that I am doing things for, which causes friction and the eventual deterioration of the relationship. And then I start all over again. How would I describe myself to myself? Pretty frustrated and a lot angrier than I admit, a lot more aggressive than I admit.

Reflecting on the virtues which comprise the conventional definition of the feminine self, a definition which she hears articulated in her mother's voice, she says, "I am beginning to think that all these virtues are really not getting me anywhere. I have begun to notice." Tied to this recognition is an acknowledgement of her power and worth, both previously excluded from the image she projected:

> I am suddenly beginning to realize that the things that I like to do, the things I am interested in, and the things that I believe and the kind of person I is not so bad that I have to constantly be sitting on the shelf and letting it gather dust. I am a lot more worthwhile than what my past actions have led other people to believe.

Her notion of a "good person," which previously was limited to her mother's example of hard work, patience and self-sacrifice, now changes to include the value that she herself places on directness and honesty. Although she believes that this new self-assertion will lead her "to feel a lot better about myself" she recognizes that it will also expose her to criticism:

> Other people may say, 'Boy, she's aggressive, and I don't like that,' but at least, you know, they will know that they don't like that. They are not going to say, 'I like the way she manipulates herself to fit right around me.' . . . What I want to do is just be a more self-determined person and a more singular person.

While within her old framework abortion had seemed a way of "copping out" instead of being a "responsible person [who] pays for his mistakes and pays and pays and is always there when she says she will be there and even when she doesn't say she will be there is there," now, her "conception of what I think is right for myself and my conception of self-worth is changing." She can consider this emergent self "also a good person," as her concept of goodness expands to encompass "the feeling of self-worth; you are not going to sell yourself short and you are not going to make yourself do things that, you know, are really stupid and that you don't want to do." This reorientation centers on the awareness that:

> I have a responsibility to myself, and you know, for once I am beginning to realize that that really matters to me . . . instead of doing what I want for myself and feeling guilty over how selfish I am, you realize that that is a very usual way for people to live . . . doing what you want to do because you feel that your wants and your needs are important, if to no one else, then to you, and that's reason enough to do something that you want to do.

Once obligation extends to include the self as well as others, the disparity between selfishness and responsibility is reconciled. Although the conflict between self and other remains, the moral problem is restructured in an awareness that the occurrence of the dilemma itself precludes nonviolent resolution. The abortion decision is now seen to be a "serious" choice affecting both self and others: "This is a life that I have taken, a conscious decision to terminate, and that is just very heavy, a very heavy thing." While accepting the necessity of abortion as a highly compromised resolution, she turns her attention to the pregnancy itself, which she now considers to denote a failure of responsibility, a failure to care for and protect both self and other.

As in the first transition, although now in different terms, the conflict precipitated by the pregnancy catches up the issues critical to development. These issues now concern the worth of the self in relation to others, the claiming of the power to choose, and the acceptance of responsibility for choice. By provoking a confrontation with these issues, the crisis can become "a very auspicious time; you can use the pregnancy as sort of a learning, teeing-off point, which makes it useful in a way." This possibility for growth inherent in a crisis which allows confrontation with a construction of reality whose acceptance previously had impeded development was first identified by Coles (1964) in his study of the children of Little Rock. This same sense of possibility is expressed by the women who see, in their resolution of the abortion dilemma, a reconstructed understanding which creates the opportunity for "a new beginning," a chance "to take control of my life."

For this woman, the first step in taking control was to end the relationship in which she had considered herself "reduced to a nonentity," but to do so in a responsible way. Recognizing hurt as the inevitable concomitant of rejection, she strives to minimize that hurt "by dealing with [his] needs as best I can without compromising my own . . . that's a big point for me, because the thing in my life to this point has been always compromising, and I am not willing to do that any more." Instead, she seeks to act in a "decent, human kind of way . . . one that leaves maybe a slightly shook but not totally destroyed person." Thus the "nonentity" confronts her power to destroy which formerly had impeded any assertion, as she consider the possibility for a new kind of action that leaves both self and other intact.

The moral concern remains a concern with hurting as she considers Kohlberg's Heinz dilemma in terms of the question, "who is going to be hurt more, the druggist who loses some money or the person who loses their life?" The right to property and right to life are weighed not in the abstract, in terms of their logical priority, but rather in the particular, in terms of the actual consequences that the violation of these rights would have in the lives of the people involved. Thinking remains contextual and admixed with feelings of care, as the moral imperative to avoid hurt begins to be informed by a psychological understanding of the meaning of nonviolence.

Thus, release from the intimidation of inequality finally allows the expression of a judgment that previously had been withheld. What women then enunciate is not a new morality, but a moral conception disentangled from the constraints that formerly had confused its perception and impeded its articulation. The willingness to express and take responsibility for judgment stems from the recognition of the psychological and moral necessity for an equation of worth between self and other. Responsibility for care then includes both self and other, and the obligation not to hurt, freed from conventional constraints, is reconstructed as a universal guide to moral choice.

The reality of hurt centers the judgment of a twenty-nine-year-old woman, married and the mother of a preschool child, as she struggles with the dilemma posed by a second pregnancy whose timing conflicts with her completion of an advanced degree. Saying that "I cannot deliberately do something that is bad or would hurt a another person because I can't live with having done that," she nevertheless confronts a situation in which hurt has become inevitable. Seeking that solution which would best protect both herself and others, she indicates, in her definition of morality, the ineluctable sense of connection which infuses and colors all of her thinking:

> [Morality is] doing what is appropriate and what is just within your circumstances, but ideally it is not going to affect—I was going to say, ideally it wouldn't negatively affect another person, but that is ridiculous, because decisions are always going to affect another person. But you see, what I am trying to say is that it is the person that is the center of the decision making, of that decision making about what's right and what's wrong.

The person who is the center of this decision making begins by denying, but then goes on to acknowledge, the conflicting nature both of her own needs and of her various responsibilities. Seeing the pregnancy as a manifestation of the inner conflict between her wish, on the one hand, "to be a college president" and, on the other, "to be making pottery and flowers and having kids and staying at home," she struggles with contradiction between femininity and adulthood. Considering abortion as the "better" choice—because "in the end, meaning this time next year or this time two weeks from now, it will be less of a personal strain on us individually and on us as a family for me not to be pregnant at this time," she concludes that the decision has

> got to be, first of all, something that the woman can live with—a decision that the woman can live with, one way or another, or at least try to live with, and that it be based on where she is at and other people, significant people in her life, are at.

At the beginning of the interview she had presented the dilemma in its conventional feminine construction, as a conflict between her own wish to have a baby and the wish of others for her to complete her education. On the basis of this construction she deemed it "selfish" to continue the pregnancy because it was something "I want to do." However, as she begins to examine her thinking, she comes to abandon as false this conceptualization of the problem, acknowledging the truth of her own internal conflict and elaborating the tension which she feels between her femininity and the adulthood of her work life. She describes herself as "going in two directions" and values that part of herself which is "incredibly passionate and sensitive"—her capacity to recognize and meet, often with anticipation, the needs of others. Seeing her "compassion" as "something I don't want to lose" she regards it as endangered by her pursuit of professional advancement. Thus the self-deception of her initial presentation, its attempt to sustain the fiction of her own innocence, stems from her fear that to say that *she* does not want to have another baby at this time would be

> an acknowledgement to me that I am an ambitious person and that I want to have power and responsibility for others and that I want to live a life that extends from 9 to 5 every day and into the evenings and on weekends, because that is what the power and responsibility means. It means that my family would necessarily come second . . . there would be such an incredible conflict about which is tops, and I don't want that for myself.

Asked about her concept of "an ambitious person" she says that to be ambitious means to be

> power hungry [and] insensitive. [Why insensitive?] Because people are stomped on in the process. A person on the way up stomps on people, whether it is family or other colleagues or clientele, on the way up. [Inevitably?] Not always, but I have seen it so often in my limited years of working that it is scary to me. It is scary because I don't want to change like that.

Because the acquisition of adult power is seen to entail the loss of feminine sensitivity and compassion, the conflict between femininity and adulthood becomes construed as a moral problem. The discovery of the principle of nonviolence begins to direct attention to the moral dilemma itself and initiates the search for a resolution that can encompass both femininity and adulthood.

## Developmental Theory Reconsidered

The developmental conception delineated at the outset, which has so consistently found the development of women to be either aberrant or incomplete, has been limited insofar as it has been predominantly a male conception, giving lip-service, a place on the chart, to the interdependence of intimacy and care but constantly stressing, at their expense, the importance and value of autonomous judgment and action. To admit to this conception the truth of the feminine perspective is to recognize for both sexes the central importance in adult life of the connection between self and other, the universality of the need for compassion and care. The concept of the separate self and of the moral principle uncompromised by the constraints of reality is an adolescent ideal, the elaborately wrought philosophy of a Stephen Daedalus, whose flight we know to be in jeopardy. Erikson (1964), in contrasting the ideological morality of the adolescent with the ethics of adult care, attempts to grapple with this problem of integration, but is impeded by the limitations of his own previous developmental conception. When his developmental stages chart a path where the sole precursor to the intimacy of adult relationships is the trust established in infancy and all intervening experience is marked only as steps toward greater independence, then separation itself becomes the model and the measure of growth. The observation that for women, identity has as much to do with connection as with separation led Erikson into trouble largely because of his failure to integrate this insight into the mainstream of his developmental theory (Erikson, 1968).

The morality of responsibility which women describe stands apart from the morality of rights which underlies Kohlberg's conception of the highest stages of moral judgment. Kohlberg (Note 3) sees the progression toward these stages as resulting from the generalization of the self-centered adolescent rejection of societal morality into a principled conception of individual natural rights. To illustrate this progression, he cites as an example of integrated Stage Five judgment, "possibly moving to Stage Six," the following response of a twenty-five-year-old subject from his male longitudinal sample:

> [What does the word morality mean to you?] Nobody in the world knows the answer. I think it is recognizing the right of the individual, the rights of other individuals, not interfering with those rights. Act as fairly as you would have them treat you. I think it is basically to preserve the human being's right to existence. I think that is the most important. Secondly, the human being's right to do as he pleases, again without interfering with somebody else's rights. (p. 29)

Another version of the same conception is evident in the following interview response of a male college senior whose moral judgment also was scored by Kohlberg (Note 4) as at Stage Five or Six:

> [Morality] is a prescription, it is a thing to follow, and the idea of having a concept of morality is to try to figure out what it is that people can do in order to make life with each other livable, make for a kind of balance, a kind of equilibrium, a harmony in which everybody feels he has a place and an equal share in things, and it's doing that—doing that is kind of contributing to a state of affairs that go beyond the individual in the absence of which, the individual has no chance for self-fulfillment of any kind. Fairness; morality is kind of essential, it seems to me, for creating the kind of environment, interaction between people, that is prerequisite to this fulfillment of most individual goals and so on. If you want other people to not interfere with your pursuit of whatever you are into, you have to play the game.

In contrast, a woman in her late twenties responds to a similar question by defining a morality not of rights but of responsibility:

> [What makes something a moral issue?] Some sense of trying to uncover a right path in which to live, and always in my mind is that the world is full of real and recognizable trouble, and is it heading for some sort of doom and is it right to bring children into this world when we currently have an overpopulation problem, and is it right to spend money on a pair of shoes when I have a pair of shoes and other people are shoeless. . . . It is part of a self-critical view, part of saying, how am I spending my time and in what sense am I working? I think I have a real drive to, I have a real maternal drive to take care of someone. To take care of my mother, to take care of children, to take care of other people's children, to take care of my own children, to take care of the world. I think that goes back to your other question, and when I am dealing with moral issues, I am sort of saying to myself constantly, are you taking care of all the things that you think are important and in what ways are you wasting yourself and wasting those issues?

While the postconventional nature of this woman's perspective seems clear, her judgments of Kohlberg's hypothetical moral dilemmas do not meet his criteria for scoring at the principled level. Kohlberg regards this as a disparity between normative and metaethical judgments which he sees as indicative of the transition between conventional and principled thinking. From another perspective, however, this judgment represents a different moral conception, disentangled from societal conventions and raised to the principled level. In this conception, moral judgment is oriented toward issues of responsibility. The way in which the responsibility orientation guides moral decision at the postconventional level is described by the following woman in her thirties:

> [Is there a right way to make moral decisions?] The only way I know is to try to be as awake as possible, to try to know the range of what you feel, to try to consider all that's involved, to be as aware as you can be to what's going on, as conscious as you can of where you're walking. [Are there principles that guide you?] The principle would have something to do with responsibility, responsibility and caring about yourself and others. . . . But it's not that on the one hand you choose to be responsible and on the other hand you choose to be irresponsible—both ways you can be responsible. That's why there's not just a principle that once you take hold of you settle—the principle put into practice here is still going to leave you with conflict.

The moral imperative that emerges repeatedly in the women's interviews is an injunction to care, a responsibility to discern and alleviate the "real and recognizable trouble" of this world. For the men Kohlberg studied, the moral imperative appeared rather as an injunction to respect the rights of others and thus to protect from interference the right to life and self-fulfillment. Women's insistence on care is at first self-critical rather than self-protective, while men initially conceive obligation to others negatively in terms of noninterference. Development for both sexes then would seem to entail an integration of rights and responsibilities through the discovery of the complementarity of these disparate views. For the women I have studied, this integration between rights and responsibilities appears to take place through a principled understanding of equity and reciprocity. This understanding tempers the self-destructive potential of a self-critical morality by asserting the equal right of all persons to care. For the men in Kohlberg's sample as well as for those in a longitudinal study of Harvard undergraduates (Gilligan & Murphy, Note 5) it appears to be the recognition through experience of the need for a more active responsibility in taking care that corrects the potential indifference of a morality of noninterference and turns attention from the logic to the consequences of choice. In the development of a postconventional ethic understanding, women come to see the violence generated by inequitable relationships, while men come to realize the limitations of a conception of justice blinded to the real inequities of human life.

Kohlberg's dilemmas, in the hypothetical abstraction of their presentation, divest the moral actors from the history and psychology of their individual lives and separate the moral problem from the social contingencies of its possible occurrence. In doing so, the dilemmas are useful for the distillation and refinement of the "objective principles of justice" toward which Kohlberg's stages strive. However, the reconstruction of the dilemma in its contextual particularity allows the understanding of cause and consequence which engages the compassion and tolerance considered by previous theorists to qualify the feminine sense of justice. Only when substance is given to the skeletal lives of hypothetical people is it possible to consider the social injustices which their moral problems may reflect and to imagine the individual suffering their occurrence may signify or their resolution engender.

The proclivity of women to reconstruct hypothetical dilemmas in terms of the real, to request or supply the information missing about the nature of the people and the places where they live, shifts their judgment away from the hierarchical ordering of principles and the formal procedures of decision making that are critical for scoring at Kohlberg's highest stages. This insistence on the particular signifies an orientation to the dilemma and to moral problems in general that differs from any of Kohlberg's stage descriptions. Given the constraints of Kohlberg's system and the biases in his research sample, this different orientation can only be construed as a failure in development. While several of the women in the research sample clearly articulated what Kohlberg regarded as a postconventional metaethical position, none of them were considered by Kohlberg to be principled in their normative moral judgments of his hypothetical moral dilemmas (Note 4). Instead, the women's judgments pointed toward an identification of the violence inherent in the dilemma itself which was seen to compromise the justice of any of its possible resolutions. This construction of the dilemma led the women to recast the moral judgment from a consideration of the good to a choice between evils.

The woman whose judgment of the abortion dilemma concluded the developmental sequence presented in the preceding section saw Kohlberg's Heinz dilemma in these terms and judged Heinz's action in terms of a choice between selfishness and sacrifice. For Heinz to steal the drug, given the circumstances of his life (which she inferred from his inability to pay two thousand dollars), he would have "to do something which is not in his best interest, in that he is going to get sent away, and that is a supreme sacrifice, a sacrifice which I would say a person truly in love might be willing to make." However, not to steal the drug "would be selfish on his part . . . he would just have to feel guilty about not allowing her a chance to live longer." Heinz's decision to steal is considered not in terms of the logical priority of life over property which justifies its rightness, but rather in terms of the actual consequences that stealing would have for a man of limited means and little social power.

Considered in the light of its probable outcomes—his wife dead, or Heinz in jail, brutalized by the violence of that experience and his life compromised by a record of felony—the dilemma itself changes. Its resolution has less to do with the relative weights of life and property in an abstract moral conception than with the collision it has produced between two lives, formerly conjoined but now in opposition, where the continuation of one life can now occur only at the expense of the other. Given this construction, it becomes clear why consideration revolves around the issue of sacrifice and why guilt becomes the inevitable concomitant of either resolution.

Demonstrating the reticence noted in the first section about making moral judgments, this woman explains her reluctance to judge in terms of her belief

> that everybody's existence is so different that I kind of say to myself, that might be something that I wouldn't do, but I can't say that it is right or wrong for that person. I can only deal with what is appropriate for me to do when I am faced with specific problems.

Asked if she would apply to others her own injunction against hurting, she says:

> See, I can't say that it is wrong. I can't say that it is right or that it's wrong because I don't know what the person did that the other person did something to hurt him . . . so it is not right that the person got hurt, but it is right that the person who just lost the job has got to get that anger up and out. It doesn't put any bread on his table, but it is released. I don't mean to be copping out. I really am trying to see how to answer these questions for you.

Her difficulty in answering Kohlberg's questions, her sense of strain with the construction which they impose on the dilemma, stems from their divergence from her own frame of reference:

> I don't even think I use the words right and wrong anymore, and I know I don't use the word moral, because I am not sure I know what it means. . . . We are talking about an unjust society, we are talking about a whole lot of things that are not right, that are truly wrong, to use the word that I don't use very often, and I have no control to change that. If I could change it, I certainly would, but I can only make my small contribution from day to day, and if I don't intentionally hurt somebody, that is my contribution to a better society. And so a chunk of that contribution is also not to pass judgment on other people, particularly when I don't know the circumstances of why they are doing certain things.

The reluctance to judge remains a reluctance to hurt, but one that stems now not from a sense of personal vulnerability but rather from a recognition of the limitations of judgment itself. The deference of the conventional feminine perspective can thus be seen to continue at the postconventional level, not as moral relativism but rather as part of a reconstructed moral understanding. Moral judgment is renounced in an awareness of the psychological and social determinism of all human behavior at the same time as moral concern is reaffirmed in recognition of the reality of human pain and suffering.

> I have a real thing about hurting people and always have, and that gets a little complicated at times, because, for example, you don't want to hurt your child. I don't want to hurt my child but if I don't hurt her sometimes, then that's hurting her more, you see, and so that was a terrible dilemma for me.

Moral dilemmas are terrible in that they entail hurt; she sees Heinz's decision as "the result of anguish, who am I hurting, why do I have to hurt them." While the morality of Heinz's theft is not in question, given the circumstances which necessitated it, what is at issue is his willingness to substitute himself for his wife and become, in her stead, the victim of exploitation by a society which breeds and legitimizes the druggist's irresponsibility and whose injustice is thus manifest in the very occurrence of the dilemma.

The same sense that the wrong questions are being asked is evident in the response of another woman who justified Heinz's action on a similar basis, saying "I don't think that exploitation should really be a right." When women begin to make direct moral statements, the issues they repeatedly address are those of exploitation and hurt. In doing so, they raise the issue of nonviolence in precisely the same psychological context that brought Erikson (1969) to pause in his consideration of the truth of Gandhi's life.

In the pivotal letter, around which the judgment of his book turns, Erikson confronts the contradiction between the philosophy of nonviolence that informed Gandhi's dealing with the British and the psychology of violence that marred his relationships with his family and with the children of the ashram. It was this contradiction, Erikson confesses,

> which almost brought *me* to the point where I felt unable to continue writing *this* book because I seemed to sense the presence of a kind of untruth in the very protestation of truth; of something unclean when all the words spelled out an unreal purity; and, above all, of displaced violence where nonviolence was the professed issue. (p. 231)

In an effort to untangle the relationship between the spiritual truth of Satyagraha and the truth of his own psychoanalytic understanding, Erikson reminds Gandhi that "Truth, you once said, 'excludes the use of violence because man is not capable of knowing the absolute truth and therefore is not competent to punish' " (p. 241). The affinity between Satyagraha and psychoanalysis lies in their shared commitment to seeing life as an "experiment in truth," in their being

> somehow joined in a universal "therapeutics," committed to the Hippocratic principle that one can test truth (or the healing power inherent in a sick situation) only by action which avoids harm—or better, by action which maximizes mutuality and minimizes the violence caused by unilateral coercion or threat. (p. 247)

Erikson takes Gandhi to task for his failure to acknowledge the relativity of truth. This failure is manifest in the coercion of Gandhi's claim to exclusive possession of the truth, his "unwillingness to learn from *anybody anything* except what was approved by the "inner voice' " (p. 236). This claim led Gandhi, in the guise of love, to impose his truth on others without awareness or regard for the extent to which he thereby did violence to their integrity.

The moral dilemma, arising inevitably out of a conflict of truths, is by definition a "sick situation" in that its either/or formulation leaves no room for an outcome that does not do violence. The resolution of such dilemmas, however, lies not in the self-deception of rationalized violence—"I was" said Gandhi, "a cruelly kind husband. I regarded myself as her teacher and so harassed her out of my blind love for her" (p. 233)—but rather in the replacement of the underlying antagonism with a mutuality of respect and care.

Gandhi, whom Kohlberg has mentioned as exemplifying Stage Six moral judgment and whom Erikson sought as a model of an adult ethical sensibility, instead is criticized by a judgment that refuses to look away from or condone the infliction of harm. In denying the validity of his wife's reluctance to open her home to strangers and in his blindness to the different reality of adolescent sexuality and temptation, Gandhi compromised in his everyday life the ethic of nonviolence to which in principle and in public he was so steadfastly committed.

The blind willingness to sacrifice people to truth, however, has always been the danger of an ethics abstracted from life. This willingness links Gandhi to the biblical Abraham, who prepared to sacrifice the life of his son in order to demonstrate the integrity and supremacy of his faith. Both men, in the limitations of their fatherhood, stand in implicit contrast to the woman who comes before Solomon and verifies her motherhood by relinquishing truth in order to save the life of her child. It is the ethics of an adulthood that has become principled at the expense of care that Erikson comes to criticize in his assessment of Gandhi's life.

This same criticism is dramatized explicitly as a contrast between the sexes in *The Merchant of Venice* (1598/1912), where Shakespeare goes through an extraordinary complication of sexual identity (dressing a male actor as a female character who in turn poses as a male judge) in order to bring into the masculine citadel of justice the feminine plea for mercy. The limitation of the contractual conception of justice is illustrated through the absurdity of its literal execution, while the "need to make exceptions all the time" is demonstrated contrapuntally in the matter of the rings. Portia, in calling for mercy, argues for that resolution in which no one is hurt, and as the men are forgiven for their failure to keep both their rings and their word, Antonio in turn foregoes his "right" to ruin Shylock.

The research findings that have been reported in this essay suggest that women impose a distinctive construction on moral problems, seeing moral dilemmas in terms of conflicting responsibilities. This construction was found to develop through a sequence of three levels and two transitions, each level representing a more complex understanding of the relationship between self and other and each transition involving a critical reinterpretation of the moral conflict between selfishness and responsibility. The development of women's moral judgment appears to proceed from an initial concern with survival, to a focus on goodness, and finally to a principled understanding of nonviolence as the most adequate guide to the just resolution of moral conflicts.

In counterposing to Kohlberg's longitudinal research on the development of hypothetical moral judgment in men a cross-sectional study of women's responses to actual dilemmas of moral conflict and choice, this essay precludes the possibility of generalization in either direction and leaves to further research the task of sorting out the different variables of occasion and sex. Longitudinal studies of women's moral judgments are necessary in order to validate the claims of stage and sequence presented here. Similarly, the contrast drawn between the moral judgments of men and women awaits for its confirmation a more systematic comparison of the responses of both sexes. Kohlberg's research on moral development has confounded the variables of age, sex, type of decision, and type of dilemma by presenting a single configuration (the responses of adolescent males to hypothetical dilemmas of conflicting rights) as the basis for a universal stage sequence. This paper underscores the need for systematic treatment of these variables and points toward their study as a critical task for future moral development research.

For the present, my aim has been to demonstrate the centrality of the concepts of responsibility and care in women's constructions of the moral domain, to indicate the close tie in women's thinking between conceptions of the self and conceptions of morality, and, finally, to argue the need for an expanded developmental theory that would include, rather than rule out from developmental consideration, the difference in the feminine voice. Such an inclusion seems essential, not only for explaining the development of women but also for understanding in both sexes the characteristics and precursors of an adult moral conception.

## Notes

1. Haan, N. *Activism as moral protest: Moral judgments of hypothetical dilemmas and an actual situation of civil disobedience.* Unpublished manuscript. University of California at Berkeley, 1971.
2. Turiel, E. *A comparative analysis of moral knowledge and moral judgment in males and females.* Unpublished manuscript, Harvard University, 1973
3. Kohlberg, L. *Continuities and discontinuities in childhood and adult moral development revisited.* Unpublished paper, Harvard University, 1973.
4. Kohlberg, L. Personal communication, August, 1976.
5. Gilligan, C., & Murphy, M. *The philosopher and the "dilemma of the fact": Moral development in late adolescence and adulthood.* Unpublished manuscript. Harvard University, 1977.

# References

Broverman, I., Vogel, S., Broverman, D., Clarkson, F., & Rosenkrantz, P. Sex-role stereotypes: A current appraisal. *Journal of Social issues*, 1972, 28, 59–78.

Coles, R. *Children of crisis*. Boston: Little, Brown, 1964.

Didion, J. The women's movement. *New York Times Book Review*, July 30, 1972, pp. 1–2; 14.

Drabble. M. *The waterfall*. Hammondsworth, Eng.: Penguin Books, 1969.

Eliot, G. *The mill on the floss*. New York: New American Library, 1965. (Originally published, 1860.)

Erikson, E. H. *Insight and responsibility*. New York: W. W. Norton, 1964.

Erikson, E. H. *Identity: Youth and crisis*. New York: W. W. Norton, 1968.

Erikson, E. H. *Gandhi's truth*. New York: W. W. Norton, 1969.

Freud, S. "Civilized" sexual morality and modern nervous illness. In J. Strachey (Ed.), *The standard edition of the complete psychological works of Sigmund Freud* (Vol. 9). London: Hogarth Press, 1959. (Originally published, 1908.)

Freud, S. Some psychical consequences of the anatomical distinction between the sexes. In J. Strachey (Ed.), *The standard edition of the complete psychological works of Sigmund Freud* (Vol. 19). London: Hogarth Press, 1961. (Originally published, 1925.)

Gilligan, C., Kohlberg, L., Lerner, J., & Belenky, M. Moral reasoning about sexual dilemmas: The development of an interview and scoring system. *Technical Report of the President's Commission on Obscenity and Pornography* (Vol. 1) [415 060–137]. Washington, D.C.: U.S. Government Printing Office, 1971.

Haan, N. Hypothetical and actual moral reasoning in a situation of civil disobedience. *Journal of Personality and Social Psychology*, 1975, 32, 255–270.

Holstein, C. Development of moral judgment: A longitudinal study of males and females. *Child Development*, 1976, 47, 51–61.

Horner, M. Toward an understanding of achievement-related conflicts in women. *Journal of Social Issues*, 1972, 29, 157–174.

Ibsen, H. *A doll's house*. In *Ibsen plays*. Hammondsworth, Eng.: Penguin Books, 1965. (Originally published, 1879.)

Kohlberg, L. From is to ought: How to commit the naturalistic fallacy and get away with it in the study of moral development. In T. Mischel (Ed.), *Cognitive development and epistemology*. New York: Academic Press, 1971.

Kohlberg, L., & Gilligan, C. The adolescent as a philosopher: The discovery of the self in a postconventional world. *Daedalus*, 1971, 100, 1051–1056.

Kohlberg, L., & Kramer, R. Continuities and discontinuities in childhood and adult moral development. *Human Development*, 1969, 12, 93–120.

Piaget, J. *The moral judgment of the child*. New York: The Free Press, 1965. (Originally published, 1932.)

Shakespeare, W. *The merchant of Venice*. In *The comedies of Shakespeare*. London: Oxford University Press, 1912. (Originally published, 1598.)

# CHAPTER 28
# A NEO-KOHLBERGIAN APPROACH TO MORALITY RESEARCH

JAMES R. REST, DARCIA NARVAEZ, STEPHEN J. THOMA, AND MURIEL J. BEBEAU

Kohlberg's work in moral judgement has been criticised by many philosophers and psychologists. Building on Kohlberg's core assumptions, we propose a model of moral judgement (hereafter the neo-Kohlbergian approach) that addresses these concerns. Using 25 years of data gathered with the Defining Issues Test (DIT), we present an overview of Minnesota's neo-Kohlbergian approach, using Kohlberg's basic starting points, ideas from Cognitive Science (especially schema theory), and developments in moral philosophy.

## Kohlberg's Legacy

Foremost in Larry Kohlberg's legacy is his modelling of openness to new developments and possibilities. When he was first formulating his theory of moral development, the work of Jean Piaget was coming to the attention of American psychologists (e.g. Flavell, 1963), and the work of John Rawls in moral philosophy (1971) was recognised as a new way for moral philosophy to say something significant (beyond clarifying moral language) about normative ethics. Kohlberg's fusion of Piaget and Rawls excited many researchers because of its interdisciplinary approach (taking seriously the questions and contributions of developmental psychology and of normative ethics), and because it addressed issues of the day (e.g. what is social justice?). Recall that in the 1960s and 1970s the US Civil Rights movement, the Vietnam War and the Watergate Scandal were all controversial issues that divided American society. Kohlberg offered a perspective that drew upon the most current work in psychology and philosophy, yet addressed these timely issues.

Kohlberg's ideas dominated the agenda of morality research for decades. In a recent analysis of Kohlberg's writings, Reed (1997) shows that Kohlberg was not particularly concerned with logical consistency among his many projects. Reed contends that Kohlberg's early ventures into moral education, based on a cognitive model of individual moral development (the Six Stage Theory), was not consistent with his later approach, which emphasised the development of community norms (the "Just Community"). Moreover, Kohlberg changed and modified his proposals for a theory of development as he went along: he changed his scoring system of stages throughout the 1970s and 1980s; in various ways he tried to relate "care" to "justice," and his debates with the Social Learning Theo-

Rest, J. R., Narvaez, D., Thoma, S. J., & Bebeau, M. J. (2000). A neo-Kohlbergian approach to morality research. *Journal of Moral Education, 29,* 381–395.

rists (e.g. Kohlberg, 1969) had many vicissitudes. Kohlberg's ideas were in constant flux. As he once confided, he was a moving target and considered himself as his own major revisionist. Therefore it would be a mistake to use his 1981 and 1984 books as the final word on a Kohlbergian approach. One wonders how Kohlberg would have changed his theory, given another decade and a normal life span.

With the benefit of hindsight, with decades of new developments in psychology and philosophy, it remains for others to decide which of Kohlberg's many ideas have turned out to be fruitful. In this article, we audaciously set out to do this and to propose some new ideas, realising, with Kohlberg, that this is an ongoing enterprise, open to revision, and likely to change.

## A Neo-Kohlbergian Viewpoint

Several factors bring us to our discussion. After 25 years of data collection, we have completed a full generation of research with the Defining Issues Test (hereafter referred to as the DIT). Advances in personal computers and technology make possible analyses that heretofore were impractical (e.g. sample sizes of 50,000). Further, the field of morality research has been fragmented and not dominated by any one approach—therefore we feel free to explore theory and research that do not employ a standard approach. In addition, the fields of psychology and philosophy are moving in directions especially congenial to our research. Much of our activity until 1997 is summarised in a recent book, *Postconventional Moral Thinking: a neo-Kohlbergian approach* (Rest et al., 1999).

We follow Kohlberg's approach to conceptualising moral judgement (see Rest et al., 1999, for fuller discussion). (a) Like Kohlberg, our starting point emphasises cognition. Kohlberg realised there were many starting points for morality research (for instance, one might start out emphasising an evolutionary biosocial perspective, and investigate certain emotions such as empathy, altruism, guilt and shame; or one might focus on the young infant's acquisition of prosocial behaviour). Everyone must begin somewhere, making assumptions and emphasising some things over other things. Despite the limitations of any starting point, the crucial question is, "Having started there, where did it lead? What important phenomena have been illuminated?" (b) Like Kohlberg, we highlight the personal construction of basic epistemological categories (e.g. "rights," "duty," "justice," "social order," "reciprocity"). This is not to deny the contribution that cultural ideologies make. Ideologies are group-derived, tools and practices of a culture. We, however, focus on the individual's attempt to make sense of his/her own social experience. (c) We portray change over time in terms of development (i.e. it is possible to talk not only of differences in moral orientation, but also of cognitive "advance" in which "higher is better" in a philosophical, normative-ethical sense). Finally, (d) we characterise the developmental change of adolescents and adults in terms of a shift from conventional to postconventional moral thinking (we think there is a sequence rather than Turiel's notion [e.g. 1983] of these being separate domains). We think these four ideas are the core assumptions of Kohlberg's "cognitive-developmental" approach. This is the Kohlbergian part of our neo-Kohlbergian approach. Because these ideas have been much discussed previously (e.g. Kohlberg, 1969, 1981, 1984, 1986; Colby et al., 1983, 1987), we will not elaborate on them here.

## Philosophers' Criticisms of Kohlberg

Over the past decades, there have been major developments in moral philosophy (e.g. Degrazia, 1992; Beauchamp & Childress, 1994; Rest et al., 1999), including the abandonment of the view that morality is primarily based on a Foundational Principle. In Kohlberg's time—in the 1960s and 1970s—many understood the business of moral philosophy as that of defining and defending the Foundational Principle of morality (be it utilitarian, or deontological, or some mix of principles, etc.). It was assumed that settling on the Foundational Principle (e.g. greatest good for the greatest number, the Categorical Imperative, Rawls's Two Principles of Justice, etc.) would provide the key for solving deductively all moral problems. Accordingly, the main job of the theoretical philosopher was to define the key Foundational Principle. The job of the applied philosopher was to articulate its application to specific cases. The job of the moral educator was to enable people to know and use this key principle in their daily lives.

However, philosophers—whom we suppose are rational, fair-minded and autonomous people—have not been able to agree on the Foundational Principle. The experience of Stephen Toulmin (1981) is instructive. Toulmin, an American bioethicist, was appointed to serve on the US National Commission for the Protection of Human Subjects along with 10 other appointees. Their job was to adopt guidelines for the use of humans in research for the US government. The 11 commissioners found that they could reach consensus on moral judgements about specific cases, but they could not agree on which abstract principles justified their judgements of specific cases. Toulmin challenged the notion that morality proceeds "top-down," from abstract principles applied to specific cases. Rather, he argued, morality is fashioned like common law by people reflecting on specific cases, reaching agreement on specific cases, then analysing similar cases to the paradigm cases, building up a "common morality" as the logical interconnections among cases are established.

Walzer (1983) presents a theoretical account of the view that morality is not based on a Foundational Principle but, rather, the morality of a community is gradually built up from the specific experiences of the community in dealing with specific cases. Walzer describes the growth of "common morality" in particular historical communities (e.g. Athens in 5 BC, and the medieval Jewish communities in Europe). Walzer describes how each community faced different moral problems, provided different services for different clienteles, had different organisational apparatuses to deal with problems, raised money in different ways, and conceptualised the practices differently in their moral ideologies. Thus, Walzer argues, the development of morality is not to be understood as an individual's applying a Foundational Principle, but rather the community's reaching agreement about how best to fulfill shareable moral ideals to suit the circumstances.

With these developments in moral philosophy, we can begin to appreciate the difficulties that philosophers have with Kohlberg's definition of Stage 6. The Kohlbergian view of Six Stages is criticised as assuming Foundational Principlism, as deductivistic rather than inductivistic, as too individually orientated rather than community-orientated, as assuming consensus for deontic principles where there is no consensus, for criticising relativism when the assumption of universality is unwarranted, and for assuming that abstract principles provide sufficient guidance for making specific moral decisions (see discussion in Rest et al., 1999).

In addition, Kohlberg is criticised for not having a fully comprehensive theory of morality or moral development (focusing on justice; using a few unrepresentative hypothetical dilemmas; emphasising rational aspects of morality while neglecting emotional aspects; claiming universality on the basis of studying a very limited sector of humanity, etc.). In his later writings, Kohlberg acknowledged the limited scope of his theory and investigations, that his theory starts out with assumptions—just as all theories must start out with limited starting points—and acknowledged that additional constructs and variables were necessary to explain the multitudinous phenomena of morality (Kohlberg, 1986, pp. 499–500). And so the criticism—Kohlberg did not tell us everything about morality—is not really a telling criticism about a theory with an acknowledged limited scope (see Rest et al., 1999).

## Differences with Kohlberg's Theory of Six Stages

We use the term moral schemas (discussed below), rather than moral stages, to signal differences with Kohlberg's conception of "hard" moral stages. Our view of the cognitive structures of moral judgement differ from Kohlberg's stages in the following five ways (the points are not discrete points but are all interconnected):

(a) "Hard" stages versus "soft" stages. We differ with Kohlberg on the concept of "stage"; we envision development as shifting distributions rather than as a staircase. Like Siegler (1997), we believe that development is a matter of changes in the frequency of usage, moving from the less to the more complex.

(b) More specific and concrete. Our schemas are more concrete than Kohlberg's stages (but are more abstract than the typical schemas of Social Cognition (e.g. person schemas, role schemas). Our schemas are conceptions of institutions and role-systems in society, whereas Kohlberg regards social institutions as "content." In other words, we have three ways of drawing the distinction between content and structure: Kohlberg's, the neo-Kohlbergian approach in the DIT and Social Cognition. All distinguish general cognitive structure from the content instantiations that can exemplify the structure, but the three draw the distinction at different levels of abstraction.

(c) Cognitive operations and the content-output of operations. Instead of Kohlberg's claim of studying "justice operations," we do not claim that our schemas directly assess cognitive operations. The Colby-Kohlberg scoring system (Colby et al., 1987) explains how one must radically purge content from structure in order to assess the operations of moral thinking. Kohlberg spent the last decade of his life working on the 1987 scoring system to radically purge content from structure. He seems to have assumed that the more abstract the analysis, the more pure the assessment of operations. In contrast, Cognitive Science has not been so eager to purge all content from structure. Gazzaniga et al. (1998) stated that mental operations are the most elusive aspect of cognitive assessment:

> A vast amount of research in cognitive science clearly shows we are conscious only of the content of our mental life, not what generates the content. It is the products of mnemonic processing, of perceptual processing, of imaging, that we are aware of—not what produced the products. Sometimes people report on what they think were the processes, but they are reporting after the fact on what they thought they did to produce the content of their consciousness (p. 532).

(d) Universality. Kohlberg postulated universality as a characteristic of stages whereas we regard cross-cultural similarity as an empirical question. He saw a universalistic morality as the bulwark against moral relativism in which a Nazi officer could defend his role in the Holocaust as simply following the relativist norms of his group. In contrast, recent moral philosophers (e.g. Beauchamp & Childress, 1994; Walzer, 1983) consider "Common Morality" as a community enterprise, relative to situation and circumstance (akin to the development of common law). According to this view, morality is a social construction, evolving from the community's experiences, particular institutional arrangements, deliberations, and the aspirations that are voiced at the time and which win the support of the community. Morality that is relative to group deliberation is not tantamount to the mindless moral relativism or moral scepticism that Kohlberg feared, nor does it pave the way to Nazi atrocities. Common morality might be different for different communities (and therefore relative), but the common morality is debated and scrutinized by members of the community and reflects an equilibrium between the ideals and the moral intuitions of the community.

(e) Articulation (interviewing task) versus tacit knowledge (multiple choice task). A common assumption in the field of morality, and one with which we disagree, is that reliable information about the inner processes that underlie moral behaviour is obtained only by asking people to explain their moral judgements. Contrary to assuming the face validity of interviews, researchers in Cognitive Science and Social Cognition contend that self-reported explanations of one's own cognitive processes have severe limitations (e.g. Nisbett & Wilson, 1977; Uleman & Bargh, 1989). People can report on the products of cognition but not on the mental operations they used to arrive at the product. A large body of research calls into question the privileged place of interview data, dependent on conscious understanding, over recognition data, dependent on implicit understanding.

By requiring participants in research to construct verbal arguments for their moral choices, and to credit someone only with cognition that they can articulate and defend, Kohlberg placed a verbal constraint that credited people with only understanding what they could explain. We believe that this is one reason why there is so little empirical evidence for Stage 5 and 6 reasoning using

Kohlberg's scoring system. One advantage of the recognition task of the DIT is that postconventional thinking is not so rarely scored as in the Kohlberg interview.

## Developmental Schemas Instead of Stages

We postulate three structures in moral thinking development: the Personal Interest schema (which derives from Kohlberg's Stage 2 and 3, referred to henceforth as "S23"); the Maintaining Norms schema (deriving from Kohlberg's Stage 4, referred to as "S4"); and the Postconventional schema (deriving from Kohlberg's Stage 5 and 6, referred to as "S56").

Developmentally, a large social-cognitive advance in adolescence (the youngest group that we study with the DIT) is the "discovery of society"—that is, that people in society are related to each other through institutions, established practices, role-systems ("the system"), and not only on a face-to-face basis (as with kin, friends, well-known acquaintances). Not only does Kohlberg speak of this development (attaining a sociocentric perspective) in adolescence (1984), but others do also (e.g. Adelson, 1971; Youniss & Yates, 1997). Awareness that society is organised in terms of a system of rules, roles and institutions raises questions about the morality of society and questions of moral authority. (How does one organise a network of co-operation on a society-wide basis, where there is full reciprocity and mutual benefit? How are power, wealth and opportunity to be distributed? What is the legitimate use of force?) These are the issues of "macro-morality" as distinct from issues of "micro-morality" (i.e. how a person interacts with others in everyday face-to-face situations). In our view, the three moral schemas are developmentally ordered ways of answering the "macro" question (how to get along with people who are not friends, kin or personal acquaintances, i.e. how to organise society-wide co-operation).

## Personal Interest Schema

We suppose that the Personal Interest schema develops in childhood and that by the time participants have sufficient reading ability to take the DIT (i.e. have a 12-year-old reading level), this schema is no longer central in their thinking. The Personal Interest schema does not entail a sociocentric perspective. Questions addressing societal co-operation are answered as if there were only "micro-moral" relationships to consider. Individuals using the Personal Interest schema analyse what each stakeholder in a moral dilemma has to gain and lose as if they did not have to worry about organising cooperation on a society-wide basis. The "Personal Interest" schema justifies a decision as morally right by appealing to the personal stake the actor has in the consequences of an action. The Personal Interest schema includes individual prudential concerns and concerns for those with whom one has an affectionate relationship. Thus it has elements described by Kohlbergian Stages 2 and 3 because the two elements fuse together as a single factor in DIT data. In DIT data, both Stage 2 and Stage 3 items are regarded as more primitive forms of thinking (see factor analysis results, discussed in Rest et al., 1999). On the whole, DIT research cannot offer insight into development in childhood, or into the distinctions within the Personal Interest schema.

## The Maintaining Norms Schema

We suppose that the Maintaining Norms schema is developmentally more advanced in attaining a sociocentric perspective (one has to consider how people who are not friends, kin or well-known acquaintances are going to cooperate). With the Maintaining Norms schema, the individual is able to identify the established practice (the existing rules and roles) and who are the de facto authorities. Functionally, the Maintaining Norms schema is a prevalent first solution to conceptualising society-wide co-operation. Examples include Kohlberg's "Law and Order" stage (1984) and Richard Nixon's "Silent Majority"; McClosky and Brill (1983) talk about the "Conservative" orientation; Adelson (1971) talked about the "Authoritarianism" of adolescence. Common to all of these, the Maintaining Norms schema has the following elements. (a) The perceived need for generally accepted social norms to govern a collective. (b) The necessity that the norms apply society-wide, to all people in a society. (c) The need for the norms to be clear, uniform, and categorical (that there is "the rule of law"). (d) The norms are seen as establishing a reciprocity (each citizen obeys the law, expecting that others will also obey). (e) The establishment of hierarchical role structures, of chains of command, of authority and duty. That is, in an organised society, there are hierarchical role structures (e.g. teacher—pupil, parent—child, general—soldier, doctor—patient, etc.). One must obey authorities, not necessarily out of respect for the personal qualities of the authority, but out of respect for the social system.

For the Maintaining Norms schema, maintaining the established social order defines morality. In the Maintaining Norms schema, "law" is connected to "order" in a moral sense. The schema leads to the expectation that without law (and duty to one's roles), there would be no order, people would instead act on their own special interests, leading to anarchy—a situation that responsible people want to prevent. For this schema, no further rationale for defining morality is necessary beyond simply asserting that an act is prescribed by the law, is the established way of doing things, or is the established Will of God. The schema, Maintaining Norms, is consonant with "Legal Positivism" (Hart, 1961, pp. 181–182, 253–254) in the sense that neither appeals to moral criteria beyond the law itself. Acquisition of this schema is what gives Conventional thinkers their sense of moral necessity for the maintenance of social order. In other words, the schema provides a sense of moral certainty ("I know I'm right for the sake of our entire society") and therefore fuels the special zeal of conventional thinkers.

## Postconventional Schema

Essential to postconventional thinking is that moral obligations are to be based on shared ideals, are fully reciprocal, and are open to scrutiny (i.e. subject to tests of logical consistency, experience of the community and coherence with accepted practice). Over the centuries, philosophers have proposed many visions for a society based on moral ideals (e.g. utilitarian, social contract, virtue-based, feminist, casuist, religious ideals). Not all moral theories fit our criteria of Postconventional schema: (a) emotivist theories of morality say that morality is nothing but the personal expression of approval or disapproval (e.g. Stevenson, 1937); (b) Nietzsche [e.g. 1886/1968] regarded cooperation as a bad idea and a ploy of the weak to hold down the strong; and (c) ethical approaches based on Fundamentalist/Orthodox religious views deny that their version of God's Will is open to scrutiny (see Beauchamp & Childress, 1994, for a discussion of the relative adequacy of various moral theories). However, most modern moral philosophies do fit our notion of postconventionality. They are based on ideals, the ideals are shareable, are open to debate and tests of logical consistency, and so on. Whereas Kohlberg was partisan to the neo-Kantian, deontological theory of John Rawls (1971), we attempt to side-step the current disputes of moral philosophy by adopting a looser, broader (less daring, more tepid) notion of cognitive advance. Instead of Kohlberg's definition of Stage 6 (in which the individual's cognitive operations achieve "ideal reciprocity," striking similarities to the theory of John Rawls), our definition of the Postconventional schema is not partial to any particular moral philosopher. Four elements comprise the Postconventional schema: primacy of moral criteria, appeal to an ideal, shareable ideals and full reciprocity (discussed in Rest et al., 1999, Ch. 3).

There has been, and still is, much dispute among moral philosophers about what ideals should govern society, how to optimise all the participants' welfare, who is a participant, what "fair-minded" and "impartial" mean, what "rational" and "equal" mean, what constitutes "logical coherence," and the relative importance of principles and paradigm cases. These issues are the unsettled business of much of current moral philosophy. Nevertheless, we focus on the gulf between conventionality and postconventionality (what Kohlberg regarded as the distinction between Stage 4 and Stage 5—Colby et al., 1987, Vol. 1, pp. 28–29). This gulf is what polarises people on so many public policy issues (e.g. rights of homosexuals, religion in public schools, euthanasia, abortion, women's roles, etc.), fuels the "Culture Wars" (Orthodoxy versus Progressivism: Hunter, 1991), and is the most important clash in ideology since the Cold War (religious fundamentalism versus secular modernism: see Marty & Appleby, 1993).

Like Kohlberg, we affirm a developmental progression from conventionality to postconventionality. A major difference between the Maintaining Norms schema and the Postconventional schema is how each attempts to establish a moral consensus: the strategy of the Maintaining Norms schema is to gain consensus by appealing to established practice and existing authority. In contrast, the strategy of the Postconventional schema is to gain consensus by appealing to ideals and logical coherence. Like Kohlberg, we assert not only that there are different cognitive structures for moral judgement, but also that they are developmentally ordered—the Postconventional schema is more advanced (in a normative ethical sense) than the Maintaining Norms schema. The cognitive developmental distinction, however, is not the same thing as the distinction in political ideology between the right-wing and left-wing. It is possible to be conventional left-wing (e.g. Political Correctness) as well as conventional right-wing (George Wallace's *Law and Order*). It is possible to be postconventional left-wing (Rawls, 1971, 1993) and postconventional Conservative (e.g. Sandel, 1982), Communitarian (Walzer, 1983) or Libertarian (Nozick, 1974).

## The Relation of Schemas to Measuring Moral Judgement

Schemas are general knowledge structures residing in long-term memory (see, for example, Rummelhart, 1980; Taylor & Crocker, 1981). Schemas (expectations, hypotheses, concepts) are formed as people notice similarities and recurrences in experiences. A schema consists of a representation of some prior stimulus phenomenon and is used to interpret new information (sometimes referred to as "top-down" processing). Schemas are evoked (or "activated") by current stimulus configurations that resemble previous stimuli. The functions of schemas are essential to human understanding. For example, schemas fill in information where information is scarce or ambiguous, provide guidance for evaluating information and for problem-solving. In short, schemas facilitate information processing.

The DIT is a device for activating moral schemas. Reading moral dilemmas and the DIT issue statements activates moral schemas (to the extent that a person has developed them). The items of the DIT are fragments of lines of reasoning; the items are not complete orations arguing for one course of action or another. (The items are often in the form of questions, without advocating one course of action or another.) The items balance "bottom-up" processing (stating just enough of a line of argument for understanding) with "top-down" processing (stating not too much of a line of argument so that the participant has to "fill in" the meaning from schemas already in long-term memory). As the participant encounters a DIT item that both makes sense and also activates a preferred schema, that item is given a high rating and ranked as being of high importance. Alternatively, when the participant encounters an item that either does not make sense or seems simplistic and unconvincing (is not activating a preferred schema), the item receives a low rating. In a sense, the DIT is a "projective test" in that the fragmented nature of the items requires the participant to supply meaning to the items that they are rating. By the patterns of ratings and rankings, we arrive at estimates of the relative strength of the three schemas.

## Measuring Moral Judgement with the DIT

The book, *Postconventional Moral Thinking* (Rest et al., 1999, Ch. 4) is devoted to citing the literature on moral judgement using the DIT, consisting of over 400 published articles plus a considerable number of studies that are not published supporting seven validity and reliability criteria. Here, we highlight our general strategy for establishing validity and give brief conclusions.

The seven criteria operationalise what we mean by "construct validity" for a test of moral judgement. That is, these criteria set forth what we believe a measure of moral judgement development must demonstrate to be viable. The seven criteria are as follows: ( 1) differentiation of various age/education groups; (2) longitudinal gains; (3) correlation with cognitive capacity measures; (4) sensitivity to moral education interventions; (5) correlation with behaviour and professional decision making; (6) predicting to political choice and attitude; and (7) reliability. Briefly, here are the conclusions from Rest et al. (1999, Ch. 4):

1. Differentiation of various age/education groups. Studies of large composite samples (thousands of subjects) show that 30–50% of the variance of DIT scores is attributable to level of education in samples ranging from junior-high education to PhDs.

2. Longitudinal gains. A 10-year longitudinal study shows significant gains of men and women, of college-attenders and people not attending college, from diverse walks of life. A review of a dozen studies of freshman to senior students in liberal arts colleges (n = 755) shows effect sizes of 0.80 ("large" gains). DIT gains are one of the most dramatic longitudinal gains in college of any variable studied in college students.

3. DIT scores are significantly related to cognitive capacity measures of moral comprehension (r = 0.60s), to recall and reconstruction of postconventional moral argument (Narvaez, 1998, 1999), to Kohlberg's measure and (to a lesser degree) to other cognitive developmental measures.

4. DIT scores are sensitive to moral education interventions. One review of over 50 intervention studies reports an effect size for dilemma discussion interventions to be 0.41 ("moderate" gains), whereas the effect size for comparison groups was only 0.09 ("small" gains).

5. DIT scores are significantly linked to many "prosocial" behaviours and to desired professional decision making. One review reports that 32 of 47 measures were statistically significant. Chapters in Rest and Narvaez (1994) link DIT scores to many aspects of professional decision making.

6. DIT scores are significantly linked to political attitudes and political choices—in a review of several dozen correlates with political attitude, DIT scores typically correlate in the range, r = 0.40–0.65. When combined in multiple regression with measures of cultural ideology, the combination predicts up to two-thirds of the variance in opinions about controversial public policy issues (such as abortion, religion in the public school, women's roles, rights of the accused, rights of homosexuals, free speech issues). Because such issues are among the most hotly debated issues of our time, the DIT's predictability to these issues is a phenomenon of importance.

7. Reliability. Cronbach's alpha is in the upper 0.70s/low 0.80s. Test-retest is about the same. In short, reliability is adequate.

Furthermore, DIT scores show discriminant validity from verbal ability/general intelligence and from conservative/liberal political attitudes (see review of more than 20 studies in Thoma et al., 1999). That is, the information in DIT scores predict to the seven validity criteria above and beyond that accounted for by scores of verbal ability/general intelligence or political attitude. Moreover, the DIT is equally valid for males and females. Sex (gender) accounts for less than one half of a per cent of the variance of the DIT, whereas education is 250 times more powerful in predicting DIT variance (Thoma, 1986).

Moreover, several developments have been made recently that increase the power of the validity trends. (a) We have devised a new developmental index for the DIT (N2 to replace the P index—Rest et al., 1999, 2000). (b) We have devised a new way to check for the reliability of data in a questionnaire (i.e. whether or not a participant is giving bogus data) (Rest et al., 1999). (c) We have completed preliminary testing of a new version of the DIT ("DIT2") with new dilemmas and new items that is more updated (Heinz is retired from active duty), is shorter, has clearer instructions, purges fewer subjects for bogus data, and is slightly more powerful on validity criteria. DIT2 indicates that new stories and items can be devised in place of the old "DIT1."

## Moving Beyond Moral Judgement Per Se

In the early 1970s, the DIT started out as a "quick and dirty" alternative to the arduous Kohlberg interview. The DIT was group-administered, multiple-choice and mechanically scored. As research began to accumulate, as the DIT provided consistent and reliable trends in moral judgement development, some of us began to think that the DIT was more than only "quick and dirty."

Recently, we have discovered that more variables can be derived from DIT data than moral judgement (measured by the P score and N2 index). In addition to tapping moral judgement development, we can regard the DIT as an information processing task. The general idea is that some people have an easier time making moral judgements than others; some people are more certain of their judgements, are more consistent and seem to approach the task of handling moral dilemmas with a definite and coherent point-of-view. What we find (Rest et al., 2000) is that the more consolidated a person is in one of the schemas we have defined (Personal Interest, Maintaining Norms or Postconventional), the greater the ease and consistency in information processing. Conversely, the greater the mix of schemas (bits and pieces of all the schemas, but not a consistent point-of-view), the more difficulty the person has in making a decision and being consistent across tasks. In other words, the schemas predict performance on the information processing variables. This links our particular definitions of moral schemas with specific effects, and thus bolsters the claim that we have defined the operative structures in people's moral thinking (otherwise, our measures of consolidation and schema predominance would have produced a meaningless jumble of numbers).

Whereas consolidation and predominance in any one schema (S23, S4 or S56) predicted ease and consistency in information processing (the schemas are alike in this regard), we also find that the different moral schemas lead to drastic differences in decision-making. In other words, while S4 and S56 are alike in leading to ease of information processing, they are different in terms of where they lead. For instance, S56 favours rights of homosexuals, S4 tends not to; S56 favours abortion rights, S4 does not. In general, S56 tends to endorse political liberal ideology; S4 tends to endorse more conservative political ideology and more religious orthodoxy.

With clearer notions about what moral judgement is, we are clearer about what moral judgement is not. Clearly in the psychology of morality, there are many variables and constructs besides moral judgement schemas (or what can be measured by the DIT). Various discussions of the multifaceted nature of morality have been written (Rest, 1983; Thoma, 1994; Narvaez & Rest, 1995; Bebeau et al., 1999). Here we will mention just two new directions that go beyond the DIT and global moral judgement schemas.

1. Intermediate constructs. Moral judgement, as studied in the Kohlbergian tradition, concerns people's conceptions about the morality of society at a global, coarse-grained, abstract level. From this highly abstract level, one may not be able to deduce solutions for problems in specific contexts. When people make moral decisions about moral dilemmas in their lives, they use concepts at a more "intermediate" level; constructs such as "due process," "informed consent," "patient-autonomy," "standards of evidence," "confidentiality," "intellectual freedom." These are often the conceptual tools emphasised in courses on professional ethics. Bebeau and Thoma (1998, 1999) identify concepts at the intermediate level of abstraction, and discuss educational programmes to instruct students in their use.

2. Theme comprehension in moral texts. Narvaez (1999) and Narvaez et al. (1998, 1999) merge traditional moral judgement research strategies with text comprehension research methods to illuminate the comprehension of moral themes in stories. Moral educators commonly assume that children understand the moral messages of moral stories, and that reading moral stories leads to moral literacy which in turn leads to moral character (Bennett, 1993). Narvaez and colleagues have found that young children do not understand the intended messages, and that there is a developmental trend in understanding beyond what can be explained by reading comprehension ability. Moral text comprehension offers a method of assessing moral cognition other than the DIT or Kohlberg's interview method.

# Conclusion

Kohlberg's ideas stimulated much research over past decades, including the development of the DIT. With 25 years of DIT research, we are able to make particular claims with some certainty. Spurred by developments in psychology and philosophy, we have moved the moral judgement enterprise towards a more complex view of moral judgement and comprehension. Our interpretations of the findings form the basis of our neo-Kohlbergian viewpoint.

# References

Adelson, J. (1971). The political imagination of the young adolescent, *Daedalus, 100*, 1010–1050.

Beauchamp, T. L. & Childress, J. F. (1994). *Principles of Biomedical Ethics*, 4th edn. (New York, Oxford University Press).

Bebeau, M. J., Rest, J. & Narvaez, D. (1999). Moving beyond the promise: a perspective for research in moral education, *Educational Researcher, 28*, pp. 18–26.

Bebeau, M. J. & Thoma, S. J. (1998). *Designing and testing a measure of intermediate level ethical concepts*, paper presented at the annual meeting of the American Educational Research Association, San Diego, CA, 13–17 April.

Bebeau, M. J. & Thoma, S. J. (1999). "Intermediate concepts" and the connection to moral education, *Educational Psychology Review, 11*, pp. 343–360.

Bennett, W. (1993). *The Book of Virtues* (New York, Simon & Schuster).

Colby, A., Kohlberg, L., Gibbs, J. & Lieberman, M. (1983). A longitudinal study of moral judgment, *Society for Research in Child Development: Monograph Series, 48*, no. 4, Chicago.

Colby, A., Kohlberg, L., Speicher, B. et al. (1987). *The Measurement of Moral Judgment, vols 1 and 2* (New York, Cambridge University Press).

Degrazia, D. (1992). Moving forward in bioethical theory: theories, cases, and specified principlism, *Journal of Medicine and Philosophy, 17*, pp. 511–539.

Flavell, J. H. (1963). *The Developmental Psychology of Jean Piaget* (Princeton, NJ, VanNostrand).

Gazzaniga, M. S., Ivry, R. B. & Mangun, G. R. (1998). *Cognitive Neuroscience: the biology of the mind* (New York, Norton).

Hart, H. L. A. (1961). *The Concept of Law* (London, Oxford University Press).

Hunter, J. D. (1991). *Culture Wars: the struggle to define America* (New York, Basic Books).

Kohlberg, L. (1969). Stage and sequence: the cognitive developmental approach to socialization, in: D.A. Goslin (Ed.) *Handbook of Socialization Theory*, pp. 347–480 (Chicago, Rand McNally).

Kohlberg, L. (1981). *Essays on Moral Development, vol. 1: The Philosophy of Moral Development* (New York, Harper & Row).

Kohlberg, L. (1984). *Essays on Moral Development: the nature and validity of moral stages, vol. 2* (San Francisco, Harper & Row).

Kohlberg, L. (1986). A current statement on some theoretical issues, in: S. Modgil & C. Modgil (Eds.) *Lawrence Kohlberg: consensus and controversy*, pp. 485–546 (Philadelphia, Falmer Press).

Marty, M. E. & Appleby, R. S. (Eds.) (1993). *Fundamentalism and the State* (Chicago, University of Chicago).

McClosky, H. & Brill, A. (1983). *Dimensions of Tolerance: what Americans believe about civil liberties* (New York, Russell Sage).

Narvaez, D. (1998). The influence of moral schemas on the reconstruction of moral narratives in eighth graders and college students, *Journal of Educational Psychology, 90*, pp. 13–24.

Narvaez, D. (1999). Using discourse processing methods to study moral thinking, *Educational Psychology Review, 11*, pp. 377–394.

Narvaez, D., Bentley, J., Gleason, T. & Samuels, S. J. (1998). Moral theme comprehension in third grade, fifth grade and college students, *Reading Psychology, 19*, pp. 217–241.

Narvaez, D., Gleason, T., Mitchell, C. & Bentley, J. (1999). Moral theme comprehension in children, *Journal of Educational Psychology, 91*, pp. 477–487.

Narvaez, D. & Rest, J. (1995). The four components of acting morally, in: W. Kurtines & J. Gewirtz (Eds.) *Moral Behavior and Moral Development: an introduction*, pp. 385–400 (New York, McGraw-Hill).

Nietzsche, F. (1986/1968). Beyond Good and Evil, W. Kaufman, (Trans.) *The Portable Nietzsche*, pp. 443–447 (New York, Viking Press).

Nisbett, R. E. & Wilson, T. D. (1977). Telling more than we can know: verbal reports on mental processes, *Psychological Review, 84*, pp. 231–259.

Nozick, R. (1974). *Anarchy, State, and Utopia* (New York, Basic Books).

Rawls, J. (1971). *A Theory of Justice* (Cambridge, MA, Harvard Press).

Rawls, J. (1993). *Political Liberalism* (New York, Columbia University Press).

Reed, D. R. C. (1997). *Following Kohlberg: liberalism and the practice of the democratic community* (Notre Dame, IN, University of Notre Dame Press).

Rest, J. (1983). Morality, in: P. H. Mussen (Series Ed.), J. Flavell & E. Markman (Vol. Eds.) *Handbook of Child Psychology: vol 3, Cognitive Development*, 4th edn, pp. 556–629 (New York, Wiley).

Rest, J., Mitchell, C., Narvaez, D. & Thoma, S. J. (2000). *How test length affects the validity and reliability of the Defining Issues Test*, manuscript submitted for publication.

Rest, J. & Narvaez, D. (Eds.) (1994). *Moral Development in the Professions: psychology and applied ethics* (Hillsdale, NJ, Lawrence Erlbaum).

Rest, J., Narvaez, D., Bebeau, M. J. & Thoma, S. J. (1999). *Postconventional Moral Thinking: a neo-Kohlbergian approach* (Mahwah, NJ, Lawrence Erlbaum).

Rest, J., Narvaez, D., Mitchell, C. & Thoma, S. J. (1999). *Exploring Moral Judgment: a technical manual for the Defining Issues Test*, manuscript available from Center, University of Minnesota.

Rest, J., Narvaez, D., Thoma, S. J. & Bebeau, M. J. (1999). DIT2: devising and testing a revised instrument of moral judgment, *Journal of Educational Psychology, 91*, pp. 644–659.

Rest, J., Thoma, S. J. & Narvaez, D. (2000). *Moral judgment: stages and schemas*, manuscript submitted for publication.

Rest, J., Thoma, S. J., Narvaez, D. & Bebeau, M. J. (1997). Alchemy and beyond: indexing the Defining Issues Test, *Journal of Educational Psychology, 89*, pp. 498–507.

Rummelhart, D. E. (1980). Schemata: the building blocks of cognition, in: R. Spino B. Bruce & W. Brewer (Eds.) *Theoretical Issues in Reading Comprehension*, pp. 33–58 (Hillsdale, NJ, Erlbaum).

Sandel, M. (1982). *Liberalism and the Limits of Justice* (Cambridge, MA, Cambridge University Press).

Siegler, R. S. (1997). Concepts and methods for studying cognitive change, in: E. Amsel & K. A. Renninger (Eds.) *Change and Development: issues of theory, method, and application*, pp. 77–98 (Mahwah, NJ, Lawrence Erlbaum).

Stevenson, C. L. (1937). *The emotive meaning of ethical terms, Mind, XLVI*, pp. 14–31.

Taylor, S. E. & Crocker, J. (1981). Schematic bases of social information processing, in: E. T. Higgins, C. P. Herman & M. P. Zanna (Eds.) *Social Cognition: the Ontario Symposium, vol. 1*, pp. 89–134 (Hillsdale, NJ, Erlbaum).

Thoma, S. J. (1986). Estimating gender differences in the comprehension and preference of moral issues, *Developmental Review, 6*, pp. 165–180.

Thoma, S. J. (1994). Moral judgment and moral action, in: J. Rest & D. Narvaez (Eds.) *Moral Development in the Professions: psychology and applied ethics*, pp. 199–211 (Hillsdale, NJ, Erlbaum).

Thoma, S., Narvaez, D., Rest, J. & Derryberry, P. (1999). The distinctiveness of moral judgment, *Educational Psychology Review, 11*, pp. 325–342.

Toulmin, S. (1981). The tyranny of principles, *Hastings Center Report, 11*, pp. 31–39.

Turiel, E. (1983). *The Development of Social Knowledge; morality and convention* (Cambridge, Cambridge University Press).

Uleman, J. S. & Bargh, J. A. (1989). *Unintended Thought* (New York, Guilford Press).

Walzer, M. (1983). *Spheres of Justice* (New York, Basic Books).

Youniss, J. & Yates, M. (1997). *Community Service and Social Responsibility in Youth* (Chicago, University of Chicago Press).

## Unit 4 Additional Recommended Readings

Belenky, M. F., Clinchy, B. M., Goldberger, N. R., & Tarule, J. M. (1986). *Women's ways of knowing: The development of self, voice, and mind.* New York, NY: Basic Books.

Durham, R. L., Hays, J. Martinez, R. (1994). Socio-cognitive development among Chicano and Anglo American college students. *Journal of College Student Development, 35*, 178–182.

Giesbrecht, N., & Walker, L. J. (2000). Ego development and the construction of a moral self. *Journal of College Student Development, 41*, 157–171.

Gilligan, C., & Attanucci, J. (1988). Two moral orientations. In C. Gilligan, J. V. Ward, & J. M. Taylor (Eds.), *Mapping the moral domain* (pp. 73–86). Cambridge, MA: Harvard University Press.

Goldberger, N., Tarule, J., Clinchy, B., & Belenky, M. (1996). *Knowledge, difference, and power: Essays inspired by women's ways of knowing.* New York, NY: Basic Books.

Jones, C. E., & Watt, J. D. (1999). Psychosocial development and moral orientation among traditional-aged college students. *Journal of College Student Development, 40*, 125–131.

Kegan, R. (2000). What "form" transforms? A constructive-developmental approach to transformative learning. In J. Mezirow (Ed.), *Learning in transformation: Critical perspectives on a theory in progress* (pp. 35–69). San Francisco, CA: Jossey-Bass.

King, P. M. (2009). Principles of development and developmental change underlying theories of cognitive and moral development. *Journal of College Student Development*, *50*, 597–620.

King, P. M., & Mayhew, M. J. (2002). Moral judgement development in higher education: Insights from the Defining Issues Test. *Journal of Moral Education*, *31*, 247–270.

King, P. M., & Mayhew, M. J. (2004). Theory and research on the development of moral reasoning among college students. In J. C. Smart (Ed.) *Higher education: Handbook of theory and research*, (Vol. XIX, pp. 375–440), The Netherlands: Kluwer Academic Publishers.

Kloss, R. J. (1994). A nudge is best. *College Teaching*, *42*, 151–158.

Knefelkamp, L. L. (2003). The influence of a classic. *Liberal Education*, *89*(3), 10–15.

Love, P. G., & Talbot, D. (1999). Defining spiritual development: A missing consideration for student affairs. *NASPA Journal*, *37*, 361–375.

Marszalek J. F. III, Cashwell, C. S., Dunn, M. S., & Jones, K. H. (2004). Comparing gay identity development theory to cognitive development: An empirical study. *Journal of Homosexuality*, *48*, 103–123.

Moore, W. S. (2001). Understanding learning in a postmodern world: Reconsidering the Perry scheme of intellectual and ethical development. In B. K. Hofer & P. R. Pintrich (eds.), *Personal epistemology: the psychology of beliefs about knowledge and knowing* (pp. 17–36). Mahwah, NJ: Lawrence Erlbaum Associates.

Parks, S. (1986). The journey toward mature adult faith: A model. In *The critical years: Young adults and the search for meaning, faith and commitment* (pp. 43–72). San Francisco: Harper Collins.

Perry, W. G. (1985). Different worlds in the same classroom: Students' evolution in their vision of knowledge and their expectations of teachers. *On Teaching and Learning: The Journal of the Harvard Danforth Center*, Retrieved from http://isites.harvard.edu/fs/html/icb.topic58474/perry.html.

Pizzolato, J. E., Chaudhari, P., Murrell, E. D., Podobnik, S., & Schaeffer, Z. (2008). Ethnic identity, epistemological development, and academic achievement in underrepresented students. *Journal of College Student Development*, *49*, 301–318.

Rest, J. R. (1982). A psychologist looks at the teaching of ethics. *The Hastings Center Report*, *12*(1), 29–36.

Rest, J. R. (1993). Research on moral judgment in college students. In A. Garrod, *Approaches to moral development: New research and emerging themes* (pp. 201–213). New York, NY: Teachers College Press.

Scheurman, G. (1997). Using principles of constructivism to promote reflective judgment: A model lesson. *Journal on Excellence in College Teaching*, *8*, 63–86.

Snarey, J., & Samuelson, P. (2008). Moral education in the cognitive developmental tradition. In L. P. Nucci & D. Narvaez (Eds.), *Handbook on Moral and Character Education* (pp. 53–79). New York, NY: Routledge.

Torres, V., & Baxter Magolda, M. (2004). Reconstructing Latino identity: The influence of cognitive development on the ethnic identity process of Latino students. *Journal of College Student Development*, *45*, 333–347.

Zhang, L. (2004). The Perry scheme: Across cultures, across approaches to the study of human psychology. *Journal of Adult Development*, *11*, 123–138.

# UNIT 5

# *CRITICAL THEORETICAL PERSPECTIVES ON DEVELOPMENT*

# CHAPTER 29
## THEORETICAL BORDERLANDS: USING MULTIPLE THEORETICAL PERSPECTIVES TO CHALLENGE INEQUITABLE POWER STRUCTURES IN STUDENT DEVELOPMENT THEORY

ELISA S. ABES

This article is an exploration of possibilities and methodological considerations for using multiple theoretical perspectives in research that challenges inequitable power structures in student development theory. Specifically, I explore methodological considerations when partnering queer theory and constructivism in research on lesbian identity development. Considerations include the dilemma of partnering contradictory theoretical perspectives; the politics of representation; and the personal and professional implications for researchers who partner theoretical perspectives.

All theoretical perspectives that guide research are incomplete. For instance, interpretivist theories may reveal a rich understanding of the phenomenon under investigation, but they do not necessarily reveal societal power structures. Postmodern theories may accomplish the latter, but sometimes mute the perspectives of the participants in the process of exploring difference through multiple stories. So what's a researcher to do? The traditional answer to this question is that the purpose of the research study and the values of the researcher guide the choice of theoretical perspectives. And the traditional way to proceed once a theoretical perspective has been selected is that it then guides the choice and application of all other aspects of the research process, such as data collection and data analysis (Crotty, 1998). The less traditional answer is that the researcher should consider experimenting with the choice and application of theoretical perspectives, bringing together multiple and even seemingly conflicting theoretical perspectives to uncover new ways of understanding the data. Rather than being paralyzed by theoretical limitations or confined by rigid ideological allegiances, interdisciplinary experimentation of this nature can lead to rich new research results and possibilities. In this article I reflect on a recent study in which a colleague and I applied, in the context of student development theory, a hybrid theoretical perspective of sorts by working in the borderland between two existing theoretical perspectives, queer theory (e.g., Butler, 1990; Sullivan, 2003) and constructivism (Baxter Magolda, 2004; Crotty). I discuss my rationale for this theoretical experimentation; the nature and results of this process in my research; and the methodological questions this

Abes, E. S. (2009). Theoretical borderlands: Using multiple theoretical perspectives to challenge inequitable power structures in student development theory. *Journal of College Student Development, 50*, 141–155.

463

process continues to raise for me. This borderland approach to research changed my way of thinking about the research process in general and the nature of student development theory in particular, especially as it relates to addressing how inequitable power structures have shaped student development theory. My hope is that my discussion of this research approach and the questions it raises will encourage more theoretical experimentation in research on student development theory. Experimentation of this nature has the potential to benefit the student affairs profession by revealing new possibilities for how student development theories can be more inclusive of marginalized student populations.

## Researching in the Borderlands of Theoretical Perspectives

A theoretical perspective is "the philosophical stance informing the methodology and thus providing a context for the [research] process and grounding its logic and criteria" (Crotty, 1998, p. 3). How then can multiple theoretical perspectives be used in combination, deviating from the typical paradigmatic categories into which studies are generally categorized, such as positivist, constructivist, critical, and poststructural? More specifically, how can one apply competing assumptions of conflicting theoretical perspectives to the same data?

Although not often raised within research on student development theory, other than philosophically through challenges to the positivist stance of the existence of one reality (e.g., Baxter Magolda, 2004; Tanaka, 2002), scholars in different academic disciplines have explored these questions. For instance, among some educational research scholars rich discussion has occurred about the emergence of multiple research paradigms, or "paradigm proliferation" (e.g., Donmoyer, 2006; Lather, 2006). With new perspectives on what knowledge is and how knowledge is accessed, numerous theoretical perspectives have emerged, such as Chicana, critical race theory, indigenous, and queer (Pillow, 2003). Lather argued that the multiplicity of paradigms is necessary given the multiplicity of reality. She encouraged the creation of multiple paradigms to guide research because "[r]ather than searching for the common elements underlying difference," there should be a "freeing of difference" that is about "divergence, dispersed multiplicities, the possibilities of that which is in excess of our categories of containment" (p. 47). She continued, explaining that she is "against the kind of methodolatry where the tail of the methodology wags the dog of inquiry" (p. 47) and therefore embraces the importance of "saying yes to the messiness, to that which interrupts and exceeds versus tidy categories. . . . thinking difference differently" (pp. 48, 52). Although I am not necessarily advocating in this article for the creation of a new paradigm, but rather researching in the borderland between multiple perspectives, Lather's notion of embracing multiple possibilities of difference is central to the approach to research for which I advocate.

In a similar vein, other scholars have urged researchers to put aside their theoretical silos to uncover the potential of using interdisciplinary theoretical perspectives in research. For instance, Kincheloe and McLaren (2005) have advocated for the border-crossing notion of bricolage, which is typically understood "to involve the process of employing . . . [multiple] methodological strategies as they are needed in the unfolding context of the research situation" (p. 316). They explained:

> The bricolage exists out of respect for the complexity of the lived world and complications of power. The task of the bricoleur is to attack this complexity, uncovering the invisible artifacts of power and culture, and documenting the nature of their influence on not only their own works but on scholarship in general. (p. 317)

Partnering multiple and contradictory theoretical perspectives to explore the power structures underlying student development theory exemplifies this notion of bricolage.

Rich examples exist of bricoleurs who have blended multiple theoretical perspectives. For instance, Tierney (1993) described how he blended critical theory and postmodernism in his research on communities of difference in higher education. The impetus behind his use of critical postmodernism was that neither perspective sufficiently addressed the realities of the individuals he was studying. For instance, in his research with gay faculty, a postmodern critique focused on differences within the participants' identities, challenging how their multiple social identities were situated, while a critical perspective facilitated the participants' ability to challenge their marginalized status. Through the combined analysis focusing on both difference and change, these two combined theoretical perspectives richly addressed the experiences of gay faculty. Tierney and Rhoads (1993) offered an insightful discussion of the merging of postmodernism and critical theory as theoretical frameworks. They explained that although critical theory is grounded in modernism, the two frameworks share several key assumptions, such as the existence of multiple social realities and the role of power in structuring subjectivity. By merging the two, critical theory, with its emphasis on praxis, offers one approach to applying postmodernism in practice (Tierney & Rhoads).

In essence, Tierney's research demonstrates how research can be conducted in the borderlands between theoretical perspectives. Anzaldua (1999) described a borderland as a third space that is neither one land nor the other but a new space that is a "both/and" location. This borderland is an environment where individuals fluctuate between two discrete worlds, participating in both and wholly belonging to neither, "none of them 'home,' yet none of them 'not home'" (p. 528). Theoretical borderlands can effectively describe diverse college students' complex understandings and experiences with their identities.

## Theoretical Borderlands in Student Development Theory Research

In the *Journal of College Student Development*'s special issue on qualitative research, Jones, Arminio, Broido, and Torres (2002) reflected on the emergence of qualitative research within the student affairs profession, and urged that the wide use of this approach necessitates an exploration of the "full epistemological and methodological landscape of qualitative methodologies" (p. 431). Beyond that introduction and further discussion in a recent textbook on qualitative research in student affairs (Jones, Torres, & Arminio, 2006), the student development literature reveals little examination regarding the complexities of using multiple theoretical perspectives such as constructivism, critical theory, or queer theory, which is an important feature of the methodological landscape. More instances in student development theory research where research is conducted within theoretical borderlands ought to push the current boundaries of how student development theory is generally understood.

I therefore present one example of how this approach might look in student development theory research. Consistent with the aims of a bricoleur, the example I offer is grounded in the notion that researchers of college student development theory must focus increased attention on inequitable power structures that result in oppressions such as racism, classism, and heterosexism (McEwen, 2003; Tanaka, 2002). Doing so is important because privilege and oppression associated with power inequities affect how college students learn and develop (e.g., Kodama, McEwen, Liang, & Lee, 2002; Pizzolato, 2003; Renn & Bilodeau, 2005). I am attempting to address some of these power dynamics through my research on the identity development of lesbian college students, but have found discrete and unidimensional theoretical approaches unsatisfactory. Restless to reap the benefits of interdisciplinary research, I recently used a hybrid approach, applying queer theory and constructivism to the same data. I brought together these two different theoretical perspectives not as a blueprint for how this interdisciplinary theoretical work ought to be done, but instead, as one possibility.

Partnering queer theory and constructivism pushes the boundaries of traditional research because the two perspectives are significantly different with regard to ontology, epistemology, and methodology. Lather (2007) described queer theory as a poststructural theory. Poststructural theories have as their purpose to deconstruct realities, including the acquisition of knowledge (Lather, 2007). Sullivan (2003) explained:

> Poststructural theorists such as Foucault argue that there are no objective and universal truths, but that particular forms of knowledge, and the ways of being that they engender, become "naturalised," in culturally and historically specific ways. . . . [Identity is] constructed in and through its relations with others, and with systems of power/knowledge. . . . We embody the discourses that exist in our culture, our very being is constituted by them. (pp. 39, 41)

Queer theory brings these poststructural concerns to sexuality studies and is effective for addressing power dynamics in college student development because of its focus on challenging the heteronormativity in identity constructions, which is the unexamined and prevalent societal assumption that normal is defined through heterosexuality (e.g., Britzman, 1997). Queer theory challenges heteronormative assumptions about how college students develop.

However, by focusing on societal dynamics rather than the particularities of individual development, queer theory does not offer an interpretation of development that necessarily resonates with how many college students describe themselves. Even though my goal was to uncover some of the power-laden assumptions in characterizations of lesbian identity development, the application of these results is enhanced by juxtaposing these findings with students' self-perceptions. Thus, I turned also to a constructivist theoretical perspective.

Constructivism is an interpretivist theory (Lather, 2007). Interpretivism and constructivism are grounded in the notions that multiple realities exist, differing in context, and knowledge is co-constructed between the researcher and participants. Methodologically, constructivist research typically seeks to understand reality through dialogue (Denzin & Lincoln, 2000). Thus, whereas poststructuralist theories seek to deconstruct reality, interpretivist theories, including constructivism, seek to understand the construction of realities (Lather). Constructivism is therefore appropriate to explore how participants made meaning of their identities, whereas queer theory challenges the very notion of identity.

Seeing value and limitations in both queer theory and constructivism, and recognizing the potential for them to uncover new possibilities when used in conjunction, I applied both of these theoretical perspectives to analyze the same data, despite their fundamental differences, and merged the results to shape my own understanding of student development theory. To describe the impetus behind my decision to do so and the results of this experiment, I discuss my evolution as a researcher and how I have come to find myself wrestling with methodological questions associated with this approach to research. I present this piece through my own evolution in part to underscore queer theory's praxis potential. It has transformed who I am as a professional and continues to change me in ways that leave me questioning how to proceed with research that does justice for lesbian college students in a heteronormative society. By addressing my own evolution, I also invite readers to consider their own journeys as researchers and to consider their own stance regarding my experimental approach.

## My Evolution Toward Researching in Theoretical Borderlands

### Where I've Been . . . My Socialization as a Constructivist Researcher of Student Development Theory

For the past 4 years, I have been conducting a longitudinal study of 10 lesbian college students' perceptions of the relationships among their multiple social identities, such as sexuality, religion, gender, race, and social class. I wanted to move beyond the developmental stage theories frequently used to describe lesbian identity development (e.g., Cass, 1979). Although these theories offer possible explanations for how college students perceive their sexual identity, they do not specifically account for how other aspects of a person's identity and the contexts in which they are situated mediate development.

To conduct the longitudinal study, which employed a narrative inquiry methodology (Lieblich, Tuval-Mashiach, & Zilber, 1998), I used a constructivist theoretical perspective. Consistent with constructivism, I conducted in-depth, conversational interviews in which the participants took the lead on the direction of the interview and considered my subjectivities when analyzing the data to allow for multiple possibilities in how students made meaning of their identities (Baxter Magolda & King, 2007). Through this framework, the results suggested that meaning-making capacity served as a filter that interpreted contextual factors prior to influencing self-perceptions of lesbian identity and its relationship with other social identities. How context influenced perceptions depended on the complexity of this meaning-making filter (Abes & Jones, 2004; Abes, Jones, & McEwen, 2007). Heterosexism emerged as a contextual influence that the participants needed to overcome to internally define their identities; the constructivist perspective, however, did not lend itself to an in-depth exploration of this power structure.

I used a constructivist theoretical perspective because that was the perspective modeled for me in much of the contemporary literature on student development theory and touted as an effective and accepted way to understand students' perceptions of their identities. Advocates of constructivism demonstrated how it lends itself to understanding students' experiences and ways of making meaning more so than positivist approaches that assumed one reality and boxed students into pre-existing developmental categories (e.g., Baxter Magolda, 2004). Although at the time there were some calls for the use of critical and poststructural frameworks in research on student development theory because of their deconstruction of power relationships (Broido & Manning, 2002), I found few published exemplars. For instance, in the *Journal of College Student Development*'s special issue on qualitative research, the featured examples of methodologically sound qualitative research on identity development employed a constructivist approach (Davis, 2002; Stewart, 2002). I was therefore socialized as a constructivist researcher.

As I moved into the second and third years of the longitudinal study, however, I became dissatisfied with my results viewed exclusively through a constructivist lens. As part of my analysis of the data collected during these phases, I considered how heterosexism mediated the three domains of development that provide a framework for understanding young adult development: cognitive (i.e., how students construct knowledge), interpersonal (i.e., how students construct relationships with others), and intrapersonal (i.e., how students understand who they are as individuals; Baxter Magolda, 2001). Maturity in each domain is necessary for self-authorship, or the ability to internally define one's beliefs, relationships, and sense of self (Baxter Magolda). When conducting this analysis, I found I was overlooking a large part of the developmental story for the lesbian college students in my study. When analyzing these follow-up interviews, my analysis initially resulted in thinking that heterosexism contributed to increased cognitive capacity because the participants encountered dissonance between external and internal perspectives about the meaning of their sexual identity. Heterosexism, however, appeared to stall interpersonal development given the participants' tendencies to define themselves though their family, peers, and personal relationships. Intrapersonal development depended on cognitive and interpersonal maturity.

The cognitive analysis seemed appropriate, but it felt terribly wrong to describe the participants' experiences as stalled interpersonal development because it located the "problem" with the individual rather than with societal power inequities. Through their intense struggles against the heterosexist norms defining their relationships, it was evident that the participants wanted to push back against dominant social structures, engaging in sophisticated interpersonal pursuits and slowly defining themselves separately from society's attempts at defining their identities for them. Characterizing their development as stalled, thereby minimizing the heterosexist obstacles they needed to shatter and scale, normalized the typical developmental patterns established through the experiences of predominantly heterosexual college students. I concluded that I needed to step outside of a constructivist framework to incorporate into their development the participants' efforts at deconstructing heteronormativity and to appreciate how development might be more complex than a constructivist perspective reveals.

## Where I Am . . . Exploring Queer Theory and Its Potential in Student Development Theory Research

Based on my dissatisfaction with characterizing the participants' development as stalled and thus reifying heterosexual privilege, I opted to explore the possibilities for using queer theory to interpret the data. Queer theory had been applied in historical and cultural analyses of higher education and college students (e.g., Dilley, 2002; Tierney, 1997), but not in the context of student development theory. I was unsure how a partnership between constructivist student development theory and queer theory would look because unlike constructivism, which focuses on how students experience their identities, queer theory challenges the notion of identity itself (Sullivan, 2003). These two theories were an unlikely and potentially problematic couple. Collaborating with a colleague who was steeped in knowledge of poststructuralism and queer theory, and less socialized in the use of constructivism as the primary perspective for researching student development, was instrumental in pushing me past some of my initial apprehensions. Still, the process of deciding how to apply queer theory within student development research was challenging. Queer theory is an eclectic theory that, true to its nature, defies definition. After much conversation about the nature of poststructuralism and queer theory, we opted to focus on three tenets of queer theory: heteronormativity, performativity, and liminality. Each of these three tenets is briefly explained here.

Queer theorists critique heteronormativity as the norm for understanding gender and sexuality (Warner, 1991). Heteronormativity is the pervasive yet invisible perception that heterosexuality defines what is natural (Britzman, 1997). A product of heteronormativity is a heterosexual and nonheterosexual binary in which nonheterosexuality is abnormal and essentialized (Muñññoz, 1999). Rather than essentializing identities, queer theorists recognize that as time and place changes, so too does identity, causing sexual and gender identities to be "multiple, contradictory, fragmented, incoherent, disciplinary, disunified, unstable, fluid" (Gamson, 2000, p. 356).

Performativity is one way in which individuals are able to deconstruct heteronormativity. Performativity describes how individuals create gender and sexual identities through everyday behaviors or performatives (Butler, 1990). As performatives, actions do not represent identity; instead, actions create identity (Butler). An individual never repeats actions precisely the same; identity is therefore always changing. The performative resistance to heternormativity is further complicated by the concept of liminality, which is a state of flux between two distinct stages of being (van Gennep, 1909/1960). It reflects how an individual may perform a seemingly contradictory performative in ever-changing ways. Liminality provides a framework for understanding the complex ways in which an individual performs sexuality in resistance to and as part of heteronormativity. The "becoming" quality of liminality emphasizes the unstable meaning of gender and sexuality (Halberstam, 2005).

## The Creation of a Queer/Constructivist Theoretical Borderland

Without one methodology to guide our use of queer theory (Gamson, 2000; Kong, Mahoney, & Plummer, 2002), my colleague and I discussed possibilities for how to apply the notions of heteronormativity, performativity, and liminality to student development research, ultimately deciding to use the data from my longitudinal study of lesbian identity development to write two narratives: one constructivist, the other queer (Abes & Kasch, 2007). We believed this approach would highlight the differences between these perspectives and how power mediates student development and the meaning of development. We first analyzed the longitudinal data using a constructivist theoretical perspective to understand how students' development toward self-authorship contributes to their understanding of the relationships among their multiple social identities. This was similar to the analysis in my original longitudinal study (Abes & Jones, 2004; Abes et al., 2007). We found that there was a somewhat linear trajectory through which students progressed to arrive at a developmental place where they were able to negotiate their multiple identities and integrate them in a manner consistent with their sense of self. For instance, for KT, the study participant we featured, development toward self-authorship contributed to her ability to challenge her mother's and society's teaching that being a lesbian prevented her from being Catholic, professionally successful, and feminine, each of which was important to KT (Abes & Kasch). As KT developed increased cognitive, interpersonal, and intrapersonal complexity, she started to challenge stereotypes and began to develop her own perspectives on the meaning of her social identities and how they relate to one another. Using this constructivist perspective, we described the development of KT's capacity to make her own meaning of her identity within a heteronormative society.

We then reanalyzed the same data using a queer theoretical perspective. Rather than focusing on how KT made meaning of her identity, a queer analysis deconstructed the meaning of identity. To conduct the queer analysis, we reread KT's interview transcripts to understand how her stories were driven by heteronormativity, performativity, and liminality. Through this queer analysis, we concluded her story was not one of a linear trajectory, but instead, was a fluid process of becoming, in which inseparable social identities were continuously changing as they interacted with each other and as they influenced and were influenced by ever-changing societal contexts. Rather than making her own meaning of her multiple identities within a heteronormative society, KT's ability to define for herself the meaning of her identities through performatives was a way of resisting and transforming heteronormativity. By doing so, she was changing the meaning of *lesbian*, *Catholic*, *feminine*, and *professional*. Through a queer perspective, student "development" for KT is a different concept than typically explained through constructivism (Abes & Kasch, 2007).

Revisiting the data to tell and retell KT's story using two different theoretical perspectives put a spotlight on some of the dominant power-laden norms underlying student development theory. We aimed to offer one possibility for queering development by presenting a perspective of the relationships among lesbian college students' multiple social identities in which each of the identities is constantly becoming; each is dependent on the other for its changing meaning; and each is forming in a manner that defies heteronormativity. Still, we were not prepared to let go of some of the ideas of developmental trajectories because they spoke to how KT described and experienced her life. We realized we needed to simultaneously embrace both theoretical perspectives, despite their contradictory nature. Thus, although we conducted two independent analyses, we merged the results, despite the contradictions of doing so, to explain how we understood KT's development as simultaneously linear and nonlinear; succumbing to and resisting heteronormativity; comprised of distinct and fused identities; and defined by and redefining societal expectations.

In essence, we created a theoretical borderland between queer theory and constructivism. Singularly, both constructivism and queer theory provide a rich, yet incomplete, perspective through which KT can be understood. Together, in a queer/constructivist theoretical borderland, they tell a richer story than either alone. This borderland, where KT is neither "home" nor "not home" (Anzaldua, 1999, p. 528) allows educators to consider both how lesbian students make meaning of their multiple identities, and how these identities are fused, performed, and becoming. The queer/constructivist borderland brings to life students' lived experiences through constructivism while simultaneously deconstructing them through queer theory. Such a combination adds a praxis component to queer theory, making it accessible and applicable in student affairs practice. As with the theoretical hybrids created by Tierney (1993), it took an experimental approach to thinking about theoretical perspectives and research to address power structures within student development theory in new ways.

## What Am I Thinking? Methodological Considerations in Creating a Queer/Constructivist Borderland

At the same time that partnering constructivism and queer theory revealed new possibilities for understanding student development, doing so also raised several methodological considerations. Among the issues it raised are whether it is appropriate to simultaneously apply theoretical perspectives that differ in fundamental assumptions, as well as to retell participants' stories through multiple theoretical perspectives, despite the potential of muting participants' voices. It also raised the more personal question of how using multiple theoretical perspectives has shaped who I am and will be as a researcher. I explore these considerations in the remainder of this paper. For each of these considerations, I discuss the strengths of the borderland approach I chose, including developing increasingly complex student development theory; engaging in student affairs practice that addresses the needs of diverse college students; and fostering reflexivity in the research process. However, given that my approach was somewhat experimental, I also challenge myself on each of these considerations. My hope is that the discussion around these considerations will further conversation and encourage research that uses multiple theoretical perspectives and other experimental approaches to study the power structures underlying student development theory.

## Consideration #1: Is It Appropriate to Partner Multiple and Contradictory Theoretical Perspectives?

Partnering queer theory and constructivism raised the consideration as to how two contradictory theoretical perspectives, one modernist and the other poststructural, can be simultaneously applied to the same data. Although nontraditional, this partnership opens new possibilities for approaching student development theory both as researched and in practice.

*Complementary, Contradictory Approaches to Research on Student Development Theory.* The paradigmatic tension of using a theoretical perspective that deconstructs identity to study identity as experienced in individuals' lives has been addressed by researchers studying higher education and other social science contexts (e.g., Britzman, 2000; Talburt, 2000). Gamson (2000) reviewed strategies that researchers have used when taking queer theory's deconstruction of identity into account in qualitative studies of identity, such as making identity the focus while highlighting the instability and fragmentation of identity, and blending the authors' multiple voices with those of the participants to challenge the authenticity of voice. Plummer (2005) explained that his aim is not to reconcile the two approaches but to live with the tensions, allowing both perspectives to be used together for the social good.

In the context of college student identity development, it is important to live with tensions to more fully describe the complexity of development. Partnering constructivism and queer theory in a student development research context brings to life students' experiences through constructivism while simultaneously deconstructing them through queer theory. For instance, in the example of KT, living with the tension within this theoretical borderland means simultaneously acknowledging that KT is developing the complexity to unlearn stereotypes, develop her own perspectives, and reconcile her previously distinct religious and sexual identities within a heteronormative context, at the same time that she is resisting and redefining the heteronormative contexts in which she is situated and that continuously reshape the meaning of these two inseparable identities that have always been fused. The simultaneous use of these two perspectives adds a praxis component to queer theory, making it more applicable in student affairs practice (Abes, 2007).

*Contradictory, Complementary Approaches to Student Development Theory and Practice.* Partnering constructivism and queer theory requires not only a shift in thinking about how to conduct student development theory research, but also the nature of student development theory in practice and what it means for educators to live with multiple realities. Consistent with Lather's (2006) notion of embracing multiple possibilities of difference, using multiple theoretical perspectives to research student development theory highlights the complexity and messiness of student development; it challenges educators to simultaneously view students from multiple perspectives and to genuinely live and work within a context of multiple realities rather than trying to understand identity through tidy frameworks. For instance, a combination of the two theoretical perspectives provides a richer picture of KT's multifaceted development: She is moving forward through a trajectory of increasingly complex meaning-making structures, while at the same time experiencing constant change and identity motion. No one theoretical perspective can describe this seemingly contradictory, yet more complete, way of looking at KT's development as simultaneously linear and spiraling.

How though is it possible to simultaneously embrace constructivism's and queer theory's contradictory perspectives on development? Constructivism seeks to understand how individuals make meaning of their identities. Queer theory challenges the notion of identity, which is not necessarily how college students perceive their experiences. The ability to live with these contradictions is a postmodern notion: embracing multiple, contradictory, and mutually informing truths and assumptions about development (Tierney & Rhoads, 1993). Living with these tensions in the borderland requires not only loosening the grip of traditional notions of student development theory as trajectories that predict and explain, but also letting go of monolithic beliefs about development and acknowledging contradictory perspectives that speak to the multiplicity of students' experiences. Rather than perceiving multiple perspectives on student development as distinct, this approach allows the possibility that all are viable perspectives that simultaneously describe the complexities of development.

*Questions Still to Be Answered.* As much as I appreciate the contributions of partnering queer theory and constructivism, it is fair to ask why my co-researcher and I didn't use only queer theory to guide the research process if our goal was to address heteronormavity in student development theory. Why did we decide to queer constructivist data rather than gathering new queer data? Would queer theory alone have more richly uncovered the influence of heteronormativity? If the developmental trajectory toward self-authorship does not fully account for lesbian college students' necessary resistance against heternormativity, why use this theory to analyze their development?

Kong et al. (2002) described possibilities for a "queer methodology" (p. 243) that problematizes and deconstructs all aspects of the inquiry process. Using queer theory as the sole theoretical perspective for a new study would have influenced all aspects of the research process, including the nature of the research question: Could I have still focused on how students perceive the meaning of their sexuality or instead would the focus be on cultural constructions of sexuality? Sampling: What difference would it have made if I sampled only female students who identified as "queer," or if I loosened my sampling criteria so that I was not limited only to women physically and emotionally attracted to other women? Might some of these students have also been straight-identified? Would there have been more gender variation? Data collection: Would the nature of the stories the participants told have been different if power differences in the interview shifted? How would I have used the term "identity" during interviews as a contested and fluid concept? Could I have discussed dimensions of identity separately or would that have implied false distinctions rather than fused differences? Data analysis: What might I have learned had I conducted a textual analysis? Writing: Might more voices have been included in the narratives? Whose voices would be privileged? Although I chose to pair queer theory with constructivism and encourage other experimental approaches of this nature, I am also eager for more published research that uses queer theory as the sole theoretical perspective for studies of college student identity development so that some of these questions might be answered and new possibilities for understanding development uncovered.

## Consideration #2: What Are the Politics of Representation Involved in Creating Theoretical Borderlands?

Another methodological consideration in using multiple theoretical perspectives to tell and retell participants' narratives relates to the notion of the "crisis of representation." Rooted in feminist research and responded to through postmodernism, the crisis of representation speaks to "the profound uncertainty about what constitutes an adequate depiction of social 'reality'" (Lather, 1991, p. 21). Representation is political because it speaks to the power that the researcher wields in all aspects of the research process (Fine, Weis, Weseen, & Wong, 2000). Fine et al. spoke to the responsibility to question how we represent ourselves as researchers choreographing the participants' stories, how we represent the participants, and how we represent how others are portrayed in the participants' stories. Among the ethical considerations involved in the politics of representation is the importance of participants seeing themselves in the stories written about them. Using multiple theoretical perspectives caused me to interrogate data analysis and writing in particular, asking whose stories are these to tell and how do I speak for and with the participants? Telling the participants' stories from multiple perspectives runs the risk of their voices becoming muted and their stories becoming only "data" distinct from the known realities of their lives. Writing multiple stories using different theoretical perspectives brings with it the risk that participants will not always readily see themselves in these stories. This concern is heightened when using a queer theoretical perspective because the cultural critiques of power inequities this theory raises might be invisible to the participants, thus minimizing how much they see themselves in "their" stories. For instance, was the queer narrative KT's queer narrative, or was it a queer narrative that my colleague and I wrote based on our poststructuralist interpretation of the data. This question, however, must be balanced against the perspective that participants are comprised of a multitude of stories, as are the researchers who write about them (Richardson & St. Pierre, 2005). The assumptions of multiple realities, multiple stories, and multiple identities underlie my approach.

Discussions about the politics of representing participants pertain to validity. What constitutes validity has been one of the most fertile places for discussion about the way different paradigms influence the research process (Guba & Lincoln, 2005). Validity debates have typically included discussions regarding the nature of criteria used to judge the rigor of methods and authenticity of interpretation. Validity, typically referred to as trustworthiness in qualitative research, includes methods such as triangulation, member checking, and peer debriefing. Talburt (2004) challenged the assumptions underlying these methods, arguing that member checking cannot verify one real story, but there will be multiple possibilities for true stories, depending on who is telling it and through what lens. Lather (2006) cautioned against "revert[ing] to romantic 'too easy' ideas about 'authenticity' in negotiating the tensions between both honoring the 'voices' of research participants and the demand for interpretive work on the part of the inquirer" (p. 50). By telling two different stories about KT, we intended both to honor the complexity of her life and to expose the invisible power system that she resisted.

Despite its modernist assumptions, we opted to use member checking to gauge KT's reactions to the narratives. At a minimum, we felt an ethical obligation for KT to be comfortable with the two narratives before others read them. I was not especially troubled by member checking the constructivist narrative, knowing that I could discuss discrepancies with her and allow multiple interpretations within the narrative. After reviewing versions of that narrative, KT commented that she readily saw herself in that portrayal of her story and was interested in the use of developmental theory to explain her experiences. She had never thought about her experiences from a developmental perspective but appreciated this explanation, which was relatively easy for her to understand (Abes & Kasch, 2007).

I was less clear on how to or whether to member check the queer narrative. KT was not familiar with queer theory, and I was skeptical that she would see herself reflected in this interpretation. In the queer narrative, we moved deeply into a theoretical story, and further away from how she knowingly experienced her life. I was confident though that this theoretical overview was one "true" story describing how KT negotiated her multiple identities. Was it necessary that she see herself in that story, especially because it described the invisibility of heteronormativity, a phenomenon she often unknowingly experienced? Our ethical obligation that at a minimum she be comfortable with the story prompted us to have her review the narrative. Not surprisingly, she found the queer theory analysis difficult to get her head around, but understood some aspects as an intriguing way to describe her experiences. KT was satisfied with this theoretical possibility and eager to have her experiences potentially shape how other educators understand lesbian college students (Abes & Kasch, 2007). Given her reaction, I was comfortable presenting two different theoretical interpretations of KT's negotiation of her multiple identities and did not feel that I silenced her voice. I also believe that KT's review of the queer story, and her new awareness of her resistance against heteronormativity, has the possibility of influencing how she perceives her identity. This is consistent with the finding from earlier work I did with another participant from my longitudinal study. Being introduced to queer theory as part of the research process had an emancipatory effect on that participant, contributing to her questioning the definition of "normal" that previously defined her, and the role of identity categories in determining the meaning of her sexuality, gender, and ethnicity (Abes, 2007).

*Questions Still to Be Answered.* In some respects, my concerns related to the politics and crisis of representation were lessened because KT was comfortable with both narratives and with her role in the research process. What if KT did not see herself in the constructivist or queer narrative or was uncomfortable with these interpretations? Had this been the case, would I have been exerting undue power by writing them and reducing her participation in the research to only a source of data? But then again, is this interpretive power any worse that the power that research interviews often wield over participants (Kong et al., 2002). Why also did we present only theoretical interpretations of KT's story? Why not also ask KT to write her own narrative, which would privilege her voice more so than do theoretical interpretations. Or why not let her comments on the queer narrative be integrated into the narrative we wrote? Would a multivoiced narrative have given KT more space to resist the power inherent in the research process?

Dilemmas related to trustworthiness and member checking become more complicated when the theoretical perspective deconstructs rather than describes or interprets the participants' experiences and identity, making it more challenging for participants to see themselves in the data. But at the same time, what does it mean that KT saw herself in the constructivist narrative? Isn't she seeing a normalized version of her development? Am I reinforcing this normalized version, thereby reinforcing power structures by presenting it as a possibility as one "true" version of her life? Clearly all interpretations are power laden, which presents an intriguing dilemma. Privileging the interpretations in which participants see themselves possibly reinforces hegemony; offering deconstructing interpretations in which participants do not see themselves challenges hegemony but reinforces researcher-participant power. These two forms of intermingled power differ in nature: concerns about power in constructivism focus on researcher-participant tensions; concerns about power in poststructuralism focus on systematic social structures. Still, this dilemma is consistent with the poststructuralist notion that power is a web in which we all are tangled (Sullivan, 2003). In this context, the researcher, participant, and heteronormativity are inseparably tied together. Researchers need to decide which of the power strings they will weave and which they will resist when working in theoretical borderlands.

## Consideration #3: What Are Researcher Implications for Partnering Queer Theory With Constructivism? (or Where Am I Going and Is It Far Enough?)

Feminist standpoint research (e.g., Wolf, 1996) teaches that researchers should engage in thoughtful reflection regarding the research decisions they make. Kincheloe and McLaren (2005) observed that bricolage "demands a new level of research self-consciousness and awareness of the numerous contexts in which any researcher is operating" (p. 316). Bringing together two divergent theoretical perspectives caused me to reflect on who I am and who I will be as a researcher. Now that I have analyzed student identity development data using queer theory, I am not sure I can go back to using only a constructivist lens. I am too aware of all of the issues I am omitting by describing only one slice of students' development and am troubled that I would be using theories that might not embrace the heteronormative realities of lesbian college students' lives. My new realizations also speak to queer theory's praxis potential. As a result of in-depth conversation with my co-researcher about the relationship between constructivist theory and queer theory, my perspective on development shifted. I am not the same teacher or researcher that I was prior to that project. As a theoretical framework then, queer theory's praxis potential goes beyond how its tenets might be applied in work with college students, but also how it can innately change who we are as professionals. Among the questions raised by my personal changes and heightened awareness are: For what purpose do researchers use theoretical perspectives? How intricately tied are a researcher's personal values and the theoretical perspectives she uses in her research? How can researchers move between perspectives and remain true to her values? Broadly considered, these are questions related to research ethics.

Certainly, I cannot let go of all that I learned about heteronormativity in student development theory through our research project with KT. So if I research and write in the future about identity development without using queer perspectives, is my research undercutting lesbian college students? By contradicting myself, am I making research only an academic endeavor rather than a meaningful story about college students through which I am committed to creating change? Can I as a researcher ever separate myself from the research, moving between theoretical perspectives without a particular agenda? As I have wrestled with these questions, I have tentatively reached the decision that I cannot turn back (tentative, knowing that contexts and circumstances change). Uncovering how heteronormativity mediates student development and theories about development requires a sustained effort to change how lesbian identity development is conceptualized and researched. Returning to only constructivist ways would undermine these efforts. Working in theoretical borderlands fosters change.

*Questions Still to Be Answered.* If I am committed to using aspects of queer theory in future research on lesbian identity development, it is fair to ask why I cannot entirely let go of constructivist theories. If they are grounded in heteronormative assumptions, why continue to use them? As asked earlier, why not subscribe only to a queer analysis of development to address heteronormativity rather than working in theoretical borderlands? I do believe theories grounded in a constructivist perspective provide one useful way of making some sense of how students perceive their identities, especially when used in conjunction with queer theory and are perceived as one incomplete perspective on truth. This approach is consistent with the postmodern perspective. It is important to view students from multiple perspectives, acknowledging that not one perspective presents a complete view of reality and that multiple realities must be simultaneously held, even when contradictory and even though the practicality of the simultaneous application of contradictory theoretical perspectives remains to be understood. Still, might letting go of constructivist theories be a possibility? Or might doing so be inconsistent with the assumption of multiple realities?

## This Isn't the End

As I move into the next phases of my research, I will continue to explore possibilities for researching in theoretical borderlands to address power structures in student development theory. Doing so addresses the limitations of singular focused theoretical perspectives, rigid adherence to particular ideological positions, and the marginalization of college students' non-normative identities. It is my hope that recounting my journey from a socialized constructivist researcher into theoretical borderlands demonstrates the benefits of a borderland approach for research, researchers, and most importantly the students with and for whom the research is conducted. I offer this approach, in particular the pairing of constructivism and queer theory as one possibility, and I continue to raise questions about the details of its implementation.

I also believe this borderland approach is appropriate for bringing together numerous other theoretical perspectives. Queer theory is just one example of a theoretical perspective that brings inequitable power structures to the forefront of thinking about student development theory. Other theoretical perspectives, such as critical race theory, critical Latino studies, and feminist poststructuralist theory, can also challenge the normalization of development (Tanaka, 2002). As with queer theory, however, each of these normative challenging perspectives is incomplete in what it illuminates about student development. Rather than turning a blind eye to these limitations or being paralyzed by them, experimenting with an interdisciplinary approach that creates theoretical borderlands has the potential to move research on student development theory in a direction that challenges power inequities and speaks to students' understandings of themselves. Whatever perspectives researchers use, researching in the borderlands is worth the challenging methodological considerations that venturing into this new territory raises.

## References

Abes, E. S. (2007). Applying queer theory in practice with college students: Transformation of a researcher's and participant's perspectives on identity. *Journal of LGBT Youth, 5*(1), 57–77.

Abes, E. S., & Jones, S. R. (2004). Meaning-making capacity and the dynamics of lesbian college students' multiple dimensions of identity. *Journal of College Student Development, 45*, 612–632.

Abes, E. S., Jones, S. R., & McEwen, M. K. (2007). Reconceptualizing the model of multiple dimensions of identity: The role of meaning-making capacity in the construction of multiple identities. *Journal of College Student Development, 48*, 1–22.

Abes, E. S., & Kasch, D. (2007). Using queer theory to explore lesbian college students' multiple dimensions of identity. *Journal of College Student Development, 48*, 619–636.

Anzaldua, G. (1999). *Borderlands: La frontera* (2nd ed.). San Francisco: Aunt Lute Books.

Baxter Magolda, M. B. (2001). *Making their own way: Narratives for transforming higher education to promote self-development* (1st ed.). Sterling, VA: Stylus.

Baxter Magolda, M. B. (2004). Evolution of a constructivist conceptualization of epistemological reflection. *Educational Psychologist, 39*(1), 31–42.

Baxter Magolda, M. B., & King, P. M. (2007). Interview strategies for assessing self-authorship: Constructing conversations to assess meaning making. *Journal of College Student Development, 48*, 491–508.

Britzman, D. P. (1997). What is this thing called love? New discourses for understanding gay and lesbian youth. In S. de Castell & M. Bryson (Eds.), *Radical in(ter)ventions: Identity, politics, and difference/s on educational praxis* (pp. 183–207). Albany: State University of New York Press.

Britzman, D. P. (2000). "The question of belief": Writing poststructual ethnography. In E. A. St. Pierre & W. S. Pillow (2000). *Working the ruins: Feminist poststructural theory and methods in education* (pp. 27–40). New York: Routledge.

Broido, E. M., & Manning, K. (2002). Philosophical foundations and current theoretical perspectives in qualitative research. *Journal of College Student Development, 43,* 434–445.

Butler, J. (1990). *Gender trouble: Feminism and the subversion of identity.* New York: Routledge.

Cass, V. C. (1979). Homosexual identity formation: A theoretical model. *Journal of Homosexuality, 4,* 219–235.

Crotty, M. (1998). *The foundations of social research: Meaning and perspective in the research process.* Thousand Oaks, CA: Sage.

Davis, T. L. (2002). Voices of gender role conflict: The social construction of college men's identity. *Journal of College Student Development, 43,* 508–521.

Denzin, N. K., & Lincoln, Y. S. (2000). The discipline and practice of qualitative research. In N.K. Denzin & Y.S. Lincoln (Eds.), *Handbook of qualitative research* (2nd ed., pp. 1–28). Thousand Oaks, CA: Sage.

Dilley, P. (2002). *Queer man on campus: A history of non-heterosexual college men, 1945-2000.* New York: Routledge-Falmer.

Donmoyer, R. (2006). Take my paradigm . . . please! The legacy of Kuhn's construct in educational research. *International Journal of Qualitative Studies in Education, 19*(1), 11–34.

Fine, M., Weis, L., Weseen, S., Wong, L. (2000). Qualitative research, representations, and social responsibilities. In N. K. Denzin & Y. S. Lincoln (Eds.), *Handbook of qualitative research* (2nd ed., pp. 107–131). Thousand Oaks, CA: Sage.

Gamson, J. (2000). Sexualities, queer theory, and qualitative research. In N. K. Denzin & Y. S. Lincoln (Eds.), *Handbook of qualitative research* (2nd ed., pp. 347–365). Thousand Oaks, CA: Sage.

Guba, E. G, & Lincoln, Y. S. (2005). Paradigmatic controversies, contradictions, and emerging confluences. In N. K. Denzin & Y. S. Lincoln (Eds.), *The Sage handbook of qualitative research* (pp. 191–215). Thousand Oaks, CA: Sage.

Halberstram, J. (2005). *In a queer time and place: Transgender bodies and subcultural lives.* New York: New York University Press.

Jones, S. R., Arminio, J., Broido, E., & Torres, V. (2002). Adding depth to an expanded horizon. *Journal of College Student Development, 43,* 431–433.

Jones, S. R., Torres, V., & Arminio, J. (2006). *Negotiating the complexities of qualitative research in higher education: Fundamental elements and issues.* New York: Routledge.

Kincheloe, J. L., & McLaren, P. (2005). Rethinking critical theory and qualitative research. In N. K. Denzin & Y. S. Lincoln (Eds.), *The Sage handbook of qualitative research* (pp. 303–342). Thousand Oaks, CA: Sage.

Kodama, C. M., McEwen, M. K., Liang, C. T. H., & Lee, S. (2002). An Asian American perspective on psychosocial student development theory. In M. K. McEwen, C. M. Kodama, A. N. Alvarez, S. Lee & C. T. H. Liang (Eds.), *Working with Asian American college students* (New Directions for Student Services No. 97, pp. 45–59). San Francisco: Jossey Bass.

Kong, T. S. K., Mahoney, D., Plummer, K. (2002). Queering the interview. In J. F. Gubrium & J. A. Holstein (Eds.), *Handbook of interview research: Context and method* (pp. 239–258). Thousand Oaks, CA: Sage.

Lather, P. (1991). *Getting smart: Feminist research and pedagogy with/in the postmodern.* New York: Routledge.

Lather, P. (2006). Paradigm proliferation as a good thing to think with: Teaching research in education as wild profusion. *International Journal of Qualitative Studies in Education, 19*(1), 35–57.

Lather, P. (2007). *Getting lost: Feminist efforts toward a double(d) science.* Albany: State University of New York Press.

Lieblich, A., Tuval-Mashiach, R., & Zilber, T. (1998). *Narrative research: Readings, analysis, interpretation.* Thousand Oaks, CA: Sage.

McEwen, M. (2003). The nature and uses of theory. In S. R. Komives, D. B. Woodard, Jr., & Associates (Eds.), *Student services: A handbook for the profession* (pp. 153–178). San Francisco: Jossey Bass.

Muñoz, J. E. (1999). *Disidentifications: Queers of color and the performance of politics.* Minneapolis: University of Minnesota Press.

Pillow, W. (2003). Race-based methodologies: Multicultural methods or epistemological shifts. In G. R. López & L. Parker (Eds.). *Interrogating racism in qualitative research methodology* (pp. 181–202). New York: Peter Lang.

Pizzolato, J. E. (2003). Developing self-authorship: Exploring the experiences of high-risk college students. *Journal of College Student Development, 44*, 797–812.

Plummer, K. (2005). Critical humanism and queer theory: Living with the tensions. In N. K. Denzin & Y. S. Lincoln (Eds). *The sage handbook of qualitative research* (pp. 357–386). Thousand Oaks, CA: Sage Publications.

Renn, K. A., & Bilodeau, B. (2005). Queer student leaders: An exploratory case study of identity development and LGBT student involvement at a Midwestern research university. *Journal of Gay & Lesbian Issues in Education, 2*(4), 49–71.

Richardson, L., & St. Pierre, E. A. (2005). Writing: A method of inquiry. In N. K. Denzin & Y. S. Lincoln (Eds.), *The Sage handbook of qualitative research* (pp. 959–978). Thousand Oaks, CA: Sage.

Stewart, D. L. (2002). The role of faith in the development of an integrated identity: A qualitative study of Black students at a White college. *Journal of College Student Development, 43*, 579–595.

Sullivan, N. (2003). *A critical introduction to queer theory*. New York: New York University Press.

Talburt, S. (2000). *Subject to identity: Knowledge, sexuality, and academic practices in higher education*. Albany: State University of New York Press.

Talburt, S. (2004). Ethnographic responsibility without the "real." *The Journal of Higher Education, 75*(1), 80–103.

Tanaka, G. (2002). Higher education's self-reflexive turn: Toward an intercultural theory of student development. *The Journal of Higher Education, 73*(2), 263–296.

Tierney, W. G. (1993). *Building communities of difference: Higher education in the 21st century*. Westport, CT: Bergin & Garvey.

Tierney, W. G. (1997). *Academic outlaws: Queer theory and cultural studies in the academy*. Thousand Oaks, CA: Sage.

Tierney, W. G., & Rhoads, R. A. (1993). Postmodernism and critical theory in higher education: Implications for research and practice. In J. C. Smart (Ed.), *Higher education: Handbook of theory and research*, v. 9 (pp. 308–343). New York: Agathon Press.

van Gennep, A. (1960). *The rites of passage*. (M. B. Vizedom & G. L. Caffe, Trans.). Chicago: University of Chicago Press. (Original work published 1909)

Warner, M. (1991). Introduction: Fear of a queer planet. *Social Text, 29*, 3–17.

Wolf, D. L. (1996). Situating feminist dilemmas in fieldwork. In D. L. Wolf (Ed.), *Feminist dilemmas in fieldwork* (pp. 1–55). Boulder, CO: Westview Press.

# CHAPTER 30
## EDUCATIONAL INEQUITIES AND LATINA/O UNDERGRADUATE STUDENTS IN THE UNITED STATES: A CRITICAL RACE ANALYSIS OF THEIR EDUCATIONAL PROGRESS

DANIEL G. SOLÓRZANO, OCTAVIO VILLALPANDO, AND LETICIA OSEGUERA

Using critical race theory (CRT) as a framework, the authors analyze the educational inequities and racialized barriers faced by Latina/o college students when navigating the educational pipeline leading to a college degree. The impact of racialized structures, policies, and practices is examined in the context of how they influence the educational attainment and academic progress of Latinas/os. The article concludes by offering CRT-based policy and practical approaches to enhancing the success of Latina/o college students.

Usando la Teoría de Raza Crítica (CRT) como marco de referencia los autores analizan las desigualdades educacionales y las barreras raciales que estudiantes universitarios Latinos encaran al navegar la tubería educacional que los lleva a obtener el grado universitario. El impacto de estructuras racializadas, políticas, y prácticas se examinan en el contexto de cómo éstas influencian el logro educacional y el avance académico para los estudiantes universitarios Latinos. El manuscrito concluye ofreciendo políticas y prácticas basadas en CRT para enriquecer el éxito de los estudiantes universitarios Latinos.

In June 2003, the Supreme Court ruled in the *Grutter v. Bollinger* (2003) case and reaffirmed the 1978 *Bakke v. Regents* case that race-based affirmative action could continue to be used as one factor in college and university admissions. However, Supreme Court Justice Sandra Day O'Connor, writing the majority opinion in *Grutter*, argued that race and ethnicity would become irrelevant characteristics for college admissions in 25 years. Clearly, one of the major outcomes of the Supreme Court's opinion in *Grutter* was to forewarn higher education institutions that race should become an irrelevant measure of the educational achievement or academic potential for students of color. The opinion further reinscribed the myth of race neutrality in higher education but, more important, set a legal

Solórzano, D. G., Villalpando, O., & Oseguera, L. (2005). Educational inequities and Latina/o undergraduate students in the United States: A critical race analysis of their educational progress. *Journal of Hispanic Higher Education, 4,* 272–294.

alarm clock that will go off in 25 years when, presumably, race will no longer play a factor in the educational experiences and conditions of students of color.

In this article, we provide an analysis of how race may indeed continue to be an important characteristic in determining students' of color educational attainment and achievement in higher education. We focus our analysis specifically on Latina/o college students, one of the largest racial/ethnic groups in American higher education yet one of the least studied populations in the field. The question guiding our analysis is: What are the educational conditions and related outcomes that exist as Latinas/os navigate the undergraduate pipeline, and why do these conditions continue to exist? We begin by reviewing educational pipeline data we have compiled on Latina/o students, focusing on the key transition points. Next, we analyze these data through a critical race theory (CRT) lens. Finally, our CRT analysis concludes with a discussion of policy and practical implications that stem from our research and analysis.

## Background

According to the 2000 Census, approximately 13% of the total U.S. population, or 35.3 million, people self-identify as Latinas/os and now represent the largest underrepresented racial/ethnic group in the United States—a category formerly ascribed to African Americans. Chicanas and Chicanos represent approximately 64% of the total Latina/o population, with Puerto Ricans (11%), Cubans (5%), Central or South Americans (14%), and other Latinas/os (7%) making up the remainder of the Latina/o population. Within the Latina/o population, there are significant subgroup differences. For instance, of the three most prominent Latina/o subgroups, Cuban Americans are the smallest, the oldest, and do much better educationally and occupationally than either Chicanas/os or Puerto Ricans. Puerto Ricans and Chicanas/os are more likely to be concentrated in urban centers, live in poverty, and experience poor educational conditions.

Chicanas/os are the youngest, the largest, and the fastest growing of the three population groups and are moving in large numbers to major metropolitan areas in the Pacific Northwest, the Midwest, and the South and on the East Coast. When one examines ethnic groups west of the Mississippi River, Chicanas/os represent the largest single group of color in almost every major metropolitan area.

Specific to education, nationally only 46% of Chicanas/os have attended at least 4 years of high school, in contrast to 84% of non-Latina/o Whites. Similarly, just 8% of Chicanas/os have acquired at least a baccalaureate degree, compared to 26% of Whites (U.S. Bureau of the Census, 2000).

## Critical Race Theory in Higher Education

To help us understand the structures, practices, and policies that led to these dismal educational attainment levels for Latina/o students, we use the interpretive framework of CRT (see Crenshaw, Gotanda, Peller, & Thomas, 1995; Delgado, 1995; Ladson-Billings, 1999; Ladson-Billings & Tate, 1995; Matsuda, Lawrence, Delgado, & Crenshaw, 1993; Parker, Deyhle, Villenas, & Crossland 1998; Solórzano, 1997; Solórzano & Delgado Bernal, 2001; Solórzano & Villalpando, 1998; Solórzano & Yosso, 2001, 2002a, 2002b; Tate, 1997; Villenas & Deyhle, 1999). Within the field of higher education, CRT is becoming an increasingly important tool to broaden and deepen the analysis of the racialized barriers erected for people of color (see Delgado Bernal & Villalpando, 2002; Solórzano & Delgado Bernal, 2001; Solórzano & Villalpando, 1998; Taylor, 1999; Villalpando, 2003; Villalpando & Delgado Bernal, 2002; Yosso, 2000). CRT in education explores the ways in which "race-neutral" laws and institutional structures, practices, and policies perpetuate racial/ethnic educational inequality. This framework emphasizes the importance of viewing policies and policy making within a proper historical and cultural context to deconstruct their racialized content (Bell, 1992; Crenshaw et al., 1995). It challenges dominant liberal ideas of color blindness and meritocracy and shows how these ideas operate to disadvantage people of color while further advantaging Whites (Delgado & Stefancic, 2001).

There are at least five defining elements that form the basic assumptions, perspectives, research methods, and pedagogies of CRT (Matsuda et al., 1993; Solórzano & Delgado Bernal, 2001; Tate, 1997; Villalpando & Delgado Bernal, 2002). These elements help to frame this examination of Latina/o college students.

*The centrality of race and racism.* CRT acknowledges as its most basic premise that race and racism are defining characteristics of American society. In American higher education, race and racism are imbedded in the structures, practices, and discourses that guide the daily practices of universities (Taylor, 1999). Race and racism are central constructs but also intersect with other components of one's identity, such as language, generation status, gender, sexuality, and class (Crenshaw, 1989; Valdes, 1996). For people of color, each of these elements of one's identity can relate to other forms of subordination (Crenshaw, 1993), yet each dimension cannot fully explain the other. For example, language oppression by itself cannot account for racial oppression nor can racial oppression alone account for class oppression.

*The challenge to dominant ideology.* CRT in higher education challenges the traditional claims of universities to objectivity, meritocracy, color blindness, race neutrality, and equal opportunity. These theoretical frameworks reveal how the dominant ideology of color blindness and race neutrality act as a camouflage for the self-interest, power, and privilege of dominant groups in American society (Calmore, 1992; Delgado, 1989).

*A commitment to social justice and praxis.* CRT has a fundamental commitment to a social justice agenda that struggles to eliminate all forms of racial, gender, language, generation status, and class subordination (Matsuda, 1996). In higher education, these theoretical frameworks are conceived as a social justice project that attempt to link theory with practice, scholarship with teaching, and the academy with the community (Solórzano & Yosso, 2000).

*A centrality of experiential knowledge.* CRT recognizes that the experiential knowledge of people of color is legitimate and critical to understanding racial subordination. The application of a CRT framework in the field of higher education requires that the experiential knowledge of people of color be centered and viewed as a resource stemming directly from their lived experiences. The experiential knowledge can come from storytelling, family history, biographies, scenarios, parables, *cuentos, testimonios,* chronicles, and narratives (Bell, 1987; Carrasco, 1996; Delgado, 1989, 1995; Olivas, 1990).

*An historical context and interdisciplinary perspective.* CRT challenges ahistoricism and the unidisciplinary focus of most analyses in educational research. In the field of higher education, this framework analyzes race and racism in both a historical and a contemporary context using interdisciplinary methods (Delgado, 1984, 1992; Garcia, 1995; Harris, 1994; Olivas, 1990).

These defining elements of CRT form a framework that can be applied to real-life problems in higher education and in broader society. It is especially applicable to the realm of higher education given how the American legal system has historically used race/ethnicity, national origin, language, class, and an ever-changing conception of justice in the construction and implementation of laws that influence higher education (Solórzano & Yosso, 2002a; Taylor, 1999). CRT provides a set of basic perspectives, methods, and pedagogy that can identify, analyze, and transform those structural and policy dimensions of higher education that maintain the racial, ethnic, gender, language, and class subordination of people of color in universities (Villalpando & Delgado Bernal, 2002). A CRT framework is useful in theorizing and examining the ways in which race and racism affect the structures, practices, and discourses within higher education by, for example, pointing to the contradictory ways in which universities operate with their potential to oppress and marginalize while also emancipating and empowering (Solórzano & Villalpando, 1998).

## The Latina and Latino Educational Pipeline

In the following section, we examine the educational pipeline for Latina/o undergraduates through a CRT framework. We begin by highlighting the educational pipeline (from elementary school to the doctorate) for the five major racial/ethnic groups and then for each of the largest Latina/o subgroups (e.g., Chicanas/os, Puerto Ricans, Cubans, Dominicans, and Salvadorans) in the United States. Then, for purposes of this article, we illustrate the aggregated Latina/o pipeline. This particular illustration includes a piece of the pipeline (i.e., community college transfer) often understudied for Latinas/os but constituting an entry point to college for the majority of Latina/o students.

The Latina/o college-age population has increased by 14% since 1994 (Carter & Wilson, 2001), contributing to a steady increase in their college enrollment during the past two decades. These gains, however, are partly driven by enrollment increases at 2-year institutions, where the numbers of Latina/o students have tripled in the past 20 years (U.S. Department of Education, 2001). In the past year alone, there was an absolute increase in college enrollment of Latina/o students of 143,000, yet 75% (108,000) of this growth occurred at 2-year colleges. This does not underscore the fact that Latina/o student enrollment in baccalaureate-granting institutions is also on the rise. Presently, Latinas/os account for 24% of undergraduates enrolled in California 4-year institutions.[1] For these reasons, an examination of students at this juncture of the pipeline is warranted.

To better understand the underrepresentation of Latinas and Latinos in postsecondary education, it is important to begin with an examination of their experiences in elementary and secondary school (Solórzano & Solórzano, 1995). Malcom (1990) has stated that "to understand the reasons for the mere trickle at the end of the . . . pipeline, . . . we must go all the way back to the headwater" (p. 249). Therefore, the underachievement and underrepresentation of Latinas and Latinos at each point in the educational pipeline might be better explained by investigating the educational conditions at the elementary and secondary "headwater."

We contend that educational researchers and policy makers need to theoretically understand the cumulative effects of inadequate educational preparation and schooling conditions of Latinas/os at the elementary and secondary levels and how that affects their educational attainment in college and beyond. This lack of achievement and attainment at each point in the educational pipeline has resulted in both a loss of talent to U.S. society and a loss of important role models for the next generation of Latina/o students who aspire to educational and professional careers.

To graphically show the leakage points in the educational pipeline, we have taken data from various sources (see Solórzano & Yosso, 2000; U.S. Bureau of the Census, 2000; Watford, Rivas, Burciaga, & Solórzano, in press). At any given point in the educational pipeline—no matter how one measures educational outcomes—Latinas/os do not perform as well as most other students (see Solórzano & Yosso, 2000; U.S. Bureau of the Census, 2000; Watford et al., in press).

Figure 1 compares the five major racial/ethnic groups in the United States along the educational pipeline from elementary school to the doctorate. The data make clear that Latinas/os do least well at each point in the educational pipeline. For example, among 100 Latinas/os who begin elementary school, a little more than one half will graduate from high school and only about 10 will complete a college degree. Eventually, less than 1 of the original 100 Latinas/os who enrolled in elementary school will complete a doctoral degree. What makes these data especially noteworthy is the fact that Latinas/os represent the largest ethnic/racial group in the United States but have the poorest educational transition rates among all groups. In fact, in Figure 2, when we disaggregate the Latina/o subgroups, we find even greater differences in educational outcomes between Latina/o groups. These low educational attainment rates are cause for concern given the youthfulness of the Latina/o population and the continued growth projections of this group in the near future (U.S. Bureau of the Census, 2000). It is critical that we begin to understand why these groups historically (as well as presently) do not attain more equal outcomes as their counterparts in the United States.

To expand and further illustrate the educational pipeline, we use Figure 3 to focus specifically on the Latina/o population. Of the 100 Latina/o students at the elementary level, 48 drop out of high school and 52 continue on to graduate. Of those 52 who graduate from high school, about 31, or 60%, continue on to some form of postsecondary education. Of those 31, about 20, or 65%, move on to community colleges and 11, or 35%, will go to a 4-year institution. Of those 20 in community colleges, only 2 will transfer to a 4-year college. Of the 11 students who went to a 4-year college and 2 who transferred, 10 will graduate from college with a baccalaureate degree. Finally, 4 students will continue on and graduate from graduate or professional school and less than 1 will receive a doctorate.

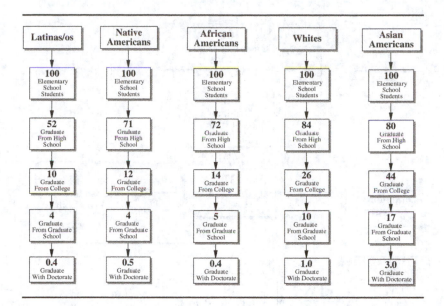

**Figure 1**  The U.S. educational pipeline.

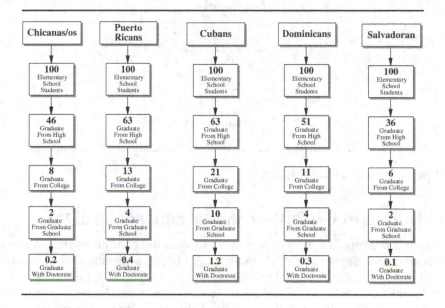

**Figure 2**  The U.S. Latina/o educational pipeline.

Clearly, investigation into the educational and social conditions at every point in the pipeline is critical to the success of one of the fastest-growing populations in the country. For this article, however, we focus primarily on the transition to college and through college, toward the attainment of a baccalaureate degree because entry and successful completion of a baccalaureate can dramatically improve the overall economic and social conditions of Latina/o groups (Dougherty, 1994). In particular, we are trying to address what we do know about the educational experiences of the few Latina and Latino students who enter postsecondary institutions, how these students survive and succeed in higher education, and what happens to students at each of the stages in the postsecondary pipeline.

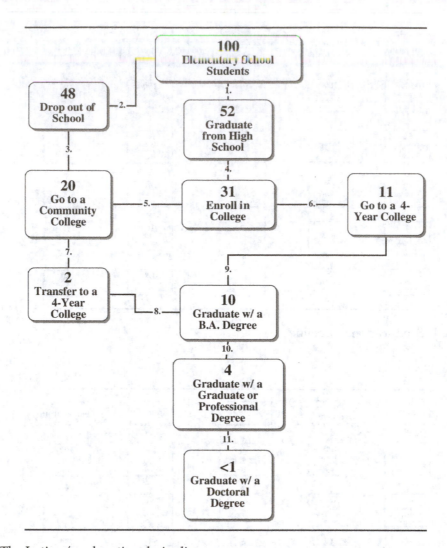

**Figure 3**   The Latina/o educational pipeline.

## Latinas and Latinos in the Postsecondary Education Sector

As we move through the pipeline, it is important to discuss the conditions that influence the completion of a baccalaureate degree among Latinas/os. To better understand the educational conditions and related outcomes that exist as Latinas/os navigate the undergraduate pipeline and why these conditions continue to exist, we present four outcomes to which higher education must attend to ensure the continued education of Latina/o college students. For each outcome, we evaluate the conditions at the leakage points that contribute to the underachievement of Latina/o undergraduate students. The three main outcomes and conditions we present include (a) the disparity between 2- and 4-year enrollments of Latina/o students, (b) the low transfer rates of Latinas/os to 4-year institutions, and (c) retention and graduation at both the 2- and 4-year level.

## Latinas/os and the Community College

In its 2003 decision on affirmative action, the U.S. Supreme Court asserted that the opportunity to attend and graduate from college has become more equitable for all students (*Grutter v. Bollinger*, 2003). As evidence, it pointed to projected increases in enrollments of low-income students and students of color and concluded that access will continue to be an attainable goal for all underrepresented students. At first glance, the Supreme Court opinion seemed to echo Clark Kerr's 1960

Master Plan for California Higher Education, which envisioned access for all students but primarily through the open admissions policies of 2-year colleges to anyone at least 18 years of age or holding a high school diploma. However, 42 years later, Kerr expressed concern about the direction and future of California higher education in the May 16, 2002, *UCLA Daily Bruin* interview (Falcone, 2002). When discussing the unequal opportunities for transfer to 4-year colleges from California's community colleges, Kerr declared,

> The good community colleges will have college preparatory courses there that you can then transfer your credits (to the UC), and the poor community colleges will have no transfer courses whatsoever. So if you want to transfer and you haven't taken any transfer courses, you can't. (p. A1)

Today, nearly half a century after the inception of the California Master Plan, we, like Clark Kerr, question whether open access to under-resourced and lower-status institutions, like community colleges, truly represents genuine access for all students. As large institutions with many part-time faculty and few resources for academic expenditures and student services, community colleges tend to serve part-time, commuting students and to offer less financial aid than 4-year institutions of any type. Their ability to develop students' cognitive and affective skills is often questioned, especially in light of their low transfer rates to 4-year institutions (Ornelas, 2002; Ornelas & Solórzano, 2004). Yet why is it that nearly two thirds of all Latinas/os begin their postsecondary education at the community college level, and to what extent does this account for their low numbers of 4-year degree attainment?

Admittedly, community colleges serve multiple and often-conflicting roles for their students. They have three primary functions that some argue have little relation to one another. Community colleges provide (a) vocational education/certificate programs, (b) terminal associate of art/science degrees, and (c) transfer opportunities to 4-year institutions. Having three separate roles often results in different outcomes for the enrolled students. For example, on one hand, community colleges are seen as spaces that are inefficient and harmful for student aspirations when their transfer and retention rates are low, yet on the other hand, they are successful at providing job training and credentialing through 2-year degrees or certificates. But it is precisely these multiple and competing functions that may serve to exacerbate the pipeline dilemma for Latina/o students who find themselves in 2-year colleges, especially because some community colleges place a stronger emphasis on one or more of these functions (see Ornelas, 2002; Ornelas & Solórzano, 2004). It is important to examine why these conditions exist at this level and what types of career and educational aspirations are being fostered in community colleges that admittedly serve a multitude of functions.

Despite these conflicting multiple functions, the largest growth in higher education has been at the community college level. First, students are unable to enroll directly into 4-year colleges because they have not met admissions requirements. This is often because of poor college preparatory counseling and the cumulative effects of having been tracked into non-college-preparatory curricula in elementary, middle, and high school (Oakes, 1985; Solórzano & Ornelas, 2004).

Second, community colleges are less expensive than 4-year colleges. Latinas/os are disproportionately found at the lowest socioeconomic sectors of U.S. society and appear to also be overrepresented in community colleges. Community colleges appear to offer the opportunity to working-class, first-generation Latinas/os to pay the low tuition while working full-time. These conditions combine to inhibit their likelihood of transferring to a 4-year institution and contribute to their inability to complete a degree.

Third, 2-year colleges are places where there is an increasing need for remediation. Faculty and institutional personnel are often confronted with the fact that most of their efforts need to be in the form of remediation for its students. The 2000 NCES-PEQIS survey indicates that 42% of public 2-year students enrolled in at least one remedial reading, writing, or math course (U.S. Department of Education, 2003). Perhaps the most central policy concern is the enrollment of underprepared students and the attendant effects of remedial programs on student achievement and matriculation through the higher education pipeline as this extends coursework and increases the likelihood that students will not persist through to a degree. In the past few years, no less than 41 state legislatures, governing boards, and higher education systems have considered or have enacted policy initiatives directed at limiting or reforming remedial education[2] in 2- and 4-year institutions (Jenkins &

Boswell, 2002; Mazzeo, 2002). Even among supporters of remedial education efforts, there are worries that requirements for remediation are not equitably enforced. In fact, the research suggests that the varying standards and definitions for remedial education from institution to institution and even within the same state or higher education system, exacerbates the dilemma of course completion and successful transfer (Grubb, 1999; Merisotis & Phipps, 2000; Perin, 2002).

Clearly, when Latinas/os begin their postsecondary education at a 2-year community college, in contrast to beginning at a 4-year institution, they face a greater possibility of not completing a baccalaureate degree. The reasons for their inability to transfer often result from institutional structures that fail to support their academic needs and professional goals and aspirations.

## Low Transfer Rates to 4-Year Institutions

One of the major ways that 2-year community colleges fail Latina/o college students is by not providing a clear and explicit method of transferring to 4-year institutions. Even though 71% of Latina/o students who enter a community college desire to transfer to a 4-year institution, only 7% to 20% end up eventually transferring (U.S. Department of Education, 2001). The absence of a "transfer culture" at 2-year community colleges leaves students without the structures, practices, and discourses that promote or facilitate transferring to a 4-year institution (Ornelas, 2002; Ornelas & Solórzano, 2004). Community colleges often lack academic guidance or clearly defined transfer procedures. Despite the growing trend of developing articulation agreements between 2- and 4-year colleges, which identify specific classes and other requirements that, once-fulfilled, guarantee students' ability to transfer, they still do not have a significant impact on Latina/o students transfer rates (Ornelas, 2002).

One example of the poor academic guidance and counseling often provided by community colleges is their inability to dispel the myth that completing the requirements of an associate of arts degree will also fulfill transfer requirements to a 4-year institution (Ornelas, 2002; Rangel, 2001; Talavera-Bustillos, 1998). The misinformation obtained by Latina/o community college students often leads them to additional coursework that both fulfills associate of arts degree and transfer requirements to a 4-year institution.

The poor academic guidance and counseling provided to Latinas/os in community colleges is often based on low expectations that instructors and counselors hold for Latinas/os (Ornelas, 2002; Ornelas & Solórzano, 2004). Deficit-based expectations about Latina/o students' culture, language, values, and ability to learn often impose structural barriers that inhibit their college-level preparation and academic success (Ornelas, 2002; Valencia, 1997). Indeed, these deficit-based stereotypes often guide the students' schooling experience prior to getting to postsecondary institutions. Jeannie Oakes (1985) has documented the effects of academic tracking and ability grouping in K-12 education, which often parallels tracking practices by community college instructors and counselors that steer Latinas/os toward vocational skills and job training programs rather than a college transfer track.

Using 2000–2001 California Postsecondary Education Commission (CPEC) data, it is no wonder that of every 100 Latina/o California high school graduates, 40 continue on to postsecondary institutions. Of these 40 students, 30 begin at one of the California Community Colleges (CCC), 3 at the University of California (UC) and 7 at the California State University (CSU) campuses. Of those 30 community college students, 3 will transfer to a CSU campus and 0.4 to a UC campus.

Clearly, data from Figure 4 confirm that practices adopted by 2-year community colleges in the state of California to increase the transfer opportunities for Latinas/os have been insufficient and ineffective. Indeed, we are losing a tremendous resource in the community college student who fails to transfer to a 4-year college or university.

## Baccalaureate Degree Retention and Attainment

This section examines the intended outcomes for Latina/o students when they do enter into higher education institutions and will highlight the programs and services that are in place to help assist in degree completion when they do enter higher education. This section will argue that even good faith efforts may often perpetuate unequal outcomes for students through the underlying messages being sent. We also speak to the factors that mitigate for and against baccalaureate degree completion.

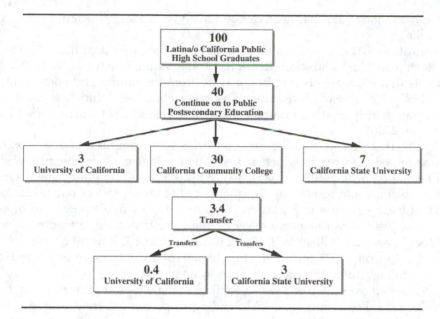

**Figure 4**    The Latina/o California postsecondary educational pipeline: 2000–2001.

There are a number of institutionalized systems in place to aid students in their degree completion. Examples include student-initiated retention programs versus university-based retention programs. Students have developed their own response to retaining fellow undergraduates through student-initiated retention efforts (Solórzano, 1999). Apparently, these students feel that the institution's programs are not serving its intended purposes. Students already have a great deal of responsibility, so agreeing to take on other students may add to their stress and workload. In addition, because these programs are student initiated and student run, there is little institutional memory, and if there is no one that can fill these roles when a student graduates, the programs cease to exist. Although it is admirable that students want to play a role in this process, the message that student-initiated and student-run programs send is that students who are serviced by these programs are really not a priority of the college and indeed should not be enrolled in those institutions.

A second condition that would advance student retention includes community college partnerships. Community college partnerships are important avenues for students to acquire knowledge of the college transfer process and other important information about the college-going experience. Community college partnerships can go a long way in developing and strengthening academic partnerships between universities and the community colleges within their area by offering such services as curricular diversity and academic advising to make students academically competitive for admission and by creating more collaborative relationships between various offices on both the community college campus and the 4-year institution, such as admission offices, academic guidance offices, transfer centers, financial aid centers, and housing offices.

A third condition that would facilitate college completion includes the financing of college for Latina/o students. Numerous studies have demonstrated that aid is a positive predictor of degree completion (Astin, 1993; Oseguera, 2004; St. John, 1991, 2003). Having the ability to finance college frees an individual from having to work and the student can spend more time devoted to college and studying. As we mentioned earlier, Latina/o students are disproportionately from low-income families. Unfortunately, low-income students are precisely the group of students most responsive to college price changes (Heller, 1997; Leslie & Brinkman, 1988). This is cause for concern given the steep rise in tuition in the past two decades coupled with the increasing shift from grant aid to loans (Price, 2003; St. John, 2003). A recent study by St. John (2003) demonstrated this phenomenon as his research identified the negative effect of reduced grant funding and overreliance on loan funding on college enrollment. In addition, Hu and St. John (2001) and Oseguera (2004) have demonstrated how financial aid that need not be repaid is also a significant positive predictor of persistence in college.

A fourth condition that can assist undergraduates in the pursuit of their degree is students receiving mentoring and/or validation (Rendon, 1994; Rendon, Jalomo, & Nora, 2000). The popular conception is that students need to break away from the family and community to be successful (Tinto, 1993), but research on students of color challenges that notion and shows that maintaining strong family and community ties enhances student success (Solórzano, 1999; Solórzano & Yosso, 2000).

A fifth condition that affects baccalaureate completion is the campus racial climate. A large body of research has explored the ways in which an institution's climate affects the lives of students and faculty. This information, when utilized, has aided campus leaders and policy makers in moving toward sustaining diversity and improving the quality of life for diverse populations. Assessing climate is important because of the implications it has on all individuals within an organization. A harsh racial climate has a direct negative effect on the recruitment and retention of minority students (Allen & Solórzano, 2001; Blackwell, 1981; Hurtado, Milem, Clayton-Pedersen, & Allen, 1999; Solórzano, Allen, & Carroll, 2002). Improving the climate for diversity, as outlined by Hurtado et al. (1999) requires (a) thoughtful reflection by campus leaders with regard to their history of inclusion and how this has carried over into the present, (b) improving the present recruitment and retention of people of color on college campuses, (c) attending to perceptions and attitudes between and among groups, and (d) enhancing inter- and intra-group relations among groups in college. Changes on all four of these dimensions are necessary and should be addressed simultaneously if we are to achieve any success in improving the racial climate and thereby the experiences of minorities within the academy (Hurtado et al., 1999).

In conclusion, a number of researchers continually demonstrate how colleges and universities can accommodate Latina/o students with services such as culturally sensitive academic advising, increased financial aid opportunities, the provision of summer and fall orientation programs for social and academic enrichment, access to learning centers, availability of school-year and summer research programs, and the alignment of diversity programs with the university's mission (Garcia, 2004; Ornelas, 2002; Solórzano, 1999).

## Discussion/Conclusion

The data we present in this article clearly show that there are persistent educational inequities for all Latina/o college students. Despite increases in their enrollment rates, our data show that Latinas/os still remain underrepresented at almost every level of the educational pipeline. In fact, as Latinas/os continue to increase their representation in the general U.S. population, it appears unlikely that higher education will achieve any measurable degree of parity either in their enrollment or educational attainment rates at any time in the near future. Despite the recent Supreme Court decision declaring that in 25 years race will no longer be a significant factor in determining access to and graduation from college for students of color, our data and analysis indicate that, for Latinas/os, their race and ethnicity will continue to be strongly related to the quality of, and equality in, their educational conditions and outcomes throughout the educational pipeline.

## What Are the Educational Conditions and Outcomes for Latina/o Undergraduates?

Our data reveal that approximately two thirds of all Latinas/os enrolling in postgraduate study begin at 2-year community colleges, and only one third enroll directly in 4-year institutions. Although the majority of Latinas/os (i.e., 70%) who enroll in 2-year community colleges aspire to transfer to 4-year campuses, the systems and support structures in place are inadequate and are often under girded by deficit-based assumptions about students' academic ability and potential.

Moreover, both 2- and 4-year institutions lack academically and culturally appropriate support systems to meet the holistic needs of Latina/o students (see Gándara & Maxwell-Jolley, 1999). Most formal, institutionally sponsored retention practices, programs, and policies continue to be centered on outdated notions of alleged race-neutral institutional integration, which insist on viewing students as academically and culturally deficient and mismatched with their campus. Rather than recognizing and nourishing the cultural wealth (Villalpando & Solórzano, 2005) that Latinas/os draw from in their pursuit of a college education, university-initiated retention efforts refuse to acknowledge the significance of these assets that have historically supported students' success in higher education (Villalpando, 2002).

Without appropriate retention efforts, our data show that graduation rates among Latinas/os at 2- and 4-year institutions will remain the weakest among all major racial/ethnic groups in the United States. In fact, when compared with their increases in the U.S. population, there actually appears to be a decline in their graduation rates given that these rates have not kept pace with their population increase. The most important point with respect to their baccalaureate degree attainment is that although their absolute numbers may have increased slightly in the past decade, this increase is entirely attributable to the increase in the college-age population and enrollment of Latina/o college students. In other words, the increase in their attainment of a bachelor's degree is not proportional to the increase in their college-aged population.

## Why Do These Conditions Continue to Exist?

To answer this question, we draw on the explanatory framework offered by CRT. One of the principal contributions of CRT is its focus on how race and racism are woven into the structures, practices, and policies of colleges and universities. Although on one hand claiming to be objective, meritocratic, and color blind in its pursuit of equal educational opportunities for all students, CRT points to how in practice, higher education adopts practices, norms, and policies that clearly inhibit the success of Latinas/os and other students of color. CRT argues that higher education in the United States cannot separate itself from the historical fact that its current identity and practices have been largely shaped by legal and sociopolitical forces that have continuously redefined concepts of race, ethnicity, national origin, language, class, and justice.

CRT provides a way of seeing and naming the contradictory ways in which higher education institutions operate. Although colleges clearly provide economic, social, political, and other benefits to the small trickle of Latina/o college graduates who can navigate them successfully, these postsecondary institutions also exercise a significant degree of oppression by sustaining a campus culture and climate that marginalizes, devalues, and silences these students.

The disparity in Latina/o student enrollments between 2- and 4-year institutions, their low transfer rates to 4-year universities, and their equally dismal retention and graduation rates at 4-year campuses illustrate the chronically persistent racial stratification of higher education in the United States. The "overrepresentation" of Latina/o students in the 2-year colleges, and their continuing underrepresentation in 4-year colleges, when viewed through a CRT framework, clearly represent the effects of the continuing manipulation of self-serving notions of racial neutrality and meritocracy by higher education institutions. A CRT analysis suggests that colleges and universities adopt concepts of alleged racial blindness in their daily norms and practices along with alleged meritocratic measures of academic potential and success to purposely maintain a racially segregated educational environment. In fact, one can argue that one of the major reasons for the disproportionate representation of Latinas/os in 2-year versus 4-year institutions, besides academic tracking and ineffective counseling, is because of the insistence of using standardized admissions exams. Despite decades of research by prominent scholars (see also Astin, 1982, 1993; Duran, 1983; Oseguera, 2004) that clearly show the lack of predictive value of standardized admissions exams for students of color, most 4-year institutions continue to insist on using these measures as admissions screening devices, in contrast to 2-year institutions that seldom, if ever, require these exams. In fact, 4-year campuses insist on using standardized admissions exams even though the testing services that create and administer these exams have consistently warned them about the limited use of these measures.

In our analysis of retention efforts designed to increase the graduation of Latina/o college students, we discovered that students have been implementing their own successful retention programs since the late 1960s—many without the official sanction or support from campus administrations. Yet we are hard-pressed to find examples of institutions that even bothered to inquire about, let alone replicate, the components of these successful retention efforts that students have been adopting. However, when viewed through a CRT framework, it should not strike us as counterintuitive that centering students' experiential knowledge within their educational experience should lead to their academic success. The challenge is in trying to persuade higher education institutions that this is an example of the types of race-conscious practices that are necessary for the success of Latina/o college students. In fact, within the current sociopolitical climate of anti-affirmative action, anti-immigration, and xenophobia, we have seen college administrators pursue a policy of retrenchment when it comes to recognizing the salience of race/ethnicity in education and the impact of racism on their campus.

Our analysis of the data through a CRT framework allows us to identify some of the racialized barriers that impede the success of Latina/o college students. Our review of these data suggest that despite an official end to de jure racial segregation, higher education continues to reflect a state of de facto racial segregation for Latina/o college students. Latina/o college students are not only concentrated in institutions considered to be of lesser prestige and with fewer resources but can expect to achieve lower levels of academic achievement—and social mobility—as a result of attending these types of institutions.

CRT suggests that if 4-year institutions were truly committed to creating equitable educational outcomes for students of color, they would not insist on adopting these practices that they claim to be racially neutral, unbiased, and represent genuine academic achievement and potential. A CRT analysis suggests that perhaps one of the reasons why 4-year institutions insist on adopting these types of tools may be related to their disinterest in seeing a greater representation of Latina/os on their campuses out of fear that they will enroll students perceived as academically unprepared and unmotivated—students who they feel would be better served by the "lesser"community college. The claims by higher education that in serving the needs of Latina/o college students, it adopts so-called "objective,""meritocratic," and "race-neutral"practices clearly do not hold up when analyzing the educational inequities that we have reviewed in our data.

We argue that rather than accept the notion that race will become irrelevant as a means of achieving greater equity, higher education needs to adopt more explicit race-conscious practices to truly enhance the success and achievement of Latina/o college students. The data suggest that although there are many factors that may have influenced the lack of educational attainment and academic progress for Latina/o college students, most of the responsibility lies on the racialized structures, policies, and practices that guide higher education.

Unfortunately, higher education has embraced the meritocratic illusion that it has been, is, and will remain objective and color blind, but we believe that its assertions of neutrality serve to maintain existing race, class, sexual, and gender privileges while clearly devaluing and marginalizing Latina/o college students.

Critical race theory proposes a contextual analysis of educational policies and practices. Our contextual analysis of the educational inequities faced by Latina/o college students points to a continuing lack of attention to how race and racism in higher education influences their educational success and achievement.

## Notes

1. These data were gathered from the Higher Education Research Institute's extensive trends file available at UCLA.

2. Remedial or developmental education at 2- and 4-year institutions focuses on the training of those students who enter college underprepared to handle college-level work. For purposes

of this article, we will refer to these practices as remedial, recognizing that the dominant discourses and bodies of research are increasingly using the term *developmental education* to refer to such practices and programs.

# References

Allen, W., & Solórzano, D. (2001). Affirmative action, educational equity and campus racial climate: A case study of the University of Michigan Law School. *La Raza Law Journal, 12,* 237–363.

Astin, A. (1982). *Minorities in higher education.* San Francisco: Jossey-Bass.

Astin, A. (1993). *What matters in college? Four critical years revisited.* San Francisco: Jossey-Bass.

Bakke v. Regents of the University of California (438 U.S. 265, 1978).

Bell, D. (1987). *And we will not be saved: The elusive quest for racial justice.* New York: Basic Books.

Bell, D. (1992). *Faces at the bottom of the well: The permanence of racism.* New York: Basic Books.

Blackwell, J. (1981). *Mainstreaming outsiders: The production of Black professionals.* Bayside, NY: General Hall.

Calmore, J. (1992). Critical race theory, Archie Shepp, and fire music: Securing an authentic intellectual life in a multicultural world. *Southern California Law Review, 65,* 2129–2231.

Carrasco, E. (1996). Collective recognition as a communitarian device: Or, of course we want to be role models! *La Raza Law Journal, 9,* 81–101.

Carter, D., & Wilson, R. (2001). *Annual status of minorities in higher education.* Washington, DC: American Council on Education.

Crenshaw, K. (1989). Demarginalizing the intersection of race and sex: A Black feminist critique of antidiscrimination doctrine, feminist theory and antiracist politics. *University of Chicago Legal Forum, 1989,* 139–167.

Crenshaw, K. (1993). Mapping the margins: Intersectionality, identity politics, and the violence against women of color. *Stanford Law Review, 43,* 1241–1299.

Crenshaw, K., Gotanda, N., Peller, G., & Thomas, K. (Eds.). (1995). *Critical race theory: The key writings that formed the movement.* New York: New Press.

Delgado, R. (1984). The imperial scholar: Reflections on a review of civil rights literature. *University of Pennsylvania Law Review, 132,* 561–578.

Delgado, R. (1989). Storytelling for oppositionists and others: A plea for narrative. *Michigan Law Review, 87,* 2411–2441.

Delgado, R. (1992). The imperial scholar revisited: How to marginalize outsider writing, ten years later. *University of Pennsylvania Law Review, 140,* 1349–1372.

Delgado, R. (Ed.). (1995). *Critical race theory: The cutting edge.* Philadelphia: Temple University Press.

Delgado, R., & Stefancic, J. (2001). *Critical race theory: An introduction.* New York: New York University Press.

Delgado Bernal, D., & Villalpando, O. (2002). The apartheid of knowledge in the academy: The struggle over "legitimate" knowledge for faculty of color [Special issue]. *Journal of Equity and Excellence in Education, 35,* 169–180.

Dougherty, K. (1994). *The contradictory college: The conflicting origins, impacts, and futures of community colleges.* Albany: State University of New York Press.

Duran, R. (1983). *Hispanics' education and background: Predictors of college achievement.* New York: College Entrance Examination Board.

Falcone, M. (2002, May 16). Former chancellor Kerr remembers UC history. *UCLA Daily Bruin,* p. A1.

Gándara, P., & Maxwell-Jolley, J. (1999). *Priming the pump: Strategies for increasing the achievement of underrepresented minority undergraduates* (College Board No. 987257). New York: College Board Publications.

Garcia, R. (1995). Critical race theory and Proposition 187: The racial politics of immigration law. *Chicano-Latino Law Review, 17,* 118–148.

Garcia, P. (2004). *Understanding obstacles and barriers to Hispanic baccalaureates.* Notre Dame, IN: Institute for Latino Policy Studies, University of Notre Dame.

Grubb, W. (1999). *Learning and earning in the middle: The economic benefits of sub-baccalaureate education.* New York: Community College Research Center, Teachers College, Columbia University.

Grutter et al. v. Bollinger et al., No. 02-241 (June 23, 2003, slip op. of the U.S. Supreme Court).

Harris, A. (1994). Forward: The jurisprudence of reconstruction. *California Law Review, 82,* 741–785.

Heller, D. (1997). Student price response in higher education: An update to Leslie and Brinkman. *Journal of Higher Education, 68,* 624–659.

Hu, S., & St. John, E. (2001). Student persistence in a public higher education system: Understanding racial and ethnic differences. *The Journal of Higher Education, 72*, 265–286.

Hurtado, S., Milem, J., Clayton-Pedersen, A., & Allen, W. (1999). *Enacting diverse learning environments: Improving the climate for racial/ethnic diversity in higher education*. San Francisco: Jossey-Bass.

Jenkins, D., & Boswell, K. (2002). *State policies on community college remedial education*. Denver, CO: Center for Community College Policy, Education Commission of the States.

Ladson-Billings, G. (1999). Preparing teachers for diverse student populations: A critical race theory perspective. *Review of Research in Education, 24*, 211–247.

Ladson-Billings, G., & Tate, W. (1995). Toward a critical race theory of education. *Teachers College Record, 97*, 47–68.

Leslie, L., & Brinkman, P. (1988). *The economic value of higher education*. New York: Macmillan.

Malcom, S. (1990). Reclaiming our past. *Journal of Negro Education, 59*, 246–259.

Matsuda, M. (1996). *Where is your body? and other essays on race, gender, and the law*. Boston: Beacon.

Matsuda, M., Lawrence, C., Delgado, R., & Crenshaw, K. (1993). *Words that wound: Critical race theory, assaultive speech, and the first amendment*. Boulder, CO: Westview.

Mazzeo, C. (2002). Stakes for students: Agenda-setting and remedial education. *The Review of Higher Education, 26*, 19–39.

Merisotis, J., & Phipps, R. (2000). Remedial education in colleges and universities: What's really going on? *The Review of Higher Education, 24*, 67–85.

Oakes, J. (1985). *Keeping track: How schools structure inequality*. New Haven, CT: Yale University Press.

Olivas, M. (1990). The chronicles, my grandfather's stories, and immigration law: The slave traders chronicle as racial history. *St. Louis University Law Journal, 34*, 425–441.

Ornelas, A. (2002). *An examination of the resources and barriers in the transfer process for Latina/o community college students: A case study analysis of an urban community college*. Unpublished doctoral dissertation, University of California, Los Angeles.

Ornelas, A., & Solórzano, D. (2004). The transfer condition of Latina/o community college students in California: Policy recommendations and solutions. *Community College Journal of Research and Practice, 28*, 233–248.

Oseguera, L. (2004). *Individual and institutional influences on the baccalaureate degree attainment of African American, Asian American, Caucasian, and Mexican American undergraduates*. Unpublished doctoral dissertation, University of California, Los Angeles.

Parker, L., Deyhle, D., Villenas, S., & Crossland, K. (Eds.). (1998). Critical race theory in education [Special issue]. *International Journal of Qualitative Studies in Education, 11*, 1–184.

Perin, D. (2002). The location of developmental education in community colleges: A discussion of the merits of mainstreaming vs. centralization. *Community College Review, 30*, 27–44.

Price, D. (2003). *Borrowing inequality: Race, class, and student loans*. Boulder, CO: Lynne Rienner.

Rangel, Y. (2001). *College immigrant students: How undocumented female Mexican immigrant students transition into higher education*. Unpublished doctoral dissertation, University of California, Los Angeles.

Rendon, L. (1994). Validating culturally diverse students: Towards a new model of learning and development. *Innovative Higher Education, 19*, 33–51.

Rendon, L., Jalomo, R., & Nora, A. (2000). Theoretical considerations in the study of minority student retention in higher education. In J. Braxton (Ed.), *Reworking the student departure puzzle* (pp. 127–156). Nashville, TN: Vanderbilt University Press.

Solórzano, D. (1997). Images and words that wound: Critical race theory, racial stereotyping, and teacher education. *Teacher Education Quarterly, 24*, 5–19.

Solórzano, D. (1999). *Navigating through college: The stages of passage for Chicana and Chicano students*. A final report on the UCLA Latino Higher Education Focus Group Study to the Inter-University Program for Latino Research, University of Texas at Austin.

Solórzano, D., Allen, W., & Carroll, G. (2002). A case study of racial microaggressions and campus racial climate at the University of California, Berkeley. *UCLA Chicano/Latino Law Review, 23*, 15–111.

Solórzano, D., & Delgado Bernal, D. (2001). Examining transformational resistance through a critical race and latcrit theory framework: Chicana and Chicano students in an urban context. *Urban Education, 36*, 308–342.

Solórzano, D., & Ornelas, A. (2004). A critical race analysis of Latina/o and African American advanced placement enrollment in public high schools. *High School Journal, 87,* 15–26.

Solórzano, D., & Solórzano, R. (1995). The Chicano educational experience: A framework for effective schools in Chicano communities. *Educational Policy, 9,* 293–314.

Solórzano, D., & Villalpando, O. (1998). Critical race theory, marginality, and the experience of minority students in higher education. In C. Torres & T. Mitchell (Eds.), *Emerging issues in the sociology of education: Comparative perspectives* (pp. 211–224). Albany: State University of New York Press.

Solórzano, D., & Yosso, T. (2000). Toward a critical race theory of Chicana and Chicano education. In C. Tejeda, C. Martinez, & Z. Leonardo (Eds.), *Demarcating the border of Chicana(o)/Latina(o) education* (pp. 35–65). Cresskill, NJ: Hampton Press.

Solórzano, D., & Yosso, T. (2001). Critical race and latcrit theory and method: Counterstorytelling Chicana and Chicano graduate school experiences. *International Journal of Qualitative Studies in Education, 14,* 471–495.

Solórzano, D., & Yosso, T. (2002a). A critical race counterstory of affirmative action in higher education. *Equity and Excellence in Education, 35,* 155–168.

Solórzano, D., & Yosso, T. (2002b). Critical race methodology: Counterstorytelling as an analytical framework for education research. *Qualitative Inquiry, 8,* 23–44.

St. John, E. (1991). What really influences minority attendance? Sequential analysis of the high school and beyond sophomore cohort. *Research in Higher Education, 32,* 141–158.

St. John, E. (2003). *Refinancing the college dream: Access, equal opportunity, and justice for taxpayers.* Baltimore, MD: Johns Hopkins University Press.

Talavera-Bustillos, V. (1998). *Chicana college choice and resistance: An exploratory study of first-generation Chicana college students.* Unpublished doctoral dissertation, University of California, Los Angeles.

Tate, W. (1997). Critical race theory and education: History, theory, and implications. *Review of Research in Education, 22,* 195–247.

Taylor, E. (1999). Critical race theory and interest convergence in the desegregation of higher education. In L. Parker, D. Deyhle, & S. Villenas (Eds.), *Race is . . . race isn't: Critical race theory and qualitative studies in education* (pp. 181–204). Boulder, CO: Westview.

Tinto, V. (1993). *Leaving college: Rethinking the causes and cures of student attrition* (2nd ed.). Chicago: University of Chicago Press.

U.S. Bureau of Census. (2000). *American fact finder, United States census 2000, summary file 4 (SF4).* Retrieved September 22, 2003, from http://www.census.gov/main/www/cen2000.html

U.S. Department of Education, National Center for Education Statistics (NCES). (2001). *Digest of education statistics, 2001.* Washington, DC: Author. Retrieved September 22, 2003, from http://nces.ed.gov/pubs2002/digest2001/

U.S. Department of Education, NCES. (2003). *Remedial education at degree-granting postsecondary institutions in fall 2000* (NCES 2004-010 by Basmat Parsad and Laurie Lewis. Project officer: Bernard Green). Washington, DC: Author.

Valdes, F. (1996). Forward: Latina/o ethnicities, critical race theory, and post-identity politics in postmodern legal culture: From practices to possibilities. *La Raza Law Journal, 9,* 1–31.

Valencia, R. (1997). *The evolution of deficit thinking: Educational thought and practice.* The Stanford Series on Education and Public Policy. London: Falmer.

Villalpando, O. (2002). The impact of diversity and multiculturalism on all students: Findings from a national study. *NASPA Journal—The Journal of Student Affairs Administration, Research, and Practice, 40,* 122–144.

Villalpando, O. (2003). Self-segregation or self-preservation? A critical race theory and Latina/o critical theory analysis of a study of Chicana/o college students. *The International Journal of Qualitative Studies in Education, 16,* 619–646.

Villalpando, O., & Delgado Bernal, D. (2002). A critical race theory analysis of barriers that impede the success of faculty of color. In W. Smith, P. Altbach, & K. Lomotey (Eds.), *The racial crisis in American higher education: Continuing challenges for the twenty-first century* (pp. 243–269). Albany: State University of New York Press.

Villalpando, O., & Solórzano, D. (2005). The role of culture in college preparation programs: A review of the research literature. In W. Tierney, Z. Corwin, & J. Colyar (Eds.), *Preparing for college: Nine elements of effective outreach* (pp. 13–28). Albany: State University of New York Press.

Villenas, S., & Deyhle, D. (1999). Critical race theory and ethnographies challenging the stereotypes: Latino families, schooling, resilience and resistance. *Curriculum Inquiry, 29,* 413–445.

Watford, T., Rivas, M., Burciaga, R., & Solórzano, D. (in press). Latinas and the doctorate: The "status" of attainment and experiences from the margin. In J. Castellanos & A. Gloria (Eds.), *Journey to a Ph.D.: The Latina/o experience in higher education.* Madison: University of Wisconsin Press.

Yosso, T. (2000). *A critical race and latcrit approach to media literacy: Chicana/o resistance to visual microaggressions.* Unpublished doctoral dissertation, University of California–Los Angeles.

# Chapter 31
# Beyond Self-Authorship
## Fifth Order and the Capacity for Social Consciousness

### Kelli Zaytoun

In this chapter, I explore the relationship between Robert Kegan's fifth-order consciousness and the capacity for social consciousness and action. I examine the role of the self in coalition work in phenomenological, postcolonial, and feminist approaches, in light of Kegan's account of self-as-system.

*When two violins are placed in a room, if a chord on one violin is struck the other violin will sound that note . . . this is for you . . . who know how powerful we are, who know we can sound the music and the people around us simply by playing our own strings.*

Activist poet Andrea Gibson, from "Say Yes"

*The conflict is potentially a reminder of our tendency to pretend to completeness when we are in fact incomplete. We may have this conflict because we need it to recover our true complexity.*

Robert Kegan, on postmodern approach to conflict and fifth-order consciousness (1994, p. 319)

In the preceding quote, Kegan captures a key feature of the evolution of consciousness: as we become aware of our unavoidable and perpetual incompleteness, we are moved to greater complexity of being over the course of our lifetimes. In fifth order, or the "self-transforming self," the major movement is of self-authorship itself from subject to object. Such movement requires the transformation of one's understanding of his or her individuation, the essence of self-formation, from that which is distinct, whole, and complete, to that which is shifting, multifaceted, interdependent, and incomplete. It is the concept of interdependence, of the relationship between self and other, in fifth-order consciousness, that I engage in this essay, not only for its usefulness to the study of individual identity development, but also to the study of collective identity and social consciousness.

Fifth-order, or "trans-systemic," consciousness is the final stage in Kegan's theory of self-evolution. In fifth order, self-authorship becomes object, or an aspect of our experience that can be reflected on and linked to something else. According to Kegan, in the transition from fourth to fifth order, "(y)ou begin to see that the life project is not about continuing to defend one formation of the self but about the ability to have the self literally *be* transformative" (Kegan as cited in Debold, 2002, p. 151, emphasis hers). In the journey beyond fourth order, one begins to see that each way of making meaning has its limits, that one's identity, or self-as-form, and system for making sense of experience, are partial. In fifth order, one holds multiple systems of thinking and identifying as object, and

Zaytoun, K. (2010). Beyond self-authorship: Fifth order and the capacity for social consciousness. In M. B. Baxter Magolda, E. G. Creamer, & P. S. Meszaros (Eds.), *Development and assessment of self-authorship: Exploring the concept across cultures* (pp. 151–166). Sterling, VA: Stylus.

develops a whole new capacity for seeing the relationship between those systems, and the systems of others. In fifth order the self is never complete, and a fixed truth cannot be known; one recognizes the tendency to pretend to be complete, but knows completeness cannot be achieved. According to Kegan, in fourth order "we take as prior the elements of a relationship (which then enter into relationship)," in fifth we take as prior "the relationship itself"; in other words, "(t)he relationship has the parts. The parts do not have the relationship" (Kegan, 1994, p. 316). Here lies the distinction between fourth and fifth orders: in fourth order, self-as-form is a priority and complete (is subject); in fifth order, the priority is the *process* of creating multiple forms; self-as(multiple)-forms becomes object.

I am interested in exploring the questions and implications that arise in consideration of what fifth-order consciousness suggests: that "it is only in relationship [with others] that we are who we are" (Love & Guthrie, 1999, p. 73). What does it mean to hold self-authorship as object and to embrace, as subject, the "interpenetration of selves" (Kegan, 1994, p. 315)? How does such a consciousness operate? What does it look like? More importantly, what is it capable of? If one's identities are understood as mutable, incomplete, and negotiated and constituted in relationship to others, might such a consciousness lend itself to an authentic investment in the well being of others and the social world in general? If so, how? I propose that it is within fifth-order consciousness that individuals find the genuine drive and quality skills to effectively work with others to address common social goals. This essay explores the function, potential, and philosophical basis of fifth-order consciousness, with other complementary accounts of the self as "selves-in-the-making," to ultimately offer a theory of the development of social consciousness and new directions for coalitions for social change.

I begin with a philosophical analysis of the importance of the notion of "self," or the psychological level of reality that is distinct from (but highly interrelated to) the social world, what Linda Martín Alcoff defines as "how we experience being ourselves" (2006, p. 93). I do this in order to engage phenomenological (e.g., Heidegger) and poststructural (e.g., Foucault, Derrida) philosophical claims that call into question the existence of a "core" self, identity, and individual agency[1]. This analysis will connect contemporary philosophical responses to such accounts, and link them to Kegan's theory of fifth-order consciousness, to ultimately expand the value and utility of the notion of "self." I explore feminist phenomenological approaches, such as the "multi-voiced, multi-cultural self" of Mariana Ortega (2001), and the relational self-account of Susan Brison (2002), as well as the feminist postcolonial approaches to self-multiplicity described by Gloria Anzaldúa (2002) and María Lugones (2006). What these theories and Kegan's fifth order have in common is the idea that the self and its identities are never complete; they are changing, situated, complex localities of consciousness constituted in association with others. This incompleteness, and the self's ability to reflect on and manipulate its own self-as-system, opens up new possibilities for understanding and acting on its relationship to the social world.

## Phenomenology and the Self

Mariana Ortega describes the goal of phenomenological theories as an attempt to provide a bridge "between how we think of the world and how we live it" (2001, p. 3). She explains that phenomenology attempts to do justice to the social, situated experiences of human beings, and argues against the notion of self put forward by traditional Cartesian accounts of persons as autonomous, unified subjects with substantive, epistemic cores. Phenomenologists do not deny the notion of *the experience* of a self, but do reject the idea of an underlying, reflective foundational subject[2]. Being is knowing, being *is* self, a self that is continually defined, then redefined, through its pre-reflective activity in the social world. Individual agency, accountability, and identity are suspect under phenomenological and other nontraditional, poststructuralist lenses, and therefore, call into question major assumptions of traditional developmental psychology (i.e., progressive, structured maturation of a core self over time and experience), including cognitive structural theories such as Kegan's. The following quote from Maurice Merleau-Ponty (1964) sums up phenomenology's criticism of psychology's individuated subject or sense of self:

What classical academic psychology calls "functions of cognition"—intelligence, perception, imaginations, etc.—when more closely examined, lead us back to an activity that is prior to cognition properly so called, a function of organizing experience that imposes on certain totalities the configurations and the kinds of equilibrium that are possible under the corporeal and social condition of the child himself. (As cited in Forrester, 2006, p. 784)

Phenomenology underscores the fundamental interrelatedness of all things; indeed, it rejects the concept of perception as "a perceiver's point of view" and asserts that the experience of perception of an object is actually property of the object; a body-subject may participate in the process of creating experience, but the subject in and of itself does not possess perspective (Forrester, 2006, p. 785). To Merleau-Ponty, experiences of the body, more specifically, prereflective, corporeal experiences intricately created with others and the world outside the body, are what constitute consciousness or self, an incarnated subjectivity. In other words, a separate consciousness does not exist outside the experience itself.

Given the preceding explanations of phenomenology's basic premises, it might appear that phenomenology and Kegan's subject/object theory are incompatible; what might be particularly problematic to phenomenology is Kegan's grounding in Piagetian principles that give primacy to the role of individual mental organization, or what Kegan calls "the work of the mind," in the ongoing construction of self[3] (Kegan, 1994, p. 29). However, I will explore how aspects of phenomenology resonate with Kegan's orders of consciousness, particularly fifth order, and how Kegan's subject/object approach complicates, yet appreciates and complements, goals of phenomenology. Next I will discuss how approaches inspired by phenomenology, like Ortega's "multi-voiced, multi-cultural self," are consistent with Kegan's understanding of consciousness and strengthen its validity.

## Feminist Negotiations of a Phenomenological Self

Ortega (2001), influenced by Heidegger's (1962) notion of *Dasein*, or self as "being-in-the-world," and postcolonial Latina feminist writers, sought to negotiate a stance between the existence of a monolithic "core" self and its dismissal by phenomenologists, and calls for a consideration of selfhood that is complex, multiplicitous, and continually evolving, but inhabits a "togetherness or continuity" (p. 17). Although she retains phenomenology's insistence that the self is conceived through its activities in the world, she takes issue with the denial of the continuity of *a* self (vs. multiple selves). For example, she is critical of María Lugones's (1990) assertion, in her explanation of "'world' traveling,"[4] that there is no underlying "I," or that individuals become different people when they travel from one context to the next. Although she admits that this approach is appealing, in that it is truly phenomenological and avoids the problems associated with the assumptions of a unified subject, a mind/self completely distinctive from the body and others' minds and bodies, she argues that the activities of memory and the ability to identify difference require a sense of a "self," not multiple "selves." She questions how one can identify and retain a sense of "me" without continuity of some sort. She calls for a more complete exploration of "selfhood," not one that revives the traditional, transcendent subject, but one that makes it possible to explain continuity and difference in our experiences and awareness of our being.

Here is where I think phenomenology and Kegan's orders of consciousness can complement each other. Kegan offers an explanation of this complex evolution of the awareness of self, its continuity, and difference from others. The selfhood that Ortega is ultimately calling for is present in Kegan's conception of fifth-order consciousness, that which recognizes the self as having multiple forms and as constituitive only in its relationship with others; it is the part of our being that is present when we keep ourselves from becoming overwhelmed by a particular identity, set of values, or stances that may have been long in the making and held as "subject" at one time (e.g., in fourth order). What is subject in fifth order is a sense of continuity of selfhood that can hold out, reflect, and act upon all our particular, multiple selves, a sense that selfhood is not complete and is constantly being created in relationship with (also incomplete) others. Kegan's concept of subject/object, particularly as it relates to fifth order, therefore provides a means to explore Ortega's suggestion that continuity in our sense of being, and difference from others, be explored more fully than what is offered in Cartesian and phenomenological accounts.

Another account of the multiplicity and relationality of self that is compatible with Ortega and Kegan's fifth order is the compelling analysis of the impact of violence on the self of Susan Brison (2002), who supports what she calls a "feminist account of the relational self," a self that is "both autonomous and socially dependent, vulnerable enough to be undone by violence and yet resilient enough to be reconstructed with the help of empathetic others" (p. 38). Indeed, this quote exemplifies the contradiction and oppositeness present in the fifth-order dialectical (Kegan, 1994, p. 29). She supports the approach that the self is positioned, situated, and, for many, operates from a "multiple consciousness" (p. 38). She explores three aspects of the self that are revealed by the impact of trauma: an embodied self, self as narrative, and the autonomous self. Regarding the embodied self, she illustrates how her relationship to her body was transformed after being violently attacked, raped, and left for dead, and discusses that her mind and her body became "indistinguishable" (p. 44). She discovered that her physical "incapacitation by fear and anxiety," insomnia, and other PTSD symptoms, or the "bodily nature of traumatic memory," merges two aspects of self traditionally seen as separate: body and mind (p. 44). Trauma not only disrupts one's relationship to the body; it disrupts memory and concept of time as well. However, according to Brison, telling the story of trauma, the act of speech itself, can serve as a vehicle for recovery and reconstructing a voice that is silenced after the experience of violence and violation. This narrative aspect of self depends on a compassionate listener or witness to take the narrative seriously; it helps the survivor to reestablish his or her identity. Lastly, Brison discusses how a survivor's sense of autonomy, or will or control over one's responses, is called into question after trauma; for example, symptoms of PTSD can trigger an overactive startle response, and survivors may feel loss of control over what once felt like a safe environment. Brison also indicates that her trauma experience emphasized to her that autonomy is relational, or interdependent with others. Trauma can evoke a loss of connection to humanity, a loss that puts one's sense of autonomy and agency in danger. But Brison insists that recovery of the self, including the aspect of autonomy, in the aftermath of trauma is possible, but only possible in the presence of empathetic others.

One of Brison's most powerful statements related to this chapter's premise is in her criticism of the poststructuralist approach that the self is a fiction (this is *not* what she means by narrative self), in the sense that it is "freely constructed by some narrator" (2002, p. 135). She remarks, tongue-in-cheek but notably, that "no one, not even Stephen King, would voluntarily construct a self so tormented by trauma and its aftermath" (p. 135). This statement underscores the process by which lived, relational experience literally makes the self, a view consistent with phenomenological thought. But Brison, like Ortega, parts ways with phenomenology in her stance that a self (not multiple selves), even after being undermined in the aftermath of violent, debilitating trauma, can retain a sense of resiliency, autonomy, and continuity.

Through the lens of Kegan's approach, hearing a survivor say "I'm not the same person I was before the rape" can be an indicator of how one might view the self-as-system, a means for holding a former form of the self as object, a self with which the survivor may have formerly overidentified, a self no longer subject, but part of the survivor nonetheless.[5] Kegan's fifth order provides a framework that captures the features and complexities of the self/other relationship put forth by Ortega and Brison. It retains appreciation for the lived experiences of the self and interactions with others as part of a dynamic cycle of the evolution of consciousness. Indeed, I believe that Kegan uses the language of "interpenetration of self and other" and "inter-individuation" to honor the depth and integrity of the process of interconnection and its power to transform and quite possibly merge self and other, a concept he hints at in an interview with Elizabeth Debold (2002), and an intriguing one to consider in future discussions about what lies beyond fifth order. Brison's (2002) account emphasizes the role of bodily experiences in the shaping of self, an aspect of meaning-making that Kegan does not stress but probably would not deny. Approaches like Brison's and others, rooted in phenomenology, open up possibilities for expanding Kegan's domains of knowing (i.e., cognitive, affective, and social) to include bodily forms of knowing as well.

For the purposes of this chapter, I lay out the observation that Ortega, Brison, and Kegan retain, that there is value in continuing to maintain but explore an assumption that is critical to cognitive structural approaches: the pattern of differentiation and integration in the evolution of consciousness. According to Kegan, this pattern is present "whether we are looking at mental development in infancy or the highly elaborated order of consciousness that underlies postmodernism" (1994, p. 326). He continues, "Before we can reconnect to, internalize, or integrate something with which we were originally fused, we must first distinguish ourselves from it" (p. 326). Indeed, this process of "distinguishing ourselves" is the central task in making something "object" in the subject/object relationship. This pattern is also a critical component of Marcia Baxter Magolda's (2001) work on development, in her exploration of internal vs. external foundation. Gloria Anzaldúa, in her work on consciousness (*conocimiento*) (2002), which I will discuss in more detail in the next section, also retains this pattern in describing how the self moves between settling within the body and inner psyche to reaching out and reconciling the demands from the outer world. She discussed how individuals move from the familiar, safe terrain of knowing and being until some experience pulls them into the unfamiliar, where they are required to negotiate the self within that context. Although Anzaldúa did not make reference to movement toward specific, qualitatively different perspectives on self as differentiated versus self as integrated, the alternating and negotiating of inner and integrated self is clearly a theme throughout her stages. On an interesting note, Anzaldúa's and Kegan's last stages of development similarly discuss moments of the merging of self and other. I find the latter concept intriguing and a worthy next step in understanding the evolution of consciousness, but I maintain that it is critical to emphasize and defend the existence and functions of a reflective, inner sense of self or continuity that, although highly interdependent on other beings and its environment, has distinct functions and potentials in the creation of highly functional relationships, communities, and social harmony.

I will now explore two more approaches to self from feminist postcolonial thought that call for and strengthen the possibility of the type of consciousness described by Kegan as fifth order. Looking at these theories together can help us more clearly visualize the functions of fifth order. More importantly, the following analysis will help ground the notion of a lived experience of consciousness in light of phenomenological and poststructural thought, but with the additional consideration of a lived sense of consistency of a self, a self that assumes responsibility for its own actions and its connectedness to the world.

## Self and Social Consciousness and Complex Communication

Chicana writer Gloria Anzaldúa (2002), in her description of the concept of *conocimiento*, explores a cyclical journey of the self's focus back and forth between "inner work" and "public acts"[6] (p. 540). She explains the stage of "shifting realities" as one that nurtures the function of consciousness that understands that "beneath individual separateness lies a deeper interrelatedness" (p. 569). I'm particularly interested in this function as it indicates that the self is a system of relational parts and can serve to mobilize individuals to act collectively. She calls the function *la naguala*, and asserts that this form of knowing is "always with you but is displaced by the ego and its perspective," suggesting that Anzaldúa viewed the self as having a sense of continuity similar to Ortega's description. Kegan might offer that "being displaced by the ego" occurs when that way of knowing is subject. Anzaldúa describes *conocimiento* as a theory of composition, a construction of an awareness that she illustrates in the following way:

> When you watch yourself and observe your mind at work you find that behind your acts and your temporary sense of self (identities) is a state of awareness that, if you allow it, keeps you from getting completely caught up in that particular identity or emotional state. (As cited in Keating, 2000, p. 177)

Anzaldúa proposes here that a function of self exists that sees relationships between parts of the self (identities) without being consumed by them. She also suggests that this function engages and monitors interactions with others as follows:

Orienting yourself to the environment and your relationship to it enables you to read and garner insight from whatever situation you find yourself in. This concocimiento gives you the flexibility to swing from your intense feelings to those of the other without being hijacked by either. When confronted with the other's fear, you note her emotional arousal, allow her feelings/words to enter your body, then you shift to the neutral place of *la naguala*. (Anzaldúa, 2002, p. 569)

This description can be viewed as an example of how fifth-order consciousness operates. The "neutral place of *la naguala*" may be consistent with what Kegan meant by the function of the dialectical in fifth order, that which allows for the ability to hold self-authorship, self-formation as object, and to hold as subject the contradictions and conflicts within the self and its relationships to others. What is subject in fifth order is the understanding of the self's incompleteness, malleability, multipleness, and interdependence with others; what Ortega would call a "complicated being in the making" (2001, p. 17). It could also be argued that *la naguala* is present in fourth-order consciousness, because self-authorship allows one the ability to be influenced but not determined by others; however, I contend that *la naguala* requires a step beyond self-authorship, more fluidity in the understanding of self; it requires the ability to hold one's identities (not just values and ideals) as objects; it requires a divestment rather than investment in self-authorship. In other words, I would argue that even in self-authorship the ego, or what is subject in fourth order—the investment in one's differentiated values, ideals, and identities—gets in the way, and the ego keeps one from becoming conscious of the function of *la naguala*, which Anzaldúa sees as a gateway to understanding relatedness. But what is missing from Anzaldúa's commentary on *la naguala* is a description of *how* the self moves its focus from the ego to a sense of deeper interrelatedness. Here I use Lugones's work to help explore this transformation.

In her theory of "complex communication," postcolonial philosopher María Lugones (2006) helps to clarify the conditions under which the shift to interrelatedness occurs. Lugones is critical of what she calls "the logic of narrow identity"; this narrow logic, that one primarily belongs to one fixed identity, is the basis for coalition work in the United States. She explains that working toward social harmony cannot occur as long as we see identities as fixed categories. She argues that complex communication "requires a movement outward toward other affiliate groups recognized as resistant" (p. 76). In order to make this move, it is necessary to understand that we cannot assume the transparencies of others, nor should our goal be to see our commonalities with them. Complex communication means meeting others in what she calls "liminal spaces," which exist in particular times and places; liminal spaces are communicative achievements that require reading the opacity of others, understanding their differences in that communicative moment, and listening to their particular strategies. According to Lugones, complex communication and coalition work require a continual reconstruction of a self, a self conceived in liminal space with others who may be unlike us but who are also resisting oppression. Like Anzaldúa, Lugones asserts that a change in self is essential to achieve interrelatedness, but she qualifies that the change can only occur in the course of understanding our own multiplicity and in reading each other's opacity. Lugones's proposal is similar to Kegan's description that fifth-order consciousness is interested in "the transformative *process* of our being, rather than the formative *products* of our becoming" (Kegan, 1994, p. 351, emphasis mine).

## On the Functions of Fifth Order

I believe there is a link between what Lugones (2006) is calling coalitional limens, the communicative achievements made with others, and what Kegan refers to as the postmodern curriculum, navigated best by fifth-order consciousness. According to Kegan, fifth order requires transcending identification with internally fixed forms, and coming to an understanding that no system of organization or its parts is ever complete. It is understanding the self-as-system as a communicative achievement, as Lugones might say. And what can come with the knowledge that the self is a shifting process of being is the understanding that others experience this process as well, and that openness to their struggles and strategies brings depth to one's own. Such a consciousness allows one to truly hear and engage others, not for what one has in common with them, but for what their different experiences and ways of being contribute to one's own ways of thinking. I believe that this is what Lugones means by reading others' opacity. Fourth-order consciousness, where one has relationships but is not consumed by them, certainly provides a foundation for the function of reading others' opacity, but it is in fifth order that one truly appreciates the value of others' roles in the construction of their own experiences of self. Understanding the deep interrelatedness of the self requires knowing that even the act of thinking itself is not an isolated process. The activities of listening and sympathizing, for example, can be considered "relational forms of thinking" (Anzaldúa, 2002). When we truly engage in them and are open to what the experience has to offer, we and others are transformed by these acts.

Fifth-order consciousness is congruent with these functions of relationship; according to Kegan, the self-transforming self "is much more friendly to contradiction . . . to being able to hold on to multiple systems of thinking . . . (it is) more about movement through different forms of consciousness than about the defending and identifying with any one form" (DeBold, 2002, p. 154). Therefore, conflict and difference are not threatening to one's views because those views (and the self-as-form itself), having moved from subject to object, are now seen as continually open to manipulation and transformation.

## Potential Contributions

> If the consciousness complexity of postmodern discourse is over our heads, how will it affect us?
> (Kegan, 1994, p. 337)

Expanding discussion of fifth order can further our understanding of our potential as individuals and our potential for creating well-functioning communities. Indeed, our future may depend on a shift to fifth-order consciousness, individually and collectively; a shift to a radical way of being that honors the inextricable link between self and other. Anzaldúa, Lugones, and others, in their work on social movements, have called for a new sense of coalition that recognizes the fluidities of identities and intersectionalities of oppression. This requires a move beyond the coalition politics most prevalent in the United States today, one in which coalitions are based on and divided by single identity group interests. M. Jacqui Alexander (2005) comments that "our oppositional politic has been necessary, but it will never sustain us" (p. 282). She explains that, although temporary gains in creating such divisions are possible, there is great risk in living segregated lives; humans are indeed interdependent and "this is why forced separations wreak havoc on our souls" (p. 282). I use Kegan's theory here to strengthen this call for a more sophisticated means of achieving social harmony. In doing so, I hope to have expanded discussion on the functions and potential of fifth-order consciousness, and on theories of coalition building as well.

In the prologue to *In Over Our Heads*, Kegan (1994) explained that "although the writer is the one who starts the book, the reader is the one who finishes it" (p. 1). He further clarified that he hoped his text would "be a context for readers' ongoing invention" (p. 2). This chapter is meant to engage us in conversation about what happens *beyond* self-authorship, and to encourage us to pick up where Kegan left off. Tracking the course of fifth-order consciousness has much to offer scholars, educators, psychologists, administrators, and activists; it has the potential to reveal how social consciousness, and other related capacities like global citizenship develop and, therefore, how they can be cultivated and supported. Incorporating feminist and postcolonial scholars' calls for attention to shifting identities, identities that are grounded in and inseparable from ever-changing experiences of the body in the social world, can be a vital contribution to exploring the capacities and possibilities of fifth order. The next steps in studying the journey beyond self-authorship will likely involve uncovering narratives of the shifting, multiplicitous, complex, resilient self, a self that is simultaneously incomplete, penetrable, and interdependent, but all the better for it. In *The Pedagogies of Crossing*, M. Jacqui Alexander (2005) sums up what I see as the major task of fifth-order consciousness in the following passage:

> When we have failed at solidarity work we often retreat, struggling to convince ourselves that this is indeed the work we have been called on to do. The fact of the matter is that there is no other work but

the work of creating and re-recreating ourselves within the context of community. Simply put, there is no other work. (p. 283)

Alexander calls for a shift in consciousness that enables the individual to see relationship as the primary source of a complex self and purpose, and means for "anchor(ing) the struggle for social justice" (p. 283). The "failures at solidarity work" to which she refers certainly could result from a variety of causes; however, I contend that they could indeed be related to our inability to move beyond self-authorship, from our investment in the hard-earned, internal, empowered sense of self, to a state in which, as Kegan says, "the self has become totally identified with the world," or, as Debold replies, "a transcendence of the limitations of the subject-object relationship itself" (Debold, 2002, p. 147). As Kegan claims, self-authorship provides a necessary foundation for the self-transforming self. As I have maintained in this chapter, the self-transforming self is necessary to recognize "the call" described previously by Alexander, the call to push through the struggles of difference, the investment in differences and identities, to work with others on common social goals and social justice concerns.

Operating in fifth-order consciousness, as individuals and as collectives, it is not so hard to see how the work of one individual could inspire a movement; it is not so hard to imagine how we ourselves can be like the violins that Andrea Gibson (2006) describes in the opening quote of this chapter, and how we might respond to her with the plea with which I close, "The world needs us more right now than it ever has before . . . pull all your strings; play every chord."

## Notes

1. For an historical overview and critique of philosophical approaches to self and identity, see Linda Martín Alcoff's *Visible Identities: Race, Gender, and the Self*, particularly Part One, Chapter Three. Post-structuralist accounts assert that self is constituted by discourse. Foucault and Derrida, for example, emphasized the effects of power on the self. Phenomenological accounts will be discussed in the next section.

2. In modern philosophy, the term "subject" was used to refer to the epistemic account of persons, which traditionally meant one's ability to reason (i.e., Descarte's "I think therefore I am"). Although some philosophers use the terms subject and self interchangeably, many make a distinction between the two, for example, those who reject the concept of "subjectivity" in its reference to the account of persons as possessing a substantial core. However, some have sought to redefine subjectivity to include alternative accounts of persons.

3. Although since his earliest theorizing about psychological growth, represented in *The Evolving Self* (1982), Kegan has expanded Piaget's focus on "thinking" to include "affective, interpersonal, and intrapersonal realms," the self is constituted by its capacity for organizing experience, by what the mind does (Kegan, 1994, p. 29). Phenomenologists would argue that the mind does not exist outside of the experience itself and meaning is instead a work of the body.

4. See María Lugones' essay, "Playfulness, 'World'-Traveling, and Loving Perception," in *Making Face, Making Soul/Haciendo Caras: Creative and Critical Perspectives by Women of Color* for a more thorough explanation of her concept of "world"-traveling.

5. A person operating from third- or fourth-order consciousness might also say that she is not the "same person" that she was before the rape; however, fifth order would provide a particular coping mechanism for constructing and managing the experience that third and fourth would not provide. In third order, one might become too dependent on others for healing; in fourth, one might become too dependent on oneself. In fifth order, one can appreciate how one's own autonomy is dependent on relationships with others, and find a balance between self-reliance and reliance on others.

6. For a detailed discussion of Anzaldúa's concept of *conocimiento* as a developmental theory, see Zaytoun (2005) "New Pathways toward Understanding Self-in-Relation: Anzaldúan (Re) Visions for Developmental Psychology," in Keating's *EntreMundos/Among Worlds: New Perspectives on Gloria E. Anzaldúa.*

# References

Alcoff, L. M. (2006). *Visible identities: Race, gender, and the self.* New York: Oxford University Press.

Alexander, M. J. (2005). *Pedagogies of crossing: Meditations on feminism, sexual politics, memory, and the sacred.* Durham, NC: Duke University Press.

Anzaldúa, G. E. (2002). Now let us shift. In G. Anzaldúa & A. Keating (Eds.), *This bridge we call home: Radical visions for transformation* (pp. 540–578). New York: Routledge.

Baxter Magolda, M. B. (2001). *Making their own way: Narratives for transforming higher education to promote self-development.* Sterling, VA: Stylus.

Brison, S. (2002). *Aftermath: Violence and the remaking of a self.* Princeton, NJ: Princeton University Press.

Debold, E. (2002). Epistemology, fourth order consciousness, and the subject-object relationship, or how the self evolves with Robert Kegan. *What is Enlightenment?* (Fall/Winter 2002): 143–154.

Derrida, J. (1984). *The margins of philosophy.* Trans. A. Bass. Chicago: University of Chicago Press.

Forrester, M. A. (2006). Projective identification and intersubjectivity. *Theory & Psychology, 16*(6) 783–802.

Foucault, M. (1983). The subject and power. In H. L. Dreyfus & P. Rabinow (Eds.). *Beyond structuralism and hermeneutics: Michel Foucault* (pp. 208–228). Chicago: University of Chicago Press.

Gibson, Andrea. (2006). Say yes. Video posted November 17, 2007 to http://www.youtube.com/watch?v=TsINiBj4pCc

Heidegger, M. (1962). *Being and time.* Trans. J. Macquarrie & E. Robinson. London: SCM Press.

Keating, A. L. (Ed.), (2000). *Gloria E. Anzaldúa: Interviews entrevistas.* New York: Routledge.

Kegan, R. (1982). *The evolving self: Problem and process in human development.* Cambridge, MA: Harvard University Press.

Kegan, R. (1994). *In over our heads: The mental demands of modern life.* Cambridge, MA: Harvard University Press.

Love, P. G., & Guthrie, V. L. (1999, Winter). Kegan's orders of consciousness. *New Directions for Student Services, 88*, 65–75.

Lugones, M. (1990). Playfulness, "world"-travelling, and loving perception. In G. Anzaldúa (Ed.), *Making face, making soul/Haciendo caras: Creative and critical perspective by women of color* (pp. 390–402). San Francisco: Aunt Lute.

Lugones, M. (2006). On complex communication. *Hypatia. 21*(3): 75–85.

Merleau-Ponty, M. (1964). The child's relations with others. In M. Merleau-Ponty (Ed.), *The primacy of perception and other essays on phenomenological psychology* (pp. 159–190). Evanston, IL: Northwestern University Press.

Ortega, M. (2001). 'New mestizas,' 'world'-travelers,' and 'Dasein': Phenomenology and the multi-voiced, multi-cultural self. *Hypatia. 16*(3): 1–29.

Zaytoun, K. (2005). New pathways toward understanding self-in-relation: Anzaldúan (re)visions for developmental psychology. In A. Keating (Ed.), *Entremundos/Among worlds: New perspectives on Gloria E. Anzaldúa* (pp. 147–159). New York: Palgrave MacMillan.

# Unit 5 Additional Recommended Readings

Abes, E. S., & Kasch, D. (2007). Using queer theory to explore lesbian college students' multiple dimensions of identity. *Journal of College Student Development, 48*, 619–636.

Brookfield, S. (2005). Contesting hegemony. In S. Brookfield *The power of critical theory for adult learning and teaching* (pp. 94–117). New York, NY: McGraw-Hill.

Dill, B. T., McLaughlin, A. E., & Nieves, A. D. (2007). Future directions of feminist research: Intersectionality. In S. N. Hesse-Biber (Ed.), *Handbook of feminist research* (pp. 629–637). Thousand Oaks, CA: Sage.

Dilley, P. (2002). Queer theory, identity development theory, and non-heterosexual students. In *Queer man on campus: A history of non-heterosexual college men, 1945-2000* (pp. 15–52). New York, NY: RoutledgeFalmer.

Harper, S. R. (2009). Niggers no more: A critical race counternarrative on Black male student achievement at predominantly White colleges and universities. *International Journal of Qualitative Studies in Education, 22,* 697–712.

McLaren, P. (2008). Critical pedagogy: A look at the major concepts. In A. Darder , M. P. Baltodan, & R. D. Torres (Eds.) *The critical pedagogy reader* (2nd ed., pp. 61–83), New York, NY: Routledge.

Ostrove, J. M., & Cole, E. R. (2003). Privileging class: Toward a critical psychology of social class in the context of education. *Journal of Social Issues, 59,* 677–692.

Patton, L. D., McEwen, M., Rendón, L., & Howard-Hamilton, M. F. (2007). Critical race perspectives on theory in student affairs. In S. R. Harper & L. D. Patton, *Responding to the realities of race on campus* (New Directions for Student Services No. 120, pp. 39–53). San Francisco, CA: Jossey-Bass.

Rhodes, R. A., & Black, M. A. (1995). Student affairs practitioners and transformative educators: Advancing a critical cultural perspective. *Journal of College Student Development, 36,* 413–421.

Solórzano, D. G., Ceja, M., & Yosso, T. (2000). Critical race theory, racial microaggressions, and campus racial climate: The experiences of African American college students. *Journal of Negro Education, 69,* 60–73.

Solórzano, D. G., & Villalpando, O. (1998). Critical race theory, marginality, and the experience of students of color in higher education. In C. A. Torres & T. A. Mitchell (Eds.) *Sociology of education: Emerging perspectives* (pp. 211–224). New York, NY: State University of New York Press.

Tanaka, G. (2002). Higher education's self-reflexive turn: Toward an intercultural theory of student development. *Journal of Higher Education, 73,* 263–296.

Villalpando, O. (2004). Practical considerations of critical race theory and Latino critical theory for Latino college students. In A. M. Ortiz (Ed.), *Addressing the unique needs of Latino American students* (New Directions for Student Services No. 105, pp. 41–50). San Francisco, CA: Jossey-Bass.

Zaytoun, K. (2006). Theorizing at the borders: Considering social location in rethinking self and psychological development. *NWSA Journal, 18*(2), 53–72.

# UNIT 6

## *THEORY TO PRACTICE*

# CHAPTER 32
# ON MODELING REALITY

## CLYDE A. PARKER

What we are to our inward vision, . . . can only be expressed by way of myth. Myth is more individual and expresses life more precisely than the science. Science works with concepts of averages which are far too general to do justice to the subjective variety of an individual life.—C. G. Jung

At the 1970 convention of this Association, I proposed (Parker 1970, 1973) the notion that what we needed in student personnel services was a comprehensive theory of the college student. That hypothesis was based on the assumption that if we were to create and adequately test such a comprehensive theory, we would then be able to devise more rational programs and provide more effective services for our college students. Today, of course, the assumption seems naive; in 1970, however, it did not. The 1960s had been a cataclysmic watershed for student personnel workers and we were in the process of redefining our roles and purposes. The ACPA project, Tomorrow's Higher Education, was stimulated by our desire for redefinition. It suggested a redirection of our energies toward the individual development of students and away from standing in loco parentis to them.

Like most academicians, we had a theory-practice orientation. If we were going to focus on student development, then what we needed was a theory of the development of college-age students. We looked to our colleagues in developmental psychology to supply us with one. If they had had such a theory on tap, it is quite likely that student personnel services would have taken a radically different direction. As it was, we discovered that if we wanted a theory we would have to create it ourselves. Many of us figuratively took off our jackets, rolled up our sleeves, and tried to form hypotheses. We found ourselves up against the question, In what way can theory—any theory—be helpful to practitioners?

At first blush, this question seemed rather straightforward and simple. After wrestling with it for several years, I have found that it is neither straightforward nor simple. In fact, I have had to wrestle with first a dilemma, second a paradox, and third a problem. The dilemma is that good research and theory building require the abstraction of a few elements from the whole of human experience. Practice, on the other hand, requires concrete and specific behavior in complex situations. The paradox is that theory dealing with abstractions from the general case cannot be applied in concrete and specific situations. Yet concrete and specific action flows from the personal theories of the actor. The problem is learning how to transform formal theory into personal theories of action. I would like to deal with each of these in turn. Then I will describe three ways in which we have found theory useful.

Parker, C. A. (1977). On modeling reality. *Journal of College Student Personnel, 18,* 419–425.

## The Dilemma

Two then students, Lee Knefelkamp and Carole Widick, joined me in the pursuit to create a comprehensive theory and to demonstrate that developmental theory could be used in practice. They devised a classroom experiment to test the applicability of William Perry's (1970) theory of intellectual development in college students. Using a quasi-experimental design, they demonstrated that the intentional structuring of both the content and process of a literature class resulted in advancing students in Perry's stages of intellectual development (Knefelkamp 1974; Widick 1975). Subsequent research (Stephenson & Hunt 1975) demonstrated that the progress stimulated with intentional developmental instruction was greater than that achieved by students in comparison classes. Sprinthall (1975), Erickson (1975), and others provide further evidence of the ability to use developmental theory in practice.

We now are fairly certain that we can demonstrate our ability to use theory to devise programs which result in developmental change under experimental conditions. But this does not give us the confidence that we should proceed with such goals and procedures in the real world of regular classes or student affairs activities. The model we have used and tested in our quasi-experimental setting does not have sufficient conformity to reality to work with people in the real world.

## Why Formal Theories Don't Work

It is not that the theory is inadequate to describe, explain, or even predict and control the intellectual development of students in general. The difficulty is that, of necessity, the theory or model captures only a small part of the whole person in the situation. In paying attention to intellectual development we have ignored much that was of equal or more importance.

Thus the dilemma. In order for us to create a researchable model of the person we must abstract from a very complex wholeness those parts which we wish to study. When we do so we ignore the rest of the person, which is interrelated in a complex and systemic way. On the other hand, the practitioner works with whole persons in real-life situations. If we attempt to preserve that wholeness we have such complexity that we cannot handle it conceptually. Workable models are too complex to research and researchable models are too simplified to be useful in practice. Sanford (1976) recently expressed the problem this way:

> The trouble is that the formulae never quite fit the concrete case. . . . It is not that the formulae are wrong, for they can be shown to hold in a general way or when specified conditions are present; it is that they are not adequate to the complexity of the real situations to which they are applied. Too many relevant factors are left out of account, too many relationships are ignored, and what is perhaps most common, there is too big a gap between abstractly conceived and mathematically manipulable variables and the real processes they are supposed to embody. . . . (p. 763)

Theories are abstractions and simplifications of the real world. They allow us to hypothesize and test relationships between elements of the real world. If we try to reverse the process and apply abstractions to a given real-life situation, we find they don't fit because no single person is Mr. Average. In Perry's (1976) language, "Any event, no matter how small, is bigger than any category or theory which may be used to enlighten our understanding of it."

## The Paradox

A paradox is a contradiction in nature. Two opposite conditions exist, each true yet contradictory. We have said that theories are not directly useful in practice. Yet the fact is we do not approach our work as practitioners without a theory, willy-nilly, without some fairly set ideas about what is important, how those elements are related to each other, and what should happen. Further, those concepts and assumptions are very powerful determinants of our behavior.

For example, we believe that intellectual development is an important part of the college experience and that classroom instruction contributes to intellectual development. Such concepts are a theory for us. So we organize institutions with faculties, course content, and classrooms. That is the use of theory in practice. Or, we believe that students need to develop interpersonally and we arrange for student governments, other student organizations, or encounter groups. Thus, our paradox: a basic contradiction in the nature of things. The nature of theory is such that it does not lead directly to practice and the nature of practice is such that it does not proceed without theory. Unlike a problem, a paradox cannot be resolved, it can only be understood.

## Reinterpreting the Paradox

Is there a way to interpret the paradox so that we are not stymied? Following Rychlak (1968), we make a distinction between formal and informal theory. By formal theory we refer to the explicit conceptualization of the essential elements of a particular phenomenon, the hypothesized relationships among those elements, and the procedures by which those relations may be validated. Such formal theories are shared in the scientific community and tested in the laboratory or in natural settings.

By informal theory we refer to the body of common knowledge that allows us to make implicit connections among the events and persons in our environment and upon which we act in everyday life. We all have such informal theories or models. In most cases these are implicit microtheories, they relate only two or three elements, seem not to be connected with one another, and contain propositions of what is valuable. These microtheories are such a part of us that we don't think of them as theories. In fact, we usually are not aware of them. Argyris (1976) has called such theories "theories in use."

Whether we retain our theories as guides to future action depends on our experience with them. Do they hold up in our everyday experience? Usually we don't ask that question systematically. Rather, we accept what supports our view and ignore other data unless there is some blatant evidence that we are wrong.

For example, suppose we believe that conducting leadership training sessions helps student leaders be more effective in their organizations. We believe they need to know *Roberts' Rules of Order*, how to file purchase orders, and how to work through the maze of room scheduling. After the seminars, three students we especially like take the time to tell us how much they learned from what we did. That is the validation we need to confirm our plans for next year! One of them even comes back two quarters later with specific examples of how much hassle our seminars helped her avoid. Our theory holds up! But we don't hear anything from the other 25. That is, until one day we are in the hall and just happen to hear five well-respected student leaders (ones we don't usually talk with) talking and one of them makes a very disparaging remark about the "waste" of those seminars and how hard it is to get us to hear that message. It is then that we might call the implicit theory into question.

It is precisely because of our tendency to not self-correct that we cannot rely solely on our informal theories. Formal theories and their validation are crucial as counterforces to our highly personal world. It is the process of formal theory building and testing that corrects and adds to the body of knowledge common to a group or a culture, in our particular case, the group of professionals who work in student affairs. Formal theory building and testing is the means of increasing our knowledge of student development in general. That is how we move the field ahead. However, just as it is formal theory that advances the body of knowledge for a professional field, it is the informal theories which each person constructs that make it possible to practice.

Before I can complete my argument I need to introduce one more element. As practitioners we are really scientists, that is, we formulate informal theories and in our everyday work we go about informally validating them. George Kelly (1955) said that the same was true of every person, including students. One way of describing student behavior is to liken it to the way a scientist works. Students also have microtheories about persons, things, and events, which Kelly called personal constructs. Our actions are based on these constructs or micromodels of reality. When events go as anticipated constructs are confirmed. When they don't, we become frustrated. If we are open, we alter our constructs to fit our experience. If we are not open, we distort our experience to fit our theories. By extending our notion of informal theory to include all persons we include the students we are attempting to help. How well our own theories work depends upon how open we are to the personal constructs of our students and their circumstances.

## The Problem

The dilemma we have described requires that we choose between abstract, simplified models of reality which are researchable and the concrete, complex reality in which we act. The paradox we have found is understandable if we distinguish between formal theory and informal theory. The problem, by contrast, can be solved if we are competent enough.

I was recently asked to meet with a group of student activities staff members to lead a discussion on "how to apply student development theory." In making the request they emphasized their frustration in knowing a great deal about various theories related to the development of students but not knowing what to do with them in practice. They were much reassured when I explained that in my 20 years of teaching counseling psychologists that has been the single most perplexing problem I have faced: how to teach students to use the theory they know when working directly with clients.

The explicit matching of practice to theory is full of all the pitfalls we have discussed. This is particularly true when working in an institutional setting where our explicit ideas about what ought to be happening to students are different from others' ideas. There is currently a strong difference of opinion whether it is possible to do so (Kohlberg 1971; Loevinger 1976). Loevinger feels that using her theory of ego development is particularly difficult:

> Furthermore, no one knows how to assist ego development effectively, nor do the advocates of higher ego level have a means of access to formative institutions. The world could be incinerated or its resources exhausted in less time than it would take to learn how to foster ego development through the public school system, and to have such a program accepted over the protests of those who would consider it radical and subversive. . . . (p. 429)

The picture is not that dismal, but I wish to emphasize that the solution to this problem requires patient thoughtfulness and creativity. It is, in my experience, among the most difficult professional tasks. It is true of other scientific fields as well.

> The step of adapting the general laws to apply to a particular situation is the hardest task for the student. That is the step that is learned by watching others do it in case after case. Kuhn states: in general, there are no rules to assist the process. Thus, by Kuhn's own testimony, the hardest step in becoming a physicist is most like the training of a psychoanalyst. (Loevinger 1976, p. 391)

## Three Ways of Using Theory

We have been successful in using theory in three ways: at the level of the college, at the level of the classroom, and with individual students. The more broad and inclusive our work has been the more useful we find formal theory. The more we focus on the individual the more we have had to rely on informal theory and personal constructs. I have chosen three examples to illustrate.

Two years ago I was asked to assist the University of Minnesota's College of Agriculture in their faculty development efforts. With the support of several graduate students, I began a three-year pilot project consulting with the faculty of that college. The first year we collected what we felt would be useful data to understand the students, faculty, and setting of the college. Our guiding theory was Perry's (1970) *Forms of Intellectual and Ethical Development in the College Years*. We were particularly interested in whether faculty were teaching at a level that matched the student's developmental level. We interviewed 80 students, 20 from each of the four undergraduate classes. Then we interviewed six faculty and observed their teaching styles. We found that in general the students were expecting to be taught by faculty who knew the right answers to important questions and to learn the facts. They expected to be rewarded for learning those facts and reproducing them on examinations. The faculty, however, were interested in students being able to use a variety of data to analyze problems, to bring together seemingly disparate knowledge into integrated syntheses, and to make important judgments.

In brief, students were in dualistic and multiplistic stages while faculty were relativistic and highly committed persons. The following illustrations from Froberg and Parker (1976) will help.

Student A: "In biology, there's really not two ways you can look at it. A bird has two feet. That's pretty conclusive" (p.22).

Professor A: "Rarely do you get a piece of information that's out there all by itself. You need to pull it into your system somewhat" (p.11).

Student B: "Things can be a hundred different ways. Both sides can bring in a ton of evidence to support their views. Both are equally right. Everybody's right. That's disillusioning" (p.25).

Professor B: "We are critical of how well an individual is able to take a subject matter area and adequately prepare and defend his position" (p.13).

Student C: "I have a fear of tests. I don't know what I'm supposed to know. Teachers say 'You should have gotten this from what I told you there.' Teachers should teach what they know. . . . A dedicated teacher would tell students what he knew" (p.23).

Professor C: "One criticism I've had is that I ask questions that don't have absolute answers . . . I give them these kinds of questions because that's what life is. There aren't nice clean answers. They must come up with alternatives, weigh things, and make a decision" (p.17).

Data confirming such a mismatch have provided us with a direction for our consultation. We were able with those data to show faculty the need for changing the ways they taught some students. At the same time we learned that we could not, as we had expected we might, prescribe specific approaches that could be used by faculty in general. Rather, we have had to turn to working with small groups of faculty on an almost individual basis.

A second way we have found theory useful is in planning activities for relatively homogeneous groups. When a group of students is similar in respect to particular needs or characteristics, then activities can be planned with those particular characteristics in mind. A recent experience of one member of our research team helps to illustrate (personal communication, J. Lawson, 1975).

She has taught for 10 years and is quite aware that classes develop their unique personalities based on the characteristics of the students, the teacher, and the interaction among them. Yet she was hopeful that one preparation would suffice for two sections. Within the first two weeks it became obvious that the two classes were so different that that would not be possible. An exercise that went well in one class just did not work in the other. She sought some help from the "Perry seminar" which met each Friday afternoon. In the seminar we made the following analysis of the two classes:

| Activities | Responses | |
| --- | --- | --- |
| | **A.M. Group** | **P.M. Group** |
| 1. Group role play. | Couldn't get into roles. | Played roles effectively. |
| 2. Discussion of guideline sheet. | Resistance to requirements. | Accepted requirements. |
| 3. Formation of base groups. | Freely chose members with whom they wanted to work. | Resistance to choosing other students. Delayed a day. Processed reactions during the next class. Formed groups reluctantly. |
| 4. Role play with me as student and class as teacher. Goal: respond to problem. | Gave good responses. Made errors but continued. Analyzed tape. Uncovered all the problems. | Few attempts made to give responses. Became frustrated with errors. Didn't uncover the problems. |

The analysis led her to provide more structure for the afternoon section in order to meet its dualistic character. At the same time she set goals for them to be better able to see alternative points of view, to take more risks, to be less dependent on the instructor. In the morning class she encouraged students to share reactions rather than asking them specific questions. Her developmental tasks for them were helping them to make choices from alternatives and encouraging them to take responsibility for what happened in class. The results of this differential approach to the two classes were most evident in the fact that the relativistic morning class did the final evaluation and grading for themselves, while the dualistic afternoon class would only accept the instructor's judgment.

When students have common characteristics, a general theory can be helpful in setting goals for the group and in determining effective procedures to reach those goals. As practitioners we are often confronted with the necessity or responsibility to assist in program development or in policy formulation. In these instances, a model which provides a description of the ends toward which students should be moving in general and the means for facilitating that movement can be very helpful. Knowing that movement from conventional morality to principled morality (Kohlberg 1971) is characteristic of the college-age period and that it is possible to create appropriate classroom experiences (Sprinthall 1975) might stimulate a student activities bureau to organize moral development seminars for student groups. The difficulty is that in most settings in which we work students are not that similar. They are highly diverse and do not fit into any general model. Working in the real world always requires an adaptation to the individual.

Formal theory and data collection add to the body of knowledge common to the profession and help us work with groups of students. It is from this body of knowledge that we form personal constructs that help us work with individuals. We have come to view students as highly diverse individuals, in need of emotional, social, intellectual, and value development, coming from a wide range of backgrounds and with divergent interests, as a result of research accumulated in the body of knowledge common to student affairs. But the problem that has plagued us has been how to use that knowledge to understand the individual (see Allport 1962). We know much about the average student but we are left (seemingly) to our own resources when it comes to working with a particular student. No student fits the average.

If our common knowledge is sufficiently broad it will allow us to enter into the diverse world of students' personal constructs and to form meaning from what is said. It will also allow us to arrive at an understanding with the student of what is needed to advance development. We do that by utilizing many theories to understand and assist an individual whose life forms its own uniqueness and whose personal constructs grow out of and make up that uniqueness.

A clear example of this process in the negative can be drawn from the experiences with minority students on our campuses. When they began to arrive in large numbers during the 60s, it was apparent that we did not know their world well enough. During the past 10 years we have tried to accommodate by employing professional and paraprofessional minority personnel whose knowledge bridged the gap between the majority and minority cultures. At the same time we have attempted to broaden the general body of knowledge so that our personal constructs would allow us to understand and meet their particular needs. I need only remind you of the personal pain that has caused for many minorities to help you see how important it is that our common knowledge be broadbased and as accurate as possible.

The spirit of what I am attempting to convey is captured in the following from C. G. Jung (1965):

> Naturally, a doctor must be familiar with the so-called "methods." But he must guard against falling into any specific, routine approach. In general, one must guard against theoretical assumptions. Today they may be valid, tomorrow it may be the turn of other assumptions. In my analysis they play no part. I am unsystematic very much by intention. To my mind, in dealing with individuals, only individual understanding will do. We need a different language for every patient. In one analysis I can be heard talking Alderian dialect, in another the Freudian. The crucial point is that I confront the patient as one human being to another. . . . (p. 131)

This ability to adapt oneself to each individual Hunt (1976) has called "reading" and "flexing." He has emphasized the point made here that one cannot apply a general theory to individuals, but rather that one must be sufficiently adaptable to *read* the student cues and *flex* in reaction to meet the particular needs of the person and the situation. Thus we have the two major uses of theory coming together—the formal and the informal, the general and the specific, the abstract and the concrete—by using a general body of knowledge, arrived at through the practice of science, in designing general programs and adapting to the needs of individual students (reading and flexing) through understanding the ways they personally construe their life and environs.

An example from our project in the College of Agriculture will serve as a final illustration of this point. Jane Lawson has been meeting in a weekly seminar with five faculty members from the College. They have shared their personal theories about teaching. She has observed their classrooms. Together they have identified particular instances of student-faculty mismatch. The challenge has been to assist the faculty to change their microtheories of students enough to be more adaptable in teaching them.

Professor Donely is an outgoing, friendly, challenging person. He values good teaching; at one point he shared his life's goal as being remembered by his students as a good teacher rather than as having a reputation as a researcher. His constructs about students uniformly stressed his preference for alive, questioning, motivated students. His approach to teaching seems predicated on the students in his classes being like that. He is informal, assumes students have read the material, and initiates the class by asking if there are any questions. He is very comfortable with this style of teaching. Yet he had become quite disillusioned because the students were unable to pass his examinations. He was contemplating asking to be relieved of his teaching load.

The discussion of his personal constructs of students identified a particular student, Roger, with whom Donely was having difficulty. Roger was quiet, didn't ask questions, and didn't seem to be learning. Clearly a mismatch of student and professor. In the seminar there were discussions of alternative ways of approaching such students in general, but it was in the individual consultation that Jane was able to provide specific help.

In one session she asked Donely if he knew anyone else like Roger. At first he said no. But Jane recognized some similarities between Roger and a faculty member in the seminar. Donely later recognized these similarities and then volunteered that he had known for some time that this professor was motivated by support and encouragement. If he were made to feel needed he produced some very good work. She also encouraged Donely to reflect on the ways he worked with one of his own children who needed more time and understanding than the others. Suddenly Donely saw the parallels. He was able to view Roger as needing structure, support, and encouragement rather than being uninterested, unmotivated, and a poor student.

Roger began taking notes, following short lectures and responding to structured questions, and finished the quarter successfully. Donely is enthusiastic about his own ability to "read" a new kind of student and to "flex" enough to provide the structure that that student needs to learn.

## Conclusion

I have confessed my naivete about the direct use of theory in the practice of student personnel work. I have shared my saga through dilemma, paradox, and problem. Hopefully, the illustrations of our work at the college, classroom, and individual levels will restore your hope that models of reality can be helpful to you. We need not return to that never-never land where imitation, random trial and error, personal bias, and frustration prevail.

## References

Allport, G. W. The general and the unique in psychological science. *Journal of Personality*, 1962, *30*, 405–422.

Argyris, C. Theories of action that inhibit individual learning. *American Psychologist*, 1976, *31*, 638–654.

Erickson, V. L. Deliberate psychological education for women: From Iphegenia to Antigone. *Journal of Counselor Education and Supervision*, 1975, *14*, 297–309.

Froberg, D., & Parker, C. P. Progress report of the developmental instruction project. Minneapolis, Minn.: University of Minnesota, 1976. (mimeo)

Hunt, D. Teacher's adaptation: "Reading" and "flexing" to students. *Journal of Teacher Education*, 1976, in press.

Jung, C. G. *Memories, dreams, reflections.* New York: Vintage Books, 1965.

Kelly, G. A. *The psychology of personal constructs.* New York: Norton, 1955.

Knefelkamp, L. *Developmental instruction: Fostering intellectual and personal growth of college students.* Unpublished doctoral dissertation, University of Minnesota, 1974.

Kohlberg, L. The concepts of developmental psychology as the central guide to education, Examples from cognitive, moral, and psychological education. In M. Reynolds (Ed.), *Psychology and the process of schooling in the next decade.* Minneapolis, Minn.: University of Minnesota, 1971.

Loevinger, J. *The meaning and measurement of ego development.* San Francisco: Jossey-Bass, 1976.

Parker, C. A. Ashes, ashes. . . Paper presented at the American College Personnel Association convention, St. Louis, Missouri, March 1970. (mimeo)

Parker, C. A. With an eye to the future. *Journal of College Student Personnel*, 1973, 14, 195–201.

Perry, W. G., Jr. *Comments regarding use of developmental theory.* Unpublished paper prepared for a conference on student development in higher education, Minneapolis, May 1976.

Perry, W. G., Jr. *Forms of intellectual and ethical development in the college years.* New York: Holt Rinehart & Winston, 1970.

Rychlak, J. F. *A philosophy of science for personality theory.* Boston: Houghton Mifflin, 1968.

Sanford, N. Graduate education then and now. *American Psychologist*, 1976, 31, 756–764.

Sprinthall, N. Moral and psychological development: A curriculum for secondary schools. In *Symposium on education and value development.* New York: Fordham University, 1975.

Stephenson, B. W., & Hunt, C. *Intellectual and ethical development: A dualistic curriculum intervention for college students.* Paper presented at the American Psychological Association convention, Chicago, September 1975.

Widick, C. C. *An evaluation of developmental instruction in a university setting.* Unpublished doctoral dissertation, University of Minnesota, 1975.

# CHAPTER 33
## THE PROFESSIONAL PRACTICE OF STUDENT DEVELOPMENT

### C. CARNEY STRANGE AND PATRICIA M. KING

## Introduction and Overview

This chapter focuses on the purposes and functions of a theoretical knowledge base for the professional practice of student development in postsecondary education. It begins with a brief statement about the character of professional work and the role of theory and research in guiding it. This is followed by a summary of the status of the student development knowledge base and its implications for practice. Problems inherent to the nature of applied educational fields are then identified and issues related to the imperfect correspondence between theory and practice are discussed. Finally, several strategies are recommended to those involved in professional preparation and staff development for successfully connecting theory to practice in the course of graduate education and in-service programs.

## Professionals at Work

"We make a difference or your money back!" the sign in bold letters says; "Call the professionals," another one reads; "Choose the experts," an advertisement suggests; "Skilled . . . certified . . . approved . . . accredited" banner lines in the yellow pages proclaim. All are claims of comfort we have come to rely upon in a consumer-oriented society. They are, in effect, promises of quality we expect from the person who changes the oil in our car to the individual who invests and manages our life savings. Attention to those assumed "to know" is more than good business or common sense, though. In a world where complexity exceeds the boundaries of any single individual's grasp, it is a matter of survival. Whatever the field or concern, it is characteristic of modern society to value and depend heavily on the input of those who are professionals at what they do.

What is the meaning of being a professional? By contrast, how does that differ from being a nonprofessional or amateur? The thesis proposed here is that professionals are clearly distinguished from nonprofessionals in reference to five criteria, and therefore, they have more to offer. Professionals can:

1. offer reasonable and believable explanations for the phenomena they purport to address (*theory*);

2. support the validity of their explanations with evidence (*research*);

3. respond to those phenomena on the basis of their explanations, and do so with methods, both unique or standard, that are generally endorsed by peers (*practice*);

Strange, C. C., & King, P. M. (1990). The professional practice of student development. In D. Creamer & Associates, *College student development: Theory and practice for the 1990s* (pp. 9–24). Alexandria, VA: ACPA Media.

4. demonstrate the success of their efforts with evidence (*evaluation*); and

5. articulate a clear sense of what is important and valuable in relation to the phenomena they address (*values*).

Each of these five criteria addresses an important component or tool of the professional at work. Explanations derive from *theory*; the validity of these explanations is supported through *research*; action flows directly from these explanations and is governed by standards of *practice*; and consequences are monitored and documented through *evaluation*. Above all, the *value* of the phenomena addressed is expressed through personal commitment.

The cyclical relationship between these elements is illustrated in Figure 1. For example, consider the familiar archetype of the professional at work—the family physician. Most of us have had the experience of limping off to the family doctor with a host of unpleasant symptoms, looking for some relief or, at the very least, a reasonable explanation for our private misery. Our choice of a doctor (rather than, say, a legal consultant) is obvious. First, we assume that, by virtue of the physician's professional preparation and training, she or he will see the connections between our

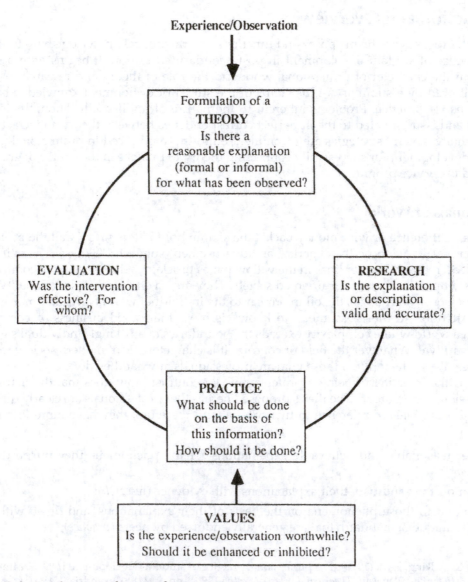

**Figure 1**    Relating theory and research to practice.

symptoms and, in this case, drawing upon a knowledge of virology and bacteriology (*theories*), will be able to identify the probable cause of our illness. Second, we may further assume that the doctor has kept up with the latest issues of the *New England Journal of Medicine* and is abreast of the recent developments in this area, particulary concerning the current endemic strains of virus (*research*). Third, we expect the doctor to treat our illness based on an appropriate diagnosis and consistent with the accepted standards of practice. For example, the doctor may prescribe an antibiotic for bacterial infections, but may offer only symptomatic relief for viral infections (*practice*). Finally, we do expect to feel better, and if not, we are likely to go back for another explanation or perhaps even seek the advice of a different physician (*evaluation*). At the core of this whole process is our assumption that this physician clearly values good health and holds it as a goal of professional efforts (*values*).

## Student Development Educators as Professionals at Work

Student development, the power and promise of formal education to enhance the growth and development of individuals encountering life transitions, constitutes a core *value* of the student affairs profession. Within the past two decades, the profession has articulated a knowledge base that more clearly enlightens the goal of student development. Student development *theories* help explain the complexities of students' behavior, change, and growth; these explanations, and the cumulative *research* that sharpens and validates them, constitute the "science of student development." Theory and research help us recognize that student behavior is not just a matter of chance and random effect; rather, many aspects of student behavior are observable, measurable, explainable, generalizable, and therefore, to some extent, predictable. The student development knowledge base has also yielded new ways of reaching the goal of intentional student development through the use of more effective strategies. The process of translating these explanations into professional *practice* by using various models, techniques, and methods constitutes the "art of student development." The notion of transforming ideas into practice is not new: Aristotle contrasted "artisans," those who did things well and knew why, from those who were "just lucky." The professional practice of student development, therefore, is an art informed by science, as is the profession of medicine.

Consider the case of a dean of students who is faced with a student considering leaving school during the first semester of her freshman year. In choosing how to respond, the dean may draw from a reservoir of knowledge about the developmental status of freshman students and the differential impact of various educational environments. The student's comments of "being confused about what to do with my life and what to major in" and about "not feeling that I belong" might quickly invoke the conceptions of Chickering's (1969) Developing Purpose and Identity vectors and Astin's (1984) involvement model that underscore the importance of a student's connection to the activities and structures of the institution. Perhaps the student's overly acquiescent manner and deference to the dean as an "authority who knows the answer" may also lead to hypotheses about developmental level, in this case, perhaps Dualistic (Perry, 1970) or Dependent/Conforming (Harvey, Hunt, & Schroder, 1961). All of these possible explanations, or *theories*, are useful for understanding this student's behavior and for anticipating her potential reaction, such as how she might respond to the dean's advice and whether or not she will stay in college. There is ample evidence in the attrition/retention *research* to suggest that, given her present characteristics and status, she is indeed a high-risk candidate for leaving school. Here, the dean is drawing from his knowledge of the science of his profession.

With the goal of student development in mind, and based upon the above explanations, several options for *practice* might be warranted. Three options the dean might consider are offered below. First, the dean could advise the student to enroll in a career decision-making class offered on campus. This recommendation might be based on two major theoretical assumptions: (a) that addressing resolution of questions of vocational purpose and direction often benefits other aspects of development, such as identity, sense of competence and self-esteem, and relationships with others (Chickering, 1969); and (b) that identification of the "ideal self," in this case one's occupational identity, provides a critical referent for evaluating the present environment (Pervin, 1968).

Second, the dean also may suggest that this student join an organization or group compatible with her interests. This second recommendation might be based on several theory-based assumptions: (a) that environmental attraction, personal satisfaction, and stability are enhanced in a congruent, differentiated environment (Holland, 1973); (b) that an individual increases his or her power to achieve a reinforcement by joining a group (Skinner, 1953); and (c) that student involvement on campus positively affects student persistence, self-esteem, and satisfaction with most aspects of college life (Astin, 1984).

A third option the dean may consider is to encourage more risk taking on the part of this student, supporting her attempts at self-reliance and judgment. The theoretical assumptions here are that tolerance of uncertainty and acknowledgment of self as a legitimate source of judgment are requisite changes in the achievement of more advanced levels of development (Harvey et al., 1961; Kitchener & King, 1981; Perry, 1970).

Each of these options incorporates elements common to the practice of intentional planned change. The student development goals to be reached are informed by theories of student development, an assessment of the current level or progress is made (formal or informal), and intervention strategies (instruction, consultation, environmental management) are planned to encourage growth (Miller & Prince, 1976; Morrill, Hurst, & Oetting, 1980). Which option or options the dean chooses and what methods of conveying and implementing the chosen option(s) will depend on his expertise in the art of student development.

*Monitoring* or *evaluating* the student's experience and progress with these recommendations may confirm the validity of the dean's response, or suggest alternative strategies. Evaluation also may suggest additional changes in policies and practices affecting other students that can be initiated in a more proactive, systematic manner, such as requiring students to complete an initial career planning assessment session as part of orientation to the freshman year, or establishing an institutional developmental transcript system to encourage and monitor student involvement on campus.

Another illustration of the student development educator as a "professional at work" might involve a program planning task such as orienting returning adult learners to a new Weekend College program on campus. Recent life-span literature (Levinson, 1978; Schlossberg, 1984) describes adult development in terms of a sequence of alternating periods of stability and transition (*theories*). The theoretical and research literature also has clarified the connection between the return to formal education and the experience of significant life transitions, most frequently those of a career or relationship nature (Aslanian & Brickell, 1980). In addition, adult learners also have been found to approach their return to school with memories of less-than-successful previous attempts, low self-esteem, and suspicion about the formal trappings of traditional classroom learning (Cross, 1981). The literature further shows that adults often expect a practical and concrete return for their efforts (*research*). These findings suggest that a successful orientation program for adults ought to acknowledge these concerns in some way. Opportunities for career interest assessment, exposure to various campus support services, and a chance to confront their reservations about returning to school in a nonthreatening, supportive atmosphere with other adults all are important components of interventions (*practice*) that are supported by theory and research. The successful matriculation, satisfaction, and retention of adult learners on campus will help determine the effectiveness of such interventions (*evaluation*).

The point of these illustrations is that theory, research, practice, and evaluation are integral components of a student development educator's professional repertoire in selecting a response that can be intentionally analyzed and implemented. Failure to effect a linkage between these components may yield a less than adequate explanation, unreasonable expectations, and, as a result, ineffective practice. Furthermore, the field itself cannot advance without the accumulated knowledge and experience of informed professional practitioners who understand these components and who communicate with each other about their successes and failures. The immediate risk is the failure of one program, but the long-term consequences are students' diminished developmental outcomes and the inability of educational institutions to fulfill their developmental mission and potential. The professional student development educator, as scientist and artisan, is an important link in addressing such questions on campus.

# Formal Theories of Student Development

Our collective knowledge about student development comes from a variety of sources, from individual informal hunches derived from personal experiences to formal theories with extensive research bases. We will focus on the formal theory base in this section. The role of informal theories will be examined later.

From the earlier writings of Erikson (1950) on identity development to current conceptions such as Kegan's (1982) charted path of the "Evolving Self," the student development literature has been enlightened by a host of theoretical models and schemes, each attempting to describe the course and processes of human development. Likewise, the pioneer works of Lewin (1936), Murray (1938), Stern (1970), and Holland (1973), as well as the more recent thinking of Moos (1979), have helped us understand more fully the power and dynamics of human environments. This accumulated body of knowledge from the behavioral and social sciences has collectively informed the student affairs field about changes in growth and development that are likely to occur across the life span, and how educational environments can either inhibit or enhance that process. Table 1 offers an overview of these theories for purposes of examining their implications for the practice of student development.

The central paradigm represented here is the differential interactionist perspective of Kurt Lewin (1936), who argued that scientific psychology must take into account the interaction of the person and the environment. Lewin's classic formula for examining and explaining human behavior is: "Behavior is a function of the interaction of person and environment," or $B = f(P \times E)$. This paradigm suggests that if we are to understand students' behavior and their progress toward the developmental goals we espouse, we must develop a language and a variety of concepts for describing both students' individual ("personological") differences and the important features of the various campus environments they experience ("environmental" characteristics). In the student

## TABLE 1

### A Theoretical Framework for the Professional Practice of Student Development

$$B = f(P \times E)$$

#### Behavior Results from an Interaction between Persons and Environments

**Personological Models** identify differences in persons.
- *Life Structures and Psychosocial Tasks* describe specific age-related developmental tasks.
- *Cognitive and Interpersonal Styles* describe differences in the way individuals approach and resolve psychosocial tasks.
- *Cognitive-Developmental Structures* describe ways individuals explain their experiences and observations.

**Environmental Models** identify differences in environments.
- *Human Aggregates* describe differences according to the collective characteristics of individuals who inhabit environments.
- *Physical Features* describe influences of specified natural and synthetic characteristics of environments on human behavior.
- *Organizational Structures* describe effects of organized features related to goals and purposes of given environments.
- *Perceptual Interpretations* describe how individuals' evaluations of their environments affect their response and behavior.

**Person-Environment Interaction Models** identify predictions about behavior that results when certain types of individuals interact with certain types of environments.
- *Challenge:* environmental characteristics individuals find differentially stimulating, invigorating, or demanding.
- *Support:* environmental characteristics individuals find differentially comforting, familiar, or stabilizing.
- *Developmental Dissonance:* the degree of balance between environmental challenges and supports.

development literature, various theoretical models have emerged that are helpful in understanding individual differences in people, differences in human environments, and the consequences of specific person-environment interactions (Table 1).

## Personological Theories

With respect to personological differences, concepts from the *life structure and psychosocial models* (e.g., Chickering, 1969; Erikson, 1950; Gould, 1978; Havighurst, 1972; Levinson, 1978) underscore the importance of the ascendancy and resolution of specific developmental tasks in individuals' lives. Cyclical periods of transition and stability, generally a function of chronological maturation, offer opportunities for teachable moments when the learning tasks are personally relevant. The *cognitive and interpersonal style models* (e.g., Heath, 1964; Holland, 1973; Kolb, 1984; Myers, 1980; Witkin, 1976) suggest that individuals approach these tasks in characteristically different ways; they tend to exhibit different styles and patterns that must be taken into account when designing and presenting learning tasks. And finally, the *structural developmental models* (e.g., Harvey et al. 1961; Kohlberg, 1969; Kitchener & King, 1981; Perry, 1970) give us a view of how individuals differ in the way they organize and assign meaning to the events around them. These qualitative, hierarchical patterns are important for understanding the goals of development (i.e., independence/self-reliance, principled reasoning, reflective judgment, commitment) as well as the stepwise paths leading to those goals. Collectively, these personological models provide a means for understanding and assessing "where students are, where they are going, and how they get there" in terms of their own growth and development.

## Environmental Theories

With respect to environmental differences, the *human aggregate models* (e.g., Astin, 1968; Holland, 1973; Myers, 1980) suggest that environments are transmitted through people and reflect the collective characteristics of the individuals who inhabit them. Environments also select and shape the behavior of individuals over time in a coercive manner, depending on the degree of differentiation and consistency of both the person and the environment. Concepts from the *physical models* (e.g., Heilweil, 1973; Michelson, 1970) note that the natural and synthetic features of environments set limits on the behavior that can occur within them. The *structural organizational models* (e.g., Blau & Scott, 1962; Etzioni, 1964; Hage & Aiken, 1970; Price, 1968) underscore the importance of the goals and purposes of environments that give rise to various organizational structures which, in turn, encourage or discourage certain behaviors (e.g., innovation, effectiveness). Finally, the *perceptual models* (e.g., Moos, 1979; Murray, 1938; Pace & Stern, 1958; Pervin, 1968; Stern, 1970) acknowledge that a critical element in understanding how individuals experience an environment is their subjective interpretation of that environment. Collectively, these environmental models help us understand how various aspects of educational environments attract, sustain, and satisfy students (Strange, in press).

## Person-Environment Interaction

A final set of theories emerging in the student development literature describes the dynamics of person-environment interaction. Sanford's (1966) principle that development occurs when challenges in the environment are balanced by environmental supports is paramount. This concept is also referred to as "developmental dissonance" (Festinger, 1957). Here, too little challenge under highly supportive conditions is assumed to result in no developmental change, as there is little or no stimulus to alter present behavior. The opposite condition, that is, too much challenge accompanied by too little support, also may result in no developmental change because of overstimulation. Each of these conditions is a function of the interaction between personological characteristics and environmental conditions which, in combination, influence how the individual evaluates and responds to the environment, and, in short, whether development occurs as a result of the interaction. In other words, as Chickering (1969) noted, the impact or effectiveness of a given learning experience depends on the characteristics of the person who encounters it. Such differences may include, for example, learning style, assumptions about knowledge and learning, self-confidence, and willingness to take personal and intellectual risks.

These dynamics hold several implications. First, there is no single best method for promoting student development: What is effective will depend on the characteristics of the individual student and the specific features of the educational environment. Second, because students differ, a single experience can have different developmental outcomes. By the same token, different experiences can have similar outcomes. Third, the impact of a given experience depends on the *time* at which it is introduced because time is related to development (e.g., readiness to learn, willingness to be challenged, being in a period of stability or transition).

In summary, according to the interactionist paradigm, the greatest opportunities for growth and development occur when students are "matched" with appropriate environmental conditions. Designing such conditions (the art of student development) requires using the knowledge of concepts about the person and about the environment and how such elements interact to influence behavior (the science of student development).

## Theory and Practice in Applied Fields

Lewin (1936) asserted that there is nothing so practical as a good theory, and Cross (1981) contended that, although theory without practice is empty, practice without theory is blind. Both claims affirm the importance of a theory and research base and its linkage to practice as essential for professional effectiveness. Yet, linking theory and practice, and incorporating a theory and research base in the professional preparation of student affairs practitioners, is problematic for several reasons. The problems with the linkages are hypothesized to be: (a) the inherently imperfect correspondence between theory and reality; (b) the difficulties of translating theory to practice; (c) the nature of applied fields; and (d) the nature of individuals attracted to people-oriented, applied fields.

### Theory and Reality

As stated above, theory is a believable explanation for reality; it serves to organize and delineate the relationships between observed facts. A theoretical concept or model is derived from an abstraction of a potentially infinite number of specific and concrete variations of a phenomenon. For example, Kolb (1984) described the complex variations in the way students learn in terms of four patterns: (a) divergence, with its emphasis on concrete experience and reflective observation; (b) assimilation, emphasizing reflective observation and abstract conceptualization; (c) convergence, with a preference for abstract conceptualization and active experimentation; and (d) accommodation, with an emphasis on active experimentation and concrete experience. No single individual's learning style can be completely captured by any one of these patterns, yet the presence of each of these is clearly evident in given populations. In this sense, theory cannot be an accurate description of any specific reality, but only an approximate representation of many.

### Theory and Practice: The Role of Informal Theories

Parker (1977) addressed succinctly the difficulty of translating theory into practice in student affairs. He stated that such a task presents a dilemma to theorists and practitioners alike, that it is, in fact, paradoxical, and that it is therefore problematic. The dilemma, according to Parker, is that:

> In order for us to create a researchable model of the person [i.e., a theory] we must abstract from a very complex wholeness those parts which we wish to study. When we do so we ignore the rest of the person, which is interrelated in a complex and systemic way. . . . Workable models are too complex to research and researchable models are too simplified to be useful in practice. (p. 420)

The paradox Parker identified is that although "the nature of theory is such that it does not lead directly to practice, . . . the nature of practice is such that it does not proceed without theory" (p. 420) or ". . . some fairly set ideas about what is important, how those elements are related to each other, and what should happen" (p. 420). To understand the paradox, he drew the distinction between formal theory and informal "theories in use" (Argyris, 1976). Formal theories comprise:

> . . . explicit conceptualization[s] of the essential elements of a particular phenomenon, the hypothe-sized relationships among those elements, and the procedures by which those relations may be vali-dated. Such theories are shared in the scientific community and tested in the laboratory or in natural settings. (Parker, 1977, p. 420)

Informal theory refers to the "body of common knowledge that allows us to make implicit connec-tions among the events and persons in our environment and upon which we act in everyday life" (Parker, 1977, p. 420). Parker suggested that:

> . . . it is precisely because of our tendency to not self-correct that we cannot rely solely on our informal theories. Formal theories and their validation are crucial as counterforces to our highly personal world. It is the process of formal theory building and testing that corrects and adds to the body of knowledge common to a group or a culture, in our particular case, the group of professionals who work in student affairs. (p. 420)

Parker's solution is to recognize the problem of learning how to translate formal theories into infor-mal theories-in-action, in effect, using formal theories to "tune our ears" and to adapt "to the needs of individual students (reading and flexing) through understanding the ways they personally con-strue their life and environs" (1977, p. 424).

## The Nature of Applied Fields

The problem of linking theory to practice, it is hypothesized, is also a function of the nature of ap-plied fields and the types of individuals attracted to them. Success in an applied field tends to be gauged in terms of what an individual has done. Accomplishments accumulated over time lead to a successful "track record" which, in turn, becomes the mark of an experienced and "seasoned practi-tioner." Individuals must "pay their dues" as an apprentice, learning from those who have "been there." Advancement is contingent upon a succession of responsibilities and assignments. Basic knowledge, such as theory, that is acquired through traditional schooling is both a source of mis-trust and perhaps even a threat to those already practicing in the field. It may be a source of mistrust for several reasons. Claims of expertise, grounded in "what you know" rather than "what you have done," will predictably be met with suspicion in an applied field. This is especially true of a field like student affairs where interaction with people is paramount. Nothing substitutes for experience and maturity in terms of learning about and responding to the complexities of human behavior. Consequently, a status claim based on "what you know" (e.g., knowledge of current theory) rather than "what you have done" is understandably threatening because it tends to undercut the experi-ential foundation of the field.

This phenomenon is exacerbated by the already imperfect relationship between theory, reality, and practice. Moreover, the debate sharpens particularly at a time when the theory and research base of the field is expanding rapidly, such as is presently the case in student affairs. It is difficult to find time to stay current with all the new developments in the literature, and, unfortunately, sup-port for continuing education and professional development is too often seen as a luxury item and therefore is the first to go when budgets tighten. Theory and practice are continually juxtaposed in an applied field, and the tension created by this dynamic is inevitable.

## Practitioners Attracted to Applied Fields

Assumptions about the nature of applied fields are also important in understanding the type of in-dividuals who are attracted to them. The notion that different occupational settings create character-istic environments that, in turn, differentially attract individuals to them is not a new idea. Holland (1973) has written extensively on this topic and claims that environments select and shape the be-havior of people within them. Those who more closely resemble the dominant type within an environment are most likely to be attracted to it, and once within it, to be more satisfied and stable. A host of other studies examining differences in psychological type (Provost & Anchors, 1987), cognitive style (Messick & Associates, 1976), and learning style (Kolb, 1984) lend additional support to the validity of the notion of person-environment congruence.

An implication of this dynamic for the present discussion is that the dominant group of individuals attracted to a people-oriented applied field like student affairs may simply not value a theory and research base because they are essentially "doers." In the parlance of the Myers-Briggs model (Myers, 1980), they may be "extroverts," "sensors," "feelers," and "judgers," each characteristic representing an aversion to abstract, logical analysis and prescription. From Witkin's (1976) vantage point, the dominant group may tend toward "field dependence," seeing the whole rather than the parts. Alternatively, according to Kolb (1984), many student affairs professionals may be "accommodators," with a preference for active experimentation and concrete experience as principal modes of learning. Furthermore, using Holland's (1973) model, the individuals in the dominant group are often characterized as "Social," "Enterprising," and "Artistic" and derive occupational satisfaction from people rather than data, ideas, or things. The point of this analysis is that student affairs may attract a dominant group of individuals who are not particularly interested in manipulating concepts and ideas, and who are skeptical about the value of theory and research components in professional preparation criteria or staff development programs.

## Theory and Practice in the Education of Student Development Professionals

The following recommendations are offered for addressing the treatment of theory in staff development opportunities and in graduate preparation of professional student development practitioners. The suggestions are derived both from formal theory and 10 years of our own accumulated informal "theories in use" as graduate faculty members. The recommendations are offered to increase students' and practitioners' awareness of the role of theory in their actual situations, not as final solutions to the four hypothesized problems just discussed. The importance of a theory and research base for professional practice is not compromised, but the inherent difficulty of transmitting such a value is acknowledged. The three basic proposed recommendations follow.

1. *Encourage the role of "personal theorist."* This strategy recognizes that theory building is a very natural activity for practitioners. To wonder how something functions, or why something worked well or did not work, is a normal step in the day-to-day decisions a practitioner must make. Encourage the role of "personal theorist" by having students or staff members first focus on identifying their informal "theories in use." Within the context of a formal course or staff development workshop, for example, appropriate activities might include addressing basic questions like: "Do college students change over the course of their undergraduate years?" "In what ways?" "To what can you attribute such changes?" "What is the connection between those changes and the programs and activities we sponsor in our office?" There is an inevitable period of struggle in addressing such questions because informal theories are never completely clear and are invariably difficult to articulate. Group discussions that focus on synthesizing disparate "hunches" and developing a consensual framework (e.g., a descriptive model of the changes that take place among students during the college years) seem to work well. It is important to do this before any formal theories are introduced. Articulating and owning a personally generated explanation is critical to successfully initiate the "personal theorist" role. This is also an important step in recognizing the need for a more adequately articulated and supported perspective, namely, formal theory. Our own experience over the years with this exercise suggests that, collectively, a group of students or staff members will generate an informal theory model in response to the above task that is very close to what they will later come to know as a formal theory. This compatibility is an affirming process and helps them gain confidence in recognizing and using their own informal theories.

2. *Move from the concrete to the abstract, from practice to theory.* This second recommendation recognizes that formal theory rarely introduces a completely new idea, but rather, it more often helps to organize and articulate better what we intuitively know or already have observed. For example,

interacting with an individual who approaches issues from an absolute, authoritarian, simplistic, and black-and-white perspective is not an uncommon experience for most of us. The concept of Dualism, as described by Perry (1970), is immediately recognizable and helps us identify more clearly the nature of that pattern of thinking, as well as its sequence in an overall scheme of development (in this case, a requisite step to Multiplicity and Relativism). Good theories allow us to incorporate extant knowledge. The best theories seem to be almost self-evident, as if anyone could have developed and written them.

The best place to start, then, in presenting theory is with the concrete experience of students and staff members. Inductive methods, where the task is to move from particulars to general principles, are most effective at this point. For example, guiding students or staff members through an actual moral dilemma and having them synthesize and organize the various choices and responses builds an important informal theory base that will leave them much more receptive to the formal stages of moral reasoning identified by Kohlberg (1969). The use of case studies, focusing on the development of an explanation for individual differences (e.g., how two students responded differently to the same class or editorial), is another effective technique.

3. *Move from the abstract to the concrete, from theory to practice.* At first glance, this seems to contradict the recommendation above. However, it is offered as a suggestion for completing the learning cycle. Going from the particular to the general, from the concrete to the abstract, from practice to theory, is important for the initial acquisition of concepts. To fully understand the concepts, though, the process must come full circle, moving from the general to the particular, from the abstract to the concrete, and from theory back to practice. Kolb (1984) addressed in greater detail the sequence and effectiveness of this cycle of learning. Kolb described a learning model in terms of four sequential points on a cycle, beginning with *concrete experience*, leading to *reflective observation*, followed by *abstract conceptualization*, and then by *active experimentation*.

A quick reference to the children's television show "Mr. Wizard" makes the model easy to remember. The classic scene begins with a curious member of the neighborhood in Mr. Wizard's kitchen-laboratory being asked to "try something out" (concrete experience). A flash of excitement occurs (many times literally!) and Mr. Wizard challenges the naive participant to think about what happened (reflective observation). Following a brief moment of puzzlement, Mr. Wizard comes to the rescue with a succinct description and explanation of the basic principles involved and proceeds to unravel the mysterious underlying elements of cause and effect (abstract conceptualization). Now having understood what is likely to happen in this situation, or even a variation thereof, the participant is challenged to "try it again" (active experimentation), and the learning cycle is complete.

Strategies that capitalize on the last two steps of this cycle (i.e., moving from abstract conceptualization to active experimentation) might include using a particular theoretical model to critique current campus policies or practices, or generating a program intervention designed to stimulate developmental growth. The focus of such a task should be on examining the implications inherent in the way a particular theory explains the phenomenon it purports to address. For example, developmental differences identified by the Conceptual Systems theory (Harvey et al., 1961) imply that a "Dependent-Conforming" individual requires more environmental structure for growth than one who is "Independent Self-Reliant." How can those structural differences be reflected in the way a class is taught? In a counseling/advising approach? In variations of a program design? In terms of critiquing policies or practices, for example, the method used to assign roommates or to deliver career counseling services might be examined in reference to a typology model like the Myers-Briggs model (Myers, 1980). Too often theory is presented as a revealed, abstract conceptualization, with little reference to the reality that initially generated it. Starting from the concrete, moving to the abstract, and then going back to the concrete can bridge the critical gap between theory and practice. These strategies are applicable to any phase of professional preparation, from an entry-level degree program to opportunities for continuing education and staff development.

In summary, the relationship between theory and practice in an applied field is not a problem to be solved; it is a concern that can be managed. Enabling practitioners to go beyond the present generation's experience and respond in more creative and informed ways in the future, and making the relationship between theory and practice more explicit, are signs of a mature profession.

# References

Argyris, C. (1976). Theories of action that inhibit individual learning. *American Psychologist, 31,* 638–654.

Aslanian, C., & Brickell, H. (1980). *Americans in transition: Life changes as reasons for adult learning.* New York: College Entrance Examination Board.

Astin, A. W. (1968). *The college environment.* Washington, DC: American Council on Education.

Astin, A. W. (1984). Student involvement: A developmental theory for higher education. *Journal of College Student Personnel, 25,* 297–308.

Blau, P. M., & Scott, W. R. (1962). *Formal organizations: A comparative approach.* San Francisco: Chandler.

Chickering, A. W. (1969). *Education and identity.* San Francisco: Jossey-Bass.

Cross, K. P. (1981). *Adults as learners.* San Francisco: Jossey-Bass.

Erikson, E. (1950). *Childhood and society.* New York: Norton.

Etzioni, A. (1964). *Modern organizations.* Englewood Cliffs, NJ: Prentice-Hall.

Festinger, L. (1957). *A theory of cognitive dissonance.* New York: Row, Peterson.

Gould, R. L. (1978). *Transformations: Growth and change in adult life.* New York: Simon & Schuster.

Hage, J., & Aiken, M. (1970). *Social change in complex organizations.* New York: Random House.

Harvey, O. J., Hunt, D. E., & Schroder, H. M. (1961). *Conceptual systems and personality organization.* New York: Wiley.

Havighurst, R. J. (1972). *Developmental tasks and education.* New York: McKay.

Heath, R. (1964). *The reasonable adventurer.* Pittsburgh: University of Pittsburgh Press.

Heilweil, M. (1973). The influence of dormitory architecture on residence behavior. *Environment and Behavior, 5,* 377–412.

Holland, J. L. (1973). *Making vocational choices: A theory of careers.* Englewood Cliffs, NJ: Prentice-Hall.

Kegan, R. (1982). *The evolving self: Problem and process in human development.* Cambridge, MA: Harvard University Press.

Kitchener, K. S., & King, P. M. (1981). Reflective judgment: Concepts of justification and their relationship to age and education. *Journal of Applied Developmental Psychology, 2,* 89–116.

Kohlberg, L. (1969). Stage and sequence: The cognitive developmental approach to socialization. In D. Goslin (Ed.), *Handbook of socialization theory and research* (pp. 347–480). Chicago: Rand McNally.

Kolb, D. A. (1984). *Experiential learning: Experience as the source of learning and development.* Englewood Cliffs, NJ: Prentice-Hall.

Levinson, D. J. (1978). *The seasons of a man's life.* New York: Ballantine.

Lewin, K. (1936). *Principles of topological psychology.* New York: McGraw-Hill.

Messick, S., & Associates (Eds.) (1976). *Individuality in learning.* San Francisco: Jossey-Bass.

Michelson, W. (1970). *Man and his urban environment: A sociological approach.* Reading, MA: Addison-Wesley.

Miller, T., & Prince, J. (1976). *The future of student affairs.* San Francisco: Jossey-Bass.

Moos, R. (1979). *Evaluating educational environments.* San Francisco: Jossey-Bass.

Morrill, W., Hurst, J., & Oetting, E. (1980). *Dimensions of intervention for student development.* New York: Wiley.

Murray, H. (1938). *Exploration in personality.* New York: Oxford University Press.

Myers, I. B. (1980). *Gifts differing.* Palo Alto, CA: Consulting Psychologists Press.

Pace, C. R., & Stern, G. G. (1958). An approach to the measurement of psychological characteristics of college environments. *Journal of Educational Psychology, 49,* 269–277.

Parker, C. A. (1977). On modeling reality. *Journal of College Student Personnel, 18*(5), 419–425.

Perry, W. G. (1970). *Forms of intellectual and ethical development in the college years: A scheme.* New York: Holt, Rinehart & Winston.

Pervin, L. (1968). Performance and satisfaction as a function of individual-environment fit. *Psychological Bulletin, 69,* 56–68.

Price, J. L. (1968). *Organizational effectiveness: An inventory of propositions.* Homewood, IL: Irwin.

Provost, J. A., & Anchors, S. (1987). *Applications of the Myers-Briggs type indicator in higher education.* Palo Alto, CA: Consulting Psychologists Press.

Sanford, N. (1966). *Self and society: Social change and individual development.* New York: Atherton.

Schlossberg, N. (1984). *Counseling adults in transition.* New York: Springer.

Skinner, B. F. (1953). *Science and human behavior.* New York: Macmillan.

Stern, G. (1970). *People in context: Measuring person-environment congruence in education and industry.* New York: Wiley.

Strange, C. (in press). Managing college environments: Theory and practice. In T. K. Miller, R. B. Winston, and W. Mendenhall (Eds.), *Administration and leadership in student affairs.* Muncie, IN: Accelerated Development.

Witkin, H. A. (1976). Cognitive style in academic performance and in teacher-student relations. In S. Messick and Associates (Eds.), *Individuality in learning* (pp. 38–89). San Francisco: Jossey-Bass.

# CHAPTER 34
# DECONSTRUCTING WHITENESS AS PART OF A MULTICULTURAL EDUCATIONAL FRAMEWORK: FROM THEORY TO PRACTICE

## ANNA M. ORTIZ AND ROBERT A. RHOADS

Based on emerging theoretical work on White racial identity, the authors argue that a central problem of multicultural education involves challenging the universalization of Whiteness. The authors propose a theoretical framework to advance a multicultural perspective in which the exploration and deconstruction of Whiteness is key.

Over the past 20 years a host of educational researchers have explored the intersections of race and schooling as part of the larger project to achieve racial equality in the United States. Such efforts have focused both on K through 12 settings as well as postsecondary educational contexts (Altbach & Lomotey, 1991; Apple, 1982; Kozol, 1991; McCarthy & Crichlow, 1993; Ogbu, 1978). More recently, and most pertinent to this article, theory and practice has focused on multicultural education and the goal of building culturally inclusive schools, colleges, and universities (Astin, 1993a; Banks, 1988; Delpit, 1995; Giroux, 1992; hooks, 1994; Rhoads & Valadez, 1996; Sleeter & Grant, 1994; Tierney, 1993). This movement is also evident in the field of student affairs where a variety of researchers have explored multiculturalism in relation to out-of-class learning as well as the preparation of student affairs practitioners (Manning & Coleman-Boatwright, 1991; McEwen & Roper, 1994; Pope, 1993; Rhoads & Black, 1995; Strange & Alston, 1998). The vast majority of multicultural research and theorizing has focused on the problems and complexities faced by students of color as members of diverse minority cultures in the United States. Although many of these findings are helpful in advancing multiculturalism, a major gap exists in this body of literature.

The gap in higher education's knowledge base relates to the limited exploration of White racial identity, or what may be termed "Whiteness." By ignoring the cultural complexities associated with White racial identity, practitioners and scholars may unwittingly contribute to the universalization of Whiteness, and consequently, the marginalization of non-White racial identities. Fusco (1988) addresses this very issue: "Racial identities are not only black, Latino, Asian, native American, and so on; they are also White. To ignore White ethnicity is to redouble its hegemony by naturalizing it. Without specifically addressing White ethnicity, there can be no critical evaluation of the construction of the other" (p. 9). And Roediger explained,

Ortiz, A. M., & Rhoads, R. A. (2000). Deconstructing Whiteness as part of a multicultural educational framework: From theory to practice. *Journal of College Student Development, 41*, 81–93.

When residents of the US talk about race, they too often talk only about African Americans, Native Americans, Hispanic Americans, and Asian Americans. If whites come into the discussion, it is only because they have "attitudes" towards nonwhites. Whites are assumed not to "have race," though they might be racists. Many of the most critical advances of recent scholarship on the social construction of race have come precisely because writers have challenged the assumption that we only need to explain why people come to be considered Black, Asian, Native American or Hispanic and not attend to . . . the "invention of the white race." (1994, p. 12)

We, along with others, concur with Roediger in seeing race largely as a social construction—meaning that little biological basis exists for grouping people by racial categories (Frankenberg, 1993, 1994, 1997; Giroux, 1997; hooks, 1992). However, we do not deny that as a social construction race has significant effects in terms of defining privilege and nonprivilege. As Roediger paradoxically notes, "Race is thus both unreal and a seeming reality" (1994, p. 6). For some, race is a very harsh reality, and this, ideologically and pragmatically, is what multiculturalism seeks to address.

Our goal in this article is to review recent scholarship on White racial identity and to suggest a theoretical framework for advancing multiculturalism in which the exploration and deconstruction of Whiteness is pivotal. Our fundamental assumption is this: If educators want to advance students' understanding of White privilege, and relatedly, racial inequality, they need to help students explore and deconstruct White racial identity, both among Whites and non-Whites. This is a pivotal step in promoting a multicultural perspective. However, placing Whiteness under the microscope is problematic; for example, significant resistance derives from the lack of consciousness among Whites about their own racial identity, and consequently, resentment is often directed at other racial groups who connect with their cultural heritage. Ultimately, our goal is to displace White racial identity as the universal norm by challenging ourselves and our students to name it. When students begin to see Whiteness as a visible aspect of society and culture, they are then in a better position to raise questions about its inequitable universalization.

## Research on White Racial Identity

Research on White racial identity tends to be rooted in one of three general areas of inquiry: psychological, cultural, and educational. Psychological research on White identity development primarily revolves around Helms' work (1984, 1990). By focusing on the racial attitudes of Whites toward self and others, Helms identified six stages that Whites may pass through on the way to a more complex and integrated view of race. More recently, Helms and Piper (1994) have suggested that the stages may be best understood as statuses that do not necessarily follow a linear trajectory. The six statuses are: contact, disintegration, reintegration, pseudo-independent, immersion/emersion, autonomy.

Movement between these statuses generally flows from "a superficial and inconsistent awareness of being White" (Helms, 1990, p. 55) to high levels of consciousness characterized by a realization of White privilege and a commitment to pursuing social change.

Rowe, Bennett, and Atkinson (1994) developed a similar conception of White racial consciousness and suggested seven types reflective of one's attitudes toward racial identity; avoidant, dissonant, dependent, dominative, conflictive, reactive, and integrative. As with later explanations of the Helms model, the White racial consciousness model is not to be treated as a linear stage theory. Also, like the Helms model, the White racial consciousness model suggests that attitudinal differences among Whites range from a lack of "consideration of one's own White identity" (p. 136) to those reflecting a "pragmatic view of ethnic/minority issues" (p. 141). Block and Carter (1996) criticized the final location in the White racial consciousness model because it implies, in their words, "that an individual characterized by a healthy White identity could be seen as being passive and free of guilt with regard to racial/ethnic issues and simply be content with the status quo in this country, suggesting that he or she would be a supporter of a racist society" (p. 329). We also assert that any developmental model of Whiteness must include a commitment to social action as a central facet of a vital identity.

A serious problem with the preceding psychological theories is that they only address a portion of what it means to be White: a sole focus on racial attitudes toward oneself and others does not constitute a holistic view of White identity. This, as Roediger (1994) has pointed out, is problematic given the fact that one's sense of White racial identity involves much more than simply how one views Whites and non-Whites. Just as ethnic identity for culturally different people includes aspects of culture (language, customs, religion, food), identifying elements of White culture is necessary for a wholistic view. For example, specific aspects of U.S. culture predominantly reflect the White experience; the racial segregation of sports and genres of music offer some examples. Equally assured is the fact that if particular aspects of culture are part of the White experience, then they also contribute to White identity. After all, as Hall (1990) has pointed out, "Cultural identities are the points of identification . . . which are made within the discourses of history and culture" (p. 226). Similarly, Rhoads (1997) has argued, "Identities are constituted within the parameters of culture" (p. 95). The classic statement from Geertz (1973) alludes to the power of culture in shaping identity as well: "Man is an animal suspended in webs of significance he himself has spun" (p. 5). Let us turn then to cultural analyses of the construction of White racial identity.

In cultural studies, incorporating mostly feminist, historical, anthropological, and sociological frameworks, researchers also have uncovered understandings linked to the construction of White racial identity which more directly illustrate the connection between White racial identity and the supremacy of Whiteness in U.S. society. For example, Winant (1997) has argued that White identity has been reinterpreted and rearticulated "in a dualistic fashion: on the one hand egalitarian, on the other privileged; on the one hand individualistic and 'color blind,' on the other hand 'normalized' and White" (p. 42). Nowhere is this dualistic framework more evident than in the 1990s debate about affirmative action. Whereas one group of Whites has supported affirmative action as part of an egalitarian measure, the other, as Winant argued, has situated Whiteness as disadvantage. Despite the lack of empirical support for claims of reverse discrimination, a deeply resistant form of White identity emerged after the dramatic social and cultural upheaval of the 1960s, and, as Winant has maintained, "provides the cultural and political 'glue' that holds together a wide variety of reactionary racial politics" (p. 42). Particular constructions of Whiteness, for Winant, have tended to fall into one of five categories ranging from a belief in the biological superiority of Whites (the far right racial project) to a belief in the need to abolish Whiteness altogether (the new abolitionist racial project).

The abolitionist project is most notable in the work of Roediger (1991, 1994), who has argued that "the idea of race is given meaning through the agency of human beings in concrete historical and social contexts, and is not a biological or natural category" (1994, p. 2). This supports our contention that race is largely socially constructed; and because race is a social construction it offers the possibility of being deconstructed and reconstructed. Intellectual efforts aimed at making Whiteness visible is for Roediger part of the political and cultural project of abolishing Whiteness altogether (something that remains largely invisible and often is deeply entrenched within the subconscious realm is hard to critique). And, of course, because Whiteness is the universal standard by which diverse others are measured, and, in turn, delimited and devalued, its abolition has the potential to be emancipatory for non-Whites.

Intellectually and pragmatically, we have concerns about the goal of abolishing Whiteness as a cultural construction and source of identity, as well as the logical conclusion of ultimately eliminating the entire category of race. The presumption underlying such a strategy suggests to us that equality cannot be achieved without complete elimination of racial identity differences and the related identity politics. We believe an alternative vision does in fact exist and is rooted in the ideals of multiculturalism and the valuing of difference. Briefly, multiculturalism advances the ideal of communities of difference in which concerns for dialogue and learning about one another's lives becomes a source of community building (Burbules & Rice, 1990; Rhoads, 1997; Rhoads & Valadez, 1996; Tierney, 1993). Hence, in terms of Whiteness, its elimination is not the only solution: Displacing Whiteness as the universal standard by which all other races are gauged is also a step toward racial and cultural equity. Frankenberg (1997) has spoken to this position when she argued for the need to "resituate Whiteness from its unspoken (perhaps unspeakable?) status; to displace and then reemplace it" (p. 3). Realistically, any movement toward denormalizing Whiteness is a positive step to be taken.

From the intellectual advances associated with the recent exploration of White racial identity have come educational research and theory aimed at exposing the underlying influences of Whiteness in teaching and learning contexts. Maher and Tetreault (1997), for example, sought to reexamine their study of college classrooms conducted from a feminist perspective. "We considered ourselves feminist researchers sharing a common perspective with the women of color that we studied," they explained, only later to discover that "as White researchers, we did not fully interrogate our social position of privilege, which made us vis à vis our subjects, oppressors as well as feminist allies" (p. 322). In the reexamination of the data that previously had formed the basis for *The Feminist Classroom* (1994), Maher and Tetreault sought to unearth racial privilege through the "excavation of Whiteness in its many dimensions and complexities" (p. 322). A key strategy they have recommended is the use of literature aimed in part at unearthing the effects of the cultural networks related to Whiteness. Examples of the literature they have recommended include Morrison's *The Bluest Eye* (1970) and *Playing in the Dark* (1993), McIntosh's (1992) work on White and male privilege, Ellsworth's (1997) pedagogical exploration of the effects of Whiteness, and Hacker's (1995) analysis of Black and White racial divisions and related discrimination.

Giroux (1997) also explored the educational implications of Whiteness and suggested that educators need to create learning opportunities that enable students to connect White ideology and identity with progressive social reform. "Central to such a task is the political and pedagogical challenge of refashioning an anti-racist politics that informs a broader, radical, democratic project" (1997, p. 315). The deconstruction of Whiteness, especially its advantages and privileges, helps students to discover the direct impact of living in a society where being White is favored in the distribution of social capital and opportunity. Concerned with advancing antiracist politics, Fine (1997) offered insight into the potential of examining institutionalized discrimination in schools (e.g.,tracking) "that renders Whiteness meritocratic and other colors deficient" (p. 64). Instead of focusing on students who continue to endure discrimination, Fine has suggested that institutional analyses may be better suited for exposing the ways that Whiteness is situated as advantage. Also concerned with unearthing advantage, Rosenberg (1997) found student autobiographies to be helpful tools in promoting understandings of privilege among White college students.

The preceding works reflect a belief in the political and cultural potential of educational interventions. In this regard, we agree with King and Shuford (1996), who have argued that a multicultural perspective actually depicts a cognitively more advanced view about cultural diversity. Ultimately, educational theory and practice concerned with unearthing Whiteness and advancing a more democratic, multicultural society needs to explore specific pedagogical strategies.

## A Theoretical Framework

Theoretical and empirical evidence supports the development of educational strategies that challenge students to give serious consideration to the construction of Whiteness. Educational strategies that assist students in exploring White racial identity are likely to promote higher levels of White racial consciousness and at the same time offer the potential to deepen student understanding of culture and privilege. The problem, as most college and university educators are well aware, is that students, especially White students, tend to shut down when issues of race and privilege are introduced to classroom and cocurricular contexts. Students often fear that they may unintentionally make ignorant or racist statements, or that they may indeed expose prejudice and stereotypes they have. Therefore, multicultural education theories and strategies are needed for addressing this problem.

The following four assumptions undergird our theoretical approach:

1. Culture is a misunderstood construct, but one that is key for helping students understand diversity and confront their own racism.

2. Students in general and White students in particular have a difficult time identifying their own cultural connections.

| | Step 1: Understanding Culture | Step 2: Learning About Other Cultures | Step 3: Recognizing and Deconstructing White Culture | Step 4: Recognizing the Legitimacy of Other Cultures | Step 5: Developing a Multicultural Outlook |
|---|---|---|---|---|---|
| Cognitive Goal | To develop a complex understanding of culture (culture shapes people's lives and people shape culture). | To develop a more advanced understanding of diverse cultures. | To develop an understanding of how White culture has been universalized as the norm and to begin to question its privileged position. | To recognize that culture other than one's own is just as valued to another individual. | To recognize that all cultures within a given society shape each other and that the inclusion of all cultures requires the reconstruction of U.S. society. |
| Beginning Problem Statement | I see culture as something a society creates. | I know that differences between cultural groups exist, but the differences are only superficial. | I see culture as something that some have, but others do not. | I understand that there are many cultures, but we should agree on a common culture. | I value living in a society that is multicultural. |
| Ending Problem Statement | Culture is something I create, but that also creates me. | I understand that many cultural groups exist within the U.S. and each reflects deeply held norms, values, beliefs, and traditions. | I see culture as something that all people have. | I see that many diverse cultures can coexist including my own and that this is a good thing. | I can work to make society an equitable place for people of all cultural backgrounds because our vitality is intricately tied to one another's. |
| Activity | Understanding Culture —Observing and critically analyzing everyday events. | Exploring Cultures —Attending cultural events and reflecting on their meaning as well as dialoguing with culturally diverse others. | Analyzing White Culture —Learning to recognize White culture and to begin to challenge its normalization. | The Impact of Culture —Students identifying aspects of own cultures that play important roles in their lives and sharing these with other students. | Multiculturalism leads to Action —Discovering how institutions shape the ways in which culture is expressed. |

**Figure 1**    Framework of multicultural education (Ortiz & Rhoads).

3. Cultural diversity is a fact of life and efforts to build a common culture inevitably privilege the dominant culture.

4. Multiculturalism is a valued and desired view for students to develop.

Our framework follows five steps which are informed by the assumptions listed above: (a) understanding culture, (b) learning about other cultures, (c) recognizing and deconstructing White culture, (d) recognizing the legitimacy of other cultures, and (e) developing a multicultural outlook (see Figure 1). Our thinking reflects not only the work on Whiteness and White privilege by Roediger (1991, 1994), Frankenberg (1994, 1997), McIntosh (1992) and others, but also the work of Sleeter and Grant (1994) on multicultural educational strategies and Garcia's (1995) work on culture as a key construct in multicultural training. The framework is not meant to be considered as an invariant linear model, but one in which each of the five steps contributes to an overall educational goal of enhancing multicultural education. Elements of each step may be incorporated in one educational intervention, used separately in individually designed educational programs, or the framework as a whole may be used to guide the development of curricula addressing multicultural issues.

Following the discussion of each step in the framework, we briefly discuss educational strategies that we have used to meet the cognitive goal of the step. We wish we could include student outcomes research verifying the effectiveness of the framework and thus demonstrating that we have helped students to progress toward multicultural understanding, but this is not the case, nor is such data likely to become available anytime soon. The fact is that altering attitudes involves much more than simply exposing students to alternative forms of thought through a 1- or 2-hour exercise. The pedagogical strategies suggested should be viewed as part of a long-term process through which increased exposure to alternative ways of viewing race, culture, and identity eventually challenge students to rethink their own views. As student outcomes research has clearly shown, oftentimes the effects of college are long term (Astin, 1993b; Pascarella & Terenzini, 1991). In the end then, the development of meaningful pedagogical strategies must rest a great deal on the logical extensions drawn from sound theories.

## Step 1: Understanding Culture

In Step 1, the overarching cognitive goal is for students to fully understand how culture shapes their lives and how they shape culture through their interactions. This is the more complex notion of culture, in which culture is much more than simply the artifacts that a society creates. Geertz's (1973) dynamic notion of culture as "webs of significance" that are in part created through human interaction and at the same time guide human interaction is the depth of understanding sought here. The beginning problem statement reads: "I see culture as something a society creates." However, the ending problem statement reads: "Culture is something I create, but that also creates me." An activity designed to promote a more advanced understanding of culture involves some type of exercise that gets at how culture shapes the human condition, but at the same time highlights the ability people have to alter culture. An advanced understanding of culture also should incorporate knowledge about how culture shapes one's worldview and hence, how one perceives others and their cultures.

For Step 1 a myriad of activities can be used to achieve the cognitive goal. Many of these come from the work of intercultural communication practitioners and scholars who train students and business personnel to sojourn abroad (Bennett, 1986; Gudyknust & Kim, 1984; Hess, 1997; Paige, 1993; Sorti, 1990; Stewart & Bennett, 1991). In Step 1 the bulk of learning comes from critical reflection and analysis of everyday events. From this examination comes the realization that culture indeed affects individuals and that individuals through social interaction also affect culture.

Because of the cognitive complexity of this stage we recommend two activities that have been particularly effective in helping students to understand culture as a dynamic and dialectical phenomenon. In the first activity, students observe a setting on campus where their attention is focused on one particular behavior or attribute. For example, a student may choose to study how students greet each other on the central quad area of campus. Before the observation, students, guided by the facilitator, generate a list of questions about the behavior and setting they are about to observe. Sample questions might be: Were the greetings loud and boisterous or more subdued? Did students use physical contact in some way? Were students walking alone or in groups? Did they stay or move on? What were the students wearing? Once the observations are complete, students are given quiet time to write down their reflections and discoveries from the exercise (this could be done as a homework assignment as well). The group then comes together and compares notes. Attention must be paid to the many "teachable moments" as students are often drawn to different attributes in the setting and will have divergent interpretations of the same setting. At this point students begin to see how culture shapes human behavior and perception. Facilitators can encourage this process by asking questions such as: What norms did you observe and did anyone violate those norms? From where do such norms come? These questions should help students to see how social lives are indeed shaped by culture, but also they come to understand how people shape cultural norms.

A more advanced activity for Step 1 is to conduct an analysis of a "critical incident." Kappler (1998) used the following critical incident in her study of intercultural perspective-taking among U.S. students:

> Mariko is a student from Japan. Although when she first arrived she was a little uneasy, she is now used to the different routines and lifestyle and is doing quite well in school and is fluent in English. She has become good friends with one of her classmates, Linda. One afternoon, their professor asked

for two volunteers to come in early the next class to help with a special project. Linda raised her hand and volunteered herself and suggested Mariko might also be willing. Mariko replied hesitantly that she did not think she could do it and that it would be better to ask someone else. Linda said that Mariko would be quite good and told the professor they would do it. The next day, Mariko did not turn up and Linda did all the work herself. The next time Linda saw Mariko she asked her rather coldly what had happened to her. Mariko apologized and said that she had to study for an exam that day and she didn't really feel capable of doing the work. Linda was frustrated and asked her why she had not said so clearly in the class at the time. Mariko looked down and said nothing.

Analysis of this critical incident challenges students to develop an explanation of what happened from Linda's point of view, from Mariko's point of view, and from the students' own points of view. The comparative analysis of the differing points of view helps to demonstrate how culture shapes our behavior and our perspectives. Additionally, the facilitator also needs to raise questions about how cultural norms might be altered by various actors in a critical incident. Of course, facilitators should be encouraged to write critical incidents that are highly relevant to the specific contexts of the students with whom they are working.

## Step 2: Learning About Other Cultures

Step 2 provides the laboratory for Step 1. Much of the multicultural education that took place on college campuses in the 1980s focused on "cultural awareness." Programs and events were designed to expose students to the traditions, food, and music of distinct cultural groups. Although such programs are important in helping students experience aspects of diverse cultures, we contend that without serious reflection about culture as a construct, the potential for a deeper understanding of cultural diversity is likely to be lost. With the orientation to understanding culture that is offered in Step 1, the cultural exploration of others' lives becomes grounded in a theoretical understanding of culture. We have found through our own pedagogical efforts that students develop an enthusiasm for cultural exploration when it is enhanced by theoretical insights about culture. They begin to make connections between cultural artifacts such as food, clothing, and music, and the complex norms, values, and beliefs associated with various cultural groups. Hence, the beginning problem statement in Step 2 reads: "I know that differences between cultural groups exist, but the differences are only superficial." The ending problem statement is: "I understand that many cultural groups exist within the U.S. and each reflects deeply held norms, values, beliefs, and traditions."

Step 2 activities should be designed to build energy and enthusiasm for learning about other cultures. Activities like this are probably a staple of multicultural education at most colleges and universities. The educational activity for this step involves motivating students to attend cultural events and programs already planned by groups on campus. Of course, an easy way to help students take the risk to attend such events is to go as a group. Although we tend to think that attending cultural events is a low-risk way to educate oneself, "I don't have anyone to go with" is a common refrain we hear from our students (and sometimes ourselves). Such outings should be accompanied by a reflection component as this will help to facilitate a more meaningful learning experience much in the way reflection adds to the community service experience.

In groups where participation is ongoing (i.e., an orientation course or student staff training), we also recommend an activity in which students engage in an ongoing dialogue with a culturally different person. We have used this strategy in courses by asking students to meet with their dialogue partner at least once a week for about 6 weeks. We do not encourage students to enter each encounter with a set of interview questions; rather, our preference is the student or facilitator determine a general topic for each meeting. We also stress that the dialogues are meant to be an exchange and not a one-way conversation in which the primary contributor is the cultural other. We have found that students learn a great deal about another culture and person through this exercise, and that their confidence level in having significant interactions with diverse others increases. The extent of this process can be quite basic or rather extensive, as in the "voice project" described by Strange and Alston (1998).

## Step 3: Recognizing and Deconstructing White Culture

In Step 3, the overarching cognitive goal is helping students to see that Whites have culture, and that White culture has become in many ways the unchallenged, universal basis for racial identity. Experience tells us that in the preceding step students primarily will focus on aspects of culture typically derived from non-Whites (both White and non-White students when asked to explore a culture different from their own will rarely select White cultural groups). Because of a general lack of recognition of White culture, students are ill-equipped for deconstructing Whiteness. Recognizing and deconstructing Whiteness is particularly challenging to White students, because of White culture being so universalized. When White students begin to recognize that they in fact are culturally positioned, they are more likely to understand that others have culture too. Thus, White students begin to see the essence of racial differences. The beginning problem statement for Step 3 is: "I see culture as something that some have, but others do not." The ending problem statement reads: "I see culture as something that all people have." We call the pedagogical exercise for Step 3, "Analyzing White Culture," and we focus on getting students to reflect on aspects of White culture as a source of identity.

Step 3 is the key contribution we offer to a comprehensive multicultural educational intervention. We need to be clear here. We are not saying that White culture is in any way more significant or of greater value than any of the many other cultural identities. However, a lack of understanding of Whiteness is a major barrier to achieving a multicultural society. Therefore, we contend that the deconstruction of Whiteness must be central to educational interventions designed to challenge White privilege and advance a multicultural perspective.

The exercise we have used for Step 3 is called Analyzing White Culture and is quite simple to implement. However, although the exercise may be simple, the complications and discomforts associated with students' explorations of race need to be thought about in advance. Because the discussion has the potential to be animated and conflictual, the facilitator should establish some communicative guidelines before beginning the activity. Guidelines might include the following: only one person speaks at a time, no heckling, participants must agree to keep an open mind, and participants must agree to stay through the debriefing phase of the program. Analyzing White Culture involves asking students to list on a sheet of paper the 10 most significant characteristics, adjectives, or statements that come to mind when asked to describe White racial identity or White culture. We use the terms "White racial identity" and "White culture" interchangeably in this exercise because some students find it easier to describe one and not the other, and both capture various characteristics associated with the diversity of White experience in the U.S.

We use two basic permutations of this exercise. One strategy is to collect the lists and then pass them back to students randomly so that each student gets someone else's. Of course, to ensure anonymity, the same kind of paper should be used by all students and they should not write their names on the paper. Another option, but one that only should be used with a diverse group of students, is to ask the students to indicate whether they are White or a person of color (specific racial or ethnic categories may compromise student anonymity, depending of course on the size and diversity of the group). This adds another dimension to the discussion in that theoretically one might expect to see some differences in the lists depending on the status of the student as White or as a person of color. For example, White students often ask, "What do you mean by White culture? There isn't one." Meanwhile, students of color may already be on item five or six. This is to be expected given the fact that the universalization of Whiteness is experienced most pointedly by people of color, while its normative status may be taken for granted by Whites. The fact that students of color may have an easier time completing their lists is an important outcome of the exercise and should be a key concern in the subsequent discussion. Again, attempting this exercise without adequate representation of both students of color and White students is not advisable because a degree of discomfort related to racial exploration is a likely result and small numbers of students from one group should not be forced to confront such psychological and emotionally challenging activities.

Once the responses have been collected and then randomly distributed, the facilitator will ask for volunteers to read their lists (and to identify the race of the person who completed the list, but only if the group is diverse!). Once several lists have been read the facilitator should solicit reactions from students. Debriefing involves the facilitator reconnecting the purpose of the Exploring White Culture exercise with the larger goal of advancing racial and multicultural understanding.

## Step 4: Recognizing the Legitimacy of Other Cultures

The cognitive goal of Step 4 is recognizing that culture other than one's own is just as valuable and meaningful to another individual. This involves getting students to see that many cultures exist at the same time and that such multiplicity is not a bad thing. The beginning problem statement reads: "I understand that there are many cultures, but we should agree on a common culture." The ending problem statement is: "I see that many diverse cultures can co-exist including my own and that this is a good thing."

In Step 4 students move from general and specific understandings of culture and cultures to the realization that multiple cultures have a legitimate place in U.S. society. The activity recommended for this step helps students to recognize the impact of culture on individuals by identifying which aspects of their individual cultures play important roles in their lives. The worksheet for this exercise has three columns. In the first column (titled Cultural Attribute) students list important aspects of their culture. In the second column (titled Contribution to Sense of Self) students explain what each attribute contributes to their identity, how they feel about and perceive themselves in reference to others. Finally, in the last column (titled Affects How I See the World by . . .) students record the ways in which each attribute might shape their perceptions of themselves, other individuals, cultures, and societies.

After students have completed the grid they should be placed in small groups that are as diverse as possible (up to four). They are instructed to notice what attributes they have in common and those that are different. Those with common attributes are likely to have different responses for the last two columns. Students need to pay close attention to these as they are the prime examples of the ways in which culture affects individuals.

## Step 5: Developing a Multicultural Outlook

The cognitive goal for Step 5 is helping students to recognize that all cultures within a given society shape each other and that the inclusion of all cultures requires the reconstruction of U.S. society. The previous steps help students to learn more about other cultures and begin to incorporate multicultural perspectives into their own identities. Step 5 offers the potential to motivate students to take action to assist creating multicultural society. The beginning problem statement reads: "I value living in a society that is multicultural." The ending problem statement reveals a more complex understanding of the interface between culture, society, and its members: "I can work to make society an equitable place for people of all cultural backgrounds because our vitality is intricately tied to one another's." Students need to focus on embracing multiculturalism and discover how societal institutions embrace or deny cultural difference and how the status of one's culture in a society affects individuals. Educational strategies used in this step help students move away from xenophobia and toward celebrating difference in such a way that they see taking social action toward the inclusion of diverse cultural perspectives as the logical next step in their own education and liberation. In this regard, we agree with Sleeter and Grant's (1994) view: The most valuable form of multicultural education is both multicultural and social reconstructionist.

In Step 5 students are encouraged to integrate a multicultural perspective that helps them to become critical consumers of culture. At this point students should be able to recognize that their culture changes over time (and their "selves" change as well) as they and their society embrace diverse cultural perspectives. In their quest to learn about other cultures, they may find that they incorporate aspects of other cultures into their own behavior and cognitive structures. They also begin to see societal consequences for the continuing marginality of diverse cultures in the U.S. Their multicultural outlook calls for them to take action on both internal and external levels.

The activity that helps students become more multiculturally oriented is an institutional analysis of how their colleges or universities support or do not support the expression of diverse cultures. This activity may be implemented two different ways. With an ongoing group such as a staff or a class, small groups of three students are given a unit or activity at the particular institution to analyze. They visit the space or context, speak with staff and students, examine the publications related to the unit or activity, and explore the connections the particular unit or activity has with other areas of campus life. Their charge is to unearth the ways in which diverse cultural expressions are present or absent from the particular environment and what might be done to enhance cultural inclusiveness.

With a group that meets only one time (i.e., a training session or one-shot educational program), the facilitator uses the same small group method, but instead of extended study of a particular unit or activity, the facilitator collects artifacts from various units or activities around campus. The artifacts may include publications, job descriptions, applications, photos, or newspaper clippings. Small groups then have the same charge as the more permanent groups: to unearth ways in which diverse cultural expressions are present or absent from the particular environment and what might be done to enhance cultural inclusiveness.

## Conclusion

We believe that this framework helps to increase the multicultural understanding of all students, but especially White students. We see multicultural understanding as a developmental journey where a multicultural outlook is created by guiding students through a process where they are confronted with more difficult challenges as they accomplish those which are less challenging. This framework also promotes attitudes that encourage cultural learning and intercultural competence as Hess (1997) outlined. These attitudes include: a high regard for culture, an eagerness to learn, a desire to make connections, and a readiness to give as well as receive.

One of the major limitations of this framework and of other frameworks or models of multicultural education or prejudice reduction is the paucity of research and evaluative findings. Although some specific interventions have been tested in small studies (Greenman & Kimmel, 1995; Suarez-Balcazar, Drulak, & Smith, 1995), we did not find widespread research on the effects of multicultural education and prejudice reduction models. We have begun to collect data for the activity described in Step 3 (Analyzing White Culture), and we will seek to examine the effectiveness of the framework and its activities in the future. We encourage other researchers and educators to collect evaluative data and share such findings through publication and conference presentations. Evaluative data need not be limited to the study of outcomes, but may also include qualitative explorations of the dynamics of facilitating such activities and reports of student reactions to them. Obviously, all theoretical frameworks should be continually refined, and we expect no less for the framework proposed here. We also encourage educators to experiment with the kinds of activities suggested for each of the theoretical steps of our framework. We have described some that have worked for us, but at the same time improvements can be made here as well. The usefulness and success of some of the activities we list will vary depending on the contexts and the students involved.

We in no way expect that this framework completes a student's multicultural journey. We see students moving from this framework to others that focus on prejudice reduction (Helms's White Racial Identity Model), ally development (Washington & Evans, 1991), and more social-action-oriented goals (Sleeter & Grant, 1994).

One lesson that we have learned in the course of our work with students in multicultural education is that if more resistant White students are to be affected by multicultural education, the intervention and facilitators must be willing to meet the students at their respective level of development. For most college-aged White students, beginning the dialogue with discussions of White privilege or White racism provide too great a challenge. We assert that our framework of multicultural understanding begins at a less threatening point (but no less important) that teaches students basics about the importance of culture. As with other forms of learning, the goal of the educator is to foster students' enthusiasm for learning in a way that motivates them to take on greater challenges. Indeed, enthusiasm for cultural learning is at the heart of building a multicultural society and is key to the success of the framework we have proposed in this article.

# References

Altbach, P. G., & Lomotey, K. (Eds.). (1991). *The racial crisis in American higher education*. Albany: State University of New York Press.

Apple, M. W. (1982). *Education and power*. Boston: Routledge and Kegan Paul.

Astin, A. W. (1993a). Diversity and multiculturalism on the campus: How are students affected? *Change, 25*(1), 44–49.

Astin, A. W. (1993b). *What matters in college: Four critical years revisited*. San Francisco: Jossey-Bass.

Banks, J. (1988). *Multicultural education: Theory and practice*. Boston: Allyn and Bacon.

Bennett, M. J. (1986). A developmental approach to training for intercultural sensitivity. *International Journal of Intercultural Relations, 2*, 179–96.

Block, C. J., & Carter, R. T. (1996). White racial identity attitude theories: A rose by any other name is still a rose. *The Counseling Psychologist, 24*(2), 326–334.

Burbules, N., & Rice, S. (1991). Dialogue across differences: Continuing the conversation. *Harvard Educational Review, 61*(4), 393–416.

Delpit, L. (1995). *Other people's children: Cultural conflict in the classroom*. New York: New Press.

Ellsworth, E. (1997). Double binds of Whiteness. In M. Fine, L. Weis, L. C. Powell, & L. M. Won (Eds.), *Off-White: Readings on society, race, and culture* (pp. 259–269). New York: Routledge.

Fine, M. (1997). Witnessing Whiteness. In M. Fine, L. Weis, L. C. Powell, & L. M. Won (Eds.), *Off-White: Readings on society, race, and culture* (pp. 57–65). New York: Routledge.

Frankenberg, R. (1993). *White women, race matters: The social construction of Whiteness*. Minneapolis: University of Minnesota Press.

Frankenberg, R. (1994). Whiteness and Americanness: Examining constructions of race, culture and nation in White women's life narratives. In S. Gregory & R. Sanjek (Eds.), *Race* (pp. 62–77). New Brunswick, NJ: Rutgers University Press.

Frankenberg, R. (1997). Introduction: Local Whitenesses, localizing Whiteness. In R. Frankenberg (Ed.), *Displacing Whiteness: Essays in social and cultural criticism* (pp. 1–33). Durham, NC: Duke University Press.

Fusco, C. (1988). Fantasies of oppositionality. *Afterimage, 16* (December), 6–9.

Garcia, M. H. (1995). An anthropological approach to multicultural diversity training. *Journal of Applied Behavioral Science, 31*(4), 490–504.

Geertz, C. (1973). *The interpretation of cultures*. New York: Basic Books.

Giroux, H. A. (1992). *Border crossings: Cultural workers and the politics of education*. New York: Routledge.

Giroux, H. A. (1997). Rewriting the discourse of racial identity: Towards a pedagogy and politics of Whiteness. *Harvard Educational Review, 67*(2), 285–320.

Greenman, N. P., & Kimmel, E. B. (1995). The road to multicultural education: Potholes to resistance. *Journal of Teacher Education, 46*, 360–368.

Gudyknust, W. B., & Kim, Y. Y. (1984). *Communicating with strangers: An approach to intercultural communication*. Reading, MA: Addison-Wesley.

Hacker, A. (1995). *Two nations: Black and White, separate, hostile, unequal*. New York: Ballantine Books.

Hall, S. (1990). Cultural identity and diaspora. In J. Rutherford (Ed.), *Identity: Community, culture, difference* (pp. 222–237). London: Lawrence & Wishart.

Helms, J. E. (1984). Toward a theoretical explanation of the effects of race on counseling: A Black and White model. *The Counseling Psychologist, 12*(4), 153–165.

Helms, J. E. (1990). *Black and White racial identity attitudes: Theory, research, and practice*. Westport, CT: Greenwood.

Helms, J. E., & Piper, R. E. (1994). Implications of racial identity theory for vocational psychology. *Journal of Vocational Behavior, 44*, 124–138.

Hess, J. D. (1997). *Studying abroad/learning abroad: An abridged edition of the whole world guide to culture learning*. Yarmouth, ME: Intercultural Press.

hooks, b. (1992). *Black looks: Race and representation*. Boston: South End Press.

hooks, b. (1994). *Teaching to transgress: Education as the practice of freedom*. New York: Routledge.

Kappler, B. J. (1998). *Refining intercultural perspective-taking*. Unpublished doctoral dissertation, University of Minnesota, Minneapolis.

King, P. M., & Shuford, B. C. (1996). A multicultural view is a more cognitively complex view: Cognitive development and multicultural education. *American Behavioral Scientist, 40*(2), 153–164.

Kozol, J. (1991). *Savage inequalities: Children in America's schools*. New York: Harper Perennial.

Maher, F. A., & Tetreault, M. K. T. (1994). *The feminist classroom: An inside look at how professors and students are transforming higher education for a diverse society*. New York: Basic Books.

Maher, F. A., & Tetreault, M. K. T. (1997). Learning in the dark: How assumptions of Whiteness shape classroom knowledge. *Harvard Educational Review, 67*(2), 321–349.

Manning, K., & Coleman-Boatwright, P. (1991). Student affairs initiatives toward a multicultural university. *Journal of College Student Development, 32*, 367–374.

McCarthy, C., & Crichlow, W. (Eds.). (1993). *Race, identity, and representation in education*. New York: Routledge.

McEwen, M. K., & Roper, L. D. (1994). Incorporating multiculturalism into student affairs preparation programs: Suggestions from the literature. *Journal of College Student Development, 35*, 46–53.

McIntosh, P. (1992). White privilege and male privilege: A personal account of coming to see correspondence through work in women's studies. In M. L. Anderson & P. Hill Collins (Eds.), *Race, class, and gender: An anthology* (pp. 70–81). Belmont, CA: Wadsworth.

Morrison, T. (1970). *The bluest eye*. New York: Holt, Rinehart & Winston.

Morrison, T. (1993). *Playing in the dark: Whiteness and the literary imagination*. New York: Vintage.

Ogbu, J. U. (1978). *Minority education and caste: The American system in cross-cultural perspective*. New York: Academic.

Paige, R. M. (Ed.) (1993). *Education for the intercultural experience*. Yarmouth, ME: Intercultural Press.

Pascarella, E. T., & Terenzini, P. T. (1991). *How college affects students*. San Francisco: Jossey-Bass.

Pope, R. L. (1993). Multicultural-organization development in student affairs: An introduction. *Journal of College Student Development, 34*, 201–205.

Rhoads, R. A. (1997). *Community service and higher learning: Explorations of the caring self*. Albany: State University of New York.

Rhoads, R. A., & Black, M. A. (1995). Student affairs practitioners as transformative educators: Advancing a critical cultural perspective. *Journal of College Student Development, 36*, 413–421.

Rhoads, R. A., & Valadez, J. R. (1996). *Democracy, multiculturalism, and the community college: A critical perspective*. New York: Garland.

Roediger, D. (1991). *The wages of Whiteness: Race and the making of the American working class*. New York: Verso.

Roediger, D. (1994). *Towards the abolition of Whiteness: Essays of race, politics, and working class history*. New York: Verso.

Rosenberg, P. M. (1997). Underground discourses: Exploring Whiteness in teacher education. In M. Fine, L. Weis, L. C. Powell, & L. M. Won (Eds.), *Off-White: Readings on society, race, and culture* (pp. 79–89). New York: Routledge.

Rowe, W., Bennett, S. K., & Atkinson, D. R. (1994). White racial identity models: A critique and alternative proposal. *The Counseling Psychologist, 22*, 129–146.

Saurez-Balcazar, J., Drulack, J. A., & Smith, C. (1995). Multicultural training practices in community psychology programs. *American Journal of Community Psychology, 22*, 785–798.

Sleeter, C. E., & Grant, C. A. (1994). *Making choices for multicultural education: Five approaches to race, class and gender* (2nd ed.). New York: Macmillan.

Sorti, C. (1990). *The art of crossing cultures*. Yarmouth, ME: Intercultural Press.

Stewart, E. C., & Bennett, M. J. (1991) (2nd ed.). *American cultural patterns: A cross-cultural perspective*. Yarmouth, ME: Intercultural Press.

Strange, C., & Alston, L. (1998). Voicing differences: Encouraging multicultural learning. *Journal of College Student Development, 39*, 87–99.

Tierney, W. G. (1993). *Building communities of difference: Higher education in the 21st century*. Westport, CT: Bergin & Garvey.

Washington, J., & Evans, N. J. (1991). Becoming an ally. In N. J. Evans & V. A. Wall (Eds.), *Beyond tolerance: Gays, lesbians, and bisexuals on campus*. Alexandria, VA: American Association of Counseling and Development.

Winant, H. (1997). Behind blue eyes: Whiteness and contemporary U.S. racial politics. In M. Fine, L. Weis, L. C. Powell, & L. M. Wong (Eds.), *Off-White: Readings on race, power, and society* (pp. 40–53). New York: Routledge.

# CHAPTER 35
## LEARNING PARTNERSHIPS MODEL
### A FRAMEWORK FOR PROMOTING SELF-AUTHORSHIP

MARCIA B. BAXTER MAGOLDA

He takes the approach that he wants you to do it on your own. He will help you plot through your ideas and he will help you sort out what you are thinking and help direct you and he still encourages you to work independently. He just makes his office setting very comfortable. He'll ask "What are you confused about?" and he will ask your opinion on the matter rather than telling you what you should do. He will ask you exactly what is happening and what you need help with and try to direct you from there rather than presenting himself in a way that is kind of intimidating.... I think the way I see it is that he wants you to feel that you are at the same level as him, not in as far as the same knowledge, he wants the atmosphere to be such that you feel comfortable asking him or talking to him in any way. (Erica, in Baxter Magolda, 1999, pp. 133–134)

Erica's comments reflect the learning partnership she experienced with Professor Snowden, the instructor of her zoology course. The course introduced scientific complexity by virtue of Professor Snowden's statement on the syllabus that he wanted students to understand the tentative nature of scientific facts, and he wanted them to learn to think like scientists. Erica's description of Professor Snowden's approach to helping students meet these goals conveys the integration of challenge and support and the blend of connection and autonomy that characterize learning partnerships. Professor Snowden challenged Erica to work through her ideas to construct her own perspective yet supported her by helping her sort through her thinking. By respecting Erica as a capable learner, Professor Snowden offered connection and support that made her comfortable exploring her thinking with him. Refraining from telling her what to do in favor of helping her figure it out through accessing her thinking conveyed to Erica that Professor Snowden wanted her to think autonomously. This chapter describes the Learning Partnerships Model conceptualized from the characteristics Erica and other learners portrayed as central to their journeys toward self-authorship.

## Origins of the Learning Partnerships Model

The Learning Partnerships Model emerged from a 17-year longitudinal study of young adults' learning and development (Baxter Magolda, 1992, 2001). Grounded in the constructivist-developmental tradition of Perry's (1970) and Belenky, Clinchy, Goldberger, and Tarule's (1986) work, the college phase of the study traced epistemological development during college. Using an inductive

Baxter Magolda, M. B. (2004). Learning partnerships model: A framework for promoting self-authorship. In M. Baxter Magolda & P. M. King (Eds.), *Learning partnerships: Theory and models of practice to educate for self-authorship* (pp. 37–62). Sterling, VA: Stylus.

approach consistent with this tradition (Piaget, 1950) yielded dialogue during the college interviews about classroom and campus conditions that promoted or hindered developmental growth. Extensive data emerged from the 432 interviews conducted during the first 5 years of the study. Of 101 students interviewed in their first year of college, 95 returned for the sophomore-year interview, 86 for the junior-year interview, 80 for the senior-year interview, and 70 for the fifth-year interview. The participants were all students at Miami University, a public liberal arts institution with an enrollment of 16,000. Two students who transferred to other institutions their junior year remained in the study. The group was balanced by gender during the first year (51 women and 50 men) and remained reasonably so throughout the study. Only three participants were members of underrepresented populations.

Because I intended the longitudinal study to explore possibilities for development, the stories and my interpretations of them offer one possible portrayal of development during college and the conditions that promote it. I provide in-depth narratives elsewhere (Baxter Magolda, 1992, 2001) to help readers judge the degree to which this portrayal is applicable to other contexts. Miami attracts primarily traditional age students who have high entrance test scores and high school grades, are highly involved, and are highly motivated to succeed. The campus culture reinforces academic success and campus involvement. The participants were enrolled in all six divisions of the University (Applied Sciences, Arts and Science, Business Administration, Education and Allied Professions, Interdisciplinary Studies, and Fine Arts), involved in various campus activities (e.g., organizations related to academic majors, service organizations, Greek life, and leadership positions), and employed in diverse settings (e.g., computer labs, recreation centers, residence life, dining halls, and local businesses). Nine studied abroad while in college.

Continuing the constructivist approach to the study in the postcollege phase broadened the contexts in which to explore conditions to promote self-authorship. Study participants moved to diverse geographic locations, enrolled in various graduate and professional schools, accepted employment in multiple fields, and engaged in the diverse complexities of young adult life. Interviews reflected the participants' intrapersonal and interpersonal growth as well as their epistemological growth due in part to their shift from college to multiple contexts and due in part to my realization that their development could be best understood by integrating the multiple dimensions of development. Thirty-five participants have remained in the study for 17 years, yielding approximately 450 interviews from the 6th to the 17th year. These postcollege interviews, taking place in the participants' 20s and early 30s, reveal a more comprehensive understanding of the Learning Partnerships Model than was evident in the college years and show that it is applicable beyond the college years.

Participants' graduate or professional educational opportunities were another major source of data to identify the conditions that promoted self-authorship. Of the 35 longitudinal participants who currently remain in the study, 24 pursued some form of graduate or professional education. Seven others who are no longer in the study but participated in the early years after college also pursued graduate or professional study. The participants collectively attended a wide range of institutions, from small, private colleges to major research universities for their graduate/professional studies. Twelve participants completed their degrees part time while working full time. The majority worked for 1 to 3 years prior to pursuing graduate degrees, whereas those going into law, medicine, and the seminary generally began immediately after college graduation. The pursuit of advanced education was equally prevalent among women (16) and men (15). Eight participants pursued master's degrees in business in either business administration (6), economics (1), or international affairs (1). Six pursued master's degrees in education: 4 in teaching, 1 in supervision, and 1 in educational technology. Five studied social sciences, resulting in 2 master's degrees in psychology, 2 in social work, and 1 PhD in organizational behavior. Eight participants studied in professional schools: 2 in medicine, 3 in law, 2 in seminary, and 1 in culinary arts. Four participants pursued continuing education in teacher licensure, computer technology, mathematics education, and art history.

Postcollege employment provided another major source of experiences that promoted self-authorship. Participants entered the workforce in numerous occupations in diverse settings. Some followed the same career path from college graduation to their 30s, whereas others frequently changed paths. Although some stayed with the same institution or company for this span of time, most moved to new institutions or companies at least once or twice over these years. The two most prevalent work settings for the 35 participants remaining in the study were business and education. Fifteen participants, 8 women and 7 men, work in the business arena. One is an accountant. The majority work in sales and services, including insurance, computers, pharmaceutical or medical equipment, advertising, marketing, real estate, and chemical sales. A few work in retail sales, primarily in clothing and furniture. One participant owns a retail business. Ten participants are educators—9 in K–12 settings and 1 in higher education. Two of these participants are men, both of whom work in K–12 where 1 is a principal. The federal government employed 1 participant (a male) as an economist. Five (3 men and 2 women) work in human services in counseling, social work, services for the blind, and the Christian ministry. The group includes 2 practicing attorneys (1 female and 1 male), 1 physician (a male), and 2 restaurant professionals.

Finally, community and personal life contexts offered insights into the conditions that promote self-authorship. Many participants pursued leadership positions and volunteer work in their communities. These experiences often involved using their business or human relations skills to help others whose lives differed significantly from those of the participants. Interaction with diverse others contributed to the conditions for self-authorship to emerge. Participants' personal lives entailed intense relationship development, such as finding life partners, having children, and coping with parental or their own divorces. Thirty-three of the participants married after college; three of those divorced and two remarried. Twenty-five had children during their twenties or early thirties. In addition, six participants encountered major health problems. Responding to and managing these life experiences yielded important insights into the conditions that promote self-authorship.

An observational study provided one more source for exploring conditions that promote self-authorship (Baxter Magolda, 1999). In the interest of directly observing the optimal learning conditions described by longitudinal participants, I observed three semester-length college courses. I chose a large education course for first- and second-year students to observe how self-authorship might be prompted in younger students and two upper-division courses (i.e., zoology and mathematics) to observe how it might be promoted for more advanced students. Attending the course sessions, interviewing the instructors, and interviewing students in the courses confirmed the insights the longitudinal participants shared and yielded more tangible possibilities for translating their insights to educational practice.

All four contexts—college education, graduate or professional education, employment, and community and personal life—not only revealed the conditions that promote self-authorship but also demonstrated how crucial achieving self-authorship in one's early to mid-20s is for success in adult life. Minimal self-authorship was often the source of struggle in all these contexts. The stories in this chapter illustrate how educators can help learners successfully resolve these struggles to internally define their belief systems, identities, and relations with others in adult life.

## The Learning Partnerships Model

I identified conditions that promote self-authorship from analyzing these multiple contexts and their influence on participants' journeys toward self-authorship (Baxter Magolda, 2001). Despite diversity across contexts, environments that promoted self-authorship consistently operated on *three key assumptions* and *three key principles*. The assumptions modeled the expectation for self-authorship in each developmental dimension, challenging learners to move toward self-authorship. The principles offered the support necessary to do so. The combination of these assumptions and principles forms the Learning Partnerships Model shown in Figure 1.

Learners were exposed to epistemological, intrapersonal, and interpersonal complexity via the three assumptions. First, these environments conveyed *knowledge as complex and socially constructed*. Whether engaged in a course assignment, job responsibility, or volunteer role, participants encountered challenges through multiple interpretations, ambiguity, and the need to negotiate what to believe with others. This complexity modeled the epistemological growth—the capacity to wisely

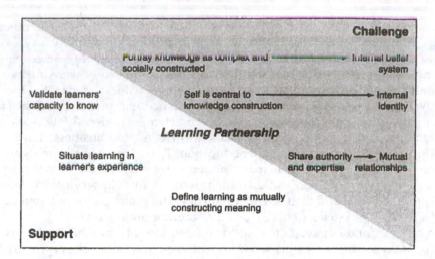

**Figure 1**    The Learning Partnerships Model.

choose from among multiple alternatives—needed for self-authorship. Framing knowledge as complex and socially constructed gave rise to the second assumption—that *self is central to knowledge construction.* Encouragement to define themselves and bring this to their way of learning, work, and relationships emphasized the intrapersonal growth, the internal sense of self, needed for self-authorship. The third assumption evident in these environments was that *authority and expertise were shared in the mutual construction of knowledge among peers.* The invitation and necessity to participate as equal partners in this mutual construction modeled the interpersonal growth, or the ability to function interdependently with others, needed for self-authorship. These three assumptions were tightly linked in environments that were most effective in promoting self-authorship.

These three assumptions were usually not explicitly stated, however. They were, instead, enacted through the approach educators, employers, or other adults used when interacting with the longitudinal participants. These assumptions complemented *three principles for educational practice* initially identified from the college phase of the study (Baxter Magolda, 1992). These principles were derived from college experiences that longitudinal participants reported as aiding intellectual development and were further supported by the observation study in which the principles' use in college courses promoted students' intellectual development (Baxter Magolda, 1999). Participants' stories in their 20s provide further evidence that these three principles help educators join learners at their current developmental place in the journey and support movement toward self-authorship. These were powerful supports because they modeled and encouraged a blend of connection and autonomy. Thus, the three assumptions challenge learners to journey toward self-authorship, while the three principles bridge the gap between their current developmental place and authoring their own beliefs, identities, and relationships.

The first principle, *validating learners' capacity to know,* was evident in employers' soliciting employees' perspectives and trusting their judgments as well as in educators' interest in learners' experiences and respect for their beliefs. This validation invited participants into the knowledge construction process, conveyed that their ideas were welcome, and offered respect that boosted their confidence in themselves. Soliciting their perspectives reinforced the importance of connection with others' perspectives yet blended it with the autonomy implied in constructing one's own ideas. The second principle, *situating learning in learners' experience,* was evident in educational and employment settings that used participants' existing knowledge and experience as the basis for continued learning and decision making. Participants perceived the use of their current knowledge and experience as a sign of respect (emphasizing connection); it simultaneously gave them a foundation for enhancing their learning or work (the potential for autonomy). The third principle, *mutually con-*

*structing meaning*, involved educators or employers connecting their knowledge to that of the participants to arrive at more complex understandings and decisions. This welcomed participants as equal partners in knowledge construction, helped them clarify their own perspectives (emphasizing autonomy), and helped them learn how to negotiate with others (emphasizing connection). The blend of connection and autonomy inherent in mutually constructing meaning supported learners in moving toward the mutuality characteristic of self-authorship.

These three principles promoted self-authorship by modeling it and providing participants the kind of support they needed to shift from external to internal self-definition. Because participants were at varying places along the journey, the company they needed varied accordingly. Situating learning in learners' experience and mutual construction of meaning helped educators and employers connect to and stay in tune with participants' development. Mutual construction helped educators and employers understand participants' journeys. This connection aided but did not overshadow learners taking initiative, learning by doing, and experiencing consequences of their choices to grow toward self-authorship.[1]

The data from which the Learning Partnerships Model were constructed suggest that it is most effective when the assumptions and principles are used intentionally to create learning partnerships. As will be evident in the exemplars that follow, however, the assumptions and principles sometimes occurred naturally. For example, situating learning in learners' experience can be done intentionally, or it can occur by virtue of being directly immersed in what one is learning, as was the case in many employment settings. Similarly the complexity and social construction of knowledge was evident in some contexts regardless of whether educators or employers explicitly emphasized it. Thus, using the Learning Partnerships Model intentionally is a matter of capitalizing on the assumptions and principles naturally occurring in a context and building in the others to achieve the combination of challenge and support that the collective set of assumptions and principles provide.

## Exemplars: The Learning Partnerships Model in Action

Participants' narratives reveal the nuances of the Learning Partnerships Model in educational, employment, and community life settings. The variations of the model within and across these contexts illustrate that the model's basic assumptions and principles can be used flexibly and creatively rather than prescriptively. Exemplars from the longitudinal participants' graduate education illustrate the nature of learning partnerships in multiple academic disciplines. Undergraduate exemplars reveal that traditional age students are capable of and appreciate participating in learning partnerships. Employment exemplars demonstrate the Learning Partnerships Model in diverse employment contexts and model types of learning partnerships that could be adopted by college educators in both academic and campus employment contexts. Community life exemplars show various forms the Learning Partnerships Model can take in everyday interactions with others and model learning partnerships college educators could translate to college community life, service learning, cultural immersion programs, and study abroad.

### Graduate Education Exemplars

After working in business for a year after college, Andrew pursued his MBA. His story recounts numerous aspects of his graduate program that model learning partnerships and how this experience affected him. The three core assumptions are evident in this story about one of his courses:

> In graduate school there was a lot more taking a position and defending it. There were a lot of things where there wasn't exactly a right answer. But you could come up with better answers and explain why you got to them. I had a management class where we were in essence running a business. We ran a simulated airline. There was no one right answer because we had nine groups and nine airlines in the class and all of them chose different philosophies in how they wanted to run their business. And three completely different airlines finished up at the top. In fact, the way our airline did it was different, the teacher said, than any other class had ever done. We just took a completely different approach,

yet it was still successful. He even said in the grading of our report that he completely disagreed with it, but it was well argued and reasoned out, and he still gave us an A. I guess I kind of respected that aspect of—you know, "We agree to disagree." I like not always thinking there was one right answer because when you go out and try to deal with a lot of things, there isn't always one right answer. I think too much as an undergraduate we're taught to believe in black and white and there is no gray. And I think there's a lot more gray than there is black and white. (Baxter Magolda, 2001, p. 197)

Rewarding multiple philosophies and approaches to running a successful business conveyed knowledge as complex and socially constructed. Students were encouraged to bring themselves into knowledge construction because the members of the group had to develop and support their approach. Taking and defending a position in the face of no right answer modeled the complexity of knowledge construction. The instructor's respect for Andrew's team, despite his disagreement with their approach, reflected sharing expertise and authority among knowledgeable peers. The instructor validated Andrew and his classmates as knowers by giving them responsibility to seek better answers and support them as well as affirming them for providing reasonable arguments for their stance. Running the simulated airline situated learning in their experience. Doing so as a team reinforced the definition of learning as mutually constructing meaning. Because Andrew had already discovered that gray prevailed over black and white in the business world, he appreciated the opportunity to explore it further in his studies. His economics course provided a similar opportunity:

We had to pick a topic and kind of take a position—we had to use economic tools, supply and demand charts, and explain why we thought is was correct or incorrect. Which was something I had *never* done in economics. Someone had to explain why supply side economics would reduce the federal deficit or would not. You had to argue it. And we weren't told what topic to choose—it was our own decision. . . . Defending your point and getting your point across is important. You are presented with a lot—you have to defend your position and why you chose something . . . people asking questions "why?" You have to reason why you did something. Every time I do something I think through it a little more. Asking that why question a lot more. (Baxter Magolda, 2001, pp. 197–198)

Again, the complexity and social construction of knowledge was evident in using economic tools to defend multiple positions. Andrew had to bring himself to the task to choose his topic, choose his position, determine how to support it, and ask himself why he believed a particular perspective. This sharing of expertise and authority helped Andrew establish the habit of reasoning in defining his beliefs. He had to make his beliefs his own and defend them with his peers. He was supported in doing so by being validated as a learner and having learning situated in his own experiences.

Sharing expertise and authority among diverse peers added another dimension to Andrew's graduate experience and modeled another component of the Learning Partnerships Model:

For graduate school, something that added a lot was dealing with the different cultures and the people from different countries and backgrounds. Graduate school was very heterogeneous, very mixed, very unlike my undergraduate. And I think it was much better just because of that. You had people who came from different backgrounds with different opinions. And I think when you're put in a class where too many are exactly the same, a lot of things are not brought out just because you don't have anybody that's being a devil's advocate. I think a little bit of antagonism is good for learning because it forces you to think why you believe what you believe and all that. It's not just a bunch of robots taking stuff in. (Baxter Magolda, 2001, p. 200)

This mutual construction of knowledge, even if it seemed somewhat antagonistic, forced Andrew to clarify why he held his beliefs. It also caused him to question perspectives he had accepted earlier without exploration:

I mean, just a lot of things we're taught in business are from an American perspective and American approach. Well, that's not necessarily the best and most correct way. In fact, at least in the manufacturing environment, we're getting our rear ends kicked. The Japanese have a much better approach that seems to be working. They challenged a lot of what we took as standard. They even argued with some of the financial theories, which supposedly aren't one of the things that you debate. But it was really good. We had people from communist countries that just had a very different perspective. And a lot of what they said made sense from the type of situations they were dealing with. (Baxter Magolda, 2001, p. 200)

Andrew's openness to questioning the "standard" approach reflected growth on all three dimensions of development. As he gained experience in constructing and defending his own beliefs, he gained epistemological complexity. Learning to value diverse perspectives, whether from classmates taking a different approach to business or from classmates from different cultural contexts, helped Andrew achieve interpersonal complexity, or the ability to meaningfully consider and appreciate others' perspectives. Being consistently asked to decide for himself and learning to connect to others and to his own internal belief system also led to intrapersonal complexity. Although it is certainly possible that Andrew's year of work experience contributed to this growth, he linked specific aspects of his graduate program to his growth toward self-authorship.

Alice pursued a master's in counseling immediately following her college graduation. Although her program differed greatly from Andrew's, it offered another exemplar of the Learning Partnerships Model. She described it like this:

> We did a lot of videotaping and audio taping that were reviewed with the professor and kind of critiqued with different counseling styles. And I thought that was real helpful. I guess just memorizing the concepts and writing them down is one thing, but then practicing them is a whole different ball game. And it helped me to find out which styles felt more natural for me, and it has kind of helped me evolve into what theoretical background that I adhere most strongly to. By doing it some of them really feel better, seem to fit better than others. And the actual doing them on tape really helped in that process, I think. (Baxter Magolda, 2001, p. 208)

Being new at counseling, Alice found learning situated in her own experience very helpful. Practicing counseling styles helped her meet the challenge her professors presented to construct her own theoretical framework. She explained this further:

> Well, you read all these hundreds of different counseling theories and it's just real overwhelming and confusing. They tell you that they want you to work with it and develop your own—not that you have to pick one theory and say, "I'm this," and never do anything else. But they kind of want you to have in the back of your mind that you should be trying to evolve and select one that you feel is going to work best for you. You know, just try them on and see which ones fit your own personal philosophy and things like that. And by actually doing them and seeing them on tape, that helped me to do that process. (Baxter Magolda, 2001, pp. 208–209)

The challenge to develop her own theoretical foundation, one that is consistent with her own personal philosophy, was a more difficult task than Alice had been accustomed to as an undergraduate. Professors in her counseling program portrayed knowledge as complex and socially constructed. Further, it was clear that she was responsible for constructing her counseling knowledge in a way that fit her as a person. She learned more about the challenge of self as central to knowledge construction, as she reported here:

> The hands-on experience through my practicum and internship has made me realize nobody else is in this room with me when I'm doing this counseling session. And so, for me to be clear on these issues, I need to figure them out for myself. Not to say that I'm ever going to figure them out, but to know where I stand on them and to think them through. And I think that's kind of encouraged that process. It's you and your client sitting there. I feel like if I'm not sure where I stand or I'm not clear on what the issues are and what the arguments are both ways and process that myself, then I don't see how I can be of any help at all to this client. So I think that's really encouraged me to do that. (Baxter Magolda, 2001, p. 209)

Learning situated in her experience brought home the realization that it was just she and her client in the counseling relationship. She realized the necessity to work out her own stance, tentative as it must be because of the multitude of counseling theories and clients' diverse therapeutic needs. The process of practicing and mutually constructing knowledge with her instructors and supervisors supported her in meeting this challenge. Validation as a learner led her to see herself as capable of constructing her own counseling style. She shared her sense of the outcome:

> I think that I'm more independent. I'm more of a self-thinker, if that makes sense, I'm questioning things more, and I'm not taking—just because I take notes and then that's the way it is and that's all

that's been written and that's law. I'm finding that I'm really questioning things and issues. Like with the dual diagnosis. I'm really sorting stuff out for myself instead of just taking notes about everybody else's opinion. In that way I think I'm a lot different. (Baxter Magolda, 2001, p. 210)

As a self-thinker, Alice established her own beliefs internally in the context of others' opinions and available knowledge, blending autonomy and connection. She had gained the intrapersonal confidence through establishing her own internal identity as a counselor to sort perspectives out for herself. Although she did not speak directly to interpersonal complexity, her growth on the epistemological and intrapersonal dimensions suggests that she could maintain her own identity and beliefs in mutual relations with others.

## Undergraduate Education Exemplars

A few longitudinal participants described conditions that promoted self-authorship during their undergraduate experience. More substantive examples, however, are available from the course observation study with its combination of observational and interview data (Baxter Magolda, 1999). The zoology course Erica spoke of at the outset of this chapter modeled learning partnerships because of Professor Snowden's emphasis on integrating multiple disciplinary perspectives, recognizing that facts are tentative and subject to revision, and engaging students in thinking like scientists. This emphasis on the complexity and social construction of knowledge was apparent to Rich, a student in the course:

> The whole focus of most of my classes in college have been just regurgitating the facts, with the exception of a few like Winter Biology where the base facts were given to you on the ground level and where the actual learning was coming in above and beyond that. The learning was coming in where he would ask, "What do you think about this?" and you couldn't just look on your notes, you couldn't just remember what he said. It is not just blatant memorization; learning comes into it when you are utilizing the ideas towards something new that hasn't been done. That kind of set-up seems to stimulate me more than just being like a computer and storing this information to really do nothing with. This class gave more interest into the applications, what is going on right now, ideas of it, theories on what they don't know. The other classes it was "here is what we know and you have to know it too." There wasn't any fairly mutual exchange between the instructor and the class, no formulations of ideas beyond. (Baxter Magolda, 1999, p. 122)

Rich had lost interest in storing facts like a computer and regurgitating them on command. He preferred to use the facts as a foundation for exploring and constructing new knowledge. He elaborated on the mutual exchange between the instructor and the class that was absent in his other classes:

> [The lecture] has got to have structure because everybody is not on the same level. And it's got to have a mediator that can guide the group idea in the right direction and that lets certain instances of false knowledge kind of seep into the fact and encourage the idea to come out—but if it is wrong, fine, subtlety set it aside so it doesn't get into the collective. It takes some serious skills dealing with people, their collective knowledge. It is the best way to utilize other students' knowledge at least for me. There is a fine line—if I say something that is fundamentally wrong, you have to isolate that response as an instructor and figure out why that student came to that conclusion instead of being like, "No that is the wrong answer." Chris [Professor Snowden] would find out why that came about and steer it over to the rest of the idea; "Okay that is not quite right, but how did you get there? Is this how you got there?" That is what I mean by subtly bringing it back or saying that I would not be wrong if I came out and said something. (Baxter Magolda, 1999, p. 126)

These comments are Rich's interpretation of the class interactions that took place. Professor Snowden routinely engaged students in thinking with him about data and possible interpretations. As Rich reported, Professor Snowden respectfully pursued the source of students' contributions and mutually constructed meaning with them in ways that helped them correct faulty assumptions. Professor Snowden modeled epistemological complexity by noting that scientific knowledge construction is fraught with assumptions that must be pursued to determine the most reasonable interpretation. Inviting students into this process of analysis situated learning in their experience, validated them as capable of constructing knowledge, and taught them how to mutually construct meaning with others. Professor Snowden also modeled the core assumption that one brings oneself to the process of deciding what to believe.

In addition to modeling the core assumptions and principles through lecture and classroom interaction, Professor Snowden did so through the assignments. Students read primary literature on a topic of their choice and presented their findings to the class to simulate scientific conference presentations. They were also asked to write a grant proposal to seek funding for the research questions they had generated. Jill shared her thoughts regarding the overall nature of the course and these assignments:

> There are some things that are left in the air but I think that is in a good sense. There are things that we don't quite understand yet, that would lend to grant proposals that would lend to further research. I think that is the key in science; you have to have questions to move further in science. It is the whole idea that science is futuristic, you are coming up with new ideas, you want to invent new things, you need to utilize other research to come up with your own. I think he sparks questions and I think that is what science is about—questioning things, pulling things together from different sources (that is what research is), everything that has been done in science, you take something that someone else has learned and you say I have an idea, this work proves this side of my project. I just did a report on cancer and cancer of the kidney. First someone develops an idea that it is in the cortex and then someone realizes that it is in the tubules that run through the cortex, and even portions outside of the cortex, and then someone takes the ideas of these portions and say I discovered it looks like these type of cells, so that limits it to just the tubules that run in the tubules. I think you have to learn from what other people have done and apply it and ask questions and that is how you move forward and make discoveries. I think by asking questions constantly you come up with ideas for research and new discoveries. (Baxter Magolda, 1999, p. 120)

Jill, too, recognized the complexity and social construction of knowledge in the constant use of questions to lead to new discoveries. She accepted that some things are always uncertain in scientific work. She also recognized how various discoveries are coordinated to lead to future questions, an example of sharing expertise and authority among members of the scientific community in knowledge construction. The assumption of self as central was evident to her as well, as revealed in these comments:

> His point was he wanted us to learn how to be scientists. I just realized that by making us write this grant proposal, we have to put what we have learned—our topic, our seminar—into a question and be a scientist about it and make a revelation. I have been sitting here talking about how science is moving forward and asking questions and that is exactly what we are doing by writing the grant proposal. That is why it is so scary, that is what science is about and if you can't do it and you can't write a proposal than maybe you shouldn't be in science. But I think the key to really being a scientist is to not just follow what other people are saying about their discoveries but to go out on your own. I think he is doing that. (Baxter Magolda, 1999, p. 130)

Although Jill was not totally confident going out on her own with discoveries, she recognized the challenge of acknowledging her own central role in constructing scientific knowledge. She felt validated by Professor Snowden's trusting that students could generate their own questions and write grant proposals. Having these experiences situated learning in her own experience and engaged her in mutually constructing knowledge with others.

In an end-of-semester interview, Professor Snowden shared his sense of the grant proposal assignment:

> The purpose of the proposal was accomplished in the sense that they [students] have a better idea now what it means to do primary research and how it is reported. Some of the things one has to think about if you are going to continue work—what it would take to write a proposal, how hard it is to define a question. Maybe a lot of what they got out of this isn't going to show up as a high quality proposal on a piece of paper and that's okay. Because in some ways they weren't ever in a position to do this and of course they found it extremely difficult, because it is extremely difficult. (Baxter Magolda, 1999, p. 133)

Professor Snowden's reflection revealed that he used the grant proposal as a process for exposing students to the nature of scientific research. Despite the fact that they had insufficient time and experience to produce a high-quality proposal, his goal of having students understand the complexity of defining questions was met. In the process, the three core assumptions and three principles were clearly evident.

This zoology course helped students learn to think like scientists. They learned how to critique primary scientific literature, identify the next step in research, prepare a professional presentation, and write a grant proposal (the learning goals specified on the syllabus). More important, they learned how to think about and interpret scientific data and construct new knowledge. Thus, the learning goals of the course were met simultaneously with promoting self-authorship. Most students in the class reported that they were actively involved in the course and were able to envision their future role in science. The course promoted their ability to internally define scientific beliefs and themselves as scientists. Students in this course were generally open to the challenge for self-authorship because they used ways of knowing at the outset of the class that were not completely dependent on authority for knowledge (Baxter Magolda, 1999).

Similar outcomes occurred in the mathematics course, where students initially used authority-dependent ways of knowing. Melissa's report of her reaction to the course shows that the Learning Partnerships Model is useful for those who have further to travel toward self-authorship:

> With Math, up until now for me, in my own personal experience, there has always been one answer and how you arrive at it. [Sam's] trying to [help us] see that there is more than one possible answer or one possible solution. It gives you an opportunity to be creative and to try things. Sure you may be discouraged at times but I think it is very rewarding when you do come up with something and get excited and a lot of times the ideas just start flowing and you don't want to stop or put it down so it's kind of exciting. (Baxter Magolda, 1999, p. 160)

Although Melissa did not achieve self-authorship at the end of the semester, she was moving in that direction and excited about trying new things in math. Most students reported increased confidence in their ability to understand mathematical structure and generate mathematical ideas. They also succeeded in achieving one of the course goals: developing their personal (as opposed to memorized) understanding of the structure and functioning of mathematics. Most held more complex perspectives about knowledge construction at the end of the course than they did at the beginning (Baxter Magolda, 1999).

The Learning Partnerships Model promoted the journey toward self-authorship in a large education class as well. At the outset of this course, the majority of students used transitional knowing—the belief that while some knowledge is certain, other knowledge is not yet known (Baxter Magolda, 1992). The goals of the course included learning to interpret, critique, and judge educational practices. The objectives of *recognizing* positions in educational discourse and *interpreting* educational practices as they related to the purpose of schooling required that students value their own perspectives or have a "mind of their own." Cheryl described coming to value her perspective in the course:

> I feel more like a part of this class. I feel less than the professor in a lecture where he is telling you his knowledge. I feel equal in this class because it is based on my experience. The students and teacher share experiences. I have something to contribute. I am usually quiet and don't speak in class. I feel like I can in here. (Baxter Magolda, 1999, p. 196)

Cheryl also reported that sharing her perspective prompted more internal self-evaluation and questioning. She noted that her family offered what she called a "one-way" background and that the class introduced her to alternative ways to think.

*Critiquing* positions in educational discourse and *evaluating* educational practices required going beyond an awareness of new perspectives. Elaine, who on a questionnaire at the outset of the course expressed interest only in students explaining material to each other, said in her interview at the end of the course that she was learning to critique:

> Hearing opinions is important to deciding my own. I read, take my opinions, ideas that have been put forth, look further into it, compare to my ideas, and think about what we should do. I combine different things, get the main idea, compare it to my idea. I become a better person by changing my views as I learn about others' experiences. (Baxter Magolda, 1999, p. 197)

Elaine's more recent view assigned greater value to what her peers think, and their views sometimes affected hers in a positive way. Elaine said that she had learned to critically analyze through the assignments and felt that the course offered a chance to evaluate her opinions.

*Judging* educational practice and *defending* positions in educational discourse required taking a stance on what information and beliefs to endorse. Hugh was confident that he could judge educational practices on the basis of the course, saying,

> I think I can make judgments about educational practice. I will be able to make judgments in the classroom setting. This class has helped me by giving me different ways of seeing things and thinking about things. My judgments will be my own; not other people who told you you should think or do this. I appreciate this. I try to make decisions that say I've examined this situation and from past experience and what I've learned—what is the best way to handle this? (Baxter Magolda, 1999, p. 198)

These comments are an indication of contextual knowing in which one decides on the basis of appropriate evidence that particular approaches are better than others, thus representing a shift from Hugh's valuing all opinions equally at the outset of the course to deciding what he believed at the end of the course. Hugh thought that his classmates had helped him decide on a viewpoint and that the instructor had allowed him to make his own judgments. These stories reinforce the value of learning partnerships for helping students move toward self-authorship.

The next story illustrates that the Learning Partnerships Model can be effectively implemented early in college. A college sophomore participating in a panel on productive learning experiences shared this story about her first year in college:

> Good Evening, My name is Erin and I am a sophomore at IUPUI. I am majoring in Social Studies Secondary Education. It was my first day in college, my first course, I was terrified. I was in a room full of people I did not know. The professor walks in wearing a sweater that says "Question Authority." I was somewhat shocked; coming from a small private school I was not expecting that to be the teacher's first statement. I was overwhelmed as he began to go over the syllabus. I just knew that I was doomed. Would college really kill me? I can remember asking myself that question as I slouched into my couch that night at home; little did I know that the next semester would hold the answer to my question. This particular professor's course would change my outlook on college and learning in general. Presenting new and thought-provoking information, creating an understanding atmosphere, and by altering the class routine this professor gave me the opportunity to gain a new perspective on learning and interpreting information.
>
> The professor would present thought-provoking information, most of which was new to me. He went about telling the story or giving the facts without drawing conclusions. This gave me the opportunity to come to my own conclusions about the situations that he presented. My entire educational background to that point told me exactly what to think but now I had the opportunity to decide for myself. At first I looked for clues from the professor so I would know the "right" way to think, but he was very good at hiding and disguising his personal beliefs. Because I was not directed by the professor I became eager to find information on my own. I wanted to read the class text and even searched for articles that addressed our topics outside of the classroom.
>
> The atmosphere created inside his classroom was one of understanding. Dividing the class into small groups the professor would initiate discussions. The small groups helped break down some of the barriers such as not knowing others in the class and allowed everyone to participate without feeling threatened. I was timid at first and I remember being reluctant to talk about my ideas and interpretations, but I quickly warmed up to group discussions. I found myself openly expressing my opinions. I always felt that my opinions were respected, not only by my classmates but also the professor. The lines of communication were always open between students and the professor. He seemed to enjoy our input and when we had error in our line of thought he never talked down to us. Through the discussions I gained new ideas and perspectives from other students. I began to have the ability to see issues from all sides of the argument. This not only helped in the classroom setting but in all other aspects of my life.
>
> The class structure would vary. There were times when the professor would lecture and on other days our group discussions filled the entire class session. This continual change kept my interest. I looked forward to going to his class. I wanted to know what type of new and controversial information he would present and what my classmates and I would discuss.

I am thankful that I enrolled in this class my first semester even though it was not recommended. It didn't kill me but much rather made me a more responsible student. I walked away at the end of the semester with a new attitude toward learning. I no longer take things as I hear them but I compile information from many sources to evaluate them in order to apply them to my life. Because of the thoughtful information, the open atmosphere, and stylistic changes in the class structure I was able to gain a new perspective on learning. I learned to question authority. (Hillenburg, 2002)

Erin encountered knowledge as complex and socially constructed through her instructor's approach to teaching. She was invited to bring her own mind and opinions to the class and felt respected as a thinker even when she and her peers had error in their thinking. The instructor organized the course in ways that invited Erin and her peers to mutually construct knowledge. Because the instructor invited and supported her in exploring ideas, learning excited Erin. Connection with her instructor and peers made questioning authority possible and educational. Her ability to question authority at the end of her first year suggests that the Learning Partnerships Model can be useful early in college with students who have not previously experienced questioning authority as a component of learning.

## Employment Setting Exemplars

The components of the Learning Partnerships Model were evident, although not usually an explicit part of the culture, in employment settings. Employers were most likely interested in maximizing employee performance to achieve success relevant to the work setting. However, in their desire to maximize employee performance or perhaps in conveying the nature of their work settings, many employers provided the conditions to promote self-authorship.

Even in highly technical fields, ambiguity, complexity, and social construction of knowledge were common. Ned accepted a position selling paper chemicals on completing his paper science degree. His job involved analyzing extensive technical data to make decisions to address complex problems occurring at the paper mill that had contracted for his services. He explained,

There are probably several hundred people working at a mill, making thousands of tons of paper a day using millions of gallons of water. So within that system there are many things that can go wrong on a day-to-day basis. So when I go into a mill, I never know what to expect. I start with a process engineer, and say, "What are the problems that you're encountering?" Then the problem-solving process starts really by asking lots of questions and just getting the feel for what their process is like. A lot of it is by drawing simple diagrams at first and just getting comfortable with "What are they doing from start to finish there?" From that point I have to, on a rough scale, judge whether we can make a change or not with my chemicals. (Baxter Magolda, 2001, p. 246)

Ned had to understand the complexity of the mill operations before he could even offer a preliminary judgment about whether his chemicals would benefit the mill. This preliminary judgment was made in the context of his experience learning that particular mill's operation. If he judged that his chemicals might help, he then conducted laboratory tests in the mill to help determine the necessary changes. But the testing did not resolve the complexity. As Ned explained, "This test by itself might be extremely complex and require a lot of interpretation because they're not always exact science." The interpretation led to physically testing potential changes by using the new chemicals in the papermaking system and gathering data about the process for a week. This data served as the foundation for Ned's recommendations to the mill:

I am responsible for deciphering—based on everything I know about the mill, all our tests that we did in the lab, based on the objections or problems the mill might have or the mill's limitations—take the data that we recorded and assimilate all that to say, "Did it work or not?" And it's not always easy to say that it did work. A lot of it is textbook kind of work—there's a certain way of running laboratory tests. But there's also a knowledge base background for knowing "How do these classes of chemicals fit into this kind of paper making and how are they going to affect what happens at the end of the machine?" You read a couple of lines in a book saying this class of polymers should do this, but it never happens that way and there's always some good reasons why it doesn't. If you've seen the reasons enough times in different applications or different situations, you're going to be alerted or aware of the potential problems before they occur or look for those opportunities when they're there. (Baxter Magolda, 2001, pp. 246–247)

Conducting laboratory tests and then physically inserting the chemicals into the paper machine further situated learning in Ned's experience. He used previous experience to analyze and interpret the tests and outcomes. His experiences, framed in a context where knowledge was complex and socially constructed, enhanced his judgment. He was responsible for conducting the tests, interpreting them, and making his own judgment, illustrating the challenge of making self central to knowledge construction. Ned also mutually constructed these interpretations with others, including his supervisor and employees at the mill. Ned's experience eventually led him to develop what he called a framework for problem solving and decision making. Developing this framework was part of the self-authorship required of employees to effectively deal with the complexity of their work. Ned found the framework useful in the challenge of bringing self to knowledge construction. He shared,

> I'm acting more like myself. The more I like the job, the more my customers like me and want to do business with me. I'm developing my own style. You might have the title of whatever—there's this preconceived image of what that person should do. After a few years of doing it, you realize you aren't that stereotype and are more successful if you don't act that way. Self-actualization, self-confidence—maybe that's it. Coming out of school I was worried about what people thought of me, how would I make the best impression. In retrospect, you say be yourself, you can be more motivated and do the best job. People judging you hopefully aren't so self absorbed that if you aren't identical to them its okay; hopefully they judge you on results. You figure out the stereotype is wrong but play that role until you change it. (Baxter Magolda, 2001, p. 257)

Ned's story illustrates movement toward self-authorship on all three dimensions. He became increasingly comfortable with the complexity of knowledge construction and adept at bringing his own experience to bear on decisions. His success led him to value his own style (i.e., intrapersonal complexity) and to be less concerned over what others thought of him (i.e., interpersonal complexity).

Complexity and social construction of knowledge were also prevalent in fields that combined artistic and technical skills. Dawn's experience in the restaurant business exemplified the Learning Partnerships Model in action. She reported,

> I'm one of the line cooks. I'm working with a certified chef—a brilliant woman—food is second nature to her. When you are cooking food, it's easiest to just watch. I've learned so much in five months that I never knew before. I pick up things in conversation, but the easiest way to pick up this skill is to watch someone who knows how to do it. Also experimentation—make this, taste it, have chef taste it, and she knows what to do with it. I thought of myself as one who learns by doing or watching rather than actively pursuing knowledge by questioning. I notice now that I ask questions. There is a wealth of information at my fingertips and I want to learn as much as I can while I have this opportunity. I never had a job like this—outside of theater—where I can actively pursue an art or craft. Acting is more of an exploratory thing—no right and wrong. That is true to some extent in culinary arts. But there are rights and wrongs—4 tablespoons rather than 2. But you taste, create, explore putting flavors together to come up with a final product that you present. It is experimentation like in theater. It is set up very much like theater is set up—work with a group of people, creating a product, give it out to the masses. Every night we look at elements we have, and we have to make something. The job appeals to my frame of mind. (Baxter Magolda, 2001, pp. 244–245)

Cooking in this setting centered on a combination of knowledge and experimentation to create flavorful foods, reflecting the social construction of knowledge. Engaging in this experimentation situated learning in Dawn's experience. Sharing expertise and authority were evident in the openness to questions and she and the chef tasting food to determine the next step. The chef validated Dawn as a contributor rather than asking her to follow a recipe. Dawn's experience of creating something with her colleagues in the theater made her appreciate the mutual construction taking place in the kitchen. Her acting experience clearly reflected the notion of self as central to constructing characters, as she reported:

> I have had opportunities to play more than one type of character. The thing that's involved in that is exploring different parts of yourself, learning about how many different types of people you are within yourself and being able to apply that to a script that someone has written. And along with your imagination, you create these different personas. As far as the character aspect—I think there's a lot of self-learning that goes on continually. And that's one of the things that I think that always fascinates

me about this business is you never stand still. You're always progressing; you're always moving forward, learning new things about yourself, learning new ways to present your ideas to a group of people. Then that kind of melts into your technique. Oftentimes you have to get to a certain emotional level that you can't just create. So there's a process that you have to go through, self-disclosure, to some extent. You combine yourself with what you're given, what you interpret about a character. The technique comes in as transferring all that is within you to this character, your abilities to speak the character's truth from, probably, your truth. There are a lot of techniques in acting that not everybody can use. You pick and choose the ones that are right for you. (Baxter Magolda, 2001, p. 151)

Dawn's description of creating the truth of a character revolves around making herself central to the task of knowledge construction. The multitude of techniques available reflected the complexity and social construction of knowledge; actors and directors shared authority and expertise. Thus, Dawn encountered conditions to promote self-authorship in both her acting and her cooking contexts, contributing to her self-authorship.

Barb, a new attorney, encountered learning partnerships in her law practice. She described translating her law school education into practice:

People are understanding. They know we are just starting out. They give samples and point you in the right direction to get started. With corporate work, I like it because it is new. You are drafting things you have no idea how to do, so you use samples. A lot of times, I'll be confident enough to know it is common sense. If there is no sample, I have friends that have worked on it so I ask them. Or look it up in reference books. Confidence is key. There is no right answer; with law you can argue both sides. You have to state your position with authority so people perceive you as knowing what you are talking about, to put clients at ease. Sometimes I tell clients both sides, but then you say which way we should go. This is all new; you don't learn everything in law school. Practicing law is doing it off-the-cuff; I have no idea how to wing it. (Baxter Magolda, 2001, p. 245)

Complexity and social construction of knowledge permeated Barb's work, as is evident in her statement that no right answer exists. She was responsible for using her resources, both written and human, to craft arguments for both sides and choose one to recommend to her clients. She relied in part on her own training and common sense and in part on mutual construction with her colleagues. Practicing law was clearly situated in her experience, and her colleagues were willing to construct arguments with her knowing she was new at corporate law.

These stories, and many others like them, demonstrate that diverse employment settings required self-authored employees. Regardless of context, these work settings required employees to be able to analyze situations, use appropriate data, interpret it effectively, develop solutions to problems, and produce some type of product. Employers required employees to use the expertise of those around them yet also required them to develop and use their own expertise. Although degrees of support varied widely, very few of the longitudinal participants found themselves in work settings that did not demand self-authorship.

## Community Life Exemplars

Similar to employment contexts, longitudinal participants' community life experiences were not intentionally structured to promote self-authorship. The conditions for promoting self-authorship were present, however, in many contexts in which participants chose to engage. One such context was Lydia's choice to live abroad for 2 years. She reported,

It has made me more independent of what I know—more willing to try new experiences and not be so hesitant about it. I was so shy when I started college; not anymore! Because if there is one thing that living in an area that is not yours teaches you, it is that you have to get out there and speak up for what you believe in and what is right. To not let others roll you over to their ideas and roll you over to their ways. (Baxter Magolda, 2001, pp. 289–290)

Living in another country challenged Lydia to express herself and her beliefs. Although she expressed not letting others "roll her over," her openness to new experience led to reinventing who she was:

> It was a fabulous experience. I did things I never would have thought I would do. It makes you feel small; there are so many other people out there! If you have experienced this much, how much more is out there? I have a thirst for more. If you stay in the same place, you get in a rut. It is so exciting! You don't know what you are capable of; you reinvent yourself as you gain new experiences. We had earthquakes; we got used to it. We had [electrical] power-sharing there. There were 6 months when between two and four hours a day you had no power. It is fun to teach when the power goes out; 85 degrees—it gets overwhelming. It got to be a joke. Everybody accepted it. Here, the power goes out and people are beside themselves. I learned to be more flexible. When you experience other things and see other people deal with things, it puts your life into perspective. The more people you know and more experiences you hear about, you get stronger. I am a strong person now; we move and redo everything. I'm fortunate; I've stumbled onto things. I'm like a cat; land on my feet. Life is too short to be bothered by little things like moving and being uprooted from job and friends. There are other jobs and friends. (Baxter Magolda, 2001, p. 290)

New experiences to use to put her life into perspective introduced Lydia to multiple ways of living. Interacting with people who responded to life differently than she had been accustomed to doing helped Lydia reinvent herself. Her story reveals that she realized that she played a central role in constructing her view of life yet openly entertained others' ideas through mutual construction of knowledge. She reported gaining strength, flexibility, and security through this process. Regarding being uprooted from a job and friends as "little things" suggests that Lydia internally defines her beliefs, identity, and relations with others such that external changes do not shake her foundation.

Anita chose to volunteer after college in both a Big Sister program and a switchboard for runaways. Her story illustrates that learning partnerships were present in both these contexts:

> The little girl I have is 9. She has very difficult problems. She was taken away from her mother, who has AIDS. The chances of her going home are nil, but she doesn't know it. We went out for her birthday and she picked out some clothes. When I took them over, she didn't want to see me, she just wanted the gift. Her therapist said I should tell her how I felt, so I did. It went over poorly, she got angry, and now she doesn't want to see me. I also work for the national runaway switchboard. On the switchboard, you have to let them figure things out for themselves; try to turn the conversation around to steer them in a direction without giving them an answer. I'm getting used to not knowing at the switchboard. Nothing you can say is wrong, as long as you are trying to help. The same call could be handled differently by different people. Like with my little sis, I feel like I shouldn't have brought it up, but others said I had to do it. I'm learning to let things go. I'm better at realizing and admitting when I've made mistakes. I'm more humble. Sometimes I hear other calls and I wouldn't have done something that way. I'm trying to figure out for myself if I have the right to an opinion. Like if someone hits them, I have a hard time saying it is wrong. It can lead to an arrest, and make a bigger mess. I have a hard time being as directive as I should. I have to figure out for myself what my own beliefs are. I do have the right to an opinion. I know molestation is wrong, but what will life be like if I make the call? (Baxter Magolda, 2001, p. 298)

Anita's struggles with her little sister and the callers to the switchboard stemmed from the complexity of making sense out of the events that were reported and deciding how to respond. There were no sure answers or no proven solutions to these complex situations. Anita mutually constructed knowledge with others in these settings yet worked hard at defining her own beliefs. Mutual construction was also expected in how she dealt with callers: she was to guide them yet let them figure things out for themselves. Learning was clearly situated in Anita's experience, and others validated her as capable in these contexts. Anita was still struggling at the time of this story to sort out her own beliefs in the face of the serious consequences of her actions for others.

## The Learning Partnerships Model's Potential for Transforming Higher Education

Following learners longitudinally from their college entrance to their mid-30s provided extensive interview data from which to conceptualize the Learning Partnerships Model. The observation study contributed to conceptualizing the model through observing learning partnerships in action in various disciplines. Interviewing learners about how these learning partnerships affected them augmented the outcome data emerging from the longitudinal study. The assumptions and principles that constitute the Learning Partnerships Model are consistent with scholarship on how to promote student development and learning. They are also inherent in scholars' descriptions of culturally inclusive pedagogy. As a result, the model holds substantial promise for transforming higher education to promote self-authorship during college.

The chapters in part 2 of this book reveal that potential by reporting specific uses of the Learning Partnerships Model in multiple contexts. Each chapter describes the implementation of the model in detail and the particular goals it is designed to achieve. Use of the model in these diverse contexts illustrates its flexibility to blend with other models and particular practice goals. Because the Learning Partnerships Model consists of a set of assumptions and principles to shape practice, it is intended to be used creatively rather than prescriptively. The authors report assessment data to indicate the model's effectiveness in promoting self-authorship in their particular contexts, adding to the growing data that support the model. We invite you to reflect on your own educational practice as you explore these exemplars.

## Note

1. Adapted from the preface of Baxter Magolda (2001).

## References

Baxter Magolda, M. B. (1992). *Knowing and reasoning in college: Gender-related patterns in students' intellectual development*. San Francisco: Jossey-Bass.

Baxter Magolda, M. B. (1999). *Creating contexts for learning and self-authorship: Constructive-developmental pedagogy*. Nashville: Vanderbilt University Press.

Baxter Magolda, M. B. (2001). *Making their own way: Narratives for transforming higher education to promote self-development*. Sterling, VA: Stylus.

Belenky, M., Clinchy, B. M., Goldberger, N., & Tarule, J. (1986). *Women's ways of knowing: The development of self, voice, and mind*. New York: Basic Books.

Hillenburg, E. (2002, November). *Response to transforming pedagogy to transform learning*. Paper presented at the Association of American Colleges and Universities Faculty Work and Student Learning Conference, Indianapolis.

Perry, W. G. (1970). *Forms of intellectual and ethical development in the college years: A scheme*. Troy, MO: Holt, Rinehart and Winston.

Piaget, J. (1950). *The psychology of intelligence* (M. Piercy and D. Berlyne, Trans.). London: Routledge & Kegan Paul.

## Unit 6 Additional Recommended Readings

Baxter Magolda, M. B. (2000). *Teaching to promote holistic learning and development*. In M. B. Baxter Magolda (Ed.), *Teaching to promote intellectual and personal maturity: Incorporating students' worldviews and identities into the learning process* (New Directions for Teaching and Learning No. 82, pp. 88–98.) San Francisco, CA: Jossey-Bass.

Baxter Magolda, M. B. (2003). Identity and learning: Student affairs' role in transforming higher education. *Journal of College Student Development, 44*, 231–247.

Baxter Magolda, M. B., & King, P. M. (2008). Toward reflective conversations: An advising approach that promotes self-authorship. *Peer Review 10*(1), 8–11.

Bell, L. A. (2007). Theoretical foundations for social justice education. In M. Adams, L. A. Bell, & P. Griffin (Eds.), *Teaching for diversity and social justice* (2nd ed., pp. 1–14). New York, NY: Routledge.

Coomes, M. D. (1994). Using student development to guide institutional policy. *Journal of College Student Development, 35*, 428–437.

Hardiman, R., & Jackson, B. W. (1992). Racial identity development: Understanding racial dynamics in college classrooms and on campus. In M. Adams (Ed.), *Promoting diversity in college classrooms: Innovative responses for the curriculum, faculty, and institutions* (New Directions for Teaching and Learning No. 52, pp. 21–37). San Francisco, CA: Jossey-Bass.

Hodge, D. C., Baxter Magolda, M. B., & Haynes, C. A. (2009). Engaged learning: Enabling self-authorship and effective practice. *Liberal Education, 95*(4), 16–23.

Kegan, R., & Lahey, L. L. (2009). Reconceiving the challenge of change. In *Immunity to change* (pp. 11–30). Boston, MA: Harvard Business Press.

Kerr, K. G., & Tweedy, J. (2006). Beyond seat time and student satisfaction: A curricular approach to residential education. *About Campus, 11*(5), 9–15.

King, P. M., & Baxter Magolda, M. B. (1996). A developmental perspective on learning. *Journal of College Student Development, 37*, 163–173.

Nash, R. J. (1997). Teaching ethics in the student affairs classroom. *NASPA Journal, 35*, 3–19.

Palmer, P. J. (2003). Teaching with heart and soul: Reflections on spirituality in teacher education. *Journal of Teacher Education, 54*, 376–385.

Piper, T. D. (1997). Empowering students to create community standards. *About Campus, 2*(3), 22–24.

Pizzolato, J. E. (2008). Advisor, teacher, partner: Using the learning partnerships model to reshape academic advising. *About Campus, 13*(1), 18–25.

Pope, R. L., Reynolds, A. L., Mueller, J. A. (2004). Multicultural competence in theory and translation. In *Multicultural competence in student affairs* (29–45). San Francisco, CA: Jossey-Bass.

Quaye, S. J., & Baxter Magolda, M. B. (2007). Enhancing racial self-understanding through structured learning and reflective experiences. In S. R. Harper & L. D. Patton (Eds.), *Responding to the realities of race on campus* (New Directions for Student Services No. 120, pp. 55–66). San Francisco, CA: Jossey-Bass.

Rodgers, R. F. (1991). Using theory in practice in student affairs. In T. K. Miller, R. B. Winston, & Associates, *Administration and leadership in student affairs: Actualizing student development in higher education* (2nd ed., pp. 203–251). Muncie, IN: Accelerated Development.

Rutledge, M. (1989). Faith development: Bridging theory and practice. In J. Butler, *Religion on Campus* (pp. 17–32). San Francisco, CA: Jossey-Bass.

Taylor, K., & Haynes, C. (2008). A framework for intentionally fostering student learning. *About Campus, 13*(5), 2–11.

Upcraft, M. L. (1994). The dilemmas of translating theory to practice. *Journal of College Student Development, 35*, 438–443.